2001
POET'S
MARKET

1,800 PLACES TO PUBLISH YOUR POETRY

EDITED BY

PAMALA SHIELDS

WRITER'S DIGEST BOOKS
CINCINNATI, OHIO

Important market listing information

- Listings are based on questionnaires and verified copy. They are not advertisements *nor* are markets necessarily endorsed by the editors of this book.
- Information in the listings comes directly from the publishers and is as accurate as possible, but publications and editors come and go, and poetry needs fluctuate between the publication date of this directory and the time you use it.
- *Poet's Market reserves the right to exclude any listing that does not meet its requirements.*

Complaint procedure

If you feel you have not been treated fairly by a listing in *Poet's Market*, we advise you to take the following steps:

- First try to contact the listing. Sometimes one phone call or a letter can quickly clear up the matter.
- Document all your correspondence with the listing. When you write to us with a complaint, provide the details of your submission, the date of your first contact with the listing and the nature of your subsequent correspondence.
- We will enter your letter into our files and attempt to contact the listing.
- The number and severity of complaints will be considered in our decision whether or not to delete the listing from the next edition.

If you are a poetry publisher and would like to be considered for a listing in the next edition of *Poet's Market*, send a SASE (or SAE and IRC) with your request for a questionnaire to *Poet's Market*—QR, 1507 Dana Ave., Cincinnati OH 45207. Questionnaires received after February 23, 2001, will be held for the 2003 edition.

Editorial Director, Annuals Department: Barbara Kuroff
Managing Editor, Annuals Department: Doug Hubbuch
Production Editor: Nancy Breen

Writer's Digest Books website: www.writersdigest.com

International Standard Serial Number 0883-5470
International Standard Book Number 0-89879-981-3

Attention Booksellers: This is an annual directory of F&W Publications. Return deadline for this edition is December 31, 2001.

Contents

RESOURCES

INDEXES

From the Editor

Nothing remains the same. We all experience changes, new beginnings and endings at different times in our lives, the inevitable starts and stops of life. The staff at *Poet's Market* has gone through just such a transition this year. Halfway through the production process on this edition, editor Chantelle Bentley resigned to embark on a new career path, and I assumed responsibility for the book. We sadly say good-bye to her. But, with this new start, I look forward to the exciting opportunity to continue bringing you the best *Poet's Market* can offer.

Again this year we present **The "Quick-Start" Guide to Publishing**. This article provides a detailed ten-step guide to locating and contacting poetry editors and publishers and offers suggestions for maximizing this book's potential. **How to Submit Your Poetry Successfully** offers handy, easy-to-use guidelines regarding submission etiquette.

Once again, helpful symbols guide you through nearly 1,800 markets for your poems. New this year is the ◘ symbol indicating a publisher accepts poetry written by children. And the ▣ symbol will appear in the **Also Offers** section of a listing when a publication also publishes an online version with original content. You'll find these symbols, in **Key to Symbols**, located on the inside covers.

Just as life changes are unavoidable, adjustments to your work will certainly be a part of the writing process. Very few poems make it from beginning to end without being altered in some fashion. That is why this year we offer an exciting and informative article on revising your work. Poet/editor Jeffrey Hillard takes you step-by-step through the revision process, providing great tips and informative examples in a relaxed, upbeat style. You will find his article, **The Art of Revision**, on page 5.

Take advantage of ten insightful, invaluable and inspirational accounts from poets and editors who provide advice on being successful poets in our **Insider Reports**. Included in this edition are interviews with poet/editors Joe Benevento and Brian Daldorph, editor Wen Stephenson and poet Richard Jackson, among others.

It is through change that work is transformed and you grow as a poet. See where your poem takes you, meander along the creative path for awhile. Then, when you feel you are ready to share your work with the world, I encourage you to use the listings in the *2001 Poet's Market* to submit your poems for publication. Take advantage of the finest guide available to help you get your poetry into print. Remember, you have the power to impact and change readers with your words.

Pamala Shields

poetsmarket@fwpubs.com

The "Quick-Start" Guide to Publishing Your Poetry

To make the most of *Poet's Market* you need to know how to use it. With more than 600 pages of poetry publishing markets and resources, a poet could easily get lost amidst the plethora of information. But, fear not. This "quick-start" guide will help you wind your way through the pages of *Poet's Market*, as well as the poetry publishing process, and emerge with your dream accomplished—a published poem.

1. Read, read, read.

Read numerous literary journals and poetry collections to determine if your poetry compares favorably with work currently being published. If your poems are at least the same caliber as the ones you're reading, then move on to step two. If not, postpone submitting your work and spend your time polishing your poetry. Writing and reading the work of others are the best ways to improve craft.

For help with craft and critique of your work:
- You'll find Conference & Workshop listings beginning on page 501.
- You'll find Organizations, including poetry societies, on pages 522-539.

2. Analyze your poetry.

Determine the type of poetry you write to best target your submissions to markets most suitable to your work. Do you write haiku, free verse, prose poems, sonnets; political verse, nature poetry, poems about your locale, feminist poetry? There are magazines and presses seeking specialized work in each of these areas as well as numerous others.

For editors and publishers with specialized interests:
- You'll find the Subject Index beginning on page 572.
- You'll find the Glossary of Poetic Forms and Styles on page 549, which provides definitions for the various styles and forms of poetry found in the Subject Index.
- Also, look for the ◎ symbol before listing titles in the Publishers of Poetry and Contests & Awards sections.

3. Learn about the market.

Read writing-related magazines such as *Poets & Writers*, *Writer's Digest*, *The Writer* and others for interviews with poets and fiction writers, help with various aspects of writing and publishing, and reviews of small press magazines. Also, don't forget to utilize the Internet. There are numerous online journals geared specifically toward writers.

For additional writing-related publications:
- You'll find Publications of Interest on pages 540-545.
- You'll find Websites of Interest on page 546.

4. Find markets for your work.

There are a variety of ways to locate markets for poetry. The publication sections of bookstores and libraries are great places to discover new journals and magazines that might be open to your type of poetry. Read writing-related magazines and newsletters for information about new markets and publications seeking poetry submissions. Online journals often have links to the websites of other journals that may publish poetry. And last but certainly not least, read about magazines, presses and contest markets in the listings found here in *Poet's Market*.

For poetry-publishing possibilities:
- You'll find the Publishers of Poetry section beginning on page 17.

- You'll find Contest & Award listings on pages 468-497.
- Also, don't forget to utilize the indexes at the back of this book to help you target your poems to the right market.

5. Send for guidelines.

In the listings in this book, we try to include as much submission information as we can glean from editors and publishers. Over the course of the year, however, editors' expectations and needs may change. Therefore, it is best to request submission guidelines by sending a self-addressed stamped envelope (SASE). You can also check the websites of magazines and presses which usually contain a page with guideline information.

6. Begin your publishing efforts with journals and contests open to beginners.

If this is your first attempt at publishing your work, your best bet is to begin with local publications or with publications that you know are open to beginning poets. Then, after you have built a publication history, you can try the more prestigious and nationally distributed magazines. For publications and contests most open to beginners, look for the ▢ symbol preceding listing titles.

- Check the Openness to Submissions Index, on pages 555-561, for a list of magazines, presses and contests organized according to their openness to submissions. (▢ beginners; ◪ beginners and experienced; ◉ mostly experienced, few beginners; ◎ specialized)

7. Submit your poetry in a professional manner.

Take the time to show editors that you care about your work and are serious about publishing. By following a publication's submission guidelines and practicing standard submission etiquette, you can better ensure your chances that an editor will want to take the time to read your poems and consider them for publication. Remember, first impressions last, and a carelessly assembled submission packet can jeopardize your chances before your poems have had a chance to speak for themselves.

For help with preparing submissions:
- You'll find the article How to Submit Your Poetry Successfully on page 10.
- Also, read the chapter on getting published in *The Poet's Companion: A Guide to the Pleasures of Writing Poetry* by Kim Addonizio and Dorianne Laux (W.W. Norton, 1997).

8. Keep track of your submissions.

Know when and where you have sent poems and how long you need to wait before expecting a reply. If an editor does not respond by the time indicated in his market listing or guidelines, wait a few more weeks and then follow up with a letter (and SASE) asking when the editor anticipates making a decision. If you still do not receive a reply from the editor within a reasonable amount of time, send a letter withdrawing your poems from consideration and move on to the next magazine on your list.

9. Learn from rejection.

Rejection is the hardest part of the publication process. Unfortunately, rejection happens to every writer and every writer needs to learn to deal with the negativity involved. On the other hand, rejection can be valuable when used as a teaching tool rather than a reason to doubt yourself and your work. If an editor offers suggestions with his or her rejection slip, take those comments into consideration. You don't have to automatically agree with an editor's opinion of your work. It may be that the editor has a different perspective on the piece than you do. Or, you may find that the editor's suggestions give you new insight into your work and help you improve your craft.

For more insight into how poetry editors think:
- You'll find interviews with editors Wen Stephenson (page 51), Alanna Webb (page 87), Lisa Cisero (page 104), Joe Benevento (page 178) and C. J. Morrison (page 270) in this edition of *Poet's Market*.

10. Don't give up.

The best advice for poets trying to get their poems published is to be persistent and always believe in themselves and their work. By continually reading other poets' work, constantly working on the craft of poetry and relentlessly submitting your work, you will eventually find that magazine or journal that's the perfect match for your poetry. And, *Poet's Market* will be here to help you every step of the way.

GUIDE TO LISTING FEATURES

Below you will find an example of the market listings contained in the Publishers of Poetry section. Also included are callouts identifying the various format features of the listings. (For an explanation of the symbols used, see the front and back covers of this book.)

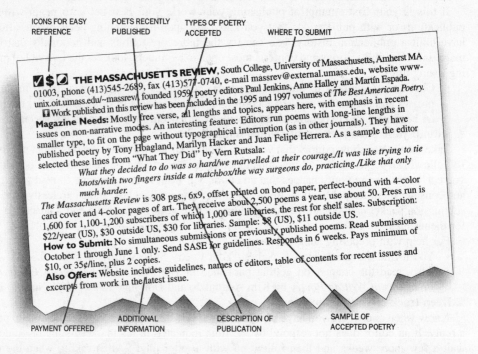

ICONS FOR EASY REFERENCE

POETS RECENTLY PUBLISHED

TYPES OF POETRY ACCEPTED

WHERE TO SUBMIT

THE MASSACHUSETTS REVIEW, South College, University of Massachusetts, Amherst MA 01003, phone (413)545-2689, fax (413)577-0740, e-mail massrev@external.umass.edu, website www-unix.oit.umass.edu/~massrev, founded 1959, poetry editors Paul Jenkins, Anne Halley and Martín Espada. Work published in this review has been included in the 1995 and 1997 volumes of *The Best American Poetry*. **Magazine Needs:** Mostly free verse, all lengths and topics, appears here, with emphasis in recent issues on non-narrative modes. An interesting feature: Editors run poems with long-line lengths in smaller type, to fit on the page without typographical interruption (as in other journals). They have published poetry by Tony Hoagland, Marilyn Hacker and Juan Felipe Herrera. As a sample the editor selected these lines from "What They Did" by Vern Rutsala:

What they decided to do was so hard/we marvelled at their courage./It was like trying to tie knots/with two fingers inside a matchbox/the way surgeons do, practicing./Like that only much harder.

The Massachusetts Review is 308 pgs., 6x9, offset printed on bond paper, perfect-bound with 4-color card cover and 4-color pages of art. They receive about 2,500 poems a year, use about 50. Press run is 1,600 for 1,100-1,200 subscribers of which 1,000 are libraries, the rest for shelf sales. Subscription: $22/year (US), $30 outside US, $30 for libraries. Sample: $8 (US), $11 outside US. **How to Submit:** No simultaneous submissions or previously published poems. Read submissions October 1 through June 1 only. Send SASE for guidelines. Responds in 6 weeks. Pays minimum of $10, or 35¢/line, plus 2 copies. **Also Offers:** Website includes guidelines, names of editors, table of contents for recent issues and excerpts from work in the latest issue.

PAYMENT OFFERED

ADDITIONAL INFORMATION

DESCRIPTION OF PUBLICATION

SAMPLE OF ACCEPTED POETRY

For More Information

If you are interested in writing for greeting card companies, *Writer's Market* (Writer's Digest Books) has a whole section dedicated to these companies, complete with contact names, addresses, phone numbers, needs and submission requirements. For poets who are also lyricists, *Songwriter's Market* (Writer's Digest Books) offers pages of opportunities in this field. Both books are available through your local library or bookstore, or can be ordered directly from the publisher by calling (800)289-0963.

The Art of Revision

BY JEFF HILLARD

Ask most poets about the beauty and depth of a poem's very first draft, and the collective answer will likely be, "What beauty, exactly?" Ask the poet if he or she is anxious to get on with revising a poem and the usual answer? A growl, or a solemn murmur, or maybe an edgy look.

Poets are not quick to revise. The first draft is always so invigorating—an oasis of creative burst—that we stare at it affectionately or else, embarrassed, we throw it away entirely. We may savor it for a few days or a week before we tinker with it; that is, if we tinker with it. There's no easy way to revise because we care too much about our "product"—the poem—to subject it to different shapes, rhythms, or word combinations. There are few key models for the practice of revision. Some of our major poets, like Elizabeth Bishop and Pablo Neruda, have left notes on what revising poems means to them. But positing a "how-to" method for revision is something poets shy away from.

Revision is an art. It is more an art and can be more creative than the first draft. It's a highly sensitive act. It could be the difference between creating a self-satisfying weak poem and a much-tweaked enthralling poem. It could be the difference between keeping a potentially terrific poem hidden forever and salvaging a weak poem by getting fruitful feedback. We poets should resolve to run toward revision rather than away from it.

Revising is a move to expand, manipulate, or congeal the original (first draft) poem. Notice I didn't use the words, "clean up grammar and mechanics of the original." I hesitate to use those words. That's not the essence of true revision. As poet Kim Addonizio suggests, it's a "*re-visioning* of the poem's potential and strategies it has used so far."

All in the attitude

Remember there is no "how-to" to a perfect revision. There's only constant exploration of what the poem can be, as Neruda says, and a final stopping point wherein you've worked as much as you can or want to on the poem. You're the gatekeeper; you're the maestro of that final stopping place. Only you can decide when the poem is polished enough and ready to submit for publication.

On the way to that decision, there are learning traits one can apply to a revision. There are useful ways to consider the task. First, think optimistically. Think of the first draft as a "feeler draft"—you're feeling your way toward what the poem might want to be. Let the poem take you where it wants to go, and so one must trust, optimistically, the whole mystery of the road ahead.

In this way, your attitude can't undertake the "I'll-only-do-one-more-draft" approach. It may take three or ten more drafts. Remain optimistic unless, after at least ten drafts, the poem is simply too daunting at this time. Then, if that's the case, put it away. (I discourage totally throwing it away; you may be able to salvage several lines for another poem. Always use what you can, any time you can, from a poem.) Come back to the poem after six months and try again.

JEFFREY HILLARD *is a poet, journalist, novelist and screenwriter who has written three books of poetry. Additionally, he is editor for* Writer Online *and is an associate professor of English at the College of Mount St. Joseph in Cincinnati, Ohio.*

With an optimistic attitude, you'll have the *pro-active* (creative) approach. You'll be thinking not about grammar but about creating a change in the poem, if necessary. The last thing on your mind should be a "cutting" (get-rid-of-poor-grammar) revision. You must always first consider its potential. It's important to realize that you can't do everything well. One of your skills such as pacing, rhyming, sound, or tone may stand out. Always capitalize on those skill strengths. Use them as widely as possible. But pay *equal* attention to weaknesses, too. Work on a weakness only *after* the strengths have permeated a draft.

If you adopt a pro-active attitude, you will be in an "exploratory mode," which is what poetry writing is about. Exploration. Discovery. This is a different approach than the one in which you resign to just "cut away" at words in the poem. A defining moment, then, in the first few drafts is this notion: revising is not about immediately reaching the ultimate, successful poem; it's about patiently exploring combinations of language *and* playing with certain elements of poetry (metaphor, imagery, form, etc.) as this particular poem calls for them.

Revising as bridge-building

Once you have the right attitude and words down on paper, then what? What if you're stuck? What if the poem doesn't mean anything yet? What if you feel it's not finished? Revising is full of "what-if's." The first order is not to worry about those things. You should not allow the appearance of a draft to alarm you. Remember—be positive. Think of one draft leading to a next, in some strange way. The number of drafts awaiting you is immaterial. The bridge (the poem) must be built.

I strongly suggest reading the poem aloud numerous times. Reading gives an authentic view of what you've accomplished so far. Even by yourself you're able to detect one strength as well as a weakness. Early on, look at individual lines. Look for flabbiness in a line. Flabbiness? If a line seems awkward, wordy, or really uninteresting, try flirting with words. For example, try removing (or adding) little words, the function words, then turn some of the prepositional phrases (*the rooms of the house*) into possessives (*the house's many rooms*), and see what happens. If this doesn't help, try to recast the ordering of words, in part or in total, to match a rhythm in other lines.

The line is the most crucial part of a poem. Know this. Remain positive about getting lines to function uniquely. Explore the way your lines appear. Try changing the length of the line, by cutting each line in half, or by doubling the length of the line, or by adding a beat or two to each line from the previous line, or by turning the draft into a prose poem (as in a whole long paragraph). Then read and listen to the poem again. Perhaps you'll find more music in these shifts. Line-lengths create different degrees of music and different expectations. They may also create or heighten tone.

Let's look at part of a poem a friend of mine wrote and revised. He worked to maximize the "movement" of the poem, i.e. the line-to-line progression. He wanted to extend one sentence as much as possible, drumming up energy and vitality from line to line. He also experimented by writing a "found poem"; a found poem is written literally using real, actual words and language from primary sources such as magazines, newspapers, brochures, and playing with that language on paper. His first draft looked like this:

> *The dove dove into the Polish soldier who, with no help*
> *from his bandage, dumped feathers, along with his hat,*
> *down a sewer. They were too close to the sewer to see*
> *the bass painted on the head of an old bass drum.*

After several revisions—one of them a very long-lined prose poem—he was still uneasy. Finally, upon his seventh draft, he realized he could draw out a sentence or two and achieve that missing energy by shortening the lines and indenting every other line. It now looks like this:

> The dove dove into the Polish soldier
>   who, with no help from his bandage,
> dumped feathers, along with his hat,
>   down a sewer. They
> were too close to the sewer
>   to see the bass
> painted on the head
>   of an old bass drum.

He wanted a more jagged, jazzy energy, and he got one in this draft. He allowed the previous six drafts to act as poetic bridge-builders, enabling him to discover the power of individual lines which came to fruition in the seventh draft. He didn't get complacent with the third or fourth drafts. He kept exploring; he dramatically changed the appearance of the poem on the page. He essentially let one draft be a bridge to the next draft.

Arriving at the true poem

The poet Elizabeth Bishop has left an enduring legacy of revising her poems. She worked tirelessly at revising and left various notes on the ways she revised. In one poem, she considered several different approaches to "arriving at the true poem" (in this case the truest line possible). Notice her sequence of revisions in just one part of her poem:

> At low tide like
> this how sheer the water is.

> At low tide
> like this
> how sheer
> the water is.

> At low tide like this how sheer
> the water is.

> At low tide like this how sheer the water is.

What worked best for her? The last example above is the actual line. Why? She did not leave a reason except to note that the "feel" of that long, almost elastic single line coincided with the mood of the speaker in the poem. Those words needed breadth, perhaps, as in a deep inhalation and then exhalation on the reader's part.

There are other ways at arriving at the true poem. For example, if the poem is meditational, as in a lyric poem, you might consider lengthening the line so that a "thought process" on the speaker's part seems to pervade the poem. Here's an example of how "thought" or consciousness might look inside longer lines:

> With soda can after empty soda can lodged deep inside
> the mouth of the rotten log, and after I cast there,
> inside the calm river pool, and waited, my shoulders jerked
> when my line snapped against the log, my hands flying off
> the reel. . . .

The speaker in this poem considers fishing as a metaphor for losing something; it could be that his bad day or week has culminated in the untimely damage to his fishing line and thus to his expectation of salvaging any goodness in a flawed day. He is meditative, and the lines seem to echo this—they are rather lengthy, mellow, and centered mainly on the workings of nature. In another revision, if the poem was geared to a more off-beat, snappy, and linguistic-type structure, without the heavy emphasis on meditation, it might look like this:

> *With soda can after*
> *empty soda can lodged*
> *deep inside*
> *the mouth*
> *of the rotten log,*
> *and after I cast*
> *there, inside the calm*
> *river pool, and waited. . . .*

This breakdown invites more linguistic pizzazz. It changes the whole mindset of the speaker, which is less meditational. The emphasis now is in fact more on the image and metaphor of the river and debris than the speaker's actual emotional state.

Only the poet knows, through experimenting, what the poem actually asks for. If, still, there is question on your part as to how far you might go in switching, shortening, or lengthening lines, feel empowered to be as radical as you'd like. Again, the poem may never be "finished." The poet Agha Shahid Ali even suggests that at times it's a good idea to look farther down in a poem and shift later lines up toward the beginning. For example, in the previous poem, you could consider this shift:

> *There, inside the calm mouth*
> *of a rotten log, where I waited*
> *with my fishing line and saw*
> *inside the deep river pool. . . .*

Does this change the context? Only experimenting with the lines will tell. The newer, immediate focus on "calm mouth/of a rotten log" is enchanting and curious, perhaps more so than soda cans. And there is a music that is derived. But Ali has an interesting point: often the poem truly starts to work, strangely enough, as the poem's middle emerges. Maybe shifting some of that energy up to the top is a good idea.

Even more startling—and adventurous—may be to reverse the entire order of a poem, sentence by sentence, and see what happens:

> *Inside the deep river pool,*
> *with my fishing line, I saw,*
> *as I waited, a rotten log*
> *whose calm mouth held*
> *soda can after empty soda can. . . .*

You never know when it's 100 percent "right"

If we abide by this dictum that we'll never know when the poem is absolutely right, then we're in danger of sometimes editing a poem far, far too much. When will it be "right"? It is a subjective call on your part. You should read it aloud numerous times, send it around to friends, listen to feedback from a writing group, and attend as much as possible to what the poem wants to express. After a set period—perhaps six weeks to six months, to give yourself a span of time—consider it finished at least for the moment.

Within this period of time, a new line or new image may crop up and want to enter the poem. This will happen. Be prepared. Dig out the poem. Add the line(s) and image(s). Don't be afraid to do so. The poem is never quite 100 percent right. This does not mean it's a failed poem to begin with. It only means that a new insight into the poem has arisen. You follow your instinct, always. The only so-called rule for realizing a poem's readiness may be the notion that the poem provides a truthful satisfaction to the writer. You're satisfied with the real work you've put into the whole process of exploring the poem.

Recently, the poet C.K. Williams won the Pulitzer Prize for Poetry (2000). A student once said to Williams, whose anecdotal poems have a conversational feel about them, "These poems must've been easy to write." Williams replied that "this particular poem took him over a year to write, and it went through over a hundred draftings."

Often this is the case with the poem that reads marvelously on the page. It never comes out that way at first on the page. One hundred drafts? That's an ungodly amount. For the novice poet, take Williams' reply seriously, in terms of the need to pay attention to a poem, but you might succeed with far, far fewer than one hundred drafts.

As long as you remember that the word "poem" derives from the Greek *poesy*, you'll know that the poem is, by definition, a "made thing." We know, too, that when something is made, the process can often be mysterious and exciting. When cooking, for instance, it's not unusual to take liberties with a recipe: more ingredients, perhaps more cooking time, more flavoring. The same is true with a poem; you may change your mind about the original poem you write in order to add more "flavoring" (more lines, less lines, more sound, etc.) Flavor the poem to sweeten the taste.

How to Submit Your Poetry Successfully

BY CHANTELLE BENTLEY

If you're a beginning poet who has yet to submit work or a veteran poet who needs a refresher course on submission procedures, this article provides the basic information you'll need to successfully submit your poetry for publication.

Before we begin discussing how to prepare poems for submission, however, determine where you want to send your work. The "Quick-Start" Guide to Publishing Your Poetry, on page 2, provides beginning poets with ways to determine if their poetry is ready for submission and ideas on how to locate suitable markets. Experienced poets should utilize the six indexes at the back of this book or go straight to the listings to find their most promising markets. In either situation, our new Openness to Submissions Index, which lists magazines, presses and contests according to their openness to unsolicited manuscripts, will make your search for markets easier by quickly identifying those markets who are open to beginners and those markets who want only experienced poets.

Once you've decided where to send your work, you can then focus on proper presentation. In the following pages, you will find specifics about approaching magazines and presses, formatting poetry manuscripts, selling the rights to your work and preparing cover letters. You'll also find suggestions about what to do if you don't receive a reply from an editor about work submitted.

Reading and following these guidelines should help you decrease the occurrence of common submission mistakes as well as increase the number of acceptance letters flowing into your mailbox.

Approaching magazine markets

If you are submitting work to a quarterly newsletter, an online magazine or an annual poetry journal, poetry editors are primarily interested in seeing how you write. Therefore, a query letter is not necessary, but a sample of your work is. Usually three to five poems with a cover letter and self-addressed stamped envelope (SASE) is preferred by most editors.

Occasionally, editors will require poets to submit in a manner other than the traditional method just mentioned. Because of this, *Poet's Market*'s Publishers of Poetry section provides the most essential submission information in its listings. Also, it's a good idea to obtain writer's guidelines by sending a SASE or visiting a magazine's website prior to submitting.

In general, agents are not needed to submit poetry to magazines. Most agents do not handle poetry because it simply does not pay. (It's hard for an agent to earn commission when a poet is paid in contributor's copies.) And because the majority of book publishers who accept unsolicited poetry are small presses—paying a small honorarium or a percentage of the print run—poets are also best to handle their own book submissions, too.

Approaching book publishers

When submitting a full-length poetry manuscript for possible publication, most editors want to first receive a query with a few sample poems and a cover letter with brief bio and publication credits. However, there are those editors who prefer to receive the complete manuscript, especially if the editor publishes chapbooks and not full-length collections. (See the discussion of chapbook publishing on page 15 of this article.)

As with approaching magazines, the best route to take when preparing to submit a manuscript to a book publisher is to send a SASE for complete guidelines or visit the publisher's website.

Proper submission format for poetry manuscripts

For the most part, a standard format exists for poetry manuscript submissions. However, as we've previously mentioned, some editors' submission guidelines deviate from the norm. For those editors, we state their submission preferences within their listings. For all others, the following list will provide you with the information needed for presenting a professional manuscript. When in doubt, however, send a SASE to the journal or press and request their writer's guidelines or check their website. To receive information from publishers outside your own country, send a self-addressed envelope (SAE) with an International Reply Coupon (IRC).

For magazine submissions:
- Submit only three to five poems at one time, positioning your best poems on top. Most editors don't have time to read more than five poems but less than three doesn't provide them with a large enough sample of your work.
- Type or print (in a legible font, e.g., Times New Roman) one poem to a page, single-spaced with double spacing between stanzas. (The only exception here may be for haiku.) Leave at least a one-inch margin on all sides of the page. *Avoid handwriting your work.*
- Use white, 8½ × 11 bond paper, preferably 16 or 20 lb. weight. The paper should be heavy enough to withstand handling by several people.
- Include your name, address, phone number and e-mail address on separate lines, single-spaced, in the upper left or right corner of each poem. (If you write under a pseudonym, you must still use your legal name here.)
- The title of your poem should appear in all caps or initial caps about six lines underneath your contact information, centered or flush left. The poem should begin one line beneath the title.
- If a poem does carry over to a second sheet, list your name in the top left margin. Underneath your name include a key word from the poem's title, the page number and information on whether the lines at the top are a continuation of the same stanza or the start of a new one (e.g., SILENCE, page 2, continue stanza or begin new stanza).

For book submissions:
- When submitting a poetry collection to a book publisher, it's best to request guidelines, because press requirements vary from a query letter with a few sample poems to the entire manuscript.
- Use a separate cover sheet for your name, address, phone number and e-mail address. Center your book title and byline about halfway down the page. Then include your last name and page number in the top left margin of the first and each subsequent manuscript page.
- If a poem, or poems, in your collection carries over to a second sheet, remember to follow the instructions from the sixth bullet of **For magazine submissions** above.

For both magazine and book submissions:
- Proofread carefully. Even the shortest poem can contain typos that elude the eye of the poet all too familiar with the lines in front of her. Also, an occasional white-out is okay, but retype (or correct and reprint) poems with numerous typos.
- Fold manuscript, five pages and under, neatly into thirds (do not fold poems individually) and mail in a business-size (#10, 4⅛ × 9½) envelope. For a manuscript over five pages, fold in half and mail in a 6 × 9 envelope. Larger manuscripts will look best mailed flat in 9 × 12 or 10 × 13 envelopes.
- To ensure a response to your submission, you must enclose a SASE (or SAE and IRCs). You can use either a #9 (4 × 9) reply envelope or a #10 business-size envelope (fold into thirds if you are also using a #10 envelope to mail your manuscript).
- To have your manuscript returned, enclose a SASE the same size as the mailing envelope

with the same amount of postage. Another option is to send a disposable manuscript. However, you must tell the editor the manuscript is disposable and the SASE you've provided is for reply only. (NOTE: One IRC is needed for one ounce by surface mail or each half-ounce by airmail. And, three pages of poetry, a cover letter and a SASE can usually be mailed for one first-class stamp. The website, http://www.usps.gov/business/calcs.htm, calculates postage for both domestic and international destinations.)

Before sending disk or e-mail submissions . . .

- Verify that the editor accepts electronic submissions. You will find a list of publications and presses open to e-mail submissions on page 547 of this book. Also, openness to fax, disk or e-mail submissions is usually noted in market listings or in writer's guidelines.
- Check market listings or writer's guidelines for specific instructions for electronic submissions, including the format in which editors prefer to receive electronic submissions (i.e., MS Word, Word Perfect, ASCII, etc.).
- Always include a printed copy with any disk submission. For e-mail submissions, it's usually best to include poems in the body of the message rather than including them as an attachment.

Concerning rights

The Copyright Law states that writers selling to magazines are primarily offering one-time rights to their work—that is, the editor or publisher may only publish your poem once—unless you and the publisher agree otherwise (in writing). Therefore, if an editor requests something different, such as the right to also later publish the work in a retrospective anthology, and you are open to such an agreement, make sure the agreement is documented.

Following is a list of various rights. Be sure you know exactly what rights you are selling before you agree to the sale. For more information on rights, refer to the revised edition of *The Writer's Legal Guide* (Allworth Press, 1998).

- **Copyright** is the legal right to exclusive publication, sale or distribution of a literary work. Since the most recent Copyright Law went into effect in 1978, your "original works of authorship" are protected as soon as they are "fixed in a tangible form of expression." As the writer or creator of a written work, you can also include your name, date and the copyright symbol (©) on your poem to establish copyright. However, copyright notices are typically considered unnecessary and, in many editors' minds, signal the work of amateurs who are distrustful of editors and publishers. If you wish, you can register your copyright with the Copyright Office for a $20 fee. If paying $20 to register each of your poems is not feasible, you can register a group of poems with one form under one title for one $20 fee.

Obtain more information about copyright from the U.S. Copyright Office, Library of Congress, 101 Independence Ave. SE, Washington DC 20559. For answers to specific questions (but not legal advice), call the Copyright Public Information Office at (202)707-3000 weekdays between 8:30 a.m. and 5:00 p.m. (EST). Copyright forms can also be ordered at that same number or downloaded from the Library of Congress website at http://lcweb.loc.gov/copyright. The website also includes information on filling out the forms, general copyright information and links to copyright-related websites.

- **First Rights (a.k.a. First Serial Rights)**—This means the poet offers a journal or magazine the right to publish the poem for the first time in any periodical. All other rights to the material remain with the writer. It's important to note that first North American serial rights means the editor will be the first to publish your work in a U.S. or Canadian periodical. Your work can still be submitted to editors outside North America, or those open to reprint rights.

• **One-time Rights**—A periodical licensing one-time rights to a work (also known as simultaneous rights) buys the *nonexclusive* rights to publish the work once. That is, there is nothing to stop the poet from submitting the work to other publications at the same time. Simultaneous submissions would typically be to periodicals without overlapping audiences.

• **Second Serial (Reprint) Rights**—Editors and publishers seeking reprint rights are open to submissions of previously published work—provided you tell them when and where the work was previously published so they can properly credit the periodical in which your work first appeared. You'll notice many poetry collections list such "credits," often on the copyright page. In essence, they've acquired reprint rights.

• **All Rights**—Some publishers require poets to relinquish all rights, which means you cannot submit that particular work for publication anywhere else—not even as part of your own collection—unless you negotiate to get reprint rights returned to you. Before you agree to this type of arrangement, ask the editor whether he is willing to buy first rights instead of all rights. If not, you can simply write a letter withdrawing your work from consideration. Also, some editors will reassign rights to a writer after a given time, such as one year.

• **Electronic Rights**—These rights cover usage in a broad range of electronic media, from online magazines and databases to CD-ROM magazine anthologies and interactive games. The editor should specify in writing if—and which—electronic rights are being requested. The presumption is that unspecified rights are kept by the writer.

Because the issue of rights is so important, almost all editors and publishers will state (in their market listing or guidelines) what rights they acquire. And once your work is accepted for publication, a number of editors and publishers will ask you to sign an agreement which not only tells you what rights are being requested, but also asks you to certify that the poetry is your own.

Including a cover letter

Though the issue of cover letters is far less serious in nature than selling rights, poets still must determine the appropriateness of including cover letters with their submissions. Some experts in the field say cover letters are unnecessary and may even impede the publication process. And a few editors agree a cover letter has never caused them to accept or reject a manuscript. However, many editors indicate a desire for cover letters in their market listings and submission guidelines.

If you do include a cover letter with your poems, the following tips will help you compose a professional letter that allows you to personally present your work to editors.

☑ Keep it brief. Your cover letter should be no more than one page.

☑ Include your name, address, phone number and e-mail address.

☑ If an editor wants biographical information for the magazine's contributors page, add two to three lines about your job, interests, why you write poetry, etc. Editors like to know there are real people behind the submissions.

☑ Avoid praising your work in a cover letter. Let your poems speak for themselves.

☑ Include the titles (or first lines) of the poems you are submitting.

☑ Include a few (no more than five) of your most recent publishing credits. If you haven't published a poem yet, either note that you have no prior credits, don't mention publication credits at all, or don't include a cover letter (unless a cover letter is required, of course). Be aware that some editors are particularly interested in new writers and make special efforts to publish beginners' work.

☑ Demonstrate some familiarity with the magazine to which you're submitting: comment on a poem in the magazine you enjoyed, tell the editor why you chose to submit to their publication, give your opinion of the magazine. More than anything, editors like to know their contributors are also their readers.

☑ Address your submission to the correct contact person. Most of the publications and presses in this directory have a particular individual to whom you should direct your submissions. If no one is listed, however, check the publication's guidelines or the masthead of a recent copy. If you are still unable to locate a specific name, simply address your letter to "Poetry Editor."

☑ Use an acceptable business-style format for your letter and make sure it is error free.

☑ Keep in mind that editors are people, too. Be brief and professional, but also personable, in your cover letter. Remember, kindness goes a long way.

Waiting for a reply

Most editors and publishers indicate (in their market listings and submission guidelines) approximately how long you must wait before you can expect to receive a reply about your submission. If an editor does not specify when you will receive a report, it is generally expected to be within three months. Many times, however, the approximate date (or three-month benchmark) will come and go without a word from the editor or publisher.

What should you do when you haven't heard from an editor within the specified time period?

1. Wait another month, then send a note inquiring about the status of your submission. Note the titles of your poems and the date sent. Ask when the editor will be making a decision. Enclose a SASE or self-addressed, stamped postcard for the editor's reply.
2. If you still do not hear from the market, send a letter or postcard withdrawing your poems from consideration. Then submit your work elsewhere.
3. If you are desperate to learn the status of your submission, you may contact an editor by phone but keep the call brief and to the point. Remember, not only is time a valuable commodity for poets eager to get published, but also for those editors who divide their time between publishing a magazine, working full-time and maintaining family obligations.

Submitting previously published poems and simultaneous submissions

When you submit your poetry to magazine editors and publishers, they not only assume the work is original (that it is yours and nobody else's), but they also assume the work has not been previously published and is not under consideration elsewhere. Before submitting a poem that has already been published or simultaneously submitting work to more than one magazine, consider the following guidelines:

- Check market listings or submission guidelines to see if an editor or publisher is willing to consider previously published poems. Some editors are simply not open to such submissions. They want to be the first to publish new work—not the second. These editors are looking to acquire first rights to your poetry—not reprint rights.
- If an editor is open to previously published work, note in your cover letter where the particular poem(s) first appeared.
- In listings and guidelines, editors should also note their preferences in regard to simultaneous submissions (i.e., sending the same package of poems to several editors at the same

time). Most poets who engage in this practice believe a batch of three to five poems submitted to two or more editors has a better chance of resulting in acceptance.

- If you choose to submit your work simultaneously and an editor accepts one of your poems, you must contact the other editor(s) immediately and withdraw your work from consideration. Be mindful that this may annoy (or even anger) the other editor(s) still in the process of making a decision. And future submissions to these markets may no longer be welcome.
- Again, even if an editor is open to simultaneous submissions, note in your cover letter that you are simultaneously submitting your work.
- If you're just beginning to submit your work or are still perfecting your craft, you are likely to quickly collect numerous rejections by simultaneously submitting your work. That can be discouraging. You may want to avoid the shortcut and submit to publications one at a time. Then you can use any rejections received to hone your craft and improve your poem before sending it on to the next editor.

Publishing a collection of poems

Once you have gathered a fair number of publication credits in literary or small press magazines, you may want to begin thinking about book publication. Book publishers, by the way, expect some of the poems in your manuscript to be previously published. And, knowing the difficulty poets face in placing a collection, they are more accepting of the practice of simultaneous submissions. Often, publishing a chapbook is a good middle step between publishing in magazines and publishing a full-length book collection.

What is a chapbook?

A chapbook is a small volume of work, usually under 50 pages in length. As such a volume is less expensive to produce than a full-length book collection (which may range from 50 to over 100 pages), a chapbook is a safe way for a publisher to take a chance on a lesser-known poet. Most chapbooks are saddle-stapled with card covers. Some are photocopied publications. Others contain professionally printed pages. While chapbooks are seldom noted by reviewers or carried by bookstores, they are good items to sell after readings or through the mail. You'll discover that, in addition to some book publishers, a number of magazine publishers also publish chapbooks (for a complete list, refer to the Chapbook Publishers Index on page 551).

Whether you're planning to submit your work to either chapbook or book publishers, you should always examine sample copies of their previously published collections. This is not only the best way to familiarize yourself with the press's offerings, but also a good way to determine the quality of the product.

Publishing contracts for book manuscripts

Various publishing arrangements exist and greatly depend on the publisher with which you are dealing. Some, in fact, are more beneficial than others. Consider the following options carefully:

- **Standard publishing**—In a standard publishing contract, the publisher usually agrees to assume all production and promotion costs for your book. You receive a 10% royalty on the retail (or sometimes wholesale) price, though with some small presses you are paid a percentage of the press run instead. Such publishers only release a few poetry volumes each year.
- **Cooperative publishing**—This arrangement is exactly that: cooperative. Although the details of such contracts vary, they require some type of investment of either time or money on your part. Some require involvement in marketing. Others specify money for production costs. In any case, know what you're signing. While cooperative publishing is respected in the literary and small press world (and many such publishers can bring your work the attention it deserves), some vanity presses try to label themselves as "cooperative." True cooperative publishing, however, shares both the risks and the profits.

- **Self-publishing**—This option may be most appealing if your goal is to publish a small collection of your work to distribute at readings or to give to family and friends. It is also a good choice for those who prefer complete control over the creative process. In this scenario, you work hand-in-hand with a local printer and invent a name for your "press." Most importantly, you pay all the costs but own all the books and net all the proceeds from any sales (which you must generate). For details, read *The Complete Guide to Self-Publishing* by Tom and Marilyn Ross (Writer's Digest Books).
- **Vanity/subsidy presses**—This is probably the least desirable option. Companies in this category usually advertise for manuscripts, lavishly praise your work, and ask for fees far in excess of costs (compare their figures to those of a local printer for a book of similar size, format and binding). These companies also make a habit of collectively advertising their books. That is, your work will simply receive a line along with 20 or so other books in an ad placed in the general media rather than a specific market. Worse yet, sometimes you own all copies of your book; sometimes you don't.

It's important to note that some anthology publications fall under "vanity/subsidy" publishing because you must pay a tidy sum to purchase the volume containing your work. If you have concerns about a particular publisher call the Poets & Writers Information Center at (212)226-3586. Calls are welcome weekdays from 11 a.m. to 3 p.m. (EST).

Tracking submissions

Once you begin submitting individual poems or manuscripts, you'll need to keep a record of all poetry submissions and correspondence with editors.

To track which poems you have submitted and where and when you submitted them, you should record such information as the title of each poem, the name of the magazine to which it was submitted, and the date your work was mailed. Also, note the date of each editor's reply, the outcome of your efforts, and any comments that may prove useful when you're next submitting to that market (such as changes in editors, reading periods or frequency of publication).

Keep current on changes and opportunities in poetry publishing

New markets are established all the time. Therefore, to keep up-to-date with new literary journals and small presses in between the yearly editions of *Poet's Market*, read such publications as *Poets & Writers Magazine* or *Writer's Digest*, both of which regularly contain information about new markets. Also, check out the Web, including our website www.writersdigest.com. Many websites for writers exist that list electronic and print publications seeking submissions. These websites may also provide direct links to those publications. (See Websites of Interest, on page 546, for a list of websites for poets seeking publication.)

The Markets

Publishers of Poetry

Containing everything from stapled newsletters published by individuals in kitchen-corner offices to perfect-bound, paperback collections produced in large suites by paid staffs, this section of *Poet's Market* provides a comprehensive look at those publishers listed within its nearly 500 pages. All the activities a publisher may conduct—whether it's publishing a quarterly magazine, maintaining a website, sponsoring a contest, or offering writing workshops—are represented within one listing to give you an overview of the publisher's operations. And for those few publishers with projects at different addresses, we've cross-referenced the listings so you still may be aware of all of a publisher's involvements.

Evaluating these publishers to determine which is right for you and your work is not an easy task—and, because our tastes and interests may differ from yours, this is something we cannot do for you. However, learning all you can about publishers and their operations is a huge step on the road toward publication. Therefore, within the following listings, we provide you with as much information as we can glean from editors and publishers—specialized interests, contact names, submission requirements, payment policies, awards received, etc.

To make the information you seek accessible and easy to locate, we include subheads using key terms in the listings to help you readily identify the type of information provided within a particular paragraph. For example, the subhead **Magazine Needs** indicates information about the type of poetry sought by a magazine or journal, a physical description of the publication and the amount of poetry received versus the amount of poetry published each year; the subhead **How to Submit** includes the magazine's submission requirements, reporting times and payment policies. For book publishers, the subheads **Book/Chapbook Needs** and **How to Submit** are used to separate their editorial needs and submission requirements. Sometimes, for very brief listings or for a listing with more than one magazine or book publishing operation, the subheads will be combined into one subhead (e.g., **Magazine Needs & How to Submit** or **Book/Chapbook Needs & How to Submit**).

The **Also Offers** subhead indicates information about contests, conferences, workshops, readings or organizations a publisher may either sponsor or be associated with. If a magazine also maintains a website, the contents of that website are noted under this subhead.

We believe letting editors speak for themselves is an excellent way for you to get an inside look at how a particular editor thinks or works. So, under the **Advice** subhead, most listings contain quotes from editors and publishers on their publishing philosophies, what types of poetry particularly interest them, any pet peeves or recurring problems they have in regard to submissions, or advice they have for poets about the poetry field or the submission process in general. You can learn much about publishers by what they choose to include in these brief statements. But, for even more insight into what makes publishers tick, read the editorial introductions included in most publications. Many editors use these first few pages of their journals to let readers know why they do what they do and exactly what kind of work they want.

LOCATE YOUR PERFECT MARKETS

The best way to approach this rather large section of information depends on what you are seeking. If you do not have a specific publisher in mind, dive right in and start reading through the listings. This will give you a good idea of what publishing opportunities are available and what types of markets exist.

However, if you are looking for a particular market, begin with the General Index. Let's say, for example, you've recently written a poem inspired by your experiences as a home healthcare nurse and you think a likely market for the poem might be *the Compleat Nurse.* You won't find *the Compleat Nurse* in this section alphabetized under C, however. The editor requested the listing be under the name of the publisher of the magazine, Dry Bones Press, and that's where you will find it. You might not have discovered that without looking in the General Index, where *the Compleat Nurse* is cross-referenced to Dry Bones Press.

The General Index also contains the names of publishers from the 2000 edition who are not included in this edition and, if known, the reasons for their absence. It also provides a way to find publishers who have changed names: though you will find a publication listed in this section under its new name, you can still find the previous name with the appropriate cross-reference in the General Index.

The Publishers of Poetry section contains 1,800 poetry publishing markets, includes 10 "Insider" interviews with editors and poets and showcases the covers of 10 diverse publications. Also worthy of mention are the roughly 300 new markets included in this edition—especially considering that new listings are often more receptive to submissions.

DISCOVER NEW LISTINGS

To locate this year's new listings, look for the new listing symbol (N) preceding the listing titles. As in years past, some new listings are publications that were in earlier editions of *Poet's Market* but not the previous one. We're happy to welcome back, for example, The Ashland Poetry Press, *The Blind Horse Review, Carnegie Mellon Magazine, The Kenyon Review,* Maypole Editions (from England), *The Pegasus Review, Xavier Review* and *Washington Review.*

Other listings new to this edition are actually "new," that is, they are magazines or presses that began publishing in the last few years. These include *Able Muse, Clay Palm Review, English Studies Forum* (online publication), *The Harlem Review, The Magnolia Quarterly, Slide* and *Red River Review* (online publication). Also new to this edition are Calypso Publications, a chapbook and anthology publisher; Piano Press, a chapbook publisher; Headlock Press, which publishes four to five paperbacks per year; and Rowan Books, which publishes two paperbacks per year from emerging Western Canadian poets.

We would also like to welcome some of the new listings from outside the United States, including *brown-bag lunch magazine* and *Rabbit Hole Press,* based in Canada; *Cyber Literature,* and *Kavya Bharati,* both published in India; *Lithuanian Papers,* from Australia; *Micropress New Zealand,* from New Zealand; *Muuna Takeena,* from Finland; *Offerta Speciale,* from Italy; and *Writing Ulster,* from Northern Ireland.

To quickly find those markets located outside the United States, look for the maple leaf symbol (■) before the titles of all listings from Canada and a globe symbol (●) before all international listings.

REFINE YOUR SEARCH FOR LOCAL AND SPECIALIZED MARKETS

One of the best ways for most poets to become a part of the literary scene is to start in their home territory. Therefore the Geographical Index, located in the back of this book, will quickly lead you to publishers with whom you have a lot in common because of either the state, region or country in which you currently live or from which you originate.

And to help poets with ties outside the United States more easily locate potential markets, we post listings from Australia, Canada, France, Japan and the United Kingdom under their own category heads in the Geographical Index. In addition, a variety of unrelated international listings are included under the category Other Countries.

For those who write specialized poetry—pertaining to a particular group or subject or poetry written in a particular form—refer to the Subject Index. This index lists publishers according to their specialties. For instance, under the heading Women/Feminism you will find a list of publishers who seek poetry written by women or focusing on issues of interest to women. Under the heading Form/Style you'll find publishers who want haiku as well as those who seek sonnets or experimental work.

DEFINE YOUR STYLE

Besides locating the publications whose interests match yours, you need to be sure your understanding of the subject matter and the editor's are the same. So, to help you be right on target with your submissions, we include a Glossary of Poetic Forms and Styles. This glossary defines the specific poetic forms and styles publishers are seeking. We have concentrated on providing definitions for those forms appearing most frequently in the Subject Index under the heading Forms/Styles. However, we have also provided definitions for many other forms not listed in the Subject Index, especially the less-known forms. For a more comprehensive list of terms, see *The Poetry Dictionary* by John Drury (Story Press, 1995) or the Glossary in *You Can Write Poetry* by Jeff Mock (Writer's Digest Books, 1998).

For any terms and abbreviations in the listings with which you are not familiar, see the Glossary of Listing Terms which follows the Glossary of Poetic Forms and Styles at the back of this book.

KEEP AN EYE ON THE DETAILS

Once you have selected the markets you feel match your interests and style, you must pay attention to submission details if you want your poetry to be given serious consideration. While a number of practices are considered standard, more and more editors are opting for variations. Thus, each year we ask editors and publishers to not only update the general information within their listings (such as reporting times and payment policies) but also to clarify specific submission details. (For a detailed discussion on preparing submissions, see *Poet's Guide: How to Publish and Perform Your Work* by Michael J. Bugeja [Story Line Press, 1995].)

For example, it is important to know if and when editors publish theme issues. While some editors develop all their issues around themes (see the Themes heading in the Subject Index for a list of these types of publications contained in *Poet's Market*), others only publish one or two theme issues a year (or even every few years). Of course, whenever an editor is reading for a theme issue, that's the type of work he or she wants to receive. If you send unrelated work, even if the editor does not normally publish theme-based material, your work will not be considered.

Once again we specifically asked editors to supply details about their upcoming themes and related deadlines. Though a number of editors were able to provide this information for 2001, many had not yet finalized their plans when we contacted them. To be sure your submission will be welcome, send a self-addressed, stamped envelope (SASE) to receive up-to-date information about themes, deadlines, and other submission guidelines.

For immediate identification of important changes to the contact information in *Poet's Market* listings, look for a check mark symbol (☑) preceding a listing's title. This symbol indicates a change in address, phone number, e-mail address or contact name from last year's edition. The dollar sign symbol (**$**) points out listings that pay a monetary amount, even if that amount is only $1. Editors also advertise contact information changes, upcoming themes and deadlines in the pages of such periodicals as *Writer's Digest, The Writer* and *Poets & Writers Magazine.* Checking these publications frequently, as well as the Market of the Day section of the Writer's Digest website (www.writersdigest.com), will keep you current on submission needs.

SNAIL MAIL VERSUS E-MAIL

As you read the listings in this section—and we encourage you to review them all—you will notice an increasing amount of fax numbers and e-mail addresses. Be careful when contacting editors by these methods. While some actually encourage electronic submissions, most still prefer manuscripts be sent via regular mail with SASEs for reply or the return of your work. Many editors simply supply fax numbers and e-mail addresses to facilitate requests for guidelines or other information.

Determining the best method for submitting your work is tricky but critical, especially because submitting material in an undesired manner may jeopardize your chances of receiving a response or even being read. Within the listings themselves, we have noted preferences for and against electronic submissions. If a listing includes a fax number or e-mail address but does not state their submission preference, or requires a reading fee, the best method is to contact the publisher before submitting your poems to verify if an e-mail or fax submission is acceptable.

To further eliminate some of the guess work, a list of those markets open to e-mail submissions appears at the end of our Websites of Interest to Poets section at the back of this book. Also, we use the computer symbol (■) to indicate online or electronic market listings. The appearance of this symbol before a listing's title should be a strong indicator of the editor's or publisher's openness to e-mail submissions.

DON'T FORGET THE REPLY ENVELOPE

For those listings not connected to the electronic world or for those requiring submissions be sent through the post, a reply envelope is, with few exceptions, an absolute necessity. Many publishers run their operations on shoe-string budgets and cannot afford to reply to every submission, query or request for information received. Including a SASE or SAE (self-addressed envelope) and IRCs (International Reply Coupons, for replies from countries outside your own) with all correspondence provides an easy way for overworked and underpaid editors to contact you.

And remember, if you want your manuscript returned, you must provide a SASE (or SAE and IRCs) large enough to contain your work and with sufficient postage. If it takes three stamps to mail material, it will take three stamps for the material to be returned—unless you are sending a disposable manuscript. But if you do not want your poems returned to you (that is, the manuscript can be discarded), the editor needs to be told the SASE is only for his or her response.

It's not surprising that editors, frustrated with receiving more and more manuscripts without SASEs, are creating policies in regard to such submissions. Many choose to include disclaimers stating that submissions without SASEs will not be acknowledged. However, some editors are not so kind; they discard submissions without SASEs before the material is even read. Other editors may require a minimal reading fee to cover postage costs. To get past this stickiest of spots in the poet/editor relationship, make a habit of sending a SASE (or SAE and IRCs) with all correspondence. Also, to make sure you are following other expected submission procedures, read (or reread) How to Submit Your Poetry Successfully on page 10.

AWARDS AND HONORS

As another way of helping you evaluate publishers, we have also included information about awards and honors that have been bestowed on editors and publishers or their magazines and books. For instance, we continue to note which publications have had poetry selected for inclusion in recent volumes of *The Best American Poetry*, an annual anthology highlighting the best poetry published in periodicals during the previous year. (This information will be set off by the trophy symbol (🏆), which indicates award-winning market listings, near the beginning of the listing). As a different guest editor compiles the anthology every year, knowing which publications have work included, especially in a number of recent volumes, can provide insight into the type and quality of material used.

In addition, *The Best American Poetry* (published by Scribner, 1230 Avenue of the Americas, New York NY 10020, 800/223-2348) can help you develop a sense for trends in the field. The 2000 volume, by the way, is published at the same time as this edition of *Poet's Market*. So, when you are ready to read the poetry that has been selected from the publications listed here, check your nearest library or bookstore.

UNDERSTAND OPENNESS TO SUBMISSIONS SYMBOLS

Finally, all listings in this section include one or more "openness" symbols preceding their titles. These symbols, selected by editors and publishers, can help you determine the most appropriate markets for your poetry. (For details see The "Quick-Start" Guide to Publishing Your Poetry on page 2.) The openness to submissions symbols and their explanations are:

- ○ **Publisher encourages beginning or unpublished poets to submit work for consideration and publishes new poets regularly.**
- ◔ **Publisher accepts quality work by beginning and established poets.**
- ◑ **Publisher seeks mostly experienced poets with previous publication credits, very few new poets; does not encourage beginners.**
- ◎ **Specialized publication encourages poets from a specific geographical area, age-group, gender, sexual orientation or ethnic background or accepts poems in specific forms or on specific themes.**
- ⦸ **Closed to unsolicited manuscripts.**

◑ **A SMALL GARLIC PRESS (ASGP); AGNIESZKA'S DOWRY (AGD)**, 5445 Sheridan #3003, Chicago IL 60640, e-mail asgp@enteract.com or marek@enteract.com or ketzle@aa.net, website www.enteract.com/~asgp/, founded 1995, co-editors Marek Lugowski, katrina grace craig.
Magazine Needs: *Agnieszka's Dowry (AgD)*, is "a magazine published both in print and as a permanent Internet installation of poems and graphics, letters to Agnieszka, and a navigation in an interesting space, all conducive to fast and comfortable reading. No restrictions on form or type. We use contextual and juxtapositional tie-ins with other material in making choices, so visiting the online *AgD* is assumed to be part of any submission." Single copy: usually $3. Make checks payable to A Small Garlic Press.
How to Submit: Submit 5-10 poems at a time. E-mail submissions strongly preferred—plain text only. "Please inform us of the status of publishing rights." Sometimes comments on rejections. Guidelines can be obtained via website. Responds online usually in 2 months. Pays 1 copy. Acquires one-time rights where applicable.
Book/Chapbook Needs & How to Submit: A Small Garlic Press (ASGP) publishes 2-7 chapbooks of poetry/year. Query with a full ms, ASCII (plain text) only.
Also Offers: "See our webpage for policies and submission guidelines. The press catalog and page of links to other markets and resources for poetry and a Broadsides section are maintained online at our website. Chat and other features are expected soon."

🌐 ◑ **AABYE; AABYE'S BABY**, 20 Werneth Ave., Gee Cross, Hyde, Cheshire SK14 5NL United Kingdom, e-mail newhope@iname.com, website www.nhi.clara.net/nhihome.htm, founded 1969 as Headland, 1980 as New Hope International, 1998 as Aabye, editor Gerald England.
Magazine Needs: *Aabye* publishes all types of poetry from traditional to avant-garde, from haiku to long poems, including collaborative poetry, translations (usually with the original), long poems, short poems, prose poems, haiku, englynion. They have published poetry by David Cobb, Graham High, Kona McPhee, Rochelle Hope Mehr, Frances Nagle and Lucien Stryk. As a sample the editor selected these lines from "On Perennial Gardens: Rocks and Holes" by Kenneth D. Smith:

> *A potted rose can survive/At least a season or two/Without a garden./But a rock without its hole,/Or*
> *a hole without its rock,/Or a perennial garden without both/Does not exist.*

Aabye is 52 pgs., digest-sized, printed offset-litho from computer typesetting, saddle-stapled, with glossy cover using color artwork. Press run is 500 for 200 subscribers of which 20 are libraries. Subscription: £10 (£13 non-

UK)/3 issues. Sample: £3.75 (£5 non-UK). Make checks payable to Gerald England. "Non-sterling cheques not accepted. Payment by International Giro (available from Post Offices worldwide), or currency notes to the sterling equivalent preferred."

How to Submit: Submit up to 6 poems at a time on separate sheets; put name and address on each sheet. Include SASE (or SAE with IRCs) or submissions will not be considered. No simultaneous submissions. Cover letter required. Translations should include copy of original. "If you do not require the ms returned (and disposable mss are preferred, especially from overseas) please advise, but do note that an SAE or IRC is still required for reply." No e-mail submissions, "except by prior arrangement." Send SASE (or SAE with IRCs) or e-mail for guidelines. Responds usually within 1 month. Always sends prepublication galleys. Pays 1 copy. Acquires first British serial rights.

Book/Chapbook Needs & How to Submit: "Only writers with a body of work already published in periodicals should consider approaching us. Always query before submitting."

Also Offers: Website (www.nhi.clara.net/nhihome.htm) includes guidelines, information on books and magazines available for sale, samples of poetry published by *New Hope International* and links to other sites. A separate website (www.nhi.clara.net/online.htm) publishes reviews of books, magazines, audio material, PC software, videos of interest to all lovers of words, arts and music. All books sent are considered for review. The associated website *Aabye's Baby* (www.aabyesbaby.ukpoets.net) publishes poetry only electronically. Its content differs entirely from that published in the printed magazine *Aabye*. Poems not selected for *Aabye* may be considered for *Aabye's Baby*. Contributors should indicate when submitting whether or not they wish their work to be considered for the website.

Advice: "Long lists of previous publications do not impress; perceptive, interesting, fresh writing indicative of a live, thinking person makes this job worthwhile."

✓ ▢ ◗ ◯ ◎ **THE AARDVARK ADVENTURER; THE ARMCHAIR AESTHETE; PICKLE GAS PRESS (Specialized: humor),** 31 Rollins Meadows Way, Penfield NY 14526, phone (716)388-6968, e-mail bypaul@netacc.net, website www.geocities.com/SoHo/Museum/1499/, founded 1996, editor Paul Agosto.

Magazine Needs: *The Aardvark Adventurer* is "a quarterly family-fun newsletter-style zine of humor, thought and verse. Very short stories (less than 500 words) are sometimes included." They prefer "light, humorous verse; any style; any 'family acceptable' subject matter; length limit 32 lines. Nothing obscene, overly forboding, no graphic gore or violence." Also accepts poetry written by children. They have published poetry by Paul Humphrey, Ray Gallucci, Harry Roman and Najwa Brax. As a sample the editor selected his poem "Squiggles and Doodles":

> wandering, pointless, meandering line/serving one purpose: to occupy time./without you i'm certain
> i'd probably find/i'd have to resort back to using my mind.

TAA is 6-12 pgs., 8½ × 14, photocopied and corner-stapled with many playful b&w graphics. They receive about 500 poems a year, accept approximately 40%. Press run is 150 for 100 subscribers. Single copy: $2; subscription: $5. Sample: $2. Make checks payable to Paul Agosto. "Subscription not required but subscribers given preference."

Magazine Needs: Also publishes *The Armchair Aesthete*, a quarterly digest-sized zine of "fiction and poetry of thoughtful, well-crafted concise works. Interested in more fiction submissions than poetry though." Line length for poetry is 30 maximum. The editor says *The Armchair Aesthete* is 40-60 pgs., 5½ × 8½, quality desktop-published, photocopied, card cover, includes ads for other publications and writers' available chapbooks. Each issue usually contains 10-15 poems and 6-9 stories. They receive about 300 poems/year, accept 25-30%. Subscription: $10/year. Sample postpaid: $3. Make checks payable to Paul Agosto.

How to Submit: For both publications, previously published poems and simultaneous submissions OK, if indicated. Cover letter preferred. E-mail and disk submissions OK, include in body of message. Time between acceptance and publication is 1 year. Seldom comments on rejections. *The Aardvark Adventurer* occasionally publishes theme issues, but *The Armchair Aesthete* does not. For both, send SASE for guidelines. Responds in 2 months. Pay 1 copy. Acquire one-time rights. The staff of *Aardvark* reviews books and chapbooks of poetry in 100 words. The staff of *Armchair* occasionally reviews chapbooks. Send books for review consideration.

Advice: "*The Aardvark Adventurer* is a perfect opportunity for the aspiring poet, a newsletter-style publication with a very playful format."

◗ **ABBEY; ABBEY CHEAPOCHAPBOOKS,** 5360 Fallriver Row Court, Columbia MD 21044, e-mail greisman@aol.com, founded 1970, editor David Greisman.

Magazine Needs & How to Submit: *Abbey*, a quarterly, aims "to be a journal but to do it so informally that one wonders about my intent." They want "poetry that does for the mind what that first sip of Molson Ale does for the palate. No pornography or politics." They have published poetry and artwork by Richard Peabody, Vera Bergstrom, D.E. Steward, Carol Hamilton, Harry Calhoun, Wayne Hogan and Cheryl Townsend. It is 20-26 pgs., magazine-sized, photocopied. They publish about 150 of 1,000 poems received/year. Press run is 200. Subscription: $2. Sample: 50¢. Send SASE for guidelines. Responds in 1 month. Pays 1-2 copies.

Book/Chapbook Needs & How to Submit: *Abbey Cheapochapbooks* come out 1-2 times a year averaging 10-15 pgs. For chapbook consideration query with 4-6 samples, bio and list of publications. Responds in 2 months. Pays 25-50 copies.

Advice: The editor says he is "definitely seeing poetry from two schools—the nit'n'grit school and the textured/ reflective school. I much prefer the latter."

✅ 📝 ◎ ABIKO ANNUAL WITH JAMES JOYCE FW STUDIES (Specialized: translations), 8-1-8 Namiki, Abiko-shi, Chiba-ken 270-1165 Japan, phone/fax 011-81-471-84-7904 or 84-5873, e-mail alp@db3 .so-net.ne.jp, website www02.u-page.so-net.ne.jp/jb3/hce, founded 1988, founding editor Laurel Willis, contact Dr. Tatsuo Hamada or Laurel Willis.

Magazine Needs: *Abiko* is a literary-style annual journal "heavily influenced by James Joyce's *Finnegan's Wake*. We publish all kinds, with an emphasis like Yeats's quote: 'Truth seen in passion is the substance of poetry!' We prefer poetry like Eliot's or Donne's. We include originals and translations from Japanese and other languages." They have published poetry by Eileen Malone, James Fairhall and Danetta Loretta Saft. It is about 800 pgs., 14.8cm×21cm, perfect-bound with coated paper cover. Press run is 500 for 50 subscribers of which 10 are libraries. Sample: $35.

How to Submit: "See *Writer's Digest, Poets & Writers* and *AWP Chronicle* for details." Open to unsolicited reviews. Writers may also send books for review consideration.

Advice: "Please remember U.S. postage does not work in Japan with SAEs! Send 2 International Reply coupons."

Ⓝ ▣ 📝 ◎ ABLE MUSE (Specialized: form/style); ERATOSPHERE, 467 Saratoga Ave., #602, San Jose CA 95129-1326, phone/fax (801)729-3509, e-mail ablemuse@plaxnet.com, website www.ablemuse.com, founded 1999, editor Alex Pepple.

Magazine Needs: *Able Muse: a review of metrical poetry* "spotlights formal poetry via a quarterly online presentation, in the supportive environment of art and photography, essays, interviews, book reviews, fiction and a literary forum. Also includes electronic books of poetry. *Able Muse* exclusively publishes formal poetry. We are looking for well-crafted poems of any length or subject that employ skillful and imaginative use of meter, or meter and rhyme, executed in contemporary idiom, that reads as naturally as your free-verse poems. Do not send us free-verse, greeting card verse or poetry campaigning for the revival of archaic language." They have published poetry by Mark Jarman, Andrea Hollander Budy, Rhina P. Espaillat, Len Krisak, John William Watkins and Patrick Daly. As a sample the editor selected these lines from "Heart Attack" by Beth Houston:

> *Even now, her last day blessed with a flood/Of roses, only one closed flower will do,/One last bud*
> *clinging to color like blood/Flowing from its thorn, her old heart's issue,/Love held so deep, so cold,*
> *that stillborn bud/In ice, that wound's child clutching one fist, two.*

They receive about 800 poems a year, accept approximately 10%. Publish 20 poems/issue.

How to Submit: Submit 1-5 poems at a time. No previously published poems or simultaneous submissions. E-mail and disk submissions OK. "E-mail is the preferred medium of submission, but we also welcome snail mail, or submit directly from the website with the automated online submission form." Cover letter preferred. Time between acceptance and publication is 4-10 weeks. Often comments on rejections. Publishes theme issues occasionally. Obtain guidelines and upcoming themes via e-mail or website. Responds in 1 month. Sometimes sends prepublication galleys. Acquires first rights. Reviews books of poetry. Open to unsolicited reviews. Poets may also send books for review consideration.

Also Offers: "*Eratosphere* is provided online for the posting and critique of poetry and other literary work. It is a 'virtual' workshop! Literary online chats also provided featuring the scheduled appearance of guest celebrity poets."

Advice: "Despite the rush to publish everything online, most of web-published poetry has been free verse. This is surprising given formal poetry's recent rise in popularity and number of print journals that exclusively publish formal poetry. *Able Muse* attempts to fill this void bringing the best contemporary formalists online. Remember, content is just as important as form."

$ ◎ ABORIGINAL SF (Specialized: science fiction), Box 2449, Woburn MA 01888-0849, website www.aboriginal.com, founded 1986, editor Charles C. Ryan, appears quarterly.

Magazine Needs: "Poetry should be 1-2 pgs., double-spaced. Subject matter must be science fiction, science or space-related. No long poems, no fantasy." The magazine is 64 pgs., with 10 illustrations. Press run is 6,000, mostly subscriptions. Subscriptions for "special" writer's rate: $14/4 issues. Sample: $6.85.

How to Submit: No simultaneous submissions. Send SASE for guidelines. Responds in 3 months, no backlog. Always sends prepublication galleys. Pays $20/poem and 2 copies. Buys first North American serial rights. Reviews related books of poetry in 100-300 words.

✅ 📝 ◎ ABOUT SUCH THINGS (Specialized: religious), 1701 Delancey St., Philadelphia PA 19103, phone (215)849-1583, e-mail aboutsuch@homepage.com, website www.aboutsuch.homepage.com, founded 1996, managing editor Laurel W. Garver.

Magazine Needs: *AST* appears twice a year. "We seek to publish poetry, fiction and arts- and culture-related essays that reflect a Christian worldview and retain a sense of wonder about God. We seek contemporary voices that speak what is noble, true, excellent and praiseworthy—that can see the possibility of healing in the midst of brokenness." They want inspirational, nature, relationship themes; contemporary free verse; "work that appeals to the senses, fresh and original, makes a lasting impression." No erotica, occult, feminist, gay/lesbian, non-

Christian religions, haiku, "anything resembling Helen Steiner Rice." They have published poetry by Timothy Hodor, R.G. Evans and Ed L. Wier. As a sample the editor selected these lines from "Broadway" by Rachel Toliver:

> *Prayer's syntax and semantics/rush warm, flush against this hour./This is the eloquence of need,/pared down to broken diction./This is the elemental, desperate language.*

AST is 28 pgs., magazine-sized, photocopied and saddle-stitched with 70 lb. text paper cover, includes grayscale original art and some clip art. They receive about 300 poems a year, accept approximately 10%. Press run is 400 for 50 subscribers, 150-200 shelf sales. Single copy: $3; subscription: $7/year. Sample: $3 plus 99¢ postage. "Purchase of a sample is highly recommended."

How to Submit: Submit up to 5 poems at a time. Line length for poetry is 4 minimum, 80 maximum. Previously published poems and simultaneous submissions OK. Cover letter preferred. Disk submissions OK. "Phone number is essential. This is how authors are contacted if accepted. One poem per page. SASE must be #10 envelope or larger with at least 2 stamps for returns." Reads submissions Spring—November through January 20; Autumn—May through July 20 only. Time between acceptance and publication is 3 months. Poems are circulated to an editorial board. "Poems are read with authors' names removed and a number assigned to them. Five or six evaluators critique each poem and score it based on set criteria. The group meets to discuss the poems, then final scores are turned in and tallied. Twelve to seventeen top poems are published." Often comments on rejections. Send SASE for guidelines or obtain via website. Responds in 1 year. Sometimes sends prepublication galleys. Pays 2 copies/accepted piece. Acquires one-time rights.

Also Offers: Website includes writing samples, art samples, submission guidelines, ordering information, contact information and a bookstore with editor's picks and writing help.

Advice: "Poetry should be much more than prose broken into stanzas. If you aren't using vivid imagery, you need to read more."

☑ $ ○ ◎ **ABOVE THE BRIDGE MAGAZINE; THIRD STONE PUBLISHING (Specialized: regional)**, P.O. Box 249, Grand Marais MI 49839, phone (906)494-2458, e-mail classen@mail.portup.com, website www.portup.com/above, founded 1985, contact poetry editor.

Magazine Needs: *Above the Bridge* is a bimonthly magazine designed to reflect life and living in Michigan's Upper Peninsula. The editor says the magazine is 60 pgs., 8½×11, and includes line art and graphics. They receive about 200 poems a year, accept approximately 10%. Press run is 4,000 for 3,000 subscribers of which 50 are libraries. Single copy: $3.50; subscription: $18. Sample: $4.

How to Submit: Submit 2-3 poems at a time. Previously published poems and simultaneous submissions OK. Cover letter preferred. Often comments on rejections. Send SASE for guidelines. Responds in 4 months. Pays $5 and 2 copies. Acquires one-time rights. Staff reviews books of poetry only if author or topic is related to Michigan's Upper Peninsula. Send related books for review consideration.

◉ ♥ **ABRAXAS MAGAZINE; GHOST PONY PRESS**, P.O. Box 260113, Madison WI 53726-0113, e-mail irmarkha@students.wisc.edu, website www.geocities.com/Paris/4614 or www.litline.org/html/ABRAXAS.html, *Abraxas* founded in 1968 by James Bertolino and Warren Woessner, Ghost Pony Press in 1980 by editor/publisher Ingrid Swanberg. Contact for both presses is Ingrid Swanberg.

Magazine Needs & How to Submit: *Abraxas* no longer considers unsolicited material, except as announced as projects arise. The editor is interested in poetry that is "contemporary lyric, experimental and poetry in translation." Does not want to see "political posing; academic regurgitations. Please include original with submissions of translation." They have published poetry by William Stafford, Ivan Argüelles, Denise Levertov, César Vallejo and Andrea Moorhead. As a sample the editor selected these lines from "the silence of lascaux" by próspero saíz:

> *in the silence of lascaux a wavering light is fading/outside the cave the bones of slaughter linger still/ traces of mass killings beneath the cliffs of stone/yet far from the equine ossuary stubby ponies tumble/ in the vanishing lines of the sacred terror of the horse . . .*

Abraxas is up to 80 pgs. (160 pgs., double issues), 6×9, flat-spined (saddle-stitched with smaller issues), litho offset, with original art on its matte card cover, using "unusual graphics in text, original art and collages, concrete poetry, exchange ads only, letters from contributors, essays." It appears "irregularly, 4- to 9-month intervals or longer." Press run is 600 for 500 subscribers of which 150 are libraries. Subscription: $16/4 issues, $20/4 issues Canada, Mexico and overseas. Sample: $4 ($8 double issues). *Abraxas* will announce submission guidelines as projects arise. Pays 1 copy plus 40% discount on additional copies.

Book/Chapbook Needs & How to Submit: To submit to Ghost Pony Press, inquire with SASE plus 5-10 poems and cover letter. Previously published material OK for book publication by Ghost Pony Press. Editor sometimes comments briefly on rejections. Responds to queries in 1-3 months, mss in 3 months or longer "We currently have a considerable backlog of mss." Payment varies per project. Send SASE for catalog to buy samples. They have published three books of poetry by próspero saíz including *the bird of nothing & other poems*; 168 pgs., 7×10, sewn and wrapped binding, paperback available for $20 (signed and numbered edition is $35), as well as *Zen Concrete Ex Etc.*, by d.a. levy; 268 pgs., 8½×11, perfect bound, illustrated, paperback for $27.50.

Also Offers: Websites include writer's guidelines and submission dates; book prices; and links to the editor.

Advice: "Ghost Pony Press is a small press publisher of poetry books; *Abraxas* is a literary journal publishing contemporary poetry, criticism and translations. Do not confuse these separate presses!"

☑ $ ☐ ◎ **ABUNDANCE—A HARVEST OF LIFE, LITERATURE AND ART; ABUNDANCE PRESS**, 265 SW Port Saint Lucie Blvd., PMB #175, Port Saint Lucie FL 34984, phone (561)336-3793, fax (561)336-4176, e-mail editor@abundancepress.com, website www.abundancepress.com, founded 1995, editor Anthony Watkins, online editor Suzanne Robinson.

Magazine Needs: *Abundance* is "a bimonthly literary magazine published and distributed throughout South Florida's Treasure Coast dedicated to promoting the arts in our community which now includes the world. We publish 1-2 poems by 4-8 poets per issue. Poems should be 20-30 lines unless haiku, do not send religious, rhyming or humorous poetry. Write honestly, use words that you might actually speak on occasion. We want a piece of your life, not a fantasy of a world you know not of." Also accepts poetry written by children, ages 0-15. As a sample the editors selected these lines from "Things I Will Tell Her" by Mariah Stewart-Hencke:

> And I will laugh with her/About the praying hands/Of church ladies/About the drunken, red-faced
> bride/And the thousands of other/Little ways they try/To cover/A woman's fire.

Abundance is about 30 pgs., published in tabloid and online formats. They receive about 40 submissions per issue and print about 8 poems. Press run is 6,000. Sample: $2 "to cover postage & handling." Make checks payable to Abundance Press. "Sample requests not encouraged, just send your work. We also use 1 piece of short fiction each issue."

How to Submit: Submit 3-4 typed poems at a time. Line length for poetry is 30 maximum. Previously published poems and simultaneous submissions OK. Cover letter preferred ("more about you, less about publishing credits"). E-mail submissions preferred, include in body of message. "Make sure your name and address are on each page if you submit by snail-mail, work is passed around to all editors and title page can get separated from poems. If you are submitting work to multiple publications, we reserve the right to publish if you do not withdraw your submission in writing within 30 days of notice of intent to publish." Time between acceptance and publication is usually 2 months. Often comments on rejections "sometimes editor will call you with suggestions, so be prepared, Anthony likes to talk to 'his' poets." Tries to respond within 1 month. Pays $5-10/poem plus copies. Overseas receive 1-2 copies, domestic 10. Buys one-time rights plus reprint rights for "Best of" Collections. Reviews books and chapbooks of poetry. Open to unsolicited reviews "must include copy of reviewed work." Poets may also send books for review consideration.

Advice: "We do not print poetry or fiction by the same author more than once per year. We do, however, consider both poetry and fiction by the same author. So if we publish your poetry, you might consider submitting fiction."

⊕ ☑ ◎ **ACID ANGEL**, 35 Falkland St. (GFL), Glasgow, Scotland G12-9QZ, phone 44(0)141-221-1223, e-mail acidangel@acidity.globalnet.co.uk, first founded 1984 (as Dada Dance), relaunched 1998, editor Dee Rimbaud.

Magazine Needs: *Acid Angel* is published "once or twice per year. The magazine is "highly visual, innovative, eclectic and visionary; and growing in popularity, both in the UK and the US. We publish poetry and prose of the highest calibre and discourage submissions from inexperienced writers. It is recommended that you buy a sample issue before sending contributions." They have published poetry by Ivor Cutler, Angela Death, Yoshi Ooshi, James Kelman, Alasdair Gray, Arthur Rimbaud, Edwin Morgan. As a sample they selected these lines from "Spindrifting" by Dee Rimbaud:

> I am featherblown in hallucinating winds/faltering in flight to falling dreams obsessions: the spirit of
> night possesses me/taking me/tying my hands, but gently, so gently/sliding its phallocentric idiocies
> into my ruby stigmata/taking me down/down into the netherworld/into the lightless void/and I am
> Innanna/sacrificing my eyes for love.

The magazine is 80-100 pgs., A4, b&w with card cover. They receive about 2,000 submissions a year, accept less than 5%. Press run is 1,000 and growing. Single copy: $15 cash (US) or £7.50 (UK); subscription: $60 cash (US) or £30 (UK). Make checks payable to Dee Rimbaud (U.S. purchasers should send cash or international money orders).

How to Submit: Submit 4-10 poems at a time with large SAE and 2 IRCs. No previously published poems or simultaneous submissions. Cover letter required. E-mail submissions OK. "If sending by e-mail, submit only 1 poem or 100 words of prose in the first instance. If these stimulate interest, we will request a larger submission." Time between acceptance and publication is at least 1 year. Seldom comments on rejections. Criticism fee: $3 per poem. "Editor will red pen suggestions on poem. Payment in advance only." Responds quickly.

Also Offers: A.A. Small Press Listings, the most accurate, in-depth and detailed UK small press listings available and the only one available by e-mail. Nearly 700 UK magazines featured including poetry, literature, science fiction, fantasy, horror, ecology and alternative lifestyles. E-mail version: $6 cash (US) or £2 international money order (UK). Send e-mail enquiry for further details.

Advice: "If you are turned on by the likes of Richard Brautigan, William Burroughs, Laurie Anderson, Patti Smith, Hermann Hesse and Sylvia Plath, you will have multiple orgasms when you leaf through the pages of Acid Angel. We mean this metaphorically but if it happens for you literally we want to know."

$ ◎ **ACM (ANOTHER CHICAGO MAGAZINE); LEFT FIELD PRESS**, 3709 N. Kenmore, Chicago IL 60613, website www.anotherchicagomag.com, founded 1977, poetry editor Barry Silesky.

Work published in *ACM* has been included in *The Best American Poetry* (1995, 1996 and 1997) and *Pushcart Prize* anthologies.

Magazine Needs: *ACM* is a literary biannual, with emphasis on quality, experimental, politically aware prose, fiction, poetry, reviews, cross-genre work and essays. No religious verse. They have published prose and poetry by Albert Goldbarth, Michael McClure, Jack Anderson, Jerome Sala, Nance VanWinkel, Nadja Tesich, Wanda Coleman (winner of the 1999 Marshall Prize from the Academy of American Poets), Charles Simic and Diane Wakoski. As a sample the editor selected these lines by Dean Shavit:

> *Just the facts. Forgotten on purpose./This is our land. Yes, you said, "ours."/A gang of teenagers, too*
> *young for the army, too stupid for respect.*

Silesky says *ACM* is 220 pgs., digest-sized, offset with b&w art and ads. Editors appreciate traditional to experimental verse with an emphasis on message, especially poems with strong voices articulating social or political concerns. Circulation is 2,000 for 500 subscribers of which 100 are libraries.

How to Submit: Submit 3-4 typed poems at a time. No previously published poems; simultaneous submissions OK. Responds in 3 months, has 3- to 6-month backlog. Sometimes sends prepublication galleys. Pays $5/page, "if funds permit," and 1 copy. Buys first serial rights. Reviews books of poetry in 250-800 words. Open to unsolicited reviews. Poets may also send books for review consideration.

Also Offers: Sponsors Chicago Literary Prize. Deadline in December. Website includes guidelines, contest guidelines, subscription info and current issues info.

Advice: "Buy a copy—subscribe and support your own work."

THE ACORN; EL DORADO WRITERS' GUILD (Specialized: regional), P.O. Box 1266, El Dorado CA 95623-1266, phone (530)621-1833, fax (530)621-3939, e-mail theacorn@visto.com, founded 1993, poetry consultant Taylor Graham, editor Kirk Colvin.

Magazine Needs: *the ACORN* is a quarterly journal of the Western Sierra, published by the El Dorado Writers' Guild, a nonprofit literary organization. It includes "fiction and nonfiction, history and reminiscence, story and legend, and poetry." They want poetry "up to 30 lines long, though we prefer shorter. Focus should be on western slope Sierra Nevada. No erotica, pornography or religious poetry." They have published poetry by Nancy Cherry, Jeanne Wagner, Joyce Odam and Edward C. Lynskey. As a sample the poetry consultant selected these lines from "Talking Water" by Blaine Hammond:

> *It has been the hawk/after it was a rat/eaten by the hawk. Listen!/It was your lover/after she breathed*
> *moist oxygen/once exhaled by the pine,/which gave its limbs a perch/to the hawk, breathed/carbon*
> *dioxide expiration.//It has passed through so many cells,/been alive so many times/without dying, by*
> *now/it has become aware./You should taste/its memory.*

The poetry consultant says *the ACORN* is 44 pgs., 5½×8½, offset-printed and saddle-stapled with light card cover. They receive about 400 poems a year, use approximately 15%. Press run is 200 for 110 subscribers. Subscription: $12. Sample: $3.

How to Submit: Submit 3-5 poems, neatly typed or printed, at a time. Previously published poems OK—indicate where published; however, no simultaneous submissions. E-mail submissions encouraged. "Prefer attachment in MSWord format. However, in body of message is acceptable." Cover letter with short (75-word) bio and publication credits preferred. "Our issues favor topical items suitable for the season." Deadlines are February 1, May 1, August 1. "December is our contest issue." Time between acceptance and publication is 1 month. "Poetry consultant screens, then five editors score the poems for content, form and suitability. Graphics editor selects to fit space available." Often comments on rejections. Responds within 1 month after deadline. Pays 2 copies.

Also Offers: Sponsors annual contest. 1st Prize: $100, 2nd Prize: $50, 3rd Prize: $20, 2 $10 honorable mentions. Entry fee: $7/3 poems, 40 lines maximum/poem. Deadline: July 31. All winning entries are published in the contest edition of *the ACORN* in December. Send SASE for complete rules.

Advice: "If your poetry is about nature, be accurate with the species' names, colors, etc. If you describe a landscape, be sure it fits our region. Metered rhyming verse had better be precise. (We have an editor with an internal metronome!) Slant rhyme and free verse are welcome. Avoid trite phrases."

ACORN WHISTLE; ACORN WHISTLE PRESS, 907 Brewster Ave., Beloit WI 53511, e-mail burwellf@lib.beloit.edu, website www.acornwhistle.com, founded 1994, first issue published in spring 1995, editor Fred Burwell.

Magazine Needs: *Acorn Whistle* appears once or twice a year. "We seek writing that moves both heart and mind. We seek accessible poetry: narrative, lyrical, prose poem. No length requirements. We are not interested in experimental, religious, erotic or New Age work. We also publish fiction, memoir and personal essay." Also accepts poetry written by children. They have published poetry by Mary Legato Brownell, Wendy Taylor Carlisle, Daniel Smith and JoAnne McFarland. As a sample the editor selected these lines from "Splicing the Rope" by Sara DeLuca:

> *There would be little rest for any crewman/on a 1950's haying day,/little respite from the growling*
> *tractors, hissing heat,/blue dust of stem and leaf baled tight,/the bite of twinestring,/sharp and throbbing*
> *through thick leather gloves.*

The editor says *AW* is 75-100 pgs., 8½×11, staple-bound, using b&w photos and art, no ads. Press run is 500. Subscription: $14. Sample: $7.

How to Submit: Include SASE with all submissions. No previously published poems; simultaneous submissions OK. Often comments on rejections. Send SASE for guidelines. Responds in 3 months. Pays 2 copies. Acquires first North American serial rights.

Also Offers: Founded in 1998, Acorn Whistle Press has published *Songs From an Inland Sea*, a collection of poems by Sara DeLuca and another collection, *Stills*, by Joanne McFarland. Website includes guidelines, table of contents of each issue, photos of covers, sample poems and prose, reviews of magazines and books, information on Acorn Whistle Press and its books. "We plan to include sample poems and stories."

Advice: "We publish no reviews, although we plan to mention publications by our past authors. We wish more writers would focus on material that matters to them, rather than trying to impress an audience of editors and teachers. We seek accessible writing for an audience that reads for pleasure and edification. We encourage a friendly, working relationship between editors and writers."

ACUMEN MAGAZINE; EMBER PRESS; THE LONG POEM GROUP NEWSLETTER, 6 The Mount, Higher Furzeham, Brixham, South Devon TQ5 8QY England, phone (01803)851098, press founded 1971, *Acumen* founded 1984, poetry editor Patricia Oxley. *The Long Poem Group Newsletter* founded 1995, editors William Oxley and Sebastian Banker.

Magazine Needs: *Acumen* appears 3 times a year (in January, May and September) and is a "small press publisher of a general literary magazine with emphasis on good poetry." They want "well-crafted, high quality, imaginative poems showing a sense of form. No experimental verse of an obscene type." They have published poetry by Elizabeth Jennings, William Oxley, Gavin Ewart, D.J. Enright, Peter Porter, Kathleen Raine and R.S. Thomas. As a sample the editor selected this poem, "Learning A Language" by Danielle Hope:

> *... And I walk to the sea/to look for messages in dunes/and sea-grass/but I find a tangle of red flowers*
> *I cannot identify./The sea shuffles/illegible scatters of sand.*

Acumen is 100 pgs., A5, perfect-bound. "We aim to publish 120 poems out of 12,000 received." Press run is 650 for 400 subscribers of which 20 are libraries. Subscription: $45 surface/$50 air. Sample copy: $15.

How to Submit: Submit 5-6 poems at a time. No previously published poems; simultaneous submissions OK, if not to UK magazines. Responds in 1 month. Pays "by negotiation" and 1 copy. Staff reviews books of poetry up to 300 words, single format or 600 words, multi-book. Send books for review consideration to Glyn Pursglove, 25 St. Albans Rd., Brynmill, Swansea, West Glamorgan SA2 0BP Wales.

Also Offers: Publishes *The Long Poem Group Newsletter* featuring short articles about long poems and reviews long poems. Free for large SASE (or SAE with IRC).

Advice: "Read *Acumen* carefully to see what kind of poetry we publish. Also read widely in many poetry magazines, and don't forget the poets of the past—they can still teach us a great deal."

ADASTRA PRESS, 16 Reservation Rd., Easthampton MA 01027-2536, founded 1980, publisher Gary Metras.

Book/Chapbook Needs: "Adastra is primarily a chapbook publisher using antique equipment and methods, i.e., hand-set type, letterpress printed, hand-sewn bindings. Any titles longer than chapbook length are by special arrangement and are from poets who have previously published a successful chapbook or two with Adastra. Editions are generally released with a flat-spine paper wrapper, and some titles have been bound in cloth. Editions are limited, ranging from 200-400 copy print runs. Some of the longer titles have gone into reprint and these are photo-offset and perfect-bound. Letterpress chapbooks by themselves are not reprinted as single titles. Once they go out of print, they are gone. Instead, I have released *The Adastra Reader, Collected Chapbooks, 1979-1986* (1987) and *The Adastra Reader II, collected Chapbooks, 1987-1992* (2000). These anthologies collect the first twelve chapbooks and the second twelve, respectively, and I am now planning the third series. I am biased against poems that rhyme and/or are religious in theme. Sequences and longish poems are always nice to present in a chapbook format. There are no guidelines other than these. Competition is keen. Less than .5% of submissions are accepted." Poets published include Linda Lee Harper (*Blue Flute*), Thomas Lux (*The Blind Swimmer: Selected Early Poems, 1970-1975*), Miriam Sagan (*Pocahontas Discovers America*) and Geoffrey Jacques (*Suspended Knowledge*). As a sample the editor selected these lines from "Neighbor" in *Leaving for a Year*, by Tom Sexton:

> *Across a stubble field his old house/is an accordian played by wind,//A life of hauling lobster traps/*
> *has worn him to the bone.//After dark we watch him carrying/a lamp from room to room//talking to*
> *shadows on the wall.*

Two to four chapbooks are brought out each year. Sample chapbook: $5.

How to Submit: Send a complete chapbook ms of 12-18 pgs., double-spaced preferred, during the month of February. Notification of acceptance/rejection by April. "I choose 1 or 2 mss to publish the following year." Query with a sample of 5 poems from a chapbook ms in the Fall. "If I like what I see, I'll ask you to submit the chapbook ms in February. Always include an SASE." Time between acceptance and publication is 1-2 years. Payment is 10% of the print run in copies with a discount on additional copies.

ADEPT PRESS; SMALL BRUSHES, P.O. Box 391, Long Valley NJ 07853-0391, founded 1999, editor Jan Epps Turner.

Magazine Needs: Published biannually, *Small Brushes* wants "to be another showcase for good poetry from many voices. Although we prefer poems of 32 lines or fewer, we will occasionally run an excellent two-page poem (up to 64 lines). We want poetry of all forms springing from important human emotions, ethics, and realizations. Sadness is acceptable, but we prefer that some catharsis, uplifting, or hope be offered with it. We do not want language or ideas that might offend anyone. We do not want maudlin sentimentality, forced rhyme, or trite greeting card verse. We do not want material that is narrowly religious, explicitly sexual or obscure in meaning." They have published poetry by Ann DeFalco, Claudia Showers Drezga, Bruce E. Litton, Jane M. Long, R. Paul Muni and John Chadsey Turner IV. As a sample the editor selected these lines from "Italia Nuovo" by Jane M. Long:

> When Fra Angelico took up his small brushes/did he dream big?/Did he want to climb through the
> monastery roof/and paint golden hosannas on the heavens?/Or did he stay below in the stable,/in the
> carefully balanced contours

SB is 32 pgs., digest-sized, desktop-published with some photocoping, saddle-stapled with parchment cover, includes b&w cartoons, or occasionally color graphics. They receive about 140 poems a year, accept approximately 40%. Publish 25-28 poems/issue. Press run is 80 for 15 subscribers, 26 shelf sales; 33 distributed free to contributors and libraries. Single copy: $3; subscription: $5/year (2 issues). Sample: $2. Make checks payable to Adept Press. "There are no requirements for contributors. The poetry stands on its own merit. Ours is a labor of love and not for profit. We do urge our regular contributors to subscribe, so that our magazine can continue."
How to Submit: Submit 3-4 poems at a time. Line length for poetry is 4 minimum, 32 maximum. No previously published poems or simultaneous submissions. Cover letter required. "Please include a brief bio in your cover letter, place your name and address at the top of each manuscript page and type or print clearly. Please send disposable copies, as well as your SASE for our comments or contact." Reads submissions January 1 through August 31 only. Submit seasonal poems 2 months in advance. Time between acceptance and publication is 2-15 months. Seldom comments on rejections. Send SASE for guidelines. Responds in 2 months. Sometimes sends prepublication galleys. Pays 1 copy/published poem. Rights remain with authors and artists.
Advice: "Read poetry, including the masters. Ignore the trends. Write from your own experiences and deep feelings."

Ⓝ Ⓞ Ⓞ ADORATION: A JOURNAL OF CHRISTIAN POETRY (Specialized: religious), P.O. Box 802954, Santa Clarita CA 91380-2954, e-mail adoration@mccullumsoftware.com, website www.mccullumsoftwa re.com/adoration, founded February 2000, editor Kurt McCullum.
Magazine Needs: *Adoration* is published quarterly in the winter, spring, summer and fall seasons. "We welcome unsolicited submissions of poetry and will accept any style or form, especially meter. While we will consider almost any subject matter, *Adoration* is a Christian publication and will reflect the views of Christianity." Subscription: $12/year, $20/2 years. Sample: $3.50. Make checks payable to Adoration Press.
How to Submit: Submit 3-5 poems at a time—typed, single-spaced, one poem/page. Simultaneous submissions OK, "but please inform us as soon as possible if your work is accepted elsewhere." Include a SASE for return of mss. E-mail submissions OK, "but must be sent as plain text." Pays 2 copies.
Advice: "We believe that there is a vast amount of quality Christian poetry which needs to be given voice. It is our prayer that *Adoration* will be the medium through which these poems can be heard. Please join us in giving adoration to our Lord."

Ⓞ Ⓞ ADRIFT (Specialized: ethnic), 46 E. First St., #3D, New York NY 10003, founded 1980, editor Thomas McGonigle.
Magazine Needs: The editor says, "The orientation of the magazine is Irish, Irish-American. I expect the reader-writer knows and goes beyond Yeats, Kavanagh, Joyce, O'Brien." The literary magazine is open to all kinds of submissions, but does not want to see "junk." They have published poetry by James Liddy, Thomas McCarthy, Francis Stuart and Gilbert Sorrentino. *Adrift* appears twice a year and is 32 pgs., magazine-sized, offset printed on heavy stock, saddle-stapled with matte card cover. Circulation is 1,000 with 200 subscriptions, 50 of which are libraries. Single copy: $4; subscription: $8. Sample: $5. Make checks payable to T. McGonigle.
How to Submit: Simultaneous submissions OK. Magazine pays, rate varies; contributors receive 1 copy. Reviews books of poetry. Open to unsolicited reviews. Poets may also send books for review consideration.

Ⓞ ADVOCATE, PKA's PUBLICATION, 301A Rolling Hills Park, Prattsville NY 12468, phone (518)299-3103, founded 1987.
Magazine Needs: *Advocate* is a bimonthly advertiser-supported tabloid, 12,000 copies distributed free, using "original, previously unpublished works, such as feature stories, essays, 'think' pieces, letters to the editor, profiles, humor, fiction, poetry, puzzles, cartoons or line drawings." They want "nearly any kind of poetry, any length, but not religious or pornographic. Poetry ought to speak to people and not be so oblique as to have meaning only to the poet. If I had to be there to understand the poem, don't send it. Now looking for horse related poems, stories, drawings and photos." They accept approximately 25% of poems received. Sample: $4.
How to Submit: No previously published poems or simultaneous submissions. Time between acceptance and publication is an average of 4-6 months. Editor "occasionally" comments on rejections. Responds in 2 months. Pays 2 copies. Acquires first rights only.
Advice: "All submissions and correspondence must be accompanied by a self-addressed, stamped envelope with sufficient postage."

Clymenza Hawkins, a frequent contributor to *African Voices*, created the cover design for the Summer/Fall 1998 issue. Publisher Carolyn A. Butts feels this cover symbolizes the rebirth of a new Black literary renaissance. "The feature article is on poet/writer/publisher Jessica Care Moore," Butts explains. "Ms. Moore represents the new generation of poets who are the leaders of our current arts movement." *African Voices*, a quarterly art and literary magazine published in New York, supports and highlights the work of emerging writers and artists of color.

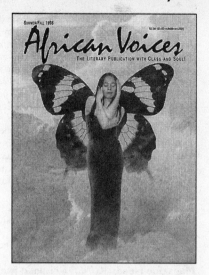

 AETHLON: THE JOURNAL OF SPORT LITERATURE (Specialized: sports/recreation), Dept. PM, English Dept., East Tennessee State University, Box 70270, Johnson City TN 37614-0270, founded 1983, general editor Don Johnson, Dean, Arts & Sciences, ETSU. Submit poems to poetry editor Robert W. Hamblin, Professor of English, Southeast Missouri State University, Cape Girardeau MO 63701.
Magazine Needs: *Aethlon* publishes a variety of sport-related literature, including scholarly articles, fiction, poetry and reviews; 12-15 poems/issue; two issues annually, fall and spring. Subject matter must be sports-related; no restrictions regarding form, length, style or purpose. They do not want to see "doggerel, cliché-ridden or oversentimental" poems. Poets published include Neal Bowers, Joseph Duemer, Robert Fink, Jan Mordenski, H.R. Stoneback and Don Welch. The magazine is 200 pgs., digest-sized, offset printed, flat-spined, with illustrations and some ads. Circulation is 1,000 for 750 subscribers of which 250 are libraries. Subscription is included with membership ($40) in the Sport Literature Association. Sample: $15.
How to Submit: "Only typed mss with SASE considered." No simultaneous submissions. Submissions are reported on in 6-8 weeks and the backlog time is 6-12 months. Contributors receive 5 offprints and a copy of the issue in which their poem appears.

N **AFFABLE NEIGHBOR**, P.O. Box 3635, Ann Arbor MI 48106-3635, founded 1994, editor-in-chief Joel Henry-Fisher, poetry editor Leigh Chalmers.
Magazine Needs: Published various times throughout the year, *Affable Neighbor* "pushes the boundaries of what a magazine is supposed to be/can be and provides a good laugh too." They want "shocking, groundbreaking work that 'pushes the envelope' whatever that means, and sometimes short." No religious, flowery, uninspired poetry. They have published poetry by Marshall Stanley, A. Huffstickler, Dave Noven and Steve Toth. The editors say *AN* is photocopied and stapled with cardstock cover, includes "photos, drawings, etc., very visual." They receive about 500-1,000 poems a year, accept approximately 1%. Single copy: $2; subscription: $20. Make checks payable to Joel Fisher.
How to Submit: Previously published poems and simultaneous submissions OK. Cover letter preferred. "If a response is desired, please say so and include a SASE." Time between acceptance and publication is "several months or years." Poems are circulated to an editorial board. "A poem must be unanimously accepted by the editors and staff of *Affable Neighbor*." Often comments on rejections. Publishes theme issues occasionally. Responds in 2 weeks. Pays copies as requested. Staff reviews other magazines.
Book/Chapbook Needs & How to Submit: Affable Neighbor Press publishes 0-5 poetry titles per year. "We publish exciting and groundbreaking work that can find no other outlet." Query first, with a few sample poems and cover letter with brief bio and publication credits. Pays royalties of 50% maximum. "We work out terms with individual authors."
Advice: "*Affable Neighbor* appreciates writing that includes or is mixed with visuals. For beginners: keep working."

 AFRICAN VOICES (Specialized: ethnic), 270 W. 96th St., New York NY 10025, phone (212)865-2982, fax (212)316-3335, e-mail annebutts@aol.com, website www.africanvoices.com, founded 1992, poetry editor Layding Kalida.
Magazine Needs: *AV* is a quarterly "art and literary magazine that highlights the work of people of color. We publish ethnic literature and poetry on any subject. We also consider all themes and styles: avant-garde, free

verse, haiku, light verse and traditional. We do not wish to limit the reader or author." Also accepts poetry written by children. They have published poetry by Reg E. Gaines, Maya Angelou, Jessica Care Moore, Asha Bandele, Tony Medina and Louis Reyes Rivera. *African Voices* is about 30 pgs., 8½×11, professionally printed and saddle-stapled with paper cover, includes b&w photos and illustrations. They receive about 100 submissions a year, accept approximately 30%. Press run is 20,000 for 5,000 subscribers of which 30 are libraries, 40% shelf sales. Single copy: $2.50; subscription: $12. Sample: $3.50.

How to Submit: Submit no more than 5 poems at any one time. Previously published poems and simultaneous submissions OK. E-mail and fax submissions OK, include in body of e-mail message. Cover letter and SASE required. Seldom comments on rejections. Send SASE for guidelines and upcoming themes. Responds in 2 months. Pays 5 copies. Acquires first or one-time rights. Reviews books of poetry in 500-1,000 words. Open to unsolicited reviews. Poets may also send books for review consideration, attn. Layding Kaliba.

Also Offers: Sponsors periodic poetry contests and readings. Send SASE for details.

Advice: "We strongly encourage new writers/poets to send in their work and not give up if their work is not accepted the first time. Accepted contributors are encouraged to subscribe."

☑ $ ⊘ **AGNI**, Boston University, 236 Bay State Rd., Boston MA 02215, phone (617)353-7135, fax (617)353-7134, e-mail agni@bu.edu, website www.bu.edu.com/agni/, founded 1972, editors Askold Melnyczuk and Colette Kelso.

　📖 Work published in *AGNI* has been included in *The Best American Poetry* (1995, 1997, 1998 and 1999) and *Pushcart Prize* anthologies.

Magazine Needs: *AGNI* is a biannual journal of poetry, fiction and essays "by both emerging and established writers. We publish quite a bit of poetry in forms as well as 'language' poetry, but we don't begin to try and place parameters on the 'kind of work' that *AGNI* selects." Editors seem to select readable, intelligent poetry—mostly lyric free verse (with some narrative and dramatic, too)—that somehow communicates tension or risk. They have published poetry by Adrienne Rich, Seamus Heaney, Maxine Scates, Rosanna Warren, Chinua Achebe and Ha Jin. *AGNI* is typeset, offset-printed and perfect-bound with about 40 poems featured in each issue. Circulation is 1,500 by subscription, mail order and bookstore sales. Subscription: $18. Sample: $9.

How to Submit: "We will not be accepting unsolicited submissions until further notice. Consult recent issue for reinstatement date of open submission reading period." Manuscripts will be returned unread. When open, submit 3 poems at a time. "No fancy fonts, gimmicks or preformatted reply cards. No work accepted via e-mail. Brief, sincere cover letters." No previously published poems; simultaneous submissions OK. Pays $10/page, $150 maximum, plus 2 copies and one-year subscription. Buys first serial rights.

Also Offers: *AGNI* also publishes Take Three, an annual series of work by three young poets in conjunction with Graywolf Press. Poets are chosen by *AGNI*'s editorial board. Website includes writer's guidelines, names of editors, poetry and interviews, plus information on back issues.

Ⓝ ◖ ◯ ◑ ◎ **AG-PILOT INTERNATIONAL MAGAZINE (Specialized: agricultural aviation)**, P.O. Box 1607, Mt. Vernon WA 98273, phone (360)336-6129 or (888)490-8206, fax (360)336-2506, e-mail agpilot@chw.com, website www.agpilot.com, publisher Tom Wood, contact Krista Salinas.

Magazine Needs: *AG-Pilot* "is intended to be a fun-to-read, technical, as well as humorous and serious publication for the ag pilot and operator. Interested in agricultural aviation (crop dusting) and aerial fire suppression (air tanker pilots) related poetry ONLY—something that rhymes and has a cadence." Also accepts poetry written by children. As a sample we selected these lines from "Freedom" by Jack B. Harvey:

> So now I dress in faded jeans/And beat up cowboy boots./My flying's done on veg'tables,/The row crops, and the fruits.//My wife now drives the flaggin' truck/And marks off all my fields./She tells me all about the crops/And talks about the yields.

It appears monthly, 64-96 pgs., 8½×10⅞, saddle-stapled, circulation 7,200.

How to Submit: Buys 1 poem/issue. E-mail submissions OK. Pays about $35.

Also Offers: Publishes a Spanish-language version of *Ag-Pilot* titled *Volando*. For more information, contact managing editor Iris Carias at the above address.

◖ ◑ ◎ **THE AGUILAR EXPRESSION (Specialized: social issues); EROS ERRANT (Specialized: love/romance/erotica)**, 1329 Gilmore Ave., Donora PA 15033, phone (724)379-8019, founded 1986, editor/publisher Xavier F. Aguilar.

Magazine Needs: *Aguilar Expression* appears 2 times/year. "In publishing poetry, I try to exhibit the unique reality that we too often take for granted and acquaint as mediocre. We encourage poetics that deal with *now*, which our readers can relate to. We are particularly interested in poetry dealing with social issues." They have published poetry by Martin Kich and Gail Ghai. As a sample the editor selected these lines from "The Water Truck" by Donna Taylor Burgess:

> But pockets are as empty/As the taps/In a government day/And water has never been free.

AE is 4-20 pgs., photocopied on 8½×11 sheets and corner stapled. They receive about 20-30 poems a month, use approximately 5-10 poems. Circulation is 300. Sample: $6. Make checks payable to *Aguilar Expression*.

How to Submit: "We insist that all writers send a SASE for writer's guidelines before submitting." Submit up to 3 poems at a time, 24-line limit, any topic/style. "Send copies; mss will not be returned." Cover letter, including writing background, and SASE for contact purposes, required with submissions. Responds in 2 months. Pays 1 copy. Open to unsolicited reviews.

Magazine Needs: *Eros Errant* appears 2 times/year (June and December) and publishes poetry, fiction and b&w line art. They want poems that "exhibit the sexual travels of various characters and situations—diversity is our call. All situations with adults considered. The more graphic the better. No fetish." As a sample the editor selected these lines from "Obsessed" by Corrine DeWinter:

I whispered to you,/told you secrets./I asked you to come,/to bring me stars,/to say my name.

EE is 4-12 pgs., photocopied on 4¼×5½ sheets. Circulation is 100. Sample: $3. Make checks payable to *Aguilar Expression*.

How to Submit: Submit up to 5 poems at a time, 20-line limit/poem. "We ask that writers send a SASE for guidelines before submitting work." No simultaneous submissions; previously published poems OK. Pays 1 copy. Acquires one-time rights.

$ 🗌 ⊘ ◎ AIM MAGAZINE (Specialized: social issues, ethnic, political), P.O. Box 1174, Maywood IL 60153, phone (773)874-6184, fax (206)543-2746, e-mail mapilado@aol.com, website www.aimmagazine.org, founded 1974, poetry editor Ruth Apilado.

Magazine Needs: *Aim* is a quarterly, "dedicated to racial harmony and peace." They use 3-4 poems ("poetry with social significance mainly"—average 32 lines) in each issue. Also accepts poetry written by high school students. They have published poetry by J. Douglas Studer, Wayne Dowdy, Ned Pendergast and Maria DeGuzman. *Aim* is magazine-sized with glossy cover, circulation 10,000. They receive about 30 submissions a year, use half. They have 3,000 subscribers of which 15 are libraries. Single copy: $3; subscription: $12. Sample: $4.

How to Submit: Simultaneous submissions OK. Send SASE for upcoming themes. Responds in 6 weeks. Pays $3/poem and 1 copy. You will not receive an acceptance slip: "We simply send payment and magazine copy."

Also Offers: Website includes advertising, subscription information.

Advice: "Read the work of published poets."

🌐 $⊘ AKROS PUBLICATIONS; ZED₂O MAGAZINE, 33 Lady Nairn Ave., Kirkcaldy, Fife KY1 2AW Scotland, United Kingdom, founded 1965, contact Duncan Glen.

Magazine Needs & How to Submit: *ZED₂O* is an annual poetry and arts magazine containing a "variety of special topics in each issue." They are open to all forms and length of poetry. The editor says *ZED₂O* is 60 pgs., 210×130mm. They accept approximately 10% of work received. Press run is 500. Single copy: £3.95. Make checks payable to Duncan Glen. Does not accept checks in US funds. Submit 6 poems at a time. No previously published poems or simultaneous submissions. Cover letter preferred. "Submit hard copy initially; disks welcomed after acceptance if compatible with IBM—high density. We get many submissions from USA and UK without SASE or SAE and IRCs." Time between acceptance and publication is 9 months. Always comments on rejections but "very briefly." Publishes theme issues. Guidelines included inside magazine. Responds monthly. Sometimes sends prepublication galleys. No payment. Acquires first United Kingdom publication rights.

Book/Chapbook Needs & How to Submit: Akros Publications is a poetry press—"often publishing Scottish poems." They publish 1 paperback and 6 chapbooks/year. Chapbooks (also called pamphlets in the U.K.) are 20 pgs., 210×130mm, offset litho printed. Replies to queries in 2 months maximum, to mss "quickly." Pays 10% royalties and/or 6 author's copies (out of a press run of 500). "No royalties given if chapbooks are by new poets." Send SAE and IRCs for catalog.

⊘ ALABAMA LITERARY REVIEW, English Dept., Troy State University, Troy AL 36082, phone (334)670-3286, fax (334)670-3519, poetry editor Ed Hicks.

Magazine Needs: *ALR*, a biannual, wants contemporary poetry that is "imagistic—but in motion." Will look at anything, but does not want to see "lyrics sent as poetry. We want serious craft." They have published poetry by David Musgrove, R.T. Smith, Ed Peaco, Joanne M. Riley, Martha Payne, Edward Byrne and Katherine McCanless. The beautifully printed 100-page, 7×10 magazine, matte cover with art, b&w art and some colored pages inside, receives 300 submissions/year, uses 30, has a 2-month backlog. Sample: $5.

How to Submit: "Not accepting submissions for 2001. Will resume in 2002." Submit 2-5 poems at a time. "SASE with appropriate postage is paramount." Simultaneous submissions OK. Reads submissions September 1 through July 31 only. Sometimes comments on rejections. Responds in 3 months. Sometimes sends prepublication galleys. Pays copies, sometimes honorarium. Acquires first rights. Open to unsolicited reviews. Poets may also send books for review consideration.

✓ ⊘ ALASKA QUARTERLY REVIEW, University of Alaska Anchorage, 3211 Providence Dr., Anchorage AK 99508, phone/fax (907)786-6916, e-mail ayaqr@uaa.alaska.edu, website www.uaa.alaska.edu/aqr, founded 1981, executive editor Ronald Spatz.

🔻 Poetry published in *AQR* has been selected for inclusion in *The Best American Poetry*, *Pushcart Prize* and *Beacon's Best* anthologies.

Magazine Needs: "A journal devoted to contemporary literary art. We publish both traditional and experimental fiction, poetry, literary nonfiction and short plays." They have published poetry by Kim Addonizio, Tom Lux,

Pattiann Rogers, John Balaban, Albert Goldbarth, Jane Hirshfield, Billy Collins and Dorianne Laux. Editors seem to welcome all styles and forms of poetry with the most emphasis perhaps on voice and content that displays "risk," or intriguing ideas or situations. They publish two double-issues a year, each using between 25-50 pgs. of poetry. The copy of *AQR* we received was 262 pgs., 6×9, professionally printed and perfect-bound with card cover containing b&w photo. They receive up to 3,000 submissions a year, accept 40-60. Circulation is 2,200 for 500 subscribers of which 32 are libraries. Subscription: $10. Sample: $6.

How to Submit: Manuscripts are *not* read from May 15 through August 15. They take up to 4 months to report, sometimes longer during peak periods in late winter. Pay depends on funding. Acquires first North American serial rights. Guest poetry editors have included Stuart Dybek, Jane Hirshfield, Stuart Dischell, Maxine Kumin, Pattiann Rogers, Dorianne Laux and Billy Collins.

✔ ⊘ ◎ **ALBATROSS; THE ANABIOSIS PRESS (Specialized: nature)**, 2 South New St., Haverhill MA 01835, phone (978)469-7085, editor Richard Smyth.

Magazine Needs: *Albatross* appears: "as soon as we have accepted enough quality poems to publish an issue. We consider the albatross to be a metaphor for an environment that must survive. This is not to say that we publish only environmental or nature poetry, but that we are biased toward such subject matters. We publish mostly free verse, 200 lines/poem maximum, and we prefer a narrative style, but again, this is not necessary. We do not want trite rhyming poetry which doesn't convey a deeply felt experience in a mature expression with words." Also publish interviews with established writers. They have published poetry by Daniel Comiskey, Fredrick Zydek, Paul B. Roth, Duane Locke and Susan Herport Methvin. As a sample the editors selected these lines by Christine Delea:

> We mended their hurt bodies,/stashed the bones of the dead/in hidden places, and purred like humans/
> when they licked us clean,/forgave us our sins.

The magazine is 28-36 pgs., 5½×8½, laser typeset with linen cover, some b&w drawings, and sometimes, in addition to the poetry, has an interview with a poet in each issue. Circulation is 300 for 75 subscribers of which 10 are libraries. Many complimentary copies are sent out to bookstores, poets and libraries. Subscription: $5/2 issues. Sample: $3.

How to Submit: Submit 3-5 poems at a time. "Poems should be typed single-spaced, with name, address and phone number in upper left corner." No simultaneous submissions. Cover letter not required; "We do, however, need bio notes and SASE for return or response." Send SASE for guidelines. Responds in 6 months, has 6- to 12-month backlog. Pays 1 copy. Acquires all rights. Returns rights provided that "previous publication in *Albatross* is mentioned in all subsequent reprintings."

Also Offers: Holds a chapbook contest. Submit 20 pgs. of poetry, any theme, any style. Deadline is June 31 of each year. Include name, address and phone number on the title page. Charges $7 reading fee (check payable to Anabiosis Press). Winner receives $100 and 25 copies of his/her published chapbook. All entering receive a free copy of the winning chapbook. "The Anabiosis Press is a nonprofit, tax-exempt organization. Membership fee is $20/year."

Advice: "We expect a poet to read as much contemporary poetry as possible. We seek deeply felt experiences expressed maturely within a unique style of writing. We want to be moved. When you read our poetry, we hope that it moves you in the same way that it moves us. We try to publish the kind of poetry that you would want to read again and again."

✔ ▣ $◯ ⊘ **ALDEN ENTERPRISES; GRACIE PUBLICATIONS; POETIC VOICES MAGAZINE**, 2206 Bailey St. NW, Hartselle AL 35640-4219, e-mail editor@poeticvoices.com (for R.C. Travis) or poetryeditor@poeticvoices.com (for Ursula T. Gibson), website www.poeticvoices.com, founded 1997, executive editor (Alden Ent.) R.C. Travis, submissions editor (Poetic Voices) Ursula T. Gibson.

Magazine Needs: E-mailed to subscribers monthly, *Poetic Voices* is "informational and educational in content. Articles include feature interviews, columns on the mechanics of writing, questions on writing and publishing, information on organizations useful to poets, contest and award opportunities, publishing opportunities, workshops and conferences, book reviews and more. We are open to most forms, styles and subjects. No pornography, scatology, racial slurs or dehumanizing poems." They have published poetry by Lyn Lifshin. As a sample the editors selected these lines from "The Created" by Sue Scalf:

> From this rough clay/pounded upon the wheel,/from this body made of dirt, spinning/like a wind lifted
> in that turning,/he is making a porcelain,/fired in the kiln and glowing,/a vessel of intricate filligree/
> planned and wrought/before the world was made,/of our bones the bone-white/light, translucent.

**FOR EXPLANATIONS OF THESE SYMBOLS,
SEE THE INSIDE FRONT AND BACK COVERS OF THIS BOOK.**

PV is an electronic magazine containing 30-60 pgs. It can be accessed at members.aol.com/gracieami/arch.htm. They receive about 1,200 poems a year, accept approximately 10%. Circulation is "over 10,000 poets in 20 countries each month."

How to Submit: Submit up to 4 poems a month by e-mail, text in body of message, to Ursula T. Gibson. Previously published poems and simultaneous submissions OK. Cover letter preferred. Often comments on rejections. Send SASE for guidelines or obtain via website. Responds in 2 months. Sometimes sends prepublication galleys. Acquires one-time rights. Reviews books and chapbooks of poetry and other magazines in 200-500 words. Open to unsolicited reviews. Poets may also send books for review consideration to R.C. Travis at above address or e-mail.

Book/Chapbook Needs & How to Submit: Gracie Publications, a division of Alden Enterprises, seeks "to promote new and talented poets, and their work, via the publication of chapbooks of poetry. All styles of poetry are welcome. . . . We are open to new writers, look for variety and excellence, are open to concrete forms, traditional, and free verse as well as other varieties. We do accept religious theme poems." They publish 6-10 chapbooks/year. Chapbooks are usually 20-40 pgs., 8½×5½, laser printed and saddle-stitched with cardstock covers containing art. Submit ms containing 20-30 poems ("no epic poetry please"), typed and double spaced on 8½×11 paper. ("We ask that you also include a disk copy of your poetry saved in text format.") No e-mail submissions. Include cover letter with address and phone number. Poems must be original; simultaneous submissions and previously published poetry OK if noted. Reading fee: $10, must be included with submission. Make checks payable to Alden Enterprises. Reads submissions March 15 through September 15. Replies to queries in 1-2 months; to mss in 3-4 months. Pays royalties of 8-15% and 10 author's copies (out of a press run of 200). Order sample books or chapbooks by sending $5 to above address.

Also Offers: Sponsors WritersClub.com, the online community for writers. The website (www.writersclub.com) includes chats, genre newsletters, searchable agents and publishers database, courses, message boards, reviews, author interviews and horoscopes for writers. The Alden website includes writer's guidelines, books published, purpose and purchasing information on books.

Advice: "Make sure you read and follow guidelines. Make sure your work is neatly presented. There is nothing worse than receiving messy work or work that does not conform to the guidelines."

☑ ◯ **ALEMBIC; TRISKELION PRESS; ALEMBIC ANNUAL POETRY CONTEST**, P.O. Box 28416, Philadelphia PA 19149, phone (610)460-0588, e-mail alembic33@yahoo.com, founded 1998, editor L.P. Farrell.

Magazine Needs: *Alembic* is a "quarterly magazine of poetry, fiction and artwork dedicated to giving a venue for publication of new poets, writers and artists." They want "all kinds with exception to typewritten gymnastics, pornography, hate works, obscure works and forced rhymes. Also, no poems over 40 lines." The editor says *Alembic* is 50 pgs., 8½×11, photocopied and side-stapled with card cover with artwork, includes b&w drawings. They receive about 500 poems a year, accept approximately 40%. Press run is 200 for 60 subscribers. Subscription: $11. Sample: $3.50. Make checks payable to L.P. Farrell.

How to Submit: Submit 3 poems at a time. Line length for poetry is 40 maximum. No previously published poems or simultaneous submissions. Cover letter required. "For cover letters, we need a short biography, a statement that the work(s) are original and not previously published or a simultaneous submission." Time between acceptance and publication is 1 year. Often comments on rejections. "I always write a couple paragraphs of suggestions, but charge $10 per story and $2 per poem for editing advice and corrections." Send SASE for guidelines. Responds in 3 months. Pays 1 copy. Acquires first North American serial rights. Staff reviews books and chapbooks of poetry in 100 words, single book format. Send books for review consideration to L.P. Farrell. "Include cover letter."

Also Offers: Sponsors the Alembic Annual Poetry Contest. Awards $50 Grand Prize. Submit maximum of 3 unpublished poems in 1 envelope. Entry fee: $3/3 poems. Award issue published in October.

Advice: "Get emotionally involved with your work. Always revise, revise and then revise again after letting your work sit between revisions. Take a chance and submit: rejection never killed anyone; getting published makes you feel very alive."

☑ ◐ ◎ **ALICE JAMES BOOKS; NEW ENGLAND/NEW YORK AWARD, BEATRICE HAWLEY AWARD, JANE KENYON CHAPBOOK AWARD (Specialized: regional, women)**, University of Maine at Farmington, 98 Main St., Farmington ME 04938, phone/fax (207)778-7071, e-mail ajb@umf.maine.edu, website www.umf.maine.edu/~ajb, founded 1973, contest coordinator Alice James Books.

Book/Chapbook Needs: *Alice James Books* is "a nonprofit author's collective which only publishes poetry. Authors are primarily from the New England Area. We emphasize poetry by women, though we now seek poetry by any contemporary voice." They publish flat-spined paperbacks of high quality, both in production and contents, no children's poetry or light verse. They publish 4-5 books, 80 pgs., each year in editions of 1,500, paperbacks— no hardbacks. They have published *Camera Lyrica* by Amy Newman; *The Kingdom of the Subjunctive* by Suzanne Wise and poetry by Jane Kenyon, Jean Valentine and B.H. Fairchild.

How to Submit: Query first (with SASE), but no need for samples: simply ask for dates of reading period, which is in early fall and winter. No phone queries. Send 2 copies of the ms. Simultaneous submissions OK, but "we would like to know when a manuscript is accepted elsewhere." Responds in 4 months.

Also Offers: Offers Beatrice Hawley Award for poets living anywhere in the US. Winners of the New England/ New York competition become members of the collective with a three-year commitment to editorial board. Each winner in both competitions receives a cash award of $1,000. Also offers the Jane Kenyon Chapbook Award every 2 years. Next chapbook competition is in 2001. Send SASE for guidelines. Website includes information on press, guidelines, sample poems and individual pages on published poets.

✓ $ ◻ ◎ ALIVE NOW (Specialized: spirituality, themes); POCKETS (Specialized: religious, children, themes); DEVO'ZINE (Specialized: religious, youth, themes); WEAVINGS; THE UPPER ROOM, 1908 Grand Ave., P.O. Box 340004, Nashville TN 37203-0004, website www.upperroom.org. This publishing company brings out about 30 books a year and 5 magazines: *The Upper Room, Alive Now, Pockets, Devo'Zine* and *Weavings.* Of these, three use unsolicited poetry.

Magazine Needs & How to Submit: *Pockets, Devotional Magazine for Children*, which comes out 11 times/year, circulation 90,000, is for children 6-12, "offers stories, activities, prayers, poems—all geared to giving children a better understanding of themselves as children of God. Some of the material is not overtly religious but deals with situations, special seasons and holidays, and ecological concerns from a Christian perspective." It uses 3-4 pgs. of poetry/issue. Sample free with 7½×10½ SAE and 4 first-class stamps. Ordinarily 24-line limit on poetry. Send SASE for themes and guidelines. Pays $25-50.

Magazine Needs & How to Submit: *Alive Now*, editor George Graham, is a bimonthly, circulation 75,000, for a general Christian audience interested in reflection and meditation. They buy 30 poems a year, avant-garde and free verse. Submit 5 poems, 10-45 lines. Send SASE for themes and guidelines. Pays $25-50.

Magazine Needs & How to Submit: *Devo'Zine: Just for Teens*, is a bimonthly devotional magazine for youth ages 13-18, offers meditations, scripture, prayers, poems, stories, songs and feature articles to "aid youth in their prayer life, introduce them to spiritual disciplines, help them shape their concept of God, and encourage them in the life of discipleship." Ordinarily 20-line limit on poetry. Send SASE for theme and guidelines. Pays $25.

Also Offers: *The Upper Room* magazine does not accept poetry.

✓ ◻ ◎ ALLEGHENY REVIEW (Specialized: undergraduate students), Box 32, Allegheny College, Meadville PA 16335, phone (814)332-6553, e-mail review@alleg.edu, website http://webpub.alleg.edu/group/review, founded 1983, faculty advisor Sonya Jones.

Magazine Needs: "Each year *Allegheny Review* compiles and publishes a review of the nation's best undergraduate literature. It is entirely composed of and by college undergraduates and is nationally distributed both as a review and as a classroom text, particularly suited to creative writing courses." In the Fall of 1995, they added a section of essays on poetry and literature or theory. (Submit 10-20 typed pgs., double-spaced.) "We will print poetry of appreciable literary merit on any topic, submitted by college undergraduates. No limitations except excessive length (2-3 pgs.) as we wish to represent as many authors as possible, although exceptions are made in areas of great quality and interest." They have published poetry by Eric Sanborn, Cheryl Connor, Rick Alley and Kristi Coulter. The *Review* appears in a 6×9, flat-spined, professionally-printed format, b&w photo on glossy card cover. Single copy: $4. Sample: $4 and 11×18 SASE.

How to Submit: Submit 3-5 poems as hard copy and on disk, if possible. Submissions should be accompanied by a letter "telling the college poet is attending, year of graduation, any background, goals and philosophies the author feels are pertinent to the work submitted." Call or e-mail for current deadlines. Responds 2 months following deadline. Poem judged best in the collection earns $50-75 honorarium.

Advice: "Ezra Pound gave the best advice: 'Make it new.' We're seeing far too much imitation; there's already been a Sylvia Plath, a Galway Kinnell. Don't be afraid to try new things. Be innovative. Also, traditional forms are coming 'back in style,' or so we hear. Experiment with them; write a villanelle, a sestina or a sonnet. And when you submit, please take enough pride in your work to do so professionally. Handwritten or poorly typed and proofed submissions definitely convey an impression—a negative one."

◻ ✎ ALLIGATOR JUNIPER, Prescott College, 220 Grove Ave., Prescott AZ 86301, phone (520)778-2090, ext. 2012, e-mail aj@prescott.edu, founded 1995, managing editor Melanie Bishop, poetry editor Sheila Sanderson.

Magazine Needs: *Alligator Juniper* is a contest publication appearing annually in May. "Aside from advertised theme issues, we publish work based only on artistic merit." They have published poetry by Elton Glaser and Fatima Lim-Wilson. The editors say *AJ* is approximately 200 pgs. with b&w photography. They receive about 1,200-1,500 poems a year, accept approximately 6-20 poems. Press run is 1,500 for 600 subscribers; 200 distributed free to other reputable journals, MFA programs and writers' colonies. Subscription: $12/2 years (2 issues). Sample: $7.50. "We publish one issue per year and it's always a contest, requiring a $10 fee which allows us to pay a $500 first prize in each category—fiction, poetry, creative nonfiction and photography. All entrants receive a copy of the next issue."

How to Submit: Submit up to 5 poems at a time with reading fee. No previously published poems; simultaneous submissions OK. Cover letter preferred. No e-mail or fax submissions. Reads submissions October 1 through December 15 only. Postmark deadline: October 1. "We read and select what we will publish from all the work submitted so far that calendar year." Reading fee: $10/entry (5 poems or 5 pages of poetry). Time between acceptance and publication is 3-5 months. "Finalists are selected in-house and passed on to a different guest judge each year." Publishes theme issues occasionally. Send SASE for guidelines or obtain via e-mail or website. Responds in 5 months. Each year, one winner receives $500 plus 4 copies; all other poets whose work is selected for publication receive payment in copies only.

☑ ◯ ◎ **ALLISONE PRESS; STAR RISING MAGAZINE; STAR RISING PUBLISHERS, (Special-ized: psychic/occult, religious, science fiction/fantasy, social issues, spirituality/inspirational)**, P.O. Box 494, Mt. Shasta CA 96067, phone (530)926-1254, fax (530)926-1830, e-mail editor@allisonepress.com, website www.allisonepress.com, founded 1996, editor Kristen B. May, publisher Robin B. May.

Magazine Needs: *Star Rising Magazine* is published biannually and contains "all types of writing—poetry, short stories and articles." They want "poetry that speaks from experience and the heart. Be creative. No pornographic material." They have published poetry by Anna Laxague and Anmol Bhagchand. As a sample the editor selected these lines from "Heaven is Falling" by Matthew Donald Wetherby:

> *Molding all within a fetish light/While the earth's very breath is transformed/Into but a shade of the universe,/Mocking mankind with an impotent fear,/Commanding all life to breathe of its tears;/Frown oh sulking stars, heaven is falling.*

SRM is about 60 pgs., magazine-sized, photocopied and glued into a folder-like card cover, includes art/graphics and ads. They receive about 200 poems a year, accept approximately 60%. Press run is 500 for 200 subscribers of which 50 are libraries, 100 shelf sales; 50 distributed free to "hospitals, rest homes, etc." Subscription: $17.95/year, $35/2 years. Sample: $8.95. Make checks payable to Odenthal, Inc.

How to Submit: Submit 5 poems at a time. Previously published poems and simultaneous submissions OK. Cover letter preferred. E-mail submissions OK. Time between acceptance and publication is 4 months. Poems are circulated to an editorial board. Often comments on rejections. Send SASE for guidelines or obtain via e-mail or website. Responds in 1 month. Pays 1 copy, more copies available at wholesale cost. Acquires one-time rights. Reviews books of poetry in single book format. Open to unsolicited reviews. Poets may also send books for review consideration to Robin B. May, publisher.

Book/Chapbook Needs & How to Submit: Star Rising Publishers considers all types and forms of poetry. They publish 2 paperbacks/year. Books are usually 60-200 pgs., 5½×8½, digitally printed and perfect-bound with cover stock, includes art/graphics.

How to Submit: Send complete ms with cover letter, list of credits and brief bio. Replies to queries in 1 month; to mss in 4 months. Pays royalties of 10-20% and 10 author's copies (out of a press run of 100). Order sample books by sending $10.

Also Offers: Website includes guidelines, submissions, poetry, monthly updates for writers, referrals to other contests, help typing submissions, advertising, books, address and subscriptions. Allisone Press publishes New Age, metaphysical and how-to titles.

Advice: "Be creative and never limit your expression. Be open to new ideas and ways of writing. We like to see new writers. They usually receive first consideration."

☑ $◑ ◯ **ALMS HOUSE PRESS; WHEAT EAR**, P.O. Box 218, Woodbourne NY 12788, fax (914)436-0099, founded 1985, poetry editors Lorraine De Gennaro and Alana Sherman, publishes the biannual *Wheat Ear* and 3-4 chapbooks/perfect-bound books per year.

Magazine Needs & How to Submit: For *Wheat Ear* (formerly *The Alms House Journal*), submit 3-5 poems at a time with $5 reading fee. Include SASE. Pays 1 copy.

Book/Chapbook Needs: "We have no preferences with regard to style as long as the poetry is high caliber. We like to see previous publication in the small press, but we are open to new writers. We look for variety and excellence and are open to experimental forms as well as traditional forms. Any topics as long as the poems are not whiny or too depressing, pornographic or religious." Also accepts poetry written by children over age 10. They have published poetry by Karen Nelson and Don Schofield. As a sample the editors selected these lines of poetry:

> *moving my arms like giant/wings breathing/minerals and sand/inhaling you/an orange and black fan*

How to Submit: For chapbooks, submit 16- to 24-page ms with $15 reading fee; for longer collections, submit up to 50 pages with $25 reading fee. All mss must be typed with 1 poem/page. No previously published poems or simultaneous submissions. Reads submissions March 15 through June 15 and September 15 through December 15 only. Send SASE for guidelines or request via fax. Responds in 2-3 months. Press pays $25 plus 10 copies and 7% of all sales over first 100 books.

Also Offers: They sponsor a poetry reading series and offer a critical and editorial service for $50.

Advice: "We treat every poem, every manuscript and every author with respect. We believe poetry should be well presented."

🄽 🌐 ◗ **AMBIT**, 17 Priory Gardens, Highgate, London N6 5QY England, phone 0181-340-3566, website www.ambit.co.uk, editor Martin Bax; poetry editors Martin Bax, Carol Ann Duffy and Henry Graham; prose editors J.G. Ballard and Geoff Nicholson; art editor Mike Foreman.

Magazine Needs: *Ambit* is a 96-page quarterly of avant-garde, contemporary and experimental work. Subscription: £22 individuals, £33 institutions (UK); £24 ($48) individuals, £35 ($70) institutions (overseas). Sample: £6.

How to Submit: Submit up to 6 poems at a time, typed double-spaced. No previously published poems or simultaneous submissions. Pay is "variable plus 2 free copies. SAE vital for reply." Staff reviews books of poetry. Send books for review consideration, attn. review editor.

Also Offers: Website includes names of editors and poetry and prose selected from the magazine's latest number.

N ⊕ **AMBITIOUS FRIENDS**, P.O. Box 435, Liverpool NSW 2170 Australia, phone (02)96013788, fax (02)96011398, e-mail editor@af.asn.au, website www.af.asn.au, literature sub-editor Marisa Cano.

Magazine Needs: *AF* produces a "quarterly multicultural magazine featuring community news, arts, recipes, poems, history and culture. All types of poetry expression are welcome." The editor says *AF* is 48 pgs., magazine-sized, professionally printed and stapled with glossy cover, includes photos, drawings, ads. Publishes theme issues.

How to Submit: Submit 1 poem at a time. "Subscribers are given priority." Previously published poems and simultaneous submissions OK. Cover letter preferred. E-mail and disk submissions OK. Reads submissions "in between deadlines." See website for more information. Poems are circulated to an editorial board. Seldom comments on rejections.

$ ⊘ ◎ **AMELIA; CICADA; SPSM&H; THE AMELIA AWARDS (Specialized: form)**, 329 "E" St., Bakersfield CA 93304 or P.O. Box 2385, Bakersfield CA 93303, phone (805)323-4064, founded 1983, poetry editor Frederick A. Raborg, Jr.

Magazine Needs & How to Submit: *Amelia* is a quarterly magazine that publishes chapbooks as well. Central to its operations is a series of contests, most with entry fees, spaced evenly throughout the year, awarding more than $3,500 annually, but they publish many poets who have not entered the contests as well. Among poets published are Pattiann Rogers, Stuart Friebert, John Millett, David Ray, Larry Rubin, Charles Bukowski, Maxine Kumin, Charles Edward Eaton and Shuntaro Tanikawa. They are "receptive to all forms to 100 lines. We do not want to see the patently-religious or overtly-political. Erotica is fine; pornography, no." The digest-sized, flat-spined magazine is offset on high-quality paper and sometimes features an original four-color cover; its circulation is about 1,642, with 702 subscribers, of which 28 are libraries. Subscription: $30/year. Sample: $10.95. Submit 3-5 poems at a time. No simultaneous submissions except for entries to the annual Amelia Chapbook Award. Responds in 2-12 weeks, the latter if under serious consideration. Pays $2-25/poem plus 2 copies. "Almost always I try to comment." The editor says, "*Amelia* is not afraid of strong themes, but we do look for professional, polished work even in handwritten submissions. Poets should have something to say about matters other than the moon. We like to see strong traditional pieces as well as the contemporary and experimental. And neatness *does* count." Fred Raborg has done more than most other editors to ensure a wide range of styles and forms, from traditional European to Asian, from lyric to narrative. Typically he is swamped with submissions and so response times can exceed stated parameters. *Amelia* continues to place in outside surveys as a top market, because of editorial openness. Brief reviews are also featured.

Magazine Needs & How to Submit: *Cicada* is a quarterly magazine that publishes haiku, senryu and other Japanese forms, plus essays on the form—techniques and history—as well as fiction which in some way incorporates haiku or Japanese poetry in its plot, and reviews of books pertaining to Japan and its poetry or collections of haiku. Among poets published are Roger Ishii, H.F. Noyes, Knute Skinner, Katherine Machan Aal, Ryah Tumarkin Goodman and Ryokufu Ishizaki. They are receptive to experimental forms as well as the traditional. "Try to avoid still-life as haiku; strive for the *whole* of an emotion, whether minuscule or panoramic. Erotica is fine; the Japanese are great lovers of the erotic." The magazine is offset on high-quality paper. Circulation is 800, with 562 subscribers of which 36 are libraries. Subscription: $18/year. Sample: $6. Submit 3-10 haiku or poems. No simultaneous submissions. Responds in 2 weeks. No payment, except three "best of issue" poets each receive $10 on publication plus copy. "I try to make some comment on returned poems always."

Magazine Needs & How to Submit: *SPSM&H* is a quarterly magazine that publishes only sonnets, sonnet sequences, essays on the form—both technique and history—as well as romantic or Gothic fiction which, in some way, incorporates the form, and reviews of sonnet collections or collections containing a substantial number of sonnets. They are "receptive to experimental forms as well as the traditional, and appreciate wit when very good." Among poets published are Margaret Ryan, Harold Witt, Sharon E. Martin, Rhina P. Espaillat and Robert Wolfkill. Perhaps it may help to know the editor's favorite Shakespearean sonnet is #29, and he feels John Updike clarified the limits of experimentation with the form in his "Love Sonnet" from *Midpoint*. The magazine is offset on high-quality paper. Circulation is 602, for 409 subscribers and 26 libraries. Subscription: $14/year. Sample: $4.95. Submit 3-5 poems at a time. No simultaneous submissions. Responds in 2 weeks. No payment, except two "best of issue" poets each receive $14 on publication plus copy. "I always try to comment on returns."

Also Offers: The following annual contests have various entry fees: The Amelia Awards (six prizes of $200, $100, $50 plus three honorable mentions of $10 each); The Anna B. Janzen Prize for Romantic Poetry ($100, annual deadline January 2); The Bernice Jennings Traditional Poetry Award ($100, annual deadline January 2); The Georgie Starbuck Galbraith Light/Humorous Verse Prizes (six awards of $100, $50, $25 plus three honorable mentions of $5 each, annual deadline March 1); The Charles William Duke Longpoem Award ($100, annual deadline April 1); The Lucille Sandberg Haiku Awards (six awards of $100, $50, $25 plus three honorable mentions of $5 each, annual deadline April 1); The Grace Hines Narrative Poetry Award ($100, annual deadline May 1); The Amelia Chapbook Award ($250, book publication and 50 copies, annual deadline July 1); The Johanna B. Bourgoyne Poetry Prizes (six awards of $100, $50, $25, plus three honorable mentions of $5 each); The Douglas Manning Smith Epic/Heroic Poetry Prize ($100, annual deadline August 1); The Hildegarde Janzen Prize for Oriental Forms of Poetry (six awards of $50, $30, $20 and three honorable mentions of $5 each, annual deadline September 1); The Eugene Smith Prize for Sonnets (six awards of $100, $50, $25 and three honorable mentions of $5 each); The A&C Limerick Prizes (six awards of $50, $30, $20 and three honorable mentions of $5 each); The Montegue Wade Lyric Poetry Prize ($100, annual deadline November 1).

☑ $☻ **AMERICA; FOLEY POETRY CONTEST**, 106 W. 56th St., New York NY 10019, phone (212)581-4640, founded 1909, poetry editor Paul Mariani.
Magazine Needs: *America* is a weekly journal of opinion published by the Jesuits of North America. They primarily publish articles on religious, social, political and cultural themes. They are "looking for imaginative poetry of all kinds. We have no restrictions on form or subject matter, though we prefer to receive poems of 35 lines or less." They have published poetry by Philip Levine, Kelly Cherry and Dabney Stuart. *America* is 36 pgs., magazine-sized, professionally printed on thin stock with thin paper cover. Circulation is 39,000. Subscription: $42. Sample: $2.25.
How to Submit: Send SASE for "excellent" guidelines. Responds in 2 weeks. Pays $2.50/line plus 2 copies.
Also Offers: The annual Foley Poetry Contest offers a prize of $500, usually in late winter. Send SASE for rules. "Poems for the Foley Contest should be submitted between January and April. Poems submitted for the Foley Contest between July and December will be returned unread."
Advice: "*America* is committed to publishing quality poetry as it has done for the past 89 years. We encourage more established poets to submit their poems to us."

◯ ◎ **THE AMERICAN COWBOY POET MAGAZINE (Specialized: cowboy)**, Dept. PM, P.O. Box 326, Eagle ID 83616, phone (208)888-9838, fax (208)888-2986, e-mail icpg@cowboyrudy.com, website www.cowboyrudy.com/icpg1.htm, founded 1988 as *The American Cowboy Poet Newspaper*, magazine format in January 1991, publisher Rudy Gonzales, editor Rose Fitzgerald.
Magazine Needs: *ACPM* is a quarterly "about real cowboys" using "authentic cowboy poetry. Must be clean—entertaining. Submissions should avoid 'like topics.' We will not publish any more poems about Old Blackie dying, this old hat, if this pair of boots could talk, etc. We do not publish free verse poetry. Only traditional cowboy poetry with rhyme and meter." They also publish articles, including a "Featured Poet," stories of cowboy poetry gatherings, and news of coming events. Subscription: $12/year US, $15 Canada, $20 Overseas. Sample: $3.50.
How to Submit: Cover letter required with submissions. Send SASE for guidelines, request via e-mail or check website. Editor always comments on rejections. Staff reviews related books and tapes of poetry. Send books and cowboy music tapes for review consideration.

☑ ◯ **THE AMERICAN DISSIDENT**, 1837 Main St., Concord MA 01742, e-mail enmarge@aol.com, website http://members.theglobe.com/ENMARGE, founded 1998, editor G. Tod Slone.
Magazine Needs: *AD* appears 2-3 times a year to "provide an outlet for critics of America." They want "well-written dissident work (non-rhyming poetry and short 250-950 word essays) in English, French or Spanish. Submissions should be iconoclastic and anti-obfuscatory in nature and should criticize some aspect of the American scene, including poet laureates, assimilated beatnik and hippy radicals, poetry slams of theatricality, artistes non-engagés, impenetrable ivory towers, state and national cultural councils, literary prizes, millionaire politicos proclaiming themselves champions of the poor, teachers, professors and deans of hypocrisy, armchair Thoreaus, media whores, medicare-bilking doctors, boards of wealthy used-car-salesmen trustees, justice-indifferent lawyers, judges and other careerists, global human rapports, the democratic sham masking the plutocracy and, more generally, the veil of charade placed upon the void of the universe to keep the current oligarchical system operational and the wealthy power elite firmly entrenched in North America." The editor says *AD* is 56 pgs., digest-sized, offset printed and perfect-bound with card cover, includes political cartoons. Press run is 200. Single copy: $7. Subscription: $14.
How to Submit: Submit 3 poems at a time. No previously published poems; simultaneous submissions OK. No e-mail submissions. "Include SASE and cover letter containing short bio (Manifest humility! Don't list credits and prizes), including de-programing and personal dissident information and specific events that may have pushed you to shed the various national skins of indoctrination and stand apart from your friends and/or colleagues to howl against corruption." Time between acceptance and publication is 3-6 months. Almost always comments on rejections. Send SASE for guidelines. Responds in 4 months. Pays 1 copy. Acquires first North American serial rights. Reviews books and chapbooks of poetry and other magazines in 250 words, single book format. Open to unsolicited reviews. Poets may also send books for review consideration.
Also Offers: Website includes guidelines, sample poems and essays, names of editors and contact information.
Advice: "Do not submit work apt to be accepted by the multitudinous valentine and academic journals and presses that clog up the piping of the nation's bowels. *AD* is concerned about the overly successful indoctrination of the citizenry and resultant happy-face fascism. It is concerned that too many citizens have become clonified teamplayers, networkers and blind institutional patriots for whom loyalty (semper fi) has overwhelming priority over the truth. *AD* is interested in unique insights and ways of looking at the national infrastructure of hypocrisy, fraud and corruption, the glue that seems to be holding America together."

◎ **AMERICAN INDIAN STUDIES CENTER; AMERICAN INDIAN CULTURE AND RESEARCH JOURNAL (Specialized: ethnic/nationality)**, 3220 Campbell Hall, Box 951548, UCLA, Los Angeles CA 90095-1548, phone (310)825-7315, fax (310)206-7060, e-mail aiscpubs@ucla.edu, website www.sscnet.UCLA.edu/esp/aisc/index.html, founded 1975.
Magazine Needs: The *American Indian Culture and Research Journal* is a quarterly which publishes new research and literature about American Indians. All work must have Native American content. The editor says

the journal is 300 pgs., 6×9, perfect-bound. They receive about 50-70 poems a year, accept approximately 30. Press run is 1,200 for 1,000 subscribers of which 400 are libraries, 10 shelf sales. Subscription: $25 individual, $60 institution. Sample: $12. Make checks payable to Regents of the University of California.

How to Submit: Submit 5-6 poems at a time. No previously published poems or simultaneous submissions. Cover letter preferred. No fax or e-mail submissions. Time between acceptance and publication is 6 months. Poems are circulated to an editorial board. Often comments on rejections. Publishes theme issues. Responds in 2 months. Always sends prepublication galleys. Pays 1 copy.

Book/Chapbook Needs & How to Submit: The American Indian Studies Center also publishes 1-2 paperback books of poetry in their Native American Literature Series. They have published *The Light on the Tent Wall: A Bridging* by Mary TallMountain and *Old Shirts & New Skins* by Sherman Alexie. Pays author's copies and offers 40% discount on additional copies. Send SASE for a complete list of the center's publications.

AMERICAN LITERARY REVIEW, University of North Texas, P.O. Box 311307, Denton TX 76203-1307, phone (940)565-2755, website www.engl.unt.edu/alr, editor Lee Martin, poetry editor Bruce Bond.

Magazine Needs: *ALR* is a biannual publishing all forms and modes of poetry and fiction. "We are especially interested in originality, substance, imaginative power and lyric intensity." They have published poetry by Christopher Howell, David Citino, Laura Kasischke, Pattiann Rogers, Eric Pankey and David St. John. *ALR* is about 120 pgs., 6×9, attractively printed and perfect-bound with color card cover with photo. Subscription: $15/year, $28/2 years. Sample: $9 (US), $10 (elsewhere).

How to Submit: Submit up to 5 typewritten poems at a time. Cover letter with author's name, address, phone number and poem titles required. Responds in 2 months. Pays copies.

Also Offers: Sponsors poetry and fiction contest in alternating years. Next poetry contest will be in 2000. Send SASE for details.

$ AMERICAN POETRY REVIEW; JEROME J. SHESTACK PRIZES; JESSICA NOBEL MAXWELL MEMORIAL POETRY PRIZE, Dept. PM, 1721 Walnut St., Philadelphia PA 19103, phone (215)496-0439, fax (215)569-0808, founded 1972.

Poetry published here has also been included in the 1995, 1997 and 1998 volumes of *The Best American Poetry*.

Magazine Needs: *APR* is probably the most widely circulated (18,000 copies bimonthly) and best-known periodical devoted to poetry in the world. Poetry editors are Stephen Berg, David Bonanno and Arthur Vogelsang, and they have published most of the leading poets writing in English and many translations. The poets include Gerald Stern, Brenda Hillman, John Ashbery, Norman Dubie, Marvin Bell, Galway Kinnell, James Dickey, Lucille Clifton and Tess Gallagher. *APR* is a newsprint tabloid with 13,000 subscriptions, of which 1,000 are libraries. They receive about 10,000 submissions a year, accept approximately 200. This popular publication contains mostly free verse (some leaning to the avant-garde) with flashes of brilliance in every issue. Editors seem to put an emphasis on language and voice. Because *APR* is a tabloid, it can feature long poems (or ones with long line lengths) in an attractive format. Translations are also welcome. In all, this is a difficult market to crack because of the volume of submissions. Sample: $3.95.

How to Submit: No simultaneous submissions. Responds in 3 months, has 12- to 18-month backlog. Always sends prepublication galleys. Pays $1/line. The magazine is also a major resource for opinion, reviews, theory, news and ads pertaining to poetry.

Also Offers: Each year the editors award the Jerome J. Shestack Prizes, 2 prizes of $1,000 for the best poems, in their judgment, published in *APR*. Also sponsors the Jessica Nobel Maxwell Memorial Poetry Prize, $2,000 awarded annually to a younger poet whose work has appeared in *APR* during the preceding calendar year. The editors also sponsor the *APR*/Honickman First Book Prize in Poetry. Award is $3,000 and publication. Entry fee: $20. Mss must be postmarked by October 31. Send SASE for complete guidelines.

AMERICAN POETS & POETRY, P.O. Box 7692, Port St. Lucie FL 34985-7692, founded 1996, editor John DeStefano.

Magazine Needs: *American Poets & Poetry* is a national magazine of contemporary poetry which appears bimonthly, except July and August. They want "high-quality poetry by new and established writers. Individuality as well as skillful crafting with respect to the art must be evident in the framework of the poem. Nothing abstract or political." They have published poetry by Alfred Dorn, Norman Leer, H.R. Coursen, June Owens. *AP&P* is 24-36 pgs., 5½×8½, offset printed on quality paper and saddle-stapled with a white card cover printed in 2 colors. They receive about 3,000-3,500 mss a year, accept 25-30% and publish 30-35 poems in each issue. Press run is 375 for 225 subscribers. Subscription: $14/5 issues. Sample: $3.50. Make checks payable to John DeStefano.

How to Submit: Submit 3-5 poems at a time. No previously published poems; simultaneous submissions OK. Cover letter with brief bio preferred. "High volume of submissions does not allow comments on rejections." Responds "usually within 15 days." Pays 1 copy.

N AMERICAN RESEARCH PRESS (Specialized: paradoxism), P.O. Box 141, Rehoboth NM 87322, e-mail M_L_Perez@yahoo.com, website www.gallup.unm.edu/~smarandache/Pit-term.htm, founded 1990, publisher Minh Perez.

Book/Chapbook Needs: American Research Press publishes 2-3 poetry paperbacks per year. They want experimental poetry dealing with paradoxism. No classical poetry. See website for poetry samples. They have published poetry by Al. Florin Tene, Anatol Ciocanu, Nina Josu and Al. Bantos.

How to Submit: Submit 3-4 poems at a time. No previously published poems or simultaneous submissions. Cover letter preferred. Submit seasonal poems 1 month in advance. Time between acceptance and publication is 1 year. Seldom comments on rejections. Replies to queries in 1 month. Pays 100 author's copies. Order sample books by sending SASE.

Also Offers: Sponsors the "Florentin Smarandache" award for Paradoxist Poetry. Website includes features of paradoxism: www.gallup.unm.edu/~smarandache/features.htm.

$ ◙ THE AMERICAN SCHOLAR, 1785 Massachusetts Ave., NW, 4th Floor, Washington DC 20036, phone (202)265-3808, founded 1932, poetry editor Robert Farnsworth, associate editor Sandra Costich.

Magazine Needs: *American Scholar* is an academic quarterly which uses about 5 poems/issue. "The usual length of our poems is 34 lines." The magazine has published poetry by John Updike, Philip Levine and Rita Dove. What little poetry is used in this high-prestige magazine is accomplished, intelligent and open (in terms of style and form). Study before submitting (sample: $6.95, guidelines available for SASE).

How to Submit: Submit up to 4 poems at a time; "no more for a careful reading. Poems should be typed, on one side of the paper, and each sheet should bear the name and address of the author and the name of the poem." Responds in 2 months. Always sends prepublication galleys. Pays $50/poem. Buys first rights only.

◎ AMERICAN TANKA (Specialized: form/style), P.O. Box 120-024, Staten Island NY 10312, e-mail editor@americantanka.com, website www.americantanka.com, founded 1996, contact editor.

Magazine Needs: *AT* appears twice a year (Spring and Fall) and is devoted to single English-language tanka. They want "concise and vivid language, good crafting, and echo of the original Japanese form." They do not want anything that is not tanka. They have published poetry by Sanford Goldstein, ai li, Jane Reichhold and George Swede. As a sample the editor included this tanka by Marianne Bluger:

> *Headed back/from good-byes at the airport/I keep checking/in rear-view the sky/where your contrail lingers.*

American Tanka is 65-85 pgs., 8½ × 5½, perfect-bound with glossy cover, b&w original drawings. Single copy: $8; subscription: $16. Sample: $8.

How to Submit: Submit 5 poems at a time. No previously published poems or simultaneous submissions. Electronic submissions OK. E-mail submissions OK. "Send submissions in the text of the e-mail." Submission deadlines: August 15 for Fall, February 15 for Spring. Send SASE for guidelines or see website. Responds in 6 weeks. Pays 1 copy. Acquires first North American serial rights.

Also Offers: Website includes guidelines, sample poems from issues, information about the tanka form and a tanka bibliography.

Advice: "The tanka form is rapidly growing in popularity in the West because of its emotional accessibility and because it is an exquisite way to capture a moment in one's life."

Ⓝ ◻ ◎ AMERICAN TOLKIEN SOCIETY; MINAS TIRITH EVENING-STAR; W.W. PUBLICA-TIONS (Specialized: science fiction/fantasy), P.O. Box 7871, Flint MI 48507-0871, phone/fax (727)585-0985, founded 1967, editor Philip W. Helms.

Magazine Needs & How to Submit: Their journal and chapbooks use poetry of fantasy about Middle-Earth and Tolkien. Also accepts poetry written by children. They have published poetry by Thomas M. Egan, Anne Etkin, Nancy Pope and Martha Benedict. *Minas Tirith Evening-Star* is magazine-sized, offset from typescript with cartoon-like b&w graphics. Press run is 400 for 350 subscribers of which 10% are libraries. Single copy: $3.50; subscription: $10. Sample: $1.50. Make checks payable to American Tolkien Society. No simultaneous submissions; previously published poems "maybe." Cover letter preferred. "We do not return phone calls unless collect." Editor sometimes comments on rejections. Publishes theme issues occasionally. Send SASE for guidelines. Responds in 2 weeks. Sometimes sends prepublication galleys. Pays contributor's copies. Reviews related books of poetry; length depends on the volume, "a sentence to several pages." Open to unsolicited reviews. Poets may also send books to Paul Ritz, Reviews, P.O. Box 901, Clearwater FL 33757 for review consideration.

Book/Chapbook Needs & How to Submit: Under the imprint of W.W. Publications they publish collections of poetry 50-100 pgs. For book or chapbook consideration, submit sample poems. Publishes 2 chapbooks/year.

Also Offers: Membership in the ATS is open to all, regardless of country of residence, and entitles one to receive the quarterly journal. Dues are $10 per annum to addresses in US, $12.50 in Canada and $15 elsewhere. They sometimes sponsor contests.

◎ AMERICAN WRITING: A MAGAZINE; NIERIKA EDITIONS (Specialized: form/style), 4343 Manayunk Ave., Philadelphia PA 19128, founded 1990, editor Alexandra Grilikhes.

   🅥 Since *American Writing* began, 20 of the authors they have published won national awards after publication in the magazine.

Magazine Needs: *American Writing* appears twice a year using poetry that is "experimental and the voice of the loner, writing that takes risks with form, point of view, language and ways of perceiving. Interested in the powers of intuition and states of being, the artist as shaman. No cerebral, academic poetry. Poets often try to make an experience 'literary' through language, instead of going back to the original experience and finding the original images. What we are interested in: the voice that speaks those images." They have published poetry by Ivan Argüelles, Antler, Eleanor Wilner, Diane Glancy and Margaret Holley. *AW* is 96 pgs., digest-sized, professionally printed and flat-spined with matte card cover. Press run is 1,800 for 1,000 subscribers. Subscription: $10. Sample: $6.

How to Submit: Submit 8 poems at a time. No previously published poems; simultaneous submissions OK. Guidelines available with SASE. Responds anywhere from 6 weeks to 6 months. Pays 2 copies/accepted submission group.

Advice: "Many magazines print the work of the same authors (the big names) who often publish 'lesser' works that way. *AW* is interested in the work itself, its particular strength, energy and voice, not necessarily in the 'status' of the authors. We like to know *something* about the authors, however. We recommend reading a sample issue before just blindly submitting work."

[N] ◯ ◎ AMETHYST & EMERALD PUBLISHING, 1556 Hatford Ave., Suite #124, Santa Clara CA 95051, fax (408)249-7646, e-mail amem@earthlink.net, website www.amethystandemerald.com, founded 1997, publisher Cathyann Ortiz.

Book/Chapbook Needs: "Amethyst & Emerald Publishing seeks to publish written works to inspire a collective change toward universal fellowship." They publish 3 poetry titles, 1 paperback and 2 chapbooks per year. They want strong images, emotions and messages. "Poetry must move the reader in content and form." No greeting card verse or pornographic material. Books are usually 70-90 pgs. (chapbooks 40 pgs.), offset printed, (chapbook photocopied), perfect-bound (chapbook saddle-stitched), paper cover, some art/graphics.

How to Submit: Submit 5 sample poems with $10 reading fee. Simultaneous submissions OK. E-mail and disk submissions OK. Cover letter preferred. "Poems are selected monthly." Reads submissions January 1 through June 30 only. Time between acceptance and publication is 6 months. Often comments on rejections. Replies to queries in 2 weeks; to mss in 1 month. Pays 20 author's copies (out of a press run of 100).

Also Offers: Publishes individual poems through a contest on their website at the Poetry Café.

◆ ◯ ◎ THE AMETHYST REVIEW, 23 Riverside Ave., Truro, Nova Scotia B2N 4G2 Canada, phone (902)895-1345, e-mail amethyst@col.auracom.com, website www.col.auracom.com/~amethyst, founded 1992, editors Penny Ferguson and Lenora Steele.

Magazine Needs: *TAR* is a biannual publication (May and November) of poetry, prose and black ink art. They want "quality, contemporary poetry to 200 lines. No bad rhyme and meter." They have published poetry by Joe Blades and Liliane Welch. As a sample the editors selected these lines from "Shade Garden of Your Bones" by Shawna Lemay:

> For me, it was not the rape itself/which leaves its trace on the body/the way espresso stains white
> linen/and on the heart which is soft and spongy and forgets/for me, it was not even the seven months
> trial,/but the sibille

TAR is 84 pgs., about 7×8½, perfect-bound with colored recycled paper cover and b&w art on the cover and inside. They receive 1,000 poems a year, accept approximately 4%. Press run is 180 for 200 subscribers of which 5 are libraries. Single copy: $6 Canadian; subscription: $12 Canadian, $14 US, $24 international. Sample (including guidelines): $4 Canadian, $6 US.

How to Submit: Submit 3-5 poems at a time. No previously published poems or simultaneous submissions. Cover letter preferred. No e-mail submissions; inquiries via e-mail OK. Send SASE (or SAE and IRC) for guidelines. "No American stamps please!" Submission deadlines: January 31 and August 31. Responds in 6 months maximum, "usually in 1-2 months." Pays 1 copy. Acquires first North American serial rights.

Also Offers: They also sponsor an annual contest. The contest fee is the cost of (and includes) a subscription. First prize is $100 Canadian. Send SASE (or SAE and IRC) for details after May. Deadline: January 31. Website features writer's and contest guidelines, contest winners, samples of prose and poetry, editors' names, links, cover of current issue, people in current issue, etc.

Advice: "Therapy is not always good poetry. The craft must be the important focus."

✓ ◎ THE AMHERST REVIEW, Box 2172, Amherst College, P.O. Box 5000, Amherst MA 01002-5000, e-mail review@amherst.edu, editors-in-chief Audrey Fan and Steven Lee.

Magazine Needs: *The Amherst Review*, appearing in April, is an annual literary magazine seeks quality submissions in fiction, poetry, nonfiction and photography/artwork. "All kinds of poetry welcome." The editor says *AR* is 50 pgs., 5×8, soft cover with photography, art and graphics. They receive 300-500 poems a year, accept around 10. Most copies are distributed free to Amherst students. Sample: $6. Make checks payable to *The Amherst Review*.

How to Submit: No previously published poems; simultaneous submissions OK. E-mail submissions OK. Reads submissions from September to March only. Magazine staff makes democratic decision. Seldom comments on rejections. Send SASE for guidelines. Responds in late March. Pays 1 copy.

$ ◨ ◎ THE AMICUS JOURNAL (Specialized: nature/rural/ecology), 40 W. 20th St., New York NY 10011, phone (212)727-4412, fax (212)727-1773, e-mail amicus@nrdc.org, website www.nrdc.org/eamicus/home.html, poetry editor Brian Swann.

Magazine Needs: The quarterly journal of the Natural Resources Defense Council, *Amicus* publishes about 15 poems a year and asks that submitted poetry be "rooted in nature" and no more than one ms page in length. They have published poetry by some of the best-known poets in the country, including Mary Oliver, Gary Snyder, Denise Levertov, Reg Saner, John Haines and Wendell Berry. As a sample the editor selected these lines from "Into the Light" by Pattiann Rogers:

> *There may be some places the sun/never reaches—into the stamen/of a prairie primrose bud burned/*
> *and withered before blooming,/or into the eyes of a fetal/lamb killed before born. I suppose . . .*

The Amicus Journal is 48 pgs., about 7½×10½, finely printed, saddle-stapled, on high quality paper with glossy cover, using art, photography and cartoons. Circulation is 400,000. Sample: $4.

How to Submit: "All submissions must be accompanied by a cover note (with notable prior publications) and self-addressed, stamped envelope. We prefer to receive submissions by mail, no fax or e-mail. However, poets can request information by e-mail." Pays $50/poem plus 1 copy and a year's subscription.

Also Offers: They publish *e-Amicus*, an online magazine.

☑ ◖ ◗ ◎ **ANALECTA (Specialized: students)**, Liberal Arts Council, FAC 17, University of Texas, Austin TX 78712, phone (512)499-8439, fax (512)471-4518, website www.utexas.edu/cola/depts/lac/analecta.html, founded 1974, editor Alice Wang.

Magazine Needs: *Analecta* is an annual of literary works and art by college/university students and graduate students chosen in an annual contest. No restrictions on type. Submissions cannot be returned. "Our purpose is to provide a forum for excellent student writing. Works must be previously unpublished." Published in the fall, it is a 150-page, digest-sized magazine, professionally printed and perfect-bound with glossy 4-color card cover, glossy plates for interior artwork in color. They receive about 800 submissions a year, accept approximately 40. Press run is 800 for 700 subscribers, 100 shelf sales. Sample: $8.

How to Submit: Entries must be typed; name should appear on cover sheet only. Send SASE for cover sheet and guidelines. Deadline is in mid-October. Prizes in each category. Pays 2 copies and $100 for each prize.

Also Offers: Website includes contest guidelines, links to other Austin literary organizations, cover sheet, upcoming events, old issues and brief description of *Analecta*.

☑ ◖ **ANAMNESIS PRESS; ANAMNESIS POETRY CHAPBOOK AWARD CONTEST**, P.O. Box 51115, Palo Alto CA 94303, phone (415)255-8366, fax (510)481-7123, e-mail anamnesis@compuserve.com, website http://ourworld.compuserve.com/homepages/Anamnesis, founded 1990, publisher Keith Allen Daniels.

Book/Chapbook Needs: Primarily publishes chapbooks selected through its annual contest, though occasionally publishes a larger volume "to preserve poetry that might otherwise be forgotten. We wish to see poems of intellectual and emotional depth that give full rein to the imagination, whether free verse or formalist. Please don't send us trite, sappy, maudlin or 'inspirational' poetry." They have published poetry by Joe Haldeman, James Blish, David R. Bunch and Steven Utley. Chapbooks are 25-40 pgs., photo offset and saddle-stapled with 2-color covers.

How to Submit: For the Anamnesis Poetry Chapbook Award Contest, submit 20-30 pgs. of poetry with a cover letter, SASE and $15 entry fee postmarked by March 15. Previously published poems (if author provides acknowledgments) and simultaneous submissions OK. "Poets can request guidelines via fax and e-mail and obtain guidelines via our website, but we do not accept poetry submissions via e-mail or fax." Winners are selected in June. Prize: $1,000, an award certificate, publication and 20 copies of winning chapbook.

Advice: "We encourage poets to purchase a sample chapbook for $6 before submitting, to get a feel for what we're looking for. We use free verse and well done formal poetry."

◖ ◎ **ANCIENT PATHS (Specialized: religious)**, 709 Coronado, Box 117, Harlingen TX 78550, e-mail skylar.burris@gte.net, website www.geocities.com/journalancient/index.html, founded 1998, editor Skylar Hamilton Burris.

Magazine Needs: *Ancient Paths* is published semiannually in February and August "to provide a forum for Christian writers in a journal that can be distributed at cost. It contains poetry, short stories and drawings." They want "traditional forms or free verse; Christian images, issues, events or themes. I seek poetry that makes the reader both think and feel. No 'preachy' poetry or obtrusive rhyme; no stream of conscious or avant-garde work; no poetry that is not accessible." They have published poetry by Giovanni Malito, Diane Glancy and April Selley. As a sample the editor selected these lines from "Obstruction of Construction" by Roger Sedarat:

> *The carpenter nailed across the plank/And started crying. He didn't know why./He did not see, as each*
> *nail sank,/The carpenter nailed across the plank.*

AP is 20-23 pgs., 8½×11, photocopied and stapled with color cardstock cover, includes clip art and b&w drawings. They receive about 300 poems a year, accept approximately 15%. Press run is 230 for 50 orders and subscriptions; 180 distributed free to churches, libraries, individuals. Subscription: $9/2 years. Sample: $2.25. Make checks payable to Skylar Burris.

How to Submit: Submit up to 5 poems at a time, single-spaced. Line length for poetry is 60 maximum; 20-50 lines preferred. Previously published poems and simultaneous submissions OK. E-mail and disk submissions OK. "Paste in body or attach as WordPerfect 6.0 or lower. Include name, address, line count and e-mail. Specify that it is a submission to the *Ancient Paths* journal." Cover letter preferred. "Name, address and line count on first page. Save as text only if submitting on disk. Note if the poem is previously published and what rights (if any) were purchased." Do not submit mss in January and July. Time between acceptance and publication is up to 6 months. Often comments on rejections. Send SASE for guidelines. Responds in "2-3 weeks if rejected, longer if being seriously considered." Pays 1 copy. Acquires first or one-time rights. Staff reviews other magazines in 50 words. "We publish submission guidelines for some other magazines if they submit them and qualify (i.e., other Christian lit journals)."

Also Offers: "All poems are automatically entered in a contest each issue. Three poems are selected. Prizes are $10, $7 and $4 plus an additional free copy of the journal."

■ The online journal contains original content not found in the print edition. "Work not accepted for printed publication will be considered for online publication in the 'Featured Works' section. Easter and Christmas poems needed for online seasonal issues. Contact Skylar H. Burriss.

�‍◯◎ **ANGEL NEWS MAGAZINE (Specialized: spirituality/inspirational, religious, themes)**, 519 W. Plantation Blvd., Lake Mary FL 32746-2530, phone (407)323-5037, e-mail dbaumbach@aol.com, founded 1980, publisher/editor Daphne C. Litke-Baumbach, membership chairman Jeanne Foley.

Magazine Needs: *Angel News* is a quarterly publication "devoted to the constant study and reflection of Angels. By sharing knowledge, it offers information on the nature and functions of Angels and Angelic beings. Poems must relate to Angels, God, Heart, Love, Heaven, Rainbows, Doves or Peace." Also accepts poetry written by children. They have published poetry by Mary E. Matthews, Dottie Melton, Marcia Ann Kolovich and Melissa Deal Forsh. *Angel News* is 70 pgs., 8½×11, computer-generated then photocopied, flat-spined with paper cover, includes b&w graphics and photos, ads. Press run is 100. Subscription/membership: $16/year. Sample: $5. Make checks payable to Daphne C. Litke-Baumbach.

How to Submit: "One poem per person can be free with purchase of sample copy. All other poems we would appreciate a donation of $2/poem to cover postage and handling costs." Previously published poems and simultaneous submissions OK. Cover letter required. E-mail and fax submissions OK. Time between acceptance and publication is 1 month or as soon as possible. Always comments on rejections. Publishes theme issues. Send SASE for guidelines and upcoming themes. Responds in 1 month or "as soon as possible." Pays 1 copy. Reviews books of poetry and other magazines, single book format. Poets may also send books for review consideration.

◉ **ANGELFLESH; ANGELFLESH PRESS**, P.O. Box 141123, Grand Rapids MI 49514, founded 1994, editor Jim Buchanan.

Magazine Needs: *Angelflesh* appears up to 2 times/year and publishes "today's best cutting-edge fiction, poetry and art." They want poetry that is "strong, real and gutsy, with vivid images, emotional and spiritual train wrecks. No taboos, no 'Hallmark' verse." They have published poetry by Elizabeth Florio, Todd Balazic, Juliet Cook, Gerald Locklin and Joseph Shields. As a sample the editor selected these lines from "When You Can't Do A Damn Thing Else" by Mark Senkus:

> I go back to my room/with sacred plans to/drink my eyeballs numb/and I hope for a life/that is just/
> long enough/to do it

The editor says *Angelflesh* is 40-50 pgs., 5½×8½, photocopied, saddle-stitched or paperback. They receive about 1,000 poems a year, accept 2-5%. Press run is up to 500. Subscription: $10. Sample: $4.

How to Submit: Submit 3-5 poems at a time. Simultaneous submissions OK. Cover letter preferred. Time between acceptance and publication is 2-12 months. Seldom comments on rejections. Responds in about 1 month. "I will respond to submissions via e-mail if the poets do not need their material returned." Pays 1 copy.

Book/Chapbook Needs & How to Submit: Under Angelflesh Press the editor also publishes 1-2 perfect-bound paperbacks/year. Replies in 1 month. Pay negotiable.

◉ **ANHINGA PRESS; ANHINGA PRIZE**, P.O. Box 10595, Tallahassee FL 32302-0595, phone (850)521-9920, fax (850)442-6323, e-mail info@anhinga.org, website www.anhinga.org, founded 1972, poetry editors Rick Campbell and Van Brock.

Book/Chapbook Needs: The press publishes "books and anthologies of poetry. We want to see contemporary poetry which respects language. We're inclined toward poetry that is not obscure, that can be understood by any literate audience." They have published *The Secret History of Water* by Silvia Curbelo; and *Conversations During Sleep* by Michele Wolf (the 1997 Anhinga Prize winner).

How to Submit: Considers simultaneous submissions. Include SASE with all submissions.

Also Offers: The Anhinga Prize for poetry awards $2,000 and publication to a book-length manuscript each year. Send SASE for rules. Submissions accepted January 1 to March 31 only. Entry fee: $20. The contest has been judged by such distinguished poets as William Stafford, Louis Simpson, Henry Taylor, Hayden Carruth, Marvin Bell, Donald Hall and Joy Harjo. "Everything we do is on our website."

◯◎ **ANNA'S JOURNAL (Specialized: childlessness issues)**, P.O. Box 341, Ellijay GA 30540, phone/fax (706)276-2309, e-mail annas@ellijay.com, founded 1995, editor Catherine Ward-Long.

Magazine Needs: *Anna's Journal* appears quarterly to offer "spiritual support for childless couples who for the most part have decided to stay that way." They want any type of poetry as long as it relates to childless issues. *AJ* is 8 pgs., 8½×11, neatly printed on colored paper and saddle-stapled, includes clip art and b&w photos. They receive about 10 poems a year, accept approximately 50%. Press run is 200 for 36 subscribers; 20 distributed free to churches, doctor's offices. Subscription: $14/1 year, $24/2 years. Sample: $3.

How to Submit: Submit 3 poems at a time. Previously published poems OK; no simultaneous submissions. E-mail submissions OK. Cover letter preferred. Time between acceptance and publication is 1-2 months. Publishes theme issues occasionally. Responds in up to 2 months. Pays 3 copies. Acquires first rights and reprint rights. Reviews books of poetry, single book format. Open to unsolicited reviews. Poets may also send books for review consideration.
Advice: "Poetry must relate to childlessness issues. It helps if writer is childless."

✓◻◯◪ **ANTHOLOGY; INKWELL PRESS**, P.O. Box 4411, Mesa AZ 85211-4411, website www.anthologymagazine.com, executive editor Sharon Skinner, publisher Bob Nelson.
Magazine Needs: *Anthology* appears every 2 months and intends to be "the best poetry, prose and art magazine." They want "poetry with clear conceit. Evocative as opposed to provocative. We do not dictate form or style but creative uses are always enjoyed. Graphic horror and pornography are not encouraged." Also accepts poetry written by children. They have published poetry by Corbet Dean, Nancy Berg and Julia Ann Delbridge. As a sample the editor selected these lines from "The Home" by Curt Sloan, 1st Place winner of the 1999 *Anthology* Poetry Contest:
> Stinging whispers and cries/Come from rolling chairs/Crammed with yesterday's roses
Anthology is 28-32 pgs., 8½×11, printed on coated glossy paper, saddle-stitched with two-color cover, b&w drawings and clip art inside. Press run is 1,000 for 100 subscribers of which 2 are libraries, with 50-75 distributed free to local coffeehouses, beauty parlors, doctors' offices, etc. Single copy: $3.95; subscription: $20 (6 issues). Make checks payable to *Anthology*.
How to Submit: Submit up to 5 poems at a time with SASE. Previously published and simultaneous submissions OK. "Please try not to send handwritten work." Time between acceptance and publication is 6-8 months. Send SASE for guidelines or obtain via website. Responds in 3 months. Pays 1 copy. Acquires one-time rights.
Also Offers: Sponsors annual contest with cash and other prizes for both poetry and short stories. Entry fee: $1/poem required. Send SASE for guidelines. Website includes submission guidelines, sample poems and prose, listings of staff members, issue availability, events, interesting links and contest information.
Advice: "Send what you write, not what you think an editor wants to hear. And always remember that a rejection is seldom personal, it is just one step closer to a yes."

◪◎ **THE ANTHOLOGY OF NEW ENGLAND WRITERS; ROBERT PENN WARREN POETRY AWARDS (Specialized: form); NEW ENGLAND WRITERS/VERMONT POETS ASSOCIATION**, P.O. Box 483, Windsor VT 05089, phone (802)674-2315, fax (802)674-5503, e-mail www.newvtpoet@aol.com, website www.hometown.aol.com/newvtpoet/myhomepage/profile.html, founded 1989, editor Frank Anthony, associate editor Susan Anthony.
Magazine Needs: *The Anthology of New England Writers* appears annually in November. All poems published in this annual are winners of their contest. They want "unpublished, original, free verse poetry only; 10-30 line limit." Open to *all* poets, not just New England. They have published poetry by Richard Eberhart, Rosanna Warren, David Kirby and Vivian Shipley. *Anthology* is 44 pgs., 5½×8½, professionally printed and perfect-bound with colored card cover, b&w illustrations. Press run is 400. Single copy: $3.95. Sample: $3. Make checks payable to New England Writers.
How to Submit: Submit 3-9 poems at a time with contest reading fee (3 poems: $6; 6 poems: $10; 9 poems: $15). Include 3×5 card with name, address and titles of poems. No previously published poems or simultaneous submissions. Reads submissions September through June 15 (post mark) only. SASE for guidelines optional; also may request via e-mail. Responds 6 weeks after June 15 deadline. Sometimes sends prepublication galleys. Pays 1 copy. All rights revert to author upon publication.
Also Offers: Sponsors an annual free verse contest with The Robert Penn Warren Poetry Awards. Awards $300 for first, $200 for second and $100 for third. They also award 10 Honorable Mentions ($20 each), 10 Commendables and 10 Editor's Choice. Entry fee: $6/3 poems. Winners announced at the New England Writers Conference in July. All submissions are automatically entered in contest. The Vermont Poets Association was founded in 1986 "to encourage precision and ingenuity in the practice of writing and speaking, whatever the form and style." Currently has 400 members. Writing information is included in the biannual newsletter, *NewScript*. Meetings are held several times a year. Membership dues: $9, $6 senior citizens and students. Send SASE for additional information. Also sponsors the annual New England Writers Conference with nationally known writers and editors involved with workshops, open mike readings and a writer's panel. 2000 date: July 22. Conference lasts one day and is "affordable," and open to the public. 1999 keynote speaker was John Kenneth Galbraith. Website includes names of the panelists, also workshop leaders, judges of poetry and fiction contests and the location of the conference and dates.

$◎ **ANTIETAM REVIEW (Specialized: regional)**, Washington County Arts Council, 41 S. Potomac St., Hagerstown MD 21740-5512, phone/fax (301)791-3132, founded 1982, poetry editor Crystal Brown.
Magazine Needs: *The Antietam Review* appears annually in May and looks for "well-crafted literary quality poems. We discourage inspirational verse, haiku, doggerel." Uses poets (natives or residents) from the states of Maryland, Pennsylvania, Virginia, West Virginia, Delaware and District of Columbia. Needs 25 poems/issue, up to 30 lines each. They have published poetry by Paul Grant, Rick Cannon and Kathy Anderson. As a sample the editor selected these lines from "The Black Fish" by Lois Marie Harrod:

> *Later that evening he took the black fish that was swimming through the air/and gave it to her to swallow so that it could grow as a pumpkin seed/in her belly, and for days she could feel it flipping inside her . . .*

AR is 72 pgs., 8½×11, saddle-stapled, glossy paper with glossy card cover and b&w photos throughout. Press run is 1,000. Sample: $3.15 back issue, $5.25 current.

How to Submit: Submit 5 typed poems at a time. "We prefer a cover letter stating other publications, although we encourage new and emerging writers. We do not accept previously published poems and reluctantly take simultaneous submissions." Do not submit mss from February through August. "We read from September 1 through February 1 annually." Send SASE for guidelines. Sends prepublication galleys, if requested. Pays between $15-25/poem, depending on funding, plus 2 copies. Buys first North American serial rights.

Also Offers: Sponsors a contest for natives or residents of DC, DE, MD, PA, VA and WV. Send SASE for details.

▓ ◐ THE ANTIGONISH REVIEW, St. Francis Xavier University, P.O. Box 5000, Antigonish, Nova Scotia B2G 2W5 Canada, phone (902)867-3962, fax (902)867-5563, e-mail TAR@stfx.ca, website www.antigoni sh.com/review, founded 1970, editor George Sanderson, poetry editor Peter Sanger.

Magazine Needs: *The Antigonish Review* appears quarterly and "tries to produce the kind of literary and visual mosaic that the modern sensibility requires or would respond to." They want poetry not over "80 lines, i.e., 2 pgs.; subject matter can be anything, the style is traditional, modern or post-modern limited by typographic resources. Purpose is not an issue." No "erotica, scatalogical verse, excessive propaganda toward a certain subject." They have published poetry by Andy Wainwright, W.J. Keith, Michael Hulse, Jean McNeil, M. Travis Lane and Douglas Lochhead. *TAR* is 150 pgs., 6×9, flat-spined with glossy card cover, offset printing, using "in-house graphics and cover art, no ads." They receive 2,500 submissions/year; accept 10%. Press run is 850 for 700 subscribers. Subscription: $24. Sample: $4.

How to Submit: Submit 5-10 poems at a time. No simultaneous submissions or previously published poems. Include SASE (or SAE and IRCs if outside Canada). E-mail and fax submissions OK. Time between acceptance and publication is 3-8 months. Editor "sometimes" comments on rejections. Send SASE for guidelines or request via e-mail. Responds in 2 months. Pays 2 copies. Acquires first North American serial rights.

$◐ THE ANTIOCH REVIEW, P.O. Box 148, Yellow Springs OH 45387, phone (937)767-6389, founded 1941, poetry editor Judith Hall.

▓ Work published in this review has also been included in *The Best American Poetry* (1995 and 1998 volumes) and *Pushcart Prize* anthologies.

Magazine Needs: *The Review* "is an independent quarterly of critical and creative thought . . . For well over 50 years, creative authors, poets and thinkers have found a friendly reception . . . regardless of formal reputation. We get far more poetry than we can possibly accept, and the competition is keen. Here, where form and content are so inseparable and reaction is so personal, it is difficult to state requirements or limitations. Studying recent issues of *The Review* should be helpful. No 'light' or inspirational verse." They have published poetry by Ralph Angel, Jorie Graham, Jacqueline Osherow and Mark Strand. They receive about 3,000 submissions/year, publish 16 pages of poetry in each issue, and have about a 6-month backlog. Circulation is 5,000, of which 70% is through bookstores and newsstands. Large percentage of subscribers are libraries. Subscription: $35. Sample: $6.

How to Submit: Submit 3-6 poems at a time. No previously published poems. Reads submissions September 1 through May 1 only. Send SASE for guidelines. Responds in 2 months. Pays $10/published page plus 2 copies. Reviews books of poetry in 300 words, single format.

$◎ ANTIPODES (Specialized: regional), 8 Big Island, Warwick NY 10990, e-mail kane@vassar.edu, founded 1987, poetry editor Paul Kane.

Magazine Needs: *Antipodes* is a biannual of Australian poetry and fiction and criticism and reviews of Australian writing. They want work from Australian poets only. No restrictions as to form, length, subject matter or style. They have published poetry by A.D. Hope, Judith Wright and Les Murray. The editor says *Antipodes* is 180 pgs., 8½×11, perfect-bound, with graphics, ads and photos. They receive about 500 submissions a year, accept approximately 10%. Press run is 500 for 200 subscribers. Subscription: $20. Sample: $17.

How to Submit: Submit 3-5 poems at a time. No previously published poems or simultaneous submissions. Cover letter with bio note required. The editor says they "prefer submission of photocopies which do not have to be returned." Seldom comments on rejections. Responds in 2 months. Pays $20/poem plus 1 copy. Acquires first North American serial rights. Staff reviews books of poetry in 500-1,500 words. Send books for review consideration.

Ⓝ ◐ ◎ APALACHEE QUARTERLY; APALACHEE PRESS (Specialized: themes), P.O. Box 10469, Tallahassee FL 32302, founded 1971, editors Laura Newton, Mary Jane Ryals and Michael Trammell.

Magazine Needs: They have published poetry by David Kirby, Peter Meinke, Alfred Corn and Virgil Suarez. *Apalachee Quarterly* is 160 pgs., 6×9, professionally printed and perfect-bound with card cover. There are 55-

95 pgs. of poetry in each issue. "Every year we do an issue on a special topic. Past issues include Dental, Revenge, Cocktail Party and Noir issues." Press run is 700 for 350 subscribers of which 75 are libraries. Subscription: $15. Sample: $5.
How to Submit: Submit clear copies of 3-5 poems, name and address on each. Simultaneous submissions OK. "We don't read during the summer (June 1 through August 31)." Sometimes comments on rejections. Publishes theme issues. Send SASE for guidelines. Pays 2 copies. Staff reviews books of poetry. Send books for review consideration.

APHASIA PRESS, P.O. Box 1626, Orange CA 92856, phone (714)663-9701, e-mail aphasiapress@hot mail.com, website www.csulb.edu/~rroden, founded 1998, editor Robert Roden.
Book/Chapbook Needs & How to Submit: Aphasia Press publishes 2 chapbooks per year, minimum. They have published *Armageddon's Garden/Between Genesis and 666* by Jerry Gordon/Robert Roden. Chapbooks are usually 24-48 pgs., digest-sized, photocopied and saddle-stapled with card cover. Submit 10 sample poems with SASE for inquiry. "Check website for some indication of appropriate material." Reads submissions June through August only. Replies in 3 months. Pays 25-50 author's copies (out of an initial press run of 50-100). Order sample chapbooks by sending $5. "I encourage poets to order a sample chapbook before sending in their completed manuscript to see the quality of the work I do."
Also Offers: Website includes chapbook information with sample poems, bios and photos of authors, ordering information.

APPALACHIA; THE APPALACHIA POETRY PRIZE (Specialized: nature), 5 Joy St., Boston MA 02108, phone (617)523-0636, founded 1876, poetry editor Parkman Howe, editor-in-chief Sandy Stott.
Magazine Needs: *Appalachia* is a "semiannual journal of mountaineering and conservation which describes activities outdoors and asks questions of an ecological nature." They want poetry relating to the outdoors and nature—specifically weather, mountains, rivers, lakes, woods and animals. "No conquerors' odes." They have published poetry by Bruce Ducker, Warren Woessner, Lucille Day, Mary Oliver and Thomas Reiter. The editor says *Appalachia* is 160 pgs., 6×9, professionally printed with color cover, using photos, graphics and a few ads. They receive about 200 poems a year, use 10-15. Press run is 10,000. Subscription: $10/year. Sample: $5.
How to Submit: Submit up to 6 poems at a time. "We favor shorter poems—maximum of 36 lines usually." No previously published poems or simultaneous submissions. Cover letter required. Time between acceptance and publication is 1 year. Seldom comments on rejections. Send SASE for guidelines. Responds in 6 weeks. Pays 1 copy. Acquires first rights. Staff reviews "some" books of poetry in 200-400 words, usually single book format.
Also Offers: An annual award, The Appalachia Poetry Prize, given since 1972. Write for details.
Advice: "Our readership is very well versed in the outdoors—mountains, rivers, lakes, animals. We look for poetry that helps readers see the natural world in fresh ways. No generalized accounts of the great outdoors."

APPALACHIAN HERITAGE; THE DENNY C. PLATTNER AWARDS, Hutchins Library, Berea College, Berea KY 40404, phone (606)986-9341 ext. 5496, fax (606)985-7300, e-mail jim_gage@berea.e du, website www.berea.edu, founded 1973, editor Jim Gage.
Magazine Needs: *AH* a literary quarterly with Southern Appalachian emphasis. The journal publishes several poems in each issue, and the editor wants to see "poems about people, places, the human condition, social issues, etc., with Southern Appalachian settings. No style restrictions but poems should have a maximum of 14 lines, prefer 8-10 lines." She does not want "blood and gore, hell-fire and damnation, or biased poetry about race or religion." She has published poetry by Jim Wayne Miller, James Still, George Ella Lyon and Robert Morgan. The flat-spined magazine is 6×9, professionally printed on white stock with b&w line drawings and photos, glossy white card cover with 4-color illustration. Issues we have scanned tended toward lyric free verse, emphasizing nature or situations set in nature, but the editor says they will use good poems of any subject and form. Sample copy: $6.
How to Submit: Submit 2-4 poems at a time, typed one to a page. No previously published poems; simultaneous submissions OK. Requires cover letter giving information about previous publications where poets have appeared. E-mail submissions OK. Prefer attached file, most formats, but will accept in body of message. Publishes theme issues occasionally. Send SASE for upcoming themes or request via fax or e-mail. Responds in 1 month. Sometimes sends prepublication galleys. Pays 3 copies. Acquires first rights. Reviews books of poetry. Open to unsolicited reviews. Poets may also send books for review consideration.
Also Offers: The Denny C. Plattner Awards go to the authors of the best poetry, article or essay, or short fiction published in the four issues released within the preceding year. The award amount in each category is $200.

APROPOS (Specialized: subscribers), Ashley Manor, 450 Buttermilk Rd., Easton PA 18042, founded 1989, editor Ashley C. Anders.
Magazine Needs: *Apropos* publishes all poetry submitted by subscribers except that judged by the editor to be pornographic or in poor taste. $25 for 6-issue subscription. As a sample the editor selected her own poem "With Pen in Hand":

*With pen in hand I can confess/my innermost unhappiness,/or wonder in the things I see—/a newborn
bird; a lovely tree.//This gift that God has given me/Allows my feelings to be free./With pen in hand I
always say/whatever's on my mind each day.*

Apropos is 90 pgs., digest-sized, plastic ring bound, with heavy stock cover, desktop-published. Sample: $3.
How to Submit: Submit 1 poem at a time. Line length for poetry is 40 maximum—50 characters/line. Editor
prefers to receive sample of poetry prior to acceptance of subscription. Samples will not be returned. No simultaneous submissions; previously published poems OK. Send SASE for guidelines. All poems are judged by subscribers. Prizes for regular issues are $50, $25, $10 and $5.

N @ Ø AQUARIUS, Flat 10, Room A, 116 Sutherland Ave., Maida-Vale, London W9 England, poetry
editor Eddie Linden.
Magazine Needs & How to Submit: *Aquarius* is a literary biannual publishing poetry, fictional prose, essays,
interviews and reviews. "Please note the magazine will not accept work unless writers have bought the magazine
and studied the style/form of the work published." Single copy: $10; subscription: $50 (US). Payment is by
arrangement.

Ø @ ARACHNE, INC. (Specialized: rural), 2363 Page Rd., Kennedy NY 14747-9717, founded 1980,
senior editor Susan L. Leach.
Book/Chapbook Needs: *Arachne* focuses on the work of "America's finest rural poets" and publishes 2
chapbooks/year (500 press run). They want "any style, as long as its theme is rural in nature. No purient subjects."
Chapbooks are usually 30 pgs., staple-bound, #10 cover, no graphics.
How to Submit: Submit 7 poems at a time. No previously published poems or simultaneous submissions.
Cover letter preferred. "Please include a SASE for return and correspondence." Reads submissions January and
June only. Time between acceptance and publication is 6 months. Poems are circulated to an editorial board.
"Poems selected initially by membership, presented to board for final decision." Seldom comments on rejections.
Replies to queries and mss within 3 months.
Advice: "We will not consider any material of a sexually questionable nature. We remain a conservative press."

N Ø ARCHITRAVE, Dept. of English, New York Institute of Technology, Old Westbury NY 11568, phone
(516)686-7557, fax (516)686-7760, e-mail cmoylan01@sprynet.com, founded 1994, editor Christopher Moylan.
Magazine Needs: Appearing 2-3 times a year, *Architrave* "focuses on ekphrastic poetry and short fiction,
meaning works with some engagement with art or architecture. We encourage microfiction and experimental
forms. No prose poems; no poems on Georgia O'Keefe, Van Gogh or Frieda Kahlo." *Architrave* is 45 pgs.,
magazine-sized, attractively printed on colored paper and saddle-stapled with light card cover with b&w artwork,
includes b&w artwork. They receive about 250 poems a year, accept approximately 20%. Press run is 500 for
100 subscribers of which 10 are libraries, 200 shelf sales; 100 distributed free to contributors, writers. Sample:
$4. Make checks payable to NYIT/English or Christopher Moylan.
How to Submit: Submit 3 poems at a time. No previously published poems; simultaneous submissions (if noted)
OK. E-mail submissions OK. Reads submissions September 1 through June 1 only. Time between acceptance and
publication is 1 month. Often comments on rejections. Send SASE for guidelines. Responds in 1 month. Sometimes sends prepublication galleys. Pays 2 copies. Acquires one-time rights. Reviews books and chapbooks of
poetry in 500 words, single and multi-book format. Open to unsolicited reviews. Poets may also send books for
review consideration.
Advice: "Read and support small presses!"

Ø ARCTOS PRESS; HOBEAR PUBLICATIONS, P.O. Box 401, Sausalito CA 94966-0401, phone
(415)331-2503, e-mail runes@aol.com, founded 1997, editor CB Follett.
Book/Chapbook Needs: Arctos Press, under the imprint HoBear Publications, publishes 1-2 paperbacks each
year. "We publish quality books and anthologies of poetry, usually theme-oriented, in runs of 1,000, paper cover,
perfect-bound." They have published poetry by Robert Hass, Kay Ryan, Brenda Hillman and Jane Hirshfield.
As a sample the editor selected these lines from "Every Day" by Ellery Akers:
*It is not impersonal, the world./Or strict. If she is awake to every stalk./If she can watch the hyacinths
hammer their green beaks/through the ground.*
How to Submit: "We do not accept unsolicited mss unless a current call has been posted in *Poets & Writers*
and/or elsewhere, at which time up to 5 poems related to the theme should be sent." Previously published poems
(if author holds the rights) and simultaneous submissions ("if we are kept informed.") OK.
Advice: "Our first title *Beside the Sleeping Maiden: Poets of Marin* has been very favorably reviewed."

Ø ◐ ARJUNA LIBRARY PRESS; JOURNAL OF REGIONAL CRITICISM, 1025 Garner St. D, Space
18, Colorado Springs CO 80905-1774, library founded 1963, press founded 1979, editor-in-chief Count Prof.
Joseph A. Uphoff, Jr.
Magazine Needs: "The Arjuna Library Press is avant-garde, designed to endure the transient quarters and
marginal funding of the literary phenomenon (as a tradition) while presenting a context for the development of
current mathematical ideas in regard to theories of art, literature and performance; photocopy printing allows for
very limited editions and irregular format. Quality is maintained as an artistic materialist practice." He publishes

"surrealist prose poetry, visual poetry, dreamlike, short and long works; not obscene, profane (will criticize but not publish), unpolished work." He has published work by Mary Evangelisto and Robert C. Blossman. As a sample the editor selected these lines from "He Always Told Me" by Diana Lee Goldman:

> He always told me to walk in the sunshine but to play in the rain;/to love the change of the seasons
> and the feel of the warm damp earth;/to understand that snow melts and sometimes the wind is meant
> to howl;/that we are all connected by an invisible silken thread/and that spirits are found where we
> want them to be, in a rock, in a tree.

Journal of Regional Criticism is published on loose photocopied pages of collage, writing and criticism, appearing frequently in a varied format. Press run: 1 copy each. Reviews books of poetry "occasionally." Open to unsolicited reviews. Poets may also send books for review consideration. "Upon request will treat material as submitted for reprint, one-time rights."

Book/Chapbook Needs: Arjuna Library Press publishes 6-12 chapbooks/year, averaging 50 pgs. Sample: $2.50.

How to Submit: He is currently accepting one or two short poems, with a cover letter and SASE to be considered for publication.

Advice: "Poets should be aware that literature has become a vast labyrinth in which the vision of the creative mind may be solitary. One can no longer depend upon an audience to entertain the storyteller. The writer may be left lonely in the presence of the creation which should, therefore, be entertainment in its own right if not for an audience then at least for the holder of the copyright."

ARKANSAS REVIEW: A JOURNAL OF DELTA STUDIES (Specialized: regional), P.O. Box 1890, State University AR 72467-1890, phone (870)972-3043, fax (870)972-2795, e-mail delta@toltec.astate.edu, website www.clt.astate/arkreview, founded 1968 (as *Kansas Quarterly*), general editor William M. Clements, creative materials editor Norman E. Stafford.

Magazine Needs: Appearing 3 times a year, the *Arkansas Review* is "a regional studies journal devoted to the seven-state Mississippi River Delta. Interdisciplinary in scope, we publish academic articles, relevant creative material, interviews and reviews. Material must respond to or evoke the experiences and landscapes of the seven-state Mississippi River Delta (St. Louis to New Orleans)." They have published poetry by Errol Miller, Mary Kennan Herbert, Lora Dunetz and Mark DeFoe. As a sample the editors selected this untitled poem:

> On her good old stove, her hardy skillet/waits, iron sentinel guarding those grim days/when her food
> stuck to the field hand's ribs./Her stove is as yellow now as an old/wedding gown. It stands, perfuming
> the air/with the just aroma of Mr. Clean.

The editors say *AR* is 92 pgs., magazine-sized, photo offset printed, saddle-stitched with 4-color cover, includes photos, drawings and paintings. They receive about 500 poems a year, accept approximately 5%. Press run is 600 for 400 subscribers of which 300 are libraries, 20 shelf sales; 50 distributed free to contributors. Subscription: $20. Sample: $7.50. Make checks payable to ASU Foundation.

How to Submit: No limit on number of poems submitted at a time. No previously published poems or simultaneous submissions. Cover letter with SASE preferred. E-mail and disk submissions OK. Time between acceptance and publication is about 6 months. Poems are circulated to an editorial board. "The Creative Materials Editor makes the final decision based—in part—on recommendations from other readers." Often comments on rejections. Publishes theme issues occasionally. Send SASE for guidelines and upcoming themes. Responds in 4 months. Pays 5 copies. Acquires first rights. Staff reviews books and chapbooks of poetry in 500 words, single and multi-book format. Send books for review consideration to William M. Clements. ("Inquire in advance.")

Also Offers: Website includes past table of contents, guidelines for contributors, list of editors.

ARSENAL PULP PRESS, 103-1014 Homer St., Vancouver, British Columbia V6B 2W9 Canada, founded 1980, publishes 1 paperback book of poetry/year. They only publish the work of Canadian poets and are *currently not accepting any unsolicited mss.*

ART TIMES: COMMENTARY AND RESOURCE FOR THE FINE & PERFORMING ARTS, P.O. Box 730, Mount Marion NY 12456-0730, phone/fax (914)246-6944, e-mail poetry@arttimesjournal.com, website www.arttimesjournal.com, poetry editor Raymond J. Steiner.

Magazine Needs: *Art Times* is a monthly tabloid newspaper devoted to the arts. It focuses on cultural and creative articles and essays, but also publishes some poetry and fiction. The editor wants to see "poetry that strives to express genuine observation in unique language; poems no longer than 20 lines each." As a sample he selected these lines from "Satin" by Paul Camacho:

> an encounter with a noticed article,/the satin of a bias smile,/which causes the novice to speak/of no
> experience save his own:/what is beauty, but articulate bone?

Art Times is 20-26 pgs., newsprint, with reproductions of artwork, some photos, advertisement-supported. They receive 300-500 poems/month, use only 40-50/year. Circulation is 21,000, of which 5,000 are by request and subscriptions; most distribution is free through galleries, theatres, etc. Subscription: $15/year. Sample: $1 with 9 × 12 SASE with 3 first-class stamps.

How to Submit: Submit 4-5 typed poems at a time, up to 20 lines each. "All topics; all forms." Include SASE with all submissions. They have an 18-month backlog. Send SASE for guidelines. Responds in 6 months. Pays 6 copies plus 1-year subscription.

ARTISAN, A JOURNAL OF CRAFT, P.O. Box 157, Wilmette IL 60091, e-mail artisanjnl@aol.com, website http://members.aol.com/artisanjnl, founded 1995, editor Joan Daugherty.

Magazine Needs: *artisan* is a quarterly publication based on the idea that "anyone who strives to express themselves with skill is an artist and artists of all kinds can learn from each other. We want poetry that is vital, fresh and true to life; evocative. Nothing trite, vague or pornographic." They have published poetry by Richard Stephens and Juliet Cook. Also accepts poetry written by children. As a sample the editor selected these lines from "Far Far Away" by Errol Miller:

> We go back again to womb/in the dry autumn cocoon/there is no answer/like a yellow butterfly/
> frantically rowing at dusk.

artisan is 36 pgs. (including cover), 8½×11, saddle-stitched with card stock cover, minimal graphics and ads. They receive about 450 poems a year, use approximately 10%. Press run is 300 for 100 subscribers, 100 distributed free to coffeehouses and local libraries. Subscription: $18. Sample: $5. Make checks payable to artisan, ink.

How to Submit: Submit 2-3 poems at a time. No previously published poems; no simultaneous submissions. E-mail submissions and queries OK (submit as part of message). Cover letter not necessary, however "if you send a cover letter, make it personal. We don't need to see any writing credentials; poems should stand on their own merit." Send SASE for guidelines. Responds in 8 months. Pays 2 copies. Acquires first rights.

Also Offers: *artisan* sponsors an annual poetry contest. First prize is $150, second is $75. Prize winners and works meriting honorable mention are published in an upcoming issue. Entry fee is $5/poem. Postmark deadline: December 31. Send SASE for guidelines. Website includes writer's guidelines, excerpts from current issue and contest announcements.

ASCENT, Dept. of English, Concordia College, Moorhead MN 56562, e-mail olsen@cord.edu, founded 1975, editor W. Scott Olsen.

Magazine Needs: *Ascent* appears 3 times/year, using poetry that is "eclectic." They have published poetry by Kate Coles, Sydney Lea, Wendy Bishop, Larry Watson and Scott Cairns. The editor describes *Ascent* as 100 pgs., 6×9, professionally printed and perfect-bound with matte card cover. They receive more than 1,000 poems a year, accept approximately 5%. Press run is 750 for 750 subscribers of which 90 are libraries. Subscription: $12/year. Sample: $5.

How to Submit: Submit 3-6 poems at a time. Always sends prepublication galleys. Pays 2 copies.

Advice: "Poems are rejected or accepted from 2 weeks to 5 months. Acceptances are usually published within the year."

SHERMAN ASHER PUBLISHING, P.O. Box 2853, Santa Fe NM 87504, phone (505)984-2686, fax (505)820-2744, e-mail 71277.2057@compuserve.com, website www.shermanasher.com, founded 1994, contact Judith Rafaela or Nancy Fay.

Book Needs: "We are dedicated to changing the world one book at a time, committed to the power of truth and the craft of language expressed by publishing fine poetry. We specialize in anthologies. We do *not* publish chapbooks." They publish 3-5 paperbacks/year. "Please see our current books as an example of what we look for in poetry. We enjoy well-crafted form. No rhymed doggerel, cowboy poetry or stiff academic work." They have published poetry by Marge Piercy, Galway Kinnell, Naomi Shihab Nye and Judyth Hill.

How to Submit: Submit 5 poems at a time with SASE only during calls for submissions. Previously published poems and simultaneous submissions OK. Cover letter preferred. No e-mail or fax submissions. "We specialize in anthologies and do not accept manuscripts for books. Also, we read submissions only during calls for submissions for our anthologies. Write for list with SASE." Time between acceptance and publication is 3-6 months. Poems are circulated to an editorial board. "Selection depends on the content/idea of the anthology and how well the poems fit together." Does not comment on rejections. Replies to queries in 2 months. Pays 1 copy/poem. Inquire for catalog or buy through local bookstores.

Also Offers: Website includes writer's guidelines, names of editors, poetry, interviews with authors and book ordering information.

Advice: "We do not take unsolicited manuscripts—only individual poems during our calls for submissions for our anthologies. Writers can check *Poets & Writers* magazine and other related magazines for these dates, or write us for a list. Enclose SASE."

ASHEVILLE POETRY REVIEW, P.O. Box 7086, Asheville NC 28802, phone (828)649-0217, founded 1994, founder/managing editor Keith Flynn.

Magazine Needs: *APR* appears biannually. "We publish the best regional, national and international poems we can find. We publish translations, interviews, essays, historical perspectives and book reviews as well." They

ALWAYS include a self-addressed, stamped envelope (SASE) when sending a ms or query to a publisher within your own country. When sending material to other countries, include a self-addressed envelope and International Reply Coupons (IRCs), available at many post offices.

want "quality work with well-crafted ideas married to a dynamic style. Any subject matter is fit to be considered so long as the language is vivid with a clear sense of rhythm." They have published poetry by Robert Bly, Yevgeny Yevtushenko, Eavan Boland and Fred Chappell. The editor says *APR* is 160-180 pgs., 6×9, perfect-bound with laminated, full-color cover with b&w art inside. They receive about 1,200 poems a year, accept approximately 10-15%. Press run is 600-750. Subscription: $22.50/1 year, $43.50/2 years. Sample: $13. "We prefer poets purchase a sample copy prior to submitting."

How to Submit: Submit 3-5 poems at a time. No previously published poems; simultaneous submissions OK. Cover letter required. Include comprehensive bio, recent publishing credits and SASE. Submission deadlines: January 15 and July 15. Time between acceptance and publication is 3-5 months. Poems are circulated to an editorial board. Seldom comments on rejections. Publishes theme issues occasionally. Send SASE for guidelines and upcoming themes. Responds in 3-5 months. Pays 1 copy. Rights revert back to author upon publication. Reviews books and chapbooks of poetry. Open to unsolicited reviews. Poets may also send books for review consideration.

N̄ $◎ THE ASHLAND POETRY PRESS (Specialized: anthologies, themes), Ashland University, Ashland OH 44805-3702, phone (419)289-5110, fax (419)289-5329, founded 1969, editor Robert McGovern.

Book/Chapbook Needs: Ashland publishes anthologies on specific themes and occasional collections. It has published the collection *American Lit* (a sonnet sequence) by Harold Witt; the anthology *And What Rough Beast: Poems at the End of the Century*; *Demons in the Diner* by David Ray; and *Little Apocalypse* by Wendy Battin.

How to Submit: "Watch publications such as *Poets & Writers* for calls for mss, but don't submit otherwise. We do not read unsolicited mss; anthology readings take quite a bit of time." Considers simultaneous submissions. On collections, poet gets 10% royalty; anthologies, poets are paid stipulated price when sufficient copies are sold. Write for catalog.

◎ ASIAN PACIFIC AMERICAN JOURNAL; ASIAN AMERICAN WRITERS' WORKSHOP (Specialized: ethnic/nationality, anthology), 37 St. Mark's Place #B, New York NY 10003, phone (212)228-6718, fax (212)228-7718, e-mail desk@aaww.org, website www.aaww.org, founded 1992, contact poetry editor.

Magazine Needs: The *APA Journal* is a biannual published by the AAWW, a not-for-profit organization. It is "dedicated to the best of contemporary Asian-American writing." They have published poetry by Arthur Sze, Mei-Mei Berssenbrugge and Sesshu Foster. *APA Journal* is 200 pgs., digest-sized, typeset and perfect-bound with 2-color cover and ads. They receive submissions from about 150 poets/year, accept about 30%. Press run is 1,500 for 400 subscribers of which 50 are libraries, 800 shelf sales. Single copy: $10; subscription/membership: $35; institutional membership: $50. Sample: $12.

How to Submit: Submit 4 copies of up to 10 pages of poetry, maximum of one poem per page. No previously published poems. Cover letter with phone and fax numbers and 1- to 4-sentence biographical statement required. Deadlines are usually August 15 and February 15 for December 1 and June 1 issues, respectively. "We will work with authors who are promising." Send SASE for guidelines. Responds in up to 4 months. Pays 2 copies. Acquires one-time rights. In 1998, they published *Watermark: Vietnamese American Poetry & Prose* and *Black Lightning: Poetry in Progress*.

Also Offers: The AAWW offers creative writing workshops, a newsletter, a bookselling service, readings and fellowships to young Asian-American writers. Write for details. Website includes general workshop information, names of editors and submission guidelines.

✓ ◐ ATLANTA REVIEW; POETRY 2001, P.O. Box 8248, Atlanta GA 31106, e-mail dan@atlantareview. com, website www.atlantareview.com, founded 1994, editor Daniel Veach.

Work published in this review has been included in the *Pushcart Prize* anthologies.

Magazine Needs: *Atlanta Review* is a semiannual primarily devoted to poetry, but also featuring fiction, interviews, essays and fine art. They want "quality poetry of genuine human appeal." They have published poetry by Seamus Heaney, Derek Walcott, Maxine Kumin, Rachel Hadas, Charles Simic and Naomi Shihab Nye. As a sample the editor selected these lines from "In the Parking Lot at Walgreen's" by Andrew Dillon:

> *Standing in the light/of the undeniably average, I feel whole again,/forgiven for missing the group photograph of eternity,/for I'm neither hungry, nor hurt, nor unemployed,/but thankful for merciful rain, this nimbus of neon,/and all the hemorrhoids of happiness.*

AR is 132 pgs., 6×9, professionally printed on acid-free paper and flat-spined with glossy color cover and b&w artwork. They receive about 10,000 poems a year, use about 1%. Press run is 3,500 for 1,000 subscribers of which 25 are libraries, 2,000 shelf sales. Single copy: $6; subscription: $10. Sample: $5.

How to Submit: No previously published poems. Issue deadlines are June 1 and December 1. Time between acceptance and publication is 3 months. Seldom comments on rejections. Each spring issue has an International Feature Section. Send SASE for guidelines. Responds in 1 month. Pays 2 copies plus author's discounts. Acquires first North American serial rights.

Also Offers: *AR* also sponsors POETRY 2001, an annual international poetry competition. Prizes are $2,000, $500 and $250, plus 50 International Merit Awards. Winners are announced in leading literary publications. All entries are considered for publication in *Atlanta Review*. Entry fee is $5 for the first poem, $2 for each additional.

No entry form or guidelines necessary. Send to POETRY 2001 at the above address. Postmark deadline: May 1, 2001. Website includes submission and contest guidelines, names of editors, poetry samples from several issues, and a free issue offer.

Advice: "We are giving today's poets the international audience they truly deserve."

$☐ THE ATLANTIC MONTHLY, Dept. PM, 77 North Washington St., Boston MA 02114, phone (617)854-7700, website www.theatlantic.com, founded 1857, poetry editor Peter Davison, assistant poetry editor David Barber.

 Poetry published here has been included in the 1995 and 1996 volumes of *The Best American Poetry.*

Magazine Needs: *The Atlantic Monthly* publishes 1-5 poems in each issue. Some of the most distinguished poetry in American literature has been published by this magazine, including work by William Matthews, Andrew Hudgins, Stanley Kunitz, Rodney Jones, May Swenson, Galway Kinnell, Philip Levine, Richard Wilbur, Jane Kenyon, Donald Hall and W.S. Merwin. The magazine has a circulation of 500,000, of which 5,800 are libraries. They receive some 50,000 poems/year, of which they use 30-35 and have a backlog of 6-12 months. Sample: $3.

How to Submit: Submit 3-5 poems with SASE. No simultaneous submissions. No fax or e-mail submissions. Publishes theme issues. Always sends prepublication galleys. Pays about $4/line. Buys first North American serial rights only.

Advice: Wants "to see poetry of the highest order; we do *not* want to see workshop rejects. Watch out for workshop uniformity. Beware of the present tense. Be yourself."

☑ ATOM MIND; MOTHER ROAD PUBLICATIONS, P.O. Box 22068, Albuquerque NM 87154-2068, first founded 1968-70, reestablished 1992, editor Gregory Smith.

Magazine Needs: *Atom Mind* is a quarterly journal of "alternative literature, mostly influenced by the Beats, Steinbeck, John Fante and Bukowski. Narrative, free verse, 20-80 lines preferred, although length restrictions are not set in stone. No light verse, inspirational poetry, doggerel, 'moon-spoon-June' rhyming verse." They have published poetry by Lawrence Ferlinghetti, Charles Plymell and Wilma Elizabeth McDaniel. The editor says *AM* is 120 pgs., 8½×11, offset, with illustrations and photographs. They receive approximately 2,000 submissions annually, publish perhaps 5%. Press run is 1,000 for 750 subscribers of which 25 are libraries. Subscription: $20/4 issues. Sample: $6.

How to Submit: Prefers to consider submissions of 5-8 poems at a time, 20-80 lines each. Poems should be typed and single-spaced, with name and address on the first page. "Do not staple or otherwise bind your manuscript; a paper clip will suffice. Do not submit low-resolution dot-matrix computer printouts." Include SASE "large enough to hold your manuscript" with sufficient postage for return of materials. Previously published poems OK; no simultaneous submissions. No electronic submissions. Time between acceptance and publication is 8-12 months. "*Atom Mind* is very much a one-man operation; therefore, submissions are subject to the whims and personal biases of the editor only." Often comments on rejections. Send SASE for guidelines. Responds in 2 months. Pays copies, number varies. Acquires first or one-time rights.

Book/Chapbook Needs & How to Submit: "Book-length poetry manuscripts considered by invitation only." Mother Road Publications publishes 2 paperback and 2 hardback collections of poetry/year. Send SASE for catalog.

🅽 ☑ AURA LITERARY/ARTS REVIEW, Dept. PM, Box 76, Hill University Center, University of Alabama at Birmingham, Birmingham AL 35294-1150, phone (205)934-3216, founded 1974, editor Steve Mullen.

Magazine Needs: *Aura* is a semiannual magazine that publishes "fiction and art though majority of acceptances are poetry—90-100 per year. Length, style, subject matter open. We want quality work. Both first-time and often-published poets are published here." *Aura* has published work by Lyn Lifshin, Adrian C. Louis, William Miller, Dori and Joseph DeCamillis. The 6×9 magazine is 120-145 pgs., perfect-bound, printed on white matte with b&w artwork and the front and back cover in color. Circulation is 5,000, of which 40-50 are subscriptions; other sales are to students and Birmingham residents. Subscription: $6. Sample postpaid: $3.

How to Submit: Writers should submit "5-7 poems, with SASE, no simultaneous submissions, will take neatly handwritten." Send SASE for guidelines. Responds in 2-3 months. Pays 2 copies.

☑ THE AUROREAN: A POETIC QUARTERLY; ENCIRCLE PUBLICATIONS, P.O. Box 219, Sagamore Beach MA 02562, phone/fax (508)833-0805 (call before faxing; sometimes used at deadline for last-minute bios or changes in proofs), e-mail cafpoet37@aol.com, press founded 1992, magazine founded 1995, editor Cynthia Brackett-Vincent.

Magazine Needs: *The Aurorean*, which appears in March, June, September and December, seeks to publish "poetry that is inspirational (but not religious), meditational or reflective of the Northeast. Strongly encouraged (but not limited to) topics: positiveness, recovery and nature. Maximum length: 38 lines. Typographical oddities are OK as long as it can be reproduced on our page. No hateful, overly religious or poetry that uses four-letter words for four-letter words' sake. Four-letter words are a rare necessity. Uses mostly free-verse; occasional rhyme; I am biased toward haiku and well-written humor. I'm *always* in need of short (2-6 lines), seasonal poems.

insider report

Going online: how one print publication found success

With Internet publications popping up all over the place, there are a lot of questions over the differences between publishing a journal online and publishing one in print. Generally, the many publications that publish online do so because they cannot afford the cost of putting their journals in print. Print publishers, on the other hand, generally do not put much of their content on the Web for fear of losing revenues because readers choose to read the Web version instead of subscribing to, or buying, the print version. However, one publication has been able to utilize the best of both worlds and with great success!

Wen Stephenson

Wen Stephenson, editorial director for *Atlantic Unbound* (www.theatlantic.com, the online journal for the prestigious *Atlantic Monthly*), has been on the forefront of web-zine success. In November 1993, the *Atlantic Monthly* launched a digital version of their magazine on AOL (America Online). Utilizing interactive features, message boards, conferences, and other technology, the *Atlantic* began uploading its entire print content each month for online readers. In November 1995, the *Atlantic* was available both on the Web and on AOL, and in December 1996, the publication moved solely to the Web. By March of 1997, not only was the *Atlantic* print version available on the Web, but so was a completely separate digital publication called *Atlantic Unbound*, where one of *Unbound*'s greatest digital features has been their use of multi-media poetry.

Surprisingly enough, *Atlantic Monthly* didn't suffer sales by this move. Stephenson says, "We put about 99 percent of the print magazine online every month. We purposely delay the appearance of the magazine online until the first of the month. By then, subscribers have already had it for two weeks and it's been on the newsstand for a week. We have found that, instead of cannibalizing our own print readership by putting the content online, it has served as a wonderful advertisement for the magazine. We sell a lot of subscriptions to the *Atlantic* through the website. Because much of the *Atlantic*'s experience is visual, The *Atlantic Monthly* isn't the type of publication people would choose to read on a computer." However, the digital *Atlantic Unbound* is a publication perfectly suited to the online experience.

Outside of a few technical issues, the inherent differences between publishing digital and print journals are minor. Stephenson, who has worked in both industries, claims there aren't many major differences. "On the Web, all deadlines are artificial," Stephenson says. "There's no issue. You don't ship. It is the eternal now, and everything can be published and updated instantly. In a way, it's liberating. But, at the same time it becomes a hard master to serve. We're not a daily publication—we're not a newspaper or a news service. But even as a literary and cultural publication, there's this sense that because you're online you should be able to react to things very quickly, that somehow you should be somewhat newsy and topical."

One of the things that digital copy does is free the editor from the physical limitations in traditional print publications. "You rarely have to fit copy on the Web. A page on the Web can go on as long as you want it to," says Stephenson. However, this freedom can also be a challenge to editors. "The online editor doesn't have strict space limitations and has to be more disciplined about keeping pieces to a reasonable length. We impose word count limits on certain kinds of pieces. It requires more of a discipline than print, where the limitations are real as opposed to arbitrary."

Also, a digital editor can do several things that a print editor can't do. "There's the interactive aspect and the multi-media aspect (of digital publishing). Good online publishing ought to take advantage of the medium. It shouldn't simply shovel words on the screen but should exploit the medium any way it can. A reader can't open a print magazine and listen to a poet reading," explains Stephenson.

Atlantic Unbound has always focused on the multi-media aspect of electronic publishing. In their digital publication, readers can find audio recordings of poets reading their own works or the works of other poets. "One of the very first things we did was a feature I put together with Robert Pinsky for our November 1995 launch," says Stephenson. "We had Pinsky reading aloud from his translation of Dante's *Inferno*. So in our very first appearance on the Web, we had multi-media poetry. It has always been an emphasis of ours." Stephenson states that another challenge is to remain up to date with the latest technological advances.

Digital and print publications also differ in the amount of time it takes to put an issue together. Stephenson explains that putting together a typical week's features in *Atlantic Unbound* takes "anywhere from hours to weeks. Certain kinds of *Unbound* features will be in development for many weeks. If we're putting together a special poetry feature that involves lining up three or four poets to read Whitman, that could be in development for months. But, a Web Citation on a new website might be assigned, written, and edited within the space of twenty-four to forty-eight hours."

He adds, "Some of what we do is timely and topical journalism and some of what we do is more like what you find in a literary quarterly. The best way to think of it is that we have multiple production rhythms or paces. There's the weekly update, but some things are on a biweekly schedule, some things are monthly, and others are on a quarterly schedule. We stagger the uploads throughout the month so that there's always something new every week."

Most print magazines and journals have a long lead time between the assignment of articles and features and the publication of them. "We don't have a long lead time like the print magazine," explains Stephenson. "Articles for *The Atlantic* are usually commissioned, conceived, and written a good six months before they appear in print. We're not tied to that kind of production schedule. Because we can publish instantly, some of our articles have lead times of forty-eight hours, while other projects have been in the works for many weeks or even months."

Many people wonder whether digital publication will take over and make print publication obsolete. Stephenson doesn't seem to think this will actually happen. "I think it depends on what kind of magazine or what kind of content you are talking about. If you're talking strictly about news information, then I think there is a fair chance that online publishing will overtake print publishing. But when we start talking about cultural publishing— literature and the arts and the kind of journalism that the *Atlantic* and other magazines do—that's a whole different topic. As far as the kind of literary journalism we are engaged in, online and print are going to continue side by side. The online side of things will continue to evolve and do the things it is more suited to do. The print side will continue to do what it does best. They can complement one another."

Every month the content of the *Atlantic Monthly* is uploaded to the Web for readers. *Atlantic Unbound*, a completely separate publication with online content only, is uploaded on a weekly basis. *Atlantic Unbound* does not accept poetry submissions but does accept submissions of fiction and other items. Most of the columns appearing in the *Unbound* edition are written by a stable of writers. Due to staff limitations, they do not accept unsolicited manuscripts, but they do consider unsolicited queries. The *Atlantic Monthly* has a separate set of guidelines for submissions of poetry, short fiction, and other forms of writing.

While there are technical differences and advantages to each separate medium, Stephenson says digital and print publications have the same goals. "The challenges and rewards of online publishing are really the same as those of traditional publishing. It's all about good writing and interesting ideas. There's the satisfaction of knowing you've put out a high quality publication and knowing that people appreciate it. I believe we make too much of the differences between online and print."

—*Robin Travis*

For seasonal poems, please note specific deadlines in our guidelines." They have published poetry by Michael R. Burch, Gary L. Edwards, ed galing and Doug Holder. As a sample the editor selected this haiku by Eleanor Brown Steele:

This morning the print/of a Red-tailed hawk's wing/still upon the snow.

The Aurorean contains 35 pgs. of poetry, 5 pgs. of contributor's bios and separate insert page for subscription information and other market information, $5\frac{1}{2} \times 8\frac{1}{2}$, professionally printed, perfect-bound with papers and colors varying from season to season. Press run is 500. Single copy: $5 US, $6 international. Subscription: $17 US, $21 international. Make checks payable to Encircle Publications or *The Aurorean*.

How to Submit: Submit 3-5 poems at a time. No previously published poems or simultaneous submissions. No fax submissions. "Make it clear what you're submitting. Type if possible; if not, write as clearly as possible." Cover letter strongly preferred (especially with first submission). Sometimes comments on rejections. Send SASE for guidelines. "I notify authors of receipt of manuscripts immediately and report on decisions in one week to three-and-a-half months maximum." Always sends prepublication galleys. Pays 3 copies/poem with an-up-to 50-word bio in the "Who's Who" section. Also features a "Poet-of-the-Quarter" each issue with publication of up to 3 poems and an extended bio (100 words). The "Poet-of-the-Quarter" receives 10 copies and a 1-year subscription.

Advice: "Study *Poet's Market*. If possible, request a sample before you submit. Always have a ms out there. Stop saying you want to be a writer. You are a writer if you write. Remember, editors are people too. What one editor rejects one day, another may jump at the next. Invest in small presses with samples. Invest in yourself with postage. Always include enough postage for the return/reply process!!! When sending requests and enclosing SASEs, just use common sense. For example, if requesting a sample copy and guidelines, no SASE is necessary as guidelines can be placed in with sample; if sending a submission and requesting guidelines, 2 SASEs are needed if guidelines are expected before reply to manuscript. When in doubt, an extra first-class stamp or SASE is appreciated. Read more poetry than you write, and read your poetry out loud. Editors: I'm open to subscription and ad-swapping with other markets."

AUSTRALIAN GOTHICA, P.O. Box 25021, Lexington KY 40524, e-mail ausgothica@hotmail.com, founded 1993, editor Rebecca Ly Kiernan.

Magazine Needs: *Australian Gothica* appears biannually. "We publish tightly crafted, impressive works of art, poetry, short stories, the exotic and erotic, and science fiction of the highest literary value." The magazine is 38-50 pgs., 6×9, professionally printed and flat spined. Press run is 1,000 for 600 subscribers, 400 distributed free at readings, caves, UFO abduction sites and eclipses.

Advice: "We have a sense of horror and humor. Tell us something we will never forget!"

AVOCET; AVOCET PRESS (Specialized: nature, spirituality), P.O. Box 8041, Calabasas CA 91372-8041, e-mail patricia.j.swenson@csun.edu, website www.csun.edu/~pjs44945/avocet.html, first issue published fall 1997, editor Patricia Swenson.

Magazine Needs: *Avocet* is a quarterly poetry journal "devoted to poets seeking to understand the beauty of nature and its interconnectedness with humanity." They want "poetry that shows man's interconnectedness with nature; discovering the Divine in nature." They do not want "poems that have rhyme or metrical schemes, cliché, abstraction and sexual overtones." The editor says *Avocet* is 30 pgs., 4¼×5½, professionally printed and saddle-stapled with card cover, some illustrations. Single copy: $2.50; subscription: $10. Make checks payable to Pat Swenson.

How to Submit: Submit up to 5 poems at a time. Previously published poems OK if acknowledged; no simultaneous submissions. Cover letter required including SASE. E-mail submissions OK with name, city, state and e-mail address. Time between acceptance and publication is 3-6 months. Responds in 4-6 weeks. Pays 1 copy.

Also Offers: Website includes writer's guidelines, editor's e-mail address, deadlines and sample poems.

AXE FACTORY REVIEW; CYNIC PRESS, P.O. Box 40691, Philadelphia PA 19107, *Axe Factory* founded 1986, Cynic Press founded 1996, editor/publisher Joseph Farley.
- We highly recommend obtaining a sample before submitting as the editor has displayed, in his answers to our questionnaire, a quirky sense of humor.

Magazine Needs: *Axe Factory* is published 1-4 times/year and its purpose is to "spread the disease known as literature. The content is mostly poetry and essays. We now use short stories too." They want "eclectic work. Will look at anything but suggest potential contributors purchase a copy of magazine first to see what we're like. No greeting card verse." Also accepts poetry written by children. "Parents should read magazine to see if they want their children in it as much material is adult in nature." They have published *River Architecture: poems from here & there* by Louis McKee and poetry by Taylor Graham, A.D. Winans, Normal and Kimberly Brittingham. As a sample the editor selected these lines from "Starting Over" by Louis McKee:

> I kept the doll I found/in the yard, a Barbie with matted/blond hair and not a stitch/of clothing. A new
> wife,/I thought, and I proposed to her

Axe Factory is 20-40 pgs., 8½×11, saddle-stitched, neatly printed with light card cover. Press run is 100. Single copy: $8; subscription: $20 for 3 issues. Sample: $3 for old issue, $8 for recent. Make checks payable to Joseph Farley.

How to Submit: Submit up to 10 poems. Previously published poems "sometimes, but let me know up front"; simultaneous submissions OK. Cover letter preferred "but not a form letter, tell me about yourself." Often comments on rejections. Pays 1-2 copies. "'Featured poet' receives more." Reserves right to anthologize poems under Cynic Press; all other rights returned. Reviews books of poetry in 10-1,000 words. Open to unsolicited reviews. Poets may also send books for review consideration.

Book/Chapbook Needs & How to Submit: Cynic Press occasionally publishes chapbooks. Published *Yellow Flower Girl* by Xu Juan and *Under The Dogwood* by Joseph Barford. Send $10 reading fee with ms. No guarantee of publication. All checks to Joseph Farley.

Advice: "Writing is a form of mental illness, spread by books, teachers, and the desire to communicate."

BABEL: The multilingual, multicultural online journal and community of arts and ideas (Specialized: bilingual/foreign language), e-mail malcolm@towerofbabel.com, website www.towerofbabel.com, founded 1995, editor-in-chief Malcolm Lawrence.

Magazine Needs: "*Babel* is an electronic zine which publishes regional reports from international stringers all over the planet, as well as features, round table discussions, fiction, columns, poetry, erotica, travelogues and reviews of all the arts and editorials. We are an online community involving an extensive group of over 50 artists, writers and programmers, and over 150 translators representing (so far) 36 of the world's languages. We encourage poetry from all over the planet, especially multicultural poetry as well as multilingual poetry or poetry which has been translated into or from another language, so long as it is in English at least. We also encourage gay/lesbian, bisexual and pansexual writers. Please, God, no more Bukowski wannabe's. Poetry is not a Darwinian competition. It is an expression of who you are. We're not interested in male-bashing or female-bashing poetry. There's a difference between the person who broke your heart and half of the human race. Please don't confuse poetry with therapy. If you do have to bash something, bash the real enemy: corporations. The more they keep us bashing each other, the more they know we won't have the energy to bash them." They have published poetry by Federico Garcia Lorca, Leila Imam-Kulieva, Yves Jaques and Suzanne Gillis. As a sample the editor selected these lines from "Jesse James Was A Virgo" by Russell C. Smith:

> I dream of robbing banks with a gang of friends by my side./What would Freud say, or is he born yet?/
> Aiming at innocent bystanders who get in my way./You can't argue with a six-gun, Buddy./I'm not such
> a bad guy./My heart is heavy with my misdeeds at times./But mainly I think about escaping the moment,
> not too unlike other just people./Instead of always daydreaming, my body and senses feel the escape./
> Ass on saddle, dust stings my eyes.

They receive about 100 poems a year, accept approximately 5%.

How to Submit: Submit no more than 10 poems at a time. Previously published poems and simultaneous submissions OK. E-mail submissions only. Cover letter required. "Please send submissions with a résumé/cv or biography as a Microsoft Word or RTF document attached to e-mail." Time between acceptance and publication varies; "usually no more than a month or two depending on how busy we are." Seldom comments on rejections. Obtain guidelines via website. Responds in 2-4 weeks. Reviews books and chapbooks of poetry and other magazines, single and multi-book format. Open to unsolicited reviews. Poets may also send books for review consideration.

Advice: "We would like to see more poetry with first-person male characters written by female poets as well as more poetry with first-person female characters written by male poets. The best advice we could give to writers wanting to be published in our publication is simply to write passionately."

○ **BABYSUE**, P.O. Box 8989, Atlanta GA 31106-8989, founded 1985, website www.babysue.com, editor/publisher Don W. Seven.

Magazine Needs: *babysue* appears twice a year publishing obtuse humor for the extremely open-minded. "We are open to all styles, but prefer short poems." No restrictions. They have published poetry by Edward Mycue, Susan Andrews and Barry Bishop. The editor says *babysue* is 32 pgs., offset printed. "We print prose, poems and cartoons. We usually accept about 5% of what we receive." Subscription: $12 for 4 issues. Sample: $3.

How to Submit: Previously published poems and simultaneous submissions OK. Deadlines are March 30 and September 30 of each year. Seldom comments on rejections. Responds "immediately, if we are interested." Pays 1 copy. "We do occasionally review other magazines."

Advice: "We have received no awards, but we are very popular on the underground press circuit and sell our magazine all over the world."

◑ **BACCHAE PRESS; SOUTH JETTY BOOKS**, No. 10 Sixth St., Astoria OR 97103, e-mail brown@pacifi c.com, founded 1992, publisher Dr. Robert Brown.

Book/Chapbook Needs: Under the imprints Bacchae Press and South Jetty Books, this press publishes poets who are in transition from smaller to larger publishers. They publish 2 paperbacks and 4 chapbooks/year. They want "high quality, literary poetry by poets who read and reflect. No greeting card verse." They have published poetry by Hal Sirowitz, Bart Baxter and Karen Braucher. Books/chapbooks are usually 28/72 pgs., 5½×8½, offset printed, saddle-stitched/perfect-bound.

How to Submit: Query first with 5 sample poems and cover letter with brief bio and publication credits. Previously published poems and simultaneous submissions OK. Time between acceptance and publication is 6-12 months. Poems are circulated to an editorial board. Seldom comments on rejections. Replies to queries and ms in 2 months. Pays 25 author's copies. Order sample books or chapbooks by sending $5.

Also Offers: Sponsors the annual Bacchae Press Poetry Chapbook Contest. Winner(s) receive 25 copies of the chapbook, which is scheduled to be published in September. Submit 16-24 typed ms pages. No more than 1 poem/page. Deadline: April 15. Entry fee: $9, includes copy of the winning chapbook. "With your submission, include a brief bio, acknowledgements, and a SASE for return of your manuscript and/or contest results." Contest winners announced in June.

○ ◑ **THE BACK PORCH; BURN BRIGHT PUBLICATIONS**, P.O. Box 376, Lawrenceburg IN 47025, phone (812)537-2903, fax (812)537-4812, founded 1997, publisher Timothy Burnett.

Magazine Needs: "*The Back Porch* is a semiannual journal which promotes art, poetry and photography with universality that appeals to every man." They want "poetry that is imaginative, real and strong. No 'Hallmark' verse or cutesy poetry; no forced rhyme." They have published poetry by Damniso Lopez, Simon Perchik, Virgie Suarez and Alexandra Beller. As a sample the publisher selected his poem "Coming Home":

> *Up the tall wooden staircase and through the door/I close it softly, 'click'/Padded footfalls upon the long carpeted corridor/I feel a creaking in the aged wood beneath/There is a scent, your scent and it permeates the/Dimness/I smile/I am Home.*

Back Porch is 160 pgs., 6×9, professionally printed and perfect-bound with glossy card stock cover, includes b&w art and photography, will consider ads. Press run is 500 for 100 subscribers of which 10 are libraries, 250 shelf sales. Single copy: $15.95; subscription: $30. Sample: $12.50. Make checks payable to Burn Bright Publications. They suggest potential contributors purchase a sample copy. Published authors are strongly encouraged to subscribe for 1 year.

How to Submit: Submit 3-5 poems at a time. Previously published poems and simultaneous submissions OK. Cover letter preferred. Reads submissions January 1 through October 1 only. Time between acceptance and publication is 4-6 months. "Acceptance at editors discretion only." Often comments on rejections. Written critiques available for $5/poem or short story. Send SASE for guidelines. Responds in 1 month. Pays 1 copy. Acquires one-time rights.

☑ ◑ **THE BALTIMORE REVIEW; BALTIMORE WRITER'S ALLIANCE**, P.O. Box 410, Riderwood MD 21139, phone (410)377-5265, fax (410)377-4325, e-mail hdiehl@bcpl.net, website http://members.aol/balto pen/index.htm, *BR* founded 1996, Baltimore Writers' Alliance founded 1980, editor Barbara Diehl.

Magazine Needs: *The Baltimore Review* appears 2 times a year (winter and summer) and showcases the "best short stories and poems of writers from the Baltimore area and beyond." They have no restrictions on poetry except they do not want to see "sentimental-mushy, loud or very abstract work; corny humor; poorly crafted or preachy poetry." They have published poetry by Fredrick Zydek, Marvin Solomon, Barbara F. Lefcowitz and

Simon Perchik. *BR* is 128 pgs., 6×9, offset lithography, perfect-bound with 10 pt. CS1 cover, back cover photo only. Publish 20-30 poems/issue. Press run is 1,000. Single copy: $7.95; subscription: $14/year (2 issues). Sample: $8. Make checks payable to Baltimore Writers' Alliance.

How to Submit: Submit up to 5 poems at a time. No previously published poems; simultaneous submissions OK. Cover letter preferred. No e-mail or fax submissions. Time between acceptance and publication is 1-6 months. "Poems and short stories are circulated to at least 2 reviewers." Sometimes comments on rejections. Send SASE for guidelines. Responds in 1-3 months. Pays 2 copies, reduced rate for additional copies.

Also Offers: The Baltimore Writers' Alliance is "a vital organization created to foster the professional growth of writers in the metro Baltimore area." The Alliance meets monthly and sponsors workshops, an annual conference, and an annual contest. It also publishes *WordHouse*, a monthly newsletter for members. Write for details. Website includes writer's guidelines and distributor information.

⊘ BANTAM DELL PUBLISHING GROUP, 1540 Broadway, New York NY 10036, phone (212)354-6500, only accepts mss from agents.

⬇ ◖ ◗ ◎ BARBARIAN PRESS (Specialized: translations), 12375 Ainsworth Rd., R.R. 8, Mission, British Columbia V2V 5X4 Canada, phone (604)826-8089, fax (604)826-8092, founded 1977, publisher Crispin and Jan Elsted.

> ⊻ Barbarian Press won the 1998 Allvin Society Citation for Excellence in Book Design in Canada for their book *Rufinus: The Completed Poems*, translated by Robin Skelton.

Book/Chapbook Needs: "We publish poetry of many kinds, but favor strong lyric poetry and accomplished translation." They publish 1 hardback and 1-2 chapbooks/year. They want "strong lyric poetry, rhymed or unrhymed, but immaculate technique essential. Translations a strong interest. No Hallmark poems, feminist/racist polemics, satirical verse, parodies, hard-nosed cynicism." They have published poetry by Robert Bringhurst, Paula Gardiner, Rachel Norton and John Carroll. Chapbooks are usually 48 pgs., 6×9, letterpress printed, sewn binding with printed paper wraps, wood engravings if any art is used.

How to Submit: "We prefer at least a chapbook-length manuscript, i.e., 30-50 pages." Previously published poems OK; no simultaneous submissions. Cover letter required. Time between acceptance and publication varies, but at least 1 year. Seldom comments on rejections. Replies to queries in 2-4 months; to mss in 4-6 weeks. Pays in copies, 10% of press run.

◖ ⊘ BARBARIC YAWP; BONEWORLD PUBLISHING, 3700 County Route 24, Russell NY 13684, phone (315)347-2609, founded 1996, editor John Berbrich.

Magazine Needs: *Barbaric Yawp*, appears quarterly, "publishing the best fiction, poetry and essays available"; encourages beginning writers. "We are not preachers of any particular poetic or literary school. We publish any type of quality material appropriate for our intelligent and wide-awake audience; all types considered, blank, free, found, concrete, traditional rhymed and metered forms. We do not want any pornography, gratuitous violence, or any whining, pissing or moaning." They have published poetry by Errol Miller, Mark Spitzer and Gary Jurechka. As a sample the editors selected these lines from "A Good Day" by Virginia Burnett:

> *He will step outside/with certainty in his boots./He will listen to his buckets,/and judge the breeze with*
> *his face./He will turn to us/with a smile/and he will tell me why/this is a good day for sugarin'.*

The editors say *BY* is a 60-page booklet, stapled with 67 lb. cover, line drawings. They receive 1,000 poems a year, accept approximately 5%. Press run is 120 for 30 subscribers. Single copy: $4; subscription: $15/year for 4 issues. Sample: $3. Make checks payable to John Berbrich.

How to Submit: Submit up to 5 poems at a time, no more than 50 lines each, and include SASE. All types considered. Previously published poems and simultaneous submissions OK. One-page cover letter preferred, include a short publication history (if available) and a brief bio. No deadlines; reads year round. Time between acceptance and publication is 2-6 months. Often comments on rejections. Send SASE for guidelines. Responds in 1-2 months. Pays 1 copy. Acquires one-time rights.

Advice: "We are primarily concerned with work that means something to the author but which is able to transcend the personal into the larger more universal realm. Send whatever is important to you. We will use yin and yang. We really like humor."

Ⓝ ◎ THE BARK (Specialized: animals), 2810 Eighth St., Berkeley CA 94710, phone (510)704-0827, fax (510)704-0933, e-mail editor@thebark.com or staff@thebark.com, website www.thebark.com, editor Claudia Kawczynska.

Magazine Needs: Published quarterly, "*The Bark* is a cultural arts magazine for the modern dog culture. We publish essays, reviews, interviews, commentary, excerpts, poetry and artwork. All work must include dogs in a prominent manner." The editor says *The Bark* is 64 pgs., magazine-sized, color throughout. Press run is 60,000. Sample: $3.50. Previously published poems OK. "Please identify dates and names of publications." E-mail submissions OK. Responds in 4 months if SASE is included. Acquires first North American serial rights.

Also Offers: Website includes content sampling, guidelines and information about magazine.

Ⓝ $◖ BARNWOOD PRESS; BARNWOOD, P.O. Box 146, Selma IN 47383, phone (765)285-8409, e-mail tkoontz@gw.bsu.edu, founded 1975, editor Tom Koontz.

Magazine Needs: *Barnwood* appears 3 times a year "to serve poets and readers by publishing excellent poems." They do not want "expressions of prejudice such as racism, sexism." They have published poetry by Bly, Goedicke and Stafford. As a sample the editor selected these lines from "Prophecy" by Alice Friman:

> *I've already told you what I want:/that sloshing sea of you turned in this direction,/my arms reaching into you like jetties./The tides taking care of the rest.*

The editor says *Barnwood* is 12 pgs., magazine-sized, photocopied and saddle-stitched with paper cover. They receive about 500 poems a year, accept approximately 4%. Press run is 200 for 150 subscribers of which 30 are libraries. Single copy: $5; subscription: $15/3 issues. Sample: $5.

How to Submit: Submit 1-3 poems at a time. No previously published poems; simultaneous submissions OK. "SASE or no response." Reads submissions September 1 through May 31 only. Time between acceptance and publication is 6 months. Poems are circulated to an editorial board. "Submissions screened by assistant editors. Editor makes final decisions." Seldom comments on rejections. Responds in 1 month. Pays $25/poem and 2 copies. Acquires one-time rights.

Book/Chapbook Needs & How to Submit: Barnwood Press publishes 1 paperback and 1 chapbook of poetry/year. Chapbooks are usually 12-32 pgs., size varies, offset printed and saddle-stitched with paper cover and cover art. Query first with a few sample poems and cover letter with brief bio and publication credits. Replies to queries and mss in 1 month. Payment varies. Order sample books or chapbooks by sending price of book plus $2.50. Website lists titles.

☑ ◎ **BARROW STREET**, P.O. Box 1015, Bowling Green Station, New York NY 10274, e-mail barrowstreet@mindspring.com, website www.barrowstreet.org, founded 1998, editors Andrea Carter Brown, Peter Covino, Lois Hirshkowitz, Melissa Hotchkiss.

⬛ Poetry published in *Barrow Street* has also been selected for inclusion in *The Best American Poetry 2000*.

Magazine Needs: "*Barrow Street*, a poetry journal appearing in the fall and spring, is dedicated to publishing award-winning, emerging, and previously undiscovered poets." They want "well-crafted poetry of the highest literary quality; open to all styles and forms." They have published poetry by Kim Addonizio, Brooks Haxton, Mark Jarman, Maureen Owen and Molly Peacock. As a sample the editors selected these lines from "The Voyage Out" by Yvette Christiansë:

> *A pipe dropped, rolling on the deck—/we looked for the bird chucking/deep in its woody throat, thought/ of trees, their shade across our bodies, not/a pipe dropped, rolling on the deck.*

The editors say *BS* is 96-120 pgs., 6×9, professionally printed and perfect-bound with glossy cardstock cover with color and photography. They receive about 3,000 poems a year, accept approximately 3%. Press run is 1,000. Subscription: $15/1 year, $18/2 years, $42/3 years. Sample: $8.

How to Submit: Submit up to 5 poems at a time. No previously published poems; simultaneous submissions OK (when notified). Cover letter with brief bio preferred. Reads submissions year round. Deadline for the fall issue is June 1; for the spring issue, December 1. Time between acceptance and publication is 3-6 months. Poems are circulated to an editorial board. Seldom comments on rejections. Publishes theme issues occasionally. Send SASE for guidelines and upcoming themes. Responds in 4 months. Always sends prepublication galleys. Pays 2 copies. Acquires first rights.

⬛ ◎ **BATHTUB GIN; PATHWISE PRESS**, P.O. Box 2392, Bloomington IN 47402, e-mail charter@blue marble.net, website www.bluemarble.net/~charter/btgin.htm, founded 1997, co-editors Christopher Harter and Tom Maxedon.

Magazine Needs: *Bathtub Gin*, a biannual, is described by its editors as "an eclectic aesthetic . . . we want to keep you guessing what is on the next page." They want poetry that "takes a chance with language or paints a vivid picture with its imagery . . . has the kick of bathtub gin, which can be experimental or a sonnet. No trite rhymes . . . Bukowski wannabes (let the man rest) . . . confessional (nobody cares about your family but you)." They have published poetry by A.D. Winans, Laurel Speer, John Grey and Patrick McKinnon. As a sample the editor selected these lines from "The Water Horses" by John Gohmann:

> *Whiskey had slit poetry's throat in a barfight/So painting was the only exorcism I could muster/And as I set out my oils and brushes,/Cubism seemed the logical tool/To pulverise two separate nightmares/ Into a communal pile of rubble*

BG is approximately 50 pgs., 8½×5½, laser-printed and saddle-stapled, 54 lb. cover stock cover, includes "eclectic" art. "We feature a 'News' section where people can list their books, presses, events, etc." They receive about 800 poems a year, accept approximately 10%. Press run is 160 for 30 subscribers, 60 shelf sales; 15 distributed free to reviewers, other editors. Subscription: $10. Sample: $5; foreign orders add $1; back issues: $3. Make checks payable to Christopher Harter.

How to Submit: Submit 4-6 poems at a time. Include SASE. Previously published poems and simultaneous submissions OK. Cover letter preferred. E-mail submissions OK (include in text of message). "Three to five line bio required if you are accepted for publication . . . if none [given], we make one up." Reads submissions July 1 through September 15 and January 1 through March 15 only. Time between acceptance and publication is 2-4 months. Often comments on rejections. Send SASE for guidelines. Responds in 2 months. Pays 1 copy. "We also sell extra copies to contributors at a discount, which they can give away or sell at full price. Reviews books and chapbooks of poetry and spoken word recordings. Open to unsolicited reviews. Poets may also send books for review consideration.

Book/Chapbook Needs & How to Submit: Pathwise Press's goal is to publish chapbooks, broadsides and "whatever else tickles us. Another part of our goal is to help create a network for writers/artists with a focus on distribution."

Also Offers: "We also publish a newsletter, *The Bent*, with reviews, ads and news items. Price is $1." Website includes guidelines, subscription and patronage info, outlets, links to small presses, resources and independent music labels.

Advice: "The small presses/magazines are where it's at. They are willing to take chances on unknown and experimental writers and because of that they are publishing the most interesting work out there—have been for years."

◎ ∅ **WILLIAM L. BAUHAN, PUBLISHER (Specialized: regional)**, P.O. Box 443, Old County Rd., Dublin NH 03444, phone (603)563-8020, fax (603)563-8026, founded 1959, editor William L. Bauhan, publishes poetry and art, especially New England regional books. *Currently accepts no unsolicited poetry.*

◯ ∅ **BAY AREA POETS COALITION (BAPC); POETALK**, P.O. Box 11435, Berkeley CA 94712-2435, e-mail poetalk@aol.com, founded 1974, direct submissions to Editorial Committee. Coalition sends quarterly poetry journal, *Poetalk*, to over 300 people. They also publish an annual anthology (22nd—180 pgs., out in Spring 2001), giving one page to each member of BAPC (minimum 6 months) who has had work published in *Poetalk* during the previous year.

Magazine Needs: *Poetalk* publishes approximately 100 poets each issue. BAPC has 150 members, 70 subscribers, but *Poetalk* is open to all. No particular genre. Short poems (under 35 lines) are preferred. "Rhyme must be well done." Membership: $15/year of *Poetalk*, copy of anthology and other privileges; extra outside US. Also offers a $50 patronage, which includes a subscription and anthology for another individual of your choice, and a $25 beneficiary/memorial, which includes membership plus subscription for friend. Subscriptions: $6/year. As a sample the editors selected this complete poem, "Mathematics of Race" by Mark States:

> We divide ourselves/to become separate ones./We attempt to achieve balance/by raising negatives./We
> belittle those carrying over positives/as being square roots./However,/we are equal in that we multiply.

Poetalk is 36 pgs., 5½×8½, photocopied, saddle-stapled with heavy card cover. Send SASE with 78¢ postage for a free complimentary copy.

How to Submit: Submit up to 4 poems, typed and single-spaced, 35 lines maximum preferred, with SASE, no more than twice a year. "Be sure to count blank lines, and add *two* for title and *two* for Author and the Address. *Too large is the number one reason for rejection.*" Simultaneous and previously published work OK, but must be noted. "All subject matter should be in good taste." No e-mail submissions. Response time is up to 4 months. Pays 1 copy. All rights revert to authors upon publication.

Also Offers: BAPC holds monthly readings, yearly contest, etc. BAPC's annual contest, established in 1980, awards a $40 1st Prize, $25 2nd Prize, $10 3rd Prize, certificates for 1st, 2nd and honorable mention, plus publication in and 1 copy of BAPC's annual anthology. Submissions must be unpublished. Submit 2 copies of up to 8 poems on any subject of 15-35 lines (blank lines count), with SASE for winners list. Include name, address and whether member or nonmember on 1 copy only. Entry fee: $1/poem for members and $1.50/poem for nonmembers. Submission period: October 1 through November 15, 2001. Winners will be announced by mail in January 2001. People from many states and countries have contributed to *Poetalk* or entered their annual contests. Send SASE in early September for contest guidelines.

Advice: "If you don't want suggested revisions you need to say so clearly in your cover letter."

◯ ∅ ◎ **BAY WINDOWS (Specialized: gay/lesbian)**, 631 Tremont St., Boston MA 02118, fax (617)266-5973, e-mail calendar@baywindows.com, founded 1983, poetry editor Rudy Kikel.

Magazine Needs: *Bay Windows* is a weekly gay and lesbian newspaper published for the New England community, regularly using "short poems of interest to lesbians and gay men. Poetry that is 'experiential' seems to have a good chance with us, but we don't want poetry that just 'tells it like it is.' Our readership doesn't read poetry all the time. A primary consideration is giving pleasure. We'll overlook the poem's (and the poet's) tendency not to be informed by the latest poetic theory, if it does this: pleases. Pleases, in particular, by articulating common gay or lesbian experience, and by doing that with some attention to form. I've found that a lot of our choices were made because of a strong image strand. Humor is always welcome—and hard to provide with craft. Obliquity, obscurity? Probably not for us. We won't presume on our audience." They have published poetry by Judith Saunders, Mina Kumar, Tom Cole, Diane Adair and Dennis Rhodes. As a sample the editor selected these lines from "This Man" by Ron Mohring:

> With his breath/fogs my skin, then watches/his traces erase. I am a window/he sees into, a house in
> which/the lamps are coming on again

THE OPENNESS TO SUBMISSIONS INDEX at the back of this book lists all publishers in this section by how open they are to submissions.

"We try to run four poems each month." They receive about 300 submissions/year, use 1 in 10, have a 3-month backlog. Press run is 13,000 for 700 subscribers of which 15 are libraries. Single copy: 50¢; subscription: $40. Sample: $3.

How to Submit: Submit 3-5 poems at a time, "up to 30 lines are ideal; include short biographical blurb and SASE. No submissions via e-mail, but poets may request info via e-mail." Responds in 3 months. Pays 1 copy. Acquires first rights. Editor "often" comments on rejections. They review books of poetry in about 750 words—"Both single and omnibus reviews (the latter are longer)."

☑ ◯ ◐ ◎ **BAYBURY REVIEW (Specialized: regional)**, 40 High St., Highwood IL 60040, e-mail baybury@flash.net, founded 1997, editor Janet St. John.

Magazine Needs: *Baybury Review* appears annually in the summer and publishes "any style or form of poetry as long as it demonstrates attention to craft and fresh insight. While we advise Midwestern writers to submit work, we also welcome poems about, or from, anywhere in the world." They have published poetry by Mary Crow, Jim Elledge, Mark Halperin, Lyn Lifshin, William Orem and Virgil Suarez. As a sample the editor selected these lines from "To an Absent Husband, After the Nightly News" by Jan Worth:

> . . . *a sound/of the desert, a survivor's keen/from somewhere parched and dangerous—/not of this overgrown yard, its green life/incessant, surging up wall and windows,/takeover green, and you not here.*

Baybury Review is 70-115 pgs., 5½×8½, professionally printed and flat-spined with card cover, b&w graphics, accepts exchange ads. They receive about 450 poems a year, accept approximately 5%. Press run is 500. Subscription: $8 (includes postage). Sample: $6.

How to Submit: Submit 3-6 poems at a time. No previously published poems; simultaneous submissions OK. Cover letter preferred. "Manuscripts should be clearly typewritten and include author's name and address on each work. Please indicate simultaneous submissions in cover letter. An adequate SASE must accompany the submission to receive a response or have work returned." Reads submissions June 1 through December 1 only. Time between acceptance and publication is 4-9 months. Poems are circulated to an editorial board. May comment on rejections. "Editors may comment on manuscripts that have passed the first round." Responds in 3 months. Pays 2 copies. Acquires first North American serial rights. Accepts reviews of very recent poetry books (350 word maximum). Poets may also send books for review consideration.

Advice: "We encourage submissions from emerging as well as established writers, but suggest that, before submitting, writers spend some time reading literary magazines to get a feel for where their work might belong."

☑ ◎ **BEACON (Specialized: regional)**, Southwestern Oregon Community College, 1988 Newmark Ave., Coos Bay OR 97420-2956, phone (541)888-7335, e-mail beacon@southwestern.cc.or.us, editor changes yearly.

Magazine Needs: *Beacon* is a small, college literary magazine that appears twice a year and publishes the work of local writers and artists. They want poetry only from those who have had their beginnings or currently reside in Southwestern Oregon. No specifications as to form, length, subject matter or style. "Submissions limited to five poems per term, prefer non-saga poems; one story per term, maximum 1,500 words." The editor says *Beacon* is 50-75 pgs., 5½×8, professionally printed with color cover and b&w art within; no ads. They receive about 400 poems a year, accept approximately 25%. Press run is 300, all shelf sales. Sample: $4.50.

How to Submit: No previously published poems or simultaneous submissions. Cover letter required. "Prefer short bio, SASE." Reads submissions December 1 through January 15 and March 1 through April 15 only. Time between acceptance and publication is 2 months. Seldom comments on rejections. Responds "on publication." Pays 1 copy. Acquires first rights.

Advice: "We encourage poets to visit for readings and bring works to offer for sale. We do not compensate in any way for these readings. The purpose of our magazine is to heighten the value of literature in our community."

☑ ◐ ◎ **BEACON STREET REVIEW (Specialized: graduate-level writers)**, 100 Beacon St., Emerson College, Boston MA 02116, e-mail beaconstreetreview@hotmail.com, founded 1986, editor Siobhan McFarland, poetry editor Jill Owens.

Magazine Needs: *BSR* appears biannually "to publish the best prose (fiction and nonfiction) and poetry we receive; to publish specifically the poetry that evidences the highest degree of creative talent and seriousness of effort and craft. Facile poetry that is not polished and crafted and poems that lack a strange sense of the 'idea' will not be ranked highly. Submissions from Emerson students as well as writers across the country are welcomed and encouraged." They have published poetry by Charlotte Pence, John McKernan and Paul Berg. As a sample the editors selected these lines from "Odysseus, Returning" by Kristi McKim:

> . . . *Distractions/Gathered into one concentrated mass and sealed shut,/Mouth closed, no other path but the familiar/Stretch of sea, separating body from origin./He savors the lotus on his parched tongue: if only/It could always enter his body with ease, the lazy comfort/Of pulling some barely seen thing into the self, loving/Indistinction, the gauzy body of possibility.*

BSR is 96-104 pgs., 5½×8½, offset printed and perfect-bound with 4-color, matte finish cover with art/photo. They receive about 300 poems a year, accept approximately 10%. Press run is 800; 200 distributed free to Emerson College students. Subscription: $5/year (2 issues), $9/2 years (4 issues). Sample: $3.

How to Submit: Submit 3-5 poems at a time. No previously published poems; simultaneous submissions OK. E-mail (in body of message) and disk submissions OK. Cover letter required. "Poets should include three copies of each poem. The poet's name and address should not appear on those copies but should appear on the cover letter with all titles clearly listed." Reads submissions year round but responds only during early November and late March. Time between acceptance and publication is 2 months. Poems are circulated to an editorial board. "We have reading boards who read and rate all poems, submitting ranks and comments to a poetry editor. The poetry editor and the editor-in-chief confer with those ranks and comments in mind and then make final decisions." Send SASE for guidelines. Responds in 2 months. Pays 3 copies. Acquires first rights. Staff reviews of poetry in 250 words, single book format. Send books for review consideration to editor-in-chief.

Also Offers: Sponsors the Editor's Choice Awards. Selected by local established poets, the award gives a cash prize for the best poems published in *BSR* during the year. Website publishes chosen works simultaneously with bound edition; also includes submission guidelines.

$ ☐ ◎ THE BEAR DELUXE (Specialized: nature/rural/ecology), P.O. Box 10342, Portland OR 97296-0342, phone (503)242-1047, fax (503)243-2645, e-mail bear@orlo.org, website www.orlo.org, founded 1993, editor Tom Webb, contact poetry editor.

● Note: *The Bear Deluxe* is published by Orlo, a nonprofit organization exploring environmental issues through the creative arts.

Magazine Needs: *Bear Deluxe*, formerly *Bear Essential*, is a quarterly that "provides a fresh voice amid often strident and polarized environmental discourse. Street-level, non-dogmatic and solution-oriented, *The Bear Deluxe* presents lively creative discussion to a diverse readership." They want poetry with "innovative environmental perspectives, not much longer than 50 lines. No rants." Also accepts poetry written by children. They have published poetry by Judith Barrington, Robert Michael Pyle, Mary Winters, Stephen Babcock, Carl Hanni and Derek Sheffield. As a sample the editor selected these lines from "Smoking" by Leanne Grabel:

> I wonder what I/think's going to/happen if I/breathe only/air.

The publication is 60 pgs., 11 × 14, newsprint with brown Kraft paper cover, saddle-stitched, with lots of original graphics and b&w photos. They receive about 400 poems a year, publish 20-30. Press run is 17,000 for 750 subscribers of which 10 are libraries, 16,000 distributed free on the streets of the Western US and beyond. Subscription: $16. Sample: $3. Make checks payable to Orlo.

How to Submit: Submit 3-5 poems at a time up to 50 lines each. Previously published poems and simultaneous submissions OK, "so long as noted." E-mail submissions OK, "in body of message. We can't respond to e-mail submissions but do look at them." Poems are reviewed by a committee of 7-9 people. Publishes 1 theme issue/ year. Send SASE for guidelines and upcoming themes. Responds in 2 months. Pays $10/poem, 5 copies (more if willing to distribute) and subscription. Buys first or one-time rights.

$ ☑ ◎ BEAR STAR PRESS; DOROTHY BRUNSMAN POETRY PRIZE (Specialized: regional), 185 Hollow Oak Dr., Cohasset CA 95973, phone (530)891-0360, founded 1996, publisher/editor Beth Spencer.

Book/Chapbook Needs: Bear Star Press accepts work by poets from Western and Pacific states. ("Those in Mountain or Pacific time zones.") "Bear Star is committed to publishing the best poetry it can attract. Each year it sponsors a contest open to poets from Western and Pacific states, although other eligibility requirements change depending on the composition of our list up to that point. From time to time we add to our list other poets from our target area whose work we admire." They publish 1-2 paperbacks and occasionally chapbooks/year. They want "well-crafted poems. No restrictions as to form, subject matter, style or purpose." They have published *On John Muir's Trail* by Gary Thompson, *Part Song* by Muriel Nelson, *The Orphan Conducts the Dovehouse Orchestra* by Deborah Woodard and poetry by George Keithley and Terri Drake. As a sample the publisher selected these lines from "Beeman" by Deborah Woodard:

> Bitten near the mouth, he keeps/completely still under his burred coat./The bees have flung a leopard
> skin/over the shoulders of a strong man./And then intractable as ivy,/they dedicate themselves to
> hanging on,

Books are usually 35-75 pgs., size varies, professionally printed and perfect-bound.

How to Submit: "Poets should enter our annual book competition. Other books are occasionally solicited by publisher, sometimes from among contestants who didn't win." Previously published poems and simultaneous submissions OK. "Prefer single-spaced manuscripts in plain font such as Times New Roman. SASE required for results. Manuscripts not returned but are recycled." Generally reads submissions August through November. Send SASE for current guidelines before submitting. Contest entry fee: $16. Time between acceptance and publication is 3-9 months. Poems are circulated to an editorial board. "I occasionally hire a judge. More recently I have taken on the judging with help from poets whose taste I trust." Seldom comments on rejections. Replies to queries regarding competitions in 1-2 weeks. Contest winner notified February 1 or before. Contest pays $1,000 and 25 author's copies (out of a press run of 500).

Advice: "Send your best work, consider its arrangement. A 'Wow' poem early on keeps me reading."

◙ THE BEATNIK PACHYDERM, P.O. Box 161, Deadwood SD 57732, founded 1998, editor Tim Brennan, editor Randall K. Rogers.

Magazine Needs: *TBP* appears 3 times a year and publishes poems, prose, artwork, letters and short stories. They want "shorter poems; poems from social philosopher poets of the everyday life; humor, experimental, slice of life poems; Beat-influenced." As a sample they selected these lines from "Bank Job" by editor Tim Brennan:

> *I had this strange dream early this morning/it was about me four or five people I work with and Bing Crosby/we were successful bank robbers/celebrating a major bank job/my dreams aren't always like this/in this one Bing kept his clothes on*

TBP is 25-30 pgs., magazine-sized, photocopied, artwork contributions desired. They receive about 400 poems a year, accept approximately 20%. Press run is 250. Single copy: $5; subscription: $13. Make checks payable to Tim Brennan.

How to Submit: Submit up to 6 poems at a time. Line length for poetry is 60 maximum. Previously published poems and simultaneous submissions OK. Cover letter preferred. "Name and address on each page; include SASE." Time between acceptance and publication is 6 months. Poems are circulated to an editorial board of 3 editors. Often comments on rejections. Responds in 6 months. Pays 1 copy. Acquires one-time rights.

Advice: "Enjoy writing, reflect, tell a unique or twisted observation."

☑️⭕🖊️ **BEAUTY FOR ASHES POETRY REVIEW**, 1000 Charles St., Mechanicsburg PA 17055-3944, e-mail creativeashes@cs.com, website www.geocities.com/paris/2729/, founded 1996, editor C.R. Cain.

Magazine Needs: *BFAPR* appears 3 times/year. "Our desire is to join the reader and the poet together; challenging the poet with a quality of language so as to cause the reader to consider it his own. We consider free verse first but this does not mean abstract. We will consider well-written rhyme. No erotica, vulgar or profane poems." They have published poetry by Deborah Ryder, Robert Cooperman, Gary Fincke, Deborah Phelps and Joyce Lazarus. As a sample the editor selected these lines from "This Is Not Death" by Alan Pucciarello:

> *This one found bone says silence./The arc of white rib/Marks no roads, hangs/like a last, loose comma—/The longest pause./You can't learn about the dead or dying/this way . . .*

BFAPR is 40 pgs., digest-sized, desktop-published and saddle-stitched with card cover with pen & ink drawings. "We are interested in receiving artwork for future covers. We will also carry ads for chapbooks. Send SASE for details. They accept approximately 5% of poems received. Press run is 200 for 50 subscribers, 75-100 shelf sales. Subscription: $10. Sample: $4.

How to Submit: Submit 3-5 poems. No previously published poems; simultaneous submissions OK if notified. Cover letter required including bio. E-mail submissions OK, no attachments. Time between acceptance and publication is 3-9 months. Often comments on rejections. Send SASE for guidelines or obtain via website. Responds in 2 months, "occasionally longer." Pays 2 copies. Acquires first or one-time rights. "Some poems are held in archive at our website. After publication in print, poets may request their poem be removed from the website." Reviews books and chapbooks of poetry. Open to unsolicited reviews. Poets may also send books for review consideration.

Also Offers: Sponsors annual contest. Contest submissions are accepted from January 1 to March 1. Subject is open. Reading fee: $10 for up to 3 poems. 1st Place: $250 and 1-year subscription. Website includes writer's guidelines, annual contest guidelines, sample poems from previous issues, editor's comments and select links for the serious poet.

Advice: "Too many poets write but don't read poetry. And all too often poets go to open readings to read and not to listen. Lastly, never submit a poem you wrote last night or last week. Work on it. Inspiration without perspective rarely produces an inspired poem."

☑️ $⭕ **BEGGAR'S PRESS; THE LAMPLIGHT; RASKOLNIKOV'S CELLAR; BEGGAR'S REVIEW**, 8110 N. 38th St., Omaha NE 68112-2018, phone (402)455-2615, e-mail beggarspress@aol.com, website http://angelfire.com/journal/begpress, founded 1977, editor Richard R. Carey, contact Danielle Staton.

Magazine Needs & How to Submit: *The Lamplight* is a semiannual (more frequent at times) publication of short stories, poetry, humor and unusual literary writings. "We are eclectic, but we like serious poetry, historically orientated. Positively no religious or sentimental poetry. No incomprehensible poetry." They have published poetry by Fredrick Zydek and Heidi von Palleske. As a sample the editor selected these lines (poet unidentified):

> *Lord, why did you curse me with doubt!/I'm a shot discharged in a wood without trees,/like a scream that began as a shout./Never too far from famine or mire;/hunger and cold, and all creatures turn bold—/But, Lord, why did you give me desire!*

The Lamplight is 40-60 pgs., 8½×11, offset printed and perfect-bound with 65 lb. cover stock. They receive about 600 poems a year, use approximately 10-15%. Press run is 500 for 300 subscribers of which 25 are libraries. Single copy: $9.50. Sample: $7 plus 9×12 SASE. No previously published poems; simultaneous submissions OK. Cover letter required—"must provide insight into the poet's characteristics. What makes this poet different from the mass of humanity?" Time between acceptance and publication is 4-12 months. Always comments on rejections. Also offers "complete appraisals and evaluations" for $4/standard sheet, double-spaced. Brochure available for SASE. Responds in 1 month or less. Pays 1 copy. Acquires first North American serial rights. *Raskolnikov's Cellar* is an irregular magazine of the same format, dimensions and terms as *The Lamplight*. However, it deals in "deeper psychologically-orientated stories and poetry. It is more selective and discriminating in what it publishes. Guidelines and brochures are an essential to consider this market." Send SASE for guidelines. Brochures require only SASE. *Beggar's Review* is 20-40 pgs., 8½×11, offset printed and saddle-stitched. It lists and reviews books, chapbooks and other magazines. "It also lists and reviews unpublished manuscripts: poetry, short stories, book-length, etc. Our purpose is to offer a vehicle for unpublished work of merit, as well as published material. We like to work with poets and authors who have potential but have not yet been recognized." Lengths of reviews range from a listing or mere caption to 1,000 words, "according to merit." Single copy: $6.

Book/Chapbook Needs & How to Submit: Beggar's Press also plans to publish 2 paperbacks/year—some on a subsidy basis. "In most cases, we select books which we publish on a royalty basis and promote ourselves. Borderline books only are author-subsidized." Query first with a few sample poems and a cover letter with brief bio and publication credits. "We also like to know how many books the author himself will be able to market to friends, associates, etc." Replies to queries in 1 month, to mss in 2½ months. Pays 10-15% royalties and 3 author's copies. Terms vary for subsidy publishing. "Depending on projected sales, the author pays from 20% to 60%."

Advice: "Our purpose is to form a common bond with distinguished poets whose poetry is marketable and worthy. Poetry is difficult to market, thus we sometimes collaborate with the poet in publishing costs. But essentially, we look for poets with unique qualities of expression and who meet our uncustomary requirements. We prefer a royalty arrangement. Beggar's Press is different from most publishers. We are impressed with concrete poetry, which is without outlandish metaphors. Keep it simple but don't be afraid to use our language to the fullest. Read Poe, Burns and Byron. Then submit to us. There is still a place for lyrical poetry."

◯ ◎ BELHUE PRESS (Specialized: gay), 2501 Palisade Ave., Suite A1, Riverdale, Bronx NY 10463, e-mail belhuepress@earthlink.net, website www.perrybrass.com, founded 1990, editor Tom Laine.

Book/Chapbook Needs: A small press specializing in gay male poetry, publishing 3 paperbacks/year—no chapbooks. "We are especially interested in books that get out of the stock poetry market." They want "hard-edged, well-crafted, fun and often sexy poetry. No mushy, self pitying, confessional, boring, indulgent, teary or unrequited love poems—yuck! Poets must be willing to promote book through readings, mailers, etc." As a sample the editor included these lines from "Two Steppin' with Mr. Right," from *The Lover of My Soul*, by Perry Brass

> *He knotted his scarf/'bout my neck like a cowboy,/then pulled me to his mouth/for one last sweet taste./ I held on to his tanned neck,/his chest and his biceps,/but he blew like the wind/to embrace his hard fate.*

"We have a $10 sample and guideline fee. Please send this before submitting any poetry. We have had to initiate this due to a deluge of bad, amateur, irrelevant submissions. After fee, we will give constructive criticism when necessary."

How to Submit: Query first with 6 pgs. of poetry and cover letter. Previously published poems and simultaneous submissions OK. Time between acceptance and publication is 1 year. Often comments on rejections. Will request criticism fees "if necessary." Replies to queries and submitted mss "fast." No payment information provided. Sample: $9.95.

Advice: "The only things we find offensive are stupid, dashed off, 'fortune cookie' poems that show no depth or awareness of poetry. We like poetry that, like good journalism, tells a story."

◖ THE BELLINGHAM REVIEW; THE SIGNPOST PRESS; 49TH PARALLEL POETRY AWARD, M.S. 9053, Western Washington University, Bellingham WA 98225, website www.wwu.edu/~bhreview/, founded 1975, editor Robin Hemley.

Magazine Needs: *The Bellingham Review* appears twice a year, runs an annual poetry competition and publishes other books and chapbooks of poetry occasionally. "We want well-crafted poetry but are open to all styles," no specifications as to form. They have published poetry by David Shields, Tess Gallagher, Gary Soto, Jane Hirshfield, Albert Goldbarth, R.T. Smith and Rebecca McClanahan. As a sample the editor selected these lines from "Sitting at Dusk in the Back Yard After the Mondrian Retrospective" by Charles Wright:

> *Form imposes, structure allows—/the slow destruction of form/So as to bring it back resheveled, reorganized,/Is the hard heart of the enterprise./Under its camouflage,/The light, relentless shill and cross-dresser, pools and deals./Inside its short skin, the darkness burns.*

The *Review* is 6×9, perfect-bound, with art and glossy cover. Each issue has about 60 pgs. of poetry. They have a circulation of 1,500 with 500 subscriptions. Subscription: $10/year, $19/2 years. Sample: $5. Make checks payable to The Western Foundation/*Bellingham Review*.

How to Submit: Submit 3-5 poems at a time with SASE. Simultaneous submissions OK with notification. Reads submissions October 1 through May 1 only. Send SASE for guidelines or obtain via website. Responds in 4 months. Pays 1 copy, a year's subscription plus monetary payment (if funding allows). Acquires first North American serial rights. Reviews books of poetry. Send books for review consideration also between October 1 and May 1.

Book/Chapbook Needs & How to Submit: Query about book publication before sending a ms.

Also Offers: The 49th Parallel Poetry Award, established in 1983, awards a $1,000 first prize, $250 second prize and $100 third prize, plus a year's subscription to the *Review*. Submissions must be unpublished and may be entered in other contests. Send any number of poems on any subject, in any form. The author's name must not appear on the ms. Enclose with each poem a 3×5 index card with the poem's title, first line of poem, author's name and address, phone/fax number, e-mail address (if any). Manuscripts will not be returned. Include SASE for winners list. Send SASE or visit website for guidelines. Entry fee: $5/poem. Submission period: October 1 through November 30. Most recent award winner was Robert A. Troyer (1999). Judge was Linda Bierds. Winners will be announced in April. Copies of previous winning poems may be obtained by sending for a sample copy of the *Review*'s winners issue ($5 postpaid). Website features submission guidelines, contest guidelines, names of editors and staff, and selections from recent issue.

◙ **BELLOWING ARK; BELLOWING ARK PRESS**, P.O. Box 55564, Shoreline WA 98155, phone (206)440-0791, founded 1984, editor Robert R. Ward.

Magazine Needs: *Bellowing Ark* is a bimonthly literary tabloid that "publishes only poetry which demonstrates in some way the proposition that existence has meaning or, to put it another way, that life is worth living. We have no strictures as to length, form or style; only that the work we publish is to our judgment life-affirming." They do not want "academic poetry, in any of its manifold forms." They have published poetry by Len Blanchard, Robert King, David Ross, Paula Milligan, Muriel Karr, Teresa Noelle Roberts and Elizabeth Biller Chapman. The paper is 32 pgs., tabloid-sized, printed on electrobright stock with b&w photos and line drawings. Circulation is 1,000, of which 275 are subscriptions and 500 are sold on newsstands. Subscription: $15/year. Sample: $3.

How to Submit: Submit 3-6 poems at a time. "Absolutely *no* simultaneous submissions." They reply to submissions in 2-12 weeks and publish within the next 1 or 2 issues. Occasionally they will criticize a ms if it seems to "display potential to become the kind of work we want." Sometimes sends prepublication galleys. Pays 2 copies. Reviews books of poetry. Send books for review consideration.

Book/Chapbook Needs & How to Submit: Bellowing Ark Press publishes collections of poetry by *invitation only.*

✔ ◖ ◯ ◙ ◎ **BELL'S LETTERS POET (Specialized: subscribers)**, P.O. Box 2187, Gulfport MS 39505-2187, e-mail jimbelpoet@aol.com, founded 1956, publisher/editor Jim Bell.

Magazine Needs: *BL* is a quarterly which you must buy ($5.50/issue, $22 subscription) to be included. The editor says "many say they stop everything the day it arrives," and judging by the many letters from readers, that seems to be the case. Though there is no payment for poetry accepted, many patrons send awards of $5-100 to the poets whose work they especially like. Poems are "four to 20 lines in good taste." Also accepts poetry written by children. They have published poetry by Denver Stull, Dolores Malaschak, Ted Turner, Marlene Meehl and Paul Pross. As a sample the editor selected these lines by Maurine Williams:

> *"The bee kisses honeysuckles and the vagrant bird sings/melodies to heal the heart."*

BL is about 64 pgs., digest-sized, photocopied on plain bond paper (including cover) and saddle-stitched. Sample (including guidelines): $5. "Send a poem (20 lines or under, in good taste) with your sample order and we will publish in our next issue."

How to Submit: Submit 4 poems a year. Ms must be typed. No simultaneous submissions. Previously published poems OK "if cleared by author with prior publisher." E-mail submissions OK. Accepted poems by subscribers go immediately into the next issue. Deadline for poetry submissions is 3 months prior to publication. Reviews books of poetry by subscribers in "one abbreviated paragraph." "The Ratings" is a competition in each issue. Readers are asked to vote on their favorite poems, and the "Top 40" are announced in the next issue, along with awards sent to the poets by patrons. *BL* also features a telephone exchange among poets and a birth-date listing.

Advice: "Tired of seeing no bylines this year? Subscription guarantees a byline in each issue."

◙ **THE BELOIT POETRY JOURNAL; CHAD WALSH POETRY PRIZE**, 24 Berry Cove Rd., Lamoine ME 04605-4617, phone (207)667-5598, e-mail sharkey@maine.edu (for information only), website www.bpj.org. founded 1950, editor Marion K. Stocking.

▼ Poetry published in *The Beloit Poetry Journal* has also been included in *The Best American Poetry* (1994 and 1996) and *Pushcart Prize* anthologies.

Magazine Needs: *The Beloit Poetry Journal* is a well-known, long-standing quarterly of quality poetry and reviews. "We publish the best poems we receive, without bias as to length, school, subject or form. It is our hope to discover the growing tip of poetry and to introduce new poets alongside established writers. We publish occasional chapbooks to diversify our offerings. These are almost never the work of one poet." They want "fresh, imaginative poetry, with a distinctive voice. We tend to prefer poems that make the reader share an experience rather than just read about it, and these we keep for up to four months, circulating them among our readers, and continuing to winnow for the best. At the quarterly meetings of the Editorial Board we read aloud all the surviving poems and put together an issue of the best we have." They have published poetry by Bei Dao, A.E. Stallings, Albert Goldbarth and Janet Holmes. As a sample the editor selected an excerpt from the poem "Alpha Images" by Karl Elder:

> *The minimalist's/gate to hell and heaven, these/corridors of light.//Blind to what's ahead,/behind, the*
> *ego takes this/pillar for a name.//What looks like a squawk/is to the ear a moth or/butterfly, clinging.*

The journal averages 48 pgs., 6×9, saddle-stapled, and attractively printed with tasteful art on the card cover. They have a circulation of 1,300 for 580 subscribers of which 328 are libraries. Subscription: individuals $18/year, institutions $23/year. Sample (including guidelines): $5. Send SASE for guidelines alone.

How to Submit: Submit any time, without query, any legible form. No e-mail submissions. "No previously published poems or simultaneous submissions. Any length of ms, but most poets send what will go in a business envelope for one stamp. Don't send your life's work." Pays 3 copies. Acquires first serial rights. Staff reviews books by and about poets in an average of 500 words, usually single format. Send books for review consideration.

Also Offers: The journal awards the Chad Walsh Poetry Prize ($4,000 in 1999) to a poem or group of poems published in the calendar year. "Every poem published in 2001 will be considered for the 2001 prize." Website includes writer's guidelines, magazine history, names of editors, sample poems, a 50-year index and table of contents of recent issues.

Advice: "We'd like to see more strong, imaginative, experimental poetry; more poetry with a global vision; and more poetry with fresh, vigorous language."

N ◎ BENJAMIN FRANKLIN LITERARY AND MEDICAL SOCIETY, INC.; HUMPTY DUMP-TY'S MAGAZINE; TURTLE MAGAZINE FOR PRESCHOOL KIDS; CHILDREN'S DIGEST; CHIL-DREN'S PLAYMATE; JACK AND JILL; CHILD LIFE (Specialized: children), 1100 Waterway Blvd., P.O. Box 567, Indianapolis IN 46206-0567.
Magazine Needs: This publisher of magazines stressing health for children has a variety of needs for mostly short, simple poems. For example, *Humpty Dumpty* is for ages 4-6; *Turtle* is for preschoolers, similar emphasis, uses many stories in rhyme—and action rhymes, etc.; *Children's Digest* is for preteens (10-13); *Jack and Jill* is for ages 7-10. *Child Life* is for ages 9-11. *Children's Playmate* is for ages 6-8. All appear 8 times/year with cartoon art, very colorful. Sample: $1.25.
How to Submit: Send SASE for guidelines. Responds within 10 weeks. Pays $15 minimum. Staff reviews books of poetry. Send books for review consideration.
Advice: "Writers who wish to appear in our publications should study current issues carefully. We receive too many poetry submissions that are about kids, not for kids. Or, the subject matter is one that adults think children would or should like. We'd like to see more humorous verse."

◎ BENNETT & KITCHEL (Specialized: form), P.O. Box 4422, East Lansing MI 48826, phone (517)355-1707, founded 1989, editor William Whallon.
Book/Chapbook Needs: Publishes 1-2 hardbacks/year of "poetry of form and meaning. No free verse or blank verse." As an example of what he admires, the editor selected these lines by Anthony Lombardy:

> *From recent fires surrounding groves are ashen,/Are like the Trojan women mad with thirst,/Who*
> *begged for water while the one accursed/Allowed the guards to fill her pool to splash in.*

Sample: $4.
How to Submit: Submit 6 poems at a time. Simultaneous submissions and previously published poems OK if copyright is clear. Minimum volume for a book "might be 750 lines." Time between acceptance and publication is 9 months. Seldom comments on submissions. Responds in 2 weeks. Terms are "variable, negotiable."
Advice: "To make a bad rhyme not from incompetence but willfully is like stubbing your toe on purpose."

$ ◻ ◎ BIBLE ADVOCATE (Specialized: religious), P.O. Box 33677, Denver CO 80233, e-mail cofgsd @denver.net, website www.baonline.org, founded 1863, associate editor Sherri Langton.
Magazine Needs: The *Bible Advocate*, published monthly, features "Christian content—to advocate the Bible and represent the church." They want "free verse, some traditional; 5-20 lines, with Christian/Bible themes." They do not want "avant garde poetry." The editor says *BA* is 24 pgs., $8\frac{3}{4} \times 11\frac{7}{8}$ with most poetry set up with 4-color art. They receive about 30-50 poems a year, accept 10-20. Press run varies for 13,500 subscribers with all distributed free.
How to Submit: Submit no more than 5 poems at a time, 5-20 lines each. Previously published poems (with notification) and simultaneous submissions OK. E-mail submissions OK (ASCII files or Microsoft Word 5.0 or 6.0 files). "No fax or handwritten submissions, please." Cover letter preferred. Time between acceptance and publication is 3-12 months. "I read them first and reject those that won't work for us. I send good ones to editor for approval." Seldom comments on rejections. Publishes theme issues. Send SASE for guidelines. Responds in 2 months. Pays $10. Buys first, reprint and one-time rights.
Also Offers: Website includes writer's guidelines. Online magazine is separate from the print and doesn't feature poetry.
Advice: "Avoid trite, or forced rhyming. Be aware of the magazine's doctrinal views (send for doctrinal beliefs booklet)."

◼ ◻ ◲ ◎ BIBLIOPHILOS (Specialized: bilingual/foreign language, ethnic/nationality, politi-cal), 200 Security Building, Fairmont WV 26554, phone (304)366-8107, fax (304)366-8461, founded 1981, editor Gerald J. Bobango.
Magazine Needs: "*Bibliophilos* is a quarterly academic journal, for the literati, illuminati, amantes artium, and those who love animals; scholastically oriented, for the liberal arts. Topics include fiction and nonfiction; literature and criticism, history, art, music, theology, philosophy, natural history, educational theory, contemporary issues and politics, sociology and economics. Published in English, French, German, Romanian." They want "tradi-tional forms, rhyme is OK; also blank verse, free verse. Aim for concrete visual imagery, either in words or on the page. No inspirational verse, or anything that Ann Landers or Erma Bombeck would publish." Also accepts poetry written by children, ages 12-17. They have published poetry by Belle Randall, Lois Greene Stone and Jack Lloyd Packard. As a sample the editor selected these lines from "Trademark" (poet unidentified):

> *superimposed on a picture too faint to see,/printed in red in English and Chinese,/concludes: ". . .*
> *should not be poured out/until five minutes have passed/when the taste will come out/in its full glory."*

Bibliophilos is 64 pgs., $5\frac{1}{2} \times 8$, laser photography printed and saddle-stapled with light card, includes clip art and ads. They receive about 60 poems a year, accept approximately 33%. Press run is 200 for 100 subscribers. Subscription: $18/year. Sample: $5. Make checks payable to The Bibliophile. West Virginia residents please add 6% sales tax.

How to Submit: Query first with SASE and $5 for sample and guidelines. Then, if invited, submit 3-5 poems at a time. Previously published poems and simultaneous submissions OK. Cover letter with brief bio preferred. Time between acceptance and publication is 3 months. Often comments on rejections. Send SASE for guidelines. Responds in 2 weeks. Pays 3 copies plus offprints. Acquires first North American serial rights. Staff reviews books and chapbooks of poetry in 750-1,000 words, single book format. Send books for review consideration.

Also Offers: Sponsors poetry contest. Send SASE for rules. 1st Prize $25 plus publication and offprints.

Advice: "There is too much maudlin over-emotionalism and instant pop psychology in this touchy-feely world. We need some good traditional, hearty, Kiplingesque poetry that stirs, inspires, and hits you between the eyes. Also, we need more peristaltic belchings of crabbed organisms arguing that malls, 'feeling everyone's pain,' and building self-esteem as opposed to educating people, should all be extinguished as blights."

☑ $◎ BILINGUAL REVIEW PRESS; BILINGUAL REVIEW/REVISTA BILINGÜE (Specialized: ethnic/Hispanic, bilingual/Spanish), Hispanic Research Center, Arizona State University, Box 872702, Tempe AZ 85287-2702, phone (480)965-3867, journal founded 1974, press in 1976, managing editor Karen Van Hooft.

Magazine Needs: "We are a small press publisher of U.S. Hispanic creative literature and of a journal containing poetry and short fiction in addition to scholarship." *BR/RB,* published 3 times/year, contains some poetry in most issues. "We publish poetry by and/or about U.S. Hispanics and U.S. Hispanic themes. We do not publish translations in our journal or literature about the experiences of Anglo-Americans in Latin America. We have published a couple of poetry volumes in bilingual format (Spanish/English) of important Mexican poets." They have published poetry by Alberto Ríos, Martín Espada, Judith Ortiz Cofer and Marjorie Agosín. The editor says the journal is 96 pgs., 7×10, offset printed and flat-spined, with 2-color cover. They use less than 10% of hundreds of submissions received each year. Press run is 1,000 for 700 subscribers. Subscriptions: $21 for individuals, $35 for institutions. Sample: $7 individuals/$12 institutions.

How to Submit: Submit "two copies, including ribbon original if possible, with loose stamps for return postage." Cover letter required. Pays 2 copies. Acquires all rights. Reviews books of US Hispanic literature only. Send books, Attn: Editor, for review consideration.

Book/Chapbook Needs & How to Submit: Bilingual Review Press publishes flat-spined paperback collections of poetry. For book submissions, inquire first with 4-5 sample poems, bio and publication credits. Pays $250 advance, 10% royalties and 10 copies. Over the years, books by this press have won 6 American Book Awards and 2 Western States Book Awards.

$◢ ◎ BIRCH BROOK PRESS (Specialized: anthology), P.O. Box 81, Delhi NY 13753, phone (212)353-3326, fax (607)746-7453, website www.birchbrookpress.com, founded 1982, contact Tom Tolnay.
  • BBP acquired the poetry publishing activities of Persephone Press in 1998.

Book/Chapbook Needs: Birch Brook "is a letterpress book printer/typesetter/designer that uses monies from these activities to publish several titles of its own each year with cultural and literary interest." Publishes 4-6 paperbacks and/or hardbacks per year. The press specializes "mostly in anthologies with specific subject matter. BBP publishes one or two books annually by individuals with high-quality literary work relating to popular culture, on a co-op basis." Books are "handset letterpress editions printed in our own shop." They have published *The Melancholy of Yorick* by Joel Chace; *Waiting On Pentecost* by Tom Smith; *The Derelict Genius of Martin M* by Frank Fagan and *Repercussions* by Marcus Rome.

How to Submit: Query by mail only or send the entire ms. "Must include SASE with submissions." Occasionally comments on rejections. Authors may obtain sample books by sending SASE for catalog. Pays from $5-20 for publication in anthology.

Advice: The editor is "interested in poetry about flyfishing."

☑ ◢ ◎ BIRMINGHAM POETRY REVIEW (Specialized: translations), English Dept., HB205, 1530 Third Ave. S, University of Alabama at Birmingham, Birmingham AL 35294, phone (205)934-4250, website www.uab.edu/english/bpr, founded 1988, co-editors Robert Collins and Adam Vines.

Magazine Needs: The review appears twice a year using poetry of "any style, form, length or subject. We are biased toward exploring the cutting edge of contemporary poetry. Style is secondary to the energy, the fire the poem possesses. We don't want poetry with cliché-bound, worn-out language." They have published poetry by Hague, Harrod, McDonald, Murawski and Steinman. They describe their magazine as 50 pgs., 6×9, offset printed, with b&w cover. Press run is 700 for 300 subscribers. Subscription: $4/year; $7/2 years. Sample: $2.

How to Submit: Submit 3-5 poems, "no more. No cover letters. We are impressed by good writing; we are unimpressed by publication credits." SASE required. No simultaneous or multiple submissions, and previously published poems only if they are translations. Editor sometimes comments on rejections. Send SASE for guidelines. Responds in 6 months. Pays 2 copies and one-year subscription.

Also Offers: Website includes guidelines, contents of current issue, submission guidelines, subscription information, list of editors and sample poems.

Advice: They say, "Advice to beginners: Read as much good contemporary poetry, national and international, as you can get your hands on. Then be persistent in finding your own voice."

◐ ◎ **THE BITTER OLEANDER; FRANCES LOCKE MEMORIAL AWARD (Specialized: transla-tions)**, 4983 Tall Oaks Dr., Fayetteville NY 13066-9776, phone (315)637-3047, fax (315)637-5056, e-mail bones44@ix.netcom.com, founded 1974, editor/publisher Paul B. Roth.

Magazine Needs: *The Bitter Oleander* appears biannually, publishing "imaginative poetry; poetry in translation; serious language." They want "highly imaginative poetry whose language is serious. We prefer short poems of no more than 25 lines. We are not interested in very long poems and prefer not to receive poems about the common values and protests of society." They have published poetry by Robert Bly, Alan Britt, Duane Locke and Ray Gonzalez. *The Bitter Oleander* is 80-125 pgs., digest-sized, offset printed, perfect-bound with glossy 2-color cover, cover art and ads. They receive about 2,500 poems a year, accept approximately 4%. Press run is 1,500, 1,000 shelf sales. Single copy: $8; subscription: $15. Make checks payable to Bitter Oleander Press.

How to Submit: Submit up to 8 poems at a time with name and address on each page. No previously published poems or simultaneous submissions. No e-mail submissions. Cover letter preferred. Does not read mss during July. Time between acceptance and publication is 4-6 months. "All poems are read by the editor only and all decisions are made by this editor." Often comments on rejections. Responds within a month. Pays 1 copy.

Also Offers: Sponsors the Frances Locke Memorial Award, awarding $500 and publication. Submit any number of poems. Entry fee: $10/5 poems, $2 each additional poem. Open to submissions March 15 through June 15 only.

Advice: "We simply want poetry that is imaginative and serious in its performance of language. So much flat-line poetry is written today that anyone reading one magazine or another cannot tell the difference."

☑ $◙ **BKMK PRESS**, University House, University of Missouri-Kansas City, 5101 Rockhill Rd., Kansas City MO 64110-2499, phone (816)235-2558, fax (816)235-2611, e-mail bkmk@umkc.edu, founded 1971, managing editor Ben Furnish, associate editor Michelle Boisseau, director/executive editor James McKinley.

Book/Chapbook Needs: BkMk Press generally publishes 4-5 full-length paperbacks. The press seeks to publish "well-known and beginning poets fairly and equally." They have no specifications regarding form, length or subject matter but do not want to see "pretentious, unserious poetry." They have published *Fall From Grace* by Christopher Buckley, *Inverted Fire* by Alice Friman and books of poetry by Howard Schwartz and Neal Bowers. Their books are generally 64 pgs., 5½×8½, professionally printed and perfect-bound with laminated covers with art and photographs.

How to Submit: Query first with sample poems and a cover letter with brief bio and publication credits. Previously published poems and simultaneous submissions OK. Occasionally comments on rejections. Replies to queries in 3 months, to mss in 3-8 months. Pays 10% royalties and 20 author's copies (out of a press run of 600). Call or write for catalog to order samples.

☑ ◐ ◎ **BLACK BEAR PUBLICATIONS; BLACK BEAR REVIEW (Specialized: social issues)**, 1916 Lincoln St., Croydon PA 19021-8026, e-mail BBReview@earthlink.net, website http://home.earthlink.net/~BBReview, founded 1984, poetry and art editor Ave Jeanne, producer Ron Zettlemoyer.

Magazine Needs: *Black Bear Review* is a semiannual international literary and fine arts magazine in print and online. "We like well-crafted poetry that mirrors real life—void of camouflage. We seek energetic poetry, avant-garde, free verse and haiku which relate to the world today. We seldom publish the beginner. No traditional poetry is used. The underlying theme of *BBR* is social and political, but the review is interested also in environmental, war/peace, ecological and minorities themes. We would like to receive more ideas on AIDS awareness, life styles and current political topics." They have published poetry by Juan Sequeira, A D Winans, John Grey, Carlos Martinez, Alan Catlin and Jay Marvin. As a sample the editor selected these lines from "The Emigrant" by Katherine Sanchez:

> I am the boy, stomach flat on sand./I reach under the barbed wire fence/for homeland dirt. The soldier's
> boot/smooths the wrinkles on my hand like an iron . . .

BBR is 64 pgs., digest-sized, perfect-bound, offset from typed copy on white stock, with line drawings, collages and woodcuts. Circulation is 500 for 300 subscribers of which 15 are libraries. Subscription: $12, $18 overseas. Sample: $6; back copies when available are $5 (overseas add $3/copy). Make checks payable to Ron Zettlemoyer.

How to Submit: Submit 5 poems at a time by e-mail only. "E-mail submissions are answered within a week. Include snail mail address. No attached files please." Simultaneous submissions are not considered. Time between acceptance and publication is 6 months. Send SASE for guidelines or visit website. Pays 1 copy. Acquires first North American serial rights and electronic rights, "as work may appear on our website."

Book/Chapbook Needs & How to Submit: They publish 2 chapbooks/year. "Publication is now on a subsidy basis." Chapbook series requires a reading fee of $5, complete ms and cover letter sent via snail mail. Send SASE for guidelines. For book publication, they require that "*BBR* has published the poet and is familiar with his/her work." Author receives one-half print run.

USE THE GENERAL INDEX, located at the back of this book, to find the page number of a specific publisher. Also, publishers that were listed in last year's edition but not included in this edition are listed in the General Index with a notation explaining why they were omitted.

Also Offers: "Our yearly poetry competition offers cash awards to poets." Deadline: November 30. Send SASE for guidelines. Website features most recent issues, complete guidelines, links and current needs. "Our website is designed and maintained by Ave Jeanne and is updated regularly to meet the diverse needs of our readers."

Advice: "We appreciate a friendly, brief cover letter. All submissions are handled with objectivity and quite often rejected material is directed to another market. We are always interested in aiding those who support small press. We frequently suggest poets keep up with the current edition of *Poet's Market*. We make an effort to keep our readers informed and on top of the small press scene. Camera-ready ads are printed free of charge as a support to small press publishers. We also run an ad page on the Internet, "InterActions," for all interested poets and writers to advertise. We do suggest poets and artists read issues before submitting to absorb the flavor and spirit of our publication. Send your best!" The editor adds, "Visit our applauded website. *Black Bear* will continue to print in our paperback format as well as art and poems online. We are financially supported by our poets, artists, readers and editors."

🍎 🌀 ◎ **$BLACK BOUGH (Specialized: haiku)**, 188 Grove St. #1., Somerville NJ 08876, founded 1991, editor Chuck Easter.

Magazine Needs: *bb* is a triannual that publishes "haiku and related poetry that uses the Eastern form in the Western milieu." They want "haiku, senryu, tanka, haibun (in particular) and sequences. No academic essays or extremely long poems." Also accepts poetry written by children. They have published work by Tom Clausen, Elizabeth Howard and Andrea Missias. As a sample the editor selected this haiku by Harry Bose:

> *in the wheel barrow/patches of rust/filled with frost*

bb is 30 pgs., digest-sized, professionally printed, saddle-stitched, with photos. They receive about 5,200 poems a year, use 5-10%. Press run is 200 for 125 subscribers. Subscription: $18. Sample: $6.50.

How to Submit: "Submit no more than 20 haiku; prefer several haiku/page." No previously published poems or simultaneous submissions. Time between acceptance and publication is 3-6 months. Comments on rejections "if requested." Responds in 10 weeks. Pays $1/verse, up to $4 for a long poem or haiku sequence. Buys first rights.

Also Offers: *black bough* books has published *Spirit Dance* by Chuck Easter and *Road Work* by Michael Ketchek. Send SASE for additional information.

🌀 **BLACK BUZZARD PRESS; BLACK BUZZARD REVIEW; VISIONS—INTERNATIONAL, THE WORLD JOURNAL OF ILLUSTRATED POETRY; THE BLACK BUZZARD ILLUSTRATED POETRY CHAPBOOK SERIES; INTERNATIONAL—VISIONS POETRY SERIES**, 1007 Ficklen Rd., Fredericksburg VA 22405, founded 1979, poetry editor Bradley R. Strahan, associate editor Shirley G. Sullivan.

Magazine Needs: *Visions*, a digest-sized, saddle-stapled magazine finely printed on high-quality paper, appears 3 times a year, uses 56 pages of poetry in each issue. Circulation 800 with 400 subscribers of which 50 are libraries. Sample: $5.50. Current issue: $5.50. They receive *well* over 1,000 submissions each year, use 150, have a 3- to 18-month backlog. "*Visions* is international in both scope and content, publishing poets from all over the world and having readers in 48 U.S. states, Canada and 24 other countries." *Black Buzzard Review* is a "more or less annual informal journal, dedicated mostly to North American poets and entirely to original English-language poems. In *BBR*, we are taking a more wide-open stance on what we accept (including the slightly outrageous)." Sample: $4.50. Current issue: $5.50. It is 36 pgs., magazine-sized, side-stapled, with matte card cover.

How to Submit: Submit 3-6 poems at a time. "Poems must be readable (not faded or smudged) and not handwritten. We resent having to pay postage due, so use adequate postage! No more than six pages, please." No previously published poems or simultaneous submissions. Publishes theme issues. Send SASE for upcoming themes. Responds in 3 weeks. Pays 1 copy or $5-10 "if we get a grant." Buys first North American serial rights. Staff reviews books of poetry in "up to two paragraphs." Send books for review consideration.

Book/Chapbook Needs & How to Submit: "We are an independent nonsubsidized press dedicated to publishing fine accessible poetry and translation (particularly from lesser-known languages such as Armenian, Gaelic, Urdu, Vietnamese, etc.) accompanied by original illustrations of high quality in an attractive format. We want to see work that is carefully crafted and exciting, that transfigures everyday experience or gives us a taste of something totally new; all styles except concrete and typographical 'poems.' Nothing purely sentimental. No self-indulgent breast beating. No sadism, sexism or bigotry. No unemotional pap. No copies of Robert Service or the like. Usually under 80 lines but will consider longer." They have published poetry by Michael Mott, Sharon Olds, Eamon Grennan, Miller Williams, Phillip Appleman, Naomi Shihab Nye and Lawrence Ferlinghetti. To submit for the chapbook series, send samples (5-10 poems) and a brief cover letter "pertinent to artistic accomplishments." Responds in 3 days to 3 weeks. Pays in copies. Usually provides criticism. Send $4 for sample chapbook. They also publish the International-Visions Poetry Series. Send SASE for flyer describing titles and order information.

Advice: The editors add that in *Visions*, "We sometimes publish helpful advice about 'getting published' and the craft of poetry, and often discuss poets and the world of poetry on our editorial page."

$ ▢ ◎ BLACK DIASPORA MAGAZINE; BLACK DIASPORA COMMUNICATIONS, LTD. (Specialized: ethnic/nationality), 298 Fifth Ave., 7th Floor, New York NY 10001, phone (212)268-8348, fax (212)268-8370, e-mail blakdias@earthlink.net, website www.blackdiaspora.net, founded 1979, executive editor Michelle Phipps, publisher Rene John-Sandy.

Magazine Needs: Published 7 times a year, *BDM* is a "general interest publication for African-Americans, Caribbeans, Africans, Hispanics. Covers general topics in all facets of their lives." They want "long and short poems—creatively done. Sonnets are good. They should all follow editorial guidelines. Be imaginative. No five-page poems." They have published poetry by Sabrina Smith and Annan Boodram. As a sample they selected these lines from "Altered Mind" by Barbara Grant-Richardson:

> *We are the family of Black/America standing at the turning/point of life/Silently absorbed in a world/ misunderstood by many./Where the human spirit and level/of admiration are steadily stripped of their luster.*

They say *BDM* is 68-84 pgs., magazine-sized, flat-spined with glossy cover, includes photos and ads. They receive about 60 poems a year, accept approximately 100%. Press run is 50,000 for 250,000 subscribers. Single copy: $2.95; subscription: $15/year. Sample: $5.

How to Submit: Submit up to 2 poems at a time. Previously published poems OK; no simultaneous submissions. Cover letter preferred. Disk submissions OK. "Format should be in Word Perfect 5.1." Time between acceptance and publication is 3 months. Seldom comments on rejections. Publishes theme issues. Send SASE for guidelines and upcoming themes. Responds in 3 weeks. Pays $15. Buys first North American serial rights or one-time rights. Reviews books of poetry in 200-300 words, single book format. Open to unsolicited reviews. Poets may also send books for review consideration to Michelle Phipps.

Also Offers: Website includes a preview of the latest issue.

Advice: "Please do not call editors. They're very busy and don't have time for all calls. Be patient. Make friends with editorial assistants and assistant editors."

◑ BLACK MOON: POETRY OF IMAGINATION, 233 Northway Rd., Reisterstown MD 21136, fax (410)833-9362, founded 1994, contact Alan Britt.

Magazine Needs: *Black Moon* appears annually in January and publishes the "most imaginative, outspoken poetry available. Experimental poetry and essays welcome." They have published poetry by Colette Inez, Marjorie Agosín, Paul B. Roth, Judy Rae, Steve Barfield, Robert Bly and John Haines. As a sample the editor selected these lines from "The Hague" by Duane Locke:

> *The moon never departs/but stays all day in a flower pot./The avenues leisurely stroll/and lovingly hold the hands of canals.*

Black Moon is about 224 pgs., 6×9, professionally printed and perfect-bound, with glossy card cover, ads. They accept 10% of work received. Press run is 4,000 for 200 subscribers of which 20 are libraries, 3,500 shelf sales. Single copy: $8.95. Sample: $10.70. "Read sample copy before submitting."

How to Submit: No previously published poems; simultaneous submissions OK. Cover letter preferred. Time between acceptance and publication is 6-12 months. "Some poems are accepted by various consultants for *Black Moon*." Often comments on rejections. Responds in 3 months. Pays 1 copy. Does not acquire rights, however, "we would like to be recognized for having published the piece."

Advice: "We would like to see more submissions that reflect political and social consciousness. Surreal, deep-image, immanentist poetry welcome."

Ⓝ ⚟ $◑ BLACK MOSS PRESS, 2450 Byng Rd., Windsor, Ontario N8W 3E8 Canada, phone (519)252-2551, fax (519)253-7809, e-mail mgervais2@home.com, founded 1969, contact Marty Gervais.

Book/Chapbook Needs: Black Moss Press publishes 12 poetry titles per year. They want rural, small town, sports related poetry. No religious work, greeting card limericks. They have published work by Robert Hilles, Rosemary Sullivan, A.L. Purdy, Irving Layton and Karen Mulhallen. Books are usually 85 pgs., 6×9, perfect-bound with 4-color cover. Query first, with 10 sample poems. Reading fee: $25. No previously published poems or simultaneous submissions. Poems are circulated to an editorial board. Often comments on rejections. Replies to queries in 5 weeks. Pays royalties of 10% plus advance of $200 and 10 author's copies.

✓ ▢ BLACK SPRING PRESS; BLACK SPRING REVIEW, 63-89 Saunders, 6G, Rego Park NY 11374, founded 1997, editor/publisher John Gallo.

Magazine Needs: *Black Spring Review* is published 4-6 times a year. "We are seeing poetry from two different camps: Those who use poetry as a form of expression and those who use poetry as a craft. We prefer poetry as expression. Don't be afraid to let it all hang out. We don't care if you have a Ph.D. in Literature or if you began writing on a napkin yesterday. Make the reader feel what you feel. No 'Sword & Sorcery'/Hallmark/Gothic Vampire Romance type poems." They have published poetry by Linda La Porte, Ana Christy, Ed Galing, A.D. Winans, Frank Lima, Raymond Mason and Kate Greene. As a sample the editor selected these lines from "Nonsense" by Laura Joy Lustig:

> *Sense is known/only/but its/non./& only 1/is/usable*

The editor says *BSR* is approximately 20 pgs., 8½×5½ chapbook, cardstock cover and saddle-stapled. They receive approximately 500-600 poems a year, uses about 30%. Press run is 200 for 50 subscribers. Single copy: $5; subscription: $20/4 issues. Make checks/money orders payable to John Gallo, not Black Spring Press. Editor also wants to comment that "there are no back issues available of the 'old' *Black Spring Review* nor will there be any in the foreseeable future. Beginning in January 2000 we will be undergoing a massive overhaul. First issue of 'new' *Black Spring Review* will arrive in January 2000."

How to Submit: Submit 6 poems maximum. Previously published poems and simultaneous submissions OK. "Please ensure that name and address appears on each page. I can't tell you how many times poems accepted for submission have gone by the wayside due to the fact that I couldn't tell who wrote it or where it came from. Writing name and address on envelope is not good enough, since there are hundreds and they tend to get torn and tossed. Also be sure to send SASE. Any submission without an SASE will be discarded." Time between acceptance and publication varies. "Please refrain from sending letter upon letter about when you will see your poem in print. If it's accepted it will be published." Sometimes comments on rejections. Send SASE for guidelines. Responds in up to 2 months. "There are a ton of submissions and only one man going through them. Please be patient." Pays 1 copy.

Book/Chapbook Needs & How to Submit: Black Spring Press wants "strong, emotional writing that isn't afraid to be bold, hard and risky" and publishes 4-6 chapbooks/year. "We also publish a small series called 'Mezzotints' for individual poets." They have published *Bloody and Living* by Ed Galing, *Naked Brunch* by Laura Joy Lustig, *Poems Not For Your Aunt Nora* by Raymond Mason, and *Suck Out the Marrow of Life* by Linda La Porte. Chapbooks are usually 20-40 pgs., 5½×8½, photocopied and saddle-stapled with card stock cover. Query first. "Please do not send the entire manuscript, especially if it's over 200 pages long. However, books and chapbooks are usually solicited, but we are open to unsolicited mss provided that the poet queries first. We do offer co-op publishing of chapbooks. Write for details." Replies to queries and mss in 2 weeks. Pays 40 author's copies (out of a press run of 100). Write to obtain sample books or chapbooks.

Advice: "Write from deep within you. Find your own voice. Bukowski already did Bukowski and Ginsberg already did Ginsberg. Black Spring Press respects the Beat tradition but is not interested in resurrecting a by-gone era. It's the 21st century now. Time to move forward. Also, take whatever you may have learned in college literature courses or writing workshops and ignore it. Good writing does not necessarily come out of the universities. Keep your ego in check. There are an awful lot of people writing out there, and a small press will not make you rich and famous beyond your wildest dreams. However small presses have been a nice stepping stone to bigger and better things. Just don't think I am going to get you the Pulitzer prize. Remember what small in 'small press' means. We feel it should be a network of independent writers and artists to share ideas and their work since none of the large houses would ever look our way unless there's a million dollars to be made."

⊘ **BLACK THISTLE PRESS**, 491 Broadway 6th Floor, New York NY 10012, phone (212)219-1898, fax (212)431-6044, e-mail bthistle@netcom.com, website www.blackthistlepress.com, founded 1990, publisher Ms. Hollis Melton. "We are no longer accepting submissions because we are not publishing new projects at this time."

◑ **BLACK TIE PRESS**, P.O. Box 440004, Houston TX 77244-0004, fax (713)789-5119, founded 1986, publisher and editor Peter Gravis.

Book/Chapbook Needs: "Black Tie Press is committed to publishing innovative, distinctive and engaging writing. We publish books; we are not a magazine or literary journal. We are not like the major Eastern presses, university presses or other small presses in poetic disposition. To get a feel for our publishing attitude, we urge you to buy one or more of our publications before submitting. Prefer the exotic, the surreal, the sensual—work that provokes, shocks . . . work that continues to resonate long after being read. Surprise us." They do not want "rhyme or fixed forms, unless remarkably well done. No nature, animal, religious, or pet themes." They have published poetry by Steve Wilson, Guy Beining, Laura Ryder, Donald Rawley, Harry Burrus and Jenny Kelly. As a sample the editor selected these lines from "Late November, Los Angeles" in *Steaming* by Donald Rawley:

> In this rubbed dusk,/the false fall sky/silvers itself/into a pale, nude witch,/a sun of mother's cologne,/
> and a neck of distanced chill

Sample: $8.

How to Submit: "We have work we want to publish, hence, unsolicited material is not encouraged. However, we will read and consider material from committed, serious writers as time permits. Query with four sample poems. Write, do not call about material. No reply without SASE." Cover letter with bio preferred. Responds in 6 weeks. Always sends prepublication galleys. Author receives percent of press run.

Advice: "Too many writers are only interested in getting published and not interested in reading or supporting good writing. Black Tie hesitates to endorse a writer who does not, in turn, promote and patronize (by actual purchases) small press publications. Once Black Tie publishes a writer, we intend to remain with that artist."

☑ $ ⊘ **BLACK WARRIOR REVIEW**, P.O. Box 862936, Tuscaloosa AL 35486-0027, phone (205)348-4518, website www.sa.ua.edu/osm/bwr, founded 1974, poetry editor Mark Neely, editor T. J. Beitelman.

▼ Poetry published in *BWR* has been included in the 1997, 1999 and 2000 volumes of *The Best American Poetry* and Pushcart prize anthologies.

Magazine Needs: *BWR* is a semiannual review. They have published poetry by W.S. Merwin, Tomaz Salamun, Nancy Eimers, Alice Notley, Thomas Rabbitt and C.D. Wright. As a sample the editor selected these lines from "The Birth of a Saint" by Bob Hicok:

> *If there's a gun in her theory of Heaven it's unloaded,/pearl-handled, graced with the feel of flesh/*
> *extending from hand to steel, the confidence/of her palm radiating to the man . . .*

BWR is 200 pgs., 6×9. Circulation is 2,000. Subscription: $14. Sample: $8.

How to Submit: Submit 3-6 poems at a time. Simultaneous submissions OK if noted. No electronic submissions. Send SASE for guidelines. Responds in 4 months. Pays $30-45/poem plus 2 copies. Buys first rights. Reviews books of poetry in single or multi-book format. Open to unsolicited reviews. Poets may also send books for review consideration to Christopher Chambers, editor.

Also Offers: Awards one $500 prize annually to a poet whose work appeared in either the fall or spring issue. Website includes guidelines, names of editors, poetry, and subscription information.

Advice: "We solicit a nationally-known poet for a chapbook section. The remainder of the issue is chosen from unsolicited submissions. Many of our poets have substantial publication credits, but our decision is based simply on the quality of the work submitted."

⊕ $ ⊘ ◎ BLACKWATER PRESS (Specialized: regional), P.O. Box 5115, Leicester LE2 8ZD Great Britain, founded 1996, contact Hilary Solanki.

Book/Chapbook Needs: Blackwater Press "aims to publish poets based in the United Kingdom who have established a reputation in journals, pamphlets, etc., but who have not yet had a full collection published." The press publishes 3-4 paperbacks/year. They have published *A Year Without Apricots* by Kate Foley and *Einstein's Bumblebee* by Colin Sutherell. Books are usually about 50 pgs., 21×15cm, professionally printed and perfect-bound with soft cover.

How to Submit: Submit "enough poems for a 50- to 60-page book. Previously published poems OK, if in journals/pamphlets; no simultaneous submissions. Cover letter required. Time between acceptance and publication is 1 year. Poems are circulated to an editorial board. Replies to queries in 1 month; to mss in 2 months. Pays 10% royalties and 6 author's copies (out of a press run of 500). Obtain sample books or chapbooks by purchasing from the press.

Ⓝ ⊘ THE BLIND HORSE REVIEW, P.O. Box 15902, Beverly Hills CA 90209-1902, founded 1992, editor Todd Kalinski.

Magazine Needs: *The Blind Horse Review* is a poetry and prose publication that appears about twice a year. They do not want poetry that is "overtly sentimental in nature. No particular qualms as to length, and subject matter or language may be what it may [and they mean that]. No academic writing for the sake of strictly writing it, and no globs of despair for no sensible reason." They have published poetry by Gerald Locklin, Barbara Peck, B.Z. Niditch, John Grey and Matt Boys. As a sample the editor selected these lines from "Locked Out" by Chris Mortenson:

> *It would be preferable to contemplate/and to discuss important things/but most people don't.//Humanity*
> *more easily accepts the insubstantial,/though some have a bit more depth,/it is not much.*

BHR is 36-48 pgs., digest-sized and saddle-stapled with heavy, colored, matte paper cover. They accept about 5% of the poetry received and feature 11-14 writers in each issue. Press run is 300 for 50 subscribers. Subscription: $11 for 2 issues, $15 for 3 issues. Sample postpaid: $6. Make checks payable to Todd Kalinski.

How to Submit: Submit 10 poems at a time. No previously published poems or simultaneous submissions. Include SASE "and, if you may, a cover letter without awards and publications, but a letter of interest, something maybe of insight." Often comments on rejections. Send SASE for guidelines. Responds in up to 1 month. Pays 1 copy. Rights revert to authors.

Advice: "Type yourself into a certain sensibility that one can actually persevere in this vocation; because it doesn't seem to come easily to most of the writers writing today."

✓ ⏱ ⊘ THE BLIND MAN'S RAINBOW, P.O. Box 1557, Erie PA 16507-0557, e-mail bmrainbow@excite.com, website www.angelfire.com/on2/blindmansrainbow, founded 1993, editor Melody Sherosky.

Magazine Needs: *Blind Man's Rainbow* is a quarterly publication "whose focus is to create a diverse collection of quality poetry and art." They want "all forms of poetry (Beat, rhyme, free verse, haiku, etc.), though excessively long poems are less likely to be accepted. All subject matter accepted." They do not want "anything graphically sexual or violent." Also accepts poetry written by children. As a sample the editor selected these lines from "Fiddlehead Harvest" by Maija Barnett:

> *Hunched over mud/and last summer's leaves/my fingers dig/into/thick clumps of ferns/curled like a*
> *fetus/inside their coppery sheaths.*

The Blind Man's Rainbow is 20-24 pgs., 8½×11, photocopied and side-stapled, paper cover with art, line drawings inside. They receive about 500 submissions a month. Subscription: $10 US, $14 foreign. Sample: $3 US, $4 foreign. Make checks payable to Melody Sherosky.

How to Submit: Submit 2-10 poems at a time with name and address on each poem. Include SASE. Previously published poems and simultaneous submissions OK, "but it is nice to let us know." Cover letter preferred. "Submissions only returned if requested and with adequate postage." Time between acceptance and publication is 1-6 months. Often comments on rejections. Send SASE for guidelines. Responds in 3 months. Pays 1 copy. Acquires one-time rights.

Also Offers: Website includes writer's guidelines, subscription information, poets and covers from latest issues.

$ ◎ BLINDSKILLS, INC.; DIALOGUE MAGAZINE (Specialized: blind or visually impaired), P.O. Box 5181, Salem OR 97304-0181, phone (800)860-4224 or (503)581-4224, fax (503)581-0178, e-mail blindskl@ teleport.com, website www.blindskills.com, founded 1983, editor Carol M. McCarl, assistant editor Richard L. Belgard.

Magazine Needs: *Dialogue*, a world of ideas for visually impaired people of all ages, appears quarterly and publishes "interviews of interest or assistance to newly blind and other visually impaired persons, examples of career and leisure experiences, fiction, humor and poetry. Material that is religious, controversial, political or contains explicit sex, is not acceptable. Our readers enjoy traditional forms of poetry such as blank verse and free verse. Submit one poem to a page, complete with title, date, name and address of author. Poems may mention a supreme being, but will not be accepted if their theme or nature is religious. We especially want submissions from visually impaired writers." *Dialogue* is published in four formats: braille, large print, 4-track cassette tape and IBM-compatible diskette. The large print (18 point) format is about 150 pgs., 8½×11, neatly printed and spiral-bound with colored paper cover. Subscription (4 issues): $28 for legally blind readers, $40 for not legally blind readers. Sample: available at no cost. "Please indicate preferred format."

How to Submit: Submit up to 5 poems at a time. Line length for poetry is 20 maximum. No previously published poems or simultaneous submissions. Disk submissions OK. "Material should be submitted on a low-density IBM-compatible diskette in WordPerfect format. Include a hard copy and a SASE if you would like your disk returned. If you do not have a computer, material may also be submitted in typed or brailled form." Receipt of ms acknowledged via postcards. SASE required for return of rejected material. Deadlines: January 1 (Spring issue), April 1 (Summer issue), July 1 (Fall issue), October 1 (Winter issue). Always comments on rejections. Send SASE for guidelines or obtain via website. Responds in 2 months. Pays $10-15 for poetry plus 1 copy. Buys all rights "with a generous reprint policy."

◐ BLOOD AND FIRE REVIEW, P.O. Box 89, Cassville GA 30123-0089, founded 1996, editor Valerie Gilreath.

Magazine Needs: *Blood and Fire* is a biannual (November and May) and "provides an outlet for quality poetry and short fiction. Contains mostly poetry with usually one short story per issue." They want "poetry that speaks from experience, but is concise with a strong sense of imagery. No limit on length, subject matter or style." No epic poetry or sentimental Hallmark verse. They have published poetry by Mildred Greear and Anselm Brocki. As a sample the editor selected these lines from "Taking in Strays" by Robert Parham:

> I think of my father, showing me a fallen sparrow/so young it could not eat, so he crushed it with
> kindness/in his hand. The myth of what is best has always eluded me.

BFR is 40-50 pgs., digest-sized, attractively printed and saddle-stapled with 2- or 3-color card cover. No artwork. They receive about 1,300 poems a year, accept approximately 5%. Press run is 75 for 25 subscribers, 20-25 shelf sales. Subscription: $8.50. Sample: $4.50. Make checks payable to Valerie Gilreath, *BFR*.

How to Submit: Submit 5 poems at a time. Include SASE. "Submissions without a SASE will not read." No previously published poems; simultaneous submissions OK. Cover letter preferred, "include a bio that can be used if work is accepted. No electronic submissions." Time between acceptance and publication is "no longer than 7 months, usually sooner." Seldom comments on rejections. Send SASE for guidelines. Responds in 10 weeks. Pays 1 copy and a discount on additional copies. Acquires first rights.

Advice: "We use a lot of free verse, but we like to see forms as well when they are done right. Just send us your best. Also, we do provide guidelines, but my advice is just to go ahead and submit or buy a sample instead."

☑ ◐ ◎ BLUE COLLAR REVIEW; PARTISAN PRESS; WORKING PEOPLE'S POETRY COMPETITION (Specialized: political, social issues), P.O. Box 11417, Norfolk VA 23517, e-mail redart@pilot.in fa.net, website www.angelfire.com/ua/brc, *BCR* founded 1997, Partisan Press founded 1993, editor A. Markowitz, co-editor Mary Franke.

Magazine Needs: *Blue Collar Review* (*Journal of Progressive Working Class Literature*) is published quarterly and contains poetry, short stories and illustrations "reflecting the working class experience, a broad range from the personal to the societal. Our purpose is to promote and expand working class literature and an awareness of the connections between workers of all occupations and the social context in which we live. Also to inspire the creativity and latent talent in 'common' working people." They want "writing of high quality which reflects the working class experience from delicate internal awareness to the militant. We accept a broad range of style and focus—but are generally progressive, political/social. Nothing racist, sexist-misogynist, right wing or overly religious. No 'bubba' poetry, nothing overly introspective or confessional, no acedemic/abstract or 'Vogon' poetry. No simple beginners rhyme or verse." They have published poetry by Maggie Jaffe, Martín Espada, Robert Edwards, Errol Miller, Valentina Gnup-Kruip and Chris Butters. As a sample the editor selected these lines from "Bulletin" by Tim Seibles:

> We must stop shopping We just/can't shop. Tomorrow keeps running/from what we're buying today.//
> The chimps should be swinging,/but big business is flinging/the whole living world away.//Who will
> tell the Earth/we love her? Who will make/the trees? Somebody give the river/back to the water. Give
> the bright birds/back to the breeze.

BCR is 56 pgs., 8½×5½, offset printed and saddle-stitched with colored card cover, includes b&w illustrations and literary ads. They receive hundreds of poems a year, accept approximately 30%. Press run is 350 for 200 subscribers of which 8 are libraries, 50 shelf sales. Subscription: $15/year. Sample: $5. Make checks payable to A. Markowitz (*BCR*).

How to Submit: Submit up to 4 poems at a time; "no complete manuscripts please." Previously published poems and simultaneous submissions OK. No e-mail submissions. Cover letter preferred. "Poems should be typed as they are to appear upon publication. Author's name and address should appear on every page. Overly long lines reduce chances of acceptance as line may have to be broken to fit the page size and format of the journal." Time between acceptance and publication is 3 months to 1 year. Poems are reviewed by editor and co-editor. Seldom comments on rejections. SASE for response. Responds in 3 months. Sends prepublication galleys only upon request. Pays 1-3 copies. Reviews of chapbooks and journals accepted. Open to unsolicited reviews.

Book/Chapbook Needs & How to Submit: Partisan Press looks for "poetry of power that reflects a working class consciousness and which moves us forward as a society. Must be good writing reflecting social/political issues, militancy desired but not didactic screed." They publish about 3 chapbooks/year and are not presently open to unsolicited submissions. "Submissions are requested from among the poets published in the Blue Collar Review." Chapbooks are usually 20-60 pgs., 5½ × 8½, offset printed and saddle-stitched with card or glossy cover. Sample chapbooks are $5 and listed on website.

Also Offers: Sponsors the Working People's Poetry Competition. Entry fee: $15 per entry. Prize: $100 and 1-year subscription to *Blue Collar Review*. Deadline: May 1. "Include cover letter with entry and make check payable to A. Markowitz." Website includes mission statement, e-mail, sample poetry, rate of publication, subscription info and list of available chapbook collections.

Advice: "Don't be afraid to try. Read a variety of poetry and find your own voice. Write about reality, your own experience and what moves you."

▣ BLUE LIGHT PRESS; THE BLUE LIGHT POETRY PRIZE AND CHAPBOOK CONTEST, P.O. Box 642, Fairfield IA 52556, phone (515)472-7882, founded 1988, chief editor Diane Frank.

Book/Chapbook Needs: Publishes 2 paperbacks, 3 chapbooks/year. "We like poems that are imagistic, emotionally honest and uplifting, where the writer pushes through the imagery to a deeper level of insight and understanding. No rhymed poetry." They have published poetry by Rustin Larson, Viktor Tichy, Tom Centolella and Diane Averill. As a sample the editor selected these lines from "Where She Goes" from *Beautiful Obstacles* by Kate Gray:

> On the river rowing blind, all I really know/is her voice, its tone and thickness consistent as/blood
> flowing through veins. In the double, she tells me/when to risk, how to jump at "Attention,/Go," to
> push through pain of breathing without/air. Each a Ruth for the other, we back away/from some
> women's warnings: we will bulge,/be fit. Last weekend she guided me/through tests on rowing machines,
> air/sucked and measured through tubes, blood/tapped evenly. Better than cox'ns, she called

That book is 88 pgs., digest-sized, professionally printed and flat-spined with elegant matte card cover, includes woodcuts by Molly Bellman: $12 plus $1.50 p&h. They have also published 3 anthologies of visionary poets.

How to Submit: Send SASE for submission deadlines. They have an editorial board, and "work in person with local poets, have an ongoing poetry workshop, give classes, and will edit/critique poems by mail—$30 for 4-5 poems."

Also Offers: Sponsors The Blue Light Poetry Prize and Chapbook Contest. "The winner will be published by Blue Light Press, receive a $100 honorarium and 50 copies of his or her book, which can be sold for $8 each, for a total of $500." Submit ms of 10-24 pages, typed or printed with a laser or inkjet printer, between March 1, 2001 and May 1, 2001. Reading fee: $10. Make checks payable to Blue Light Press. Include SASE. No ms will be returned without a SASE. Winner will be announced on or before September 1, 2001, and the book will be published in December, 2001. Send SASE for more information.

▣ ◎ BLUE UNICORN, A TRIQUARTERLY OF POETRY; BLUE UNICORN POETRY CONTEST (Specialized: translations), 22 Avon Rd., Kensington CA 94707, phone (510)526-8439, founded 1977, poetry editors Ruth G. Iodice, Martha E. Bosworth and Fred Ostrander.

Magazine Needs: *Blue Unicorn* wants "well-crafted poetry of all kinds, in form or free verse, as well as expert translations on any subject matter. We shun the trite or inane, the soft-centered, the contrived poem. Shorter poems have more chance with us because of limited space." They have published poetry by James Applewhite, Kim Cushman, Charles Edward Eaton, Patrick Worth Gray, Joan LaBombard, James Schevill, John Tagliabue and Gail White. As a sample the editors selected this poem, "White Pages" by Charles Edward Eaton:

> What is more subtle than a book of white?—/All the passions written down in black, the print elite:/
> The wings are folded now, will not take flight.//We come at last to some pure sense of testament:/It is
> all in the book from early start to laggard finish,/All except some final thing you may have meant.//
> On the table, dahlias, pink and glorious, call for sequel./When the letter was folded, sealed, something
> was left out—/was it more than what was said or merely equal?

Blue Unicorn is "distinguished by its fastidious editing, both with regard to contents and format." It is 56 pgs., narrow digest-sized, finely printed, saddle-stapled, with some art. It features 40-50 poems in each issue, all styles, with the focus on excellence and accessibility. They receive over 35,000 submissions a year, use about 200, have a year's backlog. Sample: $5.

How to Submit: Submit 3-5 typed poems on 8½×11 paper. No simultaneous submissions or previously published poems. "Cover letter OK, but will not affect our selection." Send SASE for guidelines. Responds in 3 months (generally within 6 weeks), sometimes with personal comment. Pays 1 copy.

Also Offers: They sponsor an annual contest with small entry fee, with prizes of $150, $75, $50 and sometimes special awards, distinguished poets as judges, publication of 3 top poems and 6 honorable mentions in the magazine. Entry fee: $6 for first poem, $3 for others to a maximum of 5. Write for current guidelines. Criticism occasionally offered.

Advice: "We would advise beginning poets to read and study poetry—both poets of the past and of the present; concentrate on technique; and discipline yourself by learning forms before trying to do without them. When your poem is crafted and ready for publication, study your markets and then send whatever of your work seems to be compatible with the magazine you are submitting to."

☑ ◎ **BLUE VIOLIN (Specialized: form/style)**, P.O. Box 1175, Humble TX 77347-1175, founded 1995, editor Mary Agnes Dalrymple.

Magazine Needs: *BV* is an annual publication of free verse poetry (month of publication varies). The editor wants "free verse poetry only, no longer than 60 lines and no rhyme please. Shorter poems have a better chance of being accepted. I tend to select poems that are drawn from life experiences but will consider any well written poem. Send only your best work. Consider, before submitting, if your work is ready for publication. If a poem has never been revised it is probably not ready. Submissions are read and considered year-round." As a sample the editor selected these lines from "Church Supper Marriage" by Jennifer B. MacPherson:

> We listen to the clock,/beating hope from the future/with its tiny hands,/rolling piecrusts/which all look
> the same.

Blue Violin is 30-40 pgs. (including cover), digest-sized, neatly printed and saddle-stapled with colored card cover and graphics done by the editor. She receives about 3,000 poems a year, accepts 25-30. Press run is 100-200. Subscription: $10. Sample: $5.

How to Submit: Submit 3-7 poems at a time, typed 1 to a page, name and address on each. "Please include letter-size SASE with proper postage for reply." Previously published poems and simultaneous submissions OK. Cover letter and letter-sized envelopes preferred. Time between acceptance and publication is 1 year. Sometimes comments on rejections. Responds within 3 months. "Poets who are accepted receive a free copy of the issue in which their poem appears."

◎ **BLUELINE (Specialized: regional)**, Dept. PM, English Dept., Potsdam College, Potsdam NY 13676, fax (315)267-2043, e-mail blueline@potsdam.edu, founded 1979, editor-in-chief Rick Henry, and an editorial board.

Magazine Needs: *Blueline* "is an annual literary magazine dedicated to prose and poetry about the Adirondacks and other regions similar in geography and spirit." They want "clear, concrete poetry pertinent to the countryside and its people. It must go beyond mere description, however. We prefer a realistic to a romantic view. We do not want to see sentimental or extremely experimental poetry." They usually use poems of 75 lines or fewer, though "occasionally we publish longer poems" on "nature in general, Adirondack Mountains in particular. Form may vary, can be traditional or contemporary." They have published poetry by Phillip Booth, George Drew, Eric Ormsby, L.M. Rosenberg, John Unterecker, Lloyd Van Brunt, Laurence Josephs, Maurice Kenny and Nancy L. Nielsen. *Blueline* is 200 pgs., 6×9, with 90 pgs. of poetry in each issue. Circulation is 600. Sample copies: $4 for back issues.

How to Submit: Submit 3 poems at a time. Include short bio. No simultaneous submissions. Submit September 1 through November 30 only. Occasionally comments on rejections. Send SASE for guidelines or request via e-mail. Responds in 10 weeks. Pays 1 copy. Acquires first North American serial rights. Reviews books of poetry in 500-750 words, single or multi-book format.

Advice: "We are interested in both beginning and established poets whose poems evoke universal themes in nature and show human interaction with the natural world. We look for thoughtful craftsmanship rather than stylistic trickery."

◉ **BOA EDITIONS, LTD.**, 260 East Ave., Rochester NY 14604, phone (716)546-3410, e-mail boaedit@fronti ernet.net, website www.info-boaeditions.org, founded 1976, poetry editor Thom Ward. They have published some of the major American poets, such as W.D. Snodgrass, John Logan, Isabella Gardner, Richard Wilbur and Lucille Clifton, and they publish introductions by major poets of those less well-known. For example, Gerald Stern wrote the foreword for Li-Young Lee's *Rose*. Send SASE for guidelines. Pays 10 copies.

◉ **BOGG PUBLICATIONS; BOGG**, 422 N. Cleveland St., Arlington VA 22201-1424, founded 1968, poetry editors John Elsberg (USA), George Cairncross (UK: 31 Belle Vue St., Filey, N. Yorkshire YO 14 9HU England), Wilga Rose (Australia: 13 Urara Rd., Avalon Beach, NSW 2107 Australia) and Sheila Martindale (Canada: P.O. Box 23148, 380 Wellington St., London, Ontario NGA 5N9 Canada).

Magazine Needs: Appearing at least twice a year, *Bogg* is "a journal of contemporary writing with an Anglo-American slant. Its contents combines innovative American work with a range of writing from England and the Commonwealth. It includes poetry (to include haiku, prose poems and experimental/visual poems), very short experimental or satirical fiction, interviews, essays on the small press scenes both in America and in England /

the Commonwealth, reviews, review essays and line art. We also publish occasional free-for-postage pamphlets." The magazine uses a great deal of poetry in each issue (with several featured poets)—"poetry in all styles, with a healthy leavening of shorts (under ten lines). Prefer original voices." They accept all styles, all subject matter. "Some have even found the magazine's sense of play offensive. Overt religious and political poems have to have strong poetical merits—statement alone is not sufficient." *Bogg* started in England and in 1975 began including a supplement of American work; it now is published in the US and mixes US, Canadian, Australian and UK work with reviews of small press publications from all of those areas. They have published work by Robert Cooperman, Robert Peters, Jon Silkin, Ron Androla, Ann Menebroker, Richard Peabody and Miriam Sagan. As a sample the editors selected these lines from "Bondi Afternoons" by Australian poet Peter Bakowski:

> *I hear children and seagulls squeal,/the clock leisurely licks its paws./There is rust and washing and*
> *tin chimneys./It's timeless, lazy, beautiful./An acoustic guitar and mist can still/break your heart.*

It's about 68 pgs., typeset, saddle-stitched, in a 6×9 format that leaves enough white space to let each poem stand and breathe alone. There are about 50 pgs. of poetry/issue. They receive over 10,000 American poems/year, use 100-150. Press run is 850 for 400 subscribers of which 20 are libraries. Single copy: $4.50; subscription: $12 for 3 issues. Sample: $3.50.

How to Submit: Submit 6 poems at a time. SASE required or material discarded ("no exceptions.") Prefer typewritten manuscripts, with author's name and address on each sheet. "We will reprint previously published material, but with a credit line to a previous publisher." No simultaneous submissions. Cover letters preferred. "They can help us get a 'feel' for the writer's intentions/slant." SASE required for return of ms. Send SASE for guidelines. Responds in 1 week. Pays 2 copies. Acquires one-time rights. Reviews books and chapbooks of poetry in 250 words, single book format. Open to unsolicited reviews. Poets may also send books to relevant editor (by region) for review consideration.

Book/Chapbook Needs & How to Submit: Their occasional pamphlets and chapbooks are by *invitation only*, the author receiving 25% of the print run, and you can get chapbook samples free for 6×9 SASE. "Better make it at least 2 ounces worth of postage."

Advice: "Become familiar with a magazine before submitting to it. Long lists of previous credits irritate me. Short notes about how the writer has heard about *Bogg* or what he or she finds interesting or annoying in the magazine I read with some interest."

☑ $ ☻ **BOMB MAGAZINE**, 594 Broadway, Suite 905, New York NY 10012, phone (212)431-3943, fax (212)431-5880, e-mail bomb@echonyc.com, website www.bombsite.com, founded 1981, editor-in-chief Betsy Sussler, associate editor Susan Sherman.

Magazine Needs: *BOMB* is a quarterly magazine that "encourages a dialogue among artists of various media. Experiments with form and language are encouraged. No limericks, inspirational verse, clever or greeting card styles." They have published poetry by Joe Osterhaus, Sidney Wade, David Mamet and Harold Pinter. *BOMB* is 112 pgs., perfect-bound with 4-color cover. "We receive about 100 manuscripts a month; we accept 2 or 3 every 4 months." Press run is 37,000 for 6,500 subscribers of which 1,000 are libraries. Single copy: $6; subscription: $18/year. Sample: $8 (by mail).

How to Submit: No previously published poems; simultaneous submissions OK. Cover letter including name, address, telephone number and previous publications required. "Poetry should be legibly typed." Time between acceptance and publication is 4-6 months. Responds in 4 months. Pays $50. Buys first North American serial rights.

Also Offers: Website includes sample of magazine's contents.

◖ **BOMBAY GIN**, Naropa University, 2130 Arapahoe Ave., Boulder CO 80302, phone (303)546-3540, fax (303)546-5297, e-mail bgin@naropa.edu, website www.naropa.edu, founded 1974, contact the editor.

Magazine Needs: "*Bombay Gin*, appearing in June, is the annual literary magazine of the Jack Kerouac School of Disembodied Poetics at Naropa University. Produced and edited by MFA students, *Bombay Gin* publishes established poets and fiction writers alongside new writers. It has a special interest in works that push conventional literary boundaries." Recent issues have included works by Lisa Jarnot, Anne Waldman, Wang Ping, Keith Abbott and Ted Berrigan. As a sample the editor selected these lines from "Evidence" by Max Regan:

> *both of us today/with an aversion to dreams/both of us stacking tasks/like cordwood/both asleep inside/*
> *the iris of an eye.*

BG is 124 pgs., 6×9, professionally printed, perfect-bound with color card cover, includes art and photos. They receive about 300 poems a year, accept approximately 5%. Press run is 500, 400 shelf sales; 100 distributed free to contributors. Single copy: $10. Sample: $5.

How to Submit: "Submit up to 3 pages of poetry or up to 8 pages of prose/fiction (12 pt. Times New Roman). Art may be submitted as slides, negatives or prints." No previously published poems or simultaneous submissions.

THE SUBJECT INDEX, located at the back of this book, can help you select markets for your work. It lists those publishers whose poetry interests are specialized ◎ .

Cover letter preferred. Disk submissions OK (PC format). Reply with SASE only. Deadline: December 1. Submissions read December 15 through March 15. Send SASE for guidelines. Notification of acceptance/rejection: April 15. Pays 2 copies. Acquires one-time rights.

Also Offers: Website includes writer's guidelines, sample poems, readings and events.

N **☺** **∅** **BONE & FLESH PUBLICATION**, P.O. Box 349, Concord NH 03302-0349, phone/fax (603)225-0521, e-mail movespring@aol.com, founded 1988, publisher/editor-in-chief Lester Hirsh.

● *"Bone & Flesh* has been listed in *Clockwatch Review* as one of the finest small press magazines in the country."

Magazine Needs: *Bone & Flesh* appears 1-2 times a year and publishes "material that touches on the lives of people and universal themes; highly crafted, original work." They have published poetry by Thomas Raine Crowe, Keith Flynn, Lyn Lifshin and Mary Winters. *B&F* is 50-75 pgs., 8×11 or 5×7, docutech printed with 70-80 lb. cover with art "mostly pen & ink." Press run is about 300. Single copy: $10; subscription: $16. Sample: $7-10.

How to Submit: "Poets and prose writers may send queries or ask about needs and subscription info only. *No submissions*. By invitation only." Publishes theme issues occasionally. Send SASE for guidelines and upcoming themes. Pays 1-2 copies. Acquires all rights. Returns rights upon publication.

Advice: "Be true to your nature—your writing—be conscious of craft, originality, the importance of each word. Know the market needs and needs of individual publications."

N **∅** **THE BOOKPRESS: THE NEWSPAPER OF THE LITERARY ARTS**, The DeWitt Bldg., 215 N. Cayuga St., Ithaca NY 14850, phone (607)277-2254, fax (607)275-9221, e-mail bookpress@thebookery.com, website www.thebookery.com/Bookpress, founded 1990, editor/publisher Jack Goldman.

Magazine Needs: *Bookpress* appears 8 times/year, each month except January and June, July and August. As for poetry, the editor says, "The only criterion is a commitment to the aesthetic power of language. Avoid the hackneyed and formulaic." They have published poetry by Phyllis Janowitz, Kathleen Gemmell and A.R. Ammons. The editor says *The Bookpress* is a 12-page tabloid. They receive about 50 poems a year, accept approximately 10%. Press run is 6,500 for 300 subscribers of which 15 are libraries. Subscription: $12/year. Sample copies free.

How to Submit: No previously published poems or simultaneous submissions. E-mail submissions OK, include in body of message. Cover letter preferred. Reads submissions August 1 through April 1 only. SASE required. Time between acceptance and publication is 1 month. Often comments on rejections. Send SASE for guidelines. Responds in 3 months. Pays 2 copies. Acquires first North American serial rights. Reviews books of poetry. Length of reviews varies, typically between 1,500-2,000 words, sometimes longer. Poets may also send books for review consideration.

✓ **∅** **BORDERLANDS: TEXAS POETRY REVIEW**, P.O. Box 33096, Austin TX 78764, e-mail cgilbert @austin.rr.com, website www.borderlands.org, founded 1992, contact editor.

Magazine Needs: *Borderlands* appears twice a year publishing "high-quality, outward-looking poetry by new and established poets, as well as brief reviews of poetry books and critical essays. Cosmopolitan in content, but particularly welcomes Texas and Southwest writers." They want "outward-looking poems that exhibit social, political, geographical, historical, feminist or spiritual awareness coupled with concise artistry. We also seek poems in two languages (one of which must be English), where the poet has written both versions. Please, no introspective work about the speaker's psyche, childhood or intimate relationships." They have published poetry by Walter McDonald, Naomi Shihab Nye, Lyn Lifshin, Kurt Heinzelman, Carol Coffee Reposa and Jill Alexander Essbaum. As a sample the editors selected these lines from "How It Happened" by Paul Martin:

> *. . . and stroke by stroke, painting away the ceiling,/slowly ascend,/singing*

Borderlands is 80-120 pgs., $5\frac{1}{2} \times 8\frac{1}{2}$, offset, perfect-bound, with 4-color cover, art by local artists. They receive about 2,000 poems a year, use approximately 120. Press run is 1,000. Subscription: $17/year; $33/2 years. Sample: $10.

How to Submit: Submit 5 typed poems at a time. No previously published poems or simultaneous submissions. Include SASE (or SAE and IRCs) with sufficient postage to return poems. Seldom comments on rejections. Responds in 6 months. Pays 1 copy. Acquires first rights. Reviews books of poetry in one page. Also uses 3- to 6-page essays on single poets and longer essays (3,500-word maximum) on contemporary poetry in some larger context (query first). Address poetry submissions to "Editors, *Borderlands*."

Also Offers: The Austin Writers' League is a state-wide group open to the general public. Founded in 1981, the purpose of the Austin Writers' League is "to provide a forum for information, support, and sharing among writers; to help members improve and market their skills; and to promote the interests of writers and the writing community." Currently has 1,600 members. Annual membership dues are $45. Send SASE for more information to: AWL, 1501 W. 5th St., Suite E-2, Austin TX 78703. Website includes history, guidelines, board of directors, staff, sample poems, order form, readings and exhibits.

☑ $ ⊘ ◎ **BORDIGHERA, INC.; VOICES IN ITALIAN AMERICANA; VIA FOLIOS; THE BORDIGHERA POETRY PRIZE; ANIELLO LAURI AWARD (Specialized: ethnic/nationality)**, P.O. Box 1374, Lafayette IN 47902-1374, phone (765)494-3839, fax (765)496-1700, e-mail tamburri@purdue.edu, founded 1990, editors Anthony Julian Tamburri, Paolo Giordano and Fred Gardaphé.

Magazine Needs: *Voices in Italian Americana* (*VIA*) is "a semiannual literary and cultural review devoted to the dissemination of information concerning the contributions of and about Italian Americans to the cultural and art worlds of North America." They are open to all kinds of poetry. They have published poetry by Daniela Gioseffi, David Citino, Felix Stefanile and Dana Gioia. As a sample the editor selected these lines from "Coming To Know Empedokles" by Diane diPrima:

> *A couple of millennia seems like a moment:/This song cd be planting rite of black Sicilians/in autumn*
> *fields behind a small house/the sounds / the colors as if/intervening greys & anglo stillness/had never*
> *entered.*

The editor says *VIA* is about 250 pgs., 8½ × 5½, docutech printed, perfect-bound with glossy paper cover, includes art and ads. They receive about 150 poems a year, accept approximately 25%. Press run is 500 for 300 subscribers of which 50 are libraries, 50 shelf sales; 50 distributed free to contributors. Subscription: $20 individual; $15 student/senior citizen; $25 institutional; $30 foreign. Sample: $10. Make checks payable to Bordighera, Inc.

How to Submit: No previously published poems or simultaneous submissions. Cover letter required. E-mail and disk submissions OK. Reads submissions October 1 through May 31 only. Time between acceptance and publication is 3 months. Poems are circulated to an editorial board. Often comments on rejections. Publishes theme issues occasionally. Send SASE for guidelines. Responds in 6 weeks. Always sends prepublication galleys. Acquires all rights. Rights returned upon publication. "But in subsequent publications, poet must acknowledge first printing in *VIA*." Reviews books and chapbooks of poetry in 500-1,000 words, single book format. Open to unsolicited reviews. Poets may also send books for review consideration to Fred Gardaphé, Center for Italian Studies, State University of New York, Stony Brook NY 11794-3358.

Book/Chapbook Needs & How to Submit: Bordighera, under the imprint *VIA* Folios, publishes 5 titles/year with the print run for each paperback being 550. Books are usually 50-75 pgs., 8½ × 5½, docutech printed and perfect-bound with glossy paper cover and art. Query first, with a variety of sample poems and a cover letter with brief bio and publication credits. Replies to queries in 2 weeks; to mss in 4-6 weeks. Pays 10% royalties. Offers subsidy arrangements. Poets are required to subsidize 50% of publishing costs. "Author regains subsidy through sales with 50% royalties up to subvention paid, 10% thereafter."

Also Offers: Sponsors the Bordighera Poetry Prize, which awards book publication and $2,000, and the Aniello Lauri Award, which awards $150 plus publication in *Voices in Italian Americana*. Send SASE for contest rules.

▓ ☑ ◎ ⊘ **BOREALIS PRESS; TECUMSEH PRESS LTD.; JOURNAL OF CANADIAN POETRY (Specialized: regional)**, 110 Bloomingdale St., Ottawa, Ontario K2C 4A4 Canada, phone (613)298-9299, fax (613)798-7974, e-mail borealis@istar.ca, founded 1972. They are presently not considering unsolicited submissions.

Also Offers: The *Journal* is an annual that publishes articles, reviews and criticism, not poetry. Sample: $15.95.

$ ◖ **THE BOSTON PHOENIX: PHOENIX LITERARY SECTION (PLS)**, 126 Brookline Ave., Boston MA 02215, phone (617)536-5390, founded 1966, poetry editor Lloyd Schwartz.

   ▓ Poems published in this review have appeared in the 1995 volume of *The Best American Poetry*.

Magazine Needs: *TBP* is a monthly book review with one poem in almost every issue. Press run is 150,000. Single copy: $1.50.

How to Submit: Submit 1-3 poems at a time, under 50 lines each. "Please include cover letter and SASE." Responds in 4 months. Pays $50. Poets may also send books for review consideration to Susan Ryan Vollmar, book editor.

▓ ◖ ⊘ **THE BOSTON POET**, McCormack Post Office, P.O. Box 863, Boston MA 02103-0863, e-mail thebostonpoet@ivillage.com, founded 1995, editor Deborah Byrne.

Magazine Needs: *The Boston Poet* is a "monthly calendar of events and poetry magazine featuring interviews, poetry, New England poetry events (and some NYC events), poetry news, special topics, young writer's page, poetry translations. We publish new and established writers and mainly publish free verse and certain form poetry such as sonnets, sestinas, villanelles, triolet, rondeau, ghazals, and pantoums. We like to receive poems with purpose, poems which trancend the 'me' or 'I' and have the ability to touch both the heart and mind. We like poems which cause a person's body to feel when they read the poem and poems which people want to remember, poems that will add to or change another person's daily grind. We also publish translations, prose poems, and have theme issues. We seldom publish rhymed poetry unless the rhyme is slant or not forced. Seldom publish center aligned poetry. We do not publish rants or poetry that is abstract or wrapped up in 'me-ism'. We do not publish inspirational poetry." They have published poetry by Anne Busby Hill, Adam Golaski, Jennifer Johnson, Jeff Male, Susan Roberts and Thomas Sterns. As a sample the editor selected these lines from "Mrs. Christian Stillings Bares Her Soul" by Jennifer Johnson:

> *The nudges at tea, whisperings at the opera—/oh, Puccini's grand finale!/Always who is doing what*
> *with whom/couldn't Mary choose a wealthier man?/Don't tell me useless stories of the heart—/it's such*
> *a small, bitter stone.*

TBP is about 46 pgs., magazine-sized, Docutech printed, includes ads. They receive about 1,000 poems a year, accept approximately 50%. Publish approximately 45 poems/issue. Press run is 700 for 120 subscribers of which 10 are libraries, 500 shelf sales; 60 distributed free to poets who have had their poetry accepted and also to shelters and girl's clubs. Subscription: $40. Sample: $4. Make checks payable to Deborah Byrne.

How to Submit: Submit up to 3 poems at a time. No previously published poems; simultaneous submissions OK. E-mail submissions OK. Cover letter required. "Poems must be typed on $8\frac{1}{2} \times 11$ clean white paper. Name, address, telephone number, e-mail address in upper right corner. If you do not wish to include an SASE and have an e-mail address, we will accept or reject by electronic mail if you request. If you wish only a reply and not the return of manuscripts, please note this in your cover letter and attach appropriate postage. If you wish a return of your manuscript if we do not accept, please attach appropriate postage for return mailing. Otherwise, we will recycle any unaccepted manuscripts. Cover letters should state the names of poems and include short bio." Submit seasonal poems 4 months in advance. Time between acceptance and publication is up to 6 months. Poems are circulated to an editorial board. "I have guest editors on board to help select poems, and I make the final decision." Seldom comments on rejections. Publishes theme issues occasionally. Send SASE for guidelines and upcoming themes. Responds in up to 6 months. Pays 1 copy. Acquires one-time rights. Staff reviews books and chapbooks of poetry and other magazines in 200-500 words, single and multi-book format. Poets may also send books for review consideration.

Advice: "Read poetry. Know who has laid the foundations for you as a writer. Invest in poetry books and journals to keep the art of writing alive. Understand that you probably will not become rich writing poetry. Edit your work. Be a master at line breaking. Learn to read your poetry out loud, but write in a way that if you aren't around to read your poetry a reader will understand the poem just by reading it to themselves."

$ ◙ BOSTON REVIEW, E53-407, MIT, 30 Wadsworth St., Cambridge MA 02139-4307, phone (617)253-3642, fax (617)252-1549, website www.polisci.mit.edu/BostonReview/, founded 1975, poetry editors Mary Jo Bang and Timothy Donnelly.

  ☒ Poetry published by this review has been included in *The Best American Poetry* (1998 and 2000 volumes).

Magazine Needs: *Boston Review* is a bimonthly tabloid format magazine of arts, culture and politics which uses about 30 poems a year, for which they receive about 3,000 submissions. "We are open to both traditional and experimental forms. What we value most is originality and a strong sense of voice." They have published poetry by Gilbert Sorrentino, Heather McHugh, Richard Howard, Allen Grossman, Cole Swenson, Tan Lin and Claudia Rankine. Circulation is 20,000 nationally including subscriptions and newsstand sales. Single copy: $3.50; subscription: $17. Sample: $4.50.

How to Submit: Submit 3-5 poems at a time. Cover letter with brief bio encouraged. Submissions and inquiries are accepted via regular mail only. They have a 6-12 month backlog. Responds in 3 months. Pays $40/poem plus 5 copies. Buys first serial rights. Reviews books of poetry. Only using *solicited* reviews. Publishers may send books for review consideration.

Also Offers: Sponsors an annual poetry contest. Awards publication and $1,000. Submit up to 5 unpublished poems, no more than 10 pgs. total, with postcard to acknowledge receipt. Deadline: June 1. Entry fee: $15. Send SASE for guidelines.

✓ ◙ BOTTOMFISH, De Anza College, 21250 Stevens Creek Blvd., Cupertino CA 95014, website www.deanza.fhda.edu/bottomfish, founded 1976, editor Randolph Splitter.

Magazine Needs: This college-produced magazine appears annually in April. It has published poetry by Chitra Divakaruni, Robert Cooperman, Walter Griffin and Tom Clark. As a sample the editor selected these lines from "The Clumsy Contest" by Kurt Brown:

> *He was good. Real good. Mama fed him/vinegar and nettles while Papa pulled his punches—/only*
> *inches from the boy's lips—to insure/a life of stumbling and dropping things.*

Bottomfish is 80 pgs., $7 \times 8\frac{1}{4}$, well-printed on heavy stock with b&w graphics, perfect-bound. Circulation is 500, free to libraries, but $5/copy to individuals.

How to Submit: Submit 3-5 poems at a time. "Before submitting, writers are strongly urged to purchase a sample copy." Best submission times: September through December. Annual deadline: December 31. Responds in 6 months, depending on backlog. Include SASE for reply. "We cannot return manuscripts." Pays 2 copies.

$ ◙ BOULEVARD, 4579 Laclede Ave. #332, St. Louis MO 63108-2103, phone (314)361-2986, founded 1985, editor Richard Burgin.

Magazine Needs: *Boulevard* appears 3 times a year. "*Boulevard* strives to publish only the finest in fiction, poetry, and nonfiction (essays and interviews; we do not accept book reviews). While we frequently publish writers with previous credits, we are very interested in publishing less experienced or unpublished writers with exceptional promise. We've published everything from John Ashbery to Howard Moss to a wide variety of styles from new or lesser known poets. We're eclectic. Do not want to see poetry that is uninspired, formulaic, self-conscious, unoriginal, insipid." They have published poetry by Amy Clampitt, Molly Peacock, Jorie Graham and Mark Strand. *Boulevard* is 200 pgs., digest-sized, professionally printed, flat-spined, with glossy card cover. Their press run is 3,500 with 1,000 subscribers of which 200 are libraries. Subscription: $15. Sample: $8 plus 5 first-class stamps and SASE.

How to Submit: Submit up to 5 poems at a time. Line length for poetry is 200 maximum. "Prefer name and number on each page. All submissions must include an SASE. Encourage cover letters but don't require them. Will consider simultaneous submissions but not previously published poems." Reads submissions October 1 through April 1 only. Editor sometimes comments on rejections. Responds in about 3 months. Pays $25-250/poem, depending on length, plus 1 copy. Buys first-time publication and anthology rights. Open to unsolicited reviews.

Advice: "Write from your heart as well as your head."

BRANDO'S HAT; TARANTULA PUBLICATIONS, 14 Vine St., Kersal, Salford, Manchester M7 3PG United Kingdom, phone/fax (0161)792 4593, e-mail tarantula_pubs@lineone.net, founded 1998, contact Sean Body.

Magazine Needs: *Brando's Hat* appears 3 times a year. They want "extremely high-quality poetry only. No restrictions on subject matter, form or style." They do not want "careless, unrhythmical, boring, unoriginal work—i.e., 90 percent of what we get." They have published poetry by Tony Curtis, Peter Sansom, Kevin Crossley-Holland and John Latham. As a sample they selected these lines from "Searching" by Gaia Holmes:

> Night falls/like you slip into my head/I smell the scent of something late./You're curled into yourself/
> like paper when it burns/and a hundred black moths

They say *Brando's Hat* is 42 pgs., A5, laser printed and saddle-stapled with color card cover. They receive about 1,300 poems a year, accept approximately 10%. Press run is 250 for 200 subscribers. Subscription: £13 Sterling. Sample: £5 Sterling. Make checks (Sterling only) payable to Tarantula Publications.

How to Submit: Submit 6 or more poems at a time. No previously published poems or simultaneous submissions. Cover letter required. "Cover letters should give brief (just a few lines) biographical details, publications, etc. Must include SAE with appropriate postage [or IRCs], otherwise discarded." Time between acceptance and publication is 3 months. Poems are circulated to an editorial board. "There are four editors (all poets). Decisions for publishing have to be unanimous." Seldom comments on rejections. Responds in 3 months or less. Pays 1 copy. Acquires first rights.

THE BREAD OF LIFE MAGAZINE (Specialized: religious), 209 Macnab St. N., P.O. Box 395, Hamilton, Ontario L8N 3H8 Canada, phone (905)529-4496, fax (905)529-5373, founded 1977, editor Fr. Peter Coughlin.

Magazine Needs: *The Bread of Life* is "a Catholic charismatic magazine, published bimonthly and designed to encourage spiritual growth in areas of renewal in the Catholic Church today." It includes articles, poetry and artwork. As a sample the editor selected these lines from "To Know His Love" by Margaret Larrivee:

> In times when all is going well/on His great love we seldom dwell./It's only when we are laid low/His
> abundant love we start to know.//It comes in cards with loving words/get well wishes, written, heard./
> Calls and visits cheerfully bring/joy to my soul, my heart to sing.

TBOL is 34 pgs., 8½×11, professionally printed and saddle-stapled with glossy paper cover, includes original artwork and photos. They receive about 50-60 poems a year, accept approximately 25%. Press run is 3,600 for subscribers only. "It's good if contributors are members of *The Bread of Life*."

How to Submit: Previously published poems and simultaneous submissions OK. Cover letter preferred. Publishes theme issues. Send SAE with IRCs for upcoming themes.

BREAKFAST ALL DAY, 43 Kingsdown House, Amhurst Rd., London E8 2AS United Kingdom, fax (33)235403326, e-mail boxall@badpress.com, website www.badpress.com, founded 1995, editor Philip Boxall, US submissions to: Mary Wraight, 709 S. Broadway, Urbana IL 61801.

Magazine Needs: *BAD* is a biannual magazine of "fiction, comment, humour, poetry and graphics, attracting contributions from Britain, mainland Europe and North America;" and publishes "satire, humor, general interest; special interest in art and language; includes short fiction and graphic work." They want "20 lines average (not more than 50 lines); any subject matter." No concrete poems, sentimental verse or long poems. As a sample the editor selected these lines from an untitled poem by Gavin Coombs:

> Free to roam for 20 feet/Lonely dogs on stakes/Gnash in frustration/Awaiting prey they'll never savor//
> Cars, strollers, school kids//And the dogs,/Bereft of all but pride and a bark//bark

BAD is 100 pgs., A4 (11½×8¼ inches approximately), perfect-bound with color cover and b&w pages, includes illustrations and cartoons. They receive about 600 poems a year, accept approximately 10-15%. Press run is 400 for 100 subscribers, 200 shelf sales. Subscription: $20/year (US), £8/year (UK). Sample: $10 (US), £4 (UK). Send US contributions for subscriptions to: Mary Wraight. Make checks payable to Bad Press.

How to Submit: Submit 5 poems at a time, "preferably on 3.5 disk, as a text (ASCII) file, or hard copy in clear black type on white paper." E-mail submissions OK (attached ASCII file). Previously published poems sometimes accepted. Cover letter required. Send SASE (or SAE and IRC) for guidelines or request via e-mail and the website. Responds in 3 months. Pays 1 copy on request. Acquires one-time rights.

Also Offers: Website includes general information about BAD Press, writers' guidelines, samples of poetry and fiction.

[N] [◎] BREAKTHROUGH INC.; THE BREAKTHROUGH INTERCESSOR (Specialized: intercessory prayer), P.O. Box 121, Lincoln VA 20160, phone (540)338-5522, fax (540)338-1934, e-mail breakthrough @intercessors.org, website www.intercessors.org, founded 1980, editor Andrea Doudera, in-house editor Trudi Schwarting.

Magazine Needs: Published quarterly, *TBI* is focused toward "encouraging people in prayer and faith; preparing and equipping those who pray." They have published poetry by Norman Vincent Peale. As a sample the editors selected these lines from "The Wise Prayer" by Eliza M. Hickok:

> *I know not by what method rare,/But this I know, God answers prayer./I know not when He sends the word/That tells us fervent prayer is heard./I know it cometh soon or late;/Therefore, we need to pray and wait.*

TBI is 32 pgs., magazine-sized, professionally printed and saddle-stitched with self cover, includes art/graphics. They receive about 12 poems a year, accept approximately 25%. Press run is 10,000 for 9,100 subscribers; 900 distributed free to requesters. Single copy: $3; subscription: $15. Sample: $2. Make checks payable to Breakthrough Inc.

How to Submit: Previously published poems OK. E-mail submissions OK. Time between acceptance and publication varies. Poems are circulated to an editorial board. Reporting time varies.

[◢] [◎] THE BRIAR CLIFF REVIEW (Specialized: regional), Briar Cliff College, 3303 Rebecca St., Sioux City IA 51104-2340, e-mail emmons@briar-cliff.edu, website www.briar-cliff.edu/administrative/publications/ bccrevie/bcreview.htm, founded 1989, managing editor Tricia Currans-Sheehan, poetry editor Jeanne Emmons.

[▼] *The Briar Cliff Review* received the 1998 Columbia Scholastic Association Gold Crown.

Magazine Needs: *The Briar Cliff Review*, appearing in April, is an attractive annual "eclectic literary and cultural magazine focusing on (but not limited to) Siouxland writers and subjects." They want "quality poetry with strong imagery; especially interested in regional, Midwestern content with tight, direct, well-wrought language. No allegorical emotional landscapes." They have published poetry by Sandra Adelmunch, William Snyder Jr. and Michael Carey. As a sample the editor selected these lines from "Eden of the New Moon" by Jonathan Stull:

> *and the apple drops, shaking the limb/that draws light from the back of the moon,/as the unpressed winesaps rise/and fall like some red,/unholy thunder*

BCR is 64 pgs., 8½×11, professionally printed on 70 lb. matte paper, saddle-stapled, four-color cover on 10 pt. coated stock, b&w photos inside. They receive about 100 poems a year, accept 12. Press run is 500, all shelf sales. Sample: $9.

How to Submit: Submissions should be typewriten or letter quality, with author's name and address on the first page, with name on following pages. No previously published poems; simultaneous submissions OK. "We will assume that submissions are not simultaneous unless notified." Cover letter with short bio required. "No manuscripts returned without SASE." Reads submissions August 1 through November 1 only. Time between acceptance and publication is 5-6 months. Seldom comments on rejections. Responds in 6 months. Pays 2 copies. Acquires first serial rights.

Also Offers: Website includes writer's guidelines, annual contest guidelines and sample contest winners.

[✓] [◢] [◎] BRICKHOUSE BOOKS, INC.; NEW POETS SERIES, INC./CHESTNUT HILLS PRESS; STONEWALL SERIES (Specialized, Stonewall only: gay/lesbian/bisexual), 541 Piccadilly Rd., Baltimore MD 21204, phone (410)830-2869 or 828-0724, fax (410)830-3999, e-mail charriss@towson.edu, website www.towson.edu/harriss/, founded 1970, editor/director Clarinda Harriss. NPS, along with Chestnut Hills Press and Stonewall, is now a division of BrickHouse Books.

Book/Chapbook Needs: BrickHouse and The New Poets Series, Inc. brings out first books by promising new poets. Poets who have previously had book-length mss published are not eligible. Prior publication in journals and anthologies is strongly encouraged. They want "excellent, fresh, nontrendy, literate, intelligent poems. Any form (including traditional), any style." BrickHouse Books and NPS pay 20 author's copies (out of a press run of 1,000), the sales proceeds going back into the corporation to finance the next volume. "BrickHouse has been successful in its effort to provide writers with a national distribution; in fact, The New Poets Series was named an Outstanding Small Press by the prestigious Pushcart Awards Committee, which judges some 5,000 small press publications annually." Chestnut Hills Press publishes author-subsidized books—"High quality work only, however. CHP has achieved a reputation for prestigious books, printing only the top 10% of mss CHP and NPS receive." CHP authors receive proceeds from sale of their books. The Stonewall series publishes work with a gay, lesbian or bisexual perspective. NPS/CHP has published books by Chester Wickwire, Ted McCrorie, Sharon White, Mariquita McManus and Jeff Mann. As a sample the editor selected these lines from *To Move Into the House* from "Just After Dawn" by Richard Fein:

> *I woke to the murmur of my words./Leaning against the headboard/I yielded to the words that took me back/to my mother's slow death, how I finally stopped wishing/I had a sister to take her off my hands,/how we worked through that long illness to embrace/and she called me Ruvn. Ruvn.*

Brickhouse publishes 64-112 page works. Chapbooks: $8. Full-length books: $10.

How to Submit: Send a 50- to 55-page ms, $10 reading fee and cover letter giving publication credits and bio. Indicate if ms is to be considered for BrickHouse, NPS, CHP or Stonewall. Simultaneous submissions OK. No e-mail submissions. Cover letters should be very brief, businesslike and include an accurate list of published work. Editor sometimes comments briefly on rejections. Responds in up to 1 year. Mss "are circulated to an editorial board of professional, publishing poets. BrickHouse is backlogged, but the best 10% of the mss it receives are automatically eligible for Chestnut Hills Press consideration," a subsidy arrangement. Send $5 and a 7×10 SASE for a sample volume.

Also Offers: Stonewall Series offers a chapbook contest whose winner is published by NPS. Send 20-30 poems with $20 entry fee, postmarked no later than August 15. Rane Arroyo's *The Naked Thief* is a recent Stonewall winner. Website features writer's guidelines, names of editors, list of in-print publications, plus sample poetry from individual books.

THE BRIDGE: A JOURNAL OF FICTION AND POETRY, 14050 Vernon St., Oak Park MI 48237, founded 1990, editor Jack Zucker, poetry editor Mitzi Alvin.

Magazine Needs: *The Bridge* appears twice a year using "exciting, largely mainstream poetry." They have published poetry by Ruth Whitman and Daniel Hughes. It is 160 pgs., digest-sized, perfect-bound. Press run is 700. Subscription: $13. Sample: $7.

How to Submit: Line length for poetry is 200 maximum. Poems are circulated to an editorial board. Three consider mss; decision made by editor and 1 special editor. Editor rarely comments at length on submissions. Pays 2 copies. Acquires first rights. Reviews books of poetry and prose in 1-10 pgs.

$BRIDGES: A JOURNAL FOR JEWISH FEMINISTS AND OUR FRIENDS (IV-Ethnic, women/feminism, social issues), P.O. Box 24839, Eugene OR 97402, phone/fax (541)343-7617, e-mail ckinberg@pond.net, website www.pond.net/~ckinberg/bridges, founded 1990, managing editor Clare Kinberg.

Magazine Needs: The biannual *Bridges* is "a showcase for Jewish women's creativity and involvement in social justice activism." They want "anything original by Jewish women, not purely religious." They have published poetry by Emily Warn, Willa Schneberg and Ellen Bass. As a sample the managing editor selected these lines from "I'll Tell You What My People Know of the Land" by Judith Arcana:

> Later, much later, who can say how it came to be, there were market stalls in Kiev, Bobroisk, the
> Ukraine, changing names and shifting borders with the decades. Every war made new rules to learn,
> new names, but still they came in the night to burn and tear at us. So we climbed on the wagon, hid
> our boxes under the straw, and rode out across the meadows by moonlight. The leather straps creaked
> all night, they made me think of something, something before.

Bridges is 128 pgs., 7×10, professionally printed on 50% recycled paper, perfect-bound, with 2-color cover, b&w photos inside. They receive about 200 poems a year, accept about 20. Press run is 3,000 for 1,500 subscribers of which 70 are libraries, 300 shelf sales; 200 distributed free to exchanges, board members, funders. Subscription: $15/year. Sample: $7.50.

How to Submit: Submit 6-10 poems at a time. No previously published poems or simultaneous submissions. Cover letter preferred with 40 word bio. Time between acceptance and publication is 6 months. Poems are circulated to an editorial board. "Two poetry readers and sometimes others decide on poems." Often comments on rejections. Publishes theme issues. Send SASE for guidelines. Responds in 9 months. Sometimes sends prepublication galleys. Pays $50 per selection plus 3 copies. Sometimes reviews books of poetry. Open to unsolicited reviews. Poets may also send books for review consideration.

BRIGHT HILL PRESS; NATIONAL POETRY BOOK COMPETITION; NATIONAL CHAP-BOOK COMPETITION, P.O. Box 193, Treadwell NY 13846, phone (607)746-7306, fax (607)746-7274, e-mail wordthur@catskill.net, website www.nyslittree.org, founded 1992, director/editor-in-chief Bertha Rogers.

Book/Chapbook Needs: Bright Hill Press publishes 2-3 paperbacks and 1 chapbook/year through their competitions. They want "intelligent, well-crafted poetry—traditional or experimental." They have published *Blue Wolves* by Regina O'Melveny; *To Fit Your Heart into the Body* by Judith Neeld; *Boxes* by Lisa Harris; and *Whatever Was Ripe* by William Jolliff. As a sample the director selected these lines from "Crystal Anniversary" by Beth Copeland:

> Those years slide by and our lives/run together. Light bends through a lens/of ice. We follow frost
> bows, mock moons,/wheels of arctic sunlight./Landmarks loom on prisms of frozen breath,/mirroring
> themselves. . .

Chapbooks are usually 24-36 pgs., 5½×8½, stapled-bound; full-length books are 48-64 pgs., 5½×8½, perfect-bound. Full-length poetry books: $12; chapbooks: $6; anthologies: $15-25.

How to Submit: Submit 48-64 pgs. including bio, table of contents and acknowledgments page. Poems may be previously published in journals or anthologies. No submissions via fax or e-mail. Mss will be judged blindly by nationally-known poet. Send SASE for complete guidelines. Entry fee: $15; $10 for Word Thursdays/Bright Hill Press members. Postmark deadline: September 15. Winner announced winter of the following year. Winner receives $500, publication and 25 copies. For the Chapbook Competition (poetry in odd-numbered years; fiction in even-numbered years), winner receives $100, publication and 25 copies. Submit 16-24 pgs. including bio, table of contents, acknowledgments page and title page. Poems may be previously published in journals or anthologies. Send SASE for complete guidelines. Entry fee: $9; $6 Word Thursday/Bright Hill Press members. Postmark deadline: May 31 of odd-numbered years. Winner announced in late fall. Obtain sample books or chapbooks by sending SASE for catalog.

Also Offers: Bright Hill Press sponsors a large variety of activities throughout the year, including a bimonthly reading series and an annual festival. Write for details. Also administers the New York State Literary Curators' website in partnership with the NYSCA.
Advice: "Revise, revise, revise! Read other poets to learn how good poetry is crafted."

⬛ ◎ **BRILLIANT CORNERS: A JOURNAL OF JAZZ & LITERATURE (Specialized: jazz-related literature)**, Lycoming College, Williamsport PA 17701, phone (570)321-4279, fax (570)321-4090, e-mail feinstei@lycoming.edu, website www.lycoming.edu/dept/bc/bcvol1.html, founded 1996, editor Sascha Feinstein.
Magazine Needs: *Brilliant Corners*, a biannual, publishes jazz-related poetry, fiction and nonfiction. "We are open to length and form, but want work that is both passionate and well crafted—work worthy of our recent contributors. No sloppy hipster jargon or improvisatory nonsense." They have published poetry by Amiri Baraka, Jayne Cortez, Philip Levine, Colleen McElroy and Al Young. As a sample the editor selected these lines from "Rhythm Method" by Yusef Komunyakaa:

> *If you can see blues/in the ocean, light & dark,/can feel worms ease through/a subterranean path/*
> *beneath each footstep,/Baby, you got rhythm.*

BC is 100 pgs., 6×9, commercially printed and perfect-bound with color card cover with original artwork, ads. They accept approximately 5% of work received. Press run is 1,800 for 200 subscribers. Subscription: $12. Sample: $7.
How to Submit: Submit 3-5 poems at a time. Previously published poems "very rarely, and only by well established poets"; no simultaneous submissions. Cover letter preferred. No e-mail or fax submissions. Reads submissions September 1 through May 15 only. Seldom comments on rejections. Responds in 2 months. Pays 2 copies. Acquires first North American serial rights. Staff reviews books of poetry. Poets may also send books for review consideration.

◎ **BRILLIANT STAR (Specialized: children, religious)**, Baha'i National Center, 1233 Central St., Evanston IL 60201.
Magazine Needs: *Brilliant Star* is a Baha'i bimonthly for children, appearing in a magazine-sized format. "Poems are always illustrated, so think about how your poem will look. Our readers are ages 6-12. Write for them not for yourself. We do not want to see Christmas themes in any form. If you are not familliar with the Baha'i Faith, research is encouraged." As a sample the editor selected these lines from "Which Wealth" by Susan Engle:

> *Now do you think our king was sad?/No! Gold was gone, but he was glad./He'd found that love was*
> *irreplaceable/And gold, mere gold, was, well, erasable./Sometimes I wonder just how much/I would*
> *enjoy the golden touch./Would I have chosen, if I could/The gold for now, or love for good?*

Sample: $3 with 9×12 SASE (sufficient postage for 5 oz.).
How to Submit: Objectives are printed in the masthead. Considers simultaneous submissions. Pays 2 copies.
Advice: The editor urges children who wish to write poetry to avoid "writing about tired subjects like 'dogs as friends' and being 'afraid of the dark.' Write about today's world in fun, exciting language. Write about a realistic fear—guns, drugs, the school dance, my ugly feet, will my parents divorce. Make your poem an engaging short story." This is also good advice for adults who wish to write children's poetry for this publication.

Ⓝ ⊕ ◎ **BRITISH HAIKU SOCIETY; HAIKU REVIEW; THE MUSEUM OF HAIKU LITERATURE; JAMES W. HACKETT HAIKU AWARD (Specialized: form/style, translations)**, P.O. Box 1974, Bristol BS99 3BB England, e-mail asummers@dircon.co.uk, founded 1990, secretary Alan J. Summers.
Magazine Needs & How to Submit: *Haiku Review*, a quarterly journal, publishes mainly haiku, senryu and tanka sent in by society members, but one section, "The Pathway," accepts originals in any language plus a translation in one of English, French or German, and is open to non-members. Submission address for all but "The Pathway" section: Hill House Farm, Knighton, Powys LD7 1NA Wales, editor Caroline Gourlay. Submission address for "The Pathway" section only: Sinodun, Shalford, Braintree, Essex CM7 5HN United Kingdom, editor David Cobb. Staff reviews books of poetry. Send books for review consideration. BHS also publishes a newsletter and other occasional publications (pamphlets, folios).
Also Offers: The Museum of Haiku Literature, Tokyo, gives a quarterly best-of-issue award (£50). In addition, BHS administers the annual James W. Hackett Haiku Award (currently £70). Rules of entry are available annually in the spring. Send SASE (or SAE and IRC from outside England) to J.W. Hackett Award, % D. Cobb, Sinodun, Shalford, Essex CM7 5HN England.

⊕ ⬜ ◯ ⬛ **THE BROBDINGNAGIAN TIMES**, 96 Albert Rd., Cork, Ireland, phone 353-21-311 227, founded 1996, editor Giovanni Malito.
Magazine Needs: *TBT* appears quarterly. "Its purpose and contents are international and eclectic. We wish to present a small sample of what is happening out there in the 'world' of poetry." They are open to all kinds of poetry of 40 lines or less. "Translations are very welcome. Not very partial to rhyming forms." Also accepts poetry written by children. They have published poetry by Miroslav Holub, Leonard Cirino, Albert Huffstickler and John Millet. It is 8 pgs., A3 sheet folded twice, photocopied from laser original. They receive about 300 poems a year, accept approximately 10%. Press run is 250 for 42 subscribers, variable shelf sales; 12 distributed free to writers' groups. Subscription: $4. Sample: $1 or postage. Make checks payable to Giovanni Malito.

How to Submit: Submit 4-8 poems at a time. Line length for poetry is 1 minimum, 40 maximum. Previously published poems and simultaneous submissions OK. Cover letter preferred. "SASE is required. If IRCs are not convenient then loose stamps for trade with Irish stamps are fine." Time between acceptance and publication is 1-3 months. Often comments on rejections. Publishes theme issues occasionally. Note: the theme issues appear as supplements. Send SASE for guidelines and upcoming themes. Responds in 1 month. Sometimes sends prepublication galleys. Pays 2 copies. Acquires one-time rights. Staff reviews books and chapbooks of poetry in 300-500 words, single book format. Send books for review consideration.

Book/Chapbook Needs & How to Submit: The Brobdingnagian Times Press is open to any type of prose and/or poetry and publishes 2-8 chapbooks/year. Chapbooks are usually "palmtop" in size, photocopied from laser original and side-stapled with slightly heavier stock colored paper, cover art only. "The palmtops are quite small. They may be one long poem (8 pages) or several (8-16) short poems (less than 6 lines) or something in between. Collections (unless haiku/senryu) must be more or less themed." Replies to queries in 1 week; to mss in 1-3 weeks. Pays 50 author's copies (out of a press run of 100). "Poets outside of Ireland are asked to cover the postage." Order sample chapbooks by sending 2 IRCs.

Advice: "Nerve and verve and the willingness to edit: these are three qualities a poet must possess."

N ○ ◑ ◎ BROKEN BOULDER PRESS; GESTALTEN; NEOTROPE (Specialized: form/style), P.O. Box 172, Lawrence KS 66044-0172, phone (785)331-0270, e-mail apowell10@hotmail.com or paulsilvia@excite.com, website www.brokenboulder.com, founded 1996, co-editor Adam Powell, co-editor Paul Silvia.

Magazine Needs & How to Submit: *gestalten* appears 2 times a year and publishes experimental poetry from new and established writers. "We want experimental, abstract, collage, visual, language, asemic, found, system, proto, non, and simply strange forms of poetry. Coherence and words are optional. No vampire poetry; religious/inspirational poetry; Bukowski rip offs; no poems containing the word 'poetry'." They have published poetry by John Lowther, Spencer Selby, Peter Ganick, John M. Bennett, Michael Lenhart and the Atlanta Poet's Group. As a sample the editors selected this poem, "24/7" by Sheila E. Murphy:

> Allow forth format, gem/The interimshot letterfest/Play to altercations/Summative in form of plenty/
> folded latitude

gestalten is a 40-page tabloid printed on newsprint, folded with full-color cover, includes "tons" of art/graphics and a few small-press ads. They receive about 750 poems a year, accept approximately 10%. Publish 70 poems/issue. Press run is 1,000 for 250 subscribers of which 50 are libraries, 250 shelf sales; 200 distributed free to friends, editors and educational/community organizations. Subscription: $4/2 issues, $7/4 issues. Sample: $3. Make checks payable to Broken Boulder Press. Submit 5-20 poems at a time. No previously published poems or simultaneous submissions. E-mail submissions OK. Cover letter preferred. "SASE required. For e-subs, we prefer to have poems pasted into the message, not attached as files. We like casual and quirky cover letters." Time between acceptance and publication is 4 months. Always comments on rejections. Send SASE for guidelines. Responds in 3 weeks. Sometimes sends prepublication galleys. Pays 5 copies. Acquires one-time rights.

Magazine Needs & How to Submit: Published annually, *neotrope* "focuses primarily on experimental fiction and drama, with some visual poetry and abstract art. We publish primarily fiction and want to see visual poetry, collages and abstract art only (Visual/text hybrids OK.) No traditional or text poetry. If you send text poems we will send them back unread." They have published poetry by Jim Leftwich, John M. Bennett, Michael Basinski and Dave Chirot. *neotrope* is 160 pgs., digest-sized, professionally printed and perfect-bound with full-color glossy cover, includes 10-20 pgs. of art per issue, some ads included on an exchange basis. They receive about 30 poems a year, accept approximately 20%. Publish 5-8 poems/issue. Press run is 1,500 for 250 subscribers of which 50 are libraries, 1,000 shelf sales; 30 distributed free to review publications. Subscription: $8/2 issues, $15/4 issues. Sample: $5. Make checks payable to Broken Boulder Press. Submit up to 10 poems at a time. No previously published poems; simultaneous submissions OK. E-mail submissions OK. Cover letter with brief bio preferred. "Electronic submissions should be sent in Quark or Pagemaker format, if possible. E-mail us to make other arrangements." Time between acceptance and publication is about 6 months. Always comments on rejections. Send SASE for guidelines. Responds in 1 month. Sometimes sends prepublication galleys. Pays 2 copies. Acquires one-time rights.

Book/Chapbook Needs & How to Submit: Broken Boulder Press publishes 6 chapbooks per year. "We want to promote experimental writing; we're biased toward work by underappreciated and beginning poets." Chapbooks are usually 24-32 pgs., 5½ × 8½, photocopied and saddle-stapled with cardstock cover, includes lots of art. "Normally we like to see the whole manuscript, but if it's a long one you can send 5-10 sample poems. Publishing in our journals is certainly not required but nearly all of our chapbook authors have done so." Replies to queries and mss in 1 month. Pays 25 author's copies (out of a press run of 100). Order sample chapbooks by sending $1.50 per title.

Also Offers: Website includes editor's information, submission guidelines, catalog, samples of previous offerings.

Advice: "You can't do anything new until you know what's already been done. For every hour you spend writing, spend five hours reading other writers."

N ◑ THE BROWN BOTTLE, 21A Grove St., Concord NH 03301, founded 1999, editor Nate Graziano.
Magazine Needs: Appearing biannually, *The Brown Bottle* publishes poetry, short fiction and essays. Each issue includes some b&w art. They want "work that cuts the vein. Open to any style/form, although rhymed

verse stands less of a chance. No sappy love poetry; poems about rabbits munching lillies in the garden; anything timid. No 'Hallmark' verse." They have published poetry by AD Winans, Mark Senkus, Ana Christy, Taylor Graham and Joseph Shields. As a sample the editor selected these lines from "Soapbox" by Joseph Verrilli:

> *I laugh and sneer at all of you/on silly little pads of paper/just like this one./Maybe it's not much of a life to you,/but to me/it's everything . . ./it's all I've got left.*

The editor says *BB* is 36 pgs., digest-sized, saddle-stitched with cardstock cover, includes b&w art. They receive about 300 poems a year, accept approximately 10%. Publish 10-15 poems/issue. Press run is 100. Single copy: $3; subscription: $6. Sample: $2. Make checks payable to Nate Graziano.

How to Submit: Submit 3-5 poems at a time. No previously published poems; simultaneous submissions OK. Cover letter preferred. "Include name and address on every page. Send an SASE with all submissions or they'll be returned unread." Time between acceptance and publication is 1-5 months. Often comments on rejections. Send SASE for guidelines. Responds in 1 month. Pays 1 copy. Acquires one-time rights. Reviews books and chapbooks of poetry in 100 words. Open to unsolicited reviews. Poets may also send books for review consideration.

Also Offers: Also publishes a broadside series titled Happy Hour. It includes poetry, articles and reviews.

Advice: "Editors are not gods. We make mistakes. A rejection letter doesn't mean your work is poorly written. It just means it doesn't fit in that particular magazine. There are thousands of others. Look at this book!"

N ⬇ ◐ BROWN-BAG LUNCH MAGAZINE, P.O. Box 29130, 3500 Fallowfield Rd., Nepean, Ontario K2J 4A9 Canada, e-mail editor@brownbaglunch.net, website www.brownbaglunch.net, founded 2000, managing editor Victoria Martin.

Magazine Needs: *brown-bag lunch magazine* biannually publishes poetry, short fiction and book reviews from around the world. *"brown-bag lunch* welcomes poems in a variety of forms with a strong voice, effective language, and fresh images. Also interested in short fiction up to 2,500 words and books reviews. No L-A-N-G-U-A-G-E poetry; religious verse; vampire/goth/science fiction and fantasy poetry or fiction; greeting card verse." As a sample the editor selected these lines from "The Fish" by Elizabeth Bishop:

> *his brown skin hung in strips/like ancient wallpaper,/and its pattern of darker brown/was like wallpaper:/shapes like full-blown roses/stained and lost through age.*

The editor says the magazine is about 80 pgs., 8½×11, photocopied and saddle-stitched with cover containing b&w photography or art, includes art inside and ads. Publish 20-25 poems/issue. Press run is 250. Single copy: $4; subscription: $8/2 issues, $12/4 issues. Sample: $4 plus 4 IRCs. "We cannot use other countries' stamps to send from Canada." Make checks (Canada only) payable to Victoria Martin. "All other countries send postal money orders; drawn in U.S. dollars."

How to Submit: Submit 6 poems at a time. Line length for poetry is 10 minimum, 100 maximum. No previously published poems or simultaneous submissions. E-mail submissions OK. Cover letter required. "Submissions must be typed, single-spaced (double-spaced for fiction and reviews) on 8½×11 paper, formatted exactly as the author wishes to see it in print. E-mail submissions should come as attachments in Word 97 or Corel Word Perfect. Cover letter should include brief bio. SASE mandatory." Submit seasonal poems 6 months in advance. Time between acceptance and publication is up to 1 year. Often comments on rejections. Publishes theme issues occasionally. Send SASE for guidelines. Responds in 6 weeks. Pays 2 copies. Acquires first North American serial rights and "electronic rights (e-rights) that revert to the author after a set period of time." Reviews books and chapbooks of poetry in 1,500 words maximum for multi-book; 500-750 words maximum for single book. Open to unsolicited reviews. Poets may also send books for review consideration.

Also Offers: Website includes writers' guidelines, subscription information, samples of poetry, short fiction and reviews from the current issue, name of editor.

Advice: "All writers should become involved in their local literary community, give readings, enroll in a creative writing workshop. If the quality of the work is there, it will receive the attention it deserves. Don't let your best writing fester in a drawer!"

✓ ◐ THE BROWNSTONE REVIEW, 335 Court St., PMB 174, Brooklyn NY 11231, phone (718)788-6220, founded 1995, poetry editor Aaron Scharf.

Magazine Needs: *BR* appears twice a year. "We will consider poems of any length or style and addressing any theme. Formal poetry is encouraged, provided the form is used for a reason. Keep your language fresh and incantatory, your imagery vivid. No workshop poems, no greeting card verse." They have published poetry by Charles Edward Mann, Mary Kennan Herbert, John Lowery, Mark DeFoe, Elizabeth Florio and Nancy Berg. As a sample the editor selected these lines from "Renoir's Onions" by Jan Weiss:

> *He fell in love with women stacking grapes,/fell in love with all the women—young ones,/faces seamless as peaches,/and the old—gnarled like figs.//He was an outsider, drunk on the glory of it—/even death was grand—sheep from whom the guts were slit,/still hanging,//But it was the onion Renoir chose to immortalize,/the lowly onion,/abandoned on its table of simple wood,//long after the market was swept clean,/the voices gone.*

The editor says *TBR* is 60 pgs., 7×8½, side-stapled. They receive 750-1,000 poems/year, use 30-40. Press run is 200. Single copy: $5; subscription: $10. Make checks payable to Dawson Publishing.

How to Submit: Submit 3-5 poems at a time. No previously published poems; simultaneous submissions OK. Cover letter preferred. Seldom comments on rejections. Send SASE for guidelines. Responds within 3 months. Pays 2 copies.

Advice: "Strive to create the poetic state in others, rather than living it yourself."

BRUNSWICK PUBLISHING CORPORATION, 1386 Lawrenceville Plank Rd., Lawrenceville VA 23868, phone (804)848-3865, e-mail brunspub@jnent.com, website www.brunswickbooks.com, founded 1978, poetry editor Dr. Walter J. Raymond.

Book/Chapbook Needs: Brunswick is a partial subsidy publisher. Books are digest-sized, flat-spined, neatly printed, glossy cover with photo. Send SASE for catalog to order samples and "Statement of Philosophy and Purpose," which explains terms. That Statement says: "We publish books because that is what we like to do. Every new book published is like a new baby, an object of joy! We do not attempt to unduly influence the reading public as to the value of our publications, but we simply let the readers decide that themselves. We refrain from the artificial beefing up of values that are not there. . . . We are not competitors in the publishing world, but offer what we believe is a needed service. We strongly believe that in an open society every person who has something of value to say and wants to say it should have the chance and opportunity to do so." Recently published . . . *only the trying.* . . . by David J. Thomas.

How to Submit: Query with 3-5 samples. Response in 2 weeks with SASE. If invited, submit double-spaced, typed ms. E-mail submissions OK in attached files. Responds in 1 month, reading fee only if you request written evaluation. Always sends prepublication galleys. Poet pays 50-80% of cost, gets same percentage of profits for market-tester edition of 500-1,000, advertised by leaflets mailed to reviewers, libraries, book buyers and bookstores.

BUDDHA EYES; INFINITE HIWAY, 1077 Brite Lane, Poteet TX 78065, phone/fax (830)276-8387, founded 1998, editor/publisher Leticia Coward.

Magazine Needs: *Buddha Eyes* appears 2 times a year and publishes "fiery, beat, underground and street poetry. Anything exciting, wild, fresh and alive. Any length. No rhyming, sweet, religious or children's poetry. Nothing boring." Editor says *BE* is 8½×11, desktop-published and side-stapled. Single copy: $3; subscription: $6. Sample: $5. Make checks payable to Leticia Coward.

How to Submit: Submit 5 poems at a time (with $3 reading fee). No previously published poems or simultaneous submissions. Cover letter required. "Prefer only mailed submissions with friendly cover letter." Time between acceptance and publication is 6 months. Always comments on rejections. Send SASE for guidelines. Responds in 3 months. Pays 1 copy. Acquires first rights.

Also Offers: Publishes *Infinite Hiway* which contains plays, prose and stories.

BUFFALO BONES (Specialized: regional), Evergreen Poets & Writers, P.O. Box 714, Evergreen CO 80437, founded 1994, contact editors (editorial staff rotates).

Magazine Needs: *Buffalo Bones* appears 4 times/year, is a nonprofit publication containing "nothing elitist. Poems by known and unknown poets stand side by side. We look for high quality." They want "any form of poetry, 40-line limit, strong imagery, narratives with a new twist, and a bit of fun once in awhile. No profanity, graphic/sexual, or woe-is-me poems." They have published poetry by Robert Cooperman, Judith Herschemeyer, Donna Park, Carolyn Campbell and Lyn Lifshin. *BB* is 50 pgs., digest-sized, nicely printed on quality paper. Sample: $5. Make checks payable to Evergreen Poets & Writers.

How to Submit: Submit 3 poems with a $5 reading fee. "Poems are not returned." Previously published poems and simultaneous submissions OK. Reads submissions September 1 through June 1. Poems are circulated to an editorial board. "We have a rotating editorship in order to ensure variety and a fresh look in every issue." Send SASE for guidelines. Responds in 3 months. Pays 1 copy.

Advice: "Every poem gets attention from several readers. There are many fine poems—so little space. Our editorial staff rotates for each issue, therefore, try us again."

$ BUGLE, JOURNAL OF ELK COUNTRY (Specialized: animals, nature/rural/ecology, conservation), Rocky Mountain Elk Foundation, P.O. Box 8249, Missoula MT 59807-8249, phone (406)523-4570, fax (406)523-4550, e-mail bugle@rmef.org, website www.rmef.org, founded 1984, editorial assistant Lee Cromrich.

Magazine Needs: *Bugle* is the bimonthly publication of the nonprofit Rocky Mountain Elk Foundation, whose mission is to ensure the future of elk, other wildlife and their habitat. "The goal of *Bugle* is to advance this mission by presenting original, critical thinking about wildlife conservation, elk ecology and hunting." They want "high quality poems that explore the realm of elk, the 'why' of hunting, or celebrate the hunting experience as a whole. Prefer one page. Free verse, cowboy poetry, etc., OK. No 'Hallmark' poetry." *Bugle* is 130 pgs., 8½×11, professionally printed on coated stock and saddle stitched with full-color glossy cover containing photos, illustrations, ads. They receive about 20 poems a year, accept approximately 30%. Press run is 195,000 for 110,000 subscribers, 85,000 shelf sales. Subscription: $30 membership fee. Sample: $4.95. Make checks payable to Rocky Mountain Elk Foundation.

How to Submit: "Poets may submit as many poems as they'd like at a time." Simultaneous submissions OK. Cover letter preferred. E-mail (prefer attached file in Word or WordPerfect), fax and disk submissions OK. Time between acceptance and publication varies. "Poems are screened by editorial assistant first, those accepted then passed to editorial staff for review and comment, final decision based on their comments. We will evaluate your poem based on content, quality and our needs for the coming year." Rarely comments on rejections. Publishes special sections. Send SASE for guidelines and upcoming themes. Responds in 3 months. Pays $100/poem plus 3 copies. Acquires first North American serial rights. Staff reviews other magazines.

Advice: "Although poetry has appeared periodically in *Bugle* over the years, it has never been a high priority for us, nor have we solicited it. A lack of high-quality work and poetry appropriate for the focus of the magazine has kept us from making it a regular feature. However, we've decided to attempt to give verse a permanent home in the magazine. . . . Reading a few issues of *Bugle* prior to submitting will give you a better sense of the style and content of the magazine. The Rocky Mountain Elk Foundation is a nonprofit conservation organization committed to putting membership dollars into protecting elk habitat. So we appreciate, and still receive, donated work. However, if you would like to be paid for your work, our rate is $100 a poem, paid on acceptance. Should your poem appear in *Bugle*, you will receive three complimentary copies of the issue."

N ⊕ ⬮ THE BURNING BUSH, 35 Glenard Crescent, Salthill, Galway, Ireland, e-mail kphiggins@hotma il.com, founded 1999, co-editor Kevin Higgins, co-editor Michael S. Begnal.

Magazine Needs: *The Burning Bush* appears biannually "to publish new contemporary poetry which is well written but not rigidly formal. We are open to the experimental." They have a "bias towards free verse, the contemporary, surrealism. No rigidly formal, pastoral or New Age poetry." They have published poetry by Sarah Berkeley, Ron Offen, Tom MacIntyre, James Liddy, Fred Johnston and Noelle Vial. As a sample the editor selected this poem "Once Upon a Time in Clare" by Michael Durack:

> For ninety percent of intents he was a four-eyed jellyfish,/a fellow who never buckled a swash in his
> life,/who if he could beat snow off a rope,/would scarely pull the socks from a dead man./And she was
> desire in the raw in a gymslip/when sex was still Latin for seven minus one.

The editors say *Burning Bush* is 56 pgs., magazine-sized, printed on Windows 98 and stapled with color cover (using Strata Studio Pro 3.53 and Photoshop). They receive about 1,000 poems a year, accept approximately 10%. Press run is 200 for 20 subscribers, 100 shelf sales; 80 distributed free to contributors, Irish literary magazines and publishers. Subscription: £10. Sample: £2.50. Make checks payable to Kevin Higgins.

How to Submit: Submit 6 poems at a time. No simultaneous submissions. Cover letter preferred. "Poems should be typed and submitted with a number of IRCs sufficient to cover return postage." Time between acceptance and publication is 4 months. Seldom comments on rejections. Send SASE for guidelines. Responds in 4 months. Pays 1 copy. Reviews books and chapbooks of poetry and other magazines in 400 words, single book format. Open to unsolicited reviews. Poets may also send books for review consideration.

Advice: "We would like to shake up Irish poetry a little. We look away from Yeats and Heaney and towards Eliot, Pound and The New York, Black Mountain and Beat poets."

N ◯ ⬮ BURNING BUSH PUBLICATIONS; PEOPLE BEFORE PROFITS POETRY PRIZE, P.O. Box 9636, Oakland CA 94613, phone (510)482-9996, e-mail editor@bbbooks.com, website www.bbbooks.com, founded 1996, contact acquisitions editor.

Book/Chapbook Needs: Burning Bush serves "voices that are underserved by mainstream presses." Publishes 1 paperback/year. They want "uplifting writing that believes in a more harmonious and equitable world with an emphasis on social justice and conscience." They do not want "any work that is degrading to humans or other lifeforms." They have published poetry by Morton Marcus, Lyn Lifshin, Patti Sirens, Opal Palmer Adisa and Grace Paley. As a sample the editor selected these lines from "like a red tail" by Abby Bogomolny:

> i scope out your canyon/clearing the ridge and view your landscape,/a shifting of your desire/steaming,
> brown, dusty/and ride the hot wind high

Books are usually 144 pgs., 5½ × 8½, offset, stapled with medium card cover and photographs.

How to Submit: "Send ten sample poems with a description of the audience you wish to reach. Explain the scope of work in a cover letter and include any previous publications including references." Previously published poems OK; no simultaneous submissions. Time between acceptance and publication is 1 year. Poems are circulated to an editorial board. "Board meets once per month and reviews all submissions that have passed our acquisitions editors approval." Seldom comments on rejections. Charges critism fees "only under special circumstances: if the author can benefit from it, agrees to it and if we love their work enough to provide it. They must first send ten-poem sample for approval." Replies to queries and mss in 2 months. Authors are paid by individual contract.

Also Offers: People Before Profits Poetry Prize awards a $100 first prize and two Honorable Mentions. Submit up to 3 poems in any style or form. Attach index card with name, title of poems, address, entry fee, phone and e-mail address. Entry fee: $10. Poems accepted through February 17. Send SASE for guidelines or obtain via website. Winners published in their e-zine. "Our website explains the inspiration behind Burning Bush Publications, lists our mail order titles, writer's guidelines, contest guidelines and features a literary e-zine." Our books are distributed to the trade by Bookpeople, Baker & Taylor and Small Press Distribution.

✔ $◯ BUTTON MAGAZINE; BUTTON 2001 POETRY CONTEST, 3 Oak Ave., Lunenburg MA 01462, e-mail buttonx26@aol.com, founded 1993, poetry editor D.E. Bell.

● Please note that the Button 2001 Poetry Contest is a new addition to this listing.

Magazine Needs: *Button* "is New England's tiniest magazine of fiction, poetry and gracious living." They want "poetry about the quiet surprises in life, not sentimental, and true moments carefully preserved. Brevity counts." They have published poetry by William Corbett, David Barber and Amanda Powell. As a sample the editor selected these lines from "Town Dump" by Brendan Galvin:

> *Muddle and rummage, and men/with a special talent for it. Take Tilton/for starters, drawing on/his*
> *White Mule gloves/so slow he won't have to/help you unload*

Button appears twice a year and is 30 pgs., 4¼×5½, saddle-stitched, card stock 4-color cover with illustrations that incorporate one or more buttons. Press run is 1,200 for more than 500 subscribers; 750 shelf sales. Subscription: $5/2 years, $25/lifetime. Sample: $2.
How to Submit: Submit up to 3 poems at a time. No previously published poems. Cover letter required. Time between acceptance and publication is 3-6 months. Poems are circulated to an editorial board. Often comments on rejections. Send SASE for guidelines or request via e-mail. Responds in 4 months. Pays honorarium, 2-year subscription and author's copies. Acquires first North American serial rights.
Also Offers: Sponsors the Button 2000 Poetry Contest. Submit poems on any topic, 25 lines or fewer, with SASE. Entry fee: $10/2 poems ($5 for each additional poem). Deadline: July 1, 2000. Awards $100 and publication. Send SASE for guidelines.
Advice: "*Button* was started so that a century from now when people read it they'll say, 'Gee, what a wonderful time to have lived. I wish I lived back then.' Our likes include wit and humanity, intelligence and eccentricity. Button tries to reflect a world one would *want* to live in."

$ ◎ BYLINE MAGAZINE; BYLINE LITERARY AWARDS (Specialized: writing), P.O. Box 130596, Edmond OK 73013-0001, phone (405)348-5591, e-mail bylinemp@aol.com, website www.bylinemag.com, founded 1981, poetry editor Sandra Soli, editor Marcia Preston.
Magazine Needs: *ByLine* is a magazine for the encouragement of writers and poets, using 8-10 poems/issue about writers or writing. As a sample the editor selected these lines from "Revise, Revise" by L.G. Mason:

> *there will be a version/left in autumn/like a darkened lantern/swinging on a limb,/like a poem/surviving*
> *a man:/let anyone/find in it what he can.*

ByLine is magazine-sized, professionally printed, with illustrations, cartoons and ads. They have more than 3,000 subscriptions and receive about 2,500 poetry submissions/year, of which they use about 100. Subscription: $22. Sample: $4.
How to Submit: Submit up to 3 poems at a time, no reprints. No e-mail or fax submissions, please. Send SASE for guidelines. Responds within 6 weeks. Pays $10/poem. Buys first North American serial rights.
Also Offers: Sponsors up to 20 poetry contests, including a chapbook competition open to anyone. Send #10 SASE for details. Also sponsors the ByLine Literary Awards. Prize: $250. Send SASE for guidelines. Website features guidelines, contest listings, subscription info and sample column or article from magazine.
Advice: "We are happy to work with new writers, but please read a few samples to get an idea of our style. We would like to see more serious poetry about the creative experience (as it concerns writing)."

Ⓝ ▣ ◻ ◯ ◪ ◎ BYTES OF POETRY; LOVESTORIES.COM; BACKUP COMPUTER RESOURCES (Specialized: anthologies), 905 S. 30th St., Broken Arrow OK 74014, phone/fax (918)251-4652, e-mail webmaster@lovestories.com, website www.lovestories.com, website founded September 1997, founder/editor Alanna Webb.
   ● Lovestories.com has received awards and mentions by USA Today Hot Site (1998), LA Times (1999), Houston Chronicle (1998), Entertainment Weekly (1999), ABCNews.com (1999), CNN.com (1998), ThirdAge.com (1999), Poetry Today Online (1999).
Book/Chapbook Needs: Under *Bytes of Poetry*, Backup Computer Resources publishes 2-4 poetry anthologies per year. "We are looking for heartfelt poetry. Our emphasis is poetry written by everyday people. We review poetry written by all ages, on a wide range of topics, and in a wide range of styles. We do not accept poetry that contains profanity, or very explicit subject matter. We do accept sensual poetry though." They have published poetry by C.J. Heck, Paula Duquette, Susan Fridkin, Randall Longshore, Max the Poet and Chuck Pool. As a sample the editor selected this poem, "Live on (Peter's Poem)" by Julia Warfel:

> *Love could not hold you,/Nor could our tears./You suffered in silence,/Enslaved by your fears./Now*
> *mortal boundaries,/Keep us apart,/But live in my memory./Live on in my heart.*

Books are usually 150-170 pgs., 5½×8½, offset printed and perfect-bound with full-color paper cover, custom designed
How to Submit: "We only print poetry anthologies of poetry posted by people on our website. Poets can post 5 poems/24 hours onto our website. To post, poets must sign up for our free Poet Account." Previously published poems and simultaneous submissions OK. Submit seasonal poems 4 months in advance. Time between acceptance and publication is 3 months. "Poetry for our books are selected by our internal staff with the help of nominations by fellow poets on the website." Seldom comments on rejections. Responds in 1 month. Pays 1 author's copy/published poem (out of a press run of 5,000). Order sample books by calling Book Clearing House at (800)431-1579 or ordering online at www.bytesofpoetry.com.
Also Offers: Sponsors weekly and monthly poetry contests, voted by visitors and staff. Winners are reviewed for possible inclusion in books. Also, visit their website to vote for the weekly Top 10 Poems. "Our staff and sponsors select the Poem of the Month winners from all poems posted on a monthly topic. Our website

Promoting poetry for everyday people

Alanna Webb, editor and founder of Lovestories.com and *Bytes of Poetry: A Lovestories.com Anthology*, began a career in chemical engineering before deciding to switch gears and pursue an interest in computers. After teaching herself to create graphics and web pages, she fused a love of romance with her computer skills to produce Lovestories.com, one of the largest poetry communities on the Internet. The website has received numerous awards and mentions from *USA Today*, *The LA Times*, *The Houston Chronicle*, CNN.com, *Entertainment Weekly*, ABCNews.com and Yahoo!.

Webb says, "Lovestories.com was one of the first Web communities to focus on real content from real people, providing a forum for people to share their stories, viewpoints, and creative talents in an interactive community." Poets from every walk of life frequent the Lovestories.com website. There are currently

Alanna Webb

more than 60,000 poems archived in their database. "Anyone with Internet access can sign up and post their original poetry. Our poetry community also offers poets a chance to communicate with other poets through chat rooms, message boards and comment forms," she says.

The popularity of the poetry section has grown to such an astonishing level, bringing in more than 400,000 visitors each month, that Webb decided to further develop the opportunities she sees for herself, her site and her poets. Thus *Bytes of Poetry: A Lovestories.com Anthology* was conceived and then published in October 1999. In this first volume, Webb's purpose was to "promote poetry written by everyday people to everyone, especially those who haven't discovered the joys of reading poetry. We wanted to spread the word about the wonderful poetry posted on Lovestories.com, and to provide a publishing opportunity to poets who may otherwise feel intimidated by the traditional publishing process. You don't have to be a scholar to be able to write poetry or to be able to enjoy it."

In spotlighting the "everyday" poet, Webb discovered the "diversity of the poets submitting that is illustrated in the short bios included in the back of the book. Among the poets in the anthology, you'll find writers, a stage and film actor, military veterans, a widow, a photographer, and two poets who met through Lovestories.com's poetry community and fell in love. Several have written poetry for years, while others started writing after visiting Lovestories.com. For most, this is their first publishing opportunity." Webb says, "I think of this book as an emotional quilt. Each poem adds color and warmth to the whole anthology. We wanted *Bytes of Poetry* to reflect as many poets, tastes, styles, and topics as possible."

The selection process for the anthology is wonderful. Poets from all over the world can freely post their poems to share with readers and be given the opportunity to appear in the book. Webb says, "We select a handful of poems from previous winners of our weekly and monthly poetry contests. We ask these poets to nominate two more poems and then ask the nominated poets to nominate two more, and so on. So the poetry selected for this book is a mix of our tastes and (that of) our poets." The following clever poem by C. J. Heck reflects the work found in the book:

". . . And He Whispered" (Dual Poems)

Warm breath
and whispers
"Sweet, sweet woman . . .
in my ear,
waking up
. . . my forever darling . . .
more than
my mind.
. . . I've never been . . .
Love's arrows
pierce through
. . . so happy.
dreams, slice
through sleep fog,
I've never known . . .
arousing the her-parts;
soft as a sigh,
. . . such love.
yet as fast as
hummingbird wings.
I now know . . .
Once awake, raw
passion takes hold of
. . . the purpose of . . .
"my life."

(originally published in *Bytes of Poetry: A Lovestories.com Anthology*, issue number 1, Fall 1999; reprinted with permisssion from the author)

Bytes of Poetry has become a force of its own, being sold in the world market to poetry writers and lovers from every corner of the globe. It contains 115 poems written by eighty poets, ranging from teens to seniors, that were selected from the thousands posted by poets at Lovestories.com. Topics include love, romance, nature, family, friendship, divorce, social issues, hope, religion, children and more.

There are two additional volumes of *Bytes of Poetry* in the works with other projects in the idea stage. The second, released in spring 2000, also contains poetry for lovers and features love poems and mild erotica that engage the sensual, loving emotions of its readers. The "family" of books published by Alanna Webb will continue to contain poems submitted to the Lovestories.com website.

—Judy Gripton

(Lovestories.com) has one of the largest poetry sections on the Internet, as part of our love and romance community. BytesofPoetry.com is our special domain that contains details on the books we publish, including sample poems, forms to contact the poets, Our News Releases and reviews and order information." They also post e-mail interviews with poets and publishers.

Advice: "We believe that there is a lot of untapped talent in everyday people who haven't studied poetry formally. Our goal is to promote poetry written at the grassroots level and to promote poetry to everyone. We encourage people to make poetry reading part of their everyday life. The Internet can be a wonderful way to learn about poetry, get feedback and recognition for your poetry, and interact with other poets. Just be wary of contest scams and check out the sites you frequent and post at."

☑ ◎ **THE CAFÉ REVIEW,** c/o Yes Books, 20 Danforth St., Portland ME 04101, e-mail all@seegerlab.com, website www.thecafereview.com, founded 1989, editor-in-chief Steve Luttrell.

Magazine Needs: *Café Review* is a quarterly which has grown out of open poetry readings held at a Portland cafe. The editors say they aim "to print the best work we can!" They want "free verse, 'beat' inspired and fresh. Nothing clichéd." They have published poetry by Charles Bukowski, Robert Creeley, Janet Hamill and Diane Wakoski. *The Review* is 70-80 pgs., 5½×8½, professionally printed and perfect-bound with card cover, b&w art, no ads. They receive over 1,000 submissions a year, accept approximately 15%. Press run is 500 for 70 subscribers of which 10 are libraries, 75-100 shelf sales. Subscription: $25. Sample: $6.

How to Submit: No previously published poems or simultaneous submissions. Cover letter with brief bio required. "Poems only may be sent via e-mail. All other requests should be sent via U.S. mail. We usually respond with a form letter indicating acceptance or rejection of work, seldom with additional comments." Responds in 4 months. Pays 1 copy.

Book/Chapbook Needs: They also publish 1-2 chapbooks/year.

Ⓝ ◯ ◎ **CALIFORNIA QUARTERLY; CALIFORNIA STATE POETRY SOCIETY,** P.O. Box 7126, Orange CA 92863-7126, phone (949)854-8024, e-mail jspalley@aol.com, founded 1972, editorial board chair Julian Palley.

Magazine Needs: *CQ* is the official publication of the California State Poetry Society (an affiliate of the National Federation of State Poetry Societies) and is designed "to encourage the writing and dissemination of poetry." They want poetry on any subject, 60 lines maximum. "No geographical limitations. Quality is all that matters." They have published poetry by Michael L. Johnson, Lyn Lifshin and Robert Cooperman. *CQ* is 64 pgs., 5½×8½, offset and perfect-bound, heavy paper cover with art. They receive 3,000-4,000 poems a year, accept approximately 5%. Press run is 500 for 300 subscribers of which 24 are libraries, 20-30 shelf sales. Membership in CSPS is $20/year and includes a subscription to *CQ*. Sample (including guidelines): $4. Send SASE for guidelines.

How to Submit: Submit up to 6 "relatively brief" poems at a time; name and address on each sheet. Include SASE. Prefer no previously published poems or simultaneous submissions. Seldom comments on rejections. Responds in up to 4 months. Pays 1 copy. Acquires first rights. Rights revert to poet after publication.

Also Offers: CSPS also sponsors an annual poetry contest. Awards vary. All entries considered for *CQ*.

Advice: "Since our editor changes with each issue, we encourage poets to resubmit. Also, we are not opposed to rhyme, but it should be used with great discretion."

Ⓝ ◎ **CALYPSO PUBLICATIONS,** 5810 Osage, #205, Cheyenne WY 82009, founded 1989.

Book/Chapbook Needs: Calypso Publications seeks to print "excellent and accessible contemporary poetry." They publish occasional chapbooks and anthologies. They want "contemporary poetry, no limitations on form, etc. No traditional rhyming or inspirational poetry." They have published poetry by William Kloefkorn, Jean Nordhaus, Lyn Lifshin, William Dickey, Barbara Crooker and Dennis Saleh. Books are usually 60-100 pgs., 6×9, perfect-bound, some with multi-color covers, includes line drawing on covers.

How to Submit: "We don't accept queries. We accept full manuscripts and only when we request them through monthly writing magazines. Poems for book publication can be previously published." No simultaneous submissions. SASE required. Time between acceptance and publication is up to 1 year. Often comments on rejections. Replies to mss in 2 months. Payment varies. Order sample books by sending $5.

Advice: "For our first three years, we published an annual magazine called *Calypso*. We now publish occasional anthologies and chapbooks. Writers should check writing magazines periodically to learn of our future projects."

◯ ◎ **CALYX, A JOURNAL OF ART & LITERATURE BY WOMEN (Specialized: women, lesbian, multicultural); CALYX BOOKS,** P.O. Box B, Corvallis OR 97339-0539, phone (541)753-9384, fax (541)753-0515, e-mail calyx@proaxis.com, founded 1976, senior editor Beverly McFarland.

Magazine Needs: *Calyx*, a journal edited by a collective editorial board, publishes poetry, prose, art, book reviews and interviews by and about women. They want "excellently crafted poetry that also has excellent content." They have published poetry by Maurya Simon, Robin Morgan, Carole Boston Weatherford and Eleanor Wilner. As a sample the editor selected these lines from "Transparent Woman" by Donna Henderson:

> in the basement of the science museum,/half-lit, naked and marvelous with her perfect/posture, lucite arms straight and slightly apart,/palms turned toward us like the Blessed Virgin's,/helplessly welcoming.

Calyx appears 3 times every 18 months and is 6×8, handsomely printed on heavy paper, flat-spined, glossy color cover, 128 pgs., of which 50-60 are poetry. Poems tend to be lyric free verse that makes strong use of image and symbol melding unobtrusively with voice and theme. Single copy: $9.50. Sample: $11.50.

How to Submit: *Calyx* is open to submissions October 1 through December 15 only. Mss received when not open to reading will be returned unread. Send up to 6 poems with SASE and short bio. "We accept copies in good condition and clearly readable. We focus on new writing, but occasionally publish a previously published piece." Simultaneous submissions OK, "if kept up-to-date on publication." Send SASE or e-mail for guidelines. Responds in 9 months. Pays 1 copy/poem and subscription. Open to unsolicited reviews. Poets may also send books for review consideration.

Book/Chapbook Needs & How to Submit: Calyx Books publishes 1 book of poetry a year. All work published is by women. Recently published: *Details of Flesh* by Cortney Davis. However, Calyx Books is closed for ms submissions until further notice.

Advice: "Read the publication and be familiar with what we have published."

● **CAMELLIA; CAMELLIA PRESS INC.**, P.O. Box 40438, Washington DC 20016-0438, editor Tomer Inbar, associate editor Beth Stevens.

Magazine Needs: *Camellia* is published biannually as a fold-out magazine/poster "available for free in New York City, the San Francisco/Oakland Bay area, Seattle, Ithaca, D.C., Northern Virginia and Baltimore, or by sending 2 first-class stamps. We publish poetry in the W.C. Williams tradition. The poetry of things, moment and sharpness. We encourage young writers and like to work with the writers who publish with us. Our main goal is to get the poetry out. We do not want to see poetry where the poem is subordinate to the poet or poetry where the noise of the poetic overshadows the voice. We look for poetry that is honest and sharp and unburdened." *Camellia*'s exact dimensions, the theme for a given issue and the mix of poetry and other art will be determined on an issue by issue basis. "We will keep the basic graphic design consistent with the style we have used for the past issues, however we will be inviting guest designers to work with that design, bringing something new to each issue. We will continue to publish special project issues from time to time using various formats and mediums." They receive approximately 300-350 poems/issue and publish about 20. Press run is 1,000-2,000. Subscription: $5/year, $7 overseas. Sample: 2 first-class stamps.

How to Submit: Submit 8 poems at a time. Simultaneous submissions and previously published poems OK. "Cover letters are helpful, but shouldn't go overboard. Sometimes the cover letters are more interesting than the poetry received." Responds "ASAP." Pays 2 copies. Editor comments on submissions "if asked for or if I want to see more but am not satisfied with the poems sent."

Also Offers: Available is a poster of poetry, photographs and design using poems from the first 6 years of *Camellia*. They send prepublication galleys only for chapbooks.

🍁 ✅ ☯ ◎ **CANADIAN DIMENSION: THE MAGAZINE FOR PEOPLE WHO WANT TO CHANGE THE WORLD (Specialized: political)**, 2B-91 Albert St., Winnipeg, Manitoba R3B 1G5 Canada, phone (204)957-1519, fax (204)943-4617, e-mail info@canadiandimension.mb.ca, website www.canadiandimension.mb.ca/~cdol/, founded 1964, editorial contact Ed Janzen.

Magazine Needs: *Canadian Dimension* appears 6 times/year, using "short poems on labour, women, native, gay/lesbian and other issues. Nothing more than one page." They have published poetry by Tom Wayman and Milton Acorn. It is 48-56 pgs., magazine-sized, slick, professionally printed, with glossy paper cover. Press run is 3,500 for 2,500 subscribers of which 800 are libraries, 1,000 shelf sales. Subscription: $34.50 US ($24.50 Canadian). Sample: $2.

How to Submit: Submit up to 5 poems at a time. Previously published poems are unlikely to be accepted. Simultaneous submissions OK, if notified. Editor comments on submissions "rarely." Publishes theme issues. Send SASE (or SAE and IRC) for upcoming themes. Reviews books of poetry in 750-1,200 words, single or multi-book format.

Advice: "We are broadly political—that is, not narrowly sloganeering, but profoundly sensitive to the connections between words and the state of the world. Topics can be personal as well as political. Also, American writers are reminded to include Canadian return postage or its equivalent in reply coupons, etc."

🍁 ✅ ☯ **THE CANADIAN JOURNAL OF CONTEMPORARY LITERARY STUFF**, P.O. Box 53106, Ottawa, Ontario K1N 1C5 Canada, fax (613)562-3542, e-mail grunge@achilles.net, founded 1997, editors Grant Wilkins and Tamara Fairchild.

Magazine Needs: *CJOCLS* appears 2-4 times a year and aims "to make Canadian literature interesting to read, interesting to read about, accessible and fun." They want "fresh, literate poetry written in a unique voice. Poetry

---

THE CHAPBOOK INDEX, located at the back of this book, lists those publishers who consider chapbook mss. A chapbook, a small volume of work (usually under 50 pages), is often a good middle step between magazine and book publication.

that actually says something. No insipid, banal pieces about broken hearts. No landscapes or navel gazing about writing. Poets should note that we prefer to publish sets of two to four poems by the same writer." They have published poetry by Bill Bissett, Stan Rogal, Sharon H. Nelson and Catherine Jenkins. As a sample we selected these lines from "where are you from, really?" by Sumana Sen-Bagchee:

> *they call this time of year, fall/yet, these aged planes and sycamores/lining the Embankment walk/have neither turned colour/nor dropped their leaves/as they are supposed to—/today's soothing sunlight/is the colour of pernod/spilling onto the pavement/where we wade through pigeons,/pass other strollers, the odd dove//the sun on our spines/tingling down to our palms/(we keep them tightfisted in pockets)/ words flutter from him/random, like pigeons/his fresh English face, eager/where are you from, really,/ I've been wondering . . .*

The editors say it is 40 pgs., magazine-sized, saddle-stapled with b&w plus third color cover, includes b&w photos and ads. They receive about 400 poems a year, accept approximately 5%. Press run is 1,000. Single copy: $4.75; subscription: $16. Sample: $6.50. Make checks payable to *CJOCLS*.

How to Submit: Submit 5 or more poems at a time. No previously published poems or simultaneous submissions. Cover letter and SASE required. E-mail and disk submissions OK. Time between acceptance and publication is 3 months. Poems are circulated to an editorial board. "We are two editors in two separate cities. We both get a copy of submissions for an issue. We each go through submissions on our own, then get together and compare notes." Seldom comments on rejections. Send SASE (or SAE and IRC) for guidelines or obtain via e-mail. Responds in 8 months. Pays 5 copies. Acquires first rights. Reviews books and chapbooks of poetry in 300-500 words. Open to unsolicited reviews. Poets may also send books for review consideration.

Advice: "We're also looking for fiction, articles, interviews, cartoons, art and photos."

CANADIAN LITERATURE (Specialized: regional), 167-1855 West Mall, University of British Columbia, Vancouver, British Columbia V6T 1Z2 Canada, phone (604)822-2780, fax (604)822-5504, website www.cdn-lit.ubc.ca, founded 1959, editor E.M. Kröller.

Magazine Needs: *CL* is a quarterly review which publishes poetry by Canadian poets. "No limits on form. Less room for long poems." They have published poetry by Atwood, Ondaatje, Layton and Bringhurst. "See recent issue for poetry sample." Each issue is professionally printed, digest-sized, flat-spined, with 175-200 pgs., of which about 10 are poetry. They receive 500 poetry submissions/year, use 10-40. Circulation is 1,200, two-thirds of which are libraries. Sample for the cover price: $15 Canadian plus postage and GST.

How to Submit: No simultaneous submissions or reprints. Cover letter and SASE (or SAE and IRC) required. Responds within the month. "Accepted poems must be available on diskette." *CL* retains full copyright for articles and reviews published. Reviews books of poetry in 500-1,000 words.

CANADIAN WOMAN STUDIES (Specialized: women), 212 Founders College, York University, 4700 Keele St., North York, Ontario M3J 1P3 Canada, phone (416)736-5356, fax (416)736-5765, e-mail cwscf@yorku.ca, website www.yorku.ca/org/cwscf/home.html, founded 1978, literary editor Marlene Kadar.

Magazine Needs: *CWS* appears quarterly and focuses on "women's studies; experiential and academic articles, poetry, book reviews and artwork." They want poetry "exploring women's lives/perspectives. No long poems (i.e., more than 50 lines)." They have published poetry by Libby Scheier, Patience Wheatley and Lyn Lifshin. The editor says *CWS* is about 152 pgs., magazine-sized, offset printed and perfect-bound with full color cover, includes art and ads. They receive about 400 poems a year, accept approximately 15%. Press run is 4,000 for 1,500 subscribers of which 500 are libraries, 1,000 shelf sales; 250 distributed free to women's groups. Single copy: $10; subscription: $36 plus $2.10 gst/year. Sample: $13.

How to Submit: Submit 5 poems at a time. No previously published poems or simultaneous submissions. Cover letter required. E-mail submissions OK. "SASE (or SAE and IRC) appreciated, bio note must accompany submission." Time between acceptance and publication is 5 months. Publishes theme issues. Responds in 5 months. Pays 1 copy. "Poets maintain copyright of their work at all times." Reviews books and chapbooks of poetry in 750 words, single and multi-book format. Open to unsolicited reviews. Poets may also send books for review consideration to Fran Beer, book review editor.

Also Offers: Website includes tables of contents, policies, order information, guidelines for submissions and calls for papers.

CANADIAN WRITER'S JOURNAL (Specialized: writing), White Mountain Publications, Box 5180, New Liskeard, Ontario P0J 1P0 Canada, phone (705)647-5424, fax (705)647-8366, e-mail cwj@ntl.sympatico.ca, website www.nt.net/~cwj/index.htm, owner Deborah Ranchuk, contact Carole Mangeau, managing editor.

Magazine Needs: *CWJ* is a digest-sized quarterly, publishing mainly short "how-to" articles of interest to writers at all levels. They use a few "short poems or portions thereof as part of 'how-to' articles relating to the writing of poetry and occasional short poems with tie-in to the writing theme. We try for 90% Canadian content but prefer good material over country of origin, or how well you're known." Subscription: $15/year, $25/2 years. Sample: $5.

How to Submit: Submit up to 5 poems (identify each form). Include SASE ("U.S. postage accepted; do not affix to envelope"). No previously published poems. E-mail and fax submissions OK. "Include in body of message, not as attachment. Write "Submission" in the subject line. Hard copy and SASE (or SAE and IRC) required if accepted." Responds in 3 months. Token payment. Pays $2-5 and 1 copy/poem.

Also Offers: Website includes writer's guidelines, names of editors and table of contents.

N ☘ ◻ ◎ CAPERS AWEIGH MAGAZINE ANNUAL ANTHOLOGY (Specialized: regional), 39 Water St., Glace Bay, Nova Scotia B1A 1R6 Canada, founded 1992, publisher John MacNeil.

Magazine Needs: *CAM* is a quarterly of poetry and short fiction "of, by and for Cape Bretoners at home and away." They want work by Cape Bretoners only. Nothing profane. The publisher says it is 50-60 pgs., 5×8, desktop-published, stapled, including computer graphics and trade ads. Press run is 500. Subscription: $20. Sample: $5.

How to Submit: No simultaneous submissions. Cover letter required. Seldom comments on rejections. Pays 1 copy.

☘ $ ◻ THE CAPILANO REVIEW, 2055 Purcell Way, North Vancouver, British Columbia V7J 3H5 Canada, phone (604)984-1712, fax (604)990-7837, e-mail tcr@capcollege.bc.ca, website www.capcollege.bc.ca/dept/TCR/, founded 1972, editor Ryan Knighton.

Magazine Needs: *The Capilano Review* is a literary and visual media review appearing 3 times/year. They want "avant-garde, experimental, previously unpublished work, poetry of sustained intelligence and imagination. We are interested in poetry that is new in concept and in execution." They have published poetry by Bill Bissett, Phyllis Webb and Michael Ondaatje. *TCR* comes in a handsome digest-sized format, 115 pgs., flat-spined, finely printed, semi-glossy stock with a glossy full-color card cover. Circulation is 1,000. Sample: $9 prepaid.

How to Submit: Submit 5-6 poems, minimum, with cover letter and SAE and IRC. Do not submit mss during June and July. No simultaneous submissions. No e-mail or disk submissions. Responds in up to 5 months. Pays $50-200, subscription, plus 2 copies. Buys first North American serial rights.

Also Offers: Website includes guidelines, excerpts, subscription info, contest info, etc.

Advice: "*TCR* receives several manuscripts each week; unfortunately the majority of them are simply inappropriate for the magazine. The best advice we can offer is to read the magazine before you submit."

✓ $ ◻ ◻ CAPPER'S, 1503 SW 42nd St., Topeka KS 66609-1265, phone (785)274-4300, fax (785)274-4305, website www.cappers.com, founded 1879, contact editor Ann Crahan.

Magazine Needs: *Capper's* is a biweekly tabloid (newsprint) going to 240,000 mail subscribers, mostly small-town and rural families. Uses 6-8 poems in each issue. They want short poems (4-10 lines preferred, lines of one-column width) "relating to everyday situations, nature, inspirational, humorous. Most poems used in *Capper's* are upbeat in tone and offer the reader a bit of humor, joy, enthusiasm or encouragement." Also accepts poetry written by children, ages 12 and under and 13-19. They have published poetry by Elizabeth Searle Lamb, Robert Brimm, Margaret Wiedyke, Helena K. Stefanski, Sheryl L. Nelms and Claire Puneky. Send $1.95 for sample. Not available on newsstand.

How to Submit: Submit 5-6 poems at a time, 14-16 lines. No simultaneous submissions. No e-mail or fax submissions. Returns mss with SASE. Publishes seasonal theme issues. Send SASE for upcoming themes. Responds in 3 months. Pays $10-15/poem. Additional payment of $5 if poem is used on website. Buys one-time rights.

Also Offers: Website includes guidelines and summary of current issue.

Advice: "Poems chosen are upbeat, sometimes humorous, always easily understood. Short poems of this type fit our format best."

✓ ◎ THE CARIBBEAN WRITER (Specialized: regional); THE DAILY NEWS PRIZE; THE CHARLOTTE AND ISIDOR PAIEWONSKY PRIZE; DAVID HOUGH LITERARY PRIZE; THE MARGUERITE COBB MCKAY PRIZE, University of the Virgin Islands, RR 02, P.O. Box 10,000, Kingshill, St. Croix, USVI 00850, phone (340)692-4152, fax (340)692-4026, e-mail ewaters@uvi.edu or qmars@uvi.edu, website www.rps.uvi.edu/CaribbeanWriter/, founded 1987, editor Dr. Erika Waters, contact submissions editor.

Magazine Needs: *The Caribbean Writer* is an annual literary magazine, appearing in July, with a Caribbean focus. The Caribbean must be central to the literary work or the work must reflect a Caribbean heritage, experience or perspective. They have published poetry by Derek Walcott, Kamau Brathwaite and Opal Palmer Odisa. The magazine is over 300 pgs., 6×9, handsomely printed on heavy stock, perfect-bound, with glossy card cover, using advertising and b&w art by Caribbean artists. Press run is 1,000. Single copy: $10 plus $1.50 postage; subscription: $18/2 years. Sample: $5 plus $1.50 postage. Send SASE for guidelines. (Note: Postage to and from the Virgin Islands is the same as within the US.)

How to Submit: Submit up to 5 poems. No previously published poems; simultaneous submissions OK. Submissions by e-mail OK. No fax submissions. Blind submissions only: name, address, phone number and title of ms should appear in cover letter along with brief bio. Title only on ms. Deadline is September 30 of each year. The annual appears in the spring. Publishes theme issues. Send SASE for guidelines. Pays 2 copies. Acquires first North American serial rights. Reviews books of poetry and fiction in 500 words. Open to unsolicited reviews. Poets may also send books for review consideration.

Also Offers: The magazine annually awards The Daily News Prize ($300) for the best poem or poems, The Marguerite Cobb McKay Prize to a Virgin Island author ($100), The David Hough Literary Prize to a Caribbean author ($500), The Canute A. Brodhurst Prize for Fiction and The Charlotte and Isidor Paiewonsky Prize ($200) for first-time publication. Website includes work from previous issues and current issue, along with biographies and photos of contributors.

N: ⊕ ◎ CARN; THE CELTIC LEAGUE (Specialized: ethnic, foreign language), 11 Hilltop View, Braddan, Isle of Man, phone/fax (UK)(0)1624-627128, website www.manxman.co.im/cleague, founded 1973, general secretary Bernard Moffatt.
Magazine Needs: *Carn* is a magazine-sized quarterly, circulation 2,000. "The aim of our quarterly is to contribute to a fostering of cooperation between the Celtic peoples, developing the consciousness of the special relationship which exists between them and making their achievements and their struggle for cultural and political freedom better known abroad."
How to Submit: "Contributions to *Carn* come through invitation to people whom we know as qualified to write more or less in accordance with that aim. We would welcome poems in the Celtic languages if they are relating to that aim. If I had to put it briefly, we have a political commitment, or, in other words, *Carn* is not a literary magazine." Reviews books of poetry only if in the Celtic languages.

N: ◑ ◎ CARNEGIE MELLON MAGAZINE (Specialized: university affiliation), Carnegie Mellon University, Bramer House, Pittsburgh PA 15213, phone (412)268-2132, editor Ann Curran.
Magazine Needs & How to Submit: *CMM* is the alumni magazine for the university and limits selections to writers connected with the university. Single copies: $2. Submit 3 poems at a time (typed, double-spaced, with SASE) to Gerald Costanzo, poetry editor. No payment. Only uses staff-written reviews.

✔ ◑ THE CAROLINA QUARTERLY; THE CHARLES B. WOOD AWARD, CB #3520 Greenlaw Hall, University of North Carolina, Chapel Hill NC 27599-3520, phone (919)962-0244, e-mail cquarter@unc.edu, website www.unc.edu/student/orgs/cquarter, founded 1948, poetry editor Christopher Windolph.
Magazine Needs: *Carolina Quarterly* appears 3 times a year publishing fiction, poetry, reviews, nonfiction and graphic art. They have no specifications regarding form, length, subject matter or style of poetry. They also consider translations of work originally written in languages other than English. They have published poetry by Denise Levertov, Richard Wilbur, Robert Morgan, Ha Jin and Charles Wright. *TCQ* is about 90 pgs., 6×9, professionally printed and perfect-bound with one-color matte card cover, a few graphics and ads. They receive about 6,000 poems a year, accept less than 1%. Press run is 1,500 for 200 library subscriptions and various shelf sales. Subscription: $12, $15 (institution). Sample: $5.
How to Submit: No previously published poems or simultaneous submissions. SASE required. Poems are circulated to an editorial board. "Manuscripts that make it to the meeting of the full poetry staff are discussed by all. Poems are accepted by majority consensus." Seldom comments on rejections. Responds in 4 months. "Poets are welcome to write or phone about their submission's status, but please wait about four months before doing so." Pays 2 copies. Acquires first rights. Reviews books of poetry. Poets may also send books for review consideration (attn: Editor).
Also Offers: The Charles B. Wood Award for Distinguished Writing is given to the author of the best poem or short story published in each volume of *The Carolina Quarterly*. Only those writers *without* major publications are considered and the winner receives $500. Website includes the history of the publication, subscription information, writer's guidelines, contents of current issue and index to poetry and fiction from 1948-present.

◎ ◑ CAROLINA WREN PRESS (Specialized: women, ethnic, gay/lesbian, social issues), 120 Morris St., Durham NC 27701, phone (919)560-2738, e-mail carolinawrenpress@compuserve.com, founded 1976.
Book/Chapbook Needs: Publishes 1 book/year, "primarily women and minorities, though men and majorities also welcome." They have published poetry by Jaki Shelton Green, Mary Kratt and Steven Blaski.
How to Submit: They currently are not accepting any unsolicited mss. Send 9½ × 12 SASE for catalog (include postage for 3 ounces).
Also Offers: "We are launching our new North American Poetry Chapbook Series with George Elliott Clarke's *Gold Indigoes*."

◐ CARPE LAUREATE DIEM; MIDDLE GEORGIA ASSOCIATION OF WORDSMITHS AND ARTISTS, 3063 Stokes Store Rd., Forsyth GA 31029, e-mail laureate@rose.net, website home.rose.net/~heidiho/, founded 1995, hard copy editor Emily Worthington, electronic editor Heidi Pehrson.
Magazine Needs: *Carpe Laureate Diem* is published quarterly to "encourage new/unpublished writers and artists and to bring poetry and art to people who don't usually see new poets and artists." They want "poetry you feel passionately about. No graphic, erotica/pornography; no harsh profanity (remember children contribute and read)." They have published poetry by Mike Catalano, Kent Clair Chamberlain, John Grey and Tim Scannell. *CLD* is 24 pgs. (printed on 1 side only), 8½ × 11, photocopied and corner-stapled, includes b&w line drawings. They receive about 400 poems a year, accept approximately 90%. Press run is 400 for 50 subscribers; the rest distributed free to area businesses. Subscription: $8. Sample: $3. Make checks payable to Emily Worthington.

How to Submit: "Will not be accepting submissions for the rest of 2000. Will begin accepting again in 2001." Submit 3 poems at a time. Previously published poems OK; no simultaneous submissions. "Cover letters are appreciated and will make a difference in the way we perceive your submission." E-mail submissions OK, prefer MS Publisher, Word Perfect or Microsoft Office formats. "One poem to a page, typed preferred—must be legible if handwritten." Time between acceptance and publication is 3-6 months. Often comments on rejections. Publishes theme issues occasionally. Send SASE for guidelines and upcoming themes or obtain via e-mail. Responds in 2 months. Sometimes sends prepublication galleys. Pays 1 copy (extra copies available at reduced rate). Acquires one-time rights. Reviews books and chapbooks of poetry and other magazines. Open to unsolicited reviews. Poets may also send books for review consideration.

Also Offers: Each issue features a Readers' Choice contest in three categories—adult writer, young writer and artist. "Person with the most reader votes wins a prize. Prize is usually writing- or art-related such as books, handheld recorders or pencil sets."

Advice: "Please be patient with us, sometimes we are slow because we have an extremely small staff."

CATAMOUNT PRESS; COTYLEDON (Specialized: anthology, nature/rural/ecology), 2519 Roland Rd. SW, Huntsville AL 35805-4147, founded 1992, editor Georgette Perry.

Magazine Needs: *Cotyledon*, founded in 1997, published 4 times a year is a miniature magazine. They want poems up to 8 lines. Nature and the environment are favorite subjects, but a variety of subject matter is needed. Poets published include Rosemary J. Wentworth, Paul Willis, Carl Mayfield and Patricia G. Rourke. It is 16 pgs., $3\frac{1}{2} \times 4\frac{1}{4}$, photocopied, saddle-stapled, with bond cover and b&w art.

How to Submit: Submit 3-6 poems at a time with cover letter and SASE. Previously published poems OK if identified as such. Send three unattached first-class stamps for a sample *Cotyledon*, guidelines and news of press offerings and plans. Responds in 2 months. Pays at least 2 copies.

Book/Chapbook Needs & How to Submit: Catamount Press publishes one to two $5\frac{1}{2} \times 8\frac{1}{2}$ chapbooks or anthologies/year. Poets who have had poems in *Cotyledon* have a better chance of acceptance. As a sample the editor selected a poem by David Gross:

> dry spell/under the log bridge/trickle of blue phlox

CAVEAT LECTOR, 400 Hyde St., Apt. 606, San Francisco CA 94109-7445, phone/fax (415)928-7431, founded 1989, editors Christopher Bernard, James Bybee and Andrew Towne.

Magazine Needs: Appearing 2 times/year, "*Caveat Lector* is devoted to the arts and to cultural and philosophical commentary. We publish visual art and music as well as literary and theoretical texts. We are looking for accomplished poems, something that resonates in the mind long after the reader has laid the poem aside. We want work that has authenticity of emotion and high craft whether raw or polished, that rings true—if humorous, actually funny, or at least witty. Classical to experimental. 500-line limit." They have published poetry by Mary Winters, Taylor Graham, Les Murray, Simon Perchik, Lee Chilcote, among others. As a sample the editor selected these lines from "To A Friend Who Has Not Written," by Christopher Hewitt:

> You must have some news./I do. The asters bloomed. There's/still no rain./Oh and I go often to/A place
> I found/Where leaves are letters falling/All of which I've written.//How I exhaust myself/Catching
> them!

The editors say *CL* is 36-64 pgs., $11 \times 4\frac{1}{4}$, photocopied and saddle-stitched with b&w card cover. They receive about 600-800 poems a year, accept less than 2%. Press run is 300 for 30 subscribers, 200 shelf sales. Single copy: $3.50; subscription: $15/4 issues. Sample: $3.

How to Submit: Submit up to 6 short poems (up to 50 lines each), 3 medium length poems (51-100 lines), or 1 long poem (up to 500 lines) at a time "on any subject, in any style, as long as the work is authentic in feeling and appropriately crafted." Place name, address, and (optional) telephone number on each page. Include SASE, cover letter, and brief bio (30 words or less). Simultaneous submissions OK, "but please inform us." Time between acceptance and publication is 1 year. Sometimes comments on rejections. Responds in 1 month. Pays 5 copies. Acquires first publication rights.

Advice: "The two rules of writing are: 1. Rewrite it again. 2. Rewrite it again. The writing level of most of our submissions is pleasingly high. A rejection by us is not always a criticism of the work, and we try to provide comments to our more promising submitters."

CC. MARIMBO COMMUNICATIONS, P.O. Box 933, Berkeley CA 94701-0933, founded 1996, editor Peggy Golden, staff Randy Fingland.

Book/Chapbook Needs: CC. Marimbo Communications "promotes the work of underpublished poets/artists by providing a well-crafted, cheap (people's prices) and therefore affordable/accessible, collection." They publish 2-3 poetry titles per year. "Books are issued as 'minichaps' to introduce underpublished poets/artists to the public. Runs done by alphabet, lettered A-Z, AA-ZZ, etc. Short poems for the small format, styles and content welcome in whatever variation. We do not want to see already published work, unless poems previously in print in magazines (attributed), i.e., poems OK, reprintable books not OK." They have published poetry by Errol Miller, Don A. Hoyt and Bert Glick. As a sample the editor selected this poem, "These Kids," from *My Back Yardstick* by Tom Plante:

Singing, these kids/kicking that eternal ball

Chapbooks are usually 40 pgs., 4¼×5¼ or 5½×4¼, offset printed and photocopied, mainly handsewn binding with matt cover, includes art/graphics according to project.

How to Submit: Query first, with a few sample poems and cover letter with brief bio and publication credits, include SASE. Line length for poetry is 25 maximum. Replies to queries in 2 weeks; to mss in 3 months. Pays 5 author's copies (out of a press run of 26), additional copies paid for larger press runs. "Author gets 10% of cover price on all copies sold, except for copies sold to author." Order sample chapbooks by sending $5 (5¢ for p&h).

Advice: "We must keep seeking."

☑ $ ◎ **CC MOTORCYCLE NEWS MAGAZINE (Specialized: sports/recreation)**, P.O. Box 808, Nyack NY 10960-0808, phone (914)353-MOTO, fax (914)353-5240, e-mail info@motorcyclenews.cc, website www.motorcyclenews.cc, founded 1990.

Magazine Needs: *CCMNM* is a monthly containing regional motorcycle news and features. They want motorcycle-related poetry. They say *CCMNM* is tabloid-sized and printed on newsprint. Circulation of 60,000; available in 1,000 motorcycle shops from Washington, DC to Rhode Island to Chicago. Sample: $3. Offers subscriptions. Make checks payable to Motomag Corp.

How to Submit: Submit up to 5 poems at a time. Previously published poems and simultaneous submissions OK. Cover letter required including SASE. Time between acceptance and publication is 1-4 months. Often comments on rejections. Publishes theme issues. Send SASE for guidelines and upcoming themes. Responds in 1 month. Pays $10-25. Buys one-time regional rights and Internet rights.

☑ $ ⊘ **CEDAR HILL PUBLICATIONS; CEDAR HILL REVIEW**, P.O. Box 15, Mena AR 71953, phone (501)394-7029, founded 1996, managing editor Gloria Doyle, senior editor Christopher Presfield, poetry editor Maggie Jaffe, editorial assistant Thom Hofman.

Magazine Needs: *Cedar Hill Review* is "eclectic in its taste (formal and free verse) but favors contemporary themes and engaged poetry. Nothing racist, sexist or anti-environment." They have published poetry by Hayden Carruth, Leonard Cirino, Yannis Ritsos, Sharon Doubiago, Adrian C. Louis, Virgil Suarez, Sara Saper Gauldin, Joanne Lowery, Michael McIrvin, Jimmy Santiago Baco and Jon Forrest Glade. As a sample the editor selected these lines from "Conversation in the Kitchen at 3 a.m." by J. Mills:

> *This is what I know about love/my father said/then he leaned forward/kissed my tense face/and left the room.*

CHR is 64 pgs., 5½×8½, professionally printed and perfect-bound with laminated cover, includes cover art. They receive about 2,000 poems a year, accept approximately 10%. Press run is 300 for 200 subscribers of which 10 are libraries; 50 distributed free to institutions. Single copy: $6; subscription: $15. Sample: $4. Make checks payable to Cedar Hill Publications.

How to Submit: Submit 5 poems at a time, September through May, to Maggie Jaffe at 3438 Villa Terrace, San Diego CA 92104-3424, (619)294-4924, e-mail mjaffe@mail.sdsu.edu. Previously published poems and simultaneous submissions OK. Cover letter required. Responds in up to 6 months. Acquires all or one-time rights. Returns rights upon publication. Reviews books of poetry and occasionally other journals.

Book/Chapbook Needs & How to Submit: Cedar Hill Publications "seeks to publish the best sound North America has to offer." They publish 10 paperbacks and 2 chapbooks/year. Books are usually 64-80 pgs., 5½×8½, professionally printed and perfect-bound with laminated cover with art. "Must appear in *Cedar Hill Review* for book consideration." Replies to queries and mss in 1 month.

☑ ◉ **CENTER PRESS; MASTERS AWARDS**, Box 17897, Encino CA 91416, e-mail news7@letterbox.com, website http://members.xoom.com/CenterPress, founded 1980, editor Gabriella Stone.

Book/Chapbook Needs & How to Submit: Center Press is "a small press presently publishing 6-7 works per year including poetry, photojournals, calendars, novels, etc. We look for quality, freshness and that touch of genius." In poetry, "we want to see verve, natural rhythms, discipline, impact, etc. We are flexible but verbosity, triteness and saccharine make us cringe. *We now read and publish only mss accepted from the Masters Award.*" They have published books by Bebe Oberon, Walter Calder, Exene Vida, Carlos Castenada and Sandra Gilbert. As a sample the editor selected these lines from "The Patriot" by Scott Alejandro Sonders:

> *Underwire bras/and other implements/of torture, are remnants of the Inquisition./It would be best to set/the breast free to hang, as a proud silk flag/on a windless day.*

Their tastes are for poets such as Adrienne Rich, Li-Young Lee, Charles Bukowski and Czeslaw Milosz. "We have strong liaisons with the entertainment industry and like to see material that is media-oriented and au courant."

Also Offers: "We sponsor the Masters Awards, established in 1981, including a $1,000 grand prize annually plus each winner (and the five runners-up in poetry) will be published in a clothbound edition and distributed to selected university and public libraries, news mediums, etc. There is a one-time only $15 administration and reading fee per entrant. Submit a maximum of five poems or song lyric pages (no tapes) totaling no more than 150 lines. Any poetic style or genre is acceptable, but a clear and fresh voice, discipline, natural rhythm and a certain individuality should be evident. Further application and details available with a #10 SASE."

Advice: "Please study what we publish before you consider submitting."

CHACHALACA POETRY REVIEW, English Dept., UT-Brownsville, Brownsville TX 78521, fax (956)544-8988, founded 1997, contact Marty Lewis.

Magazine Needs: *CPR* is "published once or twice a year, depending on number of submissions. We are looking for thematic substance and crafted lines in the poetry we publish. That doesn't often mean standard stanza pattern or any particular style, but there should be some connection between form and content. We don't accept poems with skinny, three syllable lines, intrusive rhymes, arbitrary line breaks, random indentation, or center justification just because the PC can do it. No haikus or prose poems. Because of space limitations, we usually can't use poems of more than 60 lines." They have published poetry by Lola Rodriquez, Vivian Shipley, Virgil Suarez and Nathan Whiting. As a sample the editor selected these lines from "What to Do with Hands" by Anne Giles Rimbey:

> My pain lets down like milk and whitens our tea./I am trying to tell you what my father/said:
> Understanding is not black or white but/surface with typography. Equal heights reached/here or there.
> I shape hands in a hill over/teapots like I am conjuring. Or praying.

Chachalaca is 50-100 pgs., professionally printed and perfect-bound with no ads. Press run is 500 with 200 distributed free to libraries, 100 shelf sales. Single copy: $8. Sample: $4.

How to Submit: Submit 5-10 poems at a time. Include SASE. No previously published poems; simultaneous submissions OK "if you alert us." Cover letter with short bio preferred. Time between acceptance and publication varies. Poems are circulated to an editorial board of 3 readers. Seldom comments on rejections. Responds in 2 months or more. Pays 2 copies. Buys all rights. Returns rights.

Advice: "*Chachalaca* is fairly new, but its editors are experienced and the journal is well supported."

CHAFF, 4400 Shamrock, Unit 1A, McHenry IL 60050, e-mail jordan5450@aol.com, founded 1996, first issue 1997, editor Jordan Taylor Young.

Magazine Needs: *Chaff* is a semiannual publication "dedicated to the Lord, for the express purpose of reaching out to a lost and hurting world, as well as uniting Christian poets through the publication of their work." They want "free verse poetry—rhyme and meter only if exceptional quality—romance, nature, aging, friendship, family life, animals, mystery, senior citizens, social issues, children and humor. Nothing satanic, obscene, violent, sensual, erotic or homosexual." Also accepts poetry written by children, ages 8 and older. As a sample the editor selected this poem, "This Miracle Mile" by Jordan Taylor Young:

> Who gives/music/to the/songbird,/feathered limbs/for flight,/what determines/when the/stars should/
> shine, and/bid the/morning night.//I often/ask/on bended/knee/by what possessed/this smile,/for I am/
> but a feeble/guest/upon/this/miracle mile.

Chaff is 20-30 pgs., 5½×8, laser-printed and stapled. Press run is 50-100. Single copy: $6. Poetry may be complemented by appropriate photographs, illustrations or scripture. In addition, *Chaff* includes a "Featured Poet" segment, consisting of a short bio and photograph.

How to Submit: Submit no more than 5 poems at a time with $2/poem reading fee. Make checks payable to Jordan Taylor Young, editor. Previously published poems and simultaneous submissions OK. Cover letter and SASE required. E-mail submissions OK. Responds in 1 month. Pays 2 copies, 3 copies to Featured Poet.

Advice: "Often poets are not recognized for their artistry, separated like chaff from wheat. The name *Chaff* stems from my deep conviction that we are like chaff, and separated from God we can do nothing. We intend to provide a stronger link to self, helping new and aspiring poets to find their own voices through the publication of their work. 'For where your treasure is, there will your heart be also.' (Matthew 6:21)."

CHALLENGER INTERNATIONAL; MCNAUGHTON EDITIONS (Specialized: teen/young adult), 440 McNaughton Ave., McNaughton Center, Quesnel, British Columbia V2J 3K8 Canada, phone (250)991-5567, e-mail lukivdan@hotmail.com, founded 1978, editor Dan Lukiv.

Magazine Needs: *Challenger international*, a literary quarterly, contains poetry, short fiction, novel excerpts, and black pen drawings. The editor says he is open to "any type of work, especially by teenagers (*Ci*'s mandate: to encourage young writers, and to publish their work alongside established writers), providing it is not pornographic, profane, or overly abstract." He has published poetry from Canada, the US and Columbia. As a sample the editor selected "At the Graveyard" by Dan Lukiv:

> An old man/On a bench coughs/As children play/Like lion cubs.//He chews lunch—/Corned beef in a
> can—/And speaks to himself/As one boy secretly/Stares.

Ci is about 20 pgs., 8½×11, photocopied and side-stapled. Press run is 100. The journal is distributed free to McNaughton Center-secondary alternate-students.

How to Submit: Previously published poems and simultaneous submissions OK. Cover letter required with list of credits, if any. E-mail submissions OK. Sometimes comments on rejections. "No SASE (or SAE and IRC) means submission goes into the garbage. Sometimes we edit to save the poet rejection." Responds in 4 months. Pays 1 copy.

SENDING TO A COUNTRY other than your own? Be sure to send International Reply Coupons (IRCs) instead of stamps for replies or return of your manuscript.

Book/Chapbook Needs & How to Submit: McNaughton Editions publishes chapbooks of work by authors featured in *Ci*. Pays 3 copies. Copyright remains with authors. They have published *Polaris*, by Nick Vair. Distribution of free copies through the Quesnel Library.

Advice: "Clarity of image and theme—that gets our attention."

⊕ ✓ $ ◎ **CHAPMAN (Specialized: ethnic); CHAPMAN PRESS**, 4 Broughton Place, Edinburgh EH1 3RX Scotland, phone (0131)557-2207, fax (0131)556-9565, e-mail editor@chapman-pub.co.uk, website www.chapman-pub.co.uk, founded 1970, editor Joy Hendry.

Magazine Needs: "*Chapman* magazine is controversial, influential, outspoken and intelligent. Founded in 1970, it has become a dynamic force in Scottish culture covering theatre, politics, language and the arts. Our highly-respected forum for poetry, fiction, criticism, review and debate makes it essential reading for anyone interested in contemporary Scotland. *Chapman* publishes the best in Scottish writing—new work by well-known Scottish writers in the context of lucid critical discussion. It also, increasingly, publishes international writing. With our strong commitment to the future, we energetically promote new writers, new ideas and new approaches." They have published poetry and fiction by Alasdair Gray, Liz Lochhead, Sorley MacLean, T.S. Law, Edwin Morgan, Willa Muir, Tom Scott and Una Flett. As a sample the editor selected these lines from Judy Steel's poem "For Nicole Boulanger" who, Steel says, "was born in the same year as my daughter and died in the Lockerbie air disaster of 1988":

> *You died amongst these rolling Border hills:/The same our daughters played and rode and walked in -/*
> *They make a nursery fit to shape and mould/A spirit swift as water, free as air.//But you, west-winging*
> *through the Christmas dark/Found them no playground but a mortuary -/Your young life poised for*
> *flight to woman's years/Destroyed as wantonly as moorland game.*

Chapman appears 4 times a year in a 6×9, perfect-bound format, 104 pgs., professionally printed in small type on matte stock with glossy card cover, art in 2 colors. Press run is 2,000 for 900 subscribers of which 200 are libraries. They receive "thousands" of poetry submissions/year, use about 200, have a 4- to 6-month backlog. Sample: £4 (overseas).

How to Submit: "We welcome submissions which must be accompanied by a SASE/IRC. Please send sufficient postage to cover the return of your manuscript. Do not send foreign stamps." Submit 4-10 poems at a time, one poem/page. "We do not usually publish single poems." Cover letter required. No simultaneous submissions. Responds "as soon as possible." Always sends prepublication galleys. Pays copies. Staff reviews books of poetry. Send books for review consideration.

Book/Chapbook Needs: Chapman Press is currently not accepting submissions.

Also Offers: Website includes sample of current issue, guidelines, back list of issues and publications.

Advice: "Poets should not try to court approval by writing poems especially to suit what they perceive as the nature of the magazine. They usually get it wrong and write badly." Also, they are interested in receiving poetry dealing with women's issues and feminism.

$ ◙ **THE CHARITON REVIEW**, Truman State University, Kirksville MO 63501, phone (816)785-4499, founded 1975, editor Jim Barnes.

Magazine Needs: *The Chariton Review* began in 1975 as a twice yearly literary magazine and in 1978 added the activities of the press (now defunct). The poetry published in the magazine is, according to the editor, "open and closed forms—traditional, experimental, mainstream. We do not consider verse, only poetry in its highest sense, whatever that may be. The sentimental and the inspirational are not poetry for us. Also, no more 'relativism': short stories and poetry centered around relatives." They have published poetry by Michael Spence, Neil Myers, Sam Maio, Andrea Budy, Charles Edward Eaton, Wayne Dodd and J'laine Robnolt. There are 40-50 pages of poetry in each issue of the *Review*, a 6×9, flat-spined magazine of over 100 pages, professionally printed, glossy cover with photographs. Circulation is about 600 for 400 subscribers of which 100 are libraries. They receive 8,000-10,000 submissions/year, of which they use 35-50, with never more than a 6-month backlog. Subscription: $9/1 year, $15/2 years. Sample: $5.

How to Submit: Submit 5-7 poems at a time, typescript single-spaced. No simultaneous submissions. Do *not* write for guidelines. Response times here are quick, and accepted poems often appear within a few issues of notification. Always sends prepublication galleys. Pays $5/printed page. Buys first North American serial rights. Contributors are expected to subscribe or buy copies. Open to unsolicited reviews. Poets may also send books for review consideration.

$ ◙ **THE CHATTAHOOCHEE REVIEW**, Georgia Perimeter College, 2101 Womack Rd., Dunwoody GA 30338, phone (770)551-3019, website www.dc.peachnet.edu/~twadley/cr/index.htm, founded 1980, editor-in-chief Lawrence Hetrick, poetry editors (Mr.) Collie Owens and Steven Beauchamp.

Magazine Needs: *The Chattahoochee Review* is a quarterly of poetry, short fiction, essays, reviews and interviews, published by Georgia Perimeter College. "We publish a number of Southern writers, but *CR* is not by design a regional magazine. All themes, forms and styles are considered as long as they impact the whole person: heart, mind, intuition, and imagination." They have published poetry by Joanne Childers, Robert Dana, Mildred Greear, Rosemary Daniell and John Frederick Nims. *The Review* is 140 pgs., 6×9, professionally printed on cream stock with b&w reproductions of artwork, flat-spined, with one-color card cover. Recent issues feature a wide range of forms and styles augmenting prose selections. Circulation is 1,250, of which 300 are complimentary copies sent to editors and "miscellaneous VIPs." Subscription: $16/year. Sample: $6.

How to Submit: Writers should send 1 copy of each poem and a cover letter with bio material. No simultaneous submissions. Time between acceptance and publication is 3-4 months. Publishes theme issues. Send SASE for guidelines and upcoming themes. Queries will be answered in 1-2 weeks. Responds in 3 months. Pays $50/poem and 2 copies. Acquires first rights. Staff reviews books of poetry and short fiction in 1,500 words, single or multi-book format. Send books for review consideration.

☑ $☑ ◎ CHELSEA; CHELSEA AWARD COMPETITION (Specialized: translations), P.O. Box 773, Cooper Station, New York NY 10276-0773, e-mail chelseamag@aol.com, founded 1958, editor Richard Foerster, senior associate editor Alfredo de Palchi, associate editor Andrea Lockett.

☑ Work published in *Chelsea* has been included in the 1995, 1997 and 1998 volumes of *The Best American Poetry*.

Magazine Needs: *Chelsea* is a long-established, high quality literary biannual, appearing in June and December, that aims to promote intercultural communication. "We look for intelligence and sophisticated technique in both experimental and traditional forms. We are also interested in translations of contemporary poets. Although our tastes are eclectic, we lean toward the cosmopolitan avant-garde. We would like to see more poetry by writers of color. Do not want to see 'inspirational' verse, pornography or poems that rhyme merely for the sake of rhyme." They have published poetry by Timothy Liu, Virgil Suarez, Reginald Shepherd, Karen Volkman, Carl Phillips and Brenda Shaughnessy. As an example of "the kind of attention to language and imagery" wanted for *Chelsea*, the editor selected these lines from "The Eye-mote" by Sylvia Plath, which first appeared in *Chelsea* in 1960:

> What I want back is what I was/Before the bed, before the knife,/Before the brooch-pin and the salve/
> Fixed me in this parenthesis;/Horses fluent in the wind,/A place, a time gone out of mind.

Chelsea is 192-240 pgs., 6×9, perfect-bound, offset printed, full-color cover art on card cover, occasional photos, ads. Circulation is 2,100 for 900 subscribers of which 200 are libraries. Subscription: $13 domestic, $16 foreign. Sample: $7.

How to Submit: Submissions of 5-7 pgs. of poetry are ideal; long poems should not exceed 10 pgs.; must be typed; include brief bio. No previously published poems or simultaneous submissions. E-mail for queries only, not for submissions. "We try to comment favorably on above-average mss; otherwise, we do not have time to provide critiques." Responds within 3 months. Always sends prepublication galleys. Pays $20/page and 2 copies. Buys first North American serial rights and one-time nonexclusive reprint rights.

Also Offers: Sponsors the annual Chelsea Award Competition (deadline December 15), $1,000 for poetry. Guidelines available by SASE to P.O. Box 1040, York Beach ME 03910 or by e-mail to chelseamag@aol.com.

Advice: "Beginners should realize editors of little magazines are always overworked and that it is necessary haste and not a lack of concern or compassion that makes rejections seem coldly impersonal."

Ⓝ ⊕ $☐ ◯ ◑ ◎ CHERRYBITE PUBLICATIONS; HELICON; REACH (Specialized: subscription), Linden Cottage, 45 Burton Rd., Little Neston, South Wirral CH64 4AE England, e-mail helicon@glo balnet.co.uk, founded 1993, editor Shelagh Nugent.

Magazine Needs: *Helicon* is a quarterly poetry journal. Poems may be any style or length. Poets are strongly advised to study the magazine before submitting. Also accepts poetry written by children. They have published poetry by Albert Russo, M. Munro Gibson, RL Cook and Fiona Curnow. *Helicon* is 40 pgs., A5, neatly printed and saddle-stitched with card cover, occasionally includes line drawings, ads. They receive about 2,000 poems a year, accept approximately 2%. Press run is 400. Single copy: 9 IRCs; subscription: 31 IRCs. "Must buy at least one copy before submitting. The standard is high."

Magazine Needs: Also publishes the bimonthly poetry magazine *Reach*. It contains "poetry and letters, sometimes short articles. *Reach* intends to encourage beginners but uses a lot of established poets." They have published poetry by Eric Holt, Denise Margaret Hargrave, K.T. Frankovitch (US) and Tara Dawn (US). Its format is similar to *Helicon*'s. They receive about 1,500 poems a year, accept approximately 20%. Press run is 400. Single copy: 6 IRCs; subscription: 30 IRCs for 4 copies. Subscription required for consideration.

How to Submit: For *Helicon* and *Reach*, submit 6 poems at a time. Previously published poems OK; no simultaneous submissions. Cover letter required. "No e-mail submissions accepted." Time between acceptance and publication is 6 months. Often comments on rejections. SAE and 2 IRCs for guidelines. Responds in 2 weeks. *Helicon* pays £2 sterling or credit vouchers for overseas work. *Reach* does not pay. For both journals, copyright remains with the author.

Also Offers: Sponsors regular competitions and "several booklets of use to poets and writers." Publishes the *Competitions Bulletin*, a bimonthly magazine containing details of UK writing competitions. Send IRC for details.

Advice: "Never send submissions without studying a magazine first. Always send a cover letter."

☑ ◎ CHICAGO REVIEW (Specialized: translations), 5801 S. Kenwood, Chicago IL 60637-1794, phone/fax (773)702-0887, e-mail org_crev@orgmail.uchicago.edu, website www.humanities.uchicago.edu/huma nities/review/, founded 1946, poetry editor Devin Johnston.

Magazine Needs: "We publish high quality poetry. About 10% of the work we select is unsolicited; the remainder is solicited from poets whose work we admire. Translations are welcome, but please include a statement of permission from the original publisher if work is not in the public domain." They have published poets as diverse as Alice Fulton, Yusef Komunyakaa, Turner Cassity, Nathaniel Mackey, August Kleinzahler, Meena Alexander and Anne Carson. Circulation is 2,800. Sample: $6.

How to Submit: Queries and guideline requests may be sent/requested via fax and e-mail. No electronic submissions. Responds in 3 months, longer in some cases. Sometimes sends prepublication galleys. Pays 3 copies and one-volume subscription. Occasionally reviews books of poetry. Open to unsolicited reviews.

☑ ◯ **CHILDREN, CHURCHES AND DADDIES; SCARS PUBLICATIONS**, P.O. Box 150, Intercourse PA 17534, e-mail ccandd96@pa.freei.net, website www.yotko.com/scars, founded 1993, editor and publisher Janet Kuypers.

Magazine Needs: *Children, Churches and Daddies (the unreligious, non-family oriented literary magazine)* is published "monthly or bimonthly depending on year and contains news, humor, poetry, prose and essays. We specialize in electronic issues and collection books. We accept poetry of almost any genre, but we're not keen on rhyme for rhyme's sake, and we're not keen on religious poems (look at our current issue for a better idea of what we're like). We like gay/lesbian/bisexual, nature/rural/ecology, political, social issues, women/feminism. We do accept longer works, but within two pages for an individual poem is appreciated. We don't go for racist, sexist (therefore we're not into pornography either), or homophobic stuff." They have published poetry by Rochelle Holt, Virginia Love Long, Pete McKinley and Janine Canan. As a sample we selected these lines from the publisher's own poem "Scars 1997":

> I wear my scars like badges./These deep marks show through from under my skin/like war paint on
> an Apache chief./Decorated with feathers, the skins of his prey.

The publisher says the print version of *CCAD* is about 100 pgs., 8 × 11, photocopied and saddle-stitched, cover, includes art and ads. They receive hundreds of poems a year, accept approximately 40%. Press run "depends." Sample: $5.50. Make checks payable to Janet Kuypers.

How to Submit: Prefers electronic submissions. Submit via e-mail in body of message, explaining in preceding paragraph that it is submission or mail floppy disk with ASCII text or Macintosh disk. Previously published poems and simultaneous submissions OK. Seldom comments on rejections. Send SASE for guidelines or obtain via e-mail or website. Responds in 2 weeks.

Also Offers: Scars Publications sometimes sponsors a book contest. Write or e-mail for information. Website includes writer's guidelines, past issues archives, past books archive, writers' work, art, awards, interactive poetry, names of editors, poetry, interviews. "The website is a more comprehensive view of what *CC&D* does. All the information is there."

☑ ◻ ◯ ◪ **CHIRON REVIEW; CHIRON BOOKS; CHIRON REVIEW POETRY CONTEST; KINDRED SPIRIT PRESS**, 702 N. Prairie, St. John KS 67576-1516, phone (316)549-6156 or (316)786-4955, e-mail chironreview@hotmail.com, website www.geocities.com/SoHo/Nook/1748/, founded 1982 as *The Kindred Spirit*, editor Michael Hathaway, assistant editor Shon Fox, contributing editor (poetry) Gerald Locklin.

Magazine Needs: *Chiron Review* is a quarterly tabloid using photographs of featured writers. No taboos. Also accepts poetry written by children. They have published poetry by John Gilgun, Douglas Airmet, Paul Snoek, Alison Pelegrin and Paul Agostino Hafiz. As a sample the editor selected this poem, "Blue Cellophane" by Melissa Huseman:

> How about that neat piece of blue/cellophane floating into your yard on the wind?///See, Lorna, God
> still loves you./God dropped his eye into your sky.//Go grab that piece of blue. To love it you gotta/
> look at the world as if you're not in it.

Each issue "contains dozens of poems." Their press run is about 1,000. Sample: $4 ($8 overseas or institutions).

How to Submit: Submit 3-6 poems at a time, "typed or printed legibly." No simultaneous submissions or previously published poems. No submissions via e-mail. Very seldom publishes theme issues. Send SASE for guidelines and upcoming themes. Responds in 2 months. Pays 1 copy. Acquires first-time rights. Reviews books of poetry in 500-700 words. Open to unsolicited reviews. Poets may also send books for review consideration.

Book/Chapbook Needs & How to Submit: For book publication submit complete ms. They publish 1-3 chapbooks/year, flat-spined, professionally printed, paying 25% of press run of 100-200 copies.

Also Offers: Their annual poetry contest offers awards of $100 plus 1-page feature in Winter issue, $50, and 5 free subscriptions and a Chiron Press book. Entry fee: $5/poet. Website includes guidelines, sample poems, contest information, news and notes, and Personal Publishing Program information. They feature their Personal Publishing Program under the Kindred Spirit Press imprint. "Through special arrangements with a highly specialized printer, we can offer extremely short run publishing at unbelievably low prices." Send SASE for information. They also host the annual Chiron Review Poetry Festival the first weekend in August each year in St. John, KS. Website includes writer's guidelines, names of editors, poetry samples, contest info and book publishing.

☑ $ ◪ ◎ **THE CHRISTIAN CENTURY (Specialized: religious, social issues)**, Dept. PM, 104 S. Michigan Ave., Suite 700, Chicago IL 60603, phone (312)263-7510, fax (312)263-7540, website www.ChristianCentury.com, founded 1884, named *The Christian Century* 1900, founded again 1908, joined by *New Christian* 1970, poetry editor Jill Peláez Baumgaertner.

Magazine Needs: This "ecumenical weekly" is a liberal, sophisticated journal of news, articles of opinion and reviews from a generally Christian point-of-view, using approximately 1 poem/issue, not necessarily on religious themes but in keeping with the literate tone of the magazine. They want "poems that are not statements but experiences, that do not talk about the world, but show it. We want to publish poems that are grounded in images and that reveal an awareness of the sounds of language and the forms of poetry even when the poems are written in free verse." They do not want "pietistic or sentimental doggerel." They have published poetry by Jeanne Murray Walker, Ida Fasel, Kathleen Norris, Luci Shaw, J. Barrie Shepherd and Wendell Berry. As a sample the editor selected this poem, "Rapture" by Ashley Mace Havird:

> In a straight-backed pew/on the balcony's front row,/I keep my distance./Still, the sunburst/of red-hot
> gladiolus,/fireball mums,/spikes me blind. . . .

The journal is magazine-sized, printed on quality newsprint, using b&w art, cartoons and ads, about 30 pgs., saddle-stapled. Sample: $3.
How to Submit: Submit poems of up to 20 lines, typed and double-spaced, 1 poem/page. Include your name, address and phone number on the first page of each poem. "Prefer shorter poems." No simultaneous submissions. Submissions without SASE or SAE and IRCs will not be returned. Pays usually $20/poem plus 1 copy and discount on additional copies. Acquires all rights. Inquire about reprint permission. Reviews books of poetry in 300-400 words, single format; 400-500 words, multi-book format.

$ 🗓 ◐ THE CHRISTIAN SCIENCE MONITOR, The Home Forum Page, One Norway St., Boston MA 02115, website www.csmonitor.com, founded 1908, poetry editor Elizabeth Lund.
Magazine Needs: *CSM* is an international daily newspaper. Poetry used regularly in The Home Forum. They want "finely crafted poems that explore and celebrate daily life. Seasonal material always needed. Especially interested in poems with an urban flavor. No violence or sensuality. Poems about illness, death or suffering are not a good fit. Short work preferred." They have published work by Diana Der-Hovanessian, Marilyn Krysl and Michael Glaser. As a sample the editor included these lines from "Carpe Diem" by Marilyn Krysl:

> Three bees seize/this opportunity to/buzz me, but see://now, instead of three,/there are many: lazy,/
> buzzing me and the blue//felicias, three convened/to please the powers that/be, bees and me and this

How to Submit: Submit up to 5 poems at a time, single-spaced. SASE must be included. "No faxed submissions please." No previously published poems or simultaneous submissions. Usually responds within 2 months. Pays varying rates, upon publication.
Also Offers: A "small (but growing) poetry section includes interviews, reviews, a teacher's guide, Poem of the Month and more. They also sponsor an annual poetry contest for children (preschool through high school). Entries are accepted from October 1 to November 30.
   📱 Website includes all of the daily paper, submission guidelines and original content.

◯ ◐ ◎ CHRISTIANITY AND THE ARTS (Specialized: religious), P.O. Box 118088, Chicago IL 60611, phone (312)642-8606, fax (312)266-7719, e-mail chrnarts@aol.com, website www.christianarts.net, founded 1994, editor/publisher Marci Whitney-Schenck, poetry editor Robert Klein Engler (and submissions should go directly to him at 901 S. Plymouth Ct., Apt. 1801, Chicago IL 60605).
Magazine Needs: *Christianity and the Arts* is a quarterly magazine designed "to celebrate the revelation of God through the arts and to encourage excellent Christian artistic expression." They want poetry of "excellence—open to all styles—with a Christian viewpoint. Although we are a Christian magazine, we will consider most types of poetry. Please no 'inspirational' verse, light verse or erotica." All submissions must be original and previously unpublished. They have published poetry by Lucy Shaw, Judith Deem Dupree and Carl Winderl. It is 72 pgs., 8½×11, professionally printed on coated stock and saddle-stapled, with b&w and color photos. They accept 20% of the poetry received. Press run is 5,500 for 4,000 subscribers. Single copy: $7; subscription: $21. Sample: $7.
How to Submit: No e-mail submissions. Simultaneous submissions OK. Time between acceptance and publication is 6 months. Publishes theme issues. Send SASE for upcoming themes. Themes for November 2000, February 2001, May 2001, August 2001 and November 2001 are Lord of the Dance, Emmaus, Popular Culture, Simple Gifts and Eve and Mary in the Arts, respectively. Responds in up to 3 months. Always sends prepublication galleys. Pays 2 copies. Acquires first or one-time rights.
Also Offers: Sponsors annual contest. See website or send SASE for details.
   📱 Website contains original content not found in print edition. Contact: Marci Johnson.
Advice: "We wish to support the efforts of Christian poets, however we get more poetry than any other type of writing. We can't publish everyone's wonderful efforts but we do try to include as many poems as possible, especially when the poems concern our themes. Many submissions read more like prayers than poems. We are looking for quality verse."

$ ◐ ◎ CHRYSALIS READER (Specialized: spirituality, themes), Rt. 1 Box 184, Dillwyn VA 23936-9616, fax (804)983-1074, e-mail chrysalis@hovac.com, founded 1985, poetry editor Robert F. Lawson, editor Carol S. Lawson,
Magazine Needs: *Chrysalis Reader* is published by the Swedenborg Foundation as a "contribution to the search for spiritual wisdom." Appearing annually, it is a "book series that draws upon diverse traditions to engage thought on questions that challenge inquiring minds using literate and scholarly fiction, essays and poetry." They want poetry that is "spiritually related and focused on the particular issue's theme. Nothing overly

religious or sophomoric." They have published work by Jan Frazier, William Kloefkorn, Linda Pastan, Julia Randall, Robert Bly, Peter Bethanis, Pat Schneider and Tom O'Grady. As a sample the editor selected these lines from "The Only Love That Lasts" by Kate Gleason:

> *I want to grow alike/in the grand tradition of great marriages,/want our faces to wrinkle like wax paper/that's been used and smoothed and used again.*

CR is 208 pgs., 7×10, professionally printed on archival paper and perfect-bound with coated cover stock, illustrations and photos. They receive about 1,000 poems a year, use 2-5%. Press run is 3,500. Sample: $10.

How to Submit: Submit no more than 5 poems at one time. No previously published poems or simultaneous submissions. Time between acceptance and publication is typically 18 months. Send SASE for themes and guidelines. Upcoming theme is Education. Responds in 3 months. Always sends prepublication galleys. Pays $25 and 3 copies. Buys first-time rights. "We expect to be credited for reprints after permission is given."

Advice: "When time permits, editorial suggestions are offered in the spirit of all good literature."

THE CHURCH-WELLESLEY REVIEW; XTRA! (Specialized: gay/lesbian), 491 Church St., Suite 200, Toronto, Ontario M4Y 2C6 Canada, fax (416)925-6503, website www.xtra.ca/cwr/.

● *Xtra!*, the review's parent magazine, has received several community awards as well as a journalism award for a column on Living with AIDS.

Magazine Needs: *The Church-Wellesley Review* is the annual supplement for *Xtra!* (Canada's largest gay/lesbian newspaper.) "We want wild humour, fast-paced drama, new takes on old themes, gays and lesbians in other contexts. Our aim is always quality, not style. Although we prefer non-traditional poetry, we have in the past published a contemporary 30-line 'up-dating' of Chaucer called 'Provincetown Tales.' Amaze us or amuse us, but just don't bore us." They have published Shyam Selvadurai, Paul Russell, Camilla Gibb, Timothy Findley, Chocolate Waters and David Watmough. The magazine receives over 1,000 submissions/year. Press run is 37,000 in Toronto plus 22,000 in Vancouver and is distributed free.

How to Submit: Poetry can be any length ("no epics, please"). Manuscripts should include up to 8 poems with name on every page, daytime phone number and 50-word bio. Submissions accepted all year round. "We respond as soon as possible." Payment is made in Canadian funds within one month of publication. Staff reviews books of poetry. Send books for review consideration to the attention of Fiction Editor.

Also Offers: Publishes a quarterly website.

CIDER PRESS REVIEW, P.O. Box 881914, San Diego CA 92168, founded 1997, co-editors Caron Andregg and Robert Wynne.

Magazine Needs: *Cider Press Review* appears twice a year and features "the best new work from contemporary poets." They want "thoughtful, well-crafted poems with vivid language and strong images. We prefer poems that have something to say. We would like to see more well-written humor. No didactic, inspirational, greeting-card verse; therapy or religious doggerel." They have published poetry by Jackson Wheeler, Janet Holmes, W.D. Snodgrass and Gary Young. As a sample the editors selected these lines from "Why My Father Smoked" by Jennifer Lesh:

> *Just before he'd shake/open a newspaper and block me from sight,/he'd blow me a ring, two, three, fat/as hoopskirts, and as these dissolved/into my laughter, my father/would slide slowly into silence/of important words and men.*

The editors say *CPR* is 120 pgs., digest-sized, offset printed and perfect-bound with 2-color coated card cover. They receive about 1,500 poems a year, accept approximately 5%. Press run is 750. Subscription: $20/2 issues. Sample: $10.

How to Submit: Submit up to 5 poems at a time. No previously published poems; simultaneous submissions OK. Cover letter with short bio preferred. "Please include two SASEs. Poets whose work is accepted will be expected to provide a copy of the poem on disk. Do not send unsolicited disk submissions." Time between acceptance and publication is 6-10 months. Poems are circulated to an editorial board. Seldom comments on rejections. Obtain guidelines via website. Responds in up to 6 months. Pays 1 copy. Acquires first North American serial rights.

$ CIMARRON REVIEW, 205 Morrill Hall, Oklahoma State University, Stillwater OK 74078-0135, founded 1967, poetry editor Lisa Lewis.

Magazine Needs: *Cimarron* is a quarterly literary journal. "We take pride in our eclecticism. We like evocative poetry (lyric or narrative) controlled by a strong voice. No sing-song verse. No quaint prairie verse. No restrictions as to subject matter. We look for poems whose surfaces and structures risk uncertainty and which display energy, texture, intelligence, and intense investment." Among poets they have published are Dorothy Barresi, Cesare Pauese, Mark Doty, Tess Gallagher, David Rivard and Albert Goldbarth. This magazine, 100-150 pgs., 6×9, perfect-bound, boasts a handsome design, including a color cover and attractive printing. Poems lean toward free verse, lyric and narrative, although all forms and styles seem welcome. There are 15-25 pages of poetry in each issue. Circulation is 500 of which most are libraries. Single copy: $5; subscription: $16/year ($20 Canada), $45/3 years ($55 Canada), plus $2.50 for all international subscriptions.

How to Submit: Submit 3-5 poems, name and address on each, typed single- or double-spaced. No simultaneous submissions. No response without SASE. Pays $15 for each poem published, 1 copy and a subscription. Buys all rights. "Permission for a reprinting is granted upon request." Reviews books of poetry in 500-900 words, single book format, occasionally multi-book. All reviews are assigned.

CITY LIGHTS BOOKS, 261 Columbus Ave., San Francisco CA 94133, phone (415)362-1901, founded 1955, edited by Lawrence Ferlinghetti and Nancy J. Peters.
Book/Chapbook Needs & How to Submit: City Lights Books is a paperback house that achieved prominence with the publication of Allen Ginsberg's *Howl* and other poetry of the "Beat" school. They publish "poetry, fiction, philosophy, political and social history." Simultaneous submissions OK. "All submissions must include SASE." Responds in 2 months. Payment varies.

CLACKAMAS LITERARY REVIEW; WILLAMETTE AWARD, 19600 South Molalla Ave., Oregon City OR 97045, phone (503)657-6958 ext. 2520, website www.clackamas.cc.or.us/cirs/b/clr, founded 1997, editors Jeff Knorr and Tim Schell.
The *Clackamas Literary Review* received the Community College Humanities Association's Best New Magazine Award.
Magazine Needs: "The *Clackamas Literary Review* is a nationally distributed magazine that publishes quality literature. It is an annual magazine produced at Clackamas Community College under the direction of the English Department. *CLR* promotes the work of emerging writers and established writers of fiction, poetry, and creative nonfiction." They consider all quality poetry. They have published poetry by Beckian Fritz Goldberg, Walt McDonald, Paul Berg, Amanda Coffey and Pamela Rice Porter. The editors say *CLR* is 150-200 pgs., 6×9, paperback. They receive about 1,800 poems a year, accept approximately 5%. Press run is 1,500 for 400 subscribers of which 20 are libraries, 420 shelf sales; 211 distributed free to graduate programs. Single copy: $6; subscription: $10/1 year, $20/2 years. Sample: $3. Make checks payable to *CLR*.
How to Submit: Submit 4 poems at a time. No previously published poems; simultaneous submissions OK. "Please inform us if your submitted work is accepted elsewhere." Cover letter with bio and SASE required. Reads submissions September 1 through June 1 only. Time between acceptance and publication is 2-6 months. Poems are circulated to an editorial board. Seldom comments on rejections. Send SASE for guidelines or obtain via website. Responds in 4 months. Acquires first North American serial rights.
Also Offers: Sponsors Willamette Award for fiction and poetry. The winning prize in each category is $500. Send no more than 6 poems or 1 story to *CLR* by June 1. Entry fee: $10. "Each contestant will receive a copy of the journal. Follow our general submission guidelines for submitting work and remember that if you wish return of the manuscript or notification you must enclose a SASE. All work submitted to the contest will also be considered for inclusion in the journal." Judges for upcoming contests will be announced.
Advice: "Always submit your best work."

THE CLAREMONT REVIEW (Specialized: teens/young adults), 4980 Wesley Rd., Victoria, British Columbia V8Y 1Y9 Canada, phone (250)658-5221, fax (250)658-5387, e-mail review@claremont.victoria.bc.ca, website 206.12.151.253, founded 1991, contact Susan Stenson.
Magazine Needs: *The Claremont Review* is a biannual review which publishes poetry and fiction written by those ages 13 to 19. Each fall issue also includes an interview with a prominent Canadian writer. They want "vital, modern poetry with a strong voice and living language. We prefer works that reveal something of the human condition. No clichéd language nor copies of 18th and 19th century work." Also accepts poetry written by children, ages 13-19. They have published poetry by Jen Wright, Erin Egan and Max Rosenblum. As a sample the editors selected these lines from "The Last Room" by Jen Wright:
> These men study death./They say it is congestive heart failure,/brain hemorrhage, invasive tumor./But
> that's not what you showed me/one child's day/after we found a robin, frozen, on the porch.

The Claremont Review is 110 pgs., 6×9, professionally printed and perfect-bound with an attractive color cover. They receive 600-800 poems a year, publish 120. Press run is 700 for 200 subscribers of which 50 are libraries, 250 shelf sales. Subscription: $12/year, $20/2 years. Sample: $6.
How to Submit: Submit poems typed one to a page with author's name at the top of each. No previously published poems; simultaneous submissions OK. Cover letter with brief bio required. Reads submissions September through June only. Always comments on rejections. Send SASE (or SAE and IRC) for guidelines. Responds in up to 6 weeks (excluding July and August). Pays 1 copy and funds when grants allow it. Acquires first North American serial rights.
Also Offers: Website include writer's guidelines.
Advice: "We strongly urge potential contributors to read back issues of *The Claremont Review*. That is the best way for you to learn what we are looking for."

THE OPENNESS TO SUBMISSIONS INDEX at the back of this book lists all publishers in this section by how open they are to submissions.

N ☻ ◎ CLARK STREET REVIEW (Specialized: form/style, narrative poetry), P.O. Box 1377, Berthoud CO 80513, phone (970)669-5175, e-mail clarkreview@earthlink.net, website www.home.earthlink.net/~clarkreview, founded 1998, editor Ray Foreman.

Magazine Needs: Appearing 6 times a year, *CSR* publishes narrative poetry and short shorts—"to give writers and poets cause to keep writing by publishing their best work. (*Clark Street Review* was previously *Coffeehouse Magazine* which published for 8 years.)" They want "narrative poetry under 150 lines that reach readers who are mostly published poets and writers. Subjects are open. No obscure and formalist work." They have published poetry by Laurel Speer, Steven Levi, Errol Miller and Ray Clark Dickson. As a sample the editor selected these lines from "those days" by Lamar Thomas:

> Through fog and smoke a long ash crooks/at my cigarette's end./It feels like a Hopper diner,/stark, sad
> eyes, a conversation stalls,/she sits steady, pieta-like in blue light./I stare through the steam of my
> coffee.

CSR is 24 pgs., digest-sized, photocopied and saddle-stitched with paper cover. They receive about 500 poems a year, accept approximately 25%. Press run is 200 for 90 subscribers; 30 distributed free to "appreciative but broke readers." Subscription: $10 for 10 issues postpaid. Sample: $1. Make checks payable to R. Foreman—"prefer cash or stamps."

How to Submit: Submit 1-10 poems at a time. Line length for poetry is 20 minimum, 150 maximum. Previously published poems and simultaneous submissions OK. "Disposable copies only—sharp copies. Maximum width—65 characters. SASE or e-mail address for reply. No cover letter." Time between acceptance and publication is 3 months. "Editor reads everything with a critical eye of 30 years of experience in writing and publishing small press work." Often comments on rejections. Publishes theme issues occasionally. Send SASE for guidelines or obtain via e-mail. "If one writes narrative poetry, they don't need guidelines. They feel it." Responds in 3 weeks. Pays 1 copy. Acquires one-time rights.

Advice: "*Clark Street Review* is geared to the more experienced poets and writer. There are tips throughout each issue writers appreciate. As always, the work we print speaks for the writer and the magazine. We encourage communication between our poets by listing their e-mail and home addresses. Publishing excellence and giving writers a cause to write is our only aim."

◎ THE CLASSICAL OUTLOOK (Specialized: themes, translations, classics, Latin), Classics Dept., Park Hall, University of Georgia, Athens GA 30602-6203, phone (706)542-9257, fax (706)542-8503, e-mail mricks@arches.uga.edu, founded 1924, editor Prof. Richard LaFleur, poetry editors Prof. David Middleton (original English verse) and David Slavitt (translations and original Latin verse).

Magazine Needs: *The Classical Outlook* "is an internationally circulated quarterly journal (4,200 subscriptions, of which 250 are libraries) for high school and college Latin and Classics teachers, published by the American Classical League." They invite submissions of "original poems in English on classical themes, verse translations from Greek and Roman authors, and original Latin poems. Submissions should, as a rule, be written in traditional poetic forms and should demonstrate skill in the use of meter, diction and rhyme if rhyme is employed. Original poems should be more than mere exercise pieces or the poetry of nostalgia. Translations should be accompanied by a photocopy of the original Greek or Latin text. Latin originals should be accompanied by a literal English rendering of the text. Submissions should not exceed 50 lines." They have published work by James Fowler and Victor Howes. As a sample the editors selected these lines from "The Swan" by Peter Huggins:

> Zeus in the clouds saw her, as he had seen/So many others, and just as he'd done before,/He hit upon
> a way to possess her/And deceive Hera too. Bird shape was more//Appealing to him and elegant as a
> swan he flew/Down to take her, not thinking of history,/Not allowing himself one glimpse of lovely
> Helen,/Or Clytemnestra, or noble Andromache

There are 2-3 magazine-sized pgs. of poetry in each issue, and they use 15% of the approximately 350 submissions they receive each year. They have a 12- to 18-month backlog, 4-month lead time. Single copy: $10.

How to Submit: Submit 2 anonymous copies, double-spaced, no more than 5 poems at a time. No previously published or simultaneous submissions. "Please include a floppy disk containing work, if possible. Also, please identify the name and version number of word-processing package used." Poetry is refereed by poetry editors. Send SASE for guidelines or request via e-mail or fax. Responds in up to 9 months. Pays 2 copies. Sample copies are available from the American Classical League, Miami University, Oxford OH 45056 for $10. Reviews books of poetry "if the poetry is sufficiently classical in nature."

Advice: "Since our policy is to have poetry evaluated anonymously, names and addresses on poems, etc., just make work at this end. Cover letters are not forwarded to the poetry editors. Also, we never knowingly publish any works which have been or will be published elsewhere."

N ◖ ◪ CLAY PALM REVIEW: ART AND LITERARY MAGAZINE, 8 Huntington St., Suite 307, Shelton CT 06484-5228, e-mail claypalm@cs.com, website www.claypalmreview.com, founded 1999 (premier issue, spring/summer 2000), founder/editor Lisa Cisero.

Magazine Needs: Published biannually, *Clay Palm Review* "aims to introduce new and already established poets. We would like to create a place for the imagination to flourish. The public needs to become culturally aware, and I feel that poets and artists understand their connection to life and one another. We accept well-crafted poetry with specific attention to detail and imagery. The poem must appeal to the senses and be full of texture, void of cliché language. Translations are always welcomed. We encourage the writer to experiment with their

insider report

What poetry is all about: finding meaning through simplicity

In the early summer of 1999, Lisa Cisero established a new art and literary magazine, *Clay Palm Review*. This slightly larger than digest-sized, perfect-bound, glossy-covered collection of art and literature features approximately eighty pages of poetry, color artwork, translations, streams of consciousness, short fiction, letters, essays and interviews. Cisero says she will also "print a featured youth page for artists and writers under the age of fourteen who would like to be introduced to the world of professional publication."

Lisa Cisero

Clay Palm Review received its title from Cisero's love of the "earth and an interest in Native American tradition and spirituality, as well as art sculptures and poetry (using your hands to form)." She believes it's "what poetry is all about: finding meaning through simplicity. *Palm* displays a connection to humankind. I have always loved the images of hands and palms in photography and magazine ads. It is my own unique creation, a line of poetry in itself."

Cisero brings to *Clay Palm Review* a BFA in Creative Writing and English Literature from Roger Williams University in Bristol, Rhode Island. Along with a certificate from The Institute of Children's Literature in West Redding, Connecticut, and a year of graduate studies, Cisero is on her way to a career as a creative writing professor. She worked closely with RWU's literary magazine, *Calliope*, and has worked as an editorial assistant for *Fairfield County Magazine*, out of Westport, Connecticut. Promoting poetry, she hosts an open mic night at a local coffee bar, offers workshops and is a member of the Connecticut Poetry Society.

This new publication promises to be an exquisite sampling of today's most talented individuals, giving both the authors/artists and their readers an enjoyable literary and visual adventure, as well as a place to let their work be seen. Cisero plans to "publish high quality writing and artwork that appeals to the senses." She says, "It is extremely hard to pinpoint the exact style I am looking for—it usually comes forth as a miracle! I am looking for the poet/writer to introduce the world in ways that have never been used before—through the use of imagery, new language, and the writer/poet's own style."

Cisero encourages the writer/poet "to avoid cliched language and to understand what cliched language is before submitting. Many people submit 'Hallmark' material, and this is what I avoid. For example, instead of blue, why not cerulean, aquamarine, topaz or indigo? The poet must breathe life into the piece, let it serve as life for the reader, let it paint a vivid scene, spark emotion within the reader, let it be their lifeblood. Some people who contribute overdo it! The talent must be within the poet in order for them to expand upon it."

Here is an example from Heather MacLeod's poem that shows Cisero's preference as an editor:

"Seven Reasons"

She comes for me in the evenings
when the sagehill blossoms on the hills,
and the smell of freshly cut grass
lifts itself up and floats like gossamer wings,
like the colour of madrigals
through my bedroom window.
She takes me to a woman, covered
in Egyptian cotton, pale, irises like tattoos
inside the palms of her hands. Maps instead
of veins, journeys instead of blood.

Last winter I photographed the Eiffel Tower;
I lie awake in the mornings dreaming
of each step, rising and falling,
the long walk up, the endless descent,
the good view.

I fell in love once, wanted to marry him,
wanted to wake each morning, in a variety
of places, with him lying, quiet, beside me.
None of that happened, he married
someone else, her breasts round and full,
her hair long and dark; I wake up alone,
photographs of Paris, Venice and Ephesus
rising like rotund orbs, full and calling;
Cairo resting in the back of my mind,
Muslims praying, holy water on my forehead,
geography all over the soles of my feet.

The train, across the river, rattles
its way through my dreams and imagination;
I wake to its hum in the night. I remember
how I was brought to this land when I was small,
carried in a basket, a light cotton blanket over me.

I feel unformed,
sometimes almost anonymous, as if who I am
is a kaleidoscope of information
and misrepresentation; and I fall forward
crushing my worries which scurry
across the floor like beetles.

Christ comes to me,
loves me in the nights,
and leaves me covered, light film
of sand from Jerusalem,
lemon markings against my pale neck.
I wear a medallion of Saint Michael
standing above the dragon; Christ comes
in cabalistic ways, has dried
my tears with his hair.

I would like to settle down in Eden,
carry water in a ceramic jug atop my head;
I'd like to settle down in the ground,
cross-legged in the dust; I'd like to be properly
adorned, tribal designs to cover my chest,
the rise and slope of breast and belly;
I'd like to settle into my clan. And I would like
a man to fill my days up with desire
and after the desire has been filled, I'd like
to find abundance; the word: plenty.

(by Heather Macleod, originally published in spring/summer 2000 issue of *Clay Palm Review*; reprinted by permission of the author)

Clay Palm Review has received submissions from writers across the globe. The first issue is filled with international poetry, an interview with longtime poet Duane Locke and more. Its second issue boasts a wonderful essay on poetry as a craft written by Professor Tim Bellows from Sierra College. Both Duane Locke and Tim Bellows have a solid publishing base and have amassed a fine list of publication credits.

Each new issue of *Clay Palm Review* promises to deliver quality art and literature with "the majority of the magazine composed of poetry, one or two short fiction pieces, one interview or essay and about six color art pieces," says Cisero.

Cisero offers a bit of her philosophy, speaking to poets and readers who will surely enjoy her new creation. "Poetry is a passageway into understanding ourselves," she says. "The less tangible aspects serve as a connector, a lifeline to those around us. I've always likened my mind to a museum, an ever-expanding gallery of words, whether spoken or born against the silence of the page. It is essential, in order to function day to day, that we discover our hidden passion, delve beneath the stress and strain of everyday life to create a balance between reality and our perception of it and discover what, in thirty, forty, fifty years down the road is most essential to our existence."

Looking at today's best upcoming talent gives direction for our artistic and literary exposure. Cisero conquers today with the best of tomorrow in *Clay Palm Review*.

—Judy Gripton

language, to be unique and different." Also accepts poetry written by children. "There will be a 'featured youth' page in every issue for aspiring writers, 14 and under, who would like to be introduced to the world of professional writing and publication. There will also be a 'special to this issue' section including featured essays or interviews." *CPR* does not accept rhyme, vulgarity, social or political content, science fiction or depressive material. They have published poetry by Duane Locke, Tim Bellows, Heather MacLeod, Ruth Daigon, Martha Christina and Trace Weatherford. As a sample the editor selected these lines from "Seven Reasons" by Heather MacLeod:

> She takes me to a woman, covered/in Egyptian cotton, pale, irises like tattoos/inside the palms of her hands. Maps instead/of veins, journeys instead of blood./. . . Muslims praying, holy water on my forehead,/geography all over the soles of my feet.

The editor says *CPR* is about 70 pgs., "a bit larger than digest-sized," offset printed and perfect-bound with glossy cover, includes colored artwork and ads. Single copy: $8; subscription: $15. Sample: $6.

How to Submit: Submit 5-6 poems at a time. Previously published poems OK "only with written consent from publisher"; no simultaneous submissions. Cover letter required. E-mail submissions OK, "but not preferred." Disk submissions OK. "Each poem must include the name and address of the poet in the upper right hand corner, along with copyright date. A SASE must always be included. No handwritten submissions." Reads submissions July through September for fall/winter issue and December through March for spring/summer issue. Submit seasonal poems 3-4 months in advance. Time between acceptance and publication is about 4 months. "Submissions are given an extensive review, in order to decide whether they meet the satisfaction of the editor. They are then accepted, rejected, or held for future use. Always comments upon the drafts, creating a working relationship with the poet." Publishes theme issues occasionally. Obtain guidelines via website. "Also welcome to e-mail any questions." Responds in up to 4 months. Sometimes sends prepublication galleys. Pays 1 copy. Acquires first North American serial rights. "The rights revert back to the poet after publication. We do need to be recognized as the first-time publisher."

Advice: "Poets should always review guidelines before submitting. Purchasing a sample copy is best to determine whether your writing style meets our needs. Revise, revise, revise! The more you write the more 'polished' you become. As long as you are passionate about what you write, you will succeed."

$ ◎ CLEANING BUSINESS MAGAZINE; CLEANING CONSULTANT SERVICES, INC. (Specialized: cleaning, self-employment), P.O. Box 1273, Seattle WA 98111, phone (206)622-4241, fax (206)622-6876, e-mail wgriffin@cleaningconsultant.com, website www.cleaningconsultants.com, founded 1976, poetry editor William R. Griffin.

Magazine Needs: *CBM* is "a monthly magazine for cleaning and maintenance professionals" and uses some poetry relating to their interests. "To be considered for publication in *Cleaning Business*, submit poetry that relates to our specific audience—cleaning and self-employment." He has published poetry by Don Wilson, Phoebe Bosche, Trudie Mercer and Joe Keppler. The editor says it is 100 pgs., 8½ × 11, offset litho printed, using ads, art and graphics. They receive about 50 poems a year, use approximately 10. Press run is 5,000 for 3,000 subscribers of which 100 are libraries, 500 shelf sales. Single copy: $5; subscription: $20. Sample: $3.

How to Submit: No previously published poems; simultaneous submissions OK. Send SASE and $3 for guidelines. Pays $5-10 plus 1 copy.

Advice: "Poets identify a specific market and work to build a readership that can be tapped again and again over a period of years with new books. Also write to a specific audience that has a mutual interest. We buy poetry about cleaning, but seldom receive anything our subscribers would want to read."

☑ ◯ ◎ CLEVELAND STATE UNIVERSITY POETRY CENTER; CSU POETRY SERIES; CLEVELAND POETS SERIES; CSU POETRY CENTER PRIZE (Specialized: regional), 1983 E. 24 St., Cleveland OH 44115-2440, phone (216)687-3986, or toll-free (888)278-6473, fax (216)687-6943, e-mail poetrycenter@csuohio.edu, website www.ims.csuohio.edu/poetry/poetrycenter.html, coordinator Rita Grabowski, editors Dave Evett, Bonnie Jacobson, Ted Lardner and Ruth Schwartz. The Poetry Center was founded in 1962, first publications in 1971.

Book/Chapbook Needs: The Poetry Center publishes the CSU Poetry Series for poets in general and the Cleveland Poets Series for Ohio poets. "Open to many kinds of form, length, subject matter, style and purpose. Should be well-crafted, clearly of professional quality, ultimately serious (even when humorous). No light verse, devotional verse or verse in which rhyme and meter seem to be of major importance." They have published *Buried Treasure* by Dan Bellm; *Fresh Kills* by David Breskin; *After the Rain, Les Barricades Mysterieuses, Pincushion's Strawberry* and *Work for the Night is Coming* by Jared Carter; *Body Betrayer* and *In the Badlands of Desire* by Beckian Fritz Goldberg; *Hammerlock* and *Hurdy-Gurdy* by Tim Seibles; *The Obsidian Ranfla* by Anthony Vigil; and *The Door Open to the Fire* by Judith Vollmer. As a sample the editors selected "Amatory Salute" from *Cocktails with Brueghel at the Museum Cafe* by Sandra Stone:

> I want to be negligent tonight in front of the eye of the fire,/that bounder with a single eye, falsely hot.//Let me be negligent as a flare for myself, that searer,/negligently to cast my shadow, a wanton,// in front of that singed eye,/lascivious in its glow.//I am stunned by its fiery narrative,/its salutary tongue.

Books are chosen for publication from the entries to the CSU Poetry Center Prize contest. (Write and send $2 for catalog of Poetry Center books.) Postmark deadline: February 1. Entry fee: $20. The winner receives $1,000 and publication. They publish some other entrants in the Poetry Series, providing 50 copies (out of a press run of 1,000) and $300 lump sum. The Cleveland Poets Series (for Ohio poets) offers 100 copies of a press run of 600.

How to Submit: To submit for all series, send ms between November 1 and February 1 only. Responds to all submissions for the year by the end of July. No e-mail submissions. Mss should be for books of 50-100 pgs., pages numbered, poet's name, address and phone number on cover sheet, clearly typed. Poems may have been previously published (listed on an acknowledgment page). Simultaneous submissions OK, if notified and "poet keeps us informed of change in status." Send e-mail or SASE for guidelines.

Also Offers: The Center also publishes other volumes of poetry, including chapbooks (20-50 pgs.), with a $15 reading fee for each submission (except for Ohio residents, who can submit without the fee). Chapbook submissions are not eligible for the $1,000 prize.

THE CLIMBING ART (Specialized: nature/rural/ecology, sports/recreation), 6390 E. Floyd Dr., Denver CO 80222, phone/fax (303)757-0541, e-mail rmorrow@dnur.uswest.net, founded 1986, editor Ron Morrow.

Magazine Needs: *The Climbing Art* is a biannual journal "read mainly by mountain enthusiasts who appreciate good writing about mountains and mountaineering. We are open to all forms and lengths. The only requirement is that the work be fresh, well-written and in some way of interest to those who love the mountains." They have published poetry by Terry Gifford, Allison Hunter, Paul Willis, Denise K. Simon and Barry Govenor. *TCA* is 160 pgs., digest-sized, professionally printed on heavy stock with glossy card cover. They use 12-20 poems/issue, receive 50 submissions/month. Press run is 1,500 for 700 subscribers of which 10 are libraries, 500 shelf sales. Subscription: $18. Sample: $4.

How to Submit: Simultaneous submissions and previously published poems OK. Responds in 6 months. Sometimes sends prepublication galleys. Pays 2 copies and subscription. Acquires one-time rights. Reviews books of poetry only if they concern mountains. Open to unsolicited reviews.

CLÓ IAR-CHONNACHTA (Specialized: bilingual/foreign language), Indreabhán, Co. Galway, Ireland, phone (091)593307, fax (091)593362, e-mail cic@iol.ie, website www.cic.ie, founded 1985, contact Deirdre O'Toole.

Book/Chapbook Needs: Publishes paperback books of Irish language poetry, one of which is selected through a competition. They have published collections of poetry by Cathal Ó Searcaigh, Nuala Ni Dhomhnaill, Gabriel Rosenstock, Michael Davitt and Liam ó Muirthile.

How to Submit: Query with 20 sample poems and a cover letter with brief bio and publication credits. Mss are read by an editorial panel. Often comments on rejections. No payment information provided. The poetry competition offers a £5,000 first prize in addition to publication. Next poetry competition 2002. Send SASE (or SAE and IRC) for details.

CLOUD RIDGE PRESS, 815 13th St., Boulder CO 80302, founded 1985, editor Elaine Kohler.

Book/Chapbook Needs: Cloud Ridge Press is a "literary small press for unique works in poetry and prose." They publish letterpress and offset books in both paperback and hardcover editions. In poetry, they publish "strong images of the numinous qualities in authentic experience grounded in a landscape and its people." The first book, published in 1985, was *Ondina: A Narrative Poem* by John Roberts. The book is 6×9¼, handsomely printed on buff stock, cloth bound in black with silver decoration and spine lettering, 131 pgs. 800 copies were bound in Curtis Flannel and 200 copies bound in cloth over boards, numbered and signed by the poet and artist. This letterpress edition, priced at $18/cloth and $12/paper, is not available in bookstores but only by mail from the press. The trade edition was photo-offset from the original, in both cloth and paper bindings, and is sold in bookstores. The press plans to publish 1-2 books/year.

How to Submit: Since they are not accepting unsolicited mss, writers should query first. Queries will be answered in 2 weeks and mss reported on in 1 month. Simultaneous submissions are acceptable. Royalties are 10% plus a negotiable number of author's copies. A brochure is free on request; send #10 SASE.

CLUBHOUSE; YOUR STORY HOUR (Specialized: children, teens), P.O. Box 15, Berrien Springs MI 49103, phone (616)471-3701, website www.yourstoryhour.com, poetry editor Elaine Trumbo.

Magazine Needs: The publication is printed in conjunction with the Your Story Hour radio program, founded 1949, which is designed to teach the Bible and moral life to children. The magazine, *Clubhouse*, started with that title in 1982, but as *Good Deeder*, its original name, it began publication in 1951. The editor says, "We do like humor or mood pieces. Don't like mushy-sweet 'Christian' poetry. We don't have space for long poems. Best—16 lines or under." They have published poetry by Lillian M. Fisher, Audrey Osofsky, Sharon K. Motzko, Bruce Bash and Craig Peters. *Clubhouse*, published monthly, is 20 pgs. The magazine has a circulation of 500, all for subscribers of which maybe 5 are libraries. Subscription: $5/year. Sample cost: 3 oz. postage.

How to Submit: They are closed to submissions until 2001. Simultaneous submissions OK. The "evaluation sheet" for returned mss gives reasons for acceptance or rejection. Writer's guidelines available for SASE. Pays about $12 for poems under 24 lines plus 2 copies. Negotiates rights.

Also Offers: Website includes general information about *Your Story Hour*, current newsletter and the current issue of *Clubhouse*.

$ ◻ ◎ CLUBHOUSE JR. (Specialized: children, religious), 8605 Explorer Dr., Colorado Springs CO 80920, phone (719)531-3400, fax (719)531-3499, founded 1988, associate editor Kim Washburn, editor Jesse Florea.

▓ *Clubhouse Jr.* won the Evangelical Press Association Award for Youth Publication.

Magazine Needs: *Clubhouse Jr.* is a monthly magazine published by Focus on the Family for 4-8 year olds. They want short poems—less than 100 words. "Poetry should have a strong message that supports traditional values. No cute, but pointless work." As a sample the editors selected this poem, "My Friend," by Mary Ryer:

> If I'm feeling very sad/And don't know what to do./If I'm feeling all alone/Or angry through and
> through./I really shouldn't worry/Or sit alone and cry./I always have a friend to help./Jesus is nearby.

Clubhouse Jr. is 16-20 pgs., magazine-sized, web printed on glossy paper and saddle-stapled with 4-color paper cover, includes 4-color art. Press run is about 90,000 for 85,000 subscribers; 500 distributed free. Single copy: $1.50; subscription: $15/year. Sample: $1 with SASE. Make checks payable to Focus on the Family.

How to Submit: Submit up to 5 poems at a time. No previously published poems; simultaneous submissions OK. Cover letter preferred. Time between acceptance and publication is 4-12 months. Seldom comments on rejections. Publishes theme issues occasionally. Send SASE for guidelines. Responds in up to 2 months. Pays $40-100. Acquires first rights.

◖ CLUTCH, 147 Coleridge St., San Francisco CA 94110, founded 1991, editors Dan Hodge and Oberc.

Magazine Needs: *Clutch* is an irregular (1 or 2 issues/year) "alternative/underground literary review." They want "poetry which explores or reveals an edge, societal edges especially. Take chances. Academic, overly-studied poems are not considered." They have published poetry by Charles Bukowski, Lorri Jackson, Todd Moore and Robert Peters. As a sample the editors selected these lines from "1492" by Mitchel Cohen:

> and the syringe is the size of a lover, O yes!/and the kisses, and the bodies,/and the fleshy zipless
> hallucinations/that pass for lovers/are no cure, no cure at all . . .

The editors describe *Clutch* as 60-70 pgs., approximately 5½×8½. "Printing, binding and graphics vary with each issue. We receive approximately 400-500 unsolicited submissions a year, but we accept less than 10% of unsolicited material. The majority of material is solicited." Press run is 200-500 for 40 subscribers of which 6 are libraries, approximately 70 shelf sales. Subscription: $5/issue for as many future issues as specified. Sample: $5. Make checks payable to Dan Hodge.

How to Submit: Simultaneous submissions OK. Cover letter required. Seldom comments on rejections. Responds in 6 months. Pays 1 copy. Rights revert to authors. "Open to publishing reviews of books/magazines from underground press." Poets may also send books for review consideration.

Advice: "Length isn't as important as impact, and I have yet to find a subject that was truly dangerous in its own right. If this doesn't clear things up, buy an issue and get a feel for what we like . . . just don't send a bunch of poems about kitties and butterflies."

◖ COAL CITY REVIEW, English Dept., University of Kansas, Lawrence KS 66045, founded 1989, editor Brian Daldorph.

Magazine Needs: Published in the fall, *CCR* is an annual publication of poetry, short stories, reviews and interviews—"the best material I can find." As for poetry, the editor quotes Pound: " 'Make it new.' " They do not want to see "experimental poetry, doggerel, five-finger exercises or beginner's verse." They have published poetry by Taylor Graham, David Ray, Gary Lechliter and Elliot Richman. As a sample the editor selected these lines from "How to Be a Gay Literary Icon" by Michael Gregg Michaud:

> Say you knew Tennessee Williams./Say you slept with him./He's dead, who'll know?/Enter your latest
> book/in the annual Lambda Literary Awards/and vote for yourself./Be sullen./Be fat with a receding
> hairline/a 44 inch waist/and a mother complex./Frequent hustler bars./Be photographed with Sandra
> Bernhard, Madonna,/or Jeff Stryker.

CCR is 80 pgs., 5½×8½, professionally printed on recycled paper and perfect-bound with light, colored card cover. They accept approximately 5% of the material received. Press run is 200 for 50 subscribers of which 5 are libraries. Subscription: $8. Sample: $5.

How to Submit: Submit 6 poems at a time. Accepts previously published poems occasionally; prefers not to receive simultaneous submissions. "Please do not send list of prior publications." Seldom comments on rejections. Send SASE for guidelines. Responds in up to 3 months. Pays 1 copy. Reviews books of poetry in 300-1,000 words, mostly single format. Open to unsolicited reviews. Poets may also send books for review consideration.

Book/Chapbook Needs & How to Submit: *CCR* also publishes occasional chapbooks as issues of the magazine but does not accept unsolicited chapbook submissions. Their most recent chapbook is *Slowly Along the Riverbeds* by Phil Wedge.

Advice: "Care more (much more) about writing than publication. If you're good enough, you'll publish."

▣ ◯ ◎ COCHRAN'S CORNER (Specialized: subscribers), 1003 Tyler Court, Waldorf MD 20602-2964, phone (301)870-1664, founded 1985, executive editor Jeanie Saunders, poetry editor Billye Keene.

Magazine Needs: *Cochran's Corner* is a "family type" quarterly open to beginners, preferring poems of 20 lines or less. You have to be a subscriber to submit. "Any subject or style (except porn)." Also accepts poetry written by children to age 14. They have published poetry by Jean B. York, Brian Duthins, C.J. Villiano and Annette Shaw. As a sample the editor selected this poem, "Journey," (poet unidentified):

> *You take me to places/Within myself/Where I have never been—/foreign places/Timidly I follow you*
> *through/Subterranian chambers/And/Undiscovered essences/to the/mainstream/that/is/I*

CC is 58 pgs., desktop-published, saddle-stapled, with matte card cover. Press run is 500. Subscription: $20. Sample: $5 plus SASE.

How to Submit: Submit 5 poems at a time. Simultaneous submissions and previously published poems OK. Send SASE for guidelines. Responds in 3 months. Pays 2 copies. Acquires first or one-time rights. Reviews books of poetry. Send books for review consideration.

Also Offers: Sponsors contests in March and July; $5 entry fee for unlimited poems "if sent in the same envelope. We provide criticism if requested at the rate of $1 per page."

Advice: "Write from the heart, but don't forget your readers. You must work to find the exact words that mirror your feelings, so the reader can share your feelings."

THE COE REVIEW, Coe College, 1220 First Ave. NE, Cedar Rapids IA 52402, phone (319)399-8760, e-mail tavandeb@coe.edu, founded 1972, contact Charles Aukema or Tracy Van DeBoom.

Magazine Needs: Published annually in April, *Coe Review* is "a diverse magazine, valuing innovation and originality, preferring well-developed and tasteful content, but eclectic in selection." They have published poetry by James Galvin and Jan Weissmiller. It is 100-150 pgs., flat-spined, digest-sized with matte card cover. "Each issue includes 4-8 reproductions of works of art, usually photographs, lithography and etched prints." Circulation is about 500. Sample: $4.

How to Submit: Submit 3-5 poems at a time. No simultaneous submissions. Include "brief cover letter with biographical information and SASE. We only accept submissions from August 31 through March 15 due to the academic school year." Send SASE for guidelines. Pays 2 copies.

COFFEE HOUSE PRESS, 27 N. Fourth St., Suite 400, Minneapolis MN 55401, phone (612)338-0125, founded 1984, managing editor Chris Fischbach.

Coffee House Press books have won numerous honors and awards. As an example, *The Book of Medicines* by Linda Hogan won the Colorado Book Award for Poetry and the Lannan Foundation Literary Fellowship.

Book Needs: The press publishes 12 books/year, 4-5 of which are poetry. They want poetry that is "challenging and lively; influenced by the Beats, the NY School or Black Mountain." They have published poetry collections by Victor Hernandez Cruz, Anne Waldman and Paul Metcalf.

How to Submit: Submit 8-12 poems at a time. Previously published poems OK. Cover letter and vita required. "Please include a SASE for our reply and/or the return of your ms." Seldom comments on rejections. Replies to queries in 1 month, to mss in 6 months. Always sends prepublication galleys. Send SASE for catalog. No phone calls.

COLD MOUNTAIN REVIEW, English Dept., Appalachian State University, Boone NC 28608, phone (828)262-3098, faculty advisor Kathryn Kirpatrick.

Magazine Needs: *CMR* is published twice a year by graduate students in the English Department at Appalachian State University and features poetry, short fiction, b&w line drawings and photographs. They have no specifications regarding form, subject matter or style of poetry. "Works longer than 15 pages in length are discouraged." They have published poetry by Charles Frazier, Donald Seachrist, Deanne Bayer, Carol Frith and Saleem Peeradina. As a sample the editors selected these lines from "Metamorphosis" by Louise Till:

> *your breath permeating the earth./I heard your soft sigh, looked out my window/To see nothing left*
> *but the strands of your hair/swaying through the plants/And the tips of your breasts/Sprouting*

The editor says *CMR* is about 72 pgs., 6×9, neatly printed with 1 poem/page (or 2-page spread), saddle-stitched, with light card stock cover. They publish about 10% of the submissions received. For sample, send SASE or make donation to ASU Cold Mountain Review.

How to Submit: No simultaneous or previously published submissions. "Please include short biographical sketch, with name, address and phone/e-mail number on each poem." Reads submissions August 25 through November 15 and January 10 through March 15 only. Send SASE for guidelines. Pays 3 copies.

COLLAGES & BRICOLAGES, THE JOURNAL OF INTERNATIONAL WRITING (Specialized: translations, feminist, political, social issues, themes), P.O. Box 360, Shippenville PA 16254, e-mail cb@penn.com, website www.angelfire.com/on2/collagesbricolages/ or www.freeyellow.com/members8/collagesbricolages, founded 1986, editor Marie-José Fortis.

Magazine Needs: *C&B* is a "small literary magazine with a strong penchant for literary, feminist, avant-garde work. We are looking for the innovative, the profound, the provocative, even the lyric. Strongly encourages poets and fiction writers, as well as essayists, whether English-speaking or foreign." (Note: Writers sending their work in a foreign language must have their mss accompanied by an English translation.) As a sample the editor selected these lines from "The Weaver Thumbs" by Gail Cerridwen:

> *The story comes back to me now like a map,/a history that belongs to me, the star sapphire//inherited*
> *and forgotten at the bottom of my jewelry box,/buried under cheap beds, dollar earrings, yellowed*
> *receipts.//Those nineteenth century weavers of India/and their lost thumbs make me want to dig in the*
> *earth,//to uncover their screams, lovingly archive/their dexterity for spinning a silk so fine*

The annual is 130-160 pgs., magazine-sized, perfect bound with card cover. They accept 7% of 900 poetry submissions/year. Press run is 800. Sample: $10 (postage not included for orders outside the U.S.), $5 for back issue.

How to Submit: Submit up to 5 poems at a time, no more (only 1 piece if poem is several pages long). Poems submitted without SASE will neither be read nor returned. Reads submissions August 15 through December 15 only. Publishes theme issues occasionally. Send SASE for upcoming themes. Responds in up to 3 months. Always sends prepublication galleys. Pays 2 copies with 50% off additional copies. Acquires first rights (rights revert to author after publication).

Advice: "It is recommended that potential contributors order a copy, so as to know what kind of work is desirable. We understand that nobody's budget is unlimited, but remember that most lit mags' back issues are half price. Be considerate to editors, as many of them work on a voluntary basis and sacrifice much time and energy to encourage writers. And please, use a SASE that is at least 9½×4″. Show me that you write as if nothing else mattered."

$Ø COLORADO REVIEW; COLORADO PRIZE FOR POETRY, Dept. of English, Colorado State University, Ft. Collins CO 80523, phone (970)491-5449, e-mail creview@vines.colostate.edu, website www.colostate.edu/Depts/English/pubs/colrev/colrev.htm, founded 1955 as *Colorado State Review*, resurrected 1967 under "New Series" rubric, renamed *Colorado Review* 1985, editor David Milofsky, poetry editors Jorie Graham and Donald Revell.

Poetry published in *Colorado Review* has been included in the 1995, 1996 and 1997 volumes of *The Best American Poetry*.

Magazine Needs: *Colorado Review* is a journal of contemporary literature which appears 3 times a year; it combines short fiction, poetry, interviews with articles about significant contemporary poets and writers, articles on literature, culture and the arts and reviews of recent works of the literary imagination. They have published poetry by Karen Volkman, Cal Bedient, Susan Wheeler and Tracy Philpot. *CR* is about 180 pgs., 6×9, professionally printed and perfect-bound with glossy card cover. Circulation is 1,500 for 300 subscribers of which 100 are libraries. They receive about 10,000 submissions a year, use approximately 2%. Subscription: $24/year. Sample: $10.

How to Submit: Submit about 5 poems at a time. Submissions must include SASE for response. No previously published poems or simultaneous submissions. No electronic or e-mail submissions. Reads submissions September 1 through May 1 only. Responds in 2 months. Pays $5/printed page for poetry. Buys first North American serial rights. Reviews books of poetry and fiction, both single and multi-book format. Poets may also send books for review consideration.

Also Offers: Also sponsors the annual Colorado Prize for Poetry, established in 1995, offering an honorarium of $1,500. Complete book must be unpublished. Submit a book-length ms on any subject in any form. Send SASE for guidelines. Entry fee: $25. Deadline: January 8. Most recent award winner was Stephen Burt (1999). Judge was Jorie Graham. Winner will be announced in May. Website includes writer's guidelines, list of editorial staff, subscription guidelines and Colorado Prize for Poetry guidelines.

✓Ø COLUMBIA: A JOURNAL OF LITERATURE AND ART, 415 Dodge Hall, Columbia University, New York NY 10027, phone (212)854-4216, e-mail arts-litjournal@columbia.edu, website www.columbia.edu/cu/arts/writing/columbiajournal/columbiafr.html, founded 1977, editor Monica Ferrell, poetry editor Audra Epstein.

Magazine Needs: *Columbia* appears semiannually and "will consider any poem that is eclectic and spans from traditional to experimental genre." They have published poetry by John Ashbery, Brenda Shaughnessy, Marie Ponset and W.S. Merwin. As a sample the editor selected these lines from "On a Mandarin Inscription" by David Yezz:

> *I have no Chinese; yet how these calligraphs/do articulate the spattered flight of swans,/or pines tortured by sleet on mountain paths./Beside this columned hand, along a pond,/an introspective couple walks in clothes/blazoned with ceremony.*

The editor says *Columbia* is 180 pgs., 6×9, offset printed with notch binding, glossy cover, includes art and ads. They receive about 2,000 poems a year, accept approximately 2%. Press run is 2,000 for 50 subscribers of which 30 are libraries. Single copy: $8. Make checks payable to *Columbia Journal*.

How to Submit: Submit up to 4 poems at a time. No previously published poems; simultaneous submissions OK, when noted. Cover letter preferred. Reads submissions September 1 through May 1 only. Poems are circulated to an editorial board. Seldom comments on rejections. Send SASE for guidelines. "Solicits theme section for each issue. Send SASE for subject and guidelines prior to submitting." Recent themes include Film and Writing; Reinventing Fairy Tales, Myth and Legends; and Beyond Sportswriting: Spectatorship, Exhaustion, Competition. Responds in 6 months. Pays 2 copies. Acquires first North American serial rights.

Also Offers: Sponsors annual contest with an award of $250. Open to submissions January 1 though April 15. Entry fee: $12. Submit no more than 5 poems/entry. All entrants receive a copy of the issue publishing the winners.

▣ ◎ COMMON THREADS; OHIO HIGH SCHOOL POETRY CONTESTS; OHIO POETRY ASSOCIATION (Specialized: membership, students), 3520 State Route 56, Mechanicsburg OH 43044, phone (937)834-2666, founded 1928, editor Amy Jo Zook. Ohio Poetry Association (Amy Renee Daniel, treasurer, 161 Crestview Lane, Tiffin OH 44883), is a state poetry society open to members from outside the state, an affiliate of the National Federation of State Poetry Societies.

Magazine Needs: *Common Threads* is their poetry magazine, appearing twice a year. Only members of OPA may submit poems. They do not want to see poetry which is highly sentimental, overly morbid or porn—and nothing over 40 lines. "We use beginners' poetry, but would like it to be good, tight, revised. In short, not first drafts. Too much is sentimental or prosy when it could be passionate or lyric. We'd like poems to make us think as well as feel something." Also accepts poetry written by children "if members or high school contest winners." They have published poetry by Yvonne Hardenbrook, Betsy Kennedy, Rose Ann Spaith and Dalene Workman Stull. As a sample the editor selected these lines from "September Light" by J.A. Totts:

> My daughters will be home soon,/laughing down the road they call/the dragon's tail, following its
> loops/and tree-cut curves. The faint mutter/of leaf smoke clings to the tall grass,/and I think the dragon
> must be breathing/easily . . .

The magazine is 52 pgs., digest-sized, computer typeset, with matte card cover. "Ours is a forum for our members, and we do use reprints, so new members can get a look at what is going well in more general magazines." Annual dues including *Common Threads*: $15. Senior (over 65): $12. Single copies: $2.

How to Submit: Previously published poems OK, if "author is upfront about them. All rights revert to poet after publication."

Also Offers: Ohio Poetry Association sponsors an annual contest for unpublished poems written by high school students in Ohio with categories of traditional, modern, and several other categories. March deadline, with 3 money awards in each category. For contest information write Ohio Poetry Association, % Elouise Postle, 4761 Willow Lane, Lebanon OH 45036. "Also, we have a quarterly contest open to all poets, entry fee, two money awards and publication. Write to Janeen Lepp, president, 1798 Sawgrass Dr., Reynoldsburg OH 43068 (#10 SASE) or e-mail janeenlepp@juno.com for dates and themes."

$ ◐ ◎ COMMONWEAL (Specialized: religious), 475 Riverside Dr., New York NY 10115, fax (212)662-4183, website www.commonwealmagazine.org, poetry editor Rosemary Deen.

Magazine Needs: *Commonweal* appears every 2 weeks, circulation 20,000, is a general-interest magazine for college-educated readers by Catholics. Prefers serious, witty, well-written poems of up to 75 lines. Does not publish inspirational poems. As a sample the editor selected these lines from "One is One," a sonnet by Marie Ponsot:

> Heart, you bully, you punk, I'm wrecked, I'm shocked/stiff. You? you still try to rule the world—though/
> I've got you: identified, starving, locked/in a cage you will not leave alive . . .

Subscription: $44. Sample: $3.

How to Submit: Considers simultaneous submissions. Reads submissions September 1 through June 30 only. Pays 50¢ a line plus 2 copies. Buys all rights. Returns rights when requested by the author. Reviews books of poetry in 750-1,000 words, single or multi-book format.

Also Offers: Website include writer's guidelines, names of editors, poetry, interviews, samples from current issue, and back issues with table of contents.

☑ ◎ COMMUNITIES (Specialized: intentional community living), 290 McEntire Rd., Tryon NC 28782, phone/fax (828)863-4425, e-mail communities@ic.org, website www.ic.org, founded 1972, editor Diana Christian.

Magazine Needs: *Communities* is a "quarterly publication on intentional communities and cooperative living," occasionally using poetry relevant to those topics. It is 80 pgs., magazine-sized, professionally printed on recycled white stock with 2-color glossy paper cover, perfect-bound. Sample: $6.

How to Submit: Submit any number of poems at a time. SASE required. Previously published poems and simultaneous submissions OK. E-mail and fax submissions OK. Publishes theme issues. Send SASE for upcoming themes. Pays 4 copies and subscription. They also publish the *Communities Directory*.

Advice: "Poets rarely 'get' who we are and what our publication is about, so I reject good poems for wrong content. We're about cooperation and intentional community living."

▣ ◎ A COMPANION IN ZEOR (Specialized: science fiction/fantasy), 307 Ashland Ave., Egg Harbor Township NJ 08234-5568, phone (609)645-6938, fax (609)645-8084, e-mail klitman323@aol.com or karenlitman@juno.com, website www.simegen.com/in-t/Virtualtecton/CZ, founded 1978, editor Karen Litman.

Magazine Needs: *A Companion in Zeor* is a science fiction/fantasy fanzine appearing irregularly on the Internet. Material used is now limited to creations based solely on works (universes) of Jacqueline Lichtenberg. No other submission types considered. Prefer nothing obscene. Homosexuality not acceptable unless very relevant to the piece. Prefer a 'clean' publication image."

How to Submit: Cover letter preferred with submissions; note whether to return or dispose of rejected mss. E-mail and faxed submissions OK. Send SASE for guidelines. Sometimes sends prepublication galleys. Pays 1 copy, "but can negotiate." Acquires first rights. "Always willing to work with authors or poets to help in improving their work." Reviews books of poetry. Open to unsolicited reviews. Poets may also send books for review consideration.

Also Offers: Website includes submission guidelines, excerpts from past issues, and current issues.

☑ ◑ **THE COMSTOCK REVIEW; COMSTOCK WRITERS' GROUP INC.; MURIEL CRAFT BAILEY MEMORIAL PRIZE**, 4958 St. John Dr., Syracuse NY 13215, phone (315)488-8077, e-mail kniles1@t wcny.rr.com, founded 1987 as *Poetpourri*, published by the Comstock Writers' Group, Inc., coordinator Kathleen Bryce Niles.
Magazine Needs: *CR* appears biannually. They use "well-written free and traditional verse. No obscene, obscure, patently religious or greeting card verse." They have published poetry by Charles Atkinson, Virgil Suarez, Susan Terris, Robert Cooperman and Katharyn Howd Machan. As a sample they selected these lines from "Extremity" by Karla Huston:
> I often study the motion/of hands, watch the way skin/and bone form the flutter of fingers,/see them
> unfold like thoughts or/shiver in the air like the thin reeds.
The Comstock Review is about 100 pgs., digest-sized, professionally printed, perfect-bound. Circulation is 600. Subscription: $15/year; $8/issue. Sample: $6.
How to Submit: Submit 3-6 poems at a time, name and address on each page, unpublished poems only. Cover letter with short bio preferred. Poems are read January 1 through February 28 and July 1 through August 31 only. Poems are held until next reading period for consideration. Editors sometimes comment on returned submissions. Pays 1 copy. Acquires first North American serial rights.
Also Offers: They offer the Muriel Craft Bailey Memorial Prize yearly with $1,000 1st Prize, $200 2nd Prize, $100 3rd Prize, honorable mentions, publication of all finalists. Entry fee: $3/poem. 40-line limit. Deadline: July 1.

◑ **CONCHO RIVER REVIEW; FORT CONCHO MUSEUM PRESS**, P.O. Box 10894, Angelo State University, San Angelo TX 76909, phone (915)942-2273, fax (915)942-2155, e-mail james.moore@angelo.edu, website www.angelo.edu, founded 1984, editor James A. Moore, poetry editor Jerry Bradley.
Magazine Needs: *Concho River Review* is a literary journal published twice a year. "Prefer shorter poems, few long poems accepted; particularly looking for poems with distinctive imagery and imaginative forms and rhythms. The first test of a poem will be its imagery." Short reviews of new volumes of poetry are also published. *CRR* is 120-138 pgs., digest-sized, professionally printed and flat-spined, with matte card cover. They use 35-40 of 600-800 poems received/year. Press run is 300 for about 200 subscribers of which 10 are libraries. Subscription: $14. Sample: $5.
How to Submit: "Please submit 3-5 poems at a time. Use regular legal-sized envelopes—no big brown envelopes; no replies without SASE. Type must be letter-perfect, sharp enough to be computer scanned." Responds in 2 months. Pays 1 copy. Acquires first rights.
Also Offers: Website includes writer's guidelines and names of editors.
Advice: "We're always looking for good, strong work—from both well-known poets and those who have never been published before."

☑ ▢ ◑ **CONCRETE ABSTRACT; THE ABSTRACT CONCRETE**, % Will Lennertz, Santiago Canyon College, 8045 E. Chapman Ave., Orange CA 92669-4512, phone (714)564-4781, e-mail concreteabstract@ho tmail.com, website www.members.tripod.com/concreteabstract, founded 1998, editor Will Lennertz.
Magazine Needs: *The Concrete Abstract* is updated bimonthly at www.members.tripod.com/concreteabstract "to publish online the best poetry we can find. Clarity, precision and concrete details are highly valued. Subject matter and form are open. We publish poetry with a strong sense of the physical world and an emphasis on the tangible materials we encounter every day. No obtuse, abstract, senseless word play." They have published poetry by Jennifer Ogle, Matthew White and Erin Brehm. They receive about 2,500 poems a year, accept approximately 7-10%.
Magazine Needs: *The Abstract Concrete* is updated quarterly at www.members.tripod.com/abstractconcrete "to publish experimental word-art, poetry, poem-art collisions. The journal explores the mystery of language and art." They receive about 1,500 poems a year, accept approximately 10%. *The Abstract Concrete* is the inverse function of the *Concrete Abstract* (its sister publication). Submissions sent to one magazine will be considered for the other."
How to Submit: For both online publications, submit 3-5 poems at a time. No previously published poems or simultaneous submissions. Cover letter preferred. E-mail submissions OK. "Prefer e-mail submissions to concreteabstract@hotmail.com. Cut and paste poetry into e-mail. Also accepts fiction and art. Jpeg and gif formats for art submissions." Time between acceptance and publication is 2 months. Seldom comments on rejections. Obtain guidelines via website. Responds in 3 months. Acquires first rights. For both, staff reviews books and chapbooks of poetry and other magazines in 300-500 words, single and multi-book format. Send books for review consideration.
Advice: "Send some poems. See what happens. Rejection is not a personal issue. This labor of love is ruled by the editor's tastes. Try me a few times and realize I am going by my vision of poetry. Yours may just clash with mine. So be it. I am not evaluating your worth as a writer."

◑ **CONDUIT**, 510 Eighth Ave. NE, Minneapolis MN 55413, e-mail conduit@bitstream.net, founded 1993, editors William D. Waltz and Brett Astor.
Magazine Needs: *Conduit* is a semiannual designed "to explore language, art, life without ulterior motives; to publish work that is 'essential.' " They want "lively, honest poetry that is attuned to language." They have

published poetry by James Tate, Mary Jo Bang, Franz Wright, Tomaz Salamun, Amy Gerstler and Noelle Kocot. *Conduit* is 64 pgs., 4¼×11, neatly printed on recycled paper and perfect bound with matte card cover and art. They receive about 3,000 poems a year, publish about 150. Press run is 1,000-1,200 for 300 subscribers, 100-400 shelf sales. Subscription: $12. Sample: $6.

How to Submit: Submit 3-5 poems at a time. No previously published work. Time between acceptance and publication is 6-12 months. Seldom comments on rejections. Send SASE for guidelines or request via e-mail. Responds in up to 6 months. Pays 3 copies. Rights revert to authors upon publication. Reviews books of poetry in 500 words. Open to unsolicited reviews. Poets may also send books for review consideration.

Advice: "*Conduit* is dedicated to the work of poets and artists who wear the stains of a life lived and whose edges are neither affected nor accidental. *Conduit* will grow and evolve, but one thing will remain constant: quality writing that risks annihilation."

CONFLUENCE; OHIO VALLEY LITERARY GROUP, P.O. Box 336, Belpre OH 45714, phone (304)422-3112, e-mail dbprather@prodigy.net, founded 1983 as *Gambit*, 1989 as *Confluence*, poetry editors James Scott Bond, Barbara D. Lou and David B. Prather.

Magazine Needs: *Confluence* is an annual "credible platform for established/emerging authors and outstanding student work. This literary magazine is published at Marietta College, Marietta, Ohio, and was named to represent the merging of the Ohio and Muskingum Rivers as well as the collaboration of the Ohio Valley Literary Group with Marietta College." They have published poetry by Daniel Bourne, Walt McDonald, Pamela Kircher and Richard Hague. *Confluence* is 80-100 pgs., digest-sized, professionally printed and perfect-bound with full color, coated card cover and b&w graphics. They receive 2,500-5,000 submissions a year, accept approximately 2%. Press run is 1,000 for 300 subscribers of which 10 are libraries, about 150 shelf sales. Single copy: $5. Sample: $4 plus $1.25 postage.

How to Submit: Submit 5-7 poems with SASE. No previously published poems or simultaneous submissions. Cover letter with brief bio required. E-mail submissions OK. Reads submissions September 1 through March 1 only. Time between acceptance and publication is 6 months. Seldom comments on rejections. Send SASE for guidelines or request via e-mail. Responds in up to 2 months. Pays 1-3 copies. Returns rights upon publication.

CONFLUENCE PRESS (Specialized: regional), 500 Eighth Ave., Lewis-Clark State College, Lewiston ID 83501, phone (208)799-2336, fax (208)799-2850, e-mail conpress@lcsc.edu, website confluencepress.com, founded 1975, poetry editor James R. Hepworth.

"We have received four Western States Book Awards and two awards from The Pacific Northwest Booksellers within the last decade."

Book/Chapbook Needs: Confluence is an "independent publisher of fiction, poetry, creative nonfiction and literary scholarship. We are open to formal poetry as well as free verse. No rhymed doggerel, 'light verse,' 'performance poetry,' 'street poetry,' etc. We prefer to publish work by poets who live and work in the northwestern United States." They have published poetry by John Daniel, Greg Keeler, Nancy Mairs and Sherry Rind. They print about 2 books a year.

How to Submit: "Please query before submitting manuscript." Query with 6 sample poems, bio and list of publications. Replies to queries in 6 weeks. Pays 10% royalties plus copies. Buys all rights. Returns rights if book goes out of print. Send SASE for catalog to order samples.

CONFRONTATION MAGAZINE, English Dept., C.W. Post Campus of Long Island University, Brookville NY 11548-1300, phone (516)299-2720, fax (516)299-2735, e-mail mtucker@liu.edu, founded 1968, editor-in-chief Martin Tucker, poetry editor K. Hill-Miller.

Magazine Needs: *CM* is "a semiannual literary journal with interest in all forms. Our only criterion is high literary merit. We think of our audience as an educated, lay group of intelligent readers. We prefer lyric poems. Length generally should be kept to two pages. No sentimental verse." They have published poetry by Karl Shapiro, T. Alan Broughton, David Ignatow, Philip Appleman, Jane Mayhall and Joseph Brodsky. *Confrontation* is about 300 pgs., digest-sized, professionally printed, flat-spined, with a circulation of about 2,000. They receive about 1,200 submissions/year, publish 150, have a 6- to 12-month backlog. Subscription: $10/year. Sample: $3.

How to Submit: Submit no more than 10 pgs., clear copy. No previously published poems. Fax submissions OK. Do not submit mss June through August. "Prefer single submissions." Publishes theme issues. Send SASE for upcoming themes. Responds in 2 months. Sometimes sends prepublication galleys. Pays $5-50 and copy of magazine. Staff reviews books of poetry. Send books for review consideration.

Also Offers: Basically a magazine, they do on occasion publish "book" issues or "anthologies." Their most recent "occasional book" is *Clown at Wall*, stories and drawings by Ken Bernard.

THE BOOK PUBLISHERS INDEX, located at the back of this book, lists those publishers who consider full-length book collections.

CONJUNCTIONS, Dept. PM, Bard College, Annandale-on-Hudson NY 12504, phone (914)758-1539, fax (914)758-2660, e-mail conjunctions@bard.edu, website www.conjunctions.com, founded 1981, managing editor Michael Bergstein, editor Bradford Morrow.

Poetry published in *Conjunctions* has also been included in *The Best American Poetry* 1998.

Magazine Needs: *Conjunctions* is an elegant journal appearing twice a year, using work that is "stylistically innovative. Potential contributors should be familiar with the poetry published in the journal." They have published poetry by John Ashbery, Robert Kelly, Charles Stein, Michael Palmer, Ann Lauterbach and Fanny Howe. This publication is distributed by Consortium. It is 350 pgs., 6×9, flat-spined, professionally printed. Poems compete with prose, with more pages devoted to the latter. Press run is 5,500 for 1,000 subscribers of which 250 are libraries. Subscription: $18. Sample: $15. Pays $100-175 plus 2 copies.

Also Offers: Website includes current and past texts, art, subscription and back issue information.

$ **THE CONNECTICUT POETRY REVIEW**, P.O. Box 818, Stonington CT 06378, founded 1981, poetry editors J. Claire White and Harley More.

Magazine Needs: *CPR* is a "small press annual magazine. We look for poetry of quality which is both genuine and original in content. No specifications except length: 10-40 lines." They have published such poets as John Updike, Robert Peters, Diane Wakoski and Marge Piercy. Each issue seems to feature a poet. As a sample the editors selected these lines from "Reel" by Claudia Buckholts:

> *A linguist after his stroke/every day lost another language/lost it whole and complete: a world/lost,*
> *the crowds in the streets speaking French,/the Etoile shining, and the great chestnuts/flowering above*
> *the avenues.*

The flat-spined, large digest-sized journal is "printed letterpress by hand on a Hacker Hand Press from Monotype Bembo." Most of the 45-60 pgs. are poetry, but they also have reviews. They receive over 2,500 submissions a year, use about 20, have a 3-month backlog. Press run is 400 for 80 subscribers of which 35 are libraries. Sample: $3.50.

How to Submit: Reads submissions April through June and September through December only. Responds in 3 months. Pays $5/poem plus 1 copy.

Advice: "Study traditional and modern styles. Study poets of the past. Attend poetry readings and write. Practice on your own."

CONNECTICUT REVIEW, Southern Community State University, 501 Crescent St., New Haven CT 06473, phone (203)392-6737, founded 1968, editor Dr. Vivian Shipley.

Poetry published in this review has been included in *The Best American Poetry* 1998, 1998 Pushcart Prizes, *XXIII* and has won the Phoenix Award for Significant Editorial Achievement from the Council of Editors of Learned Journals (CELJ).

Magazine Needs: *CR*, published biannually, contains essays, poetry, articles, fiction, b&w photographs and color artwork. They have published poetry by Robert Phillips, Ron Wallace, Colette Inez, Dave Smith, Pattiann Rogers, Alberto Ríos, Leo Connellan and Walt McDonald. *Connecticut Review* is 176 pgs., digest-sized, offset printed, perfect bound, with glossy 4-color cover and 8-color interior art. They receive about 2,500 poems a year, accept approximately 5%. Press run is 3,000 of which 400 are libraries, with 1,000 distributed free to Connecticut State libraries and high schools. Sample: $6. Make checks payable to Connecticut State University.

How to Submit: Submit 3-5 typed poems at a time with name, address and phone in the upper left-hand corner on 8½×11 paper with SASE for return only. Publishes theme issues. Send SASE for guidelines and upcoming themes. Pays 2 copies. Acquires first or one-time rights.

CONNECTICUT RIVER REVIEW; BRODINE CONTEST; WINCHELL CONTEST; LYNN DECARO HIGH SCHOOL COMPETITION; CONNECTICUT POETRY SOCIETY, P.O. Box 4053, Waterbury CT 06704-0053, website http://pages.prodigy.net/mmwalker/cpsindex.html, founded 1978, editor Kevin Carey.

Magazine Needs: *CRR* appears biannually. They are looking for "original, honest, diverse, vital, well-crafted poetry; any form, any subject. Translations and long poems accepted." They have published poetry by Jana Harris, Lewis K. Parker, Alyce Miller, Walt McDonald and Miguel Torga. As a sample the editor selected these lines from "Bicycler's Sonnet" by Fileman Waitts:

> *On pedals I have climbed as steep as spires,/have sweated fiercely in the glaring noon;/and coasted*
> *straight down into sunset fires/to hang my handlebars upon the moon.*

The editor says *CRR* is attractively printed, digest-sized and contains about 40 pgs. of poetry, has a circulation of about 500 with 175 subscriptions of which 5% are libraries. They receive about 2,000 submissions a year, use approximately 80. Subscription: $12. Sample: $6.

How to Submit: Submit up to 3 poems at a time. Include SASE for return of mss. Cover letter with current bio appreciated. "SASE must be sufficient for additional communication. SASE with insufficient postage will not be returned." No previously published poems or simultaneous submissions. Guidelines available with SASE and online. Responds in up to 6 weeks. Pays 1 copy. International submissions must be accompanied by a minimum of 2 IRCs.

Also Offers: The Brodine Contest has a $2 entry fee/poem and 3 cash awards plus publication in the *Connecticut River Review*. Entries must be postmarked between May 1 and July 31. The Winchell Contest has a $2 entry fee/

poem and 3 cash awards plus publication in the *Connecticut River Review*. Entries must be postmarked between October 1 and December 31. The Lynn DeCaro Competition for Connecticut high school students only has no entry fee and 3 cash prizes plus publication in the *Connecticut River Review*. Entries must be postmarked between September 1 and February 27. Connecticut Poetry Society (203 Hanover Rd., Newtown CT 06470, president Faith Vicinanza) was founded in 1974 to encourage the art of poetry. State-wide organization open to all who are interested in poetry. Affiliated with the National Federation of State Poetry Societies. Currently has 150 members. Sponsors conferences, workshops. Publishes *Poets at Work*, for members only, appearing irregularly; and *Newsletter*, a bimonthly publication, also available to nonmembers for SASE. Members or nationally known writers give readings that are open to the public. Sponsors open-mike readings. Membership dues are $25/year. Members meet monthly. Send SASE for additional information.

⊕ $☐ CONNECTIONS, THE LITERARY SCENE IN THE SOUTH EAST, 13, Wave Crest, Whitstable, Kent CT5 1EH United Kingdom, editor Narissa Knights.

Magazine Needs: *Connections* is a quarterly magazine. "Just producing its twentieth issue, it aims to encourage new writers and provides an outlet for aspiring writers to see their work alongside articles, reviews and critiques from professionals. Each issue carries at least six poems and one short story up to 2,500 words." *Connections* is 32 pgs., A4, printed on coated paper and saddle-stapled with 2-color glossy cover, includes b&w photos. Press run is 350. Single copy: £4.25 (12 IRCs); subscription: £14 (33 IRCs).

How to Submit: Submit up to 6 poems at a time. "Nothing longer than those which will fit on a single page of A4." Responds in 3 months. Pays £5. Enclose SASE (SAE and IRCs). "Our competitions for the year 2000 were for short stories up to 2,500 words and poetry up to 50 lines." Closing date: June.

♻ ✓ $☐ CONTEMPORARY VERSE 2; THE LENA CHARTRAND AWARD, P.O. Box 3062, Winnipeg, Manitoba R3C 4E5 Canada, phone (204)949-1365, fax (204)942-1555, founded 1975, managing editors Janine Tschuncky and Clarise Foster.

Magazine Needs: *CV2* appears quarterly. "We publish poetry, prose, essays, interviews, reviews and art by women and men." They want "writing which in its diversity represents a range of social and cultural experience, with a particular focus on the experience of women." They have published poetry by Di Brandt, Gail Scott, Catherine Hunter and others. As a sample the editor selected these lines from "Brave" by Jeanette Lynes:

> You've been watching her for years, only/now see her, a brave woman with lilacs/picking her way
> along the white, gnarled path,/the vertebrae of love.

CV2 is 76 pgs., 6×9, with cover art, inside art, exchange ads. They receive about 800-1,000 poems a year, accept approximately 160. Press run is 700 for 480 subscribers of which 50 are libraries, 130 shelf sales; 80 distributed free at readings and events. Subscription: $23.98. Sample: $7.

How to Submit: Submit 4-6 poems at a time. No previously published poems or simultaneous submissions. Fax submissions OK, "as long as poets send a SASE by mail." Cover letter required with a 3-line bio and SASE. Time between acceptance and publication is 6 weeks. Poems are circulated to an editorial board. Poems go to the editorial collective; usually 3 out of 6 editors work on an issue and make those decisions. Often comments on rejections. Publishes theme issues. Send SASE (or SAE and IRC) for guidelines and upcoming themes. Responds in 6 weeks. Always sends prepublication galleys. Pays $20/poem. Reviews books and chapbooks in 800 words. Open to unsolicited reviews. Poets may also send books for review consideration.

Also Offers: Sponsors 2 annual contests, and administers The Lena Chartrand Award recognizing the outstanding work of one poet over the year. The award is around $300/year.

Advice: "Familiarize yourself with the publication you are submitting to."

✓ ◐ COPPER CANYON PRESS; HAYDEN CARRUTH AWARD, P.O. Box 271, Port Townsend WA 98368, phone (360)385-4925, fax (360)385-4985, e-mail poetry@coppercanyonpress.org, website www.copperca nyonpress.org, founded 1972, editor Sam Hamill.

Book/Chapbook Needs: Copper Canyon publishes books of poetry. They have published books of poetry by Lucille Clifton, Hayden Carruth, Carolyn Kizer, Olga Broumas and Jim Harrison. As a sample, the editor selected these lines from "Comice" in *Below Cold Moutain* by Joseph Stroud:

> I think of Issa often these days, his poems about the loneliness/of fleas, watermelons becoming frogs
> to escape from thieves./Moon in solstice, snowfall under the earth, I dream of a pure life./Issa said of
> his child, She smooths the wrinkles from my heart./Yes, it's a dewdrop world. Inside the pear there's
> a paradise/we will never know, our only hint the sweetness of its taste.

How to Submit: Query first with sample poems and cover letter with brief bio and publication credits. Include SASE. No queries via e-mail or fax. Replies to queries and mss (if invited) in 1 month. Time between acceptance and publication is 2 years. Write for catalog to order samples.

Also Offers: Copper Canyon Press publishes 1 volume of poetry each year by a new or emerging poet through its Hayden Carruth Award. "For the purpose of this award an emerging poet is defined as a poet who has published not more than two books." Winning poet receives a book contract with Copper Canyon Press and $1,000. Send SASE for contest guidelines.

Ⓝ ⊕ ☐ ◑ CORE LITERARY JOURNAL, P.O. Box 419, Geelong, Victoria 3213 Australia, founded 1996, co-editors Paul AR Howie or Cameron Lowe.

Magazine Needs: *core* appears 3 times a year in autumn, winter and spring. "We sincerely publish all that is poetry and poetic and are open to any and all means to achieving that style, type, genre, sense—from 1 line to 20 pages; from visual to concrete; political to postmodern; from the past, to the future." They want "radical, traditional, streetwise." They have published poetry by Charles Bernstein, Jesse Glass and Paul Hardacre. The editor says *core* is 75 pgs., professionally printed and perfect-bound with card cover, includes art/graphics. They receive about 1,000 poems a year, accept approximately 10-15%. Press run is 250 for 60 subscribers. Single copy: $5 (Australian); subscription: $15.
How to Submit: Submit 5 poems at a time, depending on length. Line length for poetry is 1 minimum, 600 maximum. Previously published poems and simultaneous submissions OK. Disk submissions OK. Cover letter preferred. Submissions can be ten words or ten thousand. Where possible, text should be presented in an A4, 12 point font, 1.5 to 2.0 line format. Always include a SASE (SAE and IRC). By all means, send a brief biography. Each edition of *core* publishes up to thirty artists and authors. *core* accepts contributions throughout the year. Reads submissions January 1 through December 31 only. Time between acceptance and publication is 2 months. Poems are circulated to an editorial board. Seldom comments on rejections. Send SASE (or SAE and IRC) for guidelines. Responds in 2 months. Pays 1 copy. "Author retains copyright." Open to unsolicited reviews.
Advice: "Whether new or old in style, make it good, not great, not the best, just good."

☑ $ ◎ CORNERSTONE MAGAZINE (Specialized: religious), Jesus People USA, 939 W. Wilson, Chicago IL 60640-5706, phone (773)561-2450 ext. 2080, e-mail poetry@cornerstonemag.com, website www.cornerstonemag.com, poetry editor Curt Mortimer.
Magazine Needs: *Cornerstone* is a mass-circulation (40,000), free publication appearing 2-4 times/year, directed at young adults (20-35), covering "contemporary issues in the light of Evangelical Christianity." They use avant-garde, free verse, haiku, light verse, rarely traditional—"no limits except for epic poetry. (We've not got the room.)" As a sample the editor selected these lines by Beth Wagler:

> she lies like a young man's tie thin and pressed/holding her own hand/open-mouthed/baby robin-like/
> waiting for Bigness to drop in/something that'll make her strong enough to fly

They buy 10-25 poems/year, use 1-2 pgs./issue, and have a 6- to 9-month backlog. Sample free with 9×12 envelope and 5 first-class stamps. "Do not send SASE for response. We will not reply unless we accept the poem(s). We will not return submitted materials."
How to Submit: Submit maximum of 5 poems at a time. Cover letter required. E-mail submissions preferred. Send SASE for guidelines. Pays 6 copies and $10 for poems having 1-15 lines, $25 for poems having 16 lines or more. Buys first or one-time rights. Open to unsolicited reviews. Poets may also send books for review consideration.

☑ ◑ CORONA, Dept. of History and Philosophy, Montana State University, P.O. Box 172320, Bozeman MT 59717-2320, phone (406)994-5200, founded 1979, poetry editors Lynda and Michael Sexson.
Magazine Needs: *Corona* "is an interdisciplinary occasional journal bringing together reflections from those who stand on the edges of their disciplines; those who sense that insight is located not in things but in relationships; those who have deep sense of playfulness; and those who believe that the imagination is involved in what we know." In regard to poetry they want "no sentimental greeting cards; no slap-dash." They have published poetry by Wendy Battin, William Irwin Thompson, Frederick Turner and James Dickey. The journal is 125-140 pgs., perfect-bound, professionally printed. They use about 20-25 pgs. of poetry/issue. Press run is 2,000. Sample: $7.
How to Submit: Submit any number of pages. No simultaneous submissions. Responds in up to 9 months. Payment is "nominal" plus 2 copies.
Advice: "Today's poet survives only by the generous spirits of small press publishers. Read and support the publishers of contemporary artists by subscribing to the journals and magazines you admire."

❧ ◯ ◎ COSMIC TREND; PARA*PHRASE (Specialized: themes, love/romance/erotica), Sheridan Mall Box 47014, Mississauga, Ontario L5K 2R2 Canada, founded 1984, Cosmic Trend poetry editor George Le Grand, *PARA*phrase editor Tedy Asponsen.
Magazine Needs: *PARA*phrase—Newsletter of Cosmic Trend (irregular: 1-2 times a year)—publishes "poetry related to our major anthologies advertised here."
Book Needs: Cosmic Trend annually publishes 1 anthology with narrated music cassettes of "New Age, and Post-New-Age, sensual and mind-expanding short material of any style, but preferably unrhymed; also: humorous, unusual or zany entries (including graphics) with deeper meaning. We ignore epics, run-of-a-mill romantic and political material. Would like to publish more free verse." They have published poetry by Joanna Nealon and Jiri Jirasek. As a sample the editor selected these lines by Jiri Jirasek:

> The speed of love is still—/no place to go but home!

How to Submit: For both Cosmic Trend and *PARA*phrase, submit up to 10 poems at a time with name and address on each sheet. Submission fee: $1 for each 2 poems submitted, plus $1 for postage. Minimum fee is $2 plus postage. ("No U.S. postal stamps, please.") They will consider simultaneous submissions and previously published poems "with accompanied disclosure and references." Publishes theme issues. Theme for Summer 2001 and 2002 are "Tomorrows Seem Forever" (deadline: November 15, 2000) and "Forgotten Future Memories" (deadline: November 15, 2001), respectively. Send $1 for guidelines and upcoming themes or $6 for sample publication, guidelines and upcoming themes. Response time is usually less than 3 weeks. Editor "often"

Heeding the voices of silence

Born in 1962 in Cuba, Virgil Suarez is a prolific writer, crossing between genres—poem, short story, novel, memoir—sometimes all in the same book. I first encountered his work when he submitted poems to *Coal City Review*. I selected two of them to publish, including the wonderful long poem "Bitterness," set in Cuba where he lived for the first eight years of his life. Suarez and his family left Cuba for Spain in 1970, then after four years in Spain, moved to Los Angeles, where he spent his teenage years and early adulthood. He now teaches at Florida State University and is the author of four novels—*Going Under*, *Havana Thursdays*, *Latin Jazz* and *The Cutter*—as well as collections of short stories and poems. So much of Suarez's writing concerns his Cuban childhood and his Cuban-American experience, that this became one of the main topics of this interview.

Virgil Suarez

© Ryan G. VanCleave

In *Spared Angola* (1997) you write of the necessity of confronting the past: "There comes a time in a man's life when he must confront his past, stare at it eye-to-eye, have a showdown." How important has this been in your own writing?

I found that I had grown tired of having to invent things for my fiction, my novels and stories. I had been writing poetry since 1980 and had never shown any of it to anyone. I felt it was too personal, meaning that it dealt with things in my own life that I (then) wasn't brave enough to show anybody. I wanted to continue writing this kind of poetry because early on I had a strong sense of voice, of place, of these things that had happened to me during the eight years that I lived in Cuba. Almost eight years ago, I decided to really take off my mask of the fiction writer, the liar, the inventor and put down more of what I had lived through. I feel strongly that I must tackle my past because we all have a need to know answers, to keep track of what has brought us this far in our own lives. I do, and daily I sit at the computer and work it out, the "little scars," as I call them.

What have been the advantages and disadvantages of writing in a "second language," English?

I've always written in English. I feel that English is the best language for me as a writer because I am not enamored by any particular aspect of it. Of course, that doesn't mean I don't follow the rules. I do. But I also like to experiment. I learned not to fall in love with any of my sentences. It was an important lesson for me as a young writer because you must learn how to revise, how to make your writing better. You can't do this if you look at your words and say, "This is damn good. I'm not changing anything because everything is perfect." I have students like this now. And I tell them they need to tear things apart in their writing. They need to assemble and disassemble if they have to. It's the only way to learn.

You write of your solitude and introversion as a boy and how this left a "sort of Grand Canyon of emotional scars" but also prepared you for the writer's life. Can you imagine writing without this "preparation?"

I am an only son. I grew up sheltered. I grew up alone, though I have many cousins and friends. I always thought my house was the place where I could be alone, and it is a feeling that I have to this day—house as temple. In Cuba I was ostracized because my parents had declared they wanted to leave the country. In Spain I was ostracized because I spoke Spanish with a Cuban accent. In Los Angeles I was ostracized because I spoke Spanish and not English and because I looked different. I sought refuge in books, in words. I read a lot when I was a kid because I found out I didn't really have to go very far or take chances with my world when I had the Count of Monte Cristo, Alice, Romeo, Ahab, Ali Baba, Madame Bovary, Lolita, Roderick Usher, and so many other wonderful characters. The training I received as an avid reader I simply translated into the training of the writer. You do both alone. You do both in a quiet, undisturbed environment. You learn to listen to so much silence. Then you begin to hear things, voices that speak to you, voices that beg you to heed them.

"Study in Shadow"

In sepia, the stilted shadow of my father
(the one taking the photograph?)
in Havana breaks where I stood
next to the hibiscus, a boy of six
hair scalloped back into the Malanguita,
a proper boy's style, my mother's
. favorite haircut for boys. This is 1968,
outside the house of light, house
of shade, the world ablaze with protest,
war, jungle orange poisons.
I fake a smile for all time, my father urges
it on my lips, of this spindly, awkward boy-me-dressed in matched shirt
and shorts, mother-sewed that summer.
Clean, pretty, sadness riddled into my eyes,
our parrot Chicharo calls out:
"Sonrisa!" Smile, my father says behind
the camera, then the flash of light
which swallows us both all that remains
of that boy is the squint of years,
the weight of memories, broken shadows
of a man, his son, that life in Cuba,
bent on the grass, greener with possibility.

(first published in *Pleaides*; reprinted by permission of the author)

You write in different genres and mix them in the same book: poems, memoirs, stories. At what point do you know what genre you'll be working in? Which genre comes most easily to you?

No particular genre comes easy. All my writing is painstaking work, but I relish it. I think of the many writers who complain about how hard it is to write, how painful. Then I think that for me it has been difficult, yes, but a gift too. I love to do it, but none of it comes easy. I often spend hours trying to figure out a sentence structure just to get it right. Or there are mornings when I meditate upon a single word. I think about what gets lost in translation when "butterfly" changes into "mariposa." I often don't know what shape the writing is going to take. For example, in *Spared Angola*, I had to make conscious decisions to make my writing into memoir and not into a poem or vice versa. I begin with ideas and go from there. When a piece yearns to become a poem, then I start to pay closer attention to rhythm, line breaks, the exactness of words, meter.

Please describe your writing process.

I write on the computer. I love computers because they allow me to focus on the energy of typing, of how words magically blink onto the screen. I write in longhand too. I keep a journal which I take with me everywhere I go. It's like one of those yute sacks my father used to carry in Cuba when he went foraging for stuff for us to eat. The process by which I move ideas from my journal to my computer is magical for me because I tend to "layer" as I go. I develop things, erase them, start from scratch at times. I write every day. I used to write at night. Now I simply write in the morning. I write in my office. I write at home. I write at the park while the girls play soccer. I write all the time, everywhere I can. Even when I'm not physically jotting things down, I'm writing.

Do you ever have writer's block?

I don't really suffer from it. When I run dry, I feed myself by reading other writers. I tell my students all the time to not be afraid of having nothing to say. Sometimes you read to fill yourself with ideas. I appreciate such breaks as pit stops, necessary for filling up again.

Which poets are you reading now?

Living in the United States is like living in a poetry candy store. There's a poet around the corner, somebody doing incredible work—Rita Dove, Billy Collins, Leroy V. Quintana, Charles Wright, Phillip Levine, hundreds of poets, thousands. It's mind-blowing.

How much is your writing affected by a sense of audience? By editors?

I've been lucky to never really know who my audience is, though I suspect it is other writers, other poets, people who have a passion for the written word. Most of my experience with editors has been positive. I appreciate their input because they can often see things in my writing that I've overlooked, not because I'm sloppy or careless but because they can look at it from a different point of view, a different angle. I couldn't write in a world that doesn't include editors.

You have already achieved so much in your writing. What are your ambitions now?

My ambitions as a writer don't change much from day to day. I want to sit down and write the best story, best poem, best essay I possibly can, given my limitations as a human being and as a writer. And I want my stuff to be read, which is the reason why I send it out. So many writers disconnect so completely from following through with their work. The first step is to write well, the next is to send the work out, let it see the light of print.

Many people I've spoken to about this interview have said, "I know Virgil's work. I've seen it in this or that journal." You're widely published. What is your approach to publishing?

My approach to writing and publishing is very simple. I sit and write. Revision is very important to me. I revise until I can't push the piece any further. At that time I make copies and send them to particular friends who are honest about my work. A few weeks will go by during which I get on to new work and forget the old. Then it comes back and I get to look at it fresh.

Recently, I've been getting invitations from editors to submit work, which is very nice indeed. But before this, I had to send out my work like everybody else. I love to do research on literary magazines: there are so many good ones, so many. For every one that folds because of lack of money, there are three new ones. If I like the magazine, I submit work to them. Of course where would I be without my "bibles," *Poet's Market* and *The International Directory of Little Magazines & Small Presses*.

Please tell us about your current projects.

I am still working on a novel, *Sonny Manteca's Blues*, which I started seven years ago and intend to finish one of these fine days. I am also working on a new collection of stories and a new collection of poems. Every day I sit down to write and to live through my writing. I look out my window, see how beautiful the day is, then I plunge in to write my heart out.

—*Brian Daldorph, editor of* Coal City Review

comments on submissions. Does not pay for poetry. However, poets may purchase a discounted copy of the publication in which their work appears. Rights revert to authors upon publication. Poets may also send books for review consideration, attn. Tedy Asponsen.

Also Offers: Cosmic Trend publishes electronic music cassette tapes in addition to their poetry/music anthology accompaniments.

Advice: "Share your adventure of poetry beyond the usual presentation! Cosmic Trend can choose your poems for narration with music and inclusion into our cassette accompaniments to our illustrated anthologies."

COTEAU BOOKS; THUNDER CREEK PUBLISHING CO-OP (Specialized: Canadian, children), 401-2206 Dewdney Ave. #401, Regina, Saskatchewan S4R 1H3 Canada, phone (306)777-0170, fax (306)522-5152, e-mail coteau@coteau.unibase.com, website http://coteau.unibase.com, founded 1975, publisher Geoffrey Ursell, managing editor Nik L. Burton, contact acquisitions editor.

Book/Chapbook Needs: Coteau is a "small literary press that publishes poetry, fiction, drama, anthologies, criticism, young adult novels—by Canadian writers only." They have published *The Long Landscape* by Paul Wilson and *The Blue Field* by Barbara Klar. As a sample they selected these lines from "Our Sullen Art" in *On Glassy Wings* by Anne Szumigalski:

> the language of poetry has something to do/with the open mouth the tongue that jumps/up and down like a child on a shed roof calling/ha ha and who's the dirty rascal now?/the same boy sent to his room for punishment/leans from his window listening for animals/far away in the woods strains his ears to catch/even the slightest sound of rage but nothing howls/even the hoot of owls in the dusk is gentle

"We publish theme anthologies occasionally."

How to Submit: Writers should submit 30-50 poems "and indication of whole ms," typed with at least 12 point type; simultaneous and American submissions not accepted. Cover letter required; include publishing credits and bio and SASE (or SAE and IRC) for return of ms. E-mail submissions OK (send as .txt file attachments maximum 20 pgs.). No fax submissions. Queries will be answered and mss responded to in 4 months. Always sends prepublication galleys. Authors receive 10% royalty and 10 copies. Their catalog is free for 9×12 SASE (or SAE and IRC), and sample copies can be ordered from it.

Also Offers: Website includes title and ordering information, author interviews, awards, news and events, submission guidelines and links.

Advice: "Generally, poets should have a number of publishing credits, single poems or series, in literary magazines and anthologies before submitting a manuscript."

COTTONWOOD; COTTONWOOD PRESS (Specialized: regional), 400 Kansas Union-Box J, University of Kansas, Lawrence KS 66045, phone (913)864-3777, e-mail cottonwd@falcon.cc.ukans.edu, website www.falcon.cc.ukans.edu/~cottonwd, founded 1965, poetry editor Philip Wedge.

Magazine Needs: For *Cottonwood* they are looking for "strong narrative or sensory impact, non-derivative, not 'literary,' not 'academic.' Emphasis on Midwest, but publishes the best poetry received regardless of region. Poems should be 60 lines or fewer, on daily experience, *perception.*" They have published poetry by Rita Dove, Virgil Suarez, Walt McDonad and Luci Tapahonso. As a sample the editors selected these lines from "The World Remade" by Lyn Plath:

> Sunlight becomes a room in the city,/an angle of windows, a bar of gold on the floor./In a white vase
> on a table in the corner/flowers open, pulling the day into themselves,/into the rush and flutter of
> yellow petals/the way one body draws another body into itself.

The magazine, published 2 times/year, is 112 pgs., 6×9, flat-spined, printed from computer offset, with photos, using 10-15 pages of poetry in each issue. They receive about 4,000 submissions/year, use about 30, have a maximum of 1-year backlog. They have a circulation of 500-600, with 150 subscribers of which 75 are libraries. Single copy: $8.50. Sample: $5.

How to Submit: Submit up to 5 pgs. of poetry at a time. No simultaneous submissions. Sometimes provides criticism on rejected mss. Responds in up to 5 months. Pays 1 copy.

Book/Chapbook Needs & How to Submit: The press "is auxiliary to *Cottonwood Magazine* and publishes material by authors in the region. Material is usually solicited." The press published *Violence and Grace* by Michael L. Johnson and *Midwestern Buildings* by Victor Contoski.

Also Offers: Website includes guidelines, names of editors and staff, information on publications and subscription order form.

Advice: "Read the little magazines and send to ones you like."

COUNTERMEASURES, Creative Writing Program, College of Santa Fe, 1600 St. Michael's Dr., Santa Fe NM 87505, phone (505)473-6448, e-mail gglazner@csf.edu, website www.csf.edu/countermeasures, editor Greg Glazner, editor Jon Davis.

  Countermeasures has received a Pushcart Prize.

Magazine Needs: *Countermeasures* is "a biannual magazine of poetry and ideas; colloquims on contemporary poetry. We look for ambition, experimentation and attention to craft. We do not want the 40-line personal lyric, flippant, breezy poems, deadened formalist exercises." They have published poetry by Dana Levin, Sandra Kohler, Aurthor Sze and Stephen Berg. The editors say *Countermeasures* is 40 pgs., 8½×11, web press printed with sewn binding, 2-color cover, includes some art/graphics. They receive about 1,000 poems a year, accept approximately 1%. Press run is 2,000 for 400 subscribers of which 20 are libraries, 300 shelf sales; 300 distributed free to writers groups, bookstores, individuals. Subscription: $5/year. Sample: $2.50.

How to Submit: Submit 3-5 poems at a time. No previously published poems; simultaneous submissions OK. Reads submissions September 1 through May 1 only. Time between acceptance and publication is 6 months. "Students review poems and discuss them. All editorial decisions are made by Greg Glazner and Jon Davis." Seldom comments on rejections. Publishes theme issues occasionally. Responds in 3 months. Pays 2 copies.

COUNTRY FOLK, HC 77, Box 608, Pittsburgh MO 65724, phone/fax (417)993-5944, founded 1994, editor Susan Salaki.

Magazine Needs: "*Country Folk* is a quarterly magazine written for, by and about people living in country and rural areas. We publish poetry that reflects the serenity and peace of mind one feels when living close to nature. We also like humorous poetry. We do not want to see poetry with images of violence or meanness." They have published poetry by Goldena Trolinger of Hermitage MO and Reed Shook of Zion IL. As a sample the editor selected these lines from "Our Small Town" by Bev Boucher:

> Friendly and warm, where I was born,/I like my small country town./No traffic light, or gangs that
> fight,/that pleases me, somehow.

The editor says *CF* is 40 pgs., magazine-sized, web offset printed, 2-color cover, includes "photos of country people" and ads. They receive about 100 poems a year, accept approximately 10%. Press run is 2,000 for 500 subscribers. Single copy: $2.75; subscription: $15/4 issues. Sample: $4.

How to Submit: Submit up to 3 poems at a time. Line length for poetry is 8 minimum, 30 maximum. Previously published poems and simultaneous submissions OK. Cover letter preferred. "Include SASE if you want your poetry returned." Time between acceptance and publication is 2 months. Seldom comments on rejections. Publishes theme issues occasionally. Send SASE for guidelines. Pays 1 copy. Acquires one-time rights. Staff reviews other magazines in 500 words, single book format.

Advice: "We strongly suggest poets read a copy of *Country Folk* to get a flavor for what we like. Your poetry may be outstanding work but if you mail it to the wrong magazine for review it will get rejected. Know your market. It's the least you can do for your poetry. Without exception, most of the poems we read could be improved with additional revisions. Yet we find that poets usually decline to revise when asked to do so because they feel it was an inspirational work and should not be tampered with. At that point, we must either reject the work, which we often do, or publish it 'as is' because it's the best we have been able to find, a sad conclusion but true."

$ ◎ COUNTRY WOMAN; REIMAN PUBLICATIONS (Specialized: women, humor), P.O. Box 643, Milwaukee WI 53201, founded 1970, executive editor Kathy Pohl.

Magazine Needs: *Country Woman* "is a bimonthly magazine dedicated to the lives and interests of country women. Those who are both involved in farming and ranching and those who love country life. In some ways, it is very similar to many women's general interest magazines, and yet its subject matter is closely tied in with rural living and the very unique lives of country women. We like short (4-5 stanzas, 16-20 lines) traditional rhyming poems that reflect on a season. No experimental poetry or free verse. Poetry will not be considered unless it rhymes. Always looking for poems that focus on the seasons. We don't want rural putdowns, poems that stereotype country women, etc. All poetry must be positive and upbeat. Our poems are fairly simple, yet elegant. They often accompany a high-quality photograph." They have published poetry by Hilda Sanderson, Edith E. Cutting and Ericka Northrop. *CW* is 68 pgs., magazine-sized, printed on glossy paper with much color photography. They receive about 1,200 submissions of poetry/year, use 40-50 (unless they publish an anthology). One of their anthologies, *Cattails and Meadowlarks: Poems from the Country*, is 90 pgs., saddle-stapled with high-quality color photography on the glossy card cover, poems in large, professional type with many b&w photo illustrations. Their backlog is 1-3 months. Subscription: $16.98/year. Sample: $2.

How to Submit: Submit up to 6 poems at a time. Photocopy OK if stated not a simultaneous submission. Responds in 3 months. Pays $10-25/poem plus 1 copy. Buys first rights (generally) or reprint rights (sometimes).

Also Offers: They hold various contests for subscribers only.

Advice: "We're always welcoming submissions, but any poem that does not have traditional rhythm and rhyme is automatically passed over."

$ ⬤ CRAB ORCHARD REVIEW; CRAB ORCHARD AWARD SERIES IN POETRY, English Dept., Faner Hall, Southern Illinois University at Carbondale, Carbondale IL 62901-4503, website www.siu.edu/~crborc hd, founded 1995, poetry editor Allison Joseph, managing editor Jon C. Tribble, editor-in-chief Richard Peterson.

 Crab Orchard Review received a 1999 Literary Award from the Illinois Arts Council. Poetry from *COR* has also appeared in *The Best American Poetry 1999*.

Magazine Needs: The *Crab Orchard Review* appears biannually in May and December. "We are a general interest literary journal publishing poetry, fiction, creative nonfiction, interviews, book reviews and novel excerpts." They want all styles and forms from traditional to experimental. No greeting card verse; literary poetry only. They have published poetry by Virgil Suarez, Kyoko Mort, R.T. Smith and Colleen J. McElroy. In response to our request for sample lines of poetry the editors say, "We'd prefer not to, since no one excerpt can convey the breadth of poetry we'd like to receive." *COR* is 250 pgs., 5½×8½, professionally printed and perfect-bound with photos, usually glossy card cover containing b&w photo. They receive about 4,000 poems a year, accept approximately 20%. Each issue usually includes 35-40 poems. Press run is 1,600 for 1,100 subscribers of which 60 are libraries, 390 shelf sales; 50 distributed free to exchange with other journals. Subscription: $10. Sample: $6.

How to Submit: Submit up to 5 poems at a time. No previously published poems; simultaneous submissions OK with notification. Cover letter preferred. "Indicate stanza breaks on poems of more than one page." Reads submissions April to October for our Spring/Summer special issue, November to April for regular, non-thematic Fall/Winter issue. Time between acceptance and publication is 6-12 months. Poems are circulated to an editorial board. "Poems that are under serious consideration are discussed and decided on by the editor-in-chief, managing editor, and poetry editor." Seldom comments on rejections. Publishes theme issues. Theme for Spring/Summer 2001 issue is "The City: Past, Present and Future." Deadline: October 15, 2000. Send SASE for guidelines and upcoming themes or obtain via website. Responds in up to 8 months. Pays $10/page, $50 minimum plus 2 copies and 1 year's subscription. Buys first North American serial rights. Staff reviews books of poetry in 500-700 words, single book format. Send books for review consideration to managing editor Jon C. Tribble.

Also Offers: Sponsors the Crab Orchard Award Series in Poetry. The publisher of the books will be Southern Illinois University Press. The competition is open from October 1 to November 16 for US citizens and permanent residents. "The Crab Orchard Award Series in Poetry, launched in 1997, is committed to publishing two book-length manuscripts each year. We also run an annual fiction/nonfiction contest." Books are usually 50-70 pgs., 9×6, perfect-bound with color paper covers. Entry fee: $20/submission. 1st and 2nd Prize winners each receive a publication contract with Southern Illinois University Press. In addition, the 1st Prize winner will be awarded a $2,000 prize and $1,000 as an honorarium for a reading at Southern Illinois University at Carbondale; also, the 2nd Prize winner will receive $1,000 as an honorarium for a reading at Southern Illinois University at Carbondale. Both readings will follow the publication of the poets' collections by Southern Illinois University Press. Recent winners were Elton Glaser's *Winter Amnesties* (1999 runner-up) and Marilene Phipps' *Crossroads and Unholy Water* (1999 winner). Send SASE for details. Website includes guidelines, details of past issues, book reviews, list of contributors, contest requirements and results, editors' biographies and calls for submissions.

☑ ⊘ **CREAM CITY REVIEW**, P.O. Box 413, Dept. of English, University of Wisconsin at Milwaukee, Milwaukee WI 53201, phone (414)229-4708, e-mail creamcity@uwm.edu, website www.uwm.edu/Dept/English/CCR, editors Peter Whalen and Kyoko Yoshida, poetry editors Brent Gohde and Karen Howland.

☑ Poetry published in this review has been included in the 1996 and 1997 volumes of *The Best American Poetry*.
Magazine Needs: *Cream City Review* is a nationally distributed literary magazine published twice a year by the university's Creative Writing Program. "We seek to publish all forms of writing, from traditional to experimental. We strive to produce issues which are challenging, diverse and of lasting quality. We are not interested in sexist, homophobic, racist or formulaic writings." They have published poetry by Audre Lorde, Marge Piercy, May Sarton, Philip Dacey, Amiri Baraka, Tess Gallagher, Cathy Song, Mary Oliver and Philip Levine. They do not include sample lines of poetry; "We prefer not to bias our contributors. We strive for variety—vitality!" *CCR* is averaging 200 pgs., 5½×8½, perfect-bound, with full-color cover on 70 lb. paper. Press run is 1,000 for 450 subscribers of which 40 are libraries. Single copy: $7; subscription: $12/1 year, $21/2 years. Sample: $5.
How to Submit: "Include SASE when submitting and please submit no more than five poems at a time." Simultaneous submissions OK when notified. "Please include a few lines about your publication history and other information you think of interest." Reads submissions September 1 through April 30 only. Editors sometimes comment on rejections. Send SASE for guidelines. Responds in 4 months. Payment includes 1-year subscription. Buys first rights. Reviews books of poetry in 1-2 pgs. Open to unsolicited reviews. Poets may also send books to the poetry editors for review consideration.
Also Offers: Sponsors an annual contest for poems under 100 lines. Submit 3-5 poems/entry. Entry fee: $15 includes 1-year subscription. Awards $100 plus publication; possible publication for second through fifth place. Website includes submission guidelines; publication index—a list of contributors, their submitted (published) essays, poems, fiction and the volume # in which their piece appears; publication/magazine overview and history; complete list of staff.

☑ ⬠ ⬡ ⊘ **CREATIVE JUICES; FORESTLAND PUBLICATIONS**, 423 N. Burnham Highway, Canterbury CT 06331, e-mail forestland@snet, website www.geocities.com/Soho/atrium/1782, founded 1989 (Forestland Publications), editor Geraldine Hempstead Powell.
Magazine Needs: *Creative Juices*, published bimonthly, features poetry, arts, photos, "something to inspire everyone's creative juices." They want "any style or subject, 50 lines or less." They do not want pornography. Also accepts poetry written by children. They receive about 100-1,000 poems a year, accept approximately 350. They have published poetry by Richard Brobst, John Allen Jaynes and Herman Slotkin. Press run is 100 for 65 subscribers, 30 shelf sales. Single copy: $3; subscription: $18 (6 issues). Sample: $1.50. Make checks payable to Geraldine Powell.
How to Submit: Submit 3-5 poems at a time. Previously published poems (with credits) and simultaneous submissions OK. E-mail submissions OK. Prefer attached file. Cover letter preferred. Time between acceptance and publication is 1-3 months. Submissions reviewed by editor. Often comments on rejections. Publishes theme issues. Send SASE or visit website for guidelines and upcoming themes. Responds in 1 month. Sometimes sends prepublication galleys. Pays 1 or more copies. Acquires first North American serial or one-time rights. Always returns rights. Reviews books of poetry. Open to unsolicited reviews. Poets may also send books for review consideration.
Book/Chapbook Needs & How to Submit: Forestland Publications publishes 3 chapbooks/year. Chapbooks are usually 5×7, 20 pgs. Query first with sample poems and cover letter with brief bio and publication credits. Replies to queries in 1 week, to mss in 1 month. Obtain sample chapbooks by sending SASE. "Beginning in 1999, non-subscribers [to *Creative Juices*] should remit a $10 reading fee for chapbook submissions."
Also Offers: Website includes guidelines, submission info and subscription forms.

☑ ⬡ ◎ **CREATIVE WITH WORDS PUBLICATIONS (C.W.W.); SPOOFING (Specialized: themes); WE ARE WRITERS, TOO (Specialized: children); THE ECLECTICS (Specialized: adults)**, P.O. Box 223226, Carmel CA 93922, fax (831)655-8627, e-mail geltrich@usa.net or cwwpub@usa.net, website http://members.tripod.com/~CreativeWithWords, founded 1975, poetry editor Brigitta Geltrich.
Magazine Needs: *C.W.W.* offers criticism for a fee. It focuses "on furthering folkloristic tall tales and such; creative writing abilities in children (poetry, prose, language art); creative writing in adults (poetry and prose)." The editors publish on a wide range of themes relating to human studies and the environment that influence human behaviors. $5 reading fee/poem, includes a critical analysis. The publications are anthologies of children's poetry, prose and language art; anthologies of 'special-interest groups' poetry and prose; *Spoofing: An Anthology of Folkloristic Yarns and Such*; and anthologies with announced themes (nature, animals, love, travel, etc.). "Do not want to see: too mushy; too religious; too didactic; expressing dislike for fellow men; political; pornographic; death and murder poetry and prose." Send SASE for guidelines and upcoming themes. They have published poetry by Claire Yeomans, Daniel Adait, Vada Overall, D.V. Sahani and Beverly Brydon Market. As a sample the editor selected these lines by Mandeep Sandhu:

> *To love is to be loved/To hate is to be hated/To possess is to be possessed/To command is to be commanded*

Spoofing! and *We are Writers, Too!* are low-budget publications, photocopied from typescript, saddle-stapled, card covers with cartoon-like art. Samples: $6 plus p&h. Single copy: $9-12, depending on length; subscription: 12 issues for $60; 6 issues for $36; 3 issues for $21. Libraries and schools receive 10% discount. Make checks payable to Brigitta Ludgate.

How to Submit: Submit poems of 20 lines or less, 46 character maximum line length, poems geared to specific audience and subject matter. No simultaneous submissions or previously published poems. No fax submissions. "Query with sample poems (one poem/page, name and address on each), short personal biography, other publications, poetic goals, where you read about us, for what publication and/or event you are submitting. SASE is a must." Queries via fax OK. They have "no conditions for publication, but C.W.W. is dependent on author/poet support by purchase of a copy or copies of publication." They offer a 20% reduction on any copy purchased.

Also Offers: Sponsors "Best of the Month" contest, awards publication certificate and 1 copy. Website includes guidelines, themes, editing information, contest and winners.

Advice: "Trend is proficiency. Poets should research topic; know audience for whom they write; check topic for appeal to specific audience; should not write for the sake of rhyme, rather for the sake of imagery and being creative with the language. Feeling should be expressed (but no mushiness). Topic and words should be chosen carefully; brevity should be employed; and author should proofread for spelling and grammar. We would like to receive more positive and clean, family-type poetry."

◻ **CREATIVITY UNLIMITED PRESS®; ANNUAL CREATIVITY UNLIMITED PRESS® POETRY COMPETITION**, 30819 Casilina, Rancho Palos Verdes CA 90275, e-mail sstockwell@earthlink.net, founded 1978, editor Shelley Stockwell.

Book/Chapbook Needs: Creativity Unlimited® publishes annually a collection of poetry submitted to their contest, $5 fee for 1-5 poems; prizes of $50, $35 and $25 and possible publication. Deadline: December 31. "Clever, quippy, humor and delightful language encouraged. No inaccessible, verbose, esoteric, obscure poetry. Limit three pgs. per poem, double-spaced, one side of page."

How to Submit: "Poems previously published will be accepted provided writer has maintained copyright and notifies us." E-mail submissions OK. They often use poems as chapter introductions in self-help books. Always comments on rejections. Publishes theme issues. Send SASE for upcoming themes. Sometimes sends prepublication galleys. Pays 2 copies.

Advice: "We are interested in receiving more humorous poetry."

[N] [⊕] [◐] [◎] **CRESCENT MOON PUBLISHING; PASSION (Specialized: anthology, gay/lesbian, love/romance/erotica, occult, religious, spirituality, women/feminism)**, P.O. Box 393, Maidstone, Kent ME14 5XU United Kingdom, founded 1988, editor Jeremy Robinson.

Magazine Needs: "We publish a quarterly magazine, *Passion* ($4 each, $17 subscription). It features poetry, fiction, reviews and essays on feminism, art, philosophy and the media. Many American poets are featured, as well as British poets such as Jeremy Reed, Penelope Shuttle, Alan Bold, D.J. Enright and Peter Redgrove. Contributions welcome."

Book/Chapbook Needs: Crescent Moon publishes about 25 books and chapbooks/year on arrangements subsidized by the poet. He wants "poetry that is passionate and authentic. Any form or length." Not "the trivial, insincere or derivative. We are also publishing two anthologies of new American poetry each year entitled *Pagan America*." They have also published studies of Rimbaud, Rilke, Cavafy, Shakespeare, Beckett, German Romantic poetry and D.H. Lawrence. Books are usually about 76 pgs., flat-spined, digest-sized. Anthologies now available ($8.95 or $17 for 2 issues of *Pagan America*) include: *Pagan America: An Anthology of New American Poetry*; *Love in America: An Anthology of Women's Love Poetry*; *Mythic America: An Anthology of New American Poetry*; and *Religious America: An Anthology of New American Poetry*.

How to Submit: Submit 5-10 poems at a time. Cover letter with brief bio and publishing credits required ("and please print your address in capitals"). Send SASE (or SAE and IRCs) for upcoming anthology themes. Replies to queries in 1 month, to mss in 2 months. Sometimes sends prepublication galleys.

Advice: "Generally, we prefer free verse to rhymed poetry."

$◎ **CRICKET; SPIDER, THE MAGAZINE FOR CHILDREN; LADYBUG, THE MAGAZINE FOR YOUNG CHILDREN; BABYBUG, THE LISTENING AND LOOKING MAGAZINE FOR INFANTS AND TODDLERS (Specialized: children); CICADA (Specialized: teens)**, P.O. Box 300, Peru IL 61354-0300, *Cricket* founded 1973, *Ladybug* founded 1990, *Spider* founded 1994, *Babybug* founded 1995, *Cicada* founded 1998, editor-in-chief Marianne Carus.

MARKETS THAT WERE listed in the 2000 edition of *Poet's Market* but do not appear this year are listed in the General Index with a notation explaining why they were omitted.

Magazine Needs: *Cricket* (for ages 9-14) is a monthly, circulation 68,000, using "serious, humorous, nonsense rhymes" for children and young adults. They do not want "forced or trite rhyming or imagery that doesn't hang together to create a unified whole." They sometimes use previously published work. *Cricket* is 64 pgs., 8 × 10, saddle-stapled, with color cover and full-color illustrations inside. *Ladybug*, also monthly, circulation 127,000, is similar in format and requirements but is aimed at younger children (ages 2-6). *Spider*, also monthly, circulation 90,000, is for children ages 6-9. Format and requirements similar to *Cricket* and *Ladybug*. *Cicada*, appearing bimonthly, is a new magazine for ages 14 and up publishing "short stories, poems, and first-person essays written for teens and young adults." They want "serious or humorous poetry; rhymed or free verse." *Cicada* is 128 pgs., 5½ × 8½, perfect-bound with full-color cover and b&w illustrations. Subscription: $32.97/6 issues. *Babybug*, published at 6-week intervals, circulation 45,000, is a read-aloud magazine for ages 6 months to 2 years; premier issue published January 1995. It is 24 pgs., 6¼ × 7, printed on cardstock with nontoxic glued spine and full-color illustrations. The magazines receive over 1,200 submissions/month, use 25-30, and have up to a 2-year backlog. Sample of *Cricket*, *Ladybug*, *Spider* or *Babybug*: $5; sample of *Cicada*: $8.50.

How to Submit: Do not query. Submit no more than 5 poems—up to 50 lines (2 pgs. max.) for *Cricket*; up to 20 lines for *Spider* and *Ladybug*, up to 25 lines for *Cicada*, up to 8 lines for *Babybug*, no restrictions on form. Guidelines available for SASE. Responds in 4 months. Payment for all is up to $3/line and 2 copies. "All submissions are automatically considered for all five magazines."

Also Offers: *Cricket* and *Spider* hold poetry contests every third month. *Cricket* accepts entries from readers of all ages; *Spider* from readers ages 10 and under. Current contest themes and rules appear in each issue.

✔ ◎ **CROSS & QUILL, THE CHRISTIAN WRITERS NEWSLETTER (Specialized: religious); CHRISTIAN WRITERS FELLOWSHIP INTERNATIONAL**, 1624 Jefferson Davis Rd., Clinton SC 29325-6401, phone (864)697-6035, e-mail cwfi@aol.com, website http://cwfi-online.org, founded 1976, editor/publisher Sandy Brooks.

Magazine Needs: *Cross & Quill* is a bimonthly newsletter published "to encourage and equip Christians in publishing at all experience levels." They want traditional, free verse, blank verse and rhymed verse. Nothing longer than 12 lines. They have published poetry by Fannie Houck, Mary Sayler, Leona Choy and Jane Lippy. As a sample the editor selected these lines (poet unidentified):

> Pen of Heaven/write to me/words of what the Master sees./Pen from Heaven/speak to me/oracles of
> sweet simplicity./Take my laughter, take my pain/and write for me as heaven's gain

The editor says *C&Q* is 16 pgs., newsletter-sized, desktop-published, folded/loose, b&w cover, includes computer-generated art and ads. They receive about 100 poems a year, accept approximately 1%. Press run is over 1,000. Single copy: $4; subscription: $20/year. Sample (including guidelines): $2. Make checks payable to CWFI.

How to Submit: Submit 3 poems at a time. Line length for poetry is 12 maximum. Previously published poems OK; no simultaneous submissions. "We will accept electronic submissions upon request. If previously published, tell me where and when it was published." Time between acceptance and publication is 3-6 months. Usually comments on rejections. Send SASE for guidelines or obtain via e-mail. Responds in 2 weeks. Pays 3 copies. Acquires first or reprint rights. Reviews books and chapbooks of poetry, "only as it applies to writing poetry."

Also Offers: "We provide critiques, online writers group, help with contracts, publicity for member books, connections with writers and groups near them." Website includes publicity for member books, links for writers, information about CWFI and sample articles.

Advice: "We lean toward informational materials rather than personal experience."

✔ ◑ ◎ **CROSS-CULTURAL COMMUNICATIONS; CROSS-CULTURAL REVIEW OF WORLD LITERATURE AND ART IN SOUND, PRINT, AND MOTION; CROSS-CULTURAL MONTHLY; CROSS-CULTURAL REVIEW CHAPBOOK ANTHOLOGY; INTERNATIONAL WRITERS SERIES (Specialized: translations, bilingual)**, 239 Wynsum Ave., Merrick NY 11566-4725, phone (516)868-5635, fax (516)379-1901, e-mail cccmia@juno.com or cccpoetry@aol.com, founded 1971, Stanley H. and Bebe Barkan.

Magazine Needs & How to Submit: *Cross-Cultural Monthly* focuses on bilingual poetry and prose. Subscription (12 issues/editions): $50. Sample postpaid: $7.50. Pays 1 copy.

Book/Chapbook Needs & How to Submit: *CCR* began as a series of chapbooks (6-12 a year) of collections of poetry translated from various languages and continues as the Holocaust, Women Writers, Latin American Writers, African Heritage, Asian Heritage, Italian Heritage, International Artists, Art & Poetry, Jewish, Israeli, Yiddish, Hebrew, Arabic, American, Bengali, Cajun, Chicano, Czech, Dutch, Finnish, Gypsy (Roma), Indian, Polish, Russian, Serbian, Sicilian, Swedish, Scandinavian, Turkish, and Long Island and Brooklyn Writers Chapbook Series (with a number of other permutations in the offing)—issued simultaneously in palm-sized and regular paperback and cloth-binding editions and boxed and canned editions, as well as audiocassette and videocassette. Cross-Cultural International Writers Series, focusing on leading poets from various countries, includes titles by Leo Vroman (Holland) and Pablo Neruda (Chile). The Holocaust series is for survivors. In addition to publications in these series, CCC has published anthologies, translations and collections by dozens of poets from many countries. As a sample the editor selected the beginning of a poem by Rainer Maria Rilke, as translated by Stephen Mitchell:

> She was no longer that woman with blue eyes/who once had echoed through the poet's songs,/no
> longer the wide couch's scent and island,/and that man's property no longer.//She was already loosened

like long hair,/poured out like fallen rain,/shared like a limitless supply.
That's from the bilingual limited poetry and art edition, *Orpheus. Eurydice. Hermes: Notations on a Landscape*, published in 1996. It is 35 pgs., 10½ × 13½, smythe-sewn cloth. Sample chapbook: $10 postpaid. All submissions should be preceded by a query letter with SASE. Send SASE for guidelines. Pays 10% of print run.
Also Offers: CCC continues to produce the International Festival of Poetry, Writing and Translation with the International Poets and Writers Literary Arts Week in New York. CCC won the Poor Richards Award "for a quarter century of high-quality publishing," presented by The Small Press Center in New York.

☑ ◻ ◐ **CRUCIBLE; SAM RAGAN PRIZE**, Barton College, College Station, Wilson NC 27893, phone (252)399-6456, e-mail tgrimes@barton.edu, founded 1964, editor Terrence L. Grimes.
Magazine Needs: The *Crucible* is an annual published in November using "poetry that demonstrates originality and integrity of craftsmanship as well as thought. Traditional metrical and rhyming poems are difficult to bring off in modern poetry. The best poetry is written out of deeply felt experience which has been crafted into pleasing form. No very long narratives." They have published poetry by Robert Grey, R.T. Smith and Anthony S. Abbott. It is 100 pgs., 6 × 9, professionally printed on high-quality paper with matte card cover. Press run is 500 for 300 subscribers of which 100 are libraries, 200 shelf sales. Sample: $6.
How to Submit: Submit 5 poems at a time between Christmas and mid-April only. No previously published poems or simultaneous submissions. Responds in up to 4 months. "We require three unsigned copies of the manuscript and a short biography including a list of publications, in case we decide to publish the work."
Also Offers: Send SASE for guidelines for contests (prizes of $150 and $100), and the Sam Ragan Prize ($150) in honor of the former Poet Laureate of North Carolina.
Advice: Editor leans toward free verse with attention paid particularly to image, line, stanza and voice. However, he does not want to see poetry that is "forced."

◐ ◎ **CUMBERLAND POETRY REVIEW; THE ROBERT PENN WARREN POETRY PRIZE (Specialized: translations)**, Dept. PM, P.O. Box 120128, Acklen Station, Nashville TN 37212, founded 1981.
Magazine Needs: *CPR* is a biannual journal presenting poetry, poetry criticism, and poets of diverse origins to a widespread audience. "We place no restrictions on form, subject, or style. Our aim is to support the poet's effort to keep up the language. We accept a special responsibility for reminding our readers that excellent poems in English are written by citizens of many counties around the world. We have published such poets as Dan Stryk, Ovid (in translation), James Sutherland-Smith and C.K. Stead." *CPR* is 75-100 pgs., 6 × 9, flat-spined. Circulation is 500. Sample: $9.
How to Submit: Send poetry, translations or poetry criticism with SASE or SAE with IRC. Submit up to 6 poems at a time. No previously published poems. "We accept, but do not like to receive simultaneous submissions." Cover letter with brief bio required. Responds in 6 months. Pays 2 copies. Acquires first rights. Returns rights "on request of author providing he acknowledges original publication in our magazine."
Also Offers: They award The Robert Penn Warren Poetry Prize annually. Winners receive $500, $300 and $200 and publication in the review. Entry fee: $28. For contest guidelines, send SASE.

⊕ ◻ ◐ ◎ **CURRENT ACCOUNTS (Specialized: membership); BANK STREET WRITERS COMPETITION**, 16-18 Mill Lane, Horwich, Bolton, Lancashire BL6 6AT England, phone/fax (01204)669858, e-mail rodriesco@cs.com, founded 1994, editor Rod Riesco.
  ● Wilderswood Press, formerly mentioned in this listing, is not currently operating.
Magazine Needs: *Current Accounts* is a biannual publishing poetry, fiction and nonfiction by members of Bank Street Writers and other contributors. They are open to all types of poetry; maximum 100 lines. Also accepts poetry written by children. They have published poetry by Pat Winslow, M.R. Peacocke and Gerald England. As a sample the editor selected these lines from "Spinal Tap" by Geoff Stevens:
> *All bronzes, and stone sculptures, are bald.//And yet backbone is a long plait/bronzed or marbled to the flesh.//It is the necessary fibre/the rhino whip lashing together head and hip.//A blind man that has never seen the Andes/can recognize the chain of the human frame.//It bumps under his fingers/from nape to coccyx.*

CA is 24-48 pgs., A5, photocopied and saddle-stapled, card cover with b&w or color photo or artwork. They receive about 40 poems a year, accept approximately 20%. Press run is 40 for 2 subscribers, 30 shelf sales; 4 distributed free to competition winners. Subscription: UK £3. Sample: UK £1.50. Make checks payable to Bank Street Writers (sterling checks only). "No requirements, although some space is reserved for members."
How to Submit: Submit up to 6 poems at a time. Previously published poems OK; no simultaneous submissions. Cover letter required. E-mail and fax submissions OK. Time between acceptance and publication is 6 months. Seldom comments on rejections. Responds in 1 month. Pays 1 copy. Acquires first rights.
Also Offers: Sponsors the annual Bank Street Writers Poetry and Short Story Competition. Submit poems up to 40 lines, any subject or style. Deadline: October 31. Entry fee: £2/poem. Send SAE and IRC for entry form. Also, the Bank Street Writers meets once a month and offers workshops, guest speakers and other activities. Write for details.

◑ ◎ CURRICULUM VITAE LITERARY SUPPLEMENT; SIMPSON PUBLICATIONS (Specialized: themes), Grove City Factory Store, P.O. Box 1309, Grove City PA 16127, e-mail simpub@hotmail.com, website www.evitae.homepage.com, founded 1995, editor Amy Dittman.

Magazine Needs: *Curriculum Vitae Literary Supplement* appears biannually. "*CVLS* is a thematic zine, but quality work is always welcome whether or not it applies to our current theme. We'd like to see more metrical work, especially more translations, and well-crafted narrative free verse is always welcome. However, we do not want to see rambling Bukowski-esque free verse or poetry that overly relies on sentimentality. We are a relatively new publication and focus on unknown poets." As a sample the editor selected these lines from "Faye's Loose Hair" by Andy Krackow:

> Grandma called you Susan,/But Mom I named you Faye/To my ninth grade classmates/Because it was
> romantic and I wanted you/To be a movie star with a murderous man.

The editor says *CVLS* is 40 pgs., digest-sized, photocopied and saddle-stitched with a 2-color card stock cover. They receive about 500 poems a year, accept about 75. Press run is 1,000 for 300 subscribers of which 7 are libraries, 200 shelf sales. Subscription: $6 (4 issues). Sample: $3.

How to Submit: Submit 3 poems at a time. "Submissions without a SASE cannot be acknowledged due to postage costs." Previously published poems and simultaneous submissions OK. Cover letter "to give us an idea of who you are" preferred. E-mail submissions OK. Time between acceptance and publication is 8 months. Poetry is circulated between 3 board members. Often comments on rejections. Publishes theme issues. Send SASE for guidelines and upcoming themes or request via e-mail. Responds within a month. Pays 2 copies plus 1-year subscription.

Book/Chapbook Needs & How to Submit: Simpson Publications also publishes about 5 chapbooks a year. Interested poets should query.

Also Offers: "We are currently looking for poets who would like to be part of our Poetry Postcard series." Interested writers should query to The *CVLS* Poetry Postcard Project at the above address for more information. Website includes writer's guidelines, masthead, standards and practices and a condensed version of the magazine.

◑ CUTBANK; THE RICHARD HUGO MEMORIAL POETRY AWARD, English Dept., University of Montana, Missoula MT 59812, phone (406)243-6156, e-mail cutbank@selway.umt.edu, website www.umt.edu/cutbank, founded 1973, contact poetry editor.

Magazine Needs: *Cutbank* is a biannual literary magazine which publishes regional, national and international poetry, fiction, reviews, interviews and artwork. They have published poetry by Jane Miller, Sheryl Noethe, Nance Van Winckel and Jane Hirshfield. There are about 100 pgs. in each issue, 25 pgs. of poetry. Circulation is 400 for 250 subscribers of which 30% are libraries. Single copy: $6.95; subscription: $12/2 issues. Sample: $4.

How to Submit: Submit 3-5 poems at a time, single-spaced with SASE. Simultaneous submissions discouraged but accepted with notification. "We accept submissions from August 15 through March 15 only. Deadlines: Fall issue, November 15; Spring issue, March 15." Send SASE for guidelines or request via e-mail. Responds in 2 months. Pays 2 copies. All rights return to author upon publication.

Also Offers: It also offers 2 annual awards for best poem and piece of fiction published in the magazine, The Richard Hugo Memorial Poetry Award and The A.B. Guthrie, Jr. Short Fiction Award. Winners are announced in the spring issue. Website includes "pretty much the whole magazine."

Ⓝ ⊕ ◑ ◎ CYBER LITERATURE (Specialized: membership/subscription), Dr. Chhote Lal Khatri, Jehanabad, Bihar 804408 India, phone 0621-363326, fax 0612-669188, founded 1997, contact Dr. Chhote Lal Khatri or Dr. Shaileshwar Sati.

Magazine Needs: *Cyber Literature* appears biannually to "nurture creativity and serve humanity by spreading the voice of muse and foster world peace and fellow-feeling." They are "open to all sorts of poems within 25 lines that have authenticity of experience and vitality of expression, well knit, compact and crisp, preference to structural verse. No sermons, prosaic, experimental work without any purpose." They have published poetry by Ruth Wildes Schuler, R.K. Singh and I.H. Rizvi. They say *CL* is 70-80 pgs., offset printed and side-stitched with paper back cover, includes ads. They receive about 200 poems a year, accept approximately 30-40%. Press run is 500 for 300 subscribers of which 20 are libraries, 100 shelf sales; 40-60 distributed free to editors, celebrities. Single copy: $5; subscription: $10. Sample: $5. Make checks payable to "The editor, Cyber Literature, Jehanabad." Membership or purchase of copy required for consideration.

How to Submit: Submit 3-6 poems at a time. Line length for poetry is 25 maximum. Previously published poems and simultaneous submissions OK. Cover letter preferred. Include SASE or IRC and a bio. Reads submissions March 1 through April 30 and September 1 through October 30 only. Time between acceptance and publication is 6 months. Poems are circulated to an editorial board. "Poems are circulated among associate editors. They are returned to the editor for final decision." Seldom comments on rejections. Responds in 1 month. Pays 1 copy. Acquires one-time rights. Reviews books and chapbooks of poetry and other magazines in 500 words, single book format. Open to unsolicited reviews. Poets may also send books for review consideration.

Also Offers: Also publishes an anthology of poetry of poets from both India and abroad.

✓ ▣ $◑ CYBER OASIS, fax (603)971-5013, e-mail eide491@earthlink.net, website www.sunoasis.com/oasis.html, founded 1996, contact David Eide.

Magazine Needs: *Cyber Oasis* is a monthly online journal containing poems, stories, personal essays, articles for writers and commentary. "The purpose is two-fold. Number one is to publish excellent writing and number two is to explore the web for all the best writing and literary venues. Not only does *Cyber Oasis* publish original material but it investigates the web each month to deliver the very best material it can find." They want "poetry that has an active consciousness and has artistic intention. Open on form, length, subject matter, style, purpose, etc. It must deliver the active consciousness and artistic intention. No sing song stuff, fluff stuff, those who write poems without real artistic intent because they haven't given the idea a thought." They have published poetry by Libby Hart (Australia), John Horvath, Jeff Crooke and Prakash. As for the format of *Cyber Oasis*, Mr. Eide says "I'm trying to find the right style for the Web. I was inspired by the literary magazine phenomena but find the Web to be a new medium. One that is terrific for poetry." They receive "hundreds" of poems a year, accept approximately 15%.
How to Submit: Submit 5 poems at a time. Previously published poems OK; no simultaneous submissions. E-mail and disk submissions OK. "Try to include submission in ASCII plain-text in body of e-mail message." Time between acceptance and publication is 2-3 months. "If I know I don't want it I'll turn it back that day. If there is something there that warrants further reading I'll put it into a review folder. As the day of publication approaches I'll get the review folder out and start to eliminate stuff. If I eliminate something that I like I'll put it into next month's folder. Then I come down to a chosen few. One or two I pick for publication, the others I schedule for another month. I then notify the writer of acceptance, I notify the others that I want to publish their poems later and give them updates on that." Often, but not always, comments on rejections. Obtain guidelines via e-mail or website. Responds in 1 month. Pays $10/poem. Buys first, first North American serial, one time and reprint rights.
Advice: "Seek to improve the writing; take poetry seriously, treat it as an art and it will treat you well."

⬜ ◎ **CYCLE PRESS; INTERIM BOOKS; CAYO MAGAZINE (Specialized: regional)**, 715 Baker's Lane, Key West FL 33040, founded 1968, contact Kirby Congdon.
Magazine Needs & How to Submit: *Cayo* is a quarterly regional literary magazine focusing on the Florida Keys. The editor says *Cayo* is 40 pgs., magazine-sized, offset printed and saddle-stitched with self-cover, includes photography. They receive about 100 poems a year, accept approximately 20%. Press run is 1,000 for 100 subscribers, 400 shelf sales; 500 distributed free to sponsors/contributors. Single copy: $3; subscription: $16. Sample: $4. Submit 3 poems at a time. Previously published poems and simultaneous submissions OK. Cover letter preferred. SASE required. Reads submissions July through August and October through April only. Time between acceptance and publication is 3-6 months. Poems are circulated to an editorial board. "The poetry editor finalizes his choices with the publisher and editor-in-chief." Often comments on rejections. Responds in 3 months. Pays 2 copies. Acquires one-time rights.
Book/Chapbook Needs: Cycle Press and Interim Books publish poems that are "contemporary in experience and thought. We concentrate on single poems, rather than more elaborate projects, for the author to distribute as he sees fit—usually in numbered copies of 50 to 300 copies." They want "provocative, uncertain queries; seeking resolutions rather than asserting solutions. No nineteenth century platitudes." As a sample Mr. Congdon selected these lines from his poem "Discus Thrower":

> *His figure, cut in silhouette/with no excess expended/nor stint in measure,/takes its careful aim.*

Books are usually 6-12 pgs., 5×8, computer-generated with hand-sewn binding, paper jackets, some photos.
How to Submit: Submit 3 poems at a time. Simultaneous submissions OK. Cover letter preferred. "If spelling, punctuation and grammer are secondary concerns to the author. I feel the ideas and experience have to be secondary too." Time between acceptance and publication is 1 year. Often comments on rejections. "No requirements except a feeling of rapport with the author's stance."

🌐 ⬜ ◎ **DANDELION ARTS MAGAZINE; FERN PUBLICATIONS (Specialized: membership/ subscription)**, 24 Frosty Hollow, East Hunsbury, Northants NN4 0SY England, fax 01604-701730, founded 1975, editor/publisher Mrs. Jacqueline Gonzalez-Marina M.A.
   ● Fern Publications subsidizes costs for their books, paying no royalties.
Magazine Needs: *Dandelion Arts Magazine*, published biannually, is "a platform for new and established poets to be read throughout the world." They want poetry "not longer than 35-40 lines. Modern but not wild." They do not want "bad language poetry, religious or political, nor offensive to any group of people in the world." They have published poetry by Andrew Duncan, Donald Ward, Andrew Pye, John Brander and Diane Moore. As a sample the editor selected these lines from her own poem:

> *. . . The human spirit without a planned path/to follow, is a sad landscape,/only grass and weeds, and nothing more/to expect.*

The editor says *Dandelion* is approximately 25 pgs., A4, thermal binding with b&w and color illustrations, original cover design, some ads. They receive about 200-300 poems a year, accept approximately 15%. Press run is up to 1,000 for 100 subscribers of which 10% are universities and libraries, some distributed free to chosen organizations. Subscription: £9 (UK), £18 (Europe and US). Sample: half price of subscription. Make checks payable to J. Gonzalez-Marina.
How to Submit: Poets must become member-subscribers of *Dandelion Arts Magazine* and poetry club in order to be published. Submit 4-6 poems at a time. No previously published poems; simultaneous submissions OK. Cover letter required. "Poems must be typed out clearly and ready for publication, if possible, accompanied by

a SAE or postal order to cover the cost of postage for the reply. Reads submissions any time of the year. Time between acceptance and publication is 2-6 months. "The poems are read by the editor when they arrive and a decision is taken straight away." Some constructive comments on rejections. Send SASE (or SAE and IRC) for guidelines. Responds "straight away." Reviews books of poetry. Open to unsolicited reviews. Poets may also send books for review consideration.

Also Offers: *Dandelion* includes information on poetry competitions and art events.

Book/Chapbook Needs & How to Submit: Fern Publications is a subsidy press of artistic, poetic and historical books and publishes 2 paperbacks/year. Books are usually 50-80 pgs., A5 or A4, "thermal bound" or hand finished. Query first with 6-10 poems. Requires authors to subscribe to *Dandelion Arts Magazine*. Replies to queries and mss in 1-2 weeks. "All publications are published at a minimum cost agreed beforehand and paid in advance."

Advice: "Consider a theme from all angles and to explore all the possibilities, never forgetting grammar! Stay away from religious or political or offensive issues."

$ ⬤ JOHN DANIEL AND COMPANY, PUBLISHER; FITHIAN PRESS, a division of Daniel & Daniel, Publishers, Inc., P.O. Box 21922, Santa Barbara CA 93121-1922, phone (805)962-1780, fax (805)962-8835, e-mail dandd@danielpublishing.com, website www.danielpublishing.com/, founded 1980, reestablished 1985.

Book/Chapbook Needs: John Daniel, a general small press publisher, specializes in literature, both prose and poetry. "Book-length mss of any form or subject matter will be considered, but we do not want to see pornographic, libelous, illegal or sloppily written poetry." He has published *Words Never Spoken*, by Doris Vanderlipp. As a sample John Daniel selected these lines from "Exhortation to a Discouraged Poet" from the book *The Shadow Heart*, by Julia Cunningham:

> Remember how it was when you had wings?/Never too easy to rise, a strained flapping/as you huffed
> yourself forward/and your feet left gravity/as you wobbled aloft, your wings/made heavy by doubt?//
> Call to the self that listens/and hear/Put your wings back on!/Put your wings back on!

He publishes about 4 flat-spined poetry paperbacks, averaging 80 pgs., each year. Press runs average between 500-1,000. For free catalog of either imprint, send #10 SASE.

How to Submit: Send 12 sample poems and bio. Responds to queries in 2 weeks, to mss in 2 months. Simultaneous submissions OK. No fax or e-mail submissions. Always sends prepublication galleys. Pays 10% royalties of net receipts. Buys English-language book rights. Returns rights upon termination of contract.

Also Offers: Fithian Press books (50% of his publishing) are subsidized, the author paying production costs and receiving royalties of 60% of net receipts. Books and rights are the property of the author, but publisher agrees to warehouse and distribute for one year if desired. Website includes writer's guidelines, author profiles, description of books and opinionated advice for writers.

Advice: "We receive over five thousand unsolicited manuscripts and query letters a year. We publish only a few books a year, of which fewer than half were received unsolicited. Obviously the odds are not with you. For this reason we encourage you to send out multiple submissions and we do not expect you to tie up your chances while waiting for our response. Also, poetry does not make money, alas. It is a labor of love for both publisher and writer. But if the love is there, the rewards are great."

N ⊕ ⬤ ◎ DARENGO; SESHAT: CROSS-CULTURAL PERSPECTIVES IN POETRY AND PHILOSOPHY (Specialized: translation), P.O. Box 9313, London E17 8XL United Kingdom, phone/fax (44)181-679-4150, Darengo founded 1989, *Seshat* founded 1997, editor/proprietor Terence DuQuesne, editor Mark Angelo de Brito.

Magazine Needs: *Seshat*, published biannually, "provides a focus for poetry enthusiasts by publishing high-quality poems in English and in translation. It also prints prose articles which highlight connections between the poetic, the philosophical, and the spiritual. *Seshat* is committed to the view that poetry and other art-forms are vitalizing and raise consciousness and thus should not be regarded as minority interests. Poetry is not merely an aesthetic matter: it can and should help to break down the barriers of class, race, gender, age, and sexual preference. *Seshat* is named for the Egyptian goddess of sacred writing and measurement." They have published poetry by Sappho, Anthony James, Martina Evans, Ellen Zaks and Dwina Murphy-Gibb. The editors say *Seshat* is 80 pgs., US standard, offset printed with stitched binding, laminated paper cover, includes graphics. Press run is 200. Single copy: £10 (payable in sterling only plus £5 postage outside UK); subscription: £20.

How to Submit: Submit up to 5 poems at a time. Previously published poems OK; no simultaneous submissions. Cover letter required. Disk submissions OK. Time between acceptance and publication is 3 months. Often comments on rejections. Send SASE (or SAE and IRC) for guidelines. Responds in 2 weeks. Always sends prepublication galleys. Pays 1 copy, more on request. Poets retain copyright. Reviews books and chapbooks of poetry and other magazines in 1,000 words. Open to unsolicited reviews. Poets may also send books for review consideration.

Book/Chapbook Needs & How to Submit: Darengo currently does not accept unsolicited mss.

✓ $ ⬤ ◎ DARK REGIONS (Specialized: horror, science fiction/fantasy), P.O. Box 6301, Concord CA 94524, phone (510)254-7442, e-mail isedmorey@aol.com, founded 1985, poetry editor Bobbi Sinha-Morey.

Magazine Needs: *Dark Regions* is a quarterly magazine "dedicated to putting out an on-time quality product that will entertain as well as make the reader think. We publish weird fantasy and horror and occasionally weird science fiction. Our magazine is intended for mature readers. We want inventive tales that push the boundaries of originality and invention. We dislike overused themes like Friday the 13th, Conan and invaders from Mars." They want "dark fantasy, disturbing horror, vampires, gothicism, psychological verse, magic and wonder. For horror poetry, make it eerie and tantalizing. Use plenty of imagery and be passionate about your writing. Use your imagination and make your work fly. More fantasy!" Free verse and traditional verse. They have published poetry by Bruce Boston, Ann K. Schwader and Kendall Evans. As a sample the editor selected these lines from "Pyramid of the Moon" by Ann K. Schwader:

> The wind off Cerro Blanco is crying/tonight with the tongues of dead warriors.

Dark Regions is 64-80 pgs., 5½×8½, offset printed and saddle-stapled with full color cover. They receive about 100 poems a year, accept approximately 25%. Press run is 1,000 for 300 subscribers of which 50 are libraries, 500 shelf sales; 150 distributed free to reviewers, writers, poets, advertising. Single copy: $3.95; subscription: $13. Make checks payable to Dark Regions Press.
How to Submit: Submit 4 poems at a time, either single-spaced or double-spaced, 1 poem/page. Line length for poetry is 35 maximum. Previously published poems OK; no simultaneous submissions. Cover letter preferred. "I take care of all poetry submissions and respond personally to each one." Often comments on rejections. Publishes theme issues occasionally. Send SASE for guidelines and upcoming themes. Responds in 3 weeks. Always sends prepublication galleys. Pays $5-10/poem plus 1 copy. Acquires first North American serial rights.

☑ ▣ $ ▢ ◐ **DEAD END STREET PUBLICATIONS, LLC**, 813 Third St., Hoquiam WA 98550, phone/fax (310)301-1818, e-mail submissions@deadendstreet.com, website deadendstreet.com, founded 1997, director of submissions John Rutledge, director of publications Ivan Black.
Book/Chapbook Needs: Dead End Street Publications publishes electronic collections of poetry and seeks "cutting edge authors who represent the world's dead end streets." Accepts poetry written by children. They have published poetry by Circe, CD Reed, T. Rening, Larry Jaffe, and Von Enemy. As a sample they offer their mission statement:

> It must be known/that where I have been,/has both things to despise/and knowledge to lend.

How to Submit: "We request complete collections so the depth and experience of the poet can be adequately judged." No previously published poems; simultaneous submissions OK. Cover letter required. "We prefer electronic submissions (disk and e-mail) in MS Word or Word Perfect." Time between acceptance and publication is 6 months. Poems are circulated to an editorial board. Seldom comments on rejections. "Complete submission guidelines provided on company website." Replies to queries in 1 month. Pays royalties of 10% minimum, 40% maximum and 10 author's copies. Obtain sample books via website.

☑ ◯ ◉ **DEAD FUN (Specialized: horror)**, P.O. Box 752, Royal Oak MI 48068-0752, e-mail deadfun@xoommail.com, website www.members.xoom.com/deadfun/zine.htm, founded 1997 as *Dead Fun*, editoress Kelli.
Magazine Needs: *Dead Fun* appears sporadically and is a "gothic horror zine with a sense of humor. Includes interviews, poetry, art, photography, editorials, fun, spooky stuff; ads, clip-art, etc." They prefer "gothic horror-related, religious/sacrilegious material." They do not want poetry that is "political, flowery." They have published poetry by David Sanders, Ben Wilensky and Rod Walker. As a sample the editor selected these lines from "After the Feast" by John Grey:

> What a meal,/no . . . a banquet:/eyes like grapes,/spaghetti veins,/flesh tender/on the bone./I lick her
> lips,/knowing she would/if she could.

Dead Fun is about 50 pgs., digest-sized, photocopied and stapled with cardstock cover, includes pen and ink drawings, charcoal art, photography and ads for zines, bands, photography, "anything relative." Accept approximately 30% of poetry submitted. Sample: $3 plus 77¢ postage (inside US) or IRC. Make money orders payable to Kelli or send well-concealed cash.
How to Submit: Submit up to 3 poems at a time. Previously published poems and simultaneous submissions OK. Cover letter strongly preferred. Time between acceptance and publication up to 6 months "unless otherwise agreed." Always comments on rejections. Send SASE or e-mail for guidelines. Responds in 6 weeks or a few days for e-mail requests. Pays 1 copy. Staff reviews books of poetry in approximately 40 words. Send books for review consideration.
Also Offers: Website includes writer's guidelines, names of editors and general informaton.

Ⓝ ◐ **DEAD METAPHOR PRESS**, P.O. Box 2076, Boulder CO 80306-2076, phone (303)417-9398, e-mail dmetaphoreP.@aol.com, founded 1992, contact Richard Wilmarth.
Book/Chapbook Needs: Publishes 3-5 chapbooks of poetry and prose a year through an annual chapbook contest. "No restrictions in regard to subject matter and style." They have published poetry by John McKernan, Patrick Pritchett, Mark DuCharme, Thomas R. Peters, Jr. and Gil Poulin. As a sample we selected these lines from "currently" by richard wilmarth:

> the refrigerator motor is my companion/we have coffee together/talk sports/interface with the phone
> system/we keep everything cold

Chapbooks are usually 24-60 pgs., sizes differ, printed, photocopied, saddle-stitched or perfect-bound, some with illustrations.

How to Submit: Submit 24 pgs. of poetry or prose with a bio, acknowledgments. Manuscripts are not returned. SASE for notification. "Entries must be typed or clearly reproduced and bound only by a clip. Do not send only copy of manuscript." Previously published poems and simultaneous submissions OK. Reading fee: $10. Deadline: October 31. Winner receives 10% of press run plus discounted copies. For sample chapbooks, send $6.

☑ ⬤ ⬤ **DEBUT REVIEW**, P.O. Box 412184, Kansas City MO 64141-2184, founded 1999, editor M.L. Acksonj.

Magazine Needs: *Debut Review* appears annually to "showcase the work of a select few talented poets. Although we favor form, we are looking for poetry of the highest order in traditional form or free verse. We prize the voice that demonstrates both objectivity and control. We look for the use of poetic devices such as: alliteration, simile, metaphor, etc. Wit is fine, but nothing overly humorous, trite, or unpolished." The editor says it is "somewhere between 25-30 pages, printed in a somewhat informal manner, but highly professsional. After a few issues, the review will be perfect-bound by a printer, and presented to contributors and libraries."

How to Submit: Submit 7-10 poems at a time. No previously published poems or simultaneous submissions. Cover letter required. Mss should be double-spaced with name and address in upper right-hand corner of each page. Reads submissions January through March only. Time between acceptance and publication is 8 months. Always comments on rejections. Send SASE for guidelines. Responds in 3 weeks. Pays 2 copies. Acquires one-time rights.

Advice: "As our title suggests, we are looking to showcase the work of emerging poets, although this is probably not the place for beginners. We are interested in poets who have honed their craft, but have not yet had a collection of poems published. We request that poets write for guidelines before submittting."

☑ ⬤ **DEFINED PROVIDENCE PRESS**, P.O. Box 16143, Rumford RI 02916, e-mail defprov@aol.com, website www.definedprovidence.com, founded 1992, editor Gary J. Whitehead.

Book/Chapbook Needs & How to Submit: "Defined Providence, which last year ceased publication of its journal, will publish two full-length volumes of poetry in 2001 in open competition to be judged by well known poets. For both contests, the author of the winning 48-120 page ms will receive a prize of $1,000 and 100 copies of a perfect-bound, professionally printed book, selling in paperback for $8. The deadlines are January 1 and June 4. For additional details, or to sample previous books, visit the website or send a SASE."

$ ⬤ **DENVER QUARTERLY; LYNDA HULL POETRY AWARD**, Dept. of English, University of Denver, Denver CO 80208, phone (303)871-2892, fax (303)871-2853, founded 1965, editor Bin Ramke.

⬤ Poetry published here has also been included in the 1997, 1998 and 1999 volumes of *The Best American Poetry*.

Magazine Needs: *DQ* is a quarterly literary journal that publishes fiction, poems, book reviews and essays. There are no restrictions on the type of poetry wanted. Poems here focus on language and lean toward the avant-garde. Length is open, with some long poems and sequences also featured. Translations are also published. They have published poetry by John Ashbery, Jorie Graham, Arthur Sze and Paul Hoover. *Denver Quarterly* is about 130 pgs., 6×9, handsomely printed on buff stock and perfect-bound with 2-color matte card cover. Press run is 1,900 for 900 subscribers of which 300 are libraries, approximately 700 shelf sales. Subscription: $20/year to individuals and $24 to institutions. Sample: $6.

How to Submit: Submit 3-5 poems at a time. Include SASE. Simultaneous submissions OK. Do not submit between May 15 and September 15 each year. Publishes theme issues. Responds in 3 months. "Will request diskette upon acceptance." Pays 2 copies and $5/page. Reviews books of poetry.

Also Offers: The Lynda Hull Poetry Award of $500 is awarded annually for the best poem published in a volume year. All poems published in the *Denver Quarterly* are automatically entered.

⬤ **DESCANSO LITERARY JOURNAL**, P.O. Box 20066, Seattle WA 98102, e-mail goyozura@earthlink.net, website home.earthlink.net/~goyozura, founded 1996, editor Gregory Zura.

Magazine Needs: *Descanso Literary Journal* is a biannual focusing on the "exploration of different issues facing Americans and people of the world through contemporary poetry, fiction and art. One topic is covered per issue." They want "contemporary and honest work; any length, subject matter or style; verse or prose. No overly romantic or gothic style." They have published poetry by Joan Fiset and Noel Franklin. The editor says *DLJ* is 58-64 pgs., 5½×8½, offset printed and saddle-stitched with 4-color cover stock, includes cover photo and photos throughout magazine, b&w ads (3-4 per issue). They receive about 300 poems a year, accept approximately 10%. Press run is 1,000 for 350 subscribers, 300 shelf sales; 50 distributed free to advertisers and contributors. Single copy: $7; subscription: $20/4 issues. Sample: $8.

How to Submit: Submit 5 poems at a time, do not exceed 5 printed pages for any 1 poem. No previously published poems or simultaneous submissions. Cover letter required—"must include brief biography with previous publishing credits." E-mail (plain text or Word attachment) and disk submissions OK. "Name and address must be included on each piece." Time between acceptance and publication is 1 month. Poems are circulated to an editorial board. "Read and discussed by a board of three people." Seldom comments on rejections. Publishes theme issues. Send SASE for guidelines and upcoming themes. Responds in 1 month. Pays 2 copies. Acquires first rights.

Also Offers: Website includes writer's guidelines, ordering information, poetry and photos from past issues, performance information and resource links.

DESCANT (Specialized: themes), Box 314, Station P, Toronto, Ontario M5S 2S8 Canada, phone (416)593-2557, e-mail descant@web.net, website www.descant.on.ca, founded 1970, editor-in-chief Karen Mulhallen.

Magazine Needs: *Descant* is "a quarterly journal of the arts committed to being the finest in Canada. While our focus is primarily on Canadian writing we have published writers from around the world." Some of the poets they have published are Lorna Crozier, Eric Ormsby and Jan Zwicky. *Descant* is 140 pgs., over-sized digest format, elegantly printed and illustrated on heavy paper, flat-spined with colored, glossy cover. They receive 1,200 unsolicited submissions/year, of which they use less than 100, with a 2-year backlog. Circulation is 1,200. Sample: $8.50 plus postage.

How to Submit: Submit typed ms of no more than 6 poems, name and address on first page and last name on each subsequent page. Include SASE with Canadian stamps or SAE and IRCs. "Please include an extra stamp, or an e-mail address, or fax number, so that we may acknowledge receipt of your submission." No previously published poems or simultaneous submissions. Send SASE (or SAE and IRC) for guidelines and upcoming themes. Responds within 4 months. Pays "approximately $100." Buys first rights.

Also Offers: Website includes writer's guidelines, editors, themes, subscription info and excerpts.

Advice: "The best advice is to know the magazine you are submitting to. Please read the magazine before submitting."

DESCANT: FORT WORTH'S JOURNAL OF POETRY AND FICTION, English Dept., Box 297270, Texas Christian University, Fort Worth TX 76129, phone (817)257-6537, fax (817)257-6239, e-mail descant@tcu.edu, founded 1956, editor Dave Kuhne.

Magazine Needs: *Descant* appears annually. They want "well-crafted poems of interest. No restrictions as to subject matter or forms. We usually accept poems 60 lines or fewer but sometimes longer poems." It is more than 100 pgs., 6×9, professionally printed and saddle-stapled with matte card cover. "We publish 30-40 pgs. of poetry per year. We receive probably 4,000-5,000 poems annually." Their press run is 500 for 350 subscribers. Double issue: $12, $18 outside US. Sample: $6.

How to Submit: No simultaneous submissions. Reads submissions September through May only. Responds in 6 weeks. Pays 2 copies.

Also Offers: The Betsy Colquitt Award for poetry, $500 prize awarded annually to the best poem or series of poems by a single author. $10 entry fee. E-mail or send SASE for complete contest rules or guidelines.

DESPERATE ACT, P.O. Box 1081, Pittsford NY 14534, e-mail desact@aol.com, founded 1995, editors Gary Wiener and Steve Engel.

Magazine Needs: *Desperate Act* appears 2 times a year and "focuses on art as something that we do not merely for enjoyment, college credit, fame or tenure, but because we are driven to do it—to keep ourselves sane perhaps. We favor regional writers but will consider good work from anywhere. Any style or content is acceptable so long as the work comes from the writer's inner impulses—some real need—and not from a M.F.A. program. We favor material that is witty, ironic, clever and original. We believe that a poem should 'mean' as well as 'be.' No rhymed or sentimental verse; Hallmark verse; L-A-N-G-U-A-G-E or meaningless poetry." They have published poetry by Thom Ward, William Heyen, Ryan G. Van Cleave and Peter Connors. As a sample the editors selected these lines from "Postmodern Wedding" by Jessy Randall:

> *My silver pattern is high density/aerodynamic steel./My dress is five dimensional./There's a veil behind*
> *my veil.*

DA is 60-100 pgs., digest-sized, desktop-published and flat-spined with 4-color card cover, includes line art and photos. They receive about 1,000 poems a year, accept approximately 1%. Press run is 200 for 20 subscribers of which 5 are libraries, 100 shelf sales. Subscription: $10/2 issues. Sample: $5.

How to Submit: Submit 3-5 poems at a time. No previously published poems; simultaneous submissions OK if informed. Cover letter preferred. E-mail (any format) and disk submissions OK. "However, we do not necessarily send rejections through e-mail. That is, e-mail contributors should not expect a response." Time between acceptance and publication is 6-12 months. Poems are circulated to an editorial board. "Interns, contributing editors and head editors read and recommend pieces." Publishes theme issues occasionally. Send SASE for guidelines and upcoming themes. Responds in 6 months. Pays 1 copy. Acquires first North American serial rights.

Advice: "Our ideal writer has a handful of previous acceptances and several hundred rejections, yet continues to toil away at the craft, convinced that just around the corner . . . are several hundred more rejections. Residence in a garret and/or nose rings are not mandatory, but a rejection slip from *The Iowa Review* is a big plus. Submissions need not be written in blood."

☑ ◑ **DEVIL BLOSSOMS**, P.O. Box 5122, Seabrook NJ 08302-3511, founded 1997, editor John C. Erianne, e-mail theeditor@asteriuspress.com, website www.asteriuspress.com.

Magazine Needs: *Devil Blossoms* appears irregularly, 1-2 times/year, "to publish poetry in which the words show the scars of real life. Sensual poetry that's occasionally ugly. I'd rather read a poem that makes me sick than a poem without meaning." They want poetry that is "darkly comical, ironic, visceral, horrific; or any tidbit of human experience that moves me." They do not want religious greetings, 'I'm-so-happy-to-be-alive' tree poetry. They have published poetry by John Sweet, T. Kilgore Splake, Dennis Saleh and Alan Catlin. As a sample the editor selected these lines from "The Big News" by Karl Wachter:

> A serpent is waiting/beneath the sewer drain/winged angels are asked/for change and the darkness/in
> a god's eyes is mistaken/for dirt.

Devil Blossoms is 24 pgs., 8½×11, saddle-staped, with a matte-card cover and ink drawings (cover only). They receive about 1,500 poems a year, accept approximately 2-3%. Press run is 500, 200 shelf sales. Single copy: $3; subscription: $8. Make checks payable to John C. Erianne.

How to Submit: Submit 2-5 poems at a time. Simultaneous submissions OK. E-mail submissions OK, include in body of message. Cover letter preferred. Time between acceptance and publication is 3-6 months. "I promptly read submissions, divide them into a 'no' and a 'maybe' pile. Then I read the 'maybes' again." Seldom comments on rejections. Send SASE for guidelines. Responds in up to 5 weeks. Pays 1 copy. Acquires first rights.

Also Offers: Website includes guidelines, publication info, contest updates, etc.

Advice: "Write from love; don't expect love in return, don't take rejection personally and don't let anyone stop you."

◑ ◎ **DIAL BOOKS FOR YOUNG READERS (Specialized: children)**, 345 Hudson St., New York NY 10014, website www.penguinputnam.com.

Book/Chapbook Needs & How to Submit: Publishes some illustrated books of poetry for children. They have published poetry by J. Patrick Lewis and Nikki Grimes. Do not submit unsolicited mss. Query first with sample poems and cover letter with brief bio and publication credits. SASE required with all correspondence. No previously published poems; simultaneous submissions OK. Send queries to Attn: Submissions. Replies to queries in 2-4 months. Payment varies.

N ⊕ ◐ **DIALOGOS: HELLENIC STUDIES REVIEW**, Dept. of Byzantine and Modern Greek Studies, King's College, Strand Campus, London WC2R 2LS England, phone/fax 020-7848-2663, e-mail david.ricks@kcl. ac.uk, founded 1994, co-editors David Ricks and Michael Trapp.

Magazine Needs: *Dialogos* is an annual of "Greek language and literature, history and archaeology, culture and thought, present and past." They want "poems with reference to Greek or the Greek world, any period (ancient, medieval, modern), translations of Greek poetry." They do not want "watery mythological musings." They have published poetry by Homer (translated by Oliver Taplin) and Nikos Engonopoulos (translated by Martin McKinsey). As a sample the editor selected these lines by C. Haim Gouri, translated by Avi Sharon:

> "Error always returns" said Odysseus to his weary heart/and came to the crossroads of the next town/
> to find that the way home was not water.

The editor says *Dialogos* is 150 pgs., professionally printed and bound. They receive about 30 poems a year, accept approximately 5%. Press run is 500 for 150 subscribers of which 100 are libraries. Sample: $45. Make checks payable to Frank Cass & Co. Ltd.

How to Submit: Submit 6 poems at a time. No previously published poems or simultaneous submissions. No e-mail submissions. Cover letter preferred. Time between acceptance and publication is 1 year. Poems are circulated to an editorial board of 2 editors. Seldom comments on rejections. Send SASE (or SAE and IRC) for guidelines. Responds within 6 weeks. Always sends prepublication galleys. Pays 1 copy and 25 offprints. Acquires all rights. Returns rights. Reviews books of direct Greek interest, in multi-book review. Open to unsolicited reviews. Poets may also send books for review consideration.

◑ ◎ **JAMES DICKEY NEWSLETTER (Specialized: membership/subscription, nature/rural/ ecology)**, 1753 Dyson Dr., Atlanta GA 30307, fax (404)373-2989, e-mail joycepair@mindspring.com. website www.jamesdickey.org, founded 1984, editor Joyce M. Pair.

Magazine Needs: *JDN* is a biannual newsletter devoted to critical articles/studies of James Dickey's works/ biography and bibliography. They "publish a few poems of high quality. No poems lacking form or meter or grammatical correctness." They have published poetry by Linda Roth, Paula Goff, John Van and Peenen. It is 30 pgs. of ordinary paper, neatly offset (back and front), with a card back-cover, stapled top left corner. The newsletter is published in the fall and spring. Subscription to individuals: $12/year (includes membership in the James Dickey Society), $14 to institutions in the US; outside the US send $14/year individuals, $15.50 institutions. Sample available for $3.50 postage.

How to Submit: Contributors should follow MLA style and standard ms form, sending 1 copy, double-spaced. Cover letter required. E-mail submissions OK (prefer attached file). Fax submissions OK. "However, if a poet wants written comments/suggestions line by line, then mail ms with SASE." Pays 3 copies. Acquires first rights. Reviews "only works on Dickey or that include Dickey." Open to unsolicited reviews.

Also Offers: Website includes biography of Dickey, bylaws of society, contacts, study help, etc.

Advice: "Acquire more knowledge of literary history, metaphor, symbolism and grammar, and, to be safe, the poet should read a couple of our issues."

⬤ THE DIDACTIC, 11702 Webercrest, Houston TX 77048, founded 1993, editor Charlie Mainze.
Magazine Needs: *The Didactic* is a monthly publishing "only, only didactic poetry. That is the only specification. Some satire might be acceptable as long as it is didactic."
How to Submit: Previously published poems and simultaneous submissions OK. Time between acceptance and publication is about a year. "Once it is determined that the piece is of self-evident quality and is also didactic, it is grouped with similar or contrasting pieces. This may cause a lag time for publication." Responds "as quickly as possible." Pay is "nominal." Buys one-time rights. Considering a general review section, only using staff-written reviews. Poets may send books for review consideration.

✤ ⬤ DIG., #2-95 Tyndall Ave., Toronto, Ontario M6K 2G1 Canada, e-mail digjen@interlog.com, founded 1997, editor/publisher j.a. LoveGrove.
Magazine Needs: Published 2 times a year, *dig.* is "an independent literary magazine committed to contemporary writing and art of varying styles and genres. We prefer work that is innovative, impactful and challenging. Nothing cliché, sexist, racist, homophobic, inspirational or boring." They have published poetry by John Barlow, Louise Bak, rob mclennan, Shannon Bramer, Paul Vermeersch, Adeena Karasick, Sherwin Tjia and Jay MillAr. The editor says *dig.* is 30-40 pgs., magazine-sized, photocopied and hand-stitched with hand-stamped covers on handmade papers, includes a couple of ads. They receive about 300 poems a year, accept approximately 12%. Press run is 200. Single copy: $5; subscription: $15/3 issue subscription. Sample: $4. Make checks payable to Jennifer LoveGrove.
How to Submit: Submit 4-6 poems at a time. No previously published poems; simultaneous submissions OK, notify if work is accepted elsewhere. Cover letter with brief bio and SASE. E-mail submissions OK (no attachments). Time between acceptance and publication is 1-6 months. Seldom comments on rejections. Publishes theme issues occasionally. Send SASE for guidelines or obtain via e-mail. Responds in up to 3 months. Pays 2 copies. Rights remain with author. Staff reviews books and chapbooks of poetry in 750 words, single book format. Send books for review consideration.
Book/Chapbook Needs & How to Submit: Publishes poetry/fiction chapbooks. Query first with sample and proposal and bio. Replies to queries in up to 3 months.

$⬤ DIM GRAY BAR PRESS, 600 W. 111th St., New York NY 10025, phone (212)866-4465, e-mail ordinarymind@erols.com, founded 1989, publisher Barry Magid.
Book/Chapbook Needs: Dim Gray Bar Press publishes letterpress limited editions marketed to the rare book/fine printing trade. They publish 1-2 hardbacks and 1-2 chapbooks/year. They have no restrictions regarding form or style. They have published poetry by William Matthews and James Laughlin. As a sample the publisher selected this poem "Favrile" by Mark Doty:

> Don't we need a word/for the luster/of things which insist/on the fact they're made,/which announce/
> their maker's bravura?

Books are letterpress printed and hand bound, both cloth and wrapper covers, include commissioned illustrations.
How to Submit: Submit 3-6 poems at a time. Previously published poems and simultaneous submissions OK. Cover letter preferred. E-mail submissions OK. Time between acceptance and publication is 6-9 months. "Almost (but not all) manuscripts are solicited by the publisher from established authors whose first editions are considered collectible by the rare book market." Seldom comments on rejections. Replies to queries and mss in 1-2 months. Pays $100 honorarium or 5-10 author's copies (out of a press run of 100).
Also Offers: The press has printed/designed winning chapbooks in the Center for Book Arts Poetry Chapbook Competition series. Send SASE for guidelines to CBA, 626 Broadway, New York NY 10012.

⬤ ◎ DIRIGIBLE (Specialized: form/style, avant-garde, translations), 101 Cottage St., New Haven CT 06511, e-mail dirigibl@javanet.com, founded 1994, co-editors David Todd and Cynthia Conrad.
Magazine Needs: "*Dirigible* is a quarterly avant-garde journal of language art which publishes prose, poetry, selective reviews, translations, and hybrid genres. We seek language-centered poetry, controlled experiments, fiction that is postmodern, paraliterary, nonlinear or subjective, and work that breaks with genre, convention or form. Hybrid forms of writing and essays on aesthetics, poetics, reader experience and writing processes are also of interest to us. No social issues, no inspirational, scatological or emotional exhibitionism." They have published poetry by Sheila E. Murphy, W.B. Keckler, Simon Perchik, Ron Padgett, Richard Kostelanetz, Scott Keeney and Dennis Holt. As a sample the editor selected these lines from "Weights and Measures" by Morgan Avery Sispoidis:

> I hold your steadfastness/like a spirit level/to keep a balance that/does not fall/to guide me past the
> worn down chairs/away from spoon-faces and kitchen knives/and things that linger in thin curtains/
> sharp and white like razor blades.

Dirigible is 40-48 pgs., 4¼×7, photocopied, saddle-stapled with buff card cover, in-house graphics; "will swap ads with similar publications." They accept approximately 10% of poems received each year. Press run is 500-800, 60% shelf sales. Subscription: $10/year. Sample: $3. Make checks payable to Dirigible.

How to Submit: Submit up to 8 poems at a time. No previously published poems or simultaneous submissions. No e-mail submissions. Cover letter preferred. Time between acceptance and publication is 1-3 months. Responds in up to 3 months. Pays 2 copies. Acquires first rights. Staff reviews books of poetry—"selective reviews; length and type vary."

Advice: "We are interested in a phenomenological lyricism which recreates the texture and logic of interior experience. We are grinding an aesthetic ax and acceptance is dependent upon our editorial vision."

☑ ◐ **THE DISTILLERY**, Motlow State Community College, P.O. Box 88100, Lynchburg TN 37352-8500, phone (931)393-1700, fax (931)393-1761, founded 1994, editor Inman Majors.

Magazine Needs: *The Distillery* appears twice a year and publishes "the highest quality poetry, fiction and criticism. We are looking for poetry that pays careful attention to line, voice and image. We like poems that take emotional risks without giving in to easy sentimentality or staged cynicism." They have published poetry by Walter McDonald, Thomas Rabbitt, Virgil Suarez and John Sisson. As a sample the editor selected these lines from "Toward a Theology of Headgear" by G.C. Waldrep:

> In the town of my youth one mansion's cupola/beckoned with its shadow, burned a darker//shade of
> night and hid the moon so perfectly/it seemed a part of space itself, wheeling,//in collusion with the
> small mean stars.

Distillery is 88 pgs., digest-sized, professionally printed on matte paper, perfect-bound, color cover, b&w photography. They receive about 800 poems a year, accept approximately 2%. Press run is 750. Subscription: $15/year (2 issues). Sample: $7.50.

How to Submit: Submit 4-6 poems at a time with SASE. No previously published poems; simultaneous submissions OK "if poet informs us immediately of acceptance elsewhere." Cover letter preferred. Reads submissions August 15 through May 15 only. Time between acceptance and publication is 6-12 months. Poems are circulated to an editorial board. "Poems are read by three preliminary readers then passed to the poetry editor." Seldom comments on rejections. Send SASE for guidelines. Responds in 3 months. Pays 2 copies. Acquires first North American serial rights.

Advice: "We continue to publish the best poetry sent to us, regardless of name or reputation. We like poets who look as if they would write poems even if there were no magazines in which to publish them."

☑ ◐ ◎ **DIXIE PHOENIX (Specialized: humor, regional, spirituality/inspirational, writing)**, P.O. Box 5676, Arlington VA 22205, e-mail jsmosby@gateway.net, website www.concentric.net/~yamyak/dixiephoenix, founded 1992, co-editor Michael Munson.

Magazine Needs: *Dixie Phoenix* is "a home-grown literary magazine featuring short stories, travel essays, poetry, history, spirituality, reviews, recipes, etc." They want "anything from free verse to sonnet in style, spiritual (your own definition) and/or sincere in subject matter; confessional to transcendentalist. No profanity or violence; no shock poetry in general." They have published poetry by John Grey and Patricia G. Rourke. As a sample the editor selected these lines from "The Would-Be Buddies" by Edward Mycue:

> nor a secret sting nor a single source/for light. You won't go against the/grain. To open the grain you
> have to/continue the assault on summer, assault/the seasons, senses, force the glistening/hasp, confront
> what still could grow again.

The editor says *DP* is 48 pgs., 5½×8½, photocopied and stapled with 20-60 lb. color paper cover, includes photocopied graphics and trades ads. They receive about 90-100 poems a year, accept approximately 1-2%. Press run is 500 for 50 subscribers of which 5-10 are libraries. Subscription: $8/4 issues. Sample: $2. Make checks payable to Michael Munson. Potential contributors are encouraged to buy sample copy.

How to Submit: Submit up to 5 poems at a time. Previously published poems and simultaneous submissions OK. Cover letter preferred. E-mail submissions OK (must be in body of message). Reads submissions August 1 through November 1 for winter issue, January 1 through June 1 for summer issue. Time between acceptance and publication is 6 months. Seldom comments on rejections. Publishes theme issues occasionally. Send SASE for guidelines. Responds in 4 months. Pays 3 copies. Acquires one-time rights. Staff reviews books and chapbooks of poetry and other magazines in 200-700 words. Send books for review consideration.

Also Offers: Website includes writer's guidelines and ordering information, as well as certain features and links.

Advice: "Develop your own style, don't copy or adhere to others. We value sincerity over shock value."

⊕ ☑ ◐ **DOC(K)S; AKENATON**, 4 Cours Grandval, F 20 000 AJACCIO France.

Magazine Needs: *Doc(k)s* uses "concrete, visual, sound poetry; performance; mail-art; metaphysical poetry." They have published work by Nani Balestrini, Bernard Heidsieck, James Koller, Julien Blaine, Philippe Castellin and Franco Beltrametti. The magazine *Doc(k)s* is published 4 times a year and has a circulation of 1,100, of which 150 are subscriptions. It is an elegantly produced volume of over 300 pgs., 7×10, flat-spined, using heavy paper and glossy full-color card covers. Most of it is in French. "We cannot quote a sample, because concrete poetry, a cross between poetry and graphic art, requires the visual image to be reproduced."

How to Submit: There are no specifications for submissions. Pays 5 copies.

Book/Chapbook Needs: Akenaton publishes collections of poetry, mostly in French.

☑ ○ **DOGGEREL; INSPECTOR J. LEE POETRY CONTEST**, 312 S. 16th Ave., Hattiesburg MS 39401, phone (601)583-7422, e-mail hrozelle@ocean.st.usm.edu, founded 1994, editor Lee Rozelle.

Magazine Needs: *Doggerel* is almost a biannual journal designed "to publish poetry with a limp. We also take short prose, reviews, photos, cartoons, etc." They have published poetry by Brian Becker, Mike Clark, Philip Heldrich, Angela Ball and Mark Cox. As a sample the editor selected these lines from "Hitch Hiker" by Wayne Sheldrake:

> *When you pass,/I search for the vocabulary/of black magic. I drive needles/made of my middle finger into the/voo doo doll of your asphalt heart.*

Doggerel is 30-50 pgs., 6½×8½ (folded 8½×11), printed by "the cheapest method possible," saddle-stapled with glossy card cover containing b&w photo or art. They receive about 250 poems a year, accept approximately 20%. Press run is 150. Subscription: $8. Sample: $4. Make checks payable to Lee Rozelle.
How to Submit: Submit 3-5 poems at a time. Previously published poems OK; no simultaneous submissions. "No e-mail submissions." Time between acceptance and publication is 6 months. Poems are circulated to an editorial board. Seldom comments on rejections. Send SASE for guidelines. Responds in 3 months. Sometimes sends prepublication galleys. Pays 1 copy. Acquires all rights. Returns rights after publication Reviews books and chapbooks of poetry and other magazines in 250 words. Open to unsolicited reviews. Poets may also send books for review consideration.
Also Offers: Sponsors the Inspector J. Lee Poetry Contest. 1st Prize: $100. Reading fee: $1. No restrictions on matter or style. Send query for deadline info.

DOLPHIN-MOON PRESS; SIGNATURES (Specialized: regional), P.O. Box 22262, Baltimore MD 21203, founded 1973, president James Taylor.
Book/Chapbook Needs: Dolphin-Moon is "a limited-edition (500-1,000 copies) press which emphasizes quality work (regardless of style), often published in unusual/'radical' format." The writer is usually allowed a strong voice in the look/feel of the final piece. "We've published magazines, anthologies, chapbooks, pamphlets, perfect-bound paperbacks, records, audio cassettes and comic books. All styles are read and considered, but the work should show a strong spirit and voice. Although we like the feel of 'well-crafted' work, craft for its own sake won't meet our standards either." They have published work by Teller, Michael Weaver, John Strausbaugh, Josephine Jacobsen and William Burroughs. Send SASE for catalog and purchase samples or send $15 for their 'sampler' (which they guarantee to be up to $25 worth of their publications).
How to Submit: To submit, first send sample of 6-10 pgs. of poetry and a brief cover letter. Replies to query or to submission of whole work (if invited) in 2-4 weeks. Always sends prepublication galleys. Pays in author's copies, negotiable, though usually 10% of the run. Acquires first edition rights.
Advice: "Our future plans are to continue as we have since 1973, publishing the best work we can by local, up-and-coming and nationally recognized writers—in a quality package."

DOVETAIL: A JOURNAL BY AND FOR JEWISH/CHRISTIAN FAMILIES (Specialized: interfaith marriage), 775 Simon Greenwell Lane, Boston KY 40107, phone (502)549-5499, fax (502)549-3543, e-mail DI-IFR@Bardstown.com, website www.dovetailpublishing.com, founded 1991, editor Mary Rosenbaum.
Magazine Needs: *Dovetail*, published bimonthly, provides "strategies and resources for interfaith couples, their families and friends." They want poetry related to Jewish/Christian marriage issues. No general religious themes." The editor says *Dovetail* is 12-16 pgs., magazine-sized, stapled, includes 1-5 ads. They receive about 10 poems a year, accept approximately 1%. Press run is 1,000 for 700 subscribers. Single copy: $4.50; subscription: $25. Sample: $5.28. Make checks payable to DI-IFR.
How to Submit: Submit 1 poem at a time. Previously published poems and simultaneous submissions OK. E-mail and disk submissions OK. Time between acceptance and publication is up to 1 year. Poems are circulated to an editorial board. "Clergy and other interfaith professionals review draft issues." Seldom comments on rejections. Publishes theme issues. Send SASE for guidelines and upcoming themes. Responds in 1 month. Pays $10-20 plus copies. Buys first North American serial rights. Reviews other magazines in 500 words, single and multi-book format. Open to unsolicited reviews.

DREAM INTERNATIONAL QUARTERLY (Specialized: dreams), 809 W. Maple St., Champaign IL 61820-2810, founded 1981, senior poetry editor Carmen M. Pursifull.
Magazine Needs: "Poetry must be dream-inspired and/or dream-related. This can be interpreted loosely, even to the extent of dealing with the transitory as a theme. Nothing written expressly or primarily to advance a political or religious ideology. We have published everything from neo-Romantic sonnets to stream-of-consciousness, ala 'the Beat Generation.'" They have published poetry by Ursula Le Guin, Errol Miller and Dr. Dimitri Mihalas. As a sample the publisher selected these lines from Ms. Pursifull's poem "Co-existing With Change in a World of Probabilities":

> *What enchants in daytime/can be menacing in the dark./Black trees rustle wind-whisper warnings,/to each other of formless monster-stalkings/in the night.*

DIQ is 120-150 pgs., 8½×11, with vellum cover and drawings. They receive 300 poems a year, accept about 30. Press run is 300 for 20 subscribers. Subscription: $50 for 1 year. Sample: $13.
How to Submit: Submit up to 3 typed poems at a time. Previously published poems and simultaneous submissions OK. Cover letter including publication history, if any. "As poetry submissions go through the hands of two readers, poets should enclose 2 loose stamps, along with the standard SASE." Do not submit mss in September

or October. Time between acceptance and publication is 1-2 years. Comments on rejections if requested. Send large SASE with 2 first-class stamps plus $2 for guidelines. Responds in 2 weeks. Sometimes sends prepublication galleys. Pays 1 copy, "less postage. Postage/handling for contributor's copy costs $3." Also, from time to time, "exceptionally fine work has been deemed to merit a complimentary subscription." Acquires first North American serial or nonexclusive reprint rights.

Advice: "We consider all types of poetry from blank verse to sonnets, from shape poems to haiku. However, nothing will turn me off more quickly on a submission than 'sing-song' greeting card style verse. Be very careful with rhyming poetry."

N **$** **☐** **◐** **◎** **DREAMS AND NIGHTMARES (Specialized: science fiction/fantasy)**, 1300 Kicker Rd., Tuscaloosa AL 35404, phone (205)553-2284, e-mail dragontea@earthlink.net, website home.earthlink.net/~dragontea/index.html, founded 1986, editor David C. Kopaska-Merkel.

● *Dreams and Nightmares* received an award from the Professional Book Center for "advancing the field of speculative poetry."

Magazine Needs: The editor says, "I want to see intriguing poems in any form or style under about 60 lines (but will consider longer poems). All submissions must be either science fiction, fantasy or horror (I prefer supernatural horror to gory horror). Nothing trite or sappy, no very long poems, no poems without fantastic content, no excessive violence or pointless erotica. Sex and/or violence is OK if there is a good reason." Also accepts poetry written by children. He has published poetry by Charlee Jacob, Herb Kauderer, D.F. Lewis, Wendy Rathbone, Greg Stewart and John Grey. As a sample the editor selected these lines from "out by the airport" by W. Gregory Stewart:

> there's a joint/called the Mobius Strip/where the girls/take it off/and take it off/and take it off again

Dreams and Nightmares, published three times a year, is 24 pgs., digest-sized, photocopied from typescript and saddle-stapled with a colored card stock cover and b&w illustrations. They accept about 80 of 1,000-1,500 poems received. Press run is 200 for 90 subscribers. Subscription: $12/6 issues (North America); $15/6 issues (outside North America). Lifetime subscription: $100 (includes available back issues). Samples: $3.

How to Submit: Submit up to 5 poems at a time. "Rarely" uses previously published poems. No simultaneous submissions. Send SASE for guidelines. Information requests and comments via e-mail are welcome; e-mail submissions are accepted in body of message. Responds in 10 weeks. Pays $5/poem plus 2 copies. Buys first North American serial rights. The editor reviews books of poetry. Send books for review consideration.

Advice: "There are more magazines publishing fantastic poetry than ever before, and more good fantastic poetry is being written, sold for good money and published. The field is doing very well."

◎ **THE DRIFTWOOD REVIEW (Specialized: regional)**, P.O. Box 700, Linden MI 48451-0700, e-mail driftwdmi@aol.com, founded 1996, poetry editor Jeff Vande Zande.

Magazine Needs: "An annual publication, *The Driftwood Review* strives to publish the best poetry and fiction being written by Michigan writers—known and unknown. We consider any style, but are particularly fond of poetry that conveys meaning through image. Rhyming poetry stands a poor chance. Give up the ghost; rhyme is dead—good riddance." They have published poetry by Daniel James Sundahl, Anca Vlasopolos, Terry Blackhawk and Joe Sheltraw. As a sample the editor selected these lines from "Tattooed" by Matthew Echelberger:

> I remember when he bought me a speed bag/for Christmas and made the red leather sing,/his sinew and muscle straining/against the anchor tattooed on his forearm

TDR is 100-125 pgs., digest-sized, professionally printed and perfect-bound with glossy card cover containing b&w artwork. They receive about 500 poems a year, accept approximately 5-7%. Press run is 200 for 75 subscribers. Subscription: $6.

How to Submit: Submit 3-5 poems at a time. No previously published poems or simultaneous submissions. Cover letter preferred. "Cover letter should include a brief bio suitable for contributors notes. No SASE? No reply." Reads submissions January 1 through October 1 only. Time between acceptance and publication is 9 months. Seldom comments on rejections. "Will comment on work that's almost there." Responds in 3 months. Pays 1 copy and includes the opportunity to advertize a book. Acquires first North American serial rights. Staff reviews chapbooks of poetry by Michigan writers only in 500 words, single book format. Send chapbooks for review consideration.

Also Offers: Sponsors a Reader's Choice Award. "Our readers vote by e-mail and the winner receives a cash award."

Advice: "There are too many writers and not enough readers."

✓ **▣** **○** **THE DRINKIN' BUDDY MAGAZINE**, P.O. Box 720608, San Jose CA 95172, e-mail kc@cfqdesign.com, website www.drinkinbuddy.com, founded 1994, contact Poetry Dept.

Magazine Needs: *The Drinkin' Buddy Magazine*, published weekly online, is "a magazine for art and words." They want "shorter, concise work." They receive about 50 poems a year, "use what we can."

How to Submit: Previously published poems and simultaneous submissions OK. Cover letter preferred. Only accepts e-mail submissions. For e-mail submissions, include text file or Word document. Time between acceptance and publication "depends on when we can use it." Seldom comments on rejections. Acquires first North American serial or one-time rights. Reviews books of poetry. Open to unsolicited reviews. Poets may also send books for review consideration.

☑ ◻ ◉ **DRY BONES PRESS; THE COMPLEAT NURSE (Specialized: nursing)**, P.O. Box 597, Roseville CA 95678-0597, voice mail/fax (415)707-2129, e-mail jrankin@drybones.com, website www.drybones .com, founded 1992 (Dry Bones Press), editor/publisher Jim Rankin, RN, MSN.

Magazine Needs: *the Compleat Nurse*, a monthly newsletter, "is a voice of independent nursing featuring matters of interest to nurses—a very broad range, indeed." They have published poetry by James Snydal. *the Compleat Nurse* is 4 pgs., 8½ × 11, desktop-published, folded with clip art; occasionally published as an anthology. They receive about 10-20 poems a year, "accept most, if in our range." Press run is 500-1,000 with all distributed free. Sample for SASE.

How to Submit: Submit 2-3 poems at a time. Previously published poems and simultaneous submissions OK. E-mail and fax submissions OK. Cover letter preferred. Time between acceptance and publication "varies greatly; 1 month to 2 years." Poems are selected by editor with consideration of space availability. Always comments on rejections. Responds "within 30 days." Sometimes sends prepublication galleys. Pays 4 copies. Acquires "one-time rights, plus right to include in anthology." Reviews books or chapbooks of poetry. Open to unsolicited reviews. Poets may also send books for review consideration.

Book/Chapbook Needs & How to Submit: Dry Bones Press seeks "to encourage nurses, or just do things we like, or want to take a flyer on." Publishes 1-3 paperbacks and 2-3 chapbooks/year as well as occasional anthologies. Books are usually 5½ × 8½, offset, stapled or "fine wire-O" bound with glossy, b&w cover. Replies to queries and mss in 1 month. Pays 10 author's copies.

☑ ◖ **THE DRY CREEK REVIEW**, Aims Community College, 5401 W. 20th St., P.O. Box 69, Greeley CO 80634, website www.aims.edu/AcademicAffairs/CHB/DCR, founded 1990, faculty advisor Tony Park.

Magazine Needs: *TDCR* is an annual. "We accept creative nonfiction, fiction, translations and quality poetry." They are open to all forms/styles. "We want poems built around vivid imagery, rich language and risk. We do not want to see the abstract based on the insignificant." They have published poetry by Carolyn Forché, Joy Harjo, Bill Tremblay and Veronica Patterson. As a sample the editor selected these lines from "Driving Home After Spanish Class" by Jane Oakley:

> *Dark as the inside of a wolf's mouth/Tenses of verbs flood my brain/The bruja empties a bucket of*
> *water/on the windshield/Estuvo lloviendo/It was raining.*

The editors say *Dry Creek Review* is 120-140 pgs., 6 × 9, professionally printed and flat-spined with glossy card cover. They receive 500-600 poems a year, accept 5-15%. Press run is 1,000.

How to Submit: No previously published poems; simultaneous submissions OK. Poems are circulated to an editorial board. Seldom comments on rejections. Responds in 6 months. Pays 2 copies. Rights revert to author on publication. Open to unsolicited reviews. Poets may also send books for review consideration.

◖ ◉ **DWAN (Specialized: gay/lesbian/bisexual, translations, bilingual/foreign language)**, Box 411, Swarthmore PA 19081-0411, e-mail dsmith3@swarthmore.edu, founded 1993, editor Donny Smith.

Magazine Needs: Published every 2 to 3 months, *Dwan* is a "queer poetry zine; some prose; some issues devoted to a single poet or a single theme ('Jesus' or 'Mom and Dad,' for instance)." The editor wants "poetry exploring gender, sexuality, sex roles, identity, queer politics, etc. Heterosexuals usually welcome." They have published poetry by Haviland Ferris, Fabián Iriarte and Alicia Gallegos. As a sample the editor selected these lines by Sappho:

> *Viniste, hiciste bien; yo te deseaba./Me refrescaste el alma que ardía de deseo.*

Dwan is 20 pgs., 5½ × 8½, photocopied on plain white paper, and stapled. They receive 400-500 pgs. of poetry/ year, accept less than 10%. Press run is 100. Sample available for $2 (free to prisoners). Make checks payable to Donny Smith.

How to Submit: Submit 5-15 poems typed. Previously published poems and simultaneous submissions OK. E-mail submissions OK, "include in body of message, no attachments." Cover letter required. Time between acceptance and publication is 6-18 months. Often comments on rejections. Send SASE for upcoming themes. Responds in 3 months. Pays copies. The editor reviews books, chapbooks and magazines usually in 25-150 words. Send books for review consideration.

Advice: "Our guidelines: Queer. Legible. You decide what that means."

☑ ◻ ◖ ◉ **EAGLE'S FLIGHT; EAGLE'S FLIGHT BOOKS (Specialized: translations)**, 1505 N. Fifth St., Sayre OK 73662, phone (580)928-2298, founded 1989, editor/publisher Shyamkant Kulkarni.

TO RECEIVE REGULAR TIPS AND UPDATES about writing and Writer's Digest publications via e-mail, send an e-mail with SUBSCRIBE NEWSLETTER in the body of the message to newsletter-request@writersdigest.com, or sign up online at www.writersdigest.com.

Magazine Needs: *EF* is a quarterly "platform for poets and short story writers—new and struggling to come forward." They want "well-crafted literary quality poetry, any subject, any form, including translations. Translations should have permission of original poets." They have published poetry by Robert O. Schulz, Amrita Kulkarni and Kim Klemm. As a sample the editor selected these lines from "Midnight" by Camille E. Torok:

> Midnight calls, I respond./The force of nature beckons/me from constraint. Dawn is a lifetime away/
> and the darkness lasts forever.

Eagle's Flight is 8-12 pgs., 7×8½, printed on colored paper and saddle-stapled, including simple art, few ads. They receive about 200 poems/year, accept 10%. Press run is 200 for 100 subscribers. Subscription: $5. Sample: $1.25.

How to Submit: Submit up to 5 poems at a time, no more than 21 lines each. No previously published poems or simultaneous submissions. Cover letter required; include short bio, up to 4 lines. Reads submissions January 1 through June 30 only. Time between acceptance and publication is 1-3 years. Seldom comments on rejections. "All material accepted for publication is subject to editing according to our editorial needs." Send SASE for guidelines. Responds in 3 months. Pays 1 copy. Acquires first publication rights. Reviews books of poetry in 250-750 words, single format.

Advice: "We expect poets to be familiar with our publication and our expectations and our limitations. To be a subscriber is one way of doing this. Everybody wants to write poems and, in his heart, is a poet. Success lies in getting ahead of commonplace poetry. To do this one has to read, to be honest, unashamed and cherish decent values of life in his heart. Then success is just on the corner of the next block."

✓ ◎ EARTH'S DAUGHTERS: A FEMINIST ARTS PERIODICAL (Specialized: women/feminism, themes), P.O. Box 41, Central Park Station, Buffalo NY 14215, website www.earthsdaughters.org, founded 1971.

Magazine Needs: The "literary periodical with strong feminist emphasis" appears 3 times a year, irregularly spaced. Its "format varies. Most issues are flat-spined, digest-sized issues of approximately 60 pgs. We also publish chapbooks, magazine-sized and tabloid-sized issues. Past issues have included broadsheets, calendars, scrolls and one which could be assembled into a box." Poetry can be "up to 40 lines (rare exceptions for exceptional work), free form, experimental—we like unusual work. All must be strong, supportive of women in all their diversity. We like work by new writers, but expect it to be well-crafted. We want to see work of technical skill and artistic intensity. We rarely publish work in classical form, and we never publish rhyme or greeting card verse." They have published poetry by Christine Cassidy, Diane di Prima, Janine Pommy Vaga, Joseph Bruchak, Lyn Lifshin, Susan Fantl Spivack, "and many fine 'unknown' poets, writers and artists." They publish poetry by men if it is supportive of women. As a sample the editor selected "Sweet Dream" by Tori Gallagher:

> I woke from dreaming the smooth arctic/wasteland of your skin which I have haunted/slowly, again
> and again. The cliffs/of your face soared above me, the sea/washing green to blue in your/tropic
> eyes . . .

"Our purpose is to publish work that otherwise might never be printed, either because it is unusual, or because the writer is not well known." Subscription: $18/3 issues for individuals; $22 for institutions. Sample: $5.

How to Submit: Reading fee: $5 for nonsubscribers. Simultaneous submissions OK. "Per each issue, authors are limited to a total of 150 lines of poetry, prose or a combination of the two. Submissions in excess of these limits will be returned unread. Business-size envelope is preferred, and use sufficient postage—we do not accept mail with postage due." Publishes theme issues. Send SASE for guidelines and upcoming themes. Length of response time is atrociously long if ms is being seriously considered for publication, otherwise within 3 weeks. Pays 2 copies and reduced prices on further copies. Editor comments "whenever we have time to do so—we want to encourage new writers."

Also Offers: Website includes writers guidelines, upcoming topics, history of *ED*, etc.

Advice: "Once you have submitted work, please be patient. We only hold work we are seriously considering for publication, and it can be up to a year between acceptance and publication. If you must contact us (change of address, notification that a simultaneous submission has been accepted elsewhere), be sure to state the issue theme, the title(s) of your work and enclose SASE."

✓ ◯ ◎ EASTERN CARIBBEAN INSTITUTE (Specialized: ethnic/nationality, regional), P.O. Box 1338, Frederiksted, U.S. Virgin Islands 00841, phone (340)772-3164, fax (340)772-3463, e-mail sjonesh@hotmail.com, website www.nvo.com/sjonesh, founded 1982, editor S.B. Jones-Hendrickson, editorial contact S.B. Jones-Hendrickson.

Book/Chapbook Needs: *Eastern Caribbean Institute* is a "small press publisher" especially interested in poetry of the Caribbean and Eastern Caribbean. As a sample the editor included these lines from "We'll Understand Why" in *A Walk Through My Mind* by Meredith Warner-Phipps:

> Sometimes our lives are filled with sorrow,/How we grown and how we cry/But in spite of our tears
> and anguish/One of these days we'll understand why.

Their books are softcover, averaging 60 pgs. Sample copies available for purchase.

How to Submit: Submit 5 sample poems with SASE and cover letter with bio and previous publications. Simultaneous submissions and previously published poems OK. Reads submissions January to May only. Publishes theme issues. Send SASE for guidelines. Responds in 1 month. Pays 50 copies.

Advice: "In our part of the world, poetry is moving on a new level. People who are interested in regional poetry should keep an eye on the Caribbean region."

◐ ECKERD COLLEGE REVIEW, Eckerd College, 4200 54th Ave. S., St. Petersburg FL 33711, phone (727)864-7859, e-mail siren@eckerd.edu, contact poetry editor, founded 1993.

Magazine Needs: Appearing annually in March, *Eckerd College Review* is the nationally-distributed literary magazine of Eckerd College which publishes high quality poetry, fiction and color and b&w artwork. "We want to see poems of a wide range of content, length and tone from poets who pay particular attention to craft (particularly line, stanza and voice). Nothing sentimental or cliché, nor poems that are needlessly obscure or Beat." They have published poetry by Dannie Abse, Betty Adcock, Ruth Schwartz and Dana Gioia. As a sample the editor selected these lines from "Postscript" by Simeon Berry:

> *This light/that falls away, from the mud in the bricks,//from the street of crushed shell, from everything/*
> *that is involuntary in your body, this light//will fall away forever.*

The editor says *ECR* is 100 pgs., perfect-bound with full-color cover and art. "We receive 800-900 poems a year and usually accept 1%." Press run is 1,400 for 800 shelf sales. Sample: $6.

How to Submit: Submit 3-5 poems at a time. Line length for poetry is 75 maximum. No previously published poems or simultaneous submissions. Cover letter with short bio and SASE required. Reads submissions September 1 through January only. Postmark deadline: January 15. Seldom comments on rejections. Send SASE for guidelines. Responds in 6 weeks. Pays 2 copies. Acquires first rights. Staff reviews books of poetry and fiction in 900 words, single format. Send books for review consideration.

Also Offers: Sponsors a yearly poetry contest with a first prize ($500 in 1999-2000); write or e-mail for guidelines on how to submit to contest.

Advice: "Editors favor authors who have studied other poets as well as their craft."

▨ $◐ ◎ ÉCRITS DES FORGES; ESTUAIRE; ARCADE; EXIT (Specialized: foreign language, women), 1497 Laviolette, Trois-Rivières, Québec G9A 5G4 Canada, phone (819)379-9813, fax (819)376-0774, e-mail ecrits.desforges@aiqnet.com, founded 1971, président Gaston Bellemare, directrice générale Maryse Baribeau.

Magazine Needs: Écrits des Forges publishes 3 poetry journals each year: *Estuaire* appears 5 times a year and wants poetry from well-known poets; *Exit* appears 4 times a year and wants poetry from beginning poets; and *Arcade* appears 3 times a year and wants poetry from women only. All three publications only accept work in French. They want poetry that is "authentic and original as a signature." "We have published poetry from more than a thousand poets coming from most of the francophone's countries: André Romus (Belgium), Amadou Lamine Sall (Sénégal), Nicole Brossard, Claudine Bertrand, Denise Brassard, Tony Tremblay and Jean-Paul Daoust (Québec)." As a sample they selected these lines from "La peau fragile du ciel" by Bernard Pozier:

> *l'infini défait ses gris hérités de la pluie/dans la brume laiteuse du soir/et l'on tente de distinguer la*
> *plage le ciel et l'océan/en flottant dans ce néant/et c'est comme essayer enfin de savoir/s'il est plus*
> *facile de faire parler le poème/ou bien faire taire la mer*

The 3 journals are 88-108 pgs., 5½×8, perfect-bound with art on cover, includes ads from poetry publishers. They receive more than 1,000 poems a year, accept less than 5%. Press run for *Estuaire* is 750 for 450 subscribers of which 250 are libraries. Press run for *Arcade* is 650 for 375 subscribers of which 260 are libraries. Press run for *Exit* is 500 for 110 subscribers of which 235 are libraries. Subscription for *Estuaire* is $45 plus p&h; for *Arcade* is $27 plus p&h; for *Exit* is $36 plus p&h. Samples: $10 each. For *Exit* make checks payable to Éditions Gaz Moutarde. For *Estuaire* and *Arcade*, make checks payable to the respective publication.

How to Submit: Submit 10 poems at a time. No previously published poems or simultaneous submissions. "We make decisions on submissions in February, May, September and December." Time between acceptance and publication is 3-12 months. Poems are circulated to an editorial board. "Nine persons read the submissions and send their recommendations to the editorial board." *Arcade* publishes theme issues. Upcoming themes are listed in the journal. Obtain guidelines via e-mail. Responds in 5 months. Pays "10% of the market price based on number of copies sold." Buys all rights for 1 year. Retains rights to reprint in anthology for 10 years. Staff reviews books and chapbooks of poetry and other magazines on 1 page, double-spaced, single book format. Send books for review consideration.

Book/Chapbook Needs & How to Submit: Écrits des Forges inc. publishes poetry only—40-50 paperbacks/year. Books are usually 80-88 pgs., 5½×8, perfect-bound with 2-color cover with art. Query first with a few sample poems and cover letter with brief bio and publication credits. Replies to queries in 3-6 months. Pays royalties of 10-20%, advance of 50% maximum, and 25 author's copies. Order sample books by writing or faxing.

Also Offers: Sponsors the International Poetry Festival. "250 poets from 30 countries based on the 5 continents read their poems over 10-day period in 70 different cafés, bars, restaurants, etc. 30,000 persons attend. All in French." For more information, see website: www.aiqnet.com/fiptr.

▨ $◐ ECW PRESS, 2120 Queen St. E., Suite 200, Toronto, Ontario M4E 1E2 Canada, phone (416)694-3348, fax (416)698-9906, e-mail ecw@sympatico.ca, website www.ecw.ca/press, founded 1979, literary editor Michael Holmes.

Book/Chapbook Needs: ECW Press typically publishes 4 Canadian-authored paperback titles/year. They want interesting—structurally challenging poetry. No greeting card doggerel. They have published poetry by Robert Priest, Sky Gilbert, David McGimpsey, Mark Sinnett and Libby Scheier. Books are usually 96-150 pgs., 5×8, perfect-bound with full color covers.

How to Submit: Query first with a few sample poems and cover letter with brief bio and publication credits. Then, when requested, submit 10 poems at a time. Previously published poems and simultaneous submissions OK. E-mail submissions OK, include as attached file. Cover letter required. Time between acceptance and publication is 12-18 months. Seldom comments on rejections. Replies to queries in 2 weeks; to mss in 2 months. Pays royalties of 10% plus advance of $300 and 20 author's copies (out of initial press run of 750). Order sample books by sending $14.

EDGAR: DIGESTED VERSE (Specialized: macabre), 486 Essex Ave., Bloomfield NJ 07003, phone (973)748-5794, e-mail dragoons5@aol.com, founded 1999, editor John Picinich, associate editor Victoria Picinich.

Magazine Needs: *EDGAR* is a "quarterly eclectic collection of the darkly bizarre, erotic and offbeat." They want "horror, gothic, surreal, science fiction. Go for the jugular, but give the reader something to chew over." They do not want "prose poems; werewolf and vampire verse; sappy sweet stuff." Accepts poetry written by teenagers. They have published poetry by Kurt Newton, Marge Simon, c.s. anderson and Marie Kazalia. As a sample the editors selected these lines from "Awake" by Lorelei K. Hickman:

> *If I were to tell you the truth/about the sorts of things/that plague my dreams—/the visions of your blood/spattering the walls/dripping from my hands and chin—/would you still/smooth back my sweaty hair in the dark/and whisper gentle words/to ease my transition/back into reality?*

The editors say *EDGAR* is 28 pgs., digest-sized, offset printed and saddle-stapled with b&w card cover with illustrations. They receive about 300 poems a year, accept approximately 30%. Press run is 150 for 75 subscribers, 30 shelf sales; 6 distributed free to reviewers. Subscription: $10. Sample: $2.50. Make checks payable to John Picinich.

How to Submit: Submit up to 3 poems at a time; "prefer disposable copies." No previously published poems or simultaneous submissions. Cover letter required. E-mail submissions OK. "For e-mail submissions, do not send poem as an attached file; keep within the body of the e-mail message along with street and e-mail addresses. Snail mail submissions must have a SASE. Also, include publishing credits, if any, and tell us a little bit about yourself in the cover letter." Time between acceptance and publication is 6-9 months. Always comments on rejections. Send SASE for guidelines. Responds in 5 weeks. Pays 1 copy. Acquires first North American serial rights.

Advice: "We recommend poets send SASE for guidelines and buy a sample copy. Each issue runs one or two Poe-ish poems and one or two food poems. We run mostly free verse. Poems of 40 lines or less have a good chance of getting accepted but have run poems of up to 75 lines. We have debuted several new poets."

THE EDGE CITY REVIEW, 10912 Harpers Square Court, Reston VA 20191, fax (703)716-5752, e-mail terryp17@aol.com, website www.edge-city.com, founded 1991, editor T.L. Ponick.

Magazine Needs: *The Edge City Review* appears 3 times a year and "publishes poetry, fiction, criticism and book reviews for a combined lay and academic audience—iconoclastic, conservative and not hospitable to left-wing crusaders." They want poetry in traditional forms (sonnets, ballads, rhyme), narrative, satire; quality verse. No free verse; no greeting card verse. They have published poetry by Dana Gioia, R.S. Gwynn, Jared Carter, Joseph Salemi and Richard Moore. As a sample the editor selected this sonnet by Peter Russell:

> *I own the freehold of my small estate/I am my sole and only mortgagee./Stranger! Look carefully at the well hung gate/That's closed between us—I Have the only key./My walls are skull and skin, my earth's my mind—/My gate, the eyes you never see behind.*

ECR is 48-52 pgs., 8½×11, neatly printed and saddle-stitched with 80 lb. colored stock cover, only occasionally includes ads. They receive about 250 poems a year, accept approximately 15%. Press run is 535 for 305 subscribers of which 25 are libraries, 75 shelf sales; 130 distributed free for promotional purposes. Sample: $5.50.

How to Submit: No previously published poems; simultaneous submissions OK "if so indicated." Cover letter preferred. E-mail and disk submissions OK. "Disk submissions can be Mac or PC, Word or WordPerfect preferred. For e-mail, send poems in the body of the message. Only send attachment if crucial to format." Do not submit mss in December. Time between acceptance and publication is 6 months. Poems are circulated to an editorial board. "Poetry editor makes first cut, final selections based on consensus." Seldom comments on rejections. Responds in 4 months. Pays 2 copies. Acquires first North American serial rights. Staff reviews books of poetry and other magazines in 800-1,000 words, single book format. Send books for review consideration.

Also Offers: Website includes reprints from hardcopy magazine, book reviews, interviews, special events, poetry, commentary, Washington, DC theater and music reviews.

Advice: "We are sometimes exasperated with the inappropriateness of submissions to our magazine. We are open to formal poetry only, and simply do not want to see free verse. We strongly encourage purchase of a sample copy."

EDGEWISE PRESS, INC., 24 Fifth Ave., #224, New York NY 10011, website www.angelfire.com/Biz/edgewisebooks. Currently accepts no unsolicited poetry.

EIDOS MAGAZINE: SEXUAL FREEDOM & EROTIC ENTERTAINMENT FOR CONSENTING ADULTS (Specialized: erotica), P.O. Box 96, Boston MA 02137-0096, phone (617)262-0096, fax (617)364-0096, e-mail eidos@eidos.org, website www.eidos.org, founded 1982, poetry editor Brenda Loew.

Magazine Needs: "Our press publishes erotic literature, poetry, photography and artwork. Our purpose is to provide an alternative to women's images and male images and sexuality depicted in mainstream publications like *Playboy*, *Penthouse*, *Playgirl*, etc. We provide a forum for the discussion and examination of two highly personalized dimensions of human sexuality: desire and satisfaction. We do not want to see angry poetry or poetry that is demeaning to either men or women. We like experimental, avant-garde material that makes a personal, political, cultural statement about sensu-sexuality." They have published poetry by Nancy Young, Miriam Carroll, Linwood M. Ross, Ann Tweedy and Mona J. Perkins. As a sample we selected this poem, "The Things We Talk About, Part II," by Gene Mahoney:

> When you say crazy things like:/"I was planning on participating/in his Ramadan,"/I break out
> laughing./I know that you've got to be kidding./"Girl," I say,/"Are you fucking nuts?/Islam doesn't
> accept chicks with dicks./You'd never make it into Mecca;/they'd cut off your head in a public square/
> and throw your remains to stray dogs./Besides, I'm guessing that this shit/wouldn't sit too well with
> your Buddha either./Your mischievous smile tells me the truth.

Eidos is 40 pgs., 8½ × 11, professionally printed with b&w photography and art. They receive hundreds of poems/year, use about 100. Readership is 12,000. Subscription: $25 for 4 issues. Sample: $7.

How to Submit: Only accepts sexually-explicit material. Length for poetry is 1-page maximum, format flexible. Must be 18 or over; age statement required. Camera-ready, "scannable" poems preferred or poems on disk. No previously published poems; simultaneous submissions OK. "Poets must submit their work via regular 'snail' mail. No faxes or e-mail submissions accepted." Publishes bio information as space permits. Comment or criticism provided as often as possible. Send SASE for guidelines. Responds in 8 months. Pays 1 copy. Acquires first North American serial rights. Open to unsolicited reviews.

Also Offers: Website features names of publisher, editor and webmaster; interviews; articles and essays; poetry and photos. The *Eidos* website was selected as the "Playboy Online Pick of the Day."

Advice: "There is so much poetry submitted for consideration that a rejection can sometimes mean a poet's timing was poor. We let poets know if the submission was appropriate for our publication and suggest they resubmit at a later date. Keep writing, keep submitting, keep a positive attitude."

1812; NEW WRITING AWARDS, P.O. Box 1812, Amherst NY 14226, e-mail info@newwriting.com, website www.newwriting.com/contest.html or members.aol.com/newwriting, founded 1993, editors Richard Lynch, Rick Lupert and Sam Meade.

Magazine Needs: *1812* is an annual electronic, literary arts publication appearing in February. They want "material with a bang." They receive about 1,000 poems a year, accept 1-3%.

How to Submit: Previously published poems OK; no simultaneous submissions. Cover letter required. E-mail submissions OK; "do not use attached files. Submit poems in the body of the e-mail only." Time between acceptance and publication is up to 1 year. Sometimes comments on rejections. Send SASE for guidelines. Payment is "arranged." Buys one-time rights. Open to unsolicited reviews.

Also Offers: Sponsors New Writing Awards with $3,000 in prizes plus publication. "See www.newwriting.com/contest.html for more information." Entry fee: $10. Send SASE or visit website for forms and guidelines. Website has complete magazine contents, including poetry, stories, artwork and music.

$ THE EIGHTH MOUNTAIN PRESS, 624 SE 29th Ave., Portland OR 97214, founded 1985, editor Ruth Gundle.

Book/Chapbook Needs: Eighth Mountain is a "small press publisher of literary works by women." They have published poetry by Lucinda Roy, Maureen Seaton, Irena Klepfisz, Almitra David, Judith Barrington and Elizabeth Woody. They publish 1 book of poetry averaging 128 pgs., every other year. "Our books are handsomely designed and printed on acid-free paper in both quality trade paperbacks and library editions." Initial press run for poetry is 2,500.

How to Submit: "We expect to receive a query letter along with a few poems. A résumé of published work, if any, should be included. Work should be typed, double-spaced, and with your name on each page. If you want to know if your work has been received, enclose a separate, stamped postcard." Responds within 6 weeks. SASE (#10 envelope) must be included for response. "Full postage must be included if return of the work submitted is desired." Pays 7-8% royalties. Buys all rights. Returns rights if book goes out of print.

EKPHRASIS (Specialized: ekphrastic verse); FRITH PRESS; OPEN POETRY CHAPBOOK COMPETITION, P.O. Box 161236, Sacramento CA 95816-1236, *Ekphrasis* founded Summer 1997, Frith Press 1995, editors Laverne Frith and Carol Frith.

● Patricia M. Bindert's "Bide-A-While Mobile Home Park" was winner of the 1999 Open Poetry Chapbook Competition.

Magazine Needs: *Ekphrasis* is a biannual "outlet for the growing body of poetry focusing on individual works from any artistic genre." They want "poetry whose main content is based on individual works from any artistic genre. Poetry should transcend mere description. Form open. No poetry without ekphrastic focus. No poorly crafted work. No archaic language." They nominate for Pushcart Prize: Best of the Small Press editions. They have published poetry by Terry Blackhawk, Peter Cooley, Rhina Espaillat, Linda Nemec Foster, William Greenway, Simon Perchik, Joseph Stanton and Stephanie Strickland. *Ekphrasis* is 40-50 pgs., digest-sized, photocopied and saddle-stapled with matte cover. Subscription: $12/year. Sample: $6. Make checks payable to Laverne Frith.

How to Submit: Submit 3-7 poems at a time with SASE. Accepts previously published poems "occasionally, must be credited"; no simultaneous submissions. Cover letter required including short bio with representative credits and phone number. Time between acceptance and publication is up to 1 year. Seldom comments on rejections. Send SASE for guidelines. Responds in 4 months. Pays 1 copy. Acquires first North American serial or one-time rights.

Book/Chapbook Needs & How to Submit: Frith Press publishes well-crafted poems—all subjects and forms considered—through their annual Open Poetry Chapbook Competition. Submit 16-24 pages of poetry with $8 reading fee. Include cover sheet with poet's name, address and phone number. Previously published poems must be credited. "No poems pending publication elsewhere." Deadline: October 31. Winner receives $100, publication and 50 copies of their chapbook.

Advice: "With the focus on ekphrastic verse, we are bringing attention to the interconnections between various artistic genres and dramatizing the importance and universality of language. Study in the humanities is essential background preparation for the understanding of these interrelations."

N ☉ EMERALD COAST REVIEW; WEST FLORIDA LITERARY FEDERATION; FRANCIS P. CASSIDY LITERARY CENTER; W.I.S.E. (WRITERS IN SERVICE TO EDUCATION); W.I.S.T.S. (WRITERS IN SERVICE TO SENIORS) PROGRAMS (Specialized: regional), 400 S. Jefferson St., Suite 212, Pensacola FL 32501, phone (850)435-0942. The WFLF was founded in 1987 and began the Francis P. Cassidy Literary Center, a regional writers' resource and special collections library.

Magazine Needs & How to Submit: The *Emerald Coast Review* is published every odd year and is usually limited to Coast regional writers and members of the West Florida Literary Federation. Sample: $11. Send SASE for guidelines. Submit with required form (included in guidelines) January 1 through May 15 only. Pays copies.

Also Offers: One ongoing WFLF program is W.I.S.E., which provides area writers who volunteer their time to share their writing and writing experiences with local students. They sponsor a Student Writers Network for students in grades 9-12 and also sponsors a PenWISE poetry contest for grades 1-12. The contest awards publication in a chapbook. They also publish *The Legend*, a monthly newsletter bringing literary arts news, events and contests to area writers and WFLF supporters. Back Door Poets, one of their subgroups, conducts open microphone poetry readings the third Saturday of each month. WFLF also hosts a writing workshop the first Saturday of every month. Their newest program is W.I.S.T.S. (Writers In Service to Seniors) which provides volunteer area writers to nursing homes and assisted living facilities to read and entertain the residents. Membership dues range from $10/year for students and senior citizens to $500 for lifetime and corporate memberships.

✓ ◗ EMOTIONS LITERARY MAGAZINE; WINGS OF DAWN PUBLISHING, 17216 Saticoy St. PMB 370, Van Nuys CA 91406, phone (818)345-9759, toll free fax (877)WINGS-90, e-mail wingsbooks@aol.com, website www.wingsofdawn.com, founded 1997, editor-in-chief Lupi Basil.

Magazine Needs: Appearing 6 times a year, *Emotions*, *"where the pen meets the heart,"* welcomes "good quality work from talented writers as they share their thoughts and emotions in their own unique style and form." They want "all styles and topics as long as they are in good taste, and not degrading to the human spirit. Each line in the poem should not exceed 65 characters in length, including spaces. We also consider fiction, short stories, essays and articles if they are between 1,000-2,500 words, b&w photos/artwork and 4×6 landscape color photos for front cover." They have published poetry by award-winning novelist Ben Bova, Dr. C. David Hay, Dave Taub, k.t. Frankovich and J.E. Dorsey (Doug Claybourne). The editor says *Emotions* is 40 pgs., $8\frac{1}{2} \times 11$, printed on 70 lb. good quality paper and saddle-stapled with glossy color cover, includes b&w photos, artwork and ads. They receive about 2,000 submissions a year, accept approximately 10%. Press run is 500 for 50% subscribers. Single copy: $4.99 US, $6 international; subscription: $25/year US, $40/year international. Make checks payable to Wings of Dawn Publishing Co. or fax credit card orders.

How to Submit: Submit 3 poems at a time. Previously published poems OK (sometimes); no simultaneous submissions unless previously notified. Cover letter with 50-word bio required. E-mail submissions OK, if mailing address and bio included. "Submission must be in body of the e-mail, no attachments." Time between acceptance and publication is 2-4 months. Rarely comments on rejections. Publishes theme issues. Send SASE for guidelines or obtain via e-mail or website. Responds in up to 5 months. Pays 1 copy. Acquires first North American serial or one-time rights.

MARKET CONDITIONS are constantly changing! If you're still using this book and it is 2002 or later, buy the newest edition of *Poet's Market* at your favorite bookstore or order directly from Writer's Digest Books (800)289-0963 or www.writersdigest.com.

Chapbook Needs & How to Submit: Wings of Dawn publishes 1 paperback and 2 chapbooks of poetry/year, averaging 50-60 pages. "We do not accept unsolicited manuscripts unless a current call is posted on our website for a certain theme. We suggest you check our website periodically for information."
Also Offers: Website includes poems, guidelines and general information.
Advice: "We are a small press but internationally acclaimed. Our magazine is distributed in 15 countries. We strongly recommend you order a sample of our magazine to get a feel for what type of material we accept."

EMPLOI PLUS; DGR PUBLICATION, 1256 Principale N. St. #203, L'Annonciation, Quebec J0T 1T0 Canada, phone (819)275-3293, fax (819)275-3293, founded 1988 (DGR Publication), 1990 (*Emploi Plus*), publisher Daniel G. Reid.
Magazine Needs: *Emploi Plus*, published irregularly, features poems and articles in French or English. They have published poetry by Robert Ott. *Emploi Plus* is 12 pgs., 7×8½, photocopied, stapled, with b&w drawings and pictures, no ads. Press run is 500 distributed free. Sample: free.
How to Submit: *They do not accept unsolicited submissions.*

EMRYS JOURNAL, P.O. Box 8813, Greenville SC 29604, founded 1982, editor Jeanine Halva-Neubauer, contact poetry editor.
Magazine Needs: *Emrys Journal* is an annual appearing in April. They want "the accessible poem over the fashionably sophisticated, the touching dramatic or narrative poem over the elaborately meditative, the humorous poem over the ponderously significant, the modest poem over the showily learned." They have published poetry by Starkey Flythe, Becky Gould Gibson and Claire Bateman. As a sample the editor selected the first stanza from "Clay of Dreams" by Joanne Clarkson:

> My children's sleep is porcelain:/Clay that takes the light;/their lids as thin as birth shell,/skin seamless
> as the bowl/from the craftsman's agile wheel/when they say the clay breathes.

EJ is up to 120 pgs., 6×9, handsomely printed, flat-spined. Press run is 400 for 250 subscribers of which 10 are libraries. "About 10 poems are selected for inclusion." Single copy: $12.
How to Submit: Submit up to 5 poems. "No individual poem may exceed three pages. Include phone number, fax and/or e-mail, if desired." Reads submissions August 15 through December 1. Responds in about 2 months. Send SASE for guidelines. Pays 5 copies.

THE EMSHOCK LETTER (Specialized: subscribers), Randall Flat Rd., P.O. Box 411, Troy ID 83871-0411, phone (208)835-4902, founded 1977, editor Steve Erickson.
Magazine Needs: *The Emshock Letter* appears 3-12 times/year, occasionally with poetry and other writings by subscribers. It is "a philosophical, metaphysical, sometimes poetic expression of ideas and events. It covers a wide range of subjects and represents a free-style form of expressive relation. It is a newsletter quite unlike any other." The editor describes it as 5-7 pgs., magazine-sized, photocopied from typescript on colored paper. Subscription: $25.
How to Submit: "Poets (who are subscribers) should submit poetry which contains some meaning, preferably centering on a philosophic theme and preferably 50 lines or less. Any good poetry (submitted by a subscriber) will be considered for inclusion and will receive a personal reply by the editor, whether or not submitted material is published in *The Emshock Letter*. Editor will promptly discard any and all material submitted by nonsubscribers. Poets must become subscribers prior to submitting any material!" Reviews books of poetry only if written by subscribers.

ENCOUNTER: MEETING GOD FACE-TO-FACE; STANDARD PUBLISHING CO. (Specialized: religious, teens), (formerly *Straight*), 8121 Hamilton Ave., Cincinnati OH 45231, phone (513)931-4050, editor Heather E. Wallace. Standard is a large religious publishing company.
Magazine Needs: *Encounter* is a weekly take-home publication (traditional magazine-sized, 8 pgs., color glossy) for teens. Poetry is by teenagers, any style, religious or inspirational in nature. No adult-written poetry. As a sample the editor selected "Why Grace to Me" by Janice Dru:

> This beat-up soul has/Not much to give,/Not much to say . . ./Not much at all./Yet through it all,/It is
> showered with Your grace.

Teen author must include birthdate and social security number.
How to Submit: Submit 1-5 poems at a time. Simultaneous submissions OK. Time between acceptance and publication is 9-12 months. Publishes theme issues. Guidelines and upcoming themes available for SASE. Responds in up to 6 weeks. Pays $10/poem plus 5 copies. Buys first or reprint rights.
Advice: "Many teenagers write poetry in their English classes at school. If you've written a poem on an inspirational topic, and your teacher's given you an 'A' on it, you've got a very good chance of having it published in *Encounter*."

ENGLISH JOURNAL, Dept. of English, Youngstown State University, Youngstown OH 44555, phone (330)742-3415, fax (330)742-2304, e-mail willgreenway@aol.com, poetry editor William Greenway.
Magazine Needs: The *English Journal* is looking for the best poems under 40 lines, and if its subject matter is teaching or learning, so much the better. Any special theme issues will be announced.

How to Submit: Submit 1 copy of no more than 5 typed poems with cover letter and SASE between September and May. No previously published poems or simultaneous submissions. E-mail (submit in Word7 or lower) and fax submissions OK. Pays 2 copies.

N □ ◉ ENGLISH STUDIES FORUM, Dept. of English, Ball State University, Muncie IN 47306, phone (765)285-8580, e-mail tkoontz@gw.bsu.edu, website www.bsu.edu/english/cwp/forum, founded 2000, editors-in-chief Tom Koontz and Patti White.

Magazine Needs: *ESF* is an online publication created with the "purpose of distributing art and ideas. It contains creative writing, scholarship and commentary." They have no specifications for poetry submissions. However, they do not want to see weak artistry or prejudiced thought.

How to Submit: Submit 1-3 poems at a time. No previously published poems or simultaneous submissions. E-mail and disk submissions OK. Cover letter preferred with SASE, brief bio and other pertinent info. Reads submissions September 1 through April 30 only. Poems are circulated to an editorial board. "Poems reviewed by editorial board of faculty and students. Editors-in-chief make final decisions." Seldom comments on rejections. Publishes theme issues. Obtain guidelines and upcoming themes via website. Responds in 1 month. Acquires first rights.

N ⊕ ⊘ ENITHARMON PRESS, 36 St. George's Ave., London N7 0HD England, phone (020)7607-7194, fax (020)7607-8694, founded 1967, poetry editor Stephen Stuart-Smith.

Book/Chapbook Needs: Enitharmon is a publisher of fine editions of poetry and literary criticism in paperback and some hardback editions, about 15 volumes/year averaging 100 pages. They have published books of poetry by John Heath-Stubbs, Ted Hughes, David Gascoyne, Thom Gunn, Ruth Pitter and Anthony Thwaite.

How to Submit: "Substantial backlog of titles to produce, so no submissions possible before 2002."

✔ □ ◯ ◐ ENTERZONE, 1440 Broadway, Suite 920, Oakland CA 94612, phone (510)451-4964, fax (510)465-1518, e-mail query@ezone.org, website ezone.org, founded 1994, poetry editor Freeman Ng.

Magazine Needs: *Enterzone* is a quarterly online publication containing writing, art and new media. They want concrete poetry. No vague poetry. They have published poetry by Janan Platt, David Hunter Sutherland and Cort Day. They receive about 80 poems a year, accept approximately 10%.

How to Submit: Submit 1 poem at a time. Previously published poems and simultaneous submissions OK. Cover letter required. E-mail and disk submissions OK. "Please query first by e-mail." Time between acceptance and publication is 6-9 months. Often comments on rejections. Publishes theme issues occasionally. Obtain guidelines via e-mail. Responds in 2 months. Acquires one-time rights. Reviews books and chapbooks of poetry in 1,500 words, single book format. Open to unsolicited reviews. Poets may also send books for review consideration.

N ⊕ ⊘ ENVOI, 44 Rudyard Rd., Biddulph Moor, Stoke-on-Trent, Staffs ST8 7JN United Kingdom, founded 1957, editor Roger Elkin.

Magazine Needs: *Envoi* appears 3 times/year using poetry, articles about poetry and poets, and reviews. "1) *Envoi* does not subscribe to any one particular stable, school or style of contemporary poetry writing and has catholic tastes; 2) To be selected, poetry must be sincere in its emotional and intellectual content, strongly integrated in form and contemporary in its subject matter—while a poem may be set in classical times or depend heavily on mythic archetypes, its overall 'texture' must have contemporary relevance; 3) *Envoi* requires writing that is daring in its subject matter and challenging in its expressive techniques—in short, work that takes risks with the form, the language and the reader; 4) *Envoi* is, however, still interested in traditional verse structures (the villanelle, pantoum, sonnet) but these must subscribe to the points listed in 2); and 5) *Envoi* is looking for writing that sustains its creative strengths over a body of poems, or sequence. These criteria are prescriptive, rather than proscriptive; gates rather than hurdles. The over-riding concern is the creation of access for writers and readers to as wide a variety of contemporary poetry as space will allow." *Envoi* is 176 pgs., digest-sized, professionally printed and perfect-bound with matte card cover. "The emphasis is on giving space to writers so the reader can begin to assess the cumulative strengths of any one author over a body of work. This means competition for space is very keen. I handle between 300 and 500 poems per week and can only feature the equivalent of 100 poems three times a year!" Press run is 1,000 including 20 library subscriptions. Single copy: £4 ($10); subscription: £15 ($30—"U.S. funds preferably in bills rather than checks because of the high cost of conversion rates"). Sample: £3 ($8).

How to Submit: Submit no more than 6 poems, or a long poem of up to 6 sides; each poem on a separate page, bearing name and address; an accompanying SAE with 3 IRCs for return. Responds in 2 months. Pays 2 copies.

Advice: "*Envoi* presents the work of any one poet by a group of poems, up to six. Space is given to long(er) poems and short sequences, or extracts from longer sequences. We have a First Publication Feature for writers who have not appeared in national publications previously, and each issue contains a 'reading' of a modern poem or an article on poetic style. The Review section has been expanded in length to feature more comprehensive articles. Each issue also features a competition with prizes totalling £200; prize-winning poems are published along with a full adjudicator's report. We also feature poems in collaboration, as well as translations."

⊘ **EPICENTER**, P.O. Box 367, Riverside CA 92502, website www.geocities.com/Athens/Delphi/2884, founded 1994.

Magazine Needs: *Epicenter* is a biannual poetry and short story forum open to all styles. *"Epicenter* is looking for ground-breaking poetry and short stories from new and established writers. No angst-ridden, sentimental or earthquake poetry. We are not adverse to graphic images if the work is well presented and contains literary merit." They have published poetry by Lon Risley, Max Berkovitz, Stan Nemeth and Vicki Solheid. *Epicenter* is 24 pgs., digest-sized and saddle-stapled with semi-glossy paper cover and b&w graphics. They receive about 1,000 submissions a year, use approximately 5%. Press run is 400 for 250 shelf sales. Single copy: $3. Sample: $3.50. Make checks payable to Rowena Silver.

How to Submit: Submit up to 5 poems. Include SASE with sufficient postage for return of materials. Previously published poems and simultaneous submissions OK. Seldom comments on rejections. Send SASE for guidelines. Pays 1 copy. Acquires one-time and electronic rights.

☑ $ ⊠ **EPOCH; BAXTER HATHAWAY PRIZE**, 251 Goldwin Smith, Cornell University, Ithaca NY 14853, phone (607)255-3385, founded 1947, poetry editor Nancy Couto Vieira.

Magazine Needs: *Epoch* has a distinguished and long record of publishing exceptionally fine poetry and fiction. They have published work by such poets as Ashbery, Ammons, Eshleman, Wanda Coleman, Molly Peacock, Robert Vander Molen and Alvin Aubert. The magazine appears 3 times/year in a 6×9, professionally printed, flat-spined format with glossy color cover, 128 pgs., which goes to 1,000 subscribers. They use less than 1% of the many submissions they receive each year, have a 2- to 12-month backlog. Mostly lyric free verse, with emphasis on voice and varying content and length, appears here (and, occasionally, avant-garde or "open" styles)—some of it quite powerful. Sample: $5.

How to Submit: "We don't read unsolicited mss between April 15 and September 15." Responds in 2 months. Occasionally provides criticism on mss. Pays $5-10/page. Buys first serial rights.

Also Offers: The annual Baxter Hathaway prize of $1,000 is awarded for a long poem or, in alternate years, a novella. At this time, however, the Baxter Hathaway Prize has been temporarily suspended.

Advice: "I think it's extremely important for poets to read other poets. I think it's also very important for poets to read the magazines that they want to publish in. Directories are not enough."

⊘ **ETHEREAL GREEN**, 238 W. Saginaw St. #106, East Lansing MI 48823-2646, e-mail EtherealGreen@aol.com, website www.angelfire.com/yt/etherealgreenpoetry/index.html, founded 1996, contact Sarah Hencsie.

Magazine Needs: *EG*, published quarterly, strives "to feed readers unknown talent." Contains poetry, art and articles. They want "the avant-garde, spiritual and the unknown. Poems should be less than 40 lines." They do not want "children's, ethnic or edited poems." As a sample the editor selected these lines by Jaime Morrison:

> *Because it's raining . . . you're/falling from the sky, from/your soul being drained . . .*

Ethereal Green is 30-70 pgs., approximately 6×8, with cover art. They receive hundreds of poems a year, accept approximately 50%. Press run is 250 for about 70 subscribers, 60% shelf sales. Subscription: $27. Sample: $7. Make checks payable to Sarah C. Hencsie.

How to Submit: Submit 3-7 printed or typed poems at a time. SASE required. Previously published poems and simultaneous submissions OK. Cover letter required. E-mail submissions OK (no attachments). Time between acceptance and publication is 3-7 months. Poems are circulated to an editorial board with "poems edited twice; once by publisher and again by select editors on board." Always comments on rejections. Send SASE for guidelines and upcoming themes. Responds in 4 months. Sometimes sends prepublication galleys. Pays 1 copy. Acquires first North American serial or one-time rights. Open to unsolicited reviews.

Also Offers: Website includes guidelines, sample poems, poet polls and prices.

⊕ ⊠ ◎ **EUROPEAN JUDAISM (Specialized: religious, ethnic)**, Kent House, Rutland Gardens, London SW7 1BX England, founded 1966, poetry editor Ruth Fainlight.

Magazine Needs: *European Judaism* is a "twice-yearly magazine with emphasis on European Jewish theology/philosophy/literature/history, with some poetry in every issue. It should preferably be short and have some relevance to matters of Jewish interest." They have published poetry by Linda Pastan, Elaine Feinstein, Daniel Weissbort and Dannie Abse. As a sample the editor selected these lines from a poem by Michael Heller:

> *I took silence into time, marking the absence/of our late vocabularies in their conspirings,/these new mythologies, as they fell from on high//through our skies and through our roofs/scouring the mind as cosmic rays leave/traceries in the cool white lime of tunnels.*

It is a glossy, elegant, 6×9, flat-spined magazine, rarely art or graphics, 110 pgs. They have a press run of 950, about 50% of which goes to subscribers (few libraries). Subscription: $27.

How to Submit: Submit 3-4 poems at a time. No material dealt with or returned if not accompanied by SASE (or SAE with IRCs). "We cannot use American stamps. Also, I prefer unpublished poems, but poems from published books are acceptable." Cover letter required. Pays 1 copy.

$ ⊘ ◎ **EVANGEL; LIGHT AND LIFE COMMUNICATIONS (Specialized: religious)**, P.O. Box 535002, Indianapolis IN 46253-5002, founded 1897, editor J. Innes.

Magazine Needs: *Evangel* is a weekly adult Sunday school paper. "Devotional in nature, it lifts up Christ as the source of salvation and hope. The mission of *Evangel* is to increase the reader's understanding of the nature

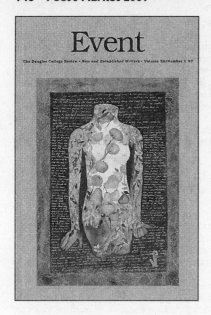

According to Calvin Wharton, editor of Canadian journal *Event*, "The cover art is intended to reflect a corresponding sense of what's inside the magazine; that is, dynamic, intriguing examples of fine contemporary writing." Vancouver artist Sharalee Regehr created the cover for Volume 28, No. 1. "She finds profound inspiration in the lives of the women she portrays," Wharton says of Regehr. Commenting on this particular cover, Wharton adds, "We were attracted first by the artwork's visual appeal: the combination of dynamic colors, intriguing presentation and the use of text in the art." Finely printed, *Event* is 6×9, runs 140 pages and is flat-spined with glossy cover.

and character of God and the nature of a life lived for Christ. Material that fits this mission that isn't more than one page will be considered." No rhyming work. *Evangel* is 8 pgs., 5½×8½ (2 8½×11 sheets folded), printed in 4 color and unbound with photos and graphics used. They accept approximately 5% of poetry received. Press run is approximately 20,000 for 19,000 subscribers. Subscription: $1.85/quarter (13 weeks).

How to Submit: Submit 3 poems at a time. Simultaneous submissions OK. Cover letter preferred. Seldom comments on rejections. Send #10 SASE for guidelines Responds in 6 weeks. Pays $10 plus 2 copies on publication. Buys one-time rights.

Advice: "Poetry is used primarily as filler. Send for sample and guidelines to better understand what and who the audience is."

THE EVANSVILLE REVIEW, 1800 Lincoln Ave., Evansville IN 47722, phone/fax (812)488-1042, founded 1989, editor-in-chief Dan Walker.

Magazine Needs: *The Evansville Review* appears annually and publishes "prose, poems and drama of literary merit." They want "anything of quality." No experimental work or erotica. They have published poetry by John Updike, Willis Barnstone, Carol Muske, Vivian Shipley, David Ignatow and Tess Galagher. As a sample the editor selected these lines from "Beckett Had Only One Student" by James Ragan:

> As a tutor, Beckett taught only one/thought to a farmer who had pushed/a stone up pasture with a leg,/
> how to add/a syllable to the name of <u>God</u>/and reverse direction in the space of letters/from the dauphin
> <u>to</u> to the expanse of <u>ot</u>,/and to skip the space that followed/as a symbol of regret.

The editor says *TER* is 200 pgs., digest-sized, perfect-bound, includes art on cover only. They receive about 1,000 poems a year, accept approximately 2%. Publish 45 poems/issue. Press run is 3,000; all distributed free to students and attendees at conferences. Sample: $5.

How to Submit: Submit 5 poems at a time. Previously published poems and simultaneous submissions OK. Cover letter required. Include SASE for reply for return and brief bio. Reads submissions September 1 through December 10 only. Time between acceptance and publication is 3 months. Poems are circulated to an editorial board. Seldom comments on rejections. Send SASE for guidelines. Responds in 5 months. Pays 2 copies. Rights remain with poet. "We are not copywritten."

EVENT, Douglas College, P.O. Box 2503, New Westminster, British Columbia V3L 5B2 Canada, phone (604)527-5293, fax (604)527-5095, e-mail event@douglas.bc.ca, founded 1971, poetry editor Gillian Harding-Russell.

Magazine Needs: *Event* appears 3 times/year and is "a literary magazine publishing high-quality contemporary poetry, short stories, creative nonfiction and reviews. In poetry, we tend to appreciate the narrative and sometimes the confessional modes. In any case, we are eclectic and always open to content that invites involvement. We publish mostly Canadian writers." They have published poetry by Tom Wayman, Lorna Crozier, Russell Thornton, Don McKay, A.F. Moritz, Marlene Cookshaw and Tim Bowling. *Event* is 140 pgs., 6×9, finely printed and flat-spined with glossy cover. Press run is 1,000 for 700 subscribers of which 50 are libraries. Subscription: $20/year, $30/2 years. Sample: $7. Prices include GST. US subscribers please pay is US funds. Overseas and institutions: $30/year, $45/2 years. Sample: $9.

How to Submit: Submit 5 poems at a time. No previously published poems. Brief cover letter with publication credits required. Include SASE (Canadian postage only) or SAE and IRCs. "Tell us if you'd prefer your manuscript to be recycled rather than returned." Time between acceptance and publication is within 1 year. Comments on some rejections. Responds in 4 months. Pays honorarium. Buys first North American serial rights.

EXIT 13 (Specialized: geography/travel), % Tom Plante, P.O. Box 423, Fanwood NJ 07023-1162, phone (908)889-5298, e-mail plante@bellatlantic.net, founded 1987, editor Tom Plante.

Magazine Needs: *Exit 13* is a "contemporary poetry annual" using poetry that is "short, to the point, with a sense of geography." They have published poetry by Charles Plymell, Errol Miller, Adele Kenny, Varese Layzer and Ken Smith. As a sample the editor selected these lines by M.E. Grow:

> *Under the trees in the wind's paw reds scream./Torn by the sun time folds into rock.*

Exit 13, #9, was 60 pgs. Press run is 300. Sample: $6.50.

How to Submit: They accept simultaneous submissions and previously published poems. E-mail submissions OK, include in body of message. Send SASE for guidelines. Responds in 4 months. Pays 1 copy. Acquires one-time and possible anthology rights. Staff reviews books of poetry and magazines in a "Publications Received" column, using 25-30 words/listing. Send books for review consideration.

Advice: "Write about what you know. Study geography. *Exit 13* looks for adventure. Every state, region and ecosystem is welcome. Send a snapshot of an 'Exit 13' road sign and receive a free copy of the issue in which it appears."

EXPEDITION PRESS, 411 Stanwood St., Apt. E, Kalamazoo MI 49006-4543, phone (616)382-6823, founded 1978, publisher Bruce W. White.

Book/Chapbook Needs: Expedition Press publishes chapbooks that are "offbeat and bohemian with egalitarian appeal." Open to any style. This press is "not for snobs." He has published poetry by J. Kline Hobbs, Robin Reish, Todd Zimmerman, Margaret Tyler, Martin Cohen and C. VanAllsburg. As a sample the publisher selected these lines from "After the Ice Storm" by Margaret Tyler:

> *. . . They shook their heads at such abandon/and warned their daughters not to be as wanton as the wild rose/that drops its petals to the earth/and comes in Spring, in Winter goes.*

Sample chapbooks: $5. Make checks payable to Bruce White.

How to Submit: Submit typed ms of 20-30 pgs. and cover letter with brief bio. Reading fee: $5. Please send SASE. Responds in 1 month. Sometimes sends prepublication galleys. Pays 100 copies. Bruce White provides "much" criticism on rejected mss.

[N:] EXPERIMENTAL FOREST PRESS, 223 A Bosler Ave., Lemoyne PA 17043, phone (717)730-2143, e-mail xxforest@yahoo.com, website www.geocities.com/paris/salon/9699, founded 1999, co-editors Jeanette Trout and Kevyn Knox.

Magazine Needs: *Experimental Forest* is published bimonthly "to show the world that there is more out there than meets the eye. Please, no sappy love poetry!" They have published poetry by John Taggart, Richard Kostelanetz, Gene Hosey, Anne Wynne, Kerry Shawn Keys and Jack Veasey. As a sample the editor selected these lines (poet unidentified):

> *E-mail is humming in pythagorean space/Chopin composes the flesh of a nocturne/Pink white apple blossoms/inner-tubes bearing naiads drift down the Delaware.*

The editor says *EF* is 60 pgs., 5½×8½, stapled, b&w artwork on cover stock, also inside art. They receive about 1,000 poems a year, accept approximately 20%. Publish 30 poems/issue. Press run is 250 for 25 subscribers of which 5 are libraries, 75 shelf sales; 25 distributed free to fellow editors. Single copy: $4; subscription: $18/1 year. Sample: $5. Make checks payable to Jeanette Trout and/or Kevyn Knox.

How to Submit: Submit up to 5 poems at a time. No previously published poems; simultaneous submissions OK. E-mail submissions OK. Cover letter preferred. "We prefer to have a short bio for our contributors page. We also require a SASE." Time between acceptance and publication is 6 months. Often comments on rejections. Publishes theme issues occasionally. Send SASE for upcoming themes. Responds in 2 months. Pays 1 copy. Acquires one-time rights.

Also Offers: Sponsors a poetry contest every fall with a $100 1st Prize and a short story contest each spring with a $100 1st Prize. Obtain rules and guidelines via SASE or e-mail request. Website includes information on submitting, subscription and back issues, contests and sample poetry.

Advice: "We accept poetry of any style or subject. We look for poetic voices that have something fresh and new to say. Remember, we are called '*Experimental*' Forest."

EXPLORATIONS; EXPLORATIONS AWARD FOR LITERATURE, UAS, 11120 Glacier Highway, Juneau AK 99801-8761, e-mail jfamp@uas.alaska.edu, founded 1980, editor Professor Art Petersen.

Magazine Needs: *Explorations* is the literary magazine of the University of Alaska Southeast and appears annually in July. "The editors respond favorably to 'language really spoken by men and women.' Standard form and innovation are encouraged as well as appropriate and fresh aspects of imagery (allusion, metaphor, simile, symbol . . .)." *Explorations* is digest-sized, nicely printed and saddle-stapled, with front and back cover illustration in one color. The editors tend to go for smaller-length poems (with small line breaks for tension) and often print two on a page—mostly lyric free verse with a focus on voice. Sample: $5.

How to Submit: An entry/reading fee is required: $6 for 1 or 2 poems (60 lines/poem maximum), $2/poem for 3-5 poems (5 maximum, no more than 60 lines each); those paying reader/contest entry fees receive a copy of the publication. Checks should be made payable to "UAS Explorations." Mss must be typed with name, address, and 3- to 4-line biography on the back of each first page. Simultaneous submissions OK. Submit January through May 15 only. Mss are not returned. Send SASE for guidelines or request via e-mail. Responds in July. Pays 2 copies. Acquires one-time rights.

Also Offers: Sponsors the Explorations Awards for Literature. First place (for a poem or short story): $1,000; second place (for best work in a genre different from first place winner): $500; and third place for poetry: $100. Submit up to 5 poems, no more than 60 lines each. Entry fee: $6 for 1-2 poems, $3/poem for 3-5 poems. Judge for 1999 contest was Richard Dauenhauer. Send SASE for guidelines.

FAMILY OF MAN PRESS, 319 S. Block Ave., Suite 17, Fayetteville AR 72701, phone (501)587-1726, e-mail drwriterguy@netscape.net, website www.familypress.com, founded 1950 (reorganized 1980), editor G.F. Hutchison.

Book/Chapbook Needs: Family of Man Press publishes full-length books on disk. They want "clean, enjoyable poetry with 'little thinking' necessary—serious to ridiculous, adult and senior; happy message. No abstract work." They have published poetry by Grampa Gray and Jeremy Hess. As a sample the editor selected these lines from "Lookin' Great!" (poet unidentified):

> *You're really lookin' great, my friend,/We say to babies new,/And mean they're cute from end to end,/*
> *As slobber there on you!/You're really lookin' great, my friend,/We say to scout at door,/As in her*
> *uniform she vends/Those cookies—"Please buy more!" . . ./You're really lookin' great, my friend,/We*
> *tell new bride and mate,/No need on that day to pretend,/Their beauty radiates! . . ./You're really*
> *lookin' great, my friend./Folks say to me today./"Well thanks! Sure hope so," I contend,/"Took years*
> *to get this way!!!"*

How to Submit: Query first, with 6-10 printed sample poems (more if on disk) and cover letter with brief bio and publication credits. Previously published poems and simultaneous submissions OK. Disk submissions preferred (MS Word, Adobe Acrobat or ASCII). Time between acceptance and publication is 2-4 months. Poems are circulated to an editorial board. "Sample poems read by editor. Then poet panel group makes final decisions." Replies to queries in 2 weeks. Pays royalties of 15%. Order sample books by sending $10.

Advice: "Our readers like poetry that is fun. Beautiful is fine if it is not abstract. Rhymes are most welcome."

FARRAR, STRAUS & GIROUX/BOOKS FOR YOUNG READERS (Specialized: children), 19 Union Square W., New York NY 10003, phone (212)741-6900, founded 1946, contact Editorial Dept./ Books for Young Readers.

Book/Chapbook Needs: They publish one book of children's poetry "every once in awhile," in both hardcover and paperback editions. They are open to book-length submissions of children's poetry only. They have published collections of poetry by Valerie Worth and Deborah Chandra.

How to Submit: Query first with sample poems and cover letter with brief bio and publication credits. Poems previously published in magazines and simultaneous submissions OK. Seldom comments on rejections. Send SASE for reply. Replies to queries in 1-2 months, to mss in 1-4 months. "We pay an advance against royalties; the amount depends on whether or not the poems are illustrated, etc." Also pays 10 copies.

FAT TUESDAY, 560 Manada Gap Rd., Grantville PA 17028, phone (717)469-7159, e-mail cotolo @excite.com, website www.mp3.com/frankcotolo, founded 1981, editor-in-chief F.M. Cotolo, other editors Kristen Cotolo and Lionel Stevroid.

Magazine Needs: *Fat Tuesday* publishes irregularly as "a Mardi Gras of literary, visual and audio treats featuring voices, singing, shouting, sighing and shining, expressing the relevant to irreverent." They want "prose poems, poems of irreverence, gems from the gut. Particularly interested in hard-hitting 'autofiction.'" Also accepts poetry written by children, ages 10 and up. They have published poetry by Mark Cramer, Mary Lee Gowland, Patrick Kelly, Gerald Locklin and Julia Solis, as well as material by unknown authors. The magazine is up to 60 pgs., typeset (large type, heavy paper), saddle-stapled, card covers, usually chapbook style (sometimes magazine-sized, unbound) with cartoons, black line art and ads. Circulation is 1,000/year with poetry on 80% of

FOR EXPLANATIONS OF THESE SYMBOLS,
SEE THE INSIDE FRONT AND BACK COVERS OF THIS BOOK.

the pages. They receive hundreds of submissions each year, use 3-5%, have a 3- to 5-month backlog "but usually try to respond with personal, not form, letters." "In 1998 *Fat Tuesday* was presented in a different format with the production of a stereo audio cassette edition. *Fat Tuesday's Cool Noise* features readings, music, collage and songs, all in the spirit of *Fat*'s printed versions. Other *Cool Noise* editions will follow. *Fat* solicits artists who wish to have their material produced professionally in audio form. Call the editors about terms and prices on how you can release a stereo audio cassette entirely of your own material. *Fat* has released *Seven Squared*, by Frank Cotolo and is looking for other audio projects. In-print magazines will still be produced as planned. You can hear Cotolo music and purchase CDs at our website." All editions are $5, postage paid.

How to Submit: Submit any number of poems at a time. No previously published poems or simultaneous submissions. E-mail submissions OK (text or attached file). "Cover letters are fine, the more amusing the better." Publishes theme issues. Send SASE for guidelines. Responds in 2 weeks. Pays 2 copies if audio. Rights revert to author after publication.

Advice: "Be yourself. Use your own voice. We don't care about trends, we listen for unique and individual voices. We rely on sales to subsidize all projects so writers should be sensitive to this hard truth and buy sample editions."

☑ ◐ **FAULTLINE,** Dept. of English & Comparative Literature, University of California—Irvine, Irvine CA 92697-2650, phone (949)824-1573, website www.humanities.uci.edu/faultline, founded 1991, managing editor Thomas Babayan.

☑ Poetry published by this journal has also been selected for inclusion in a *Pushcart Prize* anthology.

Magazine Needs: *Faultline* is an annual journal of art and literature occasionally edited by guest editors and published at the University of California, Irvine. "We are looking for top, top quality poetry from poets who are obviously acquainted with contemporary poetry." They have published poetry by Thomas Lux, Heather McHugh and Sabina Grogan. As a sample we selected the opening lines of "Gravediggers" by Linda Thomas:

> At first I am sure/the sea once covered our backyard./With each spadeful of dirt/come cones and sea
> slippers,/the dry dishes of scallops and jackknives,/and I am sure/this neglected plot of hard clay/once
> served as the ocean floor.

Faultline is approximately 120 pgs., 6×9, professionally printed on 60 lb. paper, perfect-bound with 80 lb. cover stock and featuring color and b&w art and photos. They receive about 1,500 poems a year, accept approximately 5%. Press run is 500 for 50 subscribers, 175 shelf sales. Single copy: $7. Sample: $5.

How to Submit: Submit up to 5 poems at a time. Simultaneous submissions OK. Cover letter preferred. Do not include name and address on ms to assist anonymous judging. Reads submissions September 15 to March 1 only. Poems are selected by a board of up to 6 readers. Seldom comments on rejections. Send SASE for guidelines. Responds in 3 months. Pays 2 copies. Buys first or one-time rights.

◐ **FAUQUIER POETRY JOURNAL,** P.O. Box 68, Bealeton VA 22712-0068, founded 1994, managing editor D. Clement.

Magazine Needs: *Fauquier Poetry Journal* is a quarterly that contains poetry, poetry commentary, editorials, contest announcements and book reviews. They want "fresh, creative, well-crafted poetry, any style. Due to format, longer poems over 40 lines are not often used. Do not want overly sentimental or religious themes, overdone subjects, or overly obscure work." They have published poetry by Sean Brendan-Brown, Daniel Green, Fredrick Zydek, Maura Ramer, Nancy Ryan and Marilyn Injeyan. As a sample the editor selected these lines from "a week" by Peter Layton:

> I can hear the fog puffs from the bay/bellying nicely/the oil boats swag low their dark loads/sag in the
> drudged waves/the light behind the house is gray/cold comes in the screen . . ./your sat-on-the-table
> note/lays there

FPJ is 40-50 pgs., digest-sized, laser-printed on plain white paper and saddle-stapled with bright colored paper cover. Press run is more than 300 for 100 subscribers, including libraries. Subscription: $20. Sample: $5.

How to Submit: The editor encourages subscriptions by requiring a reading fee for nonsubscribers ($5 for 1-5 poems only per month); no reading fee for subscribers. Submit up to 5 poems with name and address in the upper left corner of each page and include SASE. Simultaneous submissions OK. Accepts previously published poems. Sometimes comments on rejections. Send SASE for guidelines and upcoming themes. Responds within 6 weeks. Offers Editor's Choice Awards of $5-25 for the best entries in each issue. Pays 1 copy to remainder of published poets. Acquires one-time rights.

Also Offers: They sponsor quarterly poetry contests, explained in the journal. Entry fee: $5. Prizes range from $15-75, and winners are published in the following issue. In addition to poetry, *FPJ* occasionally prints articles by guest columnists. Articles should deal with some aspect of poetry, the writing experience, reactions to particular poems or poets, the mechanics (how to), etc. No reading fee, no guidelines other than word limit (around 1,000 words). "Pretty much anything goes as long as it's interesting and well-written." Pays 2¢/word.

Advice: "Let us see a variety in your submission; what one editor likes, another won't. Send a range of work that illustrates the breadth and depth of your talent; this helps us decide if there's something we like. We encourage submissions from anyone who is writing mature, well-crafted poetry."

⊕ ☑ ◯ ◎ **FEATHER BOOKS; THE POETRY CHURCH MAGAZINE; CHRISTIAN HYMNS & SONGS (Specialized: anthology, humor, religious),** Fairview, Old Coppice, Lyth Bank, Shrewsbury,

Shropshire SY3 0BW United Kingdom, phone/fax (01763)872177, e-mail john@waddysweb.freeuk.com, website www.waddysweb.com, Feather Books founded 1982, *Poetry Church Magazine* founded 1996, contact Rev. John Waddington-Feather.

Magazine Needs: *The Poetry Church Magazine* appears quarterly and contains Christian poetry and prayers. They want "Christian or good religious poetry—usually around 20 lines, but will accept longer." They do not want "unreadable blasphemy." They have published poetry by M.A.B. Jones, Joan Smith, Bruce James, Idris Caffrey and Walter Nash. *TPCM* is 40 pgs., digest-sized, photocopied, saddle-stapled with laminated cover and b&w cover art. They receive about 1,000 poems a year, accept approximately 500. Press run is 1,000 for 400 subscribers of which 10 are libraries. Single copy free; subscription: £7 ($15 US). Sample: $5. Make checks payable to Feather Books. Payment can also be made through website.

How to Submit: Submit 2 typed poems at a time. Previously published poems and simultaneous submissions OK. E-mail submissions OK in attached file. Cover letter preferred with information about the poet. All work must be submitted by mail with SASE (or SAE and IRC). Time between acceptance and publication is 4 months. "The editor does a preliminary reading; then seeks the advice of colleagues about uncertain poems." Always comments on rejections. Send SASE (or SAE and IRC) for guidelines or request via e-mail or fax. Responds within 1 week. Pays 1 copy. Poets retain copyright.

Book/Chapbook Needs & How to Submit: Feather Books publishes the Feather Books Poetry Series, books of Christian poetry and prayers. Books are usually photocopied and saddle-stapled with laminated covers. "Poets' works are selected for publication in collections of around 20 poems in our Feather Books Poetry Series. We do not insist, but most poets pay for small run-offs of their work, e.g., around 50-100 copies for which we charge $200 per fifty. If they can't afford it, but are good poets, we stand the cost. We expect poets to read our *Poetry Church Magazine* to get some idea of our standards." Pays 5% royalty "where we sell copies of poetry" or 1 author's copy (out of a press run of 50) "if we pay cost."

Also Offers: Feather Books also publishes *Christian Hymns & Songs*, a quarterly supplement by Grundy and Feather. And, each fall, selected poems that have been published throughout the year in *Poetry Church Magazine* appear in *The Poetry Church Anthology*, the leading Christian poetry anthology used in churches and schools. Website includes directors and editors and their specialized areas. Also lists publications and the top twenty most popular works sold.

Advice: "We find it better for poets to master rhyme and rhythm before trying free verse. Many poets seem to think that if they write 'down' a page they're writing poetry, when all they're doing is writing prose in a different format."

✔️ ◎ **FEMINIST STUDIES (Specialized: women/feminism)**, % Dept. of Women's Studies, P.O. Box 30507, University of Maryland, College Park MD 14603-0507, phone (301)405-7415, fax (301)314-9190, e-mail femstud@umail.umd.edu, website www.inform.umd.edu/femstud, founded 1969, poetry editor Shirley Geok-Lin Lun.

Magazine Needs: *Feminist Studies* "welcomes a variety of work that focuses on women's experience, on gender as a category of analysis, and that furthers feminist theory and consciousness." They have published poetry by Janice Mirikitani, Paula Gunn Allen, Cherrie Moraga, Audre Lorde, Valerie Fox and Diane Glancy. The elegantly printed, flat-spined, 250-page paperback appears 3 times a year in an edition of 8,000, goes to 7,000 subscribers, of which 1,500 are libraries. There are 4-10 pgs. of poetry in each issue. Sample: $15.

How to Submit: No simultaneous submissions; will only consider previously published poems under special circumstances. Manuscripts are reviewed twice a year, in May and December. Deadlines are May 1 and December 1. Authors will receive notice of the board's decision by June 30 and January 30. Always sends prepublication galleys. Pays 2 copies. Commissions reviews of books of poetry. Poets may send books to Claire G. Moses for review consideration.

🌱 💲◻️◿️◎ **THE FIDDLEHEAD (Specialized: regional, students)**, Campus House, University of New Brunswick, P.O. Box 4400, Fredericton, New Brunswick E3B 5A3 Canada, founded 1945, poetry editors Ross Leckie, Julie Dennison and Eric Hall.

Magazine Needs: From its beginning in 1945 as a local little magazine devoted mainly to student writers, the magazine retains an interest in poets of the Atlantic region and in young poets but prints poetry from everywhere. It is open to excellent work of every kind, looking always for vitality, freshness and surprise. They have published poetry by James Gurley and Thomas O'Grady. As a sample, the editors selected these lines by Al Moritz:

> As if you erased the city where the house/where I was born was standing. As if I/had gone away a minute, just to see what lies beyond,/as if anything does, and you swept away my path/with your broom and rubbed it out/with your wheels, crisscrossing it into chaos

The Fiddlehead is a handsomely printed, 6×9, flat-spined paperback (120 pgs.) with b&w graphics, colored cover, paintings by New Brunswick artists. They use less than 10% of submissions. Circulation is 1,000. Subscription: $20/year plus $6 postage (US). Sample: $7 (US).

How to Submit: Submit 3-10 poems at a time. No simultaneous submissions. For reply or return of ms, send SAE with Canadian stamps, IRCs or cash. Response time is 6 months, backlog 6-18 months. Pay is $10-12/ printed page. Reviews books of poetry by Canadian authors mainly.

$ ▨ ◎ FIELD; FIELD TRANSLATION SERIES; FIELD POETRY PRIZE; FIELD POETRY SE-RIES; OBERLIN COLLEGE PRESS (Specialized: translations), Rice Hall, Oberlin College, Oberlin OH 44074, phone (440)775-8408, fax (440)775-8124, e-mail oc.press@oberlin.edu, website www.oberlin.edu/~ocpress, founded 1969, editors David Young, Alberta Turner, David Walker, Martha Collins and Pamela Alexander.

🔲 Work published in *Field* has also been included in the 1992, 1993, 1994, 1995 and 1998 volumes of *The Best American Poetry*.

Magazine Needs: *Field* is a literary journal appearing twice a year with "emphasis on poetry, translations and essays by poets." They want the "best possible" poetry. They have published poetry by Marianne Boruch, Miroslav Holub, Charles Simic and Sandra McPherson. The handsomely printed, digest-sized journal is flat-spined, has 100 pgs., rag stock with glossy card color cover. Although most poems fall under the lyrical free verse category, you'll find narratives and formal work here on occasion, much of it sensual, visually appealing and resonant. Circulation is 2,500, with 800 library subscriptions. Subscription: $14/year, $24/2 years. Sample: $7.

How to Submit: Submit up to 5 poems at a time. Cover letters preferred. Reads submissions year-round. No previously published poems, simultaneous submissions, e-mail or disk submissions. Seldom comments on rejections. Responds in 1 month. Time between acceptance and publication is 1-6 months. Always sends prepublication galleys. Pays $15-20/page plus 2 copies. Staff reviews books of poetry. Poets and publishers may send books for review consideration.

Book/Chapbook Needs & How to Submit: They publish books of translations in the Field Translation Series, averaging 150 pgs., flat-spined and hardcover editions. Query regarding translations. Pays 7½-10% royalties with some advance and 10 author's copies. They also have a Field Poetry Series. They have published *Ill Lit* by Franz Wright; *A Saturday Night at the Flying Dog* by Marcia Southwick. This series is by invitation only. Write for catalog to buy samples.

Also Offers: Sponsors the *Field* Poetry Prize, the winning ms will be published in their poetry series and receive $1,000 award. Submit mss of 50-80 pgs. with a $22 reading fee in May only. Contest guidelines available for SASE. Website includes information on all publications, including excerpts and ordering information.

▨ ✔ ▨ FILLING STATION, P.O. Box 22135, Bankers Hall, Calgary, Alberta T2P 4J5 Canada, phone (403)234-0336, e-mail housepre@telvsplanet.net, founded 1993, co-managing editors Derek Beaulieu and Courtney Thompson.

Magazine Needs: Appearing 3 times/year (February, June and October), *filling Station* is a magazine of contemporary writing featuring poetry, fiction, interviews, reviews and other literary news. "We are looking for all forms of contemporary writing. No specific objections to any style." They have published poetry by Fred Wah, Larissa Lai and Paula Tatarunis. As a sample the editor selected these lines from "Breath Ghazal 53" by Douglas Barbour:

> To say it all You need big lungs./That heavy intake then a slow rush.

fS is 56 pgs., 8½×11, saddle-stapled with card cover and includes photos, artwork and ads. They receive about 100 submissions for each issue, accept approximately 10%. Press run is 500 for 100 subscribers, 250 shelf sales. Subscription: $20/1 year, $35/2 years. Sample: $7.

How to Submit: Submit typed poems with name and address on each page. No previously published poems; simultaneous submissions OK. E-mail submissions OK (include mailing address). Cover letter required. Deadlines are November 15, March 15 and July 15. Seldom comments on rejections. Send SASE (or SAE with IRC) for guidelines. Responds in 3 months. Pays 1-year subscription. Acquires first North American rights. Reviews books of poetry in both single and multi-book format. Open to unsolicited reviews. Poets may also send books for review consideration.

Advice: "You stop between these 'fixed' points on the map to get an injection of something new, something fresh that's going to get you from point to point. . . . We want to be a kind of connection between polarities: a link. We'll publish any poem or story that offers a challenge: to the mind, to the page, to writers and readers."

✔ ▨ FINE MADNESS, P.O. Box 31138, Seattle WA 98103-1138, website www.scn.org/arts/finemadness, founded 1982, editors Sean Bentley, John Malek, Judith Skillman, Anne Pitkin and Alan Wald.

Magazine Needs: *Fine Madness* aims to publish 3 issues every 2 years (a new issue roughly every 8 months). They want "contemporary poetry of any form and subject. We look for the highest quality of thought, language and imagery. We look for the mark of the individual: unique ideas and presentation; careful, humorous, sympathetic. No careless poetry, greeting card poetry, poetry that 10,000 other people could have written." They have published poetry by Pattiann Rogers, Albert Goldbarth and Caroline Knox. As a sample we selected these lines from "Sugar" by Alan Ridenour:

> The piñata explodes like a beehive./Amid the sound of clubs,/its candy is trampled into diamonds/ while paper crowns are whirled through/blind rage and love of chocolate.

Fine Madness is 64 pgs., digest-sized, offset printed and perfect-bound with color card cover. They accept about 40 of 1,500 poems received each year. Their press run is 1,000 for 100 subscribers of which 10 are libraries. Subscription: $9. Sample: $4.

How to Submit: Submit 2-5 poems, preferably originals, not photocopies, 1 poem/page. No previously published poems or simultaneous submissions. Send SASE for guidelines. Responds in 4 months. Pays 1 copy plus subscription.

Also Offers: Website includes guidelines, subscription and back issue information and samples of work published.

Advice: "If you don't read poetry, don't send us any."

⊕ ▢ ◔ FIRE, Field Cottage, Old Whitehill, Tackley, Kidlington, Oxfordshire OX5 3AB United Kingdom, founded 1994, editor Jeremy Hilton.

Magazine Needs: *Fire* appears 3 times a year "to publish little-known, unfashionable or new writers alongside better known ones." They want "experimental, unfashionable, demotic work; longer work encouraged." Also accepts poetry written by children. No rhyming verse. They have published poetry by Marilyn Hacker, Adrian C. Louis, Tom Pickard, Allen Fisher, Gael Turnbull and David Hart. The editor says *Fire* is 150 pgs., A5. They receive about 400 poems a year, accept approximately 35%. Press run is 250 for 180 subscribers of which 20 are libraries. Single copy: £4, add £1 postage Europe, £2 postage overseas. Subscription (3 issues): £7, add £2 postage Europe, £4 postage overseas.

How to Submit: Previously published poems OK; no simultaneous submissions. Cover letter preferred. Disk submissions OK. Time between acceptance and publication "varies enormously." Often comments on rejections. Send SASE for guidelines. Responds in 2 months. Sometimes sends prepublication galleys, "but rarely to overseas contributors." Pays 2 copies.

$ ◎ FIREBRAND BOOKS (Specialized: feminist, lesbian, ethnic), 141 The Commons, Ithaca NY 14850, phone (607)272-0000, website www.firebrandbooks.com, founded 1984, editor/publisher Nancy K. Bereano.

Book/Chapbook Needs: Firebrand "is a feminist and lesbian publishing company committed to producing quality work in multiple genres by ethnically diverse women." They publish both quality trade paperbacks and hardbacks. Books are usually 94 pgs., flat-spined, elegantly printed on heavy stock with a glossy color card cover, a photo of the author on the back.

How to Submit: Simultaneous submissions acceptable with notification. Replies to queries within 2 weeks, to mss within 1 month. Pays royalties. Send for catalog to buy samples.

⊕ ✓ ◑ FIREWATER PRESS INC.; VARIOUS ARTISTS; WORKING TITLES, 34, Northleaze, Long Ashton, Bristol BS41 9HT United Kingdom, founded 1989, contact editor Tony Lewis-Jones for *Various Artists* and editor Claire Williamson for *Working Titles*.

Magazine Needs: Both *Various Artists* and *Working Titles* appear annually and intend "to encourage good accessible poetry by new and established writers. *Working Titles* also has a brief to encourage women's writing." They want any format/style "so long as the work is not anti-minority. Prefer short poems (up to 40 lines)." They have published poetry by Sophie Hannah, Robert Etty, Michael Daugherty and Martin Holroyd. As a sample, editor Tony Lewis-Jones selected his own haiku:

> Mist on the river/Skies are as fickle/As love, as snow.

The editors say *VA* is approximately 30 pgs., A5, saddle-stitched with graphics; *WT* is approximately 30 pgs., A5, saddle-stitched. Both publications accept 10% of poems received a year (2,000 for *VA*, 1,500 for *WT*). Press runs are 250 for 100 subscribers of which 10 are libraries. Single copy: $5; subscription: $10. Sample: $3. Make checks payable to A. Lewis-Jones (they prefer currency from the US).

How to Submit: Submit 6 poems at a time. No previously published poems or simultaneous submissions. Cover letter preferred. Time between acceptance and publication is 1-12 months. Always comments on rejections. Send SASE (or SAE and IRC) for guidelines. *VA* responds in 2 weeks; *WT* in less. Pays 2 copies. Returns rights upon publication. Staff reviews books of poetry. Send books for review consideration.

Also Offers: Firewater Press also sponsors a number of awards for poets working in the United Kingdom.

Advice: "Write from the heart, don't compromise and keep trying. If you're good enough, you'll make it."

✴ ✓ $ ◎ FIREWEED: A FEMINIST QUARTERLY (Specialized: women), P.O. Box 279, Station B, Toronto, Ontario M5T 2W2 Canada, phone (416)504-1339, e-mail fireweed@web.net, founded 1978, contact editorial collective.

Magazine Needs: *Fireweed*, edited by the Fireweed editorial/collective, is a feminist journal of writing, politics, art and culture that "especially welcomes contributions by women of color, working-class women, native women, lesbians and women with disabilities." As a sample they selected the opening lines of "Remembering My Voice" by Treena Kortje:

> Today the baby discovers sound under water./It is my own voice she recognizes,/how it reached her
> once through soft folds of skin,/to the swell in my belly where she began

Fireweed is 88 pgs., 6¾×9¾, professionally printed and perfect-bound with 3- or 4-color glossy cover, includes b&w art. Press run is 1,500. Subscription: $22 individuals, $35 institutions in Canada; $30 individuals, $45 institutions in US. Sample: $5-15 (double issues), Canadian or US funds.

How to Submit: Submit up to 5 poems, single-spaced. Simultaneous submissions OK. Send cover letter with brief bio and publication credits, if any. Publishes theme issues. Send SASE (or SAE and IRC) for upcoming themes. Responds in up to 1 year. "Please include SAE and IRC for reply." Pays 1 year subscription and 2 copies of issue in which work appears.

FIREWEED: POETRY OF WESTERN OREGON (Specialized: regional), 2917 NE 13th, Portland OR 97212, phone/fax (503)460-9063, e-mail jazzpo@iccom.com, founded 1989.
Magazine Needs: *Fireweed* is a quarterly publishing the work of poets living in Western Oregon or having close connections to the region. However, poems need not be regional in subject; any theme, subject, length or form is acceptable. They have published poetry by Stephanie Van Horn, James Grabill, Paulann Petersen and Lex Runciman. As a sample they selected these lines from "Memory for a City Dweller" by Michael Spurlin:

> *Recall this day when the world/spoke its center in you,/when a glacier's movement into water/was the*
> *rapid motion of earth/and your eye roved around/the world's stillness, bounded/by mountain, river*
> *and open range.*

Fireweed is 44 pgs., digest-sized, laser printed and saddle-stapled with card cover. "We receive several hundred poems and publish about ¼ or ⅓ of them." Press run is 250 for 180 subscribers of which 20 are libraries, 25 shelf sales. Subscription: $10. Sample: $4.
How to Submit: Submit 3-5 poems at a time, name and address on each page. No previously published poems; simultaneous submissions OK. Cover letter with brief bio required. Often comments on rejections. They do not publish guidelines for poets but will answer inquiries with SASE. Responds in up to 4 months. Pays 2 copies. Acquires first North American serial rights. Reviews books of poetry by Oregon poets in 500-750 words, single format. Open to unsolicited reviews. Oregon poets may also send books for review consideration.
Advice: "Try to examine a copy before submitting."

FIRM NONCOMMITTAL: AN INTERNATIONAL JOURNAL OF WHIMSY (Specialized: humor), 5 Vonda Ave., Toronto, Ontario M2N 5E6 Canada, e-mail firmnon@idirect.com (queries only), website http://webhome.idirect.com/~firmnon, founded 1995, editor Brian Pastoor, assistant editor Vince Cicchine.
Magazine Needs: *FN* is an annual forum, published in August, for international light verse and humorous, short fiction and nonfiction. "Short poems under 40 lines are preferred, in all forms and styles from visual to villanelle. There is a morass of morose writing out there. We seek writers who find the sunshine in the saturnine, who 'take the utmost trouble to find the right thing to say and then say it with the utmost levity'—G.B. Shaw." They have published "levity" by bill bissett (Canada), K.V. Skene (England), Michael Shuval (Israel) and haiku by Francine Porad (U.S.). *Firm Noncommittal* is 40-48 pgs., 6¼×8¼, professionally printed and perfect-bound with matte card cover, using mirthful, b&w art. They accept "nearly 10%" of the submissions received. Circulation is 100 and growing, "thanks to support from *Krax* and other light-minded magazines." Sample: $5 (Canadian funds). Make checks payable to Brian Pastoor.
How to Submit: Submit up to 6 poems in *May or June only*. Previously published poems OK; no simultaneous submissions. Cover letter required; include a brief bio, "preferably under 50 words, preferably factual. Unless of edificial genius, mss without SASE or SAE and IRCs will be binned (sorry)." Obtain guidelines via website. Responds in 2 months. Pays 1 copy.
Also offers: Website includes writer's guidelines, sample writing from back issues, professional affiliations and names of editors.
Advice: "While we do admit a bias to the ironist here, we shy away from satire that is too heavy. We're after light, perspicuous writing that reveals a quickness of mind about the spiritual or mundane (all themes universal), writing that is characterized by imagination, ingenuity and/or self-conscious verbal artifice. Tom Robbins, as always, put it best: 'Those who fail to see the whimsy of things will experience rigor mortis before death.' "

FIRST CLASS; FOUR-SEP PUBLICATIONS, P.O. Box 12434, Milwaukee WI 53212, website www.exe cpc.com/~chriftor, founded 1994, editor Christopher M.
Magazine Needs: *First Class* appears 3 times/year and "publishes excellent/odd writing for intelligent/creative readers." They want "short post-modern poems, also short fiction." No traditional work. They have published poetry by Bennett, Locklin, Fitzsimmons, Splake, Catlin and Huffstickler. *FC* is 46-48 pgs., 8½×11, printed, saddle-stitched with colored cover. They receive about 1,000 poems a year, accept approximately 30. Press run is 200-400. Sample (including guidelines): $5 or mini version $1. Make checks payable to Christopher Meyer.
How to Submit: Submit 5 poems at a time. Previously published poems and simultaneous submissions OK. Cover letter preferred. Time between acceptance and publication is 2-4 months. Often comments on rejections. Responds in 3 weeks. Pays in 1 copy. Acquires one-time rights. Reviews books of poetry. Open to unsolicited reviews. Poets may also send books for review consideration.
Also Offers: Chapbook production available. Website includes guidelines, recent books and chapbooks, current issue information, etc.
Advice: "Belt out a good, short, thought-provoking, graphic, uncommon piece."

FIRST OFFENSE (Specialized: form/style), Syring, Stodmarsh, Canterbury, Kent CT3 4BA England, founded 1985, contact Tim Fletcher.

Magazine Needs: *First Offense* is published 1-2 times a year. "The magazine is for contemporary poetry and is not traditional, but is received by most ground-breaking poets." They want "contemporary, language and experimental poetry and articles. No traditional work." Mr. Fletcher says *FO* is photocopied. "So we need well typed manuscripts, word processed." Press run is 300. Subscription: £2.50 plus 75¢ p&h. Make checks payable to Tim Fletcher.

How to Submit: No previously published poems. "No reply without SASE or SAE and IRC." Reviews books and chapbooks of poetry and other magazines.

Advice: "Always buy a copy before submitting for research so as not to waste everyone's time."

☑ ◌ ◐ **FIRST STEP PRESS; STEPPING STONES MAGAZINE: A LITERARY MAGAZINE FOR INNOVATIVE ART; CRIMSON RIVERS**, P.O. Box 902, Norristown PA 19404-0902, e-mail firststeppress@excite.com, founded 1996, editor/publisher Michael D. Ross, Sr.

Magazine Needs: "*Stepping Stones Magazine* is published quarterly to showcase established talent as well as the aspiring poet; to provide a means of helping poets with their craft." They want any style, any length, any genre "so long as it's good." No first drafts. They have published poetry by Lisa M. Brennan, Michael Rinehart and Ed Galing. *SSM* is 60 pgs., 5½ × 8½, photocopied and saddle-stapled with cardstock cover, includes b&w clip art. They receive about 720 poems a year, accept approximately 30%. Press run is 300 for 100 subscribers; 100 distributed free to coffeehouses. Single copy: $5; subscription: $15. Sample: $3. Make checks payable to Michael D. Ross, Sr.

How to Submit: Submit 7 poems at a time. Previously published poems and simultaneous submissions OK. Cover letter preferred. E-mail submissions OK. Disk submissions in ASCII, WordPerfect or MSWord formats OK. Time between acceptance and publication is up to 1 year. Always comments on rejections. Send SASE for guidelines. Responds in 1 month. Always sends prepublication galleys. Pays 1 copy. Acquires first or one-time rights. Reviews books and chapbooks of poetry and other magazines in 250-500 words, single book format. Open to unsolicited reviews. Poets may also send books for review consideration.

Also Offers: Publishes in October, *Crimson Rivers*, a yearly anthology of splatter punk poetry and short fiction. "This publication will provide a forum for those wishing to express the darkness that resides in the deepest regions of the soul. Here, there are no limits, no boundaries, there is no turning back." For poetry, send 1-30 poems "any style is fine, so long as it can chill the marrow in the reader's bones. Poems about unseen fears are especially desired." Also sponsors contests. Send SASE for details.

Advice: "There are no proven methods for success, the best thing to do is to keep writing and believe in your work because if you can't—nobody else will."

☑ $ ◑ **FIRST THINGS**, 156 Fifth Ave., Suite 400, New York NY 10010, phone (212)627-1985, fax (212)627-2184, e-mail poetry@firstthings.com, website www.firstthings.com, founded 1990, poetry editor J. Bottum.

Magazine Needs: *FT* contains "social commentary with a special interest in issues of religion and public life: ethics, law, education, mores, politics." They have published poetry by Marjorie Maddox, Laurance Wieder, Luci Shaw and Atar Hadari. *FT* is 64-84 pgs., magazine-sized, web offset printed and perfect-bound with 80 lb. text paper cover, includes display and classified ads. They receive about 500 poems a year, accept approximately 5%. Subscription: $29/year.

How to Submit: Line length for poetry is 40 maximum. No previously published poems or simultaneous submissions. Cover letter preferred. Time between acceptance and publication is 2-6 months. Publishes theme issues occasionally. Responds in up to 3 weeks. Pays $50 plus 2 copies.

◑ **FISH DRUM**, P.O. Box 966, Murray Hill Station, New York NY 10156, website www.fishdrum.com, founded in 1988 by Robert Winson (1959-1995), editor Suzi Winson.

Magazine Needs: *Fish Drum* is a literary magazine appearing once a year. They want "West Coast poetry, the exuberant, talky, often elliptical and abstract 'continuous nerve movie' that follows the working of the mind and has a relationship to the world and the reader. Philip Whalen's work, for example, and much of *Calafia, The California Poetry*, edited by Ishmael Reed. Also magical-tribal-incantatory poems, exemplified by the future/primitive *Technicians of the Sacred*, ed. Rothenberg. *Fish Drum* has a soft spot for schmoozy, emotional, imagistic stuff. Literate, personal material that sings and surprises, OK?" They have published poetry by Philip Whalen, Arthur Sze, Nathaniel Tarn, Alice Notley, John Brandi, Steve Richmond, Jessica Hagedorn and Leo Romero. As a sample the editor selected these lines from "Glossalalia" by Kate Bremer:

> Everywhere I look I see amino acids on the ground./When I close my eyes, I see molecules and pieces
> of Sanskrit:/I hear syllables and alphabets.

FD is approximately 80 pgs., professionally printed, perfect-bound. Press run is 2,000 for subscribers, libraries and shelf sales. Subscription: $24/4 issues. Sample: $6.

How to Submit: Publishes theme issues. Sends prepublication galleys. Pays 2 copies. Acquires first serial rights. Reviews books or chapbooks of poetry in long essays and/or capsule reviews. Open to unsolicited reviews. Poets may also send books for review consideration.

Advice: "We're looking for prose, fiction, essays, what-have-you, and artwork, scores, cartoons, etc.—just send it along. We are also interested in poetry, prose and translations concerning the practice of Zen. We publish chapbooks, but solicit these from our authors." She also adds, "It is my intention to complete Robert's work and to honor his memory by continuing to publish *FishDrum*."

☑ ◉ **5 AM**, P.O. Box 205, Spring Church PA 15686, founded 1987, editors Ed Ochester and Judith Vollmer. **Magazine Needs:** *5 AM* is a poetry publication that appears twice a year. They are open in regard to form, length, subject matter and style. However, they do not want poetry that is "religious or naive rhymers." They have published poetry by Rita Dove, Edward Field, Jesse Lee Kercheval, Billy Collins, Alicia Ostriker and Alberto Rios. *5 AM* is a 24-page, offset tabloid. They receive about 3,000 poems a year, use approximately 2%. Press run is 1,000 for 550 subscribers of which 25 are libraries, about 300 shelf sales. Subscription: $12/4 issues. Sample: $4.
How to Submit: No previously published poems or simultaneous submissions. Seldom comments on rejections. Responds within 2 months. Pays 2 copies. Acquires first rights.

☑ $◻ **FIVE POINTS; JAMES DICKEY PRIZE FOR POETRY**, Georgia State University, University Plaza, Atlanta GA 30303-3083, phone (404)651-0071, fax (404)651-1710, website www.webdelsol.com/Five-Points, founded 1996, managing editor Megan Sexton.
Magazine Needs: *Five Points* appears 3 times a year and "publishes quality poetry, fiction, nonfiction, interviews and art by established and emerging writers." They want "poetry of high quality which shows evidence of an original voice and imagination." They have published poetry by Charles Wright, Kate Daniels and Philip Levine. As a sample the editor selected these lines from "Talc" by Jane Hirschfield:

> When you phoned I was far, and sleeping,/but they brought me the message and I ran,/I ran to the
> phone where you were,/You were speaking, we two were speaking,/When I ran back to the room I no
> longer/knew we would speak again.

Five Points is about 200 pgs., 6½×9, professionally printed and perfect-bound with 4-color card cover, includes b&w photos and ads. They receive about 2,000 poems a year, accept approximately 5%. Press run is 2,000 for about 1,000 subscribers of which 10% are libraries, 40% shelf sales. Single copy: $6. Sample: $5.
How to Submit: Submit no more than 3 poems at a time. No previously published poems or simultaneous submissions. Cover letter preferred. Reads submissions September 1 through May 30 only. Time between acceptance and publication is 3 months. Poems are circulated to an editorial board. "First reader culls poems then send them to the final reader." Seldom comments on rejections. Send SASE for guidelines. Responds in 3 months. Always sends prepublication galleys. Pays $50/poem plus 2 copies and 1-year subscription. Acquires first North American serial rights.
Also Offers: Sponsors the James Dickey Prize for Poetry which awards $1,000 and publication in the Spring issue. Reading fee: $10 for up to 3 poems, no more than 50 lines each. Entries must be typed. Fee includes 1-year subscription. Deadline: November 30. Send SASE for complete contest guidelines.

🌐 ◉ **FLAMBARD**, Stable Cottage, East Fourstones, Hexham NE47 5DX England, phone +44 1434 674360, fax +44 1434 674178, founded 1990, contact Peter Lewis.
Book/Chapbook Needs: Flambard "is particularly sympathetic to new or neglected writers from the North of England, and is keen to nourish developing talent." But open to all. They have published *Stepping on the Cracks* by Amanda White and *The Apple Exchange* by S.J. Litherland. They publish 5 paperbacks/year. Books are usually 64 pgs., 234×156mm, disk to plate printing, limp-sewn binding, 4-color cover, art work sometimes included.
How to Submit: "Books only considered." Submit at least 15 poems at a time. Previously published poems and simultaneous submissions OK. Cover letter required. "If accepted, we expect the text on a disk we can read." Time between acceptance and publication is 12-15 months. Often comments on rejections. Replies to queries and mss in 1 month. Pays honorarium and 6 author's copies. Obtain samples of books or chapbooks "by direct mail purchase or through shops."
Advice: "Not much point thinking about book publication until a reasonable level of magazine publication has been achieved."

🌐 ◉ **FLAMING ARROWS**, County Sligo VEC, Riverside, Sligo, Ireland, phone (+353)7145844, fax (+353)7143093, website www.artspark.com/home/sligovec, founded 1989, editor Leo Regan, A.E.O.
Magazine Needs: *Flaming Arrows*, published annually in January, features poetry, prose, interviews, graphics and photographs. They want "cogent, lucid, coherent, technically precise poetry. Poems of the spirit, mystical, metaphysical but sensuous, tactile and immediate to the senses." They do not want "loose rambling emotional release." They have published poetry by Sydney Bernard Smith, Medbh McGuckian, James Liddy and Ciaran O'Driscoll. As a sample the editor selected these lines from "The Summons" by Peter Van Belle:

> Sacred hawk, descend from your heights,/star clenched in beak, your eyes, my diamonds,/your mind,
> a twine of steel./From this roof I speak to you,/holding one foot over the abyss./I relish the dizziness.

Flaming Arrows is 80-102 pgs., A5, offset printed, perfect-bound or saddle-stapled, with 2-color cover stock, and b&w interior photos and graphics used in conjunction with the written work. They receive about 500 poems a year, accept 6%. Press run is 500 for 150 subscribers of which 30 are libraries, 180 shelf sales; 100 distributed free to writer's groups, contributors, literary events. Sample: $6. Make checks payable to Co. Sligo VEC.

How to Submit: Submit 5 poems "typed, A4, in 10 or 12 pt. for scanning or discs for Word 7 in Windows 95." Previously published poems and simultaneous submissions OK. Cover letter required. Time between acceptance and publication is 10 months. Responds in 3 months. Pays 1 copy, additional copies at cost. They receive financial assistance from the Arts Council of Ireland.

Advice: "Inspection of previous issues, especially 2, 3, 5 or 6 will inform prospective contributors of style and standard required."

🌐 $⃝⃝ ◕ **FLARESTACK PUBLISHING; OBSESSED WITH PIPEWORK,** 15 Market Place, Redditch, Worcestershire B98 8AR England, phone (01527)63291, fax (01527)68571, e-mail flare.stack@virgin.net or redditchlib@worcestershire.gov.uk, founded 1995, editor Charles Johnson.

Magazine Needs: *Obsessed with Pipework* appears quarterly. "We are very keen to publish strong new voices— 'new poems to surprise and delight' with somewhat of a high-wire aspect. We are looking for original, exploratory poems—positive, authentic, oblique maybe—delighting in image and in the dance of words on the page." They do not want "the predictable, the unfresh, the rhyme-led; the clever, the sure-of-itself. No formless outpourings, please." They have published "Searching For Salsa" by Jennifer Ballerini and poetry by David Hart, Jennifer Compton, Susan Wicks and Vuyelwa Carlin. As a sample the editor selected these lines from "Fixtures and Fittings" by Dianne Neoh:

> That summer/we folded up the contents of our lives/and placed them into boxes./Even I became of use/
> sanctioning the closure of the dolls house/and removal of toys.

The editor says *OWP* is 49 pgs., A5, photocopied and stapled with card cover, ads "by arrangement." They receive about 1,500 poems a year, accept approximately 10%. Press run is 70-100. Single copy: £3.50; subscription: £12. Sample: £2 if available. Make checks payable to Flarestack Publishing.

How to Submit: Submit maximum of 6 poems at a time. No previously published poems or simultaneous submissions. Cover letter preferred. E-mail and fax submissions OK. "If sending by e-mail, send a maximum 3 poems in the body of the message, as attached files may become lost or corrupted." Time between acceptance and publication is 4 months maximum. Often comments on rejections. Send SASE for guidelines or request via fax or e-mail. Responds in 2 months. Pays 1 copy. Acquires first rights.

Book/Chapbook Needs & How to Submit: Flarestack Publishing ("talent to burn") aims to "find an audience for new poets, so beginners are welcome, but the work has to be strong and clear." They publish 12 chapbooks/year. Chapbooks are usually 12-50 pgs., A5, photocopied and stapled with card cover.

How to Submit: Query first with a few sample poems and cover letter with brief bio and publication credits. "Normally we expect a few previous magazine acceptances, but no previous collection publication." Replies to queries in 6 weeks; to mss in 2 months. Pays royalties of 25% plus 6 author's copies (out of a press run of 50-100). Order sample chapbooks by sending £3.50.

Advice: "Most beginning poets show little evidence of reading poetry before writing it! Join a poetry workshop. For chapbook publishing, we are looking for coherent first collections that take risks, make leaps and come clean."

Ⓝ $◕ **FLESH AND BLOOD: QUIET TALES OF DARK FANTASY & HORROR,** 121 Joseph St., Bayville NJ 08721, e-mail Ahhh@webtv.net, website www.geocities.com/soho/lofts/3459/Fnb.html, founded 1997, senior editor Jack Fisher, associate editor Matt Doeden.

Magazine Needs: Appearing 3 times a year, *Flesh and Blood* publishes work of dark fantasy and the supernatural. They want surreal, bizarre and avant-garde poetry. No "rhyming or love poems, epics, killers, etc." They have published poetry by Charles Jacob, Mark McLaughlin, Kurt Newton, Wendy Rathbone, JW Donnelly and Donna Taylor Burgess. The editor says *FAB* is 44-52 pgs., 5½×8½, saddle-stapled with glossy 2-color cover, includes art/graphics and ads. They receive about 200 poems a year, accept approximately 10%. Publish 4-6 poems/issue. Press run is 500 for 400 subscribers, 100 shelf sales; 50 distributed free to reviewers. Subscription: $11. Sample: $4. Make checks payable to John Fisher.

How to Submit: Submit up to 5 poems at a time. Line length for poetry is 3 minimum, 30 maximum. Previously published poems OK; no simultaneous submissions. E-mail submissions OK. Cover letter preferred. "Poems should be on separate pages, each with the author's address. Cover letter should include background credits." Time between acceptance and publication is 5-10 months. Often comments on rejections. Send SASE for guidelines or obtain via website. Responds in 2 months. Pays $5/poem.

Also Offers: Website includes guidelines, updates, news, editors, issue contents, etc.

Advice: "Be patient, professional, tactful and courteous."

◯ ◕ **FLINT HILLS REVIEW,** Division of English, Box 4019, Emporia State University, Emporia KS 66801, phone (316)341-5216, fax (316)341-5547, e-mail heldricp@emporia.edu or webbamy@emporia.edu, website www.emporia.edu/fhr, founded 1995, editors Phil Heldrich and Amy Sage Webb.

FOR AN EXPLANATION of symbols used in this book, see the Key to Symbols on the front and back inside covers.

Magazine Needs: Published annually in June, *Flint Hills Review* is "a regionally focused journal presenting writers of national distinction alongside burgeoning authors." They are open to all forms except "rhyming, sentimental or gratuitous verse." They have published poetry by E. Ethelbert Miller, Elizabeth Dodd, Vivian Shipley and Gwendolyn Brooks. *FHR* is about 100 pgs., digest-sized, offset printed and perfect-bound with glossy card cover with b&w photo, also includes b&w photos. They receive about 2,000 poems a year, accept approximately 5%. Single copy: $5.50.

How to Submit: Submit 3-5 poems at a time. No previously published poems; simultaneous submissions OK. Disk submissions OK. Cover letter with SASE required. Reads submissions January through March only. Time between acceptance and publication is about 1 year. Seldom comments on rejections. Publishes theme issues occasionally. Send SASE for guidelines and upcoming themes. Pays 1 copy. Acquires first rights.

Also Offers: Sponsors the annual Bluestem Press Award. See listing in the Contests & Awards section of this book. Website includes guidelines, samples, "a comprehensive web presence."

Advice: "Subscribe for examples of what we publish, understand our guidelines and see our website."

☑ ◉ **FLOATING BRIDGE PRESS (Specialized: regional)**, P.O. Box 18814, Seattle WA 98118, e-mail ppereira5@aol.com, website www.scn.org/arts/floatingbridge, founded 1994, contact editor.

Book/Chapbook Needs: The press publishes chapbooks and anthologies by Washington state poets, selected through an annual contest. They have published chapbooks by Bart Baxter, James Gurley, Molly Tenenbaum and Donna Waidtlow. In 1997 they began publishing *Pontoon*, an annual anthology featuring the work of Washington state poets. That anthology is 96 pgs., digest-sized, offset-printed and perfect-bound with matte cardstock cover. For a sample chapbook or anthology, send $7 postpaid.

How to Submit: For consideration, Washington poets (only) should submit a chapbook ms of 20-24 pgs. of poetry with $10 reading fee and SASE (for results only). The usual reading period is November 1 to February 15. Previously published individual poems and simultaneous submissions OK. Author's name must not appear on the ms; include a separate page with title, name, address, telephone number and acknowledgments of any previous publication. Mss are judged anonymously and will not be returned. In addition to publication, the winner receives $500 (minimum), 50 copies and a reading in the Seattle area. All entrants receive a copy of the winning chapbook. All entrants will be considered for inclusion in *Pontoon*, a poetry anthology. Send SASE for complete guidelines or visit website.

Also Offers: Website includes guidelines, sample poems, poet bios, ordering information and links to other sites of interest to poets.

◖ **THE FLORIDA REVIEW**, Dept. of English, University of Central Florida, Box 25000, Orlando FL 32816, phone (407)823-2038, website pegasus.cc.ucf.edu/~english/floridareview/home.htm, founded 1972, contact editors.

Magazine Needs: *FR* is a "literary biannual with emphasis on short fiction and poetry." They want "poems filled with real things, real people and emotions, poems that might conceivably advance our knowledge of the human heart." They have published poetry by Knute Skinner, Elton Glaser, Silvia Curbelo and Walter McDonald. It is 128 pgs., professionally printed, flat-spined, with glossy card cover. Press run is 1,000 for 500 subscribers of which 50 are libraries, 300 shelf sales. Subscription: $10. Sample: $6.

How to Submit: Submit no more than 6 poems at a time. No correspondence, including mss, will be read or acknowledged unless accompanied by a SASE. Simultaneous submissions OK. Editor comments on submissions "occasionally." Send SASE for guidelines. Responds in 3 months. Always sends prepublication galleys. Pays 3 copies, small honorarium occasionally available. Acquires all rights. Returns rights "upon publication, when requested." Reviews books of poetry in 1,500 words, single format; 2,500-3,000 words, multi-book format. Send books for review consideration.

Also Offers: Website includes contents of past issues, information about Editors' Awards competition and submission guidelines.

Advice: "We would like more formal verse."

☑ ◖ **FLYWAY, A LITERARY REVIEW**, 206 Ross Hall, Iowa State University, Ames IA 50011-1201, fax (515)294-6814, e-mail flyway@iastate.edu, website www.engl.iastate.edu/main/flyway/flyway.html, founded 1961, editor Stephen Pett.

Magazine Needs: Appearing 3 times a year, *Flyway* "is one of the best literary magazines for the money; it is packed with some of the most readable poems being published today—all styles and forms, lengths and subjects." The editor shuns elite-sounding free verse with obscure meanings and pretty-sounding formal verse with obvious meanings. It is 112 pgs., 6×9, professionally printed and perfect-bound with matte card cover with color. Circulation is 600 for 400 subscribers of which 100 are libraries. Subscription: $20. Sample: $7.

How to Submit: Submit 4-6 poems at a time. Cover letter preferred. "We do not read mss between the end of May and mid-August." May be contacted by fax. Publishes theme issues (Chicano, Latino). Responds in 6 weeks (often sooner). Pays 1 copy. Acquires first rights.

Also Offers: Sponsors an annual award for poetry, fiction and nonfiction. Send SASE for details.

◖ ◖ **FOOTPRINTS; WRITER'S WORKS CHAPBOOKS**, 604 Crabill Rd., Toutle WA 98649, phone (360)274-4372, founded 1998, editor Larry Stewart.

Magazine Needs: *Footprints* appears quarterly and is "a forum for poets and writers containing poetry and short stories." They want "quality poetry. Shorter poems are preferred, but, if a long poem says a lot, we will be interested." No "vulgar or suggestive language. Quality works can be produced without sexually explicit scenes. Controversial political opinions are to be avoided. Then there is religion. Leave out references to denominations, specific doctrines or people." They have published poetry by Dolores Malaschak, Ezra Cardiff and Virginia Cole Veal. As a sample the editor selected these lines from his poem "Of Chance Encounters":

> *Among the peaks of Olympia, heavy were the snows,/ in the days when the winter kept our souls*
> *imprisoned./ It was the time of our great longing, our reaching out/ to touch each other, to explore the*
> *regions of our youth;/ the uncharted wilderness—like this improbable place,/chosen, by our parents,*
> *to put down roots . . .*

The editor says *Footprints* is 40-50 pgs., 8½×11, offset printed and saddle-stapled with glossy color cover and b&w and color illustrations. Press run is 100 for 54 subscribers of which 15 are libraries. Single copy: $7.50; subscription: $19.50. Sample: $6. Make checks payable to Larry Stewart.
How to Submit: Submit up to 10 poems at a time. Previously published poems OK; no simultaneous submissions. Cover letter preferred. Time between acceptance and publication is 1-3 months. Often comments on rejections. Send SASE for guidelines. Responds in 3 weeks. Pays 1 copy. Acquires first rights. Reviews chapbooks of poetry. Poets may send books for review consideration.
Book/Chapbook Needs & How to Submit: Writer's Works Chapbooks publishes chapbooks of 24-40 pgs., digest-sized, offset printed and saddle-stapled. Query first with a few sample poems and cover letter with brief bio and publication credits. Replies to queries in 4 weeks, to mss in 2 months. Pays 10% royalties. "Expect poet to subsidize cost! Help in sales!"

■ Ⓜ **FOR POETRY.COM**, e-mail editor@forpoetry.com, website www.forpoetry.com, founded March 1999, editor Jackie Marcus.
Magazine Needs: *For Poetry.Com* is a web magazine with daily updates. "We wish to promote new and emerging poets, with or without MFAs. We will be publishing established poets, but our primary interest is in publishing excellent poetry, prose, essays, reviews, paintings and photography. We are interested in lyric poetry, vivid imagery, open form, natural landscape, philosophical themes but not at the expense of honesty and passion: model examples: Robert Hass, James Wright, Charles Wright's *The Other Side of the River*, Montale, Neruda, Levertov and Karen Fish. No city punk, corny sentimental fluff or academic workshop imitations." They have published poetry by Charles Simic, Marilyn Hacker and Karen Fish. As a sample the editor selected these lines from "Elegy" by Joseph Duemer:

> *Wind lifts the curtains/in an empty room./I'm somewhere else—/a line storm moving up from the Gulf/*
> *meaning a downpour in Tennessee./Like all the weather—a blessing & a curse.*

"We receive lots of submissions and are very selective about acceptances, but we will always try to send a note back on rejections."
How to Submit: Submit no more than 2 poems at a time. No previously published poems; simultaneous submissions OK. Cover letter preferred. Accepts e-mail submissions only. Reads submissions September through May only. Time between acceptance and publication is 2-6 weeks. Poems are circulated to an editorial board. "We'll read all submissions and then decide together on the poems we'll publish." Comments on rejections "as often as possible." Obtain guidelines via website. Responds in 2 weeks. Reviews books and chapbooks of poetry and other magazines in 800 words. Open to unsolicited reviews.
Advice: "As my friend Kevin Hull said, 'Get used to solitude and rejection.' Sit on your poems for several months or more. Time is your best critic."

☑ Ⓜ **FORKLIFT, OHIO: A JOURNAL OF POETRY, COOKING & LIGHT INDUSTRIAL SAFETY**, P.O. Box 19650, Cincinnati OH 45219-0650, website www.hubcapart.nu, founded 1994, editor Matt Hart, editor Eric Appleby.
Magazine Needs: *Forklift, Ohio* is a biannual journal seeking "language that does work." They want "poems, recipes, light industrial safety tips; also artwork, essays and short stories. No literal, natural or political work; nothing 'experimental,' spiritual, erotic or gothic." They have published poetry by Terri Ford, Cornelius Eady, Nancy Bonnell-Kangas and Forrest Griffen. As a sample the editor selected these lines from "BP Station Employee Restroom, 2 a.m." by Terri Ford:

> *Here are some words/we use toward love: Crush Flame./Arrow. Torch. Fallen. I//fell. Maintain eye/*
> *contact with each incoming//person. Greet them. Hi.*

Forklift is 30-40 pgs., uses eclectic artwork, ads on back page only. A recent issue was bound with a bolt and sandpaper. They receive about 300 poems a year, accept approximately 15%. Press run is 300; distributed free in Cincinnati and across the US and to other journals. Single copy: $3 plus SASE; subscription: $12/4 issues. Sample for SASE. Make checks payable to Eric Appleby.
How to Submit: "*Forklift* is temporarily suspending publication for 2 years." When publication resumes submit 3-5 poems at a time, 1 poem/page. No previously published poems; simultaneous submissions OK. Cover letter preferred with brief bio. E-mail submissions OK, "plain text, MS Word." Time between acceptance and publication is 1 month. Poems are circulated to an editorial board—"two editors, occasional guest editor." Often comments on rejections. Send SASE for guidelines. Responds in 6 months. Pays 2 copies. Staff reviews books and chapbooks of poetry and other magazines in 30 words. Send books for review consideration.

Also Offers: Forklift Press has also released broadsheets, chapbooks and cassette recordings of selected poets who have been published in *Forklift, Ohio*. Website includes back issues, submission guidelines and recipes from the *Forklift, Ohio* test kitchen.

Advice: "Request a sample before submitting and include SASE for response from editors."

◐ ◎ **THE FORMALIST; HOWARD NEMEROV SONNET AWARD (Specialized: form, translations)**, 320 Hunter Dr., Evansville IN 47711, founded 1990, editor William Baer.

Magazine Needs: *The Formalist*, appears twice a year, "dedicated to contemporary *metrical* poetry written in the great tradition of English-language verse. We're looking for well-crafted poetry in a contemporary idiom which uses meter and the full range of traditional poetic conventions in vigorous and interesting ways. We're especially interested in sonnets, couplets, tercets, ballads, the French forms, etc. We're not, however, interested in haiku (or syllabic verse of any kind) or sestinas. Only rarely do we accept a poem over 2 pages, and we have no interest in any type of erotica, blasphemy, vulgarity or racism. Finally, we suggest that those wishing to submit to *The Formalist* become familiar with the journal beforehand. We are also interested in metrical translations of the poetry of major, formalist, non-English poets—from the ancient Greeks to the present." They have published poetry by Richard Wilbur, Donald Justice, Mona Van Duyn, Derek Walcott, John Updike, Maxine Kumin, James Merrill, Karl Shapiro, X.J. Kennedy, May Swenson, W.S. Merwin, W.D. Snodgrass and Louis Simpson. As a sample the editor selected the opening stanza from "The Amateurs of Heaven" by Howard Nemerov:

> Two lovers to a midnight meadow came/High in the hills, to lie there hand in hand/Like effigies and
> look up at the stars,/The never-setting ones set in the North/To circle the Pole in idiot majesty,/And
> wonder what was given them to wonder.

The Formalist is 128 pgs., digest-sized, offset printed on bond paper and perfect-bound, with colored card cover. Subscription: $12/year; $22/2 years (add $4/year for foreign subscription). Sample: $6.50.

How to Submit: Submit 3-5 poems at a time. No simultaneous submissions, previously published work, or disk submissions. A brief cover letter is recommended and a SASE is necessary for a reply and return of ms. Responds within 2 months. Pays 2 copies. Acquires first North American serial rights.

Also Offers: The Howard Nemerov Sonnet Award offers $1,000 and publication in *The Formalist* for the best unpublished sonnet. The final judge for 2000 was W.D. Snodgrass. Entry fee: $3/sonnet. Postmark deadline: June 15. Send SASE for guidelines. See also the contest listing for the World Order of Narrative and Formalist Poets. Contestants must subscribe to *The Formalist* to enter.

🌐 ✅ 💲◎ **FORUM (Specialized: erotic poetry)**, Northern & Shell Tower, City Harbour, London E14 9GL England, phone (0207)308 5090, fax (0207)308 5075, e-mail forum@marshall.co.uk, founded 1967, editor Elizabeth Coldwell.

Magazine Needs: Appearing 13 times a year, *Forum* is "a magazine which deals with all aspects of human sexuality." Poetry has to be short (16 lines maximum) and erotic in nature. The editor says *Forum* is 196 pgs. and magazine-sized. They receive about 200 poems a year, accept approximately 5%. Press run is 40,000 for 100 subscribers; 35,000 distributed free. Single copy: £3.60.

How to Submit: Submit 1 poem at a time. No previously published poems or simultaneous submissions. Fax and e-mail submissions OK (e-mail submissions submit in body of message). Cover letter preferred. Pays £10/poem. Buys one-time rights. Staff reviews books of erotic poetry. Send books for review consideration.

✅ ▢ ◖ ◯ ◐ ◎ **4*9*1 IMAGINATION (Specialized: soul experience)**, P.O. Box 91212, Lakeland FL 33804-1212, phone/fax (863)688-1226, e-mail stompdncr@aol.com, website www.fournineone.com, founded 1997, editor Donald Ryburn, assistant editor Rhonda Rozell.

Magazine Needs: *4*9*1 Imagination* appears continuously as an online publication and publishes poetry, art, photography, essays and interviews. They want "poetry of soul experience. No academic poetry, limited and fallacious language." Also accepts poetry written by children. They have published poetry by Rhonda Roszell and Donald Ryburn. As a sample the editor selected this poem "Poem from the North" by Stephen Sleboda:

> A fragile finger/Dressed in wood/Reminds me/of taste/from/an/ancient tomb

How to Submit: Submit 3-6 poems at a time. Previously published poems and simultaneous submissions OK. Cover letter with picture and SASE preferred. E-mail, fax, disk and CD-ROM submissions preferred. Note "submission" in subject area. "Would like to hear the poets own words not some standard format." Time between acceptance and publication varies. Response time varies. Payment varies. Acquires first or one-time rights. Reviews books and chapbooks of poetry and other magazines. Open to unsolicited reviews. Poets may also send books for review consideration.

Also Offers: Sponsors a series of creative projects. Write for details or visit the website.

Ⓝ ◎ **FOURTEEN HILLS: THE SFSU REVIEW**, Creative Writing Dept., San Francisco State University, 1600 Holloway Ave., San Francisco CA 94132, (415)338-3083, fax (415)338-7030, e-mail hills@sfsu.edu, website www.mercury.sfsu.edu/~hills/14hills.html, founded 1994, contact poetry editor.

Ⓥ Work published in this review has been included in *The Best American Poetry 1996*.

Magazine Needs: *Fourteen Hills* is a biannual. "We are seeking high quality, innovative work." They have published poetry by Alice Notley, Kate Braverman, Leslie Scalapino and Jane Hirshfield. As a sample the editor selected these lines from "Striptease #3" by Kate Braverman:

> *Full moon in New York./I am three days without you./I decipher dialects of stone/and the gestures of boulevards/in a granite autumn.*

FH is 170 pgs., 6×9, professionally printed and perfect-bound with glossy card cover. They receive about 600 poems a year, accept approximately 5-10%. Press run is 600 for 125 subscribers of which 25 are libraries. Single copy: $7; subscription: $12/year, $21/2 years. Sample: $5.

How to Submit: Submit 5 poems at a time. No previously published poems; simultaneous submissions OK. Cover letter preferred. Reads submissions August-September for the fall issue; January-February for the spring. "The editorial staff is composed entirely of graduate students from the Creative Writing Program at SFSU." Seldom comments on rejections. Send SASE for guidelines. Responds in 6 months. Always sends prepublication galleys. Pays 2 copies.

Advice: "Please read an issue of *Fourteen Hills* before submitting."

✔ ◎ **FOX CRY REVIEW**, University of Wisconsin-Fox Valley, 1478 Midway Rd., Menasha WI 54952-1297, phone (920)832-2600, e-mail lmills@uwc.edu, founded 1974, editor Laurel Mills.

Magazine Needs: *Fox Cry Review* is a literary annual, published in August, using poems of any length or style, include brief bio, deadline February 15. They have published poetry by David Graham, Doug Flaherty, Daniel J. Weeks, Carol Hamilton and Estella Lauter. As a sample the editor selected these lines from "Let the Words of My Mouth" by Beverly Voldseth, which was nominated for a Pushcart Prize:

> *We take comfort in these lines/that wait on our tongues—/to be rolled out to bank tellers//neighbors we pass on the street/strangers in the post office./What little boredoms our lives//are made up of, how they stand/in the mouth like truth.*

Fox Cry is 86 pgs., digest-sized, professionally printed and perfect-bound with light card cover with b&w illustration, also contains b&w illustrations. Their press run is 300. Single copy: $6 plus $1 postage.

How to Submit: Submit maximum of 3 poems from September 1 through February 15 only. Include SASE. "Include name, address and phone number on each poem." No previously published poems. Request guidelines via e-mail. Pays 1 copy.

Ⓝ ◎ **BENJAMIN FRANKLIN LITERARY AND MEDICAL SOCIETY, INC.; HUMPTY DUMPTY'S MAGAZINE; TURTLE MAGAZINE FOR PRESCHOOL KIDS; CHILDREN'S DIGEST; CHILDREN'S PLAYMATE; JACK AND JILL; CHILD LIFE (Specialized: children)**, 1100 Waterway Blvd., P.O. Box 567, Indianapolis IN 46206-0567.

Magazine Needs: This publisher of magazines stressing health for children has a variety of needs for mostly short, simple poems. For example, *Humpty Dumpty* is for ages 4-6; *Turtle* is for preschoolers, similar emphasis, uses many stories in rhyme—and action rhymes, etc.; *Children's Digest* is for preteens (10-13); *Jack and Jill* is for ages 7-10. *Child Life* is for ages 9-11. *Children's Playmate* is for ages 6-8. All appear 8 times/year with cartoon art, very colorful. Sample: $1.25.

How to Submit: Send SASE for guidelines. Responds within 10 weeks. Pays $15 minimum. Staff reviews books of poetry. Send books for review consideration.

Advice: "Writers who wish to appear in our publications should study current issues carefully. We receive too many poetry submissions that are about kids, not for kids. Or, the subject matter is one that adults think children would or should like. We'd like to see more humorous verse."

Ⓝ ◯ ◎ **FREE FOCUS (Specialized: women/feminist); OSTENTATIOUS MIND (Specialized: form/style)**, P.O. Box 7415, JAF Station, New York NY 10116, *Free Focus* founded 1985, *Ostentatious Mind* founded 1987, poetry editor Patricia D. Coscia.

Magazine Needs: *Free Focus* "is a literary magazine only for creative women, who reflect their ideas of love, nature, beauty and men and also express the pain, sorrow, joy and enchantment that their lives generate. *Free Focus* needs poems of all types on the subject matters above. Nothing X-rated, please. The poems can be as short as two lines or as long as two pages. The objective of this magazine is to give women poets a chance to be fullfilled in the art of poetry, for freedom of expression for women is seldom described in society." They have published poetry by Helen Tzagoloff, Elizabeth Hahn Ph.D., Patricia A. Pierkowski, D.R. Middleton, Crystal Beckner, Carol L. Clark and Mary Anderson. *Ostentatious Mind* "is a co-ed literary magazine for material of stream of consciousness and experimental poems. The poets deal with the political, social and psychological." They have published poetry by Paul Weinman, Rod Farmer, L. Mason, Dr. John J. Soldo, Carl A. Winderl, James W. Penha and Joe Lackey. Both magazines are printed on 8×14 paper, folded in the middle and stapled to make a 10-page (including cover) format, with simple b&w drawings on the cover and inside. The two magazines appear every 6-8 months. Sample of either is $4.

How to Submit: Submit only 3 poems at a time. Poems should be typed neatly and clearly on white typing paper. Simultaneous submissions and previously published poems OK. Publishes theme issues. Send SASE for guidelines and upcoming themes. Responds "as soon as possible." Sometimes sends prepublication galleys. Pays 1 copy.

Advice: "I think that anyone can write a poem who can freely express intense feelings about their experiences. A dominant thought should be ruled and expressed in writing, not by the spoken word, but the written word."

FREE LUNCH, P.O. Box 7647, Laguna Niguel CA 92607-7647, founded 1988, editor Ron Offen.

Magazine Needs: *Free Lunch* is a "poetry journal interested in publishing the whole spectrum of what is currently being produced by American poets. Occasionally offers a 'Reprise Series' in which an overlooked American poet is reexamined and presented. Among those who have been featured are Kenneth Patchen, Maxwell Bodenheim, Stephen Vincent Benet, Kenneth Fearing and Lola Ridge. Also features a 'Mentor Series,' in which an established poet introduces a new, unestablished poet. Mentors have included Maxine Kumin, Billy Collins, Lucille Clifton, Donald Hall, Carolyn Forché, Wanda Coleman, Lyn Lifshin and Stephen Dunn. Especially interested in experimental work and work by unestablished poets. Hope to provide all serious poets living in the US with a free subscription. For details on free subscription send SASE. Regarding the kind of poetry we find worthwhile, we like metaphors, similes, arresting images, and a sensitive and original use of language. We are interested in all genres—experimental poetry, protest poetry, formal poetry, etc. No restriction on form, length, subject matter, style, purpose. No aversion to form, rhyme." Poets published include Neal Bowers, Thomas Carper, Jared Carter, Billy Collins, Donald Hall, D. Nurkse and Marge Piercy. As a sample the editor selected this poem, "Even Long After Grief" by Judy Kronenfeld:

> how busy/the living are,/waving from trains,/at airport gates,/how busy the crows/on their flight paths,
> even/the dry pods of the leafless silk tree—rubbing/shoulders, clicking hips, ticticticking/like
> schizophrenics—and the long/fingers of the eucalyptus,/untangling the tresses/of air

FL, published 2-3 times a year, is 32-40 pgs., digest-sized, attractively printed and designed, saddle-stapled, featuring free verse that shows attention to craft with well-knowns and newcomers alongside each other. Press run is 1,200 for 1,000 free subscriptions and 200 paid of which 15 are libraries. Subscription: $12 ($15 foreign). Sample: $5 ($6 foreign).

How to Submit: "Submissions must be limited to three poems and are considered only between September 1 and May 31. Submissions sent at other times will be returned unread. Although a cover letter is not mandatory, I like them. I especially want to know if a poet is previously unpublished, as I like to work with new poets." No previously published poems; simultaneous submissions OK. Editor comments on rejections and tries to return submissions in 2 months. Send SASE for guidelines. Pays 1 copy plus subscription.

Advice: "Archibald MacLeish said, 'A poem should not mean/ But be.' I have become increasingly leery of the ego-centered lyric that revels in some past wrong, good-old-boy nostalgia, or unfocused ecstatic experience. Poetry is concerned primarily with language, rhythm and sound; fashions and trends are transitory and to be eschewed; perfecting one's work is often more important than publishing it."

$ FREEFALL MAGAZINE, Alexandra Writers' Centre Society, 922 Ninth Ave. SE, Calgary, Alberta T2G 0S4 Canada, phone/fax (403)264-4730, e-mail awcs@writtenword.org, website www.writtenword.org/awcs, founded 1990, editor Catherine Fuller, managing editor Sherring Amsden.

Magazine Needs: "Published biannually, *FreeFall's* mandate is to encourage the voices of new, emerging and experienced writers and provide an outlet for their work. Contains: fiction, nonfiction, poetry, interviews related to writers/writing; artwork and photographs suitable for b&w reproduction." They want "poems in a variety of forms with a strong voice, effective language and fresh images." They have published poetry by Anne Burke, David Groulx, Norma Linder, Julie Lockhart, T.M. McDade and Renee Norman. The editor says *FreeFall* is 40-44 pgs., magazine-sized, "xerox digital" printing and saddle-stitched with 60 lb. paper cover, includes art/graphics. They receive about 50-60 poems a year, accept approximately 20%. Publish 12-18 poems/issue. Press run is 350 for 270 subscribers of which 20 are libraries, 80 shelf sales; 30 distributed free to contributors, promotion. Single copy: $8.50 US, $7.50 Canadian; subscription: $14 US, $12 Canadian. Sample: $6.50 US, $5.50 Canadian.

How to Submit: Submit 2-5 poems at a time. Line length for poetry is 60 maximum. No previously published poems or simultaneous submissions. Disk submissions (ASCII, text format) OK with hard copy. Cover letter with 2-line bio and SASE required. Reads submissions March through April and October through November only. Time between acceptance and publication is 6 months. Poems are circulated to an editorial board. "All submissions read by four editors." Seldom comments on rejections. Publishes theme issues occasionally. Send SAE and IRC for guidelines and upcoming themes or obtain via e-mail or website. Responds in 3 months. Pays $5 Canadian/page and 1 copy. Buys first North American serial rights.

Also Offers: See website for information about the Alexandra Writers' Centre Society activities and services and for additional information about *FreeFall* magazine.

Advice: "Check guidelines carefully before submitting material."

FREEHAND, 5 Island Court, Riversdale Rd., West Kirby, Wirral CH48 4E2, United Kingdom, phone (44)0151-625-0969, e-mail josephinewood@compuserve.com, founded 1996, editor Jo Wood.

Magazine Needs: *Freehand* appears bimonthly "to spread availability and access to those starting out in writing and to offer a platform for promising writers." They do not want "foul language." As a sample the editor selected these lines from "For Dad—The Seasons of Life" by Jo Burns:

> In early spring you rocked me in your arms/The world was far too big for me/And so your rose lay
> cradled in her green and leafy gown/But you were there, and frost and snow/Could never penetrate
> that blanket love had thrown around her

The editor says *Freehand* is 36 pgs., magazine-sized, stapled with 100g paper cover, includes various ads. They receive about 300 poems a year, accept approximately 70%. Press run is 250 for 220 subscribers. Single copy: £2; subscription: £18 overseas, £12 UK. Sample: £2 plus postage. "Prefer subscribers."

How to Submit: Submit 5 poems at a time. Previously published poems and simultaneous submissions OK. E-mail and disk submissions OK. Cover letter preferred. "SAE's especially from overseas." Reads submissions all year. Time between acceptance and publication is 2 months. "Sole member of staff reads submissions." Often comments on rejections. Publishes theme issues occasionally. Send SASE (or SAE and IRC) for guidelines or obtain via e-mail. Responds in 2 weeks. Acquires first British serial rights. Reviews books of poetry and other magazines in 300 words. Open to unsolicited reviews. Poets may also send books for review consideration.

Also Offers: Offers free reviews of subscribers books and free ads for subscribers.

Advice: "Try a sample copy."

N ⊕ ◯ ◐ **FREEXPRESSION**, P.O. Box 4, West Hoxton NSW 2171 Australia, phone (02)9607 5559, fax (02)9826 6612, e-mail frexprsn@bigpond.com.au, founded 1993, managing editor Peter F. Pike.

Magazine Needs: *FreeXpresSion* is a monthly publication containing "creative writing, how-to articles, short stories and poetry including cinquain, haiku, etc., and bush verse." They are open to all forms. "Christian themes OK. Humorous material welcome. No gratuitous sex; bad language OK. We don't want to see anything degrading." They have published poetry by Ron Stevens, John Ryan and Ken Dean. As a sample the editor selected these lines from "The Riding of Tearaway" by Ellis Campbell:

> I wasn't scared of any horse—or of the ringer's jeers—/I'd rode the worst to come my way since early
> childhood years./While droving with my father—since the day my mother died—/I'd often bested older
> men and showed them how to ride./But years diminish glory and I'm weary of the fray;/I had no
> inclination for the scalp of Tearaway.

FreeXpresSion is 24 pgs., magazine-sized, offset printed and saddle-stapled with paper cover, includes b&w graphics. They receive about 1,500 poems a year, accept approximately 50%. Press run is 500 for 300 subscribers of which 20 are libraries. Single copy: $2.50 AUS; subscription: $25 AUS ($40 overseas airmail). For sample, send large SAE with $1 stamp.

How to Submit: Submit 3-4 poems at a time. Previously published poems and simultaneous submissions OK. E-mail and disk submissions OK. Cover letter preferred. "Very long poems are not desired but would be considered." Time between acceptance and publication is 2 months. Seldom comments on rejections. Publishes theme issues. Send SAE and IRC for guidelines. Responds in 2 months. Sometimes sends prepublication galleys. Pays 1 copy, additional copies available at half price. Acquires first Australian rights only. Reviews books of poetry in 500 words. Open to unsolicited reviews. Poets may also send books for review consideration.

Also Offers: Sponsors annual contest with 2 categories for poetry: blank verse (up to 40 lines), traditional verse (up to 80 lines). 1st Prize (in both categories): $200, 2nd Prize: $100. *FreeXpresSion* also publishes books up to 200 pgs. through subsidy arrangements with authors.

Advice: "Enter some of the many competitions listed in *FreeXpresSion*; compare your work with competition winners."

◯ ◎ **FRISSON: DISCONCERTING VERSE; SKULL JOB PRODUCTIONS (Specialized: form/ style)**, 1012 Pleasant Dale Dr., Wilmington NC 28412-7617, founded 1995, editor Scott H. Urban.

Magazine Needs: *frisson: disconcerting verse*, published quarterly, "presents poetry that is disturbing, haunting, macabre, yet subtle—poetry that attempts to elicit 'frisson.'" They want "poetry that takes readers past the edge of comfort and into disturbing realms of experience. Poems should attempt to elicit the delicate sensation of 'frisson.' Any form or length, although shorter poems stand better chance." They do not want "light verse, romantic verse, inspirational verse, humorous verse." They have published poetry by Tom Piccirilli, Wendy Rathbone, Lee Ballentine and Steve Sneyd. As a sample the editor selected these lines from "Arabesque" by Richard Geyer:

> death is sweeter than a kiss,/a blooming rose/or waves of bliss./there is no veil to be pierced,/just a
> lantern/and a wish.

frisson is 20-24 pgs., digest-sized, photocopied, saddle-stapled with cardstock cover, original artwork on cover and in interior with limited ads. They receive about 150-200 poems a year, accept approximately 10-15%. Press run is 100 for 50 subscribers, with 15 distributed free to reviewers. Subscription: $10. Sample: $2.50. Make checks payable to Scott H. Urban.

How to Submit: Submit 4-10 poems at a time in standard poem ms format. "Shorter ones (50 lines or less) stand a better chance of acceptance." No previously published poems; simultaneous submissions OK. No e-mail submissions. Cover letter preferred. Time between acceptance and publication is 3-5 months. Poems chosen

---

ALWAYS include a self-addressed, stamped envelope (SASE) when sending a ms or query to a publisher within your own country. When sending material to other countries, include a self-addressed envelope and International Reply Coupons (IRCs), available at many post offices.

"solely according to editor's personal taste—how well each individual poem is applicable to the concept of 'disconcerting verse.'" Often comments on rejections. Send SASE for guidelines. Responds within a week. Sometimes sends prepublication galleys. Pays 2 copies or "short" subscription. Acquires first North American serial rights. There is no review column as such, although editor recommends material in the introductory 'Foreshadowings' article. Send books for review consideration.

Advice: "Open others' perceptions to that shadowy, half-glimpsed world that you as a poet are aware lurks just at the edge of each dream. . . .'"

FROGMORE PAPERS; FROGMORE POETRY PRIZE, 18 Nevill Rd., Lewes, East Sussex BN7 1PF England, founded 1983, poetry editor Jeremy Page.

Magazine Needs: *Frogmore Papers* is a biannual literary magazine with emphasis on new poetry and short stories. "Quality is generally the only criterion, although pressure of space means very long work (over 100 lines) is unlikely to be published." They have published "Other Lilies" by Marita Over and "A Dozen Villanelles" by Matthew Mead and poetry by Carole Satyamurti, John Mole, Linda France, Elizabeth Garrett, John Harvey and John Latham. As a sample the editor selected these lines by Tobias Hill:

> *if I stand just here, just right/and look up, I can see the rain/coming, and light on aeroplanes/high and*
> *certain, crossing time zones.*

The magazine is 42 pgs., saddle-stapled with matte card cover, photocopied in photoreduced typescript. They accept 3% of the poetry received. Their press run is 300 for 120 subscribers. Subscription: £7 ($20). Sample: £2 ($5). (US payments should be made in cash, not check.)

How to Submit: Submit 5-6 poems at a time. Considers simultaneous submissions. Editor rarely comments on rejections. Responds in 6 months. Pays 1 copy. Staff reviews books of poetry in 2-3 sentences, single book format. Send books for review consideration to Sophie Hannah, reviews editor, Flat 3, Dryden House, 16A Newton Road, Cambridge CB2 2AL England.

Also Offers: Sponsors the annual Frogmore Poetry Prize. Write for information.

Advice: "My advice to people starting to write poetry would be: Read as many recognized modern poets as you can and don't be afraid to experiment."

FROGPOND: INTERNATIONAL HAIKU JOURNAL; HAIKU SOCIETY OF AMERICA; HAIKU SOCIETY OF AMERICA AWARDS/CONTESTS (Specialized: form/style, translation), P.O. Box 2461, Winchester VA 22604-1661, phone (540)722-2156, fax (708)810-8992, e-mail redmoon@shentel.net, website www.octet.com/~hsa/, founded 1978, editor Jim Kacian.

Magazine Needs: *Frogpond* is the international journal of the Haiku Society of America and is published triannually. They want "contemporary English-language haiku, ranging from 1-4 lines or in a visual arrangement, focusing on a moment keenly perceived and crisply conveyed, using clear images and non-poetic language." They also accept "related forms: senryu, sequences, linked poems, and haibun. It welcomes translations of any of these forms." Also accepts poetry written by children. As a sample the editor selected these poems by Harriet Axelrad, Chuck Easter and Dimitar Anakiev:

> *Snowflakes glued/to the kindergarten window—/no two alike—Harriet Axelrad//close lightning/the*
> *metallic taste/in my mouth—Chuck Easter//garden work—/talking to each other/back to back—*
> *Dimitar Anakiev*

Frogpond is 96 pgs., 5½×8½, perfect-bound, and has 60 pgs. of poetry. They receive about 20,000 submissions/year and use about 500. *Frogpond* goes to 800 subscribers, of which 15 are libraries, as well as to over a dozen foreign countries. Sample back issues: $7. Make checks payable to Haiku Society of America.

How to Submit: Submit 5-10 poems, with 5 poems per 8½×11 sheet, with SASE. (Send submissions to Jim Kacian at address mentioned above.) No simultaneous submissions. E-mail submissions OK (include in body of message). Send SASE for submission guidelines and information on the HSA. Responds "usually" in 3 weeks or less. Pays $1/accepted item. Poetry reviews usually 1,000 words or less. Open to unsolicited reviews. "Authors are urged to send their books for review consideration."

Also Offers: The *Supplement* publishes longer essays, articles and reviews from quarterly meetings and other haiku gatherings. It is 96 pgs., 5½×8½, perfect-bound. The *HSA Newsletter*, edited by Charles Trumbull, appears 6 times a year and contains reports of the HSA Quarterly meetings, regional activities, news of upcoming events, results of contests, publications activities and other information. A "best of issue" prize is awarded for each issue through a gift from the Museum of Haiku Literature, located in Tokyo. The Society also sponsors The Harold G. Henderson Haiku Award Contest, the Gerald Brady Senryu Award Contest, The Bernard Lionel Einbond Memorial Renku Contest, The Nicholas A. Virgilio Memorial Haiku Competition for High School Students and the Merit Book Awards for outstanding books in the haiku field.

Advice: "Submissions to *Frogpond* are accepted from both members and nonmembers, although familiarity with the magazine will aid writers in discovering what it publishes."

FRONTIERS: A JOURNAL OF WOMEN STUDIES (Specialized: feminist), % Susan Armitage, Wilson 12, Washington State University, Pullman WA 99164-4007, founded 1975.

Magazine Needs: *Frontiers* is published 3 times/year and uses poetry on feminist themes. They have published work by Audré Lorde, Janice Mirikitani, Carol Wolfe Konek and Opal Palmer Adisa. The journal is 200-208 pgs., 6×9, flat-spined. Circulation is 1,000. Sample: $9.

How to Submit: No simultaneous submissions. Responds in 5 months. Pays 2 copies. "We are not currently publishing reviews of books, poetry, essays or otherwise."

◐ **FUGUE**, Brink Hall, Room 200, University of Idaho, Moscow ID 83844-1102, website www.uidaho.edu/LS/Eng/Fugue, founded 1989.

Magazine Needs: *Fugue* is a biannual literary digest of the University of Idaho. They have "no limits" on type of poetry. "We're not interested in trite or quaint verse. Nothing self-indulgent or overly metaphoric to the point of being obscure." They have published poetry by Raymond Federman and Stephen Dann. As a sample the editor selected these lines from "The Burned Diary" by Sharon Olds:

> . . . And when the dawn came up/on the black water of the house, they found it/by the side of her bed,
> its pages scorched,/a layer of them arched, the corners curled up/like the tips of wings, a messenger/
> from the other world, the solitary heart.

The editor says *Fugue* is 80 pgs., digest-sized, perfect-bound. They receive approximately 400 poems/semester, use 5-10 poems/issue. Press run is 250 plus an electronic version on the World Wide Web. Sample: $5.

How to Submit: No previously published poems or simultaneous submissions. Submit with #10 SASE or submission will not be considered. No e-mail submissions. Reads submissions September 1 through May 1 only. Time between acceptance and publication is up to 1 year. "Submissions are reviewed by staff members and chosen by consensus with final approval by the editorial board. No major changes are made to a manuscript without author approval." Responds in 3 months. Pays at least 1 copy and honorarium. Buys first North American serial rights.

Also Offers: Website includes writer's guidelines, names of editors, poetry samples and cover art.

Advice: "Proper manuscript format and submission etiquette are expected; submissions without proper SASE will not be read or held on file."

✓ ▢ $ ▢ ◐ ◎ **THE FUNNY PAPER; F/J WRITERS SERVICE (Specialized: children/teen/young adult/humor, senior citizen, students, writing)**, P.O. Box 22557, Kansas City MO 64113-0557, e-mail felix22557@aol.com, website angelfire.com/funnypaper, founded 1985, editor F.H. Fellhauer.

Magazine Needs: *The Funny Paper* appears 4 times a year "to provide readership, help and the opportunity to write for money to budding authors/poets/humanists of all ages." Also accepts poetry written by children, ages 8-15. They want "light verse; space limited; humor always welcome. No tomes, heavy, dismal, trite work." As a sample we selected this poem, "Farewell" by Betty R. Cevoli:

> Roughly grasping at my fingers,/They pull at my tee-shirt/My arms scratched as I/clutch them//Bright,
> sunny orange with/dark hills and valleys/covering their skin.//Roadmaps—promising tender,/juicy, rich
> flavor—/The last canteloupes of summer.

The Funny Paper is 10 pgs., 8½×11, photocopied on colored paper and unbound, includes clip art and cartoons. They receive about 300 poems a year, accept approximately 10%. Single copy: $2. Make checks payable to F/J Writers Service.

How to Submit: Submit 1-2 poems at a time. E-mail submissions OK (include in body of message). "We encourage beginners; handwritten poems OK. Submissions not returned." Seldom comments on rejections. Publishes contest theme issues regularly. Send SASE for guidelines and upcoming themes or obtain via website. Pays $5-25/published poem and 1 copy. Acquires one-time rights.

Also Offers: Sponsors contests with $100 prize. Send SASE for guidelines or visit website. Website includes guidelines, jokes, descriptive page and bulletin board.

Advice: "When trying for $100 prize, take us seriously. The competition is fierce."

◐ **FUTURE TENSE PRESS**, P.O. Box 42416, Portland OR 97242, e-mail futuret@teleport.com, website www.teleport.com/~futuret, founded 1990, publisher/editor Kevin Sampsell.

Book/Chapbook Needs: Future Tense Press publishes "some poetry by unique poets, but mostly fiction that displays edge and style and craft." They publish 1 paperback and 4-6 chapbooks/year. The publisher wants "bold, brave, challenging work. I like funny, sexy, experimental and rule breaking writing. Mostly short fiction, some poetry. Nothing too political or sentimental or workshop dull. No Hallmark or rhyming verse either." They have published poetry by Brandon Freels, Richard Meltzer and Carl Miller Daniels. As a sample the publisher selected these lines from "Independence" by Verlena Orr:

> She trains like a prizefighter,/Drinks brewer's yeast and orange juice./Children follow her to breakfast,/
> try to please her. One calls her mom.

Books are usually 36 pgs., 4¼×5½, with either cardstock cover or "something unique."

How to Submit: Submit 4 poems or 2 stories at a time. Previously published poems and simultaneous submissions OK. Cover letter required. "E-mail query with bio if you like before submitting work." Time between acceptance and publication is 8 months. Often comments on rejections. Replies to queries in 2 weeks; to mss in 2 months. Pays 30 author's copies (out of a press run of about 200). "Other payment negotiable." 25% of books are author-subsidy published each year. "If an author can help with money it will probably be helpful in speeding up the publication." Order sample books or chapbooks by sending a $5 check to Kevin Sampsell.

Ⓝ $ ◐ **FUTURES MAGAZINE**, 3039 38th Ave. S, Minneapolis MN 55406-2140, phone (612)724-4023, e-mail barbl@tela.com, website www.firetowrite.com, founded 1997, poetry editor RC Hildebrandt.

Magazine Needs: *Futures* is a bimonthly magazine containing short stories, essays, poetry, artwork and "inspiration for artists of all kinds." They have "no specific poetry needs—everything considered." However, they do not want to receive gratuitous profanity or pornography. They have published poetry by John Bennett, Karen Davenport, Nancy Austring, Matt Welter and Ally Reith. The editor says *Futures* is 75-80 pgs., 8½×11, with 4-color semigloss cover, includes art and ads. They receive about 250 poems a year, accept approximately 10%. Publish 5-10 poems/issue. Press run is 2,000. Single copy: $6.95; subscription: $35. Sample (including guidelines): $4.

How to Submit: Submit up to 5 poems at a time. Previously published poems OK. E-mail submissions OK. Cover letter preferred. "Send SASE for our response—originals not returned." Reads submissions January 31 through October 31 only. Submit seasonal poems 6 months in advance. Time between acceptance and publication is 2-6 months. Often comments on rejections. "If you want to assure a critique of your work, you may enclose a SASE and $3 with your request." Publishes theme issues occasionally. Obtain guidelines via website. Pays up to $50. Buys first North American serial rights or one-time rights. "We prefer first time rights."

Also Offers: Website includes writer's guidelines, names of editors, artwork and illustrations, greeting cards for writers, cover art, contests, etc.

Advice: "If it is flat on the page, it is not a poem. You have to make an impact in few words. In poetry the line is really all—like a commercial—you have to make an emotional statement in a flash."

◎ FUTURIFIC (Specialized: optimistic poems of the future), Futurific Inc., Foundation for Optimism, 305 Madison Ave., New York NY 10165, phone/fax (212)297-0502, e-mail keytonyc@aol.com, founded 1976, publisher Balint Szent-Miklosy.

Magazine Needs: *Futurific* is a monthly magazine published to "improve our understanding of the future and show our readers the direction of development. **Optimistic only.**" The publisher says it is 32 pgs., 8½×11, glossy cover, b&w throughout. They receive about 12 poems a year, accept approximately 1%. Press run is 10,000. Single copy: $15; subscription: $70/year individual, $140/year institutional. Sample: $10.

How to Submit: Previously published poems and simultaneous submissions OK. Disk submissions OK (PC compatible disks in WordPerfect 5.0, 6.0 and MS Word) Time between acceptance and publication is 1 month. Send SASE for guidelines or obtain via e-mail. Responds in 1 month. Pays 5 copies. Acquires one-time rights.

✓ ◐ G.W. REVIEW, Marvin Center Box 20, 800 21st St. NW, Washington DC 20052, phone (202)994-7779, fax (202)994-6102, e-mail gwreview@gwu.edu, website www.gwu.edu/~gwreview, founded 1980, contact Casey Reivich.

Magazine Needs: *G.W. Review* appears twice a year publishing unconventional, solid work and some translations. The magazine is published for distribution to the George Washington University community, the Washington D.C. metropolitan area and an increasing number of national subscribers. They have published poetry by Anne Caston, Maxine Clair, Judy Bolz and Cornelius Eady. As a sample the editor selected these lines from "On Muranowska Street" by Myra Sklarew:

> I have always loved particulars: the angels/bearing a martyr's palm, the way the hair/of the
> worshippers forms waves or/filaments, the flowers embroidered/on your sleeve.

It is 64 pgs., perfect-bound with b&w illustration or photo on the cover. They receive about 3,300 poems a year and accept 20-30. Their annual press run averages 4,000 copies. Subscription: $9/year, $16/2 years. Sample: $4.50.

How to Submit: Submit up to 5 poems at a time. They consider simultaneous submissions but not previously published poems. E-mail and fax submissions OK (send e-mail submissions to gwreview@gwis2.circ.gwu.edu). Cover letter, including bio, list of enclosures, recent publications and phone number, required. The staff does not read manuscripts from April 15 through August 15. Editor sometimes comments on rejections when the staff likes the work but thinks it needs to be revised. Responds in 3 months. Pays 5 copies.

⊕ ◐ GAIRM; GAIRM PUBLICATIONS (Specialized: ethnic, foreign language), 29 Waterloo St., Glasgow G2 6BZ Scotland, phone/fax (0141)221-1971, editor Derick Thomson, founded 1952.

Magazine Needs: *Gairm* is a quarterly that uses modern/cosmopolitan and traditional/folk verse in Scottish Gaelic only. It has published the work of all significant Scottish Gaelic poets, and much poetry translated from European languages. An anthology of such translations, *European Poetry in Gaelic*, is available for £7.50 or $15. A recent collection is Derick Thomson's *Meall Garbh/The Rugged Mountain*, £7.50 or $15. *Gairm* is 96 pgs., digest-sized, flat-spined with coated card cover. Circulation is 1,000. Sample: $3.50.

How to Submit: Submit 3-4 poems at a time, Gaelic only. Staff reviews books of poetry in 500-700 words, single format; 100 words, multi-book format. Occasionally invites reviews. Send books for review consideration. All of the publications of the press are in Scottish Gaelic. Catalog available.

⊕ ◒ GALAXY PRESS, 71 Recreation St., Tweed Heads N.S.W., 2485 Australia, phone (07)5536-1997, founded 1978, editor Lance Banbury.

Book/Chapbook Needs: Galaxy Press publishes "high seriousness about the opportunities of culture at the latter end of the twentieth century, including personal or experimental responses." They want "poetry equally concerned with form and content." They have published work by Sheila Williams. As a sample the editor selected these lines by Maud Tennyson:

> *Come into the garden, Maud,/For the black bat, Night, has flown,/Come into the garden, Maud,/I am*
> *here at the gate alone;/And the woodbine spices are wafted abroad,/And the musk of the roses blown.*

Books are usually 16-20 pgs., 15×21cm, offset/lithograph printed, glossy color card cover, includes art. Press run is 100.

How to Submit: Previously published poems and simultaneous submissions OK. Cover letter preferred. Often comments on rejections. Replies to queries in 2 weeks. Obtain sample books or chapbooks by "written request."

☑ ◐ **GARGOYLE MAGAZINE; PAYCOCK PRESS**, % Atticus Books, 2308 Mt. Vernon Ave., Alexandria VA 22301, phone (703)548-7580, fax (703)837-1783, e-mail atticus@atticusbooks.com, website www.atticus books.com, founded 1976, co-editors Richard Peabody and Lucinda Ebersole.

Magazine Needs: *Gargoyle Magazine* appears annually "to publish the best literary magazine we can. We generally run short one page poems. We like wit, imagery, killer lines. Not big on rhymed verse or language school." They have published poetry by Nicole Blackman, Wayne Koestenbaum and Jeremy Reed. As a sample the editors selected these lines from "Abortion Elegy: What I Know About Her" by Rose Solari:

> *There are times I can see her face as if/she were here, as if she had lived—hair darker/than yours or*
> *mine, your cheeks, my mouth./She stands over my bed as she did almost/a full year before we knew of*
> *her, or runs/through the living room, both hands spread,/chasing a shadow.*

The editors say *Gargoyle* is 365 pgs., 6×9, offset printed and perfect-bound, color cover, includes photos, artwork and ads. Accept approximately 10% of the poems received each year. Press run is 3,000. Subscription: $20 for 2; $25 to institutions. Sample: $10. Make checks payable to Atticus Books. "We have international distribution through Bernhard DeBier, Airlift Book Co. and Perigo Distribution."

How to Submit: Submit 5 poems at a time. Simultaneous submissions OK. E-mail and disk submissions OK in Microsoft Word or WordPerfect format. Reads submissions Memorial Day through Labor Day only. Time between acceptance and publication is 4-5 months. Poems are circulated to an editorial board. "The two editors make some concessions but generally concur." Often comments on rejections. Responds in 2 months. Always sends prepublication galleys. Pays 1 copy and ½ off additional copies. Acquires first rights

Book/Chapbook Needs & How to Submit: Paycock Press has published 9-10 books since 1976. However, they are not currently seeking mss.

◐ **GARNET**, P.O. Box 655, Hampden-Sydney VA 23943, phone (804)223-6462, e-mail somervillen@hsc.edu, website www.hsc.edu, founded 1937, editor Nate Somerville.

Magazine Needs: *Garnet* is a semiannual journal of literature and the creative arts published by Hampden-Sydney College. "We like to see most anything—forms, free verse, light verse. Poems must, of course, be of the highest quality. No trash. No erotica, juvenile, religious or romantic work." They have published poetry by Craig Challender, Jaroslav Seifert, Grace Simpson and Louis Simpson. As a sample the editor selected these lines from "Who Knows" by Richard Stern:

> *Such the enzymes that decayed/the sugars of life and laid/him youthful in the ground, amazed, decayed.*

Garnet is 80-100 pgs., 6×9, professionally printed, perfect-bound with glossy card cover, photography and art included. They receive about 500 poems a year, accept approximately 5-10%. Press run is 1,000 for 400 subscribers of which 20 are libraries, 100-200 shelf sales; about 500 distributed free to students, professors, alumni and contributors. Single copy: $3.95; subscription: $6. Sample: $5.

How to Submit: Submit no more than 3 poems at a time, "two page limit to any poetry." No previously published poems; simultaneous submissions OK. Cover letter required. "Include name, address and phone number on ms; include 50-word bio; electronic submissions accepted—contact editor for details." Time between acceptance and publication is 6-8 months. Poems are circulated to an editorial board. Often comments on rejections. Send SASE for guidelines and upcoming themes or request via e-mail. Responds in 2 months. Sometimes sends prepublication galleys. Pays 1 copy. Acquires one-time rights. Reviews books or chapbooks in 1,000-2,000 words, single book format. Open to unsolicited reviews. Poets may also send books for review consideration.

Also Offers: Sponsors several contests awarding a total of $1,000. All submissions are automatically eligible.

Advice: "We have published both beginners and Pulitzer Prize recipients. We're not looking for names; we're looking for outstanding poetry. Show us you care for your work."

☑ ◑ **A GATHERING OF THE TRIBES; FLY BY NIGHT PRESS**, P.O. Box 20693, New York NY 10009, phone (212)674-3778, e-mail info@tribes.org, website www.tribes.org, founded 1991, managing editor Steve Cannon.

Magazine Needs: *A Gathering of the Tribes*, published biannually, "showcases established and emerging poets, writers, artists and forums." They want poetry 30 lines maximum. They do not want "third-rate poetry." They have published poetry by Jayne Cortez, Nikki Giovanni, Victor Cruz and Kimiko Hahn. The editor says *A Gathering of the Tribes* is 96 pgs., 8×10, glossy cover, with ads in back pages. They receive about 600 poems a year, accept approximately 5%. Press run is 2,000 for 100 subscribers of which 10 are libraries, 100 shelf sales; 200 distributed free. Subscription: $30. Sample: $15.

How to Submit: Submit 3 poems at a time. Previously published poems and simultaneous submissions OK. Cover letter preferred. No e-mail submissions. Time between acceptance and publication is 3 months. Always comments on rejections. Send SASE for guidelines. Responds immediately. Always sends prepublication galleys. Pays 1 copy. Staff reviews books of poetry or other magazines. Send books for review consideration.

Book/Chapbook Needs & How to Submit: Fly By Night Press is a subsidy press publishing "excellence in poetry from a diverse perspective (topics of the author's choosing)." Books are usually 70 pgs., 5½×7½. Replies to queries in 3 months. Pays 12-15% royalties and 500 author's copies (out of a press run of 1,000). Offers subsidy arrangements: Fly By Night Press puts up 50% fee, author puts up 50% and sells their half. Obtain sample books by writing to the above address.

Also Offers: Sponsors annual poetry contest. Deadline is in April. Send up to 3 poems, no poem to exceed 30 lines with a $10 entry fee. 1st Place prize of $500 and publication.

Advice: "We believe the United States should celebrate its diversity from a global perspective. *Tribes* tries to achieve the same through excellence in the arts."

GAZELLE PUBLICATIONS, 11650 Red Bud Trail, Berrien Springs MI 49106, phone (616)471-4717 or (800)650-5076 (orders only), e-mail kivu@juno.com, website www.hoofprint.com, founded 1976, editor Ted Wade, is a publisher for home schools and compatible markets including books of verse for children but is not currently considering unsolicited manuscripts.

GECKO, P.O. Box 25021, Lexington KY 40524, phone (606)271-4028, e-mail geckogalpoet@hotmail.com, founded 1998, editor Rebecca Lu Kiernan.

Magazine Needs: Published annually, *Gecko* "is an ambitious literary journal desirous of showcasing exciting new talent as well as established writers. A featured writer is chosen for each issue. All writers submitting will be treated with respect! Give me vivid imagery; make me feel like I am in the work, not outside looking in. Make me laugh, cry, pound my fists. Say it in a fresh, new way that no one else could have expressed. Knock me out!" The editor does not wish to see "anything degrading to women. Also no haiku, no rhyme and please, God, no limerick! Please don't put a gecko in your work just for me." They have published poetry by Bright Majikay, Grant Logan Jambors, Chaney Keblusek, Neal Bowers, Aleksey Katkov and Chelsea Rummaway. As a sample the editor selected these lines from her poem "Intrepid Vagina":

> *Does my desire unnerve you?/Unblinking, lips parted/my breath/condensating in your ear/down on my haunches/like a jaguar/muscled for the strike./Are you happier to hunt me/over a half scrubbed toilet/in yellow gloves,/pinned hair/woefully accommodating you/like wet, underfoot grass?*

Gecko is 32-40 pgs., 5½×8½, professionally printed and flat-spined, color card cover with art/graphics. They receive about 2,000 poems a year, accept under 3%. Press run is 1,000 for 450 subscribers; 250 distributed free to writers, libraries, media, colleges.

How to Submit: Submit 3-5 poems at a time. Line length for poetry is 12 minimum, 42 maximum. No previously published poems; simultaneous submissions OK. Cover letter required. "Writers must enclose SASE." Reads submissions year-round, slow during summer months. Time between acceptance and publication is 3-10 months. Seldom comments on rejections. Responds in 4 months. Pays 1 copy. Acquires first North American serial rights.

Advice: "I choose the best of the best. If I must reject, don't give up until you have been rejected by every appropriate listing in *Poet's Market*. If you have any talent, I promise you someone will discover it."

GENERATOR; GENERATOR PRESS, 3503 Virginia Ave., Cleveland OH 44109, phone (216)351-9406, founded 1987, editor John Byrum.

Magazine Needs: *Generator* is an annual magazine "devoted to the presentation of all types of experimental poetry, focusing on language poetry and 'concrete' or visual poetic modes."

Book/Chapbook Needs: Generator Press also publishes the Generator Press chapbook series. Approximately 1 new title/year.

How to Submit: They are currently not accepting unsolicited manuscripts for either the magazine or chapbook publication.

GENEWATCH (Specialized: ecology/biotechnology/genetics), 1600 Newton St. NE, Washington DC 20018-2318, phone (202)529-0003, e-mail aheutte@toad.net, website www.gene-watch.org, founded 1987, poetry editor Anne Heutte.

Magazine Needs: "*GeneWatch*, published bimonthly by the Council for Responsible Genetics, monitors the social impact of biotechnology, featuring scientifically reliable articles and book reviews." The newsletter is looking for "poems to help anchor its readers in the real world of struggle for the well-being of Gaea and her children, in opposition to an illusory one of false promises and comforts, and to reflect the diversity and sanctity of all life, from plants to people." They have published poetry by Jean Nordhaus. As a sample the editor selected these lines from "Torturing Her Secrets From Her" by Don Ogden:

> *Remaking the Creator in their own image/in the vicinity of six billion human souls/ghosts of fiction wrestle ghosts of science/Oppenhiemer, Frankenstein/looking over their shoulders/back to Francis Bacon, back to Descartes/putting nature in constraints/"torturing her secrets from her."*

The editor says *GeneWatch* is 16-20 pgs., 8½×11. They receive about 20-30 poems a year, accept 6 per year. Press run is 2,500 for 1,500 subscribers of which 15 are libraries. Subscription: $29 individual, $30 libraries, $100 corporations. Sample: free. Make checks payable to CRG and mail to CRG, 5 Upland Rd., Suite 3, Cambridge MA 02140.

How to Submit: Submit 1-3 poems at a time with SASE for response/return. Line length for poetry is 8 minimum, 1 ms page maximum. Previously published poems and simultaneous submissions OK. E-mail submissions OK. Cover letter preferred. Time between acceptance and publication is 6 weeks. Poems are circulated to an editorial board. "However, editor of magazine gives final approval." Often comments on rejections, but "comments are applied sparingly." Publishes theme issues. Send SASE for guidelines and upcoming themes. Responds in 1 month. Pays 1 copy. Acquires first rights.

Ⓝ ⊕ ◯ ◔ GENTLE READER, 8 Heol Pen-y-Bryn, Penyrheol, Caerphilly, Mid Glam, South Wales CF83 2JX United Kingdom, phone (029)20 886369, e-mail lynne_jones@hotmail.com, founded 1994, editor Lynne E. Jones.
Magazine Needs: Published quarterly, *Gentle Reader* is "a short story magazine to encourage mostly new and unpublished writers worldwide. Poems provide food for thought and sometimes light relief." The editor wants "general easy to read verse, not too long, that appeals to a wide audience. Nothing obscure, odd or esoteric. As a sample the editor selected these lines from "A Coffee-Shop Conversation" by Yvonne Eve Walus:

> You say I'm brooding/my clock is talking/the age old instinct/emerging/from the sea of documents/and references

GR is 48 pgs., A5, desktop-published and stapled with paper cover, includes clip art and scanned photos, reciprocal ads from other small presses. They receive about 50 poems a year, accept approximately 80%. Press run is 80 for 65 subscribers of which 5 are libraries; 10 distributed free to writers, other presses. Single copy: £2, overseas £2.50; subscription: £7, overseas £9.50. Sample: £1.65. Make checks payable (in sterling) to L.E. Jones.
How to Submit: Submit 2-3 poems at a time. Line length for poetry is 12 minimum, 30 maximum. Previously published poems and simultaneous submissions OK. E-mail and disk submissions OK. Cover letter preferred. "E-mail in body of document message with/for lines; disks, save file as text, use slashes for lines. IRCs please for reply and return of work." Time between acceptance and publication is up to 1 year. Send SAE and IRC for guidelines. Responds in 2 months. Pays 1 copy. Acquires first British serial rights. Staff reviews other magazines in 50 words, single book format. Send books for review consideration.
Advice: "Keep it simple."

Ⓝ ◯ ◯ ◔ ◎ THE GENTLE SURVIVALIST (Specialized: ethnic, nature, inspirational), Gen Del, Arroyo Seco NM 87514, website www.infowest.com/gentle/, founded 1991, editor/publisher Laura Martin-Bühler.
Magazine Needs: Publishes 6 issues per year. *The Gentle Survivalist* is a newsletter of "harmony—timeless truths and wisdom balanced with scientific developments for Native Americans and all those who believe in the Great Creator." They want poetry that is "positive, inspirational, on survival of body and spirit, also man's interconnectedness with God and all His creations. Nothing sexually oriented, occult, negative or depressing." Also accepts poetry written by children. They have published poetry by Keith Moore and C.S. Churchman. *TGS* is 9 pgs. (two 11×17 sheets folded in half plus insert). The issues we have received discuss environmental illness, Eastern medicine, and list common household toxins to avoid. They also offer money-saving tips and ideas on writing a personal history. "We print four poems average per issue." Press run is 200. Subscription: $22. Sample: $3.
How to Submit: Submit 4 poems at a time. Previously published poems and simultaneous submissions OK. Cover letter required; "just a note would be fine. I find noteless submissions too impersonal." Time between acceptance and publication is 3-4 months. Send SASE and $3 for sample and guidelines, no guidelines sent without sample request. "Folks need to see what they are getting into and I need to weed out frivolous submitters." Responds within 2 months. Does not return poetry. Pays 1 copy.
Also Offers: Sponsors annual contest. Awards a 1-year subscription to the winner. Winner announced in January issue.
Advice: "To succeed, one must not seek supporters, but seek to know whom to support. *TGS* receives a great deal of poetry that is too general in nature. We seek poems of inspiration about God, Man and our interconnectedness with all living."

$ ◔ GEORGE & MERTIE'S PLACE: ROOMS WITH A VIEW, P.O. Box 10335, Spokane WA 99209-1335, phone (509)325-3738, founded 1995, editors George Thomas and Mertie Duncan.
Magazine Needs: Appearing monthly except for January, *GMP* is "a monthly journal of opinion and imagination or any realm between. We are open to any form but our limited format prohibits long poetry." They have published poetry by Simon Perchik, Dennis Saleh and Eric Howard. As a sample the editors selected these lines from "Why I Don't Vote" by Geoff Peterson:

> Some columnist said it best./He said remember the shiny boys and girls/who courted your vote/to be president/when you were horny and failing math/and too crazy to drive a car? . . .

GMP is a 4- to 8-page, 8½×11, "micromagazine," printed (unbound) on colored paper with b&w graphics. In addition to poetry it may contain essays, short short stories, letters, opinions and "tidbits with a twist." Press run is 100 for 60 subscribers, 20 shelf sales. Subscription: $15/year. Sample: $2.
How to Submit: Submit 3-5 poems at a time. No previously published poems or simultaneous submissions. Cover letter preferred, "but not a long list of credits; we're looking for historical comments to personalize your

"We strive to present writing that is fresh, distinctive, and appealing to a wide range of readers," says Stephen Corey, acting editor of *The Georgia Review*. "So we try to find visual art that will have the same kind of immediate and memorable impact." On the Winter 1999 cover, a double image shows both the interior and exterior of Kathleen Holmes' work titled, "Billie Jewel." The Florida artist creates these "books" which are inspired by registries often kept in old Southern family Bibles. Holmes uses materials as diverse as crocheted pieces, printed texts, and corrugated tin to suggest forgotten stories in works meant to be "opened." *The Georgia Review* is 208 pages, 7 × 10, professionally printed, flat-spined with glossy card cover.

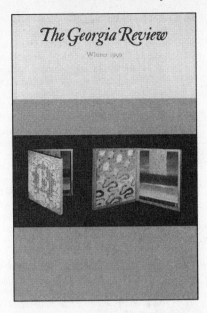

submission." Time between acceptance and publication is 3 months. Comments on rejections. Responds in 2 months. Pays 1¢/word ($2 minimum) and 1 copy. A $25 "The Dick Diver Best of Issue" prize is awarded each month; poetry, fiction and essays compete.

Also Offers: Sponsors contest. No more than 3 poems per entry. One entry per person. Entries to be postmarked no later than July 1, 2001. All entries will be considered for publication in monthly issues of George & Mertie's Place and, if used, will receive GMP's normal 1¢ a word payments, a contributor's copy and, in addition, will be eligible for that month's customary $25 Richard Diver Prize. These honoraria, for the final award recipient, are in addition to the $100 prize. SASE for return on mss.

Advice: "As Baudelaire says, 'Be always drunken—with wine, with poetry or with virtue—as you will—but be always drunken.' "

$ 🖊 **THE GEORGIA REVIEW**, The University of Georgia, Athens GA 30602-9009, phone (706)542-3481, website www.uga.edu/garev, founded 1947, contact editor.

Magazine Needs: *Georgia Review* appears quarterly. "We seek the very best work we can find, whether by Nobel laureates and Pulitzer Prize-winners or by little-known (or even previously unpublished) writers. All manuscripts receive serious, careful attention." They have published poetry by Peter Davison, Rita Dove, Stephen Dunn, Philip Levine, Linda Pastan and Pattiann Rogers. "We have featured first-ever publications by many new voices over the years, but encourage all potential contributors to become familiar with past offerings before submitting." As a sample the editor selected these lines from "The Voice of the Light" by John Engels:

> thins and hurls itself away./I've begun to starve/for memories, and memory/is beginning to speak/ another language, difficult/to understand; but I think/it likely to be telling me/we've all flown from one another,/and in every direction at once.

GR is 208 pgs., 7 × 10, professionally printed, flat-spined with glossy card cover. They use 60-70 poems a year, less than one-half of one percent of those received. Circulation is 6,000. Subscription: $18/year. Sample: $6.

How to Submit: Submit 3-5 poems at a time. No simultaneous submissions. Rarely uses translations. No submissions accepted during June, July and August. Publishes theme issues occasionally. Responds in 3 months. Always sends prepublication galleys. Pays $3/line, 1-year subscription and a copy of issue in which work appears. Buys first North American serial rights. Reviews books of poetry. "Our poetry reviews range from 500-word 'Book Briefs' on single volumes to 5,000-word essay reviews on multiple volumes."

Also Offers: Website includes writer's guidelines, names of the *GR* staff, subscription and advertising information, and samples of work published in *The Review*.

Advice: "Needless to say, competition is extremely tough. All styles and forms are welcome, but response times can be slow during peak periods in the fall and late spring."

🖊 🔲 **GERBIL: A QUEER CULTURE ZINE; GERBIL PRESS** (Specialized: **gay/lesbian/bisexual**), P.O. Box 10692, Rochester NY 14610, e-mail gerbilzine@aol.com, founded 1994, editor Tony Leuzzi.

Magazine Needs: *Gerbil*, published occasionally, is designed to provide "an open forum for lesbian/gay-identified writers and artists to express themselves and their work." They seek poetry with gay/lesbian content but are not limited to that. They are "open to all forms as long as the poetic voice is honest and clear. We look for lively, personal material of literary merit. No angst, pointless experimentation or abstraction." They have published poetry by Dave Trinidad, Beth Bailey, Deb Owen, Glenn Sheldon and Ken Pobo. As a sample the editors selected these lines from "French Lessons" by Darrel Borque:

> he will feel the world plumb/to his toes/he will feel it course through/the top of his head/scramble back
> inside him/go straight for the trapdoor/at the back of his throat

Gerbil is 28 pgs., about 7½×9½, offset and saddle-stitched with coated paper cover and b&w photos and graphics and lots of spot color inside. They receive about 750 poems a year, accept about 20. Press run is 3,000 for 100 subscribers, 1,000 shelf sales. Subscription: $10/4 issues. Sample: $3.

How to Submit: Submit 3-5 poems at a time. No previously published poems. "Friendly" cover letter preferred. Disk submissions (for Mac) welcome. E-mail submissions OK. Time between acceptance and publication is up to 1 year. Always comments on rejections. Publishes theme issues occasionally. Responds usually in up to 5 months. Pays 2 copies. Acquires first rights. Reviews books of poetry and other magazines. Open to unsolicited reviews. Poets may also send books for review consideration.

Also Offers: Occasionally sponsors poetry contests; watch magazine for details. Gerbil Press also occasionally publishes chapbooks on a cooperative basis. They usually work with poets who first published in the magazine, and their publishing arrangements vary based on the writer and project.

Advice: "If you're a beginning writer, don't be afraid to submit work! We publish a wide range of work of literary merit."

$ ☑ THE GETTYSBURG REVIEW, Gettysburg College, Gettysburg PA 17325, phone (717)337-6770, fax (717)337-6775, website www.gettysburgreview.com, founded 1988, editor Peter Stitt.

Work appearing in *The Gettysburg Review* has been included in *The Best American Poetry* (1995, 1997 and 1998) and *Pushcart Prize* anthologies. As for the editor, Peter Stitt won the first PEN/Nora Magid Award for Editorial Excellence.

Magazine Needs: *TGR* is a multidisciplinary literary quarterly considering "well-written poems of all kinds." They have published poetry by Rita Dove, Donald Hall, Susan Ludvigson, Pattiann Rogers, Charles Wright and Paul Zimmer. As a sample the editor selected these lines by Thomas Rabbitt:

> My father nods again and does not speak./This is Boston. He is thirty-six. The war is over./The good
> times have begun. And yet, overhead,/Floating in the oaks above Hyde Park, there is/This blimp, round
> as a breast, gray as death,/Slow as a mortgage, going nowhere overhead.

They accept 1-2% of submissions received. Press run is 4,500 for 2,700 subscriptions. Subscription: $24/year. Sample: $7.

How to Submit: Submit 3-5 poems at a time, with SASE. No previously published poems or simultaneous submissions. Cover letter preferred. Reads submissions September through May only. Publishes theme issues occasionally. Response times can be slow during heavy submission periods, especially in the late fall. Pays 1 copy plus subscription plus $2/line. Essay-reviews are featured in each issue. Open to unsolicited essay-reviews. Poets may also send books for review consideration.

Also Offers: Website includes guidelines, current masthead and staff bios, ordering information and forms, and most importantly, reprints of works published in recent issues. Works—poems, stories, essays—appear in their entirety.

☑ ☑ GINGER HILL, c/o English Dept., Room 312, Spotts World Cultures Building, Slippery Rock University, Slippery Rock PA 16057, fax (724)738-2188, e-mail vcain@sru.edu, faculty advisors Vernice Cain and Penny Kelly, founded 1963.

Magazine Needs: *Ginger Hill* is an annual literary magazine of poetry, short fiction, essay, miniplays, artwork and photography. It is digest-sized, "varies in format and layout every year," perfect-bound, with 2,000 distributed free.

How to Submit: Submit 3 poems at a time in duplicate. "One copy should have your name and address; leave the second copy blank for blind jurying." Average length for poetry is 57. Accepts only queries via e-mail. No previously published poems. Submissions must be postmarked on or before December 1 of each year. Send SASE for guidelines. Pays in copies. Only artwork is returned. After publication, all rights revert to author.

Advice: "We choose about 5-10% of all submissions. Excellence in technical skill is stressed."

Ⓝ ⊕ $ ☑ GINNINDERRA PRESS, P.O. Box 53, Charnwood ACT 2615 Australia, e-mail gp@dynamite .com.au, website www.netinfo.com.au/gp, founded 1996, publisher Stephen Matthews.

Book/Chapbook Needs: Ginninderra Press works "to give publishing opportunities to new writers." They have published poetry by Alan Gould and Geoff Page. Books are usually up to 56 pgs., A5, laser printed and saddle-stapled with board cover, sometimes includes art/graphic.

How to Submit: Query first, with a few sample poems and cover letter with brief bio and publication credits. Previously published poems OK; no simultaneous submissions. Time between acceptance and publication is 2 months. Seldom comments on rejections. Replies to queries in 1 week; to mss in 2 months. Pays royalties of 12½%.

N ✿ ◯ ◑ ◎ **GIRL CULT GIRLKULTURZINE (Specialized: gay/lesbian/bisexual)**, 48 Craig St., London, Ontario N6C 1E8 Canada, e-mail girlcult@execulink.com, founded 1995, editor/publisher Joan Brennan.
Magazine Needs: The zine is published quarterly to "promote writing and reading; to connect like minded individuals; to provide an alternative to mainstream media. No set form—quality/lucidity of thought and expression is everything. Interested in lesbian, gay, bi, queer poetry but not rigidly so! Sex, gender and the humor of them is paramount." They have published poetry by Geri MacRae, Claire Ani Reyes, Vernon Maulsby and Sullivan Haye. As a sample the editor selected these lines from "Advice" by Pamela Brown:

> he says/what strong people/have to look out for/is/the needle and thread/someone hands them/to mend/
> a hundred thousand/tiny tears/in their old worn out/coat.

The editor says *Girl Cult* is 40-50 pgs., 5½×8½, offset printed and stapled with cardstock cover, includes art/graphics. They accept approximately 50% of poetry received. Publish 3-5 poems/issue. Press run is 550; 200 distributed free to trades with other zines/contributors. Sample: $2. Make checks payable to Joan Brennan.
How to Submit: Previously published poems and simultaneous submissions OK. E-mail and disk submissions OK. Cover letter required. "Send SASE if returns requested." Seldom comments on rejections. Publishes theme issues occasionally. Send SASE for guidelines. Pays 2 copies. Acquires one-time rights. May review other magazines in 150-200 words, single and multi-book format. Open to unsolicited reviews. Poets may also send books for review consideration.
Advice: "This is a one woman operation: be patient with me but don't hesitate to write again if you don't hear from me."

✓ $ ◯ ◑ ◎ **GLB PUBLISHERS (Specialized: gay/lesbian/bisexual)**, P.O. Box 78212, San Francisco CA 94107-8212, phone (415)621-8307, e-mail glbpubs@mindspring.com, website www.glbpubs.com, founded 1990, associate editor John Hanley.
Book/Chapbook Needs: "We are a cooperative publisher founded for gay, lesbian and bisexual writers. Authors share cost of printing and promotion but have much control over cover design, typefaces, general appearance." They publish 2-4 paperbacks and 1-2 hardbacks/year. They want "book-length collections from gay, lesbian or bisexual writers. Nothing antagonistic to gay, lesbian or bisexual life-styles." They have published poetry by Robert Peters, Paul Genega, Thomas Cashet and Winthrop Smith.
How to Submit: Request author guidelines before submission. E-mail submissions OK—"WordPerfect or PDF (format is important)." Previously published poems OK; no simultaneous submissions. Cover letter required. "Author should explain intention for poems and expectations for sales of books." Often comments on rejections. Replies to queries in 10 days, to mss in 1 month. Always sends prepublication galleys. Pays 15-25% royalties and 20 author's copies. Check bookstores for samples.
Also Offers: Website includes poetry excerpts, guidelines and author bios. They also offer services for electronic publication of chapbooks and full-volumes. See the Per Pub Poetry section of their website.

◎ **DAVID R. GODINE, PUBLISHER**, 9 Hamilton Place, Boston MA 02108, website www.godine.com. They say, "Our poetry program is completely filled through 2001, and we do not accept any unsolicited materials."

✓ $ ◑ ◎ **GOLDEN ISIS MAGAZINE; GOLDEN ISIS PRESS; PAGAN POETS SOCIETY (Specialized: pagan/wiccan)**, P.O. Box 4263, Chatsworth CA 91313, e-mail poetrywitch@usa.net, website www.clubs.yahoo.com/clubs/paganpoetssociety, founded 1980, editor Gerina Dunwich.
Magazine Needs: "*Golden Isis* is a biannual New Age/Neo-Pagan journal of Goddess-oriented poetry, Pagan art, Wiccan news and announcements, reviews, networking services, witchy recipes, ritual outlines and ads. Positive magick for solitaries and covens of all traditions, and a literary forum in which individuals from around the world can share poetic visions and their special love for the Goddess and Horned God. Occult, Egyptian, mystical haiku and magickal chants are published. We are also interested in New Age spiritual poetry and astrological verses. All styles considered; under 60 lines preferred. We do not want to see pornographic, Satanic, sexist or racist material." They have published poetry by Lee Prosser, Reed Dunwich, Sheryl J. Miller and Anne Wilson. As a sample the editor selected these lines from "Transformation (A Circle Prayer)" by Gerina Dunwich:

> Learn, learn, the magick of the Earth,/the spiral dance of life,/the cauldron of re-birth./Yearn, yearn,
> for the old forgotten days;/return, return to our ancient Pagan ways.

The newsletter is about 10 pgs., desktop published. International circulation is 5,000. Single copy: $5; subscription: $10/year.
How to Submit: Submit 1 poem/page, typed single-spaced, name and address on upper left corner and the number of lines on upper right corner. No limit on number of poems submitted. Previously published poems and simultaneous submissions OK. E-mail submissions OK. Occasionally comments on rejected material. Responds

---

OPENNESS TO SUBMISSIONS: ◯ beginners; ◑ beginners and experienced;
◐ mostly experienced, few beginners; ◎ specialized; ◒ closed to unsolicited mss.

in 3 weeks. "Payment varies from contributor copies up to $5 per published poem." All rights revert to author upon publication. Reviews books of poetry, "length varies." Open to unsolicited reviews. Poets may also send books for review consideration.

Book/Chapbook Needs & How to Submit: Golden Isis Press currently accepts mss for chapbook publication. Send complete ms and $5 reading fee. "Make checks payable to Golden Isis. We offer a small advance, ten free copies of the published work, and 10% royalty on every copy sold for as long as the book is in print."

Also Offers: Website includes a literary circle for writers, publishers, readers and reviewers of pagan/wiccan poetry. Membership in the Pagan Poets Society is free. Members are encouraged to post poetry, reviews and related announcements on the club's message board. Other features available to members include a chat room, photo page, calendar of events, and links. A "Year of the Dragon" poetry contest is planned for 2000. Free guidelines available.

GOOSE LANE EDITIONS (Specialized: regional), 469 King St., Fredericton, New Brunswick E3B 1E5 Canada, phone (506)450-4251, acquisitions editor L. Boone, founded 1956.

Book/Chapbook Needs: Goose Lane is a small press publishing Canadian fiction, poetry and literary history. Writers should be advised that Goose Lane considers mss by Canadian poets only. They receive approximately 400 mss/year, publish 10-15 books yearly, 2 of these being poetry collections. Writers published include Gary Geddes and Claire Harris.

How to Submit: They are not currently reading submissions. "Call to inquire whether we are reading submissions." Always sends prepublication galleys. Authors may receive royalty of up to 10% of retail sale price on all copies sold. Copies available to author at 40% discount.

GOSPEL PUBLISHING HOUSE; LIVE (ADULT); DISCOVERY TRAILS (Specialized: religious, children/teens), The General Council of the Assemblies of God, 1445 Boonville Ave., Springfield MO 65802-1894, phone (417)862-2781 ext. 4356, fax (417)862-6059.

Magazine Needs & How to Submit: *Live* is a weekly take home paper for adults in Assemblies of God Sunday Schools, circulation 115,000. Wants traditional free and blank verse, 12-20 lines. "Please do not send more than three poems at one time. Submit seasonal material 1 year in advance; do not mention Santa Claus, Halloween or Easter bunnies." Sample copy and writer's guidelines for #10 SASE with first class stamp. Pays $35-60 on acceptance. Buys first and/or second rights. *Discovery Trails* (formerly *Junior Trails*) is a Sunday School take home paper containing religious fiction and biographical, historical and scientific articles with a spiritual emphasis for boys and girls ages 10-11, circulation 38,000. Buys 10-15 poems/year. Wants free verse and light verse. Submit seasonal/holiday material 15 months in advance. Simultaneous and previously published submissions OK. Sample copy and writer's guidelines for #10 SASE. Responds within 1 month. Pays $5-15 on acceptance. Buys first and/or second rights.

Advice: "We like poems showing contemporary children positively facing today's world. For all our publications, submit not more than one to two poems at a time."

GOTTA WRITE NETWORK LITMAG; MAREN PUBLICATIONS (Specialized), 515 E. Thacker, Hoffman Estates IL 60194, phone/fax (847)882-8054 (nights only), e-mail netera@aol.com or gwnlitmag@aol.com, website http://members.aol.com/gwn/amag, founded 1988, editor/publisher Denise Fleischer.

Magazine Needs: *GWN* features "contemporary poetry, articles, short stories and market listings. *GWN* now spans 40 states, Canada, England and Japan. Half of the magazine is devoted to science fiction and fantasy in a section called 'Sci-Fi Galleria.' A short checklist of what I look for in all poems and stories would be: drawing the reader into the protagonist's life from the beginning; presenting a poem's message through powerful imagery and sensory details; and language that is fresh and dynamic. I prefer free verse. Would also like to receive experimental, multicultural, feminist, humor, contemporary and translations. The poetry I publish expresses today's society with a tell-it-like-it-is voice. Contributors dive into subjects where others turn away. They speak of rape, suicide, the lives of Native Americans, the Holocaust and the sign of the times." *Gotta Write* has published poetry by Debbi McIntyre, Priscilla Wichrowski, Tim DiVita and Mariana Berner. As a sample the editor has selected the poem "I am the daughter of Crazy Horse and Black Buffalo Woman" by Raven:

> I came from that mad morning/dash across Yellowstone Country,/I came from the loins of that strange/
> man sprang from the belly of that/woman "warm and good as May/earth," I am the love that blood/
> could not kill the love that no/bullets could end . . .

The semiannual is 48-76 pgs., magazine-sized, desktop-published, saddle-stapled. "Gotta Write Network subscribers receive more than a magazine. In subscribing, they become part of a support group of both beginners and established poets. Readers are from all walks of life. I'm striving to give beginners a positive starting point (as well as promote the work of established writers and editors) and to encourage them to venture beyond rejection slips and writer's block. Publication can be a reality if you have determination and talent. There are over a thousand U.S. litmags waiting for submissions. So take your manuscripts out of your desk and submit them today!" Subscription: $15. Sample: $6. Overseas add $3.

How to Submit: Submit up to 5 poems at a time. Name and address on each page. No previously published poems or simultaneous submissions. Fax and e-mail submissions OK (no attachments). Include a cover letter and SASE. "No SASE, no response!" Accepts poetry submissions via fax "at night" or via e-mail "any hour."

Responds in 4 months. Sometimes sends prepublication galleys. Pays 1 copy, offers second copy at a discount. Acquires first North American serial rights and "now asking electronic rights." Pays $10 for assigned by-mail interviews with established big press authors and small press editors.

Advice: "Write the way you feel the words. Don't let others mold you into another poet's style. Poetry is about personal imagery that needs to be shared with others."

✓ ◯ ◙ **GRAFFITI RAG; GRAFFITI RAG POETRY AWARD; HELEN YOUNG/LINDA ASHEAR PRIZE**, 5647 Oakman Blvd., Dearborn MI 48126, phone (313)624-8794, e-mail hayan.charara@worldnet.att.net, founded 1995, editor Hayan Charara, co-editor Erik Fahren Kopf, west coast editor Bayla Winters.

Magazine Needs: *Graffiti Rag*, published annually, is a "poetry journal that seeks to publish work of well-known and gifted unknown poets on the urban experience." They want "poetry of the highest quality that brings a unique perspective on the shifting and limitless themes of urban life—economic, ethnic, intellectual, political, sexual." They have published poetry by Khaled Mattawa, Catherine Bowman, Wang Ping, Jim Daniels and Chase Twichell. As a sample the editor selected these lines from "A Last Look Back" by Chase Twichell:

> So strange, to inhabit a space/and then leave it vacant, standing open.//Each change in me is a stone
> step/beneath the blur of snow./In spring the sharp edges cut through.//When I look back, I see my
> former selves,/numerous as the trees.

Graffiti Rag is approximately 96 pgs., 6×9, perfect-bound, professionally printed with a colored matte cover. They receive about 900-1,500 poems a year, accept less than 10%. Press run is 750, 400 shelf sales. Single copy: $9.95; subscription: $9.95 plus $1.50 p&h. Sample issue: $7.95 plus $1.50 p&h.

How to Submit: Submit 3-5 poems at a time. No previously published poems or simultaneous submissions. Cover letter preferred. Time between acceptance and publication varies. Poems are circulated to an editorial board. "Guest editor (usually poets) assist in editorial process. Final decisions are made by main editor, Charara." Often comments on rejections. Send SASE for guidelines. Responds in 4 months. Pays 1 copy. Acquires first North American serial or one-time rights.

Also Offers: Sponsors the annual Graffiti Rag Poetry Award. Submit 3-5 unpublished poems from February 1 through June 30. Enclose reading fee of $10 (check or money order) and a SASE. Winning poet is featured in the anthology and receives cash award of $1,000. Also sponsors the Helen Young/Linda Ashear Prize for poets between the ages 14-19. No entry fee. Submit 3-5 poems with SASE. 1st Prize: $250 plus publication; 2nd Prize: $150 plus publication; and 3rd Prize: $100 plus publication.

Advice: "Read literary journals to better gauge their 'likes.' "

🖾 ◙ **GRAFFITO, THE POETRY POSTER**, Dept. of English, Dept. PM, University of Ottawa, Ottawa, Ontario K1N 6N5 Canada, fax (613)738-1929, e-mail graffito@uottawa.ca, website www.webapps.com/graffito, founded 1994, managing editor b stephen harding.

Magazine Needs: *graffito* is a monthly poster/zine. They want any style of poetry, maximum 32 lines. They have published poetry by R.M. Vaughan, George Elliot Clark, Michael Dennis, John B. Lee and Susan McMaster. *graffito* is an 11×17 sheet of colored paper folded in half to allow for a front cover and back cover containing reviews. Press run is 250; half distributed free within the local area of Ottawa. Subscription: $12 in Canada, $20 in US. Sample: $1. Make checks payable to b stephen harding.

How to Submit: Submit 5-8 poems at a time. No simultaneous submissions. Cover letter preferred. Time between acceptance and publication is 6-8 months. "We have a guest editor who is responsible for the content of their issues. However, final approval rests with the managing editor." Send SASE (or SAE and IRC) for guidelines or obtain via website. Responds in up to 8 months. Pays 3 copies. "We review books and chapbooks with preference for chapbooks." Poets may also send books for review consideration.

🖾 $◙ **GRAIN; SHORT GRAIN CONTEST**, Box 1154, Regina, Saskatchewan S4P 3B4 Canada, phone (306)244-2828, fax (306)244-0255, e-mail grain.mag@sk.sympatico.ca, website www.skwriter.com, founded 1973, editor Elizabeth Philips, poetry editor Séan Virgo.

Magazine Needs: "*Grain*, a literary quarterly, strives for artistic excellence and seeks poetry that is well-crafted, imaginatively stimulating, distinctly original." *Grain* is 128-144 pgs., digest-sized, professionally printed. Press run is 1,300 for 1,100 subscribers of which 100 are libraries. They receive about 1,200 submissions of poetry/year, use 80-140 poems. Subscription: $26.95/1 year, $39.95/2 years, for international subscriptions provide $4 postage for 1 year, $8 postage for 2 years in US dollars. Sample: $7.95 plus IRC.

How to Submit: Submit up to 8 poems, typed on 8½×11 paper, single-spaced, one side only. No previously published poems or simultaneous submissions. Cover letter required. Include "the number of poems submitted, address (with postal or zip code) and phone number. Submissions accepted by regular post only. No e-mail submissions." Reads submissions August through May only. Send SASE (or SAE and IRC) for guidelines or request via e-mail or website. Responds in 3 months. "Response by e-mail if address provided (ms recycled). Then IRCs or SASE not required." Pays over $30/poem plus 2 copies. Buys first North American serial rights.

Also Offers: Holds an annual Short Grain Contest. Entries are either prose poems (a lyric poem written as a prose paragraph or paragraphs in 500 words or less), dramatic monologues, or postcard stories (also 500 words or less). Also sponsors the Long Grain of Truth contest for nonfiction and creative prose (5,000 words or less). Prizes for all categories are $500 first, $250 second, $125 third; also honorable mentions. All winners and honorable mentions receive regular payment for publication in *Grain*. Entry fee of $22 allows up to two entries in the same category, and includes a 1-year subscription. Additional entries are $5 each. "U.S. and international entrants send fees in U.S. funds ($22 for two entries in one category plus $4 to help cover postage)." Entries are normally accepted between September 1 and January 31. Website includes contest winners, submission guidelines, sample work from current issue, back issues available, contest rules, subscription information/online ordering and mandate.

Advice: "Only work of the highest literary quality is accepted. Read several back issues."

■ ◉ **GRAND STREET**, 214 Sullivan St., 6C, New York NY 10012, phone (212)533-2944, fax (212)533-2737, poetry editor Michael Schmidt.

Work published in *Grand Street* has been included in the 1995 and 1997 volumes of *The Best American Poetry*.

Magazine Needs: *Grand Street* is now an online magazine publishing poetry, fiction, nonfiction and art (with one printed anthology printed each year). "We have no writer's guidelines, but publish the most original poetry we can find—encompassing quality writing from all schools." They have published poetry by John Ashbery, Nicholas Christopher, Fanny Howe, Robert Kelly, August Kleinzahler and Charles Simic.

How to Submit: Submit 5 poems at a time. Publishes theme issues. Send SASE for list of upcoming themes. Responds in 2 months.

◯ ◿ **GRASSLANDS REVIEW**, P.O. Box 626, Berea OH 44017, e-mail lkennelly@aol.com, website members.aol.com/GLReview/index.html, founded 1989, editor Laura B. Kennelly.

Magazine Needs: *Grasslands Review* is a biannual magazine "to encourage beginning writers and to give adult creative writing students experience in editing fiction and poetry; using any type of poetry; shorter poems stand best chance." They have published poetry by Virgil Suarez, James Doyle, Jane McClellan, Ed Orr, Ruth C. Holzer and Edward Mycue. As a sample the editor selected these lines from "The Reagan Years" by Allison M. Heim:

> It began with the lascivious crickets'/great spill, grated love lessons//the Impala's back seat//crickets
> scoring in the glove box, spreading/to the spare tire due to over population, prolific//as their robust
> love songs ignored the consequences/and we squashed everyone we caught.

GR is 80 pgs., digest-sized, professionally printed, photocopied, saddle-stapled with card cover. They accept 30-50 of 600 submissions received. Press run is 200. Subscription (2 issues): $10 for individuals, $20 institutions. Sample: $4.

How to Submit: Submit only during October and March, no more than 5 poems at a time. No previously published poems or simultaneous submissions. No e-mail submissions. Short cover letter preferred. Send #10 SASE for response. Editor comments on submissions "sometimes." Responds in 4 months. Sometimes sends prepublication galleys. Pays 1 copy.

Also Offers: Sponsors annual Editors' Prize Contest. Prize: $100 and publication. Deadline: April 30. Entry fee: $12 for 5 poems, $1/poem extra for entries over 5 poems. Entry fee includes 1-year subscription. Send SASE for reply. Website includes writer's guidelines and information on contests.

☑ $◿ **GRAVITY PRESSES; NOW HERE NOWHERE; VOICES ON THE WIND**, 27030 Havelock, Dearborn Heights MI 48127-3639, phone (313)563-4683, e-mail kingston@gravitypresses.com, website www.bignet.net/~blank/gravity/gphome.html, founded 1998, publisher Michael J. Barney, editor-in-chief Paul Kingston.

Magazine Needs: *NOW HERE NOWHERE* is a quarterly magazine publishing "the best poetry and short prose (fiction and nonfiction) that we can find. We are primarily a poetry magazine but will publish one to two prose pieces per issue. We have no restrictions or requirements as to form, content, length, etc. We publish what we like and what we think is good. No greeting card verse or song lyrics (unless by Leonard Cohen and Tom Waits)." They have published poetry by John Carle, Laurence W. Thomas, C.C. Russell and T. Kilgore Splake. As a sample the editor selected these lines from "Communication" by Patti Couture:

> Sometimes my words seemed carved/with the dull clumsy chisels barely scratching/the granite air/I
> long for sharp clean edges/to cut precisely/deep through the silent stone

NOW HERE NOWHERE is 48-52 pgs., 6¾×8½, offset printed or photocopied, saddle-stapled with glossy card cover, includes b&w illustrations. They receive about 500 poems a year, accept approximately 30%. Press run is 100 for 10 subscribers, 85 shelf sales. Single copy: $5.50; subscription: $20/4 issues. Sample: $6. Make checks payable to Gravity Presses.

How to Submit: Submit 5 poems at a time. No previously published poems; simultaneous submissions OK. Disk submissions OK. "International submissions only will be accepted in ASCII format via e-mail." Cover letter preferred. "SASEs should accompany all submissions." Time between acceptance and publication is 6-12 months. Poems are circulated to an editorial board. "All work is seen by at least two editors (of four) and must be accepted by at least two editors. Controversies are settled by the editor-in-chief with no appeals." Seldom comments on rejections. Publishes theme issues occasionally. Send SASE for guidelines and upcoming themes. Responds in 6 months. Sometimes sends prepublication galleys. Pays $3-5/issue plus 1 copy. Buys first North American serial rights.

Book/Chapbook Needs & How to Submit: Gravity Presses seeks to "publish the best work we can find for the broadest audience we can." They publish 3-5 chapbooks per year, plus 1 anthology titled *Voices on the*

Wind. Chapbooks are usually 64-76 pgs., 8½ × 7, offset printed or photocopied, saddle-stapled with glossy cardstock cover, includes art/illustrations "if appropriate." Recent publications: *Used Books*, by Mark Maurus; *Petals, Mountains, Heartz*, by Patricia Sullivan; *Under a Crescent Sun*, by Michael Marcus.

How to Submit: Query first with 5 sample poems and cover letter with brief bio and publication credits. Replies to queries within 1 year. Pays 200 author's copies (out of a press run of 250). Obtain sample chapbooks by sending "requests to our address."

Also Offers: Website includes samples of *Now Here Nowhere's* current issue, writer's guidelines, and contact information.

Advice: "The only advice we have for beginners is to write well and submit fearlessly and unrelentingly."

[N] [O] GRAYWOLF PRESS, 2402 University Ave., Suite 203, Saint Paul MN 55114, website www.graywolfp ress.org, founded 1974, editor Jeffrey Shotts.

Book/Chapbook Needs & How to Submit: Graywolf Press does not read unsolicited mss. They have published poetry by Jane Kenyon, David Rivard, Vijay Seshadri, John Haines, Eamon Grennan, Tess Gallagher, Tony Hoagland, William Stafford, Linda Gregg, Carl Phillips and Dana Gioia. Sometimes sends prepublication galleys. No e-mail submissions. Pays 7½-10% royalties, 10 author's copies, advance negotiated.

Also Offers: In conjunction with *Agni* magazine (see listing in this section), they also publish *Take Three*, a new annual series introducing emerging poets. Graywolf does not take direct submissions for this series.

[✓] [O] GREEN BEAN PRESS, P.O. Box 237, Canal Street Station, New York NY 10013, phone/fax (718)302-1955, e-mail gbpress@earthlink.net, website http://home.earthlink.net/~gbpress, founded 1993, editor Ian Griffin.

• Their journal, *Brouhaha*, is no longer being published.

Book/Chapbook Needs: Green Bean Press publishes 1-2 chapbooks and 1-2 full-length books/year. Chapbooks are usually 20-30 pgs., priced $3-5, no graphics, occasional cover art, "but each one is different." Average press run is 125. "Chapbook arrangements consist of payment in copies only." Full-length books can range from 78-300 pgs., usually 5½ × 8½, list prices $10-20, catalog available upon request. Average press run is 600. They have published *Long Live the 2 of Spades*, by Daniel Crocker and *North Beach Revisited*, by A.D. Winans.

How to Submit: No unsolicited mss are read for full-length books. For chapbooks query first, with 5-10 sample poems and cover letter with brief bio and publication credits by mail, fax or e-mail. "Not the entire manuscript, please." E-mail submissions preferred in attached RTF file. Replies to queries and mss in 1 month. Pays 35% author's copies (out of a press run of "whatever.") "Each arrangement is different. Some authors have helped with costs, others have not."

[O] GREEN HILLS LITERARY LANTERN, P.O. Box 375, Trenton MO 64683, phone (660)359-3948 ext. 324, fax (660)359-3202, e-mail jsmith@mail.ncmc.cc.mo.us, editors Jack Smith and Ken Reger, poetry editor Joe Benevento.

Magazine Needs: *Green Hills* is the annual journal of North Central Missouri College and the North Central Missouri Writer's Guild and is open to short fiction and poetry of "exceptional quality." They want "the best poetry, in any style, preferably understandable. There are no restrictions on subject matter, though pornography and gratuitous violence will not be accepted. Obscurity for its own sake is also frowned upon. Both free and formal verse forms are fine, though we publish more free verse overall. No haiku, limericks or anything over two pages." They have published poetry by R. Nikolas Macioci, Jim Thomas, Marilyn Shelton and Yvette A. Schnoeker-Shorb. As a sample the editor selected these lines from "Snowstorm" by Francine Tolf:

> *A man's black eyes/roll over me,/cool basalt across/shoulders, thighs,/slide/from my knees/back to a*
> *newspaper/of sickled alphabet/I do not understand.*

Green Hills is 200 pgs., 6 × 9, professionally printed and perfect-bound with glossy, 4-color cover. They receive work by more than 200 poets a year and publish about 10% of the poets submitting—less than 10% of all poetry received. Press run is 500. Sample: $7.

How to Submit: Send submissions to Joe Benevento, Truman State University, Division of Language and Literature, McClain Hall 310, 100 E. Normal, Kirksville MO 63501-4221. Submit 3-7 poems at a time, typed, 1 poem/page. No previously published poems; simultaneous submissions OK but not preferred. No fax or e-mail submissions. Cover letter with list of publications preferred. Often comments on rejections. Send SASE for guidelines or request via e-mail. Responds within 4 months. Always sends prepublication galleys. Pays 2 copies. Acquires one-time rights.

Advice: "Read the best poetry and be willing to learn from what you encounter. A genuine attempt is made to publish the best poems available, no matter who the writer. First time poets, well-established poets, and those in-between, all can and have found a place in the *GHLL*. We try to supply feedback, particularly to those we seek to encourage."

[O] GREENHOUSE REVIEW PRESS, 3965 Bonny Doon Rd., Santa Cruz CA 95060, founded 1975, publishes a series of poetry chapbooks and broadsides. "Unsolicited mss are not accepted."

[✦] [O] GREEN'S MAGAZINE, P.O. Box 3236, Regina, Saskatchewan S4P 3H1 Canada, founded 1972, editor David Green.

insider report

Editor shines literary lantern on poetry

"When Jack Smith first started publishing *Green Hills Literary Lantern*, he was looking mostly for 'local' writers and I was local enough to qualify," says Joe Benevento, poetry editor of the Trenton, Missouri, journal. "I got published in its pages two or three years running, so when he decided to expand it to a national journal that would actively seek submissions from all over, he got so inundated that he needed help. I'd never met him before, but when he called and offered me the post of poetry editor, I had already come to admire what he had done with *GHLL* and what he might now be able to do, so I agreed."

Since 1983, Benevento has worked at Truman State University (formerly Northeast Missouri State University) where he was recently promoted to full professor. In addition to his editing responsibilities at *GHLL*, he also serves as associate editor of

Joe Benevento

fiction for *The Chariton Review*. As a noted author of poetry, fiction and nonfiction (his fiction has been nominated three times for the Pushcart Prize, and he was one of seven writers featured in the "New Decade, New Writers" issue of *The MacGuffin*), Benevento brings a working writer's perspective to his editorial relationship with poets.

Benevento's collection, *Holding On*, was published in 1996 by Warthog Press. "I saw Warthog's entry in *Poet's Market*, liked their emphasis on 'understandable poetry,' and sent the sample they requested. The editor, Patricia Fillingham, initially sent a note saying she liked my work, but I should wait six months, and if I still hadn't found a publisher to then send my manuscript." It took another year before *Holding On* was actually accepted for publication, so Benevento understands the patience that the submission process demands of poets.

"I remind myself how upset it makes me for someone to hold onto my stuff for six months or a year and then cavalierly send me a form rejection without even a signature," he says. "So I make sure I get poets their stuff back within three months." Although *GHLL* is an annual (coming out in June or July), Benevento reads poems all year. "I usually stop accepting poems for that year's issue in March," he says, "then I start reading for the next year's issue immediately in April."

There are certain qualities Benevento appreciates in the work he considers. "I like poems that are unpretentious, which is not to say simple. I like poems that have strong voice, wonderful use of language, and a striking sensibility of some sort, whether it be a humaneness that shines through the persona, or perhaps something quite different—it could be cynicism or anger, so long as it comes through honestly, with grace or maybe humor." He cites Jim Thomas, Philip Miller, Mary Winters, Francine Tolf, R. Nikolas Macioci, and Marilyn Shelton as among those poets "who have touched me and impressed me more than once with beautiful, fully realized poems" that he admires for being "skilled, profound and yet largely accessible."

As an example, Benevento picked the following poem by Jim Thomas:

"Lovers"

Naked and unashamed, rapturously
singing, dozens of toads and tiny frogs
line ragged edges of this huge puddle
beside a timber road. So long as I
stand back to watch and listen, they ignore
me; only when I come near does my shadow,
ungainly size and movement cause them fear,
set off an eruption of leaping
and splashing like coiled springs come unwound.
Even then, farther down the pool as yet
undisturbed choristers keep the glade loud
with passionate melody. As soon
as I move away, the displaced rejoin
this glad din of flautists gone mad again.
I move on, crunching pale leaves left over
from last winter, my eyes filled up with sweet
williams and dutchmen's breeches and set
for morels and copperheads, locust thorns.

(Originally published in *Green Hills Literary Lantern*, Issue No. 9, 1998; reprinted with permission of the author)

As a creative writing teacher, Benevento has a wealth of advice to share with his fellow poets. "Beginning poets should write a lot and certainly understand that rewriting is the most important thing they can do to make a fair poem good and a good poem very good," he says. "They need to get self-critical, without losing the nerve it takes to be a writer in the first place, the pride it takes to believe that strangers will be moved by what you have to say and how you say it." Benevento also believes poets should take their time. "I think the best advice I can give my students is not to be in a hurry to publish, especially at the level of a book. I want them to value small press publication—especially if they mostly want to publish poetry and probably even if they seek to publish fiction."

Benevento's own fiction includes his recently completed novel, *The Odd Squad*, which "treats a half year in the life of three teens—one black, one white and one Hispanic—and their attempts to maintain a close friendship in the face of all kinds of peer pressure to 'stick to their own kind.'" The novel is based on his experiences in the 60s and 70s growing up in a working-class, post-white-flight Queens neighborhood. "I think lots of readers would find it fascinating to read about a white who was a 'minority' among Hispanics and blacks, and I think my own fluency in Spanish and my own biography make me an ideal voice for that story."

In the classroom, Benevento often finds himself learning along with his students. "We do lots of workshopping, and they critique my work, as I do theirs, and they do each other's. Students actually find it a lot easier to be harder on my writing than on each other's, which I find amusing. However, if they really like something, then I know they probably mean it."

Benevento also does assignments along with his students, participating in the "brainstorming, list-making and other basic heuristics that I ask for them to use. And these methods have led to published poems for me.

"When I'm not with my students, I revert to my older method, just sit with a blank piece of paper in some quiet setting and see if a poem is ready to start. I get maybe eight or ten false starts for every one I finish. Only some of the ones I finish are even halfway decent, yet that's still how I come to write a poem, more times than not," he explains.

Benevento turns to literary masters for inspiration as well. "By far and away my favorite poet is Walt Whitman," he says. "His identification with and belief in the reader, his seeing the miraculous in the ordinary, his undervalued mastery of language are all things I love about him. I also like Neruda, Frank O'Hara, Keats and a Spanish Romantic poet, Gustavo Adolfo Becquer." Drawing on past musical and songwriting experience, Benevento has set Whitman's "Song of Myself" and many of Becquer's "Rimas" to music.

In addition to *Holding On* and the literary journals in which his work appears, Benevento shares his poetry through readings. "I've given a few dozen readings over the years," he says, "about half of those here at Truman, under one auspice or another, and the other half on campuses like Northern Illinois University or 'The Writer's Place' in Kansas City." He concedes that we've all suffered through readings from poets who write better than they read. "But if you can read your work with enthusiasm and help set up the sound of the poems with explanatory or amusing anecdotes, you'll almost certainly have a good experience. And certainly you'll learn things about your own work: how it sounds aloud, which poems go over best, etc., that you otherwise might not know."

—Nancy Breen

Magazine Needs: *Green's Magazine* is a literary quarterly with a balanced diet of short fiction and poetry. They publish "free/blank verse examining emotions or situations." They do not want greeting card jingles or pale imitations of the masters. They have published poetry by David Conford, Penny Ferguson and Bernadette Higgins. As a sample the editor selected these lines from "Mr. Weed Killer" by Robert D. Hoeft:

> I was spraying weeds recently,/directing poison to their leaves/so they could direct it/to their roots
> where they could die.//Something in this world is skewed/when your only crime is being green

The magazine is 96 pgs., digest-sized, typeset on buff stock with line drawings, matte card cover, saddle-stapled. Circulation is 300. Subscription: $15. Sample: $5.

How to Submit: Submit 4-6 poems at a time. The editor prefers typescript, complete originals. No simultaneous submissions. "If © used, poet must give permission to use and state clearly the work is unpublished." Time between acceptance and publication is usually 3 months. Comments are usually provided on rejected mss. Send SASE (or SAE and IRCs) for guidelines. Responds in 2 months. Pays 2 copies. Acquires first North American serial rights. Occasionally reviews books of poetry in "up to 150-200 words." Send books for review consideration.

Advice: "Would-be contributors are urged to study the magazine first."

THE GREENSBORO REVIEW; GREENSBORO REVIEW LITERARY AWARDS, English Dept., Room 134, McIver Bldg., University of North Carolina, P.O. Box 26170, Greensboro NC 27402, phone (336)334-5459, fax (336)334-3281, e-mail jlclark@uncg.edu, website www.uncg.edu/eng/mfa, founded 1966, editor Jim Clark.

Work published in this review has been included in a *Pushcart Prize* anthology.

Magazine Needs: *The Greensboro Review* appears twice yearly and showcases well-made verse in all styles and forms, though shorter poems (under 50 lines) seem preferred. They have published poetry by Brendan Galvin, Stanley Plumly, Adrienne Su and Michael Collier. As a sample the poetry editor selected these lines from "Double Life" by Daniel Tobin:

> To have driven along blue levitating roads/this far into land's end, golden, rumpled,/these humps that
> could be the goddess's bedclothes,/and the red broach of a bridge pinning the continent/together, it is
> all ample and errant

The magazine is 128 pgs., digest-sized, professionally printed and flat-spined with colored matte cover. Uses about 25 pgs. of poetry in each issue, about 1.5% of the 2,000 submissions received for each issue. Subscription: $10. Sample: $5.

How to Submit: "Submissions (no more than five poems) must arrive by September 15 to be considered for the Spring issue (acceptances in December) and February 15 to be considered for the Fall issue (acceptances in May). Manuscripts arriving after those dates will be held for consideration with the next issue." No previously published poems or simultaneous submissions. No fax or e-mail submissions. Cover letter not required but helpful. Include number of poems submitted. Responds in 4 months. Always sends prepublication galleys. Pays 3 copies. Acquires first North American serial rights.

Also Offers: They sponsor an open competition for *The Greensboro Review* Literary Awards, $250 for both poetry and fiction each year. Deadline: September 15. Send SASE for guidelines. Website includes writer's guidelines, subscription information and literary award information.

⦰ GROVE ATLANTIC, 841 Broadway, New York NY 10003. They do not accept unsolicited mss.

⦿ GSU REVIEW; GSU REVIEW ANNUAL WRITING CONTEST, Georgia State University, Campus Box 1894, Atlanta GA 30303, phone (404)651-4804, fax (404)651-1710, e-mail mnewcome@mindspring.com, website www.gsu.edu, founded 1980, poetry editor Katie Chaple, editor Michelle Newcome.

Magazine Needs: *GSU Review* is a biannual literary magazine publishing fiction, poetry and photography. They want "original voices searching to rise above the ordinary. No subject or form biases." They do not want pornography or Hallmark verse. They have published poetry by Bert Hedin, Gary Sange and Dana Littlepage Smith. The editors say *GSU Review* is 112 pgs. Press run is 2,500 for 500 subscribers, 600 shelf sales; 500 distributed free to students. Single copy: $5; subscription: $8. Sample: $3.

How to Submit: Submit 3 poems at a time. No previously published poems; simultaneous submissions OK. Cover letter with 3- to 4-line bio preferred. Time between acceptance and publication is 3 months. Seldom comments on rejections. Send SASE for guidelines. Responds in 1 month. Pays 1 copy.

Also Offers: Sponsors the *GSU Review* Annual Writing Contest, an annual award of $1,000 for the best poem; copy of issue to all who submit. Submissions must be previously unpublished. Submit up to 3 poems on any subject or in any form. "Specify 'poetry' on outside envelope." Send SASE for guidelines. Inquiries via fax and e-mail OK. Postmark deadline: January 31. Competition receives 200 entries. Past judges include Sharon Olds, Jane Hirschfield and Phil Levine. Winner will be announced in the Spring issue. Website includes guidelines and sample poems.

Advice: "Avoid cliched and sentimental writing but as all advice is filled with paradox—write from the heart. We look for a smooth union of form and content."

▨ ✓ ◎ GUERNICA EDITIONS INC.; ESSENTIAL POET SERIES, PROSE SERIES, DRAMA SERIES; INTERNATIONAL WRITERS (Specialized: regional, translations, ethnic/nationality), P.O. Box 117, Toronto, Ontario M5S 2S6 Canada, fax (416)657-8885, e-mail guernicaeditions@cs.com, website www.guernicaeditions.com, founded 1978, poetry editor Antonio D'Alfonso.

Book/Chapbook Needs: "We wish to bring together the different and often divergent voices that exist in Canada and the U.S. We are interested in translations. We are mostly interested in poetry and essays on pluricultur- alism." They have published work by Mary Melfi, Vittorio Sereni, Laura Boss, Maria Mazziotti Gillan (US); Karen Shenfeld and Maria Luzi (Italy).

How to Submit: Query with 1-2 pgs. of samples. Send SASE (Canadian stamps only) or SAE and IRCs for catalog.

Advice: "We are interested in promoting a pluricultural view of literature by bridging languages and cultures. Besides our specialization in international translation."

▧ ⦿ GULF COAST: A JOURNAL OF LITERATURE AND FINE ART, Dept. of English, University of Houston, Houston TX 77204-3012, phone (713)743-3223, fax (713)743-3215, founded 1986, poetry editors Michael Theune, Julie Chisolm and Matt Otremba.

Magazine Needs: *Gulf Coast* is published twice a year in May and December. While the journal features work by a number of established poets, editors are also interested in "providing a forum for new and emerging writers who are producing well-crafted work that takes risks." Each issue includes poetry, fiction, essays, interviews, and color reproductions of work by artists from across the nation. They have published poetry by Heather McHugh, Robert Pinsky, Marilyn Nelson, William Logan, Lisa Lewis, Gail Mazur and Asha Shahid Ali. As a sample the editors selected these lines from "Answer to Crowd" by Ed Skoog:

> *You have to ask, what was your war crime?/This is social work, walking around the crowd,/wanting to tell the woman who left hours ago/that her scarf still lies across the bench,/another coworker at a crossroad like yours./At the end of the world one feels worldlier.*

The editor says *Gulf Coast* is 140 pgs., 6×9, offset printed, perfect-bound. Single copy: $7; subscription: $12/ year, $22/2 years.

How to Submit: Submit up to 4 poems at a time. No previously published poems; simultaneous submissions OK with notification. Cover letter with previous publications, "if any," and a brief bio required. Does not read submissions June through August. Send SASE for guidelines. Responds in 6 months. Pays 2 copies and $15 per poem. Returns rights upon publication.

☑ ⊘ **GULF STREAM MAGAZINE**, English Dept. Florida International University, 3000 NE First St., North Miami Campus, North Miami FL 33181, phone (305)919-5599, website http://as/1s.fiu.edu/cwp/gulfstream .htm, founded 1989, editor Lynne Barrett, associate editors Lissette Mendez and Brandt Ryan.

Magazine Needs: *Gulf Stream* is the biannual literary magazine associated with the creative writing program at FIU. They want "poetry of any style and subject matter as long as it is of high literary quality." They have published poetry by Gerald Costanzo, Naomi Shihab Nye, Jill Bialosky and Catherine Bowman. The handsome magazine is 96 pgs., digest-sized, flat-spined, printed on quality stock with glossy card cover. They accept less than 10% of poetry received. Press run is 750. Subscription: $9. Sample: $5.

How to Submit: Submit no more than 5 poems and include cover letter. Simultaneous submissions OK (with notification in cover letter). Reads submissions September 15 through April 30 only. Editor comments on submissions "if we feel we can be helpful." Publishes theme issues. Send SASE for guidelines. Responds in 3 months. Pays 2 copies and 2 subscriptions. Acquires first North American serial rights.

◐ ◎ **HABERSHAM REVIEW (Specialized: regional)**, P.O. Box 10, Demorest GA 30535, fax (706)776-2811, e-mail swhited@piedmont.edu, founded 1991, poetry editor Dr. Stephen R. Whited.

Magazine Needs: *Habersham Review* is a biannual, general interest, regional journal published by Piedmont College. "While we are interested in publishing regional poets, we will publish a good poem no matter where the poet lives. We accept all styles, and we prefer a range of subject matter." They have published poetry by Judson Mitcham, R.T. Smith, William Miller and James Baker Hall. As a sample we selected these lines from "When I Survey the Wondrous Cross" by David Bottoms:

> A heavy odor of flowers/rode the fans,/and I sat with my bare feet dangling over a bench./Light from
> an open window fell across the face/of a brown guitar, dust twisting like worms in that light,/as the
> pail of water/slid across the splintered floor.

HR is about 100 pgs., 6×9, perfect-bound, offset, with color art and photographs on the cover, some b&w art and photographs inside, and ads. It receives 250 poems a year, accepts 25. Press run is 1,000 for 300 subscribers of which 10% are libraries, 50-100 shelf sales. Subscription: $12. Sample: $6. Make checks payable to Piedmont College.

How to Submit: Submit up to 5 poems at a time. No previously published poems or simultaneous submissions. Cover letter preferred. Time between acceptance and publication is 1-2 years, "in some cases." Send SASE for guidelines. Responds in up to 6 months. Pays 5 copies. Acquires first rights. Requires acknowledgment if reprinted elsewhere. Staff reviews books of poetry in 200-500 words, single or multi-book format. Send books for review consideration.

N $ ◻ **HADROSAUR TALES**, P.O. Box 8468, Las Cruces NM 88006-8468, phone (505)527-4163, e-mail Billosaur@mindspring.com, website http://hadrosaur.com, founded 1995, editor David L. Summers.

Magazine Needs: "*Hadrosaur Tales* is a literary journal that appears 2 times a year and publishes well written, thought-provoking science fiction and fantasy." They want science fiction and fantasy themes. "We like to see strong visual imagery; strong emotion from a sense of fun to more melancholy is good. We do not want to see poetry that strays too far from the science fiction/fantasy genre." They have published poetry by Keith Allen Daniels, Jim Dunlap, Steve Sneyd and Gary Every. As a sample the editor selected these lines from "Iggy Guards Her Secrets" by Keith Allen Daniels:

> Here on the table top/I have constructed Stonehenge/from several dominoes./I seem to remember/a
> circlet of lights in the sky.//a starship growing brighter and brighter/as it descended./But just before
> the mysteries unfold,/our resident green iguana//flicks her tail imperiously/and the cromlechs scatter
> in all directions./Iggy guards her secrets/like a dragon guards its treasure.

HT is about 100 pgs., digest-sized, "high quality photocopy," perfect-bound with black drawing on card stock cover, uses cover art only, includes minimal ads. They receive about 100 poems a year, accept approximately 25%. Press run is 100 for 25 subscribers. Single copy: $5.95; subscription: $10/year. Sample: $6.95. Make checks payable to Hadrosaur Productions.

How to Submit: Submit 1-5 poems at a time. Previously published poems and simultaneous submissions OK. E-mail submissions OK. Cover letter preferred. "For electronic mail submissions, please place the word, 'Hadrosaur' in the subject line. Poetry will not be returned unless sufficient postage is provided." Time between acceptance and publication is 1 year. Often comments on rejections. Publishes theme issues occasionally. Send SASE for guidelines and upcoming themes. Responds in 1 month. Sends prepublication galleys on request. Pays $2/poem plus 2 copies. Buys one-time rights.

Also Offers: Website includes writer's guidelines, a staff description and company history, links to authors websites and an online bookstore through Amazon.com.

Advice: "Unfortunately, science fiction/fantasy poetry doesn't appear to have a strong 'main stream' market. However, science fiction poetry often provides the most evocative images and intriguing ideas."

⬤ ◎ HAIGHT ASHBURY LITERARY JOURNAL (Specialized: social issues, themes), 558 Joost Ave., San Francisco CA 94127, founded 1979-1980, editors Indigo Hotchkiss, Alice Rogoff and Conyus.

Magazine Needs: *Haight Ashbury* is a newsprint tabloid that appears 1-3 times/year. They use "all forms including haiku. Subject matter sometimes political, but open to all subjects. Poems of background—prison, minority experience—often published, as well as poems of protest and of Central America. Few rhymes." They have published poetry by Molly Fisk, Laura del Fuego, Dancing Bear, Lee Herrick, Janice King and Laura Beausoleil. As a sample the editors selected these lines from "in the lines" by Tia Blassingame:

> *color boys and girls/leaves the trees in flower/triggers the metal from which year olds drop/drug addict*
> *babes born on/crack open their skulls/on the ground/color boys and girls/does not become men and*
> *women*

The tabloid uses graphics, ads, 16 pgs., circulation 2,000-3,000. $35 for a lifetime subscription, which includes 3 back issues. Subscription: $12/4 issues. Sample: $3.

How to Submit: Submit up to 6 poems. "Please type one poem to a page, put name and address on every page and include SASE." No previously published poems. Each issue changes its theme and emphasis. Send SASE for guidelines and upcoming themes. Upcoming themes include "Jazz Poetry" and "Millennium." Responds in 4 months. Pays 3 copies, small amount to featured writers. Rights revert to author. An anthology of past issues, *This Far Together*, is available for $15.

Also Offers: "Millennium" writing contest with cash award. Deadline: December 31, 2000.

Ⓝ 🗋 ◯ ⬤ ◎ HAIKU HEADLINES: A MONTHLY NEWSLETTER OF HAIKU AND SEN-RYU (Specialized: Form), 1347 W. 71st St., Los Angeles CA 90044-2505, phone (323)778-5337, founded 1988, editor/publisher Rengé/David Priebe.

Magazine Needs: *HH*, "America's only monthly publication dedicated to the genre," uses haiku and senryu only. The editor prefers the 5/7/5 syllabic discipline, but accepts irregular haiku and senryu which display pivotal imagery and contrast. Also accepts poetry written by children. They have published haiku by Dorothy McLaughlin, Jean Calkins, Günther Klinge and Mark Arvid White. Here are examples of haiku and senryu by Rengé:

> *HAIKU: By the very sound/of the splash in the water/—invisible frog!*
> *SENRYU: The silent facades/of the tall city buildings/teeming with people.*

The newsletter is 8 pgs., 8½ × 11, corner-stapled and punched for a three-ring binder. "Each issue has a different color graphic front page. The back page showcases a Featured Haiku Poet with a photo-portrait, biography, philosophy and six of the poet's own favorite haiku." *HH* publishes 100 haiku/senryu a month, including, on the average, work from 6 newcomers. They have 225 subscribers of which 3 are libraries. Single copy: $2 US and Canada, $2.50 overseas; subscription: $24 US and Canada, $30 overseas.

How to Submit: Haiku/senryu may be submitted with 12 maximum/single page. Unpublished submissions from subscribers will be considered first. Nonsubscriber submissions will be accepted only if space permits and SASE is included. Responds in 2 months. Pays subscribers half price rebates for issues containing their work; credits applicable to subscription. Nonsubscribers are encouraged to prepay for issues containing their work.

Also Offers: Monthly Readers' Choice Awards of $25, $15 and $10 are shared by the "Top Three Favorites." The "First Timer" with the most votes receives an Award of Special Recognition ($5).

Ⓝ ⬤ HALF TONES TO JUBILEE, English Dept., Pensacola Junior College, 1000 College Blvd., Pensacola FL 32504, phone (904)484-1418, founded 1986, faculty editor Walter Spara.

> 🏆 *Half Tones to Jubilee* has received 2 national awards, a 1st Place with merit from the American Scholastic Press Association, and 1st Place, Southern division, literary magazine competition, Community College Humanities Association.

Magazine Needs: *HTTJ* is an annual literary journal appearing in the fall that features poetry and short fiction. They have published poetry by R.T. Smith, Sue Walker, Larry Rubin and Simon Perchik. *HTTJ* is 100 pgs., digest-sized, perfect-bound with matte card cover, professionally printed. They receive about 1,000 poems a year, use 50-60. Press run is 500. Subscription: $4. Sample: $4.

How to Submit: Submit 5 poems at a time. No previously published work or simultaneous submissions. SASE mandatory. Cover letter with bio and/or publication history preferred. Reads submissions August 1 through May 15 only. Responds in 3 months, faster when possible. Pays 1 copy. Acquires first rights.

Also Offers: *HTTJ* sponsors an annual poetry competition, 1st Place $300, 2nd $200, Third $100. Entry fee: $3/poem. Send SASE for rules and deadlines.

🌐 ◎ HANDSHAKE; THE EIGHT HAND GANG (Specialized: science fiction), 5 Cross Farm, Station Rd., Padgate, Warrington, Cheshire WA2 OQG United Kingdom, founded 1992, contact J.F. Haines.

USE THE GENERAL INDEX, located at the back of this book, to find the page number of a specific publisher. Also, publishers that were listed in last year's edition but not included in this edition are listed in the General Index with a notation explaining why they were omitted.

Magazine Needs: *Handshake*, published irregularly, "is a newsletter for science fiction poets. It has evolved into being one side of news and information and one side of poetry." They want "science fiction/fantasy poetry of all styles. Prefer short poems." They do not want "epics or foul language." They have published poetry by Margaret B. Simon, Fleming A. Calder and Jacqueline Jones. As a sample the editor selected these lines from "A Home in Space" by Jacqueline Jones:

> *Blueish splinters and a lightning beauty/Saw us through the orbits throat on earth*

Handshake is 1 sheet of A4 paper, photocopied with ads. They receive about 50 poems a year, accept approximately 50%. Press run is 60 for 30 subscribers of which 5 are libraries. Subscription: SAE with IRC. Sample: SAE with IRC.

How to Submit: Submit 2-3 poems, typed and camera-ready. No previously published poems or simultaneous submissions. Cover letter preferred. Time between acceptance and publication varies. Editor selects "whatever takes my fancy and is of suitable length." Seldom comments on rejections. Publishes theme issues. Responds ASAP. Pays 1 copy. Acquires first rights. Staff reviews books or chapbooks of poetry or other magazines of very short length. Send books for review consideration.

Also Offers: *Handshake* is also the newsletter for The Eight Hand Gang, an organization for British science fiction poets, established in 1991. They currently have 60 members. Information about the organization is found in their newsletter.

🌐 ◐ **HANDSHAKE EDITIONS; CASSETTE GAZETTE**, Atelier A2, 83 rue de la Tombe Issoire 75014, Paris, France, phone 33-1-4327-1767, fax 33-1-4320-4195, e-mail jim_haynes@wanadoo.fr, founded 1979.

Magazine Needs & How to Submit: *Cassette Gazette* is an audiocassette issued "from time to time. We are interested in poetry dealing with political/social issues and women/feminism themes." Poets published include Ted Joans, Yianna Katsoulos, Judith Malina, Elaine Cohen, Amanda Hoover, Jayne Cortez, Roy Williamson and Mary Guggenheim. Single copy: $10 plus postage. Pays in copies.

Book/Chapbook Needs & How to Submit: Handshake Editions does not accept unsolicited mss for book publication. New Book: *Just Say "No" to Family Values* by David Day and *What's Wrong? What's Right?* by John Calder.

Advice: Jim Haynes, publisher, says, "I prefer to deal face to face."

$ ◻ ◐ **HANGING LOOSE PRESS; HANGING LOOSE**, 231 Wyckoff St., Brooklyn NY 11217, founded 1966, poetry editors Robert Hershon, Dick Lourie, Mark Pawlak and Ron Schreiber.

🏆 Poetry published in *Hanging Loose* has been included in the 1995, 1996 and 1997 volumes of *The Best American Poetry.*

Magazine Needs: *Hanging Loose* appears 3 times/year. The magazine has published poetry by Sherman Alexie, Paul Violi, Donna Brook, Kimiko Hahn, Ron Overton, Jack Anderson and Frances Phillips. *Hanging Loose* is 120 pgs., flat-spined, offset on heavy stock with a 2-color glossy card cover. One section contains poems by high-school-age poets. The editor says it "concentrates on the work of new writers." Sample: $9.

How to Submit: Submit 4-6 "excellent, energetic" poems. No simultaneous submissions. "Would-be contributors should read the magazine first." Responds in 3 months. Pays small fee and 2 copies.

Book/Chapbook Needs & How to Submit: Hanging Loose Press does not accept unsolicited book mss or artwork.

☑ $ ◻ ◐ **HANOVER PRESS, LTD.; THE UNDERWOOD REVIEW**, P.O. Box 596, Newtown CT 06470-0596, phone (203)426-3388, fax (203)426-3398, e-mail faith@hanover-press.com, website www.hanover-press.com, founded 1994, editor Faith Vicinanza.

Magazine Needs: *The Underwood Review* biannually publishes poetry, short stories, essays, reviews and b&w artwork including photographs. They want "cutting-edge fiction, poetry and art. We are not afraid of hard issues, love humor, prefer personal experience over nature poetry. We want poetry that is strong, gutsy, vivid images, erotica accepted. No religious poems; no 'Hallmark' verse." Also accepts poetry written by children. They have published poetry by Patricia Smith ("Queen of Performance Poetry"), Marc Smith ("father of slam poetry") and Michael Brown. As a sample the editor selected these lines from "Mommy's Hubby" by Leo Connellan (Poet Laureate of Connecticut):

> *Yes, it's Fisk tellin' you split./Imagine it, Fisk tellin' you leave!/Because now I'm Mommy's Hubby and we've got our coffins/picked out/plots and perpetual flowers.*

TUR is 120-144 pgs., 6×9, offset printed and perfect-bound with card cover with computer graphics, photos, etc. They receive about 600 poems a year, accept approximately 10%. Press run is 1,000. Subscription: $24. Sample: $13. Make checks payable to Hanover Press, Ltd./Faith Vicinanza.

How to Submit: Submit up to 6 poems at a time. No previously published poems; simultaneous submissions OK. Cover letter with short bio (up to 60 words) preferred. Disk submissions OK. No e-mail submissions. Reads and responds to submissions twice a year—January/February and June/July. Time between acceptance and publication is 1-6 months. Send SASE for guidelines. Responds in 5 months. Pays 2 copies. Acquires one-time rights. Reviews books and chapbooks of poetry and other magazines in 500 words, single book format. Open to unsolicited reviews. Poets may also send books for review consideration.

Book/Chapbook Needs & How to Submit: Hanover Press, Ltd. seeks "to provide talented writers with the opportunity to get published and readers with the opportunity to experience extraordinary poetry." They have published *Crazy Quilt* by Vivian Shipley; *Short Poems/City Poems* by Leo Connellan; *We Are What We Love* by Jim Scrimgeour; *Full Circle* by Elizabeth Thomas; *Dangerous Men* by David Martin. They publish 5 paperbacks/ year. Books are usually 6×9, offset printed and perfect-bound with various covers, include art/graphics. Query first with a few sample poems and cover letter with brief bio and publication credits. Replies to queries in 2 months; to mss in 6 months. Pays royalties of 3-7% or 100 author's copies (out of a press run of 1,000). Order sample books by sending $11.

Also Offers: Website includes poetry calendar, mission statement, guidelines, online bookstore and online poetry newsletter.

⊘ **HARCOURT, INC.; HARCOURT CHILDREN'S BOOKS; GULLIVER BOOKS; SILVER WHIS- TLE**, 525 B St., Suite 1900, San Diego CA 92101, phone (619)231-6616. Harcourt Children's Books, Gulliver Books and Silver Whistle publish hardback and trade paperback books for children. They do not accept unsolicited material.

◯ ◎ **HARD ROW TO HOE; MISTY HILL PRESS (Specialized: nature/rural/ecology)**, P.O. Box 541-I, Healdsburg CA 95448, phone (707)433-9786, editor Joe E. Armstrong.

Magazine Needs: *Hard Row to Hoe,* taken over from Seven Buffaloes Press in 1987, is a "book review newsletter of literature from rural America with a section reserved for short stories (about 2,000 words) and poetry featuring unpublished authors. The subject matter must apply to rural America including nature and environmental subjects. Poems of 30 lines or less given preference, but no arbitrary limit. No style limits. Do not want any subject matter not related to rural subjects." As a sample the editor selected these lines from "A Good Man" by Deborah Quigley Smith:

> *In the spring he watched the maple moon/take the frost from the ground/and run it up the trees in sapsickles. . . .*

HRTH is 12 pgs., magazine-sized, side-stapled, appearing 3 times a year, 3 pgs. reserved for short stories and poetry. Press run is 300. Subscription: $7/year. Sample: $2.

How to Submit: Submit 3-4 poems at a time. No simultaneous submissions. Previously published poems OK only if published in local or university papers. Send SASE for guidelines. Editor comments on rejections "if I think the quality warrants." Pays 2 copies. Acquires one-time rights. Reviews books of poetry in 600-700 words. Open to unsolicited reviews. Poets may also send books for review consideration.

Ⓝ ⊘ **THE HARLEM REVIEW**, 420 E. 70th St., Apt. 5H, New York NY 10021, phone (212)794-1732, e- mail dwgalarn@mail.med.cornell,edu, founded 1999, editor David Galarneau.

Magazine Needs: *The Harlem Review* appears 3 times a year and is "dedicated solely to poetry, will publish any high quality work. This publication is dedicated to the memory of Langston Hughes and looks favorably upon pieces that emulate his style. Looking for poetry that moves the soul. Open to any genre of poetry. "We smile upon poetry in the style of Hughes, Bukowski, or Thomas. We do not want to see anything where the meaning/symbolism is not readily apparent." They have published poetry by Shamim Islam. As a sample the editor selected these lines from "always, my love" by D. Frazier:

> *a copper wind subsiding/that day I do recall/forewarned glances not withdrawn/tears, more mindful words between//something*

The editor says *THR* is 40 pgs., laser printed, includes ads. They receive about 100 poems a year, accept approximately 20%. Press run is 100 for 20 subscribers. Subscription: $12. Sample: $5. Make checks payable to David Galarneau.

How to Submit: Submit up to 7 poems at a time. Previously published poems and simultaneous submissions OK. E-mail submissions OK, "but prefer submission by mail." Cover letter preferred. Time between acceptance and publication is 3 months. Seldom comments on rejections. Send SASE for guidelines or obtain via e-mail. Responds in 1 month. Sometimes sends prepublication galleys. Pays 1 copy. Acquires one-time rights.

Advice: "Beginners—don't give up the fight—if you can't join them, beat them."

⚘ $ ⊘ **THE HARPWEAVER; CANADIAN AUTHORS ASSOCIATION PRIZE FOR POETRY**, Dept. of English, 500 Glenridge Ave., St. Catharines, Ontario L2S 3A1 Canada, phone (905)688-5550 ext. 3469, fax (905)688-5550 ext. 4492, e-mail harpweav@spartan.ac.BrockU.ca, founded 1996. Contact editor.

Magazine Needs: *"the Harpweaver* biannually publishes the creative work of emerging and established artists. We want poetry embodying the best words in the best order. This poetry is always consistent with innovation in form and content." They have published poetry by George Elliott Clarke and James Reaney. *Harpweaver* is 75- 100 pgs., 5½×8½, offset printed and perfect-bound with card cover, includes artwork. They receive about 200 poems a year, accept approximately 8-10%. Press run is 1,000. Subscription: $10. Sample: $4.

How to Submit: Submit up to 12 poems at a time. No previously published poems or simultaneous submissions. Cover letter required. E-mail and disk submissions OK. Reads submissions February through March and May through October only. Time between acceptance and publication is 2 months. Poems are circulated to an editorial board—"student board to faculty editor to journal editors." Often comments on rejections. Send SASE for guidelines or request via fax or e-mail. Responds in 3 months. Pays $10. Reviews books and chapbooks of poetry in 5,000 words, single book format. Open to unsolicited reviews. Poets may also send books for review consideration.

Also Offers: Sponsors the Canadian Authors Association Prize for Poetry, a cash award of $50 given "to the author of the poem that our judges consider to be the most noteworthy among the many fine poems *the Harpweaver* has the opportunity to publish in its two yearly issues."

✓ ◎ **THE HARVARD ADVOCATE (Specialized: university affiliation)**, 21 South St., Cambridge MA 02138, phone (617)495-0737, fax (617)496-9470, e-mail soudavar@fas.harvard.edu/~advocate, website www.hcs .harvard.edu/~advocate, founded 1866, president Saadi Soudavar.

Magazine Needs: *The Harvard Advocate* is a quarterly literary and arts review, circulation 4,000, that publishes poetry, fiction and art only by undergraduate and graduate students currently enrolled at Harvard University. Sample: $5.

How to Submit: In submitting state your exact relationship to Harvard. Submissions should be typed and single-sided. Use only 10 point or larger font. No previously published work. E-mail submissions OK. "Submissions are considered anonymously; write the title of your poem, your name, class, address, telephone number, and e-mail address on an index card. Place the index card inside an envelope and seal it. Upon the envelope write only the title of your work. Use a paper clip to attach the envelope to your manuscript." Does not pay. Reviews books, including poetry.

Also Offers: Website includes full magazine text as well as submission policies and the magazine's history.

◖ **HAWAII PACIFIC REVIEW**, 1060 Bishop St., Honolulu HI 96813, phone (808)544-1107, fax (808)544-0862, founded 1986, poetry editor Patrice Wilson.

Magazine Needs: *HPR* is an annual literary journal appearing in September. They want "quality poetry, short fiction and personal essays from writers worldwide. Our journal seeks to promote a world view that celebrates a variety of cultural themes, beliefs, values and viewpoints. We wish to further the growth of artistic vision and talent by encouraging sophisticated and innovative poetic and narrative techniques." They have published poetry by Wendy Bishop, B.Z. Niditch, Sandra Kohler and Willie James King. *HPR* is 80-120 pgs., 6×9, professionally printed on quality paper, perfect-bound, with coated card cover; each issue features original artwork. They receive 800-1,000 poems a year, accept 30-40. Press run is approximately 1,000 for 200 shelf sales. Single copy: $7. Sample: $5.

How to Submit: Submit up to 5 poems, maximum 100 lines each. 1 submission/issue. "No handwritten manuscripts." No previously published poems; simultaneous submissions OK with notification. No e-mail submissions. Cover letter with 5-line professional bio including prior publications required. "Our reading period is September 1 through December 31 each year." Seldom comments on rejections. Send SASE for guidelines or request via e-mail. Responds within 3 months. Pays 2 copies. Acquires first North American serial rights.

Advice: "We'd like to receive more experimental verse. Good poetry is eye-opening; it investigates the unfamiliar or reveals the spectacular in the ordinary. Good poetry does more than simply express the poet's feelings; it provides both insight and unexpected beauty."

◖◖ **HAWAI'I REVIEW**, 1733 Donaghho Rd., Honolulu HI 96822, founded 1973, poetry editor Lisa Kanae, editor Kyle Koza.

Magazine Needs: *Hawai'i Review* is a biannual literary journal. "We publish high quality poetry, fiction, nonfiction and some visual art." They want "mostly free verse; all topics as long as they are interesting, provocative, insightful and skillfully crafted. No rhymed verse, traditional forms. Please, no self-indulgent poems, or song lyrics." Also accepts poetry written by children. They have published poetry by Juliana Spahr, Joe Balaz and Dan Rodhe. The editors say *HR* is 150-250 pgs., digest-sized, web offset printed and perfect-bound with coated card stock cover. They receive about 1,000 poems a year, accept approximately 5%. Press run is 1,000 for 200 subscribers of which 100 are libraries, 75 shelf sales. Subscription: $20/year; $30/2 years. Sample: $10. Make checks payable to University of Hawaii.

How to Submit: Submit 5 typed poems at a time. No previously published poems; simultaneous submissions OK if noted. Cover letter preferred. "SASE required for response." Poems are circulated to an editorial board. Seldom comments on rejections. Publishes theme issues occasionally. Send SASE for guidelines and upcoming themes. Responds in 5 months. Always sends prepublication galleys. Pays 4 copies. Acquires first North American serial rights.

✓ ◖ **HAYDEN'S FERRY REVIEW**, Box 871502, Arizona State University, Tempe AZ 85287-1502, phone (480)965-1243, founded 1986.

Magazine Needs: *Hayden's Ferry* is a handsome literary magazine appearing twice a year. They have published poetry by Dennis Schmitz, Raymond Carver, Maura Stanton, Ai, and David St. John. *HFR* is 6×9, 120 pgs., flat-spined with glossy card cover. Press run is 1,300 for 200 subscribers of which 30 are libraries, 800 shelf sales. They accept about 3% of 5,000 submissions annually. Subscription: $10. Sample: $6.

How to Submit: "No specifications other than limit in number (six) and no simultaneous submissions." Submissions circulated to two poetry editors. Editor comments on submissions "often." Send SASE for guidelines. Responds in 3 months of deadlines. Deadlines: February 28 for Spring/Summer issue; September 30 for Fall/Winter. Sends contributors page proofs. Pays $25/page (maximum $100) and 2 copies.

◑ ◎ HAYPENNY PRESS; IPSISSIMA VERBA (THE VERY WORDS) (Specialized: poetry written in first-person singular), 32 Forest St., New Britain CT 06052, e-mail ipsiverba@aol.com, founded 1989 (press), 1991 (magazine), editor/publisher P.D. Jordan.
Magazine Needs: *ipsissima verba (the very words)* appears twice yearly, with special issues, and publishes fiction and poetry in the first person. They want poetry of "any length, topic, format, etc., as long as it's written in first person." They have published poetry by Laurel Speer, Ron Watson and the late Joe Singer. As a sample the editor selected this poem by Tony Lewis-Jones:

> I kept no photographs of you; I wanted/to erase you from my life, my memory./Impossible I've realized,
> for now/Some nights you appear to me in dreams

The editor says *ipsissima verba* is about 65 pgs., magazine-sized, offset and digitally printed, binding varies (usually glue), cover varies, includes illustrations or photos and ads. They receive about 200 poems a year, accept approximately 30%. Subscription: $15. Sample: $8. Make checks payable to P.D. Jordan.
How to Submit: Submit up to 5 poems at a time. Previously published poems OK; no simultaneous submissions. Cover letter preferred. "All submissions, correspondence, etc., must include SASE." Time between acceptance and publication averages 3 months. Seldom comments on rejections. Publishes theme issues occasionally. Send SASE for guidelines and upcoming themes. Responds in 1 month (on average). Pays 2 copies. Acquires one-time rights. Staff reviews books and chapbooks of poetry and other magazines, multi-book format. "Sometimes only a 'Top Picks' list depending on space and reviewer's time." Send books for review consideration.
Also Offers: "We will be sponsoring contests (probably with entry fees) in the future. We also will be going to a cash payment format for published submissions."

◪ ◐ HAZ MAT REVIEW; CLEVIS HOOK PRESS, P.O. Box 30507, Rochester NY 14603-0507, founded 1996, editor Norm Davis, fiction editor Nick DiChario.
Magazine Needs: The *Haz Mat Review* is a biannual literary review, "about 70% poetry; 25% short story; 5% misc. (essays, review, etc.). *Haz Mat* stands for 'hazardous material,' which we believe poetry most definitely may be!" They want "your best material; take chances; political pieces welcome; also experimental and/or alternative; especially welcome pieces that show things are not what they appear to be. We think poetry/fiction of the highest quality always has a chance. New Age, witches, ghosts and goblins, vampires, probably not." They have published poetry by Marc Olmstead, Bruce Sweet, Jim Cohn, Bobby Johnson, Thom Ward, Lawrence Ferlinghetti and Richard Cambridge. As a sample the editor selected this untitled poem by Larry Hilf:

> full moon/hides/in cloud thicket/ambush.

Haz Mat is 96 pgs., digest-sized, professionally printed and perfect-bound with glossy color or b&w cover, includes photographs or original art. They receive about 500 poems a year, accept approximately 60%. Press run is 400 for 25 subscribers of which 5 are libraries, 100 shelf sales; 100 distributed free to coffee house publicity. Single copy: $7; subscription: $14/year. Sample: $5.
How to Submit: Submit 3 poems at a time. Previously published poems OK; no simultaneous submissions. Disk submissions OK. Cover letter preferred. SASE requested. Time between acceptance and publication is up to 1 year. Poems are circulated to an editorial board. "Editors pass promising material to staff readers for second opinion and suggestions, then back to editors for final decision." Often comments on rejections. Send SASE for guidelines. Responds in 3 months. Pays 1-2 copies. Acquires one-time rights. Staff reviews chapbooks of poetry. "Best chance for fiction, 2,500 words or less."
Advice: "We are encouraged by the renewed interest in poetry in recent years. If at all possible, read the magazine first before submitting to get a feel for the publication."

◪ ⊕ ◐ HEADLOCK PRESS, Old Zion Chapel, The Triangle, Somerton, Somerset TA11 6QP United Kingdom, phone/fax (01458)272962, founded 1994, editor Tony Charles.
Book/Chapbook Needs: Headlock Press publishes 4-5 paperbacks per year. They want "new writing, both traditional and experimental. Originality essential. No performance poetry, rap." They have published poetry by Pam Bridgeman, Geoff Hattersley, Jim Lindop and Gordon Wardman. As a sample the editor selected these lines from "Soul Kitsch/Stealth Fighter" by Kerry Sowerby:

> If the walls are composed of old/faces, paper over the cracks.//It's just words, you convince yourself,/
> carving out layer after layer,//but you're drowned by insane babble/as you have yet to cut out the
> tongues.

Books are usually 48-80 pgs., A5, photocopied and perfect-bound with card cover, sometimes includes art/graphics.
How to Submit: Query first, with 6 sample poems and cover letter with brief bio and publication credits. Previously published poems OK; no simultaneous submissions. Disk submissions OK. "Tell me about yourself and why you want Headlock to publish your collection." Time between acceptance and publication is 6 months. Poems are circulated to an editorial board. "Four or five readers are involved in the final acceptance process." Seldom comments on rejections. Replies to queries in 6 weeks; to mss in 2 months. Pays 10% author's copies out of a variable press run. Order sample books by sending SAE for price list.
Also Offers: Sponsors an annual book competition for unpublished poetry. Winners receive publication. Send SAE and IRC for full details.
Advice: "We publish around four book a year; so are very selective. Do not send whole collections unsolicited; always include SAE. Work from abroad, send disposable copies, we send reply only. Don't give up hope."

☑ $ ⊘ ◎ **THE HEARTLANDS TODAY (Specialized: regional, themes)**, Firelands College, 1 University Rd., Huron OH 44839, phone (419)433-5560, fax (419)433-9696, e-mail lsmithdog@aol.com, founded 1990, editors Larry Smith and Nancy Dunham.

Magazine Needs: *The Heartlands Today* is an annual publication of the Firelands Writing Center at Firelands College. They want work by Midwestern writers about the Midwest Heartlands, "writing and photography that is set in the Midwest today and deals revealingly and creatively with the issues we face—good writing and art that documents our lives." Each issue has a specific theme. They have published poetry by Alberta Turner, Chris Llewellyn and Lawrence Ferlinghetti. The editors describe it as 160 pgs., 6×9, perfect-bound with 20 b&w photos. They accept 10-20% of the poetry received. Press run is 800. Single copy: $8.50. Sample: $5.

How to Submit: Submit up to 5 poems at a time. Simultaneous submissions OK. No e-mail submissions, only queries. Cover letter with brief bio required. Reads submissions January 1 to June 1 only. Often comments on rejections. Send SASE for guidelines and upcoming themes. Responds in 2 months once reading period begins. Pays $10 and 2 copies. Buys first or second rights.

☑ ⊘ ◎ **HEAVEN BONE MAGAZINE; HEAVEN BONE PRESS; HEAVEN BONE PRESS INTERNATIONAL CHAPBOOK COMPETITION (Specialized: spiritual, nature/rural/ecology)**, P.O. Box 486, Chester NY 10918, phone (914)469-9018, e-mail heavenbone@aol.com, founded 1986, poetry editor Steve Hirsch.

Magazine Needs: *Heaven Bone* publishes poetry, fiction, essays and reviews with "an emphasis on spiritual, metaphysical, surrealist, experimental, esoteric and ecological concerns." They have published poetry and fiction by Richard Kostelanetz, Charles Bukowski, Marge Piercy, Kirpal Gordon, Diane di Prima and Michael McClure. As a sample the editor selected these lines from "Message of Hope" by G. Sutton Breiding:

> The screech owl's call/Is vertical: a tower/Rippling in the mist,/A door of oracles/Hung between night/
> And dawn that opens/And shuts softly/In the white places/Of sleep.

Heaven Bone is approximately 144 pgs., magazine-sized, perfect-bound, using b&w art, photos on recycled bond stock with glossy 4-color recycled card cover. They receive 700-1,000 poems a year, accept 18-30. Press run is 2,000. Sample: $10.

How to Submit: Submit 3-10 poems at a time. "I will not read submissions without SASEs." Simultaneous submissions and previously published poems OK, "if notified." E-mail submissions OK (PDF, Microsoft Word). Time between acceptance and publication is up to 1 year. Occasionally publishes theme issues. Send SASE for upcoming themes. Responds in up to 6 months. Sometimes sends prepublication galleys. Pays 2 copies. Acquires first North American serial rights. Reviews books of poetry. Open to unsolicited reviews. Poets may also send books for review consideration.

Also Offers: The press sponsors the biannual Heaven Bone Press International Chapbook Competition which awards $100 plus publication to an original, unpublished poetry ms of 30 pgs. or less. Reading fee $10. Send SASE for guidelines.

Advice: Editor advises, "Please be familiar with the magazine before sending mss. We receive too much religious verse. Break free of common 'poetic' limitations and speak freely with no contrivances. No forced end-line rhyming please. Channel the muse and music without being an obstacle to the poem."

⊕ ⊘ ◎ **HEIST MAGAZINE (Specialized: men)**, P.O. Box 2, Newcastle University Union, Callaghan NSW 2308 Australia, e-mail matthew@mockfrog.com, website www.mockfrog.com/heist, founded 1998, submissions editor Matt Ward.

Magazine Needs: *Heist Magazine* appears bimonthly and "aims to encourage men to write and get themselves published. *Heist* is mostly short fiction, with a section devoted to quality poetry." They want poetry of any form (except haiku) and any theme. "We take both amusing and serious work. No haiku, no cut-and-paste surrealist poems. No 'revenge' on my ex-girlfriend/wife poems." They have published poetry by Timothy Hodor, Austria; Robert Dunn, New York; and Frank Finney, Thailand. They receive about 50 poetry submissions a year, accept approximately 50%. Press run is 1,000 for 100 subscribers, 700 shelf sales; 200 distributed free to contributors and various Australian writing societies. Single copy: $2.50 AUS, $1.50 US; subscription: $5 AUS, $10 US. Sample (including postage): $2.50. Those outside Australia should send cash only.

How to Submit: Submit 6 poems at a time. No previously published poems or simultaneous submissions. Disk submissions OK (PC or Mac). Cover letter required. "Poems should be single-spaced. Also, include a floppy disk saved in Word or Word Perfect or Clarisworks; IRCs and cover letter." Time between acceptance and publication is 4 months. Seldom comments on rejections. Send SASE for guidelines or obtain guidelines via e-mail or website. Responds in 3 months. Pays 1 copy. Acquires first Australian rights.

Advice: "Be brave in what you write, but do not take yourself too seriously. If your poetry is serious, throw in one or two amusing, satirical poems as well."

Ⓝ ⓥ **HELICON NINE EDITIONS; MARIANNE MOORE POETRY PRIZE**, 3607 Pennsylvania Ave., Kansas City MO 64111, phone (816)753-1095, fax (816)753-1016, e-mail twpkcmo@aol.com, website www.heliconnine.com, founded 1977, editor Gloria Vando Hickok.

Book/Chapbook Needs & How to Submit: Helicon Nine publishes poetry, including winners of the annual Marianne Moore Poetry Prize. "We do not accept unsolicited mss for Helicon Nine Editions without prior inquiry." They have published *One Girl* by Sheila Kohler and *Flesh* by Susan Gubernat. As a sample the editor selected these lines from "Night Ritual" by Marjorie Stelmach from her book *Night Drawings*:

> *Finger things: a silver hook/lifted and lowered on the screen-porch door,/a lamp-key turned to lower the flame,/a gown's hem lifted for stairs, one/slippered foot suspended.*

No electronic submissions.

Also Offers: The Marianne Moore Poetry Prize awards $1,000 and publication for an unpublished poetry ms of at least 50 pgs. Manuscripts are not returned, and there is a $20 reading fee for all contest entries. Deadline for entry: May 1. Send SASE for guidelines.

✪ **HELIKON PRESS**, 120 W. 71st St., New York NY 10023, founded 1972, poetry editors Robin Prising and William Leo Coakley, "try to publish the best contemporary poetry in the tradition of English verse. We read (and listen to) poetry and ask poets to build a collection around particular poems. We print fine editions illustrated by good artists. Unfortunately we cannot encourage submissions."

✔ ✪ **HELIOTROPE**, P.O. Box 20037, Spokane WA 99204, e-mail gribneal@ior.com, founded 1996, editors Tom Gribble, Iris Gribble-Neal and Jan Strener.

Magazine Needs: *Heliotrope*, published annually in January, is "an outlet for poetry, fiction, prose and criticism." They want "poetry of any form, length, subject matter, style or purpose with no restrictions." They have published poetry by Nance Van Winckel, Christopher Howell, James Grabill and Kris Christensen. As a sample the editors selected these lines from "Butterflies" by John Whalen:

> *Don't bring up butterflies/Unless you're willing to lend me/An afternoon of butterflies/That won't depend on personality alone.*

The editor says *Heliotrope* is 100 pgs., 6×9, perfect-bound with glossy cover with art. Press run is 200-300 for 75 subscribers. Subscription: $7. Make checks payable to Tom Gribble/*Heliotrope*.

How to Submit: Submit 5 poems at a time. No previously published poems or simultaneous submissions. Cover letter preferred. E-mail submissions OK. Reads submissions June 21 through September 21 only. Poems are circulated to an editorial board. Seldom comments on rejections. Send SASE for guidelines. Responds 2 months after end of reading period. Sometimes sends prepublication galleys. Pays 1 copy.

Advice: "We are open to all writers."

✪ ◎ **HELLAS: A JOURNAL OF POETRY AND THE HUMANITIES; THE HELLAS AWARD; THE ALDINE PRESS, LTD.; THE NEW CLASSICISTS (Specialized: form)**, 304 S. Tyson Ave., Glenside PA 19038, phone (215)884-1086, e-mail harnett@aldinepress.com, website www.aldinepress.com, founded 1988, editor Gerald Harnett.

Magazine Needs: *Hellas* is a semiannual published by Aldine Press that wants poetry of "any kind but especially poems in meter. We prize elegance and formality in verse, but specifically encourage poetry of the utmost boldness and innovation, so long as it is not willfully obscurantist; no ignorant, illiterate, meaningless free verse or political poems. If we don't understand it, we don't print it. On the other hand, we don't want obvious, easy, clichéd or sentimental verse." They have published poetry by Hadas, Steele, Moore, Bowers, Conquest, Gioia and many others. *Hellas* is 172 pgs., 6×9, flat-spined, offset printed, using b&w art. Press run is 1,000. Subscription: $16/year, $28/2 years. Sample: $9.

How to Submit: Submit 3-5 poems at a time. No simultaneous submissions or previously published poems. No e-mail submissions. Editor comments on rejections "happily if requested." Send SASE for guidelines. Responds in 4 months. Pays 1 copy. Acquires first North American serial rights.

Also Offers: The *Hellas* Award ($100) is open to *Hellas* subscribers only and is awarded annually to the finest poem entered in the contest. Poems may be submitted to both *Hellas* and the contest simultaneously at any time throughout the year, but the annual deadline is December 31. Winner is published in spring issue of *Hellas*. Enclose SASE if submission is to be returned. In addition, they sponsor the *Hellas* readings, held at various locations in Philadelphia, New York and elsewhere. Send SASE for guidelines.

Advice: "*Hellas* is a lively and provocative assault on a century of modernist barbarism in the arts. A unique, Miltonic wedding of *paideia* and *poiesis*, engaging scholarship and original poetry, *Hellas* has become the forum of a remarkable new generation of poets, critics and theorists committed to the renovation of the art of our time . . . Meter is especially welcome, as well as rhymed and stanzaic verse. We judge a poem by its verbal artifice and its truth. Lines should not end arbitrarily, diction should be precise: We suggest that such principles can appear 'limiting' only to an impoverished imagination. To the contrary, we encourage any conceivable boldness and innovation, so long as it is executed with discipline and is not a masquerade for self-indulgent obscurantism. . . . We do not print poems about Nicaragua, whales or an author's body parts. We do specifically welcome submissions from newer authors."

✪ **HELLP!**, P.O. Box 38, Farmingdale NJ 07727, founded 1997, editors Joe Musso and Rick Silvani.

Magazine Needs: *HELLP!* "rears its ugly head at will—no set schedules here." Includes poetry, fiction, interviews, drawings and articles. "The purpose of *HELLP!* is to give freedom of expression yet another forum. Everyone needs a little *HELLP!*." They want "edgy, thought-provoking work with depth—challenge us. Send

Keeping writing at the center of her life: poet Patty Seyburn

If you like to keep abreast of emerging writers who produce dynamic poetry, you may be familiar with Patty Seyburn's debut volume *Diasporadic*. Or, if you're a reader of quality literary journals such as the *Paris Review, New England Review*, and *Crazyhorse*, among others, no doubt you've already come across Seyburn's strikingly intelligent poems.

Patty Seyburn

As its title suggests, *Diasporadic* engages in tribal reflection. One of the primary strengths of this collection is the manner in which the poems arrive at their subject from radically different perspectives and provide the reader the experience of traveling the expanse of both the individual and collective history. The poetic range of Seyburn's work is apparent in the various modes she employs in exploring the rootlessness of the exile; this subject is passionately sought in poems that address personal experience, as well as those which undertake the retelling of stories in the voices of lost women from the Bible.

Seyburn's poetic range extends to her excellent craftsmanship. She employs a variety of traditional forms while maintaining such an easy tone that even the more complicated pieces strike one as naturally and effortlessly achieved. As the title poem suggests, the overarching movement of Seyburn's book is aligned to the dispersion of the Jewish people.

"Diasporadic"

When I saw the Jews floating, I knew
it was time to pack up, when the water
struck their oak boxes, the small stones
placed atop their graves in memory
scattering, the great slabs engraved
like charms on a bracelet swept
downstream as though the rocks were
driftwood, rocks were feathers—
in our game, paper bested rocks
which crippled scissors, anyway—
and I put on my tall rubber boots,
zipped my duffel that could be lifted
high as a child overhead and made
my way toward the flume—now dry,

> *water rising on both sides, resembling*
> *the Red Sea's cinematic parting, smudged*
> *extras trudging a swath of sand, pretending*
> *that God split the sea for them clean*
> *as a perfect center part in wet hair,*
> *while De Mille's technicians shot jello*
> *at high-speed. I saw Jews' caskets freed*
> *from cemetery Beth Yeshurun meandering*
> *downtown, bumping into names, dates*
> *and epitaphs, a few trees, I thought*
> *oh, we're wandering, again. . . .*

(reprinted by permission of the author)

As Seyburn remarks on her work, "I love how writing brings you to other parts of life and brings them to you. The dialectical nature of Judaism—constructing a God, arguing a God, people's responsibility to God as well as the reverse—filters into my work and how I approach constructing the world I live in. Questioning, doubt, interrogation, humor are all part of this cultural heritage. Too many people see criticism as an act of 'negation.' I believe it's an act of engagement and therefore the highest compliment. So the ways and practices of Judaism—including ritual, to a small degree—are vital to my writing."

Born and raised in Detroit, Michigan, Seyburn pursued her love for writing. She earned degrees from Northwestern University and worked for seven years as a journalist, after which she decided to complete an M.F.A. in poetry at the University of California, Irvine. Seyburn states, "Obviously one does not 'need' to be in a writing program in order to write. All that changed was that I found a way to put writing at the center of my life and to learn from people already committed to the project of writing. I did not suddenly become a kid (I was thirty) nor did all of my prior life experience simply disappear."

Indeed, Seyburn's experience as a reporter clearly influenced the investigative nature of her work. "The journalist in me demands a beginning that will at least compel the reader to make it to line two," she says. In addition to life experience, Seyburn values what she terms a "poetry education." Seyburn attended the University of Houston's creative writing program and is in the process of completing her English Ph.D. Currently she teaches poetry writing at CalArts in Los Angeles. "In the pursuit of a poetry education, ideally a student will read and write outside his or her comfort zone," she says. "Young writers should allow themselves to be influenced by other writers—those they read, as well as those they study with."

Seyburn doesn't take much stock in the claim that writing workshops manufacture writers whose voices are indistinct from one another's. "If a student ends up sounding like someone else, they'll come out of it— or they won't. Not everyone in a program will end up a poet, but this doesn't mean it's not a valuable education or pursuit." She argues that writers shouldn't resist what school has to offer them: "It's a wholly different level of commitment, when you have to fit writing into an already full life."

In addition to being an educator, Seyburn recently assumed the editorship at Helicon Nine Editions and also works as a freelance journalist. She admits, "Sometimes it feels like too many hats—aside from the most important, that of the poet—but it's what must be done." She adds, "Whatever you do, you have to find time to write. If your job distracts you from your writing, then find something different."

Once a collection of poems is composed, Seyburn advises writers trying to publish their first books to submit work to contests. "While the book contests are such an arcane way to bring up a generation of poets, thank God for the contests, since so few publishers will take a chance on a new poet." She adds, "Send your work to all publishers. Many young, small presses are putting out great-looking books." Seyburn's one to know. After sending her manuscript to contests for two years, and two years before she became affiliated with Helicon Nine Editions, Seyburn's book was chosen as the winner of the 1997 Marianne Moore Prize, and her book was published by the small press.

As far as the poetry market is concerned, Seyburn admits that "eminently marketable poetry" is not something she aspires to. "That seems like an oxymoron to me," she laughs. Yet the success of her first book demonstrates that readers appreciate and recognize quality poetry. *Diasporadic* received the Notable Book Award for 2000, given by the Notable Book Council of Reference and User Services Association, a division of the American Library Association. This award recognizes books for "their significant contribution to the expansion of knowledge or for the pleasure they can provide for readers." The only other poet to receive this award was Seamus Heaney, winner of the 1996 Nobel Prize for Literature, for his collection *Opened Ground: Selected Poems* 1966-1996.

Seyburn is now at work on her second book of poems. While she notes that the poems have "fewer references to family and friends (most of which were made up anyway)," her writing process hasn't really changed. "I'm a big fan of the conceit, or extended metaphor, like Louise Glück's *The Wild Iris*, where every poem is in direct dialogue with other poems. The poems in my second book definitely talk to each other more than those in *Diasporadic*."

Seyburn also hopes her poems speak to a broad audience; this includes readers who are not necessarily familiar with poetry. "Many of my friends and family may not participate in literary culture, but they are people who read, who think, who are willing to delve beneath the surface, which is what's necessary for poetry. It's vital to me that poets are not the only ones reading my work or attending my readings. Poetry, however, is intimidating to people, which is not something I completely understand but have learned to accept. People want to like poetry; they don't want to feel intimidated. That's part of our/my job—to help them find a way in," she says.

Seyburn's work offers several points of entry, as noted by the poet and critic Richard Howard: "A woman, a Jew and a poet!" Seyburn affirms that her perspective as a female writer informs her work: "If someone told me I wrote like a man or they thought that I was a man from my writing, I would consider it a misread."

Seyburn also considers it vital that poets work to build their own community of writers. "You need to find a couple of people who are good readers—ideally with different strengths and aesthetics. Whatever you do to make a living, you need to keep writing at the center and one way to do this is through human interactions—relationships, friendships," she says. "In addition, I value feedback from friends and family who are not writers. I need their outlook, their 'languages,' their perspective."

And we, as readers, need the gift of articulation that Patty Seyburn's poetry so generously provides.

—Cate Marvin

your best." They have published poetry by Koon Woon, Richard Quatrone, Stepan Chapman, Elizabeth Priebe, Bill Lambdin and Richard Houff. *HELLP!* is 40-48 pgs., 5½×8½, photocopied on white or colored paper and saddle-stapled with paper cover, b&w drawings, includes ads. They receive a lot of poems, accept "what we dig." Press run is 150 for 32 subscribers. Subscription: $20, includes issues of *Threesome* and one chapbook. Sample: $3. Make checks payable to Joe Musso

How to Submit: Submit a few pieces at a time. Previously published poems and simultaneous submissions OK, if notified. Cover letter preferred. Responds ASAP. Comments on rejections only if asked. Don't send for guidelines. "I like everything except rhyme. Send work you believe in. If I believe in it too, I'll print it." Pays 1 copy.

Book/Chapbook Needs & How to Submit: *By invitation only.* "But if you think you've got something I can't turn away, give me a shot. Chances are slim, but I'll give it a look."

Also Offers: "We also publish *Threesome*, featuring two writers and one artist in each issue. At a slim 12 pages, it is a taut, easy-to-circulate forum spot-lighting several pieces at a time, by an individual, allowing a more comprehensive display of one's creative output." Sample: $1 and one first-class stamp. Included in subscription to *HELLP!*

Advice: "Don't make the mistake of writing for anyone but yourself. If you feel it, others will too. Be kind to animals. And, as always, don't eat the yellow snow."

$ ◎ HERALD PRESS; PURPOSE; STORY FRIENDS; ON THE LINE; WITH; CHRISTIAN LIV-ING (Specialized: religious, children), 616 Walnut Ave., Scottdale PA 15683-1999, phone (724)887-8500. Send submissions or queries directly to the editor of the specific magazine at address indicated.

Magazine Needs & How to Submit: *Herald Press*, the official publisher for the Mennonite Church in North America, seeks also to serve a broad Christian audience. Each of the magazines listed has different specifications, and the editor of each should be queried for more exact information. *Purpose*, editor James E. Horsch, a "religious young adult/adult monthly in weekly parts," circulation 13,000, its focus: "action oriented, discipleship living." It is 5⅜×8⅜, with two-color printing throughout. They buy appropriate poetry up to 12 lines. *Purpose* uses 3-4 poems/week, receives about 2,000/year of which they use 150, has a 10- to 12-week backlog. Send SASE for guidelines and free sample. Mss should be typewritten, double-spaced, one side of sheet only. Simultaneous submissions OK. Responds in 2 months. Pays $7.50-20/poem plus 2 copies. *On the Line*, edited by Mary C. Meyer, a monthly religious magazine, for children 9-14, "that reinforces Christian values," circulation 6,000. Sample free with SASE. Wants poems 3-24 lines. Submit poems "each typed on a separate 8½×11 sheet." Simultaneous submissions and previously published poems OK. Responds in 1 month. Pays $10-25/poem plus 2 copies. *Story Friends*, edited by Rose Mary Stutzman, is for children 4-9, a "monthly magazine that reinforces Christian values," circulation 6,500, uses poems 3-12 lines. Send SASE for guidelines/sample copy. Pays $10. *With*, Editorial Team, Box 347, Newton KS 67114, phone (316)283-5100, is for "senior highs, ages 15-18," focusing on empowering youth to radically commit to a personal relationship with Jesus Christ, and to share God's good news through word and actions." Circulation 4,000, uses a limited amount of poetry. Poems should be 4-50 lines. Pays $10-25. *Christian Living*, edited by Levi Miller, published 8 times/year, is "for family, community and culture," uses poems up to 30 lines. They have published poetry by Julia Kasdorf. As a sample the editor selected these lines from "Sometimes Hope" by Jean Janzen:

> *But sometimes hope/is a black ghost/in a fantastic twist,/an old dream that flickers/in the wind.*

The editor says *Christian Living* is 28-44 pgs., 8×10, 1-3 color with photos and artwork. They receive about 75 poems a year, accept approximately 15-20. Press run is 4,000 for 4,000 subscribers of which 8-10 are libraries, 10-20 shelf sales; 100-300 distributed free. Single copy: $3; subscription: $23.95. Sample free with 9×12 SASE ($1). Make checks payable to *Christian Living*. Submit 3-5 poems at a time. Previously published poems and simultaneous submissions OK. Cover letter preferred with information about previous publications. Time between acceptance and publication is 2-14 months. Seldom comments on rejections. Publishes theme issues. Send SASE for guidelines. Responds within 6 months. Pays $1/line plus 2 copies. Buys first or one-time rights. Staff reviews books or chapbooks of poetry in 200-800 words. Poets may also send books for review consideration.

✓ ▣ ◯ ◎ THE HERB NETWORK (Specialized: herbs), P.O. Box 752, Alpharetta GA 30009, e-mail editor@herbnetwork.com, website www.herbnetwork.com, founded 1995, editor Kathleen O'Mara.

Magazine Needs: *The Herb Network* is a quarterly newsletter of information for herbal enthusiasts. They want poetry related to herbs or plants—real or folklore. Short poems to 250 words. Also accepts poetry written by children. They have published poetry by Nancy L'enz and Anne Wilson. As a sample the editor selected "Dandelions" by Elizabeth Willis DeHuff:

> *Slim little girls with green flounced dresses,/Dandelions stand with yellow shaggy hair./Soon they grow*
> *to gray haired ladies,/Whose locks sail away through the air./Ashamed of their baldness, each of these*
> *dears,/Fringes a cap which she always wears.*

The newsletter is 16 pgs., 8½×11, neatly printed on plain white paper with a few b&w graphics. The issue we received included recipes, information about herbs used by midwives, an article focusing on lavender, book reviews and classified ads. Press run is 5,500 for 5,000 subscribers. Subscription: $35/year; student rate; $27/year; international: $45/year.

How to Submit: "Contact first with short query before submitting material." Submit up to 3 poems at a time, typed double-spaced, one poem/page, name and address on each. Line length for poems is 25 maximum. Pre-

viously published poems and simultaneous submissions OK. Submissions via e-mail OK. Submit in body of message. Cover letter preferred. Send e-mail or SASE for guidelines. Publishes theme issues. Send SASE for guidelines. Responds in 6 months. Sometimes sends prepublication galleys. Pays with 1 copy and 2 tearsheets and by barter, offering free advertisements or copies or $1-5 as budget allows. Acquires first or one-time rights.
Also Offers: Website includes writer's guidelines, membership information, articles and an interview with the editor.

○ **HEY, LISTEN!; SEAWEED SIDESHOW CIRCUS**, 3820 Miami Rd., Apt. 3, Cincinnati OH 45227, phone (513)271-2214, e-mail sscircus@aol.com, website hometown.aol.com/SSCircus/sscweb.html, founded 1994, editor Andrew Wright Milam.
Magazine Needs: *Hey, listen!* is an annual "small press magazine created to bring personal response back into publishing." They are open to all poetry, except rhyme. They have published poetry by Jim Daniels, Susan Firer, James Liddy and Sarah Fox. As a sample the editor selected these lines from "he found being in love/more difficult than driving/52 hours home" by Erich Ebert:

> no one wants to be sad/from saying "in 52 hours I'll be home."/especially since we should be/asking
> someone "Do the leaves change/when I touch your skin?"

The editor says *Hey, listen!* is 30 pgs., magazine-sized, photocopied and saddle-stapled with cardstock cover. They receive about 50-100 poems a year, accept approximately 20-30%. Press run is 100. Subscription: $5/2 years. Sample: $2. Make checks payable to Seaweed Sideshow Circus.
How to Submit: Submit 3-5 poems at a time. No previously published poems or simultaneous submissions. Cover letter preferred. E-mail submissions OK (include in body). Include SASE and name and address on each page. Time between acceptance and publication is 1-2 months. Often comments on rejections. Send SASE for guidelines. Responds in 2 months. Pays 1 copy. Rights revert to author upon publication.
Book/Chapbook Needs & How to Submit: Seaweed Sideshow Circus is "a place for young or new poets to publish a chapbook." They publish 1 chapbook/year. Chapbooks are usually 30 pgs., 8½×5½, photocopied and saddle-stapled with cardstock cover. Send 5-10 sample poems and cover letter with bio and credits. Replies to queries in 1-3 weeks; to mss in 2-3 months. Pays royalties of 50% plus 10 author's copies (out of a press run of 100). Order sample chapbooks by sending $6.

☑ ○ **THE HIGGINSVILLE READER; THE HIGGINSVILLE WRITERS**, P.O. Box 141, Three Bridges NJ 08887, phone (908)788-0514, e-mail hgvreader@yahoo.com, founded 1990, editors Amy Finkenaur, Frank Magalhaes, Kathe Palka.
Magazine Needs: *The Higginsville Reader* is a "quarterly litmag for a general adult audience. *HR* prints poetry, short fiction and essays; also b&w artwork and photographs." They want "work rich in imaginative language. We are open to all forms and styles, accept both very short poems and longer works and are always more concerned with quality than name. We do not want poems that wander without aim, overt sentimentality, assaultive negativism." They have published poetry by Robert Cooperman, Taylor Graham, Bertha Rogers, Russel Rowland and P.E. Steward. As a sample the editor selected these lines from "Ghost Carousel" by Do Gentry:

> Night has become the favorite toy/you've forgotten how to play with./You go to sleep imagining its
> hours/like scuffed wooden horses/turning round and round.

HR is 16 pgs., 7×8½, laser-printed, unbound, b&w artwork and photography inside only—no cover art. They receive about 750-1,000 poems a year, accept approximately 8-10%. Press run is 150-200 for 125 subscribers. Subscription: $5/year. Sample (including guidelines): $1.50. Make checks payable to The Higginsville Writers.
How to Submit: Submit 3-6 poems at a time. Previously published poems ("but prefer new work") and simultaneous submissions (if advised and notified) OK. E-mail submissions OK, as attached Microsoft Word file or plain text in body of message. Time between acceptance and publication is 6-12 months. Poems are circulated to an editorial board. "Two editors (out of three) must agree on a piece for it to be accepted." Seldom comments on rejections. Send SASE for guidelines or obtain via e-mail. Responds in 2 months. Pays 1 copy. Acquires one-time rights.

☑ $ ◎ **HIGH PLAINS PRESS (Specialized: regional)**, P.O. Box 123, Glendo WY 82213, phone (307)735-4370, fax (307)735-4590, website www.highplainspress.com, founded 1985, poetry editor Nancy Curtis.
Book/Chapbook Needs: High Plains considers books of poetry "specifically relating to Wyoming and the West, particularly poetry based on historical people/events or nature. We're mainly a publisher of historical nonfiction, but do publish one book of poetry every year." They have published *Close at Hand* by Mary Lou Sanelli and *Bitter Creek Junction* by Linda Hasselstrom. As a sample the editor selected these lines from "Gathering Mint" from the book *Glass-eyed Paint in the Rain* by Laurie Wagner Buyer:

> He returned at dusk, drunk on solitude, singing/in time with the gelding's rocky trot,/moccasined feet
> wet with mud,/the burlap bag he tossed me/stuffed full of mint/from the beaver slough.

How to Submit: Query first with 3 sample poems (from a 50-poem ms). Fax submissions OK. Responds in 2 months. Time between acceptance and publication is 18-24 months. Always sends prepublication galleys. Pays 10% of sales. Buys first rights. Catalog available on request; sample books: $5.

$ ◎ HIGH/COO PRESS; MAYFLY (Specialized: form), 4634 Hale Dr., Decatur IL 62526, phone (217)877-2966, e-mail brooksbooks@q-com.com, website www.family-net.net/~brooksbooks, founded 1976, editors Randy and Shirley Brooks.

Their books have received the Haiku Society of America Merit Awards.

Magazine Needs: High/Coo is a small press publishing nothing but haiku in English. "We publish haiku poemcards, minichapbooks, anthologies and a bibliography of haiku publications in addition to paperbacks and cloth editions and the magazine *Mayfly*, evoking emotions from contemporary experience. We are not interested in orientalism nor Japanese imitations." They want "well-crafted haiku, with sensual images honed like a carved jewel, to evoke an immediate emotional response as well as a long-lasting, often spiritual, resonance in the imagination of the reader." They publish no poetry except haiku. They have published haiku by Virgil Hutton, Lee Gurga and Wally Swist. *Mayfly* is 16 pgs., 3½×5, professionally printed on high-quality stock, saddle-stapled, one haiku/page. It appears in January and August. They publish 32 of an estimated 1,800 submissions. Subscription: $8. Sample: $4; or send $17 (Illinois residents add 7½% tax) for the *Midwest Haiku Anthology* which includes the work of 54 haiku poets. A Macintosh computer disk of haiku-related stacks is available for $10.

How to Submit: Submit no more than 5 haiku/issue. No previously published poems or simultaneous submissions. E-mail submissions OK. Deadlines are March 15 and October 15. Send SASE for guidelines. Pays $5/poem; no copies.

Book/Chapbook Needs & How to Submit: High/Coo Press considers mss "by invitation only."

Also Offers: Website includes sample poetry, book reviews, featured haiku writers and online collections.

Advice: "Publishing poetry is a joyous work of love. We publish to share those moments of insight contained in evocative haiku. We aren't in it for fame, gain or name. We publish to serve an enthusiastic readership."

☑ ☐ ◎ HIGHLIGHTS FOR CHILDREN (Specialized: children), 803 Church St., Honesdale PA 18431, phone (570)253-1080, fax (570)253-0179, e-mail editorial@highlights-corp.com, founded 1946, contact Rich Wallace.

Magazine Needs: *Highlights* appears every month using poetry for children ages 2-12. They want "meaningful and/or fun poems accessible to children of all ages. Welcome light, humorous verse. Rarely publish a poem longer than 16 lines, most are shorter. No poetry that is unintelligible to children, poems containing sex, violence or unmitigated pessimism." Note: Although *Highlights* is a monthly magazine, they only publish 6-10 poems a year. Also accepts poetry written by children. "We print, but do not purchase, from individuals under age 16." They have published poetry by Bobbi Katz, Myra Cohn Livingston and Carl Sandburg. As a sample the editor selected "No Trespassing" by Nancy West:

> *Moles live below all the ice and the snow/And seldom come up for air./They tunnel and dig, don't get*
> *very big,/And couldn't care less what they wear./They have their own houses—adore their own spouses,/*
> *And don't feel the need to compare./So leave all us moles right down here in our holes—/And mind*
> *your own business up there!*

It is generally 42 pgs., magazine-sized, full-color throughout. They receive about 300 submissions/year, accept 6-10. Press run is 3.3 million for approximately 2.8 million subscribers. Subscription: $29.64/year (reduced rates for multiple years).

How to Submit: Submit typed ms with very brief cover letter. Please indicate if simultaneous submission. Fax submissions OK. Editor comments on submissions "occasionally, if ms has merit or author seems to have potential for our market." Responds "generally within 1 month." Always sends prepublication galleys. Payment: "money varies" plus 2 copies. Buys all rights.

Advice: "We are always open to submissions of poetry not previously published. However, we purchase a very limited amount of such material. We may use the verse as 'filler,' or illustrate the verse with a full-page piece of art. Please note that we do not buy material from anyone under 16 years old."

⊕ ◎ HILLTOP PRESS (Specialized: science fiction), 4 Nowell Place, Almondbury, Huddersfield, West Yorkshire HD5 8PB England, website (online catalog) www.bbr-online.com/catalogue, founded 1966, editor Steve Sneyd.

Book/Chapbook Needs: Hilltop publishes "mainly science fiction poetry nowadays." Publications include *Star-Spangled Shadows* and *Kin To the Far Beyond*, between the two publications they cover poetry in US SFanzines from the 1930s to 1990s, including A-Z of writers/publications and poem extracts; and Fierce Far Suns—Proto-SF&SF Poetry in America: the 1750s to 1960s. As a sample the editor selected these lines from the book *Skip Trace Rocks, poems from inside the heads of blue-collar future Mars terrafarmers*, by Peter Layton:

> *the digi-meters are screaming spinning/I'm tumbled blind chute toward/an orchid sky, banks of liquid*
> *metal/drink vacuum suct from exhaust jets*

THE SUBJECT INDEX, located at the back of this book, can help you select markets for your work. It lists those publishers whose poetry interests are specialized ◎ .

Hilltop titles are distributed in the USA by the New Science Fiction Alliance. For full list of UK publications NSFA distributes, send SAE/IRC to A. Marsden, 31192 Paseo Amapola, San Juan Capistrano CA 92675-2227 or see website.

How to Submit: Does not accept unsolicited mss. Query (with SAE/IRC) with proposals for relevant projects.

Advice: "My advice for beginning poets is (a) persist—don't let any one editor discourage you. 'In poetry's house are many mansions,' what one publication hates another may love; (b) be prepared for long delays between acceptance and appearance of work—the small press is mostly self-financed and part time, so don't expect it to be more efficient than commercial publishers; (c) *always* keep a copy of everything you send out, put your name and address on *everything* you send and *always* include adequately stamped SAE."

🌐 $ ▨ ◎ **HIPPOPOTAMUS PRESS (Specialized: form); OUTPOSTS POETRY QUARTERLY; OUTPOSTS ANNUAL POETRY COMPETITION**, 22 Whitewell Rd., Frome, Somerset BA11 4EL England, phone/fax 01373-466653, *Outposts* founded 1943, Hippopotamus Press founded 1974, poetry editor Roland John.

Magazine Needs: "*Outposts* is a general poetry magazine that welcomes all work either from the recognized or the unknown poet." They want "fairly mainstream poetry. No concrete poems or very free verse." They have published poetry by Jared Carter, John Heath-Stubbs, Lotte Kramer and Peter Russell. As a sample we selected these lines from "The Lotus-Eaters" by Ashleigh John:

> Our lives are one long Sunday, when it rained./There were so many things we might have done—/We
> watched the television-set instead,/And the day ended as it had begun./We are the quick who may as
> well be dead:/The nothing-ventured, and the nothing gained.

Outposts is 60-120 pgs., A5, litho printed and perfect-bound with laminated card cover, includes occasional art and ads. They receive about 46,000 poems a year, accept approximately 1%. Press run is 1,600 for 1,200 subscribers of which 400 are libraries, 400 shelf sales. Single copy: $8; subscription: $26. Sample (including guidelines): $6. Make checks payable to Hippopotamus Press. "We prefer credit cards because of bank charges.

How to Submit: Submit 5 poems at a time. "IRCs must accompany U.S. submissions." No previously published poems; simultaneous submissions OK. Disk and fax submissions OK. Cover letter required. Time between acceptance and publications is 9 months. Seldom comments on rejections, "only if asked." Publishes theme issue, occasionally. Send SASE (or SAE and IRC) for upcoming themes. Responds in 2 weeks plus post time. Sometimes sends prepublication galleys. Pays £8/poem plus 1 copy. Copyright remains with author. Staff reviews books of poetry in 200 words for "Books Received" page. Also uses full essays up to 4,000 words. Send books for review consideration, attn. M. Pargitter.

Book/Chapbook Needs & How to Submit: Hippopotamus Press publishes 6 books a year. "The Hippopotamus Press is specialized, with an affinity with Modernism. No Typewriter, Concrete, Surrealism." For book publication query with sample poems. Simultaneous submissions and previously published poems OK. Responds in 6 weeks. Pays 7½-10% royalties plus author's copies. Send for book catalog to buy samples.

Also Offers: The magazine also holds an annual poetry competition.

▣ ○ ◪ **HIRAM POETRY REVIEW**, P.O. Box 162, Hiram OH 44234, founded 1967, poetry editor Hale Chatfield.

Magazine Needs: *HPR* is an annual publication appearing in October. "We favor new talent—and except for one issue every three to four years, read only unsolicited mss." They are interested in "all kinds of high quality poetry" and have published poetry by Grace Butcher, David Citino, Michael Finley, Peter Wild, Jim Daniels, Peter Klappert and Harold Witt. *Hiram Poetry Review* is now a multimedia CD-Rom for Windows or Macintosh computers. The CD-Rom is enclosed in a 5½×8½ binder with printed supplement of poetry text. Circulation is 400 for 300 subscriptions of which 150 are libraries. They receive about 5,000 submissions/year, use 20, have up to a 6-month backlog. Although most poems appearing here tend to be lyric and narrative free verse under 50 lines, exceptions occur (a few longer, sequence or formal works can be found in each issue). Single copy: $15; subscription: $15. Sample (of printed back issues): $5.

How to Submit: "Send 2-4 of your best poems. We scan poetry text electronically, directly from the typed manuscripts." No simultaneous submissions. Responds in up to 6 months. Pays 2 copies. Acquires first North American serial rights; returns rights upon publication. Reviews books of poetry in single or multi-book format, no set length. Send books for review consideration.

🌐 $ ◪ **HOBO POETRY & HAIKU MAGAZINE; HOBO PUBLISHERS, INC.**, P.O. Box 166, Hazelbrook NSW 2779 Australia, founded 1993, editor Dane Thwaites.

Magazine Needs: *Hobo* appears quarterly and publishes "poems, haiku, articles and reviews relating to both. All kinds of poetry considered. Very rigorous standards are applied." They have published poetry by Eric Beach and Colleen Burke. As a sample the editor selected these lines from "postcards from lounge lizard isle" by Joanne Burns:

> interior decoration runs through her fingertips/like a frisson through a thigh, the way a design/concept
> flows through the whole envelope of an/apartment, loft style, art deco, or harbourside/high rise, the
> way lift out self enhancement runs/through the glossy print of a lifestyle magazine . . .

Hobo is 68 pgs., digest-sized, offset printed and saddle-stapled with paper cover. They receive about 4,000 poems a year, accept approximately 2%. Press run is 750. Subscription: $20 AUS/$30 US/$25 NZ. Sample: $5.50 AUS/ $7 others. Make checks payable to Inkstream.

How to Submit: Submit up to 6 poems at a time. No previously published poems or simultaneous submissions. Cover letter preferred. SASE (or SAE and IRC) required. Time between acceptance and publication is about 6 weeks. Send SASE for guidelines. Responds in 6 weeks on average. Pays $12/page. Buys one-time rights. Staff reviews books and chapbooks of poetry and other magazines, single book format. Open to unsolicited reviews. Poets may also send books for review consideration.

$ ☐ ☐ ◎ HODGEPODGE SHORT STORIES & POETRY (Specialized: subscribers), P.O. Box 6003, Springfield MO 65801, e-mail fictionpub@aol.com, website http://members.aol.com/fictionpub/hppub.ht ml, founded 1994, editor Vera Jane Goodin, contact poetry editor.

Magazine Needs: *Hodgepodge* appears quarterly to "provide a showcase for new as well as established poets and authors; to promote writing and offer encouragement." They are open to all kinds of poetry. Also accepts poetry written by children (but makes no special allowance for them). They have published poetry by Delphine LeDoux and Tom Padgett. As a sample the editor selected these lines from "The Toddler We Knew" by Carol Meeks:

> *A toddler, short in years;/the salute, engraved/into the minds of a nation*

The editor says *Hodgepodge* is a 24- to 32-page chapbook, photocopied and saddle-stitched with self cover, includes clip art. They receive about 100 poems a year, accept approximately 50%. Press run is about 100 for about 100 subscribers. Single copy: $3; subscription: $10. Sample: $1. Make checks payable to Goodin Communications. "Potential contributors either need to purchase a copy or be annual subscribers."

How to Submit: Submit up to 4 poems at a time. Previously published poems and simultaneous submissions OK. SASE required for return of poems. Time between acceptance and publication is 2 months. Seldom comments on rejections. Publishes theme issues occasionally. Send SASE for guidelines and upcoming themes. Responds in 2 months. Pays $1/poem. Acquires one-time rights. Staff reviews books and chapbooks of poetry and other magazines in 250 words, single and multi-book format. Send books for review consideration to Review Editor.

Also Offers: Sponsors a Best-of-the-Year Contest. Any poem published in *Hodgepodge* is eligible for the contest. 1st Place $30, 2nd Place $15, 3rd Place free subscription. Also awards honorable mentions and certificates. "Judging is done by staff, but readers are asked for input." Sponsors the Sunny Edition contest; deadline: June 30, 2001—poems and short stories that are uplifting, touching or funny. Reading fee of $5 covers up to 3 entries. Awards: work published and 1st Place: $25, 2nd Place: $10, 3rd Place: $6, 4th and 5th Place: certificates. Published in fall. Also co-sponsors the annual Poetry From Planet Pissantium International Contest. Send SASE for details.

◖ ◎ HOLIDAY HOUSE, INC. (Specialized: children), 425 Madison Ave., New York NY 10017, founded 1936, editor-in-chief Regina Griffin, is a trade children's book house. They have published hardcover books for children by Myra Cohn Livingston and John Updike. They publish 1 poetry book a year averaging 32 pages. The editor says, "the acceptance of complete book manuscripts of high-quality children's poetry is limited." Send a query with SASE before submitting.

$ ◙ THE HOLLINS CRITIC, P.O. Box 9538, Hollins University, Roanoke VA 24020-1538, phone (540)362-6275, website www.hollins.edu/academics/critic, founded 1964, editor R.H.W. Dillard.

Magazine Needs: *THC*, appears 5 times/year, publishing critical essays, poetry and book reviews. They use a few short poems in each issue, interesting in form, content or both. They have published poetry by John Engels, Lyn Lifshin, George Garrett, Dara Wier. As a sample the editor selected these lines from "Carving the Salmon" by John Engels:

> *And then it is recognizable, a fish,/and ready for finishing. It quivers//a little at the skew chisel, flinches/ at the spoonbit. With the straight gouge/I give it eyes, and with the veiner, gills,//and it leaps a little in my hand.*

The Hollins Critic is 24 pgs., magazine-sized. Circulation is 500. Subscription: $6/year ($7.50 outside US). Sample: $1.50.

How to Submit: Submit up to 5 poems, must be typewritten with SASE, to Cathryn Hankla, poetry editor. Responds in 6 weeks (slower in the summer). Pays $25/poem plus 5 copies.

◙ HENRY HOLT & COMPANY, 115 W. 18th St., New York NY 10011, accepts no unsolicited poetry.

ℕ ◙ HOME PLANET NEWS, Box 415, Stuyvesant Station, New York NY 10009, founded 1979, co-editor Enid Dame, co-editor Donald Lev.

Magazine Needs: *Home Planet News* appears 3 times a year. "Our purpose is to publish lively and eclectic poetry, from a wide range of sensibilities, and to provide news of the small press and poetry scenes, thereby fostering a sense of community among contributors and readers." They want "honest, well-crafted poems, open or closed form, on any subject. Poems under 30 lines stand a better chance. We do not want any work which seems to us to be racist, sexist, agist, anti-Semitic or imposes limitations on the human spirit." They have published poetry by Layle Silbert, Robert Peters, Lyn Lifshin and Gerald Locklin. As a sample the editor selected these lines from "Milk" by Barry Wallenstein:

> *In my tired hand—milk/in my memory—it glows/a white shadow/smear around my younger mouth/ around what I used to know*

HPN is a 24-page tabloid, web offset printed, includes b&w drawings, photos, cartoons and ads. They receive about 1,000 poems a year, accept approximately 3%. Press run is 1,000 for 300 subscribers. Subscription: $10/ 4 issues, $18/8 issues. Sample: $3.

How to Submit: Submit 3-6 poems at a time. No previously published poems or simultaneous submissions. Cover letter preferred. "SASEs are a must." Reads submissions February 1 through May 31 only. Time between acceptance and publication is 1 year. Seldom comments on rejections. Publishes theme issues occasionally. "We announce these in issues." Send SASE for guidelines. "However, it is usually best to simply send work." Responds in 4 months. Pays 1-year gift subscription plus 3 copies. Acquires first rights. All rights revert to author on publication. Reviews books and chapbooks of poetry and other magazines in 1,200 words, single and multi-book format. Open to unsolicited reviews. Poets may also send books for review consideration to Enid Dame. "Note: we do have guidelines for book reviewers; please write for them. Magazines are reviewed by a staff member."

Advice: "Read many publications, attend readings, feel yourself part of a writing community, learn from others."

$ ☐ ◯ HOME TIMES, 3676 Collins Dr. #12, West Palm Beach FL 33406, phone (561)439-3509, website www.hometimes.org, founded 1988, editor/publisher Dennis Lombard.

Magazine Needs: *Home Times* is a monthly "independent, conservative, pro-Christian, pro-Jewish," 24-page newsprint tabloid of local, national and world news and views, including information in the areas of home and family, arts and entertainment, and religion. *HT* tries not to moralize but to just be positive and Biblical in perspective. Our goal is to publish godly viewpoints in the marketplace, and to counteract the culturally elite of media and politics who reject Judao-Christian values, traditional American values, true history, and faith in God." They want poetry that is "short or humorous or spiritual—not 'religious'; for a general audience. Prefer traditional or light verse up to 16 lines." Also accepts poetry written by children. They receive about 200 poems a year, accept 5%. Press run is 5,000. Single copy: $1.50. Samples: $3 for 2 current issues.

How to Submit: Submit 3 poems at a time. Previously published poems and simultaneous submissions OK. Time between acceptance and publication is 1-6 months. Sometimes comments on rejections. Send SASE for guidelines. Responds in 1 month. Pays $5 "generally" or a 6-month subscription, if requested. Buys one-time rights.

Advice: "*Home Times* is very different! Please read guidelines and sample issues." Also, the editor has written a 12-chapter report for new writers entitled "101 Reasons Why I Reject Your Mss"—which is "an effective training course for new freelancers, easy to understand and written with lots of humor."

✓ $ ◎ HOPSCOTCH: THE MAGAZINE FOR GIRLS; BOYS' QUEST (Specialized: children, themes), P.O. Box 164, Bluffton OH 45817-0164, phone (419)358-4610, fax (419)358-5027, website www.hops cotchmagazine.com or www.boysquest.com, founded 1989, editor Marilyn B. Edwards, associate editor Virginia Edwards.

Magazine Needs: *Hopscotch* is a bimonthly magazine for girls 6-12. "In need of short traditional poems for various holidays and seasons. (Limit to 21 lines if possible, 700-1,000 words.) However, we do not want Halloween-related material. Nothing abstract, experimental." The few poems in this children's magazine occasionally address the audience, challenging young girls to pursue their dreams. To see how, order a sample copy (or check one out at the library) because it is too easy for poets who write children's verse to forget that each magazine targets a specific theme . . . in a specific way. They have published poetry by Lois Grambling, Judy Nichols, Leila Dornak, Judith Harkham Semas and Maggie McGee. The editor describes *Hopscotch* as "full-color cover, 50 pgs. of 2-color inside, 7×9, saddle-stapled." They use about 30-35 of some 2,000 poems received/year. Press run is 16,000 for 10,000 subscribers of which 7,000 are libraries, 200 to inquiring schools and libraries, 2,000 shelf sales. Subscription: $17.95. Sample: $4, $5 outside US.

How to Submit: Submit 3-6 poems/submission. Cover letter preferred; include experience and where published. Publishes theme issues. Send SASE for upcoming themes. Themes include Bugs (August/September 2000), Poetry (October/November 2000), Sisters (December 2000/January 2001), Pets (February/March 2001), Rabbits (April/May 2001), Inventions (June/July 2001), Different Schools (August/September 2001). Responds in 1 month. Pays $10-40. Buys first North American serial rights.

Magazine Needs & How to Submit: They also publish *Boys' Quest*, a bimonthly magazine for boys 6-13. Similar in format to *Hopscotch*, the magazine premiered in June/July 1995. Upcoming themes include: Astronomy (August/September 2000), Unique & Unusual (October/November 2000), Winter Sports (December 2000/January 2001), Trains (February/March 2001), Flying & Planes (August/September 2001), Boats (December 2001/January 2002). Send SASE for details. Sample: $3.95, $4.95 outside US.

🌐 ☻ HORIZON, Stationsstraat 232A, 1770 Liedekerke, Belgium, founded 1985, editor Johnny Haelterman.

Magazine Needs & How to Submit: *Horizon*, published annually in December, is a "cultural magazine with prose and illustrations, in Dutch and a few pages in English." Preference is given to "poems with punctuation, metre and rhyme but that is not a hard and fast rule. If a poem is not published after a year, it means that it couldn't be used. *Horizon* takes poems only as a filler." They have published poetry by Lawrence Schimel, Marci Del Mastro, Michael Pendragon and David Aivaz. The editor says *Horizon* is 29.7×21cm, "reprographic," saddle-stapled with color cover. They receive about 50 poems (in English), used 4 in 1999. Press run is 120. Single copy: $10. Pays 1 copy.

N ◯ **HORSE LATITUDES PRESS**, P.O. Box 294, Rhododendron OR 97049, phone (503)622-4798, founded 1982, publisher Michael P. Jones.
Book/Chapbook Needs: The publisher of Horse Latitudes Press says, "Those which are unique—poetry, short stories, manuscripts, etc.—can find a home with us." They publish 15 paperbacks, 5 hardbacks and 25 chapbooks per year. Books are usually 50-125 pgs., 5½×8½ or 8½×11, offset printed, perfect-bound and Veloboard, includes b&w art/graphics.
How to Submit: Query first, with sample poems ("the more the better") and cover letter with brief bio and publication credits. Previously published poems and simultaneous submissions OK. Cover letter preferred. Poems are circulated to an editorial board. "They are read by a panel of 3. If we like them, we'll try to find a slot for them in a project." Seldom comments on rejections. Replies to queries in 2 weeks. Pays 5 author's copies (out of a press run of 500). Order sample books by writing and requesting a list with prices.
Advice: "We need enough poems to conduct a review of your work, so please send us enough samples."

$ ◯ **HOUGHTON MIFFLIN CO.**, 222 Berkeley St., Boston MA 02116, founded 1850.
Book/Chapbook Needs: Houghton Mifflin is a high-prestige trade publisher that puts out both hardcover and paperback books. They have published poetry books by Donald Hall, May Swenson, Rodney Jones, Geoffrey Hill, Galway Kinnell, Thomas Lux, Erica Funkhouser, William Matthews, Margaret Atwood, Linda Gregerson, Mary Oliver, Glyn Maxwell and Andrew Hudgins.
How to Submit: *Poetry submission is by invitation only* and they are not seeking new poets at present. Always sends prepublication galleys. Authors are paid 10% royalties on hardcover books, 6% royalties on paperbacks (minimum), $1,000 advance and 12 author's copies.

♣ $ ◯ ◎ **HOUSE OF ANANSI PRESS (Specialized: regional)**, 34 Lesmill Rd., Toronto, Ontario M3B 2T6 Canada, phone (416)445-3333, fax (416)445-5967, e-mail info@anansi.ca, website www.anansi.ca, founded 1967, publisher Martha Sharpe, assistant editor Adrienne Leahey.
Book/Chapbook Needs: House of Anansi publishes literary fiction and poetry by Canadian writers. "We seek to balance the list between well-known and emerging writers, with an interest in writing by Canadians of all backgrounds. We publish Canadian poetry only, and poets must have a substantial publication record—if not in books, then definitely in journals and magazines of repute. No children's poetry and no poetry by previously unpublished poets." They have published *Power Politics* by Margaret Atwood and *More Watery Still* by Patricia Young. As a sample they selected these lines from "The Ecstasy of Skeptics" in the book *The Ecstasy of Skeptics* by Steven Heighton:

> *This tongue/is a moment of moistened dust, it must learn/to turn the grit of old books/into hydrogen,*
> *and burn/The dust of the muscles must burn/down the blood-fuse of the sinews, . . .*

Their books are generally 96-144 pgs., trade paperback with French sleeves, a matte finish cover and full-color cover art.
How to Submit: Canadian poets should query first with 10 sample poems (typed double-spaced) and a cover letter with brief bio and publication credits. Previously published poems and simultaneous submissions OK. Poems are circulated to an editorial board. Often comments on rejections. Replies to queries within 3 months, to mss (if invited) within 4 months. Pays 8-10% royalties, a $750 advance and 10 author's copies (out of a press run of 1,000).
Also Offers: Website includes submission guidelines, front list, back list, contact info.
Advice: To learn more about their titles, check their website or write to the press directly for a catalog. "We strongly advise poets to build up a publishing résumé by submitting poems to reputable magazines and journals. This indicates three important things to us: One, that he or she is becoming a part of the Canadian poetry community; two, that he or she is building up a readership through magazine subscribers; and three, it establishes credibility in his or her work. There is a great deal of competition for only three or four spots on our list each year—which always includes works by poets we have previously published."

⊕ ◖ ◗ **HQ POETRY MAGAZINE (THE HAIKU QUARTERLY); THE DAY DREAM PRESS**, 39 Exmouth St., Kingshill, Swindon, Wiltshire SN1 3PU England, phone 01793-523927, founded 1990, editor Kevin Bailey.
Magazine Needs: *HQ* is "a platform from which new and established poets can speak and/or experiment with new forms and ideas." They want "any poetry of good quality." Also accepts poetry written by children. They have published poetry by Peter Redgrove, Alan Brownjohn, James Kirkup and Cid Corman. The editor says *HQ* is 48-64 pgs., A5, perfect-bound with art, ads and reviews. They accept approximately 5% of poetry received. Press run is 500-600 for 500 subscribers of which 30 are libraries. Subscription: £10 UK, £13 foreign. Sample: £2.70.

How to Submit: No previously published poems or simultaneous submissions. Cover letter and SASE (or SAE and IRCs) required. Time between acceptance and publication is 3-6 months. Often comments on rejections. Responds "as time allows." Pays 1 copy. Reviews books of poetry in about 1,000 words, single book format. Open to unsolicited reviews. Poets may also send books for review consideration.

Also Offers: Sponsors "Piccadilly Poets" in London, and "Live Poet's Society" based in Bath, Somerset England. Website includes poetry from past and present issues of *HQ*.

🌐 $ ⊘ ◎ **HU (HONEST ULSTERMAN) (Specialized: regional)**, 49 Main St., Greyabbey, County Down BT22 2NF United Kingdom, founded 1968, editor Tom Clyde.

Magazine Needs: *HU* is a literary magazine appearing 3-4 times a year using "technically competent poetry and prose and book reviews. Special reference to Northern Irish and Irish literature. Lively, humorous, adventurous, outspoken." They have published poetry by Seamus Heaney, Paul Muldoon, Gavin Ewart, Craig Raine, Fleur Adcock and Medbh McGuckian. As a sample the editor selected these lines from "Badger With Ursa Minor" by Frankie McGurk:

> You can see this fire in a badger's eyes,/it blazes in the white of his mask./The pole star is in his nose./
> With a bouncing gait/he moves through space/in the vast and fertile/galaxy of a field.

HU is 128 pgs., A5 (digest-sized), photolithographic, phototypeset, perfect-bound with photographs and line drawings and loose, inserted ads with an "occasional color cover." Press run is 1,000 for 350 subscribers. Subscription: $30. Sample: $10.

How to Submit: "Potential contributors are strongly advised to read the magazine before submitting their work." Submit 6 poems at a time. Editor comments on submissions "occasionally." Publishes theme issues. Send SAE and IRCs for upcoming themes. Pays "a nominal fee" plus 2 copies. Reviews books of literary and cultural interest in 500-1,000 words, single or multi-book format. Open to unsolicited reviews. Poets may also send books for review consideration.

Also Offers: They also publish occasional poetry pamphlets, and a separate index ($15).

✪ **HUBBUB, VI GALE AWARD; ADRIENNE LEE AWARD**, 5344 SE 38th Ave., Portland OR 97202, founded 1983, editors L. Steinman and J. Shugrue.

Magazine Needs: Appearing once a year (in July/August), *Hubbub* is designed "to feature a multitude of voices from interesting contemporary American poets. We look for poems that are well-crafted, with something to say. We have no single style, subject or length requirement and, in particular, will consider long poems. No light verse." They have published poetry by Madeline DeFrees, Cecil Giscombe, Carolyn Kizer, Primus St. John, Shara McCallum and Alice Fulton. The editors describe *Hubbub* as 60-65 pgs., 5½ × 8½, offset printed and perfect-bound, cover art only, usually no ads. They receive about 1,200 submissions/year, use approximately 2%. Press run is 350 for 100 subscribers of which 12 are libraries, about 150 shelf sales. Subscription: $5/year. Sample: $3.35 (back issues), $5 (current issue).

How to Submit: Submit 3-6 typed poems (no more than 6) with SASE. No previously published poems or simultaneous submissions. Send SASE for guidelines. Responds in 4 months. Pays 2 copies. Acquires first North American serial rights. "We review two to four poetry books a year in short (three-page) reviews; all reviews are solicited. We do, however, list books received/recommended." Send books for consideration.

Also Offers: Outside judges choose poems from each volume for two awards: Vi Gale Award ($100) and Adrienne Lee Award ($50). There are no special submission procedures or entry fees involved.

✔ $ ✪ **THE HUDSON REVIEW**, 684 Park Ave., New York NY 10021, contact Emily D. Montjoy.

  ✪ Work published in this review has been included in the 1997 and 1998 volumes of *The Best American Poetry*.

Magazine Needs: *The Hudson Review* is a high-quality, flat-spined quarterly of 176 pgs., considered one of the most prestigious and influential journals in the nation. Editors welcome all styles and forms. However, competition is extraordinarily keen, especially since poems compete with prose. Subscription: $28 ($32 foreign)/ 1 year, institutions $34 ($38 foreign)/1 year. Sample: $8.

How to Submit: Nonsubscribers may submit poems between April 1 and July 31 only. "Simultaneous submissions are returned unread." Responds in 2 months. Always sends prepublication galleys. Pays 2 copies and 50¢/ line.

◖ **HUNGER MAGAZINE; HUNGER PRESS**, P.O. Box 505, Rosendale NY 12472, phone (914)658-9273, fax (914)658-7044 (5**), e-mail hungermag@aol.com, founded 1997, publisher/editor J.J. Blickstein.

Magazine Needs: *Hunger Magazine* is an international zine based in the Hudson Valley and appears 2 times a year (January and June). "*Hunger* publishes mostly poetry but will accept some short fiction, essays, translations, cover art drawings and book reviews. Although there are no school/stylistic limitations, our main focus is on language-image experimentation with an edge. We publish no names for prestige and most of our issues are dedicated to emerging talent. Well known poets do grace our pages to illuminate possibilities. No dead kitty elegies; Beat impersonators; Hallmark cards; 'I'm not sure if I can write poems'. All rhymers better be very, very good. We have published poetry by Amiri Baraka, Paul Celan, Robert Kelly, Ray Gonzalez, Anne Waidman, Janine Pommy Vega and Lyn Lifshin. *Hunger* is 52-80 pgs., magazine-sized, saddle-stitched with glossy full-color card cover, uses original artworks and drawings. They receive about 1,300 poems a year, accept approximately 10%. Press run is 250-500. Single issue: $7, $10 (foreign); subscription: $14, $20 foreign. Back issue: $7. Chapbooks: $5. Make checks payable to Hunger Magazine & Press.

How to Submit: Submit 3-10 poems at a time. No previously published poems; simultaneous submissions OK, if notified. Brief cover letter with SASE preferred. E-mail submissions and queries OK. Query first for attached files. "Manuscripts without SASEs will be recycled. Please proof your work and clearly indicate stanza breaks." Time between acceptance and publication is 1-6 months. Full critiques available for $1 per page/poem (10 pages maximum). Publishes theme issues. Send SASE for guidelines and upcoming themes. Responds in 2 months. Sends prepublication galleys upon request. Pays 1-5 copies depending on amount of work published. "If invited to be a featured poet we pay a small honorarium and copies." Acquires first North American serial rights.

Also Offers: Sponsors a chapbook contest. Reading fee: $10. Accepting original mss, 25 pgs. maximum between January and May only. Chapbooks are 5½×8½, photocopied, saddle-stitched with full color card stock cover. Pays $25-50 and at least 20% of press run. Send SASE or e-mail for guidelines. Chapbooks from Richard Rizzi (*the monkey in his body; the highest paid gun in America*) and Susan G. McKechnie (*The Sailor Poems*) are available for $4.

Advice: "Read, read, read."

THE HUNTED NEWS; THE SUBOURBON PRESS, P.O. Box 9101, Warwick RI 02889, phone (401)826-7307, founded 1990, editor Mike Wood.

Magazine Needs: *The Hunted News* is an annual "designed to find good writers and give them one more outlet to get their voices heard." As for poetry, the editor says, "The poems that need to be written are those that need to be read." They do not want to see "the poetry that does not need to be written or which is written only to get a reaction or congratulate the poet." Also accepts poetry written by children. The editor says *THN* is 25-30 pgs., 8½×11, photocopied, unstapled. "I receive over 200 poems per month and accept perhaps 10%." Press run is 150-200. Sample free with SASE.

How to Submit: Previously published poems OK; no simultaneous submissions. E-mail submissions OK. Always comments on rejections. Publishes theme issues. Send SASE for guidelines and upcoming themes. Responds in 1 month. Pays 3-5 copies, more on request. "I review current chapbooks and other magazines and do other random reviews of books, music, etc. Word count varies."

Advice: "I receive mostly beginner's poetry that attempts to be too philosophical, without much experience to back up statements, or self-impressed 'radical' poems by poets who assume that I will publish them because they are beyond criticism. I would like poets to send work whose point lies in language and economy and in experience, not in trite final lines, or worse, in the arrogant cover letter."

HURRICANE ALICE (Specialized: feminist), Dept. of English, Rhode Island College, Providence RI 02908, phone (401)456-8377, fax (401)456-8379, e-mail mreddy@ric.edu, founded 1983, submissions manager Joan Dagle.

Magazine Needs: *Hurricane Alice* is a quarterly feminist review. Poems should be "infused by a feminist sensibility (whether the poet is female or male)." Also accepts poetry written by children. They have published poetry by Alice Walker, Ellen Bass, Patricia Hampl, Nellie Wong, Edith Kur and Barbara Hendryson. As a sample the editor selected these lines from "The Gift" by Marjorie Roemer:

> I would give you my right hand/My mother always said/Too many times/As if she really wanted to/As if she needed to.

The magazine is a "12-page folio with plenty of graphics." Press run is 500-1,000, of which 350 are subscriptions and about 50 go to libraries. Subscription: $12 (or $10 low-income). Sample: $2.50.

How to Submit: Submit no more than 3 poems at a time. Considers simultaneous submissions. Time between acceptance and publication is 3-6 months. Publishes theme issues. Send SASE for upcoming themes. Responds in 1 year. Pays 6 copies. Reviews books of poetry.

IBBETSON ST. PRESS, 33 Ibbetson St., Somerville MA 02143, phone (617)628-2313, founded 1999, editor Doug Holder, co-editor Dianne Robitaille, art editor Richard Wilhelm.

Magazine Needs: Appearing 3 times a year, *Ibbetson St. Press* is "a poetry magazine that wants 'down to earth' poetry that is well-written; has clean, crisp images; with a sense of irony and humor. We want mostly free verse, but open to rhyme. Poetry with vivid images, irony and humor. No maudlin, trite, overly political, vulgar for vulgar's sake, poetry that tells but doesn't show." They have published poetry by Dianne Robitaille, Robert K. Johnson, Joanne Holdridge, Don Divecchio and Ed Chaberek. As a sample the editors selected these lines by Ed Chaberek:

> It's down a curving brick/stair, where the cool beer-stale/air gets thick; it's past/the piss-stains and the cracks/left by some wise guy's skull.

THE GEOGRAPHICAL INDEX, located at the back of this book, can help you discover the publishers in your region. Publishers often favor poets (and work) from their own areas.

ISP is 30 pgs., 8½×11, desktop-published with plastic binding and cream cover stock cover, includes b&w prints and classified ads. They receive about 300 poems a year, accept approximately 40%. Press run is 100 for 20 subscribers. Single copy: $4; subscription: $7. Sample: $2. Make checks payable to Ibbetson St. Press.

How to Submit: Submit 3-5 poems at a time. Previously published poems and simultaneous submissions OK. Cover letter required. Time between acceptance and publication is 3-5 months. Poems are circulated to an editorial board. "Three editors comment on submissions." Send SASE for guidelines. Responds in 2 weeks. Pays 1 copy. Acquires one-time rights. Reviews books and chapbooks of poetry and other magazines in 250-500 words. Open to unsolicited reviews. Poets may also send books for review consideration.

Book/Chapbook Needs & How to Submit: "We also publish chapbooks by newer, little exposed poets of promise. In some cases we pay for all expenses, in others the poet covers publishing expenses." Chapbooks are usually 20-30 pgs., 8½×11, photocopied with plastic binding, white coverstock cover, includes b&w prints. "Send complete manuscript for consideration, at least 20-30 poems with or without artwork." Replies to queries in 1 month. Pays 50 author's copies (out of a press run of 100). Order sample books or chapbooks by sending $4.

Advice: "Please buy a copy of the magazine you submit to—support the small press."

☉ THE ICONOCLAST, 1675 Amazon Rd., Mohegan Lake NY 10547-1804, founded 1992, editor/publisher Phil Wagner.

Magazine Needs: *The Iconoclast* is a general interest literary publication appearing 7 times/year. They want "poems that have something to say—the more levels the better. Nothing sentimental, obscure or self-absorbed. Try for originality; if not in thought, than expression. No greeting card verse or noble religious sentiments. Look for the unusual in the usual, parallels in opposites, the capturing of what is unique or often unnoticed in an ordinary, or extraordinary moment. What makes us human—and the resultant glories and agonies. Our poetry is accessible to a thoughtful reading public." They have published poetry by Ben Wilensky, Kevin Meaux and Reeves Marcus. *The Iconoclast* is 32-64 pgs., journal-sized, photo offset on #45 white wove paper, with b&w art, graphics, photos and ads. They receive about 2,000 poems a year, use 3%. Press run is 500-2,000 for 340 subscribers. Subscription: $13 for 8 issues. Double issue: $3. Sample: $2.

How to Submit: Submit 3-4 poems at a time. Previously published poems and simultaneous submissions OK, when noted, though they say "previously published and simultaneous submissions must be demonstrably better than others. No simultaneous publication!" Time between acceptance and publication is 4-12 months. Sometimes comments on rejections. Responds in 1 month. Pays 1 copy per published page or poem, 40% discount on extras. In addition, subscribers receive $2-10 per poem for first North American rights on acceptance. Otherwise, acquires one-time rights. Reviews books of poetry in 250 words, single format.

◎ THE IDIOT (Specialized: humor), 1706 S. Bedford St., Los Angeles CA 90035, e-mail purple-hayes@juno.com, founded 1993, editor Sam Hayes.

Magazine Needs: *The Idiot* is a biannual humor magazine. "We mostly use fiction, articles and cartoons, but will use anything funny, including poetry. Nothing pretentious. We are a magazine of dark comedy. Death, dismemberment, and the Talmud are all subjects of comedy. Nothing is sacred. But it needs to be funny, which brings us to . . . Laughs! I don't want whimsical, I don't want amusing, I don't want some fanciful anecdote about childhood. I mean belly laughs, laughing out loud, fall on the floor funny. If it's cute, give it to your sweetheart or your puppy dog. Length doesn't matter, but most comedy is like soup. It's an appetizer, not a meal. Short is often better. Bizarre, obscure, and/or literary references are often appreciated but not necessary." They have published poetry by Mark Romyn, Dan Medeiros, Ralph Gamelli and Todd Balazic. As a sample the editor selected these lines from "Messiah Complex" by Mark Lafferty:

> *Die once/Die twice/My life was nice.*

The Idiot is 48 pgs., 5½×8½, professionally printed and staple-bound with glossy cover. They receive about 100 submissions a year, accept 3-4. Press run is 300. Single copy: $4. Sample: $5.

How to Submit: Previously published poems and simultaneous submissions OK. E-mail submissions OK if included in body of message. Seldom comments on rejections. Responds in 6 months. Pays 1 copy. Acquires one-time rights.

Advice: "If it ain't funny, don't send it! I mean it! We're talkin' belly laughs, damn it!"

◙ ILLUMINATIONS, AN INTERNATIONAL MAGAZINE OF CONTEMPORARY WRITING, % Dept. of English, College of Charleston, 66 George St., Charleston SC 29424-0001, phone (843)953-1993, fax (843)953-3180, e-mail lewiss@cofc.edu, website www.cofc.edu/~lewis/illums.html, founded 1982, editor Simon Lewis.

Magazine Needs: *Illuminations* is published annually "to provide a forum for new writers alongside already established ones." They are open as to form and style. Do not want to see anything "bland or formally clunky." They have published poetry by Peter Porter, Michael Hamburger, Geri Doran and Anne Born. As a sample the editor selected these lines from "For Stephen Spender" by Louis Bourne:

> *Old romantic, imprisoned in your speech,/Steeled in a world racing to its doom,/We've taken in the news from your compass-points./You've given us some signs that still can teach.*

Illuminations is 64-88 pgs., 8×5, offset printed and perfect-bound with 2-color card cover, includes photos and engravings. They receive about 1,500 poems a year, accept approximately 5%. Press run is 400. Subscription: $20 for 3 issues. Sample: $10.

How to Submit: Submit up to 6 poems at a time. No previously published poems or simultaneous submissions. E-mail and fax submissions OK. Brief cover letter preferred. Time between acceptance and publication "depends on when received. Can be up to a year." Publishes theme issues occasionally. Obtain guidelines via e-mail. Responds within 2 months. Pays 2 copies plus one subsequent issue. Acquires all rights. Returns rights on request.

☑ $ ✿ ◎ **IMAGE: A JOURNAL OF ARTS & RELIGION (Specialized: religious)**, P.O. Box 674, Kennett Square PA 19348, e-mail image@imagejournal.org, website www.imagejournal.org, founded 1989, publisher Gregory Wolfe.

Magazine Needs: *Image*, published quarterly, "explores and illustrates the relationship between faith and art through world-class fiction, poetry, essays, visual art, and other arts." They want "poems that grapple with religious faith, usually Judeo-Christian." They have published poetry by Philip Levine, Scott Cairus, Annie Dillard and Kathleen Norris. As a sample we selected these lines from "Receptionism" by Marjorie Maddox:

> Does our kneeling/bring him down/again, from the wood,/unhinge his stone,/trumpet for ourselves/our catalytic salvation?

Image is 136 pgs., 10×7, perfect-bound, acid free paper with glossy 4-color cover, averages 10 pgs. of 4-color art/issue (including cover), ads. They receive about 800 poems a year, accept approximately 2%. They have 4,700 subscribers of which 100 are libraries. Subscription: $30. Sample: $10.

How to Submit: Submit up to 4 poems at a time. No previously published poems. Cover letter preferred. No e-mail submissions. Time between acceptance and publication is 1 year. Responds in 3 months. Always sends prepublication galleys. Pays 4 copies plus $2/line ($150 maximum). Acquires first North American serial rights. Reviews books of poetry in 1,000-1,300 words, single or multi-book format. Open to unsolicited reviews. Poets may also send books for review consideration.

Also Offers: Website includes sample material from all back issues; info on The Glen Workshop, an annual writers workshop sponsored by *Image*; guidelines; The *Image* Artist of the Month; as well as information on advertising; back issue and subscription ordering.

Ⓝ 🖳 ◎ **IMAGES INSCRIPT**, P.O. Box 44894, Columbus OH 43204-4894, e-mail submit@imagesinscript .com or comments@imagesinscript.com, website www.imagesinscript.com, founded 1998, publisher Roger Baker II, editor Carla Radwanski.

Magazine Needs: *Images Inscript* is a bimonthly online publication "to provide a showcase of poetry and short stories. *Images Inscript* is a place for writers to submit and comment on poetry and interact with other writers. We want to see creative well-written poetry that showcases the writer's talent. We do not want to see excessive use of 'adult' language." They have published poetry by Julie Rogers, Maryann Hazen, David Hunter Sutherland and Cindy O'Connor. As a sample they selected these lines from "Breasts" by Maryann Hazen:

> A man will glance at breasts before/he decides whether or not/to continue on up to the face./Will it be worth the effort? Or not?

They receive about 400 poems a year, accept approximately 15%.

How to Submit: Submit 1 poem at a time. Line length for poetry is 60 maximum. Previously published poems and simultaneous submissions OK. E-mail submissions OK. Cover letter preferred. "Electronic submissions preferred, subject line should read 'Images Inscript submission' with name, address and age included in 75 word maximum biography—sent to submit@imagesinscript.com." Reads submissions in December, February, April, June, August and October only. Time between acceptance and publication is 5 weeks. Seldom comments on rejections. Obtain guidelines via e-mail or website. Responds in 5 weeks. Sometimes sends prepublication galleys. Acquires "right to appear in *Images Inscript*."

Also Offers: Sponsors a yearly contest where the best poetry and short story writers are awarded $50. Website includes writer's guidelines, names of staff, best poem, best short story, subscription information, latest edition and back issues.

Advice: "With the gradual acceptance of online publishings, more quality Internet publications will be established to compete with the traditional print industry."

☑ 🌐 $ ◎ ◎ **IMAGO: NEW WRITING (Specialized: regional)**, School of Media & Journalism, Q.U.T., GPO Box 2434, Brisbane 4001 Queensland, Australia, e-mail imago@gut.edu.au, website www.maj.arts.g ut.edu.au/writing/imago.asp, founded 1988, managing editor Helen Horton.

Magazine Needs: *Imago*, appears three times a year, publishing "the best Australian writing, placing particular emphasis on Queensland writing and culture, but also welcoming submissions from overseas. Poems preferably short—up to about 50 lines, most from 12-25 lines. Our main criterion is good writing." They have published poetry by Tom Shapcott, Peter Rose and Philip Hammial. *Imago* is 160 pgs., digest-sized, with glossy card cover. They accept about 10% of 500 poems from about 150 writers. Press run is 1,000 for 450 subscribers of which 36 are libraries. Subscription: $A25 in Australia; $A40, overseas (airmail). Sample: $A10.50.

How to Submit: Submit 6-8 poems at a time. E-mail submissions OK. "A brief biography (few lines) of the writer accompanying the submission saves time if the work is accepted. We have a Notes on Contributors column." Responds in 6 months. Never sends prepublication galleys "unless specifically asked for by contributor." Pays $A30-40 plus 1 copy. Buys first Australian serial rights. Reviews books of poetry in 600 words—"usually commissioned. Unsolicited reviews would have to be of books relevant to *Imago* (Queensland or writing)." Send books for review consideration.

☑ ☐ ◯ ◓ ◎ IMPLOSION PRESS; IMPETUS (Specialized: erotica, women), 4975 Comanche Trail, Stow OH 44224-1217, phone/fax (330)688-5210, e-mail impetus@aol.com, founded 1984, poetry editor Cheryl Townsend.

Magazine Needs: Publishes *Impetus*, a "somewhat" quarterly literary magazine, chapbooks and special issues. The editor would like to see "strong social protest with raw emotion. Material should be straight from the gut, uncensored and real. Absolutely no nature poetry or rhyme for the sake of rhyme, oriental, or 'Kissy, kissy I love you' poems. Any length as long as it works. All subjects OK, providing there are no 'isms.' *Impetus* is now also publishing annual erotica and all-female issues. Material should reflect these themes." Also accepts poetry written by children. They have published poetry by Ron Androla, Kurt Nimmo, Lyn Lifshin and Lonnie Sherman. The magazine varies in size and is photocopied from typescript, saddle-stapled. Press run is about 1,000, with 300 subscriptions. Subscription: $15 for 4 issues; $20 for 4 issues plus chapbooks. Sample: $5; make checks payable to Implosion Press.

How to Submit: Submit 3-8 poems at a time. The editor says, "I prefer shorter, to-the-point work." Include name and address on each page. Previously published work OK if it is noted when and where. "I always like a cover letter that tells me how the poet found out about my magazine." E-mail submissions OK. Generally a 5-month backlog. Send SASE for guidelines. Usually responds within 4 months. Pays 1 copy. Acquires one-time rights. Reviews books of poetry. Open to unsolicited reviews. Poets may also send books for review consideration.

Also Offers: Implosion Press hosts "The Impecunious Poetry Project" with nationwide readings.

Advice: "Know your market. Request guidelines and/or a sample copy."

☑ ▣ ◯ IMPROVIJAZZATION NATION, 532 Yorkshire, #66, Rochester MI 48307, phone (248)852-4527, e-mail rotcod@tm.net, website http://users.tm.net/rotcod, founded 1991, editor Dick Metcalf.

Magazine Needs: *Improvijazzation Nation* is a webzine "devoted to networking; prime focus is tape/music reviews, includes quite a bit of poetry." They want "experimental, visual impact and non-establishment poetry, no more than 15 lines. No hearts and flowers, shallow, epic." They have published poetry by John M. Bennett, Joan Payne Kincaid and Anthony Lucero. They receive 50-100 poems a year, use approximately 50%.

How to Submit: Submit 3 poems at a time. Previously published poems and simultaneous submissions OK. E-mail submissions preferred. Often comments on rejections. Responds within a week or two. No payment. Reviews books of poetry. Also accepts short essays/commentary on the use of networking to void commercial music markets, as well as material of interest to musical/artist improvisors.

$ ◎ IN THE FAMILY (Specialized: gay/lesbian/bisexual), P.O. Box 5387, Takoma Park MD 20913, phone (301)270-4771, fax (301)270-4660, e-mail lmarkowitz@aol.com, website www.inthefamily.com, founded 1995, fiction editor Helena Lipstadt.

Magazine Needs: *In the Family* is a quarterly "therapy magazine exploring clinical issues for queer people and their families." We're open to anything but it must refer to a gay/lesbian/bisexual theme. No long autobiography. No limericks." They have published poetry by Benjamin Goldberg, Susan Spilecki, Alden Reimonenq and Susan Landers. As a sample the editor selected these lines from "Haiku" by Shoshana T. Daniel:

> Smoke and whiskey sours,/whatever it takes to make/your mouth taste like hers./Idiot splashes/grown
> dumb with her absence. Blue/pool no orange koi./Thumbs shoved under rind/you split the orange.
> Your hands/sting me everywhere

The editor says *In the Family* is 32 pgs., 8½ × 11, offset printed and saddle-stitched with 2-color cover, includes art and ads. They receive about 50 poems a year, accept approximately 10%. Press run is 10,000 for 8,000 subscribers of which 10% are libraries, 5% shelf sales; 10% distributed free to direct mail promos. Subscription: $22. Sample: $5.50. Make checks payable to ITF.

How to Submit: Submit 5 poems at a time. No previously published poems; simultaneous submissions OK. Cover letter required. No e-mail submissions. "Do not attach document. Paste poems into e-mail text." Time between acceptance and publication is 3-4 months. Poems are circulated to an editorial board. "Fiction editor makes recommendations." Publishes theme issues. Responds in 2 months. Always sends prepublication galleys. Pays $25 and 5 copies. Acquires first rights. Reviews books of poetry in 1,000 words, multi-book format. Open to unsolicited reviews. Poets may also send books for review consideration to attn. Reviews.

◑ ◎ IN THE GROVE (Specialized: regional), P.O. Box 16195, Fresno CA 93755, phone (559)442-4600 ext. 8105, fax (559)265-5756, e-mail inthegrove@rocketmail.com, website www.freeyellowcom/members7/lherrick/inthegrove.html, founded 1996, editor Lee Herrick, poetry editor Optimism One.

Magazine Needs: *In the Grove* appears 3 times/year and publishes "short fiction, essays and poetry by new and established writers born or currently living in the Central Valley and throughout California." They want "poetry of all forms and subject matter, no more than three pages in length (each). We seek the originality, distinct voice and craftsmanship of a poem. No greeting card verse or forced rhyme. Be fresh. Take a risk." They have published poetry by Gillian Wegener, Andres Montoya, Amy Uyematsu and Renny Christopher. As a sample the editor selected these lines from "Husk Girl" by M. Jennings:

because when that one slip occurs/as it did/when we were tumbled out as we was/like a weed through the dust of my marionette mouth/I knew what they was thinking/that I'd proved em right

The editors say *ITG* is 80-100 pgs., 5½×8½, photocopied and perfect-bound with heavy card stock cover, 4-5 pgs. of ads. They receive about 500 poems a year, accept approximately 10%. Press run is 150 for 50 subscribers, 75 shelf sales; 25 distributed free to contributors, colleagues. Subscription: $16. Sample: $6.

How to Submit: Submit 3-5 poems at a time. Previously published poems and simultaneous submissions OK. Cover letter preferred. Time between acceptance and publication is 2-4 months. "Poetry editor reads all submissions and makes recommendations to editor, who makes final decisions." Seldom comments on rejections. Send SASE for guidelines. Responds in 3 months. Pays 1 copy. Acquires first or one-time rights. Rights return to poets upon publication.

Also Offers: Website includes writer's guidelines, submission deadlines, samples from recent issues.

IN 2 PRINT MAGAZINE (Specialized: children/teen/young adult, national), P.O. Box 102, Port Colborne, Ontario L3K 5V7 Canada, phone (905)834-1539, fax (905)834-1540, founded 1994, publisher Jean Baird.

Magazine Needs: *In 2 Print*, a national forum for emerging artists, is a quarterly, award-winning, glossy color magazine which promotes and showcases the creativity of young Canadians: the magazine publishes original works by young adults ages 12-21 including poetry, short stories, plays, painting, photography, computer art and cartoons. *In 2 Print* also publishes an eclectic array of interviews and reviews of books, music and theatre." They are open to all forms and styles. "No mush, no gush! No class assignments or work produced to please teachers." As a sample we selected these lines from "angelfish" by Amelinda Berube:

i cast my nets every day,/trying so desperately to capture you,/stars in a winter sky//ever remote, you are also fire/in a hearth i left so long ago to stand/here where everything is gray as ice/sea sky ropes/ whose bite leaves blood on my hands//every day my nets come back/empty—

In 2 Print is 48 pgs., magazine-sized, web offset printed and saddle-stitched with color paper cover, includes b&w and color photos and artwork, ads. They receive about 5,000 poems a year, accept approximately 1%. Press run is 25,000 for 9,000 subscribers of which 300 are libraries, 2,000 shelf sales; balance distributed free to qualified lists. Sample: $4.

How to Submit: Submit 4 poems at a time with SASE (or SAE and IRC). No previously published poems or simultaneous submissions. Cover letter with brief bio required. "Submissions can only be made by the author, artist or photographer. While the magazine is delighted by all the teachers and educators who encourage their students to submit work for publication, the submission must be made by the creator(s) of the work. Bulk submissions from teachers or schools are not accepted." Time between acceptance and publication is 4 months. Poems are circulated to an editorial board. "Peer review to short-list. Short-list goes to six of Canada's finest poets—including Susan Musgrave, Christopher Dewdney, Lorna Crozier, Patrick Lane—for final recommendation." Send SASE (or SAE and IRC) for guidelines. Responds in 4 months. Sometimes sends prepublication galleys. Pays $50. Buys first rights. Reviews books and chapbooks of poetry and other magazines in 500-1,200 words. Open to unsolicited reviews. Poets may also send books for review consideration.

Advice: "Great writers are great readers."

INDIAN HERITAGE PUBLISHING; INDIAN HERITAGE COUNCIL QUARTERLY; NATIVE AMERICAN POETRY ANTHOLOGY (Specialized: ethnic/nationality); P.O. Box 2302, Morristown TN 37816, phone (423)581-4448, founded 1986, CEO Louis Hooban.

Indian Heritage Publishing's Native American Poetry Anthology won first prize in literature from the Green Corn Festival 1999.

Magazine Needs: *Indian Heritage Council Quarterly* devotes 1 issue to poetry with a Native American theme. They want "any type of poetry relating to Native Americans, their beliefs or Mother Earth." They do not want "doggerel." They have published poetry by Running Buffalo and Angela Evening Star Dempsey. As a sample the editor selected these lines from his poem "the Pow-wow":

And listen! You can/hear it/as the drum beats tune in/to the heartbeats of/Mother Earth/giving birth to life/in the center/of the Dance Circle.

IHCQ is 6 pgs., 5½×8½ (8½×11 folded sheet with 5½×8½ insert), photocopied. They receive about 300 poems a year, accept approximately 30%. Press run and number of subscribers vary, 50% shelf sales; 50 distributed free to Indian reservations. Subscription: $10. Sample: "negotiable." Make checks payable to Indian Heritage Council.

How to Submit: Submit up to 3 poems at a time. Previously published poems (author must own rights only) and simultaneous submissions OK. Cover letter required. Time between acceptance and publication is 3 months to 1 year. Poems are circulated to an editorial board. "Our editorial board decides on all publications." Seldom comments on rejections. Charges criticism fees "depending on negotiations." Publishes theme issues. Send SASE for guidelines and upcoming themes. Responds within 3 weeks. Pay is negotiable. Acquires one-time rights. Staff reviews books or chapbooks of poetry or other magazines. Send books for review consideration.

Book/Chapbook Needs & How to Submit: Indian Heritage Publishing publishes chapbooks of Native American themes and/or Native American poets. Format of chapbooks varies. Query first, with a few sample poems and cover letter with brief bio and publication credits. Replies to queries within 3 weeks, varies for mss. Pays 33-50% royalties. Offers subsidy arrangements that vary by negotiations, number of poems, etc. For sample chapbooks, write to the above address.

Also Offers: Sponsors a contest for their anthology, "if approved by our editorial board. Submissions are on an individual basis—always provide a SASE."

Advice: "Any poet interested in Native American themes or any Native American poet expressing poems of any theme is invited to submit to us. If you have strong feelings for Native American people, culture, religion or ideas, express yourself through your poetry and let us help you get published."

☑ $ ◎ INDIANA REVIEW, Ballantine Hall 465, 1020 E. Kirkwood, Bloomington IN 47405-7103, phone (812)855-3439, e-mail inreview@indiana.edu, website www.indiana.edu/~inreview/ir.html, founded 1982, contact poetry editor.

➥ Poetry published in *IR* has been selected for inclusion in the 1996 and 1997 volumes of *The Best American Poetry.*

Magazine Needs: *Indiana Review* is a biannual of prose, poetry and visual art. "We look for an intelligent sense of form and language, and admire poems of risk, ambition and scope. We'll consider all types of poems— free verse, traditional, experimental. Reading a sample issue is the best way to determine if *IR* is a potential home for your work. Any subject matter is acceptable if it is written well." They have published poetry by Philip Levine, Taslimā Nāsreen, Campbell McGrath, Charles Simic, Mark Strand and Alberto Rios. The magazine uses about 40-60 pgs. of poetry in each issue (6×9, flat-spined, 160 pages, color matte cover, professional printing). They receive about 5,000 submissions a year, use approximately 60. The magazine has 500 subscriptions. Sample: $8.

How to Submit: Submit 4-6 poems at a time, do not send more than 8-10 pages of poetry per submission. No electronic submissions. Pays $5/page ($10 minimum/poem), plus 2 copies and remainder of year's subscription. Buys first North American serial rights only. "We try to respond to manuscripts in 2-3 months. Reading time is often slower during summer and holiday months." Brief book reviews are also featured. Send books for review consideration. Holds yearly contests. Send SASE for guidelines.

Also Offers: Website includes writer's guidelines, current news, sample poetry and fiction from current and past issues.

$ ◎ ◎ INDIGENOUS FICTION, P.O. Box 2078, Redmond WA 98073-2078, e-mail deckr@earthlink.net (no e-mail submissions), founded 1998, publisher/managing editor Sherry Decker.

Magazine Needs: *Indigenous Fiction* appears 3 times a year and publishes "literary mainstream and genre fiction and poetry to provide a market for accomplished writers of 'unusual' or cross-genre fiction and poetry. We prefer poems that tell at least a story or part of a story; usually serious poems but have accepted two amusing 'spoof' type submissions. We do not want poetry that is so obscure and 'high literary' no one except the poet knows what it's about. No 'love' poems, unless they're odd or unusual." They have published poetry by Errol Miller, James S. Dorr, Margo Solod and Holly Day. As a sample the publisher selected these lines from "The Chupacabra" by Scott Francis:

> Water-light and rippling up the wet tangled nighttime branches, we clothe each other in our/naked cries. Hooking scarlets from the dark, our horns become the fires of our/cries. We're gorging on blood-thick petals. It has begun to rain, each drop's/touch flaming us more and more alive. Alone, we coo, far from the/stench called men

IF is 64-84 pgs., digest-sized, digitally published and saddle-stitched with full color 30-60 lb. cover, includes drawings/watercolors/ink. They receive about 650 poems a year, accept approximately 2%. Press run is 300 for 100 subscribers, 50 shelf sales; 25 distributed free to critics/reviewers. Subscription: $15. Sample: $6. Make checks payable to Sherry Decker.

How to Submit: Submit 5 poems at a time. Line length for poetry is 30 maximum. Previously published poems and simultaneous submissions OK. Cover letter preferred. "Listing credits will get my attention but will not sell me your work. Do not explain your work in your cover letter. Even though we accept previously published work, we accept very little of it. Must be truly exceptional." Time between acceptance and publication is up to 6 months. Seldom comments on rejections. Send SASE for guidelines or request via e-mail. Responds in 2 weeks. Pays $5/poem or contributor's copy (author's choice). Buys first North American serial rights or one-time rights for reprints. "Contributor's copies are provided for work of at least 1,500 words. All contributors are qualified to purchase copies at the discounted rate, as explained in contract."

☑ $ ◯ ◎ INKLINGS, 1650 Washington St., Denver CO 80203, phone (303)861-8191, fax (303)861-0659, e-mail inklings@paradoxpub.com, website www.paradoxpub.com, founded 1994, poetry submissions editor Susan Adams Kauffman.

Magazine Needs: *Inklings* is "a bimonthly literary magazine and arts discussion bridging classic literature and art with popular culture in the spirit of the Inklings of Oxford: C.S. Lewis, J.R.R. Tolkien, Charles Williams and friends. *Inklings* exists as a vital catalyst to encourage honest dialogue and affecting stories relating from the common human experience—by writers who approach their craft truthfully irrespective of their religion, nationality, race or political worldview. *Inklings* publishes poetry, essays, reviews, interviews and fiction of lasting merit, honestly written with depth of plot, characterization and meaning, with thoughtful insight into the human condition." They want "serious poetry, free verse, sonnet, haiku and traditional work that corresponds with quarterly themes or addresses the universal human experience. We tend not to publish poetry that is tritely religious." They have published poetry by Luci Shaw, Albert Haley and Jon Trott. As a sample the editor selected these lines from "A Leaf Landing in a Well" by Walt McDonald:

> Rock, club, fistful of mud, something to fling/and swing again, again, until flat prose/lies battered, abstractions crushed, bleeding,/cheap rhymes scattered like rubies. Venus rose/dripping and blissful from the foam

Inklings is up to 64 pgs., magazine-sized, professionally printed on 4-color glossy paper and saddle-stapled with 4-color glossy paper cover, includes b&w photos and ads. They receive about 500 poems a year, accept approximately 10%. Press run is 10,000 for 3,500 subscribers; the remaining 6,500 go to libraries, bookstores and complimentary copies distributed mostly in Colorado. Subscription: $15/year (4 issues), $28/2 years (8 issues). Sample: $5.

How to Submit: Submit up to 10 poems at a time. Line length for poetry is 2 minimum, 100 maximum. No previously published poems or simultaneous submissions. Cover letter required. E-mail (preferred) and disk submissions OK. "Please enclose SASE [with regular mail submissions] and any background information that would be helpful." Time between acceptance and publication is up to 1 year. Poems are circulated to an editorial board. "All poems are handled by the poetry submissions editor who selects intial 6-8 poems for an issue and then involves other editors in final selection process." Often comments on rejections. Publishes theme issues. Send SASE for guidelines and upcoming themes or obtain via website. Responds in 3 months. Pays $25/poem. Buys first North American serial rights or one-time rights. Reviews books and chapbooks of poetry in 300 words. Open to unsolicited reviews. Poets may also send books for review consideration.

Also Offers: Sponsors regular poetry contests with cash awards. Contests advertised in *Inklings* or call or write to *Inklings* for details. Website includes writer's guidelines, names of editors, poetry, book reviews, articles, fiction and upcoming events.

Advice: "Read poems that have already been accepted by *Inklings*. We are looking for fresh, original (as opposed to clichéd or trite) work. Most of the poetry we publish is free verse."

THE INKWELL., % C.S. McDowell, 24031 Griffin House Lane, Katy TX 77493, fax (281)347-2568, founded 1999, contact C.S. McDowell.

Magazine Needs: *The Inkwell.* appears 3 times a year and "strives to discover and expose talent, new or old. A love of literature and a firm belief that practically nothing is stronger than the written word is my bread and butter. All forms and styles of poetry are accepted, from 1-100 lines. Also, prose and short fiction up to 1,000 words are included in each issue. The editor tends to stray towards well-worded, sound poetry with rhyme included, whether irregular or traditional. Free verse, haiku and all other forms are of equal importance, though. No forced rhyme. 'Tender skies at twilight', etc., tend to sour one's stomach. Nature and the environment are of significance to us all, but when writing on the subject try not to neuter it. Erotica may be stimulating, but please, all you ex-porn stars, exhibit your wares elsewhere." The editor says the journal is 15-30 pgs., digest-sized, high-quality print and saddle-stapled with cardstock or heavy weight paper cover with b&w illustration. "I receive 300-500 pieces a year of which 15-25% are accepted." Press run is 250-1,000. Sample: 50¢ (for postage).

How to Submit: Submit up to 5 pieces at a time (poetry, prose and short fiction). Line length for poetry is 1 minimum, 100 maximum. Previously published poems and simultaneous submissions OK. Cover letter "not mandatory, but appreciated. If cover letter is included, please send a few words about oneself, life, interests (brief bio)." Include SASE for reply or return. Reading fees: $1/piece. Make checks payable to C.S. McDowell. Time between acceptance and publication varies. "The author should be notified of their acceptance within 1-3 months. Actual publication may be from 3-6 months." Always comments on rejections. "As a writer, I have often tired of the dreaded Form Letter Rejection. As an editor, I will always personally respond to my rejections with criticism and reason. The aforementioned reading fee covers any criticism fee there may be." Send SASE for guidelines. Responds in 3 months. Pays 1 copy. If response is large enough, a "Best of Each Issue" cash prize (around $10-25) may be awarded. All rights remain with the author. Byline given.

Also Offers: "*The Inkwell.* is interested in producing 4-6 chapbooks/year. The reading fee for these is $20, of which 50% is returned if the manuscript is rejected." Follow same submission guidelines as given for the journal. Chapbook runs will be 100, of which 10 are paid to the author. The remaining 90 will be sold at $2 each, of which 50% returns to the author. Those remaining after 1 year will be given free to libraries and/or bookstores.

Advice: "It is a great thing to pull from an envelope a poet's thoughts and musings. Much better than anything in the theatres or on TV. Remembers, children, without the written word, governments fall, society falters and we couldn't tell our paycheck from the light bill. Make your words powerful."

INKWELL MAGAZINE, Manhattanville College, Box 1379, 2900 Purchase St., Purchase NY 10577, phone (914)323-7239, fax (914)323-3122, founded 1995, editor Steve Kerneklian (June 2000-June 2001).

Magazine Needs: "*Inkwell* is published biannually by Manhattanville College and publishes work by new poets and writers side by side with known poets and writers." They are open to all types. They have published poetry by April Bernard, Dan Masterson and Christian Nagle. As a sample the editor selected these lines from "The Rain-Soaked Trail" by Ace Boggess:

> The raining season kept to the clock this year./A new father tells me he misses the sun/waiting at the nearest horizon on the outskirts of May./Thai afternoons give forests their definition,/that mythical

gray text one often only reads about/in books. Such clear boundaries.
Inkwell is about 100 pgs., 6¾×10, professionally printed and perfect-bound, with 4-color card cover, includes b&w art and photos. Press run is 1,000 for 60 subscribers. Single copy: $10.50; subscription: $20. Sample: $7.
How to Submit: Submit 5 poems at a time. Simultaneous submissions OK. Disk submissions OK, if accompanied by hard copy. Cover letter required. Name, address, phone, title, word count on cover page. SASE required for response. Reads submissions May 15 through January 15 only. Time between acceptance and publication is 3-4 months. Poems are circulated to an editorial board. "The editor and selected readers read all manuscripts." Seldom comments on rejections. Send SASE for guidelines. Responds in 3 months. Pays 2 copies. Acquires first North American serial rights.
Also Offers: Sponsors annual poetry competition with $1,000 Grand Prize and 2 Honorable Mentions ($50) plus publication. Entry fee: $10 for first poem, $5 each additional. Postmark deadline in August. Send SASE for complete contest guidelines.
Advice: "*Inkwell* is dedicated to discovering new talent and to encouraging and bringing the talents of working writers and artists to a wider audience. The magazine encourages diverse voices and has an open submission policy for both art and literature."

■ ○ ◎ **INSECTS ARE PEOPLE TWO; PUFF 'N' STUFF PRODUCTIONS (Specialized),** P.O. Box 146486, Chicago IL 60614-6400, founded 1989, publisher H.R. Felgenhauer.
Magazine Needs: *Insects* is an infrequent publication focusing solely on "poems about insects doing people things and people doing insect things." Also accepts poetry written by children. They have published poetry by Bruce Boston, Steve Sneyd, Paul Wieneman and Lyn Lifshin. As a sample the editor selected these lines from an untitled poem by Steve Sneyd:
> *Is time/of insect moon—/Dry chittering comes down/to us promising hour soon we/too saved*
Insects is 8½×11, with card cover, b&w art and graphics. Press run is 1,000. Sample: $6.
How to Submit: Previously published poems and simultaneous submissions OK. Often comments on rejections. Publishes theme issues. "Next issue scheduled to be 'Insects Are People 2001,' will accept 2001 parodies involving insect behavior or bugs." Responds "immediately." Pay varies. Open to unsolicited reviews. Send books for review consideration.
Book/Chapbook Needs & How to Submit: Puff 'N' Stuff Productions publishes 1 chapbook/year. Replies to queries and mss in 10 days. Pay is negotiable.
Advice: "Hit me with your best shot. Never give up—editors have tunnel-vision. The *BEST* mags you almost *NEVER* even hear about. Don't believe reviews. Write for yourself. Prepare for failure, not success."

○ ◪ **INTERBANG; BERTYE PRESS, INC.,** P.O. Box 1574, Venice CA 90294, phone (310)450-6372, e-mail editors@interbang.net, website www.interbang.net, founded 1995, editor Heather Hoffman.
Magazine Needs: *Interbang*, published quarterly, is "Dedicated to Perfection in the Art of Writing." They want "enticing poetry of any length on any subject. Although we do not have strict standards regarding substance, texture, or structure, your craft, in tandem with your subject matter, should elicit a strong response in the reader: love, hate, shock, sorrow, revulsion, you name it. Write your name, address and phone number on each page of your submission." They have published poetry by Rob Lipton, John Thomas, Linda Platt Mintz, David Centorbi and Jessica Pompei. As a sample the editor selected these lines from "Clutter Can Manipulate So Much Wisdom" by David Centorbi:
> *The sidewalk holds nothing but wandering bodies,/life cycles without preparation./Believing in annihilation/means looking into their eyes.//So, dislocating myself/becomes the easiest response./Leaving the sidewalk is no longer walking,/but just another way of seeing.*
Interbang is 30 pgs., 7½×8½, offset printed and saddle-stitched with colored card stock cover, includes line art and photos. They receive about 500 poems a year, accept approximately 50%. Press run is 2,000 for 100 subscribers of which 10 are libraries, 20 shelf sales; 40 distributed free to other magazines, the rest distributed free at coffeehouses and bookstores in L.A. Send two stamps for a free sample copy.
How to Submit: Submit 5-15 poems at a time. Previously published poems and simultaneous submissions OK. Comments on rejections on request. Obtain the *Interbang Writer's Guide* via e-mail (writersguide@interbang.net) or website. Responds in 6 months. Always sends prepublication galleys. Pays 5 copies. Reviews chapbooks of poetry and other magazines in 350-400 words, single book format. Open to unsolicited reviews. Poets may also send books for review consideration.

◫ ▣ ○ ◪ **THE INTERFACE; BUTTERMILK ART WORKS,** % GlassFull Productions, P.O. Box 57129, Philadelphia PA 19111-7129, phone/fax (215)722-2711, e-mail interface@baworks.com, website www.baworks.com/interface, founded 1997, publisher Earl Weeks, art director Willie S. McCoy.
Magazine Needs: *The INTERFACE* is published quarterly on the Internet. They want "all kinds of work—romantic, political, social commentary. We want poetry that comes from your heart, that makes tears come to the eye or forces one to want to mobilize the troops. No poems of hate or discrimination." They have published poetry by Mike Emrys, Sheron Regular, Cassandra Norris, Willie McCoy and Monique Frederick. As a sample the publisher selected his poem "Love is":

> *Love is forever until death do we part/Love is when we never send arrows through each others hearts/*
> *Love is me snuggled warmly against your breasts./Love is when you can sleep peacefully at rest.*

They receive about 20 poems a year, accept approximately 90%. Publish 5 poems/issue.

How to Submit: Submit 7 poems at a time. Previously published poems and simultaneous submissions OK. E-mail and disk submissions OK. Cover letter preferred. "We will consider accompanying illustration." Submit seasonal poems 2 months in advance. Time between acceptance and publication is 2 months. Poems are circulated to an editorial board. Publishes theme issues occasionally. Obtain guidelines and upcoming themes via e-mail or website. Responds in 3 weeks. Acquires one-time rights. Reviews books and chapbooks of poetry and other magazines. Open to unsolicited reviews. Poets may also send books for review consideration.

Also Offers: "Under Buttermilk Art Works, we publish poetry, essays, videogame reviews, book reviews, fashion, science fiction, art and more. We are trying to make *The INTERFACE* a meeting place for idea exchanges. We need your opinions and views, so submit them to us."

INTERIM, Dept. of English Box 5011, University of Nevada—Las Vegas, Las Vegas NV 89154, phone (702)895-3333, fax (702)895-4801, e-mail keelanc@nevada.edu, editor Claudia Keelan.
• Member CLMP, New York. Indexed in *Index of American Periodical Verse*.

Magazine Needs: *Interim* is an annual magazine, appearing in December, that publishes poetry, short fiction, essay and book reviews. "We seek submissions from writers who are testing the boundaries of genre." They have published poetry by Walter McDonald, Faye George, Stephen Stepanchev and Mary Winters. As a sample the editor selected this poem, "The Paragraph She gives me to Live In" by Martha Ronk:

> *"The paragraph she gives me to live in is I don't know how./Description is a phenomenon of walks as*
> *obvious as rain./All the outcroppings in a brownish moss I can't get over/The undulation of columns*
> *one after another/Through which the distance is an extension of how we think/How someone walks*
> *into the room or sits in a chair./She says again you are where you should have begun./She offers copses*
> *and seclusion./Or you don't listen to what I say how could I foresee/"bitterns crying I the lintels" or*
> *her inner being/whatever insists is what she says I have to do.*

Interim is 100 pgs., 6×9, professionally printed and perfect-bound with coated card cover. Press run is 400. Individual subscription: $12/year, $24/2 years. Single copy: $12.

How to Submit: Submit 3-5 poems at a time, SASE and brief biographical note. No simultaneous submissions. Responds in 3 months. Pays 2 copies. Acquires first serial rights. Poems may be reprinted elsewhere with a permission line noting publication in *Interim*.

$ INTERLINK BBS, P.O. Box 2757, Springfield IL 62708-2757, phone (217)753-2471, fax (217)753-5573, e-mail info@interlink-bbs.com, website interlink-bbs.com, founded 1995, system administrator Rachel Link.

Magazine Needs: *InterLink BBS* is a weekly web page. "The purpose is entertainment. We want anything interesting, unusual or thought provoking. We especially like fun poetry. No trash. If you wouldn't read it, don't send it to us. Don't send us your English assignments." As a sample the editor selected these lines from "Final Scrimmage" by Sparrow:

> *Jesus was born at half-time/In the great Football game of history./That's why we're all dressed as*
> *linebackers now:/Prepare for the Final Scrimmage!*

They receive about 10 poems a year, accept approximately 50%.

How to Submit: Submit up to 5 poems at a time. Previously published poems and simultaneous submissions OK. Cover letter preferred. E-mail and disk submissions preferred. "Since we publish on the Web, we need to know how the author would like the poem(s) to appear on our menu." Time between acceptance and publication is 1 week. Often comments on rejections. Publishes theme issues occasionally. Obtain guidelines and upcoming themes via e-mail or website. Responds in 1 week. Pays $0-50. Buys first rights.

Advice: "Since we operate on a visual medium, including pictures or graphics greatly improves your odds of acceptance. We like fun poems, not long, somber, moody pieces about your depression. Cheer up! Also, we would be willing to run a regular column, if someone wanted to do that, and if we liked the idea."

INTERNATIONAL POETRY REVIEW (Specialized: translations), Dept. of Romance Languages, UNC-Greensboro, Greensboro NC 27412, phone (336)334-5655, fax (336)334-5358, e-mail kmather@uncg.edu, website www.uncg.edu/rom/ipr, founded 1975, editor Kathleen Mather.

Magazine Needs: *IPR* is a biannual primarily publishing translations of contemporary poetry with corresponding originals (published on facing pages) as well as original poetry in English. They have published work by Jasha Kessler, Lyn Lifshin, Pureza Canelo, Jaime Sabines and Fred Chappell. *IPR* is 100 pgs., 5½×8½, profes-

---

THE CHAPBOOK INDEX, located at the back of this book, lists those publishers who consider chapbook mss. A chapbook, a small volume of work (usually under 50 pages), is often a good middle step between magazine and book publication.

sionally printed and perfect-bound with 2-3 color cover. "We accept 5% of original poetry in English and about 30% of translations submitted." Press run is 500 for 250 subscribers of which 100 are libraries. Subscription: $10 individuals, $15 institutions. Sample: $5.

How to Submit: Submit no more than 5 pages of poetry. No previously published poems; simultaneous submissions OK. Seldom comments on rejections. Publishes theme issues. Send SASE for guidelines and upcoming themes. Responds in up to 6 months. Pays 1 copy. All rights revert to authors and translators. Occasionally reviews books of poetry. Open to unsolicited reviews. Poets may also send books for review consideration.

Advice: "We strongly encourage contributors to subscribe. We prefer poetry in English to have an international or cross-cultural theme."

✔ ▣ ◧ ◎ **INTERNATIONAL QUARTERLY; CROSSING BOUNDARIES CONTEST (Specialized: translations)**, P.O. Box 10521, Tallahassee FL 32302-0521, website www.internationalquarterly.org, founded 1993, editor-in-chief Van K. Brock.

Magazine Needs: "We welcome outstanding writing in all genres, in original English and in translation, quality work that transcends cultural givens. No one-dimensional views of people or place, work that is amateurish or lacks complexity. Poetry in translation appears in original and in English." *IQ* is a webzine. They receive about 800 mss/year, accept a quarter.

How to Submit: "Please contact website for information."

🌐 ◧ ◎ **INTERPRETER'S HOUSE; BEDFORD OPEN POETRY COMPETITION (Specialized: regional)**, 10 Farrell Rd., Wootton, Bedfordshire MK43 9DU United Kingdom, founded 1996, contact Merryn Williams.

Magazine Needs: *IH* appears 3 times/year (February, June, October) and publishes short stories and poetry. They want "good poetry (and short stories), not too long. No Christmas-card verse or incomprehensible poetry." They have published poetry by Dannie Abse, Tony Curtis, Pauline Stainer, Alan Bronnjohn, Peter Redgrove and R.S. Thomas. As a sample the editor selected these lines from "Metrics" by R.S. Thomas:

> There should be no/introit into a poem.//The listener should come/to and realize/verse has been going
> on/for some time. . . .

Merryn Williams says *IH* is 74 pgs., A5 with attractive cover design. They receive about 1,000 poems a year, accept approximately 10%. Press run is 300 for 200 subscribers. Subscription: £8.50. Sample: £2.50 plus 38 p.

How to Submit: Submit 5 poems at a time. No previously published poems or simultaneous submissions. Cover letter preferred. Time between acceptance and publication is 2 weeks to 8 months. Often comments on rejections. Send SASE (or SAE and IRC) for guidelines. Responds "fast." Pays 1 copy.

Also Offers: Sponsors the Bedford Open Poetry Competition. Send SAE and IRC for details.

✔ $ ◎ ◧ **INTERTEXT (Specialized: translations)**, 149 Water St., #35, Norwalk CT 06854, founded 1982, editor Sharon Ann Jaeger.

Book/Chapbook Needs & How to Submit: Intertext publishes "full-length collections by poets of demonstrated achievement" electronically, in on-demand editions, and is "devoted to producing lasting works in every sense. We specialize in poetry, translations and short works in the fine arts and literary criticism." In 2000-2001 we will not be reading unsolicited material.

✔ ◎ **INTRO (Specialized: students)**, AWP, Tallwood House, MS 1E3, George Mason University, Fairfax VA 22030, website http://awpwriter.org, founded 1970, publications manager David Sherwin.

• See Associated Writing Programs in the Organizations section of this book.

Magazine Needs & How to Submit: Students in college writing programs belonging to AWP may submit to this consortium of magazines publishing student poetry, fiction and plays. They are open as to the type of poetry submitted except they do not want "non-literary, haiku, etc." As to poets they have published, they say, "In our history, we've introduced Dara Wier, Carolyn Forché, Greg Pope, Norman Dubie and others." Circulation is 9,500. All work must be submitted by the writing program. Programs nominate *Intro* works in the fall. Ask the director of your writing program for more information.

◧ **INVERTED-A, INC.; INVERTED-A HORN**, 900 Monarch Way, Northport AL 35473-2663, founded 1977, editors Amnon Katz and Aya Katz.

Magazine Needs: *Inverted-A Horn* is an irregular periodical, usually 9 pages, magazine-sized, offset printed; circulation is 300. The editors do not want to see anything "modern, formless, existentialist." As a sample the editor selected these lines by Delta Zahner:

> Within a boarded-up arcade/Which some dead mason's trowel laid,/The voice of law and order said:/
> "Just run. We want to shoot you dead."

How to Submit: Simultaneous submissions OK. Replies to queries in 1 month, to mss in 4 months. Pays 1 copy plus a 40% discount on additional copies. Samples: SASE with postage for 2 ounces (subject to availability).

Book/Chapbook Needs & How to Submit: Inverted-A Inc. is a very small press that evolved from publishing technical manuals for other products. "Our interests center on freedom, justice and honor." They publish 1 chapbook/year.

Advice: "I strongly recommend that would-be contributors avail themselves of this opportunity to explore what we are looking for. Most of the submissions we receive do not come close."

🌐 🍎 🞉 **IOTA**, 67 Hady Crescent, Chesterfield, Derbyshire S41 0EB Great Britain, phone 01246-276532, founded 1988, editor David Holliday.

Magazine Needs: *Iota* is a quarterly wanting "any style and subject; no specific limitations as to length, though, obviously, the shorter a poem is, the easier it is to get it in, which means that poems over 40 lines can still get in if they seem good enough. No concrete poetry (no facilities) or self-indulgent logorrhea." Also accepts poetry written by children (but they have to take their chance with the rest). They have published poetry by Ian Caws, Edmund Harwood, Fiona Curnow, Judy Klass and Edmund Prestwich. As a sample the editor selected this poem, "Exploring the Past" by Tim Love:

> Just to see if I could, I dreamt that I dreamt that/another country whose lovesick King whose ancient
> forest/whose mighty oaks whose greener leaves/fell, fell, fell, fell, fell.

Iota is 44 pgs., professionally printed and saddle-stapled with light colored card cover. They publish about 300 of 6,000 poems received. Their press run is 500 with 250 subscribers of which 6 are libraries. Subscription: $15 (£8). Sample: $2 (£1) "but sometimes sent free."

How to Submit: Submit 4-6 poems at a time. The editor prefers name and address on each poem, typed, "but provided it's legible, am happy to accept anything." Simultaneous submissions OK, but previously published poems "only if outstanding." First response in 3 weeks (unless production of the next issue takes precedence) but final acceptance/rejection may take up to a year. Pays 2 copies. Acquires first British serial rights only. Editor usually comments on rejections, "but detailed comment only when time allows and the poem warrants it." Reviews books of poetry in about 200 words, single or multi-book format. Open to unsolicited reviews. Poets may also send books for review consideration.

Advice: "I am after crafted verse that says something; self-indulgent word-spinning is out. All editors have their blind spots; the only advice I can offer a beginning poet is to find a sympathetic editor (and you will only do that by seeing their magazines) and not to be discouraged by initial lack of success. Keep plugging!"

💲🞉 **THE IOWA REVIEW; THE TIM McGINNIS AWARD**, 308 EPB, University of Iowa, Iowa City IA 52242, phone (319)335-0462, e-mail iowa-review@uiowa.edu, website www.uiowa.edu/~iareview, founded 1970, editor David Hamilton, contact poetry editor.

📖 Poetry published in *The Iowa Review* has also been included in the 1995, 1996 and 1997 volumes of *The Best American Poetry* and the *Pushcart Prize* anthology for 1995.

Magazine Needs: *IR* appears 3 times/year and publishes fiction, poetry, essays, reviews, interviews and autobiographical sketches. The editors say, "We simply look for poems that at the time we read and choose, we admire. No specifications as to form, length, style, subject matter or purpose. There are around 40 pgs. of poetry in each issue and we like to give several pages to a single poet. Though we print work from established writers, we're always delighted when we discover new talent." *IR* is 200 pgs., professionally printed, flat-spined. They receive about 5,000 submissions/year, use about 100. Press run is 2,900 with 1,000 subscribers of which about half are libraries; 1,500 distributed to stores. Subscription: $18. Sample: $6.

How to Submit: Submit 3-6 poems at a time. No e-mail submissions. Cover letter (with title of work and genre) and SASE required. Reads submissions September 1 through January 31 "or until we fill our next volume year's issues." Time between acceptance and publication is "around a year. Sometimes people hit at the right time and come out in a few months." Occasionally comments on rejections or offers suggestions on accepted poems. Responds in up to 4 months. Pays $1/line, 2-3 copies and a 1-year subscription. Buys first North American serial rights, non-exclusive anthology rights and non-exclusive electronic rights.

Also Offers: Sponsors The Tim McGinnis Award. "The award, in the amount of $500, is given irregularly to authors of work with a light or humorous touch. We have no separate category of submissions to be considered alone for this award. Instead, any essay, story, or poem we publish which is charged with a distinctly comic vision will automatically come under consideration for the McGinnis Award." Also offers Iowa Award for the single work judged best of the year. Outside judge, any genre. Website includes excerpts, download guidelines, table of contents, etc.

✅ 🞉 ◎ **IRIS: A JOURNAL ABOUT WOMEN (Specialized: women/feminism)**, P.O. Box 800588, University of Virginia, Charlottesville VA 22908, phone (804)924-4500, fax (804)982-2801, e-mail Iris@virginia. edu, website http://minerva.acc.virginia.edu/~womenctr/pubs/iris/irishome.html, founded 1980, poetry editor Nura Yingling.

Magazine Needs: *Iris* is a semiannual magazine that "focuses on issues concerning women worldwide. It features quality poetry, prose and artwork—mainly by women, but will also accept work by men if it illuminates some aspect of a woman's reality. It also publishes translations. Form and length are unspecified. The poetry staff consists of experienced poets with a diversity of tastes who are looking for new and original language in well-crafted poems." Poets who have appeared in *Iris* include Sharon Olds, Patricia Fargnoli, Mary Oliver, Lois Marie Harrod, Linda Pastan, Naomi Shihab Nye, Christina Hutchins and Gregory Orr. As a sample the editor selected these lines from "The Lost Daughter" by Susan Imhof:

> Seven years dead and still she grows,/copper hair a strange fin/rippling through the furnace of desert
> noon,/your dream of oil spills:/birds descending/on the airstream, wings/tucked, legs unfolded to meet/

their reflections before/the black gold swallows them,/wing tips rising a brief moment toward heaven/
through the shimmering heat, a slow/explosion of blue flame. . . .

Iris is 78 pgs., magazine-sized, professionally printed on heavy, glossy stock, saddle-stapled with a full-color glossy card cover, using graphics and photos. Press run is over 2,000 for about 40 library subscriptions, 1,000 shelf sales. Single copy: $5; subscription: $9/year; $17/2 years. Sample: $6.50.

How to Submit: Submit up to 5 poems at a time. Simultaneous submissions are discouraged. Name, address, phone number should be listed on every poem. Cover letter should include list of poems submitted and a brief bio. Publishes theme issues. Send SASE for guidelines. Responds in 6 months. Pays 1 copy and subscription. Acquires first rights.

Also Offers: Website includes info on latest issue, back issues, submission guidelines and contacts.

Advice: "Because *Iris* is a feminist magazine, it receives a lot of poetry focusing on the political experience of coming to consciousness. The editor is interested in *all* aspects of the reality of women's lives and, because many poems are on similar topics, freshness of imagery and style are even more important."

ITALIAN AMERICANA; JOHN CIARDI AWARD (Specialized: ethnic), URI/CCE, 80 Washington St., Providence RI 02903-1803, phone (401)277-5306, fax (401)277-5100, website www.uri.edu/prov/italian/italian.html, founded 1974, editor Carol Bonomo Albright, poetry editor Dana Gioia.

Magazine Needs: *IA* appears twice a year using 16-20 poems of "no more than three pgs. No trite nostalgia; no poems about grandparents." They have published poetry by Mary Jo Salter and Joy Parini. It is 150-200 pgs., 7×9, professionally printed and flat-spined with glossy card cover. Press run is 1,000 for 900 subscribers of which 175 are libraries, 175 shelf sales. Singly copy: $10; subscription: $20. Sample: $6.

How to Submit: Submit 3 poems at a time. No previously published poems or simultaneous submissions. Cover letter not required "but helpful." Name on first page of ms only. Do not submit poetry in July, August or September. Occasionally comments on rejections. Responds in 6 weeks. Acquires first rights. Reviews books of poetry in 600 words, multi-book format. Poets may send books for review consideration to Prof. John Paul Russo, English Dept., University of Miami, Coral Gables FL 33124.

Also Offers: Along with the National Italian American Foundation, *IA* co-sponsors the annual $1,000 John Ciardi Award for Lifetime Contribution to Poetry. *IA* also presents $500 fiction or memoir award annually; and $1,000 in history prizes. Website includes writer's guidelines, names of editors, poetry, historical articles and fiction.

Advice: "Single copies of poems for submissions are sufficient."

ITALICA PRESS (Specialized: bilingual/foreign language), 595 Main St., #605, New York NY 10044-0047, phone (212)935-4230, fax (212)838-7812, e-mail inquiries@italicapress.com, founded 1985, publishers Eileen Gardiner and Ronald G. Musto.

Book/Chapbook Needs: Italica is a small press publisher of English translations of Italian works in Smyth-sewn paperbacks, averaging 175 pgs. They have published *Guido Cavalcanti, The Complete Poems*, a dual-language (English/Italian) book with English translation and introduction by Marc Cirigliano, and *Women Poets of the Italian Renaissance*, a dual-language anthology, edited by Laura Anna Stortoni and translated by Laura Anna Stortoni and Mary Prentice Lillie.

How to Submit: Query with 10 sample translations of medieval and Renaissance Italian poets. Include cover letter, bio and list of publications. Simultaneous submissions OK, but translation should not be "totally" previously published. E-mail submissions OK. Responds to queries in 3 weeks, to mss in 3 months. Always sends prepublication galleys. Pays 7-15% royalties plus 10 author's copies. Buys English language rights. Sometimes comments on rejections.

JAPANOPHILE (Specialized: form, ethnic), P.O. Box 7977, Ann Arbor MI 48107, phone (734)930-1553, e-mail susanlapp@aol.com or jpnhand@japanophile.com, website www.japanophile.com, founded 1974, editor Susan A. Lapp, poetry editor Ashby Kinch.

Magazine Needs: *Japanophile* is a literary quarterly about Japanese culture (not just in Japan). Issues include articles, photos, art, a short story and poetry. They want haiku or other Japanese forms ("they need not be about Japanese culture") or any form if the subject is about Japan, Japanese culture or American-Japanese relations. (Note: Karate and ikebana in the US are examples of Japanese culture.) They have published poetry by Renee Leopold, Nancy Corson Carter, Jean Jorgensen, Mimi Walter Hinman and reprints of Bashō. As a sample the editor selected this haiku (poet unidentified):

first snowstorm/our old cat rediscovers/the warm airduct

There are 10-15 pgs. of poetry in each issue (digest-sized, about 58 pgs., saddle-stapled). They have a circulation of 800 with 200 subscriptions of which 30 are libraries. They receive about 500 submissions a year, use 70, have a 2-month backlog. Sample: $4.

How to Submit: Summer is the best time to submit. E-mail and fax submissions OK. Cover letter required; include brief bio and credits if any. Send SASE for guidelines and upcoming themes or request via e-mail. Responds in 2 months. Pays $3 for haiku and up to $15 for longer poems. Open to unsolicited reviews. Poets may also send books for review consideration, attn. Ashby Kinch.

Book/Chapbook Needs & How to Submit: They also publish books under the Japanophile imprint, but so far only one has been of poetry. Query with samples and cover letter (about 1 pg.) giving publishing credits, bio.

Also Offers: Website includes guidelines, sample material, information on the magazine and brief blurbs on the editors.

Advice: "This quarterly is out as each season begins. Poems that name or suggest a season, and are received two or three months before the season, get a good look."

N ◯ ◉ JEWEL AMONG JEWELS ADOPTION NETWORK, INC.; JEWEL AMONG JEWELS ADOPTION NEWS (Specialized: adoption), P.O. Box 502065, Indianapolis IN 46256, phone/fax (317)849-5651, e-mail adoptjewel@aol.com, website http://adoptionjewels.org, founded 1994, editor Sherrie Eldridge.

Magazine Needs: *Jewel Among Jewels* is published "to celebrate the sovereignty of God through adoption, to educate about the realities of relinquishment and to help each person touched by adoption to embrace God's opinion of them—a jewel among jewels." They want "adoption-related poetry, showing the perspectives of adoptees, birth parents and adoptive parents. We also look for a biblical perspective. No work unrelated to adoption." The editor says *Jewel Among Jewels* is an 8-page newsletter with 2-color cover, includes art/graphics. They receive about 25 poems a year, accept approximately 10%. Press run is 2,000 for 1,600; distributed free to anyone who requests. Subscription: $15 suggested donation. Make checks payable to Jajani.

How to Submit: Line length for poetry is 10 minimum, 15 maximum. Previously published poems OK. E-mail and disk submissions OK. Cover letter preferred. Reads submissions quarterly—January, April, June, September. Poems are circulated to an editorial board. "Poems go to our advisory board of adoption professionals prior to publication." Publishes theme issues occasionally. Send SASE for guidelines or obtain via website. Responds in 1 month. Acquires first or one-time rights.

Also Offers: Website includes history of organization, past issues of newsletters, writer's guidelines, services offered.

◖ ◢ ◉ JEWISH CURRENTS (Specialized: themes, religious), 22 E. 17th St., Suite 601, New York NY 10003-1919, phone/fax (212)924-5740, founded 1946, editor Morris U. Schappes.

Magazine Needs: *Jewish Currents* is a magazine appearing 11 times a year that publishes articles, reviews, fiction and poetry pertaining to Jewish subjects or presenting a Jewish point of view on an issue of interest, including translations from the Yiddish and Hebrew (original texts should be submitted with translations). Also accepts poetry written by children. The editor says it is 36 pgs., 8½×11, offset, saddle-stapled. Press run is 2,500 for 2,100 subscribers of which about 10% are libraries. Subscription: $30/year. Sample: $3.

How to Submit: Submit 1 poem at a time, typed, double-spaced, with SASE. Include brief bio. No previously published poems or simultaneous submissions. Fax submissions OK. Cover letter required. Publishes theme issues. Upcoming themes include November: Jewish Book Month; December: Honuka; February: Black History Month; March: Jewish Music Season, International Women's Day; April: Holocaust Resistance, Passover; May: Israel; July through August: Soviet Jewish History. Deadlines for themes are 6 months in advance. Time between acceptance and publication is 2 years. Seldom comments on rejections. Responds in up to 1 year. Always sends prepublication galleys. Pays 6 copies plus 1-year subscription. Reviews books of poetry.

✓ ◯ ◉ JEWISH SPECTATOR (Specialized: religious), 9107 Wilshire Blvd., Beverly Hills CA 90210, fax (310)475-8015, e-mail isdev@ix.netcom.com, founded 1935, literary editor Avi Davis.

Magazine Needs: *Jewish Spectator* is a 68-page Judaic scholarly quarterly that welcomes poetry on Jewish themes. They have published poetry by Rodger Kamenetz, Louis Daniel Brodsky, Barbara Brent Brower, Lynn Levin and Robert Deluty. Subscribers: 1,400.

How to Submit: Cover letter with brief bio (2-3 lines) required. E-mail submissions OK. Responds in up to 4 months. Returns mss only with SASE. Pays 2 copies. Open to unsolicited reviews. Poets may also send books for review consideration.

✓ $ ◉ JEWISH WOMEN'S LITERARY ANNUAL; JEWISH WOMEN'S RESOURCE CENTER (Specialized: ethnic, women), 820 Second Ave., New York NY 10017, phone (212)751-9223, fax (212)935-3523, founded 1994, editor Henny Wenkart.

Magazine Needs: *JWLA* appears annually in April and publishes poetry and fiction by Jewish women. They want "poems by Jewish women on any topic, but of the highest literary quality." They have published poetry by Alicia Ostriker, Savina Teubal, Grace Herman, Enid Dame, Marge Piercy and Lesléa Newman. As a sample the editor selected these lines from "A Yiddish Poet in Winter" by Layle Silbert:

> in this winter of my life/I invent two children/scampering in snow/nourished on remains/of my past
> they say/we'll be alive for you/may they burst into a spill/of my dimming language/with last stories/of
> Vilna/take what is left/in my memory/tramped by war exile/finish children/before my winter ends

The annual is 160 pgs., 6×9, perfect-bound with a laminated card cover, b&w art and photos inside. They receive about 500 poems a year, publish approximately 15%. Press run is 1,500 for 480 subscribers. Subscription: $18/3 issues. Sample: $7.50.

How to Submit: No previously published poems. No fax submissions. Poems are circulated to an editorial board. Often comments on rejections. Responds in up to 5 months. Pays 3 copies plus a small honorarium. Rights remain with the poet.

Book/Chapbook Needs & How to Submit: The Jewish Women's Resource Center holds a monthly workshop, sponsors occasional readings and also publishes a few books of poetry. "We select only 1 or 2 manuscripts a year out of about 20 submitted. But although authors then receive editing help and publicity, they bear the cost of production. Members of the workshop we conduct and poets published in our annual receive first attention."
Advice: "It would be helpful, but not essential, if poets would send for a sample copy of our annual before submitting."

☑ THE JOHNS HOPKINS UNIVERSITY PRESS, 2715 N. Charles St., Baltimore MD 21218, website www.press.jhu.edu, founded 1878. "One of the largest American university presses, Johns Hopkins is a publisher mainly of scholarly books and journals. We do, however, publish short fiction and poetry in the series Johns Hopkins: Poetry and Fiction, edited by John Irwin. Unsolicited submissions are not considered."

🌱 ☑ ◯ ☑ JONES AV.; OEL PRESS, 88 Dagmar Ave., Toronto, Ontario M4M 1W1 Canada, phone (416)461-8739, e-mail oel@interlog.com, website www.interbg.com/~oel, founded 1994, editor/publisher Paul Schwartz.
Magazine Needs: *Jones Av.* is published quarterly and contains "poems from the lyric to the ash can; starting poets and award winners." They want poems "up to 30 lines mostly, concise in thought and image. Prose poems sometimes. Rhymed poetry is very difficult to do well these days, it better be good." They have published poetry by Stan Rogal, Edward Mycue, rob mclennan and Peter Bakowski. As a sample the editor selected this poem, "the red apple" by Claudia K. Grinnell:

> the red apple/sliced in/two redeems/spilling flesh/surrenders/to fingertips/inviting deep/ascension
> when/halves meet

Jones Av. is 24 pgs., 5½×8½, photocopied and saddle-stapled with card cover, uses b&w graphics. They receive about 300 poems a year, accept approximately 40-50%. Press run is 100 for 40 subscribers. Subscription: $8. Sample: $2. Make checks payable to Paul Schwartz
How to Submit: Submit 5-8 poems at a time. No previously published poems or simultaneous submissions. Cover letter required. E-mail and disk submissions OK. Include e-mail submissions in body of message. Time between acceptance and publication is 6-9 months. Often comments on rejections. Publishes theme issues occasionally. For 2001 "Emily Dickinson/Dorothy Livesay" issue of poet's responses to these two writers. Deadline: September 2001. Remember, US stamps cannot be used in Canada. Responds in 3 months. Pays 1 copy. Acquires first rights. Staff reviews books and chapbooks of poetry and other magazines in 50-75 words, multi-book format. Poets may also send books for review consideration.

Ⓝ ⊕ ☑ THE DAVID JONES JOURNAL; THE DAVID JONES SOCIETY, 48 Sylvan Way, Sketty, Swansea, W. Glam SA2 9JB Wales, phone (01792)206144, fax (01792)205305, e-mail anne.price-owen@sihe.ac.uk, founded 1997, editor Anne Price-Owen.
Magazine Needs: *The David Jones Journal* annually publishes "material related to David Jones, the Great War, mythology and the visual arts." They want "poetry which evokes or recalls themes and/or images related to the painter/poet David Jones (1895-1974)." They have published poetry by John Mole, R.S. Thomas, Seamus Heaney and John Montague. As a sample we selected this poem, "Good Bye" by John Montague:

> René Hague, you endured your hospital bed/with thin rolled cigarettes, and mild soldier's curses/until
> they informed you that your wife was dead/and your own disease, terminal. Then you turned/your lean
> face to the wall, after a formal farewell://You gave me back the books you had borrowed,/George
> Herbert's The Temple, and Dante's Paradiso,/then, lifting my hand to your sere lips,/breathed Good
> bye. The gift of such grace/is like a rare liqueur from which memory sips.

The journal is about 160 pgs., 5½×8½, camera-ready printed and perfect-bound with full cover card cover, includes b&w illustrations. They receive about 12 poems a year, accept approximately 8%. Press run is 400 for 300 subscribers. Single copy: $12; subscription: $35. Sample: $10. Make checks payable to The David Jones Society.
How to Submit: Submit 1 poem at a time. No previously published poems; simultaneous submissions OK. E-mail and disk submissions OK. Cover letter preferred. Time between acceptance and publication is 6 months. Poems are circulated to an editorial board. "Two editors agree on publication." Publishes theme issues occasionally. Obtain guidelines via e-mail. Responds in 6 weeks. Sometimes sends prepublication galleys. Pays 2 copies. Acquires first rights. Reviews books and chapbooks of poetry and other magazines in 750 words, single book format. Open to unsolicited reviews. Poets may also send books for review consideration.

$☑ THE JOURNAL, Dept. of English, Ohio State University, 164 W. 17th Ave., Columbus OH 43210, phone (614)292-4076, fax (614)292-7816, e-mail thejournal05@postbox.acs.ohio-state.edu, website www.cohums.ohio-state.edu/english/journals/the_journal/, founded 1972, co-editors Kathy Fagan and Michelle Herman.
● Also see the listing for Ohio State University Press/*The Journal* Award in Poetry in this section.
Magazine Needs: *The Journal* appears twice yearly with reviews, essays, quality fiction and poetry. "We're open to all forms; we tend to favor work that gives evidence of a mature and sophisticated sense of the language." They have published poetry by Brigit Kelly, Lucia Perillo, Timothy Liu and Heather McHugh. *The Journal* is

6×9, professionally printed on heavy stock, 128-144 pgs., of which about 60 in each issue are devoted to poetry. They receive about 4,000 submissions a year, use approximately 200, and have a 3- to 6-month backlog. Press run is 1,900. Subscription: $12. Sample: $7.

How to Submit: No submissions via fax. On occasion editor comments on rejections. Pays 2 copies and an honorarium of $25-50 when funds are available. Acquires all rights. Returns rights on publication. Reviews books of poetry.

Advice: "However else poets train or educate themselves, they must do what they can to know our language. Too much of the writing we see indicates poets do not in many cases develop a feel for the possibilities of language, and do not pay attention to craft. Poets should not be in a rush to publish—until they are ready."

JOURNAL OF AFRICAN TRAVEL-WRITING (Specialized), P.O. Box 346, Chapel Hill NC 27514, website www.unc.edu/~ottotwo, founded 1996, contact poetry editor.

Magazine Needs: *JATW*, published biannually, "presents and explores past and contemporary accounts of African travel." They want "poetry touching on any aspect of African travel. Translations are also welcome." Published poets include José Craveirinha, Theresa Sengova, Charles Hood and Sonia Gomez. As a sample the editor selected these lines from "Warthog Music" by Lynn Veach Sadler:

> Who cannot believe there is a God/has not the Kenyan warthog seen,/for in the delicacy of its going—/ gossamer strings plucked by divining being.

JATW is 96 pgs., 7×10, professionally printed, perfect-bound, coated stock cover with cover and illustrative art, ads. Press run is 600. Subscription: $10. Sample: $6.

How to Submit: Submit up to 6 poems at a time. Include SASE. No previously published poems; simultaneous submissions OK. Cover letter preferred. Time between acceptance and publication is 3-12 months. "The poetry editor usually makes these selections." Sometimes comments on rejections. Send SASE for guidelines. Publishes theme issues. Responds in up to 6 weeks. Always sends prepublication galleys. Pays 5 copies. Acquires first international publication rights. Reviews books, chapbooks or magazines of poetry. Open to unsolicited reviews. Poets may also send books for review consideration.

Also Offers: Website includes submission guidelines, poetry, reviews, articles and interviews.

$ ◎ JOURNAL OF ASIAN MARTIAL ARTS (Specialized: sports/recreation), 821 W. 24th St., Erie PA 16502-2523, phone (814)455-9517, fax (814)526-5262, e-mail info@goviamedia.com, website www.goviamedia.com, founded 1991, editor-in-chief Michael A. DeMarco.

Magazine Needs: *JAMA* is a quarterly "comprehensive journal on Asian martial arts with high standards and academic approach." They want poetry about Asian martial arts and Asian martial art history/culture. They have no restrictions provided the poet has a feel for, and good understanding of, the subject. They don't want poetry showing a narrow view. "We look for a variety of styles from an interdisciplinary approach." As a sample the editor selected these lines from "Cloudburst" by R.E. Mitchell, Jr.:

> When a person strikes another/Is he hurting the other or himself . . ./Is he angry with another/Or with his own shortcomings?//Whether you are killed by flood or lightning,/A storm is still a storm.

The journal is 124 pgs., 8½×11, professionally printed on coated stock and perfect-bound with soft cover, b&w illustrations, computer and hand art and ads. Press run is 12,000 for 1,500 subscribers of which 50 are libraries, the rest mainly shelf sales. Single copy: $9.75; subscription: $32/year, $55/2 years. Sample: $10.

How to Submit: Previously published poems OK; no simultaneous submissions. E-mail submissions OK. Cover letter required. Often comments on rejections. Send SASE for guidelines or request via e-mail or fax. Responds in 2 months. Sometimes sends prepublication galleys. Pays $1-100 and/or 1-5 copies on publication. Buys first world and reprint rights. Reviews books of poetry "if they have some connection to Asian martial arts; length is open." Open to unsolicited reviews. Poets may also send books for review consideration.

Advice: "We offer a unique medium for serious poetry dealing with Asian martial arts. Any style is welcome if there is quality in thought and writing."

⊕ ✓ ◖ ◒ ◎ JOURNAL OF CONTEMPORARY ANGLO-SCANDINAVIAN POETRY; ORIGINAL PLUS (Specialized: translations), 11 Heatherton Park, Bradford on Tone, Taunton, Somerset TA4 1EU England, phone 01823 461725, e-mail smithsssj@aol.com, website http://members.aol.com/smithsssj/index.html, founded 1994, contact Sam Smith.

Magazine Needs: *JoCA-SP*, published biannually, features English poetry or English translations of Scandinavian poems and interviews with Scandinavian poets. They want "new poetry howsoever it comes, translations from Scandinavian and original English language poems." They do not want "staid, generalized, all form no content." Also accepts poetry written by children. They have published poetry by Richard Wonnacott, Tomas Tranströmer, Staffan Söderblom, Olav H. Hauge and Alexis Lykiard. As a sample the editor selected these lines from "We Too Are Laymen, Said the Waves" by Werner Aspenström, translated by Robin Fulton:

> Two nights in a row setting out from Stavanger/I made my way on foot over the Atlantic/between icebergs and oil-rigs/to the accompaniment/of excited conversations with the waves/who comforted me saying:/"We too are laymen."

JoCA-SP is 60-70 pgs., A5, offset printed, perfect-bound with CS1 cover stock. They receive about 1,000 poems a year, accept approximately 5%. Press run is 100-150 for 70 subscribers of which 12 are libraries. Single copy: £6; subscription: £11. Sample: £2 or £3 (sterling). Make checks payable to Sam Smith.

How to Submit: Submit up to 6 poems. Previously published poems and simultaneous submissions OK. E-mail submissions OK but only from outside UK. Cover letter preferred. "Please send hard copy submissions with 2 IRCs." Time between acceptance and publication is 6-8 months. Often comments on rejections. Send SASE (or SAE and IRC) for guidelines. Responds in 1 month. Always sends prepublication galleys. Pays 1 copy.
Also Offers: In 1997, original plus began publishing collections of poetry. They have published books by Don Ammons, Idris Caffrey and RG Bishop. Send SASE (or SAE and IRC) for details.

JOURNAL OF NEW JERSEY POETS (Specialized: regional), English Dept., County College of Morris, 214 Center Grove Rd., Randolph NJ 07869-2086, phone (973)328-5471, fax (973)328-5425, e-mail szulauf@ccm.edu, website www.garden.net/users/swaa/JrnlNJPoets.html, founded 1976, editor Sander Zulauf.
Magazine Needs: This biannual periodical uses poetry from current or former residents of New Jersey. They want "serious work that is regional in origin but universal in scope." They do not want "sentimental, greeting card verse." They have published poetry by Amiri Baraka, X.J. Kennedy, Brigit Pegeen Kelly, Kenneth Burke, Gerald Stern, Renée and Ted Weiss, and Rachel Hadas. As a sample the editor selected these lines from "How I Learned to Kiss" by Tina Kelley:

> Perhaps each time I took a dare I got imperceptibly better—/the rowboat on the reservoir, the bell tower over Old Campus,/the night spent stowed away on top of the Empire State/Building,/abandoned fort at Corinth, breakdown lane of I-95,/bathroom on the train to Portland,/dressing room in the sporting goods store.

JNJP is published in summer and winter and is digest-sized, offset printed, with an average of 64 pgs. Press run is 900. Subscription: $10/2 issues, $16/4 issues; institutions: $12/2 issues, $20/4 issues; students/senior citizens: $10/4 issues. Sample: $5.
How to Submit: There are "no limitations" on submissions; SASE required. E-mail and fax submissions OK. Electronic submissions will not be returned. Responds in up to 1 year. Time between acceptance and publication is within 1 year. Pays 5 copies and 1-year subscription. Acquires first North American serial rights. Only using solicited reviews. Send books for review consideration.
Also Offers: Website includes cover picture of latest issue, names of editors and links to the editors.

JOURNAL OF THE AMERICAN MEDICAL ASSOCIATION (JAMA) (Specialized: health concerns, themes), 515 N. State, Chicago IL 60610, phone (312)464-2417, fax (312)464-5824, e-mail charlene_breedlove@ama_assn.org, website www.jama.org, founded 1883, associate editor Charlene Breedlove.
Magazine Needs: *JAMA* has a "Poetry and Medicine" column and publishes poetry "in some way related to a medical experience, whether from the point-of-view of a health care worker or patient, or simply an observer. No unskilled poetry." They have published poetry by Aimée Grunberger, Floyd Skloot and Walt McDonald. As a sample the editor selected these lines from "Forensics" by Paula Tatarunis:

> Bodies are embarrassing, sci-Freud,/all orifice, tentacle and slime./We try to bundle them in haute couture./the alibi, disingenue, of mind//but there's always something left to rat us out—/hair in the comb, toenailclippings, pus,/a countertop aseethe with DNA,/sophisticated spoor, shorthand for us.//We're spirit, we insist. We're noumenal./Blackjacks spritz our lofty skulls with stars./But when we wake we're back where we belong:/mug shot, booked, embarrassed. Behind bars.

JAMA is magazine-sized, flat-spined, with glossy paper cover, has 360,000 subscribers of which 369 are libraries. They accept about 7% of 750 poems received/year. Subscription: $66. Sample free. "No SASE needed."
How to Submit: No previously published poems; simultaneous submissions OK, if identified. "I always appreciate inclusion of a brief cover letter with, at minimum, the author's name and address clearly printed. Mention of other publications and special biographical notes are always of interest." Fax submissions OK. "Poems sent via fax will be responded to by postal service." E-mail submissions OK (include in body of message with postal address). Publishes theme issues. Theme issues include AIDS, violence/human rights, tobacco, medical education, access to care and end-of-life care. "However, we would rather that poems relate obliquely to the theme." Pays 1 copy, more by request. "We ask for a signed copyright release, but publication elsewhere is always granted free of charge."
Also Offers: Website includes published poems; one poem per poet.

JUNCTION PRESS, P.O. Box 40537, San Diego CA 92164, founded 1991, publisher Mark Weiss.
Book/Chapbook Needs: Junction Press aims to publish "overlooked non-mainstream poetry." The press publishes 2 paperback books of poetry a year. They want "modern or postmodern formally innovative work, any form or length. No academic, Iowa school or formal poetry." They have published poetry by Armand Schwerner, Susie Mee, Richard Elman, José Kozer and Mervyn Taylor. They say their books are typically 72-96 pgs., 5½×8½, offset printed and perfect-bound with coated covers with graphics.

SENDING TO A COUNTRY other than your own? Be sure to send International Reply Coupons (IRCs) instead of stamps for replies or return of your manuscript.

How to Submit: Query first with 10-15 pgs. of poetry and a cover letter (bio unnecessary). Previously published poems OK; no simultaneous submissions. Often comments on rejections. Replies to queries in 6 months, to mss (if invited) "immediately." Pays 100 copies (out of a press run of 1,000).

Advice: "While I don't dismiss the possibility of finding a second Rimbaud, please note that all of my authors have been in their 50s and have written and published for many years."

✔️▢◯◑◉ **JUPITER'S FREEDOM (Specialized: science fiction/fantasy, horror, surreal)**, P.O. Box 110217, Palm Bay FL 32911-0217, phone (319)725-6243, fax (419)844-8388, e-mail contact@scifi.cjb. net, website www.scifi.cjb.net, founded 1998, editor Christine Smalldone.

Magazine Needs: *Jupiter's Freedom* is a quarterly online journal featuring fiction, poetry, art and articles. The editor is looking for "works which span the regions of science fiction—from speculative fiction to horror, fantasy and works of the surreal. I want poetry with edge, style and innovative thinking; with the ability to paint a visual landscape and go in new directions. Nothing sweet and sappy. I don't mind happy endings, just do them in an interesting way." As a sample we selected these lines from "A Bed Time Story" by Cs:

> I stand in silence, mezmerized by the story that/unfolds before my eyes. Like a child's fairy tale/being
> read by its mother, who sits at the edge of/our bed and subdues our eyes into sleep./Only to awaken
> in the midst of rest with fears of/dragons and monsters running in the dark places.

They receive about 100 poems a year, accept 50-60%. They also have a printed version of *Jupiter's Freedom*. The editor says it is 8½×11, desktop-published, brass fastened, 70 lb. card cover, includes b&w and color art. Subscription: $18/year. Sample: $5.

How to Submit: Submit 1-3 poems at a time. Previously published poems OK; no simultaneous submissions. E-mail, fax and disk submissions OK. Cover letter preferred. Publishes theme issues. Send SASE for guidelines and upcoming themes. Time between acceptance and publication is 1-2 months. Often comments on rejections. Send SASE for guidelines and specifications on electronic or disk submissions or request via e-mail. Responds in 3 weeks. Pays 1 copy and "3.5 inch floppy (no Mac)."

Advice: "Remember, the longer it is the better it must be. Please try to stay away from overused and abused genre stereotypes such as vampire redemption, time travel, dragons, fairies, or robots gone mad. We don't accept any submissions having to do with sex, racism, sexism, overly gory (just for the sake of it) or anything that demeans, slanders or belittles anyone or anything. Be yourself and your own voice. Dare to be bold and different, take chances. Learn from others, but don't be like others. Break the mold and break it hard if you have to."

🌐▢▢◑ **K.T. PUBLICATIONS; THE THIRD HALF; KITE BOOKS; KITE MODERN POETS; KITE YOUNG WRITERS**, 16 Fane Close, Stamford, Lincolnshire PE9 1HG England, founded 1987, editor Kevin Troop.

Magazine Needs: *The Third Half* is a literary magazine published irregularly. It contains "free-flowing and free-thinking material on most subjects." Also accepts poetry written by children. They are "open to all ideas and suggestions. No badly written or obscene scribbling." As a sample we selected this poem, "Without Words," by Isabel Cortan:

> a savage sound,/sharp crack of a man's hand/across a woman's chin//a ritual sound,/her weeping in
> the dark/burying her love

TTH is over 100 pgs., A5, neatly printed and perfect-bound with glossy card cover, includes line drawings and occasionally ads. They receive about 3,000 poems a year, accept approximately 20%. Press run is 100-500. Single copy: £5.50 in UK. Sample: £10 overseas. Make checks payable to K.T. Publications.

How to Submit: Submit 6 poems at a time. No previously published poems. Cover letter preferred. Time between acceptance and publication "depends on the work and circumstances." Seldom comments on rejections. Publishes theme issues occasionally. Responds in 2 weeks. Always sends prepublication galleys. Pays 1-6 copies. "Copyright belongs to the poets/authors throughout."

Book/Chapbook Needs & How to Submit: Under K.T. Publications and Kite Books, they publish 6 paperbacks and 6 chapbooks/year of poetry, short stories and books for children—"at as high a standard as humanly possible." Books are usually 50-60 pgs., A5, perfect-bound with glossy cover, and art ("always looking for more.") Query first, with up to 6 sample poems and a cover letter with brief bio and publication credits. "Also include suitable SAE—so that I do not end up paying return postage every time."

Also Offers: Offers a "reading and friendly help service to writers." Write for details.

Advice: "Be patient—and never give up writing."

🅽◑☻ **KAEDEN BOOKS**, P.O. Box 16190, Rocky River OH 44116, phone (440)356-0030, fax (440)356-5081, website http://kaeden.com, founded 1990, vice president Karen Evans, editor Craig Urmston.

• Kaeden Books is a member of the American Association of Publishers.

Book/Chapbook Needs: "*Kaeden Books* is a publisher of supplementary reading and educational materials designed for early and emergent readers, ages 5-9. It is our goal to produce materials that have high story/character interest for the student, as well as structure suitable for instruction. Our books are 12-24 pages in length. Remember, our readers are beginners or early readers in pre-kindergarten through third grade, so vocabulary and sentence structure must be appropriate for the early reading levels. Kaeden Books are used in many reading programs such as Reading Recovery (R), English as a Second Language (ESL) and many Title I programs.

Familiarity with these programs and methodologies will help you understand what we need from our authors." They publish 24 poetry titles per year. Books are usually 12-24 pgs., offset-printed and saddle-stitched, includes illustrations. Press run is usually 3,000-5,000.

How to Submit: Submit 5-6 sample poems. Previously published poems and simultaneous submissions OK. Cover letter preferred. "Submissions should be typed and accompanied with a brief bio." Reads submissions July, August and December only. Time between acceptance and publication is up to 1 year. Poems are circulated to an editorial board. "Submissions are first reviewed for appropriateness to published line, then reviewed by editorial board." Obtain guidelines via website. Responds in up to 1 year. "Although, we do not reply unless interested." Pay is negotiable. Buys all rights.

Advice: "We do not return submissions. We retain them and could (and have) 'rediscovered' new authors many years later."

KAIMANA: LITERARY ARTS HAWAII; HAWAII LITERARY ARTS COUNCIL (Specialized: regional), P.O. Box 11213, Honolulu HI 96828, founded 1974, editor Tony Quagliano.

Poets in *Kaimana* have received the Pushcart Prize, the Hawaii Award for Literature, Cades Award and the John Unterecker Award.

Magazine Needs: *Kaimana*, an annual, is the magazine of the Hawaii Literary Arts Council. Poems with "some Pacific reference are preferred—Asia, Polynesia, Hawaii—but not exclusively." They have published poetry by Howard Nemerov, John Yau, Reuben Tam, Reuel Denney, Tony Friedson, Lyn Lifshin, Haunani-Kay Trask, Anne Waldman and Joe Stanton. *Kaimana* is 64-76 pgs., 7½ × 10, saddle-stapled, with high-quality printing. Press run is 1,000 for 600 subscribers of which 200 are libraries. Subscription: $15, includes membership in HLAC. Sample: $10.

How to Submit: Cover letter with submissions preferred. Sometimes comments on rejections. Responds with "reasonable dispatch." Pays 2 copies.

Advice: "Hawaii gets a lot of 'travelling regionalists,' visiting writers with inevitably superficial observations. We also get superb visiting observers who are careful craftsmen anywhere. *Kaimana* is interested in the latter, to complement our own best Hawaii writers."

$ KALEIDOSCOPE: INTERNATIONAL MAGAZINE OF LITERATURE, FINE ARTS, AND DISABILITY (Specialized: disability themes), 701 S. Main St., Akron OH 44311-1019, phone (330)762-9755, fax (330)762-0912, founded 1979, senior editor Gail Willmott, editor-in-chief Dr. Darshan C. Perusek.

Magazine Needs: *Kaleidoscope* is based at United Disability Services, a nonprofit agency. Poetry should deal with the experience of disability but not limited to that when the writer has a disability. "*Kaleidoscope* is interested in high-quality poetry with vivid, believable images and evocative language. Works should not use stereotyping, patronizing or offending language about disability." They have published poetry by Sheryl L. Nelms. As a sample the editors selected these lines from "Stopping" by Sandra J. Lindow:

> Her silver hair, a startling halo,/Radiant above storm-worm face,/High cheek bones, a smile/Like the
> yard light going on,/A beacon in the dark,/A smile like coming home.

Kaleidoscope is 64 pgs., 8½ × 11, professionally printed and saddle-stitched with 4-color semigloss card cover, b&w art inside. Circulation is 1,500, including libraries, social service agencies, health-care professionals, universities and individual subscribers. Single copy: $5; subscription: $9 individual, $14 agency. Sample: $4.

How to Submit: Submit up to 5 poems at a time. Send photocopies with SASE for return of work. Previously published poems and simultaneous submissions OK, "as long as we are notified in both instances." Fax submissions OK. Cover letter required. All submissions must be accompanied by an autobiographical sketch. Deadlines: March and August 1. Publishes theme issues. Send SASE for upcoming themes. Themes for 2000 included "Disability and the Created Environment" and "Disability and Memoir/Biography." Responds in 3 weeks; acceptance or rejection may take 6 months. Pays $10 plus 2 copies. Rights return to author upon publication. Staff reviews books of poetry. Send books for review consideration to Gail Willmott, senior editor.

☑ $ KALLIOPE, A JOURNAL OF WOMEN'S LITERATURE & ART (Specialized: women, translations, themes); SUE SANIEL ELKIND POETRY CONTEST, 3939 Roosevelt Blvd., Jacksonville FL 32205, phone (904)381-3511, website www.fccj.org/kalliope, founded 1978, editor Mary Sue Koeppel.

Magazine Needs: *Kalliope* is a literary/visual arts journal published by Florida Community College at Jacksonville; the emphasis is on women writers and artists. The editors say, "We like the idea of poetry as a sort of artesian well—there's one meaning that's clear on the surface and another deeper meaning that comes welling up from underneath. We'd like to see more poetry from Black, Hispanic and Native American women. Nothing sexist, racist, conventionally sentimental. We will have one special theme issue each year. Write for specific guidelines." Poets published include Denise Levertov, Marge Piercy, Martha M. Vertreace, Karen Subach, Maxine Kumin and Tess Gallagher. As a sample the editor selected the following lines by Melanie Richards:

> With dried orange rind,/fragrant sage, and a blue//branch of coral, I seal/this package full of artifacts//
> in case the wild horses/all vanish from the earth,//or the red throat of the hummingbird/lies to us about
> summer;

Kalliope calls itself "a journal of women's literature and art" and publishes fiction, interviews, drama and visual art in addition to poetry. The magazine, which appears 3 times/year, is 7¼ × 8¼, flat-spined, handsomely printed on white stock, glossy card cover and b&w photographs of works of art. Average number of pages is 80. Press run is 1,600 for 400-500 subscribers of which 100 are libraries, 800 shelf sales. Subscription: $14.95/year or $24.95/2 years. Sample: $7.

How to Submit: Submit poems in batches of 3-5 with brief bio note, phone number and address. No previously published poems. Reads submissions September through April only. SASE required. Because all submissions are read by several members of the editing staff, response time is usually 3-4 months. Publication will be within 6 months after acceptance. Criticism is provided "when time permits and the author has requested it." Send SASE for guidelines and upcoming themes. Usually pays $10 or subscription. Acquires first publication rights. Reviews books of poetry, "but we prefer groups of books in one review." Open to unsolicited reviews. Poets may also send books for review consideration.

Also Offers: They sponsor the Sue Saniel Elkind Poetry Contest. 1st Prize: $1,000; runners up published in *Kalliope*. Deadline: November 1. Send SASE for details. Website includes writer's guidelines, names of editors, poetry contest guidelines, back issues list, table of contents of recent issues, "Lollipops, Lizards and Literature," special events, poetry.

Advice: "*Kalliope* is a carefully stitched patchwork of how women feel, what they experience, and what they have come to know and understand about their lives . . . a collection of visions from or about women all over the world. Send for a sample copy, to see what appeals to us, or better yet, subscribe!"

KARAMU, Dept. of English, Eastern Illinois University, Charleston IL 61920, founded 1966, co-editors Olga Abella and Lauren Smith.

Karamu has received grants from the Illinois Arts Council and has won recognition and money awards in the IAC Literary Awards competition.

Magazine Needs: *Karamu* is an annual, usually published by May, whose "goal is to provide a forum for the best contemporary poetry and fiction that comes our way. We especially like to print the works of new writers. We like to see poetry that shows a good sense of what's being done with poetry currently. We like poetry that builds around real experiences, real images and real characters and that avoids abstraction, overt philosophizing and fuzzy pontifications. In terms of form, we prefer well-structured free verse, poetry with an inner, sub-surface structure as opposed to, let's say, the surface structure of rhymed quatrains. We have definite preferences in terms of style and form, but no such preferences in terms of length or subject matter. Purpose, however, is another thing. We don't have much interest in the openly didactic poem. If the poet wants to preach against or for some political or religious viewpoint, the preaching shouldn't be so strident that it overwhelms the poem. The poem should first be a poem." They have published poetry by Allison Joseph, Katharine Howd Machan and Joanne Mokosh Riley. As a sample the editor selected these lines from "Climbing the Eiffel Tower at Night" by Barbara Crooker:

> *flood-lit, so the traceries of girder and beam/seem even more insubstantial, a conjurer's vision,/an airy web spun out of light. It's a pyramid of X's,/row on row of kisses curving up to the sky,/meeting at the vanishing point, where all things come/together.*

The format is 120 pgs., 5 × 8, matte cover, handsomely printed (narrow margins), attractive b&w art. They receive submissions from about 500 poets each year, use 40-50 poems. Sometimes about a year—between acceptance and publication. Press run is 350 for 300 subscribers of which 15 are libraries. Sample: $7.50.

How to Submit: Poems—in batches of no more than 5—may be submitted to Olga Abella or Lauren Smith. "We don't much care for simultaneous submissions. We read September 1 through April 1 only, for fastest decision submit February through April. Poets should not bother to query. We critique a few of the better poems. We want the poet to consider our comments and then submit new work." Publishes occasional theme issues. Send SASE for upcoming themes. Pays 1 copy. Acquires first serial rights.

Advice: "Follow the standard advice: Know your market. Read contemporary poetry and the magazines you want to be published in. Be patient."

KARAWANE: OR, THE TEMPORARY DEATH OF THE BRUITIST (Specialized: open mic/spoken word performers), (formerly *Voices From the Well*), 402 S. Cedar Lake Rd., Minneapolis MN 55405, e-mail fluffysingler@prodigy.net, founded 1997 as *Voices From the Well*, editor/publisher Laura Winton.

Magazine Needs: *Karawane* appears 2 times a year and "features poets, playwrights, fiction and nonfiction writers who perform their work in public. We want innovative, thoughtful, well-crafted poetry. Poetry that needs to be poetry, rather than short stories and essays with line breaks. We are spoken word, but more in the manner of Cabaret Voltaire than a poetry slam. Slam poetry rarely holds up on the page. No poems that tell stories; no doggerel. I don't mind formal poetry, but do it well." They have published poetry by Terrence J. Folz, Dave Okar and Richard Kostelanetz. As a sample the editor selected these lines from "As the Ground Breaks Upward" by Jeff Mores:

> *What was it that began this madness/changing our garden to war/lay down your devices . . ./even as the ground breaks upward/the sky will not fall.*

The editor says *Karawane* is 16-28 pgs., 8½ × 11, printed on newsprint, some inside art, ads. They receive about 100 poems a year, accept approximately 50%. Press run is 1,000 for 10 subscribers, 30 shelf sales; the remainder distributed free to festivals, open mics, inquiries, reviewers. Single copy: $3; subscription: $7/4 issues. Sample: $1, "donations of more appreciated." Make checks payable to Laura Winton. "To be considered poets must read at an open mic in their community. I prefer people be an ongoing part of their spoken word scene."

How to Submit: Submit 3-6 poems at a time. Previously published poems and simultaneous submissions OK. E-mail submissions OK. Cover letter preferred. "SASEs essential! I encourage simultaneous submissions and previously published poems if you retained subsequent rights. E-mail gets a faster response from me—try any format as long as it's PC compatible." Time between acceptance and publication is up to 6 months. Seldom comments on rejections. Responds in 6 months. Pays copies. Acquires one-time rights. Reviews books and chapbooks of poetry and other magazines in 500 words. Open to unsolicited reviews. Poets may also send books for review consideration. "Don't just send books though. Enclose a letter indicating that you want a review and a SASE or SASE postcard for a reply."

Advice: "Make your own scene! Don't wait for someone else to 'find' you. You can be a 'working poet,' with a little ingenuity and ambition. Poets should use every avenue available—lit mags, readings, self-publishing, cable access, leaving pamphlets on the bus, etc., to make themselves visible."

Ø KATYDID BOOKS, 1 Balsa Rd., Santa Fe NM 87505, founded 1973, editors/publishers Karen Hargreaves-Fitzsimmons and Thomas Fitzsimmons.

Book/Chapbook Needs & How to Submit: Katydid Books publishes 3 paperbacks and 3 hardbacks/year. "We publish two series of poetry: Asian Poetry in Translation (distributed by University of Hawaii Press) and American Poets." They are currently not accepting submissions.

N ⊕ Ø ◎ KAVYA BHARATI; STUDY CENTRE FOR INDIAN LITERATURE IN ENGLISH AND TRANSLATION (SCILET) (Specialized: poetry from India or on Indian themes), SCILET, P.O. Box 63, American College Madurai, Madurai, Tamil Nadu 625002 India, phone (091)0452-533609, fax (091)0452-531056, e-mail scilet@md2.vsnl.net.in, website www.scilet.org, founded 1988, director Paul L. Love, editor R.P. Nair.

Magazine Needs: *Kavya Bharati* annually publishes "Indian poetry originally written in English and English translations from regional languages of India. We want to see poetry that makes you see life with a new pair of eyes and affirms values." As a sample they selected this poem, "Memory" by Jayanta Mahapatra:

> Out there, a line of gray windows./black spaces in them./Something is supposed to be hidden there,/
> but it just won't fit./It's like the clock—/No one disturbs it.//Does every man have to bear his./for him
> to go on?/At times it's a scar from another's,/staring moodily at the twilight body./Sometimes a wisp
> of high cirrus/that can't see its way in impossible skies.//This evening, maybe/it will stand by my bed
> again,/a hollow word, an old harlot./There was never any choice,/proof perhaps of some human grace/
> before we escape its curses.

They say *KB* is 5½×8½, photo typeset and hard-bound with cardboard cover. They receive about 90 poems a year, accept approximately 20%. Publish 30 poems/issue. Press run is 1,000 for 200 subscribers of which 60 are libraries. Sample (including guidelines): $12. Make checks payable to Study Centre, *Kavya Bharati*.

How to Submit: Submit 6 poems at a time. No previously published poems. Cover letter required. Reads submissions January through June only. Submit seasonal poems 6 months in advance. Time between acceptance and publication is 6 months. Poems are circulated to an editorial board. "A three member advisory board selects all poems." Often comments on rejections. Publishes theme issues occasionally. Send SASE (or SAE and IRC) for upcoming themes. Responds in 6 months. Pays 2 copies. Acquires first rights. Reviews books of poetry. Open to unsolicited reviews. Poets may also send books for review consideration.

Also Offers: Conducts an annual creative writing workshop. Write for details.

Advice: "Keep writing."

⊕ Ø Ø KAWABATA PRESS; SEPIA POETRY MAGAZINE, Knill Cross House, Millbrook, Torpoint, Cornwall, United Kingdom, founded 1977, poetry editor Colin David Webb.

Magazine Needs: *Sepia Poetry Magazine* publishes "nontraditional poetry, prose and artwork (line only), open to all original and well thought-out work. I dislike rhymes, traditional poems and 'genre' stories. I want original and thought-provoking material." *Sepia* is published 3 times/year in an inexpensively produced, 32-page, digest-sized, saddle-stapled format, photoreduced from typescript, with narrow margins and bizarre drawings. They receive 500 submissions a year, use approximately 50. Press run is 150 for 75 subscribers of which 5-6 are libraries. Subscription: £2 ($10) a year. Sample: 75p. ($2).

How to Submit: Submit 6 poems at a time, typed. Prefers not to use previously published poems. Simultaneous submissions OK. "Letter with poems is polite." Always comments on rejections. Responds in 3 weeks. Pays 1 copy. Reviews books of poetry in 50-100 words. Open to unsolicited reviews. Poets may also send books for review consideration.

Advice: "Strike out everything that sounds like a cliché. Don't try any tricks. Work at it, have a feeling for what you write, don't send 'exercise' pieces. Believe in what you send."

Ø ◎ KELSEY REVIEW (Specialized: regional), Mercer County Community College, P.O. Box B, Trenton NJ 08690, phone (609)586-4800, ext. 3326, fax (609)586-2318, e-mail kelsey.review@mccc.edu, website www.mccc.edu, founded 1988, editor-in-chief Robin Shore.

Magazine Needs: *KR* is an annual published in September by Mercer County Community College. It serves as "an outlet for literary talent of people living and working in Mercer County, New Jersey only." They have no specifications as to form, length, subject matter or style, but do not want to see poetry about "kittens and puppies." Also accepts poetry written by children. They have published poetry by Valerie Egar, Betty Lies, Vida Chu and Helen Gorenstein. As a sample the editor selected this poem "The Whistler" by Nancy Scott:

> *A young man came to rent a room,/told me he had no job, no money./How do you live? I asked./I barter, he replied. I bet/you'd like a widescreen TV./I shook my head./Perhaps a new refrigerator?/I'd like the rent in cash./A year's supply of frozen meat?/I'm a vegetarian./He rapped his knuckles on the door,/I'll be back, he said,/and bounded down the front steps,/whistling.*

Kelsey Review is about 80 glossy pgs., 7×11, with paper cover and line drawings; no ads. They receive about 60 submissions a year, accept 6-10. Press run is 2,000. All distributed free to contributors, area libraries, bookstores and schools.

How to Submit: Submit up to 6 poems at a time, typed. No previously published poems or simultaneous submissions. Deadline: May 1. Always comments on rejections. May request information via e-mail. Responds in June of each year. Pays 5 copies. All rights revert to authors.

Also Offers: Website includes address, deadlines, encouragement and announced publication.

N $⃝ THE KENYON REVIEW; THE WRITERS WORKSHOP, Kenyon College, Gambier OH 43022, phone (740)427-5208, fax (740)427-5417, e-mail kenyonreview@kenyon.edu, website www.KenyonReview.org, founded 1939, editor David Lynn.

Poetry published in *The Kenyon Review* was also selected for inclusion in the 1996, 1997 and 1998 volumes of *The Best American Poetry* and they have received, for the second consecutive year, the *Pushcart Prize* in each of the three considered genres: poetry, fiction and nonfiction. *Kenyon Review* was the only literary magazine to win in all above categories in 1999.

Magazine Needs: *Kenyon Review* is a triquarterly review containing poetry, fiction, essays, criticism, reviews and memoirs. It features all styles and forms, lengths and subject matters. But this market is more closed than others because of the volume of submissions typically received during each reading cycle. Issues contain work by such poets as Erin Belieu, Judith Ortiz Cofer, Joy Harjo, Robert Dana, Katharine Whitcomb, Alicia Ostriker, Sherod Santos and Quincy Troupe. The elegantly printed, flat-spined, 7×10, 180-page review has a circulation of 4,000 for 3,200 subscribers of which 1,100 are libraries. They receive about 3,000 submissions a year, use about 50 pgs. of poetry in each issue, have a 1-year backlog. The editor urges poets to read a few copies before submitting to find out what they are publishing. Sample: $9 includes postage.

How to Submit: Unsolicited submissions are typically read from September 1 through March 31. Writers may contact by phone, fax or e-mail, but may submit mss by mail only. Responds in 3 months. Pays $15/page for poetry, $10/page for prose. Buys first North American serial rights. Reviews books of poetry in 2,500-7,000 words, single or multi-book format. "Reviews are primarily solicited—potential reviewers should inquire first."

Also Offers: Also sponsors The Writers Workshop, an annual 9-day event. 2000 dates: June 24 through July 2. Location: the campus of Kenyon College. Average attendance is 12 per class. Open to writers of fiction, nonfiction and poetry. Conference is designed to provide intensive conversation, exercises and detailed readings of participants' work. Past speakers have included Erin Belieu, Allison Joseph, P.F. Kluge, Wendy MacLeod, Pamela Painter, Nancy Zafris, David Baker and Reginald McKnight. Other special features include a limited-edition anthology produced by workshop writers and *The Kenyon Review* that includes the best writing of the session. College and non-degree graduate credit is offered. Cost for summer 2000 conference was $1,450, including meals, a room and tuition. Send SASE for application. Early application is encouraged as the workshops are limited. Website includes submission policy, guidelines, excerpts from recent issues, interviews, "weekly feature" and soon an index to Kenyon Review back issues.

◐ ⃝ ◎ THE KERF (Specialized: animals, nature/ecology), College of the Redwoods, 883 W. Washington Blvd., Crescent City CA 95531, founded 1995, editor Ken Letko.

Magazine Needs: *The Kerf*, annually published in May, features "poetry that speaks to the environment and humanity." They want "poetry that exhibits an environmental consciousness." Also accepts poetry written by children. They have published poetry by Ruth Daigon, Meg Files, James Grabill and George Keithley. As a sample the editor selected these lines from "The Stones" by Janine Canan:

> *Along the beach, stones/exposed by the retreating tide/greet me like friends from long ago./And I bend to gather eggs/mounds, ovals, crescents/smoothed by life in the tumbling sea.*

The Kerf is 40 pgs., 8½×5½, printed via Docutech, saddle-stitched with CS2 cover stock. They receive about 2,000 poems a year, accept approximately 1-3%. Press run is 400, 150 shelf sales; 100 distributed free to contributors and writing centers. Sample: $5. Make checks payable to College of the Redwoods.

How to Submit: Submit up to 5 poems (up to 7 pgs.) at a time. No previously published poems; simultaneous submissions OK. Reads submissions January 15 through March 31 only. Time between acceptance and publication is 3 months. Poems are circulated to an editorial board. "Our editors debate (argue for or against) the inclusion of each manuscript." Seldom comments on rejections. Send SASE for guidelines. Responds in 2 months. Sometimes sends prepublication galleys. Pays 1 copy. Acquires first North American serial rights.

N: ◯ ⊘ **KESTREL: A JOURNAL OF LITERATURE AND ART**, P.O. Box 1797, Clarksburg WV 26302-1797, phone (304)367-4815, fax (304)367-4896, e-mail kestrel@mail.fscwv.edu, website www.fscwv.edu/pubs/pubs_hp.html, founded 1993, editor Mary Dillow Stewart.

Magazine Needs: *Kestrel* appears 2 times a year and publishes "living literature and art . . . a larger selection of a writer's work (typically a minimum of three poems) with an author's preface. Normally, each poem is given its own page." *Kestrel* contains poetry, fiction, creative nonfiction, translations and artwork. They have published poetry by Michael Harper, Seamus Heaney, Lucille Clifton, Jean Valentine, Robert Bly and Shara McCallum. As a sample the editor selected this poem, "Dispersed Light" by Angela Ball:

> It shoots into the bedroom/sidelong to land/on a lover's chest/a strange slip of the tongue/about two
> inches square./Freshly composed,/modest and spectacular,/lively but unalive,/not one or a selection/
> but all: red orange yellow green blue/indigo violet and vice versa, insisting/and diving into each other,
> plus/extensions and undetectable/by the human eye. It can't be cut;/what tries to cover it/becomes its
> screen. Transitory,/permanent. Not diffuse but/spectral and actual.

The editor says *Kestrel* is 6×9, perfect-bound with glossy cover, includes art/graphics. They accept approximately 10% of poems received. Press run is 700 for 275 subscribers of which 75 are libraries, 300 shelf sales. Single copy: $6; subscription: $10. Sample: $5. Make checks payable to Fairmont State College.

How to Submit: Submit 6-10 poems, or 2-3 longer poems at a time. No previously published poems or simultaneous submissions. Cover letter preferred. "SASE recommended if response is desired." Time between acceptance and publication is 6 months. Poems are circulated to an editorial board. "Conscensus on every acceptance." Often comments on rejections. Publishes theme issues occasionally. Send SASE for guidelines or obtain via website. Responds in 4 months. Pays 5 copies. Acquires one-time rights.

Also Offers: Sponsors the Kestrel Writing Contest, a $500 award in both poetry and fiction. Entry fee: $15/submission (includes a one-year subscription to *Kestrel*). Send SASE for contest guidelines or obtain via website. Website includes guidelines, contest information, festival information.

■ ⊘ **KIMERA: A JOURNAL OF FINE WRITING**, 1316 Hollis, Spokane WA 99201, e-mail kimera@js.spokane.wa.us, website www.js.spokane.wa.us/kimera/, founded 1996, publisher Jan Strever.

Magazine Needs: *Kimera* is a biannual online journal (appears yearly in hard copy) and "attempts to address John Locke's challenge—'where is the head with no chimeras.' " They want poetry that "attempts to 'capture the soul in motion.' No flabby poems." They have published poetry by Gayle Elen Harvey, Janet McCann, Dennis Collins Johnson and C.E. Chaffin. They accept approximately 10% of poems/year. Press run is 300 for 200 subscribers. Single copy: $7; subscription: $14. Sample: $7.

How to Submit: Submit 3-6 poems at a time. No previously published poems; simultaneous submissions OK. Cover letter required. E-mail submissions in ASCII text OK. Poems are circulated to an editorial board. Seldom comments on rejections. Obtain guidelines via website. Responds in 3 months. Pays 1 copy. Acquires first rights.

⊕ ◎ ⊘ **KINGFISHER PUBLICATIONS PLC (Specialized: anthologies, children)**, New Penderel House, 283-288 High Holborn, London WC1V 7HZ United Kingdom, phone (0171)903-9999, fax (0171)242-4979.

Book/Chapbook Needs & How to Submit: Kingfisher Publications Plc publishes very little poetry. "We currently have six titles in print, anthologies of verse for children either on particular themes or for particular age-groups, compiled by leading British poets. Because our anthologies are compiled by outside editors, we do not accept unsolicited poetry."

✓ ⊘ **KINGS ESTATE PRESS**, 870 Kings Estate Rd., St. Augustine FL 32086-5033, phone (800)249-7485, e-mail kep@aug.com, founded 1993, publisher Ruth Moon Kempher.

Book/Chapbook Needs & How to Submit: "Publishes the best contemporary poetry available; all books are illustrated." They publish about 3 paperbacks/year. "Currently overstocked, not accepting submissions until after the year 2001."

✓ ⊘ **KIOSK**, 306 Clemens Hall, SUNY, Buffalo NY 14260, phone (716)645-2578, e-mail eng-kiosk@acsu.buffalo.edu, founded 1985, poetry editor Nathan Goldberg, fiction editor Kevin Grauke.

Magazine Needs: *Kiosk* is an annual literary magazine using poetry of "any length, any style, especially experimental." They have published poetry by Robert Creeley, Carl Dennis, Colette Inez, Jon Anderson, Ron Padgett and Charles Bernstein. The editor describes *Kiosk* as flat-spined, digest-sized. They receive about 1,000 poems a year, accept approximately 40. Subscription: $6. Sample: $5. Make checks payable to SUNY at Buffalo.

How to Submit: Submit poems in batches of 5. No simultaneous submissions. Cover letter not required, "but we suggest one be included." Reads submissions September 1 through May 1 only. Responds within 4 months. Pays in copies.

$ ⬚ ◯ ⊘ **THE KIT-CAT REVIEW; THE KIT-CAT REVIEW ANNUAL POETRY AWARD**, 244 Halstead Ave., Harrison NY 10528-3611, phone (914)835-4833, founded 1998, editor Claudia Fletcher.

Magazine Needs: *The Kit-Cat Review* appears quarterly and is "named after the 18th century Kit-Cat Club whose members included Addison, Steele, Congreve, Vanbrugh, Garth, etc. Purpose: to promote/discover excellence and originality." They want quality work—traditional, modern, experimental. Also accepts poetry written by children. They have published poetry by Romola Robb Allrud, Harriet Zinnes, Louis Phillips and Romania's Nobel Prize nominee Marin Sorescu. As a sample the editor selected these lines from "Poet's Day Off" by Mary Kennan Herbert:

> *sleep till the rooster/has left for work/read the morning paper very slowly/sip coffee in a desultory*
> *way/imagine ostrich plumes languidly/fanning a breeze just for me*

The editor says the *Review* is 75 pgs., 5½×8½, laser printed/photocopied, saddle-stitched with colored card cover, includes b&w illustrations. They expect to receive about 1,000 poems a year. Press run is 500 for 200 subscribers. Subscription: $25. Sample: $7. Make checks payable to Claudia Fletcher.

How to Submit: Submit any number of poems at a time. Previously published poems and simultaneous submissions OK. "Cover letter should contain relevant bio." Time between acceptance and publication is 2 months. Responds within 2 months. Pays up to $100 a poem and 2 copies. Buys first or one-time rights.

Also Offers: Sponsors The Kit-Cat Review Annual Poetry Award of $1,000.

⊘ ALFRED A. KNOPF, 201 E. 50th St., New York NY 10022. Over the years Knopf has been one of the most important and distinguished publishers of poetry in the United States. "The list is closed to new submissions at this time."

🖐 ⊘ ◎ KOJA (Specialized: form/style), 7314 21st Ave. #6E, Brooklyn NY 11204, e-mail mikekoja@aol.com, website www.monkeyfish.com/koja, founded 1996, editor Michael Magazinnik.

Magazine Needs: *Koja* is published annually and "interested in experimental poetry but also publishes experimental prose and b&w artwork." They want "visual/concrete poetry, avant-garde poetry and experimental poetry. No religious or classical work." Also accepts poetry written by children. They have published poetry by Eileen Myles, David Burlyuk, K.K. Kuzminsky, I. Weiss, Richard Kostelanetz and Bruce Andrews. The editor says *Koja* is 64 pgs., 8½×11, various printing and binding methods, glossy color cover. They receive about 300 poems a year, accept approximately 10%. Press run is 300 for 30 subscribers of which 5 are libraries, 200 shelf sales; 50 distributed free to contributors/reviewers. Subscription: $14. Sample: $7. Make checks payable to Michael Magazinnik.

How to Submit: Submit up to 10 poems at a time. No previously published poems or simultaneous submissions. "All unsolicited submissions should be accompanied by money order/check in the amount of $7 for a sample copy of the latest issue." Cover letter preferred. E-mail submissions OK in ASCII text or .jpg files. Time between acceptance and publication is 1-8 months. Seldom comments on rejections. Responds in up to 1 year. Pays 1 copy. Acquires first North American serial rights.

Also Offers: Website includes excerpts from previous issues—poetry and artworks, list of all the authors.

🌐 ✓ ⊘ KONFLUENCE; KONFLUENCE PRESS, Bath House, Bath Rd., Nailsworth, Stroud, Gloucestershire GL6 0JB United Kingdom, phone (01453)835896, fax (01453)835587, e-mail floherus@aol.com, founded 1998, editor Mark Floyer.

Magazine Needs: *Konfluence* is "an annual platform for poetry—mainly from the west country, United Kingdom, but accept anything from across the United Kingdom and the globe if it is suitable." They are "open to a wide variety of poetry. It must have a content/form equation which is successfully true unto itself. No stream of consciousness ranting! We want to see some craft." They have published poetry by Sam Smith, Geoff Stevens and Elizabeth Hawkins. As a sample the editor selected these lines from his poem "Circle Line":

> *Slumped across his seat (a Madame/Tussaud's escapee!) he circles/Marble Arch, Baker street,/round*
> *and round and round he must/re-cycle flesh to wax, devolve-/dissolve at last to powdered dust.*

The editor says *Konfluence* is 50 pgs., magazine-sized, printed and staple bound with cardboard cover. They accept approximately 10% of poems received. Press run is 100, 50% shelf sales; 50% distributed free to contributors. Single copy: $6. Make checks payable to Konfluence Press.

How to Submit: Submit 6 poems at a time. Line length for poetry is 10 minimum, 80 maximum. Previously published poems and simultaneous submissions OK. Fax and e-mail submissions OK. Cover letter preferred. Time between acceptance and publication is 9 months. Often comments on rejections. Responds in 1 month. Pays 1 copy.

Advice: "Do send your material in! This is an 'open' publishing venture. No rules—just quality content at the editor's whim/judgement."

✓ ⊘ KONOCTI BOOKS, 23311 County Rd. 88, Winters CA 95694, phone (530)662-3364, e-mail nrpeattie@earthlink.net, founded 1973, editor/publisher Noel Peattie, publishes poetry by invitation only.

Ⓝ 🔲 ◯ ⊘ KOTA PRESS; KOTA PRESS POETRY JOURNAL, phone (206)297-1012, e-mail editor@kotapress.com, website www.kotapress.com, founded 1999, editor Kara L.C. Jones.

Magazine Needs: *Kota Press Poetry Journal* is a quarterly online e-zine "seeking to publish new as well as seasoned poets. We seek to publish the best poetry that comes to us and then to support the poet in whatever ways she may need. While form is sometimes important, we are more interested in content. We want to know what you have to say. We are interested in the honesty and conviction of your poems. Give us accessibility over form any day. Seeing tankas, for instance, in 5-7-5-7-7 form can be interesting and accessible, but do not send us words that you have stuffed into a form just to say you could write in form." They have published poetry by Claudia Mauro, Charles Fishman and Nancy Talley. As a sample the editor selected these lines by Claudia Mauro from *Reading the River*:

> You must know the/value of story and carry a library in each clear eye/the fine art of butch is to take
> your seat at the fire/and unfold your own story—then toss it in, to rise/as heat and light.

How to Submit: Submit 4 poems at a time. Previously published poems OK; no simultaneous submissions. E-mail submissions only. Cover letter required. "Previously published poems must include credit to prior publication. We accept e-mail submissions only. Please include bio info in e-mail message. Be sure to give us contact info so we can get back to you." Reads submissions December 1 through January 30 for March issue; March 1 through April 30 for June issue; June 1 through July 30 for September issue; September 1 through October 30 for December issue. Time between acceptance and publication is 1-2 months. Publishes theme issues. Obtain guidelines and upcoming themes via website. Responds in 2 months. Acquires one-time electronic rights.

Also Offers: "Because we are an Internet magazine, we are able to provide writers with resources and support through links, articles and services—as well as producing a high-quality poetry journal. Please see our website at www.kotapress.com to find out more about us and about what we offer. We look forward to hearing from you and reading your poetry."

Advice: "If you want to be a published writer you must submit your work again and again and again to anywhere and everywhere. For every 100 rejections, you will quite possibly get 1 or 2 acceptances, but you won't get rejected or accepted if you don't submit in the first place!"

KRAX (Specialized: humor), 63 Dixon Lane, Leeds, Yorkshire LS12 4RR England, founded 1971, poetry editor Andy Robson.

Magazine Needs: *Krax* appears twice yearly, and publishes contemporary poetry from Britain and America. They want poetry which is "light-hearted and witty; original ideas. Undesired: haiku, religious or topical politics." 2,000 words maximum. All forms and styles considered. They have published poetry by Julia Darling, Bernard Young, Mandy Precious and Steve Sneyd. As a sample the editor selected these lines from "Rude Names" by Julia E. Fay:

> Would someone please try to explain/why elbows only have one name?/when our naughty bits have
> two or three,/it doesn't seem quite fair to me!

Krax is 6×8, 64 pgs. of which 30 are poetry, saddle-stapled, offset printed with b&w cartoons and graphics. They receive up to 1,000 submissions a year of which they use approximately 6%, have a 2- to 3-year backlog. Single copy: £3.50 ($7); subscription: £10 ($20). Sample: $1 (75p).

How to Submit: "Submit maximum of six pieces. Writer's name on same sheet as poem. Sorry, we cannot accept material on disk. SASE or SAE with IRC encouraged but not vital." No previously published poems or simultaneous submissions. Brief cover letter preferred. Responds in 2 months. Pays 1 copy. Reviews books of poetry (brief, individual comments; no outside reviews). Send books for review consideration.

Advice: "All editors have differing tastes so don't be upset by early rejection but please ensure you always send an address for response, whatever it may turn out to be."

KUMQUAT MERINGUE; PENUMBRA PRESS, P.O. Box 736, Pine Island MN 55963, phone (507)367-4430, e-mail moodyriver@aol.com, website www.geostar.com/kumquatcastle, founded 1990, editor Christian Nelson.

Magazine Needs: *Kumquat Meringue* appears on an irregular basis, using "mostly shorter poetry about the small details of life, especially the quirky side of love and sex. We want those things other magazines find just too quirky. Not interested in rhyming, meaning of life or high-flown poetry." Also accepts poetry written by children. The magazine is "dedicated to the memory of Richard Brautigan." They have published works by Gina Bergamino, T. Kilgore Splake, Antler, Monica Kershner, Lynne Douglass and Ianthe Brautigan. As a sample the editor selected these lines from "Leaping Lizards" by Emile Luria:

> After we made love . . . Kate said,/"You're so weird, really,/Even weirder than I thought."/And I
> thought, could she taste the salt,/Feel the sea lapping on my back?/I went to sleep wondering/About
> dinosaurs and lungfish/And the deepest reaches of the sea

KM is 40-48 pgs., digest-sized, "professionally designed with professional typography and nicely printed." Press run is 600 for 250 subscribers. Subscription: $10/3 issues. Sample: $5.

How to Submit: "We like cover letters but prefer to read things about who you are, rather than your long list of publishing credits. Previously published and simultaneous submissions are OK, but please let us know." Often comments on submissions. "Please don't forget your SASE or you'll never hear back from us. E-mail address is for 'hello, praise, complaints, threats and questions' only." Send SASE for guidelines. Usually responds in 3 months. Pays 1 copy. Acquires one-time rights.

THE OPENNESS TO SUBMISSIONS INDEX at the back of this book lists all publishers in this section by how open they are to submissions.

Also Offers: "Our website includes guidelines, poetry samples and all information about *Kumquat Meringue* and our other projects."

Advice: "Read *Kumquat Meringue* and anything by Richard Brautigan to get a feel for what we want, but don't copy Richard Brautigan, and don't copy those who have copied him. We just want that same feel. We also have a definite weakness for poems written 'to' or 'for' Richard Brautigan. Reviewers have called our publication iconoclastic, post-hip, post-beat, post-antipostmodern; and our poetry, carefully crafted imagery. When you get discouraged, write some more. Don't give up. Eventually your poems will find a home. We're very open to unpublished writers, and a high percentage of our writers had never been published anywhere before they submitted here."

☑ �‍◌ ◎ **KUUMBA (Specialized: ethnic, gay/lesbian/bisexual, love/romance/erotica)**, Box 83912, Los Angeles CA 90083-0912, phone (310)410-0808 or (770)306-0889, fax (310)410-9250 or (770)306-8846, e-mail newsroom@blk.com, website www.blk.com, founded 1991, editor Reginald Harris.

Magazine Needs: *Kuumba* is a biannual poetry journal of the black lesbian and gay community. They want subject matter related to black lesbian and gay concerns. "Among the experiences of interest are: coming out, interacting with family and/or community, substance abuse, political activism, oral histories, AIDS and intimate relationships." They do not want to see "gay-only subjects that have no black content, or black-only subjects with no gay content." They have published poetry by Robert Earl Penn Jr., Sharon Bridgforth, Mistinguette and Assotto Saint. As a sample we selected these lines from "The Sweetest Taboo" (for Gene) by Richard D. Gore:

> *Forbidden,/But I loved you anyway/Dark, smouldering, and sweet/Luminous Black skin and Sloe-eyes . . .*

Kuumba is 48 pgs., 8½×11, offset and saddle-stitched, with b&w cover drawing and ads. They receive approximately 500 poems a year, accept approximately 25%. Press run is 3,000 for 750 subscribers of which 25 are libraries, 2,000 shelf sales. Subscription: $7.50/year. Sample: $4.50. Make checks payable to BLK Publishing Company.

How to Submit: Submit no more than 5 poems at a time. No previously published poems; simultaneous submissions OK, if notified. Cover letter preferred. Seldom comments on rejections. Send SASE for guidelines or obtain via e-mail or website. Responds in 6 weeks. Pays 4 copies. Acquires first North American serial rights and right to anthologize.

Also Offers: Website includes writer's guidelines.

Advice: "Named for one of the Nguzo Saba (Seven Principles) which are celebrated at Kwanzaa, Kuumba means creativity." This poetry journal is not only dedicated to the celebration of the lives and experiences of black lesbians and gay men, but it is also intended to encourage new and experienced writers to develop their poetic craft.

Ⓝ ◌ ◌ ◌ ◌ **KWIL KIDS PUBLISHING; THE KWIL CAFÉ NEWSLETTER; KWIL KIDS NEWSLETTER; THE KWIL CLUB**, Box 29556, Maple Ridge, British Columbia V2X 2V0 Canada, phone/fax (604)465-9101, e-mail kwil@telus.net, founded 1996, publisher Kwil.

Magazine Needs: *Kwil Kids* is a quarterly newsletter "publishing stories/poems to encourage and celebrate writers in the Kwil Club." They want poetry that is "gentle; with compassionate truth and beauty; peace; humor; for children, by children, about children. No profane, hurtful, myopic, violent, political or satirical work. They have published poetry by Darlene Slevin (adult), Gord Brandt (adult), Wendy Matthews (adult), Torrey Janzen (age 10), Carol McNaughton (age 6) and Ben Stoltz (age 11). As a sample they selected this poem by Kwil:

> *I know that I'd sigh and grimace/When you'd fight about your play/But let peace spread from the playground/Throughout the world one day.*

Kwil Kids is 8 pgs., (two 11×17 pages folded in half), includes b&w graphics. They receive about 400 poems a year, accept approximately 80%. Publish 8 poems/issue. Press run is 200 for 150 subscribers. Subscription: $20/individual, $25/family (cost includes membership to the Kwil Club). Sample: SASE (or SAE and IRC) and $2. Make checks payable to Kwil Kids Publishing.

How to Submit: Submit 5 poems at a time. Cover letter preferred. "Submit work by mail, e-mail or fax." Submit seasonal poems 3 months in advance. Time between acceptance and publication is 3-6 months. Always comments on rejections. "Kwil always provides encouragement and personalized response with SASE (or SAE and IRC)." Publishes theme issues occasionally. Send SASE for guidelines. Responds in April, August and December. Pays 1 copy. Acquires one-time rights.

Also Offers: "Offers 5¢ royalty (rounded to nearest dollar) on poems turned into cards for 'The Kwil Collection' sold at a local cafe, at the 'Kwil Kids Publishing Centre' and by mail order." They also sponsor The Kwil Club—a club for readers, writers, and artists of all ages. Membership features include 4 quarterly issues of the Kwil Kids newsletter, 4 quarterly issues of "Letters from the Kwil Cafe" newsletter; newsletter, newspaper, and greeting card publishing opportunities; a free subscription to Kwil's e-mail poetry list; reading, writing, and publishing tips and encouragement galore. Membership fees: $20 individual, $25 family.

Advice: "Kwil's motto: Keep your pencil moving (and your keyboard tapping!) Just be who you are, and do what you do. Then all of life's treasures will come to you."

◉ **LA JOLLA POET'S PRESS; NATIONAL POETRY BOOK SERIES; SAN DIEGO POET'S PRESS; AMERICAN BOOK SERIES**, P.O. Box 8638, La Jolla CA 92038, editor/publisher Kathleen Iddings.

Book Needs & How to Submit: La Jolla Poet's Press and San Diego Poet's Press are nonprofit presses that publish only poets who "have published widely. No beginners here." They have published 35 individual poet's books and 5 poetry anthologies featuring poetry by Allen Ginsberg, Carolyn Kizer, Galway Kinnell, Tess Gallagher, Robert Pinsky and Carolyn Forche. As a sample the editor included these lines from "Hester's Grammer" in *Curved Space* by Susan Terris:

> *He laid his boots beside my slippers and they lay there./(Past.)/He has laid his body next to mine and*
> *it has lain there./(Perfect.)//Lay, lies/laid, lay/laid, lain./All quite grammatically correct and, still, it*
> *is not/the lay or laid that bothers him but the lies.//He may love to lie with me, yet to lie about me is*
> *for him/a tense not coped with in any text of standard usage./(Imperfect.)*

The editor says most books are approximately 100 pgs., 5½ × 8½, perfect-bound, with laminated covers. Sample: $10.

⬤ **THE LAIRE, INC.,** P.O. Box 5524, Ft. Oglethorpe GA 30742, fax (706)858-1071, founded 1995, editor Kim Abston.

Magazine Needs: *the LAIRE* is a quarterly "newsletter for poets and poetry lovers, dedicated to bringing to our readers quality poetry, and related subject matter which is both creatively and/or socially aware. Open to all forms of poetry, provided it is well executed, both creatively and technically. Poetry may be of any length or subject, but we tend to prefer poems that are 40 lines or less and socially and/or politically aware." As a sample the editor selected these lines from a poem by Gregory Fiorini:

> *In that line of neglect stand revolutionaries/portable to their cause/of wings sans feathers/among*
> *debris/and all other ways akimbo*

the LAIRE is 8 pgs., 8½ × 11, photocopied, corner-stapled with line drawings and clip art. They receive about 1,500 poems a year, accept approximately 9%. Press run is 1,000 for 300-400 subscribers of which 50 are libraries, 400 shelf sales; 100 distributed free to schools, prisons, etc. Subscription: $10. Sample: $2.

How to Submit: Submit up to 5 poems at a time. No previously published poems or simultaneous submissions. Cover letter preferred. Disk submissions OK. "Author's name, address, and telephone number must appear on each page. One poem per page. We accept 1.44meg IBM formatted floppy disk submissions, provided name, address, and phone are on label. Nothing returned without SASE." Time between acceptance and publication is 1-6 months. Poems are circulated to an editorial board. "Poems are reviewed by the editorial board with the editor having final approval." Seldom comments on rejections. Publishes theme issues occasionally. Send SASE for guidelines. Responds in 2 months. Pays 1 copy. Reviews books and chapbooks of poetry and other magazines in 150-200 words, single or multi-book format. Open to unsolicited reviews. Poets may also send books for review consideration.

Also Offers: Sponsors poetry contests. Send SASE for details. They also accept article submissions on any subject related to poetry, including critiques, biographies, book reviews, and F.Y.I. pieces.

N ◯ ◎ **LAKE SHORE PUBLISHING; SOUNDINGS (Specialized: anthology)**, 373 Ramsay Rd., Deerfield IL 60015, phone (847)945-4324, founded 1983, poetry editor Carol Spelius.

Magazine Needs: *Soundings* is an effort "to put out decent, economical volumes of poetry." Reading fee: $1/ page. They want poetry which is "understandable and moving, imaginative with a unique view, in any form. Make me laugh or cry or think. I'm not so keen on gutter language or political dogma—but I try to keep an open mind. No limitations in length." They have published poetry by Bob Mills, Gertrude Rubin and June Shipley. The editor selected these sample lines from "It Used To Be So Easy" by Constance Vogel:

> *The night before your wedding/you looked across the table/at almost-in-laws waiting for their meal/*
> *and wondered if, in time,/you'd be their main course.*

The first 253-page anthology, including over 100 poets, is a paperback, at $7.95 (add $1 p&h), which was published (in 1985) in an edition of 2,000. It is flat-spined, photocopied from typescript, with glossy, colored card cover with art.

How to Submit: Submit 5 poems at a time, with $1/page reading fee, and a cover letter telling about your other publications, biographical background, personal or aesthetic philosophy, poetic goals and principles. Simultaneous submissions OK. Any form or length. "Reads submissions anytime, but best in fall." Send SASE for upcoming themes. Responds in 1 year. Pays 1 copy and half-price for additional copies. "All rights return to poet after first printing."

Book/Chapbook Needs & How to Submit: The editor will read chapbooks, or full-length collections, with the possibility of sharing costs if Lake Shore Publishing likes the book ($1/page reading fee). "I split the cost if I like the book." Sample copy of anthology or random choice of full-length collections to interested poets: $5.

⊕ **$** ◎ **LANDFALL: NEW ZEALAND ARTS AND LETTERS (Specialized: regional)**, University of Otago Press, P.O. Box 56, Dunedin, New Zealand, phone 0064 3 479 8807, fax 0064 3 479 8385, e-mail university.press@stonebow.otago.ac.nz, founded 1947, originally published by Caxton Press, then by Oxford University Press, now published by University of Otago Press, editor Chris Price.

Magazine Needs: *Landfall* appears twice a year (in May and November). They say, "Apart from occasional commissioned features on aspects of international literature, *Landfall* focuses primarily on New Zealand literature and arts. It publishes new fiction, poetry, commentary, and interviews with New Zealand artists and writers, and reviews of New Zealand books." Single issue: NZ $21.95; subscription: $39.95 NZ for 2 issues for New Zealand subscribers, $30 A for Australian subscribers, $30 US for other overseas subscribers.

How to Submit: Submissions must be typed and include SASE. "Once accepted, contributions should if possible also be submitted on disk." Publishes theme issues. Send SASE for upcoming themes and guidelines. Pays (for poetry) $15 NZ/printed page and 1 copy. New Zealand poets should write for further information.

⊕ ◯ ◑ ◎ **LAPWING PUBLICATIONS (Specialized: ethnic/nationality)**, 1 Ballysillan Dr., Belfast BT14 8HQ United Kingdom, phone/fax (01232)391240, founded 1989, director/editor Dennis Greig, director/editor Rene Greig.

Book/Chapbook Needs: Lapwing publishes "emerging Irish poets and poets domiciled in Ireland, plus the new work of a suitable size by established Irish writers." They publish 6-10 chapbooks/year. They want poetry of all kinds. But, "no crass political, racist, sexist propaganda even of a positive or 'pc' tenor." They have published poetry by Robert Greacen, James Simmons, Padraig Fiacc, Jack Holland and Desmond O'Grady. As a sample the editor selected these lines from "The Only Emperor" by Robert Greacen:

> I knock, I knock/I challenge the silence./Knock! Knock! Knock!/I open the door into the room.

Chapbooks are usually 44-52 pgs., A5, Docutech printed and saddle-stitched with colored card cover, includes occasional line art.

How to Submit: "Submit 6 poems in the first instance, depending on these, an invitation to submit more may follow." No previously published poems; simultaneous submissions OK. Cover letter required. Poems are circulated to an editorial board. "All submissions receive a first reading. If these poems have minor errors or faults, the writer is advised. If poor quality, the poems are returned. Those 'passing' first reading are retained and a letter of conditional offer is sent." Often comments on rejections. Replies to queries in 1 month; to mss in 2 months. Pays 25 author's copies (out of a press run of 250).

Also Offers: Sponsors the new imprint Ha'Penny Press and Prize. Send SASE for details.

Advice: "Due to limited resources, material will be processed well in advance of any estimated publishing date. All accepted material is strictly conditional on resources available, no favoritism. The Irish domestic market is small, the culture is hierarchical, poet/personality culture predominates, literary democracy is limited."

Ⓝ ⊕ ◑ **LATERAL MOVES; AURAL IMAGES**, 5 Hamilton St., Ashley Bridge, Bolton BL1 6RJ United Kingdom, phone (01204)596369, *Lateral Moves* founded 1995, Aural Images founded 1993, general editor Alan White, poetry editor Nick Britton.

Magazine Needs: *Lateral Moves* appears 6 times a year and includes poetry, stories, criticism, reviews, interviews, etc. They want "dangerous, challenging, subversive, transgressive poetry. No new romantic, doggerel, sappy stuff, or work about seasons." They have published poetry by Dave Ward, Gerald England, Sam Smith and Stephen Blyth. As a sample the editor selected these lines (poet unidentified):

> We let them sleep. All day, all night. We tell/the new ones: here you sleep until you're well./We wake them up a bit for Sunday visits./Food we don't bother with. They can't sit up,/their backs are raw. You see the flies. Nurse sometimes/gives them a wash. The way you'd wash a back.

The editor says *LM* is 48-52 pgs., magazine-sized, photocopied and stapled with card cover, includes art/graphics. They receive about 500-1,000 poems a year, accept approximately 10-15%. Press run is 150 for 75 subscribers. Subscription: £12/1 year, £24/2 years (sterling only). Sample: £2.50 and £35 p&h (sterling only). "Payment of equivalent in U.S. dollar bills is acceptable."

How to Submit: Submit 6 poems maximum at a time. Line length for poetry is around 80 maximum. Previously published poems OK; no simultaneous submissions. Cover letter optional. "All submissions should be typed, where possible, and should be clearly accompanied by your name and address. If you have no access to a typewriter, please write as legibly as possible." Reads submissions "4 times per year at 3 monthly internals." Time between acceptance and publication is up to 1 year. Seldom comments on rejections. Publishes theme issues occasionally. Send SASE for guidelines. Responds in 3 months. Pays 1 copy. Acquires one-time rights. Reviews books and chapbooks of poetry and other magazines in 1,500 words, single book format. Open to unsolicited reviews. Poets may also send books for review consideration.

Book/Chapbook Needs & How to Submit: Aural Images publishes 0-1 paperbacks and 0-2 chapbooks per year. However, they are not currently accepting ms submissions. They also publish occasional anthologies. Send SAE and IRC for details.

Advice: "We echo the standard advice given by all small magazines—consider buying at least one copy of the mag itself or (dare we say it) a subscription before submitting. We get a lot of material from different sources and standards are high, although new writers are also warmly encouraged. Buying a magazine or two means that you get a feel for the kinds of things we like, and that we can carry on publishing cool new literature on a nonprofitmaking basis."

◖ **LAUREL REVIEW; GREENTOWER PRESS**, Dept. of English, Northwest Missouri State University, Maryville MO 64468, phone (816)562-1265, founded 1960, co-editors William Trowbridge, David Slater, Beth Richards and Catie Rosemurgy.

Magazine Needs: *LR* is a literary journal appearing twice a year using "poetry fiction, and creative nonfiction of the highest literary quality." They have published poetry by Patricia Goedicke, Paul Zimmer, Miller Williams, Albert Goldbarth, David Citino and Nancy Willard. As a sample the editors selected these lines from "Wheel" by Jim Simmerman:

> *Don't fall in love before you've made the wheel/your study. See how it crushes and churns/unsullied*
> *on to the next disaster./See how it burns like the hoop an animal/learns to leap through for its supper.*
> *Study/the heart and its demolition derby.*

This handsome journal (128 pgs., 6×9) features excellent poems—usually more than 20 each issue—in all styles and forms. Press run is 900 for 500 subscribers of which 53 are libraries, 100 shelf sales. Subscription: $8/year. Sample: $6.

How to Submit: Submit 4 poems at a time. No previously published poems or simultaneous submissions. Reads submissions September 1 through May 31 only. Editor "does not usually" comment on submissions. Responds in up to 4 months. Always sends prepublication galleys. Pays 2 copies plus 1-year subscription. Rights revert to author upon publication.

📷 ▢ ◑ ◎ **LAURELS; WEST VIRGINIA POETRY SOCIETY (Specialized: membership)**, Rt. 2, Box 13, Ripley WV 25271, e-mail mbush814@aol.com, founded 1996, editor Jim Bush.

Magazine Needs: *Laurels* is the quarterly journal of the West Virginia Poetry Society containing 95% poetry/ 5% art. Only considers work from WVPS members. They want traditional forms and good free verse. "If it's over 100 lines it must be very, very good. No porn, foul language, shape poems; no 'broken prose.'" Also accepts poetry written by children, if members. They have published poetry by Jane Stuart, JeanPaul Jenack and Thomas Downing. The editor says *Laurels* is 50 pgs., digest-sized, mimeographed and saddle-stapled with paper cover, some pen-and-ink art, no ads. They receive about 2,000 poems a year, accept approximately 50%. Press run is 250 for 150 subscribers. Membership: $12. Sample: $4. Make checks payable to the West Virginia Poetry Society for a subscription, to Jim Bush for a sample.

How to Submit: Requires contributors be members. For membership in WVPS, send $12 to Linda Poe, Rt. 1, Box 25, Gay WV 25244. Submit 4-5 poems at a time. Previously published poems and simultaneous submissions OK. Cover letter preferred including brief bio. E-mail submissions OK (submit in body of message). Time between acceptance and publication is 3-12 months. Always comments on rejections. Publishes theme issues March 15, May 15, August 15 and November 15. Send SASE for guidelines. Responds "next day, usually." Sometimes sends prepublication galleys. Pays 1 copy. Acquires one-time rights. Staff briefly reviews 3-4 books a year if author is a member. Send books for review consideration.

Also Offers: Sponsors a 35-category annual contest for members. Entry fee: no fee to current WVPS members or K-12 students, $1/poem for nonmembers, maximum of $12 for 12 or more categories. Send SASE for guidelines.

Advice: "Our purpose is to encourage and aid amateur poets who believe that words can be used to communicate meaning and to create beauty."

✓ ▢ ▢ **LEAPINGS LITERARY MAGAZINE; LEAPINGS PRESS**, 2455 Pinercrest Dr., Santa Rosa CA 95403, fax (707)568-7531, e-mail 72144.3133@compuserve.com, website home.inreach.com/editserv/, founded 1998, editor S.A. Warner.

Magazine Needs: *Leapings* is a semiannual literary magazine that publishes essays, book reviews, b&w artwork, literary and genre fiction, and poetry. They are "open to any form, but prefer shorter verse. No rhymed for rhyming sake; no pornography." Also accepts poetry written by children. They have published poetry by Kit Knight, Kenneth Pobo, Anselm Brocki, John Grey, Leslie Woolf Hedley and John Taylor. As a sample we selected these lines from "Her love in a widened margin" by G.E. Coggshall:

> *She rises at five a.m. unrebuked/for her nightgown's raveled hem. Each day/wrinkles like skin. The*
> *corners of her/wallpaper curl away from the plaster.//Her hindsight is clouded from cataracts,/yet she*
> *believes in all her layered-up/experience, her brick-and-mortar regrets.*

The editor says *Leapings* is 35-50 pgs., digest-sized, laserjet printed and saddle-stapled with cardstock cover, uses b&w graphics. They receive about 1,000 poems a year, accept approximately 10%. Press run is 200 for 25 subscribers of which 5 are libraries, about 50 shelf sales. Single copy: $6; subscription: $10/year. Sample: $5. Make checks payable to S.A. Warner.

How to Submit: Submit up to 6 poems at a time. No previously published poems or simultaneous submissions. Cover letter preferred. E-mail (poetry, only in body of message) and fax submissions OK. "Poetry manuscripts may be submitted single-spaced and e-mailed." SASE with sufficient postage required for return of ms sent via regular mail. Time between acceptance and publication is 6 months. Often comments on rejections. Send SASE for guidelines or obtain via e-mail or website. Responds in 2 months. Pays 2 copies. Acquires first rights. Reviews books and chapbooks of poetry and other magazines in 300 words, single book format. Open to unsolicited reviews. Poets may also send books for review consideration.

Also Offers: *Leapings* sponsors an annual poetry competition to "encourage poets, and to recognize and reward excellence. Any poet residing in the U.S. is eligible to submit manuscripts." The competition has 3 categories: general, diversity of cultures and residents of the Pacific Coast states. Submit no more than 6 poems total. Entry fee: $5 for the first poem, $1 for each additional poem up to a maximum of six poems. Awards: $25 for 1st

Place, $15 for 2nd Place, $10 for 3rd Place, plus publication. Postmark deadline: May 1. Awards announced by June 1. Send SASE for details or visit website. Website includes writer's guidelines, competition guidelines, subscription information and online featured poem.

THE LEDGE, 78-44 80th St., Glendale NY 11385, founded 1988, editor-in-chief/publisher Timothy Monaghan, co-editors George Held and Laura M. Corrado.

Magazine Needs: "We publish the best poems we receive. We seek poems with purpose, poems we can empathize with, powerful poems. Excellence is the ultimate criterion." Contributors include Sherman Alexie, Kurt Brown, Tony Gloeggler, Barry Seiler, Hal Sirowitz and Brooke Wiese. As a sample the editor-in-chief selected these lines from "Crossed Lines" by Elton Glaser:

> *If you were at hand, and the night warm,/And all the crossed lines clear,/Would we undo Newton and*
> *confuse the physical,//Proving that two bodies can enclose/The same space at the same time,/As in*
> *that hybrid gift, that tourist curio//Where the Midwest finds itself/Suddenly at sea: a sand dollar/Set*
> *in the smooth belly of a buckeye burl.*

The Ledge is 128 pgs., digest-sized, typeset and perfect-bound with b&w glossy cover. They accept 5% of poetry submissions. Press run is 1,000, including 400 subscribers. Single copy: $7; subscription: $13/2 issues, $24/4 issues or $32/6 issues.

How to Submit: Submit 3-5 poems at a time. Include SASE. No previously published work. Simultaneous submissions OK. Reads submissions September through May only. Responds in 4 months. Pays 2 copies. Acquires one-time rights.

Also Offers: *The Ledge* sponsors an annual poetry chapbook contest, as well as an annual poetry contest. Send SASE for details.

Advice: "I believe the best poems appeal to the widest audience and consider *The Ledge* a truly democratic publication in that regard."

LEFT CURVE (Specialized: ethnic/nationality, political, social issues), P.O. Box 472, Oakland CA 94604-0472, phone (510)763-7193, e-mail leftcurv@wco.com, website www.ncal.verio.com/~leftcurv, founded 1974, editor Csaba Polony.

Magazine Needs: *Left Curve* appears "irregularly, about every ten months." The journal "addresses the problem(s) of cultural forms, emerging from the crisis of modernity, that strives to be independent from the control of dominant institutions, and free from the shackles of instrumental rationality." They want poetry that is "critical culture, social, political, 'post-modern,' not purely formal, too self-centered, poetry that doesn't address in sufficient depth today's problems." They have published poetry by Devorah Major, W.K. Buckley and Seamus Carraher. As a sample the editor selected these lines by Christos Tsiokas:

> *The great God money has dominion all over this globe. West, East. North,/South. Air, fire, water, earth.*
> *I could walk this planet, roam the last desert,/sail the lost sea searching for my Authentic Man. And*
> *find instead/Only Narcissus gazing into my reflection.*

Left Curve is about 140 pgs., 8½×11, offset printed, perfect-bound with Durosheen cover, photos and ads. Press run is 2,000 for 200 subscribers; 50 are libraries, 1,500 shelf sales. Subscription: $30/3 issues (individuals). Sample: $10.

How to Submit: Submit up to 5 poems at a time. E-mail submissions OK. Cover letter stating "why you are submitting" required. Publishes theme issues. Send SASE for guidelines and upcoming themes. Responds in up to 6 months. Pays 3 copies. Open to unsolicited reviews. Poets may also send books for review consideration.

Also Offers: Website includes a statement of the editorial position, recent issues, poetry, guidelines and contact information.

LIBIDO: THE JOURNAL OF SEX AND SEXUALITY (Specialized: erotica, humor, gay/lesbian/bisexual), P.O. Box 146721, Chicago IL 60614-6721, phone (773)275-0842, fax (773)275-0752, e-mail rune@mcs.com, founded 1988, editors Marianna Beck and Jack Hafferkamp, contact J.L. Beck.

Magazine Needs: *Libido* is published 4 times/year. "Form, length and style are open. We want poetry of any and all styles as long as it is erotic and/or erotically humorous. We make a distinction between erotica and pornography. We want wit, not dirty words." They have published poetry by William Levy, Nigel Hazeldine and Robert Perchan. *Libido* is 88 pgs., digest-sized, professionally printed, flat-spined, with 4-color varnished card cover. They accept about 2% of poetry received. Press run is 9,500 for 3,500 subscribers, 3,500 shelf sales and 1,500 single issues by mail. Subscription: $30 in US, $33 in Canada (US funds), $40 in Mexico, $50 in Europe and $60 elsewhere. Sample: $9.

How to Submit: Submit 2-3 poems at a time. Cover letter including "a one-sentence bio for contributors' page" required with submission. "Please, no handwritten mss and do not submit via fax or e-mail." Responds in 3 months. Pays $10-25 plus 1 copy. Send books for review consideration "only if the primary focus is love/eroticism."

LIBRA PUBLISHERS, INC., 3089C Clairemont Dr., PBM 383, San Diego CA 92117, phone/fax (858)571-1414, poetry editor William Kroll.

Book/Chapbook Needs: Publishes two professional journals, *Adolescence* and *Family Therapy*, plus books, primarily in the behaviorial sciences but also some general nonfiction, fiction and poetry. "At first we published books of poetry on a standard royalty basis, paying 10% of the retail price to the authors. Although at times we were successful in selling enough copies to at least break even, we found that we could no longer afford to publish poetry on this basis. Now, unless we fall madly in love with a particular collection, we offer professional services to assist the author in self-publishing." They have published books of poetry by Martin Rosner, William Blackwell, John Travers Moore and C. Margaret Hall.

How to Submit: Prefers complete ms but accepts query with 6 sample poems, publishing credits and bio. Replies to query in 2 days, to submissions in 2-3 weeks. Mss should be double-spaced. Sometimes sends prepublication galleys. Send 9×12 SASE for catalog. Sample books may be purchased on a returnable basis.

THE LICKING RIVER REVIEW, Dept. of Literature and Language, Northern Kentucky University, Highland Heights KY 41099, e-mail lrr@nku.edu, founded 1991, faculty advisor Andrew Miller, mail submissions to poetry editor.

Magazine Needs: *TLRR* is an annual designed "to showcase the best writing by Northern Kentucky University students alongside work by new or established writers from the region or elsewhere." They have no specifications regarding form, subject matter or style of poetry. "No long poems (maximum 75 lines)." They have published poetry by Elizabeth Howard, Errol Miller and Judi A. Rypma. The review is 96 pgs., 7×10, offset printed on recycled paper and perfect-bound with a 16-page artwork inset (all art solicited). They accept 5% of the poetry received. Press run is 1,500. Sample: $5.

How to Submit: Submit up to 5 poems at a time. No previously published poems, no multiple or simultaneous submissions. Reads submissions September through November only. Publishes in June or July. Poems are circulated to an editorial board. Responds in up to 6 months. Pays in copies. Rights revert to author. Requests acknowledgment if poem is later reprinted.

LIFTOUTS MAGAZINE; PRELUDIUM PUBLISHERS, Dept. PM, 1414 S. Third St., Suite 102, Minneapolis MN 55454-1172, fax (612)305-0655, e-mail barcass@mr.net, founded 1971, poetry editor Barry Casselman, is a "publisher of experimental literary work and work of new writers in translation from other languages." Currently not accepting unsolicited material. *Liftouts* appears irregularly.

LIGHT, Box 7500, Chicago IL 60680, founded 1992, editor John Mella.

Magazine Needs: *Light* is a quarterly of "light and occasional verse, satire, wordplay, puzzles, cartoons and line art." They do not want "greeting card verse, cloying or sentimental verse." The editor says *Light* is 64 pgs., perfect-bound, including art and graphics. Single copy: $5; subscription: $18. Sample: $4.

How to Submit: Submit 1 poem on a page with name, address, poem title and page number on each page. No previously published poems or simultaneous submissions. Seldom comments on rejections. Send #10 SASE for guidelines. Responds in 3 months or less. Always sends prepublication galleys. Pays 2 copies to domestic contributors, 1 copy to foreign contributors. Open to unsolicited reviews; query first. Poets may also send books for review consideration.

LILITH MAGAZINE (Specialized: women, ethnic), 250 W. 57th St., Suite 2432, New York NY 10107, phone (212)757-0818, fax (212)757-5705, e-mail lilithmag@aol.com, website www.lilithmag.com, founded in 1976, editor-in-chief Susan Weidman Schneider.

Magazine Needs: *Lilith* "is an independent magazine with a Jewish feminist perspective" which uses poetry by Jewish women "about the Jewish woman's experience. Generally we use short rather than long poems. Run four poems/year. Do not want to see poetry on other subjects." They have published poetry by Irena Klepfisz, Lyn Lifshin, Marcia Falk and Adrienne Rich. It is 48 pgs., magazine-sized, glossy. "We use colors. Covers are very attractive and professional-looking (one has won an award). Generous amount of art. It appears 4 times a year, circulation about 10,000, about 6,000 subscriptions." Subscription: $18 for 4 issues. Sample: $6.

How to Submit: Send up to 3 poems at a time; advise if simultaneous submission. Editor "sometimes" comments on rejections. Send SASE for guidelines.

Advice: "(1) Read a copy of the publication before you submit your work. (2) Be realistic if you are a beginner. The competition is *severe*, so don't start to send out your work until you've written for a few years. (3) Short cover letters only. Copy should be neatly typed and proofread for typos and spelling errors."

LILLIPUT REVIEW (Specialized: form), 282 Main St., Pittsburgh PA 15201-2807, website http://donw714.tripod.com/lillieindex.html, founded 1989, editor Don Wentworth.

THE BOOK PUBLISHERS INDEX, located at the back of this book, lists those publishers who consider full-length book collections.

Magazine Needs: *Lilliput* is a tiny (4½×3.6 or 3½×4¼), 12- to 16-page magazine, appearing irregularly and using poems in any style or form no longer than 10 lines. They have published *What is Born* by Jen Besemer and *Footprints and Fingerprints* by Gary Hotham and poetry by Cid Corman, Lonnie Sherman, Lyn Lifshin and Miriam Sagan. As a sample the editor selected this poem, "#380" by M. Kettner:

> end of the day . . ./parking lots deserted/buildings only things/holding up the sky

LR is laser-printed on colored paper and stapled. Press run is 250. Sample: $1 or SASE. Make checks payable to Don Wentworth.

How to Submit: Submit up to 3 poems at a time. Currently, every fourth issue is a broadside featuring the work of one particular poet. Send SASE for guidelines. Responds within 3 months. Pays 2 copies/poem. Acquires first rights. Editor comments on submissions "occasionally—always try to establish human contact."

Book/Chapbook Needs & How to Submit: Started the Modest Proposal Chapbook Series in 1994, publishing 1 chapbook/year, 18-24 pgs. in length. Chapbook submissions are by invitation only. Query with standard SASE. Sample chapbook: $3. Chapbook publications include *The Kingdom of Loose Board & Rusted Nail* by Christien Gholson.

Advice: "A note above my desk reads 'Clarity & resonance, not necessarily in that order.' The perfect poem for *LR* is simple in style and language and elusive/allusive in meaning and philosophy. *LR* is open to all short poems in approach and theme, including any of the short Eastern forms, traditional or otherwise."

LIME GREEN BULLDOZERS, P.O. Box 4333, Austin TX 78765, e-mail oysterpubs@mindspring.com, founded 1986.

Magazine Needs: *LGB* is a publication whose purpose is "to expose new, young writers and to communicate." They want "anything honest and without pretense. No boring academic crap." They have published poetry by Judson Crews, Lyn Lifshin, Edward Mycue and Alan Catlin. They say the format "depends on the number of submissions that make it in." Press run is 500 for 50 subscribers, 400 shelf sales. Sample: $5. Make checks payable to Alaina Duro.

How to Submit: "It is recommended that contributors purchase a sample copy before contributing." Submit 5 poems at a time. Previously published poems and simultaneous submissions OK. Cover letter preferred. Reads submissions November through January 1 only. Has a large backlog of work. Seldom comments on rejections. Publishes theme issues. Send SASE for upcoming themes. Obtain guidelines via e-mail. Responds "as soon as I can." Pays 1 copy. Acquires one-time rights.

Advice: "I'm very choosy about what I include. I'm struggling to maintain a personal publication that has a 'community' feel to it. I can't stand getting an envelope full of poetry from someone who has no idea or care for what *Lime Green Bulldozers* is about."

LIMESTONE: A LITERARY JOURNAL (II), Dept. of English, 1215 Patterson Office Tower, University of Kentucky, Lexington KY 40506-0027, phone (606)257-7008, founded as *Fabbro* in 1979, as *Limestone* in 1986, editor Dan Elkinson.

Magazine Needs: *Limestone* is a literary annual edited by University of Kentucky graduate students showcasing "poetry that matters, poetry that shows attention to content and form. We're interested in all poetics, but we do watch for quality of thought and a use of language that will wake up readers and resonate in their minds." They have published poetry by T. Crunk, Nikky Finney, Wendell Berry, Frank X. Walker and James Baker Hall. It is 5½×8½, offset printed and perfect-bound. They receive about 1,100 poems a year, use approximately 40-50. Press run is 500. Single copy: $5; 3-year subscription: $12; 3-year (institution): $20. Sample: $5.

How to Submit: Submit up to 10 pgs. at a time. Include cover letter and SASE. Simultaneous submissions OK. No previously published material. Responds in up to 6 months or more. Pays 2 copies.

Advice: "Send your best work."

LIMESTONE CIRCLE, P.O. Box 453, Ashburn VA 20146-0453, e-mail renjef@earthlink.net, founded 1998, editor Renee Carter Hall.

Magazine Needs: *Limestone Circle* appears quarterly. "We publish artistic, accessible poetry. Free verse is preferred, but we will read formal, experimental, Oriental forms, etc., in hopes of publishing a variety of styles and voices. We will consider poems containing adult language and subjects but nothing gratuitous, please." They have published poetry by M.C. Bruce, John Grey, Una Nichols Hynum and Anne Wilson. As a sample the editor selected these lines from "Leaving" by Ric Kasini Kadour:

> The leaves fall and bury summer. Mounds/upon mounds of them like pages//of my journal, used and past. I think/of the leaves and what I have written://weeks on the cape, afternoons/at the cafes, arguments over how we sleep.

LC is approximately 40 pgs., 8½×5½, digitally copied and saddle-stapled with matte cardstock cover, includes b&w artwork and photos. They print approximately 20-30% of poems received. Press run is 100 for 30 subscribers, 20 shelf sales. Single copy: $4; subscription: $12/1 year (4 issues). Sample: $2. Make checks payable to Renee Carter Hall.

How to Submit: Submit 3-5 poems at a time, typed with name and address on each page. No previously published poems or simultaneous submissions. Cover letter preferred. E-mail submissions OK "provided they are in the body of the message, not as attached files." If poems have odd spacing, indents, etc., please submit hard copy instead. Time between acceptance and publication is 1-4 months. Sometimes comments on rejections. Send SASE for guidelines or obtain via e-mail. Responds in 2 months for postal submissions; usually within 1 week for e-mail submissions. Pays 1 copy; additional copies available at a discount. Acquires first rights.

Also Offers: Also accepts submissions of b&w artwork and photos; send SASE for art guidelines or obtain via e-mail.

Advice: "I give respectful consideration to all submissions. That said, please remember that editors are human beings. This implies two things: first, that we like to be treated in a friendly, polite, and professional manner, and second, that any editor's decision is just one person's opinion. Keep sending out your best work and eventually someone will publish it."

LIMITED EDITIONS PRESS; ART: MAG, P.O. Box 70896, Las Vegas NV 89170, phone (702)734-8121, founded 1982, editor Peter Magliocco.

Magazine Needs: They "have become, due to economic and other factors, more limited to a select audience of poets as well as readers. We seek to expel the superficiality of our factitious culture, in all its drive-thru, junk-food-brain, commercial-ridden extravagance—and stylize a magazine of hard-line aesthetics, where truth and beauty meet on a vector not shallowly drawn. Conforming to this outlook is an operational policy of seeking poetry from solicited poets primarily, though unsolicited submissions will be read, considered and perhaps used infrequently. Sought from the chosen is a creative use of poetic styles, systems and emotional morphologies other than banally constricting." They have published poetry by Richard D. Houff, Alan Catlin, James Purdy, Donald Ryburn, T. Kilgore Splake, Wendell Metzger and Duane Locke and normal. As a sample the editor selected these lines from "Icelandic Urban Poets" by Nathan Whiting:

> Icelandic urban poets know/gasoline, scenery lovable/at population zero./They live in Oslo/or Manhattan. Let God freeze.

ART: MAG, appearing in 1-2 large issues of 100 copies/year, is limited to a few poets. Subscription: $10. Sample: $5 or more. Make checks payable to Peter Magliocco.

How to Submit: Submit 5 poems at a time with SASE. "Submissions should be neat and use consistent style format (except experimental work). Cover letters are optional." No previously published poems; simultaneous submissions OK. Sometimes comments on rejections. Publishes theme issues. Send SASE for guidelines and upcoming themes. Responds within 3 months. Pays 1 copy. Acquires first rights. Staff occasionally reviews books of poetry. Send books for review consideration.

Book/Chapbook Needs & How to Submit: "A recently published chapbook for '99-00 is: *4-On-4 (The Neo(N) VERS(O)* by selected poets (Richard D. Houff, Alan Catlin, James Purdy and the mag man). For any other press chapbook possibilities, query the editor before submitting any manuscript."

Advice: "The mag is seeking a futuristic aestheticism where the barriers of fact and fiction meet, where inner- and outer-space converge in the realm of poetic consciousness in order to create a more productively viable relationship to the coming 'cyberology' of the 21st century."

THE LINK & VISITOR (Specialized: nationality, religious, women), 30 Arlington Ave., Toronto, Ontario M6G 3K8 Canada, phone (416)651-7192, fax (416)651-0438, e-mail linkvis@idirect.com, founded 1878, editor Esther Barnes.

Magazine Needs: *The Link & Visitor* provides monthly "encouragement, insight, inspiration for Canadian Christian women; Baptist, mission and egalitarian slant. Poetry must relate to reader's experience; must be grounded in a biblical Christian faith; contemporary in style and language; upbeat but not naive. We do not want to see anything that has already been better said in the Bible or traditional hymns. No rhymes. No whines or rank." They have published poetry by Barbara Mitchell and Joan Bond. *L&V* is 16 pgs., magazine-sized, offset printed with self cover. They receive about 20 poems a year, accept approximately 30%. ("We have a few poets we use regularly because their work fits our mix.") Press run is 4,500. Subscription: $14 (Canadian), $16 (US). Sample: $1.50 (Canadian).

How to Submit: Submit up to 5 poems at a time. Line length for poetry is 8 minimum, 30 maximum. Previously published poems and simultaneous submissions OK. E-mail submissions OK. Cover letter required. Include SASE with Canadian stamps. Time between acceptance and publication is up to 2 years. Seldom comments on rejections. Publishes theme issues occasionally. Send SASE for guidelines and upcoming themes. Pays $10-25 (Canadian). Buys one-time rights.

Advice: "Canadian writers only, please."

LINKS, Bude Haven, 18 Frankfield Rise, Tunbridge Wells TN2 5LF United Kingdom, e-mail bill.headd on@nationwideisp.net, founded 1992, editor Bill Headdon.

Magazine Needs: *Links* is published biannually in April and October and contains good quality poetry and reviews. They want "contemporary, strong poetry; must relate to the 'real' world; up to 80 lines. No chopped-up prose; no bleeding heart first-person confessions; no mock Shelley." They have published poetry by Gross, Bartlett and Shuttle. As a sample the editor selected these lines from "Masterpiece" by Barbara Daniels:

> I am a transparent woman,/My lover looks through me,/into a collaged landscape,/where any man can see/tamed hills and perfect pastures,/ego ego running free.

Links is up to 32 pgs., A5, photocopied and saddle-stitched with card cover. They receive about 1,000 poems a year, accept approximately 7%. Press run is 200 for 100 subscribers of which 5 are libraries, 30 shelf sales. Subscription: £4/year (overseas £6), £7.50/2 years (overseas £10). Sample (with guidelines): £2 (£3 outside UK). **How to Submit:** Submit 5-6 poems at a time. No previously published poems or simultaneous submissions. Fax and e-mail submissions OK. Cover letter preferred. "No long bios or list of previous publications." Time between acceptance and publication is 1-6 months. Seldom comments on rejections. Send SASE for guidelines. Responds in 2 weeks. Pays 1 copy. Acquires first rights. Reviews books and chapbooks of poetry and other magazines in 100-200 words, single or multi-book format. Open to unsolicited reviews. Poets may also send books for review consideration.

N ⊕ 🗂 ◯ LINKWAY MAGAZINE, The Shieling, The Links, Burry Port, Curms SA16 0H6 S. Wales United Kingdom, founded 1995, editor Fay C. Davies.
Magazine Needs: "*Linkway* is a quarterly general interest magazine for writers and friends. It publishes new writers alongside established ones and includes poetry, articles, stories, tips and other items." They want all types of poetry, any topic or style. No erotica or crude language. Also accepts work by children. "Please state age." They have published poetry by Ken Ross (Scotland), Andy Boteril (UK) and Siona Kham (South Africa). As a sample the editor selected her poem "February into March":
> *February rain drips/through leafless trees/Crocus open purple heads/to a pale watery sun/Snowdrop groups ring/silent bells in the westerly breeze.*
The editor says *Linkway* is up to 60 pgs., magazine-sized, cardboard cover, includes illustrations. They receive about 300 poems a year, accept approximately 50%. Press run is 300 for 140 subscribers. Subscription: £15 (sterling). Sample for postage. Make checks payable to F. C. Davies.
How to Submit: Submit 1-4 poems at a time. Line length for poetry is 42 maximum. No previously published poems. Cover letter preferred. "Poem must be clearly typed or printed, can be hand printed. Writer's notes requested, name and address on each submission. Please send brief details for writers notes." Time between acceptance and publication is 3 weeks. Often comments on rejections. Publishes theme issues occasionally. Send SASE (or SAE and IRC) for guidelines. Responds in 3 weeks. Reviews books and chapbooks of poetry and other magazines in 500 words. Open to unsolicited reviews. Poets may also send books for review consideration.
Also Offers: "Prizes awarded for the best item in each category. All children receive a prize."

✓ $ ◯ LINTEL, 24 Blake Lane, Middletown NY 10940, phone (914)344-1690, founded 1977, poetry editor Walter James Miller.
Book/Chapbook Needs: "We publish poetry and innovative fiction of types ignored by commercial presses. We consider any poetry except conventional, traditional, cliché, greeting card types, i.e., we consider any artistic poetry." We have published poetry by Sue Saniel Elkind, Samuel Exler, Adrienne Wolfert, Edmund Pennant, and Nathan Teitel. "Typical of our work" is Teitel's book, *In Time of Tide*, 64 pgs., digest-sized, professionally printed in bold type, flat-spined, hard cover stamped in gold, jacket with art and author's photo on back.
How to Submit: Query with 5 sample poems. Reads submissions January and August only. "We reply to the query within a month, to the ms (if invited) in 2 months. We consider simultaneous submissions if so marked and if the writer agrees to notify us of acceptance elsewhere." Ms should be typed. Always sends prepublication galleys. Pays royalties after all costs are met and 100 copies. Buys all rights. Offers usual subsidiary rights: 50%/50%. To see samples, send SASE for catalog and ask for "trial rate" (50%).
Advice: "Form follows function! We accept any excellent poem whose form—be it sonnet or free verse—suits the content and the theme. We like our poets to have a good publishing record in literary magazines, before they begin to think of a book."

✓ ◐ LIPS, Box 1345, Montclair NJ 07042, phone (201)662-1303, founded 1981, poetry editor Laura Boss.
Magazine Needs: *Lips* "is a quality poetry magazine that is published twice a year and takes pleasure in publishing previously unpublished poets as well as the most established voices in contemporary poetry. We look for quality work: the strongest work of a poet; work that moves the reader; poems take risks that work. We prefer clarity in the work rather than the abstract. Poems longer than six pages present a space problem." They have published poetry by Allen Ginsberg, Gregory Corso, Michael Benedikt, Maria Gillan, Stanley Barkan, Lyn Lifshin, Marge Piercy, Warren Woessner, David Ignatow and Ishmael Reed. As a sample the editor selected these lines from "The Dark" by Ruth Stone:
> *In the dark of the moon/under the shadow of our local hydrogen fluff,/I look out of my worn eyes/and see the bright new Pleiades/My sister lies in a box/in a New England graveyard.*
Lips is 70 pgs. (average), digest-sized, flat-spined. They receive about 8,000 submissions/year, use less than 1%, have a 6-month backlog. Circulation is 1,000 for 200 subscriptions, approximately 100 are libraries. Sample: $6. Occasional double issues are $10.
How to Submit: Poems should be submitted between September and March only, 6 pgs., typed, no query necessary. She tries to respond in 1 month but has gotten backlogged at times. Sometimes sends prepublication galleys. Pays 1 copy. Acquires first rights. Send SASE for guidelines.
Advice: "Remember the 2 T's: Talent *and* Tenacity."

☑ ⬜ ⊘ **THE LISTENING EYE**, Kent State Geauga Campus, 14111 Claridon-Troy Rd., Burton OH 44021, e-mail graceb@geocities.com, website www.geocities.com/Athens/3716, founded 1970 for student work, 1990 as national publication, editor Grace Butcher, assistant editors Jim Wohlken and Joanne Speidel.

Magazine Needs: *TLE* is an annual publication, appearing in late summer/early fall, of poetry, short fiction, creative nonfiction and art that welcomes both new and established poets and writers. They want "high literary quality poetry. Prefer shorter poems (less than two pages) but will consider longer if space allows. Any subject, any style. No trite images or predictable rhyme." Also accepts poetry written by children if high literary quality. They have published poetry by Walter McDonald, Lyn Lifshin and Simon Perchik. As a sample the editor selected these lines from "Casualties" by Dean Blehert:

> Some conversations are like sending my best men/on suicide missions.//Afterwards I must write hurtful
> letters/to their Greek, Latin, Sanskrit,/Hebrew and Old English parents,/and I just don't know what to
> say.

The Listening Eye is 52-60 pgs., 5½×8½, professionally printed and saddle-stapled with card stock cover with b&w art. They receive about 200 poems a year, accept approximately 5%. Press run is 300. Single copy: $4. Sample: $4. Make checks payable to Kent State University.

How to Submit: Submit up to 4 poems at a time, typed, single-spaced, 1 poem/page, name and address in upper left-hand corner of each page, with SASE for return of work. Previously published poems occasionally accepted; no simultaneous submissions. Cover letter required. No e-mail submissions. Reads submissions January 1 through April 15 only. Time between acceptance and publication is 4-6 months. Poems are circulated to the editor and 2 assistant editors who read and evaluate work separately, then meet for final decisions. Occasionally comments on rejections. Send SASE for guidelines or obtain via e-mail or website. Responds in 3 months. Pays 2 copies. Acquires first or one-time rights. Also awards $30 to the best sports poem in each issue.

Advice: "I look for tight lines that don't sound like prose, unexpected images or juxtapositions; the unusual use of language, noticeable relationships of sounds; a twist in viewpoint, an ordinary idea in extraordinary language, an amazing and complex idea simply stated, play on words and with words, an obvious love of language. Poets need to read the 'Big 3'—cummings, Thomas, Hopkins—to see the limits to which language can be taken. Then read the 'Big 2'—Dickinson to see how simultaneously tight, terse, and universal a poem can be, and Whitman to see how sprawling, cosmic and personal. Then read everything you can find that's being published in literary magazines today and see how your work compares to all of the above."

⊘ **LITERAL LATTÉ; LITERAL LATTÉ POETRY AWARDS**, 61 E. Eighth St., Suite 240, New York NY 10003, phone (212)260-5532, e-mail litlatte@aol.com, website www.literal-latte.com, founded 1994, editor Jenine Gordon Bockman, contact Lisa Erdman.

● Amy Holman's poem "Man Script" was just reissued in Best American Poetry.

Magazine Needs: *Literal Latté* is a bimonthly tabloid of "pure prose, poetry and art," distributed free in coffeehouses and bookstores in New York City, and by subscription. They are "open to all styles of poetry—quality is the determining factor." They have published poetry by Allen Ginsberg, Carol Muske, Amy Holman and John Updike. As a sample we selected these lines from "What The Screech Owl Knows" by John Sokol, 1st Place winner of the annual *Literal Latté* Poetry Awards:

> That, here, in the woods/of western Pennsylvania,/life burgeons by the hour/while death rides a pig;/
> that larvae open like popcorn/and everything living/feasts on last year's detritus; . . .

LL is 24-28 pgs., 11×17, neatly printed on newsprint and unbound with b&w art, graphics and ads. They receive about 3,000 poems a year, accept approximately 1%. Press run is 25,000 for distribution in over 200 bookstores and coffeehouses in New York City and nationwide. Subscription: $11. Sample: $3.

How to Submit: No previously published poems; simultaneous submissions OK. Cover letter with bio and SASE required. E-mail submissions OK. "No attachments." Time between acceptance and publication is 6 months. Often comments on rejections. Send SASE for guidelines or request via e-mail. Responds in 3 months. Pays 10 copies and 3 subscriptions (2 gift subscriptions in author's name). All rights return to author upon publication.

Also Offers: They also sponsor the *Literal Latté* Poetry Awards, an annual contest for previously unpublished work. Offers $1,500 in awards and publication. They have added a "Food Verse" award; 1st Prize $500. Entry fee: $10 for 6 poems (or buy a subscription and the entry fee for 6 poems is included). A past contest was judged by Carol Muske. Send SASE or e-mail for current details. Website includes excerpts, guidelines, information on events and contests.

Ⓝ 💲⬜ ◎ **LITERALLY HORSES**, Equestrienne Ltd., P.O. Box 51554, Kalamazoo MI 49005, phone (616)345-5915, founded 1999, editor Laurie A. Cerny.

Magazine Needs: *Literally Horses* is "a quarterly venue for creative poetry/fiction and essays that have a horse/western lifestyle theme. Any style is acceptable. Nothing sexually explicit; nothing offensive; no curse words or racial overtones." They have published poetry by Tena Bastian. As a sample the editor selected these lines from Tena Bastian:

> For in the horse's eyes, she saw a reflection of her own fear/She looked into the horse's soul/And
> understood what brought her here/God had brought the two together/The only way he could/This horse
> was not a renegade/Simply misunderstood.

LH is about 20 pgs., 5½×8½, desktop-published and saddle-stitched with b&w paper cover, includes simple drawings, classified ads. They receive about 50 poems a year, accept approximately 75%. Press run is 1,000. Single copy: $2.25; subscription: $7.95. Sample (including guidelines): $2.75. Make checks payable to Equestrienne Ltd.

How to Submit: Submit 1-3 poems at a time. Line length for poetry is 5 minimum, 30 maximum. Previously published poems and simultaneous submissions OK. Cover letter required. "Cover letters with bio and release/permission to use poems. Include SASE for return of poems and acceptance." Time between acceptance and publication is 3 months. Often comments on rejections. Responds in 3 months. Pays $3/poem and 5 copies. Buys one-time rights. Reviews books and chapbooks of poetry in 150 words. Open to unsolicited reviews. Poets may also send books for review consideration.

Advice: "Know the topic of horses . . . terminology, etc. Don't try to fake it."

LITERARY FOCUS POETRY PUBLICATIONS; ANTHOLOGY OF CONTEMPORARY POETRY; INTERNATIONAL POETRY CONTESTS: FALL CONCOURS, SPRING CONCOURS, SUMMER CONCOURS (Specialized: anthology), P.O. Box 36242, Houston TX 77236-6242, phone/fax (281)568-8780, e-mail dprince1@swbell.net, website www.literaryfocus.com, founded 1988, editor-in-chief Adrian A. Davieson.

Magazine Needs: Purchase of anthology may be required of poets accepted for publication. Literary Focus publishes anthologies compiled in contests, 3 times/year, with prizes of $200, $100 and $50, plus "Distinguished Mention" and "Honorable Mention." "Contemporary poetry with no restriction on themes. 20-line limit. No abusive, anti-social poetry." As a sample we selected these lines from the editor's own poem "My Deep Fears":

> Out came the fears of yester-years/Eroding my very being. As I looked/The stream of tears cascaded my/Cheeks, reminding me the journey/Was not over.//Only yesterday I thought of my arrival/At shore, but now I know it was just a/Mirage, that to be thus is nothing but/To be safely thus!

The digest-sized anthologies are either flat-spined or saddle-stapled, 70 pgs., typeset.

How to Submit: Submit maximum submission 15 poems, minimum three poems. Previously published poems and simultaneous submissions OK. E-mail submissions OK. "In order to evaluate serious entries, a $5 entry fee is required for the first three poems. Poems are evaluated on an individual basis by a panel of five editors chaired by editor-in-chief. Poets are notified of acceptance two weeks after deadlines." Send SASE for guidelines or obtain via website. Pays up to 5 copies. Reviews books of poetry.

LITERARY MOMENTS, P.O. Box 30534, Pensacola FL 32503-1534, founded 1999, publisher/editor Larnette Phillips.

Magazine Needs: "*Literary Moments* is a quarterly journal suitable for the entire family; bringing back quality literature, nostalgia and storytelling to the written page. Publishes only unpublished or minimally published writers. I am open to all kinds of poetry. Although, I print more short stories and vignettes than poetry. There are no specific requirements except I will not use material with profanity, graphic sex or graphic violence." They have published poetry by Lindsey Kelly and Kevin Sanders. As a sample the editor selected these lines by Lindsey Kelly:

> The heart broken becomes/The heart open/To the eternal flame of love/That burns away/All grief, all rage, all suffering

The editor says *LM* is 30-50 pgs., 8½×11, professionally printed and saddle-stitched with b&w soft cover. They receive about 5 poems a year. Publish 1 poem/issue. Press run is 2,200 for 2,000. "Publication is distributed directly to subscribers only." Subscription: $40/year. Sample: $12.50. Make checks payable to Larnette Phillips or *Literary Moments*.

How to Submit: "Because this publication is new, I prefer that people enter their submissions through my writing competitions. Reading fees are $15 each (per entry). I hold three annual writing competitions per year for short stories, vignettes and poetry. Deadlines are in February, May and September. Each entrant should include his or her name, address and telephone number in the upper left hand corner of first manuscript page. All manuscripts should be double-spaced and SASE is required. No response or acknowledgement without SASE. Regardless of whether participants have written poetry, short story or vignette, cash prizes are as follows: 1st Prize: $500; 2nd Prize: $250; 3rd Prize: $100. Winners also receive byline, author's bio and two complimentary copies. Honorable Mentions are given. Awards are paid on publication at this time." Send SASE for guidelines. Responds in 2 months. Acquires one-time rights.

Advice: "I am looking only for the unpublished or minimally published writer of fiction (short stories, poetry, vignettes). This publication is a forum for those seeking to break into print."

THE LITERARY REVIEW: AN INTERNATIONAL JOURNAL OF CONTEMPORARY WRITING, Fairleigh Dickinson University, 285 Madison Ave., Madison NJ 07940, phone/fax (973)443-8564, e-mail tlr@fdu.edu, website www.webdelsol.com/tlr/, founded 1957, editor-in-chief Walter Cummins, contact William Zardes.

Magazine Needs: *The Literary Review*, a quarterly, seeks "work by new and established poets which reflects a sensitivity to literary standards and the poetic form." No specifications as to form, length, style, subject matter or purpose. They have published poetry by Thomas Halloran, Joanna Goodman and Dale M. Kushner. The magazine is 128 pgs., 6×9, professionally printed and flat-spined with glossy color cover, using 20-50 pgs. of poetry in each issue. Press run is 2,500 with 900 subscriptions of which one-third are overseas. They receive about 1,200 submissions a year, use approximately 100-150, have a 8- to 16-month backlog. Sample: $5 domestic, $6 outside US, request a "general issue."

How to Submit: Submit up to 5 poems at a time, clear typed. Simultaneous submissions OK. Do not submit during the summer months of June, July and August. At times the editor comments on rejections. Publishes theme issues. Send SASE for upcoming themes or request via e-mail. Responds in 3 months. Always sends prepublication galleys. Pays 2 copies. Acquires first rights. Reviews books of poetry in 500 words, single book format. Open to unsolicited reviews. Poets may also send books for review consideration.

Advice: "Read a general issue of the magazine carefully before submitting."

LITERATURE AND BELIEF (Specialized: religious), 3076-E Jesse Knight Humanities Building, Brigham Young University, Provo UT 84602, phone (801)378-3073, fax (801)378-8724, e-mail richard~cracr oft@email.byu.edu, founded 1981, editors Richard H. Cracroft and John J. Murphy, poetry editor Lance Larsen.

Magazine Needs: *Literature and Belief* is the "biannual journal of the Center for the Study of Christian Values in Literature." It uses "carefully crafted, affirmation poetry in the Judeo-Christian tradition." They have published poetry by Ted Hughes, Donnel Hunter, Leslie Norris, Susan Elizabeth Howe and Lance Larsen. As a sample the editor selected these lines from "Cycle" by Cyd Adams:

> The air bears the heaviness/of creation's spawning,/for Christ has borne the dogwood/to scale the last escarpment/so a risen sun can silver/the cobalt sky.

It is handsomely printed and flat-spined. Single copy: $5, $7 outside US; subscription: $10, $14 outside US.

How to Submit: Submit 3-4 poems at a time. No previously published poems. Responds within 6 weeks. Pays 5 copies and 10 "offprints."

Also Offers: The center also publishes religious monographs, such as *Toward the Solitary Star*, selected poems by Östen Sjöstrand. "Values in Literature" monograph series invites queries for scholarly studies of authors (C.S. Lewis, W. Cather, Leslie Norris) or works which combine fine literature and religious values and faith in God. Currently in progress: "Willa Cather and Religion" and "The York Cycle of Morality Plays"; in print: Bruce L. Edwards, C.S. Lewis *A Rhetoric of Reaching*; *Willa Cathor: Family, Community, History*.

LITHUANIAN PAPER (Specialized: nationality), P.O. Box 777, Sandy Bay, Tasmania 7006 Australia, phone (+3)62252505, e-mail A.Taskunas@utas.edu.au, founded 1987, editor Al Taskunas.

Magazine Needs: *Lithuanian Papers* is "an annual English-language journal aimed at fostering research into all aspects of Lithuania and its people." They want "high-standard poetry dealing with Lithuanian topics or any topics by Lithuanian poets (in English)." Nothing unethical or offensive. They have published poetry by Bruce Dawe, J. Reilly and Julius Keleras/Vyt Bakaitis. As a sample the editor selected these lines:

> It's then that the map of dreams/soaked through and through, caves in/like a child's balloon filled with water.

LP is 80 pgs., 5½×8½, offset printed and saddle-stitched with light card cover, includes b&w photos and art, ads. They receive about 25 poems a year, accept approximately 10%. Press run is 2,000 for 1,500 subscribers of which 100 are libraries, 100 shelf sales; 400 distributed free to members, students, etc. Subscription: $20/3 years (US). Sample: $8 (US) if available. Make checks payable to Lithuanian Studies Society (LSS).

How to Submit: Submit 2-3 poems at a time. "If translation, the originals are also required." Line length for poetry is 4 minimum, 20 maximum. No previously published poems or simultaneous submissions. E-mail and disk submissions OK. "Must be Mac-compatible." Cover letter required. "The cover letter must contain a concise c.v. and be accompanied by 2 letters of recommendation." Reads submissions December 1 through June 30 only. Time between acceptance and publication is 4-6 months. Poems are circulated to an editorial board. "Short list read by at least 2 referees—more if in disagreement." Pays 4 copies, "but may ask for more." Acquires all rights. Rights returned by negotiation.

Advice: "The Chinese say that even the longest journey starts with a single step. We are open to that step—or any advanced strides along the way."

LITRAG, P.O. Box 21066, Seattle WA 98111, e-mail litrag@hotmail.com, website www.litrag.com, founded 1997, editor Derrick Hachey, co-editor AJ Rathbun.

Magazine Needs: *LitRag* appears 3 times a year. "We strive to publish high-quality poetry, fiction and art from established and up-and-coming writers and visual artists. We look for poetry that is strong in both image and intelligence, and we admit to no thematic bias. We do not want poetry from writers who do not actually read books of contemporary poetry." Also accepts poetry written by children. They have published poetry by Ed Skoog, Barbara F. Lefkowitz and Mark Halliday. As a sample the editor selected this poem, "What Dying Might Be Like For You," by Kathleen McCarthy:

> Now, a man rumbles through the house asking, Where's/my oboe?, as he tosses pillows aside that land/ with the soft thud of a bird/confused into a window. But this can't be/right. Where's the transcendence/ in chaos?

The editors say *LitRag* is 40 pgs., magazine-sized, laser printed and staple bound, screenprint cover, includes photos, ink drawings and illustrations. They receive about 4,000 poems a year, accept approximately 10%. Press run is 500 for 150 subscribers, 125 shelf sales; 150 distributed free to random people. Subscription: $12/4 issues. Sample: $3.

How to Submit: Submit 3 poems at a time. No previously published poems; simultaneous submissions OK. Cover letter preferred. E-mail with attachments and disk submissions OK. "We require a SASE." Time between acceptance and publication is 3 months. Poems are circulated to an editorial board. "One original reader who makes the initial decision to submit it to the editorial board, which makes the final decision." Seldom comments on rejections. Send SASE for guidelines or obtain via e-mail or website. Responds in 6 weeks. Sometimes sends prepublication galleys. Pays "commemorative gift" and 4 copies. Acquires first North American serial rights. Reviews books and chapbooks of poetry and other magazines in 300 words, single book format. Open to unsolicited reviews. Poets may also send books for review consideration.

Also Offers: Website features selections from back issues and current issue, guidelines, editors, art and information on current issues, availability and upcoming events. "We host release parties for each issue."

N ◉ **LITTLE BROWN POETRY**, P.O. Box 4533, Portsmouth NH 03802, e-mail editor@littlebrownpoetry.com, website www.littlebrownpoetry.com, founded 1998, editor Sam Siegel.

Magazine Needs: *Little Brown Poetry* is a quarterly poetry journal of all lengths and styles. They want "deep emotional poetry, any style, any form. No profanity or detailed writing on killing and suicide." They have published poetry by Lynn Mooncrow, Debbie Dixon and Kim Waterbury. As a sample the editor selected these lines by Agnes Makar:

> on december barren trees/you, man of suits and cigars/disturb the peacocks/from their far off nests,/ on some transparent glow/they fluff tails/paint eyes and lips all for the/hate of tomorrow/the consistency/day in and day out/you hear them cry/among the ruins of empty cages/vacant eyes/not belonging,/peacock woman,/a wasteland of youth.

The editor says *LBP* is 35 pgs., digest-sized, stapled, color cardstock cover, includes original cover art. They receive about 500 poems a year, accept approximately 25%. Press run is 300 for 150 subscribers. Single copy: $6; subscription: $24/1 year, $40/2 years. Sample: $4.

How to Submit: Submit 3 plus poems at a time. Previously published poems and simultaneous submissions OK. E-mail and disk submissions OK. Cover letter preferred. Often comments on rejections. Publishes theme issues. Obtain guidelines and upcoming themes via e-mail or website. Responds in 1 month. Pays 4 copies. Acquires one-time rights.

Also Offers: Website includes writer's guidelines, submissions page, submissions e-mail address, about the editor, subscription info.

🌐 ◯ ◉ **LOCHS MAGAZINE; WORLD PUBLISHING; THE INDEPENDENT PRESS; KIMBO PUBLISHING**, Kimbo International, P.O. Box 12412, London SW18 5SG United Kingdom, founded 1996, publisher/editor Rafaël Kimberley-Bowen.

Magazine Needs: *Lochs* is a quarterly "comedy publication, aiming to cover a maximum of different genres of comedy." They want humorous and short poems and limericks. "Nothing too long or too serious (i.e., not light-hearted enough)." They have published poetry by Neil K. Henderson, Tony Lake, Jan O'Hansen and Brian Pastdor. As a sample the publisher selected this poem "The Ballad of a Clumsy Nurse and an Intensive Care Patient" by Dave Bryan:

> Drip/Drip/Trip/Rip/Rip

The publisher says *Lochs* is 30-40 pgs., magazine-sized, staple bound, black and red on blue cover with picture and text, includes b&w photos, cartoons, drawings. They receive about 100 poems a year, accept approximately 10%. Press run is 400 for 150 subscribers, 50 shelf sales. Single copy: $2; subscription: $10/6 issues. Sample: $1. Make checks payable to Kimbo International.

How to Submit: Submit up to 5 poems at a time. Line length for poetry is 20 maximum. Previously published poems and simultaneous submissions OK. Cover letter preferred. Disk submissions OK. "Bio appreciated, SAE/IRC as well." Time between acceptance and publication is up to 6 months. Always comments on rejections. Publishes theme issues occasionally. Send SASE (or SAE and IRC) for guidelines. Responds in up to 4 months. Pays 1-3 copies. Acquires one-time rights. Reviews books and chapbooks of poetry and other magazines in 50-250 words, single book format. Open to unsolicited reviews. Poets may also send books for review consideration.

Also Offers: "We will be launching a nationwide (UK) student magazine. Anyone interested in participating in any aspect of the venture should contact publisher R. Kimberley-Bowen."

🌐 **$**◉ **LONDON MAGAZINE**, 30 Thurloe Place, London SW7 England, founded 1954, poetry editor Alan Ross.

Magazine Needs: *LM* is a literary and art monthly using poetry "the best of its kind." Editors seem open to all styles and forms, including well-made formal works. Some of the best poems in England appear here. It is a 6×8½, perfect-bound, elegant-looking magazine, with card cover, averaging about 150 pages and appearing six times/year. They accept about 150 of 2,000 poems received each year. Press run is 5,000 for 2,000 subscribers. Subscription: £28.50 or $67. Sample: £4.75.

How to Submit: Cover letter required. Responds "very soon." Pays £20/page. Buys first British serial rights. Reviews books of poetry in up to 1,200 words. Open to unsolicited reviews. Poets may also send books for review consideration.

Advice: "Quality is our only criterion."

◎ ◢ **LONE STARS MAGAZINE; "SONGBOOK" POETRY CONTEST**, 4219 Flinthill, San Antonio TX 78230, founded 1992, editor/publisher Milo Rosebud.

Magazine Needs: *Lone Stars*, published 3 times/year, features "contemporary poetry." They want poetry that holds a continuous line of thought. No profanity. They have published poetry by Ralph E. Martin, Sheila Roark and Lisamarie Leto. As a sample the editor selected these lines from "Let Life Decide" by Terry Lee:

> *A midnight rainbow, a tear never cried, words spoken in silence: a light that does not shine.*

Lone Stars is 25 pgs., 8½×11, photocopied, with some hand-written poems, saddle-stapled, bound with tape, includes clip art. Press run is 200 for 100 subscribers of which 3 are libraries. Single copy: $5; subscription: $15. Sample: $4.50.

How to Submit: Submit 3-5 poems at a time with "the form typed the way you want it in print." Charges reading fee of $1 per poem. Previously published poems and simultaneous submissions OK. Cover letter preferred. Time between acceptance and publication is 2 months. Publishes theme issues. Send SASE for guidelines and upcoming themes. Responds within 3 months. Acquires one-time rights.

Also Offers: Sponsors annual "Songbook" (song-lyric poems) Poetry Contest. Send SASE for details.

✔ ♥ **LONE WILLOW PRESS**, P.O. Box 31647, Omaha NE 68131-0647, e-mail lonewillowpress@aol.com, founded 1993, editor Fredrick Zydek.

Book/Chapbook Needs: Publishes 2-3 chapbooks/year. "We publish chapbooks on single themes and are open to all themes. The only requirement is excellence. However, we do not want to see doggerel or greeting card verse." They have published *Cave Poems* by Marjorie Power, *Monsters We Give Our Children* by Carolyn Riehle and *From the Dead Before* by Clif Mason. That book is 36 pgs., digest-sized, neatly printed on gray paper and saddle-stapled with a light, gray card stock cover.

How to Submit: Query first with 5 sample poems and cover letter with brief bio and publication credits. Previously published poems OK; no simultaneous submissions. E-mail submissions OK. Time between acceptance and publication is 6 months. Seldom comments on rejections. Send SASE for guidelines. Replies to queries in 1 month, to mss (if invited) in 2-3 months. Pays 25 author's copies. "We also pay a small royalty if the book goes into a second printing." For a sample chapbook, send $7.95 in check or money order.

Advice: "If you don't know the work of Roethke, DeFrees and Hugo, don't bother sending work our way. We work with no more than two poets at a time."

◎ **LONG ISLAND QUARTERLY (Specialized: regional)**, P.O. Box 114, Northport NY 11768, founded 1990, editor/publisher George Wallace.

Magazine Needs: *Long Island Quarterly* uses poetry (mostly lyric free verse) by people on or from Long Island. "Surprise us with fresh language. No conventional imagery, self-indulgent confessionalism, compulsive article-droppers." They have published poetry by Edmund Pennant and David Ignatow. As a sample the editor selected this poem, "The Willow," by William Heyen:

> *Crazy Horse counted the leaves of willows along the river./He realized one leaf for each buffalo,/& the leaves just now appearing in the Moon of Tender Grass/were calves being born. If he could keep the trees/from the whites, the herds would seed themselves./He watched the buffalo leaves for long, & long,/how their colors wavered dark & light in the running wind./If he could keep his rootedness within this dream,/he could shade his people to the end of time.*

LIQ is 28 pgs., digest-sized, professionally printed on quality stock and saddle-stapled with matte card cover. Press run is 250 for 150 subscribers of which 15 are libraries, 50-75 shelf sales. Subscription: $15. Sample: $4.

How to Submit: Submit 3 poems at a time. Name and address on each page. Cover letter including connection to Long Island region required. Submissions without SASE are not returned. Responds in 3 months. Sometimes sends prepublication galleys. Pays 1 copy.

Book/Chapbook Needs & How to Submit: Wants serious contemporary poetry of merit. Publishes 3-5 chapbooks per year. Chapbooks are usually 24-32 pgs. Reviews books and chapbooks of poetry. Send books for review consideration. Terms vary.

Advice: "(1) Go beyond yourself; (2) Don't be afraid to fictionalize; (3) Don't write your autobiography—if you are worth it, maybe someone else will."

♥ **LONG SHOT**, P.O. Box 6238, Hoboken NJ 07030, website www.longshot.org, founded 1982, edited by Dan Shot, Nancy Mercado, Andy Clausen and Lynne Breitfeller.

Magazine Needs: Published biannually, *Long Shot* is, they say, "writing from the real world." They have published poetry by Wanda Coleman, Gregory Corso, Jayne Cortez, Diane diPrima, Amiri Baraka, Reg E. Gaines and Pedro Pietri. As a sample the editors selected these lines from "No Mona Lisa" by Penny Arcade:

> *I never learned how to simmer contentedly/I boil over continuously/Hot sweet syrup between my legs/ My hands never stay still*

Long Shot is 192 pgs., professionally printed and flat-spined with glossy card cover using b&w photos, drawings and cartoons. Press run is 2,000. Subscription: $24/2 years (4 issues). Sample: $8.

How to Submit: No previously published poems; simultaneous submissions OK. Responds in 2 months. Pays 2 copies.

Also Offers: They have published *The Original Buckwheat* by Reg E. Gaines; *Sermons from the Smell of a Carcass Condemned to Begging* by Tony Medina; *Night When Moon Follows* by Cheryl Boyce Taylor; and *I Have No Clue* by Jack Wiler.

Advice: "Unlike other publishers, we receive too many requests for writer's guidelines. Just send the poems."

[N] [◐] [◯] LONGHOUSE; SCOUT; ORIGIN PRESS, 1604 River Rd., Guilford VT 05301, e-mail poetry @sover.net, website www.sover.net/~poetry, founded 1973, editor Bob Arnold.

Magazine Needs & How to Submit: *Longhouse* is a literary annual using poems "from the serious working poet" from any region in any style. They have published poetry by Hayden Carruth, Janine Pommy Vega, Bobby Byrd, Sharon Doubiago, George Evans, Marie Harris, John Martone and James Koller. *Longhouse* appears as a thick packet of looseleaf 8½ × 14 sheets, photocopied from typescript, in a handsomely printed matte cover. Press run is 100-300. Sample: $12. Pays 2 copies. Reviews books of poetry.

Book/Chapbook Needs & How to Submit: They publish chapbooks and books (solicited manuscripts only) under the imprints of Longhouse and Scout.

Also Offers: "We are also a bookshop and mail-order business for modern first editions and modern poetry and small presses. We encourage poets and readers looking for collectible modern first editions and scarce—and not so scarce—books of poetry and small press magazines to locate our website."

Advice: "Origin Press is best known as Cid Corman's press. One of the quiet giants in American poetry plus the wide scope of international work. Established in the early 1950s in Boston, it has moved around as Cid went with his life: France, Italy, Boston, for many years now in Kyoto, Japan. Cid has merged with Longhouse in that we now edit and publish a few items together. He continues to edit, translate and publish from Kyoto. His own books are heavily based in our bookshop and mail-order catalog."

[✓] [◯] [◎] LONZIE'S FRIED CHICKEN℠ LITERARY MAGAZINE; SOUTHERN ESCARPMENT CO. (Specialized: regional), P.O. Box 189, Lynn NC 28750, e-mail lonziesfriedchic@hotmail.com, website www.lonziesfriedchicken.com, founded 1998, editor E.H. Goree.

Magazine Needs: *Lonzie's Fried Chicken*℠ is "a journal of accessible southern fiction and poetry—an opportunity for writers and poets to show their stuff and satisfy readers. Our focus is well-written short fiction, self-contained novel excerpts, and poetry with a feel for the South. We welcome the best contemporary, mainstream, and historical work by published and unpublished poets and writers." Charles F. Price's *Freedom Altar* won the 1999 Sir Walter Raleigh Fiction Award. They have published poetry by Keith Flynn, Errol Miller, Patricia Johnson, C.C. Wharton, Sallie Page and Charles F. Price. As a sample we selected this haiku, "Dog Barks As Car Stops," by Karen Wade:

> Dog barks as car stops/Silence ends with jingling keys/Doors close, steps echo/Sigh with an exhalation/
> Waiting wife closes her eyes

LFC is about 100 pgs., digest-sized, offset printed and perfect-bound with light card cover containing b&w photo, ads. They receive over 500 poems a year, accept approximately 10%. Press run is 1,000 for about 200 subscribers, 500 shelf sales; 100 distributed free to newspapers, reviewers and contributors. Single copy: $8.95; subscription: $14.95/year, $26.95/2 years. Sample (including guidelines): $8.95.

How to Submit: Submit up to 3 poems at a time. Line length for poetry is 40 maximum. No previously published poems; simultaneous submissions OK. Cover letter preferred. Time between acceptance and publication is up to 5 months. Poems are circulated to an editorial board. Seldom comments on rejections. Send SASE for return or reply. Responds in 3 months or less. Pays 3 copies. Acquires first rights and one-time anthology rights.

Also Offers: Website includes guidelines, contributors, list of bookstores, order form and contest rules and guidelines.

Advice: "We enjoy publishing subtle, accessible southern fiction and poetry. Not interested in essays, bleak, or 'too quaint' (i.e., we're from the south an' we eat grits, love sweet 'tater pie, etc.') pieces."

[$] [✉] LOOM PRESS, P.O. Box 1394, Lowell MA 01853-1394, founded 1978, editor/publisher Paul Marion.

Book/Chapbook Needs: Loom Press is a small press publisher of books with an emphasis on publishing poets from New England. Poets published include Marie Louise St. Onge, Susan April, Michael Casey, Eric Linder and Hilary Holladay. Books are usually perfect-bound, 6×9, with an average page count of 64. Sample: $10.

How to Submit: Writers should query first for book publication, sending cover letter, credits, 5 sample poems and bio. "Do not send book-length mss." Queries will be answered in 2 months, mss responded to in 3 months. Simultaneous submissions will be considered. Time between acceptance and publication is 18-24 months. The editor comments on mss "when time allows." Always sends prepublication galleys. Pays royalties of 10%, plus 5% of print run.

Advice: "We are especially interested in poems that address issues related to place, nature, history and cultural identity."

MARKETS THAT WERE listed in the 2000 edition of *Poet's Market* but do not appear this year are listed in the General Index with a notation explaining why they were omitted.

✓ ◐ ◎ **LOONFEATHER ANNUAL; LOONFEATHER PRESS (Specialized: regional)**, P.O. Box 1212, Bemidji MN 56619-1212, phone (218)444-4869, e-mail brossi@paulbunyan.net, founded 1979, poetry editors Betty Rossi, Mark Christensen and Gail Rixen.

Magazine Needs & How to Submit: The literary magazine *Loonfeather* appears annually, "primarily but not exclusively for Minnesota writers. Prefer short poems of not over 42 lines, accepts some traditional forms if well done, no generalizations on worn-out topics." *Loonfeather* is 98 pgs., 5½ × 8½, professionally printed in small type with matte card cover, using b&w art and ads. Subscription: $10/year. Pays 2 copies.

Book/Chapbook Needs & How to Submit: Loonfeather Press publishes a limited number of quality poetry books. They published *Feast* by Carol Ann Russell, *Faith in Ice Time* by Mark Christensen and *A Few Questions About Paradise* by Lynn Levin. "Currently have a backlog of accepted material for publication." Poetry submissions accepted October, November and December only. Query with 2-3 sample poems, cover letter and previous publications. Upcoming themes: 2001, Celebrations; 2002, Neighbors. Replies to queries in 6 months. Time between acceptance and publication is 1-1½ years. Pays 10% royalties.

◐ ◎ **LOS**, 150 N. Catalina St., No. 2, Los Angeles CA 90004, founded 1991, editors Virginia M. Geoffrey, I.B. Scrood, P.N. Bouts and M. Peel.

Magazine Needs: *Los*, published 4 times a year, features poetry. Also accepts poetry written by children. They have published poetry by Ahmed Balfouni, David Chorlton, Thomas Feeny, Gregory Jerozal, Peter Layton and Ed Orr. As a sample the editors selected these lines from "a tale of a fateful trip" by C. Mulrooney:

> permit me to give you an illustration/poetry dear editor's expensive a proposition/thrives not merely
> ahoy a natch ahoy/must servèd be trellis'd scudded film'd/all as befits the sacred Muse impartings

The editors say *Los* is 5 × 8½ and saddle-stapled. Press run is 100 for 25 subscribers; 15 distributed free to local bookstores. Sample: $2. Make checks payable to Heather J. Lowe.

How to Submit: Submit any number of poems at a time. Previously published poems and simultaneous submissions OK. Time between acceptance and publication is up to 6 months. Responds in 2 weeks. Pays 1 copy.

✓ ◎ **LOTUS PRESS, INC.; NAOMI LONG MADGETT POETRY AWARD (Specialized: ethnic)**, P.O. Box 21607, Detroit MI 48221, phone (313)861-1280, fax (313)861-4740, e-mail lotuspress@aol.com, founded 1972, editor Naomi Long Madgett.

Book/Chapbook Needs & How to Submit: "We occasionally publish sets of poster-poems on related subjects, including 'The Fullness of Earth' and 'Hymns Are My Prayers.' However, we are already committed through 2000 on book publications except for award-winning manuscripts." Query about status for 2001.

Also Offers: They sponsor the Naomi Long Madgett Poetry Award. The award goes to a ms by an African-American poet. "Under the new guidelines, poets who have already had a book published by Lotus Press are ineligible. However, inclusion in a Lotus Press anthology, such as *Adam of Ifé: Black Women in Praise of Black Men*, does not disqualify them. Those who have worked over a period of years at developing their craft will have the best chance for consideration. The work of novices is not likely to be selected. Poems submitted by another person, anthologies, or collaborations by more than one poet are not eligible." Awards $500 and publication by Lotus Press, Inc. Submit 3 complete copies of approximately 60-80 pages of poetry, exclusive of a table of contents or other introductory material, with a $15 reading fee paid by money order or cashiers check. Any number of poems in the collection may be previously published individually in newspapers, magazines, journals or anthologies. Do not include author's name on any page of the ms. Include with each copy a cover sheet with the title of the collection only and no other information. Also enclose a sheet with the title of the ms, author's name, address, phone and brief statement, signed, indicating all the poems are original and uncollected and the author is an American of African descent. Mss will not be returned. Include a stamped, self-addressed postcard for acknowledgement of receipt. Submission period: April 1 through June 30. Winners will be announced no later than September 1. Send SASE or e-mail for more information.

◐ ◎ **LOUISIANA LITERATURE; LOUISIANA LITERATURE PRIZE FOR POETRY (Specialized: regional)**, SLU-792, Southeastern Louisiana University, Hammond LA 70402, phone (504)549-5022, fax (504)549-5021, e-mail lalit@selu.edu, website www.sclu.edu/orgs/lalit, editor Jack Bedell.

Magazine Needs: *Louisiana Literature* appears twice a year. They say they "receive mss year round although we work through submissions more slowly in summer. We consider creative work from anyone though we strive to showcase our state's talent. We appreciate poetry that shows firm control and craft, is sophisticated yet accessible to a broad readership. We don't use highly experimental poetry." They have published poetry by Claire Bateman, Kate Daniels, Elton Glaser, Gray Jacobik, Al Maginnes, Vivian Shipley, Richard Katrovas, D.C. Berry and Judy Longley. As a sample the editor selected these lines from "Notre Dame" by Alison T. Gray:

> Today Grandmama is as wide as Paris/and engulfs the city like smoke./She is looking for you, sister./
> You think for a moment it's raining.//but it's a trick of the dead: how/in certain light smoke can seem
> water. . . .

The magazine is 150 pgs., 6¾ × 9¾, flat-spined, handsomely printed on heavy matte stock with matte card cover. Single copies: $8 for individuals; subscription: $12 for individuals, $12.50 for institutions.

How to Submit: Submit up to 5 poems at a time. Send cover letter, including bio to use in the event of acceptance. No simultaneous submissions. Enclose SASE specifying whether work is to be returned or discarded. No submissions via fax. Publishes theme issues. Send SASE for details. Sometimes sends prepublication galleys. Pays 2 copies. Open to unsolicited reviews. Send books for review consideration; include cover letter.
Also Offers: The Louisiana Literature Prize for Poetry offers a $400 award. Send SASE for guidelines. Website includes submission guidelines, special announcements, journal contents and notes from editor.
Advice: "It's important to us that the poets we publish be in control of their creations. Too much of what we see seems arbitrary."

✓ ◐ ◎ **THE LOUISIANA REVIEW (Specialized: regional),** Division of Liberal Arts, Louisiana State University at Eunice, P.O. Box 1129, Eunice LA 70535, phone (318)550-1328, e-mail mgage@lsue.edu, founded 1999, editors Dr. Maura Gage and Ms. Barbara Deger.
Magazine Needs: *The Louisiana Review* appears annually in the summer. "We wish to offer Louisiana residents a place to showcase their most beautiful, poignant pieces. Others may submit Louisiana-related poems. We want to publish the highest-quality poetry, fiction and drama we can get. For poetry we like imagery, metaphor and craft, but we do not wish to have sing-song rhymes, abstract, religious or overly sentimental work." They have published poetry by William Major, Michael E. Saucier and Tammy Evans. As a sample the editor selected these lines from "The Way We Used to Believe" by Sandra Meek:

> *if death is a shell to split open, I want to hear/the rocking inside.*

The editor says *TLR* is 100-125 pgs. "depending on number of excellent poems received," magazine-sized, professionally printed and saddle-stapled with glossy cover, includes 15 photographs/artwork. They receive about 200-500 poems a year, accept 40-50 poems. Press run is 300-600. Single copy: $3.
How to Submit: Submit 5 poems at a time. Previously published poems OK. Disk (Word) submissions OK. Cover letter preferred. "Send typed poems with SASE, include name and address on each poem. If including a cover letter, please tell us your association with Louisiana: live there, frequent visitor, used to live there." Reads submissions January 1 through March 31 only. Time between acceptance and publication is up to 8 months. Poems are circulated to an editorial board. "Our board 'votes' yes or no, may request revision of a 'close' submission; it is done democratically." Seldom comments on rejections. Responds in 5 months. Sometimes sends prepublication galleys. Pays 2 copies. "Poets retain the rights to their works."
Advice: "Be true to yourself as a writer. Hard work will reap its own rewards."

✓ ◐ **LOUISIANA STATE UNIVERSITY PRESS,** P.O. Box 25053, Baton Rouge LA 70894-5053, phone (225)388-6294, fax (225)388-6461, founded 1935, poetry editor L.E. Phillabaum, is a highly respected publisher of collections by poets such as Lisel Mueller, Margaret Gibson, Fred Chappell, Marilyn Nelson and Henry Taylor. Currently not accepting poetry submissions; "fully committed through 2002."

✓ ◐ ◎ **THE LOUISVILLE REVIEW (Specialized: children/teen),** College of Arts and Science, Spalding University, 851 S. Fourth St., Louisville KY 40203, phone (502)585-7122 ext. 232, founded 1976, editors Sena Jeter Naslund and David Garrison.
Magazine Needs: *The Louisville Review* appears twice a year. They use any kind of poetry except translations, and they have a section of children's poetry (grades K-12). They have published poetry by Richard Jackson, David Ray, Jeffrey Skinner, Maura Stanton, Richard Cecil, Roger Weingarten, Michael Burkhard and Greg Pape. *TLR* is 100 pgs., flat-spined, 6×9. They receive about 700 submissions a year, accept approximately 10%. Subscription: $14. Sample: $6.
How to Submit: "We look for the striking metaphor, unusual imagery and fresh language. Submissions are read by three readers; time to publication is two to three months after acceptance. Poetry by children must include permission of parent to publish if accepted." Pays 2 copies.

◐ **LOW-TECH PRESS,** 30-73 47th St., Long Island City NY 11103, founded 1981, editor Ron Kolm. "We only publish solicited mss."

🄽 ◐ ◎ **LSR (LATINO STUFF REVIEW) (Specialized: bilingual/foreign language),** P.O. Box 440195, Miami FL 33144, founded 1990, editor/publisher Nilda Cepero.
Magazine Needs: "Appearing 2 times per year, *LSR* is a bilingual (English or Spanish) magazine that publishes poetry, book reviews, interviews, and line artwork. Style, subject matter, and content of poetry open; we prefer contemporary with meaning and message. No surrealism, no porn or religious poetry. Reprints are accepted." They have published poetry by Catfish McDaris, Mike Catalano, Janine Pommey-Vega, Margarita Engle and Evangeline Blanco. As a sample the editor selected these lines by Duane Locke:

> *Death is dressed/like an old-fashioned clown/in caps and bells./Death wears silk upturned shoes./The out-of-date costume/leaves death unrecognized . . .*

The editor says *LSR* is 20 pgs., 8½×11, offset printed and saddle-stapled with a 60 lb. cover, includes line work, with very few ads. They receive about 300 poems a year, accept approximately 30%. Publish 40-50 poems/issue. Press run is 3,000 for more than 100 subscribers of which 20 are libraries; the rest distributed free to selected bookstores in the US, Europe and Latin America. Single copy: $4; subscription: $8. Sample: $5, including postage.

How to Submit: Submit 4 poems at a time. Line length for poetry is 5 minimum, 45 maximum. Previously published poems and simultaneous submissions OK. Disk submissions OK. Cover letter required. "We only accept disk submissions with print-out. Include SASE and bio." Reads submissions February 1 through October 31 only. Time between acceptance and publication is 1 year. Poems are circulated to an editorial board. "Three rounds by different editors. Editor/Publisher acts on recommendations." Send SASE for guidelines. Responds in 9 months. Pays 2 copies. Acquires one-time rights. Reviews books. "We will not write reviews; however, will consider those written by others to 750 words." Open to unsolicited reviews.

Advice: "Read as many current poetry magazines as you can."

LUCID MOON, 67 Norma Rd., Hampton NJ 08827, founded 1997, e-mail lucidmoon@worldnet.att.net, website www.lucidmoonpoetry.com, editor Ralph Haselmann Jr.
  ● As the *2001 Poet's Market* was going to press, the editor notified us that *Lucid Moon* will no longer be published.

Magazine Needs: *Lucid Moon*, published monthly, aims "to publish lively, moving, heartfelt poems and to keep the magazine in the public eye." Also includes essays, articles and chapbook reviews. They want "post Beat, independent, modern poetry—no restrictions." They have published poetry by Antler, Allen Ginsberg, Gerald Locklin, Catfish McDaris, Tony Moffeit and Charles Plymell. As a sample the editor selected these lines from his poem "Lucid Moon":

> *Traveling across America in all its terrible beauty, hitchhiking through history/the miles of highways*
> *and open roads a typewriter ribbon of future stories we could tell . . .*

Lucid Moon is 200 pgs., 8½×11, photocopied, side-stapled with some hand-written poems, cartoons and line drawings. They receive about 5,000 poems a year, accept approximately 30%. Press run is 140 for 120 subscribers. Single copy: $10. Make checks payable to Ralph Haselman Jr.

How to Submit: "Contributors are encouraged to buy a subscription." Submit up to 6 poems at a time, must be "photocopy ready." Previously published poems and simultaneous submissions OK. E-mail submissions OK (in attached file). Disk submissions OK. "Put name and address under each poem. Send Beat underground poems or enchanted love/nature/moon themed poems for Moon Beams section." Cover letter with 3- to 6-sentence bio and SASE required. Time between acceptance and publication is 5-6 months. "I choose poems that are honest and moving in some way. Humor is good." Responds same day. Rights revert to author upon publication. Poets may send poetry chapbooks, audio tape cassettes and broadsides for possible review.

Advice: "Read other poets and back issues of *Lucid Moon* to get a feel for the style wanted. Send poems you are proud of. Check out my Lucid Moon website and sign my guestbook!"

THE LUCID STONE, P.O. Box 940, Scottsdale AZ 85252-0940, founded 1994, managing editor Pauline Mounsey.

Magazine Needs: *The Lucid Stone* is a quarterly publishing "quality poetry and a small amount of quality artwork. We focus on poetry with complimentary artwork." They want "unpublished quality poetry of any style and length. We are interested in poetry in the full poetic range, including formal, traditional and experimental poems." Nothing trite or didactic. Also accepts poetry written by children. They are looking for quality poetry and do not select according to age. They have published poetry by Alan Catlin, Maureen Tolman Flannery, Albert Huffstickler and Mariana G. Warner. As a sample the editor selected these lines from "Crossing Toward X" by Lollie Butler:

> *Somewhere, a mine shaft/exhales its coppered breath,/a ghost-town line of fence posts/picks the wind's*
> *teeth/and a nightjar settles on a rusted wagon wheel/going nowhere under this come-lately light—/*
> *still, attesting to the fact that time was squandered/panning for a dream west of everything.*

LS is 56-72 pgs., 7×8½, offset printed and saddle-stitched with 80 lb. Tahoe dull cover with one halftone of artwork, 5-7 b&w pieces of artwork and photography, no ads. They receive about 5,000 poems a year, accept less than 200. Press run is 250-300 for 125 subscribers. Subscription: $16/4 issues. Sample: $6.

How to Submit: Submit 3-5 poems at a time. No previously published poems or simultaneous submissions. Cover letter preferred including "short personal biographical sketch other than the usual vita. No manuscripts or art will be returned nor queries answered unless accompanied by an SASE with adequate postage." Time between acceptance and publication is 1-6 months. Poems are circulated to an editorial board. "We have a staff of readers who individually review a group of approximately 50 poems at a time." Seldom comments on rejections. Send SASE for guidelines. Responds in 4 months. Pays 1 copy. Acquires first rights.

Advice: "We look for fresh language and use of images."

$ LUCIDITY; BEAR HOUSE PUBLISHING, 398 Mundell Rd., Eureka Springs AR 72631-9505, phone (501)253-9351, e-mail tbadger@ipa.net, website www.ipa.net/~tbadger, founded 1985, editor Ted O. Badger.

Magazine Needs: *Lucidity* is a quarterly of poetry. Submission fee required—$1/poem for "juried" selection by a panel of judges or $2/poem to compete for cash awards of $15, $10 and $5. Other winners paid in both cash and in copies. They also publish 10 pgs. of Succint Verse—poems of 12 lines or less—in most issues. "We expect them to be pithy and significant and there is no reading/entry fee if sent along with Cash Award or Juried poems. Just think of all poetic forms that are 12 lines or less: the cinquain, limerick, etheree, haiku, senryu, lune, etc., not to mention quatrain, triolet and couplets." In addition, the editor invites a few guest contributors to submit to each issue. Contributors are encouraged to subscribe or buy a copy of the magazine. The magazine is called *Lucidity* because, the editor says, "I have felt that too many publications of verse lean to obscurity." They are "open as to form, 36-line limit due to format. No restriction on subject matter except that something definitive be given to the reader. We look for poetry that is life-related and has clarity and substance." Purpose: "We dedicate our journal to publishing those poets who express their thoughts, feelings and impressions about the human scene with clarity and substance. We are open to poetry dealing with the good, bad and ugly . . . if done with finesse and style." He does not want "religious, nature or vulgar poems." Published poets include Barbara Vail, Tom Padgett, John Gorman, Penny Perry and Katherine Zauner. As a sample the editor selected these lines by Dorothy Trautfield:

> *Love like fire in grate/snuffed—turns to ash then dies as/heart and hearth grow cold.*

The magazine is 76 pgs., digest-sized, photocopied from typescript and saddle-stapled with matte card cover. They publish about 60 poems in each issue. Press run is 350 for 220 subscribers. Subscription: $11. Sample (including guidelines): $2.75.

How to Submit: Submit 3-5 poems at a time. Simultaneous submissions OK. No e-mail submissions. Time between acceptance and publication is 4 months. Send SASE for guidelines or request via e-mail. Responds in 4 months. Pays 1 copy plus "cash." Buys one-time rights.

Book/Chapbook Needs & How to Submit: Bear House Press is a self-publishing arrangement by which poets can pay to have booklets published in the same format as *Lucidity,* prices beginning at 100 copies of 32 pgs. for $288. Publishes 10 chapbooks/year.

Also Offers: Sponsors the Lucidity Poets' Ozark Retreat, a 3-day retreat held during the month of April.

Advice: "Small press journals offer the best opportunity to most poets for publication."

N ☑ **LULLWATER REVIEW; LULLWATER PRIZE FOR POETRY**, Emory University, P.O. Box 22036, Atlanta GA 30322, phone (404)727-6184, founded 1990, editor-in-chief Leah Wolfson, fiction editor Brianne Gorod, poetry editor Jennie Law.

Magazine Needs: "Appearing 2 times a year, the *Lullwater Review* is Emory University's nationally distributed literary magazine publishing poetry, short fiction and artwork." They seek poetry of any genre with strong imagery, original voice, on any subject. No profanity or pornographic material. They have published poetry by Lyn Lifshin, Nadine Estroff, Ryan Van Cleave and Ha Jin. The editors say *LR* is 104-120 pgs., magazine-sized, full color cover, includes b&w pictures. Press run is 2,500. Subscription: $10. Sample: $5.

How to Submit: Submit 5 poems at a time. No previously published poems; simultaneous submissions OK. Cover letter preferred. "We must have a SASE with which to reply. Poems may not be returned." Reads submissions September 1 through May 15 only. Time between acceptance and publication is 5-6 months. Poems are circulated to an editorial board. "A poetry editor selects approximately 14-16 poems per week to be reviewed by editors, who then discuss and decide on the poem's status." Seldom comments on rejections. Send SASE for guidelines. Responds in 5 months maximum. Pays 3 copies. Acquires first North American serial rights.

Also Offers: Sponsors the annual Lullwater Prize for Poetry. Award is $500 and publication. Deadline: March 15. Send SASE for guidelines. Entry fee: $8.

Advice: "Keep writing, find your voice, don't get frustrated. Please be patient with us regarding response time. We are an academic institution."

☑ **$** ☐ ○ ☑ **LUMMOX PRESS; LUMMOX JOURNAL; LITTLE RED BOOK SERIES**, P.O. Box 5301, San Pedro CA 90733-5301, e-mail lumoxraindog@earthlink.net, founded 1994 (press), 1996 (journal), editor/publisher D. Armstrong.

Magazine Needs: *Lummox Journal* appears monthly and "explores the creative process through interviews, articles and commentary." The editor wants "genuine and authentic poetry that makes me think 'uh huh!'— socially conscious, heartfelt, honest, insightful, experimental. No angst-ridden confessional poetry; no pretentious, pompous, racist and/or sexist work." Also accepts poetry written by children. They have published poetry by Gerald Locklin, Todd Moore, René Diedrich and Scott Wannberg. As a sample the editor selected a poem in *The Wren Notebook* by Rick Smith:

> *In celebration of St. Stephen's Day,/Wren is hung by the legs./The Wren Boys wander through Dublin/*
> *chanting and holding a mobile/of dead wrens.//The wren is tiny/like the red still fist/of a sleeping child.*

The editor says *LJ* is 24 pgs., digest-sized, photocopied and saddle-stitched with 24 lb. paper cover, includes art and ads. They receive about 100 poems a year, accept approximately 10-20%. Press run is 200 for 100 subscribers, 50 shelf sales; 25 distributed free to reviews/trades. Subscription: $20/12 issues. Sample: $2. Make checks payable to *Lummox Journal.*

How to Submit: Submit 3-5 poems at a time. Previously published poems and simultaneous submissions OK. Cover letter with bio preferred. E-mail (include in body) and disk (PC compatible) submissions OK. Include bio and introduction year round for the journal. Time between acceptance and publication is 3-6 months. Seldom comments on rejections. Criticism fees: $10 to critique, $25 to advise, $50 to tutor. Publishes theme issues. Send SASE for guidelines or obtain via e-mail. Responds in 2 weeks. Always sends prepublication galleys. Pays 1 copy. Acquires first or one-time rights. Reviews books and chapbooks of poetry and other magazines in 50-100 words, single or multi-book format. Open to unsolicited reviews. Poets may also send books for review consideration.

Book/Chapbook Needs & How to Submit: Lummox Press publishes avant-garde and concrete poetry under the imprint Little Red Book. "We are creating limited edition, hand crafted artifacts that are testaments to the book as an art form." They publish 12 books per year. Books are usually 48-72 pgs., digest-sized, photocopied/offset printed, saddle-stitched/perfect-bound. Query first with a few sample poems and cover letter with brief bio and publication credits. Reading fee: $5/submission. Replies to queries in 1 month; to mss in 2-3 weeks. Pays royalties of 10% plus 10 author's copies (out of a press run of 100). Offers subsidy arrangements for the cost of printing and distribution plus ISBN #, $1.25 to $1.50 per book (e.g., 100 copies = $150 to $200). Send check for $5 to Lummox for sample package or $2 for *Lummox Journal*.

LUNA BISONTE PRODS; LOST AND FOUND TIMES (Specialized: style), 137 Leland Ave., Columbus OH 43214-7505, founded 1967, poetry editor John M. Bennett.
Magazine Needs: May be the zaniest phenomenon in central Ohio. John M. Bennett is a publisher (and practitioner) of experimental and avant-garde writing, sometimes sexually explicit, and art in a bewildering array of formats including the magazine, *Lost and Found Times*, postcard series, posters, chapbooks, pamphlets, labels and audiocassette tapes. You can get a sampling of Luna Bisonte Prods for $10. Numerous reviewers have commented on the bizarre *Lost and Found Times*, "reminiscent of several West Coast dada magazines"; "This exciting magazine is recommended only for the most daring souls"; "truly demented"; "Insults . . . the past 3,000 years of literature"; "revolution where it counts, in the dangerous depths of the imagination," etc. Bennett wants to see "unusual poetry, naive poetry, surrealism, experimental, visual poetry, collaborations—no poetry workshop or academic pabulum." He has published poetry by J. Berry, J. Leftwich, S.S. Nash, Peter Ganick, S.E. Murphy and B. Heman. As a sample the editor selected these lines from a poem by Ivan Argüeller:

> as we all must come down from the trees/inhabiting what we have killed a writing/system to trap
> "words" as you in belief/hemerologion deposits seed (dries) polit-/the city radiating from Yr mind is
> like/No Other and yet this hi atu s yawnin g

The digest-sized, 52-page magazine, photoreduced typescript and wild graphics, matte card cover with graphics, has a circulation of 350 with 75 subscribers of which 30 are libraries. Subscription: $25 for 5 numbers. Sample: $6.
How to Submit: Submit anytime—preferably camera-ready (but this is not required). Responds in 2 days. Pays copies. All rights revert to authors upon publication. Staff reviews books of poetry. Send books for review consideration.
Book/Chapbook Needs & How to Submit: Luna Bisonte also will consider book submissions: query with samples and cover letter (but "keep it brief"). Chapbook publishing usually depends on grants or other subsidies and is usually by solicitation. He will also consider subsidy arrangements on negotiable terms.
Advice: "I would like to see more experimental and avant-garde material in Spanish and Portuguese, or in mixtures of languages."

LUNA NEGRA, Box 26, % Office of Campus Life/Student Activities or English Dept., Kent State University, Kent OH 44242, e-mail luna-negra@listserv.kent.edu, website www.studentmedia/lunanegra.kent.edu, editor Kathy Davis.
Magazine Needs: *Luna Negra* is a student-run, biannual literary and art magazine of the KSU main campus appearing in May and December, open to all forms of poetry and prose. Also accepts poetry written by children. The editor says it is 36-42 pgs., 7½×7½, with art and photography throughout. They receive 400-450 poems a year, accept 40 or 50. Press run is 2,000, most distributed to KSU students. Sample: $3. Submission fee: $2.
How to Submit: Submit up to 3 poems at a time with $5 reading fee. "Must request sample if in the published book." Line length for poetry is 100 maximum. Also accepts prose up to 1,000 words. Simultaneous submissions OK. E-mail submissions OK. Reads submissions September 1 through March 30 only. Responds in 3 months. "All rights revert to author immediately after publication."
Also Offers: Website includes past submissions and information on submitting poetry, prose and artwork.

LUNGFULL! MAGAZINE, 126 E. Fourth St., #2, New York NY 10003, e-mail lungfull@interport.net, founded 1994, website www.interport.net/~lungfull, editor/publisher Brendan Lorber.
● *LUNGFULL!* was the recipient of a multi-year grant from the New York State Council for the Arts.
Magazine Needs: *LUNGFULL!*, published biannually, prints "the rough draft of each poem, in addition to the final so that the reader can see the creative process from start to finish." They want "any style as long as its urgent, immediate, playful, probing, showing great thought while remaining vivid and grounded. Poems should be as interesting as conversation." They do not want "empty poetic abstractions." They have published poetry by Alice Notley, Allen Ginsberg, Lorenzo Thomas, Tracie Morris, Hal Sirowitz, Sparrow, Eileen Myles and Bill Berkson. As a sample the editor selected this poem, "Jung and Restless: A Waitress Dreaming on Ernest Borgnines Birthday," by Julie Reid:

> Your hair is combed differently than you ever wore it and a man in gray and/green with his hands up
> inside the working of a clock flirts lightly with the woman/beside him who's applying pink lotion from
> a travel size bottle to her hands./The woman ahead of you lifts her hair off her neck so you can read
> her tattoo . . ./She says 'To the maximum 36 . . . emotions, add umbrellas, bent and broken . . ./Add
> anticipation and dread, which . . . are both forms of dread . . .

LUNGFULL! is 170 pgs., 8½×7, offset printed, perfect-bound, desktop-published, glossy 2 color cover with lots of illustrations and photos and a few small press ads. They receive about 1,000 poems a year, accept approximately 5%. Press run is 1,000 for 150 subscribers, 750 shelf sales; 100 distributed free to contributors. Single copy: $6.95; subscription: $27.80/4 issues, $13.90/2 issues. Sample: $8.50. Make checks payable to Brendan Lorber.

How to Submit: "We recommend you get a copy before submitting." Submit up to 6 poems at a time. Previously published poems and simultaneous submissions (with notification) OK. "However, other material will be considered first and stands a much greater chance of publication." Cover letter preferred. E-mail submissions OK. "We prefer hard copy by USPS—but e-submissions can be made in the body of the e-mail itself or in a file saved as text." Time between acceptance and publication is 1-8 months. "The editor looks at each piece for its own merit and for how well it'll fit into the specific issue being planned based on other accepted work." Obtain guidelines via e-mail. Responds in 4 months. Pays 2 copies.

Also Offers: "Each copy of *LUNGFULL! Magazine* now contains a short poem, usually from a series of six, printed on a sticker—they can be removed from the magazine and placed on any flat surface to make it a little less flat. Innovatively designed and printed in black & white, previous stickers have had work by Sparrow, Mike Topp, Julie Reid, Donna Cartelli, Joe Maynard and Jeremy Sharpe, among others."

Advice: "Don't just read books, mark them up, write between the lines, make your own cover, transcribe the pages you love and burn the originals, get paper cuts kissing it, massage its spine, use only the words from the book you're reading in your speech, or none of them."

THE LUTHERAN DIGEST (Specialized: humor, nature/rural/ecology, religious, inspirational), P.O. Box 4250, Hopkins MN 55343, phone (612)933-2820, fax (612)933-5708, founded 1953, editor David Tank.

Magazine Needs: *The Lutheran Digest* appears quarterly "to entertain and encourage believers and to subtly persuade non-believers to embrace the Christian faith. We publish short poems (24 lines or less) that will fit in a single column of the magazine. Most are inspirational, but that doesn't necessarily mean religious. No avant-garde poetry or work longer than 25 lines." They have published poetry by Kathleen A. Cain, William Beyer, Margaret Peterson, Florence Berg and Erma Boetkher. As a sample we selected these lines from "Easter Has Arrived" by Kathleen A. Cain:

> Sun rays streak across the rugged/mountains in the east,/Sweet warblings of the finch, wren and/
> cardinal break through the morning peace./All of God's creation arrayed in its/spring beauty begins
> to unfold,/The desert is a bright splash of purple verbena and/daisies of orange and gold.

TLD is 72 pgs., digest-sized, offset printed and saddle-stitched with 4-color paper cover, includes b&w photos and illustrations, local ads to cover cost of distribution. They receive about 200 poems a year, accept approximately 20%. Press run is 125,000; 118,000 distributed free to Lutheran churches. Subscription: $22/2 years. Sample: $3.

How to Submit: Submit 3 poems at a time. Line length for poetry is 30 maximum. Previously published poems and simultaneous submissions OK. Cover letter preferred. "Include SASE if return is desired." Time between acceptance and publication is 3-9 months. Poems are circulated to an editorial board. "Selected by editor and reviewed by publication panel." Send SASE for guidelines. Responds in 3 months. Pays credit and 1 copy. Acquires one-time rights.

Advice: "Poems should be short and appeal to senior citizens. We also look for poems that can be sung to traditional Lutheran hymns."

LUZ EN ARTE Y LITERATURA; CARPETAS DE POESÍA LUZ; CARPETAS DE POESÍA LUZ BILINGÜE; LUZ BILINGUAL PUBLISHING, INC. (Specialized: translations, biligual/spanish), 5008 Hazeltine Ave., #16, Sherman Oaks CA 91423, phone (818)907-1454, e-mail luzve8@aol.com, founded 1991, director Veronica Miranda.

Magazine Needs: *Luz en Arte y Literatura*, published annually in May, is an "international bilingual magazine with the purpose to promote art and literature throughout U.S.A. and foreign countries." They want "Latin American literature, poetry translation from Spanish to English and English to Spanish." They have published poetry by Luis Benitez, Alima Galliano, Martha Cerda and Eduardo Liendo. As a sample the editor selected these lines from "El silencio del viento" by Juan Miguel Asensi:

> El escritorio/la mosca en el tintero/zapatos negros//and translated by Kirk Anderson:/The writing
> table/the fly in the inkpot/little black shoes

Luz en Arte y Literatura is 100-200 pgs., 8½×6½, professionally printed, perfect-bound, CS1 cover stock with art, photos and ads. They receive about 1,000 poems a year, accept approximately 10%. Press run is 1,000 for 500 subscribers of which 300 are libraries, 200 shelf sales; 300 distributed free to reviewers, collaborators, cultural institutions. Single copy: $19; subscription: $25. Sample: $8. Make checks payable to Luz Bilingual Publishing, Inc.

How to Submit: Submit up to 10 poems at a time. Previously published poems and simultaneous submissions OK. Cover letter required with curriculum vitae. Time between acceptance and publication is 6-12 months. Poems are circulated to an editorial board. "There is a preselection a year before publication and a final selection upon publication." Publishes theme issues. Send SASE for guidelines and upcoming themes. Responds in up to 1 year. Pays 1 copy. Staff reviews books or chapbooks of poetry or other magazines in 1-3 pages. Send books for review consideration.

Winter 1999, Vol. VI, No. 1 $7.95

LYNX EYE

Lynx Eye, the quarterly publication of the ScribbleFest Literary Group in Los Angeles, California, features bold, inviting artwork and strong images with an element of whimsy. "These complement our poetry and prose offerings," says Pam McCully, co-editor and co-publisher. "Whether lyric or narrative, the poetry in each issue of *Lynx Eye* creates vivid, evocative images for our readers." Wayne Hogan, a Tennessee freelance artist and poet, created the eye-catching cover for the Winter 1999 issue. McCully believes the car "suggests taking a journey—a fanciful trip through the insightful writing in the pages of *Lynx Eye*." The magazine is 5½×8½, about 120 pages, perfect-bound, with black and white artwork.

Book/Chapbook Needs & How to Submit: Luz Bilingual Publishing, Inc., publishes poetry translations: Spanish/English, English/Spanish and Spanish poetry in the form of poetry folders as the result of 2 annual poetry contests, Carpetas de Poesía Luz and Carpetas de Poesía Luz Bilingüe. Send SASE for entry form and guidelines. Entry fee: $10. Deadline for entry, February 15. Winners will be announced in *Luz en Arte y Literatura*, the works will be published in the spring and distributed with the magazine and made available to the public. The translator and/or author will receive a copy. Poetry folders are 20-40 pgs., 9×7½, professionally printed. Replies to queries and mss in 3-6 months. Pays author's copies. For sample books or chapbooks, write to the above address.

☑ $☐ ◑ **LYNX EYE; SCRIBBLEFEST LITERARY GROUP**, 1880 Hill Dr., Los Angeles CA 90041-1244, phone (323)550-8522, fax (323)550-8243, e-mail pamccully@aol.com, founded 1994, contact Pam Mc-Cully.

Magazine Needs: *Lynx Eye* is the quarterly publication of the ScribbleFest Literary Group, an organization dedicated to the development and promotion of the literary arts. *Lynx Eye* is "dedicated to showcasing visionary writers and artists, particularly new voices." Each issue contains a special feature called Presenting, in which an unpublished writer of prose or poetry makes his/her print debut. They have no specifications regarding form, subject matter or style of poetry. They have published poetry by Bruce Curley, Simon Perchik and Susan Terris. As a sample the editors selected these lines from "To Aliza . . ." by Mel C. Thompson:

> The first man is every man/who was every woman's lover/since Brahman split in two/and became you and I.

Lynx Eye is about 120 pgs., 5½×8½, perfect-bound with b&w artwork. They receive about 2,000 poetry submissions a year and have space for about 75. Press run is 500 for 250 subscribers, 200 shelf sales. Subscription: $25/year. Sample: $7.95. Make checks payable to ScribbleFest Literary Group.

How to Submit: Submissions must be typed and include phone number, address, and an SASE. No previously published poems; simultaneous submissions OK. Name, address and phone number on each piece. Always comments on rejections. Send SASE for guidelines. Responds in 3 months. Pays $10/piece and 3 copies. Buys first North American serial rights.

◎ **M.I.P. COMPANY (Specialized: foreign language, erotica)**, P.O. Box 27484, Minneapolis MN 55427, phone (612)546-7578, fax (612)544-6077, e-mail mp@mipco.com, website www.mipco.com, founded 1984, contact Michael Peltsman.

Book/Chapbook Needs & How to Submit: M.I.P. Company publishes 3 paperbacks/year. They only publish Russian erotic poetry and prose written in Russian. They have published poetry collections by Mikhail Armalinsky and Aleksey Shelvakh. No previously published poems; simultaneous submissions OK. Replies to queries in 1 month. Seldom comments on rejections.

◖ **THE MACGUFFIN; NATIONAL POET HUNT**, Schoolcraft College, 18600 Haggerty Rd., Livonia MI 48152-2696, phone (734)462-4400 ext. 5292, e-mail alindenb@schoolcrft.cc.mi.us, website www.schoolcraft. cc.mi.us, founded 1983, editor Arthur Lindenberg.

Magazine Needs: *"The MacGuffin* is a literary magazine which appears three times each year, in April, June and November. We publish the best poetry, fiction, nonfiction and artwork we find. We have no thematic or stylistic biases. We look for well-crafted poetry. Long poems should not exceed 300 lines. Avoid pornography, trite and sloppy poetry. We do not publish haiku, concrete or light verse." They have published poetry by Gary Gildner, Carrie Hines and Rustin Larson. *The MacGuffin* is 160 pgs., digest-sized, professionally printed on heavy buff stock, with matte card cover, flat-spined, with b&w illustrations and photos. Press run is 600 for 215 subscribers and the rest are local newsstand sales, contributor copies and distribution to college offices. Single copy: $6; subscription: $15. Sample: $5.

How to Submit: "The editorial staff is grateful to consider unsolicited manuscripts and graphics." Submit up to 5 poems at a time of no more than 300 lines; poems should be typewritten. "We discourage simultaneous submissions." Prefers submissions to be sent through the mail. Publishes theme issues. Send SASE for guidelines and upcoming themes or request via fax or e-mail. Responds in 3 months; publication backlog is 6 months. Pays 2 copies, "occasional money or prizes."

Also Offers: Also sponsors the National Poet Hunt, established in 1996, offering annual awards of $500 1st Prize, $250 2nd Prize, $100 3rd Prize, 3 honorable mentions and publication. Submissions may be entered in other contests. Submit 5 typed poems on any subject in any form. Put name and address on separate 3×5 index card only. Send SASE for guidelines. Entry fee: $15/5 poems. Deadline: May 31. Judge for 1999 contest was Alice Fulton. Winners will be announced August 8, and in *Poets and Writers* in the fall. Website includes writer's guidelines, names of editors, current/upcoming contest information.

Advice: "We will always comment on 'near misses.' Writing is a search, and it is a journey. Don't become sidetracked. Don't become discouraged. Keep looking. Keep traveling. Keep writing."

MACMILLAN, 1633 Broadway, New York NY 10019. Prefers not to share information.

◖ **MAD POETS REVIEW; MAD POETS REVIEW POETRY COMPETITION; MAD POETS SOCIETY**, P.O. Box 1248, Media PA 19063-8248, founded 1987, editor Eileen M. D'Angelo, associate editor Camelia Nocella.

Magazine Needs: *Mad Poets Review* is published annually in October/November. "Our primary purpose is to promote thought-provoking, moving poetry, and encourage beginning poets. We don't care if you have a 'name' or a publishing history, if your poetry is well-crafted." They are "anxious for work with 'joie de vivre' that startles and inspires." No restrictions on subject, form or style. "We are not interested in porn or obscenities used for the sake of shock value." They have published poetry by B.Z. Niditch, Molly Russakoff, Sue Walker, Jennifer MacPherson, Margaret Holley and Louis McKee. As a sample the editor selected these lines from "For Bob Forster: In Memoriam" by Lamont B. Steptoe:

> *My Vietnam poems made him leave the room/he was the undead who purchased his tears in bottles/*
> *slaughtered in a bamboo war,/he was burning like a Vietcong Village/exploding like boobytraps,*
> *collapsing like a punji pit/who or what could save him?*

MPR is about 70 pgs., digest-sized, attractively printed and perfect-bound with textured card cover. They receive about 500-700 poems a year, use approximately 50-60. Press run is 250. Single copy: $10. Sample: $11.50. Make checks payable to either Mad Poets Society or *Mad Poets Review.*

How to Submit: Submit 6 poems at a time. "Poems without an SASE with adequate postage will not be returned or acknowledged." Previously published poems and simultaneous submissions OK. Cover letter preferred, "include 3-4 sentences about yourself suitable for our Bio Notes section. Mark envelope 'contest' or 'magazine.' " Reads submissions January 1 through June 1 only. Time between acceptance and publication is 7-8 months. Often comments on rejections. Responds in 3 months. Pays 1 copy. Acquires one-time rights.

Also Offers: Sponsors the annual *Mad Poets Review* Poetry Competition. "All themes and styles of poetry are welcome, no line limit, previously unpublished work only. Send SASE for complete contest guidelines. Winners published in *MPR*. Cash prizes awarded—amount depends on number of entries. "The Mad Poets Society is an active organization in Pennsylvania. We run six poetry series; have monthly meetings for members for critique and club business; coordinate a children's contest through Del. Co. School system; run an annual poetry festival the first Sunday in October; sponsor Mad Poets Bonfires for local poets and musicians; publish an annual literary calendar and newsletters that offer the most comprehensive listing available anywhere in the tri-state area. We send quarterly newsletters to members, as well as PA Poetry Society news covering state and national events." Membership fee: $20.

Advice: "It is advised that if someone is going to submit they see what kind of poetry we publish. We sometimes receive poetry that is totally inappropriate of our mag and it is obvious the poet does not know *MPR*."

◖ **MAD RIVER PRESS**, State Road, Richmond MA 01254, phone (413)698-3184, founded 1986, editor Barry Sternlieb. Mad River publishes 1 broadside and 2 chapbooks/year, "all types of poetry, no bias," but none unsolicited.

✓ 🅐 **MAELSTROM**, P.O. Box 7, Tranquility NJ 07879, e-mail imaelstrom@aol.com, website www.geocitie s.com/~readmaelstrom, founded 1997, editor Christine L. Reed, art editor Jennifer Fennell.

Magazine Needs: *Maelstrom*, a bimonthly, "tries to be a volatile storm of talents throwing together art, poetry, short fiction, comedy and tragedy." They want any kind of poetry, "humor appreciated. No pornography." They have published poetry by Grace Cavalieri, Mekeel McBride, Daniela Gioseffi and B.Z. Niditch. As a sample the editor selected this poem, "Hemingway" by John Nettles:

> Life. Too short to live/Forever in Pamplona./I'd eat my gun too.

Maelstrom is 40-50 pgs., 7 × 8½, laser printed or photocopied, saddle-stitched with glossy paper cover, includes b&w art. They receive about 600 poems a year, accept approximately 20%. Press run is 1,500 for 100 subscribers; 200 distributed free to libraries, bookstores, colleges. Single copy: $4; subscription: $20. Sample: $3.

How to Submit: Submit up to 4 poems at a time. Previously published poems and simultaneous submissions OK. Cover letter preferred. Include name and address on every page. Send sufficient SASE for return of work. E-mail submissions OK "in the body of the e-mail message. Please do not send attached files." Time between acceptance and publication is 1-3 months. Seldom comments on rejections. Obtain guidelines via e-mail. Responds in 1 month. Pays 1 copy. Acquires first North American serial or one-time rights. Staff reviews chapbooks of poetry and other magazines in 500 words, single book format. Send books for review consideration. "Materials cannot be returned."

Also Offers: "Our award winning website includes samples of past publications, writer's guidelines, editors bios and samples of some regular features." Also publishes a year anthology, "Poetography."

$🅐 🄾 **THE MAGAZINE OF SPECULATIVE POETRY (Specialized: horror, science fiction)**, P.O. Box 564, Beloit WI 53512, founded 1984, editor Roger Dutcher.

Magazine Needs: *MSP* is an irregularly published magazine that features "the best new speculative poetry. We are especially interested in narrative form, but interested in variety of styles, open to any form, length (within reason). We're looking for the best of the new poetry utilizing the ideas, imagery and approaches developed by speculative fiction and will welcome experimental techniques as well as the fresh employment of traditional forms." They have published poetry by Terry A. Garey, Bruce Boston and Steve Rasnic-Tem. As a sample Roger Dutcher selected these lines from "Braids of Glass" by Michael Bishop:

> We step onto a plain of braided glass,/which rattles on its topographic loom/Like a million shattered vials of valium/Spilling everywhere the stench of emptiness.

MSP is 24-28 pgs., digest-sized, offset printed, saddle-stapled with matte card cover. They accept less than 5% of some 500 poems received/year. Press run is 100-200, going to nearly 100 subscribers. Subscription: $11. Sample: $3.50.

How to Submit: Submit 3 poems at a time, double-spaced. No previously published poems or simultaneous submissions. "We like cover letters but they aren't necessary. We like to see where you heard of us; the names of the poems submitted; a statement if the poetry ms is disposable; a big enough SASE; and if you've been published, some recent places." Editor comments on rejections "on occasion." Send SASE for guidelines. Responds in 2 months. Pays 3¢/word, minimum $3, maximum $25, plus copy. Buys first North American serial rights. Reviews books of speculative poetry. Query on unsolicited reviews. Send speculative poetry books for review consideration.

🅝 🄾 **MAGIC CHANGES (Specialized: themes)**, 237 Park Trail Court, Schaumburg FL 60173, phone (847)517-1690, e-mail thesenate@home.com, website http://members.home.net/thesenate, founded 1978, poetry editor John Sennett.

Magazine Needs: *Magic Changes* is published every 18 months, in an unusual format. Photocopied from typescript on many different weights and colors of paper, magazine-sized along the long side (you read it both vertically and horizontally), taped flat spine, full of fantasy drawings, pages packed with poems of all varieties, fiction, photos, drawings, odds and ends—including reviews of little magazines and other small press publications. It is intended to make poetry (and literature) fun and predictable. Each issue is on an announced theme. "*Magic Changes* is divided into sections such as 'The Order of the Celestial Otter,' 'State of the Arts,' 'Time,' 'Music' and 'Skyscraper Rats.' A magical musical theme pervades." They have published poetry by Sue Standing, Caleb Bullen, Hugh Odgen, Lauren Sennett, Chris Robbins, Kaela Sennett, Patricia A. Davey and Walt Curtis. As a sample the editor selected these lines from his poem "Mourning Friend":

> Did I hear/The dying dove's song?//Today, I promise myself/To listen to pace://Footsteps/Wind in cracks/Wings.

There are about 100 pgs. of poetry/issue. Circulation is 500 for 28 subscriptions of which 10 are libraries. Sample: $7 US, $10 foreign.

How to Submit: Submit 3-5 poems anytime. Send SASE for upcoming themes. Sometimes comments on rejections and offers criticism for $5/page of poetry. Responds in 4 months. Pays 1-2 copies. Acquires first North American serial rights. Reviews books of poetry in 500 words. Open to unsolicited reviews. Poets may also send books for review consideration.

🌐 ✔ ◯ ◑ **MAGMA POETRY MAGAZINE**, 43 Keslake Rd., London NW6 6DH United Kingdom, e-mail magmapoems@aol.com, website www.champignon.net/Magma, founded 1994, editorial secretary David Boll.

Magazine Needs: *Magma* appears 3 times a year and contains "modern poetry, reviews and interviews with poets." They want poetry that is "modern in idiom and shortish (two pages maximum). Nothing sentimental or old fashioned." They have published poetry by Thom Gunn, Diane di Prima and Selima Hill. Mr. Boll says *Magma* is 72 pgs., 8½×6, photocopied and stapled, includes b&w illustrations. They receive about 1,500 poems a year, accept approximately 4-5%. Press run is about 500. Subscription: £8/year. Sample: £3. "Add postage per copy; UK: £0.50; Europe: £0.75; Far East/Pacific Rim: £1.50; rest of world, including USA: £1.30." Make checks payable to Stukeley Press. For subscriptions contact Helen Nicholson, distribution secretary, 82 St. James's Dr., London SW17 7RR.

How to Submit: Submit up to 6 poems at a time. Simultaneous submissions OK. Cover letter preferred. E-mail submissions OK (ASCII only, no attachments). Reads submissions September through November and February through July only. Time between acceptance and publication is maximum 3 months. Poems are circulated to an editorial board. "Each issue has an editor who submits his/her selections to a board for final approval. Editor's selection very rarely changed." Publishes theme issues occasionally. Responds in 4 months. Always sends prepublication galleys. Pays 1 copy.

Also Offers: "We hold a public reading in London three times a year, to coincide with each new issue, and poets in the issue are invited to read." Website includes contact details, information about *Magma* and its policies and method of operating, as well as some examples of sumissions (poetry and prose—i.e., interviews/reviews) for recent issues.

Ⓝ ◯ ◑ **THE MAGNOLIA QUARTERLY; GULF COAST WRITERS ASSOCIATION; "LET'S WRITE CONTEST,"** P.O. Box 6445, Gulfport MS 39506, e-mail gcwriters@aol.com or ddvined@aol.com, website www.gcwriters.org, founded 1999, editor-in-chief Victoria Olsen, poetry editor John Freeman (10648 Red Bud Court, Gulfport MS 39503).

Magazine Needs: "*The Magnolia Quarterly* is primarily a newsletter and publication vehicle for GCWA members and/or magazine subscribers. It publishes members' creative writings—essays, poetry, articles, opinions—as well as a calendar of meetings and upcoming events. No restrictions on form. Erotica OK but no pornography or gratuitous profanity. They have published poetry by Leonard Cirino, Larry Johnson, Jessica Simmons and Trish Shearer. The editors say *TMQ* is 36 pgs., 8½×7, stapled, includes art/graphics. Publish 20-25 poems/issue. Press run is 200 for 85 subscribers. Single copy: $2.50; subscription: $15/year. Sample: $2. Make checks payable to Gulf Coast Writers Association. "Nonrefundable reading fee of $5 is required from nonmembers and/or nonsubscribers."

How to Submit: Submit 2-4 poems at a time with $5 reading fee (if applicable). Previously published poems and simultaneous submissions OK. E-mail submissions OK. "SASE required for response and return of unused material." Time between acceptance and publication is 1 year. Seldom comments on rejections. Responds in 3 weeks. Pays 1 copy. Acquires one-time rights. Reviews books and chapbooks of poetry, single book format. Open to unsolicited reviews. Poets may also send books for review consideration to John Freeman.

Also Offers: Sponsors the annual "Let's Write" Literary Contest for poetry, fiction and nonfiction. Also offers The Young Writers contest limited to two categories, poetry and short stories and is open only to teens—ages 13 through 18. Send SASE for complete details or visit website. "The Gulf Coast Writers Association invites you to participate in an interesting, informative and inspiring organization. GCWA membership offers: networking, to promote writing as a skill, an art, and a profession; monthly meetings, fascinating speakers present a variety of writing and publishing topics; the GCWA Newsletter—*The Magnolia Quarterly*, information on upcoming meetings, contests, classes, conferences and seminars; critique groups, meeting at various MS Coast locations for all genres and levels of writing experience." Website includes reviews and contest information and guidelines; membership information; sales of members' published books; samples of members' writing; calendar of GCWA events; links to other writing organizations.

Ⓒ ◑ ◎ **MAIL CALL JOURNAL (Specialized: American Civil War); DISTANT FRONTIER PRESS**, P.O. Box 5031, Dept. P1, South Hackensack NJ 07606, e-mail mcj@historyonline.net, website www.historyonline.net, founded 1990, managing editor Anna Pansini.

Magazine Needs: *MCJ* is published 6 times/year with the purpose of "keeping the spirit of the Civil War soldier alive." Also accepts poetry written by children. They want poetry with unique Civil War themes in first or third person. As a sample the editor selected these lines from "Colors" by Jim Boring:

> *"Now," he said/And the boys fell down/Down fell the blue and the gray/Down fell the stars/From the noble stripes/Down from the proud blue bars.*

Mail Call Journal is 8 pgs., 8½×11, offset printed on colored paper and corner stapled. They receive about 100 poems a year, accept approximately 10. Subscription: $24.95/year. Sample: $5.

How to Submit: "We prefer contributors order a writer's packet for $5 which includes submission guidelines and a sample copy before submitting, but it is not required." Previously published poems and simultaneous submissions OK. E-mail submissions OK. Submit in body of message. Cover letter optional. "If poet is a descendant of a Civil War soldier or a member of any Civil War organizations, please provide details for publication." Time between acceptance and publication is 6-12 months. Often comments on rejections. Send SASE for guidelines or request via e-mail. Responds in up to 1 year. Pays 2 copies.

Book/Chapbook Needs & How to Submit: Distant Frontier Press publishes book excerpts, narratives, diary entries, poems and editorial think pieces. Send SASE for details.

Also Offers: Sponsors an annual history poetry competition, established in 1997. Awards 3 prizes of "publication on website plus percentage of proceeds." Submissions may be entered in other contests. Two categories—American Civil War and general history. Indicate whether the poem is fictional or non-fictional. Entry fee: $5/category (3 poems). Deadline: September 15.

Advice: "Don't make a Civil War movie into a poem. Write with feeling from your heart."

MAIN STREET RAG POETRY JOURNAL; INDEPENDENCE BOULEVARD (Specialized: regional), P.O. Box 25331, Charlotte NC 28229-5331, phone (704)535-1918, e-mail mainstrag@mindspring.com, website www.MainStreetRag.com, founded 1996, publisher/editor M. Scott Douglass.

Magazine Needs: *Main Street Rag*, published quarterly, aims "to bring poetry back to the main streets and living rooms of America." They want "any style, any subject, with emphasis on grittier material (open raincoats and unnecessary foul language are not grit, they're stupid)." They do not want "poetry containing derogatory language directed toward race, religion, gender or sexual orientation." They have published poetry by Robert Cooperman, Adrian C. Louis, Leslie Ann McIlroy, Jo Nelson and A.D. Winans. As a sample the editor selected these lines from "An Hour of Freedom Clear as Light" by Mbembe Milton Smith:

> the stars that night/were cool, bright deaths,/impossibly themselves,/self-endowed/expostulating/
> beyond any empires or equations/our enemies could ever erect, . . .

The editor says *MSR* is at least 72 pgs., digest-sized, perfect bound with 80 lb. stock coated cover, photos, art, ads and now includes short fiction, reviews and essays. They receive about 3,000 poems a year, accept approximately 350-500. Press run is 500 for 200 subscribers. Subscription: $15. Sample: $5. "Sampling recommended."

How to Submit: Submit 6 pages of poetry at a time. No previously published poems or simultaneous submissions. No e-mail submissions. Cover letter preferred with a brief bio "about the poet, not their credits." Has backlog of 6-12 months. Send SASE for guidelines. Responds within 6 weeks. Pays 1 copy and contributor's discount for the issue in which they appear. Acquires one-time rights.

Magazine Needs & How to Submit: *Independence Boulevard* is "a free monthly regional tabloid—residents of NC, SC, GA, TN, VA are eligible for publication. Full color cover and centerfold featuring local visual artists. Our goal here is to create a 'coffee-table friendly' publication financed by advertising (not grants) so we can provide our contributors with a larger audience, pay them, and help to remove government from the 'funding of the ARTS' debate." Publishes poetry, short stories, essays, creative nonfiction, arts-related articles, cartoons, graphic images, photography. They have published poetry by Anthony Abbott, Ann Campanella, Don Mager and Diana Pinckney. As a sample the editor selected these lines from "Smithsonian Riff" by R.T. Smith (editor of *Shenandoah*):

> When they banished the buffalo/from the nickel in favor of Jefferson/and the silhouette of Montecello,/
> where did the great herds go?/In stampede their cleft hooves could/alter the landscape, their wallows/
> were bare as landing sites for aliens.

Press run is 10,000, distributed predominantly in Charlotte/Western NC region. Subscription: $24. Samples (several): $2. "Sampling recommended." No previously published poems or simultaneous submissions. No e-mail submissions. Responds in 6 weeks. Pays cash (varies by amount of advertising).

Also Offers: Website includes subscription information, submission guidelines, editorial from current issue, poetry teasers from current and next issue and online advertising section. Also offers poetry and chapbook contests. Deadline: January 31 for poetry contest. 1st Prize: $100, no word limit. Entry fee: $10. Deadline: May 31 for chapbook contest. 32 page limit. 1st Prize: $100 and 200 copies. Entry fee: $15. Each entrant will receive a copy of winning chapbook. Details on all contests are available via website.

Advice: "Rejection is an obstacle in the road—nothing personal—just drive around it. Always drive around it."

MALAFEMMINA PRESS; LA BELLA FIGURA (Specialized: ethnic), 4211 Fort Hamilton Pkwy., Brooklyn NY 11219-1237, founded 1988, editor Rose Romano.

Magazine Needs: *La Bella Figura* is published quarterly and contains "poetry by Italian-Americans concerning Italian-American history, culture and issues." They want poetry "on the history, culture and concerns of Italian-Americans. No stereotypes." They have published poetry by Jennifer Lagier, Barbara Crooker, Grace Cavalieri and Eileen Spinelli. The editor says *LBF* is 20 pgs., 5½×8½, offset printed and stapled with paper cover. They receive about 100 poems a year, accept approximately 50%. Press run is 200 for 150 subscribers of which 27 are libraries. Subscription: $8. Sample: $2. Make checks payable to Rose Romano. "Must be Italian-American and proud of it."

How to Submit: Submit 3-5 poems at a time. Previously published poems OK; no simultaneous submissions. Cover letter preferred. Time between acceptance and publication is 3 months. Seldom comments on rejections.

Publishes theme issues occasionally. Responds in 1 month. Pays 3 copies. Acquires first or one-time rights. Reviews books and chapbooks of poetry in 200 words, single book format. Open to unsolicited reviews. Poets may also send books for review consideration.

Book/Chapbook Needs & How to Submit: Malafemmina Press publishes 3 chapbooks/year of poetry "by and about Italian-Americans to promote awareness of our culture." Chapbooks are usually 20 pgs., 5½×8½, offset printed and saddle-stapled with paper cover. Query first, with a few sample poems and a cover letter with brief bio and publication credits. Replies to queries and mss in 3-4 months. Pays 50 author's copies (out of a press run of 200) plus 50% discount. Obtain sample books or chapbooks by sending inquiry. "Malafemmina Press will be moving to Italy soon, to publish bilingual English/Italian poetry chapbooks. Write now to be put on mailing list."

N ✄ $⃠ THE MALAHAT REVIEW; LONG POEM PRIZES, P.O. Box 1700, STN CSC, University of Victoria, Victoria, British Columbia V8W 2Y2 Canada, phone (250)721-8524, e-mail malahat@uvic.ca, website http://web.uvic.ca/malahat, founded 1967, editor Marlene Cookshaw.

Magazine Needs: *The Malahat Review* is "a high quality, visually appealing literary quarterly which has earned the praise of notable literary figures throughout North America. Its purpose is to publish and promote poetry and fiction of a very high standard, both Canadian and international. We are interested in various styles, lengths and themes. The criterion is excellence." They have published poetry by Margaret Atwood and P.K. Page. As a sample the editor selected these lines from "relay" by Jan Zwicky and Don McKay:

> . . . *Sleep/is a ship whose rigging keeps coming/undone in the rain,/and the self who wakes is the self who walks/its deck, its pockets stuffed/with all the letters you have never mailed.*

They use 50 pgs. of poetry in each issue, have 1,500 subscribers of which 300 are libraries. They receive about 2,000 poems a year, use approximately 100. Subscription: $35 Canadian (or US equivalent). Sample: $8 US.

How to Submit: Submit 5-10 poems, addressed to editor Marlene Cookshaw. Include SASE with Canadian stamps or IRC with each submission. The editors comment if they "feel the ms warrants some attention even though it is not accepted." Send SASE (or SAE and IRC) for guidelines. Responds within 3 months. Pays $30/anticipated magazine page plus 2 copies and reduced rates on others. Acquires first world serial rights. Reviews Canadian books of poetry.

Also Offers: Sponsors the Long Poem Prizes of $400, plus publication and payment at their usual rates (entry fee is a year's subscription), is for a long poem or cycle 5-15 pgs. (flexible minimum and maximum), deadline March 1 of alternate years (1999, 2001, etc.). Entry fee: $25 Canadian, $25 US/poem. Include name and address on a separate page. Website includes competition guidelines and contents of current issues.

✓ ⃠ MAMMOTH BOOKS; MAMMOTH PRESS INC., 7 South Juniata St., DuBois PA 15801, e-mail mammothbooks@hotmail.com, website http://cac.psu.edu/~dwm7/mammoth.htm, founded 1997, publisher Antonio Vallone.

Book/Chapbook Needs: MAMMOTH books, an imprint of MAMMOTH press inc., publishes 2-4 paperbacks/year of creative nonfiction, fiction and poetry through annual competitions. "We are open to all types of literary poetry." They have published *The House of Sages* by Philip Terman; *The Never Wife* by Cynthia Hogue; *These Happy Eyes* by Liz Rosenberg; and *Subjects for Other Conversations* by John Stigall. Books are usually 5×7 or 6×9, offset printed and perfect-bound, covers vary (1-4 color), include art.

How to Submit: Send mss to contest. Not currently reading outside of contests. For poetry mss, submit a collection of poems or a single long poem. Translations are accepted. "Manuscripts as a whole must not have been previously published. Some or all of each manuscript may have appeared in periodicals, chapbooks, anthologies, or other venues. These must be identified. Authors are responsible for securing permissions." Simultaneous submissions OK. No e-mail submissions. Poetry mss should be single-spaced, no more than 1 poem/page. Reads submissions September 1 through February 28/29. Entry fee: $20. Make checks payable to MAMMOTH press inc. Time between acceptance and publication is 18 months. Poems are circulated to an editorial board. "Finalists will be chosen by the staff of MAMMOTH press inc. and an outside editorial board and/or guest editor. Manuscripts will be selected based on merit only." Seldom comments on rejections. Pays royalties (10% of sales) and a least 25 free copies. Other finalist manuscripts may be selected for publication and offered a standard royalty contract and publication of at least 500 trade paperback copies. Finalists will be announced within 6 months from the end of each submission period. MAMMOTH press inc. reserves the right not to award a prize if no entries are deemed suitable. Send SASE for complete rules. Order sample books by sending for information to their mailing address or e-mail.

Advice: "Read: literary magazines, good books of poetry (both old and new) and magazines and books seemingly unconnected to poetry. Don't learn about the world by watching TV. Go out into it, too!"

✓ ⃠ ◎ MANDRAKE POETRY REVIEW; THE MANDRAKE PRESS (Specialized: translations), Box 792, Larkspur CA 94977-0792, e-mail mandrake@polbox.com, website www.angelfire.com/pe/TheMandrakePress, founded 1993 in New York, editor Leo Yankevich, editor David Castleman.

Magazine Needs: *MPR* appears at least twice a year. They have published poetry by Michael Daugherty, George Held, Hugh Fox, Errol Miller, Simon Perchik and Joan Peternel. As a sample the editor selected these lines from "By A Philosopher's Tomb" by Cornel (Adam) Lengyel:

> *How may one thank in fitting terms the maker/of new and taller windows for the soul?/I turn my*
> *transient eyes without and see/the world's great ghostly wheels of change reduce/our mortal home to*
> *essences eternal—/the terror and the grandeur, all within.*

Mandrake Poetry Review is 76-150 pgs., A5, offset printed and flat-spined with glossy white card cover. The editors say they accept about 10% of the poetry received. Press run is 500 for 100 subscribers from 3 continents. Single copy: $5 (by airmail); subscription: $20/2 years. Make checks payable to David Castleman.

How to Submit: Submit up to 7 poems at a time. "Send only copies of your poems, as we do not return poems with our reply." Previously published poems and simultaneous submissions OK. E-mail submissions OK. Cover letter preferred. Responds in 2 months. Pays 2 copies "sometimes more." All rights revert to author. "Poets are encouraged to send their books for review consideration to David Castleman. All editors and publishers whose books/chapbooks are selected for review will receive one copy of the issue in which the review appears. We publish 50-100 reviews yearly."

Also Offers: Website includes magazine in its entirety.

◑ ◎ THE MANHATTAN REVIEW (Specialized: translations), 440 Riverside Dr., Apt. 45, New York NY 10027, phone (212)932-1854, founded 1980, poetry editor Philip Fried.

Magazine Needs: *The Manhattan Review* "publishes American writers and foreign writers with something valuable to offer the American scene. We like to think of poetry as a powerful discipline engaged with many other fields. We want to see ambitious work. Interested in both lyric and narrative. Not interested in mawkish, sentimental poetry. We select high-quality work from a number of different countries, including the U.S." They have published poetry by Zbigniew Herbert, D. Nurkse, Baron Wormser, Penelope Shuttle and Peter Redgrove. The *MR* is now "an annual with ambitions to be semiannual." The magazine is 64 pgs., digest-sized, professionally printed with glossy card cover, photos and graphics. Press run is 500 for 400 subscribers of which 250 are libraries. It is also distributed by Bernhard DeBoer, Inc. They receive about 300 submissions a year, use few ("but I do read everything submitted carefully and with an open mind"). "I return submissions as promptly as possible." Single copy: $5; subscription: $10. Sample: $6.25 with 6×9 envelope.

How to Submit: Submit 3-5 pgs. of poems at a time. No simultaneous submissions. Cover letter with short bio and publications required. Editor sometimes comments "but don't count on it." Responds in 3 months if possible. Pays copies. Staff reviews books of poetry. Send books for review consideration.

Advice: "Don't be swayed by fads. Search for your own voice. Support other poets whose work you respect and enjoy. Be persistent. Keep aware of poetry being written in other countries."

☑ ◑ MANKATO POETRY REVIEW, English Dept., AH230, Minnesota State University, Mankato MN 56001, phone (507)389-5511, e-mail roger.sheffer@mankato.msus.edu, founded 1984, editor Roger Sheffer.

Magazine Needs: *MPR* is a semiannual magazine that is "open to all forms and themes, though we seldom print 'concrete poetry,' religious, or sentimental verse. We frequently publish first-time poets." They have published poetry by Edward Micus, Gary Fincke, Judith Skillman and Walter Griffin. The magazine is 30 pgs., 5×8, typeset on 60 lb. paper, saddle-stapled with buff matte card cover printed in one color. It appears usually in May and December and has a circulation of 200. Subscription: $5/year. Sample: $2.50.

How to Submit: Submit up to 6 poems at a time. Line length for poetry is 60 maximum. "Please include biographical note on separate sheet. Poems not accompanied by SASE will not be returned." However, do not submit mss in summer (May through August). No previously published poems or simultaneous submissions. Cover letter required. Send SASE for guidelines. Deadlines are April 15 (May issue) and November 15 (December issue). Responds in about 2 months; "We accept only what we can publish in next issue." Pays 2 copies.

Advice: "We're interested in looking at longer poems—up to 60 lines, with great depth of detail relating to place (landscape, townscape)."

$ ◑ MĀNOA: A PACIFIC JOURNAL OF INTERNATIONAL WRITING, 1733 Donaghho Rd., Honolulu HI 96822, fax (808)956-7808, e-mail mjournal-l@hawaii.edu, website www.hawaii.edu/mjournal (editorial office), founded 1989, poetry editor Frank Stewart.

☑ Poetry published in *Mānoa* has also been selected for inclusion in the 1995 and 1996 volumes of *The Best American Poetry.*

Magazine Needs: *Mānoa* appears twice a year. "We are a general interest literary magazine, open to all forms and styles. We are not for the beginning writer, no matter what style. We are not interested in Pacific exotica." They have published poetry by Arthur Sze, Linda Hogan and John Haines. It is 240 pgs., 7×10, offset printed, flat-spined using art and graphics. They receive about 3,000 poems a year, accept approximately 2%. Press run is 2,000 for 1,000 subscribers of which 30 are libraries, 700 shelf sales. Subscription: $22/year. Sample: $10.

How to Submit: Query by mail or e-mail. Submit 3-5 poems at a time. Send SASE for guidelines. Responds in 6 weeks. Always sends prepublication galleys. Pay "competitive" plus 2 copies. Seldom comments on rejections. They review current books and chapbooks of poetry. Open to unsolicited reviews. Poets may also send books for review consideration, attn. reviews editor.

Also Offers: Website includes writer's guidelines, names of editors, short fiction and poetry, RealAudio readings by authors, lists of back issues and future issues, subscription info, author index and awards received.

Advice: "We welcome the opportunity to read poetry from throughout the country. We are not a regional journal, but we do feature work from the Pacific and Asia, especially in our reviews and essays. We are not interested in genre or formalist writing for its own sake, or picturesque impressions of the region."

☑ ⊘ **MANY MOUNTAINS MOVING; MANY MOUNTAINS MOVING LITERARY AWARDS**, 420 22nd St., Boulder CO 80302, phone (303)545-9942, fax (303)444-6510, e-mail mmm@mmminc.org, website www.mmminc.org, founded 1994, poetry editor Debra Bokur.

Poetry published in *Many Mountains Moving* has also been included in the 1996, 1997 and 1999 volumes of *The Best American Poetry*.

Magazine Needs: Published biannually, *Many Mountains Moving* is "a literary journal of diverse contemporary voices that welcomes previously published fiction, poetry, nonfiction, and art from writers and artists of all walks of life. We publish the world's top writers as well as emerging talents." They are open to any style of poetry, but they do not want any "Hallmark-y" poetry. They have published poetry by Robert Bly, Allen Ginsberg and Adrienne Rich. As a sample they selected these lines from "Bathing Susan" by Sarah Wolbach:

> Her vertebrae are little apples softening in the heat, rocks on the river/bottom that shimmer and dissolve in the light, little tumors like the/ones within her, spreading through her lungs and glands like a flood/of mold, a village of tiny fists. Touching her body is like reading/Braille, but nothing is explained. Lifted from the water, she is wood/dripping life, she is air with light breathing through.

MMM is about 200 pgs., 6×8¾, web offset and perfect-bound with four-color cover and b&w art and photos inside. They receive 4,000 poems a year, accept about 1%. Press run is 2,000 for 400 subscribers. Single copy: $6.50; subscription: $18/year, $15/year for students and teachers.

How to Submit: Submit 3-10 poems at a time, typed with SASE. No e-mail submissions. No previously published poems; simultaneous submissions OK. Cover letter preferred. Poems are circulated to an editorial board. "Poems are first read by several readers. If considered seriously, they are passed to the poetry editor for final decision." Seldom comments on rejections. Publishes theme issues occasionally. Send SASE for guidelines. Responds within 1 month, "if we are seriously considering a submission, we may take longer." Sends prepublication galleys upon request. Pays 3 copies, additional copies available at $3/copy. Acquires first North American serial rights and "rights to publish in a future edition of the *Best of Many Mountains Moving Anthology*."

Also Offers: They sponsor the annual Many Mountains Moving Literary Awards which awards $200 plus publication in the categories of poetry, fiction and essay. Entry fee: $15 (includes subscription). Send SASE for details.

Advice: "Although we have featured a number of established poets, we encourage new writers to submit. However, we recommend that poets read through at least one issue to familiarize themselves with the type of work we generally publish."

⊘ **THE MARLBORO REVIEW; MARLBORO PRIZE FOR POETRY**, P.O. Box 243, Marlboro VT 05344, website www.marlbororeview.com, founded 1995, editor Ellen Dudley, poetry editor Ruth Anderson Barnett.

"We have won a Pushcart Prize every year since we began publishing."

Magazine Needs: *The Marlboro Review*, published biannually, is a "literary magazine containing poetry, fiction, essays, reviews and translations." They want long poems. They do not want greeting card verse. They have published poetry by William Matthews, Jean Valentine, Bill Knott and Chana Bloch. The *MR* is 80-112 pgs., 6×9, offset printed and perfect-bound with laminated colored cover and ads. They receive about 1,000 poems a year, accept approximately 7%. Press run is 1,000 for 350 subscribers of which 25 are libraries, 300 shelf sales; 50-70 distributed free to writers and institutions. Single copy: $8; subscription: $16. Sample: $8.75.

How to Submit: Submit up to 5 typed, near letter quality or better poems at a time with SASE. No previously published poems; simultaneous submissions OK "if we are notified." Send SASE for guidelines. Responds in up to 3 months. Sometimes sends prepublication galleys. Pays 2 copies. Acquires all rights. Returns rights on publication. Reviews books of poetry in 500-1,000 words, single book format. Open to unsolicited reviews. Poets may also send books for review consideration.

Also Offers: Sponsors the Marlboro Prize for Poetry. Awards a $1,000 honorarium and publication. Submit $10 reading fee for up to 5 poems. Deadline: March 15, 2001. Include name on cover letter only, not on ms. All entrants receive the Marlboro Prize issue and are considered for publication.

▣ ◻ ⊘ **MARYLAND POETRY REVIEW; MICHAEL EGAN MEMORIAL CONTEST; MARYLAND STATE POETRY AND LITERARY SOCIETY**, P.O. Drawer H, Catonsville MD 21228, website members.aol.com/mdstpoetry, founded 1985, edited by Rosemary Klein.

Magazine Needs: The *Maryland Poetry Review* "is interested in promoting the literary arts in Maryland as well as nationally and internationally. We are interested in strong, thoughtful poetry with a slight bias to free verse. All submissions are read carefully. *MPR* is open to good poets who have not published extensively as well as to those who have." Also accepts poetry written by children only for website publication. They have published poetry by Josephine Jacobsen, Richard Jackson, Gary Finke and Walter McDonald. As a sample the editor selected these lines from "Domestic Rhythm: A Pantoum" by Georgia Kreiger:

Let us sip tea together, our knees touching/Under the oak table whose legs you carved/To crouch like
the daunting legs of lions;/You always loved the thundering themes of nature.

MPR is 75 pgs., 7×11, professionally printed in small type on quality eggshell stock, perfect-bound with a glossy color cover. Current issue: $12; back issue: $8.

How to Submit: Submit up to 5 poems at a time with brief bio. No simultaneous submissions. "We read submissions only in January, April and September but accept all year." Publishes theme issues. Theme for the year 2000: Art & Technology. Send SASE for guidelines and upcoming themes. Responds in up to 6 months. Pays 1 copy. Staff reviews books of poetry. Send books for review consideration, attn. Hugh Burgess.

Also Offers: MSPLS sponsors the Michael Egan Memorial Contest for poetry of any length. Entry fee: $3/poem, $12/5 poems. Contest runs from July 1 through October 28 only. Cash prizes of $100, $50 and $25 and magazine publication. Also sponsors an annual chapbook contest. Prize includes $100 and 50 copies of winning ms. Submit mss between 20-30 pgs. Entry fee: $10/ms. Contest runs from January to June. Winners notified by Christmas. Send SASE for guidelines. Website includes writer's guidelines, names of editors, poetry samples and is "a changing, interactive site." Also have a "Kids' Page." Steve Cunningham is webmaster, esker@earthlink.net.

✔ ◑ ◎ **MARYMARK PRESS (Specialized: form/style)**, 45-08 Old Millstone Dr., East Windsor NJ 08520, phone (609)443-0646, website www.experimentalpoet.com, founded 1994, editor/publisher Mark Sonnenfeld.

Book/Chapbook Needs: Marymark Press's goal is "to feature and promote experimental poets. I will most likely be publishing only broadsides and samplers; no books at this time. I want to see experimental poetry of the outer fringe. Make up words, sounds, whatever, but say something you thought never could be explained. Disregard rules if need be." No traditional, rhyming or spiritual verse; no predictable styles. They have published poetry by Steve Andrews, Joe Verrilli, T.K. Splake, Pete Lee and Colin Cross. As a sample the editor selected his poem, "3-7," from the broadside, *With Conceptual Mistakes By:*

It's to me image 222/Thought it is good/appropriate chant (semi-coma)/I so suppose, smoke, dust, oil,
mist, etc./monday with clinical fabrics/OUT-the side a ha-street free, or gone, or barely

How to Submit: Submit 3 poems at a time. Previously published poems and simultaneous submissions OK. Cover letter preferred. "Copies should be clean, crisp and camera-ready. I do not have the means to accept electronic submissions. A SASE should accompany all submissions, and a telephone number if at all possible." Time between acceptance and publication is 2 months. Seldom comments on rejections. Replies to queries and mss in 1-2 months. Pays 1-20 author's copies (out of a press run of 200-300). May offer subsidy arrangements. "I am new at this. And so it all depends upon my financial situation at the time. Yes, I might ask the author to subsidize the cost. It could be worth their while. I have good connections in the small press." Order sample publications by sending a 6×9 SAE. "There is no charge for samples."

Also Offers: Website includes the waiting and self-published chapbooks, broadsides, samples of Mark Sonnenfeld.

Advice: "My advice is to find your writing voice, then go with it. Never give up trying to get published. A good alternative is to self-publish, then distribute anywhere and everywhere."

✔ $ ◑ **THE MASSACHUSETTS REVIEW**, South College, University of Massachusetts, Amherst MA 01003, phone (413)545-2689, fax (413)577-0740, e-mail massrev@external.umass.edu, website www-unix.oit.umass.edu/~massrev/, founded 1959, poetry editors Paul Jenkins, Anne Halley and Martín Espada.

▓ Work published in this review has been included in the 1995 and 1997 volumes of *The Best American Poetry*.

Magazine Needs: Mostly free verse, all lengths and topics, appears here, with emphasis in recent issues on non-narrative modes. An interesting feature: Editors run poems with long-line lengths in smaller type, to fit on the page without typographical interruption (as in other journals). They have published poetry by Tony Hoagland, Marilyn Hacker and Juan Felipe Herrera. As a sample the editor selected these lines from "What They Did" by Vern Rutsala:

What they decided to do was so hard/we marvelled at their courage./It was like trying to tie knots/
with two fingers inside a matchbox/the way surgeons do, practicing./Like that only much harder.

The Massachusetts Review is 308 pgs., 6×9, offset printed on bond paper, perfect-bound with 4-color card cover and 4-color pages of art. They receive about 2,500 poems a year, use about 50. Press run is 1,600 for 1,100-1,200 subscribers of which 1,000 are libraries, the rest for shelf sales. Subscription: $22/year (US), $30 outside US, $30 for libraries. Sample: $8 (US), $11 outside US.

How to Submit: No simultaneous submissions or previously published poems. Read submissions October 1 through June 1 only. Send SASE for guidelines. Responds in 6 weeks. Pays minimum of $10, or 35¢/line, plus 2 copies.

Also Offers: Website includes guidelines, names of editors, table of contents for recent issues and excerpts from work in the latest issue.

N ◑ **MATCHBOOK; MATCHBOOK PRESS; LCPH MEDIA SERVICES**, 242 N. Broad St., Doylestown PA 18901, e-mail matchgirl8@aol.com, website www.matchbookpress.com, founded 1994, editor Debrie Stevens.

insider report

Japanese culture shapes an American poet

From student to hostess in a Yakuza (Japanese Mafia bar) to poet-in-residence at Northern Kentucky University, Leah Maines has immersed herself in a colorful life that offers a rich, diverse collection of experiences on which she draws to fashion her musings, thoughts, and feelings into lyrical words. With talent and a knack for self-promotion, Maines has developed her poetry into a successful career.

Leah Maines

Maines has truly led the life of an artist, living on grant money, family money and the meager earnings she receives from readings. As a student at Northern Kentucky University, Maines was awarded a grant from the Mazak Corporation to study Japanese language and poetry at Gifu University in Gifu, Japan. Being a tall blond in a small town of diminutive people, Maines was sometimes treated as a celebrity, while at other times she seemed invisible when members of the community failed to realize she could understand Japanese. Thus, she says, "I really got to see Japan from the inside. I heard language that was less formal and saw a side of culture, particularly when I worked at the Yakuza, that no college classroom could have possibly taught me. I got to see the real Japanese people, being themselves."

The year spent in Gifu provided the tender inspiration for her chapbook, *Looking to the East with Western Eyes*, published by Finishing Line Press. When she began writing the collection she found she was influenced by the sparse Japanese language, the art of putting punch in a few lines, like haiku. Many of the poems from her chapbook reflect this style, particularly these short, sensual lines that create a sense of intimacy:

"Feeling Fireworks"

Fireflowers blooming
in the warm summer air
your hand
　unaware
brushes my breast

(reprinted with permission from the author)

During her stay in Japan, Maines kept a journal, ultimately acquiring about 1,500 pages of copious detail. Maines likes to draw ideas for poetry from observation. "I'm one of these strange people one sees sitting alone and staring at people. I observe language and interaction, and I write about what I see." As she sat in a garden in Gifu one afternoon, she watched a man chopping on a tree. He cut the branches so severely Maines thought he was killing it, but soon she realized he was creating a work of art, beautiful and majestic. A poem was shaped that afternoon and took graceful form.

"In the Garden in Gifu"

Green leaves and brown branches fall to the ground,
Trimmed back by a pruner's scissors, shaped into
Something seemly, unnatural, but beautiful.

I watch the old Japanese man at his art.

The weathered tree gives up her limbs. What choice
Does she have but to comply? Can she walk away
From his wrinkled hand?

I've heard that trees are always humming but we are
Too distant to hear their songs. Our lives can be
Thunderous. But, I wonder, if the trees hum, do they
Weep when cut?

Green leaves and brown aged branches hit the grass
The old man at work. The tree may be
Crying.

Our lives are like this tree. We are

Sometimes transformed by things that are out of our
Own control. Life shapes us into what we
Have become and what we will be—pruned by

Experiences, transformed by the hand of God or
Circumstance while sometimes shouting and
Sometimes just whispering the song of life.

(reprinted with permission from the author)

Maines entered *Looking to the East with Western Eyes* in three contests before Finishing Line Press published it. Since then Maines has worked diligently promoting the book through networking, appearing on countless radio and cable shows and poetry readings. The book is now being taught in college classrooms in Northern Kentucky and Cincinnati and is in its second printing. It hit no. 10 on the Cincinnati Tristate Best-Sellers list in nonfiction.

However, she advises poets not to wait for publishers to get them book-signing gigs—small press publishers don't always have the time. Maines got a book-signing at a bookstore by sending a copy to an events coordinator, who liked it, heavily promoted it and set up the event. Maines sold a number of books. This appearance led to a half-page interview with a local newspaper. She also gives out business cards bearing a picture of *Looking to the East with Western Eyes* at every opportunity. Maines says, "Do you think I would have had all this success if I would have stayed home and hoped the book would have sold itself? I don't think so.

I am fully convinced that writers must promote their work in order for it to be a success."

Networking, she says, is also crucial. "I talk to people and let them know I am available to head workshops, to give readings, host events." Being a member of several writing groups is another avenue Maines traverses on the networking road and this keeps her connected with the writing community and events. "It is vital for writers to toss a lifeline to each other, to help and encourage one another. When one member gets published, we can all rejoice in their success and hopefully be more motivated to continue our craft," she says.

Workshops and conferences can also afford opportunities to network and get great feedback. But, at the same time, Maines feels it is important to keep other people's opinions in perspective. You should ask yourself some important questions: Do you respect and admire the work of the person who is critiquing your work? Does their opinion matter to you? One of Maines's poems had once been offered for workshop discussion. Some members pulled it apart with negative comments. However, the workshop leader liked the poem. He advised her to leave the poem "as is." Since she valued his opinion, she took his advice and that poem, "Japanese Girl on Coming of Age Day," included in *Looking to the East with Western Eyes*, was nominated for the Pushcart Prize. Maines tries to get something down on paper every day and doesn't wait for the muse to whisper words of inspiration. She has continued keeping a daily journal. "Writing frees my mind to be creative and get at the meat of my thoughts. I write all my emotions away until I can tap into my creative side, and then I get serious with a poem." After writing the first draft, Maines walks away from it for a few days. When she returns with red pen in hand, she gets critical with her work. She may compose several drafts before feeling comfortable with sending the poem to publishers.

To Maines the submission process is a tug-of-war. The trick, she says, "is to be persistent with the tugging. As soon as a rejection letter comes in, (and they do come in) send out another batch of poems to the next group of editors. Don't give up. Keep submitting no matter how many times you are rejected. But keep in mind, a poem should somehow move the reader. I want to intrigue the reader with my words. I like poetry that makes me feel like I've joined in some common ground with the poet. I like to be seduced with language and tone. I strive to accomplish that and hope editors feel the same way."

Currently, Maines is working on a new book, *Beyond the River*. The collection focuses on transitions and changes occurring in life. Testing it out at poetry readings, she has received favorable feedback. She is considering submitting the work to contests and hopes to find a publisher soon.

—*Pamala Shields*

Magazine Needs: *Matchbook,* published biannually, "presents intriguing poetry and reviews to readers interested in same." They want "most any form, length, subject, style with the following restrictions, query first on long poems or translations." They do not want "rhymed verse, traditional forms, concrete poems." They have published poetry by Simon Perchik, Cid Corman and Robert Peters. The editor says *Matchbook* is 64 pgs., tabloid-sized, offset printed with cover art and ads. They receive about 500 poems a year, accept approximately 20%. Press run is 300 for 12 subscribers; 25 distributed free to area bookstores. Subscription: $11.95. Sample: $6.95. Make checks payable to LCPH Media Services.

How to Submit: "Copy purchase suggested but not mandatory." Submit 5-6 poems at a time typewritten, printed out, or legible copies. No previously published poems; simultaneous submissions OK "if noted." Cover letter preferred. Time between acceptance and publication is 6 months. Seldom comments on rejections. Publishes theme issues, "announced in previous issues, plus on website." Send SASE for guidelines or obtain via e-mail or website. Responds in 1 month. Sometimes sends prepublication galleys. Pays 2 copies. Acquires first North American serial rights. Staff reviews books, chapbooks, magazines and zines in 200 words, single book format. Send books for review consideration.

MATRIARCH'S WAY, JOURNAL OF FEMALE SUPREMACY; ARTEMIS CREATIONS (Specialized: women/feminism), 3395-2J Nostrand Ave., Brooklyn NY 11229, phone (718)648-8215, e-mail artemispub@aol.com, founded 1994, editor S. Oliveira.

Magazine Needs: *Matriarch's Way* is a biannual "matriarchal feminist" publication. They want "powerful fem" poetry. The editor says *MW* is 125-200 pgs., digest-sized, offset printed and perfect-bound, includes art. Single copy: $8.50 US, $10/issue; domestic subscription: $20. Sample: $10. Make checks payable to Artemis Creations.

How to Submit: Previously published poems and simultaneous submissions OK. Time between acceptance and publication is 1 week. Comments on rejections. Publishes theme issues occasionally. Send SASE for guidelines and upcoming themes. Responds in 1 week. Sometimes sends prepublication galleys. "Book reviews needed." Open to unsolicited reviews.

Also Offers: Annual writer's contest. "Would like to see a synopsis and 3 sample chapters." Unpublished book accepted; maximum 1,500 words.

MATTOID, School of Literary & Communication Studies, Deakin University, Geelong, Victoria, Australia 3217, fax (035)227 2484, e-mail bje@deakin.edu.au, founded 1977, contact Dr. Brian Edwards.

Magazine Needs: *Mattoid* appears 2 or 3 times/year. "No special requirements but interesting complexity, quality, experimentation." They have published poetry by Lauris Edmond, Kevin Hart, Judith Rodriguez, Fred Wah, Robert Kroetsch and Pamela Banting. It is 200 pgs., flat-spined with 2-color cover. They receive about 800 poems a year, publish 10-15%. Press run is 650 for 400 subscribers of which 10 are libraries, 50-100 shelf sales. Sample: $18 overseas.

How to Submit: E-mail and fax submissions OK. Publishes theme issues. Send SASE (or SAE and IRC) for upcoming themes. Responds in 3 months. Pays 1 copy. Reviews books of poetry in 1,000-2,000 words, single book format.

$ MATURE YEARS (Specialized: senior citizen, religious), P.O. Box 801, 201 Eighth Ave. S., Nashville TN 37202, phone (615)749-6292, fax (615)749-6512, e-mail mcrepsey@umpublishing.org, founded 1954, editor Marvin W. Cropsey.

Magazine Needs: *Mature Years* is a quarterly. "The magazine's purpose is to help persons understand and use the resources of Christian faith in dealing with specific opportunities and problems related to aging. Poems are usually limited to 16 lines and may, or may not, be overtly religious. Poems should not poke fun at older adults, but may take a humorous look at them. Avoid sentimentality and saccharine. If using rhymes and meter, make sure they are accurate." *MY* is 112 pgs., magazine-sized, perfect-bound, with full-color glossy paper cover. Circulation is 70,000. Sample: $5.

How to Submit: Line length for poetry is 16 lines of up to 50 characters maximum. E-mail and fax submissions OK. Submit seasonal and nature poems for spring during December through February; for summer, March through May; for fall, June through August; and for winter, September through November. Send SASE for guidelines. Responds in 2 months; sometimes a year's delay before publication. Pays $1/line upon acceptance.

MAYPOLE EDITIONS, 22 Mayfair Ave., Ilford, Essex IG1 3DQ England, (0181)252-0354.

Book/Chapbook Needs: Maypole Editions publishes 3 hardbacks/year of fiction and poetry, as well as anthologies. They want "poems broadly covering social concerns, ethnic minorities, feminist issues, romance, lyric." They do not want "politics." They have published poetry by A. Lee Firth, Samantha Willow, Brian Jeffry, Mindy Cresswell, Denise Bell and Paul Amphlet.

How to Submit: Query first with a few sample poems approximately 30 lines long and cover letter with brief bio and publication credits. Obtain samples of books by sending £1 and an A5 SAE for a catalog.

MEADOWBROOK PRESS (Specialized: anthologies, children, humor), 5451 Smetana Dr., Minnetonka MN 55343, website www.meadowbrookpress.com, founded 1975, contact Joseph Gredler.

Book/Chapbook Needs: Meadowbrook Press publishes one anthology a year as part of a series of funny poetry books for children. They want humorous poems aimed at children ages 6-12. "Poems should be fun, light and refreshing. We're looking for new, hilarious, contemporary voices in children's poetry that kids can relate to." Also accepts poetry written by children "only on the website—not for publication in books." They have published poetry by Shel Silverstein, Jack Prelutsky, Jeff Moss and Bruce Lansky. Anthologies have included *Kids Pick the Funniest Poems*; *A Bad Case of the Giggles*; and *Miles of Smiles*.

How to Submit: "Send your best work." Submit 1 poem to a page, name and address on each. Line length for poetry is 45 maximum. Include SASE with each submission. Previously published poems and simultaneous submissions OK. Cover letter required "just to know where the poet found us." Time between acceptance and publication is 1-2 years. Poems are tested in front of grade school students before being published. Send SASE for guidelines. Pays $50-100/poem plus 1 copy.

Also Offers: Website includes samples, guidelines, poetry contests for kids and educational info for kids and teachers.

MEDICINAL PURPOSES LITERARY REVIEW; MARILYN K. PRESCOTT MEMORIAL POETRY CONTEST; POET TO POET, INC., 86-37 120th St., #2D, Richmond Hill NY 11418, phone

(718)776-8853 or (718)847-2150, e-mail scarptpmp@netscape.net or robert.dunn17@ste.net, founded 1994, executive editor Robert Dunn, managing editor Thomas M. Catterson, prose editor Anthony Scarpantonio, associate poetry editor Leigh Harrison.

Magazine Needs: *Medicinal Purposes* appears biannually and wants "virtually any sort of quality poetry (3 poems, up to 60 lines/poem). Please, no pornography, gratuitous violence or hate mongering." Also accepts poetry written by children. They have published poetry by D.H. Melhem, X.J. Kennedy, Rhina P. Espaillat, Chocolate Waters, Paul Polansky, Robert Cooperman and George Dickerson. *Medicinal Purposes* is 80 pgs., 8½×5½ (landscape format), professionally printed and perfect-bound with card stock cover with b&w illustration, b&w illustrations also inside. They receive 1,200 poems a year, accept 10%. Press run is 1,000 for 270 subscribers of which 6 are libraries, 30% shelf sales. Subscription: $16/year. Sample: $9. Make checks payable to Poet to Poet.

How to Submit: Submit 3 poems at a time, up to 60 lines per poem, typed with SASE. E-mail submissions OK (1 poem per electronic page). No previously published poems or simultaneous submissions. Cover letter preferred. Time between acceptance and publication is 4-16 months. Often comments on rejections. Send SASE for guidelines or obtain via e-mail. Responds in 3 months. Always sends prepublication galleys. Pays 2 copies. Acquires first rights.

Also Offers: They produce a poetry/folk music public access cable show called "Poet to Poet." They also sponsor an annual poetry contest, 1st Prize $100. Submit 3 poems of 6-16 lines each with a $5 entry fee by June 15. Winners will be published in the year's end issue. Additionally they sponsor a chapbook contest. Also administers The Marilyn K. Prescott Memorial Poetry Contest. Send SASE for details.

Advice: "Poetry cannot be created out of a vacuum. Read the work of others, listen to performances, and most important—Get A Life! Do Things! If you get struck by lightning, then share the light. Only then do you stand a chance of finding your own voice."

MEDIPHORS (Specialized: health concerns), P.O. Box 327, Bloomsburg PA 17815-0327, e-mail mediphor@ptd.net, website www.mediphors.org, founded 1992, editor Eugene D. Radice, M.D.

Magazine Needs: *Mediphors* is a biannual literary journal of the health professions that publishes literary work in medicine and health, including poetry, short story, humor, essay, drawing, art/photography. They want "fresh insights into illness and those caregivers with the burden and joy of working in the fields of medicine and health. Optimism in the face of adversity and overwhelming sorrow. The day-to-day feelings of healthcare workers in diverse settings from hospitals in cities to war zones in military hot spots." *Mediphors* is 72 pgs., 8½×11, offset printed and saddle-stapled with color cover and b&w art, graphics and photos throughout. They receive about 2,000 poetry submissions a year, accept approximately 100. Press run is 1,200 for 300 subscribers of which 20 are libraries, 450 shelf sales. Single copy: $6.95; subscription: $15. Sample: $6.

How to Submit: Submit "2 copies of each poem that we can keep; 6 poems maximum, 30 lines each. We do not accept previously published poems or simultaneous submissions, and it is upsetting to find out that this has occurred when we accept a poem." Cover letter not required "but helpful." No e-mail submissions. Time between acceptance and publication is 10-12 months. Seldom comments on rejections. Send SASE for guidelines. Responds in 3 months. Pays 2 copies. "We require authors to sign a very tight contract for first North American serial rights that makes them legally responsible for plagiarism, libel, copyright infringement, etc."

Also Offers: Website includes writer's guidelines, sample poems, essays and short stories, letters to the editor, cover and contents, editorials, art, photographs and staff listing/editors.

Advice: "Our goal is to place in print as many new authors as possible, particularly those working within the health/medical fields (such as doctors, nurses, technologists, therapists, etc.). We encourage unsolicited manuscripts."

MEDUSA'S HAIRDO, 2631 Seminole Ave., Ashland KY 41102, e-mail medusashairdo@yahoo.com, website http://victorian.fortunecity.com/brambles/4/mh, founded 1994, contact Beverly Moore.

Magazine Needs: *Medusa's Hairdo* appears biannually, and is a "literary zine, specifically not dealing with classical myth but rather work that represents the 'mythology' of our generation." They want "poems no longer than one page. We publish a wide range of poetry." They do not want "humorous poetry or sex/violence." They have published poetry by Gary Every and Lyn Lifshin. As a sample the editor selected these lines from "The Tale of a Rock" by Mary Winters:

I was a bully, a conqueror, a captor/I sneered: I want you lovely/in my dark dank airless room

The editor says *Medusa's Hairdo* is 30 pgs., 8½×11, with b&w art and ads. They receive about 400 poems a year, accept approximately 5%. Press run is 50 for 25 subscribers. Subscription: $8.70. Sample: $4.50. Make checks payable to Beverly Moore. "Purchase of a sample copy strongly encouraged."

How to Submit: Submit up to 10 poems at a time. Previously published poems and simultaneous submissions OK. Cover letter required. E-mail submissions as text and queries preferred. Time between acceptance and publication is 6 months. Often comments on rejections. Send SASE for guidelines or obtain via website. Responds in 1 month. Pays 1 copy. Buys first North American serial rights.

Also Offers: Website includes "virtual sample copy", guidelines, news, publication schedule, writers' aids, links, mailing list, etc.

Advice: "Beginners are welcome to try us though our acceptance rate is very low. Let us know in the cover letter that you are a beginner."

MEKLER & DEAHL, PUBLISHERS; UNFINISHED MONUMENT PRESS; HAMIL-TON HAIKU PRESS (Specialized: form); THE ACORN-RUKEYSER CHAPBOOK CONTEST; THE SANDBURG-LIVESAY ANTHOLOGY CONTEST; HERB BARRETT AWARD, 237 Prospect St. S., Hamilton, Ontario L8M 2Z6 Canada, phone (905)312-1779, fax (905)312-8285, e-mail meklerdeahl@globalserve .net, website www.meklerdeahl.com, founded 1978 (Unfinished Monument Press), 1983 (Hamilton Haiku Press), managing partner James Deahl.

Book/Chapbook Needs: Unfinished Monument Press and Hamilton Haiku Press, with their 2 imprints UnMon Northland (in Canada), UnMon America (in the USA), publish 3 paperbacks and 6 chapbooks/year with 1 chapbook and 2 anthologies published as the result of contests. They want "for Unfinished Monument Press: people's poetry; for Hamilton Haiku Press: haiku." They do not want "racist or sexist poetry." They have published poetry by Linda Rogers and Ronnie R. Brown. As a sample the editor selected these lines from "The Hands" by Milton Acorn:

> *Why man, those hands, dyed/earth and tobacco brown, tough/as an old alligator suitcase, fissured/a dozen extra ways, have/a grip all courtesy, a touch/delicate and sure as a young woman's.*

Books are usually 32-128 pgs., 6×9, offset printed with art and/or graphics.

How to Submit: "Always query first with 5 sample poems." Previously published poems and simultaneous submissions OK. "We like e-mail submissions." Fax submissions OK. Cover letter required. "U.S. poets may use our Pittsburgh address: Mekler & Deahl, Publishers, P.O. Box 4279, Pittsburgh PA 15203." Has backlog of 3-4 years. Time between acceptance and publication "varies greatly." "I publish what I like and what I think will sell." Seldom comments on rejections. Replies to queries in 6 months, to mss in 1 month. Pays 10-12% royalties and 10-20 author's copies (out of a press run of 500-1,000). Obtain sample books or chapbooks by writing to the above address.

Also Offers: Sponsors The Acorn-Rukeyser Chapbook Contest, awarding 1 prize of $100 (US), publication and 50 copies. Runner-Up receives $100 (US). Submissions may be entered in other contests. Submit a poetry ms of up to 30 pgs., poems must be within the People's Poetry tradition, as exemplified by the work of Milton Acorn and Muriel Rukeyser. Send SASE for guidelines. Entry fees: $10 (US). All entrants receive a copy of the winning chapbook. Postmark deadline: September 30. Winner will be notified in January. Also sponsors The Sandburg-Livesay Anthology Contest, awarding a $200 1st Prize and publication; a $100 (US) 2nd Prize and anthology publication; a $50 (US) 3rd Prize and anthology publication; and anthology publication for other prizes. Submit up to 10 poems of up to 70 lines; poems must be within the People's Poetry tradition, as exemplified by the work of Carl Sandburg and Dorothy Livesay. Send SASE for guidelines. Entry fees: $12 (US). All entrants receive a copy of the anthology. Postmark deadline: October 31. Winners will be notified in January. Also sponsors the Herb Barrett Award for short poetry in the haiku tradition, awarding publication and a $150 1st Prize; a $100 2nd Prize; a $50 3rd Prize; and anthology publication for other prizes. Winning poems will be published in an anthology. "What is most important is that each haiku be a concise image of life." Send SASE for guidelines. Entry fees: $10 (US). "Up to 10 poems may be submitted per entry." Postmark deadline: November 30.

MELLEN POETRY PRESS, P.O. Box 450, Lewiston NY 14092-0450, phone (716)754-2266, fax (716)754-4056, e-mail mellen@wzrd.com, founded 1973, poetry editor Patricia Schultz.

Book/Chapbook Needs: Mellen Poetry Press is a scholarly press. "We do not have access to large chain bookstores for distribution, but depend on direct sales and independent bookstores." They pay 5 copies, no royalties. "We require no author subsidies. However, we encourage our authors to seek grants from Councils for the Arts and other foundations because these add to the reputation of the volume." They want "original integrated work—living unity of poems, preferably unpublished, encompassable in one reading." They have published poetry by W.R. Elton and Albert Cook. Their books are 64 pgs., 6×9, softcover binding, no graphics. Price: $14.95.

How to Submit: Submit 30-60 sample poems with cover letter including bio and publications. "We do not print until we receive at least 50 prepaid orders. Successful marketing of poetry books depends on the author's active involvement. We send out free review copies to journals or newspapers when requested. An author may, but is not required to, purchase books that count toward the needed pre-publication sales."

Advice: "We seek to publish volumes unified in mood, tone, theme."

N ○ ◐ ◎ MELTING TREES REVIEW (Specialized: ecology, social issues), P.O. Box 240268, Eclectic AL 36024, e-mail meltingtreesreview@excite.com, founded 1995, editor Mike Catalano, editor Suzanne Strickland.

Magazine Needs: *Melting Trees Review*, "The Peoples' Park of Poetry," appears quarterly and "encourages the disillusioned ecologists and bizarre nontraditionalists to explore their wild side." They want "free verse only. No academic poetry or prose. No gay/lesbian poetry—no offense." They also accept book, music and movie reviews, essays, short plays, lyrics and freelance writing. They encourage b&w artwork drawn in ink. Also accepts poetry written by children. They have published poetry by John Grey, Daniel Green, Tim Scannell, Mike Catalano and Lyn Lifshin. As a sample they selected these lines from "Death in San Jose" by Suzanne Catalano:

> *I will die in San Jose/A city with much pollution/On a Saturday night after a blind date/It will be a week or two after college starts/And my friends and I will be kidnapped at gunpoint/by a group of drunk maniacs/They will brainwash me like Patty Hearst*

MLTR is 52 pgs. (or less), digest-sized, saddle-stapled. They receive about 2,000 poems a year, use around 15%. Press run varies. Sample: $5 postpaid. Make checks or money orders payable to Suzanne Strickland. No more back issues available.

How to Submit: Submit 3-5 typed poems at a time. Published poems and simultaneous submissions OK. E-mail submission in body of message OK. Comments on rejections by request only. Responds in 1 month. Pays 1 copy. Acquires first rights.

Advice: "I want intense stuff you can't read in a classroom. In fact, I want something you wouldn't read to your best friend. We want poems that speak from the places of your heart and mind that nobody knows about. We want to know your fetishes, pet peeves and the things that really 'keep you awake.' Please, do not send poems about daisies or cute babies or cheesy love poems. Send the bizarre—send the intense. Your mother is not judging these."

$ ◎ THE MENNONITE (Specialized: religious), P.O. Box 347, Newton KS 67114-0347, phone (316)283-5100, fax (316)283-0454, e-mail gordonh@gcmc.org, website www.themennonite.org, founded 1885, associate editor Gordon Houser.

Magazine Needs: *The Mennonite* is published weekly and wants "Christian poetry—usually free verse, not too long, with multiple layers of meaning. No sing-song rhymes or poems that merely describe or try to teach a lesson." They have published poetry by Jean Janzen and Julia Kasdorf. As a sample we selected these lines from "The matchbox" by Suzanne Lawrence:

> *The empty matchbox/looks like an empty cradle.//Since Frieda died,/I will always have emptiness.// This fall I hear the children/pass our farm to school.//They belong to others,/but have some claim on me.//I fill matchboxes with candy,/a trinket, a new hankie,//peppernuts, and when I have enough,/wrap them for the Christmas program.//I will walk the mile/and a half under the stars.*

The editor says *Mennonite* is 16-24 pgs., 8½×11, 2-color cover, includes art and ads. They receive about 100 poems a year, accept approximately 10%. Press run is 18,500 for 18,000 subscribers. Single copy: $1.25; subscription: $34.95. Sample: $1.

How to Submit: Submit up to 4 poems at a time. Previously published poems and simultaneous submissions OK. Cover letter preferred. E-mail submissions preferred. Time between acceptance and publication is 1-2 months. Seldom comments on rejections. Publishes theme issues occasionally. Send SASE for guidelines and upcoming themes. Responds in 2 weeks. Pays $25-50 plus 2 copies. Buys first or one-time rights.

✓ $ ◎ MERLYN'S PEN: FICTION ESSAYS AND POEMS BY AMERICA'S TEENS, GRADES 6-12 (Specialized: students, young adults), Dept. PM, Box 1058, East Greenwich RI 02818, phone (401)885-5175, fax (401)885-5222, e-mail merlinspen@aol.com, website www.merlynspen.com, founded 1985, editor R. Jim Stahl.

Magazine Needs & How to Submit: *MP* appears annually and is 100 pgs., magazine-sized, professionally printed with matte finish paper, color cover. Press run is 6,000 for 4,000 subscribers of which 2,000 are libraries. Subscription: $29, plus 10% shipping. Send SASE or visit website for guidelines. Responds in 9 weeks. Pays 3 copies plus $20-200/piece.

✓ ♥ MESECHABE: THE JOURNAL OF SURRE(GION)ALISM, 1539 Crete St., New Orleans LA 70119-3006, phone (504)944-4823, e-mail mesechabe@hotmail.com, website www.resodance.com/mesechabe, founded 1988, editor Dennis Formento.

Magazine Needs: *Mesechabe*, published annually, exists "to surre(gion)alize the earth." They want "poetry seriously committed to changing the language, the world, or both." They do not want "poetry by poets who don't read the publications they submit to." They have published poetry by John Sinclair, Eileen Myles, Robert Creeley, Dave Shortt and A. di Michele. *Mesechabe* is 24 pgs., 8½×11, saddle-stapled with b&w photos, collages, computer graphics and drawings. They accept approximately 5% of poems received. Press run is 700 for 200 subscribers, 250-400 shelf sales; 50 distributed free to writers, friends and artists. Subscription: $20 individual, $35 institution. Sample: $5.

How to Submit: Submit 5-10 poems at a time. No previously published poems; simultaneous submissions OK. Cover letter required. Time between acceptance and publication is "unpredictable." Always comments on rejections. Publishes theme issues. Send SASE for guidelines and upcoming themes. Responds in up to 6 weeks. Sometimes sends prepublication galleys. Pays 2 copies. Staff reviews books in 200-700 words. Send books for review consideration.

✓ ⊘ MIAMI UNIVERSITY PRESS, English Dept., Miami University, Oxford OH 45056, phone (513)529-5110, website www.muohio.edu/mupress/, founded 1992, editor James Reiss. Publishes 2 books/year in paperback and cloth editions by poets who have already published at least one full-length book of poems. Recent titles include *The Disappearing Town* by John Drury, Spring 2000; *Wind Somewhere, and Shade* by Kate Knapp Johnson, Spring 2001; and *The Printer's Error* by Aaron Fogel, Spring 2001. *Currently closed to unsolicited poetry.*

✓ $ ⊙ MICHIGAN QUARTERLY REVIEW, Dept. PM, 3032 Rackham Bldg., University of Michigan, Ann Arbor MI 48109, phone (734)764-9265, e-mail mqr@umich.edu, website www.umich.edu/~mqr, founded 1962, editor-in-chief Laurence Goldstein.

⟩ Poetry published in the *Michigan Quarterly Review* was also selected for inclusion in the 1994, 1995 and 1998 volumes of *The Best American Poetry.*

Magazine Needs: *MQR* is "an interdisciplinary, general interest academic journal that publishes mainly essays and reviews on subjects of cultural and literary interest." They use all kinds of poetry except light verse. No specifications as to form, length, style, subject matter or purpose. They have published poetry by Susan Hahn, William Heyen, Joan Murray and Yusef Komunyakaa. As a sample the editor selected these lines from "Bill Evans" by Bruce Bond:

> What is dissonance, he thought, if not/a seam in the body, a sweet dread./So when you lean into the
> sound and through,/the mind is a pupil floating in its eye,/descending into an unlit hallway.

The *MQR* is 160 pgs., 6×9, flat-spined, professionally printed with glossy card cover, b&w photos and art. They receive about 1,400 submissions a year, use approximately 30, have a 1-year backlog. Circulation is 2,000, with 1,200 subscribers of which half are libraries. Single copy: $5; subscription: $18. Sample: $2.50 plus 2 first-class stamps.

How to Submit: They prefer typed mss. No previously published poems or simultaneous submissions. Cover letter preferred; "it puts a human face on the manuscript. A few sentences of biography is all I want, nothing lengthy or defensive." Publishes theme issues. Theme for winter 2001 is "Reimagining Place." Responds in 6 weeks. Always sends prepublication galleys. Pays $8-12/page. Buys first rights only. Reviews books of poetry. "All reviews are commissioned."

Also Offers: Website includes information about the current and forthcoming issues, special issues (previously published), subscription information, guidelines and Lawrence Foundation Prize information.

Advice: "There is no substitute for omnivorous reading and careful study of poets past and present, as well as reading in new and old areas of knowledge. Attention to technique, especially to rhythm and patterns of imagery, is vital."

$ ⊙ MICHIGAN STATE UNIVERSITY PRESS, 1405 S. Harrison Rd., 25 Manly Miles Bldg., East Lansing MI 48823-5202, phone (517)355-9543, fax (800)678-2120, e-mail msupress@pilot.msu.edu, website pilot.msu.edu/unit/msupress, founded 1947, acquisitions editor Martha Bates.

Book/Chapbook Needs: Michigan State University Press publishes 4-6 paperbacks/year. "We publish poetry of literary quality, with an emphasis on poets living and writing in Michigan." Books are usually 80-125 pgs., 6×9.

How to Submit: Send 5-10 sample poems and brief cover letter. Include SASE "large enough to hold all materials you wish returned." Replies to queries in about 2 months, to mss in 2 years. Pays royalties and author's copies.

𝕹 ⊕ ◯ ◎ MICROPRESS NEW ZEALAND (Specialized: subscription); HILDEGAARD PRODUCTIONS SLIM VOL. SERIES, 75 Brunner St., Bishopdale, Nelson, New Zealand, phone/fax (03)5481459, founded 1997, editor Kate O'Neill.

Magazine Needs: *Micropress New Zealand* is published 10 times a year and promotes "the growth of modern popular poetry. We publish 60-70 poems a month, February through November." They want fresh, contemporary, accessible poetry. "No convoluted, precious, sentimental, preachy, cute or nobly highminded work." They have published poetry by John O'Connor, Leicester Kyle, Patricia Prime and Catherine Mair. As a sample the editor selected these lines from "I Can't Believe Myself" by Simon Lewis:

MARKET CONDITIONS are constantly changing! If you're still using this book and it is 2002 or later, buy the newest edition of *Poet's Market* at your favorite bookstore or order directly from Writer's Digest Books (800)289-0963 or www.writersdigest.com.

> *Somehow I'm here/a grumpy would-be saint/weeping at a shut door/but I won't blame you/only the Most High/who always knew my game.*

MNZ is 16 pgs., 5¾×8⅓, photocopied and saddle-stapled with paper cover with b&w photos. They receive about 1,200 poems a year, accept approximately 60%. Press run is 150 for 110 subscribers; 40 distributed free to other editors of literary magazines. Subscription: $20 (US). Sample: $2 (US). "Contributing poets must become subscribers."

How to Submit: Submit 3-6 poems at a time. Line length for poetry is 40 maximum. Previously published poems and simultaneous submissions OK. Cover letter preferred. "All poems on single sheet, name and address on all sheets. SASE (or SAE and IRC) required." Time between acceptance and publication is 1 month. Often comments on rejections. Responds in 2 weeks. Acquires one-time rights.

Advice: "The current poetry scene in NZ is appalling—a few elite poets get published in prestigious journals resulting in a widespread rejection of poetry among nonacademic readers."

$ ◖ ◩ ◎ THE MID-AMERICA PRESS, INC.; THE MID-AMERICA POETRY REVIEW; THE MID-AMERICA PRESS WRITING AWARD COMPETITION (Specialized: regional), P.O. Box 575, Warrensburg MO 64093-0575, e-mail rnjones@iland.net, press founded 1976, editor Robert C. Jones.

Magazine Needs: *Mid-America Poetry Review* appears 3 times a year and publishes "well-crafted poetry primarily from—but not limited to—poets living in Missouri, Illinois, Arkansas, Oklahoma, Kansas, Nebraska and Iowa. We are open to all styles and forms; what we look for is poetry by writers who know both what they are doing and why. We have a prejudice against work with content that is primarily self-indulgent or overly private." They have published poetry by Ceclie M. Franking, Greg Field, Judith Towse Roberts, Elizabeth Jones Hanley and Maryfrances Wagner. As a sample the editor selected the poem "Survivors, Hiroshima, August 1945" from *The Holocaust and Hiroshima* by Brian Daldorph:

> *I suppose they are looking for food,/or for loved ones,/as they wander/like smoke in hot ruins,/their arms stretched out before them,/skin dangling from their hands./They wear hoods over absent faces./ They often stop/to look at/nothing,/and sometimes to peer at scribbled messages/on bridges, on walls,/ on the remains of homes./They say nothing./I suppose that I am looking for food,/or for loved ones.*

The editor says the *Review* is 60-70 pgs., 6×9, offset printed and perfect-bound with matte-paper cover. They receive about 900-1,000 poems a year, accept approximately 20%. Press run is 1,000. Single copy: $6; subscription: $30/2 years. Sample: $6. Make checks payable to The Mid-America Press, Inc.

How to Submit: Submit 1-3 poems at a time. No previously published poems or simultaneous submissions. Cover letter useful. "Type submissions, single- or double-spaced, on 8½×11 white paper; name, address, telephone number and e-mail address (if available) in top left or right corner. Keep copy of your manuscript—unused submissions will be recycled; send SASE for notification. One-page cover letter (if included) should list items to be considered; contain brief paragraphs of information about author and previous publications." Time between acceptance and publication is 1-6 months. Sometimes comments on rejections. Send SASE for guidelines. Responds within 2 months. Sends prepublication galleys. Pays $5/poem and 2 copies. Buys first North American serial rights. Staff occasionally reviews books of poetry. Send books for review consideration.

Book/Chapbook Needs & How to Submit: The Mid-America Press, Inc. was founded "to encourage writers and the appreciation of writing." They publish 4-6 paperbacks per year with 1 book selected through The Mid-America Press Writing Award Competition. "At present—with the exception of entries for the competition—the Press is not reading unsolicited book-length poetry mss. The competition is limited to 48- to 148-page poetry mss by poets living in Missouri, Arkansas, Oklahoma, Kansas, Nebraska, Iowa or Illinois. Mss must be unpublished in book form." Reading fee: $20. Send SASE for deadline and entry guidelines. The winner of Writing Award 1997 was *The Longest Breath* (1998) by Greg Field. Other Mid-America Press publications include *From Ink and Sandalwood* (1998) by Cecile M. Franking (winner of the 1999 Thorpe Menn Poetry Award for Writing Excellence); *Chrysanthemums I Once Thought Sweet* (1998) by Judith Towse Roberts (1999 Thorpe Menn Writing Award finalist); *Telling of Bees and Other Poems* (1998) by Ronald W. McReynolds; *The Art of Making Tea* (1998) by Elizabeth Jones Hanley; *Pointing Toward Home,* poems by Carrie Allison and *Song of Yasuka,* poems by Stacey Starr (1999); *Red Silk* (1999) by Maryfrances Wagner. Obtain sample books by sending $13.95

☑ $ ◩ ◎ MID-AMERICAN REVIEW; JAMES WRIGHT PRIZE FOR POETRY (Specialized: translations), Dept. of English, Bowling Green State University, Bowling Green OH 43403, phone (419)372-2725, website www.bgsu.edu/midamericanreview, founded 1981, editor-in-chief Michael Czyzniejewski, poetry editor Karen Craigo.

Magazine Needs: *Mid-American Review* appears twice a year. "Poetry should emanate from strong, evocative images; use fresh, interesting language; and have a consistent sense of voice. Each line must carry the poem, and an individual vision should be evident. We encourage new as well as established writers. There is no length limit." They have published poetry by Stephen Dunn, Susan Ludvigson, Albert Goldbarth, Naomi Shihab Nye, Richard Jackson, James Tate and Philip Levine. The review is 160 pgs., offset printed and flat-spined with laminated card cover using full-color artwork. They receive over 2,000 mss a year, use approximately 40-50 poems. Press run is 1,000. Single copy: $7; subscription: $12. Sample: $5.

How to Submit: Submit up to 6 poems at a time. Reads submissions September 1 through May 30 only. Send SASE for guidelines. Sometimes sends prepublication galleys. Pays $10/printed page when possible plus 2 copies. Rights revert to authors on publication. Reviews books of poetry. Open to unsolicited reviews.

Also Offers: They also publish chapbooks in translation and award the James Wright Prize for Poetry. "To be considered for the prize, send $10 fee and three poems addressed to the James Wright Prize, or write for complete guidelines."

◎ **MIDDLE EAST REPORT (Specialized: regional, ethnic, themes)**, 1500 Massachusetts Ave. NW, Suite 119, Washington DC 20005, phone (202)223-3677, website www.merip.org, founded 1971, editor Chris Toensing.
Magazine Needs: *MER* is "a magazine on contemporary political, economic, cultural and social developments in the Middle East and North Africa and U.S. policy toward the region. We occasionally publish poetry that addresses political or social issues of Middle Eastern peoples. Preference given to poets from the region or Western poets who have spent extensive time in the region." They have published poetry by Dan Almagor (Israeli) and Etel Adnan (Lebanese). It is 48 pgs., magazine-sized, saddle-stapled, professionally printed on matte finish stock with glossy paper cover, 4 issues/year. Press run is 4,800. Subscription: $35. Sample: $6 domestic; $8 airmail overseas.
How to Submit: Simultaneous submissions and previously published poems OK. Editor sometimes comments on submissions. Responds in 2 months. Pays 3 copies.
Advice: "We key poetry to the theme of a particular issue. Could be as long as 6 months between acceptance and publication."

Ⓝ **MIDMARCH ARTS PRESS**, 300 Riverside Dr., New York NY 10025.
Book/Chapbook Needs & How to Submit: Midmarch Arts Press publishes 4 paperbacks/year. Query before submission. They have recently published *Solo Crossing* by Meg Campbell; *Sight Lines* by Charlotte Mandel; and *Whirling Round the Sun* by Suzanne Noguerre.

☑ $◎ **MIDSTREAM: A MONTHLY ZIONIST REVIEW (Specialized: ethnic)**, 633 Third Ave., 21st Floor, New York NY 10017, phone (212)339-6040, e-mail info@midstream.org, website www.midstream.o rg, editor Joel Carmichael.
Magazine Needs: *Midstream* is an international journal appearing 8 times a year. They want short poems with Jewish themes or atmosphere. They have published poetry by Yehuda Amichai, James Reiss, Abraham Sutzkever, Liz Rosenberg and John Hollander. The magazine is 48 pgs., approximately 8½×11, saddle-stapled with colored card cover. Each issue includes 4 to 5 poems (which tend to be short, lyric and freestyle expressing seminal symbolism of Jewish history and Scripture). They receive about 300 submissions a year, use approximately 5-10%. Circulation is 10,000. Single copy: $3; subscription: $21.
How to Submit: Submit 2 poems at a time. Time between acceptance and publication is within 1 year. Publishes theme issues. Responds in 6 months. Pays $25/poem. Buys first rights.

$◻ ◙ **MIDWEST POETRY REVIEW**, P.O. Box 20236, Atlanta GA 30325-0236, phone (404)350-0714, fax (404)352-8417, founded 1980, editor/publisher John K. Ottley, Jr.
Magazine Needs: *MPR* is a quarterly, with no other support than subscriptions, contest entry fees and an occasional advertisement. They are looking for "quality, accessible verse. Evocative and innovative imagery with powerful adjectives and verbs. Poetry that opens the door to the author's feelings through sensory descriptions. We are attempting to encourage the cause of poetry by purchasing the best of modern poetry. No jingly verses or limericks. Any subject is considered, if handled with skill and taste. No pornography. Nothing which arrives without SASE is read or gets reply. We are open to new poets, but they must show talent." Also accepts poetry written by children. "Must be good writing." They have published poetry by Rukmini Callamchi, B.R. Culbertson, Junette Fabian, Glenna Holloway, Mikal Lofgren and Bettie Sellers. As a sample the editor selected these lines from "Picking" by Rukmini Callamchi:

> In your yard, we are picking blackberries:/strong, blue, and full of voice./It's the thinness of this
> summer I remember,/its cliff./its way of ending before the stains/wash off my dress//I do not want your
> mother to see this:/her hands, soft and restless/in the kitchen sink.//She is watching, waiting,/like the
> summer,/for something to snap, unravel/like the breaking of clouds before rain

MPR is 40 pgs., professionally printed in Univers type, digest-sized, saddle-stapled with matte card cover. Subscription: $20. Sample: $5.78 (when available).
How to Submit: Submit up to 5 poems at a time, 1 poem/page. Line length for poetry is 40 maximum. No previously published poems or simultaneous submissions. No bios or credit lists. Fax submissions OK. Send SASE and $1 for guidelines. "We will critique up to 10 of your poems at a time." Criticism fee: $20 plus SASE. Responds in 1 month. Pays $5/poem. Buys first rights.
Also Offers: They have varied contests in each issue, with prizes ranging from $10-250, with "unbiased, non-staff judges for all competitions." Contests have entry fees. Send SASE for details. A 20-point self-analysis survey to assist poets in analyzing their own work is offered free to new subscribers.

◙ **THE MIDWEST QUARTERLY**, Pittsburg State University, Pittsburg KS 66762, phone (316)235-4689, fax (316)235-4686, e-mail smeats@pittstate.edu (queries only, no submissions), founded 1959, poetry editor Stephen Meats.

Magazine Needs: *Midwest Quarterly* "publishes articles on any subject of contemporary interest, particularly literary criticism, political science, philosophy, education, biography and sociology, and each issue contains a section of poetry usually 15 poems in length. I am interested in well-crafted, though not necessarily traditional poems that explore the inter-relationship of the human and natural worlds in bold, surrealistic images of a writer's imaginative, mystical experience. Sixty lines or less (occasionally longer if exceptional)." They have published poetry by David Baker, Fleda Brown Jackson, Kathleen Norris, Pattiann Rogers, Jeanne Murray Walker and Ted Kooser. The magazine is 130 pgs., digest-sized, professionally printed and flat-spined with matte cover. Press run is 650 for 600 subscribers of which 500 are libraries. They receive about 4,000 poems a year, use approximately 60. "My plan is to publish all acceptances within 1 year." Subscription: $12. Sample: $3.
How to Submit: Mss should be typed with poet's name on each page, 10 poems or fewer. No previously published poems; simultaneous submissions OK. Publishes theme issues occasionally. Send SASE for guidelines and upcoming themes or request via fax or e-mail. Responds in 2 months, usually sooner. "Submissions without SASE cannot be acknowledged." Pays 3 copies. Acquires first serial rights. Editor comments on rejections "if the poet or poems seem particularly promising." Reviews books of poetry by *MQ* published poets only.
Advice: "Keep writing; read as much contemporary poetry as you can lay your hands on; don't let the discouragement of rejection keep you from sending your work out to editors."

◎ ∅ **MIDWEST VILLAGES & VOICES (Specialized: regional)**, P.O. Box 40214, St. Paul MN 55104, phone (612)822-6878, founded 1979.
Book/Chapbook Needs & How to Submit: MVV is a cultural organization and small press publisher of Midwestern poetry and prose. "We encourage and support Midwestern writers and artists. However, at this time submissions are accepted by invitation only. Unsolicited submissions are not accepted."

✓ ◎ **MIDWIFERY TODAY (Specialized: childbirth)**, P.O. Box 2672, Eugene OR 97402-0223, phone (541)344-7438, fax (541)344-1422, e-mail editorial@midwiferytoday.com, website www.midwiferytoday.com, founded 1986, editor-in-chief Jan Tritten, editor Alice Evans.
Magazine Needs: *Midwifery Today* is a quarterly that "provides a voice for midwives and childbirth educators. We are a midwifery magazine. Subject must be birth or profession related." They do not want poetry that is "off subject or puts down the subject." *MT* is 75 pgs., 8½×11, offset printed, saddle-stapled, with glossy card cover with b&w photos and b&w artwork photos, and ads inside. They use about 1 poem/issue. Press run is 5,000 for 3,000 subscribers, 1,000 shelf sales. Subscription: $50. Sample: $10.
How to Submit: No previously published poems or simultaneous submissions. Fax and e-mail submissions OK. Cover letter required. Time between acceptance and publication is 1-2 years. Seldom comments on rejections. Publishes theme issues. Send SASE for guidelines and upcoming themes. Responds in 6 months. Pays 2 copies. Acquires first rights.
Also Offers: Website includes writer's guidelines, articles and products.
Advice: "With our publication *please* stay on the subject."

✓ ◐ **MILKWEED EDITIONS**, 430 First Ave. N., Suite 668, Minneapolis MN 55401-1743, phone (612)332-3192, fax (612)332-6248, website www.milkweed.org, founded 1979, poetry editor Elisabeth Fitz.
Book/Chapbook Needs: One to two collections published annually. One to two poetry anthologies published each year. Unsolicited mss are only accepted from writers who have previously published a book-length collection of poetry or a minimum of 6 poems in commercial or literary journals. One of the leading literary presses in the country, Milkweed publishes some of the best poets composing today in well-made, attractively designed collections. Published books of poetry include: *Butterfly Effect* by Harry Humes; *Eating Bread and Honey* by Pattiann Rogers; and *Outsiders: Poems about Rebels, Renegades and Exiles* edited by Laure-Anne Bosselaar.
How to Submit: Submit 60 plus page ms with SAS return bookmailer (or the ms will not be returned). Include SAS postcard for notification of ms arrival. Indicate in cover letter if ms is to be recycled. Unsolicited mss read in January and June; please include return postage. Send submissions to Poetry Readers. Send SASE for guidelines. Responds in up to 6 months. Catalog available on request, with $1.50 in postage.
Also Offers: Website includes writer's guidelines, catalog, info on publishing programs and "e-verse."

Ⓝ $◐ **MILLER'S POND; LOELLA CADY LAMPHIER PRIZE FOR POETRY; H&H PRESS**, RR 2, Box 241, Middlebury Center PA 16935, phone (570)376-2821, fax (570)376-2674, e-mail cjhoughtaling@usa.net, website http://millerspond.tripod.com, founded 1987, editor C.J. Houghtaling.
Magazine Needs: *miller's pond* is an annual magazine featuring contemporary poetry, interviews, reviews and markets. "We want contemporary poetry that is fresh, accessible, energetic, vivid and flows with language and rhythm. No religious, horror, pornographic, vulgar, rhymed, preachy, lofty, trite or overly sentimental work." They have published poetry by Colette Inez, Barbara Crocker, Elaine Preston, Hayden Carruth, Frank van Zant and C.S. Fuqua. As a sample the editor selected these lines from "On the Shore" by Gail Winther Peterson:

Wrapped in purple dusk/The cottage crumples/West wind/Feathers shingles/To trap the sand.

miller's pond is 48 pgs., 5½×8½, offset printed and saddle-stapled with cardstock cover. They receive about 200 poems a year. Publish 20-25 poems/issue. Press run is 200. Single copy: $5 and $3 p&h. Sample (back issue) including guidelines: $5. Make checks payable to H&H Press.

How to Submit: Submit 3-5 poems at a time. Line length for poetry is 40 maximum. Previously published poems and simultaneous submissions OK. Disk submissions OK. Cover letter preferred. "No returns without SASE." Reads submissions June 1 through October 1 only. Time between acceptance and publication is up to 1 year. Seldom comments on rejections. Send SASE for guidelines or obtain via website. Responds in 4 months. Sometimes sends prepublication galleys. Pays $2/poem and 1 copy for work that appears in hard copy version. Acquires one-time rights. Reviews books of poetry in 150-200 words, single book format. Open to unsolicited reviews.

Also Offers: H&H Press sponsors the Loella Lamphier Prize for Poetry. Awards $250 for 1st Place, $100 for 2nd Place and $50 3rd Place. Guidelines available on website. Send SASE. Website includes submission guidelines, contest guidelines, sample poems (including the contest winners), editorial comments, links of interest to poets and writers.

Website contains original content not found in the print edition. Poetry needs same as that for print version. "Electronic submissions accepted for our website only."

Book/Chapbook Needs & How to Submit: "H&H Press is a micro-publisher of poetry chapbooks and how-to-write books, with plans to expand into nonfiction and specialty books." They publish 1 paperback and 1 chapbook per year. Books are usually 24-36 pgs., $8\frac{1}{2} \times 5\frac{1}{4}$, offset printed and saddle-stapled with cardstock cover, includes some art. "Query first for publication schedule and needs. Open to all, regardless of previous publication credits. My requirements are simple—the poem/poetry must speak to me on more than one level and stay with me for more than just those few brief moments I'm reading it." Replies in 4 months. Pays royalties of 7% minimum, 12% maximum and 25 author's copies (out of a press run of 200). Books are available for sale via website, phone or fax.

Advice: "Believe in yourself. Perseverance is a writer's best 'tool.' Study the contemporary masters: Billy Collins, Maxine Kumin, Colette Inez, Hayden Carruth. Please check our website before submitting."

JOHN MILTON MAGAZINE; DISCOVERY MAGAZINE (Specialized: children/teen, religious, visual impairment), John Milton Society for the Blind, 475 Riverside Dr., Room 455, New York NY 10115, phone (212)870-3335, fax (212)870-3229, e-mail order@jmsblind.org, website www.jmsblind.org, founded 1928, executive director Darcy Quigley.

Magazine Needs: The *John Milton Magazine* is "a quarterly digest of more than 50 Christian periodicals, produced in large print (20 point) and sent free to visually impaired adults." The executive director says *JMM* is 24 pgs., tabloid-sized, contains clip art. They receive about 30 poems a year, accept approximately 5%. Press run is 5,188 for 3,776 subscribers. Subscription is free.

Magazine Needs: *Discovery* is "a quarterly Braille magazine for blind youth (ages 8-18). Articles selected and reprinted from over 20 Christian and secular periodicals for youth." Also accepts poetry written by children. The executive director says *Discovery* is 44 Braille pgs. They receive about 30 poems a year, accept approximately 15%. Press run is 2,041 for 1,878 subscribers. Subscription is free (only available in Braille).

How to Submit: For both publications, they want "Christian themes and holidays (not exclusive), seasonal poems, subjects of interest and encouragement to blind and visually impaired persons." Submit up to 5 poems at a time. Line length for poetry is 5 minimum, 30 maximum. Previously published poems and simultaneous submissions OK. Cover letter preferred. E-mail (include in body of message) and disk submissions OK. "Please enclose a SASE with regular mail submissions." Time between acceptance and publication is 3-12 months. Seldom comments on rejections. Publishes theme issues. Send SASE for guidelines. Responds in 3 months. *JMM* pays 1-3 copies. *Discovery* pays 1 Braille copy. Acquires one-time or reprint rights.

Also Offers: Website includes writer's guidelines, publications brochure, history of society, staff names, board of directors' names.

Advice: "Review list of magazines we typically reprint from (available with writer's guidelines). The bulk of our material is reprinted from other periodicals."

MIND MATTERS REVIEW, 2040 Polk St., #234, San Francisco CA 94109, founded 1988, phone (415)775-4545, e-mail openbook@earthlink.com, website www.home.earthlink.net/~openbook, editor Carrie Drake.

Magazine Needs: *Mind Matters Review* is a "literary annual with emphasis on use of science as a tool for responsible organization of information; analysis of the role of language in consciousness, knowledge and intelligence; and social criticism particularly of metaphysics. Also includes book reviews, poetry, short stories, art and essays." They want "short poems for fillers." They have published poetry by Russell Eisenmann and Robert L. Brimm. As a sample the editor selected these lines from "Heraclitus Was Right" by T.N. Turner:

> *Heraclitus was right about physical law, I mean/that the universe is an ever changing river of fire—/*
> *Everything and everyone becoming, not being*

MMR is magazine-sized, desktop-published, includes graphics, sketches, b&w photos. Subscription: $10 US, $15 foreign. Sample: $3.50.

How to Submit: Poets are encouraged to buy a copy before submitting. Submit 3 poems at a time. E-mail submissions OK. No simultaneous submissions; previously published poems OK. Cover letter required; include publishing credits and note if submissions have been previously published or accepted for publication elsewhere. Publishes theme issues. Send SASE for guidelines and upcoming themes. Sometimes sends prepublication galleys. Pays 1 copy.

◯ ◪ **MIND PURGE**, NT Box 305471, Denton TX 76203, e-mail jivan@anet-dfw.com, founded 1994, editor Jason Hensel.

Magazine Needs: *Mind Purge* is a biannual literary and art magazine appearing in April and October that publishes poetry, short fiction, one-act plays, short screenplays, essays, book reviews and art. They want poetry that is "well-crafted, insightful, imagistic. No specifications as to form, length, subject matter or style. However no greeting card verse, hackneyed themes or poetry that says nothing or goes nowhere." They have published poetry by Lyn Lifshin, Danny Daniels, Wayne Hogan, B.Z. Niditch and Ryan G. Van Cleave. As a sample the editors selected these lines from "The Last Days Of" by Holly Day:

> *Harvest. Cultivation. The words fall alien and pleasing/from our lips, songs of summers past/of a people long since dead. Practice. The round gearshift cupped/smooth in your confused palm. The wide flat pedals creak/with rust beneath your sandaled feet. Someday/the machines will work again./ Someday, it will rain.*

Mind Purge is 36-52 pgs., 7×8½, neatly printed and saddle-stapled with matte card stock cover with b&w photo and b&w photos inside. They receive about 100 poems a year, accept approximately 10%. Press run is 100 for 10 subscribers. Subscription: $10. Sample: $4. Make checks payable to Jason Hensel.

How to Submit: Submit up to 5 poems or 10 pages at a time, name and address on each page. No previously published poems or simultaneous submissions. Cover letter preferred. E-mail submissions OK, no attachments, include in body of message. Seldom comments on rejections. Responds within 3 months. Pays 1 copy. Reviews books of poetry in 200 words, single book format. Open to unsolicited reviews. Poets may also send books for review consideration.

Advice: "Don't give up, just keep submitting. And read, not only poetry, but everything you can get your hands on."

◪ **THE MINNESOTA REVIEW: A JOURNAL OF COMMITTED WRITING**, English Dept., University of Missouri-Columbia, 110 Tate Hall, Columbia MO 65211, founded 1960, editor Jeffrey Williams.

Magazine Needs: *TMR* is a biannual literary magazine wanting "poetry which explores some aspect of social or political issues and/or the nature of relationships. No nature poems, and no lyric poetry without the above focus." *TMR* is about 200 pgs., digest-sized, flat-spined, with b&w glossy card cover and art. Press run is 1,500 for 800 subscribers. Subscription: $20 to individuals, $36 to institutions. Sample: $10.

How to Submit: Address submissions to "Poetry Editor" (not to a specific editor). Cover letter including "brief intro with address" preferred. SASE with sufficient postage required for return of mss. Publishes theme issues. Send SASE for upcoming themes. Responds in up to 4 months. Pays 2 copies. Acquires all rights. Returns rights upon request. Reviews books of poetry in single or multi-book format. Open to unsolicited reviews.

☑ ◻ ◯ ◎ **MINORITY LITERARY EXPO (Specialized: membership, minorities)**, 317 Third Ave. SW, Apt. 2E, Birmingham AL 35211, phone (205)297-9816, e-mail kervin4@hotmail.com, founded 1990, editor/publisher Kervin Fondren.

Magazine Needs & How to Submit: *MLE* is an annual literary professional publication featuring minority poets, novices and professionals. "Organization membership open to all minority poets nationally. I want poems from minority poets that are holistic and wholesome, less than 24 lines each, no vulgar or hate poetry accepted, any style, any form, any subject matter. Poetry that expresses holistic views and philosophies is very acceptable. Literary value is emphasized. Selected poets receive financial awards, certificates, honorable mentions, critiques and special poetic honors." No fee is charged for inclusion. Also accepts poetry written by children ages 12 and up. As a sample the editor selected his poem "It's Lonely at the Top":

> *No Man Can/Reach the Top of the Mountain/With Hate, Greed and Despair.//Because in Reaching the Top/He Soon Will Find Out that/he is the only one There.*

Single copy: $16. Send SASE for guidelines and upcoming themes. Pays 1 copy. E-mail submissions OK, include in body of message with e-mail address for reply. "Send edited copy, no more than one page via e-mail."

Also Offers: They also sponsor an annual poetry chapbook contest and an annual "Analyze the Poem" contest. Send SASE for details.

Advice: "We seek novices and unpublished poets to breathe the new life every poetry organization needs."

$ ◎ **THE MIRACULOUS MEDAL (Specialized: religious)**, 475 E. Chelten Ave., Philadelphia PA 19144-5785, phone (215)848-1010, founded 1928, editor Rev. William J. O'Brien, C.M.

Magazine Needs: *MM* is a religious quarterly. "Poetry should reflect solid Catholic doctrine and experience. Any subject matter is acceptable, provided it does not contradict the teachings of the Roman Catholic Church. Poetry must have a religious theme, preferably about the Blessed Virgin Mary." They have published poetry by Gladys McKee. The editor describes it as 32 pgs., digest-sized, saddle-stapled, 2-color inside and cover, no ads. *The Miraculous Medal* is used as a promotional piece and is sent to all clients of the Central Association of the Miraculous Medal. Circulation is 250,000.

How to Submit: Sample and guidelines free for postage. Line length for poetry is 20 maximum, double-spaced. No simultaneous submissions or previously published poems. Responds in up to 3 years. Pays 50¢ and up/line, on acceptance. Buys first North American rights.

N **$◯◐** **THE MISSING FEZ; THE RED FELT AWARD**, 1720 N. Dodge Blvd., Tucson AZ 85716, e-mail missing1fez@hotmail.com, founded 1999, poetry editor Alan Brich.

Magazine Needs: *The Missing Fez* is "a quarterly forum for the abnormal in literature. We want poems that embody some form of strangeness or oddity in either style, content or language. Give us something different. No poems that rhyme or are about pets, or would meet parental approval." They have published poetry by Jonathon Earney, Michael Blackwell, Jane Rhinehart, Dawn Miller, Liz Keefe and Ian Gill. As a sample the editor selected these lines from "A Woman's Husband" by Jonathon Earney:

> Everyone hid things, even his mother/Good catholic that she was, hid things./Not in her mustache, of
> course,/it was much too thin/to keep anything a secret for very long

The editor says *TMF* is 36 pgs., 7×8½, photocopied on laser quality paper and saddle-stapled with glossy card cover, includes b&w photos and illustrations. They receive about 150 poems a year, accept approximately 15%. Publish 3-5 poems/issue. Press run is 1,000 for 800 subscribers, 600 shelf sales; 100 distributed free to sponsored reading series. Single copy: $2; subscription: $8. Sample: $3. Make checks payable to Red Felt Publishing.

How to Submit: Submit 3-5 poems at a time with $3 reading fee. Previously published poems and simultaneous submissions OK. Cover letter preferred. "We do require $3 reading fee and SASE since we comment on all submissions and pay on acceptance." Time between acceptance and publication is 3-6 months. Always comments on rejections. Publishes theme issues occasionally. Send SASE for guidelines and upcoming themes. Responds in 6 weeks. Pays $15/poem plus 2 copies. Acquires one-time rights.

Also Offers: Sponsors the annual Red Felt Award. 1st Prize winner receives $250. Send SASE for complete guidelines.

Advice: "Don't write safe poetry—if you do, don't send it to us."

$◐ **MISSISSIPPI MUD**, 7119 Santa Fe Ave., Dallas TX 75223, founded 1973, editor Joel Weinstein.

Magazine Needs: *Mississippi Mud*, published irregularly, features fiction, poetry and artwork which "portray life in America as the 20th century crashes and burns." As for poetry they want "smart, contemporary themes and forms, free verse preferred." They do not want "anything stodgy, pathetic or moralistic; the self-consciously pretty or clever; purely formal exercises." They have published poetry by Tino Villanueva, Diane Averill and Simon Perchik. *MM* is 96 pgs., 7¾×10, perfect-bound, with 4-color glossy paper cover, full-page graphics and display ads. They receive 100-200 poems a year, accept less than 10%. Press run is 1,500 for 150 subscribers of which 16 are libraries, 1,000 shelf sales; about 200 distributed free to galleries, museums and critical media. Subscription: $12/2 issues. Sample: $6.

How to Submit: Submit up to 6 poems at a time. No previously published poems; simultaneous submissions OK. Time between acceptance and publication is a year or more. Seldom comments on rejections. Responds in 6 months. Pays $25 and 2 copies. Buys first North American serial rights.

◐ **MISSISSIPPI REVIEW**, University of Southern Mississippi, Box 5144, Hattiesburg MS 39406-5144, phone (601)266-4321, fax (601)266-5757, e-mail fb@netdoor.com, website www.sushi.st.usm.edu\mrw, editor Frederick Barthelme, managing editor Rie Fortenberry.

Magazine Needs & How to Submit: Literary publication for those interested in contemporary literature. Poems differ in style, length and form, but all have craft in common (along with intriguing content). Sample: $8. Query first, via mail, e-mail or their website. Does not read manuscripts in summer. Pays 3 copies. Sponsors contests. Send SASE for guidelines.

$◐ **MISSOURI REVIEW; TOM MCAFEE DISCOVERY FEATURE; LARRY LEVIS EDITORS' PRIZE CONTEST IN POETRY**, 1507 Hillcrest Hall, University of Missouri, Columbia MO 65211, phone (573)882-4474, fax (573)884-4671, website www.missourireview.org, founded 1978, poetry editor Greg Michalson, general editor Speer Morgan.

Magazine Needs: *Missouri Review* is 6×9, 208 pgs., and appears 3 times/year, publishing poetry features only—6-12 pages for each of 3 to 5 poets/issue. "By devoting more editorial space to each poet, *MR* provides a fuller look at the work of some of the best writers composing today." They have published poetry by Laura Kasichke, Davis McCombs, Charles Simic and Jeffrey Levine.

How to Submit: Submit 6-12 poems at a time. No previously published poems or simultaneous submissions. Responds in up to 10 weeks. Sometimes sends prepublication galleys. Pays $125-250/feature. Buys all rights. Returns rights "after publication, without charge, at the request of the authors." Staff reviews books of poetry.

Also Offers: Awards the Tom McAfee Discovery Feature once or twice a year to an outstanding young poet who has not yet published a book; poets are selected from regular submissions at the discretion of the editors. Also offers the Larry Levis Editors' Prize Contest in Poetry. Deadline: October 15. $1,500 1st Prize and publication. Three finalists named in addition. Write for details. Website includes guidelines, staff photos, poetry, interviews and discussion forum.

Advice: "We think we have enhanced the quality of our poetry section and increased our reader interest in this section. We remain dedicated to publishing at least one younger or emerging poet in every issue."

☑ **$◐◉** **MKASHEF ENTERPRISES; PRISONERS OF THE NIGHT (Specialized: psychic/occult, science fiction/fantasy, horror, erotica); POETIC LICENSE**, P.O. Box 688, Yucca Valley CA 92286-0688, e-mail alayne@inetworld.net, website www.asidozines.com, founded 1987, poetry editor Alayne Gelfand.

Magazine Needs: *Prisoners of the Night*, focusing on vampire erotica, uses poetry that is "erotic, unique, less horrific and more romantic, non-pornographic, original visions of the vampire." They have published poetry by Charlee Jacob, Tippi Blevins, Bobbi Sinaha-Morey, Elizabeth Wein and Della Van Hise. As a sample the editor selected these lines from "Evolution" by Wendy Rathbone:

> In the echo of June/children grow wings/and are carried off/by unexpected winds./We bury our dead/
> but they linger/in dracula shadows.

POTN is 70-90 pgs., 8½×11, comb-bound with artful cover, produced by high-speed photocopying. Most poems are illustrated. It appears annually, usually in September. They receive about 300 poems a year, accept approximately 10-20. It has an initial press run of 3,000, but each issue is kept in print. Sample: $15 each (for #1-4), $12 (#5), $9.95 each (#6-9), $7.95 (#10 and #11).

How to Submit: Beginning in September 2000, they will be accepting submissions for the 2001 issue. Send SASE for guidelines. When *POTN* is open to submissions, submit up to 6 poems at a time. No simultaneous submissions or previously published poems, "unless they've only appeared in your own chapbook." E-mail submissions OK. Editor sometimes comments on rejections. Responds "within 1 month." Pays $5/poem plus 1 copy. Buys first serial rights. *POTN* wants unusual visions of the vampire, not stereotypical characterizations.

Also Offers: Also sponsors Poetic License, a biannual poetry contest awarding $500 1st Prize, $100 2nd Prize and $50 3rd Prize, plus publication in anthology and 1 copy. Five honorable mentions receive 1 copy; other poems of exceptional interest will also be included in the anthology. Send SASE for themes and deadlines. Submit any number of poems, any style, of up to 50 lines/poem. Include name, address and phone on each poem. Enclose an SASE, for notification of winners. "Judges prefer original, accessible and unforced works." Entry fee: $1/poem. Website includes detailed contents of each issue of *Prisoners of the Night*, guidelines, sample poetry, story excerpts, editor's biography, deadlines and art samples.

Advice: "Be original! Find new ways of saying things, explore the infinite possibilities of words and images. Do not rely on stereotypical visions of the vampire; the use of clichés is the quickest road to rejection. I'm not looking for your typical 'count' or 'countess,' no loners in ruined castles. I'm looking for the unusual image and sharp word usage. I want you to make my heart race with both the structure and subject of your poem. Non-rhyming, unstructured poems much preferred."

MM REVIEW; MUTANT MULE; FINISHING LINE PRESS; NEW WOMEN'S VOICES CHAPBOOK SERIES, P.O. Box 1016, Cincinnati OH 45201-1016, e-mail finishingl@aol.com, website http://members.aol.com/FinishingL/index.html, founded 1998, editor C.J. Morrison.

Magazine Needs: *MM Review* is a biannual literary arts magazine publishing mostly poetry, but also short stories, short drama, essays and, sometimes, reviews. "We hope to discover new talent." They want "quality verse. We are open to any style or form, but prefer free verse." They have published poetry by Errol Miller, Dennis Saleh, Denise Brennan Watson, Mark McCloskey, Rane Arroyo and Alexandra Grilikhes. As a sample the editor selected these lines from "Feeling Fireworks" by Leah Maines:

> Fireflowers bloom/in the warm summer air/your hand/unaware/brushes my breast

The editor says *MM Review* is 40 pgs., digest-sized, laser-printed and saddle-stapled with glossy cover, includes b&w photos. They receive about 1,000 poems a year, accept approximately 4%. Press run is 500 for 300 subscribers. Single copy: $6; subscription: $10. Sample: $5. Make checks payable to Finishing Line Press.

How to Submit: Submit up to 3 poems at a time. Include SASE. No previously published poems; simultaneous submissions OK. Brief cover letter with 50- to 75-word bio required, include past publication credits. Time between acceptance and publication is 6 months. Poems are circulated to an editorial board. Often comments on rejections. Publishes theme issues occasionally. Send SASE for guidelines. Responds in 4 months. Sometimes sends prepublication galleys. Pays 1 copy. Acquires all rights. Returns rights upon publication. Staff reviews books and chapbooks of poetry in 200 words, multi-book format. Send books for review consideration to Finishing Line Press.

Book/Chapbook Needs & How to Submit: Finishing Line Press seeks to "discover new talent" and through their New Women's Voices Series publishes 2 chapbooks/year by women who have not previously published a book or chapbook of poetry. They have published *Looking to the East with Western Eyes* by Leah Maines; *Like the Air* by Joyce Sidman; *Startling Art* by Dorothy Sutton; *The Undertow of Hunger* by Denise Brennan Watson. Chapbooks are usually 25-30 pgs., digest-sized, laser-printed and saddle-stapled with card cover with textured matte wrapper, includes b&w photos. Submit ms of 16-24 pgs. with cover letter, bio, acknowledgements and $10 reading fee. Replies to queries in 3-4 weeks, to mss in 3-4 months. Pays 50 author's copies (out of a press run of 300). "Sales profits, if any, go to publish the next new poet." Obtain sample chapbooks by sending $5.

Also Offers: Sponsors New Women's Voices chapbook competition. Entry fee: $12. Deadline: December 31. Website includes guidelines.

Advice: "We are very open to new talent. If the poetry is great, we will consider it for a chapbook."

MÖBIUS, P.O. Box 7544, Talleyville DE 19803-0544, founded 1982, editor Jean Hull Herman, e-mail mobiusmag@aol.com.

Magazine Needs: *Möbius* is published twice a year, at Memorial Day and Thanksgiving. The editor looks for "the informed mind responding to the challenges of reality and the expression of the imagination in poetry that demonstrates intelligence and wit. Poets should say significant, passionate things about the larger world outside themselves, using all the resources of the English language. Preference is given to poetry that pleases the ear as

insider report

Finishing Line Press gives new poets a post at the starting gate

C.J. Morrison

C. J. Morrison majored in biology and was on her way to a career in medicine when marriage and motherhood sidetracked her ambitions. However, a love for writing and an appreciation for good writers led her to the publishing world. After witnessing the intense competition for publication writers face, she founded Finishing Line Press and *MM Review* to help women writers accomplish dreams. "I have friends who are struggling writers, and this just seemed like a way to do something I enjoy." Although the original focus was on women writers, she has published equal amounts of men's writing in *MM Review*, which publishes poetry, short-short stories, essays and dramas. Later this year, Finishing Line Press will publish their first chapbook by a male poet.

Finishing Line Press is not self-supporting, and her staff members work for a small honorarium. But Morrison has been fortunate in finding good editors and judges and attracting good writers such as Errol Miller and Kevin Walzer to *MM Review*.

In 1998, Morrsion introduced the New Women's Voices Series to launch new poets through a chapbook competition, publishing poets who have never published a book of poetry. *Looking to the East with Western Eyes* by Leah Maines was the first book of the series. Morrison says, "A lot depended on that book. If it did well, I planned to keep the series going. If it failed, I probably would have closed up shop." However, the chapbook did phenomenally well, and the series is now in its third year with manuscripts arriving from all over the world. For each series a winner is chosen and often honorable mentions are selected for publication.

Later in 1998, the manuscript for *The Undertow of Hunger* by Denise Brennan Watson was brought to Morrison's attention. Morrison published it in 1999 and says, "If I had to go with an example of what I like in a chapbook, it would be this work. I look for collections that are tightly thumbed and of an even tone and loaded with metaphors." The collection, centered on the sights, smells, taste and feel of food, is incredibly sensual and lyrical. Nancy Conger, author of *Sensuous Living*, says, "These poems are to savor. They are ripe, real and delicious. Watson embraces the divine senses, the stark churn of hunger, and the connections we make over food." Finishing Line Press nominated *The Undertow of Hunger* for the Pushcart Prize and the William Carlos Williams Book Award (sponsored by the Poetry Society of America). In one poem from the collection, Watson turns the simple garlic clove into sumptuous, erotic imagery.

"Ode To A Garlic Clove"

Let me unpetal you
and roll you between
my hands,
which have swollen
plump as spring.

Leave no line or print
Or grid of skin
Unperfumed
by your secretions.

Seep into me. Kiss me
with the odor
of sap
that remains
long after
the pounding
has stopped.

(reprinted with permission from the author)

Morrison reaps tremendous satisfaction from finding and having the means to publish manuscripts by little-known authors like Maines and Watson. However, a writer's success hinges on self-promotion. Morrison says, "I'm excited about how the careers of these authors have taken off. They each had really good manuscripts and they each did their part in promoting their books. I only have so much time, so I need to let writers know it is important for them to get the word out about their books." Morrison cannot emphasize enough the need for writers to network by attending readings and other poetry events and by following up on any other avenue that presents itself. "One never knows who they might meet or how one thing can lead to another in this business," she says.

One of the downsides to publishing is the necessity of reading numerous manuscripts to, according to Morrison, "find the diamonds in the coal." Submissions vary each month, but hundreds arrive for *MM Review* while less than ten chapbook manuscripts are submitted for the competition.

For both *MM Review* and the press, Morrison looks for quality. "It doesn't matter to me if the poet or writer has been published before, as long as what they wrote is excellent," she says. For beginning poets looking to get published, Morrison has emphatic but sound advice. She insists on clean manuscripts on plain white paper. "I don't want to see any graphics on the page nor do I want the poet's life story in the bio." A professional-looking cover letter with past publication credits listed in a short three-to-five line bio are preferred. A lack of publication credits should not deter the writer. But, Morrison advises, "Don't tell me the names of your cats or any jokes." Additionally, she does not "like cover letters that give guilt trips either. I once had a poet write a cover letter that said, 'If you don't publish my poems, and think they suck, I'll never write or submit anything again!' I didn't publish her." Morrison also recommends

> new poets "take care with line breaks. Consider why you are stopping one line and starting another. Does it flow better if I do short or long breaks?" And always title your work. To Morrison, untitled poems signal to her the poem is unfinished.
> —*Pamala Shields*

well as the intellect and soul; strong preference is given to work that is fine, structured, layered, as opposed to untitled, unpunctuated jottings. General topics include usage of language and the forms of poetry; the great philosophical questions; romance; relationships; war; science and technology; and humor (the editor has a weakness for humorous lines). The magazine claims no rights to poems. Delaware's only poetry magazine, Möbius has published poetry not only from 50 states but also from all seven continents." They have published poetry by Ace Boggess, Ward Kelley, Susan S. Hahn, Sandra Seaton Michel, Richard Wakefield and JeanPaul Jenack. As a sample the editor selected these lines from "36 Down (With 5 Across)" by Dennis Upper:

> *with crossword puzzles I'm obsessed/robbing me of needed rest/nightly as I lie abed/arcane factoids fill my head*

Möbius is 60-80 pgs., magazine-sized, professionally printed and perfect-bound. Subscription: $14/year. Sample: $8.

How to Submit: Submit up to 3 poems at a time, typed with name and address on each poem, 1 submission/issue. No electronic submissions. Submissions read year-round. Responds in 3 months. Comments on rejections. Pays 1 copy. Send SASE for guidelines.

$ 🖸 ◎ MODERN HAIKU; FOUR HIGH SCHOOL SENIOR SCHOLARSHIPS (Specialized: form, students), P.O. Box 1752, Madison WI 53701-1752, phone (608)233-2738, founded 1969, poetry editor Robert Spiess.

Magazine Needs: *Modern Haiku* appears 3 times/year in February, June and October and "is the foremost international journal of English language haiku and criticism. We are devoted to publishing only the very best haiku being written and also publish articles on haiku and have the most complete review section of haiku books. Issues average 112 pages." They want "contemporary haiku in English (including translations into English) that incorporate the traditional aesthetics of the haiku genre, but which may be innovative as to subject matter, mode of approach or angle of perception, and form of expression. Haiku, senryu and haibun only. No tanka or other forms." Also accepts poetry written by children. They have published haiku by Michael Dylan Welch, Bruce Ross and Yvonne Hardenbrook. As a sample the editor included this haiku by Ruth Yarrow:

> *cliff cataract/braiding water, breeze, and sun—/winter wren's song*

The digest-sized magazine appears 3 times/year, printed on heavy quality stock with cover illustrations especially painted for each issue by the staff artist. They receive about 12,000-14,000 submissions a year, use approximately 800. There are over 260 poems in each issue. Circulation is 700. Subscription: $18.50. Sample: $6.25.

How to Submit: Submit on "any size sheets, any number of haiku on a sheet; but name and address on each sheet." Include SASE. No previously published haiku or simultaneous submissions. Send SASE for guidelines. Responds in 2 weeks. Pays $1/haiku (but no contributor's copy). Buys first North American serial rights. Staff reviews books of haiku in 350-1,000 words, single book format. Send books for review consideration.

Also Offers: They offer 4 annual scholarships for the best haiku by high school seniors. Scholarships range from $200-500 (total $1,400). Deadline is mid-March. Send SASE for rules. Also offers $200 Best of Issue Awards.

Advice: "Haiku achieve their effect of felt-depth, insight and intuition through juxtaposition of perceived entities, not through intellective comment or abstract words."

🌐 ✓ $ ◻ ◎ MODERN POETRY IN TRANSLATION (Specialized: translations), King's College London, Strand, London WC2 R2LS United Kingdom, phone (171)842-2360, fax (171)848-2415, website: www.kcl.ac.uk/mpt/, founded 1965 (original series), 1992 (new series), advisory and managing editor Professor Norma Rinsler, editor Daniel Weissbort.

Magazine Needs: *Modern Poetry in Translation*, published biannually, features "translations of poems from any language into English, and essays on translation (practice rather than theory). Our aim is to further international cultural understanding and exchange and to awaken interest in poetry." They want "only translations from any language into English—'modern' refers to translation (which should be unpublished), not to original." They do not want "self-translation by those not familiar with English; work by translators who are not poets or not familiar with a range of works in the original language rarely succeed (unless they work with original authors)." *MPT* averages 240 pgs., 5⅝ × 8½, offset printed, perfect-bound with illustrated 2-color cover on scanchip board, matte laminated. Accept approximately 50% of the poems they receive. Press run is 500 for 350 subscribers of which 50% are libraries, 50 shelf sales. Single copy: £10 (UK/EU); £12 (foreign). Subscriptions (2 issues): £20 (UK/EU); £24 (foreign), inc. surface mail (airmail extra). Sample: £7.50. Make checks payable to King's College London (*MPT*).

How to Submit: Submit 5-6 poems at a time "unless very long, in which case 1 or 2". Disk submissions (in Word) preferred. Originals should accompany translation. No previously published poems or simultaneous submissions. Cover letter required. No fax submissions. Time between acceptance and publication is 3-9 months. The editor and managing/advisory editor discuss submissions and consult individual members of advisory board if expertise required. Often comments on rejections. Publishes theme issues. Send SASE (or SAE and IRC) for upcoming themes. Responds "as soon as possible—within weeks." Sometimes sends prepublication galleys. Pays £12/poem or £15/page plus 1 copy to translator, 1 for original author. "Copyright on selection as printed— general rights remain with contributors." Features reviews of poetry books often commissioned from experts in the field. Poets may also send books for review consideration (translations only).

Also Offers: Website includes contents of all issues from *Modern Poetry in Translation* (1992) onwards plus submissions forms.

 **MOJO RISIN'; JOSH SAMUELS BIANNUAL POETRY COMPETITION**, P.O. Box 268451, Chicago IL 60626-8451, founded 1995, editor Ms. Josh Samuels.

Magazine Needs: *mojo risin'* published quarterly, features "poetry, prose, short stories and some sort of contest in each issue." She wants "any form or style." She does not want "incest, racism, blatant sex or anything written for shock value." She has published poetry by Lyn Lifshin, Joan Payne Kincaid, Mary Hale Jackson and J.M. Segriff. As a sample the editor selected these lines from "The Old Man Speaks" by John Grey:

> When he lectures,/I think of scarecrows,/all poles and straw,/waving their wind driven arms/at the
> dark intentions of crows,/with a flap and a frozen grin

mojo risin' is 32 pgs., 8½×11, photocopied, saddle-stapled with colored cardstock cover and b&w artwork. She receives about 300 poems a year, accepts ⅓. Press run is 300 for 200 subscribers. Subscription: $20/year; $30/2 years. Sample: $7.

How to Submit: Subscription not required for acceptance. Submit 3-5 poems (2 pages maximum) at a time. No previously published poems or simultaneous submissions. Cover letter preferred. Time between acceptance and publication is 1-3 months. The editor is solely responsible for all aspects of editing and publishing. Send SASE for guidelines. Responds within 10 days. Manuscripts not returned. Acquires first North American serial rights.

Also Offers: Sponsors the Josh Samuels Biannual Poetry Competition. 1st Place: $100; 2nd Place: $75; 3rd Place $50. Entry fee: $10/5 poems maximum. Any form, style or subject. No previously published poems or simultaneous submissions. Mss not returned. Deadlines: May 31 and November 30. Submissions read March through May and September through November only. Winners published and paid in February and August. Send SASE for guidelines.

MONAS HIEROGLYPHICA, 58 Seymour Rd., Hadleigh, Benfleet, Essex SS7 2HL United Kingdom, e-mail monas_hieroglyphica@postmaster.co.uk, website www.geocities.com/SoHo/Museum/9668, founded 1994, contact Mr. Jamie Spracklen.

Magazine Needs: *MH* appears quarterly and "supports the Gothic music movement, but aims to provide an eclectic mix of material." For their poetry needs they say, "Send for sample copy and see." No racist or sexist work. Also accepts poetry written by children. They have published poetry by Sean Russell Friend and Steve Sneyd. As a sample Mr. Spracklen selected this poem, "The Passing of Life & Death," by S.R. Friend:

> Come, join the game of death;/My sweet black butterfly:/There is only cloud where/The fire should be,
> sun where/We should love the moon.

The editor says *MH* is 30 pgs., magazine-sized, photocopied and bound with paper cover, includes art/graphics and ads. They receive about 100 poems a year, accept approximately 25%. Press run is 500 for 400 subscribers. Single copy: $4; subscription: $15. Sample: $3. Make checks payable to Jamie Spracklen.

How to Submit: Submit 3 poems at a time. Line length for poetry is 60 maximum. No previously published poems; simultaneous submissions OK. E-mail submission OK, include in body of text. Cover letter required. "Poems must be typed on size A4 paper and in English." Time between acceptance and publication is 3 months. Seldom comments on rejections. Publishes theme issues occasionally. Send SASE for guidelines and upcoming themes. Responds in 2 weeks. Pays 1 copy. "Rights stay with author." Reviews books and chapbooks of poetry and other magazines in 20 words, multi-book format. Open to unsolicited reviews. Poets may also send books for review consideration.

Also Offers: Website includes guidelines and links to other sites.

■ ○ ◐ **MONKEY FLOWER: SANTIAGO CANYON COLLEGE REVIEW**, % Will Lennertz, 8045 E. Chapman Ave., Orange CA 92669-4512, phone (714)564-4781, e-mail themonkeyflower@hotmail.com, website www.rsccd.org/home/scceng/mkflower, founded 1999, faculty advisor Will Lennertz.

Magazine Needs: *Monkey Flower* is a "biannual online literary magazine dedicated to publishing the best literature and art we can." They are open in form and subject matter. "Our desire is to publish quality poetry, fiction and art. No doggerel or greeting card verse." They receive about 1,500 poems a year, accept approximately 7-10%.

How to Submit: Submit 3-5 poems at a time. No previously published poems or simultaneous submissions. Cover letter preferred. E-mail submissions OK. "Cut and paste poems, fiction and nonfiction into e-mail submissions." Reads submissions August through December and February through May. Time between acceptance and publication is 2 months. Poems are circulated to an editorial board. "Collectively editors reach the decision to publish poetry, fiction, nonfiction and art." Seldom comments on rejections. Obtain guidelines via e-mail or website. Responds in 2 months. Acquires first North American serial rights. Staff reviews books and chapbooks of poetry and other magazines in 300-500 words, single or multi-book format. Send books for review consideration.

Also Offers: Website includes poetry, guidelines, fiction, nonfiction and art.

Advice: "We are open to a great variety of poetry. Try us."

◐ **WILLIAM MORROW AND CO.**, 1350 Avenue of the Americas, New York NY 10019, phone (212)261-6500, publishes poetry on standard royalty contracts but accepts no unsolicited mss. Queries with samples should be submitted through an agent.

[N] ○ **MOTHER EARTH INTERNATIONAL JOURNAL; NATIONAL POETRY ASSOCIATION; POETRY FILM FESTIVAL**, % National Poetry Association, Box 886, Bolinas CA 94924, phone (415)552-9261, fax (415)552-9271, e-mail gamuse@slip.net, website www.nationalpoetry.org, *ME* founded 1991, NPA in 1976, editor/publisher Herman Berlandt.

Magazine Needs: "*Mother Earth International* is the only on-going anthology of contemporary poetry in English translation from all regions of the world. *MEI* provides a forum to poets to comment in poetic form on political, economic and ecological issues." They want "bold and compassionate poetry that has universal relevance with an emphasis on the world's current political and ecological crisis. No self-indulgent or prosaic stuff that lacks imagination." They have published poetry by Lawrence Ferlinghetti, Lyn Lifshin, Diane di Prima and Margaret Atwood. As a sample the editor selected these lines from "Four Untitled Poems" by George Jones (Canada):

> Let me put it this way:/If I were a German/I could say to myself Mozart & Rolke/But I would also
> have to say/Goebbels & Bergen-Belsen/words I could not pronounce lightly.

MEI is 40-48 pgs., tabloid-sized, offset printed, includes graphics and photographs. They receive about 4,000 poems a year, accept approximately 15%. Press run is 2,000 for 1,200 subscribers of which 280 are libraries. Subscription: $12/year. Sample: $3.75. Make checks payable to Uniting the World Through Poetry. "We encourage the purchase of a copy or a year's subscription."

How to Submit: Submit 4 poems at a time. Previously published poems and simultaneous submissions OK. Cover letter preferred. Time between acceptance and publication is 4 months. Publishes theme issues occasionally. Send SASE for guidelines and upcoming themes. Responds in 3 months. Sometimes sends prepublication galleys. Pays 2 copies. All rights revert to the author. Staff reviews books of poetry in 600 words, single book format. Send books for review consideration to H. Berlandt, Box 886, Bolinas CA 94924.

Also Offers: Sponsors a $50 prize to the best of "Your Two Best Lines," a benefit collage poem which will list all entries as a collective poem.

Advice: "*Mother Earth International* is an ongoing anthology of world contemporary poetry. For subscribers we reduced the subscription from $18 to $12/year. While all future issues will include an American section, we hope that all who send in entries will subscribe to *MEI* to get a truly world perspective of universal concerns."

❀ ✓ ◎ ◐ **(m)ÖTHÊR TØÑGUÉ PRESS (Specialized: regional)**, 290 Fulford-Ganges Rd., Salt Spring Island, British Columbia V8K 2K6 Canada, e-mail mothertongue@saltspring.com, website www.saltspring.com/art/mothertongue.htm, founded 1990, editor/publisher Mona Fertig.

Book/Chapbook Needs: "Private literary press. Specializing in beautiful chapbooks of poetry and prose, broadsides and book art. Limited and signed editions. Large letterpress printing studio. Custom die-cuts, lino cuts, debossing. Catalog available."

How to Submit: No unsolicited mss.

◐ **MOUNT OLIVE COLLEGE PRESS; MOUNT OLIVE REVIEW; LEE WITTE POETRY CONTEST**, 634 Henderson St., Mount Olive NC 28365, phone (919)658-2502, founded 1987 (*Mount Olive Review*), 1990 (Mount Olive College Press), editor Dr. Pepper Worthington.

Magazine Needs: *Mount Olive Review*, features "literary criticism, poetry, short stories, essays and book reviews." They want "modern poetry." The editor says *Mount Olive Review* is 7½×10. They receive about 2,000 poems a year, accept approximately 8%. Press run is 1,000. Single copy: $25. Make checks payable to Mount Olive College Press.

How to Submit: Submit 6 poems at a time. No previously published poems or simultaneous submissions. Cover letter preferred. Time between acceptance and publication varies. Poems are circulated to an editorial board. Seldom comments on rejections. Publishes theme issues. Send SASE for guidelines and upcoming themes. Responds in 3 months. Sometimes sends prepublication galleys. Acquires first rights. Reviews books and chapbooks of poetry and other magazines. Open to unsolicited reviews. Poets may also send books for review consideration.

Book/Chapbook Needs & How to Submit: Mount Olive Press publishes 2 books/year and sponsors the Lee Witte Poetry Contest. Write to above address for guidelines. Books are usually 5½×8. Submit 12 sample poems. Replies to queries and mss in 3 months. Obtain sample books by writing to the above address.

☑ ⊘ **MOVING PARTS PRESS**, 10699 Empire Grade, Santa Cruz CA 95060-9474, phone (831)427-2271, fax (831)458-2810, e-mail frice@movingpartspress.com, website www.movingpartspress.com, founded 1977, poetry editor Felicia Rice. They do not accept unsolicited mss.

Ⓝ ▣ ⊘ **MUDLARK: AN ELECTRONIC JOURNAL OF POETRY & POETICS**, Dept. of English, University of North Florida, Jacksonville FL 32224-2645, phone (904)620-2273, fax (904)620-3940, e-mail mudlark@unf.edu, website www.unf.edu/mudlark, founded 1995, editor William Slaughter.
Magazine Needs: *Mudlark* appears "irregularly but frequently. *Mudlark* has averaged, from 1995-1999, three issues and six posters per year. *Mudlark* publishes in three formats: 'issues' of *Mudlark* are the electronic equivalent of print chapbooks; 'posters' are the electronic equivalent of print broadsides; and 'flash' poems are poems that have news is them, poems that feel like current events. The poem is the thing at *Mudlark* . . . and the essay about it. As our full name suggests, we will consider accomplished work that locates itself anywhere on the spectrum of contemporary practice. We want poems, of course, but we want essays, too, that make us read poems (and write them?) differently somehow. Although we are not innocent, we do imagine ourselves capable of surprise. The work of hobbyists is not for *Mudlark*." They have published poetry by Sheila E. Murphy, Andrew Schelling, Frances Driscoll, Van K. Brock, Robert Sward and Diane Wald. As a sample the editor selected these lines from "The Viewing" by David Swoyer:
I envy the scavengers/being able to eat the dead/and make it alive in themselves.
They publish 15-99 poems in their "issues" and from 1-7 poems in their "posters." *Mudlark* is archived and permanently on view at www.unf.edu.
How to Submit: Submit any number of poems at a time. No simultaneous submissions. E-mail and disk submissions OK. "Previously published poems: Inasmuch as 'issues' of *Mudlark* are the electronic equivalent of print chapbooks, some of the individual poems in them might, or might not, have been previously published; if they have been, that previous publication must be acknowledged. Only poems that have not been previously published will be considered for *Mudlark* 'posters,' the electronic equivalent of print broadsides, or for *Mudlark* 'flash poems.' " Cover letter optional. Time between acceptance and publication is 1-3 months. Seldom comments on rejections. Send SASE for guidelines or obtain via e-mail or website. Responds in 1 month. Always sends prepublication galleys, "in the form of inviting the author to proof the work on a private website that *Mudlark* maintains for that purpose." Does not pay. However, "one of the things we can do at *Mudlark* to 'pay' our authors for their work is point to it here and there. We can tell our readers how to find it, how to subscribe to it, and how to buy it . . . if it is for sale. Toward that end, we maintain A-Notes (on the authors) we publish. We call attention to their work." Acquires one-time rights.
Advice: "*Mudlark* has been reviewed well and often. At this early point in its history, *Mudlark* has established itself, arguably, as one of the few serious rivals in the first generation of the electronic medium, to print versions of its kind. Look at *Mudlark*, visit the website (www.unf.edu/mudlark), spend some time there. Then make your decision: to submit or not to submit."

☑ $ ◎ **MURDEROUS INTENT (Specialized: mystery)**, Deadly Alibi Press Ltd., P.O. Box 5947, Vancouver WA 98668-5947, phone (360)695-9004, e-mail madison@teleport.com, website www.murderousintent.com, founded 1994, editor Margo Power.
Magazine Needs: *MI* is a quarterly magazine of mystery and suspense using mystery-related poetry, limericks and such as fillers. The editor says all poetry (including humorous verse) must be mystery-related and must easily entertain. They do not want poetry with "deep, convoluted meaning" and the shorter the work, the better. "Four-liners are always good though we occasionally buy a longer, ballad-type poem—always mystery-related." The editor says *Murderous Intent* is 64 pgs., 8½×11, saddle-stapled, with 2-color cover and b&w interior including art, graphics and ads. Press run is 5,500, 85% shelf sales. Single copy: $5.95; subscription: $20. Sample: $7.19. Make checks payable to Madison Publishing Company.
How to Submit: Submit 6-10 poems at a time. No previously published poems or simultaneous submissions. E-mail submissions only; no fax or US mail submissions. Send poetry in body of e-mail message. Occasionally comments on rejections. Pays $2. Buys first or one-time rights.

▨ ▣ ⊘ **MUSE JOURNAL; THE ANNUAL LOVE POEM AWARD**, 226 Lisgar St., Toronto, Ontario M6J 3G7 Canada, e-mail love@musejournal.com, website www.musejournal.com, founded 1990, editor-in-chief Manny Goncalves.

Magazine Needs: *Muse Journal* is "a quarterly online literary magazine of the arts." They have published poetry by Linda Stitt, Giovanni Malito, Ronnie Brown and Joe Blades. They receive about 1,500 poems a year, accept approximately 10%.

How to Submit: Line length for poetry is 60 maximum. No previously published poems or simultaneous submissions. E-mail submissions only. "Poets may only submit online (not by mail)." Time between acceptance and publication is 2 months. Poems are circulated to an editorial board. "Poems are read by at least two editors." Seldom comments on rejections. Charges a reading/submission fee. Publishes theme issues occasionally. Obtain guidelines via website. Responds in 2 months. Acquires one-time rights. Reviews books of poetry and art. Open to unsolicited reviews. Poets may also send books for review consideration.

Also Offers: Website includes all "pertinent" information, including information about The Annual Love Poem Award.

N ◎ MUSE WORLD MEDIA GROUP (Specialized: form/style), P.O. Box 55094, Madison WI 53705, phone (608)238-6681.

Book/Chapbook Needs: "Our goals are to publish extreme poetry and cutting-edge poetry. We want extreme poetry and poets who have a difficult time getting published anywhere else." They publish 5-15 books per year plus anthologies.

How to Submit: Submit up to 10 poems. Simultaneous submissions OK. Time between acceptance and publication is up to 1 year. "Payment agreements depend on press run and are negotiated with each author."

✓ ▣ ✿ ⊘ MUSE'S KISS WEBZINE, P.O. Box 703, Attn: L.S. Bush, Lenoir NC 28645, fax (603)761-7162, e-mail museskiss@aol.com or museskiss@yahoo.com, website http://members.aol.com/museskiss, founded 1998, publisher L.S. Bush, editor Alex Reeves.

Magazine Needs: "*Muse's Kiss* is a free webzine by writers and poets. It contains experimental and traditional poetry and short stories. We will consider general fiction, science fiction, historical fiction, and mystery for short stories and anything except erotica for poetry. Open to rhyme, free verse, etc. Please do not send nonfiction, religious, romance, gay/lesbian, children's stories or anything explicit." Also accepts poetry written by children 12 and older. They have published poetry by Lauran Sedlacek and Angela Contino Donshes. As a sample the editor selected these lines from "Why?" by C.J. Katz, Jr.:

> Why does she stay outside, always/looking in; staring, staring with those eyes/reaching in, but never
> moving forward—/always afraid, afraid of something;/maybe of me.

They receive about 200 poems a year, accept approximately 15%. Sample: $3 (by mail, online version free). Make checks payable to L.S. Bush.

How to Submit: Submit 3 poems at a time via e-mail. Line length for poetry is 8 minimum, 40 maximum. No previously published poems or simultaneous submissions. Cover letter with brief bio preferred. "Poems must be typed in body of e-mail—no attachments. If you prefer, you may submit offline by sending your poems and a cover letter. If you submit offline, there is a reading fee of $2 for up to 10 poems. Please e-mail museskiss@aol.com for offline submission details." Time between acceptance and publication is 3 months. Obtain guidelines via website. Responds in 3 months. Acquires one-time rights. Payment is publication; small honorarium when possible. Staff reviews chapbooks of poetry in 100 words, multi-book format. Send books for review consideration to L.S. Bush.

Also Offers: New e-zines: *9 Sisters* for poetry and *Storyfoam* for short stories have been added. Free subscriptions. Website includes current issues that are available online. Information about *Muse's Kiss* and how to support it is also on our webpage, plus, submission guidelines, how to subscribe to our free e-zines, and how to advertise with us.

Advice: "New poets feel free to submit and give us a try."

N ❖ ◎ MUSICWORKS (Specialized: music), 179 Richmond St. W., Toronto, Ontario M5V 1V3 Canada, phone (416)977-3546, fax (416)204-1084, e-mail sound@musicworks-mag.com, website www.musicworks-mag.com, founded 1978, editor Marisa Iacobucci.

Magazine Needs: *Musicworks* is a triannual journal of contemporary music. The editor says, "The poetry we publish only relates directly to the topics discussed in the magazine or relates to contemporary sound poetry—usually it is poetry written by the (music) composer or performers we are featuring." Poets published include bpnichol, Colin Morton and Jackson Mac Low. The magazine is 64 pgs., 8½×11, with b&w visuals, b&w photography, some illustrative graphics and scores and accompanied by 60-minute cassette. Circulation is 1,600 for 500 subscribers. Price is $5/issue and $12 for the CD. Sample: $15 for magazine and CD.

How to Submit: Simultaneous submissions OK. E-mail submissions OK in attached file. Responds within 2 months, and there is no backlog before publication. The magazine pays Canadian contributors variable rate.

N ⊕ ⊎ MUUNA TAKEENA, Hepokuja 6B26, FIN-01200 Vantaa Finland, e-mail lahtinen.palonen@meg abaud.fi, founded 1987, editor Timo Palonen.

Magazine Needs: Appearing 2 times a year, *Muuna Takeena* publishes "reviews of underground books, zines, music and videos. Poetry is used only to fill excess space. In every issue, I publish one or two poems that are near my hand." They do not want to see experimental poems. As a sample we selected these lines from "From Armitage to Ovid" by Rob Morrow:

*From Armitage to Ovid,/It's all been done before,/To go to the house/Of the one you love/And sleep at
her front door.//From palace to the poorhouse,/Sometimes against the law,/From the super rich/To the
common rag,/Classless while we snore.//From lunatic to lover,/For those we cannot keep,/We think
about you/And dream about you/When we are lost in sleep.*

The editor says *MT* is about 30 pgs., magazine-sized, photocopied and stapled, cover includes photo/drawing,
also includes photos/drawings inside, some paid ads. They receive about 50 poems a year, accept approximately
2%. Press run is 400 for 40% subscribers. Sample: $3. "No checks."
How to Submit: Submit 3 poems at a time. No previously published poems; simultaneous submissions OK.
E-mail submissions OK. Cover letter required. Time between acceptance and publication is 6 months. Pays 1
copy. Staff reviews books and chapbooks of poetry and other magazines in up to 100 words, single book format.
Send books for review consideration.
Advice: "I read, if I like, it could be printed. If I do not like, I send forward to other zine makers."

**$☐ ◎ MYSTERY TIME (Specialized: mystery, humor); RHYME TIME (Specialized: subscrib-
ers); WOMEN IN THE ARTS CONTEST**, P.O. Box 2907, Decatur IL 62524, *Mystery Time* and *Rhyme
Time* founded 1983, *Spring Fantasy* and Women in the Arts founded 1994, poetry editor and vice president Linda
Hutton.
Magazine Needs & How to Submit: *Mystery Time* is a semiannual containing 3-4 pages of humorous poems
about mysteries and mystery writers in each issue. As a sample the editor selected the poem "Epitaph" by
Elizabeth L. Hawn:

> *As a hired killer, he did his best,/So when, at last, he was laid to rest,/They wrote on the stone at his
> burial plot:/He always gave it his very best shot.*

Mystery Time is 44 pgs., digest-sized, stapled with heavy stock cover. They receive up to 15 submissions a year,
use approximately 4-6. Circulation is 100. Sample: $4. Submit 3 poems at a time, up to 16 lines, "typed in proper
format with SASE." Previously published poems OK. No fax or e-mail submissions. Does not read mss in
December. Guidelines available for #10 SASE. Pays $5 on acceptance.
Magazine Needs & How to Submit: *Rhyme Time*, is a quarterly newsletter publishing only the work of
subscribers. No length limit or style restriction. Subscription: $24. Sample: $4. Cash prize of $10 awarded to the
best poem in each issue. No fax or e-mail submissions.
Also Offers: Sponsors an annual poetry contest that awards a $25 cash prize for the best poem in any style or
length. Submit typed poem with SASE. No entry fee; one entry/person. Deadline: November 1. Sponsors annual
Women in the Arts Contest. 1st Prize: $30; 2nd Prize: $25; and 3rd Prize: $15. Submit poems, up to 32 lines
each, on any topic, in any form, no name or address on entry, include cover sheet. Entry fee: $2/poem. Make
checks payable to Women in the Arts. Deadline: November 1. Send SASE for guidelines. "WITA is a group of
100 women who share and encourage creative ideas through art, literature, music, crafts, dance, photography,
etc. Most of our members live in Illinois; those out-of-state send their work for critique by pen-palling. Follow
the rules carefully; half the entries are disqualified for some infraction."
Advice: "Always send for guidelines before submitting."

☐ ◐ NANNY FANNY; FELICITY PRESS, 2524 Stockbridge Dr. #15, Indianapolis IN 46268-2670, e-
mail nightpoet@prodigy.net, founded 1998, editor Lou Hertz.
Magazine Needs: *Nanny Fanny* appears 3 times/year and "publishes poetry accessible by the common person,
but of high quality. Some artwork wanted (b&w line art); may expand to include commentary, reviews and
contests." They want "external, extroverted observations and character studies. Happy or sad, rhyme or not,
okay. Formal poetry discouraged. Prefer 30 lines or less. No internalized, self-pitying poetry. Nothing under 8
lines or over 30 unless exceptional. No pornography, extremes of violence or language. No political poems."
Also accepts poetry written by children. They have published poetry by B.Z. Niditch, Ella J. Cvancara and John
Grey. As a sample the editor selected these lines from "Between the Sea and the Sweat" by Lamar Thomas:

> *And I start to feel the memories rocking, rocking,/rising with white flash of moon on the ridge,/on tide
> heavy winds that smell of evolution and urchin./The far Pacific in my opium years of mist and storm/
> is always captured in these dreams, in these green house days.*

The editor says *NF* is 32 pgs., $5\frac{1}{2} \times 8\frac{1}{2}$, laser-printed and side-stapled with colored 67 lb. cover, includes cover
art and some b&w line drawings inside. They receive about 800 poems a year, accept approximately 10%. Press
run is 100 for 25 subscribers; 40 distributed free to contributors, etc. Subscription: $9/3 issues. Sample: $3.50.
Make checks payable to Lou Hertz.
How to Submit: Submit 3-8 poems at a time, 1 poem/page with name and address on each. Previously published
poems OK; no simultaneous submissions. No e-mail submissions. Cover letter with brief bio preferred. Disk
submissions OK. Time between acceptance and publication is 1-6 months. Sometimes comments on rejections.
Send SASE or e-mail for guidelines. Responds in up to 2 months. Sends prepublication galleys on request. Pays
1 copy. Acquires one-time rights.
Book/Chapbook Needs: Felicity Press is not currently open for submissions.
Advice: "I want good quality poetry that the average person will be able to understand and enjoy. Let's use
poetic imagery to draw them in, not scare them away."

Nanny Fanny
POETRY MAGAZINE

Winter 2000

What kind of cover art best suits a magazine dedicated to accessible, high quality poetry? Lou Hertz, editor and publisher of *Nanny Fanny*, cites the Winter 2000 issue as a good example. Like the magazine's poetry, "this cover makes a clear statement without being overly complicated or trendy," says Hertz. Leah Biggs, contributing illustrator from Vancouver, British Columbia, created the artwork which Hertz describes as "a beautiful rendition of a seasonal theme that I was seeking for the winter issue." Published in Indianapolis, Indiana, *Nanny Fanny* is 5½ × 8½, 32 pages, laser-printed and stapled with colored 67-lb. cover. It includes some internal black and white line drawings in addition to the cover illustration.

NASSAU REVIEW, English Dept., Nassau Community College, Garden City NY 11530-6793, phone (516)572-7792, founded 1964, contact editorial board.
Magazine Needs: *Nassau Review* is an annual "creative and research vehicle for Nassau College faculty and the faculty of other colleges." They want "serious, intellectual poetry of any form or style. No light verse or satiric verse." Submissions from adults only. "No college students; graduate students acceptable. Want only poems of high quality." They have published poetry by Patti Tana, Dick Allen, Louis Phillips, David Heyen and Simon Perchik. *NR* is about 190 pgs., digest-sized, flat-spined. They receive over 1,500 poems a year, use approximately 20-25. Press run is 1,200 for about 1,200 subscribers of which 300 are libraries. Sample free.
How to Submit: Submit only 3 poems per yearly issue. No previously published poems or simultaneous submissions. Reads submissions November 1 through March 1 only. Responds in up to 8 months. Pays copies.
Also Offers: They sponsor occasional contests with $200 poetry award. Deadline: March 31.
Advice: "Each year we are more and more overwhelmed by the number of poems submitted, but most are of an amateur quality."

$ **NATIONAL ENQUIRER (Specialized: humor)**, Lantana FL 33464, filler editor Kathy Martin.
Magazine Needs: *NE* is a weekly tabloid which uses short poems, most of them humorous and traditional rhyming verse. "We want poetry with a message or reflection on the human condition or everyday life. Avoid sending obscure or 'arty' poetry or poetry for art's sake. Also looking for philosophical and inspirational material. Submit seasonal/holiday material at least three months in advance. No poetry over eight lines will be accepted."
How to Submit: Submit up to 5 poems at a time. Requires cover letter from first-time submitters; include name, address, social security and phone numbers. "Do not send SASE; filler material will not be returned." Pays $25 after publication; original material only. Buys first rights.

NATIONAL FORUM: THE PHI KAPPA PHI JOURNAL, 129 Quad Center, Mell St., Auburn University, Auburn AL 36849-5306, phone (334)844-5200, e-mail kaetzjp@mail.auburn.edu, website www.auburn.edu/academic/societies/phi_kappa_phi/natforum.html, founded 1915, editor James P. Kaetz, contact poetry editors.
Magazine Needs: *National Forum* is the quarterly publication of Phi Kappa Phi using quality poetry. *NF* is 48 pgs., magazine-sized, professionally printed, saddle-stapled, with full-color paper cover and interior. They receive about 300 poems a year, accept approximately 20. Press run is 120,000 for 117,000 subscribers of which 300 are libraries. Subscription: $25.
How to Submit: Submit 3-5 short (one page) poems at a time, including a biographical sketch with recent publications. E-mail and fax submissions OK. Reads submissions approximately every 3 months. Responds in about 4 months. Pays 10 copies.

$ **NATURALLY: NUDE RECREATION FOR ALL AGES; EVENTS UNLIMITED PUBLISHING CO. (Specialized)**, P.O. Box 317, Newfoundland NJ 07435-0317, phone (973)697-3552, fax (973)697-8313, e-mail naturally@nac.net, website www.internaturally.com, founded 1981, editor/publisher Bern Loibl.

Magazine Needs: *Naturally* is a quarterly magazine devoted to family nudism and naturism. They want poetry about the naturalness of the human body and nature, any length. As a sample the editor selected these lines from "On a Woman who is Busy Deliberating her Liberation" by Wolfgang Somary:

> *I bet: you wouldn't dare yet/to walk bare in the wet/glare of the moon/or just for fun/under the sun/in the nudeness of noon—*

Naturally is 60 pgs., 8½×11, printed on glossy paper and saddle-stitched with full-color photos throughout. They receive about 30 poems a year, use 4. Press run is 16,000 for 6,500 subscribers, 8,500 shelf sales. Single copy: $6.50; subscription: $21.95. Sample: $9 postpaid.

How to Submit: Previously published poems and simultaneous submissions OK. E-mail and fax submissions OK. "Name and address must be submitted with e-mail." Often comments on rejections. Send SASE for guidelines or obtain via e-mail. Responds in 2 months. Pays $20 and 1 copy. Buys first North American serial or one-time rights.

$ 🗑 NAZARENE INTERNATIONAL HEADQUARTERS; STANDARD; LISTEN; (Specialized: religious, children), 6401 The Paseo, Kansas City MO 64131, phone (816)333-7000.

Magazine Needs & How to Submit: Each of the magazines published by the Nazarenes has a separate editor, focus and audience. *Standard*, circulation 177,000, is a weekly inspirational "story paper" with Christian leisure reading for adults. Send SASE for free sample and guidelines. Uses 2 poems each week. Submit maximum of 5 poems, no more than 50 lines each. Pays 25¢ a line. For *Listen* and *Holiness Today*, write individually for guidelines and samples.

◻ NEBO: A LITERARY JOURNAL, English Dept., Arkansas Tech University, Russellville AR 72801-2222, phone (501)968-0256, website www.atu.edu/acad/schools/lfa/english/nebo.html, founded 1982, poetry editor Michael Ritchie.

Magazine Needs: *Nebo* appears in May and December. Regarding poetry they say, "We accept all kinds, all styles, all subject matters and will publish a longer poem if it is outstanding. We are especially interested in formal poetry." They have published poetry by Jack Butler, Turner Cassity, Wyatt Prunty, Charles Martin, Julia Randall and Brenda Hillman. *Nebo* is 50-70 pgs., digest-sized, professionally printed on quality matte stock with matte card cover. Press run "varies." Sample: $6.

How to Submit: Submit 3-5 poems at a time. Simultaneous submissions OK. "Please no offbeat colors." Cover letter with bio material and recent publications required. Do not submit mss between May 1 and August 15. Editor comments on rejections "if the work has merit but requires revision and resubmission; we do all we can to help." Responds at the end of November and February respectively. Pays 1 copy. Staff reviews books of poetry. Send books for review consideration.

◖ THE NEBRASKA REVIEW; TNR AWARDS, Creative Writing Program, FA, University of Nebraska, Omaha NE 68182-0324, phone (402)554-3159, fax (402)554-3436, founded 1973, fiction and managing editor James Reed, poetry editor Susan Aizenberg.

Magazine Needs: *The Nebraska Review* is a semiannual literary magazine publishing fiction and poetry with occasional essays. The editors want "lyric poetry from 10-200 lines, preference being for under 100 lines. Subject matter is unimportant, as long as it has some. Poets should have mastered form, meaning poems should have form, not simply 'demonstrate' it." They don't want to see "concrete, inspirational, didactic or merely political poetry." They have published poetry by Erin Belieu, Michael Bugeja, Stuart Dybek and Carl Phillips. As a sample the editors selected these lines from "Crickets" by Pamela Stewart:

> *In every small place the eye, toe, or caught breath turns,/crickets are singing. From that shin/just above the ground they fling an edge of sound/straight through what's left of wilderness./It swings out across the trees and yards,/up to the warm sills of September.*

The magazine is 60 pgs., 6×9, nicely printed and flat-spined with glossy card cover. It is a publication of the Writer's Workshop at the University of Nebraska. Press run is 500 for 380 subscribers of which 85 are libraries. Single copy: $6; subscription: $11/year. Sample: $3.50.

How to Submit: Submit 4-6 poems at a time. "Clean typed copy strongly preferred." Reads open submissions January 1 through April 15 only. Responds in 4 months. Time between acceptance and publication is 3-12 months. Pays 2 copies and 1-year subscription. Acquires first North American serial rights.

Also Offers: Submissions for The Nebraska Review Awards are read from September 1 through November 30 only. The TNR Awards of $500 each in poetry and fiction are published in the spring issue. Entry fee: $9, includes discounted subscription. You can enter as many times as desired. Deadline: November 30.

Advice: "Your first allegiance is to the poem. Publishing will come in time, but it will always be less than you feel you deserve. Therefore, don't look to publication as a reward for writing well; it has no relationship."

FOR AN EXPLANATION of symbols used in this book, see the Key to Symbols on the front and back inside covers.

◐ **NEDGE**, P.O. Box 2321, Providence RI 02906, website wings.buffalo.edu/epc/mags/nedge, founded 1994, co-editors Henry Gould and Janet Sullivan.

Magazine Needs: *Nedge* is a biannual published by The Poetry Mission, a nonprofit arts organization. It includes poetry, fiction, reviews and essays. They want work that "exhibits originality, talent, sincerity, skill and inspiration." Circulation is 300. Subscription: $12/2 issues. Sample: $6.

How to Submit: No simultaneous submissions. SASE required. Responds in 3 months. Pays 1 copy plus 1 free copy of following issue.

Also Offers: Website includes "a partial list of content of issues."

◻ ◐ **THE NEOVICTORIAN/COCHLEA**, P.O. Box 55164, Madison WI 53705, e-mail eacam@execpc.com, founded 1995, editor Esther Cameron.

Magazine Needs: *N/C* appears biannually and "seeks to promote a poetry of introspection, dialogue and social concern." They want "poetry of beauty and integrity with emotional and intellectual depth, commitment to subject matter as well as language, and the courage to ignore fashion. Welcome: well-crafted formal verse, social comment (including satire), love poems, philosophical/religious poems, poems reflecting dialogue with other writers (in particular: responses to the work of Paul Celan)." Also accepts poetry written by children. They have published poetry by Ida Fasel, Mark Halperin, W.K. Buckley, Carolyn Stoloff and Hadassah Haskale. As a sample the editor selected the poem "Astronomers" by Richard Moore:

> Seeking the origin, man hopes/through ever larger telescopes/to probe a universe more vast/each year
> and deeper in its past./As they discover, so do I,/still watching with the naked eye.

N/C is 28-32 pgs., 8 × 11, photocopied and saddle-stapled with cardstock cover, occasional graphics, no ads. "In the near future, the magazine will be supplemented by an electronic forum. E-mail the editor for details." Press run is 250 for 50 subscribers. Single copy: $6; subscription: $10.

How to Submit: Submit 3-5 poems at a time. Previously published poems and simultaneous submissions OK. Cover letter "not necessary. Poets whose work is accepted will be asked for titles of books available, to be published in the magazine." Time between acceptance and publication is 6-12 months. Often comments on rejections. Does not offer guidelines because "the tradition is the only 'guideline.' We do encourage contributors to write for a sample." Responds in up to 2 months. Pays 2 copies. Acquires first rights. *N/C* publishes the addresses of poets who would welcome correspondence.

Advice: "Like all our social functioning, poetry today suffers from a loss of community, which translates into a lack of real intimacy with the reader. Poets can work against this trend by remaining in touch with the poetry of past generations and by forming relationships in which poetry can be employed as the language of friendship. Publication should be an afterthought."

☑ ◻ ◐ **NERVE COWBOY; LIQUID PAPER PRESS**, P.O. Box 4973, Austin TX 78765, website www.onr.com/user/jwhagins/nervecowboy.html, founded 1995, co-editors Joseph Shields and Jerry Hagins.

Magazine Needs: *Nerve Cowboy* is a biannual literary journal featuring contemporary poetry, short fiction and b&w drawings. The editors are "open to all forms, styles and subject matter preferring writing that speaks directly, and minimizes literary devices. We want to see poetry of experience and passion which can find that raw nerve and ride it." They have published poetry by Rene Diedrich, Todd Moore, Celeste Bowman, David Zauher and Charles H. Webb. As a sample the editors selected these lines from "In Praise of the Penis" by Allison Joseph:

> Funny little fellow,/all our slang for you/is harsh—prick, dick, sock—/hard consonants erupting/from
> our mouths, jutting like/the bulge of the school jock.

Nerve Cowboy is 64 pgs., 7 × 8½, attractively printed and saddle-stapled with matte card cover with b&w cover art. They currently accept 5-10% of the submissions received. Press run is 250 for 85 subscribers. Subscription: $14/4 issues. Sample: $4.

How to Submit: Submit 3-7 poems at a time, name on each page. Previously published poems with notification OK; no simultaneous submissions. Informal cover letter with bio credits preferred. Seldom comments on rejections. Send SASE for guidelines. Responds in 2 months. Pays 1 copy. Acquires first or one-time rights.

Book/Chapbook Needs & How to Submit: Liquid Paper Press publishes 3-4 chapbooks/year but will not be accepting unsolicited chapbook mss in the foreseeable future. Only chapbook contest winners and solicited mss will be published in the next couple of years. For information on *Nerve Cowboy*'s annual chapbook contest, please send a SASE. Deadline is January 15 of each year. Entry fee: $10. Cash prizes and publication for 1st and 2nd place finishers. Chapbooks are 24-40 pgs., 5½ × 8½, photocopied with some b&w artwork. Recent winners include Belinda Subraman, Christopher Jones and Dave Newman. Publications include *Grappling* by Susanne R. Bowers; *The Back East Poems* by Gerald Locklin; and *Butchers and Brain Surgeons* by Fred Voss. Send SASE for a complete list of available titles.

$ ◐ **THE NEW CRITERION**, The Foundation for Cultural Review, Inc., 850 Seventh Ave., New York NY 10019, poetry editor Robert Richman.

Magazine Needs: *New Criterion* is a monthly (except July and August) review of ideas and the arts, which uses poetry of high literary quality. They have published poetry by Donald Justice, Andrew Hudgins, Elizabeth Spires and Herbert Morris. It is 90 pgs., 7 × 10, flat-spined. Poems here truly are open, with structured free verse and formal works. Sample: $4.75.

How to Submit: Cover letter required with submissions. Responds in 3 months. Pays $2.50/line ($75 minimum).
Advice: "To have an idea of who we are or what we stand for, poets should consult back issues."

⬤ NEW DELTA REVIEW; THE EYSTER PRIZE, English Dept., Louisiana State University, Baton Rouge LA 70803-5001, phone (225)388-4079, website www.lsu.edu:80/guests/wwwndr, contact poetry editor.
Magazine Needs: They "publish works of quality, many of them by young writers who are building their reputations." They have published poetry by Ann F. Walker, George Looney and Doug Martin. *NDR* appears twice a year, 90-120 pgs., 6×9, flat-spined, typeset and printed on quality stock with matte card cover with art. Press run is 500 for 100 subscribers of which 20 are libraries; the rest are for shelf sales. Subscription: $12. Sample: $7. Back issue: $4. Make checks payable to *New Delta Review*.
How to Submit: Submit up to 5 poems "and specify on the outside of the envelope that you are submitting poetry." No previously published poems. Cover letter with author's name, address, phone number, social security number and biographical information required. Include SASE for reply and return of work. Poetry editor sometimes comments on rejections, often suggesting possible revisions. Responds in 4 months. Pays 2 copies. Acquires first North American serial rights. Reviews books of poetry in no more than 2,000 words, single or multi-book format. Poets may also send books to poetry editor for review consideration.
Also Offers: The Eyster Prize of $50 is awarded to the best story and best poem in each issue. Website includes guidelines, names of editors and examples of work from the latest issue.
Advice: "Make sure two things are present in your poems: do the heart work and attend to craft."

$⬤ NEW ENGLAND REVIEW, Middlebury College, Middlebury VT 05753, phone (802)443-5075, fax (802)443-2088, e-mail nereview@mail.middlebury.edu, website www.middlebury.edu/~nereview/, founded 1978, editor Stephen Donadio.
⬤ Work published in this review was included in the 1998 and 1999 volumes of *The Best American Poetry*.
Magazine Needs: *New England Review* is a prestigious, nationally distributed literary quarterly, 180 pgs., 7×10, flat-spined, elegant make-up and printing on heavy stock, glossy cover with art. Receives 3,000-4,000 poetry submissions/year, uses 70-80 poems/year, has a 3-6 month backlog between time of acceptance and publication. The editors urge poets to read a few copies of the magazine before submitting work. They have published poetry by Agha Shahid Ali, Carol Frost, Brigit Pegeen Kelly, Carl Phillips and Elizabeth Spires. Subscription: $23. Sample: $7.
How to Submit: Submit up to 6 poems at a time. Address submissions to Poetry Editor. No previously published poems. "Brief cover letters are useful. All submissions by mail. Questions by e-mail OK." Reads submissions September 1 through May 31 only. Response time is 12 weeks. Always sends prepublication galleys. Pays $10/page, $20 minimum, plus 2 copies. Also features essay-reviews. Send books for review consideration.
Also Offers: Website includes guidelines, editorial staff, sample poetry from current and recent issues, ordering information and secure online ordering.

$◻ ◎ NEW ERA MAGAZINE (Specialized: religious, teen/young adult), 50 E. North Temple St., Salt Lake City UT 84150-3225, phone (801)240-2951, fax (801)240-5997, founded 1971, managing editor Larry Hiller.
Magazine Needs: *New Era* appears monthly and is an "official publication for youth of The Church of Jesus Christ of Latter-day Saints; it contains feature stories, photo stories, fiction, news, etc." They want "short verse in any form, particularly traditional—must pertain to teenage LDS audience (religious and teenage themes). No sing-songy doggerel, gushy love poems or forced rhymes." *New Era* is 52 pgs., approximately 8×10½, 4-color offset printed, saddle-stitched, quality stock, top-notch art and graphics, no ads. They receive 200-300 submissions a year, accept approximately 2-5%. Press run is 226,000 for 205,000 subscribers, 10,000 shelf sales. Single copy: $1.50; subscription: $8/year. Sample: $1.50 plus postage.
How to Submit: Send up to 5 poems at one time. No previously published poems or simultaneous submissions. Time between acceptance and publication is a year or longer. "We publish one poem each month next to our photo of the month." Sometimes comments on rejections. Publishes 1-2 theme issues each year, one of which is geographically themed (LDS youth in one country). Theme deadlines are 6 months minimum to 1 year in advance. Send SASE, fax or e-mail for guidelines and upcoming themes. Responds in 2 months. Sometimes sends prepublication galleys. Pays $10 minimum. "LDS church retains rights to publish again in church publications—all other rights returned."
Also Offers: They also offer an annual contest—including poetry—for active members of the LDS church between ages 12-23. Poetry entries should consist of one entry of 6-10 different original poems (none of which exceeds 50 lines) reflecting LDS values. Deadline: January. Winners receive either a partial scholarship to BYU or Ricks College or a cash award. Send SASE for rules.
Advice: "Study the magazine before submitting. We're a great market for beginners, but you must understand Mormons to write well for us. Just because a subject is noble or inspirational doesn't mean the poetry automatically is noble or inspirational. Pay attention to the craft of writing. Poetry is more than just writing down your thoughts about an inspirational subject. Poetry needs to communicate easily and be readily understood—it's too easy to mistake esoteric expression for true insight."

☑ ◐ NEW ISSUES PRESS; NEW ISSUES PRESS POETRY SERIES; NEW ISSUES PRESS FIRST BOOK POETRY PRIZE; THE GREEN ROSE PRIZE IN POETRY FOR ESTABLISHED POETS, Dept. of English, Western Michigan University, Kalamazoo MI 49008-5092, phone (616)387-8185, fax (616)387-2562, e-mail herbert.scott@wmich.edu, website www.wmich.edu/english/fac/nipps, founded 1996, editor Herbert Scott.

Book/Chapbook Needs: New Issues Press First Book Prize publishes 3-6 first books of poetry per year, one through its annual New Issues Poetry Prize. Additional mss will be selected from those submitted to the competition for publication in the series. "A national judge selects the prize winner and recommends other manuscripts. The editors decide on the other books considering the judge's recommendation, but are not bound by it." Past judges include Chase Twichell, Philip Levine and Marianne Boruch. The editor says books are published on acid free paper in editions of 1,500.

How to Submit: Open to "poets writing in English who have not previously published a full-length collection of poems in an edition of 500 or more copies." Submit 48- to 72-page ms with 1-paragraph bio, publication credits (if any) and $12 reading fee. No e-mail or fax submissions. Reads submissions June 1 through November 30 only. Send SASE for complete guidelines. Winner will be notified the following April. Winner receives $1,000 plus publication of manuscript. "We offer 33⅓% discounts on our books to competition entrants."

Also Offers: New Issues Press also sponsors The Green Rose Prize in Poetry. Award is $1,000 and publication for a book of poems by an established poet who has published one or more full-length collections of poetry. Reading fee: $20/ms. Mss accepted May 1 through September 30. Winner announced in January. Four Green Rose books were selected for publication from the 1999 competition, including the prize winner *Perfect Disappearance* by Martha Rhodes. Send SASE for complete guidelines or obtain via website.

Advice: "Our belief is that there are more good poets writing than ever before. Our mission is to give some of the best of these a forum. Also, our books have been reviewed in *Publishers Weekly*, *Booklist*, and the *Library Journal*. New Issues books are advertised in *Poetry*, *Poets & Writers*, *APR*, *American Poet*, *The Bloomsbury Review*, etc. We are publishing 12 books of poems during the year 2000. New Issues Press is profiled in the May/June 2000 issue of *Poets & Writers*."

◐ ◎ THE NEW LAUREL REVIEW (Specialized: translations), 828 Lesseps St., New Orleans LA 70117, phone (504)947-6001, founded 1971, editor Lee Meitzen Grue, poetry editor Lenny Emmanuel.

Magazine Needs: *The New Laurel Review* "is an annual independent nonprofit literary magazine dedicated to fine art. Each issue contains poetry, translations, literary essays, reviews of small press books, and visual art." They want "poetry with strong, accurate imagery. We have no particular preference in style. We try to be eclectic. We're looking for original work, without hackneyed phrases or tired thinking." They have published poetry by Jared Carter, Kalamu Ya Salaam, Melody Davis, Sue Walker and Keith Cartwright. The *Review* is 6×9, laser printed, 115 pgs., original art on cover, accepts 30 poems out of 300 mss received. It has a circulation of 500. Single copy: $10 individuals, $12 institutions. Sample (back issue): $8.

How to Submit: Submit 3-5 poems with SASE and a short note with previous publications. No simultaneous submissions. Reads submissions September 1 through May 30 only. Guidelines for SASE. Responds to submissions in 3 months, publishes in 10 months. Pays contributor's copies. Acquires first rights. Reviews books of poetry in 1,000 words, single or multi-book format.

Advice: "Read our magazine before submitting poetry."

$ ◐ NEW LETTERS; NEW LETTERS POETRY PRIZE, University of Missouri-Kansas City, Kansas City MO 64110, phone (816)235-1168, fax (816)235-2611, website www.umkc.edu/newletters, founded 1934 as *University Review*, became *New Letters* in 1971, managing editor Robert Stewart, editor James McKinley.

▼ Work published in *New Letters* appeared in the 1997 volume of *The Best American Poetry*.

Magazine Needs: *New Letters* "is dedicated to publishing the best short fiction, best contemporary poetry, literary articles, photography and artwork by both established writers and new talents." They want "contemporary writing of all types—free verse poetry preferred, short works are more likely to be accepted than very long ones." They have published poetry by Joyce Carol Oates, Amiri Baraka, Nancy Willard, Margaret Randall, Gary Gildner and Trish Reeves. The 6×9, flat-spined, professionally printed quarterly, glossy 2-color cover with art, uses about 40-45 (of 120) pgs. of poetry in each issue. Circulation is 2,500 with 1,800 subscriptions of which about 40% are libraries. They receive about 7,000 submissions a year, use less than 1%, have a 6-month backlog. Poems appear in a variety of styles exhibiting a high degree of craft and universality of theme (rare in many journals). Subscription: $17. Sample: $5.50.

How to Submit: Send no more than 6 poems at a time. No previously published poems or simultaneous submissions. Short cover letter preferred. "We strongly prefer original typescripts and we don't read between May 15 and October 15. No query needed." Responds in up to 10 weeks. Pays a small fee plus 2 copies. Occasionally James McKinley comments on rejections.

Also Offers: The New Letters Poetry Prize is given annually for a group of 3-6 poems. Send SASE for entry guidelines. Deadline: May 15. They also publish occasional anthologies, selected and edited by McKinley.

◯ ◐ THE NEW MIRAGE QUARTERLY; GOOD SAMARITAN PRESS; THE MIRAGE PRIZE; THE MIRAGE GROUP, P.O. Box 803282, Santa Clarita CA 91380-3282, phone/fax (213)383-3447, e-mail adorxyz@aol.com, founded 1996, editor Jovita Ador Lee, publisher Jerome Vallens Brooke.

Magazine Needs: *The New Mirage Quarterly* contains poetry and reviews. They want all types of poetry. They have published poetry by Linda Herring, Sharon Siekaniec, Devorie Franzwa and Amy Jo Huffman. As a sample the editor selected this poem, "Mirage" (poet unidentified):

> *Layers of false illusion lie,/Veils of lies that bind and tie./Choice returns; hope shall remain/Love returns, and love shall remain.*

The editors say *TNMQ* is 12 pgs., 5½×8½, photocopied and saddle-stapled with bond paper cover, includes clip art and ads. They receive about 100 poems a year, accept approximately 50%. Press run is 100 for 40 subscribers, 10 shelf sales; 20 distributed free to general public. Subscription: $26. Sample: $7. Make checks payable to Good Samaritan Press. "Writers are encouraged to subscribe to TNMQ."

How to Submit: Submit up to 3 poems at a time. Previously published poems and simultaneous submissions OK. Cover letter preferred. Reads submissions September 1 through June 30 only. Time between acceptance and publication is 6 weeks. Poems are circulated to an editorial board. "Reviewed by board and editors." Seldom comments on rejections. Send SASE for guidelines. Responds in 6 weeks. Pays 1 copy. Acquires all rights. Returns rights upon publication. Reviews books and chapbooks of poetry and other magazines in 200-300 words, single book format. Open to unsolicited reviews. Send books for review consideration to Jovita Ador Lee.

Book/Chapbook Needs & How to Submit: Good SAMARitan Press publishes chapbooks of verse in several series including the New Mirage Series and the Bright Dawn Series. They publish 10 chapbooks per year. Chapbooks are usually 50-120 pgs., 5×8, saddle-stitched with glossy cardstock cover. "Writers may send samples or complete manuscripts. The New Mirage Series is intended as a resource for subscribers. The Bright Dawn Series is designed to give members of the Mirage Group a resource for their work." Replies to queries in 6 weeks. Pays 1 author's copy (out of a press run of 100). Order sample chapbooks (packet of 3) by sending $7. Good Samaritan Press also publishes an annual poetry anthology. The anthology is 50-100 pgs., 5½×8½, photocopied and perfect-bound, hard cover with art prints.

Also Offers: The Mirage Group offers the annual Mirage Prize for poets of special merit. Members of the Mirage Group may nominate poets for consideration. The Mirage Group offers many services to its members including mentoring. "Members may choose to work with a more experienced writer to improve their work." Membership dues (including subscription to *TNMQ*): $26. Also offers the New Laureate Series for Laureate Members of the Mirage Group. The series publishes chapbooks and requires mss of 5 to 40 poems. The Group also provides press support. Members may also participate in our Speakers Bureau. Additionally, the Mirage Group publishes *Bright Dawn Review*, a journal for young and new poets and *Royal Avalon Review*, poetry that has a fantasy theme, such as poems set in the Middle ages.

◎ ⊘ NEW NATIVE PRESS (Specialized: translations), P.O. Box 661, Cullowhee NC 28723, phone (828)293-9237, founded 1979, publisher Thomas Rain Crowe.

Book/Chapbook Needs: New Native Press has "selectively narrowed its range of contemporary 20th century literature to become an exclusive publisher of writers in marginalized and endangered languages. All books published are bilingual translations from original languages into English." They publish on average 2 paperbacks/year. Their last 4 titles have included poetry by Philip Daughtry (Geordie); Danielle Truscott (Cornish-American); and Gaelic, Welsh, Breton, Cornish and Manx poets in an all-Celtic language anthology of contemporary poets from Scotland, Ireland, Wales, Brittany, Cornwall and Isle of Man entitled *Writing The Wind: A Celtic Resurgence (The New Celtic Poetry)*. Books are sold by distributors in four foreign countries and in the US by library vendors and Small Press Distribution. Books are typically 80 pgs., offset printed and perfect-bound with glossy 120 lb. stock with professionally-designed color cover.

How to Submit: Not currently accepting submissions. For specialized translations only—authors should query first with 10 sample poems and cover letter with bio and publication credits. Previously published poems and simultaneous submissions OK. Time between acceptance and publication is 6-12 months. Always comments on rejections. Responds in 2 weeks. Pays copies, "amount varies with author and title."

Advice: "We are still looking for work indicative of rare talent—unique and original voices using language experimentally and symbolically, if not subversively."

■ ▯ ◯ ⊘ NEW ORLEANS POETRY FORUM; GRIS-GRIS PRESS; DESIRE STREET, 257 Bonnabel Blvd., Metairie LA 70005-3738, poetry forum founded 1971, press and magazine founded 1994, president Andrea S. Gereighty, editor Jonathan Laws.

Magazine Needs: *Desire Street* is the quarterly electronic magazine of the New Orleans Poetry Forum. "The Forum, a non-profit entity, has as its chief purpose the development of poets and contemporary poetry in the New Orleans area. To this end, it conducts a weekly workshop in which original poems are presented and critiqued according to an established protocol which assures a non-judgmental and non-argumentative atmosphere. A second aim of the NOPF is to foster awareness and support for poetry in the New Orleans area through readings, publicity, and community activities. Promotion is emphasized in order to increase acceptance and support for contemporary poetry." They want "modern poetry on any topic—1 page only. No rhyming verse; no porn, obscenity or child molestation themes." Also accepts poetry written by children. They have published poetry by Jonathan Laws, Andrea GereijhtyYusef Komunyakaa, Beverly Matherne and Yevgeny Yevtushenko. As a sample we selected these lines from "Bottled Mosaic" by Rebecca Morris:

> *Swirls of turbulent blue/Depression spread across the canvas/Words travel around the edges/Never touching empty spaces//Shadows/Created by a single harsh stroke/Splashes of red/And anger enter the*

picture.//The color of whisky fills gaps/Blends the whole to a blur
DS is 8-10 pgs., desktop-published, downloaded photocopied and distributed, uses clip art. They receive about 550 poems a year, accept approximately 10%. Press run is 200 hard copies for 200 subscribers. Single copy: $3; subscription: $12/year. Sample (including guidelines): $5. Make checks payable to New Orleans Poetry Forum. **How to Submit:** Submit 2 poems at a time, 10 poem limit/year. Line length for poetry is one 8½×11 page only. Previously published poems OK; no simultaneous submissions. Cover letter required. Disk submissions OK, in ASCII or MS Dos text. Membership in the New Orleans Poetry Forum is required before submitting work. Annual fee: $25, includes 4 issues of *Desire Street*, 52 3-hour workshops and 1 year's free critique of up to 10 poems. Time between acceptance and publication is up to 1 year. Poems are circulated to an editorial board. "First, poems are read by Andrea Gereighty. Then, poems are read by a board of five poets." Comments on rejections. Publishes theme issues occasionally. Responds in 1 year. Pays 10 copies. Acquires one-time rights. **Also Offers:** The Forum conducts weekly workshops on Wednesday nights at the Broadmoor Library. They also conduct workshops at schools and in prisons. Send SASE for details.

NEW ORLEANS POETRY JOURNAL PRESS, 2131 General Pershing St., New Orleans LA 70115, phone (504)891-3458, founded 1956, publisher/editor Maxine Cassin, co-editor Charles deGravelles. **Book/Chapbook Needs:** "We prefer to publish relatively new and/or little-known poets of unusual promise or those inexplicably neglected." They do not want to see "cliché or doggerel, anything incomprehensible or too derivative, or workshop exercises. First-rate lyric poetry preferred (not necessarily in traditional forms)." They have published books by Vassar Miller, Everette Maddox, Charles Black, Malaika Favorite, Raeburn Miller, Martha McFerren and Ralph Adamo. **How to Submit:** *Query first.* They do not accept unsolicited submissions for chapbooks, which are flat-spined paperbacks. Unsolicited mss will not be returned. The editors report on queries in 2-3 months, mss in the same time period, if solicited. Simultaneous submissions will possibly be accepted. Sometimes sends prepublication galleys. Pays copies, usually 50-100. The press does not subsidy publish at present and does not offer grants or awards. **Advice:** "1) Read as much as possible! 2) Write only when you must, and 3) Don't rush into print! No poetry should be sent without querying first! Publishers are concerned about expenses unnecessarily incurred in mailing manuscripts. *Telephoning is not encouraged.*"

NEW ORLEANS REVIEW, Box 195, Loyola University, New Orleans LA 70118, phone (504)865-2295, fax (504)865-2294, e-mail noreview@loyno.edu, founded 1968, editor Sophia Stone. **Magazine Needs:** *New Orleans Review* publishes "lyric poetry of all types, fiction that is strongly voiced and essays." They have published poetry by Jack Gilbert, Rodney Jones, Besmilr Brigham and Moira Crone. It is 120-200 pgs., perfect-bound, elegantly printed with glossy card cover. Circulation is 1,700. Sample: $10. **How to Submit:** Submit 3-6 poems at a time. No previously published work. Brief cover letter preferred. Publishes some theme issues. Send SASE for upcoming themes. Responds in 3 months. Pays 3 copies. Acquires first North American serial rights.

NEW ORPHIC REVIEW; NEW ORPHIC PUBLISHERS, 1095 Victoria Dr., Vancouver, British Columbia V5L 4G3 Canada, phone (604)255-9074, founded New Orphic Publishers (1995), New Orphic Review (1998), editor-in-chief Ernest Hekkanen. **Magazine Needs:** "Appearing 2 times a year, *The New Orphic Review* is run by an opinionated visionary who is beholden to no one, least of all government agencies like the Canada Council or institutions of higher learning. He feels Canadian literature is stagnant, lacks daring and is terribly incestuous." *NOR* publishes poetry, novel excerpts, mainstream and experimental short stories and articles on a wide range of subjects. Each issue also contains a *Featured Poet* section. "*NOR* publishes authors from around the world as long as the pieces are written in English and are accompanied by an SASE with proper Canadian postage and/or US dollars to offset the cost of postage." They prefer "tight, well-wrought poetry over leggy, prosaic poetry. No 'fuck you' poetry; no rambling pseudo Beat poetry." They have published poetry by Catherine Owen, Steven Michael Berzensky (aka Mick Burns), Robert Wayne Stedingh, John Pass and Susan McCaslin. The editor says *NOR* is 120-140 pgs., magazine-sized, laser printed and perfect-bound with color cover, includes art/graphics and ads. They receive about 400 poems a year, accept approximately 10%. Press run is 500 for 250 subscribers of which 20 are libraries. Subscription: $25 (individual), $30 (institution). Sample: $15. **How to Submit:** Submit 6 poems at a time. Line length for poetry is 5 minimum, 30 maximum. No previously published poems; simultaneous submissions OK. Cover letter preferred. "Make sure a SASE (or SAE and IRC) is included." Time between acceptance and publication is up to 8 months. Poems are circulated to an editorial board. The managing editor and associate editor refer work to the editor-in-chief. Seldom comments on rejections. Publishes theme issues occasionally. Send SASE (or SAE and IRC) for guidelines. Responds in 2 months. Pays 1 copy. Acquires first North American serial rights. **Also Offers:** New Orphic Publishers publishes 4 paperbacks per year. However, all material is solicited.

THE NEW PRESS LITERARY QUARTERLY; THE NEW PRESS POETRY CONTEST, 65-39 108th St., Suite E-6, Forest Hills NY11375, phone (718)459-6807, founded 1984, editor-in-chief Victoria Figuereda.

Magazine Needs: *TNPLQ* is a quarterly magazine using poems "less than 100 lines, accessible, imaginative. No doggerel, sentimentality." They include a multilingual section for poetry. They want poems in Spanish, Italian, Czechoslovakian, Portuguese, Japanese, Chinese, Russian, Hungarian, German, Icelandic and French, accompanied by their English versions/translations. Each poem must list the author's and translator's names, phone numbers and addresses. They have published poetry by Allen Ginsberg, Lawrence Ferlinghetti, Louise Jaffe, Mary Winters, D.H. Melhem, Les Bridges and Gina Bergamino. It is 16-48 pgs., magazine-sized, desktop-published, with glossy cover, saddle-stapled. They receive 500-1,000 poems a year, accept approximately 10%. Press run is 2,000 for 350 subscribers. Subscription: $15/year, $29/2 years (add $5/year for overseas). Sample: $5.50. "Payable by check or money order in U.S. funds only."
How to Submit: Submit no more than 6 poems at a time. Nonsubscribers are required to pay a reading fee of $2 (1-3 poems) or $4 (4-6 poems). "Include name and address on the top of each page." Publishes theme issues. Send SASE for upcoming themes. Responds in 4 months. Always sends prepublication galleys. Pays 2 copies. Acquires first-time rights.
Also Offers: The New Press Poetry Contest is annual, deadline is July 1, entry fee of $5 for up to 3 poems or 100 lines, has prizes of $100, $75 and five 2-year subscriptions. They also sponsor poetry readings. Send SASE for details.

$ 🖉 ◎ THE NEW RENAISSANCE (Specialized: translations, bilingual/foreign language), 26 Heath Rd. #11, Arlington MA 02474-3645, e-mail wmichaud@gwi.net, founded 1968, editor-in-chief Louise T. Reynolds, poetry editor Frank Finale.
Magazine Needs: *the new renaissance* is "intended for the 'renaissance' person—the generalist, not the specialist. Publishes the best new writing and translations and offers a forum for articles on political, sociological topics; features established as well as emerging visual artists and writers, and highlights reviews of small press. Open to a variety of styles, including traditional." They have published poetry by Jane Mayhall and Daniel Tobin, and translations of de Andrade (by A. Levitin) and Ernst Herbeck (by Melissa Monroe). As a sample the editor selected these lines from "Dandelion" by Marion Steele:

> Spring's outcast, evil-smelling lawn pest, you/have the last word: little sun, free spirit,/driven on the
> seamless wind, your seeds/inherit the earth.

tnr is 144-186 pgs., 6×9, flat-spined, professionally printed on heavy stock, glossy, color cover, using 24-40 pgs. of poetry in each issue. They receive about 670 poetry submissions a year, use 22-35 have about a 1½- to 2-year backlog. Usual press run is 1,500 for 710 subscribers of which approximately 132 are libraries. Subscriptions: $26/3 issues US, $28 Canada, $30 all others. "A 3-issue subscription covers 18-22 months."
How to Submit: "Until January 1, 2001, we are accepting only bilingual translations." Submit 3-6 poems at a time, "unless a long poem—then one." No previously published poems "unless magazine's circulation was under 250"; simultaneous submissions OK, if notified. Always include SASE or SAE and IRC. No e-mail submissions. "All poetry submissions are tied to our Awards Program for best poetry published in a three-issue volume and judged by independent judges. Entry fee: $15 for nonsubscribers, $10 for subscribers, for which they receive the following: two back issues or a recent issue or an extension of their subscription. Submissions without entry fee are *returned unread*." Send SASE for guidelines. Responds in 5 months. Pays $18-30, more for the occasional longer poem, plus 1 copy/poem. Buys all rights. Returns rights provided *tnr* retains rights for any *tnr* collection. Reviews books of poetry. The Awards Program gives 3 awards of $250, $125 and $50, with 3 Honorable Mentions of $30.
Advice: "Read, read, read, and not just poetry but literature in general. Stay aware of what is happening in the world as well as what's happening nationally. Be familiar with the best poets of the 20th century, including, at least, the major poets from abroad. Always read those magazines, especially the literary ones, that you want to submit to, so that you know what they've been publishing, what their philosophy is and what their guidelines are. Remember that good writing is often rewriting and don't be satisfied with your first or second draft. Try to be your own best editor and don't overwrite a poem."

☑ ◻ NEW RIVERS PRESS; MINNESOTA VOICES PROJECT; HEADWATERS LITERARY COMPETITION, 420 N. Fifth St., Suite 1180, Minneapolis MN 55401, phone (612)339-7114, fax (612)339-9047, e-mail newrivpr@mtn.org, website www.newriverspress.org, founded 1968, editor Eric Braun.
Book/Chapbook Needs: Publishes collections of poetry, novels or novellas, translations of contemporary literature, collections of short fiction. Write for free catalog or send SASE for guidelines/inquiries. New and emerging authors living in Minnesota are eligible for the Minnesota Voices Project.
How to Submit: Book-length mss of poetry, short fiction, novellas or familiar essays are all accepted. New Rivers Press does not accept general submissions. "Writers should submit to one of our existing programs: The Minnesota Voices Project, open to new and emerging writers residing in Minnesota; the Headwaters Literary Competition, open to new and emerging writers residing in North America and the Marie Alexander Prose Poetry Series, open to any writer of a prose poetry collection. New River Press defines 'emerging writer' as any writer who has not published more than two books (exclusive of chapbooks) in that genre. Both competitions are also open to mss of creative prose. We accept submissions to the Minnesota Voices Project in March, the Headwaters Competition in September and October, and the Marie Alexander Series in July. Winners of the Minnesota Voices

Project and the Headwaters Competition receive $1,000 and publication. The Headwaters Competition has a $20 reading fee. Please send SASE for guidelines and entry form before submitting, or check our website. No fax or e-mail submissions. Send SASE for entry form and guidelines."

Also Offers: Website includes writer's guidelines, contest entry forms and book catalog.

◎ **A NEW SONG: THE POETRY OF GOD'S PEOPLE; NEW SONG PRESS; NEW SONG CHAP-BOOK COMPETITION (Specialized: spirituality)**, P.O. Box 629, W.B.B., Dayton OH 45409-0629, e-mail nsongpress@aol.com, founded 1995, editor/publisher Susan Jelus.

Magazine Needs: *A New Song* is published 2 times a year, in June and December, and "exhibits contemporary American poetry that speaks to endeavors of faith and enriches the spiritual lives of its readers. Includes poetry that takes a fresh approach and uses contemporary, natural language." They want "free verse that addresses spiritual life through a wide-range of topics and vivid imagery. No rhyming, sing-song, old-fashioned 'religious' poetry; or difficult-to-follow poetry." They have published poetry by Claude Wilkinson, Janet McCann, Herbert W. Martin and John Grey. As a sample the editor selected these lines from "Getting the Call" by Robert Hasselblad:

> At noon the day after/tearing down the K Mart sign/he rotated the AM dial/on his cattle guard,/seeking
> angels on talk radio./Hanging his lamb's shirt/on the left front fender/he stepped onto gravel,/threw
> car keys into the sky,/entered a conversation/with the ghost of a voice/caught in a brush fire/along the
> interstate.

ANS is 40-50 pgs., 5½×8½, usually Docutech or offset printed, saddle-stitched, cardstock cover, photo or artwork on cover. They receive about 600 poems a year, accept approximately 20%. Press run is 300 for 150 subscribers, 100 shelf sales; 50-75 distributed free to reviewers, bookstores, editors, professors, pastors. Single copy: $5; subscription: $10. Sample back issue: $3. Make checks payable to New Song Press.

How to Submit: Submit 3-5 poems at a time with short bio and SASE. No previously published poems. Simultaneous submissions OK. E-mail submissions OK, "up to 3 poems only and must have a mailing address and bio." Send SASE with regular mail submissions. Time between acceptance and publication is 6-12 months. Poems are circulated to an editorial board. Often comments on rejections. Publishes theme issues occasionally. Send SASE for guidelines. Responds in 3 months. Pays 1 copy. Acquires first North American serial rights. Sometimes reviews books of poetry in 750-1,000 words, single book format. Open to unsolicited reviews. Poets may also send books for review consideration.

Book/Chapbook Needs & How to Submit: New Song Press's goals are "to help develop a genre of contemporary spiritual poetry." They publish 1-2 chapbooks per year. They have published *Remembered into Life* by Maureen Tolman Flannery. Chapbooks are usually 20-40 pgs., 5½×8½, usually Docutech printed, sometimes offset printed color cover, saddle-stitched, cardstock cover, include art/graphics. Query first, with a few sample poems and a cover letter with brief bio and publication credits. Replies to queries in 3 months; to mss in 6 months. Payment varies.

Also Offers: Sponsors annual chapbook contest. Prize: $150 plus copies. Deadline: July 1st and 2 runners-up also recognized. Reading fee for chapbook contest entries: $15, which includes a one-year subscription to *A New Song*.

⊕ $ ◎ **THE NEW WRITER; THE NEW WRITER POETRY PRIZES**, P.O. Box 60, Cranbrook TN17 2ZR England, phone 01580 212626, fax 01580 212041, website freespace.virgin.net/ignotus.press/index.html, founded 1996, poetry editor Abi Hughes-Edwards.

Magazine Needs: Published 10 times a year, "*The New Writer* is the magazine you've been hoping to find. It's *different* and it's aimed at writers with a serious intent; who want to develop their writing to meet the high expectations of today's editors. The team at *The New Writer* are committed to working with their readers to increase the chances of publication. That's why masses of useful information and plenty of feedback is provided. More than that, we let you know about the current state of the market with the best in contemporary fiction and cutting-edge poetry backed up by searching articles and in-depth features in every issue. We are interested in short fiction, 2,000 words max.; subscribers' only; short and long unpublished poems, provided they are original and undeniably brilliant; articles that demonstrate a grasp of contemporary writing and current editorial/publishing policies; news of writers' circles, new publications, competitions, courses, workshops, etc." The poetry editor says submitted poems "must keep my heart beating. I don't have any problems with length/form but anything over two pages (150 lines) needs to be brilliant. Cutting edge shouldn't mean inaccessible. No recent disasters—they date. No my baby/doggie poems; no God poems that sound like hymns, dum-dum rhymes or comic rhymes (best left at the pub). *New Writer* is 48 pgs., A4, professionally printed and saddle-stapled with paper cover, includes clipart and b&w photos. Press run is 1,500 for 1,350 subscribers; 50 distributed free to publishers, agents. Single copy: £2.95; subscription: £42.50 in US. Sample: £4.25.

How to Submit: Submit up to 6 poems at a time. Previously published poems OK. Time between acceptance and publication is up to 6 months. Often comments on rejections. Offers criticism service: £12/6 poems. Send SASE (or SAE and IRC) for guidelines. Pays £3 voucher plus 1 copy. Buys first British serial rights. Reviews books and chapbooks of poetry and other magazines. Open to unsolicited reviews. Poets may also send books for review consideration.

Also Offers: Sponsors The New Writer Poetry Prizes. An annual prize, "open to all poets writing in the English language, who are invited to submit an original, previously unpublished poem or collection of six to ten poems.

Up to 25 prizes will be presented as well as publication for the prize-winning poets in an anthology plus the chance for a further 10 shortlisted poets to see their work published in *The New Writer* during the year." Write for contest rules.

$◻◪◎ NEW WRITER'S MAGAZINE (Specialized: humor, writing), P.O. Box 5976, Sarasota FL 34277-5976, phone (941)953-7903, e-mail newriters@aol.com, website www.newriters.com, founded 1986, editor George J. Haborak.
Magazine Needs: *New Writer's Magazine* is a bimonthly magazine "for aspiring writers, and professional ones as well, to exchange ideas and working experiences." They are open to free verse, light verse and traditional, 8-20 lines, reflecting upon the writing lifestyle. "Humorous slant on writing life especially welcomed." They do not want poems about "love, personal problems, abstract ideas or fantasy." *NWM* is 28 pgs., 8½×11, offset printed, saddle-stapled, with glossy paper cover, b&w photos and ads. They receive about 300 poems a year, accept approximately 10%. Press run is 5,000. Subscription: $15/year, $25/2 years. Sample: $3.
How to Submit: Submit up to 3 poems at a time. No previously published poems or simultaneous submissions. Time between acceptance and publication is up to 1 year. Send SASE for guidelines or request via e-mail. No e-mail submissions. Responds in 2 months. Pays $5/poem. Buys first North American serial rights. Each issue of this magazine also includes an interview with a recognized author, articles on writing and the writing life, tips and markets.

◪ NEW YORK QUARTERLY, P.O. Box 693, Old Chelsea Station, New York NY 10113, founded 1969, poetry editor William Packard.
Magazine Needs: *New York Quarterly* appears 3 times/year. They seek to publish "a cross-section of the best of contemporary American poetry" and, indeed, have a record of publishing many of the best and most diverse of poets, including W.D. Snodgrass, Gregory Corso, James Dickey and Judson Jerome. It appears in a 6×9, flat-spined format, thick, elegantly printed, glossy color cover. Subscription: $15.
How to Submit: Submit 3-5 poems at a time with your name and address; include SASE. Simultaneous submissions OK with notification. Responds within 2 weeks. Pays copies.

✓ $◙ THE NEW YORKER, 4 Times Square, New York NY 10036, founded 1925, contact poetry editor.
◪ Poems appearing in *The New Yorker* have also been selected for inclusion in the 1996, 1997 and 1998 volumes of *The Best American Poetry*.
Magazine Needs: *The New Yorker*, circulation 800,000, uses poetry of the highest quality (including translations). Sample: $3 (available on newsstands).
How to Submit: Mss are not read during the summer. Responds in up to 3 months. Pays top rates.

✓◙ NEW ZOO POETRY REVIEW; SUNKEN MEADOWS PRESS, P.O. Box 36760, Richmond VA 23235, website http://members.aol.com/newzoopoet, founded 1997, editor Angela Vogel.
Magazine Needs: *New Zoo Poetry Review* is published annually in September/October and "tends to publish free verse in well-crafted lyric and narrative forms. Our goal is to publish established poets alongside lesser-known poets of great promise. *NZPR* wants serious, intellectual poetry of any form, length or style. Rhyming poetry only if exceptional. No light verse, song lyrics or greeting card copy. If you are not reading the best of contemporary poetry, then *NZPR* is not for you." They have published poetry by Heather McHugh, Diane Glancy, DC Berry and Martha Collins. As a sample the editor selected these lines from "Cityscape with pink rose" by Richard Bear:

> As he turns away, he sees in his mind's/eye, himself turning back to buy for her/one of her own roses,
> or bloom of her choice./Idiotic! Blooms she has, and no doubt/must throw away many; wouldn't she/
> be sick, by now, of flowers?/Trading, as she does, in these symbols/of the happiness of others, what
> would be/happiness to her, here, today?

The editor says *NZPR* is 36 pgs., digest-sized, photocopied and saddle-stapled with glossy card cover with b&w photography. They receive about 2,000 poems a year, accept approximately 5%. Press run is 200. Subscription: $7 for 2 consecutive issues. Sample: $4.
How to Submit: Submit 3-5 poems at a time. No previously published poems; simultaneous submissions OK. Cover letter with brief bio required. Seldom comments on rejections. Responds in 2 months. Pays 1 copy. Acquires first North American serial rights. "Poets are discouraged from submitting more than once in a 12-month period. Please do not write to us for these submission guidelines."
Advice: "It's not enough to report something that happened to you. A great poem involves the reader in its experience. It surprises us with fresh language."

ALWAYS include a self-addressed, stamped envelope (SASE) when sending a ms or query to a publisher within your own country. When sending material to other countries, include a self-addressed envelope and International Reply Coupons (IRCs), available at many post offices.

◑ NEWSLETTER INAGO, P.O. Box 26244, Tucson AZ 85726-6244, phone (520)294-7031, founded 1979, poetry editor Del Reitz.

Magazine Needs: *NI* is a monthly newsletter. "Free verse and short narrative poetry preferred. Rhymed poetry must be truly exceptional (nonforced) for consideration. Due to format, 'epic' and monothematic poetry will not be considered. Cause specific, political or religious poetry stands little chance of consideration. A wide range of short poetry, showing the poet's preferably eclectic perspective is best for *NI*. No haiku, please." They have published poetry by Susan B. Marshall, Mark Petry, Joshua Bodwell, Steve Fay, Curtis Nelson and Jennifer A. Grier. As a sample the editor selected these lines from "Up Before Dawn" by Richard J. Weekley:

> *but the man/says he's going/poeming though it may/be a day/without a nibble*

NI is 4-5 pgs., corner-stapled. Press run is approximately 200 for subscriptions. No price is given for the newsletter, but the editor suggests a donation of $3.50 an issue or $17.50 annually ($3.50 and $21 Canada, £8 and £21 UK). Make checks payable to Del Reitz. Copyright is retained by authors.

How to Submit: Submit 10-15 poems at a time. "Poetry should be submitted in the format in which the poet wants it to appear, and cover letters are always a good idea." Simultaneous submissions and previously published poems OK. Sometimes comments on rejections. Send SASE for guidelines. Responds ASAP (usually within 2 weeks). Pays 4 copies.

◑ NEXUS, WO16A Student Union, Wright State University, Dayton OH 45435, phone (937)775-5533, founded 1967, editors Tom Poole and Andrea O. Hoilette.

Magazine Needs: "*Nexus* is a student operated magazine of mainstream and street poetry; also essays on environmental and political issues. We're looking for truthful, direct poetry. Open to poets anywhere. We look for contemporary, imaginative work." *Nexus* appears 3 times a year—fall, winter and spring, using about 40 pgs. of poetry (of 80-96) in each issue. They receive about 1,000 submissions a year, use approximately 30-50. Circulation is 1,000. For a sample, send a 10×15 SAE with 5 first-class stamps and $5.

How to Submit: Submit 4-6 pgs. of poetry with bio. Reads submissions September through May only. Simultaneous submissions OK, "but due to short response time we want to be told it's a simultaneous submission." Editor sometimes comments on rejections. Send SASE for guidelines. Responds in 5 months except summer months. Pays 2 copies. Acquires first rights.

◑ ◑ ◎ NIGHT ROSES (Specialized: teen/young adult, love/romance, nature, students, women/feminism), P.O. Box 393, Prospect Heights IL 60070-0393, phone (847)392-2435, founded 1986, poetry editor Allen T. Billy.

Magazine Needs: *Night Roses*, appears 2-4 times/year. They want "poems about dance, bells, clocks, nature, ghost images of past or future, romance and flowers (roses, wildflowers, violets, etc.). We look for women/feminism themes for our *Cocktail Shakers* series. Do not want poems with raw language." Also accepts poetry written by teens. They have published poetry by Emma J. Blanch, M. Riesa Clark, Joan Payne Kincaid, Lyn Lifshin and Alice Rogoff. As a sample the editor selected these lines from "secret light" by Cathy Drinkwater Better:

> *she looked into his eyes/and saw all of eternity/staring back at her/with the face of an enchanter*

Night Roses is 44 pgs., saddle-stapled, photocopied from typescript on offset paper with tinted matte card cover. Press run is 200-300. Subscription: $10/3 issues. Sample: $4.

How to Submit: Submit up to 8 poems at a time with #10 SASE. "Desire author's name and address in top left corner on all sheets of ms. If previously published—an acknowledgment must be provided by author with it." No simultaneous submissions; some previously published poems used. "I prefer submissions between March and September only." Publishes theme issues. Send SASE for guidelines. Responds in up to 4 months. "Material is accepted for current issue and two in progress." Sometimes sends prepublication galleys. Pays 1 copy. Acquires first or reprint rights. Staff reviews books of poetry. Send books for review consideration.

Advice: "We are more interested in items that would be of interest to our teen and women readers and to our readership in the fields of dance, art and creative learning. We are interested in positive motives in this area."

☑ ◑ NIGHTSUN, Dept. of English, Frostburg State University, Frostburg MD 21532, phone (301)687-4221, Fax (301)687-3099, founded 1981, contact poetry editor.

Magazine Needs: *Nightsun* is a literary annual of poetry, fiction and interviews. They want "highest-quality poetry." Subject matter open. Publishes mostly free verse. Prefers poems not much longer than 40 lines. Not interested in "sentimental, obvious poetry." They have published poetry by Maxine Kumin, Marge Piercy, Bruce Jacobs and Wendy Bishop. Interviews include Lucille Clifton, Sharon Olds, Carol Frost, Roland Flint and W.D. Snodgrass. As a sample the editor selected these lines from "What the White Horse Said" by Grace Butcher:

> *We had to be dream horses,/blue with the moon, black against snow/while you were gone. Never real./*
> *We were as lucky as horses in a painting./Our colors didn't matter.*

Nightsun is 68 pgs., 6×9, printed on 100% recycled paper and perfect-bound with card cover, b&w print on front. This attractive journal features well-known poets alongside relative newcomers. They accept about 1% of poetry received. Subscription/sample: $6.50.

How to Submit: Submit 3-5 poems at a time. No simultaneous submissions. Do not submit mss during summer months. Responds within 6 months. Pays 2 copies. Acquires first rights. "Contributors encouraged to subscribe."

◐ ◉ **NIMROD: INTERNATIONAL JOURNAL OF CONTEMPORARY POETRY AND FIC-TION; RUTH G. HARDMAN AWARD: PABLO NERUDA PRIZE FOR POETRY**, University of Tulsa, 600 S. College, Tulsa OK 74104-3189, phone (918)631-3080, fax (918)631-3033, e-mail nimrod@utulsa.edu, website www.utulsa.edu/nimrod/, founded 1956, editor-in-chief Francine Ringold.

   Poetry published in *Nimrod* has been included in *The Best American Poetry 1995*.

Magazine Needs: *Nimrod* "is an active 'little magazine,' part of the movement in American letters which has been essential to the development of modern literature. *Nimrod* publishes 2 issues/year, an awards issue in the fall featuring the prize winners of their national competition and a thematic issue each spring." They want "vigorous writing that is neither wholly of the academy nor the streets, typed mss." They have published poetry by Sarah Flygare, Jennifer Ward, Ruth Schwartz and Luci Getsi. The journal is 160 pgs., 6×9, flat-spined, full-color glossy cover, professionally printed on coated stock with b&w photos and art, uses 50-90 pgs. of poetry in each issue. Poems in non-award issues range from formal to freestyle with several translations. They receive about 2,000 submissions a year, accept approximately 1%, have a 3- to 6-month backlog. Press run is 3,500 of which 200 are public and university libraries. Subscription: $17.50/year inside USA; $19 outside. Sample: $10. Specific back issues available.

How to Submit: Submit 5-10 poems at a time. Request submission guidelines via e-mail or with SASE. Publishes theme issues. Send SASE for upcoming themes. Responds in up to 6 weeks. Pays 2 copies plus reduced cost on additional copies. "Poets should be aware that during the months that the Ruth Hardman Awards Competition is being conducted, reporting time on non-contest manuscripts will be longer."

Also Offers: Send business-sized SASE for guidelines and rules for the Ruth G. Hardman Award: Pablo Neruda Prize for Poetry ($2,000 and $1,000 prizes). Entries accepted January 1 through April 30 each year. The $20 entry fee includes 2 issues. Also sponsors the Nimrod/Hardman Awards Workshop, a 1-day workshop held annually in October. Cost is $30. Send SASE for brochure and registration form. Website includes writer's guidelines, names of editors, contest rules, subscription information and excerpts of published poetry.

☑ ♻ ◐ ◉ **96 INC MAGAZINE; 96 INC'S BRUCE P. ROSSLEY LITERARY AWARDS**, P.O. Box 15559, Boston MA 02215, phone (617)267-0543, fax (617)262-3568, founded 1992, editors Julie Anderson, Vera Gold and Nancy Mehegan.

Magazine Needs: *96 Inc* is an annual literary magazine appearing in July that focuses on new voices, "connecting the beginner to the established, a training center for the process of publication." They want all forms and styles of poetry, though "shorter is better." Also accepts poetry written by teens. They have published poetry by Jennifer Barber, Peter Desmond, Dana Elder, Gary Duehr, Eugene Gloria and Judy Katz-Levine. As a sample the editors selected this poem, "Haiku," by Peter Desmond:

   early April/buried receipts burst forth/deductions blossom

96 Inc is 38-50 pgs., 8½×11, saddle-stapled with coated card cover and b&w photos and graphics. They receive around 2,000 submissions a year, accept approximately 5%. Press run is 3,000 for 500 subscribers of which 50 are libraries, 1,500 shelf sales. Single copy: $4; subscription: $13. Sample: $5.50.

How to Submit: No previously published poems; simultaneous submissions OK. Time between acceptance and publication is 1 year or longer. Poems are circulated to an editorial board. Send SASE for guidelines. Responds in 6 months. Pays 4 copies, subscription and modest fee (when funds are available). Copyright reverts to author 2 months after publication. Occasionally, staff reviews books of poetry. Send books for review consideration, attn: Andrew Dawson.

Also Offers: The *96 Inc's* Bruce P. Rossley Literary Awards are given to previously under-recognized writers (of poetry or fiction). Writers can be nominated by anyone familiar with their work. Send SASE for further information.

Advice: "*96 Inc* is an artists' collaborative and a local resource. It often provides venues and hosts readings in addition to publishing a magazine."

◉ ◉ **NINETY-SIX PRESS (Specialized: regional)**, Furman University, Greenville SC 29613-0438, phone (864)294-3156, fax (864)294-2224, e-mail bill.rogers@furman.edu, website www.furman.edu/~wrogers/ 96Press/HOME.htm, founded 1991, editors William Rogers and Gilbert Allen.

Book/Chapbook Needs & How to Submit: Publishes 1-2 paperback books of poetry/year. "The name of the press is derived from the old name for the area around Greenville, South Carolina—the Ninety-Six District. The name suggests our interest in the writers, readers and culture of the region." Books are usually 45-70 pgs., 6×9, professionally printed and perfect-bound with coated stock cover. For a sample, send $10. "We currently accept submissions by invitation only. At some point in the future, however, we hope to be able to encourage submissions by widely published poets who live in South Carolina."

◐ ◉ **NITE-WRITER'S INTERNATIONAL LITERARY ARTS JOURNAL**, 137 Pointview Rd. #300, Pittsburgh PA 15227-3131, phone (412)885-3798, founded 1993, executive editor/publisher John A. Thompson Sr., associate editor Bree Ann Orner.

Magazine Needs: A quarterly open to beginners as well as professionals, *Nite-Writer's* is " 'dedicated to the emotional intellectual' with a creative perception of life." They want strong imagery and accept free verse, avant-garde poetry, haiku and senryu. Open to length and subject matter. No porn or violence. They have published poetry by Lyn Lifshin, Rose Marie Hunold, Peter Vetrano, Carol Frances Brown and Richard King Perkins II. As a sample the editors selected this poem, "Love Child," by Dianne Borsenik:

> make incense from the flower/dance naked in the light/weave a blanket/fringed with stars/to cover you at night/breathe kisses to the morning/braid songs into your hair/blow wishes on the feathered/spores that surf the curls of air/and if a storm should hurt you/pour honey on the pain/chase the clouds and catch them/then laugh/and drink the rain

The editors say the journal is 30-50 pgs., 8½×11, laser-printed, stock cover with sleeve, some graphics and artwork. They receive about 1,000 poems a year, use approximately 10-15%. Press run is about 100 for more than 60 subscribers of which 10 are libraries. Single copy: $6; subscription: $20. Sample (when available): $4.
How to Submit: Previously published poems and simultaneous submissions OK. Cover letter preferred. "Give brief bio, state where you heard of us, state if material has been previously published and where. Always enclose SASE if you seek reply and return of your material." Time between acceptance and publication is within 1 year. Always comments on rejections. Send SASE for guidelines. Responds in 1 month.
Advice: "Don't be afraid to submit your material. Take rejection as advice—study your market. Create your own style and voice, then be heard. 'I am a creator, a name beneath words' (from my poem, 'unidentified-Identified')."

◯ NO EXIT, P.O. Box 454, South Bend IN 46624-0454, fax (801)650-3743, e-mail no_exit@usa.net, founded 1994, editor Mike Amato.
Magazine Needs: *No Exit* is a quarterly forum "for the experimental as well as traditional excellence." The editor says he wants "poetry that takes chances in form or content. Form, length, subject matter and style are open. No poetry that's unsure of why it was written. Particularly interested in long (not long-winded poems)." They have published poetry by Paul Weinman, Simon Perchik and Anthony Redisi. *NE* is 32 pgs., saddle-stapled, digest-sized, card cover with art. They accept 10-15% of the submissions received. Press run is less than 500 for 65 subscribers of which 6 are libraries. Subscription: $12. Sample: $4.
How to Submit: Submit up to 5 poems ("send more if compelled, but I will stop reading after the fifth"), 1 poem/page on 8½×11 paper. "No handwritten work, misspellings, colored paper, multiple type faces, typos, long-winded cover letters and lists of publication credits." No previously published poems; simultaneous submissions OK. No e-mail submissions. Time between acceptance and publication can vary from 1 month to 1 year. Sometimes comments on rejections, "if the poem strikes me as worth saving. No themes. But spring issues are devoted to a single poet. Interested writers should submit 24 pgs. of work. Don't bother unless of highest caliber." Send SASE for guidelines. Responds in up to 3 months. Pays 1 copy plus 4-issue subscription. Acquires first North American serial rights plus right to reprint once in an anthology. Reviews books of poetry. "Also looking for articles, critical in nature, on poetry/poets." Open to unsolicited reviews. Poets may also send books for review consideration.
Advice: "Presentation means something; namely, that you care about what you do. Don't take criticism, when offered, personally. I'll work with you if I see something solid to focus on."

◯ NOMAD'S CHOIR, % Meander, 30-15 Hobart St. F4H, Woodside NY 11377, founded 1989, editor Joshua Meander.
Magazine Needs: *Nomad's Choir* is a quarterly. "Subjects wanted: love poems, protest poems, mystical poems, nature poems, poems of humanity, poems with solutions to world problems and inner conflict. 9-30 lines, poems with hope. Simple words, careful phrasing. Free verse, rhymed poems, sonnets, half-page parables, myths and legends, song lyrics. No curse words in poems, little or no name-dropping, no naming of consumer products, no two-page poems, no humor, no bias writing, no poems untitled." They have published poetry by Steven J. Stein, Madeline Artenberg, Wayne Wilkinson and Jill Dimaggio. *Nomad's Choir* is 10 pgs., 8½×11, typeset and saddle-stapled with 3 poems/page. They receive about 150 poems a year, use approximately 50. Press run is 400; all distributed free. Subscription: $5. Sample: $1.25. Make checks payable to Joshua Meander.
How to Submit: Responds in 2 months. Pays 1 copy. Publishes theme issues. Send SASE for guidelines and upcoming themes.
Advice: "Stick to your guns; however, keep in mind that an editor may be able to correct a minor flaw in your poem. Accept only minor adjustments. Go to many open poetry readings. Respect the masters. Read and listen to other poets on the current scene. Make pen pals. Start your own poetry journal. Do it all out of pure love."

$ ◯ NORTH AMERICAN REVIEW, University of Northern Iowa, Cedar Falls IA 50614, phone (319)273-6455, fax (319)273-6455, e-mail nar@uni.edu, website www.webdelsol.com/NorthAmReview/NAR, founded 1815, poetry editor Peter Cooley.
> Work published in the *North American Review* has been included in the 1995, 1996 and 1997 volumes of *The Best American Poetry*.

Magazine Needs: *NAR* is a slick magazine-sized bimonthly of general interest, 48 pgs. average, saddle-stapled, professionally printed with glossy full-color paper cover, publishing poetry of the highest quality. They have published poetry by Francine Sterle, Cynthia Hogue and Marvin Bell. They receive about 15,000 poems a year, use approximately 20-30. Press run is 4,400 for 1,700 subscribers of which 1,070 are libraries, some 1,850 newsstand or bookstore sales. Subscription: $18. Sample: $5.

How to Submit: Include SASE. No simultaneous submissions or previously published poems. Time between acceptance and publication is up to 1 year. Send SASE for guidelines. Responds in 2 months. Always sends prepublication galleys. Pays $1/line and 2 copies. Buys first North American serial rights only. Returns rights after publication.

$⊚ NORTH CAROLINA LITERARY REVIEW (Specialized: regional), English Dept., East Carolina University, Greenville NC 27858-4353, phone (252)328-1537, fax (252)328-4889, e-mail bauerm@mail.ecu.edu, founded 1992, editor Margaret Bauer.
Magazine Needs: *NCLR* is "an annual publication that contains articles and other works about North Carolina topics or by North Carolina authors." They want "poetry by writers currently living in North Carolina, those who have lived in North Carolina or those using North Carolina for subject matter." They have published poetry by Betty Adcock, James Applewhite and A.R. Ammons. The editor says *NCLR* is 200 pgs. and magazine-sized. They receive about 40-50 submissions a year, accept approximately 20%. Press run is 1,000 for 500 subscribers of which 150 are libraries, 100 shelf sales; 50 distributed free to contributors. Subscription: $20/2 years, $36/4 years. Sample: $10-15.
How to Submit: Submit 3-5 poems at a time. Previously published poems OK. Cover letter required. No e-mail submissions. Disk submissions OK. "Submit 2 copies and include SASE or e-mail address for response." Reads submissions August 1 through April 30 only. Time between acceptance and publication is up to 1 year. Often comments on rejections. Publishes theme issues. Send SASE for guidelines and upcoming themes. Responds in 2 months. Sometimes sends prepublication galleys. Pays $25-50 plus 1-2 copies. Buys first or one-time rights. Reviews books of poetry in 2,000 words, multi-book format. Open to unsolicited reviews. Poets may also send books for review consideration.

◉ NORTH DAKOTA QUARTERLY, Box 7209, University of North Dakota, Grand Forks ND 58202-7209, founded 1910, poetry editor Jay Meek.
Magazine Needs: *North Dakota Quarterly* is a literary quarterly published by the University of North Dakota that includes material in the arts and humanities—essays, fiction, interviews, poems and visual art. "We want to see poetry that reflects an understanding not only of the difficulties of the craft, but of the vitality and tact that each poem calls into play." They have published poetry by Edward Kleinschmidt, Alane Rollings and Robert Wrigley. The poetry editor says *NDQ* is 6×9, about 200 pgs., perfect-bound, professionally designed and often printed with full-color artwork on a white card cover. You can find almost every kind of poem here—avant-garde to traditional. Typically the work of about 5 poets is included in each issue. Press run is 850 for 650 subscribers. Subscription: $25/year. Sample: $8.
How to Submit: Submit 5 poems at a time, typed, double-spaced. No previously published poems or simultaneous submissions. Time between acceptance and publication varies. Responds in up to 6 weeks. Always sends prepublication galleys. Pays 1 copy.

✓ ◉ ⊚ NORTHEAST; JUNIPER PRESS; JUNIPER BOOKS; THE WILLIAM N. JUDSON SERIES OF CONTEMPORARY AMERICAN POETRY; CHICKADEE; INLAND SEA SERIES; GIFTS OF THE PRESS (Specialized: form), 1310 Shorewood Dr., La Crosse WI 54601, phone (207)778-3454, website www.ddgbooks.com, founded 1962, contact editors.
    ⚑ "Poets we have published won The Pulitzer Prize, The Posner Poetry Prize, and The Midwest Book Award."
Magazine Needs & How to Submit: *Northeast* is an annual little magazine appearing in January. They have published poetry by Mary Kay Rummel, John Glowney and Ronald Moran. The editors say *Northeast* is digest-sized and saddle-stapled. Subscription: $33/year ($38 for institutions), "which brings you one issue of the magazine and the Juniper Books, Chickadees, WNJ Books and some gifts of the press, a total of about 3-5 items." (See our website or send SASE for catalog to order individual items; orders can be placed by calling the Order Dept. at (207)778-3454.) Sample: $3. No submissions by fax or e-mail. Responds in up to 4 months. Pays 2 copies.
Book/Chapbook Needs & How to Submit: Juniper Press does not accept unsolicited book/chapbook mss.
Advice: "Please read us before sending mss. It will aid in your selection of materials to send. If you don't like what we do, please don't submit."

✓ ◉ NORTHEAST ARTS MAGAZINE, P.O. Box 4363, Portland NE 04102, founded 1990, publisher/editor Mr. Leigh Donaldson.
Magazine Needs: *NEAM* is a biannual using poetry that is "honest, clear, with a love of expression through simple language, under 30 lines. Care for words and craftsmanship are appreciated." They have published poetry by Steve Lutrell, Eliot Richman, Elizabeth R. Curry and Alisa Aran. *NEAM* is 32 or more pgs., digest-sized, professionally printed with 1-color coated card cover. They accept 20-25% of submissions. Press run is 500-1,000 for 150 subscribers of which half are libraries, 50 to arts organizations. An updated arts information section and feature articles are included. Subscription: $10. Sample: $4.50.
How to Submit: Reads submissions September 1 through February 28 only. "A short bio is helpful." Send SASE for guidelines. Responds in 3 months. Pays 2 copies. Acquires first North American serial rights.

$ ◻ ◎ **NORTHEAST CORRIDOR (Specialized: regional)**, English Dept., Beaver College, Glenside PA 19038, phone (215)947-6732, founded 1993, poetry editor Janna King, editor Susan Balée.

Magazine Needs: *Northeast Corridor* is published semiannually. Ms. King dislikes "obscurity and sloppy estimations buried in pseudo-intellectualism. She wants poetry that employs brilliance of language to trigger and convey genuine emotion. In the end, the poem must be about the reader, or it is not effective." They have published poetry by Ted Kooser, Dana Gioia, Charity Hume and Stephen Dobyns. The editor says *NC* is 120-180 pgs., 8½×5½, perfect-bound, with color cover. They receive about 500 poems a year, use approximately 30-40. Press run is 1,000 for 200 subscribers of which 5 are libraries, 700 shelf sales; a few distributed free to contributors and donors. Single copy: $7; subscription: $20. Sample: $6.

How to Submit: Submit 3-5 poems with name and address on each page/poem. No previously published poems; simultaneous submissions OK. Cover letter preferred. Reads submissions September through May only. Time between acceptance and publication is 9 months. Poems are circulated to an editorial board. Often comments on rejections. Publishes theme issues. Send SASE for guidelines and upcoming themes. Responds in 4 months. Always sends prepublication galleys. Pays $10/poem plus 2 copies. Buys first rights. Occasionally sponsors contest issues.

✓ ◼ **$** ◎ **THE NORTHERN CENTINEL (Specialized: nature/ecology/environment, ethics, legal/jurisprudence, political, social issues)**, e-mail Northern.Centinel@valley.net, website www.Centinel.org, founded 1788, poetry editor Peter J. Gardner.

Magazine Needs: *The Northern Centinel* is an online publication focusing on "political/cultural essays and analyses on matters of national interest." They publish 12-24 poems annually. They have published poetry by Molly Peacock, Allen Ginsberg and Martin Tucker.

How to Submit: No previously published poems; simultaneous submissions OK. All submissions by e-mail only. Time between acceptance and publication is up to a year. Seldom comments on rejections. Responds within 4 months. Pays $10.

✓ ◻ ◯ ◿ **NORTHERN STARS MAGAZINE**, N17285 Co. Rd. 400, Powers MI 49874, website membe rs.aol.com/WriterNet/NorthStar.html or users.aol.com/WriterNet/, founded 1997, editor Beverly Kleikamp.

Magazine Needs: *Northern Stars* is published bimonthly and "welcomes submissions of fiction, nonfiction and poetry on any subject or style. The main requirement is good clean family reading material. Nothing you can't read to your child or your mother. No smut or filth." Also accepts poetry written by children. They have published poetry by Terri Warden, Julie Sanders, Najwa Salam Brax and Gary Elam. As a sample the editor selected these lines from "Flights of Fancy" by Gary S. Elam:

> *A raven looks mysterious/With feathers black as night/An eagle perching on a cliff/Is such an awesome sight.*

NS is 32 pgs., 8½×11, photocopied and saddle-stapled with cardstock cover, may include b&w line drawings and photographs. "Send SASE for subscription information." Sample: $4. Make checks payable to Beverly Kleikamp or *Northern Stars Magazine*.

How to Submit: Submit up to 10 poems at a time, no more than 25 lines each. Previously published poems and simultaneous submissions OK. Cover letter preferred. "Manuscripts must be typed—please do not submit handwritten material." Often comments on rejections. Publishes theme issues occasionally. Pays either tearsheets or copy of *NS*—except in contests where winner receives half of all reading fees—minimum $10. No fee for regular subscribers. All rights return to authors on publication.

Also Offers: Sponsors monthly alternating issues contest for poetry and fiction/nonfiction (i.e., poetry contest in March-April issue, fiction/nonfiction in May-June). Reading fee: $2.50/poem for non-subscribers, $1/poem for subscribers. Deadline: 25th of month preceding publication. Publishes an annual chapbook of contest winners and honorable mentions. "I do publish a limited number of chapbooks for others now for an 'affordable' price to the writer." 100 copies or less available; sample available $5. Also has a "Somewhere In Michigan" regular column featuring people/places/events, etc., tied in with Michigan. Also includes adventures which have happened in Michigan. Website includes brief guidelines, poetry, and books available through North Star Publishing.

◿ **NORTHWEST REVIEW**, 369 PLC, University of Oregon, Eugene OR 97403, phone (503)346-3957, founded 1957, poetry editor John Witte.

Magazine Needs: They are "seeking excellence in whatever form we can find it" and use "all types" of poetry. They have published poetry by Alan Dugan, Olga Broumas and Richard Eberhart. *NR*, a 6×9, flat-spined magazine, appears 3 times/year and uses 25-40 pgs. of poetry in each issue. They receive about 3,500 submissions a year, use approximately 4%, have up to a 4-month backlog. Press run is 1,300 for 1,200 subscribers of which half are libraries. Sample: $4.

How to Submit: Submit 6-8 poems clearly reproduced. No simultaneous submissions. The editor comments "whenever possible" on rejections. Send SASE for guidelines. Responds within 10 weeks. Pays 3 copies.

Advice: "Persist."

☑ $⬜ ⊘ **NORTHWOODS PRESS, THE POET'S PRESS; NORTHWOODS JOURNAL, A MAGAZINE FOR WRITERS; C.A.L. (CONSERVATORY OF AMERICAN LETTERS)**, P.O. Box 298, Thomaston ME 04861-0298, phone (207)354-0998, fax (207)354-8953, e-mail cal@americanletters.org, website www.americanletters.org, Northwoods Press founded 1972, *Northwoods Journal* 1993, editor Robert Olmsted.

Magazine Needs & How to Submit: *Northwoods Journal* is a quarterly literary magazine. "The journal is interested in all poets who feel they have something to say and who work to say it well. We have no interest in closet poets, or credit seekers. All poets seeking an audience, working to improve their craft and determined to 'get it right' are welcome here. Also accepts poetry written by children. Please request submission guidelines before submitting." *Northwoods* is about 40 pgs., digest-sized, desktop-published, flat-spined with matte card cover with b&w illustration. Subscription: $12.50/year. Sample: $5.50. Reading fee: $1.50/poem for nonmembers of C.A.L., 50¢/poem for members. One free read per year when joining or renewing membership in C.A.L. "Submission must accompany membership order." Send SASE for guidelines. Deadlines are the 1st of April, July, October and January for seasonal publication. Responds within 2 weeks after deadline, sometimes sooner. Pays $4/page, average, on acceptance.

Book Needs & How to Submit: "For book-length poetry manuscripts, submit to Northwoods Press. Our program is designed for the excellent *working poet* who has a following which is likely to create sales of $3,000 or more. Without at least that much of a following and at least that level of sales, no book can be published. Send SASE for our 15 pt. poetry program. Please do not submit manuscripts until you have read our guidelines." They have published *Hog Killers and Other Poems* by Vernon Schmid and *Knotted Stems* by Sylvia Relation. Northwoods Press will pay a minimum of $250 advance on contracting a book. The editors "rarely" comment on rejections, but they offer commentary for a fee, though they "strongly recommend *against* it."

Advice: "Poetry must be non-trite, non-didactic. It must never bounce. Rhyme, if used at all, should be subtle. One phrase should tune the ear in preparation for the next. They should flow and create an emotional response."

🌐 ☑ ⊘ **NORTHWORDS**, The Stable, Long Rd., Avoch, Ross-Shire Scotland IV9 8QR United Kingdom, e-mail northwords@cromness.demon.co.uk, founded 1991, editor Angus Dunn.

Magazine Needs: Published 3 times a year, *Northwords* is "a literary journal focusing on material relevant to the North of Scotland, the geographical North generally, fiction (short) and poetry." They do not want "vague New Age poetry; philosophical poetry without physical referents. No trite sentiments in rhyme or otherwise." They have published poetry by Gael Turnbull, Sheena Blackhall, Tom Pow and Raymond Friel. As a sample the editor selected these lines from "Burnt River" by Betty Munnoch:

> *Return at dawn./Touch ancient rocks worn smooth/and smell the heavy orchid-bearing mulch/of northern woods. Listen to the lost soul cry of loons,/looking can come later. Slip into peat brown water/ and swim the warming shallows to cooler deeps.*

The editor says *Northwords* is 64 pgs., B5, perfect-bound, illustrations often used. They receive about 500 poems a year, accept approximately 10%. Press run is 500 for 200 subscribers of which 10 are libraries, 250 shelf sales. Subscription: £12. Sample: £4 pounds sterling (international money order preferred if overseas).

How to Submit: Submit 4-6 poems at a time. No previously published poems or simultaneous submissions. Cover letter required. Reads submissions the first week of each month only. Time between acceptance and publication is 4 months. Poems are circulated to an editorial board. "All submissions are read by the editorial board, who advise acceptance or rejection. Final decision rests with the editor." Seldom comments on rejections. Responds in 2 months. Pays 1 copy and a small fee. Acquires first rights. Reviews books and chapbooks of poetry in 500-1,200 words, single and multi-book format. Open to unsolicited reviews. Poets may also send books for review consideration to Robert Davidson at the above address.

⊘ **NOSTALGIA: A SENTIMENTAL STATE OF MIND**, P.O. Box 2224, Orangeburg SC 29116, website www.nospub.com, founded 1986, poetry editor Connie Lakey Martin.

Magazine Needs: *Nostalgia* appears spring and fall using "content at whim of poet, style open, prefer modern prose, but short poems, never longer than one page, no profanity, no ballads." *Nostalgia* is 24 pgs., digest-sized, offset typescript, saddle-stapled, with matte card cover. Press run is 1,000. Subscription: $8. Sample: $5.

How to Submit: "Most poems selected from contest." There are contests in each issue with award of $200 and publication for outstanding poem, publication and $25 for Honorable Mentions. Entry fee of $5 reserves future edition, covers 3 entries. Include SASE and put name and address on each poem. Deadlines: June 30 and December 31 each year. No previously published poems or simultaneous submissions. Guidelines available for SASE. Sometimes sends prepublication galleys. All rights revert to author upon publication.

Also Offers: Website includes updates on awards, deadlines and general guidelines for submission and contests.

Advice: "I offer criticism to most rejected poems, but I suggest sampling before submitting."

⊘ **NOTRE DAME REVIEW**, Dept. of English, University of Notre Dame, 356 O'Shaughnessy Hall, Notre Dame IN 46556-5639, phone (219)631-6952, fax (219)631-4268, e-mail english.ndreview.1@nd.edu, website www.nd.edu/~ndr/review.htm, founded 1994, poetry editor John Matthias.

Magazine Needs: *NDR* is "a biannual eclectic magazine of the best poetry and fiction." They are open to all types of poetry. They have published poetry by Ken Smith, Robert Creeley and Denise Levertov. As a sample the editor selected these lines from "The Watchman at Mycenae" by Seamus Heaney:

> *Some people wept, and not for sorrow-joy/That the king had armed and upped and sailed for Troy,/*
> *But inside me life struck sound in a gong/That killing-fest, the life-warm and world wrong/It brought*
> *to pass still argued and endured*

The editor says *NDR* is 170 pgs., magazine-sized, perfect-bound with 4-color glossy cover, includes art/graphics and ads. They receive about 400 poems a year, accept approximately 10%. Press run is 2,000 for 500 subscribers of which 150 are libraries, 1,000 shelf sales; 350 distributed free to contributors, assistants, etc. Single copy: $8; subscription: $15/year. Sample: $6. "Read magazine before submitting."

How to Submit: Submit 3-5 poems at a time. No previously published poems; simultaneous submissions OK. Cover letter required. Reads submissions September through May only. Time between acceptance and publication is 3 months. Seldom comments on rejections. Publishes theme issues. Obtain guidelines and upcoming themes via website. Responds in 3 months. Always sends prepublication galleys. Pays 2 copies. Acquires first rights. Staff reviews books of poetry in 500 words, single and multi-book format. Poets may also send books for review consideration.

Also Offers: Sponsors the Ernest Sandeen Prize for Poetry, a book contest open to poets with at least one other book publication. Send SASE for details. Website includes writer's guidelines, names of editors, poetry and interviews.

NOVA EXPRESS (Specialized: science fiction/fantasy, horror), P.O. Box 27231, Austin TX 78755, e-mail lawrence@bga.com, website www.delphi.com/sflit/NovaExpress, founded 1987, editor Lawrence Person.

Magazine Needs: *Nova Express* appears "irregularly (at least once a year) with coverage of cutting edge science fiction, fantasy and horror literature, with an emphasis on post-cyperpunk and slipstream. We feature interviews, reviews, fiction, poetry, and serious (but nonacademic) critical articles on important issues and authors throughout the entire science fiction/fantasy/horror/slipstream field." They want "poetry relating to literature of the fantastic in some way." They have published poetry by Alison Wimsatt and Mark McLaughlin. As a sample we selected these lines from "The Weatherworn Banshee Declares Her Undying Love For Some Accountant She Met At A Party" by Mark McLaughlin:

> *The others threw dip and salsa at me/until you, my darling, told them to stop./These hands, callused*
> *and scarred/from climbing rocks and tearing apart/wild dogs, long to hold you—and these lips,/puffy*
> *from sucking cracked rib-bones,/burn to slather you with love.*

The editor says *Nova Express* is 48 pgs., 8½×11, stapled, desktop-published with b&w graphics and line art. They receive about 20-30 poems a year, use approximately 1-2. Press run is 750 for 200 subscribers, 200 shelf sales; 200-300 distributed free to science fiction industry professionals. Subscription: $12. Sample: $5.

How to Submit: Submit up to 5 poems at a time. No previously published poems or simultaneous submissions. Cover letter preferred. E-mail submissions (in body of message) preferred, "they get the quickest response." Time between acceptance and publication is 3 months. Often comment on rejections. Publishes theme issues. Send SASE for guidelines or obtain via e-mail. Responds in 3 months. "Response will be slow until the slush pile is cleaned out." Sometimes sends prepublication galleys. Pays 2 copies plus 4-issue subscription. Acquires one-time rights.

Advice: "We are not interested in any poetry outside the science fiction/fantasy/horror genre. *Nova Express* is read widely and well regarded by genre professionals."

$ NOW & THEN (Specialized: regional, themes), ETSU, P.O. Box 70556, Johnson City TN 37614-0556, phone (423)439-5348, fax (423)439-6340, e-mail woodsidj@etsu.edu, website www.cass.etsu.edu/n&t/N&T.htm, founded 1984, editor-in-chief Jane Woodside, poetry editor Linda Parsons.

Magazine Needs: *Now & Then* is a regional magazine that covers Appalachian issues and culture. It contains fiction, poetry, articles, interviews, essays, memoirs, reviews, photos and drawings. The editor specifically wants poetry related to the region. "Each issue focuses on one aspect of life in the Appalachian region (anywhere hilly from Northern Mississippi on up to Southern New York). Previous theme issues have featured architecture, Appalachian lives, transportation, poetry, food and religion. We want genuine, well-crafted voices, not sentimentalized stereotypes." They have published poetry by Fred Chappell, Maggie Anderson, Robert Morgan and Lynn Powell. *Now & Then* appears 3 times/year and is 42 pgs., magazine-sized, saddle-stapled, professionally printed, with matte card cover. Its press run is 1,250-1,500 for 900 members of the Center for Appalachian Studies and Services, of which 100 are libraries. They accept 6-10 poems an issue. Center membership is $20; the magazine is one of the membership benefits. Sample: $7.50 postage.

How to Submit: They will consider simultaneous submissions; they occasionally use previously published poems. Submit up to 5 poems, with SASE and cover letter including "a few lines about yourself for a contributor's note and whether the work has been published or accepted elsewhere." Put name, address and phone number on every poem. Fax submissions OK. No e-mail submissions. Deadlines: March 1, July 1 and November 1. Publishes theme issues. Upcoming themes include "Rivers & Valleys" (deadline November 1), "Appalachian Accents" (deadline March 1) and "Museums & Archives" (deadline July 1). Send SASE for guidelines and upcoming themes or obtain via website. Editor prefers fax or e-mail to phone calls. Responds within 6 months. Sends prepublication galleys. Pays $10/poem plus 2 copies. Acquires all rights. Reviews books of poetry in 750 words. Open to unsolicited reviews. Send poetry directly to poetry editor Linda Parsons Marion, 2909 Fountain Park Blvd., Knoxville TN 37917. E-mail for correspondence lpmarion@utk.edu. Poets may also send books for review consideration to Sandy Ballard, book review editor, Dept. of English, Carson-Newman College, Box 2059, Jefferson City TN 37760, e-mail ballard@cncacc.cn.edu.

Also Offers: Sponsors a biennial poetry competition. Guidelines can be found at www.cass.etsu.edu/n&t/contest. htm. Website includes writer's guidelines, upcoming themes and contact information for submissions.

◻ ◎ **NUTHOUSE; TWIN RIVERS PRESS (Specialized: humor)**, P.O. Box 119, Ellenton FL 34222, website members.aol.com/Nuthous499/index.html, press founded 1989, magazine founded 1993, editor Ludwig Von Quirk.

Magazine Needs: *Nuthouse*, "amusements by and for delightfully diseased minds," appears every 6 weeks using humor of all kinds, including homespun and political. They simply want "humorous verse; virtually all genres considered." They have published poetry by Holly Day, Daveed Garstenstein-Ross and Don Webb. The editor says *Nuthouse* is 12 pgs., digest-sized and photocopied from desktop-published originals. They receive about 500 poems a year, accept approximately 100. Press run is 100 for 50 subscribers. Subscription: $5/5 issues. Sample: $1.

How to Submit: Previously published poems and simultaneous submissions OK. Time between acceptance and publication is 6-12 months. Often comments on rejections. Responds within 1 month. Pays 1 copy/poem. Acquires one-time rights.

✓ ♥ ◎ **O!!ZONE (Specialized: visual poetry, photography, collage)**, 1266 Fountain View, Houston TX 77057-2204, phone (713)784-2802, fax (713)789-5119, e-mail HarryBurrus@juno.com, founded 1993, editor/ publisher Harry Burrus.

Magazine Needs: *O!!Zone* is "an international literary-art zine featuring visual poetry, travel pieces, interviews, haiku, manifestos, and art. We are particularly intrigued by poets who also do photography (or draw or paint). We also do broadsides, publish small, modest saddle-stitched collections, and will consider book-length collections (on a collaborative basis) *as time and dinero permits*." They want visual poetry and collage. "I am interested in discovery and self-transcendence." No academic, traditional or rhyming poetry. They have published poetry by Demitry Babcuko, Willi Melnikov, Laura Ryder and Joel Lipman. The editor did not offer sample lines of poetry because he says, "*O!!Zone* needs to be seen." The editor says *O!!Zone* is 80-100 pgs., 8½×11, desktop-published, loaded with graphics. "Write for a catalog listing our titles. Our *O!!Zone 97, International Visual Poetry* ($25) and *O!!Zone 98* ($25) and *O!!Zone 99-00* ($25) are three anthologies that cover what's going on in international visual poetry."

How to Submit: Submit 3-6 poems at a time. No previously published poems or simultaneous submissions. No fax submissions. "Submissions of visual poetry via snail mail; textual poems may come by e-mail." Cover letter preferred. They have a large backlog, "but always open to surprises." Seldom comments on rejections. Send SASE for guidelines. Responds "soon." Pays 1-2 copies.

◻ ◻ ◎ **THE OAK (Specialized: fantasy, soft horror, mystery); THE ACORN (Specialized: children); THE GRAY SQUIRREL (Specialized: senior citizens); THE SHEPHERD (Specialized: inspirational)**, 1530 Seventh St., Rock Island IL 61201, phone (309)788-3980, poetry editor Betty Mowery.

Magazine Needs & How to Submit: *The Oak*, founded 1990, is a "publication for writers with poetry and fiction." They want poetry of "no more than 35 lines and fiction of no more than 500 words." No restrictions as to types and style, but no pornography. Also takes fantasy and soft horror." *The Oak* appears quarterly. Founded 1991, *The Gray Squirrel* is now included in *The Oak* and takes poetry of no more than 35 lines only from poets 60 years of age and up. They take more than half of about 100 poems received each year. Include a SASE or mss will not be returned. Press run is 250, with 10 going to libraries. Subscription: $10. Sample: $3. Make all checks payable to *The Oak*. Submit 5 poems at a time. Simultaneous submissions and previously published poems OK. Responds in 1 week. "*The Oak* does not pay in dollars or copies but you need not purchase to be published." Acquires first or second rights. *The Oak* holds several contests. Send SASE for guidelines.

Magazine Needs & How to Submit: *The Acorn*, founded 1988, is a "newsletter for young authors and teachers or anyone else interested in our young authors. Takes mss from kids K-12th grades. Poetry no more than 35 lines. It also takes fiction of no more than 500 words." It appears 4 times/year and "we take well over half of submitted mss." Press run is 100, with 6 going to libraries. Subscription: $10. Sample: $3. Make all checks payable to *The Oak*. Submit 5 poems at a time. Simultaneous submissions and previously published poems OK. Responds in 1 week. "*The Acorn* does not pay in dollars or copies but you need not purchase to be published." Acquires first or second rights. Young authors, submitting to *The Acorn*, should put either age or grade on manuscripts. *The Shepherd*, founded 1996, is a quarterly publishing inspirational poetry from all ages. Poems may be up to 35 lines. "We want something with a message but not preachy." Subscription: $10. Sample: $3. Include SASE with all submissions.

Also Offers: Sponsors numerous contests. Send SASE for guidelines.

Advice: "Beginning poets should submit again as quickly as possible if rejected. Study the market: don't submit blind. Always include a SASE or rejected manuscripts will not be returned. Please make checks for *all* publications payable to *The Oak*."

$ ▯ ◩ OASIS, P.O. Box 626, Largo FL 33779-0626, phone (727)449-2186, e-mail oasislit@aol.com, website www.litline.org, founded 1992, editor Neal Storrs.

Magazine Needs: *Oasis* is a quarterly forum for high quality literary prose and poetry written almost exclusively by freelancers. Usually contains 6 prose pieces and the work of 4-5 poets. They want "to see poetry of stylistic beauty. Prefer free verse with a distinct, subtle music. No superficial sentimentality, old-fashioned rhymes or rhythms." Also accepts poetry written by children. They have published poetry by Carolyn Stoloff, Fredrick Zydek and Kim Bridgford. As a sample the editor selected these lines from "The Lightning Speech of Birds" by Corrine DeWinter:

> But now I must comply, twisting away from the clawed/lovers, shrinking from the familiar habits/of all three wives who have built cities and spires/under my skin/from the expectant crucifixions on the shoulder of the roads,/from the blessed damned on Venus' blushing sands.

Oasis is about 75 pgs., 7 × 10, attractively printed on heavy book paper, perfect-bound with medium-weight card cover, no art. They receive about 2,000 poems a year, accept approximately 1%. Press run is 300 for 90 subscribers of which 5 are libraries. Subscription: $20/year. Sample: $7.50.

How to Submit: Submit any number of poems. Rarely accepts previously published poems; simultaneous submissions OK. E-mail submissions OK (include in body of message). Cover letter preferred. Time between acceptance and publication is usually 4 months. Seldom comments on rejections. Send SASE for guidelines. Responds "the same or following day more than 99% of the time." Sometimes sends prepublication galleys. Pays 1 copy and $5/poem. Buys first or one-time rights.

Ⓝ ⊕ ◩ OASIS BOOKS; OASIS MAGAZINE (Specialized: translations), 12 Stevenage Rd., London SW6 6ES England, founded 1969, editor/publisher Ian Robinson.

Magazine Needs: *Oasis Magazine* is a bimonthly of short fiction and poetry as well as occasional reviews and other material. "No preference for style or subject matter; just quality. No long poems; *Oasis* is a very short magazine. Also, usually no rhyming poetry." They have published *Among Memory's Ruins* by Zdenek Vanicek; *From Far Away* by Harry Gilonis and Tony Baker and poetry by Andrea Moorhead, Peter Riley and Aline Willen. The editor says *Oasis* is international A5 size, litho, folded sheets. They receive 500-600 poems a year, use about 4 or 5. Press run is 500 for 400 subscribers of which 10 are libraries. Subscription: $20/6 issues. Sample: $3.50 (US). Make checks payable to Robert Vas Dias.

How to Submit: Submit up to 6 poems at a time. Previously published poems sometimes OK; simultaneous submissions OK "if work comes from outside the U.K." Include SAE and 4 IRCs for return (US postage is not valid). Seldom comments on rejections. Publishes theme issues. Send SAE and IRC (US postage is not valid) for a list of upcoming themes. Responds in 1 month. Pays up to 5 copies. Staff reviews books of poetry. Send books for review consideration.

Book/Chapbook Needs & How to Submit: Oasis Books publishes 2-3 paperbacks and 2-3 chapbooks/year. They have published *Flecks* by Ralph Hawkins; *Anxious to Please* by Nicholas Moore; and *3,600 Weekends* by Ken Edwards. Replies to queries and mss in 1 month. For sample books or chapbooks, write for catalog. "No more book or chapbook publications are planned for the next two years."

Advice: "One IRC (U.S. postage is not valid) is not enough to ensure return airmail postage; four will, provided manuscript is not too thick. No return postage will ensure that the ms is junked. It's best to write first before submitting (include 2 IRCs for reply)."

$ ▣ OBLATES (Specialized: religious, spirituality/inspirational), Missionary Association of Mary Immaculate, 9480 N. De Mazenod Dr., Belleville IL 62223-1160, phone (618)398-7640, ext. 3333, editor Christine Portell, mss editor Mary Mohrman.

Magazine Needs: *Oblates* is a bimonthly magazine circulating free to 500,000 benefactors. "We use well-written, perceptive traditional verse, average 12 lines. Avoid heavy allusions. We prefer a reverent, inspirational tone, but not overly 'sectarian and scriptural' in content." They have published poetry by Jean Conder Soule, Carlton J. Duncan and Jeanette M. Land. *Oblates* is 24 pgs., digest-sized, saddle-stapled, using color inside and on the cover. Sample and guidelines for SAE and 2 first-class stamps.

How to Submit: Submit up to 2 poems at a time. Considers simultaneous submissions. Time between acceptance and publication "is usually within 1 to 2 years." Editor comments "occasionally, but always when ms 'just missed or when a writer shows promise.' " Responds within 6 weeks. Pays $50 plus 3 copies. Buys first North American serial rights.

Advice: "We are a small publication very open to mss from authors—beginners and professionals. We do, however, demand professional quality work. Poets need to study our publication, and to send no more than one or two poems at a time. Content must be relevant to our older audience to inspire and motivate in a positive manner."

$ ⬖ ◎ OCEAN VIEW BOOKS (Specialized: form/style, science fiction), P.O. Box 102650, Denver CO 80250, fax (780)413-1538, founded 1981, editor Lee Ballentine.

Book/Chapbook Needs: Ocean View Books publishes "books of poetry by poets influenced by surrealism and science fiction." They publish 2 paperbacks and 2 hardbacks/year. No "confessional/predictable, self-referential poems." They have published poetry by Anselm Hollo, Janet Hamill and Tom Disch. Books are usually 100 pgs., $5\frac{1}{2} \times 8\frac{1}{2}$ or 6×9, offset printed and perfect-bound with 4-color card cover, includes art. "Our books are distinctive in style and format. Interested poets should order a sample book for $5 (in the US) for an idea of our focus before submitting." Subscription: $18/year.

How to Submit: Submit a book project query including 5 poems. Previously published poems and simultaneous submissions OK. Cover letter preferred. Time between acceptance and publication is 1-3 years. "If our editors recommend publication, we may circulate manuscripts to distinguished outside readers for an additional opinion. The volume of submissions is such that we can respond to queries only if we are interested in the project. If we're interested we will contact you within 4 months." Pays $100 honorarium and a number of author's copies (out of a press run of 500). "Terms vary per project."

Advice: "In 15 years, we have published about 40 books—most consisted of previously published poems from good journals. A poet's 'career' must be well-established before undertaking a book."

☑ ▣ ⬖ OCTAVO; THE ALSOP REVIEW, e-mail manaster@alsopreview.com, website www.alsoprevie w.com/, founded 1998, editor Jamie Wasserman, founder Jaimes Alsop.

Magazine Needs: *Octavo* is a monthly Web publication and "contains 8 poems/stories per issue. It aims to merge the print and Web world, to bring established print writers to the Web and highlight those writers whose reputations are still word-of-mouth." They want "well-crafted verse with a strong voice. No pornography; overtly religious work, greeting card verse or sloppy writing." They have published poetry by Dorianne Laux, Kim Addonizio, Lola Haskins and Peter Johnson. As a sample the editors selected these lines from "Medievalism" by Ronald Donn:

> And the great theme is great/because you run from it,/in this world like water,/like skin—rush over
> muscle,/settle at the bottom into/the shape of a man.

They receive about 1,000 poems a year, accept approximately 2%.

How to Submit: Submit 3-5 poems at a time. No previously published poems; simultaneous submissions OK. Cover letter preferred. "Submissions may only be sent via e-mail in body of message." Time between acceptance and publication is 1 month. Seldom comments on rejections. Obtain guidelines via e-mail. Responds in 1 month. Acquires first rights.

Also Offers: "*Octavo* is a monthly magazine of the *Alsop Review*, a website that showcases literary works by some of today's premiere writers, including Carolyn Kizer, Barry Spacks, Andrew Hudgins and Roberts Ward." Website includes guidelines, writer's workshop, poetry chat room and book reviews.

Advice: "The Web is rapidly becoming the new medium of choice for some of today's top writers. Take Internet submissions seriously and support the online literary community by exploring the myriad of sites out there."

☑ $ ◻ ◎ OF UNICORNS AND SPACE STATIONS (Specialized: science fiction/fantasy), P.O. Box 200, Bountiful UT 84011-0200, e-mail gene@genedavis.com, website www.genedavis.com/magazine, founded 1994, editor Gene Davis.

Magazine Needs: *OUASS*, published biannually, features science fiction/fantasy literature. "Material written in traditional fixed forms are given preference. Poetry of only a scientific slant or that only uses science fiction/ fantasy imagery will be considered." Also accepts poetry written by children. *OUASS* is 60 pgs., digest-sized, digital press, saddle-stitched with "spot color" illustrated card cover. They receive about 200 poems a year, accept approximately 2%. Press run is 100 for 100 subscribers; 2-3 distributed free to convention organizers and critics. Subscription: $16/4 issues. Sample: $4. Make checks payable to Gene Davis.

How to Submit: Submit 3 poems, with name and address on each page. "Manuscripts should be paper-clipped, never stapled." Previously published poems OK; no simultaneous submissions. E-mail submissions are only accepted from subscribers. Cover letter preferred. "If sending fixed form poetry, mention what form you used in your cover letter. Editors pulling 16-hour shifts don't always spot poem types at 1 a.m." Time between acceptance and publication is 6-9 months. Poems are circulated to an editorial board of 2 editors. "Both have veto power over every piece." Seldom comments on rejections. Send SASE for guidelines. Responds in 3 months. Pays 1 copy and "$5 flat rate for poetry." Acquires one-time rights.

Also Offers: The magazine is available on the website along with writer's guidelines.

☑ ◎ OFF THE ROCKS (Specialized: gay/lesbian), 921 West Argyle #1 West, Chicago IL 60640, e-mail offtherocks@home.com, website www.newtownwriters.org/, founded 1980, president (Newtown Writers) Randy Gresham, editor (*Off The Rocks*) Larry Lesperance.

Magazine Needs: *Off The Rocks*, a publication of Newtown Writers, is an annual and publishes poetry focused on gay/lesbian subjects. They want "all forms, 30 lines or less." They have published poetry by Robert Klein Engler, Adrian Ford, Gerald Wozek and Judy McCormick. As a sample the editor selected these lines from "Door Colmel" (poet unidentified):

> You rang my bell/later on we lay/in the light of the alien t.v./at 5:00/alone I heard the self-same note/
> float in my dream . . .

The editor says *OTR* is about 50 pgs., 8×11, staple-bound with art/graphics, no ads. They receive about 100 poems a year, accept approximately 20%. Press run is 1,000, almost all shelf sales. Single copy: $5. Sample: $2. Make checks payable to Newtown Writers, Inc.

How to Submit: Submit 5 poems at a time. Previously published poems and simultaneous submissions OK. Cover letter preferred including bio and list of previously published work. Time between acceptance and publication is 1 year. Poems are circulated to an editorial board. "There is discussion of poem's merits, debate, rebuttal, then voting on poems to be published." Often comments on rejections. Obtain guidelines via e-mail or website. Responds in 3 months. Sometimes sends prepublication galleys. Pays 2 copies.

◯ ◑ OFFERINGS, P.O. Box 1667, Lebanon MO 65536-1667, founded 1994, editor Velvet Fackeldey.
Magazine Needs: *Offerings* is a poetry quarterly. "We accept traditional and free verse from established and new poets, as well as students. Prefer poems of less than 30 lines. No erotica." They have published poetry by Michael Estabrook, Kent Braithwaite, Jocelyne Kamerer and Robert Hentz. As a sample the editor selected these lines from "Life Moves" by Joan Ritty:

> *Promotion-proud, he tells me/we're moving to Detroit./With a kiss, a glass of celebration,/I swallow*
> *friends again/and ice shards in my heart./Good-bye to all my buried bones:/doctors, dentists, churches,*
> *schools.//The world is full of/the same skies and other clouds,/the same people and other crowds,/*
> *spilled milk and curdled cream—/things are never what they seem . . .//the same sermon in other*
> *words/preached to my same other selves.*

Offerings is 50-60 pgs., digest-sized, neatly printed (one poem to a page) and saddle-stapled with paper cover. They receive about 500 poems a year, accept approximately 25%. Press run is 100 for 75 subscribers, 25 shelf sales. Single copy: $5; subscription: $16. Sample: $3.
How to Submit: Submit typed poems with name and address on each page. Students should also include grade level. SASE required. No simultaneous submissions. Seldom comments on rejections. Send SASE for guidelines. Responds in 2 weeks. All rights revert to author after publication.
Advice: "We are unable to offer payment at this time (not even copies) but hope to be able to do so in the future. We welcome beginning poets."

⟦N⟧ ⊕ ◑ ◎ OFFERTA SPECIALE; BERTOLA CARLA PRESS (Specialized: form/style), Corso De Nicola 20, 10-128 Torino Italy, website www.comune.torino.it/~gioco, founded 1988, director/editor Bertola Carla, co-director Vitacchio Alberto.
Magazine Needs: *Offerta Speciale* is a biannual international journal of experimental and visual poetry. They have published poetry by Federica Manfredini (Italy), Bernard Heidsieck (France), Richard Kostelanetz and E. Mycue (US). As a sample the editor selected these lines from "My lower back" by Sheila Murphy:

> *My lower back likes to be liquid/Dose of sugar ringside/And the thought of frost/As sacrosanct as*
> *meerschaum*

OS is 56 pgs., digest-sized, neatly printed and saddle-stitched with glossy card cover. They receive about 300 poems a year, accept approximately 40%. Press run is 500 for 60 subscribers. Single copy: $25; subscription: $100. Make checks payable to Carla Bertola.
How to Submit: Submit 3 poems at a time. No previously published poems or simultaneous submissions. Time between acceptance and publication is 1 year. Often comments on rejections. Send SASE (or SAE and IRC) for guidelines. Pays 1 copy.

⟦🍎⟧ ◑ ◎ OFFICE NUMBER ONE (Specialized: form), 1708 S. Congress Ave., Austin TX 78704, e-mail onocdingus@aol.com, founded 1988, editor Carlos B. Dingus.
Magazine Needs: Appearing 2-4 times/year, *ONO* is a "humorous, satirical zine of news information and events from parallel and alternate realities." In addition to stories, they want limericks, 3-5-3 or 5-7-5 haiku and rhymed/metered quatrains. "Poems should be short (2-12 lines) and make a point. No long rambling poetry about suffering and pathos. Poetry should be technically perfect." Also accepts poetry written by children. As for a sample, the editor says, "No one poem provides a fair sample." *ONO* is 12 pgs., 8½×11, computer set in 10 pt. type, saddle-stitched, with graphics and ads. They use about 40 poems a year. Press run is 2,000 for 75 subscribers, 50 shelf sales; 1,600 distributed free locally. Single copy: $1.85; subscription: $8.82/6 issues. Sample: $2.
How to Submit: Submit up to 5 pgs. of poetry at a time. Previously published poems and simultaneous submissions OK. E-mail submissions included in body of message OK. "Will comment on rejections if comment is requested." Publishes theme issues occasionally. Send SASE for guidelines and upcoming themes or request guidelines via e-mail. Responds in 2 months. Pays "23¢" and 1 copy. Buys "one-time use, and use in any *ONO* anthology."
Advice: "Say something that a person can use to change his life."

☑ $ ◐ THE OHIO REVIEW; OHIO REVIEW BOOKS, 344 Scott Quad, Ohio University, Athens OH 45701-2979, phone (740)593-1900, fax (740)597-2967, e-mail The.Ohio.Review@ohiou.edu, website www.ohiou.edu/theohioreview/, founded 1971, editor Wayne Dodd.
Magazine Needs: *The Ohio Review* appears 2 times/year and attempts "to publish the best in contemporary poetry, fiction and nonfiction. "Only criterion is excellence." Published poets include W.S. Merwin, Jane Miller,

Bin Ramke, Mary Oliver, Charles Wright, David St. John and Rosmarie Waldrop. *The Ohio Review* is professionally printed, flat-spined format of 200 pgs., 4-color glossy cover with art, circulation 3,000, featuring about 28 poets/issue. Receives about 3,000 submissions a year, uses approximately 1% of them. Subscription: $16. Sample: $6.

How to Submit: Include SASE with submissions and type name and address on each page of ms. Reads submissions September 15 through May 30 only. Editor sometimes comments on rejections. Send SASE for guidelines. Responds in 1 month. Always sends prepublication galleys. Pays $1/line for poems and $5/page for prose plus 2 copies. Buys first North American serial rights. Reviews books of poetry in 5-10 pgs., single or multi-book format. Send books to Review Editor for review consideration.

Also Offers: Website includes writer's guidelines, names of editors, table of contents from every issue, listings for Ohio Review Books, order information for subscriptions, back issues and special offers.

OHIO STATE UNIVERSITY PRESS/THE JOURNAL AWARD IN POETRY, 1070 Carmack Rd., Columbus OH 43210-1002, phone (614)292-4856, fax (614)292-2065, e-mail ohiostatepress@osu.edu, website www.ohiostatepress.org, poetry editor David Citino.

Book/Chapbook Needs & How to Submit: Each year *The Journal* (see listing also in this section) selects for publication by Ohio State University Press one full-length (at least 48 pgs.) book ms submitted during September, typed, double-spaced, $20 handling fee (payable to OSU). They have published *Heroic Measures* by David Bergman and *Troubled Lovers in History* by Albert Goldbarth. Send SASE for confirmation of ms receipt. Mss will not be returned. Some or all of the poems in the collection may have appeared in periodicals, chapbooks or anthologies, but must be identified. Along with publication, *The Journal* Award in Poetry pays $1,000 cash prize. Each entrant receives a subscription (2 issues) to *The Journal.*

OHIO TEACHERS WRITE (Specialized: work by teachers), English Dept., Youngstown State University, One University Plaza, Youngstown OH 44555-1001, phone (330)742-3421, fax (330)742-2304, e-mail htmccrac@cc.ysu.edu, founded 1995, *OTW* 2000 editor H. Thomas McCracken.

Magazine Needs: *Ohio Teachers Write* is published "to provide an annual collection of fine literature, to encourage teachers to compose literary works along with their students, and to provide Ohioans a window into the world of teaching." They want poems on any subject and in any style. Nothing X-rated. They have published poetry by Lou Suarez and Kathleen Burgess. As a sample the editor selected these lines from "fraternity summer" by Bill Newby:

> things in profusion/clothing that had multiplied in floor piles and on chairs/desk tops buried beneath
> last week's programs and yesterday's messages/and a wounded couch saved from a salvation suicide/
> waiting for one last couple to couple

OTW is 48 pgs., 5×8, offset printed and flat-spined with cardstock cover, includes original drawings, photos. They receive about 100 poems a year, accept approximately 30%. Press run is 2,000. Subscription: $6. Sample: $4. Make checks payable to Ohio Council of Teachers of English Language Arts. "Contributors must be in-training, active or retired Ohio teachers."

How to Submit: Submit 2 poems at a time, maximum. No previously published poems or simultaneous submissions. E-mail and disk submissions OK. "Please mail five copies and a SASE." Submissions must be received by June 1 for publication each October. Time between acceptance and publication is 3 months. Poems are circulated to an editorial board. "Members of an editorial board read work independently and then confer together to select work for publication." Seldom comments on rejections. Send SASE for guidelines. Responds in July or August. Pays 1 copy. Acquires first rights..

Advice: "*Ohio Teachers Write* is a ready vehicle for Ohio teachers to share their creative writing with the teaching community and others. Submission also prepares teachers to better help students with the challenges of writing and publication."

OLD CROW REVIEW, P.O. Box 403, East Hampton MA 01027-0403, founded 1990, editors John Gibney and Tawnya Kelley.

Magazine Needs: *Old Crow* is a biannual magazine with mythic concerns, "visions or fragments of visions of a new myth." It includes novel fragments, short stories, poems, essays, interviews, photography and art. They have no specifications regarding form, length, subject matter or style of poetry. They have published poetry by Michael Ventura, Simon Perchick and Patricia Martin. *Old Crow* is 100 pgs., digest-sized, neatly printed and perfect-bound with card cover. They receive about 1,000 submissions a year, accept 2-3%. Press run is 500. Subscription: $10/year. Sample: $5. Make check payable to John Gibney.

USE THE GENERAL INDEX, located at the back of this book, to find the page number of a specific publisher. Also, publishers that were listed in last year's edition but not included in this edition are listed in the General Index with a notation explaining why they were omitted.

How to Submit: Submit 3-6 poems at a time. Previously published poems and simultaneous submissions OK. Cover letter with brief bio (for Contributor's Notes) required. Reads submissions February 1 through July 30 and October 1 through December 15. Poems are screened by editorial assistants then the editorial board then the editor-in-chief (John Gibney). Seldom comments on rejections. Responds in 2 months. Pays 1 copy. Copyright reverts to poet at publication. Open to unsolicited reviews.

N **O** **THE OLD RED KIMONO**, Humanities Division, P.O. Box 1864, Floyd College, Rome GA 30162, phone (706)295-6312, founded 1972, poetry editors Jeffrey Mack, Dr. Nancy Applegate and Kelly Doegg.

Magazine Needs: *The Old Red Kimono* has the "sole purpose of putting out a magazine of original, high-quality poetry and fiction. *ORK* is looking for submissions of three to five short poems. Poems should be very concise and imagistic. Nothing sentimental or didactic." They have published poetry by Walter McDonald, Peter Huggins, Midred Greear, John C. Morrison, Jack Stewart, Kirsten Fox and Al Braselton. The magazine is an annual, circulation 1,400, 72 pgs., 8½×11, professionally printed on heavy stock with b&w graphics, colored matte cover with art, using approximately 40 pgs. of poetry (usually 1 or 2 poems to the page). They receive about 1,000 submissions a year, use approximately 60-70. Sample: $3.

How to Submit: Reads submissions September 1 through March 1 only. Responds in 3 months. Pays 2 copies. Acquires first publication rights.

$ **ON SPEC: MORE THAN JUST SCIENCE FICTION (Specialized: regional, science fiction/fantasy, horror)**, P.O. Box 4727, Edmonton, Alberta T6E 5G6 Canada, e-mail onspec@earthling.net, website www.icomm.ca/onspec/, founded 1989, poetry editor Barry Hammond.

Magazine Needs: *On Spec* is a quarterly featuring Canadian science fiction writers and artists. They want work by Canadian poets only and only science fiction/speculative poetry; 100 lines maximum. They have published poetry by Sandra Kasturi and Alice Major. As a sample the editor selected these lines from "Wild Things" by Eileen Kernaghan:

> you can sing small songs to soothe them/make them soft and secret beds to lie in//still you will wake
> in winter dawns/to find them crouched upon your pillow/their sharp claws unravelling/the frayed edges
> of your dreams

On Spec is 112 pgs., digest-sized, offset printed on recycled paper and perfect-bound with color cover, b&w art and ads inside. They receive about 100 poems a year, accept approximately 5%. Press run is 1,750 for 800 subscribers of which 10 are libraries, 600 shelf sales. Single copy: $4.95; subscription: $19.95 (both in Canadian funds). Sample: $6.

How to Submit: Submit up to 5 poems of up to 100 lines at a time with SASE (or SAE and IRC). No previously published poems or simultaneous submissions. No submissions via fax or e-mail. Cover letter with poem titles and 2-sentence bio required. Deadlines: February 28, May 31, August 31 and November 30. Responds in 4 months maximum. Time between acceptance and publication is 6 months. Usually comments on rejections. Publishes theme issues. Send SASE for guidelines and upcoming themes or check website. Pays $20/poem and 1 copy, pays on acceptance. Acquires first North American serial rights.

Also Offers: Website includes writer's guidelines, names and bios of editors, past editorials, excerpts from back issues, links for writers and announcements.

N **ONCE UPON A TIME (Specialized: poetry about writing or illustrating)**, 553 Winston Court, St. Paul MN 55118, phone (651)457-6223, fax (651)457-9565, e-mail audreyouat@aol.com, website http://members.aol.com/ouatmag, founded 1990, editor/publisher Audrey B. Baird.

Magazine Needs: Published quarterly, *Once Upon A Time* is a support magazine for children's writers and illustrators. Poetry should be 20 lines maximum—writing or illustration-related. "No poems comparing writing to giving birth to a baby. Very overdone!" As a sample the editor selected this poem, "Writer at Work" by Anita Hunter:

> Spent the morning in my writing room/Sharpened pencils/Threw out stencils/Cleaned up some files/
> And then, all smiles/Brought my latest manuscript to bloom./By adding one small comma./After lunch,
> for inspiration/I read some books/Thought up new "hooks"/Made out long lists/Cleared mental mists/
> And with true, keen dedication/Took out the one small comma.

The editor says *OUAT* is 32 pgs., magazine-sized, stapled with glossy cover, includes art/graphics and a few ads. They receive about 40 poems a year, accept approximately 60%. Press run is 1,000 for 900 subscribers. Single copy: $6; subscription: $24.25. Sample: $5. Make checks payable to Audrey B. Baird.

How to Submit: Submit no more than 6 poems at a time. Previously published poems and simultaneous submissions OK. Cover letter preferred. "Please advise if you can submit by e-mail if asked." Time between acceptance and publication "can be up to 2 years. Short poems usually printed in less than 1 year. Often comments on rejections. Send SASE for guidelines. Responds in 1 month. Pays 2 copies. Acquires one-time rights.

Also Offers: Website includes general subscription information, sample article snippets, description of magazine, representative artwork, sample covers, comments by subscribers, guidelines, etc., plus how to get a free 4-page brochure.

Advice: "Don't send your piece too quickly. Let it sit for a week or more. Then re-read it and see if you can make it better. If you're writing rhyming poetry, the rhythm has to work. Count syllables! Accents, too, have to fall in the right place! Most rhyming poetry I receive has terrible rhythm. Don't forget SASE!"

✔ ◐ **ONE TRICK PONY; BANSHEE PRESS**, P.O. Box 11186, Philadelphia PA 19136, phone (215)331-7389, e-mail lmckee4148@aol.com, founded 1997, editor Louis McKee.

Magazine Needs: *One Trick Pony* is published biannually and contains "poetry and poetry related reviews and essays (for reviews, essays, interviews, etc.—please query)." No limitations. They have published poetry by William Heyen, Naomi Shihab Nye, Denise Duhamel and Michael Waters. *OTP* is 60 pgs., 5½×8½, offset printed and saddle-stapled, glossy cover with art. They receive about 750 poems a year, accept approximately 10%. Press run is 400 for over 150 subscribers of which 12 are libraries, 150 shelf sales. Single copy: $5; subscription: $10/3 issues. Sample: $4. Make checks payable to Louis McKee.

How to Submit: Submit 3-6 poems at a time. No previously published poems; simultaneous submissions OK. Responds in 1 month. Pays 2 copies. Acquires first rights. Reviews books and chapbooks of poetry. Open to unsolicited reviews. Poets may also send books for review consideration.

Book/Chapbook Needs: Banshee Press publishes 1 chapbook/year. Chapbooks are *by invitation only*.

✔ ◐ **THE ONSET REVIEW**, P.O. Box 3157, Wareham MA 02571, phone/fax (508)291-1188, e-mail susnp @aol.com, website www.word-studio.com/the-onset-review, founded 1994, editors Susan Pizzolato and Scott Withiam.

Magazine Needs: *The Onset Review* is published biannually "to showcase the best new writing by new and published poets and writers." They are "interested in poetry that takes risks, experiments with language and provokes the imagination. No obviously rhymed poems, early drafts or work unsure of voice; no clichéd imagery." They have published poetry by Carole Simmons Oles, Mark Cox, Martha Collins, Michael Burkard, Kristin Lund, Marsha de laO and Joyce Peseroff. The editors say *TOR* is 76-150 pgs., magazine-sized, offset printed and perfect-bound with cover photo and artwork. They receive about 1,000 submissions a year, accept approximately 10%. Press run is 1,000.

How to Submit: No previously published work; simultaneous submissions OK. Disk submissions OK. Cover letter with bio notes preferred. Time between acceptance and publication is 3 months. Occasionally comments on rejections. Send SASE for guidelines. Sometimes sends prepublication galleys. Pays 2 copies. Acquires first rights. Staff reviews books and chapbooks of poetry in 500 words. Send books for review consideration. Sample copy: $5.

Also Offers: Website includes editors' address, copy of cover photo, brief description of journal and guidelines.

Advice: "Read as much as you can, then do something different."

◐ **ONTHEBUS; BOMBSHELTER PRESS**, P.O. Box 481266, Bicentennial Station, Los Angeles CA 90048, founded 1975, *ONTHEBUS* editor Jack Grapes, Bombshelter Press poetry editors Jack Grapes and Michael Andrews.

Magazine Needs: *ONTHEBUS* uses "contemporary mainstream poetry—no more than six (ten pgs. total) at a time. No rhymed, 19th Century traditional 'verse.'" They have published poetry by Charles Bukowski, Albert Goldbarth, Ai, Norman Dubie, Kate Braverman, Stephen Dobyns, Allen Ginsberg, David Mura, Richard Jones and Ernesto Cardenal. As a sample Jack Grapes selected "Splitting Hairs" by Joyce Elaine Ross:

> After I poured my blocks onto the floor and shuffled them,/then made one last attempt to attain some
> form of poetic/fusion, like William Grant Still's Afro-American Symphony/of classical blues on jazz, I
> realized that I've never been/able to get others to understand me; that my words always/seem to turn
> into fishbones and sawdust whenever I tried/to talk about it. And if I could, I would drink my own/
> skin, erase the stain of my colors.

ONTHEBUS is a magazine appearing 2 times/year, 275 pgs., offset printed, flat-spined, with color card cover. Press run is 3,500 for 600 subscribers of which 40 are libraries, 1,200 shelf sales ("500 sold directly at readings"). Subscription: $28/3 issues; Issue #8/9, special double issue: $15. Sample (including guidelines): $12.

How to Submit: Submit 3-6 poems at a time to the above address (send all other correspondence to: 6684 Colgate Ave., Los Angeles CA 90048). Simultaneous submissions and previously published poems OK, "if I am informed where poem has previously appeared and/or where poem is also being submitted. I expect neatly-typed, professional-looking cover letters with list of poems included plus poet's bio. Sloppiness and unprofessional submissions do not equate with great writing." Do not submit mss between November 1 and March 1 or between June 1 and September 1. Submissions sent during those times will be returned unread. Responds in "anywhere from two weeks to two years." Pays 1 copy. Acquires one-time rights. Reviews books of poetry in 400 words (chapbooks in 200 words), single format. Open to unsolicited reviews. Poets may also send books for review consideration.

Book/Chapbook Needs & How to Submit: Bombshelter Press publishes 4-6 flat-spined paperbacks and 5 chapbooks/year. Query first. Primarily interested in Los Angeles poets. "We publish very few unsolicited mss." Responds in 3 months. Pays 50 copies. They also publish the *ONTHEBUS* Poets Anthology Series. Send SASE for details.

Advice: "My goal is to publish a democratic range of American poets and ensure they are read by striving to circulate the magazine as widely as possible. It's hard work and a financial drain. I hope the mag is healthy for poets and writers, and that they support the endeavor by subscribing as well as submitting."

"Our name, *Open Spaces*, stands for openness of mind and thought," says Penny Harrison, president of the Portland, Oregon, quarterly. The cover illustration on Volume 2, Issue 1 is by Deborah DeWit Marchant, a Northwest artist who exhibits in galleries as well as her own studio. With her husband, Marchant also publishes her work in note card form under the company name "Simple Minds." To Harrison, Marchant's cover depicts "one of those comfortable moments in life that encourages good conversation and an open exchange of ideas." Poetry is highly valued at *Open Spaces*, says Harrison. "We try to present it with respect—on separate pages with appropriate graphics." *Open Spaces* is magazine-sized, 64 pages, sheet-fed printed, with cover art as well as graphics and original art throughout.

✔ ⊘ **OPEN HAND PUBLISHING INC.**, P.O. Box 22048, Seattle WA 98122-0048, phone (206)323-2187, fax (206)323-2188, e-mail openhand@jps.net, website www.openhand.com, founded 1981, publisher P. Anna Johnson. Open Hand is a "literary/political book publisher bringing out flat-spined paperbacks as well as cloth cover editions about African-American and multicultural issues." They do not consider unsolicited mss.

✔ ◉ **OPEN SPACES**, 6327 C SW Capitol Hwy., Suite 134, Portland OR 97201-1937, phone (503)227-5764, fax (503)227-3401, website www.open-spaces.com, founded 1997, poetry editor Susan Juve-Hu Bucharest.
Magazine Needs: "*Open Spaces* is a quarterly which gives voice to the Northwest on issues that are regional, national and international in scope. Our readership is thoughtful, intelligent, widely read and appreciative of ideas and writing of the highest quality. With that in mind, we seek thoughtful, well-researched articles and insightful fiction, reviews and poetry on a variety of subjects from a number of different viewpoints. Although we take ourselves seriously, we appreciate humor as well." The editor says the magazine is 64 pgs., magazine-sized, sheet-fed printed, cover art and graphics and original art throughout. "We have received many submissions and hope to use 3-4 per issue." Press run is 5,000-10,000. Subscription: $25/year. Sample: $10. Make checks payable to Open Spaces Publications, Inc.
How to Submit: Submit 3-5 poems at a time. Previously published poems and simultaneous submissions OK. Cover letter required. Time between acceptance and publication is 2-3 months. Poems are circulated to an editorial board. Seldom comments on rejections. Responds in 3 months. Payment varies. Reviews books and chapbooks of poetry and other magazines in 300 words, single book format. "We solicit reviews."
Also Offers: Website includes submission guidelines, table of contents, covers, sample articles and literary essays and overview.
Advice: "Poets we have published include Vern Rutsala, Pattiann Rogers, Lou Masson and William Jolliff. Poetry is presented with care and respect."

⬛ ◎ **OPEN UNIVERSITY OF AMERICA PRESS; OPEN UNIVERSITY OF AMERICA (Specialized: religious, nature, distance learning, English pedagogy)**, 3916 Commander Dr., Hyattsville MD 20782-1027, phone/fax (301)779-0220, e-mail openuniv@aol.com, website www.openuniversityofamerica.com, founded 1965, co-editors Mary Rodgers and Dan Rodgers.
Book/Chapbook Needs: "We buy artistic work outright before copyright or publication by the author. We include these literary pieces always with the author's name in our university publications, catalogues, lists, etc." They publish 4 paperbacks and 4 hardbacks/year. They have "no restrictions on poetry. Shorter is better. One page set up for 6×9 is good. A set of poems (short chapbook) should be uniform." They are interested in receiving work on the topics of "Catholic faith and culture; morality; nature; open learning and English pedagogy (teaching English) K-Ph.D. Pre-published or pre-copyrighted or book-length poems are beyond our capability." Also accepts poetry written by children (negotiations only with parent, however). They have published poetry by Castina Kennedy, John Tormento, Emebeat Bekele and Raphael Flores. As a sample the editors selected this poem, "Reality," by Rosalee Dansan in *Catholic Teacher Poems, 1945-1995:*

> Yesterday/I had dreams of tomorrow./Somewhere in tomorrowland,/Life with you./But dreams shatter/
> Like glass;/Like mine did when halfway to my mouth,/Before I could taste the sweetness of the wine./
> Today/I do not dream./I have no guarantee of tomorrow/For today I have only today.

Books are usually 100-200 pgs., 6×9, computer/laser printed, perfect-bound (some sewn in library binding), soft cover, includes art.

How to Submit: Submit up to 10 poems at a time. No previously published poems or simultaneous submissions. Cover letter preferred. "We buy poems and small sets of poems outright (price negotiable), so we need pre-copyrighted, pre-published literary work. No whole books. When we publish compilations, we always list the name of the artist/author. Literary work is accepted on its own merit and its usefulness in perpetuity to the Press and to Open University of America. Make sure you want to put your poem for final and irrevocable sale." Reading fee: $1/poem. Time between acceptance and publication is 1-2 years. Poems are circulated to an editorial board. "Two editors plus one consultant select work to be purchased for publication. Note that we purchase all rights for publication, total rights." Seldom comments on rejections. Replies to queries and mss in 2-3 weeks. Order sample books by sending $10 or order off the web.

Advice: "Today electronic publishing, overseas sales, and other mass selling mechanisms are running rough-shod over the rights of writers. We buy your verbal art at a fair, negotiated price before copyright and publication. We use your poem/poems always with your name attached to enhance our literary productions. We keep it in perpetuity in our Literary Trust. This is an effective way to get publicity for your name and your work, as well as to earn income."

[N] ◯ ◒ OPENED EYES POETRY & PROSE MAGAZINE; KENYA BLUE POETRY AWARD CONTEST; OPENED EYES AWARD CONTEST; HAIKU CONTEST, P.O. Box 21708, Brooklyn NY 11202-1708, phone (917)921-5662, e-mail kenyablue@excite.com or openedeyes@juno.com, website www.kenyablue.com, founded 1998, editor-in-chief Kenya Blue.

Magazine Needs: Appearing 3 times a year, *Opened Eyes* is a "venue for seniors, known poets, novice poets and minority poets; offering a supportive environment and challenging environment." They want "free verse, traditional forms; prose—all styles; all subject matter; short, poetic stories. No hate or sexually explicit/graphic poetry." They have published poetry by Lynette Grant, Jay Chollick, Evie Ivy, Sol Rubin, Jihad Qasim and Tom Oleszczuk. As a sample the editor selected these lines from "Inspiration" by Kenya Blue:

> Inspiration is what you give me/Because of you I dare to soar/Dare to be adventuresome/Dare to be
> me/You are my sunrise/My sunset.

The editor says *Opened Eyes* is 8½×11, photocopied and either strip-bound or comb-bound with cardstock cover, includes art/graphics and ads. They receive about 40 poems a year, accept approximately 95%. Publish 15 poems/issue. Press run is 100 for 45 subscribers of which 5 are libraries, 24 shelf sales; 4 distributed free to Poet's House. Subscription: $18/year. Sample: $7. Make checks payable to Y. Walker.

How to Submit: Submit 1-3 poems at a time with $3 reading fee if nonsubscriber. Line length for poetry is 30 maximum. Previously published poems and simultaneous submissions OK. E-mail submissions OK. "Type name, address and e-mail in upper left hand corner. Submit typed poem in desired format for magazine and editor will try to accommodate." Time between acceptance and publication is 1-2 months. "Poems are circulated to editor and poetry consultant." Publishes theme issues occasionally. Send SASE for guidelines and upcoming themes. Responds in 3 weeks. Sometimes sends prepublication galleys. Acquires one-time rights.

Also Offers: "We sponsor one contest per issue, i.e., Kenya Blue Poetry Award (open to subscribers only) contest, haiku contest, and Opened Eyes Award contest. One winner per contest paid in one year subscription and featured write-up. Opened Eyes Award, Kenya Blue Award and haiku contest topics change yearly. In addition to a 1-year subscription and featured write-up, Kenya Blue Poetry Award offers a monetary prize to 1st- and 2nd-place winners."

Advice: "Challenge yourself and take a first step in being creative via literature and via poetry."

☑ ◯ ◒ ◎ ORACLE POETRY; ASSOCIATION OF AFRICAN WRITERS; RISING STAR PUB-LISHERS (Specialized: ethnic), 2105 Amherst Rd., Hyattsville MD 20783, founded 1989, contact Sam Okere.

Magazine Needs: *Oracle Poetry* appears quarterly using works "mainly of African orientation; must be probing and must have meaning—any style or form. Writers must have the language of discourse and good punctuation. No gay, lesbian or erotic poetry." Membership in the Association of African Writers is $20/year. *Oracle Poetry* is 46 pgs., digest-sized, saddle-stapled, print run 500. Subscription: $20/year.

How to Submit: No previously published poems or simultaneous submissions. "Poets may submit materials by fax; however, we prefer submissions by disk in WordPerfect 5.1, or in copies." Responds in up to 6 weeks. Pays 1 copy. Acquires first North American serial rights. Reviews books of poetry.

Also Offers: Sponsors contests. Send SASE for details.

Advice: "Read widely, write well and punctuate right."

◒ ORANGE WILLOW REVIEW, P.O. Box 768, Island Lake IL 60042, fax (847)487-6619, e-mail changeling@ameritech.net, founded 1998, editor/publisher Cynthia Warryn Leffner.

Magazine Needs: The *OWR* appears 2-4 times a year and "is a magazine of the arts, literature and psychology which strives to publish work reflecting creativity, originality, craft, intelligence and the ability to take risks with literature. The magazine was founded for humanity about humanity and attempts to show the value of the human experience. We like the surreal, the eclectic, and the deeply psychological. We want to see poetry that utilizes language and vivid, visual imagery to convey an involuntary, inherent response to the world; moments of 'poetic seizure.' The *Orange Willow Review* is a magazine published in memory of Van Gogh and others like him." No pornography or greeting card verse. They have published poetry by Ray Greenblatt and Thomas Catterson. As a sample the editor selected these lines from "China Sequence" by Ray Greenblatt:

> *Rain draws maps on windows/tea leaves swim in green cups/crows feet walk/across newspapers./*
> *Wearing caps of mist/rice paddies lie green and silent/by water subdivided,/a person bookmarking/*
> *each field./Buildings with pagoda roofs/and yards of rubbish/crumbling beside high rises/town after*
> *town.*

The editor says *OWR* is 100-122 pgs., 5½×8½, offset printed and perfect-bound with glossy color text weight cover, includes pen & ink, sketches, computer graphics, oil paint (fine art on cover), ads. Press run is 500. Subscription: $14. Sample: $3. Make checks payable to Cynthia Warryn Leffner.

How to Submit: Submit 6-10 poems at a time. No previously published poems; simultaneous submissions OK. Cover letter with bio and SASE preferred. Disk submissions OK. "We accept poems written in any style, any form, any length. If poems are more than 4 double-spaced pages please only send 3." Time between acceptance and publication is 3 months, "usually sooner. Presently, all work is reviewed by myself and one other assistant. However, we are in the process of adding a review board from members of our writer's groups and workshops." Always comments on rejections. Publishes theme issues occasionally. Send SASE for guidelines and upcoming themes. Responds in 3 months. Sometimes sends prepublication galleys. Pays 2 copies. Acquires first North American serial rights.

Also Offers: Sponsors contests. "We will publish a special issue on 'the artistic experience, mental illness and transcending suffering through art.' We may pay cash awards if funds allow. We are a nonprofit organization. Also, we will expand in the year 2000 to publishing chapbooks."

Advice: "We encourage beginners to keep writing and many times comment on rejections. If we especially see promise in a group of poems or a fiction piece, we often ask writers to send us more of his/her best."

🌐 $🖸 ORBIS: AN INTERNATIONAL QUARTERLY OF POETRY AND PROSE, 27 Valley View, Primrose, Jarrow, Tyne-and-Wear NE32 5QT United Kingdom, phone 44 0191-489-7055, fax 44 0191-430-1297, e-mail mikeshields@compuserve.com, founded 1968, editor Mike Shields.

Magazine Needs: *Orbis* considers "all poetry so long as it's genuine in feeling and well executed of its type." They have published poetry by Sir John Betjeman, Ray Bradbury, Seamus Heaney and Naomi Mitchison, as well as US poets Levertov, Piercy, Bell, Geddes, Wilbur, Kumin and many others, "but are just as likely to publish absolute unknowns." The quarterly is 64 pgs. minimum, 6×8½, flat-spined with glossy card cover. They receive "thousands" of submissions a year, use "less than 2%." Press run is 1,000 for 600 subscribers of which 50 are libraries. Single copy: £3.95 ($6); subscription: £15 ($28). Sample: $2 (or £1).

How to Submit: Submit 1 poem/sheet, typed on 1 side only. No bio, no query. No fax or e-mail submissions. Enclose IRCs for reply, not US postage. Responds in 2 months. Pays $10 or more/acceptance plus 1 free copy. Each issue carries £50 in prizes paid on basis of reader votes. Editor comments on rejections "occasionally—if we think we can help. *Orbis* is completely independent and receives no grant-aid from anywhere."

$🖸 ORCHISES PRESS, P.O. Box 20602, Alexandria VA 22320-1602, e-mail rlathbur@osf1.gmu.edu, website http://mason.gmu.edu/~rlathbur, founded 1983, poetry editor Roger Lathbury.

Book/Chapbook Needs: Orchises is a small press publisher of literary and general material in flat-spined paperbacks and in hardcover. "Although we will consider mss submitted, we prefer to seek out the work of poets who interest us." Regarding poetry he states: "No restrictions, really; but it must be technically proficient and deeply felt. I find it increasingly unlikely that I would publish a ms unless a fair proportion of its contents has appeared previously in respected literary journals." He has published *What She Knew* by Peter Filkins and *Believe It or Not* by Jean Monahan. He publishes about 4 flat-spined paperbacks of poetry a year, averaging 96 pgs., and some casebound books. Most paperbacks are $12.95. Hardbacks are $20-21.95 each.

How to Submit: Submit 5-6 poems at a time. No e-mail submissions. Poems must be typed. When submitting, "tell where poems have previously been published." Brief cover letter preferred. Obtain guidelines via website. Responds in 1 month. Pays 36% of money earned once Orchises recoups its initial costs and has a "generous free copy policy."

Also Offers: Website includes submission guidelines, sample poems, book covers and online catalog.

◪ ◎ OSIRIS, AN INTERNATIONAL POETRY JOURNAL/UNE REVUE INTERNATIONALE (Specialized: translations, bilingual), P.O. Box 297, Deerfield MA 01342-0297, founded 1972, poetry editor Andrea Moorhead.

Magazine Needs: *Osiris* is a semiannual that publishes contemporary poetry in English, French and Italian without translation and in other languages with translation, including Polish, Danish and German. They want poetry which is "lyrical, non-narrative, multi-temporal, post-modern, well-crafted. Also looking for translations from non-IndoEuropean languages." They have published poetry by Robert Marteau (France), D.G. Jones (Canada), Vassilis Amanatidis (Greece), Flavio Ermini (Italy) and Ingrid Swanberg (US) As a sample the editor selected these lines from "Abstract As Air" by D.G. Jones:

> *the whorl of intricate grass/in the grass, almost nothing, an/abstraction from song.*

Osiris is 40 pgs., 6×9, saddle-stapled with graphics and photos. There are 15-20 pgs. of poetry in English in each issue of this publication. Print run is 500 with 50 subscription copies sent to college and university libraries, including foreign libraries. They receive 200-300 submissions a year, use approximately 12. Single copy: $6; subscription: $12. Sample: $3.

How to Submit: Submit 4-6 poems at a time. "Poems should be sent regular mail." Include short bio and SASE with submission. "Translators should include a letter of permission from the poet or publisher as well as copies of the original text." Responds in 1 month. Sometimes sends prepublication galleys. Pays 5 copies.

Advice: "It is always best to look at a sample copy of a journal before submitting work, and when you do submit work, do it often and do not get discouraged. Try to read poetry and support other writers."

$ ☑ ◎ THE OTHER SIDE MAGAZINE (Specialized: political, religious, social issues), 300 W. Apsley St., Philadelphia PA 19144, phone (215)849-2178, website www.theotherside.org, founded 1965, poetry editor Jeanne Minahan.

Magazine Needs: *The Other Side* is an independent ecumenical magazine that seeks to advance a broad Christian vision that's biblical and compassionate, appreciative of the creative arts, and committed to the intimate intertwining of personal spirituality and social transformation. We weave together first-person essays, insightful analyses, biblical reflection, interviews, fiction, poetry, and an inviting mix of visual art. We strive to nurture, uplift, and challenge readers with personal, provocative writing that reflects the transformative, liberating Spirit of Jesus Christ." The magazine publishes 1-2 poems/issue. "Poetry submissions should include strong imagery, fresh viewpoints, and lively language, while avoiding versifications of religious instruction or syrupy piety. Be warned that only 0.5% of the poems reviewed are accepted." They have published poetry by Kathleen Norris, Paul Ramsey, Carol Hamilton and John Knoepfle. *The Other Side* is magazine-sized, professionally printed on quality pulp stock, 64 pgs., saddle-stapled, with full-color paper cover. Circulation is 13,000 to that many subscriptions. Subscription: $24. Sample: $4.50.

How to Submit: Submit 3 poems at a time. Line length for poetry is 50 maximum. No previously published poems or simultaneous submissions. Editor "almost never" comments on rejections. Send SASE for guidelines. Responds in 2 months. Pays $15 plus 2 copies and 2-year subscription.

🍁 ✔ $ ◎ OUR FAMILY (Specialized: religious, social issues, spirituality/inspirational, themes, family/marriage/parenting), Box 249, Battleford, Saskatchewan S0M 0E0 Canada, phone (306)937-7771, fax (306)937-7644, e-mail editor@ourfamilymagazine.com, website www.ourfamilymagazine.com, founded 1949, editor Marie-Louise Ternier-Gommers.

Magazine Needs: *Our Family* is a monthly religious magazine for Roman Catholic families. "Any form of poetry is acceptable. In content we look for simplicity and vividness of imagery. The subject matter should center on the human struggle to live out one's relationship with the God of the Bible in the context of our modern world. We do not want to see science fiction poetry, metaphysical speculation poetry, or anything that demeans or belittles the spirit of human beings or degrades the image of God in him/her as it is described in the Bible." They have published poetry by Nadene Murphy and Arthur Stilwell. *Our Family* is 40 pgs., magazine-sized, glossy color paper cover, using drawings, cartoons, two-color ink. Circulation is 10,000 of which 48 are libraries. Single copy: $2; subscription: $17.95 Canada, $23.95 US. Sample: $3.

How to Submit: Will consider poems of 4-30 lines. Simultaneous submissions OK. E-mail and fax submissions OK. "Please include submission in the body of the e-mail. No attachments!" Send SASE or SAE with IRC or personal check for $1.25 (American postage cannot be used in Canada) for writer's guidelines and upcoming themes. Responds within 1 month after receipt. Pays 75¢/line.

Advice: "The essence of poetry is imagery. The form is less important. Really good poets use both effectively."

▣ ◯ ◪ ◎ OUR JOURNEY (Specialized: recovery issues), PMB #327, 16016 SE Division, Portland OR 97236, e-mail wendy@zzz.com, website www.geocities.com/HotSprings/Spa/1416/ourjourney.htm, founded 1994, editor Wendy Apgar.

● *Our Journey* is interested in receiving poetry about hope and healing which are topics included in every issue.

Magazine Needs: Published by Our Journey, Inc., a 501(c)(3) tax deductable, nonprofit corporation, *Our Journey* is a quarterly newsletter featuring "poetry, articles, original art, and occasional book reviews by those involved or interested in the recovery process." They want "recovery-based poetry; all inclusive, not limited to recovery of only one (e.g., addictions, incest, pain, abuse, anger, healing, etc.); will consider any length. Each issue has specific topics. No poetry which is not easily understood or which is inappropriately sexually graphic (query editor if unsure about specific poem or essay)." Also accepts poetry written by children. They have published poetry by Marge Rogers, Sheila Roark and Heidi Sands. As a sample the editor selected this poem, "Charm" by Nancy Martindale:

> *Without a word he stole/her eight-year-old, unformed,/untried soul./Why did he desire such a trinket?/*
> *Just another charm/for his bracelet.*

Our Journey is 14-18 pgs., neatly printed on bond paper and corner stapled, no cover, contains clip art. They receive about 250-300 poems a year, accept approximately 70%. Press run is 225 for 70 subscribers. Single copy: $2.50; subscription: $10/year, $12 Canada, $15 overseas. Sample: $1.50.

How to Submit: Submit any number of poems; 1/page, typed with name and address in upper left corner. "Only mss with #10 SASE will be acknowledged or returned." Previously published poems and simultaneous submissions OK. E-mail submissions OK (include in body of message). Cover letter preferred. "Material may also be submitted via e-mail. Two poems per each e-mail, but may send as many e-mail submissions as desire (i.e., 3 e-mails total 6 poems). If accepted for publication a hard copy must then be submitted via US mail with the completed release form which will be e-mailed upon acceptance." Time between acceptance and publication is within 1 year. If asked, will offer feedback. Publishes theme issues. Upcoming themes: March 2001: Addictions, Faith, Guilt & Shame; June 2001: Abuse, Masks, Grief; September 2001: Daily Struggle, Pain, Fear; December 2001: Depression, Loneliness, Anger. Send #10 SASE for guidelines. Responds in 6 weeks, "usually sooner." Pays 2 copies. Acquires one-time rights. Open to unsolicited reviews. Poets may send books for review consideration, if published.

Also Offers: Sponsors 2-4 annual contests for subscribers. Awards: 1st Prize-$20, 2nd Prize-$10, 3rd Prize-$5. Entry fee: $2/poem. Send #10 SASE for details. Website includes writer's guidelines, upcoming issue topics, contest guidelines, non-profit information and links to other recovery-based pages.

OUTER DARKNESS: WHERE NIGHTMARES ROAM UNLEASHED (Specialized: horror, mystery, science fiction, dark fantasy), 1312 N. Delaware Place, Tulsa OK 74110, phone (918)832-1246, founded 1994, editor Dennis J. Kirk.

Magazine Needs: *Outer Darkness* is a quarterly magazine featuring short stories, poetry and art in the genres of horror, mystery, dark fantasy and science fiction. They want "all styles of poetry, though traditional rhyming verse is preferred. Send verse that is dark and melancholy in nature. Nothing experimental—very little of this type of verse is published in *Outer Darkness*." They have published poetry by John Grey, Nancy Bennett, John Maclay and Corrine De Winter. *OD* is 40-60 pgs., 8½ × 5½, photocopied, saddle-stitched, glossy cover, includes cover art, cartoons and illustrations and runs ads for other publications. They receive about 200 poems a year, accept approximately 20%. Press run is 200, 25% to subscribers, 25% to contributors, 25% sample copy sales, 25% to advertisers, free copies, etc. Single copy: $3.95; subscription: $11.95.

How to Submit: Submit up to 3 poems at a time, no longer than 60 lines each. No previously published poems; simultaneous submissions OK. Cover letter preferred. "Poets are encouraged to include cover letters with their submissions, with biographical information, personal interests, past publishing credits, etc. I strongly prefer hardcopy submissions rather than disks." Always comments on rejections. Send SASE for guidelines. Responds in up to 6 weeks. Sends prepublication galleys, when requested. Pays 2 copies. Acquires one-time rights.

Advice: "I've noticed that interest in traditional metered verse is increasing. This is the type of poetry I feature most frequently in *OD*. Take time and care in writing verse. Maintain a consistent mood and tone; get the most you can out of each line, each word. This obviously takes more time; but, in the end, it will pay off."

OUTERBRIDGE, English A324, The College of Staten Island, 2800 Victory Blvd., Staten Island NY 10314, phone (718)982-3651, founded 1975, editor Charlotte Alexander.

Magazine Needs: *Outerbridge* publishes "the most crafted, professional poetry and short fiction we can find (unsolicited except special features—to date rural, urban and Southern, promoted in standard newsletters such as *Poets & Writers*, *AWP*, *Small Press Review*), interested in newer voices. Anti loose, amateurish, uncrafted poems showing little awareness of the long-established fundamentals of verse; also anti blatant PRO-movement writing when it sacrifices craft for protest and message. Poems usually one to four pgs. in length." They have published poetry by Walter McDonald, Thomas Swiss and Naomi Rachel. The digest-sized, flat-spined annual is 100 pgs., about half poetry. Press run is 500-600 for 150 subscribers of which 28 are libraries. They receive about 500-700 submissions a year, use approximately 60. Sample: $6.

How to Submit: Submit 3-5 poems only, anytime except June and July. Include name and address on each page. "We dislike simultaneous submissions and if a poem accepted by us proves to have already been accepted elsewhere, a poet will be blacklisted as there are many good poets waiting in line." Cover letter with brief bio preferred. Publishes theme issues. Send SASE for guidelines and upcoming themes. Responds in 2 months. Pays 2 copies (and offers additional copies at half price). Acquires first rights.

Advice: "As a poet/editor I feel magazines like *Outerbridge* provide an invaluable publication outlet for poets (particularly since publishing a book of poetry, respectably, is extremely difficult these days). As in all of the arts, poetry—its traditions, conventions and variations, experiments—should be studied. One current 'trend' I detect is a lot of mutual backscratching which can result in loose, amateurish writing. Discipline!"

OUTRIDER PRESS (Specialized: women/feminism, gay/lesbian/bisexual, anthology, humor), 937 Patricia Lane, Crete IL 60417-1362, fax (708)672-5820, e-mail outriderpr@aol.com, website www.outriderpress.com, founded 1988, senior editor Whitney Scott, president Phyllis Nelson.

Book/Chapbook Needs: Outrider publishes 1-3 novels/anthologies/chapbooks annually. They want "poetry dealing with the terrain of the human heart and plotting inner journeys; growth and grace under pressure. No bag ladies, loves-that-never-were, please." They have published poetry by Pamela Miller, Margo Tamez and Cynthia Gallaher. As a sample we selected these lines from "Geese in Coming Rain" by Lyn Lifshin, from the anthology *Feathers, Fins & Fur*:

THE SUBJECT INDEX, located at the back of this book, can help you select markets for your work. It lists those publishers whose poetry interests are specialized .

only a few blood/leaves on the maple./Grass nibbled closer//to the house. The/geese move in waves/
toward pewter, a/clot on the edge./Sky colorless on/the skin of water.

That book is 256 pgs., digest-sized, attractively printed and perfect-bound with glossy card cover, $15.95.

How to Submit: Submit 3-4 poems at a time with SASE. Include name, address and phone/fax number on every poem. Simultaneous submissions OK, if specified. Cover letter preferred. Responds to queries in 3 months, to mss in 6 months. Sometimes sends prepublication galleys. Pays 1 copy.

Also Offers: Outrider publishes a themed anthology annually in August, with cash prizes for best poetry and short fiction. Submit up to 4 poems, no longer than 1 page in length (single spacing OK). Reading fee: $16, $12 for Tallgrass Writers Guild members. Send SASE for guidelines. Deadline: January 31, 2001. Published in August 2001. Our 2001 theme: Romantic Love. The press is affiliated with the Tallgrass Writers Guild, an international organization open to all who support equality of voices in writing. Annual membership fee: $30. Send SASE for information or visit website. Website includes publication titles, prices, ordering information, general guidelines/ themes, address for complete guidelines, Tallgrass Writers Guild information and membership.

Advice: "We look for visceral truths expressed without compromise, coyness or cliché. Go for the center of the experience. Pull no punches."

$ ◎ "OVER THE BACK FENCE" MAGAZINE (Specialized: regional), P.O. Box 756, Chillicothe OH 45601, phone (740)772-2165, fax (740)773-7626, founded 1994, managing editor Sarah Williamson.

Magazine Needs: A quarterly regional magazine "serving nineteen counties in southern Ohio and 10 counties in Northern Ohio, *'Over The Back Fence'* has a wholesome, neighborly style that is appealing to readers from young adults to seniors." They want rhyming or free verse poetry, 24 lines or less; open to subject matter, "but seasonal works well"; friendly or inspirational work. "Since most of our readers are not poets, we want something simple and likeable by the general public. No profanity or erotic subject matter, please." As a sample the editor selected these lines from "Etchings of the Heart" by Charles Clevenger:

I carved a heart upon this tree/With cupid's arrow aimed at thee./'Tho time and space keep us apart,/
This etching holds you in my heart.

The editor says it is 68 pgs., published on high gloss paper, saddle-stapled with b&w and color illustrations and photos, includes ads. They receive less than 200 poems a year, publish approximately 4-10. Press run is 15,000 for about 4,000 subscribers in Southern Ohio and 2,000 in Northern Ohio, 40% shelf sales. Single copy: $2.95; subscription: $9.97/year. Sample: $4. Make checks payable to Back Fence Publishing, Inc.

How to Submit: Submit up to 4 poems at a time. Previously published poems and simultaneous submissions OK, "if identified as such." Cover letter preferred. "Since we prefer reader-submitted poetry, we would like for the cover letter to include comments about our magazine or contents." Computer disk submissions should be saved in an ASCII text format, Word Perfect or Microsoft Word file. Disk should be labeled with your name, address, daytime phone number, name of format and name of file. Time between acceptance and publication is 6-12 months. Seldom comments on rejections. "We do not publish theme issues, but do feature specific Ohio counties quarterly. Send or call for specific areas." Send SASE for guidelines. Responds in up to 3 months. Pays 10¢/word, $25 minimum. Buys one-time North American print rights.

Advice: "While we truly appreciate the professional poet, most of our published poetry comes from beginners or amateurs. We strive for reader response and solicit poetry contributions through the magazine."

◖ OWEN WISTER REVIEW, Box 3625, University of Wyoming, Laramie WY 82071, phone (307)766-3819 or (307)766-6109, fax (307)766-4027, e-mail owr@uwyo.edu, founded 1978.

Magazine Needs: *OWR* is the annual literary and art magazine (appearing in April) of the University of Wyoming. They have published poetry by Sam Western, C.C. Russell and joshua loveland. The editor says *OWR* is 100-120 pgs., 6×9, professionally printed and perfect-bound with art on the cover and inside and spoken word CD. They receive more than 500 submissions a year, accept 4-6%. Press run is 500. Single copy: $7.95; subscription: $15 for 2 years/2 issues. Sample: $5. Back issues: $5 each.

How to Submit: Submit up to 5 poems. No previously published poems; simultaneous submissions discouraged. Cover letter required. May query or submit by fax; must include mailing address. E-mail submissions in attached file OK. "5 poems per e-mail. Spacing between poems." Submission deadline December 1. Send spoken word submissions on cassette tape or CD. Poems are circulated to an editorial board. Send SASE for guidelines. Responds in 3 months. Pays 1 copy and 10% discount on additional copies. Acquires first rights.

Ⓝ ◖ OXYGEN, 537 Jones St., PMB 999, San Francisco CA 94102, phone (415)776-9681, e-mail Oxygen@s lip.net (no e-mail submissions!), website www.oxygeneditions.net, founded 1991, editor Richard Hack.

Magazine Needs: *Oxygen* is published 1-2 times a year. "We are open to many forms in many categories (e.g., surrealist, expressionist, narrative, devotional, et al.). We do not like poetry that smacks too much of workshop blandness and compromise, nor do we generally like academic poetry, uninformed cafe poetry, and some others. But we are not averse to hermetic poetry, allusive poetry, or simple, clear verse. Deeper delving and passion are hoped for." They have published poetry by Bill Knott, David Fisher, John Mueller, Victor Martinez, Ana Rosetti and Christina Bruckner. The editor says *Oxygen* is 100 pgs., 5½×8½, offset printed and perfect-bound with laminated solid color cover, includes drawings and photos. They receive about 6,000 poems a year, accept approximately 1%. Publish 50 poems/issue. Press run is 500. "We sell about 300-350 in stores and on newsstands in the Bay Area and nationally through DeBoer." Subscription: $18/4 issues. Sample: $5.

How to Submit: Submit up to 10 poems at a time. Previously published poems ("as long as previous venue and its circulation are made known") and simultaneous submissions OK. Always send SASE for response. No electronic submissions. Time between acceptance and publication is up to 6 months. Send SASE for guidelines. Responds in 2 months or less. Always sends prepublication galleys. Pays 2 copies. Acquires one-time rights, "plus right to post on our website and to use in future anthologies (spelled out in acceptance letter)." Occasionally reviews books and chapbooks of poetry and other magazines. Open to unsolicited reviews. Poets may also send books for review consideration.

Also Offers: Website includes selections from current and past issues, as well as material of interest that has not been published as hard copy.

✓ ◻ **OYEZ REVIEW**, Roosevelt University, 430 S. Michigan Ave., Chicago IL 60605, phone (312)341-3818, founded 1965/66, administrative advisor Jeff Helgeson.

Magazine Needs: *Oyez Review* is an annual designed "to publish the works of the students as well as veteran and beginning writers." Seeks traditional forms and blank verse; does not want "sexually graphic poetry or racially offensive poetry." As co-sponsors of the 1999 National Poetry Slam, *Oyez Review* has published poetry by Maria McCray and Marc Smith. As a sample the editor selected these lines from "Last Lovin' Blues" by Reggie Gibson:

> this night/which is our last my beloved, let us resurrect the embers of dead memory/and recall that
> faded dream/this last night

The editor says *Oyez* is 90 pgs., magazine-sized, includes photos and drawings. Press run is 500. Single copy: $4; subscription: $8/2 issues.

How to Submit: Submit 3 poems at a time. Previously published poems and simultaneous submissions OK. Disk submissions OK. Reads submissions September through March only. Time between acceptance and publication is 7 months. Seldom comments on rejections. Publishes theme issues occasionally. Send SASE for guidelines. Responds in 3 months.

Advice: "Our major goal is to foster the development of student and beginning authors."

◖ **P.D.Q. (POETRY DEPTH QUARTERLY)**, 5836 N. Haven Dr., North Highlands CA 95660, phone (916)331-3512, e-mail poetdpth@aol.com, founded 1995, publisher G. Elton Warrick, editor Joyce Odam, web manager Lori Smaltz.

Magazine Needs: *P.D.Q.* wants "original poetry that clearly demonstrates an understanding of craft. All styles accepted." However, they do not want to see "poetry which is overtly religious, erotic, inflammatory or demeans the human spirit." They have published poetry by Jane Blue, Taylor Graham, Simon Perchik and Danyen Powell. As a sample the editor selected these lines from "Dream of Breaking" by Ann Menebroker:

> Do you know the meaning/of this oldness?/The ancient quality/Of time that this/clay pot holds?/Listen
> to it./The earth is there/The sky is there./Hold it in your hands./Drink from it./Dream about being/
> Molded dream/Of breaking/and being found.

P.D.Q. is 35-60 pgs., digest-sized, coated and saddle-stapled with a color cover of original art. They receive 1,800-2,000 poems a year, accept approximately 10%. Press run is 200 of which 5 subscribers are libraries. Single copy: $4; subscription: $16/1 year, $31/2 years, $40/3 years (add $4/year for foreign subscriptions). Make checks payable to G. Elton Warrick.

How to Submit: Submit 3-5 poems of any length, "typewritten and presented exactly as you would like them to appear," maximum 49 characters/line, with name and address on every page. All submissions should include SASE (or SAE with IRC) and cover letter with short 3-10 line bio and publication credits. No simultaneous submissions; previously published poems "occasionally" accepted with publication credits. E-mail submissions OK. Send SASE for guidelines. Responds in 3 months. Pays 1 copy.

Also Offers: Sponsors an annual Open Poetry Contest. 1st Prize: $100; 2nd Prize: $50; and 3rd Prize: $25. Entry fee: $3/poem. Deadline: December 15, 2000. Send SASE for contest guidelines. *P.D.Q.* also submits nominations for the Pushcart Prize.

✓ $ ◻ ◰ **PACIFIC COAST JOURNAL; FRENCH BREAD AWARDS; FRENCH BREAD PUB-LICATIONS**, P.O. Box 23868, San Jose CA 95153-3868, e-mail paccoastj@bjt.net, website www.bjt.net/~stgraham/pcj, founded 1992, editor Stillson Graham.

Magazine Needs: *PCJ* is a quarterly "unprofessional literary magazine that prints first-time authors, emerging authors, established authors, and authors who are so visible that everyone's sick of them." They want "offbeat poetry, visual poetry, poetry that is aware of itself. We don't rule out rhyming poetry, but rarely do we accept it." They have published poetry by B.Z. Niditch, Gale Acuff and Charles Rommelkamp. As a sample the editor selected these lines by Duane Locke:

> The night will always be a slot machine/that never stops spinning,/the night won't let you win/the night
> won't let you lose,/the night just goes on spinning.

PCJ is 56 pgs., 5½×8½, photocopied and saddle-stitched with a card stock cover and b&w photos and artwork. They receive 400-500 poems a year, accept approximately 15%. Press run is 200 for 100 subscribers. Single copy: $3; subscription: $12. Sample: $2.50.

How to Submit: Submit up to 6 poems or 12 pages at a time. No previously published poems; simultaneous submissions OK. Cover letter preferred. Time between acceptance and publication is 6-18 months. Seldom comments on rejections. Send SASE for guidelines or request via e-mail. Responds in 4 months. Pays 1 copy. Acquires one-time rights. Reviews novels, short story collections and chapbooks of poetry in 1,500 words, single format. Open to unsolicited reviews (and pays $5 if accepted). Poets may also send books for review consideration.

Book/Chapbook Needs & How to Submit: French Bread Publications also occasionally publishes chapbooks of poetry, short story collections and short novellas. Books are similar to the journal in format. They have published *Literary Junkies* by Errol Miller. Query first with 5-8 sample poems, a cover letter and a list of credits for all the poems in the ms. Replies to queries in 1-2 months, to mss (if invited) in 3-4 months. Pays royalties and 10% of press run.

Also Offers: They also sponsor the French Bread Awards for short fiction/poetry. Entry fee: $6 for a group of up to 4 poems (no longer than 8 pgs. total). 1st Prize: $50. 2nd Prize: $25. Deadline: August 1. Send SASE for details. Website includes guidelines, poetry and contest information.

Advice: "Most poetry looks like any other poetry. We want experiments in what poetry is."

PACIFIC ENTERPRISE MAGAZINE, P.O. Box 1907, Fond du Lac WI 54936-1907, phone (920)922-9218, e-mail rudyled@vbe.com, founded 1998, editor Rudy Ledesma.

Magazine Needs: Appearing 6 times a year, *PEM* is "a literary magazine that combines subjects dealing with entrepreneurial/enterprising ideas. Focus is on poems and personal essays that are autobiographical in nature—that our children's children may know us through our writing and stories." They have no limitations on style or form. "Poems written in a foreign language are welcome as long as the English translation comes with it. No racy themes or content; please, no four-letter words." They have published poetry by Gemino Abad and Jon Pineda. As a sample we selected these lines from "Dear _____," by Eileen Tabios:

> I could be smoking a Cuban lit by a buxom blonde who offered/a pale cleavage with a piece of cedar
> to light my cigar, surrounded/by mahogany walls in a dim bar on Manhattan's Upper East Side. And//
> I could be gliding over pregnant vineyards in Napa Valley/in a hot air balloon, its hide stitched from
> pieces of a rainbow,/a V of birds and a two-seater plane interrupting the horizon. And,//still, I only
> would be considering how rarely a smile/sits on your lips, and yet that it sits there with ease/when
> you look at me: Thus, you make all my spaces sunlit.

PEM is 36 pgs., magazine-sized, web offset printed and saddle-stitched with 4-color glossy paper cover, includes b&w photos, cartoons and ads. They receive about 300-400 poems a year, accept approximately 20%. Press run is over 2,500 for 500 subscribers of which 10 are libraries; remainder distributed free to potential subscribers. Single copy: $2.95; subscription: $19.95. Sample: $4. Make checks payable to *Pacific Enterprise Institute*.

How to Submit: Submit no more than 5 poems at a time. Previously published poems and simultaneous submissions OK. Cover letter undesired, "but short bio required." E-mail and disk submissions OK. "When submission is by e-mail, include poems in message or attach as text file." Time between acceptance and publication is 2-6 months. Seldom comments on rejections. Send SASE for guidelines. Responds in up to 6 months. Always sends prepublication galleys. Pays 2 copies. Acquires first or one-time rights. Reviews books of poetry. Open to unsolicited reviews. Poets may also send books for review consideration.

PAINTBRUSH: A JOURNAL OF POETRY & TRANSLATION (Specialized: translation, themes, writing); EZRA POUND POETRY AWARD, Division of Language & Literature, Truman State University, Kirksville MO 63501, phone (660)785-4185, fax (660)785-7486, e-mail pbrush@truman.edu, website www.truman.edu/Paintbrush, founded 1974, editor Ben Bennani.

Magazine Needs: *Paintbrush* appears annually in the Fall and is 250-300 pgs., 5½×8½, using quality poetry. Circulation is 500. Sample: $15.

How to Submit: No submissions June, July and August. No e-mail submissions. Send SASE with inquiries and request for samples. Pays 2 copies. Reviews books of poetry.

Also Offers: Sponsors the Ezra Pound Poetry Award. "It's on our website. $2,000 for the best collection of poems." Website includes general information, names of editors, contributors, critical acclaim and competition information.

$ PAINTED BRIDE QUARTERLY, 230 Vine St., Philadelphia PA 19106, website www.libertynet.org, editors Kathy Volk Miller and Marion Wrenn, founded 1973.

Magazine Needs: "We have no specifications or restrictions. We'll look at anything." They have published poetry by Robert Bly, Charles Bukowski, S.J. Marks and James Hazen. "*PBQ* aims to be a leader among little magazines published by and for independent poets and writers nationally." The 80-page, digest-sized, perfect-bound magazine uses 40 pgs. of poetry/issue. They receive over 1,000 submissions a year, use approximately 150. Neatly printed, it has a circulation of 1,000 for 850 subscribers, of which 40 are libraries. Subscription: $16. Sample: $6.

How to Submit: Submit up to 6 poems, any length, typed; only original, unpublished work. "Submissions should include a short bio." Seldom comment on rejections. They have a 6- to 9-month backlog. Pays 1-year subscription, 1 half-priced contributor's copy and $5/accepted piece. Publishes reviews of poetry books. "We also occasionally publish critical essays."

Also Offers: Sponsors annual poetry contest and chapbook competition. Entry fee required for both. Send SASE for details.

PALANQUIN; PALANQUIN POETRY SERIES, Dept. of English, University of South Carolina-Aiken, 171 University Pkwy., Aiken SC 29801, e-mail phebed@aiken.sc.edu, founded 1988, editor Phebe Davidson.

Book/Chapbook Needs: The press sponsors annual Fall and Spring chapbooks contests and publishes occasional longer books of poetry. They do not want "sentimental, religious, consciously academic" poetry. They have published poetry by Robert Parham and Dana Wildsmith. As a sample the editor selected these lines by Laura Lee Washburn:

> the clouds come down from the sky./They climb monkey-fashion on slick strings./They come leaving
> bruises/against the pale spots of where they have been.

How to Submit: Contest deadlines are May 15 and October 15 annually. Submissions should include 20-25 pages of poetry plus bio and acknowledgements. Include SASE for reply. Responds in 3 months. The $10 reading fee includes a copy of the winning chapbook. Make checks payable to Palanquin Press. The winning ms is published by Palanquin Press and the poet receives $100 and 50 copies of the chapbook. Samples are $5.

PALO ALTO REVIEW (Specialized: themes), 1400 W. Villaret Blvd., San Antonio TX 78224, phone (210)921-5443 or 921-5017, fax (210)921-5115, e-mail eshull@accd.edu, founded 1992, editors Ellen Shull and Bob Richmond.

Magazine Needs: *PAR* is a biannual publication of Palo Alto college. "We invite writing that investigates the full range of education in its myriad forms. Ideas are what we are after. The *Palo Alto Review* is interested in connecting the college and the community. We would hope that those who attempt these connections will choose startling topics and find interesting angles from which to study the length and breadth of ideas and learning, a lifelong pursuit." The review includes articles, essays, memoirs, interviews, book reviews, fiction and poetry. They want "poetry which has something to say, literary quality poems, with strong images, up to 50 lines. No inspirational verse, haiku or doggerel." They have published poetry by Walt McDonald, Diane Glancy, Virgil Suárez and Wendy Bishop. *PAR* is 60 pgs., 8½×11, professionally printed on recycled paper and saddle-stapled with enamel card cover with art; b&w photos, art and graphics inside. They publish about 8 poems in each issue (16 poems/year). Press run is 700 for 400 subscribers of which 10 are libraries, 200 shelf sales. Subscription: $10. Sample: $5.

How to Submit: Submit 3-5 poems at a time. No previously published poems; simultaneous submissions OK. Poems are read by an advisory board and recommended to editors, who sometimes suggest revisions. Always comments on rejections. "Although we frequently announce a theme, the entire issue will not necessarily be dedicated to the theme." Fall 2000, unthemed (deadline: July 1, 2000); Spring 2001, Beginnings (deadline: December 1, 2000). Send SASE for guidelines and upcoming themes. Responds in 3 months. Pays 2 copies. Acquires first North American serial rights. "Please note poems as first published in *Palo Alto Review* in subsequent printings."

Advice: "There are no requirements for submission, though we recommend the reading (purchase) of a sample copy."

PANDALOON; SMALL POTATOES PRESS, P.O. Box 210977, Milwaukee WI 53221, phone (800)642-9050, e-mail pandaloon@azml.com, website www.azml.com, founded 1997, editor David L. White.

Magazine Needs: *PandaLoon* is a monthly pocket poetry anthology. "Exactly by its portable pocket size, *PandaLoon* favors the shorter poem. If 'it' cannot be expressed in twenty short lines or less, adding more words will not help. Rhymes are fine. They have to work. Don't bruise the words shoving them into place. This is not a place for 'concrete' poetry. Editing is 'hands-off.' *PandaLoon* considers that a poem is evidence to the outside world that a poet has grappled with the truth and that intentional obscurity is counterproductive to the poet's overall message." *PandaLoon* is 16 pgs., 4×7, laser printed, saddle-stitched, card cover. Press run is 100. Subscription: $10 for 12 issues. Sample is free with #10 SASE.

How to Submit: Submit up to 3 poems at a time. No previously published poems or simultaneous submissions. Cover letter preferred. E-mail submissions OK. Seldom comments on rejections. Send SASE for guidelines or obtain via e-mail or website. Responds within 3 months. Sometimes sends prepublication galleys. Pays 2 copies. Acquires first North American serial rights.

PANJANDRUM BOOKS; PANJANDRUM POETRY JOURNAL (Specialized: translations), 6156 Wilkinson Ave., North Hollywood CA 91606, founded 1971, editor Dennis Koran, associate editor David Guss.

Magazine Needs & How to Submit: *Panjandrum Poetry Journal* is published occasionally. Submit no more than 10 poems at a time. No simultaneous submissions. Staff also reviews books of poetry. Send books for review consideration to Dennis Koran.

Book/Chapbook Needs & How to Submit: The press publishes a distinguished list of avant-garde books. They are interested in translations (especially European) of modern poetry, surrealism, dada and experimental poetry and accept book-length mss only with SASE. Query first. Cover letter listing previous publications is requested.

PANTHEON BOOKS INC., 201 E. 50th St., 25th Floor, New York NY 10022, editorial director Dan Frank. Prefers not to share information.

ⓃⒺ◻ⓞ PAPER WASP: A JOURNAL OF HAIKU (Specialized: form/style); SOCIAL ALTER-NATIVES (Specialized: social issues); POST PRESSED, The Graduate School of Education, The University of Queensland, Queensland 4072 Australia, e-mail jwk@powerup.com.au, *PW* founded 1972, *SA* founded 1971, editor Jacqui Murray, editor John Knight.
Magazine Needs: "*Paper Wasp* quarterly publishes haiku, senryu, renga and tanka in a range of fresh tones and voices. We acknowledge a range of forms and styles from one-liners to the conventional 5-7-5 form, and variations such as development or neglect of seasonal words for regional contexts." They want to receive haiku, senryu, tanka, renga, linked verse and haibun. They have published poetry by Janice Bostok, Carla Sari, Cornelis Vleeskens, Ross Clark, Tony Beyer and Bernard Gadd. As a sample the editor selected these lines by Alan J. Summers:
> late september rain/cutting through the lane/and the mist.
The editors say *PW* is 16 pgs., digest-sized, desktop-published and saddle-stapled, cardboard cover, includes art/graphics. They receive about 2,000 submissions a year, accept approximately 15%. Publish about 50 haiku/issue. Press run is 200 for 67 subscribers of which 12 are libraries. Single copy: $AUD6 within Australia, $US8 elsewhere. Subscription: $AUD20 within Australia, $US26 elsewhere. Make checks payable to *Paper Wasp*. "Due to very high bank charges on overseas cheques, we prefer cash or IRCs for single copies. Copies of relevant pages only are sent to published contributors who are not subscribers or who do not pay for the relevant copy."
Magazine Needs: "*Social Alternatives* is a quarterly multidisciplinary journal which seeks to analyse, critique and review contemporary social, cultural, economic and economic developments and their implications at local, national and global levels." They have published poetry by MTC Cronin, Jules Leigh Koch, ouyang yu, John O'Connor, Gina Mercer and Michael Sariban. As a sample the editor selected these lines from "Awaiting the Barbarians (after Cavafy)" by Ron Pretty:
> It was the golden age: they were there, sure./the barbarians, but on the borders,/the northern marches,
> walled out, or so/we were told, and kept in check. The city/prospered and its merchants. the constant
> flow/of captives kept the mines and circuses in action
The editors say *SA* is 76 pgs., magazine-sized, desktop-published, saddle-stapled with cardboard cover, includes art/graphics, ads. They receive approximately 1,200 submissions, accept approximately 15%. Publish about 30 poems/issue. Press run is about 800 for 587 subscribers of which 112 are libraries. Single copy: $8. Subscription: $30, plus $40 for overseas airmail.
How to Submit: Submit up to 12 poems at a time for *PW*, up to 6 poems (36 lines maximum) for *SA*. No previously published poems or simultaneous submissions. E-mail and disk submissions (IBM format with Word files, plus hard copy) OK. Cover letter required. "If mailed within Australia, send SASE, otherwise SAE plus IRCs. Unless requested with SASE, copy is not returned." Time between acceptance and publication is up to 6 months. Poems are circulated to an editorial board. "Read by two editors." Sometimes comments on rejections. Responds within 6 months. *PW* does not pay. *SA* pays 1 copy. Copyright remains with authors.

⬕▣⬿ PAPERPLATES, 19 Kenwood Ave., Toronto, Ontario M6C 2R8 Canada, phone (416)651-2551, fax (416)651-2910, e-mail paper@perkolator.com, website www.perkolator.com, founded 1990, publisher/editor Bernard Kelly, poetry editor Suzanne Hancock.
Magazine Needs & How to Submit: *paperplates* is a quarterly online magazine of general interest featuring short stories, poetry, one-act plays, reviews, travel pieces, essays and interviews. They have no preference for submissions, however they do not want religious poetry. They have published poetry by Richard Outram, Fraser Sutherland, Lyn Lifshin, Deirdre Dwyer, Colleen Flood and Maja Bannerman.
How to Submit: Submit 5 poems at a time. Simultaneous submissions OK. Cover letter preferred. E-mail submissions OK with mailing address and phone number. Time between acceptance and publication is up to 1 year. Seldom comments on rejections. Send SASE (or SAE and IRCs) for guidelines. Responds ASAP. Pays 1 hardcopy. Reviews books of poetry. Open to unsolicited reviews. Poets may also send books for review consideration.

ⓞ PARADOXISM; XIQUAN PUBLISHING HOUSE; THE PARADOXIST MOVEMENT ASSOCI-ATION (Specialized: form), University of New Mexico, Gallup NM 87301, e-mail smarand@unm.edu, founded 1990, editor Florentin Smarandache.
Magazine Needs: *Paradoxism*, (formerly *The Paradoxist Literary Movement Journal*), is an annual journal of "avant-garde poetry, experiments, poems without verses, literature beyond the words, anti-language, non-literature and its literature, as well as the sense of the non-sense; revolutionary forms of poetry." They want "avant-garde poetry, one to two pages, any subject, any style (lyrical experiments). No classical, fixed forms." They have published poetry by Paul Georgelin, Titu Popescu, Ion Rotaru, Michéle de LaPlante and Claude LeRoy.

Paradoxism is 52 pgs., digest-sized, offset printed, soft cover. Press run is 500. "It is distributed to its collabora-tors, U.S. and Canadian university libraries and the Library of Congress as well as European, Chinese, Indian and Japanese libraries."

How to Submit: No previously published poems or simultaneous submissions. Do not submit mss in the summer. "We do not return published or unpublished poems or notify the author of date of publication." Responds in up to 6 months. Pays 1 copy.

Book/Chapbook Needs & How to Submit: Xiquan Publishing House also publishes 2 paperbacks and 1-2 chapbooks/year, including translations. The poems must be unpublished and must meet the requirements of the Paradoxist Movement Association. Replies to queries in 1-2 months, to mss in 3-6 months. Pays 50 author's copies. Inquire about sample books.

Advice: They say, "We mostly receive traditional or modern verse, but not avant-garde (very different from any previously published verse). We want anti-literature and its literature, style of the non-style, poems without poems, non-words and non-sentence poems, very upset free verse, intelligible unintelligible language, impersonal texts personalized, transformation of the abnormal to the normal. Make literature from everything; make literature from nothing!"

THE PARIS REVIEW; BERNARD F. CONNORS PRIZE, 541 E. 72nd St., New York NY 10021, phone (212)861-0016, fax (212)861-4504, website parisreview.com, founded 1953, poetry editor Richard How-ard.

Poetry published in *The Paris Review* was selected for inclusion in the 1995, 1996, 1997 and 1998 volumes of *The Best American Poetry.*

Magazine Needs & How to Submit: This distinguished quarterly (circulation 15,000, digest-sized, 300 pgs.) has published many of the major poets writing in English. Though form, content and length seem open, free verse—some structured, some experimental—tends to dominate recent issues. Because the journal is considered one of the most prestigious in the world, competition is keen and response times can lag. Subscription: $46 (US); $48 (outside US). Sample: $13. Study publication before submitting.

Also Offers: The Bernard F. Connors prize of $1,000 is awarded annually for the best previously unpublished long poem (over 200 lines).

PARIS/ATLANTIC, The American University of Paris, 31 Avenue Bosquet, Paris 75007, France, phone (33 1)01 40 62 05 89, fax (33 1)01 45 89 13, e-mail auplantic@hotmail.com, founded 1982, contact the editor.

Magazine Needs: *Paris/Atlantic* appears biannually and is "a forum for both new and established artists/writers that is based in Paris and is distributed internationally. The contents vary; we publish poetry, prose, paintings, sculpture, sketches, etc." They have published poetry by Ben Wilensky, Ryan G. Van Cleave, Margo Berdeshev-sky and Susan Maurer. *Paris/Atlantic* is 80-130 pgs., professionally published with sewn binding and softcover, includes ads. They receive about 400-500 poems a year, accept approximately 40%. Press run is 1,000-1,500; distributed free to bookstores, universities, literary societies, other poets, etc.

How to Submit: Submit any number of poems at a time. "There are no requirements aside from a biography and international postage so we can forward 2 free copies of *Paris/Atlantic* if your work is published." Previously published poems and simultaneous submissions OK. Cover letter including author's name, return address with telephone number, e-mail address or fax number and a short biography required. E-mail (include in body of message) and disk submissions OK. "Please cut and paste e-mail submissions. No attachments!" Reads submis-sions September 1 through November 1 and January 1 through April 1 only. Poems are circulated to an editorial board. "The editorial board reviews work in a roundtable discussion." Send SASE (or SAE and IRC) for guidelines or request via fax or e-mail. Pays 2 copies. Acquires first rights. Rights revert to author upon publica-tion.

Advice: "Be heard! The *Paris/Atlantic* Reading Series of Poetry and Prose takes place once a month, for which we invite two poets to perform their work in the Amex Café of The American University of Paris, followed by open mikes. Take advantage to listen and he heard in this international forum, and contact us if you would like to participate."

PARNASSUS LITERARY JOURNAL, P.O. Box 1384, Forest Park GA 30298-1384, phone (404)366-3177, founded 1975, editor Denver Stull.

Magazine Needs: "Our sole purpose is to promote poetry and to offer an outlet where poets may be heard. We welcome well-constructed poetry, but ask that you keep it uplifting, and free of language that might be offensive to one of our readers. We are open to all poets and all forms of poetry, including Oriental, 24-line limit,

THE GEOGRAPHICAL INDEX, located at the back of this book, can help you discover the publishers in your region. Publishers often favor poets (and work) from their own areas.

maximum 3 poems." Also accepts poetry written by children. They have published poetry by t.k. splake, B.Z. Niditch, Simon Perchik, William Dauenhauer and H.F. Noyes. As a sample the editor selected these lines by Denny Marshall:

> The wind is gusting/Up to Sixty miles an hour/Turning dead, dry leaves/Into swarms/Of flying brown butterflies/Dancing off some time ago/Swimming back to life/For a brief reincarnation.

PLJ, published 3 times/year, is 84 pgs., photocopied from typescript, saddled-stapled, colored card cover, with an occasional drawing. They receive about 1,500 submissions a year, use approximately 350. Currently have about a 1-year backlog. Press run is 300 for 200 subscribers of which 5 are libraries. Circulation includes Japan, England, Greece, India, Korea, Germany and Netherlands. Single copy: $6 US and Canada, $9.50 overseas; subscription: $18 US and Canada, $25 overseas. Sample: $5. Offers 20% discount to schools, libraries and for orders of 5 copies or more. Make checks or money orders payable to Denver Stull.

How to Submit: Submit up to 3 poems, up to 24 lines each, with #10 SASE. Include name and address on each page of ms. "I am dismayed at the haphazard manner in which work is often submitted. I have a number of poems in my file containing no name and/or address. Simply placing your name and address on your envelope is not enough." Previously published poems OK; no simultaneous submissions. Cover letter including something about the writer preferred. "Definitely" comments on rejections. "We do not respond to submissions or queries not accompanied by SASE." Send SASE for guidelines. Responds within 1 week. Pays 1 copy. Acquires all rights. Returns rights to author on publication. Readers vote on best of each issue. Staff reviews books of poetry by subscribers only.

Also Offers: Conducts a contest periodically.

Advice: "Write about what you know. Study what you have written. Does it make sense? A poem should not leave the reader wondering what you are trying to say. Improve your writings by studying the work of others. Be professional."

N $ PARNASSUS: POETRY IN REVIEW; POETRY IN REVIEW FOUNDATION (V), 205 W. 89th St., #8F, New York NY 10024-1835, phone (212)362-3492, fax (212)875-0148, founded 1972, poetry editor Herbert Leibowitz.

Magazine Needs: *Parnassus* provides "comprehensive and in-depth coverage of new books of poetry, including translations from foreign poetry. We publish poems and translations on occasion, but we solicit all poetry. Poets invited to submit are given all the space they wish; the only stipulation is that the style be non-academic." They have published work by Alice Fulton, Eavan Boland, Ross Feld, Debora Greger, William Logan, Tess Gallagher, Seamus Heaney and Rodney Jones. Subscriptions are $27/year, $46/year for libraries; they have 1,100 subscribers, of which 550 are libraries.

How to Submit: Not open to unsolicited poetry. However, they do consider unsolicited essays. In fact, this is an exceptionally rich market for thoughtful, insightful, technical essay-reviews of contemporary collections. However, it is strongly recommended that writers study the magazine before submitting. Multiple submissions disliked. Cover letter required. Send SASE for upcoming themes. Responds to essay submissions within 10 weeks (response takes longer during the summer). Pays $25-250 plus 2 gift subscriptions—contributors can also take one themselves. Editor comments on rejections—from 1 paragraph to 2 pages. Send for a sample copy (prices of individual issues can vary) to get a feel for the critical acumen needed to place here.

Advice: "Contributors are urged to subscribe to at least one literary magazine. There is a pervasive ignorance of the cost of putting out a magazine and no sense of responsibility for supporting one."

PARTING GIFTS; MARCH STREET PRESS; FATAL EMBRACE, 3413 Wilshire, Greensboro NC 27408, e-mail rbixby@aol.com, website users.aol.com/marchst/, founded 1987, editor Robert Bixby.

Magazine Needs: "I want to see everything. I'm a big fan of Jim Harrison, C.K. Williams, Amy Hempel and Janet Kauffman." He has published poetry by Eric Torgersen, Lyn Lifshin, Elizabeth Kerlikowske and Russell Thorburn. *PG* is 72 pgs., digest-sized, photocopied, with colored matte card cover, appearing twice a year. Press run is 200. Subscription: $12. Sample: $6.

How to Submit: Submit in groups of 3-10 with SASE. No previously published poems, but simultaneous submissions OK. "I like a cover letter because it makes the transaction more human. Best time to submit mss is early in the year." Send SASE for guidelines or obtain via website. Responds in 2 weeks. Sometimes sends prepublication galleys. Pays 1 copy.

Book/Chapbook Needs & How to Submit: March Street Press publishes chapbooks. Reading fee: $10.

Also Offers: Website features bookstore advice, links, guidelines, sample issues, book catalog and "fun things" like a name generator and a metaphor generator.

$ PARTISAN REVIEW (Specialized: translations, themes), Dept. PM, 236 Bay State Rd., Boston MA 02215, phone (617)353-4260, fax (617)353-7444, e-mail partisan@bu.edu, website www.webdelsol/partisan_review/, founded 1934, editor Edith Kurzweil, editor-in-chief William Phillips, poetry editor Don Share.

Work published in this review has also been selected for inclusion in *The Best American Poetry* (volumes 1995 and 1998).

Magazine Needs: *PR* is a distinguished quarterly literary journal using poetry of high quality. "Our poetry section is very small and highly selective. We are open to fresh, quality translations but submissions must include poem in original language as well as translation. We occasionally have special poetry sections on specified themes." They have published poetry by Charles Wright, Glyn Maxwell, Debora Greger and Wislava Szymbov-ska. The journal is 160 pgs., 6×9, flat-spined. Circulation is 8,200 for 6,000 subscriptions and shelf sales. Sample: $7.50.

How to Submit: Submit up to 6 poems at a time. No simultaneous submissions. Responds in 2 months. Pays $50 and 50% discount on copies.

N ⊕ ◯ ⊘ PARTNERS WRITING GROUP; THE WORD—LIFE JOURNAL AND POETRY MAGAZINE; A BARD HAIR DAY, 289 Elmwood Ave., Feltham, Middlesex TW13 7QB United Kingdom, website www.partnersinpoetry.freeserve.co.uk, founded *The Word* 1997, *A Bard Hair Day* 1999, editor Ian Deal.

Magazine Needs: "*The Word* is the quarterly life journal that deals with the mysteries surrounding the Spirit. We offer a spiritual Renaissance for the 21st century–an ongoing romantic movement. If it moves me I will print it, especially alongside an article. I advise seeing the magazine first." They have published poetry by Professor Desmond Tarrant, Pamela Constantine, David Cobb, Toni Jehan and Nicki Griffin. The editor says *The Word* is 30 pgs., 5½×8½, stapled, softback cover, includes color art/graphics and ads. Publish 6-12 poems/issue. Sample: £3.50 sterling. Make checks payable to I. Deal. "Must include IRCs for return."

How to Submit: Submit 5 poems at a time, single-spaced—"save paper." Line length for poetry is 30 maximum. Previously published poems and simultaneous submissions OK. Cover letter required. Often comments on rejections. Send SASE (or SAE and IRC) for guidelines. Always sends prepublication galleys. Pays 1 copy. Acquires one-time rights. Staff reviews books and chapbooks of poetry and other magazines in 50-100 words. Send books for review consideration.

Magazine Needs & How to Submit: "*A Bard Hair Day* is published quarterly and features short stories, articles and poetry. "It offers a friendly forum where writers can exchange views, gain critique and advice." They want "any kind of poems as long as they show imagination—from washing up to alien abduction. Certain categories would have to be very special to be properly considered (i.e., war poetry). They have published poetry by Ian Whitely, Andrew Detheridge, John Hirst, Michele Glazer, Toni Jehan and Nicki Griffin. The editor says *ABHD* is 38 pgs., stapled with softback cover, includes ads. Publish 25-40 poems/issue. Sample: £2.50 sterling and IRCs. Make checks payable to I. Deal.

How to Submit: Submit 2 single-spaced poems at a time with required submission forms (see inside magazine). Line length for poetry is 100 maximum. Previously published poems and simultaneous submissions OK. Cover letter required. Often comments on rejections. Send SASE (or SAE and IRC) for guidelines. Acquires one-time rights.

Also Offers: Sponsors poetry contest. Send SAE and IRC for details. "Poetry chosen for *The Word's* 'Poet Showcase' is selected from the end of Partners in Poetry Competition 'honors list'."

◯ ⊘ ◎ PASSAGER: A JOURNAL OF REMEMBRANCE AND DISCOVERY (Specialized: senior citizen, themes), School of Communications Design, University of Baltimore, 1420 N. Charles St., Baltimore MD 21201-5779, e-mail kkopelke@ubmail.ubalt.edu, founded 1989, editors Kendra Kopelke and Mary Azrael.

Magazine Needs: *Passager* is published semiannually and publishes fiction, poetry and interviews that give voice to human experience. "We seek powerful images of remembrance and discovery from writers of all ages. One of our missions is to provide exposure for new older writers." The journal is 32 pgs., 8×8, printed on white linen recycled paper and saddle-stitched. Includes photos of writers. Sample: $5.

How to Submit: Submit 3-5 poems at a time, each 30 lines maximum; fiction, 3,000 words maximum. "We like clean, readable typed copy with name, address and phone number on each page." Simultaneous submissions acceptable if notified. No reprints. "We prefer cover sheets because it makes it personal. We hate pushy cover letters, 'I'm sure you'll find your readers will love my story.' " Does not read mss June through August. Occasionally does special issues. Send SASE for guidelines and upcoming themes. Responds in 3 months. Pays 2 copies.

Also Offers: They sponsor an annual spring poetry contest for new poets over 50 years old, with a $500 1st Prize and honorable mentions; and publication in *Passager*.

⊘ PASSAGES NORTH; ELINOR BENEDICT PRIZE, English Dept., 1401 Presque Isle Ave., Northern Michigan University, Marquette MI 49855, phone (906)227-2715, founded 1979, editor-in-chief Kate Myers Hanson

Magazine Needs: *Passages North* is a biannual magazine containing short fiction, poetry, creative nonfiction, essays, interviews and visual art. "The magazine publishes quality work by established and emerging writers." They have published poetry by Jim Daniels, Jack Driscoll, Vivian Shipley and Michael Delp. *PN* is 100 pgs., perfect-bound. Circulation is at 1,000 "and growing." Single copy: $7; subscription: $13/year, $18/2 years, add $10 for international mail. Sample: $2.

How to Submit: Prefers groups of 3-6 poems, typed single-spaced. Simultaneous submissions OK. "Poems over 100 lines seldom published." Time between acceptance and publication is 6 months. Reads submissions September through May only. Responds in 2 months. Pays 1 copy.

Also Offers: Sponsors the Elinor Benedict Prize in poetry and the Waasmode Fiction Contest. "We have published fiction by W.P. Kinsella, Bonnie Jo Campbell and Lisa Stolley." Send SASE for details.

$ ⬤ ◎ PASSEGGIATA PRESS (Specialized: ethnic, regional, translations, women/feminism), P.O. Box 636, Pueblo CO 81002, phone (719)544-1038, fax (719)576-4689, founded 1973, poetry editor Donald Herdeck.

Book/Chapbook Needs: "Published poets only welcomed and only non-European and non-American poets . . . We publish literature by creative writers from the non-western world (Africa, the Middle East, the Caribbean and Asia/Pacific)—poetry only by non-western writers or good translations of such poetry if original language is Arabic, French, African vernacular, etc." They have published *An Ocean of Dreams* by Mona Saudi, *Sky-Break* by Lyubomir Levchev, *The Right to Err* by Nina Iskreuko and *The Journey of Barbarus* by Ottó Oubán. They also publish anthologies and criticisms focused on relevant themes.

How to Submit: Query with 4-5 samples, bio, publication credits. Replies to queries in 2-4 weeks, to submissions (if invited) in 1-2 weeks. Always sends prepublication galleys. Offers 7.5% royalty contract (5% for translator) with $100-200 advance plus 10 copies. Buys worldwide English rights. Send SASE for catalog to buy samples.

⬤ ◎ THE PATERSON LITERARY REVIEW; HORIZONTES; ALLEN GINSBERG POETRY AWARDS; THE PATERSON POETRY PRIZE; THE PATERSON PRIZE FOR BOOKS FOR YOUNG PEOPLE; PASSAIC COUNTY COMMUNITY COLLEGE POETRY CENTER LIBRARY (Specialized: regional, bilingual/foreign language), Poetry Center, Passaic County Community College, Cultural Affairs Dept., 1 College Blvd., Paterson NJ 07505-1179, phone (973)684-6555, e-mail mgellan@pccc.cc.nj.us, website www.pccc.cc.nj.us/poetry.

Magazine Needs & How to Submit: A wide range of activities pertaining to poetry are conducted by the Passaic County Community College Poetry Center, including the annual *The Paterson Literary Review* (formerly *Footwork: The Paterson Literary Review*), founded 1979, editor and director Maria Mazziotti Gillan, using poetry of "high quality" under 100 lines; "clear, direct, powerful work." They have published poetry by David Ray, Diane Wakoski, Sonia Sanchez, Laura Boss and Marge Piercy. *TPLR* is 240 pgs., magazine-sized, saddle-stapled, professionally printed with glossy card 2-color cover, using b&w art and photos. Circulation is 1,000 for 100 subscribers of which 50 are libraries. Sample: $10. Send up to 5 poems at a time. Simultaneous submissions OK. Reads submissions September through January only. Responds in 1 year. Pays 1 copy. Acquires first rights.

Magazine Needs & How to Submit: *Horizontes*, founded in 1983, editor José Villalongo, is an annual Spanish language literary magazine using poetry of high quality no longer than 20 lines. Will accept English translations, but Spanish version must be included. They have published poetry by Nelson Calderon, Jose Kozer and Julio Cesar Mosches. *Horizontes* is 120 pgs., magazine-sized, saddle-stapled, professionally printed with full-color matte cover, using b&w graphics and photos. Circulation is 800 for 100 subscribers of which 20 are libraries. Sample: $4. Accepts simultaneous submissions. "On occasion we do consider published works but prefer unpublished works." Reads submissions September through January only. Responds in 4 months. Pays 2 copies. Acquires first rights. Staff reviews books of poetry. Send books for review consideration.

Also Offers: The Poetry Center of the college conducts The Allen Ginsberg Poetry Awards Competition each year. Entry fee: $12. Prizes of $1,000, $200 and $100. Deadline: April 1. Send SASE for rules. They also publish a *New Jersey Poetry Resources* book, the *PCC Poetry Contest Anthology* and the *New Jersey Poetry Calendar*. The Paterson Poetry Prize of $1,000 is awarded each year (split between poet and publisher) to a book of poems published in the previous year. Also sponsors The Paterson Prize for Books for Young People. Awards $500 to one book in each category (Pre-K-Grade 3, Grades 4p6, Grades 7-12). Books must be published in the previous year and be submitted by the publisher. Publishers should write with SASE for application form to be submitted by February 1 (for Poetry Prize) and March 15 (for Books for Young People Prize). Passaic County Community College Poetry Center Library has an extensive collection of contemporary poetry and seeks small press contributions to help keep it abreast. The Distinguished Poetry Series offers readings by poets of international, national and regional reputation. Poetryworks/USA is a series of programs produced for UA Columbia-Cablevision.

✓ ◯ ◎ PATH PRESS, INC. (Specialized: ethnic), P.O. Box 2925, Chicago IL 60690, phone (847)424-1620, fax (847)424-1623, e-mail pathpressinc@aol.com, founded 1969, president Bennett J. Johnson.

Book/Chapbook Needs & How to Submit: Path Press is a small publisher of books and poetry primarily "by, for and about African-American and Third World people." The press is open to all types of poetic forms; emphasis is on high quality. Submissions should be typewritten in ms format. Writers should send sample poems, credits and bio. The books are "hardback and quality paperbacks."

✓ ⬤ ⬤ PAVEMENT SAW; PAVEMENT SAW PRESS; PAVEMENT SAW PRESS CHAPBOOK AWARD; TRANSCONTINENTAL POETRY AWARD; BLOODY TWIN PRESS, P.O. Box 6291, Columbus OH 43206-0291, e-mail baratier@megsinet.net, founded 1992, editor David Baratier.

Magazine Needs: *Pavement Saw*, which appears annually, wants "letters and short fiction, and poetry on any subject, especially work. Length: one or two pages. No poems that tell, no work by a deceased writer and no translations." Dedicates 10-15 pgs. of each issue to a featured writer. They have published poetry by Will Alexander, Sandra Kohler, Naton Leslie, Jendi Reiter, Beth Anderson, Scan Killian and Tracy Philpot. The editor says *PS* is 64 pgs., 6×9, perfect-bound. They receive about 14,500 poems a year, publish less than 1%. Press run is 500 for about 250 subscribers, about 250 shelf sales. Single copy: $4; subscription: $7, $10 for libraries/institutions. Sample: $3.50. Make checks payable to Pavement Saw Press.

How to Submit: Submit 5 poems at a time. "No fancy typefaces." No previously published poems; simultaneous submissions OK, "as long as poet has not published a book with a press run of 1,000 or more." No e-mail submissions. Cover letter required. Seldom comments on rejections. Send SASE for guidelines. Responds in 6 months. Sometimes sends prepublication galleys. Pays 2 copies. Acquires first rights.

Book/Chapbook Needs & How to Submit: The press also occasionally publishes books of poetry. "Most are by authors who have been published in the journal." Recent titles include *Magnolia Hall* by Errol Miller, *The Numbers* by Gordon Massman, *Pants* by Shelley Stenhouse, and *Collected Hands, 1949-1999* by Simon Perchik.

Also Offers: Sponsors the Transcontinental Poetry Award. "Each year, Pavement Saw Press will seek to publish at least one book of poetry and/or prose poems from manuscripts received during this competition. Competition is open to anyone who has not previously published a volume of poetry or prose. Writers who have had volumes of poetry and/or prose under 40 pgs. printed or printed in limited editions of no more than 500 copies are eligible. Submissions are accepted during June and July only." Entry fee: $15. Awards publication, $1,000 and a percentage of the press run. Include stamped postcard and SASE for ms receipt acknowledgement and results notification. Send SASE for guidelines. Also sponsors the Pavement Saw Press Chapbook Award. Submit up to 32 pgs. of poetry with a cover letter. Entry fee: $7. Awards publication, $500 and 10% of print run. "Each entrant will receive a copy of the winning chapbook provided a 9 × 12 SAE with 5 first-class stamps is supplied." Deadline: December 20. Send SASE for guidelines. Pavement Saw Press also distributes books for Bloody Twin Press. Send SASE for details.

☑ ◉ PEARL; PEARL POETRY PRIZE; PEARL EDITIONS, 3030 E. Second St., Long Beach CA 90803-5163, phone (562)434-4523 or (714)968-7530, e-mail mjohn5150@aol.com, website www.pearlmag.com, founded 1974, poetry editors Joan Jobe Smith, Marilyn Johnson and Barbara Hauk.

Magazine Needs: *Pearl* is a literary magazine appearing 2 times/year. "We are interested in accessible, humanistic poetry that communicates and is related to real life. Humor and wit are welcome, along with the ironic and serious. No taboos stylistically or subject-wise. We don't want to see sentimental, obscure, predictable, abstract or cliché-ridden poetry. Our purpose is to provide a forum for lively, readable poetry, the direct, outspoken type, variously known as 'neo-pop' or 'stand-up,' that reflects a wide variety of contemporary voices, viewpoints and experiences—that speaks to real people about real life in direct, living language, profane or sublime. Our Fall/Winter issue is devoted exclusively to poetry, with a 12-15 page section featuring the work of a single poet." They have published poetry by Fred Voss, Allison Joseph, Frank X. Gaspar, Denise Duhamel, Ed Ochester and Nin Andrews. As a sample they selected these lines from "Beginning at the End" by David Hernandez:

> *A gravedigger unearths your casket,/opens the creaky lid,/and welcomes you to the world/of the living,*
> *to the smiling nurse/who escorts you to a convalescent home.*

Pearl is 96-121 pgs., digest-sized, perfect-bound, offset printed, with glossy cover. Press run is 700 for 150 subscribers of which 7 are libraries. Subscription: $18/year includes a copy of the winning book of the Pearl Poetry Prize. Sample: $7.

How to Submit: Submit 3-5 poems at a time. No previously published poems. "Simultaneous submissions must be acknowledged as such." Prefer poems no longer than 40 lines, each line no more than 10-12 words to accommodate page size and format. "Handwritten submissions and unreadable printouts are not acceptable." E-mail submissions OK. "Cover letters appreciated." Reads submissions September through May only. Time between acceptance and publication is 6-12 months. Send SASE for guidelines. Responds in 2 months. Sometimes sends prepublication galleys. Pays 1 copy. Acquires first serial rights. Each issue contains the work of 80-100 different poets and a special 10- to 15-page section that showcases the work of a single poet.

Book/Chapbook Needs: Pearl Editions "only publishes the winner of the Pearl Poetry Prize. All other books and chapbooks are *by invitation only*."

Also Offers: "We sponsor the Pearl Poetry Prize, an annual book-length contest, judged by one of our more well-known contributors. Winner receives publication, $1,000 and 25 copies. Entries accepted during the months of May, June and July. There is a $20 entry fee, which includes a copy of the winning book." Send SASE or visit website for complete rules and guidelines. Recent books include *Fluid in Darkness, Frozen in Light* by Robert Perchan, *Shelter* by Lisa Giatt, *Transforming Matter* by Donna Hilbert, *One on One* by Tony Gloeggler, *Oyl* by Denise Duhamel and Maureen Seaton and *Man Climbs Out of Manhole* by David Hernandez. Website includes current issue, back issues, submission guidelines for magazine and contests, subscription information, books and chapbooks in print, sample poems, about the editors, book ordering information, links.

Advice: "Advice for beginning poets? Just write from your own experience, using images that are as concrete and sensory as possible. Keep these images fresh and objective. Always listen to the music."

◉ PECAN GROVE PRESS; CHILI VERDE REVIEW, Box AL 1 Camino Santa Maria, San Antonio TX 78228-8608, phone (210)436-3441, fax (210)436-3782, e-mail palmer@netxpress.com, website library.stmarytx.edu/pgpress/index.html, founded 1988, editor H. Palmer Hall, co-editor Cynthia J. Harper (*Chili Verde Review*).

Magazine Needs & How to Submit: Published biannually by Pecan Grove Press and Chili Verde Press, *Chili Verde Review* is "a new magazine that welcomes only original poems by established poets and new voices." They want "poems that are carefully crafted, original, with bright things to say." They have published poetry by John Gilgun, Laurel Speer, Colin Morton, Jenny Browne and Naomi Shihab Nye. The editors say *CVR* is professionally printed and saddle-stitched with cardstock cover featuring a poet walking down a street. Press run is 300 for 97 subscribers. Single copy: $5; subscription: $8/year. "If you want to be our cover poet, send a b&w photo from the back. The editors do like to know a little about you, so do include a cover letter with brief (3-5 line) bio." Sometimes comments on rejections. Responds in up to 6 months. Pays 2 copies and 1-year subscription.

Book/Chapbook Needs: Pecan Grove Press is "interested in fine poetry collections that adhere. A collection should be like an art exhibit—the book is the art space, the pieces work together." They publish 4-6 paperbacks and 2-3 chapbooks/year. They want "poetry with something to say and that says it in fresh, original language. Will rarely publish books of more than 110 pages." They do not want "poetry that lets emotion run over control. We too often see sentiment take precendence over language." They have published poetry by Rick Mulkey, Glen Alyn and Sandra Gail Teichmann. As a sample the editor selected these lines from "This Natural History" by Gwyn McVay:

> *Three deer feed in a line at the edge of the wood/And red sky, the spike-buck lifts his head, his weight/*
> *Suspended on three sinews from the hanging earth,/The does mythical, rounding to white, one/Held*
> *breath, the space between two trees/And for that reason mostly people can't return/The buck's slight*
> *black look when he swivels/his head to take in observers, shagbark oak*

Books or chapbooks are usually 50-96 pgs., offset, perfect-bound, one-color plus b&w graphic design or photographic cover on index stock.

How to Submit: Submit complete ms. Previously published poems and simultaneous submissions OK. Cover letter required, with some indication of a poet's publication history and some ideas or suggestions for marketing the book. Time between acceptance and publication is 8-12 months. "We do circulate for outside opinion when we know the poet who has submitted a manuscript. We read closely and make decisions as quickly as posisble." Seldom comments on rejections. "We do expect our poets to have a publication history in the little magazines with some acknowledgments." Replies to queries and mss in 1-3 months. After the book has paid for itself, authors receive 50% of subsequent sales and 10 author's copies (out of a press run of 500). "We have no subsidy arrangements, but if author has subvention funds, we do welcome them. Obtain sample books by checking BIP and making purchase. We will send chapbook at random for a fee of $5; book for $10."

Advice: "We welcome submissions but feel too many inexperienced poets want to rush into book publication before they are quite ready. Many should try the little magazine route first instead of attempting to begin a new career with book publication."

$ PEER POETRY MAGAZINE; PEER POETRY INTERNATIONAL, 26 (PM) Arlington House, Bath St., Bath, Somerset BA1 1QN United Kingdom, (01225)445298, founded 1995, editor Paul Amphlett.

Magazine Needs: *Peer Poetry Magazine*, published biannually (usually January and July), "is intended to provide poets who have not yet succeeded in 'making their name,' a platform in which they can publish enough of their poetry to allow a number of people in the field to see the quality of their work and at the same time gain for themselves an idea of the informed view of a number of poets currently practicing their talent providing a wide range of views." They want "poetry with natural rhythm, fluent and flowing, having shape and plan; cherishing the sound and beauty of words and ideas. 'Noble sentiments are no substitute for technique and originality.' Highflown language does not make poetry fly high, prose in short lines remains prose; obtrusive rhymes, marching rhythms, produce doggerel!" They have published poetry by Richard Bonfield (UK), Joan Shenidan Smitt (UK), Paul Sohan (US) and Spándov Kányádi (Romania). *Peer Poetry Magazine* is 80 pgs., A4, photocopied, perfect-bound, with b&w card cover. They receive about 750 poems a year, accept approximately 33%. Press run is 300 for 100 subscribers. Single copy: UK £5 plus p&h; subscription: £12 plus p&h.

How to Submit: Submit several poems displaying range but not less than 4. "We require a sufficient quantity of poems to fill 2 A4 'foolscap' pages within a double column set-up, using approximately 50-60 lines per single column in 10 or 12 pt. font in clear black type." Previously published poems where copyright held by poet. Cover letter preferred. Time between acceptance and publication is 3-6 months. Poems are circulated to an editorial board. "Selection is based on originality, comprehensibility and quality of imagination." Often comments on rejections. Send SASE (or SAE and IRC) for guidelines. "Without charge we will publish in hardback (for the winner) and softback (for the runner-up) a colelction of the poems of two poets voted by our readers to be the best of those printed in each issue of *Peer Poetry*." Details of voting reactions and editorial comment are given in succeeding issue. Send 2 copies of submission with SASE (or SAE and IRC). Include name, address, phone and provide a list of titles on the back of each page. Payment in dollar notes or IRCs. No checks unless drawn on a UK bank.

PEGASUS, P.O. Box 61324, Boulder City NV 89006, founded 1986, editor M.E. Hildebrand.

Magazine Needs: *Pegasus* is a poetry quarterly "for serious poets who have something to say and know how to say it using sensory imagery." Avoid "religious, political, pornographic themes." They have published poetry by Kerri Brostrom, Robert K. Johnson and Nikolas Macioci. As a sample the editor selected these closing lines from "Desert Bedlam" by Elizabeth Perry:

> *The lone jacaranda tree below droops its clusters/of purple flowers as if in shame until the amber*
> *stretch/of land facing it once again assumes the mask of silence.*

Pegasus is 32 pgs., digest-sized, desktop-published, saddle-stapled with colored paper cover. Publishes 10-15% of the work received. Circulation is 200. Subscription: $18. Sample: $5.

How to Submit: Submit 3-5 poems, 3-40 lines. Previously published poems OK, provided poet retains rights; no simultaneous submissions. Send SASE for guidelines. Responds in 2 weeks. Publication is payment. Acquires first or one-time rights.

N ◖ ◯ THE PEGASUS REVIEW (Specialized: themes), P.O. Box 88, Henderson MD 21640-0088, phone (410)482-6736, founded 1980, editor Art Bounds.

Magazine Needs: *The Pegasus Review* is a 14-page (counting cover) pamphlet entirely in calligraphy, illustrated on high-quality paper, some color overlays. Editor Art Bounds says, *"The Pegasus Review* is a bimonthly, in a calligraphic format and each issue is based on a specific theme. Since themes might be changed it is suggested to inquire as to current themes. With a magazine in this format, strictly adhere to guidelines—brevity is the key. Poetry—not more than 24 lines (the shorter the better); fiction (short short—about 2½ pages would be ideal); essays and cartoons. All material must pertain to indicated themes only. Poetry may be in any style (rhyming, free verse, haiku)." Also accepts poetry written by teenagers. They have published poetry by Madeline Wise, Carol Raker Collins, P.R. Fiedler, Leslie Foster and Jill Williams. As a sample the editor selected these lines from "Naughty October" by Anthony G. Herles:

> Naughty October,/in golden gowns/dances on variegated ballroom lawns/dresses up in scarlets and browns/winks today with a sunlit complexion/masking the truth of her frosty tomorrows/naughty, naughty October/undresses in the wind/to become/naked November.

Press run is 150 for 100 subscribers, of which 4 are libraries. Subscription: $12. Sample: $2.50.

How to Submit: Submit 3-5 poems with name and address on each page. "Previously published poems OK, if there is no conflict or violation of rights agreement. Simultaneous submissions OK, but author must notify proper parties once specific material is accepted. Brief cover letter with specifics as they relate to one's writing background welcome." January/February: Civilization; March/April: Words; May/June: Childhood; July/August: Heroes; September/October: Old Age; and November/December: Traditions. Responds within a month, often with a personal response. Pays 2 copies.

Also Offers: Offers occasional book awards throughout the year.

Advice: "There are major changes in the writing market, such as electronic publishing. Keep abreast of changes but stick to the tried and true (magazines, book publishers, contests, etc.). Use *Poet's Market* and *Writer's Market* as your reliable source for information. Write daily, get involved with a local writers' group and continue, with enthusiasm, to market your work. Take pride in this time honored craft."

$ ◖ ◎ ⊘ PELICAN PUBLISHING COMPANY (Specialized: children, regional), Box 3110, Gretna LA 70054-3110, website www.pelicanpub.com, founded 1926, editor-in-chief Nina Kooij.

Book/Chapbook Needs: Pelican is a "moderate-sized publisher of cookbooks, travel guides, regional books and inspirational/motivational books," which accepts poetry for "hardcover children's books only, preferably with a regional focus. However, our needs for this are very limited; we do twelve juvenile titles per year, and most of these are prose, not poetry." Also accepts poetry written by children. They have published *Christmas All Over*, by Robert Bernardini. As a sample the editor selected these lines from *An Irish Hallowe'en* by Sarah Kirwan Blazek:

> Long ages ago/On an isle all green,/We started a feast/now called Hallowe'en

These are 32-page, large-format (magazine-sized) books with illustrations. Two of their popular series are prose books about Gaston the Green-Nosed Alligator by James Rice and Clovis Crawfish by Mary Alice Fontenot. They have a variety of books based on "The Night Before Christmas" adapted to regional settings such as Cajun, prairie, and Texas. Typically their books sell for $14.95. Write for catalog to buy samples.

How to Submit: They are *currently not accepting unsolicited mss*. Query first with 2 sample poems and cover letter including "work and writing backgrounds and promotional connections." No previously published poems or simultaneous submissions. Responds to queries in 1 month, to mss (if invited) in 3 months. Always sends prepublication galleys. Pays royalties. Buys all rights. Returns rights upon termination of contract.

Also Offers: Website includes writer's guidelines, catalog and company history.

Advice: "We try to avoid rhyme altogether, especially predictable rhyme. Monotonous rhythm can also be a problem."

◖ PEMBROKE MAGAZINE, UNCP, Box 1510, Pembroke NC 28372-1510, phone (910)521-6358, fax (910)521-6688, founded 1969 by Norman Macleod, edited by Shelby Stephenson, managing editor Fran Oxendine.

Magazine Needs: *Pembroke* is a heavy (460 pgs., 6×9), flat-spined, quality literary annual which has published poetry by Fred Chappell, Stephen Sandy, A.R. Ammons, Barbara Guest and Betty Adcock. Press run is 500 for 125 subscribers of which 100 are libraries. Sample: $8.

How to Submit: Sometimes comments on rejections. Responds within 3 months. Pays copies.

Advice: Stephenson advises, "Publication will come if you write. Writing is all."

✓ ◖ ◐ ⊘ PENMANSHIP: A CREATIVE ARTS CALENDAR, P.O. Box 338, Waynesboro VA 22980, e-mail penmanship@hotmail.com, website www.angelfire.com/me2/norris/index.html, founded 1998, editor Tameka Norris.

Magazine Needs: "I would like to see poetry, short stories, photography, drawings, quotes, any original work of art that one can think of. Looking for all types of work—but clean work! If you know an artist tell them to submit to Penmanship. Give our address to writers, your friends, people interested in getting their work published in a classy calendar." Also accepts poetry written by children. They have published poetry by Lisa Marie Brennan, Kevin Hibshman, Timothy Hodor, Bryon Howell and Rosemary Wentworth. As a sample the editor selected these lines from her poem "We Could've Talked All Day":

> There is much to be talked about/but most of us don't talk about much,/It's what we don't say/that reveals one to the other./At first our paths cross,/at last our paths stray./We hid behind ourselves,/we could've talked all day . . .

Penmanship is a 15 plus-page calendar, saddle-stapled in b&w. Single copy: $5.
How to Submit: Submit 3 poems at a time. Length for poetry is 2 pages maximum. Previously published poems and simultaneous submissions OK. Cover letter preferred. "Some type of letter describing ambitions is greatly desired. Don't forget SASE for response. Fillers are also needed." Reading fee: $5/3 poems. "Each additional group of three requires another $5 reading fee. The reading fee serves as purchase of the calendar for those who aren't chosen for publication." Time between acceptance and publication is 1-12 months. Often comments on rejections. Send SASE for guidelines. Responds in up to 1 month. Pays at least $5 refund "or more" and 2 copies ($5 value). Acquires first or one-time rights or second serial reprint rights. Reviews books and chapbooks of poetry. Open to unsolicited reviews. Poets may also send books for review consideration.
Also Offers: *Penmanship* also publishes an audio cassette series, broadside series and postcard series. Currently no submissions accepted for bookmark series. Send SASE for details. Website includes guidelines, editor's book of poetry, fan club and more.
Advice: "No one's going to listen to you if you don't make them listen!"

PENNINE PLATFORM, 7 Cockley Hill Lane, Kirkheaton, Huddersfield HD5 OHW England, phone (0)1484-516804, founded 1973, poetry editor K.E. Smith.
Magazine Needs: *PP* appears 2 times a year. The editor wants any kind of poetry but concrete ("lack of facilities for reproduction"). No specifications of length, but poems of less than 40 lines have a better chance. "All styles—effort is to find things good of their kind. Preference for religious or sociopolitical awareness of an acute, not conventional kind." They have published poetry by Elizabeth Bartlett, Anna Adams, John Ward, Ian Caws, John Latham and Geoffrey Holloway. As a sample the editor selected these lines from "A Vision of Cabez De Vaca" by Cal Clothier:

> Blanched to a skin manned by bones,/we have blood and our breathing/to prove we are men, and the hungry light/jerking our eyes. We are down to mercy,/gratitude, love, down to humanity.

The 6×8, 48-page journal is photocopied from typescript, saddle-stapled, with matte card cover with graphics. Circulation is 400 for 300 subscribers of which 16 are libraries. They receive about 300 submissions/year, use about 60, have about a 6-month backlog. Subscription: £8.50 for 2 issues (£12 abroad; £25 if not in sterling). Sample: £4.50.
How to Submit: Submit up to 6 poems, typed. Responds in about 3 months. No pay. Acquires first serial rights. Editor occasionally comments on rejections. Reviews books of poetry in 500 words, multi-book format. Open to unsolicited reviews. Poets may also send books for review consideration.

PENNSYLVANIA ENGLISH, Penn State DuBois, DuBois PA 15801-3199, phone (814)375-4814, e-mail ajv2@psu.edu, founded 1988 (first issue in March, 1989), editor Antonio Vallone.
Magazine Needs: *Pennsylvania English*, appearing annually in September, is "a journal sponsored by the Pennsylvania College English Association." They want poetry of "any length, any style." They have published poetry by Liz Rosenberg, Walt MacDonald, Amy Pence, Jennifer Richter and Jeff Schiff. The journal is up to 180 pgs., 5½×8½, perfect-bound with a full color cover. Press run is 300. Subscription: $10/year.
How to Submit: Submit 3 or more typed poems at a time. Include SASE. They consider simultaneous submissions but not previously published poems. Send SASE for guidelines. Responds in 3 months. Pays 3 copies.

PENNY DREADFUL: TALES & POEMS OF FANTASTIC TERROR (Specialized: horror), P.O. Box 719, Radio City Station, Hell's Kitchen NY 10101-0719, founded 1996, editor/publisher Michael Pendragon.
"Works appearing in *PD* have received Honorable Mention in *The Year's Best Fantasy and Horror*." Penny Dreadful nominates best tales and poems for Pushcart Prizes.
Magazine Needs: *Penny Dreadful* is a triannual publication (Autumn, Winter, Midsummer) of goth-romantic poetry and prose. Publishes poetry, short stories, essays, letters, listings, reviews and b&w artwork "which

---

THE CHAPBOOK INDEX, located at the back of this book, lists those publishers who consider chapbook mss. A chapbook, a small volume of work (usually under 50 pages), is often a good middle step between magazine and book publication.

celebrate the darker aspects of Man, the World, and their Creator. We're looking for literary horror in the tradition of Poe, M.R. James, Shelley, M.P. Shiel and LeFanu—dark, disquieting tales and verses designed to challenge the readers' perception of human nature, morality and man's place within the Darkness. Stories and poems should be set prior to 1910 and/or possess a timeless quality. Avoid references to 20th century personages/events, graphic sex, strong language, excessive gore and shock elements." They have published poetry by Nancy Bennett, Michael R. Burch, Lee Clark, Holly Day, K.S. Hardy and David Kablack. As a sample the editor selected these lines from "Destiny" by Tamara B. Latham:

> Sand which fills the hourglass/Scattered densely thru the sky/Blown by some eternal wind/Into some mere mortal's eye

Penny Dreadful is 80 pgs., 5½×8½, desktop-published, saddle-stapled with b&w line art. Includes market listings "for, and reviews of, kindred magazines." Press run is 250 copies. Subscription: $12/year (3 issues). Sample: $5. Make checks payable to Michael Pendragon.

How to Submit: Submit 3-5 poems with name and address on opening of each page, and name, title and page number appearing on all following pages. Poems should not exceed 3 pages rhymed, metered verse preferred. Previously published poems and simultaneous submissions OK. Include cover letter and SASE. Reads submissions all year. Time between acceptance and publication is up to 1 year. Poems reviewed and chosen by editor. Often comments on rejections. Responds in up to 3 months. Always sends prepublication galleys. Pays 1 copy. Acquires one-time rights.

$⊘ PENNYWHISTLE PRESS, P.O. Box 734, Tesuque NM 87574, phone (505)982-0066 or (505)982-2622, fax (505)982-6858 or (505)982-8116, e-mail pnywhistle@aol.com, founded 1986, publisher Victor di Suvero.

Book/Chapbook Needs: Pennywhistle Press "was started as a way to present the work of notable poets to the reading public. Known for its Poetry Chapbook Series, which currently features 24 titles by some of the strongest voices of our time: Francisco X. Alarcón, Dennis Brutus, Joyce Jenkins, Jerome Rothenberg, Suzanne Lummis, Judyth Hill and Sarah Blake, the Press has branched out into the anthology market with the publication of *Saludos! Poemas de Nuevo Mexico*, a bilingual collection of 66 poets presenting their diverse views of this unusual tricultural state, which is also a state of being. Poèts in this collection run the spectrum from N. Scott Momaday, Luci Tapahonso and Carolyn Forché to Janet Holmes, Reneé Gregorio and Keith Wilson." The press also has a series entitled Sextet, "an anthology of poetry comprised of six chapbooks by new and established voices." They publish 2 paperbacks and 6 chapbooks a year. They want poetry with "deep, rich imagery; confessional, solid, strong and experimental—generally one page in length." As a sample the editor selected these lines from "A Love Song from the Chimayó Landfill" by Janet Holmes from the anthology, *Saludos! Poemas de Nuevo Mexico*:

> . . . I had merely/two bags of garbage to heave into the heap,/a minor offering beside that of the men/ emptying their truckbeds with shovels. They/were happy, too; yes, everyone was laughing,/as if it were Fiesta, not the dump. I wanted to tell you:/this is how you make me feel, my darling.

Chapbooks are usually 32 pgs., 5¼×8⅜, perfect-bound; anthologies are about 200 pgs., 6×9, perfect-bound. **How to Submit:** Submit 10 poems at a time. Previously published poems and simultaneous submissions OK. Cover letter preferred. Poems are circulated to an editorial board. "Reviewed by editorial board and then submitted to managing editor and publisher for approval." Replies to queries in 2-4 months, to mss in 1 month. Pays $100 honorarium and 25 author's copies (out of a press run of 1,500).

✓ ⊘ ◎ THE PENWOOD REVIEW (Specialized: spirituality), P.O. Box 862, Los Alamitos CA 90720-0862, e-mail bcame39696@aol.com, website: http://members.aol.com/bcame39696/penwood.htm, founded 1997, editor Lori M. Cameron.

Magazine Needs: *The Penwood Review*, published biannually, "seeks to explore the mystery and meaning of the spiritual and sacred aspects of our existence and our relationship to God." They want "disciplined, high-quality, well-crafted poetry on any subject. Prefer poems be less than two pages. Rhyming poetry must be written in traditional forms (sonnets, tercets, villanelles, sestinas, etc.)" They do not want "light verse, doggerel or greeting card-style poetry. Also, nothing racist, sexist, pornographic or blasphemous." They have published poetry by Carol Kauffman, Jack Niewold, Ellen Hyatt, and Mark Aveyard. As a sample the editor selected these lines from "Mount Kenya" by Michael McManus:

> Village elders told me,/if you love something immense/and beyond your reach, if your faith/is never diminished by famine or flood/one night the stars will turn/into white talons, and lift me to your summit./I believe them.

The editor says *TPR* has approximately 40 pgs, 8½×11, saddle-stapled with heavy card cover. Press run is 50-100. Single copy: $6; subscription: $12.

How to Submit: Submit 3-5 poems, 1/page with the author's full name, address and phone number in the upper right hand corner. No previously published poems or simultaneous submissions. E-mail submissions OK in body of message. Cover letter preferred. Time between acceptance and publication is 6-12 months. "Submissions are circulated among an editorial staff for evaluations." Seldom comments on rejections. Responds in 2 months. Offers subscription discount of $10 to published authors and one additional free copy in which author's work appears. Acquires one-time rights.

$ ▢ ▢ ◉ THE PEOPLE'S PRESS, 4810 Norwood Ave., Baltimore MD 21207-6839, phone/fax (410)448-0254, press founded 1997, firm founded 1989, contact submissions editor.
Book/Chapbook Needs: "The goal of the types of material we publish is simply to move people to think and perhaps act to make the world better than when we inherited it." They want "meaningful poetry that is mindful of human rights/dignity." They have published *2000: Here's to Humanity* (includes the work of 89 poets). Also accepts poetry written by children. However, parental consent is mandatory for publication. As a sample they selected these lines from "Lament for Imelda" by Zyskandar A. Jaimot:

> *Shoe colour as well as conviction/Changes with circumstance/because it must/Have been someone else who ordered all/Those/pairs of pumps sent to your suite/At the posh Plaza Hotel/while those creatures/Back in the Philippines went without*

Books are usually 50 pgs., 5½×8, photocopied, perfect-bound and saddle-stitched with soft cover, includes art/graphics.
How to Submit: Query first with 1-5 sample poems and a cover letter with brief bio and publication credits. Previously published poems and simultaneous submissions OK. SASE required for return of work and/or response. Time between acceptance and publication is 6-12 months. Seldom comments on rejections. Publishes theme issues. Send SASE for guidelines. Replies to queries in 2-6 weeks; to mss in 1-3 months. Pays royalties of 5-20% and 50 author's copies (out of a press run of 500). Order sample books by sending $6.
Also Offers: The People's Press sponsors an annual Poetry Month Contest in April. Entries accepted April 1-15. "Prizes and/or publication possibilities vary from contest to contest." Send SASE for details.

☑ ▢ ◎ PEP PUBLISHING; LOVING MORE (Specialized: "ethical multiple relationships"), P.O. Box 4358, Boulder CO 80306, phone/fax (303)543-7540, e-mail lmm@lovemore.com, website www.lovemore.com, founded 1984, editor Ryam Nearing.
Magazine Needs: *Loving More* is a quarterly that "publishes articles, letters, poems, drawings and reviews related to polyfidelity, group marriage and multiple *intimacy*." They use "relatively short poems, though a quality piece of length would be considered, but topic relevance is essential. Please no swinger or porno pieces. Group marriage should not be equated with group sex." It is 40 pgs., magazine-sized, professionally printed on recycled paper and saddle-stapled with 4-color paper cover and a few ads. Circulation is 2,500. Subscription: $24/year. Sample: $6.
How to Submit: Submit up to 10 poems at a time. Ms should be "readable." Considers previously published poems. E-mail ("plain text, no attachments") and fax submissions OK. Also accepts mss on disk (Mac text, PC text, Word or Wordperfect). Time between acceptance and publication is 2-6 months. Editor comments on rejections "sometimes—if requested." Publishes theme issues. Send SASE for upcoming themes. Guidelines available via e-mail at writers@lovemore.com. Responds "ASAP." Pays 2 copies. Open to unsolicited reviews. Poets may also send books for review consideration.
Also Offers: Website includes writer's guidelines, articles, frequently asked questions, links.
Advice: "We're always looking for good poetry related specifically to our topic. Our readers love it when we find some to include. Writers should read our publication or visit our website before submitting, and I emphasize no swinger or porno pieces will be published."

◐ PEQUOD: A JOURNAL OF CONTEMPORARY LITERATURE AND LITERARY CRITICISM, Dept. of English, New York University, 19 University Place, Room 200, New York NY 10003, phone (212)998-8843, fax (212)995-4019, e-mail pequod.journal@nyu.edu, website www.nyu.edu/gsas/dept/eng/journal/pequod, contact poetry editor.
Magazine Needs: *Pequod* is a semiannual literary review publishing quality poetry, fiction, essays and translations. They have published poetry by Sam Hamill, Donald Hall and John Updike. It is 200 pgs., digest-sized, professionally printed, flat-spined with glossy card cover. Subscription: $14. Sample: $10.
How to Submit: Reads submissions September 15 through April 15 only. Always sends prepublication galleys.

◐ PEREGRINE: THE JOURNAL OF AMHERST WRITERS & ARTISTS PRESS; THE PEREGRINE PRIZE, P.O. Box 1076, Amherst MA 01004-1076, phone/fax (413)253-7764, e-mail awapress@javanet.com, website www.javanet.com/~awapress, founded 1984, managing editor Nancy Rose.
Magazine Needs: *Peregrine*, published annually in October, features poetry and fiction. Open to all styles, forms and subjects except greeting card verse. They have published poetry by Naomi Ayala, H. Shaw Cauchy, Willie James King and Valerie Lavender. As a sample the editor selected these lines from "Dance of the Dervish" by Lee Price:

> *. . . I am the wink of the firefly/who turns and burns,/insides red as passionfruit,/blinking, whirling,/ swirling in a cloud of sparkled lust./I am the thirst that quenches,/the Coefficient of two. . . .*

Peregrine is 104 pgs., digest-sized, professionally printed, perfect-bound with glossy cover. Each issue includes at least one poem in translation and reviews. Press run is 1,000. Single copy: $10; subscription: $20/3 issues; $30/5 issues. Sample: $8. Make checks payable to AWA Press.
How to Submit: Submit 3-5 poems, no more than 70 lines (and spaces) each. No previously published work; simultaneous submissions OK. Include cover letter with bio, 40 word maximum. No e-mail submissions. "No!

No! No!" "Each ms is read by several readers. Final decisions are made by the poetry editor." Send #10 SASE or visit website for guidelines. Reads submissions October through April only. Postmark deadline: April 1. Pays 2 copies. Acquires first rights.

Also Offers: The Peregrine Prize, an annual fiction and/or poetry contest. 1st Prize: $500, publication in *Peregrine*, and copies. Entry fee: $10. Submit 1-3 poems, limited to 70 lines (and spaces) per poem. *"Very specific contest guidelines!"* Send #10 SASE or visit website for guidelines. After the winners of the Peregrine Prize have been chosen by an outside judge, the editorial staff will select one entry from Western Massachusetts to receive the "Best of the Nest" Award. The AWA Chapbook Series is *closed* to unsolicited submissions. Website includes guidelines, staff/editors, contest winners and announcements.

☑ ◔ ◎ **PERSPECTIVES (Specialized: religious)**, P.O. Box 1196, Holland MI 49422-1196, co-editors Roy Anker, Leanne Van Dyk and Dave Timmer, poetry editor Francis Fike (send poetry submissions to Francis Fike at Dept. of English, Hope College, Holland MI 49422-9000), founded 1986.

Magazine Needs: *Perspectives* appears 10 times/year. The journal's purpose is "to express the Reformed faith theologically; to engage issues that Reformed Christians meet in personal, ecclesiastical, and societal life, and thus to contribute to the mission of the church of Jesus Christ." They want "both traditional and free verse of high quality, whether explicitly 'religious' or not. Prefer traditional form. Publish one or two poems every other issue, alternating with a Poetry Page on great traditional poems from the past. No sentimental, trite, or inspirational verse, please." They have published poetry by Len Krisak, Nancy Nicodemus and Frederick Lewis Allen. As a sample the editor selected these lines from "Entering the Kingdom" by Julia Guernsey:

> So she found Dakota Street, a heap/of trash out back, containers grimed with food,/the third floor
> balcony on which she stood,/remembering Wordsworth's ode to the shrill beep/of a forklift, which came
> to strip the mound/and struck a nest of rats. Their whiplike tails/slithered, their bodies scratching
> separate trails/like dice, a chaos over icy ground.

Perspectives is 24 pgs., 8½×11, web offset and saddle-stapled, with paper cover containing b&w illustration. They receive about 50 poems a year, accept 6-10. Press run is 3,300 for 3,000 subscribers of which 200 are libraries. Subscription: $24.95. Sample: $3.50.

How to Submit: No previously published poems or simultaneous submissions. Cover letter preferred. Include SASE. Time between acceptance and publication is 8 months or less. Seldom comments on rejections. Responds in up to 3 months. Pays 5 copies. Acquires first rights.

☑ ◔ ◎ **PERUGIA PRESS (Specialized: women)**, P.O. Box 108, Shutesbury MA 01072, e-mail perugia @valinet.com, founded 1997, director Susan Kan.

Book/Chapbook Needs: "Perugia Press publishes one collection of poetry each year, by a woman at the beginning of her publishing career. The poems that catch our attention use simple language and recognizable imagery to express complex issues, events and emotions. Our books appeal to people who have been reading poetry for decades, as well as those who might be picking up a book of poetry for the first time. Slight preference for narrative, personal work." They have published poetry by Gail Thomas, Almitra David and Janet E. Aalfs. As a sample the director selected these lines from "Ascent" by Almitra David in *Impulse to Fly*:

> Witnesses saw the children plummet,/but she watched them fly, saw each one/soar and ride the wind,/
> then tucked her baby under her wings/and took off.

Books are usually 88 pgs., 6×9, offset printed and perfect-bound with 2-color card cover with photo or illustration.

How to Submit: Query first with 10 sample poems and cover letter with brief bio and publication credits. Previously published poems and simultaneous submissions OK. Cover letter preferred. Send SASE for response. Annual deadline is January 1. Time between acceptance and publication is 9 months. Seldom comments on rejections. Replies to queries in 1 month; to mss in 6 weeks. Pay is negotiable. Order sample books by sending $10.

☑ ◕ **PHILOMEL BOOKS**, 345 Hudson St., New York NY 10014, phone (212)414-3610, fax (212)414-3395, an imprint founded in 1980, editorial director Patricia Gauch, senior editor Michael Green.

Book/Chapbook Needs: Philomel Books publishes 15-20 hardbacks and 5-7 chapbooks/year. They say, "Since we're a children's book imprint, we are open to individual poem submissions—anything suitable for a picture book. However, publication of poetry collections is usually done on a project basis—we acquire from outside through permissions, etc. Don't usually use unpublished material." They have published poetry by Edna St. Vincent Millay and Walt Whitman.

How to Submit: Query first with 3 sample poems and cover letter including publishing history. Previously published poems and simultaneous submissions OK. Replies to queries in 1 month, to mss in 2. Pay is negotiable.

☑ ◔ **PHOEBE; GREG GRUMMER POETRY AWARD**, George Mason University, 4400 University Dr., Fairfax VA 22030, phone (703)993-2915, e-mail phoebe@gmu.edu, website www.gmu.edu/pubs/phoebe, founded 1970, editor Rebecca Dunham.

Magazine Needs: *Phoebe* is a literary biannual "looking for imagery that will make your thumbs sweat when you touch it." They have published poetry by C.D. Wright, Russell Edson, Yusef Komunyakaa, Rosemarie Waldrop and Leslie Scalapino. As a sample the editor selected these lines from "Why I Cannot Write At Home" by Jeffrey Schwarz:

> *Does the moon yank a black comb/through the sun?/No, Mother does that.// . . .//Then where's the*
> *moon all morning?//Knocking and knocking on the outhouse door.*

Circulation is 3,000, with 35-40 pgs. of poetry in each issue. *Phoebe* receives 4,000 submissions a year. Single copy: $6; subscription: $12/year.

How to Submit: Submit up to 5 poems at a time; submission should be accompanied by SASE and a short bio. No simultaneous submissions. Responds in 3 months. Pays 2 copies or one year subscription.

Also Offers: Sponsors the Greg Grummer Poetry Award. Awards $1,000 and publication for winner, publication for finalists and a copy of awards issue to all entrants. Submit up to 4 poems, any subject, any form, with name on cover page only. No previously published submissions. Entry fee: $10/entry. Deadline: December 15. Contest receives 400-500 submissions. Back copy of awards issue: $6. Send SASE for guidelines.

PHOEBE: JOURNAL OF FEMINIST SCHOLARSHIP THEORY AND AESTHETICS (Specialized: women/feminism), Women's Studies Dept., Suny-College at Oneonta, Oneonta NY 13820-4015, phone (607)436-2014, fax (607)436-2656, e-mail omarakk@oneonta.edu, founded 1989, poetry editor Marilyn Wesley, editor Kathleen O'Mara.

Magazine Needs: *Phoebe* is published semiannually. They want "mostly poetry reflecting women's experiences; prefer 3 pages or less." They have published poetry by Barbara Crooker, Graham Duncan and Patty Tana. As a sample we selected these lines from "Rosh Hodesh, In the Room of Mirrors" by Lyn Lifshin:

> *eyes over crystal/that a great aunt/might have polished/reflected in a/hall mirror,/candles float/like the*
> *moon,/a reflection of a/reflection.*

Phoebe is 120 pgs., 7×9, offset printed on coated paper and perfect-bound with glossy card cover, includes b&w art/photos and "publishing swap" ads. They receive about 500 poems a year, accept approximately 8%. Press run is 500 for 120 subscribers of which 52 are libraries. Single copy: $7.50; subscription: $15/year or $25/year institutional. Sample: $5.

How to Submit: No previously published poems. Fax submissions OK. Cover letter preferred. Reads submissions October through January and May through July only. Time between acceptance and publication is 3 months. Seldom comments on rejections. Publishes theme issues occasionally. Send SASE for guidelines. Responds in up to 14 weeks. Sometimes sends prepublication galleys. Pays 1 copy. Staff reviews books and chapbooks of poetry in 500-1,000 words, single book format. Send books for review consideration.

PIANO PRESS; "THE ART OF MUSIC" ANNUAL WRITING CONTEST (Specialized: music-related topics), P.O. Box 85, Del Mar CA 92014-0085, phone (858)481-5650, fax (858)755-1104, e-mail pianopress@aol.com, website http://pianopress.iuma.com, founded 1999, owner Elizabeth C. Axford, M.A.

Book/Chapbook Needs: "Piano Press publishes poems on music-related topics to promote the art of music." They publish 50-100 poems per year. "We are looking for poetry on music-related topics only. Poems can be of any length and in any style. We do not want song lyrics." As a sample they selected these lines:

> *Friends close to home bring to mind/The times tuned to a cello or a flute/When I trace the fine vines/*
> *And glare at the candle with the brass root/Lighting the lazy throws.*

Chapbooks are usually 80 pgs., 5×7, photocopied and saddle-stitched with 110 lb. paper cover, includes some art/graphics.

How to Submit: Query first, with a few sample poems and cover letter with brief bio and publication credits. Previously published poems and simultaneous submissions OK. E-mail submissions OK. SASE required for reply. Reads submissions September 1 through June 30 only. Submit seasonal poems 6-10 months in advance. Time between acceptance and publication is 6-18 months. Poems are circulated to an editorial board. "All submissions are reviewed by several previously published poets." Often comments on rejections. Replies to queries in 1 month; to mss in 3 months. Pays 5 author's copies (out of a press run of 500). Order sample chapbooks by sending SASE for order form.

Also Offers: Sponsors an annual writing contest for poetry, short stories and essays on music. Open to ages 4 and up. Entry fee: $20/poem. Send SASE for guidelines and entry form. Website includes description of company, lists current and upcoming publications and information on annual writing contest.

PIF MAGAZINE; PIF PRIZE FOR POETRY, PMB 248, 4820 Yelm Hwy. SE, Suite B, Lacey WA 98503-4903, phone (360)459-7289, fax (360)459-4496, e-mail poetry@pifmagazine.com, website www.pifmagazine.com, founded 1995, poetry editor Anne Doolittle, managing editor Richard Luck, senior editor Camilla Renshaw.

- Richard Luck says, "*Yahoo Internet Life* recently praised *Pif Magazine* as 'The Next Wave. With writers-only classifieds and regular fiction and poetry contests, Pif targets hungry scribes eager for the chance to submit original work.' David Lehman, in the prelude to *The Best American Poetry* mentioned *Pif* as one of the 'hot new' online literary magazines."

Magazine Needs: *Pif Magazine* appears monthly and is "your home on the Internet for the best poetry, fiction, interviews and commentary available. We are fast becoming 'the' litmus test for new authors on the Net." They are open to any form or style. "We want to see poetry that is innovative and takes chances. We're plotting the course for American poetry, not following someone else's example. No stale, staid work that lacks courage or creativity." They publish an annual print version in March. They have published poetry by Liam Rector, Robert McDowell, David Lehman, Gail Hosking Gilberg and Allison Jenks. *Pif* is 30-36 electronic pgs. They receive about 750 poems a year, accept approximately 15%.

How to Submit: Submit 3-5 poems at a time. No previously published poems; simultaneous submissions OK. "Please submit all poems via our online submission form at www.pifmagazine.com/email.shtml. This will ensure that we receive your submission in the proper format." Cover letter with short bio preferred. "Tell us a little about the writing of the poem—as well as a brief bio." Time between acceptance and publication is 1 month. Seldom comments on rejections. Publishes theme issues. Send SASE or "e-mail rules@pifmagazine.com or visit website for the latest listing of upcoming themes. Responds in 2 months. Sometimes sends prepublication galleys. Pays $5-50/poem. Acquires first rights. Reviews books and chapbooks of poetry and other magazines in 250-1,000 words, single book format. Open to unsolicited reviews. Poets may also send books for review consideration to Richard Luck.

Also Offers: Sponsors the Pif Prize for Poetry, an annual award of $150 for the best poem. Also awards Honorable mention prizes. Submit 3 poems/entry, no more than 100 lines each. Poems must be unpublished but may be on any subject or in any form. Send SASE for guidelines only. Entry fee: $10/entry (3 poems). Deadline: December 31. Competition receives 50-100 entries. Winners announced March 1 in online issues of *Pif* (all winners are notified in advance by e-mail or phone). "*Pif* is home to Pilot-Search.com, the Net's premier literary search engine. Find the exact poem, interview or book review you've been looking for. Pilot-Search—the Starting Point for Literary Web Searches."

Advice: "Electronic publishing will revolutionize the art of writing as profoundly as did the printing press—and we aim to lead the way. *Pif Magazine* is a premier showcase for new and established poets on the Internet. Many of the poets published in *Pif* have gone on to have collections published by mainstream publishers. Read a couple of issues to get a feel for the type of work we admire. If we love strawberries and you're sending watermelons, well . . .?"

$ ◱ ◎ PIG IRON; KENNETH PATCHEN COMPETITION (Specialized: themes), P.O. Box 237, Youngstown OH 44501, phone (330)747-6932, fax (330)747-0599, founded 1975, poetry editor Jim Villani.

Magazine Needs: *Pig Iron* is a literary annual devoted to special themes. They want poetry "up to 300 lines; free verse and experimental; write for current themes." They do not want to see "traditional" poetry. They have published poetry by Frank Polite, Larry Smith, Howard McCord, Andrena Zawinski, Juan Kincaid and Coco Gordon. As a sample the editors included these lines from "Cat Call" by Andrenna Zawinski:

> Curled in the corner of your couch,/like your amber eyed calico cat,/I dove when the earth quaked,
> fell/into the expanse of space stretched/between your arms. You caught me,/held me there,/hair on end,
> claws out, screeching./You held me to to your breast, your heart/beat my own rhythm; and I,/star struck
> and bewitched,/I purred in your ear.

Pig Iron is 128 pgs., magazine-sized, flat-spined, typeset on good stock with glossy card cover using b&w graphics and art, no ads. Press run is 1,000 for 200 subscribers of which 50 are libraries. Single copy: $12.95. Subscription: $12.95/year. Sample: $5. (Include $1.75 postage.)

How to Submit: Include SASE with submission. Fax submissions OK. Send SASE for guidelines. Responds in 3 months. Time between acceptance and publication is 12-18 months. Publishes theme issues. Next theme issue: "Religion in Modernity." Deadline: September 2000. Send SASE for guidelines and upcoming themes. Pays $5/poem plus 2 copies (additional copies at 50% retail). Buys one-time rights.

Also Offers: They sponsor the annual Kenneth Patchen Competition. Send SASE for details.

Advice: "Reading the work of others positions one to be creative and organized in his/her own work."

◱ PIKEVILLE REVIEW, Humanities Dept., Pikeville College, Pikeville KY 41501, phone (606)432-9612, fax (606)432-9328, e-mail eward@pc.edu, website www.pc.edu, founded 1987, editor Elgin M. Ward.

Magazine Needs: "There's no editorial bias though we recognize and appreciate style and control in each piece. No emotional gushing." *PR* appears once yearly in July, accepting about 10% of poetry received. *PR* is 94 pgs., digest-sized, professionally printed and perfect-bound with glossy card cover with b&w illustration. Press run is 500. Sample: $4.

How to Submit: No simultaneous submissions or previously published poems. Editor sometimes comments on rejections. Send SASE for guidelines. Pays 5 copies.

Also Offers: They also sponsor contests. Website includes names of editors, guidelines and most recent editions.

$ ◱ ◎ PINE ISLAND JOURNAL OF NEW ENGLAND POETRY (Specialized: regional), P.O. Box 317, West Springfield MA 01090-0317, founded 1998, editor Linda Porter.

Magazine Needs: *Pine Island* appears 2 times a year "to encourage and support New England poets and the continued expression of New England themes." They want poems of "up to thirty lines, haiku and other forms welcome, especially interested in New England subjects or themes. No horror, no erotica. They have published poetry by Larry Kimmel, Roy P. Fairfield and Carol Purington. As a sample the editor selected this poem, "Trinity," by Linda Porter:

a trinity of apples/grace the handturned bowl/in the parlor.//just in case the pastor should call/or God himself stop by

Pine Island is 50 pgs., digest-sized, desktop-published and saddle-stitched, cardstock cover with art. Press run is 200 for 80 subscribers. Subscription: $10. Sample: $5. Make checks payable to Pine Island Journal.
How to Submit: "Writers must be currently residenced in New England." Submit 5 poems at a time. Line length for poetry is 30 maximum. No previously published poems or simultaneous submissions. Cover letter preferred. "Include SASE, prefer first time submissions to include cover letter with brief bio." Time between acceptance and publication is 6 months. Seldom comments on rejections. Responds in 1 month. Pays $1/poem and 1 copy. Buys first rights.

⊞ ⦿ PINK CADILLAC: THE MAGAZINE OF CREATIVE THOUGHT, 2822 Beale Ave., Altoona PA 16601-1708, e-mail ikey95@aol.com or poet29@wrta.com, website http://hometown.aol.com/ikey95/myhom epage/business.html, founded 1996, editor Alice Balest.
Magazine Needs: *Pink Cadillac* is a quarterly forum for new and established writers. They want any style, up to 50 lines. "No vulgar, pornographic or overly sentimental, sappy drivel." They have published poetry by Tom Hendrix, Patricia G. Rourke, Elizabeth Fuller, Ace Boggess, Ann A. Boger and Bess Kemp. As a sample the editor selected these lines from "Notions" by Bess Kemp:
> *Plowingfields of/reverie/deep age-furrows/appeared/in neat even rows/uninvited*
The editor says *PC* is 20 pgs., 8½×11, includes line art and reading/writing related ads. Subscription: $10. Sample: $2.50.
How to Submit: Submit 4-8 typed poems at a time. "Nothing handwritten." Line length for poetry is 3 minimum, 50 maximum. Previously published poems and simultaneous submissions OK. E-mail submissions OK. Cover letter preferred. Time between acceptance and publication is 2-4 months. Send SASE for guidelines or obtain via e-mail. Responds in 4 months. Pays 1 copy. Acquires one-time rights. Reviews books and chapbooks of poetry and other magazines. Open to unsolicited reviews. Poets may also send books for review consideration.

⦿ PINYON POETRY, Dept. of Languages, Literature & Communications, Mesa State College, Grand Junction CO 81502, phone (970)248-1123, founded 1995, managing editor Michele Gonzales, editor Randy Phillis.
Magazine Needs: *Pinyon Poetry* appears 2 times a year and publishes "the best available contemporary American poetry and b&w artwork." They have "no restrictions other than excellence. We appreciate a strong voice. No inspirational, light verse or sing-song poetry." They have published poetry by Mark Cox, Barry Spacks, Wendy Bishop and Anne Ohman Youngs. As a sample the editor selected these lines from "The Approved Poem" by John McKernan:
> *The Approved Poem sits in an oak rocker on the/front porch of a sharecropper's cabin in Logan North/ Dakota arranging the words alphabetically in a/scrapbook.*
The editors say *Pinyon* is about 48 pgs., magazine-sized, offset printed and saddle-stitched, cover varies, includes 8-10 pgs. of b&w art/graphics. They receive about 4,000 poems a year, accept approximately 2%. Press run is 200 for 50 subscribers of which 5 are libraries, 50 shelf sales; 100 distributed free to contributors, friends, etc. Subscription: $8/year. Sample: $4.50. Make checks payable to *Pinyon Poetry*, MSC.
How to Submit: Submit 3-5 poems at a time. No previously published poems or simultaneous submissions. Cover letter preferred. "Name, address and phone number on each page. SASE required." Time between acceptance and publication is 3-12 months. Poems are circulated to an editorial board. "Three groups of assistant editors, led by an associate editor, make recommendations to the editor." Seldom comments on rejections. Send SASE for guidelines. Responds in up to 3 months, "slower in summer." Pays 1 copy/printed page. Acquires one-time rights.
Also Offers: "Each issue contains a 'Featured Poet.' We generally publish 8-15 pages of this one poet's work."
Advice: "Send us your best work!"

◯ ◎ THE PIPE SMOKER'S EPHEMERIS (Specialized), 20-37 120th St., College Point NY 11356-2128, founded 1964, editor/publisher Tom Dunn.
Magazine Needs: "The *Ephemeris* is a limited edition, irregular quarterly for pipe smokers and anyone else who is interested in its varied contents. Publication costs are absorbed by the editor/publisher, assisted by any contributions—financial or otherwise—that readers might wish to make." They want poetry with themes related to pipes and pipe smoking. Issues range from 76-96 pgs., and are 8½×11, offset from photoreduced typed copy, saddle-stitched, with colored paper covers and illustrations. The editor has also published collections covering the first and second 15 years of the *Ephemeris*.
How to Submit: Cover letter required with submissions; include any credits. Pays 1-2 copies. Staff reviews books of poetry. Send books for review consideration.

▨ ⊕ SENDING TO A COUNTRY other than your own? Be sure to send International Reply Coupons (IRCs) instead of stamps for replies or return of your manuscript.

○ ◎ ◉ **PIRATE WRITINGS: TALES OF FANTASY, MYSTERY & SCIENCE FICTION (Special-ized: science fiction/fantasy, mystery)**, P.O. Box 329, Brightwaters NY 11718, founded 1992, editor Edward J. McFadden. (Published by DNA Publications. Send all business-related inquiries and subscriptions to DNA Publications, P.O. Box 2988, Radford VA 24143.)

Magazine Needs: *Pirate Writings* is a quarterly magazine "filled with fiction, poetry, art and reviews by top name professionals and tomorrow's rising stars." They want all forms and styles of poetry "within our genres— literary (humorous or straight), fantasy, science fiction, mystery/suspense and adventure. Best chance is 20 lines or less. No crude language or excessive violence. No pornography, horror, western or romance. Poems should be typed with exact capitalization and punctuation suited to your creative needs." They have published poetry by Nancy Springer, Jane Yolen and John Grey. *Pirate Writings* is 72 pgs., magazine-sized and saddle-stapled with a full-color cover, interior spot color and b&w art throughout. They receive about 150 poetry submissions a year, use approximately 15-25 poems. Subscription: $16/4 issues, $27/8 issues. Sample: $4.95.

How to Submit: Simultaneous submissions OK. Cover letter required; include credits, if applicable. Often comments on rejections. Send SASE for guidelines. Responds in 4 months. Pays 1-2 copies and 50¢ a line. Acquires first North American serial rights. Also "reserves the right to print in future volumes of *The Best of Pirate Writings* anthology."

○ ◑ **PITCHFORK; PITCHFORK PRESS**, 2002 A Guadalupe St. #461, Austin TX 78705, founded 1998, editor Christopher Gibson.

Magazine Needs: *Pitchfork* is a biannual publishing "freaky goodness." They want "erotic, psychotic and surreal poetry. No hack work." They have published poetry by Albert Huffstickler, Thomas Michael McDade and Lyn Lifshin. As a sample the editor selected these lines from "Cupid Pro-Creator" by Robert O'Neal:

> *tawdry pink hearts &/blue moons give the feathers to/foreskin, a plump-assed/cherub who splits hairs*
> *with his/feckless aim—love or/lust that quickens eggs into/raspberry-shellaced tadpoles?*

Pitchfork is 60 pgs., digest-sized, photocopied and saddle-stapled with colored paper cover. Press run varies. Subscription: $6. Sample: $3. Make checks payable to Christopher Gibson.

How to Submit: Submit 3-7 poems at a time. Previously published poems and simultaneous submissions OK "but let us know." Cover letter preferred. "Include name and address on each page; always include SASE." Time between acceptance and publication is 6 months. Seldom comments on rejections. Response time varies. Pays 1 copy. Acquires all rights. Returns rights.

Book/Chapbook Needs & How to Submit: Pitchfork Press publishes 2 chapbooks per year. Chapbooks are usually 40-60 pgs., digest-sized, photocopied and side-stapled. However, they are not accepting unsolicited mss at this time.

◑ **PITT POETRY SERIES; UNIVERSITY OF PITTSBURGH PRESS; AGNES LYNCH STARRETT POETRY PRIZE**, 3347 Forbes Ave., Pittsburgh PA 15261, phone (412)383-2456, fax (412)383-2466, website www.pitt.edu/~press, founded 1968, poetry editor Ed Ochester.

Book/Chapbook Needs: Publishes 6 books/year by established poets, and 1 by a new poet—the winner of the Starrett Poetry Prize competition. They want "poetry of the highest quality; otherwise, no restrictions—book mss minimum of 48 pages." Poets who have previously published books should query. Simultaneous submissions OK. Always sends prepublication galleys. They have published books of poetry by Lynn Emanuel, Larry Levis, Billy Collins and Alicia Ostriker. Their booklist also features such poets as Etheridge Knight, Sharon Olds, Ronald Wallace, David Wojahn and Toi Derricotte.

How to Submit: Unpublished poets or poets "who have published chapbooks or limited editions of less than 750 copies" must submit through the Agnes Lynch Starrett Poetry Prize (see below). For poetry series, submit "entire manuscripts only." Disk submissions OK with hard copy. Cover letter preferred. Reads submissions from established poets in September and October only. Seldom comments on rejections.

Also Offers: Sponsors the Agnes Lynch Starrett Poetry Prize. "Poets who have not previously published a book should send SASE for rules of the Starrett competition ($20 handling fee), the only vehicle through which we publish first books of poetry." The Starrett Prize consists of cash award of $5,000 and book publication. Reads in March and April only. Competition receives 1,000 entries. Website includes guidelines for poetry series and Agnes Lynch Starrett Poetry Prize, names of editors and descriptions of recently published poetry titles.

◑ **PLAINSONGS**, Dept. of English, Hastings College, Hastings NE 68902-0269, phone (402)463-2402 or 461-7352, founded 1980, editor Dwight C. Marsh.

Magazine Needs: *Plainsongs* is a poetry magazine that "accepts manuscripts from anyone, considering poems on any subject in any style but free verse predominates. Plains region poems encouraged." They have published award poems by Connie Donovan, John Fritzell, Ruth Harrison, Charles Helzer, Scott Lumbard, Matt Mason, John Sweet, Michael Vaughn and Gwen Williams. As a sample the editor selected these lines from "A Fable" by Bruce Tindall:

> *The stars flew up so long ago/no one remembers what they are./Their children, left behind in the*
> *woods,/come out only to the edge,/only in summer, as tentative/as field mice after an owl-fright.*

Plainsongs is 40 pgs., digest-sized, set on laser, printed on thin paper and saddle-stapled with one-color matte card cover with generic black logo. "Published by the English department of Hastings College, the magazine is partially financed by subscriptions. Although editors respond to as many submissions with personal attention as they have time for, the editor offers specific observations to all contributors who also subscribe." The name suggests not only its location on the Great Plains, but its preference for the living language, whether in free or formal verse. It is committed to poems only, to make space without visual graphics, bio or critical positions. Subscription: $10/3 issues. Sample: $3.

How to Submit: Submit up to 6 poems at a time with name and address on each page. Deadlines are August 15 for fall issue; November 15 for winter; March 15 for spring. Notification is mailed 5-6 weeks after deadlines. Pays 2 copies and 1-year subscription, with 3 award poems in each issue receiving $25. "A short essay in appreciation accompanies each award poem." Acquires first rights.

🌐 **$** 🖂 **PLANET: THE WELSH INTERNATIONALIST**, P.O. Box 44, Aberystwyth, Ceredigion SY23 3ZZ, Wales, phone 01970-611255, fax 01970-611197, founded 1970, editor John Barnie.

Magazine Needs: *Planet* is a bimonthly cultural magazine, "centered on Wales, but with broader interests in arts, sociology, politics, history and science." They want "good poetry in a wide variety of styles. No limitations as to subject matter; length can be a problem." They have published poetry by Gillian Clarke and R.S. Thomas. As a sample the editor selected these lines from "On Home Beaches" by Les Murray:

> Back, in my fifties, fatter than I was then,/I step on the sand, belch down slight horror to walk/a
> wincing pit edge, waiting for the pistol shot/laughter. Long greening waves cash themselves, foam
> change/sliding into Ocean's pocket. She turns: ridicule looks down,/strappy, with faces averted, or is
> glare and families.

Planet is 128 pgs., A5 size, professionally printed and perfect-bound with glossy color card cover. They receive about 500 submissions a year, accept approximately 5%. Press run is 1,550 for 1,500 subscribers of which about 10% are libraries, 200 shelf sales. Single copy: £2.75; subscription: £13 (overseas: £14). Sample: £3.56.

How to Submit: No previously published poems or simultaneous submissions. SASE or SAE with IRCs essential for reply. Time between acceptance and publication is 6-10 months. Seldom comments on rejections. Send SASE (or SAE and IRCs if outside UK) for guidelines. Responds within a month or so. Pays £25 minimum. Buys first serial rights only. Reviews books of poetry in 700 words, single or multi-book format.

🗖 🖉 **THE PLASTIC TOWER**, P.O. Box 702, Bowie MD 20718, founded 1989, editors Carol Dyer and Roger Kyle-Keith.

Magazine Needs: *The Plastic Tower* is a quarterly using "everything from iambic pentameter to silly limericks, modern free verse, haiku, rhymed couplets—we like it all! Only restriction is length—under 40 lines preferred. So send us poems that are cool or wild, funny or tragic—but especially those closest to your soul." Also accepts poetry written by children. They have published poetry by "more than 400 different poets." It is 38-54 pgs., digest-sized, saddle-stapled; "variety of typefaces and b&w graphics on cheap photocopy paper." Press run is 200. Subscription: $8/year. Copy of current issue: $2.50. "We'll send a back issue free for a large (at least 6×9) SAE with 2 first-class stamps attached."

How to Submit: Submit up to 10 poems at a time. Previously published poems and simultaneous submissions OK. Editors "often" comment on submissions. Send SASE for guidelines. Responds in 6 months. Pays 1 copy. Open to unsolicited reviews. Poets may also send books for review consideration.

Advice: "*PT* is an unpretentious little rag dedicated to enjoying verse and making poetry accessible to the general public as well as fellow poets. We don't claim to be the best, but we try to be the nicest and most personal. Over the past several years, we've noticed a tremendous upswing in submissions. More people than ever are writing poetry and submitting it for publication, and that makes it tougher for individual writers to get published. But plenty of opportunities still exist (there are thousands of little and literary magazines in the U.S. alone), and the most effective tool for any writer right now is not talent or education, but persistence. So keep at it!"

🌐 ✓ 🖥 🖉 ◎ **THE PLAZA (Specialized: bilingual)**, U-Kan, Inc., Yoyogi 2-32-1, Shibuya-ku, Tokyo 151-0053, Japan, phone 81-3-3379-3881, fax 81-3-3379-3882, e-mail plaza@u-kan.co.jp, website http://u-kan.co.jp, founded 1985, contact editor.

Magazine Needs: *The Plaza* is a quarterly currently published only on the website (http://u-kan.co.jp) which "represents a borderless forum for contemporary writers and artists" and includes poetry, fiction and essays published simultaneously in English and Japanese. They want "highly artistic poetry dealing with being human and interculturally related. Nothing stressing political, national, religious or racial differences. *The Plaza* is edited with a global view of mankind." They have published poetry by Al Beck, Antler, Charles Helzer, Richard Alan Bunch, Morgan Gibson and Bun'ichirou Chino. As a sample the editors selected these lines from "The Constitutional" by Charles Helzer:

> I will walk this year more slowly than the last,/pausing to observe the crumbling mortar, thrust//of
> crocus, shale, wind-scoured, and laughter/of young women, hysterical with confidence,//not here when
> I had closed my doors on winter./It fills the air, a smoldering compost of the past,//mingled with a
> bright conjunction of contraries,/of yea and nay; and for this I will walk this year.

The Plaza is 50 full color pgs. It is available free to all readers on the Internet. They receive about 2,500 poems a year, accept approximately 8%. Proofs of accepted poems are sent to the authors 1 month before online publication.

How to Submit: No previously published poems; simultaneous submissions OK. Cover letter required. E-mail and fax submissions OK. "No attachments. Please include telephone and fax numbers or e-mail address with submissions. As *The Plaza* is a bilingual publication in English and Japanese, it is sometimes necessary, for translation purposes, to contact authors. Japanese translations are prepared by the editorial staff." Seldom comments on rejections. Responds within 1 month. Reviews books of poetry, usually in less than 500 words. Open to unsolicited reviews. Poets may also send books for review consideration.

Also Offers: Website includes the current issue of the quarterly, contributor's guidelines, publisher's information, introduction of authors, a collection of selected poems, artist's gallery and intercultural events.

Advice: "*The Plaza* focuses not on human beings but humans being human in the borderless world. It is not international, but intercultural. And it is circulated all over the world—in the American continents, Oceania, Asia, the Middle East, Europe and Africa."

☑ $◙ **PLEIADES; PLEIADES/LENA-MILES WEVER TODD POETRY SERIES; PLEIADES PRESS**, Dept. of English and Philosophy, Central Missouri State University, Warrensburg MO 64093, phone (660)543-8106, e-mail kdp8106@cmsu2.cmsu.edu, website www.cmsu.edu/englphil.pleiades.edu, founded as *Spring Flight* in 1939, reestablished in its present format in 1990, editors R.M. Kinder and Kevin Prufer.

Magazine Needs: *Pleiades*, a semiannual journal which publishes poetry, fiction, literary criticism, belles lettres (occasionally) and reviews. It is open to all writers. They want "avant-garde, free verse and traditional poetry, and some quality light verse. Nothing pretentious, didactic or overly sentimental." They have published poetry by Campbell McGrath, Brenda Hillman, Kevin Young, Rafael Campo and Carl Phillips. As a sample the editor selected these lines from "How tailors are made" by Graham Foust:

> *Cipher the rate at which things are put/Together. You will discover a love for light//Sleepers who dream*
> *they are the only ones/With hands. I'll get lost on the way to your mouth.//If I could have anything I*
> *wanted, I would have/Less than I do now. Maybe your blood on a textbook,//Or your breath like some*
> *ancient hinge.*

The editor says *Pleiades* is 160 pgs., 5½ × 8½, perfect-bound with a heavy coated cover and color cover art. They receive about 3,000 poems a year, accept approximately 1-3%. Press run is 2,500-3,000, about 200 distributed free to educational institutions and libraries across the country, several hundred shelf sales. Single copy: $6; subscription: $12. Sample: $5. Make checks payable to Pleiades Press.

How to Submit: Submit 3-5 poems at a time. No previously published poems; simultaneous submissions OK with notification. Cover letter with brief bio preferred. Time between acceptance and publication can be up to 1 year. Each poem published must be accepted by 2 readers and approved by the poetry editor. Seldom comments on rejections. Send SASE for guidelines. Responds in up to 3 months. Payment varies. Buys first and second serial rights and requests rights for *Wordbeat*, a TV/radio show featuring work published in *Pleiades*. "We are always interested in short reviews of new books of poetry."

Also Offers: Sponsors the Pleiades/Lena-Miles Wever Todd Poetry Series. "We will select one book of poems in open competition and publish it in our Pleiades Press Series. Louisiana State University Press will distribute the collection." Entry fee: $15. Postmark deadline: March 31, 2001. Send SASE for complete guidelines. Website includes new poems and stories, guidelines, masthead, contributors' notes and contents for current issues.

$◙ **PLOUGHSHARES**, Emerson College, 100 Beacon St., Boston MA 02116, phone (617)824-8753, founded 1971.

▼ Work published in *Ploughshares* appears in the 1995, 1996, 1997 and 1998 volumes of *The Best American Poetry*.

Magazine Needs: The magazine is "a journal of new writing guest-edited by prominent poets and writers to reflect different and contrasting points of view." Editors have included Carolyn Forché, Gerald Stern, Rita Dove, Chase Twichell and Marilyn Hacker. They have published poetry by Donald Hall, Li-Young Lee, Robert Pinsky, Brenda Hillman and Thylias Moss. The triquarterly is 250 pgs., 5½ × 8½. Circulation is 6,000. They receive approximately 2,500 poetry submissions a year. Subscription: $21 domestic; $26 foreign. Sample: $9.95 current issue, $8 sample back issue.

How to Submit: "We suggest you read a few issues before submitting." Simultaneous submissions acceptable. Do not submit mss from April 1 to July 31. Responds in up to 5 months. Always sends prepublication galleys. Pays $50 minimum per poem, $25/printed page per poem, plus 2 copies and a subscription.

◖ $☐ ◙ **THE PLOWMAN**, Box 414, Whitby, Ontario L1N 5S4 Canada, phone (905)668-7803, founded 1988, editor Tony Scavetta.

Magazine Needs: *The Plowman* appears semiannually using "didactic, eclectic poetry; all forms. We will also take most religious poetry except satanic and evil. We are interested in work that deals with the important issues in our society. Social and environment issues are of great importance." They have published *Rough Edge* by Don Hogan, *Once Upon a Lifetime* Volume I by Rita F. Lynch and *Comes the New Dawn* by Scott Hallam. *The Plowman* is 20 pgs., 8½ × 11 (17 × 11 sheet folded), photocopied, unbound, contains clip art and market listings. They accept 70% of the poetry received. Press run is 15,000 for 1,200 subscribers of which 500 are libraries. Single copy: $5; subscription: $10. Sample free.

How to Submit: Previously published poems and simultaneous submissions OK. Cover letter required. No SASE necessary. Always comments on rejections. Guidelines available free. Responds in 1 week. Always sends prepublication galleys. Pays 1 copy. Reviews books of poetry.

Book/Chapbook Needs & How to Submit: They also publish 125 chapbooks/year. Replies to queries and mss in 1 month. Requires $25 reading fee/book. Pays 20% royalties. They have published *Whispers From the Soul: Volumes I and II* by Ida-May Wagner; *Dark Images* by Irene Kruk; and *Life Is Full of Poetry* by Irene Kruk.

Also Offers: They offer monthly poetry contests. Entry fee: $2/poem. 1st Prize: 50% of the proceeds; 2nd: 25%; 3rd: 10%. The top poems are published. "Balance of the poems will be used for anthologies."

☑ ⦿ **POCAHONTAS PRESS, INC.; MANUSCRIPT MEMORIES**, P.O. Drawer F, Blacksburg VA 24063-1020, phone (540)951-0467, fax (540)961-2847, e-mail pocahontas.press@vt.edu, founded 1984, president Mary C. Holliman. They are not considering new mss at this time.

⦿ **POEM; HUNTSVILLE LITERARY ASSOCIATION**, English Dept., University of Alabama at Huntsville, Huntsville AL 35899, founded 1967, poetry editor Nancy Frey Dillard.

Magazine Needs: *Poem*, appears twice a year, consisting entirely of poetry. "We are open to traditional as well as non-traditional forms, but we favor work with the expected compression and intensity of good lyric poetry and a high degree of verbal and dramatic tension. We equally welcome submissions from established poets as well as from less-known and beginning poets." They have published poetry by Robert Cooperman, Andrew Dillon and Scott Travis Hutchison. *Poem* is a flat-spined, 4⅜×7¼, 90-page journal that contains more than 60 poems (mostly lyric free verse under 50 lines) generally featured 1 to a page on good stock paper with a clean design and a classy matte cover. Circulation is 400 (all subscriptions, including libraries). Sample: $5.

How to Submit: "We do not accept translations, previously published works or simultaneous submissions. Best to submit December through March and June through September. We prefer to see a sample of three to five poems at a submission, with SASE. We generally respond within a month. We are a nonprofit organization and can pay only in copy to contributors." Pays 2 copies. Acquires first serial rights.

◖ ⦿ **POEM DU JOUR**, P.O. Box 416, Somers MT 59932, founded 1999, editor Asta Bowen.

Magazine Needs: *Poem du Jour* is a "weekly one-page broadside circulated in the retail environment." They want "accessible but not simplistic poetry; seasonal work encouraged; humorous, current events, slam favorites; topical work (rural, mountain, outdoors, environmental, Northwest). No erotica, forced rhyme or poems of excessive length." As a sample the editor selected these lines from "Dandelions" by Lacie Jo Twiest:

> she called them flowers but I knew that they weren't/and I watched as she rubbed yellow on her cheeks
> and her lips/her entire face was the color of the sun and she beamed/and I watched her carefully craft
> the wreath that she placed atop her head/she was a princess though I knew she was too old to pretend . . .

Press run is 20-50. Sample: $2. Make checks payable to Asta Bowen—PDJ.

How to Submit: Submit up to 5 poems at a time. Line length for poetry is 50 maximum. Previously published poems and simultaneous submissions OK. Cover letter preferred. "Prefer poems typed with name, address and phone on each page." Time between acceptance and publication varies. Seldom comments on rejections. Send SASE for guidelines. Responds in 2 months. Sometimes sends prepublication galleys. Pays 1 copy. Acquires one-time rights.

Advice: "New/young writers encouraged."

⦿ **POEMS & PLAYS; THE TENNESSEE CHAPBOOK PRIZE**, English Dept., Middle Tennessee State University, Murfreesboro TN 37132, phone (615)898-2712, founded 1993, editor Gaylord Brewer.

Magazine Needs: *Poems & Plays* is an annual "eclectic publication for poems and short plays," published in April. They have no restrictions on style or content of poetry. They have published poetry by Stephen Dobyns, David Kirby, Vivian Shipley, Charles Bukowski and Ron Koertge. *Poems & Plays* is 88 pgs., 6×9, professionally printed and perfect-bound with coated color card cover and art. "We receive 1,500 poems per issue, typically publish 30-35." Press run is 750. Subscription: $10/2 issues. Sample: $6.

How to Submit: No previously published poems or simultaneous submissions (except for chapbook submissions). Reads submissions October 1 through January 15 only. "Work is circulated among advisory editors for comments and preferences. All accepted material is published in the following issue." Usually comments on rejections. Responds in 2 months. Pays 1 copy. Acquires first publication rights only.

Also Offers: "We accept chapbook manuscripts (of poems or short plays) of 20-24 pages for The Tennessee Chapbook Prize. Any combination of poems or plays, or a single play, is eligible. The winning chapbook is printed as an interior chapbook in *Poems & Plays* and the author receives 50 copies of the issue. SASE and $10 (for reading fee and one copy of the issue) required. Dates for contest entry are the same as for the magazine (October 1 through January 15). Past winners include Maureen Micus Crisick, David Stark, Steven Sater, Angela Kelly and Rob Griffith. The chapbook competition annually receives over 100 manuscripts from the U.S. and around the world."

☑ ⦿ **POET LORE; POET LORE NARRATIVE POETRY COMPETITION**, The Writer's Center, 4508 Walsh St., Bethesda MD 20815, phone (301)654-8664, fax (301)654-8667, e-mail postmaster@writer.org, website www.writer.org, founded 1889, managing editor Jo-Ann Billings, executive editors Geraldine Connolly and Liz Poliner.

Magazine Needs: *Poet Lore* is a quarterly dedicated "to the best in American and world poetry and objective and timely reviews and commentary. We look for fresh uses of traditional form and devices, but any kind of excellence is welcome. The editors encourage narrative poetry and original translations of works by contemporary world poets." They have published poetry by William Matthews, Denise Duhamel, Susan Terris, R.T. Smith and Cornelius Eady. *Poet Lore* is 6×9, 80 pgs., perfect-bound, professionally printed with glossy card cover. Circulation includes 600 subscriptions of which 200 are libraries. They receive about 3,000 poems a year, use approximately 125. Single copy: $5.50; subscription: $18. Sample: $4.50.

How to Submit: Submit typed poems, author's name and address on each page, SASE required. No simultaneous submissions. Responds in 3 months. Pays 2 copies. Reviews books of poetry. Poets may send books for review consideration.

Also Offers: Sponsors the Poet Lore Narrative Poetry Competition for unpublished poems of 100 lines or more. The annual competition awards $350 and publication in *Poet Lore*. Deadline: November 30. Send SASE for entry form and guidelines. Website includes magazine and contest guidelines, table of contents, subscription info, current issue and back-issue archives.

N ⊕ ○ ◑ POETCRIT (Specialized: membership), Maranda, H.P. 176 102 India, phone 01894-31407, founded 1988, editor Dr. D.C. Chambial.

Magazine Needs: *Poetcrit* appears each January and July "to promote poetry and international understanding through poetry. Purely critical articles on various genres of literature are also published." They want poems of every kind. They have published poetry by Ruth Wilder Schuller (US), Danae G. Papastratau (Greece), Shiv K. Kumar (India), Joy B. Cripps (Australia) and O.P. Bhatnagar (India). As a sample the editor selected these lines from "An Existential Question" by Manas Bakashi:

> For some days/I have lived/weaving thoughts around/All that's intractable/But poised for/An apocalypse.

The editor says *Poetcrit* is 100 pgs., magazine-sized, offset printed with simple paper cover, includes ads. They receive about 1,000 poems a year, accept approximately 20%. Press run is 1,000 for 500 subscribers of which 100 are libraries, 200 shelf sales; 400 distributed free to new members. Single copy: $9; subscription: $15. Sample: $10. Make checks payable to Dr. D.C. Chambial. Membership required for consideration.

How to Submit: Submit 3 poems at a time. Line length for poetry is 25 maximum. No previously published poems; simultaneous submissions OK. Cover letter required. Reads submissions September 1 through 20 and March 1 through 20. Poems are circulated to an editorial board. "All poems reviewed by various editors and selected for publication." Publishes theme issues occasionally. Send SASE (or SAE and IRC) for guidelines and upcoming themes. Responds in about 1 month. Pays 1 copy. Acquires one-time rights. Reviews books and chapbooks of poetry and other magazines in 1,000 words, single book format. Open to unsolicited reviews ("accompanied with book").

Advice: "Beginners should meditate well on their themes before writing."

⊕ ○ POETIC HOURS, 43 Willow Rd., Carlton, Nolts NG4 3BH England, e-mail erran@arrowgroup.freeserve,co.uk, founded 1993, editor Nicholas Clark.

Magazine Needs: *Poetic Hours*, published biannually, "is published solely to encourage and publish new poets, i.e., as a forum where good but little known poets can appear in print and to raise money for Third World charities. The magazine features articles and poetry by subscribers and others." They want "any subject, rhyme preferred but not essential; suitable for wide ranging readership, 30 lines maximum." They do not want "gothic, horror, extremist, political, self-interested." As a sample the editor selected these lines from his poem "School Report: Human Race":

> Does the western world now stand for judgement/Before a clock?/There's a thought!/Whole nations check two thousand years of progress/Waiting for teachers Millennium Report

The editor says *Poetic Hours* is 36 pgs., A4, printed, saddle-stapled and illustrated throughout with Victorian woodcuts. They receive about 500 poems a year, accept up to 40%. Press run is 400 of which 12 are for libraries, 300 shelf sales. Subscription: £5, overseas payments in sterling or US dollars ($20). For a subscription send bankers checks or cash. Sample: £3. Make checks payable to Erran Publishing.

How to Submit: "Poets are encouraged to subscribe or buy a single copy, though not required." Submit up to 5 nonreturnable poems at a time. Previously published poems OK; no simultaneous submissions. Cover letter required. Time between acceptance and publication is 2-3 months. "Poems are read by editors and if found suitable, are used." Always comments on rejections. Publishes theme issues. Upcoming themes listed in magazine. Responds "immediately, whenever possible." Acquires one-time rights. Staff reviews books or chapbooks of poetry. Send books for review consideration.

Also Offers: *Poetic Hours* is non-profit-making and all proceeds go to various national charities, particularly Oxfam and Amnesty International. A page of *Poetic Hours* is set aside each issue for reporting how money is spent.

Advice: "We welcome newcomers and invite those just starting out to have the courage to submit work. The art of poetry has moved from the hands of book publishers down the ladder to the new magazines. This is where all the best poetry is found."

○ **POETIC LICENSE POETRY MAGAZINE; BOOKS BY DESIGN**, P.O. Box 311, Kewanee IL 61443-0311, e-mail poeticlicense99@hotmail.com, founded 1996, editor Denise Felt, children's editor James Shelton.
Magazine Needs: *PLPM* is a monthly publication with "the purpose of giving new and experienced poets a chance to be published. It includes articles and contests that challenge poets to grow in their craft. We want the best free verse and rhymed poetry by adults and children. No profane, vulgar, pornographic or sloppy work accepted." They have published poetry by Linda Creech, Terri Warden, Elizabeth Fuller and Robert Hentz. As a sample the editor selected these lines from "The Apartment" by Tracy Kreher:

> *My comfortable couch hugs me tenderly./It knows my needs./The book in my hands has caught my mind/but my ears tend to deceive.*

PLPM is 35-40 pgs., 8½×11, magazine-bound with full color cover, includes graphic art and ads. They receive over 1,000 poems a year, accept approximately 95%. Press run is 60/issue. Subscription: $49/year, $94/2 years. Sample: $5.50. Make checks payable to *Poetic License*.
How to Submit: Submit up to 5 poems at a time. Previously published poems and simultaneous submissions OK. Cover letter preferred. "Send double-spaced typed poems with name and address in upper right hand corner. Age required if poet is 18 or younger." Time between acceptance and publication is 1 month. "I judge poems on a 25-point system. Adult submissions with 12 points or less are rejected. Children's submissions with 10 points or less are rejected." Seldom comments on rejections. Publishes theme issues. Send SASE for guidelines and upcoming themes. Responds in 2 weeks. Acquires one-time rights.
Book/Chapbook Needs & How to Submit: They offer chapbook publication services through their press, Books By Design. "We publish quality 8½×11 chapbooks for poets to sell or share with family and friends. We ask poets wishing to publish their chapbook to send for our brochure detailing styles, sizes and cost." They also sponsor an annual chapbook competition through Books By Design. "75% of our publications are subsidized entirely by the poet. The other 25% are won through our chapbook contest." Send SASE for details on chapbook contest.
Also Offers: Sponsors a quarterly contest anthology on a different theme each February, May, August and November. Anthology chapbooks available at the end of each contest. Send SASE for contest rules. "Magazine and contest anthology winners throughout the year are published in an annual poetry volume called *100 Best Poems*. These are some of the best poems to be found by contemporary poets." Past volumes available.
Advice: "The most important thing poets should concern themselves with is excellence. Whether a poem is rewritten twice or twenty times, it shouldn't matter. The goal is to bring the poem to life. Then it's fit for publication. There is more talent in literate people of all ages than the poets of past centuries could have dreamed. Our goal is to encourage that talent to grow and flourish through exposure to the public."

N ○ ◐ **POETIC PAGE**, P.O. Box 71192, Madison Heights MI 48071-0192, e-mail poeticpage@earthlink.net, founded 1989, editor Denise Martinson.
Magazine Needs: *Poetic Page* appears quarterly. "All forms are used except explicit sex, violence and crude. No line limit and no fees. In addition to the regular poetry used, contests in each issue." They have published poetry by MacDonald Carey, Lyn Lifshin, T. Kilgore Splake and John Grey. As a sample the editor selected these lines from "Nocturne" from *Rosario Castellanos* by Leonard J. Cirino:

> *A woman sleeps, happily knowing/that she is, for a moment, awake./Her child is a stone.//The mother speaks, the child turns./Not far away the words/lie in the stones.//Their dreams fill my unspoken poems./ They won't lie still.*

Poetic Page is 28-32 pgs., magazine-sized, spiral-bound with coated card cover, desktop-published. Press run varies.
How to Submit: Simultaneous submissions and previously published poems OK. Cover letter is preferred. E-mail is for information only; no submissions. Send SASE for guidelines. Pays 1 copy.
Advice: "Only the best poetry accepted. Have something to say. If you want to write a poem about a flower, go ahead. But make that flower unique—surprise us. No trite rhyme here. However, we will publish a well-written rhyme if the rhyme is the poem, not the word endings. Free verse is what we prefer."

○ **POETIC REALM; OMNIFIC; THE WRITER'S ADVOCATE**, HC-13, Box 21-AA, Artemas PA 17211-9405, phone (814)458-3102, editor/publisher Kay Weems.
Magazine Needs & How to Submit: *Poetic Realm* is a quarterly of poetry using 36-line, sometimes longer, poems, "anything in good taste" with an Editor's Choice small cash award for each issue. No contributor copies. Subscription: $12/year; $3.50/copy. *Omnific*, a "family-type" quarterly publishes poetry only, 36 lines, sometimes longer; readers vote on favorites, small cash award or copy to favorites. Send SASE for guidelines. No contributor copies. Single copy: $4.50; subscription: $16/year.
Also Offers: She also publishes an annual Christmas anthology. Published/unpublished poetry, 36 lines maximum, Christmas themes. Address to "Christmas Anthology." Deadline: September 30. *The Writer's Advocate*,

---

THE OPENNESS TO SUBMISSIONS INDEX at the back of this book lists all publishers in this section by how open they are to submissions.

founded 1988, is a bimonthly newsletter listing over 50 publications and contests for writers, reproducing guidelines of still others. Information is presented in chronological order by deadline date, and then in alphabetical order. Circulation 200-300. Subscription: $12/year; $3.50/copy. Her other publication, *My Legacy*, is still published but now uses only short stories.

⭕ POETIC SPACE: POETRY & FICTION, P.O. Box 11157, Eugene OR 97440, fax: (541)683-1271, e-mail: poeticspac@aol.com, founded 1983, editor Don Hildenbrand.

Magazine Needs: *Poetic Space*, published annually in the fall, is a nonprofit literary magazine with emphasis on contemporary poetry, fiction, reviews (including film and drama), interviews, market news and translations. Accepts poetry and fiction that is "well-crafted and takes risks. We like poetry with guts. Would like to see some poetry on social and political issues. We would also like to see gay/lesbian poetry and poetry on women's issues. Erotic and experimental OK." Prefers poems under 1,000 words. They have published poetry by Simon Perchik, Paul Weinman, Sherman Alexie, Albert Huffstickler and Lyn Lifshin. The magazine is 30 pgs., 8½×11, saddle-stapled, offset from typescript and sometimes photoreduced. They receive about 200-300 poems a year, accept approximately 25%. Press run is 800 for 50 subscribers of which 12 are libraries. Single copy: $4; subscription: $7/2 issues, $13/4 issues. Send SASE for list of available back issues ($4).

How to Submit: Ms should be typed, double-spaced, clean, name/address on each page. "Submissions without SASE will not be considered." Simultaneous submissions and previously published poems OK. Editor provides some critical comments. Send SASE for guidelines. Responds in up to 4 months. Pays 1 copy, but more can be ordered by sending SASE and postage. Reviews books of poetry in 500-1,000 words. Open to unsolicited reviews. Poets may also send books for review consideration.

Book/Chapbook Needs & How to Submit: Also publishes one chapbook each spring. Their first chapbook was *Truth Rides to Work and Good Girls*, poetry by Crawdad Nelson and fiction by Louise A. Blum ($5 plus $1.50 p&h).

Advice: "We like poetry that takes risks—original writing that gives us a new, different perspective."

⭘⭕ POETIC VOICES JOURNAL, P.O. Box 1684, Durant OK 74702-1684, e-mail poeticvoices76@hotmail.com, founded 1998, editor/publisher Brandi Ballew.

Magazine Needs: "*Poetic Voices* is a biannual journal dedicated to giving poets and artists a voice. It includes poetry and artwork by some of today's most talented (though unknown) poets and artists. I want to see poetry full of emotion and imagery. Any style or form accepted. No racist, homophobic or pornographic material." Also accepts poetry written by children. They have published poetry by Richard Heisler, Ron Wallace, Joe Landau, Elizabeth Fuller, Tim Scannel and Samantha Van Laarhoven. *PV* is 20-30 (possibly more) pgs., 8½×11, neatly printed and saddle-stapled with card cover, includes b&w artwork, ads. They accept approximately 75% of work received. "I try to accept something from each contributor. *Poetic Voices* strives to make the unknown heard." Press run is 125; most distributed free to bookstores and coffeehouses throughout the US. Single copy: $5; subscription: $10/2 issues. Sample (including guidelines): $4.

How to Submit: Submit 3-8 poems at a time with SASE for response. Previously published poems and simultaneous submissions OK. E-mail submissions OK. "Include information about the poet and mailing address." Cover letter required, "containing publication credits, if any." Time between acceptance and publication is 1-6 months. Always comments on rejections. Responds in 1 month. Pays 1 copy. Poets and artists retain all rights. "Request acknowledgement if work is later printed elsewhere."

Also Offers: Sponsors an annual poetry and art contest. Send SASE for guidelines.

Advice: "Support the local poetry and art scene—not to mention the small press—letters of encouragement and donations are greatly appreciated.'"

$⭘ POETRY; THE MODERN POETRY ASSOCIATION; BESS HOKIN PRIZE; LEVINSON PRIZE; EUNICE TIETJENS MEMORIAL PRIZE; FREDERICK BOCK PRIZE; GEORGE KENT PRIZE; UNION LEAGUE PRIZE; J. HOWARD AND BARBARA M.J. WOOD PRIZE; RUTH LILLY POETRY PRIZE; RUTH LILLY POETRY FELLOWSHIP; JOHN FREDERICK NIMS PRIZE, 60 W. Walton St., Chicago IL 60610-3380, e-mail poetry@poetrymagazine.org, website www.poetrymagazine.org, founded 1912, editor Joseph Parisi.

⭘ Work published in *Poetry* was also selected for inclusion in the 1995, 1996, 1997, 1998 and 1999 volumes of *The Best American Poetry.*

Magazine Needs: *Poetry* "is the oldest and most distinguished monthly magazine devoted entirely to verse. Founded in Chicago in 1912, it immediately became the international showcase that it has remained ever since, publishing in its earliest years—and often for the first time—such giants as Ezra Pound, Robert Frost, T.S. Eliot, Marianne Moore and Wallace Stevens. *Poetry* has continued to print the major voices of our time and to discover new talent, establishing an unprecedented record. There is virtually no important contemporary poet in our language who has not at a crucial stage in his career depended on *Poetry* to find a public for him: John Ashbery, Dylan Thomas, Edna St. Vincent Millay, James Merrill, Anne Sexton, Sylvia Plath, James Dickey, Thom Gunn, David Wagoner—only a partial list to suggest how *Poetry* has represented, without affiliation with any movements or schools, what Stephen Spender has described as 'the best, and simply the best' poetry being written." As a sample the editor selected the opening lines of "The Love Song of J. Alfred Prufrock" by T.S. Eliot, which first appeared in *Poetry* in 1915:

*Let us go then, you and I,/When the evening is spread out against the sky/Like a patient etherized upon
a table;/Let us go, through certain half-deserted streets . . .*

Poetry is an elegantly printed, flat-spined, 5½×9 magazine. They receive over 90,000 submissions a year, use
approximately 300-350, have up to a 9-month backlog. Press run is 10,000 for 7,000 subscribers of which 53%
are libraries. Single copy: $3.50; subscription: $30, $33 for institutions. Sample: $5.

How to Submit: Submit up to 4 poems at a time with SASE. Send SASE for guidelines. Responds in 4
months—longer for mss submitted during the summer. Pays $2 a line. Buys all rights. Returns rights "upon
written request." Reviews books of poetry in multi-book formats of varying lengths. Open to unsolicited reviews.
Poets may also send books to Stephen Young, senior editor, for review consideration.

Also Offers: Eight prizes (named in heading) ranging from $200 to $3,000 are awarded annually to poets whose
work has appeared in the magazine that year. Only verse already published in *Poetry* is eligible for consideration
and no formal application is necessary. *Poetry* also sponsors the Ruth Lilly Poetry Prize, an annual award of
$75,000, and the Ruth Lilly Poetry Fellowship, two annual awards of $15,000 to undergraduate or graduate
students to support their further studies in poetry/creative writing. Website includes contents of recent issues,
poems by featured poets of the week, writer's guidelines, subscription information, announcement of prize awards
and lists of winners, brief history of the magazine and announcements of readings and events.

✔ ◉ **POETRY & PROSE ANNUAL**, P.O. Box 541, Manzanita OR 97130, e-mail poetry@poetryproseann
ual.com, website www.poetryproseannual.com, founded 1996, editor Sandra Claire Fousheé.

Magazine Needs: *Poetry & Prose Annual* "publishes work that focuses on the nature of consciousness and
enlightens the human spirit each winter quarter. A general selection of poetry, fiction, nonfiction and photography.
We are looking for excellence and undiscovered talent in poems of emotional and intellectual substance. Poems
should be original with rhythmic and lyric strength. Innovation and fresh imagery encouraged. Metrical ingenuity
recognized. Open to all forms." They have published poetry by Anita Endrezze, Tom Crawford, Mary Legato
Brownell and Carlos Reyes. As a sample the editor selected these lines from "All Evening" by Mary Crow:

*Beautiful to be slipping toward a greater/and greater whiteness as if moving/into invisibility or as if
the whiteness/were a curtain that would open into/some other world, once again green, and new.*

PPA is approximately 72 pgs., 7×8½, offset-printed and perfect-bound with glossy card cover, cover photograph,
contains line art and photos inside. Press run is about 1,000. Subscription: $15.

How to Submit: "A $20 submission fee is required. Includes subscription and reader's fee. Any work submitted
without submission fee or SASE will not be returned or read. " Submit no more than 200 lines of poetry at a
time, typed, with line count, name, address and phone number on first page. Include SASE and brief bio.
Previously published poems and simultaneous submissions OK. E-mail submissions OK. "Submit text from any
platform as an attached file." Cover letter preferred with short bio. Send SASE for guidelines. Responds after
deadline. Sometimes sends prepublication galleys. Pays 2 copies. Acquires one-time and reprints rights. Staff
reviews books of poetry. Poets may send books for review consideration. Work may also appear in the *Poetry
& Prose Annual* website.

Also Offers: Sponsors the annual "Gold Pen Award" contest in poetry and prose. Website includes writer's
submission guidelines, names of editors and work from previous editions.

◼ The online journal contains original content not found in the print edition. "From poetry submissions we may
use some original material on the website which may/may not be published in the Annual. Poetry needs are the
same as for the journal. Writers can indicate if they wish to be considered for the website. Contact the editor.

Advice: "Several new writers will also be chosen from the general selection to be featured in *American Portfolio*—a special selection within the journal showcasing work of several authors in a portfolio."

◉ **POETRY BONE**, 12 Skylark Lane, Stony Brook NY 11790, e-mail poetrybone@geocities.com, website
www.geocities.com/Athens/Styx/5635, founded 1997, editor Kiel Stuart.

Magazine Needs: *Poetry Bone* is a biannual journal publishing "general poetry of the highest quality we can
find." They want poetry with a maximum length of 29 lines (including title). "Rhyming poetry has to be
exceptional." They have published poetry by Simon Perchik. The editors say *PB* is 24 pgs., 5½×8½, laser-
printed and saddle-stitched with vellum cover. They receive about 500 poems a year, accept approximately 10%.
Press run is 200 for 100 subscribers of which 20 are libraries, 50 shelf sales. Subscription: $8. Sample: $4.50.
Make checks payable to Howard Austerlitz.

How to Submit: Submit 3 poems at a time. No previously published poems or simultaneous submissions.
Cover letter undesired. Seldom comments on rejections. Send SASE for guidelines. Responds in about 1 month.
Pays 1 copy. Acquires first North American serial rights.

Also Offers: Website includes poetry, notices, editorial, guidelines and mailing address.

▣ ◯ ◉ ◎ **THE POETRY EXPLOSION NEWSLETTER (THE PEN) (Specialized: ethnic, love,
subscription, nature)**, P.O. Box 4725, Pittsburgh PA 15206-0725, phone (412)886-1114, e-mail aford@hillhous
e.ckp.edu. website: www.incor.com (password: poetry) founded 1984, editor Arthur C. Ford.

Magazine Needs: *The Pen* is a "quarterly newsletter dedicated to the preservation of poetry." Arthur Ford
wants "poetry—40 lines maximum, no minimum. All forms and subject matter with the use of good imagery,
symbolism and honesty. Rhyme and non-rhyme. No vulgarity." Also accepts poetry written by children; "if
under 18 years old, parent or guardian should submit!" He has published poetry by Lisa Cave, Margaret A.

Brennan and Iva Fedorka. *The Pen* is 12-16 pgs., saddle-stitched, mimeographed on both sides. They receive about 300 poems a year, accept approximately 80. Press run is 850 for 400 subscribers of which 5 are libraries. Subscription: $20. Send $4 for sample copy and more information. Make checks payable to Arthur C. Ford.

How to Submit: Submit up to 5 poems, maximum 40 lines, at a time with $1 reading fee. Also include large SASE if you want work returned. Simultaneous submissions and previously published poems OK. No e-mail submissions. Sometimes publishes theme issues. "We announce future dates when decided. July issue is usually full of romantic poetry." Send SASE or visit website for guidelines and upcoming themes. Editor comments on rejections "sometimes, but not obligated." Pays 2 copies. He will criticize poetry for 15¢ a word. Open to unsolicited reviews. Poets may also send books for review consideration.

Also Offers: Website includes writer's guidelines. Use code word poetry.

Advice: "Even though free verse is more popular today, we try to stay versatile."

⬜⬜⬜◎ **POETRY FORUM; THE JOURNAL (Specialized: subscription); HEALTHY BODY-HEALTHY MINDS (Specialized: health concerns),** 5713 Larchmont Dr., Erie PA 16509, phone (814)866-2543 (also fax: 8-10 a.m. or 5-8 p.m.), e-mail 75562.670@compuserve.com, editor Gunvor Skogsholm.

Magazine Needs: *Poetry Forum* appears 3 times/year. "We are open to any style and form. We believe new forms ought to develop from intuition. Length up to 50 lines accepted. Would like to encourage long themes. No porn or blasphemy, but open to all religious persuasions." Also accepts poetry written by children ages 10 and under. They have published poetry by Ray Greenblatt, Jan Haight and Mark Young. As a sample the editor selected these lines from his poem "Tear":

> Because the tear down the cheek of a son is the reward of a lifetime of concern, the tear down the
> cheek of a brother was what I came for

The magazine is $7 \times 8\frac{1}{2}$, 38 pgs., saddle-stapled with card cover, photocopied from photoreduced typescript. Sample: $3.

How to Submit: Simultaneous submissions and previously published poems OK. Electronic submissions OK. Submissions via fax and e-mail (include in body) OK. Editor comments on poems "if asked, but respects the poetic freedom of the artist." Publishes theme issues. Send SASE for guidelines and upcoming themes or request via fax or e-mail. Sometimes sends prepublication galleys. Gives awards of $25, $15, $10 and 3 honorable mentions for the best poems in each issue. Acquires one-time rights. Reviews books of poetry in 250 words maximum. Open to unsolicited reviews. Poets may also send books for review consideration.

Magazine Needs & How to Submit: *The Journal*, which appears twice a year, accepts experimental poetry of any length from subscribers only. Sample: $3. *Healthy Body-Healthy Minds* is a biannual publication concerned with health issues. They accept essays, poetry, articles and short-shorts on health, fitness, mind and soul. Send SASE for details.

Also Offers: They offer a poetry chapbook contest. Handling fee: $12. Prize is publication and 20 copies. Send SASE for information.

Advice: "I believe today's poets should experiment more and not feel stuck in the forms that were in vogue 300 years ago. I would like to see more experimentalism—new forms will prove that poetry is alive and well in the mind and spirit of the people."

💲⬜⬜◎ **POETRY HARBOR; NORTH COAST REVIEW (Specialized: regional),** P.O. Box 103, Duluth MN 55801-0103, phone (218)733-1294, website www.poharb.toofarnorth.com, founded 1989, director Patrick McKinnon.

Magazine Needs: Poetry Harbor is a "nonprofit, tax-exempt organization dedicated to fostering literary creativity through public readings, publications, radio and television broadcasts, and other artistic and educational means." Its main publication, *North Coast Review*, is a regional magazine appearing 2 times a year with poetry and prose poems by and about Upper Midwest people, including those from Minnesota, Wisconsin, North Dakota, and the upper peninsula of Michigan. "No form/style/content specifications, though we are inclined toward narrative, imagist poetry. We do not want to see anything from outside our region, not because it isn't good, but because we can't publish it due to geographics." They have published poetry by Mark Vinz, Joe Paddock, Susan Hauser and Jim Northrup. *NCR* is 56 pgs., $7 \times 8\frac{1}{2}$, offset and saddle-stapled, paper cover with various b&w art, ads at back. They receive about 500 submissions a year, use 100-150. Press run is 1,000 for 300 subscribers of which 20 are libraries, 300 shelf sales. Subscription: $21.95/6 issues. Sample: $4.95.

How to Submit: Submit 3-5 pgs. of poetry, typed single-spaced, with name and address on each page. Previously published poems and simultaneous submissions OK, if noted. Cover letter with brief bio ("writer's credits") required. "We read three times a year, but our deadlines change from time to time. Write to us for current deadlines for our various projects." Send SASE for guidelines. Responds in up to 5 months. Pays $10 plus 2-4 copies. Buys one-time rights.

Book/Chapbook Needs & How to Submit: Poetry Harbor also publishes 1 perfect-bound paperback of poetry and 4-8 chapbooks each biennium. "Chapbooks are selected by our editorial board from the pool of poets we have published in *North Coast Review* or have worked with in our other projects. We suggest you send a submission to *North Coast Review* first. We almost always print chapbooks and anthologies by poets we've previously published or hired for readings." Anthologies include *Poets Who Haven't Moved to St. Paul* and *Days of Obsidian, Days of Grace*, selected poetry and prose by four Native American writers. Complete publications list available upon request.

Editor Fran Moramarco wanted an eye-catching cover for *Poetry International*, Issue III. "This was our first issue to be nationally distributed in bookstores and newsstands," he explains, "and I wanted something that would stand out from the pack." Artist Wendy Colin Sorin's "Trajectory" impressed Moramarco as "striking, unique, fresh and original." He cites its eclectic mix of shapes, echoes of punctuation, and subtle use of actual words "floating in the background." Cover designer Guillermo Nericcio Garcia further enhanced the impact by making the magazine's logo the same red as the oval in the center of the artwork, giving it "a real visual brightness," says Moramarco. *Poetry International*, published annually, is 200 pages, perfect bound, with coated card stock cover.

Also Offers: Poetry Harbor also sponsors a monthly reading series ("poets are paid to perform"), a weekly TV program (4 different cable networks regionally), various radio programming, a prison workshop series and other special events.

Advice: "Poetry Harbor is extremely committed to cultivating a literary community and an appreciation for our region's literature within the Upper Midwest. Poetry Harbor projects are in place to create paying, well-attended venues for our region's fine poets. Poets are now OK to people up here, and literature is thriving. The general public is proving to us that they *do* like poetry if you give them some that is both readable and rooted in the lives of the community."

POETRY INTERNATIONAL, Dept. of English, San Diego State University, San Diego CA 92182-8140, phone (619)594-1523, fax (619)594-4998, e-mail fmoramar@mail.sdsu.edu, website www-rohan.sdsu.edu:80/dept/press/poetry.html, founded 1996, editor Fred Moramarco.

Magazine Needs: *PI*, published annually, is "an eclectic poetry magazine intended to reflect a wide range of poetry being written today." They want "a wide range of styles and subject matter. We're particularly interested in translations." They do not want "cliché-ridden, derivative, obscure poetry." They have published poetry by Robert Bly, Thomas Lux, Diane Wakoski, Hayden Carroth, Kim Addonizio, Maxine Kumin and Gary Soto. As a sample the editor selected these lines from "My Life In Over" by Al Zolynas:

> my life, I mean that life/defined by narrow boundaries/narrow concerns, by survival/and whining and
> looking over/my shoulder, that life/of the bag of skin and bones/with the little fascist ego bitching/all
> day long/That little Mussolini is dead—or/if not dead—at least stripped of his shiny/black uniform,
> insignia cut/off pockets and collars,/epaulettes popped off shoulders./Not yet fully naked/but on the
> way, down/to T-shirts, shorts, and socks.

The editor says *Poetry International* is 200 pgs, perfect bound, with coated card stock cover. Press run is 1,000. Single copy: $12; subscription: $24/2 years.

How to Submit: Submit up to 5 poems at a time. No previously published poems; simultaneous submissions OK "but prefer not to." No e-mail submissions. Reads submissions September 1 through December 30 only. Time between acceptance and publication is 6-8 months. Poems are circulated to an editorial board. Seldom comments on rejections. Responds in 3 months. Pays 2 copies. Acquires all rights. Returns rights "50/50," meaning they split with the author any payment for reprinting the poem elsewhere. "We review anthologies regularly."

Also Offers: Website includes subscription information and samples from each issue.

Advice: "We're interested in new work by poets who are devoted to their art. We want poems that matter—that make a difference in people's lives. We're especially seeking good translations and prose by poets about poetry."

POETRY IRELAND REVIEW; POETRY IRELAND, Bermingham Tower, Dublin Castle, Dublin 2, Ireland, phone 353.1.6714632, fax 353.1.6714634, e-mail poetry@iol.ie, founded 1979, general manager Niamh Morris.

Magazine Nees: *Poetry Ireland Review*, the magazine of Ireland's national poetry organization, "provides an outlet for Irish poets; submissions from abroad also considered. No specific style or subject matter is prescribed.

We strongly dislike sexism and racism." They have published poetry by Seamus Heaney, Michael Longley, Denise Levertov, Medbh McGuckian and Charles Wright. Occasionally publishes special issues. The 6×8 quarterly uses 60 pgs. of poetry in each issue, circulation 1,200, with 800 subscriptions. They receive about 2,000 submissions/year, use 10%, have a 2-month backlog. Single copy: IR£5.99; subscription: IR£24 Ireland and UK; IR£32 overseas (surface). Sample: $10.

How to Submit: Submit up to 6 poems at a time. Include SASE (or SAE with IRC). "Submissions not accompained by SAEs will not be returned." No previously published poems or simultaneous submissions. Time between acceptance and publication is 1-3 months. Seldom comments on rejections. Send SASE (or SAE with IRCs) for guidelines. Responds in 2 months. Pays IR£10/poem or 1-year subscription. Reviews books of poetry in 500-1,000 words.

Also Offers: *PIR* is published by Poetry Ireland, an organization established to "promote poets and poetry throughout Ireland." Poetry Ireland offers readings, an information service, library and administrative center, and a bimonthly newsletter giving news, details of readings, competitions, etc. for IR£6/year. They also sponsor an annual poetry competition. Send SASE (or SAE with IRCs) for details.

Advice: "Keep submitting: Good work will get through."

POETRY KANTO, Kanto Gakuin University, Kamariya-cho 3-22-1, Kanazawa-Ku, Yokohama 236-8502, Japan, founded 1984, editor William I. Elliott.

Magazine Needs: *Poetry Kanto* appears annually in August and is published by the Kanto Poetry Center, which also sponsors an annual poetry conference. It publishes well-crafted original poems in English and in Japanese. The magazine publishes "anything except pornography, English haiku and tanka, and tends to publish poems under 30 lines." They have published work by A.D. Hope, Peter Robinson, Naomi Shihab Nye, Nuala Ni Dhomhnaill and Christopher Middleton. The magazine is 60 pgs., digest-sized, nicely printed (the English poems occupy the first half of the issue, the Japanese poems the second), saddle-stapled, matte card cover. Circulation is 700, of which 400 are distributed free to schools, poets and presses; it is also distributed at poetry seminars. The magazine is unpriced. For sample, send SAE with IRCs.

How to Submit: Interested poets should query from October through December with SAE and IRCs before submitting. No previously published poems or simultaneous submissions. Often comments on rejections. Responds to mss in 2 weeks. Pays 3 copies.

Advice: "Read a lot. Get feedback from poets and/or workshops. Be neat, clean, legible and polite in submissions. SAE with IRCs absolutely necessary when requesting sample copy."

POETRY LIFE (Specialized: subscription), 1 Blue Ball Corner, Water Lane, Winchester, Hampshire SO23 OER England, e-mail adrian.abishop@virgin.net, website freespace.virgin.net/poetry.life/, founded 1994, editor Adrian Bishop.

Magazine Needs: *Poetry Life*, published 3 times/year, describes itself as "Britain's sharpest poetry magazine with serious articles about the poetry scene." They want "poets who have passion, wit, style, revelation and loads of imagination." They do not want "poems on pets." They have published articles on James Fenton, Carol Ann Duffy, Les Murray, Benjamin Zephaniah and Simon Armitage. The editor says *Poetry Life* is A4. They accept approximately 1% of the poems they receive. Press run is 1,500. Single copy: £3, £5 overseas.

How to Submit: Previously published poems and simultaneous submissions OK. Cover letter required. "In common with most poetry magazines we now only accept recordings of the poets work on CD. Please do not send manuscripts. If we like what we hear then we will ask for a manuscript." Time between acceptance and publication is 6 months. Poems are circulated to an editorial board. Send SAE with IRCs for guidelines. Responds in 6 months. Reviews books or other magazines. Open to unsolicited reviews. Poets may also send books for review consideration.

Also Offers: Sponsors open poetry competitions. Send SAE with IRCs for guidelines.

THE POETRY MISCELLANY, English Dept., University of Tennessee at Chattanooga, Chattanooga TN 37403, phone (423)755-4629, e-mail suobodni@aol.com or Richard-Jackson@utc.edu, website www.utc.edu/~engldept/PM/PMHP.HTML. founded 1971 (in North Adams, MA), poetry editor Richard Jackson.

Magazine Needs: "We publish new and established writers—poems, interviews, essays, translations in January. We are truly a miscellany: We look at all schools, types, etc." They have published poetry by Mark Halliday, Bill Olsen, Paula Rankin, Tomaž Šalmun and Donald Justice. As a smaple the editor selected these lines from "Elvis Poem" by Regina Wilkins:

> But the big things come into your life/only through the little things that give you identity./That's when things like Love beome real./We spent a lot of the fifty dollars in the Snack Bar./We spent a little more at the souvenir shop./The preacher at grandfather's funeral said he could/explain the Bible as plainly as if he had spoken/to Paul himself. I knew when Janis turned down/the Elvis impersonator he'd hit on me. So everything was/back to normal. The world wasn't ending./And we had ten dollars left, which was enough.

The 16-page tabloid appears annually, professionally printed, with black ink on grey paper. Circulation is 750 for 400 subscribers of which 100 are libraries. They receive about 10,000 submissions a year, use approximately 20, have a 6-12 month backlog. Subscription: $3. Sample: $3.

How to Submit: Submit 3-4 clear copies/submission. Editor "rarely" comments on rejections. Send SASE for guidelines or obtain via e-mail. Responds in 4 months. Pays 2 copies.
Also Offers: Publishes chapbooks of translations. Sometimes holds contests "when grants allow." Website includes list of issues, editor's page and conference info.

POETRY NORTHWEST, University of Washington, P.O. Box 354330, Seattle WA 98195, phone (206)685-4750, founded 1959, editor David Wagoner.
Poetry published here has also been included in *The Best American Poetry 1996*.
Magazine Needs: *Poetry Northwest* is a quarterly featuring all styles and forms. For instance, lyric and narrative free verse has been included alongside a sonnet sequence, minimalist sonnets and stanza patterns—all accessible and lively. The magazine is 48 pgs., 5½×8½, professionally printed with color card cover. They receive 10,000 poems a year, use approximately 160, have a 3-month backlog. Circulation is 1,500. Subscription: $15. Sample: $4.
How to Submit: Occasionally comments on rejections. Responds in 1 month maximum. Pays 2 copies. Awards prizes of $500, $200 and $200 yearly, judged by the editors.

POETRY NOTTINGHAM INTERNATIONAL; NOTTINGHAM OPEN POETRY COMPETITION; NOTTINGHAM POETRY SOCIETY, 71 Saxton Ave., Heanor, Derbyshire DE75 7PZ England, founded 1946, editor Cathy Grindrod.
Magazine Needs: Nottingham Poetry Society meets monthly for readings, talks, etc., and publishes quarterly its magazine, *Poetry Nottingham International*, which is open to submissions from anyone. "We wish to see poetry that is intelligible to and enjoyable by the intelligent reader." Also accepts poetry written by children. They have published poetry by Frank Van Zant, Aidan Rooney-Céspedes and Kim Bridgford. As a sample the editor selected these lines from "Playing With Flowers" by Michael Tolkien:

> *Just when everything's tidy and needs no/coaxing you come up with packets of seeds/I might like to try; and I can't resist./They've a life of their own like fireworks/I'd fondle for days before the event,/ entranced by the touched-up promise/of colour, the crisp or fizzy rattle . . .*

There are at least 44 pgs. of poetry in each issue of the 6×8 magazine, professionally printed with articles, letters, news, reviews, glossy art paper cover. They receive about 1,500 submissions a year, use approximately 120, usually have a 1- to 3-month backlog. Press run is 275 for 200 subscribers. Single copy: £2.75 ($9.75 US); subscriptions: £17 sterling or $34 US.
How to Submit: Submit up to 6 poems at any time, or articles up to 500 words on current issues in poetry. No previously published poems. Send SAE and 3 IRCs for stamps. No need to query but requires cover letter. Responds in 2 months. Pays 1 copy. Staff reviews books of poetry. Send books for review consideration.
Book/Chapbook Needs & How to Submit: Nottingham Poetry Society publishes collections by individual poets who are members of Nottingham Poetry Society.
Also Offers: Nottingham Open Poetry Competition offers cash prizes, annual subscriptions and publication in *Poetry Nottingham International*. Open to all.
Advice: "We want originality, a 'surprise', apt imagery, good sense of rhythm, clear language. Poems most often rejected due to: use of tired language and imagery, use of clichés and inversions, old treatment of an old subject, sentimentality, poor rhythm and scansion, incorrect use of set forms."

POETRY OF THE PEOPLE (Specialized: bilingual/foreign language, humor, love, nature, fantasy, themes), P.O. Box 298, Micanopy FL 32667-0298, phone (352)466-3743, e-mail poetryforaquarter@yahoo.com, website www.angelfire.com/fl/poetryofthepeople, founded 1986, poetry editor Paul Cohen.
Magazine Needs: *Poetry of the People* is a leaflet that appears 3 times/year. "We take all forms of poetry but we like humorous poetry, love poetry, nature poetry and fantasy. No racist or highly ethnocentric poetry will be accepted. I do not like poetry that lacks images or is too personal or contains rhyme to the point that the poem has been destroyed. All submitted poetry will be considered for posting on website which will be updated every month." They are also accepting poetry written in French and Spanish. Also accepts poetry written by children. They have published poetry by Max Lizard, Prof. Jerry Reminick, Ian Ayers and Noelle Kocot. As a sample the editor selected these lines from "Lunar" by David Vetterlein:

> *"I stumble blindly/in coated forests/bound by/howling wolves/I stagger/wandering endless/in that lunar maze/called emotion*

Poetry of the People varies from 8-32 pgs., 5½×8 to 5½×4⅜, stapled, sometimes on colored paper. Issues are usually theme oriented. It has a circulation between 300 and 2,300. Copies are distributed to Gainesville residents for 25¢ each. Samples: $4 for 11 pamphlets. "Please send donations, the magazine bank account is overdrawn. Suggested donation: $2."
How to Submit: Submit up to 10 poems at a time. Include SASE. Cover letter with biographical information required with submissions. E-mail submissions OK. "I feel autobiographical information is important in understanding the poetry." Poems returned within 6 months. Editor comments on rejections "often." Publish theme issues. Theme for January 2000: "Y2K." Send SASE for upcoming themes. Takes suggestions for theme issues. Sometimes sends prepublication galleys. Pays 10 copies for poetry published in leaflet. Acquires first rights.
Also Offers: Website includes guidelines, poetry and a list of back issues. Also includes original content, please contact editor.

Revealing new discoveries through poetry

"Maybe it is impossible to live in one moment at a time," Richard Jackson writes in "Hope." His poems embrace this notion, layering the emotional, ideological, political, historical, and scientific into a graceful and sweeping poetry that transports its readers to new realms of discovery and understanding. It is not surprising, given the scope of Jackson's work, that his early interest in poetry coincided with his interest in science, that he was for a while an economics and history major, or that he chose writing as a vocation while attending Columbia University on an engineering scholarship and learning, not very well he says, to play the guitar. Although Jackson's style may best be described as "discontinuous narrative," an unmistakable coherence shapes his poems.

Richard Jackson

Photo by Terri Harvey

"A poem is a rhythm of thought and feeling," Jackson explains. "It's a question of where the poem begins and where it ends, where it starts us emotionally and where it leaves us. This movement and how it carries the reader is the subject of the poem. Poetry is not the use of language to record an event or object or scene or feeling already known, but rather an exploration of language to reveal new discoveries, new relationships. Anything we see or say has a story behind it waiting to be discovered. I have a poem where I talk about the blind spot in the middle of our eyes: technically, we don't really see what is exactly in front of us, but sort of see around it and fill in the gaps mentally. The subject that holds the poem together is that blind spot, sort of a poetic black hole," he adds.

As such, material Jackson gathers for his poems comes from a variety of sources. However, he still reads extensively in science and history. "I'm always writing in my notebook bits and pieces of things I read in books, newspapers, science journals, as well as images I see, metaphors, scenes, scraps of language. I think of these things as sort of a vocabulary of my subconscious," he says. "Usually, I start with a first line, a rhythmic push, some sort of dramatic situation or intrigue, and then I start gathering these little bits and pieces and any new things that come up as I'm writing. I don't discover what the poem is about until I'm well into it."

Jackson has published poems and essays in a number of journals, including *Georgia Review*, *Poetry*, *Ploughshares* and *Kenyon Review*. His books include four collections of poetry: *Part of the Story* (Grove Press, 1983), *Worlds Apart* (University of Alabama Press, 1987), *Alive All Day* (Cleveland State University Poetry Center, 1992) and *Heartwell* (University of Massachusetts Press, 2000); two books of criticism: *Acts of Mind: Conversations with Contemporary American Poets* (University of Alabama Press, 1983) and *Dismantling Time in Contemporary Poetry* (University of Alabama Press, 1988); and a book of poems based on Petrarch entitled *Heart's Bridge* (Aureole Press, 1999).

"The work I've done with Petrarch began in a difficult time for me," says Jackson. "I found a kind of soul mate in him and at first did straightforward translations. Later I was intrigued by what the language must have been like to the people of his day, traditional and yet filled with what were at the time new metaphors and attitudes. So I started to adapt my own language to his traditional forms and came up with a series of poems based on Petrarch, sort of surreal sonnets. In a way they are a more accurate account of my life than many of the regular poems, more, in a strange way, autobiographical. At the same time I had in mind poems I think Petrarch might have written if he wrote today."

"The Exile" (based on Petrarch)

Grief frames the doorway to that room I used to call my port
against whatever storms came careening down my street,
that room with its memories now crumpled on the table, a fleet
of hopes wrecked by words that regret what they alone distort.
Thorns fill the bed. A taunting night shakes its keys to closets
of desire I can no longer open. Who sleeps there, indiscreet
rival, while I flee his shadows that loiter like a disease
which waits for a soul to pummel, a love to perfectly thwart?
The doorknob of the night is always turning, but it is myself I flee—
my dreams, my rhymes, that lifted me towards a heaven
I thought was the love these words might finally create.
Maybe now I'll hide in those city crowds I've come to hate
since I can no longer face myself, no longer be alone.
Longing rings the doorbell, but the house is empty

(reprinted with permission from the author)

Jackson's poetry, criticism and translations have been recognized with such awards as four Pushcart Prizes, NEA and NEH fellowships, and the Juniper Prize in Poetry. He is on the faculty of the Vermont College MFA Program and teaches at the University of Tennessee-Chattanooga, where he has won several teaching awards.

"My creative writing workshop is known ironically as 'the chop-shop,'" Jackson laughs. "We are incredibly honest, and there are few pats on the back. Everyone realizes we wouldn't be so honest, sometimes deadly honest, if we didn't care about our art, and about each other. There's no coddling here. We care enough about our art to fight over it. And we are ironic enough to joke around a lot. So, while we hold high standards, we are being ruthless about our own poems before someone else is, to cite John Berryman. We are also exploring the possibilities for the poem, what Marvin Bell calls the ghost poem. We try to follow other logics for the metaphors in a potential poem to see where they might lead. In the midst of all this there is an incredible, close-knit sense of camaraderie and honest encouragement. And the students read a great deal that we discuss even more than their own poems: poets from the classical time to the present around the globe."

Jackson continues, "I think two major problems in workshops today—especially in many graduate workshops I've seen—are first, that many students primarily want validation and approval (which usually leads to stagnation) rather than honest criticism they can use to improve. Second, they don't read anything earlier than the last few years and so have no real idea of the immense possibilities their art is based upon, the immense possibilities that have been accomplished, so they end up imitating themselves or the latest fad. I can understand why anyone needs approval, but I'd rather it be honest encouragement."

Aside from the workshop, Jackson's undergraduate writing program is unique in that his students participate in the biannual Meacham Writer's Workshop, which features between eighteen and twenty-five guest writers each year who conduct workshops, lectures, and individual conferences with students and other attendees. Jackson also takes his students to Slovenia each year, where they attend the annual PEN Conference and travel to cities in neighboring Italy, an experience that "expands their vision dramatically."

Jackson's interest in central Europe began in 1986 when he was a Fulbright exchange poet in Yugoslavia. "Over the years, I've met a lot of poets in Slovenia who I've had long and interesting talks with; I started reading their poems and we had more talks. Then, I got involved in some of the issues around there and began to understand the country and feel, even now, closer to Slovenia than any place else except my own home," he says.

Jackson notes that poetry is far more important in Europe, particularly in eastern and central Europe. "It was a way of expressing one's individuality under systems that often tried to suppress it. It was a way for both the poet and the reader to stay alive. In America we think of poetry as a sideshow and a trivial one at that." Jackson feels that Slovenian poetry has a "great deal of resonance. There is a sense that each thing and gesture has meaning, a sense that if we lived the life described in the poems we would live more intensely, as Rilke says, than we could ever now imagine. So there is a richness, a concentration, an evocative power. Slovenia, situated between east and west, has been able to tap into both the empirical traditions of the west and the mystical traditions of the east to produce the vision," he says.

"There are only about two and a half million Slovenes, and their poetry is very valuable, so I try to publicize it as much as I can." To date, Jackson has published nearly thirty-five chapbooks of Slovenian poetry translated into English, as well as individual translations in the *mala revija* and *Poetry Miscellany*, both of which he edits. "The aim of *Poetry Miscellany*, true to its title, is to be miscellaneous; we don't subscribe to any school and might publish a formalist next to a surrealist next to a famous person next to an unknown next to a language poet, as long as the poems are 'discoveries'," Jackson explains.

Over the years Jackson has defined new territory of his own, such as the political edge in many of his poems that can be traced to his experiences in central Europe. "With 'political' poems there are a couple of things you have to keep in mind. One is that you shouldn't get a sense that the poet luxuriates in the pain of other people. 'Gee, isn't it lucky that all these people died because now I got a poem out of it.' That's poetry of witnessing, of reporting, which is not transforming it imaginatively into anything else," he says. "The narrator of the poem also has to realize that any one of us is capable of the most atrocious acts, given different circumstances—where you were born, where you were brought up, anything like that. I think any one of us could do any of the worst things we've read about or heard about. This applies to any poetry that classifies itself by theme—abuse poems, feminist protest poems, racial or ethnic protestations. This isn't to say that the poem shouldn't offer judgments, only that the speaker shouldn't pretend to be God in doing so. Otherwise you're preaching in the poem or setting yourself up as the morally righteous person, and to me that's a lie."

Jackson continues, "There is always this question of truth in poetry. The words in a poem have to be true to one another, even if they betray themselves as irony. Then they have to be true to the imagination, to where the poet's imagination has taken a scene or image. The poet might start with one scene, and the poem is true not if it is true to that one scene, but if it is true to where it leads the poet. In the end, the poem is true to the experience of the poem the poet has while writing it, which may include the original scene and wherever the poem has transported the poet."

—*Michelle Moore*

Advice: "Be creative; there is a lot of competition out there."

$ POETRY REVIEW; NATIONAL POETRY COMPETITION; THE POETRY SOCIETY, 22 Betterton St., London WC2H 9BU United Kingdom, phone (0044)171 420 9880, fax (0044)171 240 4818, e-mail poetrysoc@dial.pipex.com, website www.poetrysoc.com, founded 1909, editor Peter Forbes.
Magazine Needs: *Poetry Review*, published quarterly, strives "to be the leading showcase of UK poetry and to represent poetry written in English and in translation." They want "poems with metaphoric resonance." They do not want "inconsequential disconnected jottings." They have published poetry by John Ashbery, Miroslav Holub, Sharon Olds and Paul Muldoon. As a sample the editor selected these lines from "Addressee Unknown— Retour à L'Expéditeur" by Hans Magnus Enzensberger:
> Many thanks for the clouds./Many thanks for the well-tempered *clavier/and, why not, for the warm winter boots./Many thanks for my strange brain/and for all manner of other hidden organs*
The editor says *Poetry Review* is 96 pgs., 6½×9, paperback, with b&w cartoons and photos. They receive about 30-50,000 poems a year, accept approximately 0.3-0.4%. Press run is 4,750 for 4,000 subscribers of which 400 are libraries, 4 shelf sales; 100 distributed free to contributors and press. Single copy: £5.95; subscription: $56. Sample: $13.
How to Submit: Submit 4 poems at a time. No previously published poems or simultaneous submissions. Time between acceptance and publication is 6 months. Poems are selected by the editor. Seldom comments on rejections. Publishes theme issues. Responds in up to 3 months. Sometimes sends prepublication galleys. Pays £40 plus 1 copy. Buys UK first publication rights. Staff reviews chapbooks of poetry or other magazines in single or multi-book format.
Also Offers: Sponsors the annual National Poetry Competition run by the Poetry Society. 1st Prize: £5,000; 2nd Prize: £1,000; 3rd Prize: £500. Entry fee: £5 for first poem, £3/poem thereafter. Deadline: October 31. Send SASE (or SAE and IRC) for guidelines. "The Poetry Society promotes poetry, assists poets and campaigns for poets wherever possible." Offers "Poetry Prescription" reading service: £40 for 100 lines.

POETRY USA; NATIONAL POETRY ASSOCIATION, SOMAR, 934 Brannan St., Second Floor, San Francisco CA 94103, phone (415)552-9261, fax (415)552-9271, e-mail poetryusa@nationalpoetry.org, website www.nationalpoetry.org, founded 1985.
Magazine Needs & How to Submit: *Poetry USA* appears in online format only and "aims to provide a common space for the diversity of voices that make up the American experience. We include poems from all over the country, and often include poetry from young people, people without a home, and people in prison. Poets from the community have been invited to serve as guest editors, choosing different themes for past issues." They publish "shorter poems (under 50 lines, please) accessible to the non-literary general public." Consult website for submission information. Poets retain all rights.
Also Offers: "The National Poetry Association, an all-volunteer organization founded in 1975, is committed to promoting the written, spoken and visual use of language in new and traditional ways." Call or e-mail for more information.

POETS AT WORK (Specialized: subscription), VAMC Box 113, 325 New Castle Rd., Box 113, Butler PA 16001, founded 1985, editor/publisher Jessee Poet.
Magazine Needs: All contributors are expected to subscribe. The editor says, "Every poet who writes within the dictates of good taste and within my 20-line limit will be published in each issue. I accept all forms and themes of poetry, including seasonal and holiday, but no porn, no profanity, horror, bilingual/foreign language, translations, feminism." He has published poetry by Dr. Karen Springer, William Middleton, Ann Gasser, Warren Jones and Ralph Hammond. As a sample he selected his poem "An Old Romance":
> I almost loved you . . . did you know?/Sometimes you still disturb my dreams./A summer romance long ago/I almost loved you . . . did you know?/We danced to music soft and low/Just yesterday . . . or so it seems/I almost loved you . . . did you know?/Sometimes you still disturb my dreams.
Poets at Work, a bimonthly, is generally 36-40 pgs., magazine-sized, saddle-stapled, photocopied from typescript with colored paper cover. Subscription: $20. Sample: $3.50.

How to Submit: If a subscriber, submit 5-10 poems at a time. Line length for poetry is 20 maximum. Simultaneous submissions and previously published poems OK. Responds within 2 weeks. Pays nothing, not even a copy. "Because I publish hundreds of poets, I cannot afford to pay or give free issues. Every subscriber, of course, gets an issue."

Book/Chapbook Needs & How to Submit: Also publishes chapbooks. Send SASE for details.

Also Offers: Subscribers also have many opportunities to regain their subscription money in the numerous contests offered in each issue. Send SASE for flyer for separate monthly and special contests. Website includes monthly contests and more than 25 themes.

Advice: "These days even the best poets tell me that it is difficult to get published. I am here for the novice as well as the experienced poet. I consider *Poets at Work* to be a hotbed for poets where each one can stretch and grow at his or her own pace. Each of us learns from the other, and we do not criticize one another. The door for poets is always open, so please stop by; we probably will like each other immediately."

☑ ▣ ◯ **POETS CORNER; CONSTAL PUBLISHING**, P.O. Box 456, Glenoma WA 98336-0456, phone/fax (360)498-5341, e-mail tldorn@lewiscounty.com, website www.lewiscounty.com/tldorn, founded 1997, publisher T.L. Dorn.

Magazine Needs: *Poets Corner* is published 6 times a year "to give new and unknown poets a place to show their art." They want original work. "No copy of old lines such as 'roses are red—I scream' etc." Also accepts poetry written by children. The publisher says *PC* is magazine-sized, desktop-published, staple-bound, colored cover, includes art/graphics and ads. They receive about 7-900 poems a year, accept approximately 90%. Press run is 1,000 ("growing daily") for 846 subscribers of which 10 are libraries, 30 shelf sales; 90 distributed free to elderly and doctors offices." Subscription: $25/year. Sample: $5. Make checks payable to Constal Publishing.

How to Submit: Submit 1-3 poems at a time. Length for poetry is 64 lines or 2 pages maximum. Previously published poems and simultaneous submissions OK. Cover letter is "OK." Time between acceptance and publication is 1-3 months. Seldom comments on rejections. Publishes theme issues occasionally. Send SASE for guidelines. Acquires first rights. Poets may also send books for review consideration to T.L. Dorn.

Also Offers: Sponsors annual contest. Cash Prize: $200 or more.

◯ ◉ **POET'S FANTASY (Specialized: fantasy)**, Dept. PM, 227 Hatten Ave., Rice Lake WI 54868-2030, e-mail staxdome@chibardun.net, founded 1991, publisher/editor Gloria Stoeckel.

Magazine Needs: *Poet's Fantasy* is a quarterly designed "to help the striving poet see his/her work in print." They want sonnets, haiku and humorous free verse, 4-16 lines. "I accept good, clean poetry. Looking for poems of fantasy, but not exclusively. No profanity or sexual use of words." They have published poetry by earl jay perel, Nawja Salam Brax and Gary Michael Lawson. *Poet's Fantasy* is 48 pgs., letter-sized, photocopied from typescript and saddle-stapled with colored graphics and ads. They receive about 400 poems a year, accept approximately 90%. Press run is 500 for 450 subscribers. Subscription: $20/year; foreign $26/year. Sample: $5.

How to Submit: Submit 3-5 poems at a time. No previously published poems or simultaneous submissions. E-mail submissions OK ("include snail mail address on submission"). Often comments on rejections. Publishes theme issues. Send SASE for guidelines. Responds within 2 weeks. Poets must purchase copy their work is in. Acquires first North American serial rights. "I do book reviews if poet sends a complimentary copy of the book and a $3 reading fee. Reviews are approximately 200 to 300 words in length."

Also Offers: Holds contests in each issue and creates greeting cards for poets. "They use verse they wrote and can design their own cover." Send SASE for details. Also publishes a yearly anthology.

▣ ◯ **THE POET'S HAVEN**, P.O. Box 1501, Massillon OH 44648, e-mail VertigoXX@PoetsHaven.com, website www.PoetsHaven.com, founded 1997, publisher/editor Vertigo Xi'an Xavier.

☑ *Poet's Haven* has received numerous small website awards including the Nocturnal Society "All-Nighter" Awards.

Magazine Needs: *Poet's Haven Digest* magazine and *The Poet's Haven* site feature poetry, artwork, stories, book reviews, essays, editorial, quotes and much more. I want to see work that is passionate, emotional, powerful, personal, and/or intimate with either the author or subject, be it fun, sad, light, deep, about love, pain, nature, insanity, or social commentary. No material that is obscene, excessively vulgar, pornographic, racist, or christian." Also accepts poetry written by children (over 12 preferred). They have published poetry by Terri A. Hateley, Elizabeth Hendricks, Jen Pezzo, Elisha Poret and Bonnie Langford. As a sample the editor selected this haiku, "Three Card Monte" by Barry Brown:

> three card monte fools/me again, love wasn't there/where it should have been.

The magazine is published in an anthology format, 32-96 pgs., saddle-stapled and includes a color cover with some interior line-art and ads. The website features an unlimited number of pages, with new work added sporadically. Work published on the website will be left on the site permanently. They receive about 3,000 poems a year, accept approximately 80%. Copies $3-8 postage paid.

How to Submit: Previously published poems and simultaneous submissions OK. Cover letter preferred. E-mail and disk submissions OK. "Electronic submissions (e-mail, website, diskette) are preferred, especially for longer works. If you are submitting by carrier mail (snail-mail) and wish to be notified if your work is accepted, include SASE." Time between acceptance and publication is 2 weeks to 1 year. Seldom comments on rejections. May publish theme issues including states of romance, states of nature, existence and horror. Obtain guidelines via e-mail or website. Responds when published by e-mail or SASE only. Pays 1 copy. Acquires rights to publish on the website and/or in the magazine. Author retains rights to have poems published elsewhere and have the poem removed from site if desired." Reviews books of poetry in single book format. Poets may also send books for review consideration.

Also Offers: "What started our as a small e-zine has expanded into an on- and off-line community. If a submitter wishes, his/her e-mail address will be included with any of their poems published so that readers can contact them. There are also Message Boards and a Chat Room available for writers and readers to meet and discuss topics of interest to them." Website has same review process as magazine. No themes, all genres accepted for each update. Contact the publisher.

Advice: "Submitting more than one poem at a time is recommended as they will give a wider display of a writer's talents and increase the chance of publication."

POETS ON THE LINE, P.O. Box 020292, Brooklyn NY 11202-0007, e-mail llerner@mindspring.com, website www.echonyc.com/~poets, founded 1995, editor Linda Lerner. Currently not accepting unsolicited work.

POETS' PODIUM, 1-3265 Front Rd., E. Hawksbury, Ontario K6A 2R2 Canada, e-mail kennyel@hotmail.com, founded 1993, associate editors Ken Elliott, Catherine Heaney Barrowcliffe, Robert Piquette.

Magazine Needs: *Poets' Podium* is a quarterly newsletter published "to promote the reading and writing of the poetic form, especially among those being published for the first time." Their poetry specifications are open. However, they do not want poetry that is gothic, erotic/sexual, gory, bloody, or that depicts violence. Publish 25 poems/issue. Subscription: $10 (US). Sample: $3 (US). "Priority is given to valued subscribers. Nevertheless, when there is room in an issue we will publish nonsubscribers."

How to Submit: Submit 3 poems at a time. Line length for poetry is 4 minimum, 25 maximum. Previously published poems and simultaneous submissions OK. Cover letter required. Include SASE (or SAE and IRC), name, address and telephone number; e-mail address if applicable. Time between acceptance and publication varies. Send SASE (or SAE and IRC) for guidelines or request via fax or e-mail or obtain via website. Pays 3 copies. All rights remain with the author.

Advice: "Poetry is a wonderful literary form. Try your hand at it. Send us the fruit of your labours."

POETS' ROUNDTABLE; POETS' STUDY CLUB OF TERRE HAUTE; POETS' STUDY CLUB INTERNATIONAL CONTEST (Specialized: membership), 826 S. Center St., Terre Haute IN 47807, phone (812)234-0819, founded in 1939, president/editor Esther Alman.

Magazine Needs: Poets' Study Club is one of the oldest associations of amateur poets. It publishes, every other month, *Poets' Roundtable*, a newsletter of market and contest information and news of the publications and activities of its members in a mimeographed, 10-page bulletin (magazine-sized, stapled at the corner), circulation 2,000. They have also published an occasional chapbook-anthology of poetry by members "but do not often do so." Dues: $10/year (includes subscription to *Poets' Roundtable*). Sample free for SASE.

How to Submit: Uses short poems by members only. Simultaneous submissions and previously published poems OK.

Also Offers: They offer an annual Poets' Study Club International Contest, open to all, with no fees and cash prizes—a $25 and $15 award in 3 categories: traditional haiku, serious poetry, light verse. Deadline: February 1. Also contests for members every 2 months.

POLYPHONIES (Specialized: translations), 8, rue des ImBergères, 92330 SCEAUX, France, founded 1985, editor Pascal Culerrier. Editorial committee: Pascal Boulanger, Laurence Breysse, François Comba, Emmanuelle Dagnaud, Jean-Yves Masson and Alexis Pelletier.

Magazine Needs: *Polyphonies* appears twice a year. "Every case is a special one. We want to discover the new important voices of the world to open French literature to the major international productions. For example, we published Brodsky in French when he was not known in our country and had not yet won the Nobel Prize. No vocal poetry, no typographic effects." They have published poetry by Mario Luzi (Italy), Jeremy Reed (Great Britain), Octavio Paz (Mexico) and Claude Michel Cluny (France). It is about 110 pgs., 6½×9½, flat-spined, with glossy card cover, printed completely in French. Press run is 850 for 300 subscribers.

How to Submit: Uses translations of previously published poems. Pays 2 copies.

Advice: "Our review is still at the beginning. We are in touch with many French editors. Our purpose is to publish together, side-by-side, poets of today and of yesterday."

THE BOOK PUBLISHERS INDEX, located at the back of this book, lists those publishers who consider full-length book collections.

◐ **PORCUPINE LITERARY ARTS MAGAZINE**, P.O. Box 259, Cedarsburg WI 53012, e-mail ppine259@ aol.com, website: members.aol.com/ppine259, founded 1996, managing editor W.A. Reed.

Magazine Needs: *Porcupine*, published biannually, contains featured artists, poetry, short fiction and visual art work. "There are no restrictions as to theme or style. Poetry should be accessible and highly selective. If a submission is not timely for one issue, it will be considered for another." They have published poetry by Bill Embly, G.K. Wuori, Kenneth Pobo and Andrew Genn-Dorian. As a sample, we selected these lines from "Under the Watchful Eyes of Great Art" by Christine Delea:

> It's not the eyes following movement,/but red lips, painted pursed or with/a slight smirk, mouths closed
> tight in custom/or opened in horror or wonder, moving/when I move.

Porcupine is 100-150 pgs., 8½×5, offset, perfect-bound with full-color glossy cover and b&w photos and art (occasionally use color inside, depending on artwork). They receive about 300 poems a year, accept approximately 10%. Press run is 1,500 for 500 subscribers of which 50 are libraries, 500 shelf sales; 100 distributed free. Single copy: $8.95; subscription: $15.95. Sample: $5.

How to Submit: Submit up to 3 poems, 1/page with name and address on each. Include SASE. "The outside of the envelope should state: 'Poetry.' " No previously published poems or simultaneous submissions. E-mail submissions OK. Time between acceptance and publication is 6 months. "Poems are selected by editors and then submitted to managing editor for final approval." Seldom comments on rejections. Send SASE for guidelines. Responds in 3 months. Pays 1 copy. Acquires one-time rights.

Also Offers: Website features writer's guidelines, cover art, table of contents and sample poetry.

✓ ◐ **PORTLAND REVIEW**, Box 347, Portland State University, Portland OR 97207-0347, phone (503)725-4533, fax (503)725-5860, e-mail review@vanguard.vg.pdx.edu, founded 1954, editor Ryan Spear.

Magazine Needs & How to Submit: *Portland Review* is a literary quarterly published by Portland State University. "Experimental poetry welcomed." The quarterly is about 128 pgs. They accept about 30 of 300 poems received each year. Press run is 500 for 100 subscribers of which many are libraries. Sample: $6. Simultaneous submissions OK. E-mail submissions in body OK. Send SASE for guidelines. Pays 1 copy.

N ○ **PORTRAITS OF THE HEART**, P.O. Box 121, San Angelo TX 76902-0121, phone (915)947-7320, e-mail cleottus@webstar.net or leyah@hotmail.com, website www.geocities.com/SouthBeach/Cove/8094, founded 1999, publisher Karna Sabean, poetry editor Will Haro.

Magazine Needs: *POTH* appears quarterly "to publish heart warming/inspirational poetry/short stories for readers of all ages. New poets are encouraged to submit their work here." They want "poetry written from the heart to warm the heart; all forms. Nothing vulgar or explicit." As a sample the editors selected these lines from "Wildflowers" by Karna Sabean:

> Smiles are like wildflowers/Plant one and an entire garden grows

The editor says *POTH* is 10-20 pgs., 8½×11, photocopied and side-stapled with color cover with art. Press run is 50. Single copy: $2.50; subscription: $8. Sample free with SASE or send $1. Make checks payable to Will Haro Jr.

How to Submit: Submit up to 5 poems at a time with $2 reading fee. Line length for poetry is 2 minimum, 50 maximum. Previously published poems (within the last 2 years) and simultaneous submissions OK. E-mail submissions OK. Cover letter preferred. Time between acceptance and publication is approximately 2-4 months. Poems are circulated to an editorial board. "Poems are voted upon and the ones which receive the most votes are published." Often comments on rejections. Publishes theme issues occasionally. Send SASE for guidelines and upcoming themes. Responds in 6 weeks. Pays 1-3 copies. Acquires first rights.

Advice: "Believe in what you write and write what you believe."

◎ ◐ **THE POST-APOLLO PRESS (Specialized: form/style, women)**, 35 Marie St., Sausalito CA 94965, phone (415)332-1458, fax (415)332-8045, e-mail tpapress@dnai.com, website www.dnai.com/~tpapress, founded 1982, publisher Simone Fattal.

Book/Chapbook Needs & How to Submit: The Post-Apollo Press publishes "quality paperbacks by experimental poets/writers, mostly women, many first English translations." They publish 2-3 paperbacks/year. "Please note we are *not* accepting manuscripts at this time due to full publishing schedule."

N ◖ ○ ◐ ◎ **POTATO HILL POETRY (Specialized: students, teachers)**, 81 Speen St., Natick MA 01760, phone (508)652-9908, fax (508)652-9858, e-mail info@potatohill.com, founded 1996, editor Andrew Green.

Magazine Needs: *Potato Hill Poetry* appears bimonthly, except in July/August, "and publishes the best student (K-12) and teacher poetry we can find and to share writing exercises." They want poems on all topics, any length, any form. As a sample the editor selected these lines (poet unidentified):

> I won't need to remember this/won't need to remember/the boys/the trench coats or guns/this closet or
> metal/shards in my arm/in my head/in my heart

The editor says *PHP* is 16 pgs., 8½×11, saddle-stitched with 60 lb. paper stock cover, includes art/graphics and ads. They receive about 1,000 poems a year, accept approximately 5%. Publish 8-12 poems/issue. Press run is 5,000 for 2,000 subscribers of which 100 are libraries; 3,000 distributed free to schools. Subscription: $17.95. Sample: $3.

How to Submit: Submit 1-5 poems at a time. No previously published poems; simultaneous submissions OK. "Please include name, address, school, grade level you are in or teach, home phone number." Reads submissions September 1 through June 30 only. Time between acceptance and publication is 2 months. Poems are circulated to an editorial board. "Several editors read and make all decisions." Often comments on rejections. Send SASE for guidelines. Responds in 2 months. Pays 2 copies. Acquires first North American serial rights and reprint rights. Reviews books of poetry in 100-300 words, single and multi-book format. Open to unsolicited reviews. Poets may also send books for review consideration.

Also Offers: Sponsors annual poetry contest. Website includes poem of the week, contest and submissions guidelines, exercises, book catalog.

N ▢ ▢ ◑ ◎ POTLUCK CHILDREN'S LITERARY MAGAZINE (Specialized: children/teen), P.O. Box 546, Deerfield IL 60015-0546, phone (847)948-1139, fax (847)317-9492, e-mail nappic@aol.com, website http://members.aol.com/nappic, founded 1997, editor Susan Napoli Picchietti.

Magazine Needs: *Potluck* is published quarterly "to provide a forum which encourages young writers to share their voice and to learn their craft. Open to all styles, forms and subjects—we just want well crafted works that speak to the reader. No works so abstract they only have meaning to the writer. Violent, profane or sexually explicit works will not be accepted." The editor says *Potluck* is 32 pgs., $5\frac{1}{2} \times 8\frac{1}{2}$, photocopied and saddle-stapled with 60 lb. paper cover, includes original artwork on covers. They receive about 350 poems a year, accept approximately 90%. Publish 10-15 poems/issue. Press run is 300 for 150 subscribers of which 5 are libraries, 150 shelf sales; back issues distributed free to hospitals/inner city schools. Single copy: $5.50; subscription: $18. Sample (including guidelines): $4.25.

How to Submit: Submit up to 3 poems at a time. Line length for poetry is 30 maximum. No previously published poems or simultaneous submissions. E-mail submissions OK. Cover letter preferred. "All works must include a SASE for reply." Submit seasonal poems 3 months in advance. Time between acceptance and publication is 4-6 weeks. Poems are circulated to an editorial board. "We each review each poem—make remarks on page then discuss our view of each—the best works make the issue." Always comments on rejections. Publishes theme issues occasionally. Send SASE for guidelines and upcoming themes or obtain via fax, e-mail or website. Responds 6 weeks after deadline. Pays 1 copy. Acquires first rights. Reviews chapbooks of poetry.

Also Offers: Website includes general information, "testimonials," guidelines, where to find and how to order *Potluck*, special events.

Advice: "Be present—now—write what you see, hear, taste, smell, observe and what you feel/experience. Be honest, clear, and choose your words with great care. Enjoy."

▢ ◑ ◎ POTOMAC REVIEW (Specialized: regional), P.O. Box 354, Port Tobacco MD 20677, website www.meral.com/potomac, founded 1994, editor Eli Flam.

Magazine Needs: *PR* is published quarterly and "explores the topography and human terrain of the Mid-Atlantic region and beyond for a growing readership." They want "poetry with a vivid, individual quality that has vision to go with competence, that strives to get at 'the concealed side' of life." They do not want "arch, banal, mannered, surface, flat, self-serving poetry." Accepts poetry written by children through high school for Young Talent Pages. They have published poetry by Josephine Jacobsen, Roland Flint and Judith McCombs. As a sample the editor selected these lines from "Lines" by Gerald R. Wheeler:

> Eyeing my rods anchored in carved/notches of the rail, he says, "Son,/like a hunter, a true angler uses/
> one gun, and keeps his finger/on the trigger. Remember:/A catch is a gift. There are/more hungry
> fishermen/than starving fish."

Potomac Review is 128 pgs., $5\frac{1}{2} \times 8\frac{1}{2}$, offset printed, perfect-bound, with medium card cover, b&w graphic art, photos and ads. They receive about 1,000 poems a year, accept approximately 5%. Press run is 2,000 for 1,000 subscribers plus about 400 shelf sales. Subscription: $18/year (MD residents add 5%), $30/2 years. Sample: $5.

How to Submit: Submit up to 3 poems, 5 pages at a time with SASE. Simultaneous submissions OK. No previously published poems. Cover letter preferred with brief bio and SASE. Time between acceptance and publication is up to 1 year. Poems are read "in house," then sent to poetry editor for comments and dialogue. Usually comments on rejections. Publishes theme issues. Send SASE for guidelines and upcoming themes. Themes for fall 2000, winter 2000, spring 2001 and summer 2001 are Beyond Museum Walls—First Americans Take Hold, A Capital Birthday, Water, Water Everywhere?, Twining Trails III, respectively. Responds in 3 months. Pays 1 copy and offers discount on additional copies. Acquires first North American serial rights. Reviews books of poetry; write first for review consideration.

Also Offers: Sponsors annual poetry contest, usually open January through March. 1st Prize: $300; winner's poem and some runners-up are published in fall. To enter, send $15 (provides 1-year subscription), up to 3 poems, any subject, any form. Deadline: March 31, 2001. Competition receives about 170 entries. Send SASE for guidelines. Website includes samplings of each issue, contents, guidelines, background on magazine.

◑ POTPOURRI; DAVID RAY POETRY AWARD, P.O. Box 8278, Prairie Village KS 66208, phone (913)642-1503, fax (913)642-3128, e-mail Potpourpub@aol.com, website www.Potpourri.org, founded 1989, poetry editor Terry Hoyland, haiku editor Jeri Ragan.

Magazine Needs: *Potpourri* is a quarterly magazine "publishing works of writers, including new and unpublished writers. We want strongly voiced original poems in either free verse or traditional. Traditional work must represent the best of the craft. No religious, confessional, racial, political, erotic, abusive or sexual preference materials unless fictional and necessary to plot or characterization. No concrete/visual poetry (because of format)." They have published poetry by X.J. Kennedy, David Ray, Richard Moore, Pattiann Rogers and Tess Gallagher. As a sample the editor selected these lines from "Angels" by Sharon Kourous:

> They are. In the moment of fracture/where atoms split or sear; where winter takes/still ice from liquid silver edge of lake;/or light becomes a rainbow.

It is 76 pgs., 8½×11, professionally printed, saddle-stapled with red & white art on glossy cover, drawings, photos and ads inside. Press run is 1,500 for 850 subscribers. Subscription: $15. Sample: $4.95 with 9×12 envelope; $7.20 overseas.

How to Submit: Submit up to 3 poems at a time, one to a page, length to 75 lines (approximately 30 preferred). Submit seasonal themes 6 months in advance. Address haiku and related forms to Jeri Ragan. No e-mail submissions. Send SASE for guidelines. Responds in up to 10 weeks at most. Pays 1 copy. Acquires first North American serial rights.

Also Offers: The David Ray Poetry Award ($100 or more, depending upon grant monies) is given annually for best of volume. Another annual award is sponsored by the Council on National Literatures and offers $100 and publication in *Potpourri* for selected poem or short story; alternating years (2000 fiction). Send SASE for official guidelines. Deadline: September 1, 2000. Website includes back issues, biographies, submission guidelines, sample writings and literary links.

Advice: "Keep your new poems around long enough to become friends with them before parting. Let them ripen, and, above all, learn to be your own best editor. Read them aloud, boldly, to see how they ripple the air and echo what you mean to say. Unrequited love, children, grandchildren, favorite pets and descriptions that seem to be written for their own sake find little chance here."

$ POTTERSFIELD PORTFOLIO; POTTERSFIELD PORTFOLIO SHORT POEM COMPETITION, P.O. Box 40, Station A, Sydney, Nova Scotia B1P 6G9 Canada, website www.pportfolio.com, founded 1979, contact poetry editor.

Magazine Needs: Appearing 3 times a year, *Pottersfield Portfolio* is a "literary magazine publishing fiction, poetry, essays and reviews by authors from all around the world. No restrictions on subject matter or style. However, we will likely not use religious, inspirational or children's poetry. No doggerel or song lyrics. And please, no stuff that splashes symbols and images all over the page." They have published poetry by David Zieroth, Don Domanski, Jean McNeil and Alden Nowlan. As a sample the editor selected these lines from "The Coves" by Steve McOrmond:

> You ask the wind/hard questions. Try to see/where the horizon lies, blue seam/between ocean and air,/ between us/and the end of history.

The editor says *Pottersfield* is 60 pgs., 8×11, professionally printed and perfect-bound with b&w cover, includes photos and ads. They receive about 1,000 poems a year, accept approximately 5%. Press run is 1,000 for 250 subscribers of which 25 are libraries, 750 shelf sales. Single copy: $7; subscription: $26. Sample: $6. "Subscribers from outside Canada please remit in U.S. dollars."

How to Submit: Submit 6 poems at a time. No previously published poems; simultaneous submissions OK. Include SAE with IRCs. Cover letter strongly preferred. "Submissions should be on white paper of standard dimensions (8½×11). Only one poem per page." Time between acceptance and publication is 2-3 months. Send SASE (or SAE with IRC) for guidelines and upcoming themes. "Note: U.S. stamps are no good in Canada." Responds in 3 months. Pays $5/printed page to a maximum of $25 plus 1 copy. Buys first Canadian serial rights.

Also Offers: Sponsors the *Pottersfield Portfolio* Short Poem Competition. Deadline: April 1 each year. Entry fee: $20 for 3 poems, which must be no more than 20 lines in length. Fee includes subscription. Write for details or consult website.

Advice: "Only submit your work in a form you would want to read yourself. Subscribe to some literary journals. Read lots of poetry."

THE PRAGUE REVUE, BOHEMIA'S JOURNAL OF INTERNATIONAL LITERATURE, V Jámě 7, 110 00 Prague 1, Czech Republic, phone (4202)2422-2383, fax (4202)2422-1783, e-mail prague_revue @yahoo.com, website www.praguepivo.com, founded 1995, poetry editors William E. Pritts and Todd A. Morimoto, managing editor Clare Wallace.

Magazine Needs: *The Prague Revue*, appearing 2-3 times a year, is a "literary journal with an international focus. We attempt to provide new, talented writers with a forum. Also publish some literary/critical essays on themed topics." They have no preferences as to subject matter, but submissions must be English. "*The Prague Revue* reserves the right to generate additional translations for publication." They do not want "epics, tear-jerkers or rhyming verse." They have published poetry by John Kinsella (Australia), Miroslav Holub (Czech Republic), Bohumil Hrabal (Czech Republic) and John Millet. As a sample the editors selected this poem, "Autobus Urbano 45 [madrid]," by Louis Armand:

> in its rainslashed headlights/i am a crouched hyena/who has here awaited the revelations/of hieronymus bosch/on the avenida of thousands murdered/forgotten unforgotten/with treacherous claws i give/to franco what is franco's/the driver sightless/slips my five coins into their coffins.

PR is 200 pgs., A5, perfect-bound with color cover, includes b&w art and some ads. They receive about 3,000 poems a year, accept approximately 1%. Press run is 2,500 for 1,000 subscribers of which 270 are libraries, 1,200 shelf sales. Four issue subscription: $39 (US). Sample: $10/issues 5 and 6, $7 issues 1 through 4.

How to Submit: Submit no more than 15 pages or 5 poems at a time, typewritten only. Previously published poems (if author holds all rights) and simultaneous submissions OK. However, "strong preference given to previously unpublished works." Cover letter with short bio required. Send SAE with IRC for response and/or return of ms. E-mail, fax and disk (formatted for Microsoft Word) submissions OK. Time between acceptance and publication is 6 months. Poems are circulated to an editorial board. Seldom comments on rejections. Publishes theme issues occasionally. Send SASE for guidelines and upcoming themes or obtain via e-mail or website. Responds in up to 6 months. Pays 2 copies. Acquires first rights.

Also Offers: Website includes *Prague Revue*'s mission, history, submission guidelines, subscription information and latest news on the review.

🍁 ☑ $ ◐ ◑ ◎ **THE PRAIRIE JOURNAL; PRAIRIE JOURNAL PRESS (Specialized: regional, themes)**, P.O. Box 61203, Brentwood Post Office, 217-3630 Brentwood Rd. NW, Calgary, Alberta T2L 2K6 Canada, e-mail prairiejournal@iname.com, website www.geocities.com/Athens/Ithaca/4336/, founded 1983, editor A. Burke.

Magazine Needs: For *The Prairie Journal*, the editor wants to see poetry of "any length, free verse, contemporary themes (feminist, nature, urban, non-political), aesthetic value, a poet's poetry." Does not want to see "most rhymed verse, sentimentality, egotistical ravings. No cowboys or sage brush." They have published poetry by Mick Burrs, Lorna Crozier, Mary Melfi, Art Cuelho and John Hicks. *Prairie Journal* is 40-60 pgs., $7 \times 8\frac{1}{2}$, offset, saddle-stitched with card cover, b&w drawings and ads, appearing twice a year. They receive about 500 poems a year, accept approximately 4%. Press run is 600 for 200 subscribers of which 50% are libraries, the rest are distributed on the newsstand. Subscription: $8 for individuals, $15 for libraries. Sample: $8 ("Use postal money order").

How to Submit: No simultaneous submissions or previously published poems. Guidelines available for postage (but "no U.S. stamps, please"—get IRCs from the Post Office) or on website. "We will not be reading submissions until such time as an issue is in preparation (twice yearly), so be patient and we will acknowledge, accept for publication or return work at that time." Sometimes sends prepublication galleys. Pays $10-50 plus 1 copy. Acquires first North American serial rights. Reviews books of poetry "but must be assigned by editor. Query first."

Book/Chapbook Needs & How to Submit: For chapbook publication, Canadian poets only (preferably from the region) should query with 5 samples, bio, publications. Responds to queries in 2 months, to mss in 6 months. Payment in modest honoraria. They have published *Voices From Earth*, selected poems by Ronald Kurt and Mark McCawley, and *In the Presence of Grace*, by McCandless Callaghan. "We also publish anthologies on themes when material is available."

Advice: "Read recent poets! Experiment with line length, images, metaphors. Innovate."

◑ **PRAIRIE SCHOONER; STROUSSE PRIZE; LARRY LEVIS PRIZE; SLOTE PRIZE; FAULKNER AWARD; HUGH J. LUKE AWARD; STANLEY AWARD; READERS' CHOICE AWARDS**, 201 Andrews, University of Nebraska, Lincoln NE 68588-0334, phone (402)472-0911, website www.unl.edu/schooner/psmain.htm, founded 1927, editor Hilda Raz.

🏆 Poetry published in *PS* has also been selected for inclusion in *The Best American Poetry 1996* and the *Pushcart Prize* anthology.

Magazine Needs: *Prairie Schooner* is "one of the oldest literary quarterlies in continuous publication; publishes poetry, fiction, personal essays, interviews and reviews." They want "poems that fulfill the expectations they set up." No specifications as to form, length, style, subject matter or purpose. They have published poetry by Alicia Ostriker, Marilyn Hacker, Radu Hotinceneasru, Mark Rudman and David Ignatow. As a sample the editor selected these lines from "How to Get in the Best Magazines" by Eleanor Wilner:

> *it is time to write/the acceptable poem—/ice and glass, with its splinter/of bone, its pit/of an olive,/the dregs/of the cup of abundance,/useless spill of gold/from the thresher, the dust/of it filling the sunlight, the chum/broadcast on the black waters/and the fish/—the beautiful, ravenous fish—/refusing to rise.*

Prairie Schooner is 200 pgs., 6×9, flat-spined and uses 70-80 pgs. of poetry in each issue. They receive about 4,800 mss (of all types) a year from which they choose 300 pgs. of poetry. Press run is 3,100. Single copy: $7.95; subscription: $22. Sample: $5.

How to Submit: Submit 5-7 poems at a time. No simultaneous submissions. "Clear copy appreciated." Considers mss from September through May only. Publishes theme issues. Send SASE for guidelines. Responds in 4 months; "sooner if possible." Always sends prepublication galleys. Pays 3 copies. Acquires all rights. Returns rights upon request without fee. Reviews books of poetry. Open to unsolicited reviews. Poets may also send books for review consideration. Editor Hilda Raz also promotes poets whose work has appeared in her pages by listing their continued accomplishments in a special section (even when their work does not concurrently appear in the magazine).

Also Offers: The $500 Strousse Prize is awarded to the best poetry published in the magazine each year. The Slote Prize for beginning writers ($500), Hugh J. Luke Award ($250), the Stanley Award for Poetry ($500) and six other *PS* prizes are also awarded, as well as the Faulkner Award for Excellence in Writing ($1,000) and the

Larry Levis Prize for Poetry ($1,000). Also, each year 5-10 Readers' Choice Awards ($250 each) are given for poetry, fiction and nonfiction. Editors serve as judges. All contests are open only to those writers whose work was published in the magazine the previous year. Website features writer's guidelines, names of editors, subscription info, history, table of contents and excerpts from current issue.

PRAIRIE WINDS, Box 536, Dakota Wesleyan University, 1200 W. University Ave., Mitchell SD 57301, editor James C. Van Oort.

Magazine Needs: *Prairie Winds* is an annual of poetry, fiction, short essays, photos and art. They are open to all forms, lengths, styles and subjects of poetry except pornographic. They have published poetry by Simon Perchik, Robert Cooperman and Robert Parham. The editor says *PW* is 50-60 pgs., $7\frac{1}{2} \times 9\frac{1}{4}$, offset, bound, gloss litho, no ads. They accept approximately 8% of the poetry received each year. Press run is 700. Sample: $4.

How to Submit: Submit 5-10 poems at a time. No previously published poems; simultaneous submissions OK. Cover letter and SASE required. "We are an annual, published in April. All submissions must arrive by January 4. We do not return submissions." Reads submissions January 4 through 31 only. Send SASE for guidelines. Responds by end of February. Pays 1 copy.

PRAKALPANA LITERATURE; KOBISENA (Specialized: bilingual, form), P-40 Nandana Park, Calcutta 700034, West Bengal, India, phone (91)(033)478-2347, *Kobisena* founded 1972, *Prakalpana Literature* press founded 1974, magazine 1977, editor Vattacharja Chandan.

Magazine Needs: "We are small magazines which publish only Prakalpana (a mixed form of prose and poetry), Sarbangin (whole) poetry, experimental b&w art and photographs, essays on Prakalpana movement and Sarbangin poetry movement, letters, literary news and very few books on Prakalpana and Sarbangin literature. Purpose and form: for advancement of poetry in the super-space age, the poetry must be really experimental and avant-garde using mathematical signs and symbols and visualizing the pictures inherent in the alphabet (within typography) with sonorous effect accessible to people. That is Sarbangin poetry. Length: within 30 lines (up to 4 poems). Prakalpana is a mixed form of prose, poetry, essay, novel, story, play with visual effect and it is not at all short story as it is often misunderstood. Better send six IRCs to read *Prakalpana Literature* first and then submit. Length: within 16 pages (up to 2 prakalpanas) at a time. Subject matter: society, nature, cosmos, humanity, love, peace, etc. Style: own. We do not want to see traditional, conventional, academic, religious, mainstream and poetry of prevailing norms and forms." They have published poetry by Dilip Gupta, John M. Bennett and Susan Smith Nash. *Prakalpana Literature*, an annual, is 120 pgs., $7 \times 4\frac{1}{2}$, saddle-stapled, printed on thin stock with matte card cover. *Kobisena*, which also appears once a year, is 16 pgs., digest-sized, a newsletter format with no cover. Both use both English and Bengali. They receive about 400 poems a year, accept approximately 10%. Press run is 1,000 for each, and each has about 450 subscribers of which 50 are libraries. Samples: 15 rupees for *Prakalpana*, 4 rupees for *Kobisena*. *Overseas: 6 IRCs and 3 IRCs respectively or exchange of avant-garde magazines.*

How to Submit: Submit 4 poems at a time. Cover letter with short bio and small photo/sketch of poet/writer/ artist required; camera-ready copy ($4 \times 6\frac{1}{2}$) preferred. Time between acceptance and publication is within a year. After being published in the magazines, poets may be included in future anthologies with translations into Bengali/ English if and when necessary. "Joining with us is welcome but not a pre-condition." Editor comments on rejections "if wanted." Send SAE with IRC for guidelines. Pays 1 copy. Reviews books of poetry, fiction and art, "but preferably experimental books." Open to unsolicited reviews. Poets, writers and artists may also send books for review consideration.

Advice: "We believe that only through poetry, fiction and art, the deepest feelings of humanity as well as nature and the cosmos can be best expressed and conveyed to the peoples of the ages to come. And only poetry can fill up the gap in the peaceless hearts of dispirited peoples, resulted from the retreat of god and religion with the advancement of hi-tech. So, in an attempt, since the inception of Prakalpana Movement in 1969, to reach that goal in the avant-garde and experimental way we stand for Sarbangin poetry. And to poets and all concerned with poetry we wave the white handkerchief saying (in the words of Vattacharja Chandan), 'We want them who want us.'"

PRAYERWORKS (Specialized: religious), P.O. Box 301363, Portland OR 97294-9363, phone (503)761-2072, fax (503)760-1184, e-mail jay4prayer@aol.com or 76753.3202@compuserve.com, founded 1988, editor V. Ann Mandeville.

Magazine Needs: *Prayer Works* appears weekly "to share prayer concerns with others and to encourage prayer. Contents: 1 devotional and prayer requests, one filler (humorous or catchy)." *PrayerWorks* is 4 pgs., $5\frac{1}{2} \times 8$, photocopied, desktop-published, folded. They receive about 50 poems a year, accept approximately 25%. Press run is 900 for 900 subscribers. Subscription: free.

How to Submit: Submit 5 poems, 1/page. Previously published poems and simultaneous submissions OK. E-mail submissions OK (Wordperfect or Microsoft Word files). Cover letter preferred. Time between acceptance and publication is 2-6 months. Seldom comments on rejections. Publishes theme issues relating to the holidays. Send SASE for guidelines. Responds in 2 months. Pays 5 or more copies.

PREMIERE GENERATION INK, P.O. Box 2056, Madison WI 53701-2056, e-mail poetry@premieregene ration.com, website www.premieregeneration.com, founded 1998, contact poetry editor.

Magazine Needs: *PGI* appears quarterly and publishes "high quality, honest poetry in a magazine/journal format and also in a multimedia format via website. We are also looking for art, photos, live recordings of poetry (audio or video) to be put on the Web. We also want experimental video poetry which can be mailed by VHS cassette. We would like to see poetry that is less concerned with being poetry than it is with being honest and true. We welcome any length, format, style or subject matter. We do not want to see pretentious and contrived poetry." They have published poetry by Yogesh Chawla, Sophia Ali, Erin Duehring and Errol Miller. As a sample they selected these lines from "Starch" by Yogesh Chawla:

> *Swollen and oily/on my brittle flesh/you bleed the/trail of words that/cut and disagree as/i wonder*
> *what broke first-/the condom or my heart*

They say *PGI* is 30-40 pgs., 8½×11, photocopied in color and saddle-stapled, cover is color or b&w "depending on issue," includes art/graphics. Single copy: $4; subscription: $12. Sample: $4.

How to Submit: Submit 5 poems at a time. Previously published poems and simultaneous submissions OK. Cover letter preferred. Disk submissions OK. E-mail submissions preferred. "All electronic submissions or disk submissions must be in a readable PC format. Cover letters need not be formal, we prefer casual and personal." Time between acceptance and publication is 4 months. Poems are circulated to an editorial board. "Three editors review all submissions and a collective decision is reached." Often comments on rejections. Send SASE for guidelines or obtain via e-mail or website. Responds in 6 weeks. Pays 5 copies. Acquires first or reprint rights.

Also Offers: "We would like to publish books in cooperation with an author. Premiere Generation Ink will chiefly be a means for writers to distribute their art to a larger audience via the Web and the poetry journal. The sales proceeds will go to cover the costs associated with production. Any net profit will be divided equally between the author and the publisher. The main goal of this company is not profit, but rather to distribute quality art to a larger audience. We expect to work closely with the author on the format and layout of the book, and we hope eventually they will become just as much a part of the company as the founders." Order sample books by inquiring via regular mail, e-mail or website. Website includes constant updates of submission criteria and company information.

THE PRESBYTERIAN RECORD (Specialized: inspirational, religious), 50 Wynford Dr., North York, Ontario M3C 1J7 Canada, phone (416)441-1111, fax (416)441-2825, e-mail tdickey@presbyterian. ca, founded 1876.

Magazine Needs: *TPR* is "the national magazine that serves the membership of The Presbyterian Church in Canada (and many who are not Canadian Presbyterians). We seek to stimulate, inform, inspire, to provide an 'apologetic' and a critique of our church and the world (not necessarily in that order!)." They want poetry which is "inspirational, Christian, thoughtful, even satiric but not maudlin. No 'sympathy card' type verse a la Edgar Guest or Francis Gay. It would take a very exceptional poem of epic length for us to use it. Shorter poems, 10-30 lines, preferred. Blank verse OK (if it's not just rearranged prose). 'Found' poems. Subject matter should have some Christian import (however subtle)." They have published poetry by Margaret Avison, Andrew Foster, Fredrick Zydek, Kevin Hadduck, T.M. Dickey and Charles Cooper. The magazine comes out 11 times/year. Press run is 55,000. Subscription: $15.

How to Submit: Submit 3-6 poems at a time; seasonal work 6 weeks before month of publication. Simultaneous submissions OK; rarely accepts previously published poems. Poems should be typed, double-spaced. Fax and e-mail submissions OK "but will not necessarily reply to unsolicited faxes or e-mails." Pays $30-50/poem. Buys one-time rights. Staff reviews books of poetry. Send books for review consideration.

PRESENCE (Specialized: form), 12 Grovehall Ave., Leeds LS11 7EX United Kingdom, e-mail martin.lucas@talk21.com, website http://members.netscapeonline.co.uk/haikupresence, founded 1995, contact Mr. Martin Lucas.

Magazine Needs: *Presence*, published 2-3 times/year, features haiku, senryu, renga, tanka, etc. They want "haiku or haiku-related/haiku-influenced work. Maximum length: 16 lines (including title and spaces)." They do not want "anything longer than 16 lines (except renga)." They have published poetry by Thom Williams, LeRoy Gorman, Helen Robinson and Brian Tasker. As a sample the editor selected this haiku by Martin Lucas:

> *a night of stars/the footpath/sparkles with frost*

The editor says *Presence* is 44 pgs., A5, photocopied, perfect-bound, with brushdrawn art on card cover and illustrations. They receive about 2,000 poems a year, accept approximately 10%. Press run is 150 for 100 subscribers of which 5 are libraries, 10 shelf sales. Subscription: £10 ($20 US) for 4 issues surface mail. £3 ($6 US) per single issue air mail. Sample: £3 ($6 US). Please pay in US bills (no checks).

How to Submit: Submit 4-12 poems at a time. "Please ensure that separate poems can be identified, and not mistaken for a sequence." No previously published poems or simultaneous submissions. E-mail submissions in body of message OK. Cover letter preferred. Time between acceptance and publication is 1-6 months. Seldom comments on rejections. Send SASE (or SAE and IRC) for guidelines. Responds within 1 month. Pays 1 copy. Copyright remains with authors. Staff reviews books or chapbooks of poetry or other magazines in 10-500 words, single format. Poets may also send books for review consideration.

Also Offers: Website includes samples of haiku, tanka, haibun, renga, articles, subscriptions and submission information.

Advice: "The more you read the better you'll write. Those who subscribe to read make better poets than those who are motivated solely by seeing their own name in print."

◎ **THE PRESS OF THE THIRD MIND (Specialized: form)**, 1301 North Dearborn #1007, Chicago IL 60610, phone (312)337-3122, founded 1985, poetry editor "Badly Steamed Lard (anagram of Bradley Lastname)."

Book/Chapbook Needs: Press of the Third Mind is a small press publisher of artist books, poetry and fiction. "We are especially interested in found poems, Dada, surrealism, written table-scraps left on the floors of lunatic asylums by incurable psychotics, etc." They have published poetry by Anthony Stark, Jorn Barger, Michael Kaspar, and Eric Forsburg. As a sample the editor selected this poem, "Bank Deposit" by Patrick Porter, from *The Intrusive Ache of Morning*:

> These sidewalk strangers all/Bloated and to the point of/Shaking/Behind a desk a clerk asks you for
> your/ID number and you are/Known by too many/Numbers you don't know which one she is/Talking
> about//All the while she smiles like a Gershwin/Tune but inside she is filled with sharp/Doddering

They have a press run of 1,000 with books often going into a second or third printing. Sample for $1.43 postage.

How to Submit: For book publication submit up to 20 sample poems. "No anthologized mss where every poem has already appeared somewhere else." Simultaneous submissions OK, if noted. "Cover letter is good, but we don't need to know everything you published since you were age nine in single-spaced detail." Send SASE for upcoming themes. "Authors are paid as the publication transcends the break-even benchmark." The press has released an 80-page anthology entitled *Empty Calories* and published a deconstructivist novel about the repetition compulsion called *The Squeaky Fromme Gets the Grease*.

$ ◻ PRIDE IMPRINTS, 7419 Ebbert Dr. SE, Port Orchard WA 98367, website www.pride-imprints.com, founded 1989, senior editor Ms. Cris Newport.

Book/Chapbook Needs: Pride Imprints publishes "thoughtful, quality work; must have some depth." They publish 12 paperbacks/year. They want "a minimum of 100 publishable, quality poems; book length. Previously published poets only: chapbooks, major magazines and journals or book-length work. No sexually explicit material. You must be familiar with our published poetry before you submit work." They have published poetry by Jack Rickard, Vacirca Vaughn and Rudy Kikel.

How to Submit: "Visit our website. Read at least two of our poetry volumes. In initial query, comment on how your work fits into what we do and indicate which volumes you have read. SASE must be included." If invited, send entire mss, 100 poems minimum. Previously published poems and simultaneous submissions OK. No e-mail queries. Cover letter preferred. "A bio with publishing history, a page about the collection's focus, theme, etc., will help in the selection process." Time between acceptance and publication is 2 years. Poems are circulated to an editorial board. "Senior editor reviews all work initially. If appropriate for our press, work given to board for review." Seldom comments on rejections. Replies to queries and to mss in 3 months. Pays 10-15% royalties.

Also Offers: Website includes writer's guidelines, complete catalog and individual book pages.

◻ ◎ **PRIMAVERA (Specialized: women)**, P.O. Box #37-7547, Chicago IL 60637, phone (773)324-5920, founded 1975, co-editor Ruth Young.

Magazine Needs: *Primavera* is "an irregularly published but approximately annual magazine of poetry and fiction reflecting the experiences of women. We look for strong, original voice and imagery, generally prefer free verse, fairly short length, related, even tangentially, to women's experience." They have published poetry by Pamela Gemin and Simone Muench. As a sample the editors selected these lines by Parween Shakir (translated from Urdu):

> Listen, downpours don't remember streets,/And sunshine can't read road signs.

The elegantly printed publication, flat-spined, generously illustrated with photos and graphics, uses 25-30 pgs. of poetry in each issue. They receive over 1,000 submissions of poetry a year, use approximately 25. Circulation is 1,000. Single copy: $10. Sample: $5.

How to Submit: Submit up to 6 poems anytime, no queries. No simultaneous submissions. Editors comment on rejections "when requested or inspired." Send SASE for guidelines. Responds in up to 3 months. Pays 2 copies. Acquires first-time rights.

◎ **PRINCETON UNIVERSITY PRESS; LOCKERT LIBRARY OF POETRY IN TRANSLATION (Specialized: translations, bilingual)**, 41 William St., Princeton NJ 08540, phone (609)258-4900, e-mail rebrown@pupress.princeton.edu.

Book Needs: "In the Lockert Library series, we publish simultaneous cloth and paperback (flat-spine) editions for each poet. Clothbound editions are on acid-free paper, and binding materials are chosen for strength and durability. Each book is given individual design treatment rather than stamped into a series mold. We have published a wide range of poets from other cultures, including well-known writers such as Hölderlin and Cavafy, and those who have not yet had their due in English translation, such as Göran Sonnevi. Manuscripts are judged with several criteria in mind: the ability of the translation to stand on its own as poetry in English; fidelity to the tone and spirit of the original, rather than literal accuracy; and the importance of the translated poet to the literature of his or her time and country." The editor says, "All our books in this series are heavily subsidized to break even. We have internal funds to cover deficits of publishing costs."

How to Submit: Simultaneous submissions OK if you tell them. Cover letter required. E-mail submissions OK. Send mss only during respective reading periods stated in guidelines. "Manuscripts returned only with SASE." Comments on finalists only. Send SASE for guidelines to submit. Responds in 3 months.

🍁 ✅ $⃝ ⊘ **PRISM INTERNATIONAL**, Creative Writing Program, University of British Columbia, Vancouver, British Columbia V6T 1Z1 Canada, phone (604)822-2514, fax (604)822-3616, e-mail prism@interchange.ubc.ca, website www.arts.ubc.ca/prism, founded 1959, editors Jennica Harper and Kiera Miller, executive editor Laisha Rosnau.

● *Prism International* is known in literary circles as one of the top journals in Canada.

Magazine Needs: "*Prism* is an international quarterly that publishes poetry, drama, short fiction, imaginative nonfiction and translation into English in all genres. We have no thematic or stylistic allegiances: Excellence is our main criterion for acceptance of mss. We want fresh, distinctive poetry that shows an awareness of traditions old and new. We read everything." They have published poetry by Di Brandt, Esta Spalding, Karen Connelly, Derk Wynand and a translation by Seamus Heaney. As a sample the editors selected these lines from "About the Spiders" by Jason Dewinetz:

> Touching your back now,/you are on the plastic lawn chair./I am spreading oil onto skin/glinting like
> trout warm/spreading this mirror into you

Prism is 80 pgs., 6×9, elegantly printed, flat-spined with original color artwork on a glossy card cover. Circulation is for 1,000 subscribers of which 200 are libraries. They receive 1,000 submissions a year, use approximately 80, have a 4- to 6-month backlog. Subscription: $18, $27/2 years. Sample: $5.

How to Submit: Submit up to 5 poems at a time, any print so long as it's typed. Include SASE (or SAE with IRCs). No previously published poems or simultaneous submissions. E-mail and fax submissions OK. Cover letter with brief introduction and previous publications required. "Translations must be accompanied by a copy of the original. Poets may submit by e-mail, or through our website. Include the poem in the main body of the message." Send Canadian SASE or SAE with IRCs for guidelines. Responds in up to 6 months. Pays $40/printed page plus subscription; plus an additional $10/printed page to selected authors for publication on the World Wide Web. Editors sometimes comment on rejections. Acquires first North American serial rights.

Also Offers: Website includes writer's guidelines, names of editors, samples from past issues and "virtually everything you'd want to know." Website also publishes a quarter of the poetry appearing in the print issue. "Excellence is our main criterion. We appreciate poetry which is distinctive and pays close attention to language."

Advice: "While we don't automatically discount any kind of poetry, we prefer to publish work that challenges the writer as much as it does the reader. We are particularly looking for poetry in translation."

⊘ **PROMETHEUS PRESS**, P.O. Box 1569, Glendale CA 91209-1569, founded 1989. They do not currently accept submissions.

⊘ **THE PROSE POEM: AN INTERNATIONAL JOURNAL**, English Dept. Providence College, Providence RI 02918, editor Peter Johnson, assistant editor Brian Johnson.

Magazine Needs: *The Prose Poem* is published annually. "Please don't send verse poems. Although we don't want to say that we can define 'prose poetry,' we do expect our contributors to at least know the difference between verse and prose poetry, so that they don't waste their time and postage."

How to Submit: Submit 3-5 poems at a time with SASE. No simultaneous submissions. Cover letter with 2-sentence bio required. Reads submissions December through March only. "Won't be accepting until December 2001." Time between acceptance and publication is 4-6 months. Subscription: $8/year, $12/2 years. Make checks payable to Providence College. Responds in 3 months. "If we publish an anthology we reserve the right to reprint your published poem in it; we also reserve the right to publish it on our web page."

🅽 ⊘ **PROSODIA**, New College of California, 766 Valencia St., San Francisco CA 94110, e-mail gmd@dnai.com, founded 1990, faculty advisor George Mattingly.

Magazine Needs: "*Prosodia* is the annual publication of the graduate Poetics Department at the New College of California. They want experimental, imaginative, adventurous and stimulating poetry. No religious or sentimental work." They have published poetry by Brenda Hillman, Anselm Hollo, Gloria Frym and David Meltzer. As a sample they selected these lines from "There are a thousand doors to let out life" by Adam Cornford:

> 1. Already in the womb in one, the placenta's aperture/like a telescope's tiny eyepiece, just opposite/
> the still locked, only door into this life

They say *Prosodia* is 160 pgs., magazine-sized, offset printed and perfect-bound with soft cover, includes art and ads. They receive about 300 poems a year, accept approximately 25%. Press run is 500 for 50 subscribers. Sample: $8. Make checks payable to Small Press Distribution.

MARKETS THAT WERE listed in the 2000 edition of *Poet's Market* but do not appear this year are listed in the General Index with a notation explaining why they were omitted.

How to Submit: No previously published poems; simultaneous submissions OK. E-mail and disk submissions OK. Cover letter required. Reads submissions October 1 through January 20 only. Time between acceptance and publication is 1 month. Poems are circulated to an editorial board. "Editorial staff changes with each issue." Publishes theme issues occasionally. Responds in 5 months. Pays 3 copies.

$ ◐ PROVINCETOWN ARTS; PROVINCETOWN ARTS PRESS, 650 Commercial St., Provincetown MA 02657-1725, phone (508)487-3167, fax (508)487-8634, founded 1985, editor Christopher Busa.

Magazine Needs: An elegant annual using quality poetry, "*Provincetown Arts* focuses broadly on the artists and writers who inhabit or visit the tip of Cape Cod and seeks to stimulate creative activity and enhance public awareness of the cultural life of the nation's oldest continuous art colony. Drawing upon a century-long tradition rich in visual art, literature and theater, *Provincetown Arts* publishes material with a view towards demonstrating that the artists' colony, functioning outside the urban centers, is a utopian dream with an ongoing vitality." They have published poetry by Bruce Smith, Franz Wright, Sandra McPherson and Cyrus Cassells. *PA* is about 170 pgs., 8¾×11⅞, perfect-bound with full-color glossy cover. Press run is 10,000 for 500 subscribers of which 20 are libraries, 6,000 shelf sales. Sample: $10.

How to Submit: Submit up to 3 typed poems at a time. All queries and submissions should be via regular mail. Reads submissions September 1 through February 1 only. Send SASE for guidelines. Responds in 3 months. Usually sends prepublication galleys. Pays $25-100/poem plus 2 copies. Buys first rights. Reviews books of poetry in 500-3,000 words, single or multi-book format. Open to unsolicited reviews. Poets may also send books for review consideration.

Book/Chapbook Needs & How to Submit: The Provincetown Arts Press has published 7 volumes of poetry. The Provincetown Poets Series includes *At the Gate* by Martha Rhodes, *Euphorbia* by Anne-Marie Levine, a finalist in the 1995 Paterson Poetry Prize, and *1990* by Michael Klein, co-winner of the 1993 Lambda Literary Award.

▢ ◐ ◎ THE PUCKERBRUSH PRESS; THE PUCKERBRUSH REVIEW (Specialized: regional), 76 Main St., Orono ME 04473-1430, phone (207)866-4868 or 581-3832, press founded 1971, *Review* founded 1978, poetry editor Constance Hunting.

Magazine Needs & How to Submit: *The Puckerbrush Review* is a literary, twice-a-year magazine. The editor looks for freshness and simplicity, but does not want to see "confessional, religious, sentimental, dull, feminist, incompetent, derivative" poetry. As a sample the editor selected these lines from "Cutting Wood with Mary" by Patric Sheron:

> When I think/of cutting wood/I see Ben 13-years old swinging/that slippery ax/in a cold/December/
> afternoon

For the review, submit 5 poems at a time. Pays 2 copies.

Book/Chapbook Needs & How to Submit: The Puckerbrush Press is a small press publisher of flat-spined paperbacks of literary quality. They have published *Young* by Miriam Colwell and *The Eternal Moment* by Angelica Garnett. For book publication, query with 10 samples. Prefers no simultaneous submissions. Offers criticism for a fee: $100 is usual. Pays 10% royalties plus 10 copies.

◐ ◎ PUDDING HOUSE PUBLICATIONS; PUDDING MAGAZINE: THE INTERNATIONAL JOURNAL OF APPLIED POETRY; PUDDING HOUSE CHAPBOOK COMPETITIONS; PUDDING HOUSE BED & BREAKFAST FOR WRITERS; PUDDING HOUSE WRITERS RESOURCE CENTER (Specialized: political, social issues, popular culture), 60 N. Main St., Johnstown OH 43031, phone (740)967-6060, e-mail pudding@johnstown.net, website www.puddinghouse.com, founded 1979, editor Jennifer Bosveld.

Magazine Needs: Pudding House Publications provides "a sociological looking glass through poems that provide 'felt experience.' Speaks for the difficulties and the solutions. Additionally a forum for poems and articles by people who take poetry arts into the schools and the human services." They publish *Pudding* every several months, also chapbooks, anthologies, broadsides. They "want experimental and contemporary poetry—what hasn't been said before. Speak the unspeakable. Don't want preachments or sentimentality. Don't want obvious traditional forms without fresh approach. Long poems OK as long as they aren't windy. Interested in receiving poetry on popular culture, rich brief narratives, i.e. 'virtual journalism.' (sample sheet $1 plus SASE)." They have published poetry by Knute Skinner, David Chorlton, Mary Winters, Robert Collins and Nita Penfold. *Pudding* is a literary journal with an interest in poetry arts in human service as well. They use about 50 pgs. of poetry in each issue—5½×8½, 70 pgs., offset composed on IBM Microsoft Works. Press run is 2,000 for 1,400 subscribers of which 40 are libraries. Subscription: $18.95/3 issues. Sample: $7.95.

How to Submit: Submit 3-10 poems at a time with SASE. "Submissions without SASEs will be discarded." No postcards. No simultaneous submissions. Previously published submissions respected but include credits. Likes cover letter. Sometimes publishes theme issues. Send SASE for general guidelines. Responds on same day (unless traveling). Pays 1 copy; to featured poet $10 and 4 copies. Returns rights "with *Pudding* permitted to reprint." Staff reviews books of poetry. Send books for review consideration. "See our website for vast calls for poems for magazine, chapbooks and anthologies; for poetry and word games, and essays and workshop announcements."

Book/Chapbook Needs & How to Submit: Chapbooks considered outside of competitions, no query. $10 reading fee. Send complete ms and cover letter with publication credits and bio. Editor sometimes comments, will critique on request for $4/page of poetry or $75 an hour in person.

Also Offers: Pudding House offers 2 annual chapbook competitions—each requires a $10 reading fee with entry. Deadlines: June 30 and September 30. The competitions award $100, publication and 20 free copies. Pudding House Bed & Breakfast for Writers offers "pretty, comfortable, and clean rooms with desk and all the free paper you can use" as well as free breakfast in large comfortable home ½ block from conveniences. Location of the Pudding House Writers Resource Center and Library on Applied Poetry. Bed & Breakfast is $75 single or double/night, discounts available. Reservations recommended far in advance. Send SASE for details. "Our website is one of the greatest poetry websites in the country—calls, workshops, publication list/history, online essays, games, guest pages, calendars, poem of the month, poet of the week, much more." The website also links to the site for The Unitarian Universalist Poets Cooperative, a national organization. Membership: $10/year.

Advice: "Editors have pet peeves. I won't respond to postcards or on them. I require SASEs. I don't like cover letters that state the obvious, poems with trite concepts, or meaning dictated by rhyme. Thoroughly review our website; it will give you a good idea about our publication history and editorial tastes."

⊕ ✔ ◐ PULSAR POETRY MAGAZINE; LIGDEN PUBLISHERS, 34 Lineacre, Grange Park, Swindon, Wiltshire SN5 6DA United Kingdom, phone (01793)875941, e-mail david.pike@virgin.net, website www.btinternet.com/~pulsarpoetry, founded 1992, editor David Pike, editorial assistant Jill Meredith.

Magazine Needs: *Pulsar*, published quarterly, "encourages the writing of poetry from all walks of life. Contains poems, reviews and editorial comments." They want "hard-hitting, thought-provoking work; interesting and stimulating poetry." They do not want "racist material. Not keen on religious poetry." They have published poetry by Merryn Williams, Joy Martin, Li Min Hua, Virgil Suarez and Wincey Willis. As a sample the editor selected these lines from "The Watcher" by Lewis Hosegood:

> Somewhere in this tall terraced house, somewhere,/somewhere lives a boy/who surely cannot see me,/
> nor speak my name aloud, yet senses/my interest in origins./He will never go away though I wait here
> and wait. . . .

Pulsar is 32 pgs., A5, professionally printed, saddle-stapled, glossy 2-color cover with photos and ads. Press run is 250 for 100 subscribers of which 40 are libraries; several distributed free to newspapers, etc. Subscription: $30 (£10 UK). Sample: $5. Make checks payable to Ligden Publishers.

How to Submit: Submit 3 poems at a time "preferably typed." No previously published poems or simultaneous submissions. Send no more than 2 poems via e-mail; file attachments will not be read. Cover letter preferred; include SAE with IRCs. "Poems can be published in next edition if it is what we are looking for. The editor and assistant read all poems." Time between acceptance and publication is about 1 month. Seldom comments on rejections. Send SASE (or SAE and IRC) for guidelines. Responds within 3 weeks. Pays 1 copy. Acquires first rights. Staff reviews poetry books and poetry audio tapes (mainstream); word count varies. Send books for review consideration.

Advice: "Give explanatory notes if poems are open to interpretation. Be patient and enjoy what you are doing. Check grammar, spelling, etc. (should be obvious). Note: we are a non-profit making society."

Ⓝ ⊕ ◯ ◐ PURPLE PATCH; THE FIRING SQUAD, 25 Griffiths Rd., West Bromwich B7I 2EH England, founded 1975, editor Geoff Stevens.

Magazine Needs: *Purple Patch* a quarterly poetry and short prose magazine with reviews, comment and illustrations. The editor says, "All good examples of poetry considered, but prefer 40 lines max. Do not want poor rhyming verse, non-contributory swear words or obscenities, hackneyed themes." They have published poetry by Alex Warner, Sam Smith, Peter Hawkins, Steve Sneyd and "Cato." As a sample the editor selected these lines by Terry Cultbert:

> i set fire/to the rainbow/& watched/the colours burn/in the wet sky

Purple Patch is 24 pgs., digest-sized, photocopied and side-stapled with cover on the same stock with b&w drawing. They receive about 2,500 poems a year, accept approximately 8%. Publish 40 poems/issue. Circulation "varies." Subscription: £12 UK/3 issues; US price is $20 (submit dollars). Make checks (sterling only) payable to G. Stevens.

How to Submit: Cover letter with short self-introduction preferred with submissions. Time between acceptance and publication is 4 months. Publishes theme issues occasionally. Send SASE (or SAE and IRCs) for upcoming themes. Response time is 1 month to Great Britain, can be longer to US. Overseas contributors have to buy a copy to see their work in print. Acquires first British serial rights. Staff reviews poetry chapbooks, short stories and tapes in 30-300 words. Send books for review consideration.

Also Offers: *The Firing Squad* is a broadsheet of short poetry of a protest or complaint nature, published at irregular intervals. "All inquiries, submissions of work, etc., must include SASE or SAE and IRCs or $1 U.S./ Canadian for return postage/reply."

◖ ◎ PYGMY FOREST PRESS (Specialized: animals, ethnic/nationality, nature/rural/ecology, political, social issues, women/feminism), P.O. Box 7097, Eureka CA 95502, phone (707)268-1274, founded 1987, editor/publisher Leonard Cirino.

● Pygmy Forest Press no longer publishes *Semi Dwarf Review.*

Book/Chapbook Needs: The press also publishes flat-spined paperbacks. "Forms of any kind/length to 96 pgs., subject matter open; especially ecology, prison, asylum, Third World, anarchist to far right. Prefer Stevens to Williams. I like Berryman, Roethke, William Bronk; dislike most 'Beats.' Open to anything I consider 'good.' Open to traditional rhyme, meter, but must be modern in subject matter. Also open to translations." He has published *Dog* by Michael McIrvin; *Sitting on the Edge of a Cow* by Charles L. Cyndian; *Where the Four Winds Blow* (including epitaphs) by Phillipe Soupault, translated by Pat Nolan; "God's Haircut'" by Kim Offen; "Medea's Demonic Grin" by Kent Kruse; and "Life, and a Letter" by Tim Lombardo.

How to Submit: Submit 10-15 poems with bio, acknowledgements, publications. Simultaneous submissions and previously published material OK. Responds to queries in 3 weeks, to submissions in 1 month. Usually pays 20% of run ("if author typesets on IBM compatible")—about 25-50 copies. Buys first rights. He comments on "almost every" ms.

Advice: "I am basically an anarchist. Belong to no 'school.' I fund myself. Receive no grants or private funding. Generally politically left, but no mainline Stalinist or Marxist. Plan to publish one to three books yearly."

$○ **QED PRESS; CYPRESS HOUSE**, 155 Cypress St., Fort Bragg CA 95437, phone (707)964-9520, fax (707)964-7531, e-mail qedpress@mcn.org, website www.cypresshouse.com, founded 1985, senior editor John Fremont.

Book/Chapbook Needs: "QED Press has no determining philosophy. We seek clear, clean, intelligent and moving work." They publish 1-2 paperbacks/year. They want "concrete, personal and spare writing. No florid rhymed verse." They have published poetry by Luke Breit, Paula Tennant (Adams) and Cynthia Frank. As a sample the editor selected this poem, "Ao Lume," by Eugenio de Andrade:

> Nem sempre o homem é um lugar triste./Há noites em que o sorriso/dos anjos/a torna habitável e leve:/com a cabeça no teu regaço/é um cão ao lume a correr às lebres.

Translated from Portuguese by Alexis Levitin:

> Man is not always a place of sorrow./There are nights in which the smile/of angels/makes him habitable and light:/with his head in your lap/he's a dog by the fire chasing after hares.

Books are usually around 100 pgs., 5½×8½, offset printed, perfect-bound, full-color CS1 10 pt. cover.

How to Submit: "We prefer to see all the poems (about 100 pages worth or 75-80 poems) to be bound in a book." Previously published poems and simultaneous submissions OK. Cover letter required. "Poets must have prior credits in recognized journals, and a minimum of 50% new material." Time between acceptance and publication is 3-6 months. Poems are circulated to an editorial board. "We publish only 1-2 poetry books each year—by consensus." Seldom comments on rejections. Replies to queries and mss in 3 months. Pays royalties of 7½-12% and 25 author's copies (out of a press run of 500-1,000). Order sample books by sending SASE for catalog.

Also Offers: Through the imprint Cypress House, they offer subsidy arrangements "by bid with author retaining all rights and inventory. We are not a vanity press." 50% of books are author-subsidy published each year.

⊕ ✓ $○○ **QUADRANT MAGAZINE**, P.O. Box 1495, Collingwood, Victoria 3066 Australia, phone (03)9417 6855, fax (03)9416 2980, e-mail quadrnt@ozemail.com.au, founded 1956, editor P.P. McGuinnes, literary editor Les Murray.

Magazine Needs: *Quadrant*, published 10 times/year, is a "magazine of literature and ideas; about 10% of pages devoted to poetry." They have published poetry by Bruce Dawe, Geoff Page and Kathleen Stewart. *Quadrant* is 88 pgs., 7⅞×10¾, professionally printed on newsprint, saddle-stapled, CS2 cover stock with some art and ads. They receive several thousand poems a year, accept approximately 5%. Press run is 8,000 for 3,000 subscribers of which 500 are libraries, 2,500 shelf sales; 130 distributed free. Subscription: $54 (in Australia). Sample: $5.50.

How to Submit: No previously published poems or simultaneous submissions. Cover letter preferred. Time between acceptance and publication is 6 months. "Assessment made by literary editor." Seldom comments on rejections. Send SASE (or SAE and IRCs) for guidelines. Pays $40/poem plus 1 copy. Buys first Australian serial rights. Reviews books of poetry. Open to unsolicited reviews.

⊕ ✓ $○ ○○ **QUANTUM LEAP; Q.Q. PRESS**, York House, 15 Argyle Terrace, Rothesay, Isle of Bute PA20 0BD Scotland, United Kingdom, founded 1997, editor Alan Carter.

Magazine Needs: *Quantum Leap* is a quarterly poetry magazine. They want "all kinds of poetry—free verse, rhyming, whatever—as long as it's well written and preferably well punctuated, too. We rarely use haiku." Also accepts poetry written by children. They have published poetry by Dr. Stella Browning, Roger Harvey, Fiona Curnow and Roger Mitchell. As a sample the editor selected these lines from "Babies in Bourbon" by Rachel Jones:

> We drink and we feel our way;/you knew how I felt/before you knew me./Talking to me gently,/when you think I'm asleep.//The skies give us time/and ways to wear it,/as babies in bourbon./We tease life when it should be/moving us.

QL is 40 pgs., digest-sized, desktop-published and saddle-stapled with card cover, includes clip art and ads for other magazines. They receive about 2,000 poems a year, accept approximately 10%. Press run is 200 for 180 subscribers. Single copy: $9; subscription: $32. Sample: $8. Make checks payable to Alan Carter. "All things being equal in terms of a poem's quality, I will sometimes favor that of a subscriber (or someone who has at least bought an issue) over a nonsubscriber, as it is they who keep us solvent."

How to Submit: Submit 6 poems at a time. Line length for poetry is 36 ("normally"). Previously published poems (indicate magazine and date of first publication) and simultaneous submissions OK. Cover letter required. "Within the UK, send a SASE, outside it, send IRCs to the value of what has been submitted." Time between acceptance and publication is usually 3 months "but can be longer now, due to magazine's increasing popularity." Sometimes comments on rejections. Send SASE (or SAE and IRC) for guidelines. Responds in 3 weeks. Pays £2 sterling. Acquires first or second British serial rights.

Book/Chapbook Needs: Under the imprint "Collections," Q.Q. Press offers subsidy arrangements "to provide a cheap alternative to the 'vanity presses'—poetry only." They charge £120 sterling for 50 32-page books (A4), US $250 plus postage. Please write for details. Order sample books by sending $12 (postage included). Make checks payable to Alan Carter.

Also Offers: Sponsors open poetry competitions and competitions for subscribers only. Send SAE and IRC for details.

Advice: "Submit well-thought-out, well-presented poetry, preferably well punctuated, too. If rhyming poetry, make it flow and don't strain to rhyme. I don't bite, and I appreciate a short cover letter, but not a long, long list of where you've been published before!"

✔ ◑ ◎ **QUARTER AFTER EIGHT; PROSE WRITING CONTEST (Specialized: form/style)**, Ellis Hall, Ohio University, Athens OH 45701, phone (740)593-2827, fax (740)593-2818, e-mail quarteraftereight @excite.com, website www.-as.phy.ohiou.edu/Departments/English/Litjournals.html, founded 1993, editors-in-chief Christina Veladota and Thom Conroy.

Magazine Needs: *Quarter After Eight* is "an annual journal of prose and commentary devoted to the exploration of prose in all its permutations. We are interested in reading fiction, sudden fiction, prose poetry, creative and critical non-fiction, interviews, reviews, letters, memoirs, translations and drama. We do not publish traditional (lineated) poetry, but we do welcome work that provocatively explores—even challenges—the prose/poetry distinction. Our primary criteria in evaluating submissions are freshness of approach and an address to the prose form." They have published poetry by Rosmarie Waldrop, Nathaniel Tarn and Diane Glancy. As a sample the editor selected these lines from "Whining Prairie" by Maureen Seaton:

> I don't want to die in this wild onion smelly belly mire of the midwest stinking marsh this drenchy
> swaly swamp but I might and who would note the fragrant corruption of my poor elan this moorish
> bog this poachy few who come from sea with salt and myrrh to burn my rotting flesh?

QAE is 310 pgs., 6×9, professionally printed and perfect-bound with glossy card cover, includes b&w photos and ads. They receive about 1,000 poems a year, accept approximately 3%. Press run is 1,000 for 200 subscribers of which 50 are libraries, 500 shelf sales. Sample: $10.

How to Submit: Submit 4-6 poems at a time. No previously published poems; simultaneous submissions OK. Disk submissions with hard copy OK. "Include publishing history. We encourage readers/submitters to obtain a copy of the magazine." Reads submissions September 15 through March 15 only. Poems are circulated to an editorial board. "Editorial board makes final decisions; a pool of readers handles first reads and commentary/ input on editorial decisions." Often comments on rejections. Send SASE for guidelines. Responds in up to 3 months. Pays 2 copies. Acquires first North American serial rights. Reviews books of poetry in 800-1,200 words, single or multi-book format. Send books for review consideration to Book Review Editor.

Also Offers: Sponsors an annual Prose Writing Contest with $500 cash award. Reading fee: $10. Winner is published in subsequent issue. Maximum length 10,000 words—can be a sequence of poems.

Advice: "*QAE* is a somewhat specialized niche. Check out the magazine and explore the boundaries of genre."

◑ ◎ **QUARTERLY REVIEW OF LITERATURE POETRY BOOK SERIES; QRL PRIZE AWARDS (Specialized: subscription, translation)**, 26 Haslet Ave., Princeton NJ 08540, website www.princeton.edu/ ~qrl, founded 1943, poetry editors T. Weiss and R. Weiss.

Book/Chapbook Needs & How to Submit: After more than 35 years as one of the most distinguished literary journals in the country, *QRL* has appeared for the last 20 years as the *QRL Poetry Book Series*, in which 4-6 poetry books and a poetic play of a book of a poet in translation are chosen in open competition. The selected poetry books are combined in one annual volume with each of the 4-6 poets receiving $1,000 and 100 copies. The resulting 300- to 400-page volumes are printed in editions of 3,000-5,000, selling in paperback for $12, in hardback for $20. Subscription—2 paperback volumes containing 10 books: $20. Send SASE for details.

✔ $ ◑ **QUARTERLY WEST**, 200 S. Central Campus Dr., Room 317, University of Utah, Salt Lake City UT 84112-9109, phone (801)581-3938, website www.quarterlywest.org, founded 1976, editor Margot Schilpp, poetry editor Heidi Czerwiec Blitch.

▼ Poetry published in *Quarterly West* has appeared in *The Best American Poetry 1997 and 2000* and has won the Pushcart Prize several times.

Magazine Needs: *Quarterly West* is a semiannual literary magazine that seeks "original and accomplished literary verse—free or formal. No greeting card or sentimental poetry." Also publishes translations. They have published poetry by Robert Pinsky, Eavan Boland, Albert Goldbarth, William Matthews, Agha Shahid Ali and

Heather McHugh. *QW* is 220 pgs., 6×9, offset printed with 4-color cover art. They receive 1,500 submissions a year, accept less than 1%. Press run is 1,900 for 500 subscribers of which 300-400 are libraries. Subscription: $12/year, $21/2 years. Sample: $7.50.

How to Submit: Submit 3-5 poems at a time; if translations, include original. No previously published poems; simultaneous submissions OK, with notification. Seldom comments on rejections. Send SASE for guidelines. Responds in up to 6 months. Pays $15-100 plus 2 copies. Buys all rights. Returns rights with acknowledgement and right to reprint. Reviews books of poetry in 1,000-3,000 words. Open to unsolicited reviews. Poets may also send books for review consideration.

Also Offers: Website includes guidelines, staff, examples of recently published poems, graphic of cover and a list of contributors.

QUEEN OF ALL HEARTS (Specialized: religious), 26 S. Saxon Ave., Bay Shore NY 11706, phone (516)665-0726, fax (516)665-4349, e-mail pretre@worldnet.att.net, founded 1950, poetry editor Joseph Tusiani.
Magazine Needs: *QOAH* is a magazine-sized bimonthly that uses poetry "dealing with Mary, the Mother of Jesus—inspirational poetry. Not too long." They have published poetry by Fernando Sembiante and Alberta Schumacher. The professionally printed magazine is 48 pgs., heavy stock, various colors of ink and paper, liberal use of graphics and photos, has approximately 2,5000 subscriptions at $20/year. Single copy: $2.50. Sample: $3. They receive 40-50 submissions a year, use approximately 2/issue.
How to Submit: Submit double-spaced mss. Responds within 1 month. Pays 6 copies (sometimes more) and complimentary subscription. Editor sometimes comments on rejections.
Advice: "Try and try again! Inspiration is not automatic!"

N **$** **QUEEN STREET QUARTERLY (Specialized: regional)**, 704 Spadina Ave., P.O. Box 311, Station P, Toronto, Ontario M5S 2S8 Canada, phone (416)657-1637, e-mail theqsq@hotmail.com, founded 1997, editor Suzanne Zeluzo.
Magazine Needs: *QSQ* aims "to cultivate cutting-edge Canadian art; however, in the interest of cross-fertilization, we welcome submissions from the U.S. and abroad." They publish poetry, fiction, essays, photography and other prints. They want "visual poetry, language poetry, sound-text scores, experimental and avant-garde writing, but also quality conventional poetry. No confessional or satirical poetry; rhyming couplets." They have published poetry by Charles Bernstein, Chris Dewdney, Karen MacCormack, bill bissett, Victor Coleman and Frank Davey. As a sample the editor selected these lines from "Hate Sonnet I" by Michael Holmes:

> The last time I thought about it, you were covered/with new moss. A mad topiary animal/truly blue-
> green flesh, rattling, absurd/fictions like you were unopened, a lost phial/of paxil! Your telephone voice
> shook like milk,/and our friendship is stifled, tranquilized by/the shattering.

QSQ is 64 pgs., 5½×8½, offset printed and perfect-bound with 4-color glossy cardstock cover, includes art and ads. They receive about 2,000 poems a year, accept approximately 5%. Publish 20 poems/issue. Press run is 800 for 200 subscribers, 550 shelf sales. Single copy: $7.25; subscription: $25. Sample: $8.
How to Submit: Submit 6 poems at a time. Line length for poetry is 3 pages maximum. No previously published poems or simultaneous submissions. E-mail and disk submissions OK. "Where possible, submissions should be accompanied by a PC-readable disk copy." Time between acceptance and publication is 1 month. Poems are circulated to an editorial board. "Submissions reviewed blindly by literary editors." Seldom comments on rejections. Send SASE for guidelines. Responds in 6 weeks. Pays $5/page. Buys first rights.
Also Offers: Sponsors annual poetry contest for Canadians only.

$ **ELLERY QUEEN'S MYSTERY MAGAZINE (Specialized: mystery)**, 475 Park Ave. S, 11th Floor, New York NY 10016, founded 1941, contact Janet Hutchings.
Magazine Needs: *EQMM*, appears 11 times/year, primarily using short stories of mystery, crime or suspense. "We also publish short limericks and verse pertaining to the mystery field." As a sample the editor selected these lines from "Coffee Olé" by Marie E. Truitt:

> But once he married, breakfasts were the nastiest of scenes;/On making coffee, Wifie didn't know a
> hill of beans./The bitter taste! . . . the inch-deep dregs! . . . he couldn't take much more!/It went from
> bad to mega-bad, till Fred let out a roar:/"I've had enough! It's Splitsville! There's just no other
> course!/And I hold within this cup, my Dear, the grounds for our divorce!"

EQMM is 144 pgs., 5¼×8⅝₆, professionally printed on newsprint, flat-spined with glossy paper cover. Subscription: $33.97. Sample: $2.95 (available on newsstands).
How to Submit: No previously published poems; simultaneous submissions OK. Include SASE with submissions. Responds in 3 months. Pays $5-50 plus 3 copies.

$ **QUEEN'S QUARTERLY: A CANADIAN REVIEW (Specialized: regional)**, Queen's University, Kingston, Ontario K7L 3N6 Canada, phone (613)533-2667, fax (613)533-6822, e-mail qquarter@post.queensu.ca, website www.info.queensu.ca/quarterly, founded 1893, editor Boris Castel.
Magazine Needs: *Queen's Quarterly* is "a general interest intellectual review featuring articles on science, politics, humanities, arts and letters, extensive book reviews, some poetry and fiction. We are especially interested in poetry by Canadian writers. Shorter poems preferred." They have published poetry by Evelyn Lau, Sue Nevill

and Raymond Souster. There are about 12 pgs. of poetry in each issue, 6×9, 224 pgs. Circulation is 3,500. They receive about 400 submissions of poetry a year, use approximately 40. Subscription: $20 Canadian, $25 US for US and foreign subscribers. Sample: $6.50 US.

How to Submit: Submit up to 6 poems at a time. No simultaneous submissions. E-mail submissions OK. Responds in 1 month. Pays usually $50 (Canadian)/poem, "but it varies," plus 2 copies.

N ☘ ○ THE RABBIT HOLE PRESS, 2 Huntingwood Crescent, Brampton, Ontario L6S 1S6 Canada, e-mail rabbithole@3web.net, founded 1999, publisher Alice A. Cobham.

Magazine Needs: "*Rabbit Hole* is a small, quarterly literary journal that publishes poetry, short fiction, short shorts, essays, original art and photography. We are eclectic, imaginative, edgy, insightful, sensual, provocative, rebellious in nature: 'how deep is the rabbit hole.' " Their specifications are open: "We want original, quality, well-crafted work which shows the poet has his/her own voice. Poetry should be accessible, provocative, poignant, vital, honest. Feel it, mean it, be it, craft it and then share it. If it's quality, professional work and it touches me, I'll publish it. No doggerel or 'Hallmark' verse. No ranting, whining or gushing. Nothing illegal or offensive. (You should know what is illegal. I'll decide what is offensive.) Erotica is okay but no porn." They have published poetry by Alex Morgan, Kevin Hoag and Nicole Ferretti. As a sample they selected these lines from "New Year's Day" by Alex Morgan:

> All the promises/I made at midnight/slip my grasp and float/downstream on the backs of mallards.//I
> wish that I could follow,/escape that hollow confection/like the honking geese/etching secret messages
> to the sun/on the icing-sugar sky.

The editor says *TRHP* is 35-50 pgs., 5½×8½, desktop-published and saddle-stapled with card cover, includes original art and photography. They expect to receive about 500 poems a year, accept approximately 20%. Publish 10 poems/issue. Press run is 300. Subscription: $20 (US). Sample: $5 (US). Make checks payable to A. Cobham. "All payment in U.S. dollars unless you are Canadian."

How to Submit: Submit 5 poems at a time. Line length for poetry is 100 maximum. No previously published poems; simultaneous submissions OK. E-mail submissions OK. Cover letter preferred. "SASE required for all submissions and correspondence. IRC requested if outside Canada. International contributors and subscribers welcomed." Time between acceptance and publication is 1-4 months. Seldom comments on rejections. Send SASE (or SAE and IRC) for guidelines. Responds in 1 month. Sometimes sends prepublication galleys. Pays 1 copy. Acquires one-time rights.

Advice: "Read, read and write, write. Join a group of kindred spirits for constructive criticism and encouragement. Believe in yourself and never give up. Subscribe to small presses and buy books of poetry; support your craft."

✓ $○ ◎ RADIANCE: THE MAGAZINE FOR LARGE WOMEN (Specialized: women), P.O. Box 30246, Oakland CA 94604, phone (510)482-0680, e-mail info@radiancemagazine.com, website www.radiancemagazine.com, founded 1984, publisher/editor Alice Ansfield.

Magazine Needs: *Radiance* appears quarterly. "Since 1984, *Radiance* has offered support, information, and inspiration for women *all* sizes of large. *Radiance* has grown to become one of the leading resources in the worldwide size acceptance movement. Each issue features dynamic large women from all walks of life, along with articles and essays on health, media, fashion, and politics. Our focus is on celebrating body acceptance. We now have a 'young activists' column—devoted to helping plus-size children feel seen, love, and vauled for who they are, whatever their size. Keeping in mind that our magazine is geared toward large women, we look for poetry from women of any size and men who don't accept society's stereotypical standards of beauty and weight—but who celebrate women's bodies, sexuality, search for self-esteem and personal growth." As a sample she quotes "Homage to My Hips" by Lucille Clifton:

> these hips are big hips/they need space to/move around in./they don't fit into little/petty places. these
> hips/are free hips./they don't like to be held back./these hips have never been enslaved,/they go where
> they want to go/they do what they want to do./these hips are mighty hips./these hips are magic hips./
> i have known them/to put a spell on a man and/spin him like a top!

Radiance is 60 pgs., magazine-sized, professionally printed on glossy stock with full-color paper cover, saddle-stapled, 4-color graphics, photos and ads. Circulation is 14,000 "and growing" for 5,000 subscriptions, 8,000 selling on newsstands or in bookstores; 2,000 distributed free to media and clothing stores for large women. Subscription: $25/year. Sample: $5.

How to Submit: Submit typed ms. Assistant Editor usually comments on rejections. Send SASE for guidelines. Responds in up to 6 months. Pays $10-15 plus contributor's copy. Buys one-time rights. Reviews related books of poetry in 500-800 words.

⬤ RAG MAG; BLACK HAT PRESS, P.O. Box 12, Goodhue MN 55027, phone (651)923-4590, founded 1982, poetry editor and publisher Beverly Voldseth.

Magazine Needs: *Rag Mag* accepts poetry of "any length or style. No pornographic SM violent crap." They have published poetry by Robert Bly, Ann Niedringhouse and Kerri Brostrom. As a sample the editor selected these lines from "What the Plants Say" by Tom Hennen:

> Weed, it is you with your bad reputation that I/love the most. Teach me not to care what anyone/has
> to say about me. Help me to be in the world/for no purpose at all except for the joy of sunlight/and

> *rain. Keep me close to the edge where every-/thing wild begins.*

Rag Mag, appearing twice a year (usually in April and October), is 80-112 pgs., perfect-bound, 6×9, professionally printed in dark type with ads for books, matte card cover. The editor says she accepts about 10% of poetry received. Press run is 250 for 80 subscribers of which 8 are libraries. Subscription: $10. Sample: $6.

How to Submit: "Send up to eight pages of your best work with brief bio. Something that tells a story, creates images, speaks to the heart. Please proofread carefully before submitting. Poetry will be published as is." *Name and address on each page. SASE required for return of work or response.* Previously published poems and simultaneous submissions OK, "but please acknowledge both." Send SASE for guidelines. Pays 1 copy. Acquires first or one-time rights. Reviews books of poetry. Open to unsolicited reviews but has room for only 1 or 2/issue. Poets may also send books for review consideration.

Book/Chapbook Needs & How to Submit: Black Hat Press is *not* considering chapbooks or book-length mss of any kind until further notice. They have published *Boom Town* by Diane Glancy and *Crawling Out the Window* (a book of prose poems) by Tom Hennen. Black Hat Press also publishes a yearly poetry calendar open to submissions from poets residing in MN. Send SASE for details to Poetry Calendar, P.O. Box 130121, Roseville, MN 55113.

THE RAINTOWN REVIEW (Specialized: form/style), P.O. Box 370, Pittsboro IN 46167, e-mail hmpeditor@hotmail.com, website sites.netscape.net/hmpoet/, founded 1996, editor Harvey Stanbrough.

Magazine Needs: *The Raintown Review* is published quarterly, in March, June, September and October, contains only poetry. They want well-crafted poems—metered, syllabic, or free-verse. They have published poetry by Andrea B. Geffner, Mary Gribble, Robert Michael O'Hearn and Ted Simmons. As a sample the editor selected these lines from "Suicide Note" by William Baer:

> *The night that she committed suicide/her brother in New Jersey played the horses,/drinking with his buddies all night long;/her friend at Yale thumbed through a recent novel/looking in vain for meaning and for love;/her mother was asleep in New Rochelle;/her father, dead, was knocking on his box,/ hoping to distract his little girl.*

TRR is about 60 pgs., chapbook-sized, desktop-published and saddle-stapled with card cover. They receive about 900 poems a year, accept approximately 10-15%. Press run is about 200 with most going to subscribers and contributors. Subscription: $24/year. Sample: $7.

How to Submit: Submit up to 6 poems at a time. Previously published poems and simultaneous submissions OK. Cover letter preferred. "We prefer contributors write for guidelines before submitting work." Often comments on rejections. Send SASE for detailed guidelines. Responds in 1 month. Pays at least 1 copy. Acquires first or one-time rights.

Also Offers: Website includes detailed guidelines, reviews of Harvey Stanbrough's poetry collections, samples of his poetry and rates for his freelance editorial services. "There is no charge, of course, for any critique or editing done in conjunction with submissions to *The Raintown Review.*"

Advice: "To help regain the poetry audience, study your craft and write accessible, aesthetic poetry."

RALPH'S REVIEW; RC'S STAMP HOT LINE (Specialized: animals, horror, nature/rural/ecology, psychic/occult, science fiction/fantasy), 129A Wellington Ave., Albany NY 12203, e-mail rcpub@albany.net, website www.dibit.com/ictoys, founded 1988, editor R. Cornell.

Magazine Needs: *Ralph's Review*, published quarterly, contains "mostly new writers, short stories and poems." They want "horror/fantasy, environmental. No more than 30 lines." They do not want "rape, racial, political poems." They have published "Moods of Madness" by R. Cornell and poetry by Kim Laico, Dan Buck and John Grey. The editor says *Ralph's Review* is 20-35 pgs., 8½×11, photocopied, sometimes with soft cover, with art, cartoons and graphics. They receive about 80-100 poems a year, accept approximately 40%. Press run is 75-100 for 35 subscribers of which 3 are libraries; 30-40 distributed free to bookstores, toy stores, antique and coffee shops. Single copy: $2; subscription: $15. Make checks payable to R. Cornell.

How to Submit: Submit up to 5 poems, with a $3 reading fee and SASE. Previously published poems and simultaneous submissions OK. Cover letter required. Time between acceptance and publication is 2-4 months. Seldom comments on rejections. Publish theme issues. Send SASE or e-mail for guidelines and upcoming themes. Responds in 3 weeks. Pays 1 copy. Acquires all rights. Returns rights 1 year after acceptance. Reviews books in up to 5,000 words in single-book format. Open to unsolicited reviews. Poets may also send books for review consideration.

Advice: "Books are selling like crazy; keep writing, check out current trends, submit to as many publications as you can afford."

RARACH PRESS (Specialized: bilingual/foreign language), 1005 Oakland Dr., Kalamazoo MI 49008, phone (616)388-5631, founded 1981, owner Ladislav Hanka. Not open to unsolicited mss.

VISIT THE WRITER'S DIGEST WEBSITE at www.writersdigest.com for books on craft, hot new markets, daily market updates, writers' guidelines and much more.

$ � RATTAPALLAX; RATTAPALLAX PRESS, 532 La Guardia Place, Suite 353, New York NY 10012, phone (212)560-7459, e-mail rattapallax@hotmail.com, website www.rattapallax.com, founded 1998, editor-in-chief George Dickerson, senior editor Judith Werner.

Magazine Needs: "A biannual journal of contemporary literature, *Rattapallax* is Wallace Steven's word for the sound of thunder." They want "extraordinary work in poetry and short fiction—words that are well-crafted and sing, words that recapture the music of the language, words that bump into each other in extraordinary ways and leave the reader touched and haunted by the experience. We do not want ordinary words about ordinary things." They have published poetry by Lamont B. Steptoe, Kate Light, Karen Swenson and James Rayan. As a sample the editors selected these lines from "This kindled by *Guade Virgo Salutata*, a motet by John Dunstable, c. 1400" by Mark Nichols:

> *Slow-spreading English music, as though/we watched a pale drawing-off of the night/from delicate*
> *fields, and heard a haunt/of griffins in a fog close by the house./How one of the griffins, without fire,*
> *has wrought,/by a concentration of time, a face in gnarled elmwood. . . .*

The editors say *Rattapallax* is 128 pgs., magazine-sized, offset printed and perfect-bound, with 12 pt. C1S cover, includes photos, drawings, and CD with poets. They receive about 5,000 poems a year, accept approximately 2%. Press run is 2,000 for 100 subscribers of which 50 are libraries, 1,200 shelf sales; 200 distributed free to contributors, reviews and promos. Single copy: $7.95; subscription: $14/1 year. Sample (including guidelines): $7.95. Make checks payable to Rattapallax.

How to Submit: Submit 3-5 poems at a time. No previously published poems; simultaneous submissions OK. Cover letter preferred. E-mail submissions outside of the US and Canada OK. "SASE is required and e-mailed submissions should be sent as simple text." Reads submissions all year; issue deadlines are June 1 and December 1. Time between acceptance and publication is 2-6 months. Poems are circulated to an editorial board. "The editor-in-chief, senior editor and associate editor review all the submissions then decide on which to accept every week. Near publication time, all accepted work is narrowed and unused work is kept for the next issue." Often comments on rejections. Obtain guidelines via e-mail or website. Responds in 2 months. Always sends prepublication galleys. Acquires first rights.

Book/Chapbook Needs & How to Submit: Rattapallax Press publishes "contemporary poets and writers with unique powerful voices." They publish 5 paperbacks and 3 chapbooks/year. Books are usually 64 pgs., 6×9, offset printed and perfect-bound with 12 pt. C1S cover, include drawings and photos. Query first with a few sample poems and cover letter with brief bio and publication credits and SASE. Requires authors to first be published in *Rattapallax*. Replies to queries in 1 month; to mss in 2 months. Pays royalties of 10-25%. Order sample books by sending SASE and $7.

Also Offers: Website includes information about the journal, submission guidelines, bios, upcoming readings, names of editors, sample poems, chat room and links.

✓ ◻ ◐ RATTLE, 13440 Ventura Blvd. #200, Sherman Oaks CA 91423, phone (818)788-3232 or (818)788-2831, fax (818)788-2831, e-mail stellasuel@aol.com, website www.rattle.com, founded 1994, editor Alan Fox, poetry editor Stellasue Lee. Address submissions to Stellasue Lee.

Magazine Needs: *Rattle* is a biannual poetry publication which also includes interviews with poets, essays and reviews. They want "high quality poetry of any form, three pages maximum. Nothing unintelligible." Also accepts some poetry written by children. They have published poetry by Charles Bukowski, Philip Levine, Yusef Komunyakaa, Colette Inez, Dorianne Laux, Virginia Hamilton Adair and Sam Hamill. As a sample the editor selected these lines from "Nouveau Richie" by Louis McKee:

> —*"The Rich are different. . . ."/Try as I might/to stay loyal to my class,/walking in poor man's shoes/*
> *from sad job to sad bed, today I am a rich man,/a moment from last night/like a wad of bills in my*
> *pocket,/an unexpected kiss that burns/every time a nip of wind/or cold rain touched my face./Sometimes*
> *all you need is a word, the right one at the right time./You can spend it anywhere,/legal tender, but*
> *more important/than anything you could buy/is the word—keep it, lucky bastard,/and walk with a rich*
> *man's smile.*

Rattle is 196 pgs., 6×9, neatly printed and perfect-bound with 4-color coated card cover. They receive about 7,000 submissions a year, accept approximately 250. Press run is 4,000. Subscription: $28/2 years. Sample: $8. Make checks payable to *Rattle*.

How to Submit: Submit up to 5 poems at a time with name, address on each page in upper right hand corner. Include SASE. No previously published work or simultaneous submissions. Cover letter and e-mail address, if possible, is required as well as a bio. E-mail (no attached files) and fax submissions OK. Reads submissions all year. Seldom comments on rejections unless asked by the author. Responds in up to 2 months. Pays 2 copies. Rights revert to authors upon publication. Welcomes essays up to 2,000 words on the writing process and book reviews on poetry up to 250 words. Send books for review consideration.

◐ ◉ RAW DOG PRESS; POST POEMS (Specialized: humor), 151 S. West St., Doylestown PA 18901-4134, phone (215)345-6838, website www.freeyellow.com/members/rawdog, founded 1977, poetry editor R. Gerry Fabian.

Magazine Needs: "Publishes Post Poems annual—a postcard series. We want short poetry (three to seven lines) on any subject. The positive poem or the poem of understated humor always has an inside track. No taboos, however. All styles considered. Anything with rhyme had better be immortal." They have published poetry by Don Ryan, Lyn Lifshin, John Grey, Wes Patterson and the editor, R. Gerry Fabian, who selected his poem, "Arc Welder," as a sample:

> *After years of burning/he pressed his lips against hers/and sealed out any doubt.*

How to Submit: Submit 3-5 poems at a time. Send SASE for catalog to buy samples. The editor "always" comments on rejections. Pays copies. Acquires all rights. Returns rights on mention of first publication. Sometimes reviews books of poetry.

Book/Chapbook Needs & How to Submit: Raw Dog Press welcomes new poets and detests second-rate poems from 'name' poets. We exist because we are dumb like a fox, but even a fox takes care of its own."

Also Offers: He says he will offer criticism for a fee; "if someone is desperate to publish and is willing to pay, we will use our vast knowledge to help steer the ms in the right direction. We will advise against it, but as P.T. Barnum said. . . ." Website includes basic Raw Dog Press information, general poets' Q and A and general writer's guidelines.

Advice: "I get more poems that do not fit my needs. At least one quarter of all poets waste their postage because they do not read the requirements."

N **☑** **◎** **RAW NERVZ HAIKU; PROOF PRESS (Specialized: form/style)**, 67 Court St., Aylmer, Quebec J9H 4M1 Canada, founded 1994, editor/publisher Dorothy Howard.

Magazine Needs: *Raw NerVZ Haiku*, published quarterly, features "haiku and related material." They want "haiku, senryu, tanka, renga, haiga and haibun." They have published poetry by Marlene Mountain, Janice M. Bostok and LeRoy Gorman. As a sample the editor selected this haiku by Marco Fraticelli:

> *knifethrower/thunderstorm*

The editor says *RNH* is 5½ × 8½, stapled with graphics and art. Press run is 250 for 150 subscribers of which 10 are libraries. Subscription: $20. Sample: $6.

How to Submit: Submit up to 10 poems at a time. Previously published poems OK; no simultaneous submissions. Cover letter preferred "without return envelopes. Cash preferred to IRCs from non-Canadian contributors for prepaid replies." Time between acceptance and publication is 1-6 months. Seldom comments on rejections. Send SASE (or SAE and IRCs) for guidelines. Responds in 2 months. Sometimes sends prepublication galleys. Acquires one-time rights. Reviews books or chapbooks of poetry or other magazines in up to 500 words. Open to unsolicited reviews. Poets may also send books for review consideration.

Book/Chapbook Needs & How to Submit: proof press publishes 6-10 chapbooks/year of haiku and renga. Chapbooks are usually under 50 pgs., 4 × 5½ to 5½ × 8½, photocopied, saddle-stapled, cover stock with b&w graphics. Query first with 10-20 sample poems and return postage. Replies to queries in 6 weeks; to mss (if invited) in 2 months. Pays 20 author's copies (out of a press run of 200).

Advice: "Reading copies of *Raw NerVZ* is useful. We are not interested in run-of-the-mill poetry."

☑ **○** **RB'S POETS' VIEWPOINT**, 2043 S. Coleman, Shepherd MI 48883, founded 1989, editor Robert Bennett.

Magazine Needs: *RB's* published bimonthly, features poetry and cartoons. They want "general and religious poetry, sonnets and sijo with a 21-line limit." They do not want "vulgar language." They have published poetry by Marion Ford Park, Ruth Ditmer Ream, Ruth Halbrooks and Delphine Ledoux. As a sample the editor selected these lines from "Star Fantasy" by Mary Strand:

> *On the hill where Will-O-Wisps camp/I danced to the chirpings of crickets/by the glow of the lightning-*
> *bug's lamp./When the stars in their celestial thickets/beckoned me with come-hither winks/I climbed a*
> *dangling moonbeam/& skipped on heavenly rinks.*

RB's is 34 pgs., digest-sized, photocopied, saddle-stapled with drawings and cartoons. They receive about 400 poems a year, accept approximately 90%. Press run is 60. Subscription: $8. Sample: $2. Make checks payable to Robert Bennett.

How to Submit: Submit 3 poems typed single space with a $1.50 per poem reading fee. Previously published poems and simultaneous submissions OK. Reads submissions February, April, June, August, October and December only. Time between acceptance and publication is 1 month. "Poems are selected by one editor." Often comments on rejections. Send SASE for guidelines. Responds in 1 month. Pays 1 copy. Acquires one-time rights.

Also Offers: Sponsors contests for general poetry, religious poetry, sonnets and sijo with 1st Prizes of $20, $6 and $5, respectively, plus publication in *RB's*. There is a $1.50 per poem entry fee, except the sijo category, which has a 50¢ per poem fee. Send SASE for guidelines.

☑ **○** **⌀** **RE:AL—THE JOURNAL OF LIBERAL ARTS**, Dept. PM, Box 13007, Stephen F. Austin State University, Nacogdoches TX 75962, phone (409)468-2059, fax (409)468-2190, e-mail f_real@titan.sfasu.edu, website www.libweb.sfasu.edu/realpublish/index.html, founded 1968, editor W. Dale Hearell.

Magazine Needs: *RE:AL* is a "Liberal Arts Forum" using short fiction, drama, reviews and interviews; contains editorial notes and personalized "Contributors' Notes"; printed in the fall and spring. They "hope to use from 90 to 110 pages of poetry per issue, typeset in editor's office. *RE:AL* welcomes all styles and forms that display craft, insight and accessibility." Also accepts poetry written by children. They receive between 60-100 poems/ week. "We need a better balance between open and generic forms. We're also interested in critical writings on poems or writing poetry and translations with a bilingual format (permissions from original author)." It is handsomely printed, "reserved format," perfect-bound with line drawings and photos. Circulation approximately 400, "more than half of which are major college libraries." Subscriptions also in Great Britain, Ireland, Italy, Holland, Puerto Rico, Brazil, Croatia, and Canada. Subscription: $40 for institutions, $30 individual. Sample: $15.

How to Submit: Submit original and copy. "Editors prefer a statement that ms is not being simultaneously submitted; however, this fact is taken for granted when we receive a ms." Writer's guidelines for SASE. They acknowledge receipt of submissions and strive for a 1-month decision. Submissions during summer semesters may take longer. Pays 2 copies. Reviews are assigned, but queries about doing reviews are welcome.

Also Offers: Website includes the entire journal.

REALITY STREET EDITIONS, 4 Howard Court, Peckham Rye, London SE15 3PH United Kingdom, phone (0171)639-7297, e-mail reality.street@virgin.net, editor Ken Edwards. They currently do not accept unsolicited mss.

RED CEDAR REVIEW, 17C Morrill Hall, Dept. of English, Michigan State University, East Lansing MI 48824, e-mail rcreview@msu.edu, website www.msu.edu/~rcreview, founded 1963, general editor Douglas Dowland.

Magazine Needs: *Red Cedar* is a literary biannual which uses poetry—"any subject, form, length; the only requirement is originality and vision." The editor encourages work from both students and professionals. They have published poetry by Margaret Atwood, Diane Wakoski, Jim Harrison and Stuart Dybek. The review is 120 pgs., digest-sized. They receive about 500 submissions a year, use approximately 20. Press run is 400 for 200 subscribers of which 100 are libraries. Single copy: $6; subscription: $10. Sample: $4.

How to Submit: Submit up to 5 poems at a time with SASE. No previously published poems. Simultaneous submissions are discouraged. Responds in up to 4 months. Pays 2 copies. Sometimes comments on rejections. Publishes theme issues. Send SASE for guidelines. Send SASE for submission guidelines.

Also Offers: Website includes guidelines, subscription information, order forms for sample copies, and biographical information about our staff.

RED CROW; REDBUD HILL PRESS (Specialized: form/style, regional), 265 Glencoe Ave., Decatur IL 62522, e-mail RedCrowPoetry@aol.com, founded 1998, managing editor Scott Goebel.

Magazine Needs: *Red Crow* is a biannual poetry journal publishing a Beat issue in autumn and an Appalachian issue in spring. For the Beat issue, they say, "Make it Beat-down but fresh." For the Appalachian issue, they want work by or about Appalachians and their descendants; all styles and forms. "No rhyming odes to late Beat icons." They have published poetry by Larry Fontenot, Richard Hague, Joe Enzweiler and Nelson Pilsner. The editor says *Red Crow* is 5½ × 8½, laser printed and perfect-bound with color card cover. They receive about 500 poems a year, accept approximately 25%. Publish over 40 poems/issue. Press run is 300 for 35 subscribers of which 8 are libraries, 100 shelf sales; 30 distributed free to reviewers and schools. Single copy: $7; subscription: $14. Sample: $5. Make checks payable to Red Crow.

How to Submit: Submit 5 poems at a time. No previously published poems; simultaneous submissions OK. E-mail submissions OK. Cover letter required. "Cover letter should be separate from manuscript. Cover letter contains name, address, e-mail, brief bio and a list of titles." Reads submissions for Beat issue May 15 through August 15; for Appalachian issue December 1 through February 1 only. Time between acceptance and publication is 3-4 months. Poems are circulated to an editorial board "then final decisions made by the managing editor." Seldom comments on rejections. Send SASE for guidelines. Responds in 10 weeks. Sometimes sends prepublication galleys. Pays 2 copies. Acquires first North American serial rights.

Book/Chapbook Needs & How to Submit: "Redbud Hill Press publishes the best modern Appalachian and Beat poetry written today. We believe poetry serves as a record of the times in which we live." They publish chapbooks by invitation only. Pays 25 author's copies (out of a press run of 100).

Also Offers: Also sponsors a contest. Send SASE for details.

Advice: "Edit, cut, edit, cut. . . ."

RED DANCEFLOOR PRESS; RED DANCEFLOOR, P.O. Box 4974, Lancaster CA 93539-4974, fax (805)946-8082, e-mail dubpoet@as.net, website www.web.as.net/~dubpoet, founded 1989, editor David Goldschlag.

Magazine Needs & How to Submit: The press publishes the magazine, *Red Dancefloor*. However, the magazine has suspended publication until further notice.

Book Needs: Red Dancefloor Press also publishes full-length books and poetry audiotapes. No restrictions on form, length or subject matter. They have published poetry by Sean T. Dougherty, Gerry Lafemina, Laurel Ann Bogen, Marc. C. Jacksina, Gary P. Walton and Michael Stephans. As a sample the editor selected these lines from "Ladybugs" in *Estrogen Power* by Nancy Ryan Keeling:

> Allergic to "pink,"/she camouflages/her exquisite figure/in layers of baggy clothes./She is content to
> live the/sexual life of a porcupine/testing and cataloging/feelings and emotions/because she knows/
> nobody is ever pure twice.

He says, the author may want to get a copy of a book, chapbook or tape before submitting. Send 5½ × 8½ SASE with first-class stamp for catalog. Sample: $10.

How to Submit: "We openly accept submissions for books and tapes, but *please* query first with ten samples and a cover letter explaining which area of our press you are interested in. Listing credits in a cover letter is fine, but don't go crazy." E-mail and fax submission OK. "E-mail submissions may be embedded in the message itself or attached as ASCII, MS Word or Wordperfect files." Queries and submissions via e-mail "strongly encouraged." Payment negotiable.

RED DEER PRESS, Box 5005, 56 Ave. & 32 St., Red Deer, Alberta T4N 5H5 Canada, phone (403)342-3321, fax (403)357-3639, e-mail kgough@rdc.ab.ca, founded 1975, poetry editor Nicole Marcotic.
Book/Chapbook Needs & How to Submit: Red Deer Press publishes 1 poetry paperback per year under the imprint Writing West. They have published poetry by Susan Holbrook, Monty Reid, Stephen Scobie and Nicole Marcotic. Books are usually 80-100 pgs. Submit 8-10 poems at a time. Simultaneous submissions OK. Cover letter required. "Must include SASE. Canadian poets only." Time between acceptance and publication is 4-6 months. Replies to queries in 4-6 months. Pays royalties.

RED DRAGON PRESS, P.O. Box 19425, Alexandria VA 22320-0425, website www.reddragonpress.com, founded 1993, editor/publisher Laura Qa.
Book/Chapbook Needs: Red Dragon Press publishes 3-4 chapbooks/year. They want "innovative, progressive and experimental poetry and prose using literary symbolism, and aspiring to the creation of meaningful new ideas, forms and methods. We are proponents of works that represent the nature of man as androgynous, as in the fusing of male and female symbolism, and we support works that deal with psychological and parapsychological topics." They have published poetry by Suzette Bishop, George Karos and Dee Snyder. As a sample the editor selected these lines from "Visitarte" by James Kerns:

> Tonight the world is awake in the moon's embrace./I have turned everywhere but cannot outrun/the
> black shadow spreading from my feet./I like the brief side late light offers,/but I am unsure of what
> lies outside the beams/in the shade of things that have already been.

Chapbooks are usually 64 pgs., 8½×5⅜, offset printed, perfect-bound on trade paper with 1-10 illustrations.
How to Submit: Submit up to 5 poems at a time with SASE. Previously published poems and simultaneous submissions OK. Cover letter preferred with brief bio. Reading fee: $5 for poetry and short fiction, $10 for novels; check or money order payable to Red Dragon Press. Time between acceptance and publication is 8 months. Poems are circulated to an editorial board. "Poems are selected for consideration by the publisher, then circulated to senior editor and/or poets previously published for comment. Poems are returned to the publisher for further action; i.e., rejection or acceptance for publication in an anthology or book by a single author. Frequently submission of additional works is required before final offer is made, especially in the process for a book by a single author." Often comments on rejections. Charges criticism fee of $10 per page on request. Responds to queries in 10 weeks, to mss in 1 year. For sample books, purchase at book stores, or mail order direct from Red Dragon Press at the above address.
Also Offers: Website includes statement of purpose, guidelines for submissions, book list, order information, sample poems, book descriptions and author biographical information.

RED HEN PRESS; RED HEN POETRY CONTEST, P.O. Box 902587, Palmdale CA 93590-2587, fax (818)831-0649, e-mail editors@redhen.org, website www.redhen.org, founded 1993, publisher Mark E. Cull, editor Kate Gale.
Book/Chapbook Needs: Red Hen Press wants "good literary fiction and poetry" and publishes 10 paperbacks, one selected through a competition. "Translations are fine. No rhyming poetry." They have published poetry by Dr. Benjamin Saltman, Dr. Angela Ball, Ricardo Means Ybarra and Marlene Pearson. Books are usually 64-96 pgs., 5×7 or 6×9, professionally printed and perfect-bound with trade paper cover, includes paintings and photos.
How to Submit: Submit 5 poems at a time. Previously published poems and simultaneous submissions OK. Cover letter preferred. E-mail submissions OK. Time between acceptance and publication is 1 year. Poems are circulated to an editorial board. "One main poetry editor plus three to four contributing editors review the work." Seldom comments on rejections. Replies to queries in 1 month. Pays 10% royalties and 50 author's copies. To obtain sample books "write to our address for a catalog."
Also Offers: Sponsors the Benjamin Saltman Poetry Contest for a full-length collection (46-68 pgs.). Deadline is October 31.
Advice: "Be willing to help promote your own book and be helpful to the press. Writers need to help small presses survive."

RED HERRING, MidNAG, East View, Stakeford, Choppington, Northumberland NE62 5TR England, fax 01670 520457, contact Nicholas Baumfield.
Magazine Needs: *Red Herring* appears 2-3 times a year and "welcomes new original poetry of all kinds." Also accepts poetry written by children. They have published poetry by W.N. Herbert, Sean O'Brien and Matthew Sweeney. As a sample they selected these lines from "Sometimes" by Tom Kelly:

He's making his point,/stabbing his fingers/at the air, his kids, I presume,/stand near the mother,/as he
seethes/intoning his hate, his troubles/to those he loves/sometimes.

RH is 1 A3 sheet folded. They receive about 350 poems a year, accept approximately 15%. Press run is 3,000.
"Most available free in Northumberland libraries." Single copy: £1. Make checks payable to MidNAG.

How to Submit: No previously published poems; simultaneous submissions OK. "Copies preferred, as submissions cannot be returned." Time between acceptance and publication is 4 months. Poems are circulated to an editorial board. Seldom comments on rejections. Responds in 4 months. Pays 5 copies.

✔ $ ▢ ◔ ◉ **RED MOON PRESS; THE RED MOON ANTHOLOGY; AMERICAN HAIBUN & HAIGA (Specialized: form/style)**, P.O. Box 2461, Winchester VA 22604-1661, phone (540)722-2156, fax (708)810-8992, e-mail redmoon@shentel.net, founded 1994, *American Haibun & Haiga* founded 1999, editor/publisher Jim Kacian.

Magazine Needs: *American Haibun & Haiga*, published annually in January, is the first western journal dedicated to these forms. *AH&H* is 128 pages, digest-sized, offset printed on quality paper with heavy stock four-color cover. They receive several hundred submissions per year, and accept about 10%. Also accepts poetry written by children. Expected print run is 1,000 for subscribers and commercial distribution. Subscription: $15 plus $3 shipping and handling. A brief sample of the form will be available for SASE.

How to Submit: Submit up to 3 haibun or haiga at a time with SASE. No previously published work or simultaneous submissions. Fax submissions OK. E-mail submissions OK (include in body of message). Submissions will be read by at least two editors. Time between acceptance and publication varies according to time of submission. Pays $1/page. Acquires first North American serial rights. "Only haibun and haiga will be considered. If the submitter is unfamiliar with the form, consult *Journey to the Interior*, edited by Bruce Ross, for samples and some discussion."

Book/Chapbook Needs: Red Moon Press "is the largest and most prestigious publisher of English-language haiku and related work in the world." They publish *The Red Moon Anthology*, an annual volume, the finest English-language haiku and related work published anywhere in the world in the previous 12 months. The anthology is 160 pgs., digest-sized, offset printed, perfect-bound, glossy 4-color heavy-stock cover. Inclusion is by nomination of the editorial board only. The press also publishes 6-8 volumes per year, usually 3-5 individual collections of English-language haiku, as well as 1-3 books of essays or criticism of haiku. They have published the following haiku from *Some of the Silence* by John Stevenson:

my son asks/casually/what a tree costs

Under other imprints the press also publishes chapbooks of various sizes and formats.

How to Submit: Query with book theme and information, and 30-40 poems, or draft of first chapter. Replies to queries in 2 weeks, to mss (if invited) in 2-3 months. "Each contract separately negotiated."

Advice: "Haiku is a burgeoning and truly international form. It is nothing like what your fourth-grade teacher taught you years ago, and so it is best if you familiarize yourself with what is happening in the form (and its close relatives) today before submitting. We strive to give all the work we publish plenty of space in which to resonate, and to provide a forum where the best of today's practitioners can be published with dignity and prestige. All our books have either won awards or are awaiting notification."

✔ ◯ ◑ **RED OWL MAGAZINE**, 35 Hampshire Rd., Portsmouth NH 03801-4815, phone (603)431-2691, e-mail RedOwlMag@aol.com, founded 1995, editor Edward O. Knowlton.

Magazine Needs: *Red Owl* is a biannual magazine of poetry and b&w art published in the spring and fall. "Ideally, poetry here might stress a harmony between nature and industry; add a pinch of humor for spice. Nothing introspective or downtrodden. Sometimes long poems are OK, yet poems which are 10 to 20 lines seem to fit best." They are also open to poems on the subjects of animals, gay/lesbian issues, horror, psychic/occult, science fiction/fantasy and women/feminism. They have published poetry by John Binns, John Grey, Albert Huffstickler, Nancy McGovern and Dawn Zapletal. As a sample the editor selected these lines from "Night Eye" by Nancy McGovern:

colors shifting to mute tones/as though the skull of earth/held a candle within whose/wax draws sun-
fire to/illuminate the center/and glow in the moon.

Red Owl is about 70 pgs., 8½×11, neatly photocopied in a variety of type styles and spiral-bound with a heavy stock cover and b&w art inside. "Out of a few hundred poems received, roughly one third are considered." Single copy: $10; subscription: $20. Sample (including brief guidelines): $10 includes shipping and handling. Make checks payable to Edward O. Knowlton.

How to Submit: Submit 4 poems at a time. No previously published poems or simultaneous submissions. E-mail submissions OK "Relay cover letter and each poem separately." Cover letter preferred. "I mostly use the 'Net to answer questions; this isn't the best home for 'noetics' or 'noetry.' I'd prefer to receive the submissions I get via the U.S.P.S. since I feel it's more formal—and I'm not in that big of a hurry, nor do I feel that this world has reached a conclusion. . . ." Seldom comments on rejections. Responds in up to 3 months. Pays 1 copy.

Advice: "Try and be bright; hold your head up. Yes, there are hard times in the land of plenty, yet we might try to overshadow them. . . ."

RED RAMPAN' PRESS; RED RAMPAN' REVIEW; RED RAMPAN' BROADSIDE SERIES, Bishop House, 518 East Court St., Dyersburg TN 38024-4714, founded 1981, poetry editor Larry D. Griffin. Presently not accepting poetry.

RED RIVER REVIEW, e-mail Editor@RedRiverReview.com, website www.RedRiverReview .com, founded 1999, editor Bob McCranie.

Magazine Needs: "Published quarterly, *Red River Review* is a fully electronic literary journal. Our purpose is to publish quality poetry using the latest technology. *Red River* is a journal for poets who have studied the craft of writing and for readers who enjoy being stirred by language." They want "poetry which speaks to the human experience in a unique and accessible way. No rhyming poetry or poetry that is annoyingly obscure." They have published poetry by Marin Sorescu, Padi Harman, Ed Madden and Jeanne P. Donovan. As a sample the editor selected this poem, "This Day" by Meghan Ehrlich:

> This is a day to wear./Grackles whistle and click in the leaves,/damp plaid flannel shirts salute, flap
> from balconies,/fragrant green horse-apples molder underfoot./I lay out my laundry, too, like an
> offering,/like a sponge. I will keep this sun in my closet/and wear it often.

They receive about 400 poems a year, accept approximately 25%.

How to Submit: Submit 4-6 poems at a time. No previously published poems or simultaneous submissions. Cover letter preferred. Electronic submissions only. Time between acceptance and publication is 3 months. Often comments on rejections. Obtain guidelines via website. Responds in 3 months. Sometimes sends prepublication galleys. Acquires first rights and anthology rights, "if we want to do a *Red River Review Anthology*." For address and query information e-mail Editor@RedRiverReview.com.

Advice: "Write about who you are and who we are in the world. Read other writers as much as possible."

RED ROCK REVIEW; RED ROCK POETRY AWARD, English Dept. J2A, Community College of Southern Nevada, 3200 E. Cheyenne Ave., North Las Vegas NV 89030, phone (702)651-4094, e-mail rich_logs don@ccsn.nevada.edu, website www.ccsn.nevada.edu/academics/departments/English/redrock.htm, founded 1994, editor-in-chief Dr. Rich Logsdon, associate editor Todd Moffett.

Magazine Needs: *RRR* appears biannually and publishes "the best poetry available." They also publish fiction, creative nonfiction and book reviews. They have published poetry by Stephen Liu, Alberto Rios, Naomi Shahib Nye and Katharine Coles. As a sample the editors selected these lines (poet unidentified):

> Oil paint, I've read/never completely dries./The breasts of Venus droop./Mona Lisa finally drops the
> smile./Glass, I've heard, is a liquid./Windows silently slide at night,/a slow motion sink, always/toward
> the floor, Christ ascending

They say *RRR* is about 130 pgs., magazine-sized, professionally printed and perfect-bound with 10 pt. cornwall, C1S cover. Accept approximately 15% of poems received a year. Press run is 1,000. Sample: $5.50.

How to Submit: Submit 2-3 poems at a time, "mailed flat, not folded, into a letter sized envelope." Line length for poetry is 80 maximum. No previously published poems; simultaneous submissions OK. Cover letter with SASE required. E-mail (in body of message) and disk submissions OK. Do not submit mss June 1 through August 31. Time between acceptance and publication is 3 months. Poems are circulated to an editorial board. "Poems go to poetry editor, who then distributes them to three readers." Seldom comments on rejections. Send SASE for guidelines. Responds in 2 months. Pays 2 copies. Acquires first North American serial rights. Reviews books and chapbooks of poetry in 500-1,000 words, multi-book format. Open to unsolicited reviews. Poets may also send books for review consideration.

Also Offers: Sponsors the annual Red Rock Poetry Award. Winner receives $500 plus publication in the *Red Rock Review*. Submit up to 3 poems of not more than 20 lines each, typed on 8½ × 11 white paper. Reading fee: $6/entry (3 poems). Deadline: October 31. Send SASE for complete rules. Website includes regular submission and contest guidelines, information on editors and archives.

REFLECT (Specialized: form/style), 1317-D Eagles Trace Path, Chesapeake VA 23320, founded 1979, poetry editor W.S. Kennedy, assistant editor Clara Holton.

Magazine Needs: They use "spiral poetry: featuring an inner-directed concern with sound (euphony), mystical references or overtones, and objectivity—rather than personal and emotional poems. No love poems, pornography, far left propaganda; nothing overly sentimental." They have published poetry by Marikay Brown, H.F. Noyes, Joe Malone, Ruth Wildes Schuler and Stan Proper. As a sample the editor selected these lines from "April Sashays in Lime Heels" by Edward C. Lynskey:

TO RECEIVE REGULAR TIPS AND UPDATES about writing and Writer's Digest publications via e-mail, send an e-mail with SUBSCRIBE NEWSLETTER in the body of the message to newsletter-request@writersdigest.com, or sign up online at www.writersdigest.com.

*April sashays across ashy mews,/in lime heels and lilac breath,/swells sappy stalks, and shoos/winter
north, the killing guest.//Hyacinths blush and daffodils/blink as a wisp of apple smoke/curlicues through
screens until/kale yards wakes in a rainy soak.*

The quarterly is 48 pgs., digest-sized, saddle-stapled, typescript. Subscription: $8. Sample: $2.
How to Submit: Submit 4 or 5 poems at a time. All submissions should be single-spaced and should fit on
one typed page. No previously published poems or simultaneous submissions. Sometimes comments on rejections.
Send SASE for guidelines. Responds within a month. Pays 1 copy to nonsubscribers, 2 copies to subscribing
contributors. Acquires first rights. Occasionally reviews books of poetry in 50 words or more.

■ ◖ ◑ **RENAISSANCE ONLINE MAGAZINE**, 168 Orient Ave., Pawtucket RI 02861, e-mail submit@
renaissancemag.com, website www.renaissancemag.com, founded 1996, editor Kevin Ridolfi, e-mail submissions
only.
Magazine Needs: "Updated monthly, *Renaissance Online* strives to bring diversity and thought-provoking
writing to an audience that usually settles for so much less. Poetry should reveal a strong emotion and be able
to elicit a response from the reader. No nursery rhymes or profane works." Also accepts poetry written by
teenagers "but still must meet the same standard as adults." They have published poetry by Seth Abramson,
Ward Kelley, David Hunter Sutherland and Doug Tanoury. As a sample the editor selected these lines from
"Dasein" by David Hunter Sutherland:

*What can't be held send/into sleep, into turn by gentle turn/if ring worn age, covetable grace/beauty,
sadness and you spread/over this air-woven awning of clouds/to defy life's strange author*

They receive about 40 poems a year, accept approximately 50%.
How to Submit: Submit 3 poems at a time. Previously published poems and simultaneous submissions OK.
Cover letter preferred. E-mail submissions OK. "We prefer e-mail submissions, include in body of message.
Renaissance Online Magazine is only published online and likes to see potential writers read previous works
before submitting." Time between acceptance and publication is 3 months. Poems are circulated to an editorial
board. "Poems are read by the editor, when difficult acceptance decisions need to be reached, the editorial staff
is asked for comments." Often comments on rejections. Publishes theme issues occasionally. Send SASE for
guidelines or obtain via website. Responds in 2 months. Acquires all online publishing rights. Reviews books of
poetry. Open to unsolicited reviews, "but inquire first."
Also Offers: Website includes the entire magazine, including content, archives, guidelines and contact information.

⊕ $ ◎ **RENDITIONS: A CHINESE-ENGLISH TRANSLATION MAGAZINE (Specialized:
translations),** Research Center for Translation, CUHK, Shatin, NT, Hong Kong, phone 852-2609-7399, fax
852-2603-5110, e-mail renditions@cuhk.edu.hk, website www.cuhk.edu.hk/renditions, editor Dr. Eva Hung.
Magazine Needs: *Renditions* appears twice a year. "Contents exclusively translations from Chinese, ancient
and modern." They also publish a paperback series of Chinese literature in English translation. They have
published translations of the poetry of Gu Cheng, Shu Ting, Mang Ke and Bei Dao. *Renditions* is about 150 pgs.,
magazine-sized, elegantly printed, perfect-bound, all poetry with side-by-side Chinese and English texts, using
some b&w and color drawings and photos, with glossy 4-color card cover. Annual subscription: $25/1 year; $42/
2 years: $58/3 years. Single copy: $17.
How to Submit: E-mail and fax submissions OK. "Chinese originals should be sent by regular mail because
of formatting problems. Include 2 copies each of the English translation and the Chinese text to facilitate referenc-
ing." Publishes theme issues. Responds in 2 months. Pays "honorarium" plus 2 copies. Use British spelling.
They "will consider" book mss, for which they would like a query with sample translations. Submissions should
be accompanied by Chinese originals. Books pay 10% royalties plus 10 copies. Mss usually not returned. Editor
sometimes comments on rejections.
Also Offers: Website includes information on *Renditions* magazine; Research Centre for Translation; ordering
information for paperback books and forthcoming issues of *Renditions*, links to related sites, authors' and translators' indexes, names and contact information of editors and sample translations. "Please address all enquiries to
the editor."

Ⓝ ◑ ◎ **RESPONSE (Specialized: ethnic, religious),** Columbia University Post Office, P.O. Box
250892, New York NY 10025, e-mail response@panix.com, founded 1967, editor Chanita Baumhaft.
Magazine Needs: *Response* is a "Jewish journal of articles and art, poetry and fiction." They look for critical,
unconventional material. As a sample the editor has selected these lines from "On the Half Shell" by Tom
Spisak:

do you suppose/the Creator of all took note tonight/a clam crept into my chowder

The journal is 6×9, professionally printed on heavy stock, flat-spined, with a glossy "varnished" cover with
artwork. Circulation is 6,000 for 1,000 subscribers of which 10% are libraries; 2,500 distributed through bookstores and newsstands. Subscription: $30 ($10 for students); $59 for institutions.
How to Submit: E-mail submissions accepted. Time between acceptance and publication is 6 months. Responds
in about 2 months. Pays 3 copies. Acquires all rights. "Unsolicited materials welcome."

N ⊘ **RE:VERSE! A JOURNAL IN POETRY; RE:PRINT! PUBLISHING COMPANY**, P.O. Box 8518, Erie PA 16505, e-mail reverse@email.com, website www.geocities.com/reversepoetry, founded 1999, editor Eric Grignol.

Magazine Needs: *"Re:Verse!* is a yearly anthology of contemporary literary poetry from American artists. We are committed to putting moving written experiences in the hands of the reading public. As the world moves into a new century, we call for a time when the American people enjoyed poetry and felt a part of the experience. We are looking for literary poetry—taut writing, which is free from affectation. Open to all forms and styles of poems; steer clear of excessively long poems. Some themes we are interested in are healing and renewal, the extraordinary in the everyday, struggles with dichotomous situations, serious explorations of social issues—but do not limit yourself to this list! No pornographic, demeaning, or vulgar poems." As a sample the editor selected these lines from "For Molly, at Two" by Dennis Doherty:

> *Maybe Molly's weird because of the time/I cooked her brain, absently backed/the car into the sun*
> *while her mother/shopped and I smoked outside, adoring/her snoozy red face while light lasered/her*
> *carseat through the rear window.*

The editor says *Re:Verse!* is 90 pgs., 5½×8½, offset printed and perfect-bound with 2-color cardstock cover, includes line illustrations and some photos. They receive about 8,000 poems a year, accept approximately 10%. Publish 65-70 poems/issue. Press run varies according to demand. Single copy: $9.99. Sample: $6. Make checks payable to Re:Print! Publishing.

How to Submit: Submit 5 poems at a time. Previously published poems and simultaneous submissions OK, "but both must be noted as such on cover letter." Cover letter preferred. "Must include SASE or no reply will be made. Please state whether you would like your manuscript returned. If they are unable to be used, we prefer to recycle them and simply send a letter of reply back. Name and address atop each page, please." Reads submissions May 1 through July 31 and October 1 through January 31 only. Time between acceptance and publication is 10 months. Seldom comments on rejections. Publishes theme issues occasionally. Send SASE or visit website for guidelines and upcoming themes. Responds in 3 months. Always sends prepublication galleys. Pays 1 copy. Acquires one-time rights.

Also Offers: "We are working on a companion volume to *Re:Verse!* which is intended to act as a workshop, or textbook so to speak, for poets looking to strengthen their craft by analysis of contemporary poetic works, poetry history, writing exercises and editors' comments. Contact us for details on this." Website contains an overview of the contents, sample work from recent artists, guidelines, and a "writer's workshop" section as a poet's resource.

Advice: "Read constantly, explore your piece of the world, observe intently, write every day, revise your work unceasingly!"

☑ **$** ◎ **REVIEW: LATIN AMERICAN LITERATURE AND ARTS (Specialized: ethnic, regional, translations)**, 680 Park Ave., New York NY 10021, phone (212)249-8950 ext. 366, fax (212)249-5868, e-mail dshapiro@as-coa.org, website www.americas-society.org, founded 1968, managing editor Daniel Shapiro.

Magazine Needs: *Review* is a biannual magazine which serves as a "major forum for Latin American literature in English translation and articles on Latin American visual and performing arts." They want contemporary Latin American poetry and fiction. They have published poetry by Alberto Blanco, Octavio Paz and Blanca Varela. It is 100 pgs., 8½×11, with b&w photos of Latin American art. They receive 50-100 submissions, accept the work of 1-2 poets. Press run is 6,000 for 3,000 subscribers of which 500 are libraries. Subscription: $19.95 for individuals, $29.95 for institutions, $31 for international. Two-year subscription: $32 for individuals, $52 for institutions, $54 for international. Sample: $9.

How to Submit: Query before submitting work. Previously unpublished poetry and fiction only. Cover letter required. Responds in 3 months. Pays $100-300. Reviews books of poetry by Latin Americans. *Review* is published by the Americas Society, a not-for-profit organization.

◎ **REVISTA/REVIEW INTERAMERICANA (Specialized: ethnic, regional)**, Inter-American University of Puerto Rico, Box 5100, San Germán, Puerto Rico 00683, phone (787)264-1912 ext. 7229 or 7230, fax (787)892-6350, e-mail reinter@sg.inter.edu, editor Anibal José Aponte.

Magazine Needs: The *Revista/Review* is a bilingual scholarly journal oriented to Puerto Rican, Caribbean and Hispanic American and inter-American subjects, poetry, short stories and reviews. Press run is 400.

How to Submit: Submit at least 5 poems, but no more than 7, in Spanish or English, blank verse, free verse, experimental, traditional or avant-garde, typed exactly as you want them to appear in publication. Name should not appear on the poems, only the cover letter. No simultaneous submissions. Fax submissions OK. Cover letter with brief personal data required. Publishes theme issues. Send SASE for guidelines and upcoming themes. Pays 2 copies. Open to unsolicited reviews.

☑ ◎ **RFD: A COUNTRY JOURNAL FOR GAY MEN EVERYWHERE (Specialized: gay)**, P.O. Box 68, Liberty TN 37095, phone (615)536-5176, e-mail mail@rfdmag.org, website www.rfdmag.org, founded 1974, poetry editor Tom Seidner.

Magazine Needs: *RFD* "is a quarterly for gay men with emphasis on lifestyles outside of the gay mainstream— poetry, politics, profiles, letters." They want poetry that "illuminates the uniqueness of the gay experience. Themes that will be given special consideration are those that explore the rural gay experience, the gay perspective

on social and political change, and explorations of the surprises and mysteries of relationships." They have published poetry by Antler, James Broughton, Gregory Woods and Winthrop Smith. *RFD* has a circulation of 3,800 for 1,300 subscribers. Single copy: $6.50; subscription: $32 first class, $20 second class. Sample: $6.50.
How to Submit: Submit up to 5 poems at a time. Simultaneous submissions OK. Send SASE for guidelines or obtain via website. Editor sometimes comments on rejections. Responds in up to 9 months. Pays 1 copy. Open to unsolicited reviews.
Advice: "*RFD* looks for interesting thoughts, succinct use of language and imagery evocative of nature and gay men and love in natural settings."

RHINO, P.O. Box 554, Winnetka IL 60093, website www.artic.edu/~ageorge/RHINO, founded 1976, editors Deborah Rosen, Alice George, Kathleen Kirk and Helen Degen Cohen.
Magazine Needs: *Rhino* "is an annual poetry journal which also includes short-shorts and occasional essays. Translations welcome. The editors delight in work which reflects the author's passion, originality and artistic conviction. We also welcome experiments with poetic form, sophisticated wit, and a love affair with language. Prefer poems under 100 lines." They have published poetry by Maureen Seaton, James Armstrong, Susan Terris, Barry Silesky and Richard Jones. *Rhino* is a 96-page journal, digest-sized, card cover with art, on high-quality paper. They receive 1,500 submissions a year, use approximately 60-80. Press run is 1,000. Sample: $5.
How to Submit: Submit 3-5 poems with SASE. No previously published submissions; simultaneous submissions OK with notification. Submissions are accepted April 1 through October 1. Send SASE for guidelines. Responds in 3 months. Pays 2 copies. Acquires first rights only.
Also Offers: Website includes writer's guidelines, ordering info, table of contents and excerpts from current issue, literary challenges and a schedule of Chicago-area workshops, events and literary links.

THE RIALTO, P.O. Box 309, Alysham, Norwich, Norfolk NR11 6LN England, founded 1984, editor Michael Mackmin.
Magazine Needs: *The Rialto* appears 3 times a year and "seeks to publish the best new poems by established and beginning poets. *The Rialto* seeks excellence and originality." They have published poetry by Les Murray, Selima Hill, Penelope Shuttle, George Szirtes, Philip Gross and Ruth Padel. The editor says *The Rialto* is 56 pgs., A4 with full color cover, occasionally includes art/graphics. They receive about 12,000 poems a year, accept approximately 1%. Publish 50 poems/issue. Press run is 1,500 for 1,000 subscribers of which 50 are libraries. Subscription: £16. Sample: £6. Make checks payable to *The Rialto*. "Checks in sterling only please."
How to Submit: Submit 6 poems at a time. No previously published poems; simultaneous submissions OK. Cover letter preferred. "SASE or SAEs with IRCs essential. U.S. readers please note that U.S. postage stamps are invalid in U.K." Time between acceptance and publication is 3 months. Seldom comments on rejections. Responds in 3 months. "A large number of poems arrive every week, so please note that you will have to wait at least 10 weeks for yours to be read." Pays £20/poem. Poet retains rights.
Advice: "It is a good idea to read the magazine before submitting to check if you write our kind of poem."

RIO: A JOURNAL OF THE ARTS, 104 Hoyt Lane, Port Jefferson NY 11777, phone (631)474-8265, e-mail cdavidson@ms.cc.sunysb.edu, website www.engl.uic.edu/rio/rio.html, founded 1997, editors Cynthia Davidson and Gail Lukasik.
Magazine Needs: *Rio* is a biannual online journal containing "poetry, short fiction, creative nonfiction, scannable artwork/photography and book reviews. Query for anything else." They want poetry of any length or form. "Experiments encouraged with voice, image or language. No greeting card verse or sentimentality; no purely therapeutic rants against mom, dad, boss, or gender." They have published poetry by Michael Anania, Liviu Ioan Stoiciu, Eleni Fourtourni, Michael Waters, Terry Wright, Ralph Mills, Jr., David Shevin and Briar Wood. As a sample the editor selected these lines from "XI. The Sun Has Wings" by Roberta Gould:

> *Each worm in the cabbage/is joyous/Each saw-toothed form/smiles freely/Even the question mark*
> *shimmers/flexed to new functions*

Accept approximately 20% of poems received a year. Back issues are available on the website.
How to Submit: Submit 5-8 poems at a time. Previously published poems and simultaneous submissions OK "as long as you inform us of publication elsewhere." Cover letter preferred. E-mail and disk submissions OK. "For electronic submissions, use text (ASCII) or Macintosh attachments, or e-mail submissions in body of e-mail message." Time between acceptance and publication is 4-6 months. Seldom comments on rejections. Obtain guidelines via website. Responds in up to 6 months. Acquires all rights. Rights revert to authors immediately upon publication. Reviews books and chapbooks of poetry in 500-1,200 words, single book format. Open to unsolicited reviews. Send books for review consideration.
Advice: "We're looking for writers who do not fall into an easy category or niche."

RIO GRANDE REVIEW, 105 East Union, El Paso TX 79968-0622, contact poetry editor.
Magazine Needs: *Rio Grande Review*, a biannual student publication from the University of Texas at El Paso, contains poetry; flash, short, and nonfiction; short drama; photography and line art. *RGR* is 95 pgs., 6×9, professionally printed and perfect-bound with card cover with line art, line art inside. Subscription: $15/year, $30/2 years.

How to Submit: Include bio information with submission. "Submissions are recycled regardless of acceptance or rejection." SASE for reply only. Send SASE for guidelines. Pays copies. "Permission to reprint material remains the decision of the author. However, *RGR* does request it be given mention."

N ⊕ ◯ RISING, 80 Cazenove Rd., Stoke Newington, London N16 6AA England, phone 0956 992974, e-mail timmywells@hotmail.com, website www.saltpetre.com, founded 1995, editor Tim Wells.
Magazine Needs: *Rising* is a "quarterly-ish journal of poetry." They want "short, pithy work, preferably nonrhyming; epigrams; analogies. No animals, fluffy, lazy, rhyming, anything that has 'like a . . .' in it." They have published poetry by Salena Saliva, Francesca Beard, Cheryl B and Tim Turnbull. As a sample we selected this poem, "Where Babies Come From" by Jeff McDaniel:

> For my eighth birthday/I got a toy train set/my father helped assemble.//My job was to hand him/
> pieces of track and re-light/the cigarettes that went out//in his mouth. Halfway/through, I asked him/
> where babies come from.//He told me that eight years/ago today I showed up/on the front stoop//in a
> cardboard box, how/he spent the whole afternoon/putting me together,//just like this train set,/that I
> was probably lucky/the box arrived on a Saturday.

Rising is 28 pgs., A5, photocopied and saddle-stapled, colored card cover, includes b&w graphics. They receive about 250 poems a year, accept approximately 30%. Press run is 500 for 30 subscribers, 100 shelf sales. Sample: £1.
How to Submit: Submit 5 poems at a time. Line length for poetry is 60 maximum. Previously published poems and simultaneous submissions OK. E-mail submissions OK. Cover letter required. Time between acceptance and publication is 6 months. Poems are circulated to an editorial board. "If I like it, it's in. If I'm not sure, I consult others who work on *Rising*." Seldom comments on rejections. Publishes theme issues occasionally. Responds in 1 month. Pays 1 copy.
Advice: "Give 'em hell."

⊕ $◯ RIVELIN GRAPHEME PRESS, Merlin House, Church St., Hungerford, Berkshire RG17OJG England, founded 1984, poetry editor Snowdon Barnett, D.F.A.
Book/Chapbook Needs & How to Submit: Rivelin Grapheme Press publishes only poetry. Query first with biographical information, previous publications and a photo, if possible. If invited, send book-length manuscript, typed, double-spaced, photocopy OK. Payment is 20 copies of first printing up to 2,000, then 5% royalties on subsequent printings.

✓ ◯ RIVER CITY, English Dept., University of Memphis, Memphis TN 38152, phone (901)678-4591, fax (901)678-2226, e-mail rivercity@memphis.edu, website www.people.memphis.edu/~rivercity, founded 1980, editor Dr. Thomas Russell.
   Poetry published here has also been included in *The Best American Poetry 1996*.
Magazine Needs: *River City* publishes fiction, poetry, interviews and essays. Contributors have included John Updike, Marvin Bell, Philip Levine, Maxine Kumin, Robert Penn Warren, Wanda Coleman and Jane Hirshfield. The biannual is 160 pgs., 7×10, perfect-bound, professionally printed with 4-color glossy cover. Publishes 40-50 pgs. of poetry in each issue. Circulation is 2,000. Subscription: $12. Sample: $7.
Also Offers: Website includes submission guidelines, samples from previous issue and staff and contact info. Contact Mark Yakich.
How to Submit: Submit no more than 5 poems at a time. Include SASE. Does not read mss June through August. Publishes theme issues. Send SASE for guidelines and upcoming themes. Responds in up to 3 months. Pays 2 copies (and cash when grant funds available).

◯ ◯ RIVER KING POETRY SUPPLEMENT, P.O. Box 122, Freeburg IL 62243, phone (618)234-5082, fax (618)355-9298, e-mail riverkng@icss.net, founded 1995, editor Wayne Lanter.
Magazine Needs: *RKPS*, published 3 times/year (April, August, December), features "all poetry with commentary about poetry." They want "serious poetry." They do not want "light verse." They have published poetry by Alan Catlin, R.G. Bishop, Phil Dacey, John Knoopfle and Lyn Lifshin. The editor says *River King* is 8 pgs., 17×11 with newsprint. They receive about 2,000 poems a year, accept approximately 8%. Press run is 5,000 of which 600 are for libraries.
How to Submit: Submit 5 poems at a time. No previously published poems; simultaneous submissions OK. Fax and/or e-mail submissions OK. Cover letter preferred. Time between acceptance and publication is 2 months. Often comments on rejections. Responds in 1 month. Pays 10 copies.

$◯ RIVER OAK REVIEW, P.O. Box 3127, Oak Park IL 60303, phone (708)524-8725, founded 1993.
Magazine Needs: *River Oak Review* is a biannual literary magazine publishing high quality short fiction, creative nonfiction and poetry. Regarding work, they say, "quality is primary, but we probably wouldn't publish poems longer than 100 lines or so." They have published poetry by Billy Collins, Kathleen Norris, Steve Lautermilch and Maureen Seaton. *ROR* is 128 pgs., 6×9, neatly printed and perfect-bound with glossy 4-color card cover with art. They receive about 1,500-2,500 poems a year, publish approximately 1-2%. Press run is 1,300 for 750 subscribers, 200 shelf sales. Single copy: $6; subscription: $12/year, $20/2 years. Sample: $5. Make checks payable to River Oak Arts.

How to Submit: Submit 4-6 poems at a time. No previously published poems; simultaneous submissions OK if notified. Cover letter preferred. Poems are circulated to readers, then an editorial board, then the editor. Seldom comments on rejections. Send SASE for guidelines. Responds in 3 months. Always sends prepublication galleys. Pays $10-50 and 2 copies. Buys first North American serial rights.

Also Offers: They also sponsor a poetry contest in December with an award of $500 and publication in the spring issue of *River Oak Review*. Submit up to 4 poems at a time (maximum 500 lines total); typed, double spaced; with name, address, phone on cover letter only. Entries are not returned. Send postcard for notification of receipt and SASE for winners. Winners will be announced in spring. Send SASE for guidelines.

Advice: "Read literary magazines; read new poetry books; only submit if it's excellent."

$ ◙ RIVER STYX MAGAZINE; BIG RIVER ASSOCIATION, 634 N. Grand Ave., 12th Floor, St. Louis MO 63103, website www.riverstyx.org, founded 1975, editor Richard Newman, managing editor Carrie Robb.

◙ Poetry published in *River Styx* has been selected for inclusion in the 1996 and 1998 volumes of *The Best American Poetry* and *Pushcart Prize* anthologies.

Magazine Needs: *River Styx*, published 3 times/year, is "an international, multicultural journal publishing both award-winning and previously undiscovered writers. We feature poetry, short fiction, essays, interviews, fine art and photography." They want "excellent poetry—original, energetic, musical and accessible. Please don't send us chopped prose or opaque poetry that isn't about anything." They have published work by Jared Carter, R.S. Gwynn, David Kirby, Marilyn Hacker, Timothy Liu and Lucia Perillo. As a sample the editor selected these lines from "The Dismal Science" by Donald Finkel:

> He could pick up an epic this morning/from the take-away rack at the local supermarket./All over the
> city young men are scribbling, scribbling,/and old women, and schoolchildren, and several
> chimpanzees.//The young man persists in his kitchen, parboiling a dithyramb/while the sows go
> farrowing on in Iowa./Welcome to the eleventh plague: plenty.

River Styx is 100 pgs., 6×9, professionally printed on coated stock, perfect-bound with color cover and b&w art, photographs and ads. They receive about 8,000 poems/year, publish 60-75. Press run is 2,500 for 1,000 subscribers of which 80 are libraries. Sample: $7.

How to Submit: Submit 3-5 poems at a time, "legible copies with name and address on each page." Time between acceptance and publication is within 1 year. Reads submissions May 1 through November 30 only. Publishes theme issues. Guidelines available for SASE. Editor sometimes comments on rejections. Responds in up to 5 months. Pays 2 copies plus 1-year subscription plus $8/page if funds available. Buys one-time rights.

Also Offers: Sponsors annual poetry contest. Past judges include Marilyn Hacker, Philip Levine, Mark Doty and Molly Peacock. Deadline: May 31. Send SASE for guidelines. Website includes writer's guidelines, masthead, samples from current and recent issues, "ask the editor" section and calendar of upcoming themes and events.

◙ RIVERRUN, Glen Oaks Community College, 62249 Shimmel Rd., Centreville MI 49032-9719, founded 1974, contact poetry editor.

Magazine Needs: *Riverrun* is a literary biannual, using 30-40 magazine-sized pages of poetry in each issue. "We are a true miscellany. We publish a variety of styles, but we do give preference to more formal verse, that is less marketable in these times. Send rhyme, send structure; send sonnets, sestinas, villanelles, and ballads. Greeting card verse, of course, has other markets. However, feel free to send all poetry. There is structured verse we hate and free verse we love. We usually avoid anything over two manuscripts pages in length." They receive 200 poems/month, use up to 200/year. Press run is 675. Sample: $5.

How to Submit: Submit 3-7 poems at a time with SASE for response. No previously published poems; simultaneous submissions OK. Send SASE for guidelines. Responds in up to 6 months. Pays 1 copy.

Advice: "We proudly publish an extremely broad range of individuals well-known to small press circles and beyond, but we also pride ourselves on devoting occasional space to local poets and as-yet-unpublished poets."

☑ ◙ RIVERSTONE, A PRESS FOR POETRY; RIVERSTONE POETRY CHAPBOOK AWARD, 7571 E. Visao Dr., Scottsdale AZ 85262, founded 1992.

Book/Chapbook Needs: Riverstone publishes 1 perfect-bound chapbook a year through an annual contest. They have published chapbooks by Gia Hansbury, Jefferson Carter, Marcia Hurlow, Margo Stever, Cathleen Calbert, Gary Myers and Anita Barrows. As a sample the editor selected these lines by Martha Modena Vertreace:

> With vertical loops/the Ferris wheel weds Navy Pier to clouds/as if the resurrection were not enough/
> to tether poor humans to shifting Earth./So whose permission/do I need to know your holy body?

That's from "Creating Space with Light" in *Dragon Lady: Tsukimi*, which won the 1999 Riverstone Poetry Chapbook Award. It is 44 pgs., digest-sized, attractively printed on 80 lb. paper and perfect-bound with spruce green endleaves and a stippled beige card stock cover.

How to Submit: To be considered for the contest, submit $8 reading fee and chapbook ms of 24-36 pgs., "including poems in their proposed arrangement, title page, contents and acknowledgments. All styles welcome." Previously published poems OK, multiple entries and simultaneous submissions. Include 6×9 SASE or larger for notification and copy of last year's chapbook. No further guidelines. Contest deadline: June 30 postmark. Winner receives publication, 50 author's copies and a cash prize of $100. Sample: $5.

The Rockford Review
Special Y2K Edition

"Moving On"   *Britomar*

When it came to selecting a cover for the Special Y2K Edition of *The Rockford Review*, Editor David Ross found much to admire in "Moving On" by Britomar. "This cover illustration captures the human condition of being faced daily with moving on to the next challenge," he explains, "or remaining stagnant with the status quo." Ross sees the image as a metaphor for "bidding farewell to hindsight of the past century and embracing the uncertainty of the future millennium." Britomar Handlon-Lathrop, PhD (a clinical psychologist, poet, and former college professor) created the linoleum block print in 1940 at the age of 19. It's one of a series she made to illustrate her childhood journal. *The Rockford Review*, a publication of the Rockford Writers' Guild, is about 50 pages, digest-sized, neatly printed and saddle-stapled with card cover with black and white illustrations.

ROANOKE REVIEW, English Dept., Roanoke College, Salem VA 24153, founded 1968, poetry editor Robert R. Walter.

Magazine Needs: *Roanoke* is a semiannual literary review which uses poetry that is "conventional; we have not used much experimental or highly abstract poetry." They have published poetry by Peter Thomas, Norman Russell, Mary Balazs. *RR* is 52 pgs., 6×9, professionally printed with matte card cover with decorative typography. They use 25-30 pgs. of poetry in each issue. Press run is 250-300 for 150 subscribers of which 50 are libraries. They receive 400-500 submissions of poetry a year, use approximately 40-60, have a 3- to 6-month backlog. Subscription: $9. Sample: $3.

How to Submit: Submit original typed mss, no photocopies. Responds in 3 months. No pay.

Advice: "There is a lot of careless or sloppy writing going on. We suggest careful proofreading and study of punctuation rules."

ROCKET PRESS, P.O. Box 672, Water Mill NY 11976, e-mail RocketUSA@delphi.com, website www.BouncePass.com, founded 1993, editor Darren Johnson.

Magazine Needs: *Rocket Press* features "styles and forms definitely for the 21st century." The editor wants "experimental and eccentric poetry that's tight and streamlined. No rhyme. Don't use the words 'poem,' 'love' or 'ode.' " They have published poetry by Ben Ohmart, Albert Huffstickler and Cheryl Townsend. As a sample the editor selected these lines from "The Bovine Photograph" by Brandon Freels:

> At the art museum/we both stood in front of the/bovine photograph.//"It's sexy," Kris said./"I think it's just a sexy photo!"//"Look at those thighs!"/Someone in the background/mumbled.//"You know,"/ I said. "It is kind of sexy."

Rocket Press is a newspaper tabloid, 20 pgs., professionally printed, with a circulation over 2,000. They receive about 1,000 poems a year, accept approximately 1-2%. Press run is 2,000 for 200 subscribers of which 2 are libraries, 400 shelf sales. Sample: $1.50.

How to Submit: Submit 3 poems at a time. E-mail submissions OK. No previously published poems; simultaneous submissions OK. Time between acceptance and publication is 6-12 months. Often comments on rejections. "Subscribers get fuller critiques." Responds in less than 3 months. Pays 1 copy. Acquires one-time rights. Editor includes his own blurb reviews "of anything cool."

Advice: "In our sixth year of publication, we've just about seen it all—please change that. Let's break all the rules in the new millennium."

THE ROCKFORD REVIEW; ROCKFORD WRITERS' GUILD, P.O. Box 858, Rockford IL 61105, e-mail dragonldy@prodigy.net, website www.welcome.to/rwg, founded 1971, editor David Ross.

Magazine Needs: *TRR* is a publication of the Rockford Writers' Guild which appears 3 times/year, publishing their poetry and prose, that of other writers throughout the country and contributors from other countries. *TRR* seeks experimental or traditional poetry of up to 50 lines. "We look for the magical power of the words themselves, a playfulness with language in the creation of images and fresh insights on old themes, whether it be poetry, satire or fiction." They have published poetry by Cindy Guentherman, Terry Hermsen and Becca Hensley. *TRR* is about 50 pgs., digest-sized, professionally printed and saddle-stapled with card cover with b&w illustration. Circulation is 750. Single copy: $5; subscription: $18 (3 issues plus the Guild's monthly newsletter, *Write Away*). **How to Submit:** Submit up to 3 poems at a time with SASE. No previously published poems; simultaneous submissions OK. No electronic submissions. "Include a cover letter with your name, address, phone number, e-mail address (if available), a three-line bio, and an affirmation that the submission is unpublished in print or electronically." Responds in 2 months. Pays 1 copy and "you will receive an invitation to be a guest of honor at a Contributors' Reading & Reception in the spring." Acquires first North American serial rights. **Also Offers:** They offer Editor's Choice Prizes of $25 for prose, $25 for poetry each issue. They also sponsor a Spring Stanzas Contest and a Fall Short Story Contest with cash prizes and publication in *TRR*. Accepts work by children for both contests. The Rockford Writers' Guild is a nonprofit, tax-exempt corporation established "to encourage, develop and nurture writers and good writing of all kinds and to promote the art of writing in the Rockford area." They offer lectures by Midwest authors, editors and publishers, conduct several workshops and publish a monthly newsletter. Membership: $30/year. Write for further information or obtain via website.

N **$** ⬜ ◪ ◎ **ROCKY MOUNTAIN RIDER MAGAZINE (Specialized: animals, regional)**, P.O. Box 1011, Hamilton MT 59840-1011, phone (406)363-4085, fax (406)363-1056, website www.rockymountainrid er.com, founded 1993, editor Natalie Riehl.
Magazine Needs: *RMRM* is a regional, monthly, all-breed horse magazine. They want "cowboy poetry; western or horse-themed poetry. Please keep length to no more than 5 verses." The editor says *RMRM* is 64 pgs., 8½×11, web offset on newsprint and stapled. Publish 1 poem/issue.
How to Submit: Submit 1-10 poems at a time. Previously published poems and simultaneous submissions OK. Cover letter preferred. Seldom comments on rejections. Publishes theme issues occasionally. Send SASE for guidelines and upcoming themes. "We'll send a free copy if requested in a letter asking for writer's guidelines." Pays $10/poem. Acquires one-time rights. Reviews books of poetry in 200 words, single book format. Send books for review consideration.

N 🌐 ⬜ **ROMANTIC OUTSIDER**, 44 Spa Croft Rd., Ossett, West Yorkshire WF5 0HE United Kingdom, phone (01924)275814, founded 1997, editor Susan Darlington.
Magazine Needs: "*Romantic Outsider* appears 2-3 times a year and provides exposure to new writers (and musicians); celebrates the social outsider." They want "anything with passion. No overly sentimental or bigoted work." They have published poetry by Steve Andrews, Jon Summers and Colin Cross. As a sample the editor selected these lines from "Three Degrees of Separation" by Tanya Savage:
> The hours when she danced with him/at her hips, bore his bruises/as the marks of belonging, swam/
> in dissipating arcs on his icy breath.
The editor says *RO* is about 40 pgs., A5, photocopied and stapled with colored paper cover and occasional illustrations. They receive about 100 poems a year, accept approximately 30%. Press run is about 100. Sample: $4 US, (£1 in UK). Make checks (sterling only) payable to Susan Darlington.
How to Submit: Submit 5 poems maximum at a time. Previously published poems and simultaneous submissions OK. Disk submissions (Word format) OK. "Reply not guaranteed unless SAE/IRC included." Time between acceptance and publication is 1-5 months. Often comments on rejections. Responds in 1 month. Pays 1 copy. Reviews books and chapbooks of poetry in 250 words, single book format. Open to unsolicited reviews. Poets may also send books for review consideration.
Advice: "More submissions from women especially welcome."

N ⬜ ◪ **ROMANTICS QUARTERLY; A.C. SWINBURNE POETRY PRIZE; ROMANTICS POETRY GROUP**, P.O. Box 321, Fairview OR 97024-0321, fax (503)222-4383, founded 2000, poetry editor Kevin, editor Stephen, assistant editor Hyacinthe.
Magazine Needs: "Our goal is to resurrect the voice of the Victorian Romantic poet and renew popular interest in traditional, rhyming, musical verse. We have no restrictions; we want to see all varieties of quality poetry. However, we are partial to traditional rhyming verse in the style of the Victorian Romantics. We do not want to see limericks, greeting card verse, political poetry, splatter—gore, children's poetry or poems containing cliché, harsh language or graphic violence." As a sample the editor selected these lines from "Ophelia" by Kevin Roberts:
> Her fierce and frantic fingers wound/and wept for every word he said,/And tore glad grasses from the
> ground/And wove a garland for her head,/The blowing of her hair unbound,/Her guilded skirts that
> billowed 'round,/composed an eerie rustling sound/like choirs of wretched restless dead.
The editor says *RQ* is 40 pgs., 5½×8½, desktop-published and saddle-stapled, includes b&w line art, considers ads from gothic and poetry-related companies/publications. They receive about 400 poems a year, accept approximately 50%. Publish approximately 50 poems/issue. Press run is 500 of which 50 are libraries, 100 shelf sales; 50 distributed free to reviewers and colleagues of university. Subscription: $20. Sample: $5 (when available). Make checks payable to K. Roberts. (Cash and money orders preferred, $25 fee for returned checks.) "No requirements for contributors, but we encourage contributors to subscribe and keep in touch or become members of the Romantics Poetry Group."

How to Submit: Submit 1-10 poems at a time with reading fee. Previously published poems and simultaneous submissions OK. Cover letter preferred. "We prefer poems to be typed with name and address of poet on each page. Include SASE for reply. Enclose reading fee in cash, check or money order made out to K. Roberts." Reading fee: $2/poem, $3/essay or story. Time between acceptance and publication is up to 1 year. Poems are circulated to an editorial board. "The poetry editor reads all submissions and passes selected works on to 2-3 members of the editorial board (made up of graduate students). Editorial board makes the final decisions." Often comments on rejections. "If a poet wants professional criticism from graduate students/professors, please include letter stating the type of guidance you require. Include $10 per piece for thorough critique and suggestions." Send SASE for guidelines. Responds in 1 month. Sometimes sends prepublication galleys. Pays 2 copies per piece accepted. Acquires one-time rights. Reviews books and chapbooks of poetry and other magazines in 35 words, multi-book format. Open to unsolicited reviews. Poets may also send books for review consideration.

Also Offers: Sponsors the annual A.C. Swinburne Poetry Prize. Submit 1 poem and $10 entry fee. Winner will receive $100, publication of poem and 5 free copies of zine. Send SASE for contest rules. Website includes writer's guidelines, names of editors, poetry, interviews, etc.

Advice: "If you really want to impress us, study the works of Romantic poets like A.C. Swinburne, E.A. Poe, S.T. Coleridge, Lord Byron and Shelley, and take your lead from them both in terms of music and subject matter. Make us feel it was written in the 1800s."

$ RONSDALE PRESS (Specialized: regional), 3350 W. 21st Ave., Vancouver, British Columbia V6S 1G7 Canada, website www.ronsdalepress.com, founded 1988, director Ronald B. Hatch.

Book Needs: Publishes 3 flat-spined paperbacks of poetry/year—by Canadian poets only—classical to experimental. "Ronsdale looks for poetry manuscripts which show that the writer reads and is familiar with the work of some of the major contemporary poets. It is also essential that you have published some poems in literary magazines. We have never published a book of poetry when the author has not already published a goodly number in magazines." They have published *Taking the Breath Away* by Harold Rhenisch, *Two Shores/Deux rives* by Thuong Vuong-Riddick, and *Cleaving* by Florence Treadwell. As a sample the director selected these lines from "Flirt" in the *Green Man* by John Donlan:

> People are such flirts. Their animal spirits/rise and quit their dreary doppelgängers/as easily as you'd
> leave a chair./I've given up even trying to figure that out:/these tracks were laid for a lot of trains to
> run on—/maybe escape is in our nature./Attention, like a dog slipped from a leash,/leaps away from
> the body's drag of grief/out the window, heading for the trees./Or it roots around in a parent's box of
> keepsakes,/sorting a scrappy inheritance/as if that could close a valve on sorrow,/as if we were as
> brave as that plum tree/and could feel her leaves yellow and fall.

How to Submit: Query first, with sample poems and cover letter with brief bio and publication credits. Previously published poems and simultaneous submissions OK. Often comments on rejections. Replies to queries in 2 weeks, to mss in 2 months. Pays 10% royalties and 10 author's copies. Write for catalog to purchase sample books.

Also Offers: Website includes catalogs, list of upcoming events, and writer's guidelines.

Advice: "Ronsdale looks for poetry with echoes from previous poets. To our mind, the contemporary poet must be well-read."

$ ROOM OF ONE'S OWN (Specialized: women), P.O. Box 46160 Station D, Vancouver, British Columbia V6J 5G5 Canada, website www.islandnet.com/Room/enter, founded 1975.

Magazine Needs: *Room of One's Own* is a quarterly using "poetry by and about women, written from a feminist perspective. Nothing simplistic, clichéd. Short fiction also accepted." It is 96 pgs., 9×6. Press run is 1,000 for 420 subscribers of which 50-100 are libraries; 350 shelf sales. Subscription: $22 ($32 US or foreign). Sample: $8 plus IRCs.

How to Submit: "We prefer to receive 5-6 poems at a time, so we can select a pair or group." Include bio note. No simultaneous submissions. The mss are circulated to a collective, which "takes time." Publishes theme issues. Send SAE with 1 IRC for guidelines and upcoming themes. Responds in 6 months. Pays honorarium plus 2 copies. Buys first North American serial rights. "We solicit reviews." Send books for review consideration, attn. book review editor.

ROSE ALLEY PRESS, 4203 Brooklyn Ave. NE #103A, Seattle WA 98105, phone (206)633-2725, e-mail rosealleypress@juno.com, founded 1995, publisher/editor David D. Horowitz. "We presently do not read unsolicited manuscripts."

N ROSE TINTED WINDOWS; CARAVAN OF LOVE, 3 Belleville Rd., London SW11 6QS England, United Kingdom, phone (0171)223 1014, founded 1998, contact Miss Arabella Millett.

Magazine Needs: "*Rose Tinted Windows* is a very irregular, but almost annual publication. Mainly a music fanzine, but I do include some poetry and some political articles. No specifications but original poetry is always good. No clichéd poetry." They have published poetry by Steve Sneyd, Jon Summers, Colin Cross and Jim Dewitt. As a sample the editor selected this poem "Irrational Minds" by Chris Clayton:

> *They send human beings to war./You can copulate at sixteen./Yet the word "cunt",/Is considered*
> *obscene and dirty./How strange and irrational humans are./They make little sense.*

RTW is 28 pgs., A5, photocopied and saddle-stapled with paper cover. They receive about 70 poems a year, accept approximately 43%. Press run is 70. Sample: £1.

How to Submit: Submit 3-6 poems at a time. Previously published poems and simultaneous submissions OK. Cover letter preferred. Include SASE or SAE and IRC. Seldom comments on rejections. Response time "depends—I try to reply ASAP." Poet retains rights. Staff reviews books and chapbooks of poetry and other magazines in 40 words. Send books for review consideration.

Also Offers: "*Caravan of Love* is a pen-friend/advertising zine, but we occasionally include a few poems."

☑ $ ⊘ ◎ **ROSEBUD (Specialized: themes)**, P.O. Box 459, Cambridge WI 53523, phone (907)822-5146 or (800)786-5669, website www.rsbd.net, founded 1993, editor Rod Clark, poetry editor John E. Smelcer.

Magazine Needs: *Rosebud* is an attractive quarterly "for people who enjoy good writing." The editor says it is "a reader's feast for the eye, ear and heart" which has rotating themes/departments. They want contemporary poetry with "strong images, real emotion, authentic voice; well crafted, literary quality. No inspirational verse." *Rosebud* is 136 pgs., 7×10, offset printed and perfect-bound with full-color coated card cover, art, graphics and ads. They receive about 700 poems a year, accept approximately 10%. Press run is 10,000 for 2,000 subscribers, 8,000 shelf sales. Subscription: $22. Sample: $6.95.

How to Submit: Submit 3-5 poems at a time. Previously published poems and simultaneous submissions OK. Often comments on rejections. Send SASE for guidelines and explanation of themes/departments. Responds in 3 months. Pays $45/piece and 3 copies. Buys one-time rights.

Also Offers: Each year they award 3 prizes of $150 for work published in the magazine.

Advice: "We are seeking stories, articles, profiles and poems of love, alienation, travel, humor, nostalgia and unexpected revelation. And something has to 'happen' in the pieces we choose."

Ⓝ ⊘ **THE ROUND TABLE: A JOURNAL OF POETRY AND FICTION**, P.O. Box 18673, Rochester NY 14618, phone (716)244-0623, founded 1984, poetry editors Alan Lupack and Barbara Lupack.

Magazine Needs: "We occasionally publish a journal of poetry and fiction. However, we are publishing primarily chapbooks which substitute for our regular issues of *TRT*. Virtually all of our publications focus on the Arthurian legends. Few restrictions on poetry—except high quality. We like forms if finely crafted. Very long poems must be exceptional." They have published poetry by Kathleene West, John Tagliabue, Wendy Mnookin and Paul Scott. *The Round Table*, now published irregularly, is 64 pgs., digest-sized, perfect-bound, professionally printed (offset) with matte card cover. Circulation is 100 for 50 subscribers of which 3 are libraries. Subscription: $7.50. Sample: $5.

How to Submit: "We like to see about five poems at a time (but we read whatever is submitted). It is best to query about chapbook submissions." Cover letter required. Simultaneous submissions OK. "But we expect to be notified if a poem submitted to us is accepted elsewhere. Quality of poetry, not format, is most important thing. We try to respond in three months, but—especially for poems under serious consideration—it may take longer." Pays copies.

Also Offers: "Usually we will publish a volume of Arthurian poetry or fiction by one author."

Ⓝ ⊡ $ ◯ ⊘ ◎ **ROWAN BOOKS (Specialized: regional)**, #410, 10113-104 St., Edmonton, Alberta T5J 1A1 Canada, phone (780)421-1544, fax (780)421-1588, e-mail jonrach@msn.com, founded 1992, publisher H. Marshall.

Book/Chapbook Needs: Rowan Books aims "to publish emerging Western Canadian poets, previously unpublished in book form. They publish 2 paperbacks per year. They want "well-written (i.e., we look for artistic quality); feminist; regional (Alberta, Western Canadian); links with the experience of a particular group (e.g., women, lesbian/gay, ethnic minorities, youth, etc.). No pornography, racist or homophobic work." They have published poetry by Mary T. McDonald, Alice Major, Jannie Edwards, Shirley A. Serviss, Anna Mioduchowska and Lori Miseck. Books are usually 64 pgs., 5½×8½, offset printed and perfect-bound with soft 4-color laminate cover, uses photo or art for cover.

How to Submit: Query first, with a few sample poems and cover letter with brief bio and publication credits. "Prefers poets be previously published in some recognized Canadian journals. Prefer typewritten, but will accept and read legible handwritten manuscripts. Submit samples by mail; accepted manuscripts may be sent electronically upon acceptance." Time between acceptance and publication is 3-6 months. Poems are circulated to an editorial committee. Replies to queries in 1 month; to mss in 3 months. Pays royalties of 8% minimum, 11% maximum and 5 author's copies (out of a press run of 500). Order sample books by sending $15 (Canadian)/book, include shipping.

Also Offers: "We occasionally publish anthologies; watch for calls for submissions."

◯ ◎ **RUAH; POWER OF POETRY (Specialized: spirituality)**, Dominican School of Philosophy/Theology, 2401 Ridge Rd., Berkeley CA 94709, e-mail cjrenz@usa.net, founded 1990, general editor C.J. Renz, O.P., editor Gregory Thielen.

Magazine Needs: *Ruah*, an annual journal published in May, "provides a 'non-combative forum' for poets who have had few or no opportunities to publish their work. Theme: spiritual poetry. The journal has three sections: general poems, featured poet, and chapbook contest winners." They want "poetry which is of a 'spiritual nature,' i.e., describes an experience of the transcendent. No religious affiliation preferences; no style/format limitations. No 'satanic verse'; no individual poems longer than four typed pages." They have published poetry by Benjamin Alire Saens, Jean Valentine, Alberto Rios and Naomi Shihab Nye. *Ruah* is 60-80 pgs., $5\frac{1}{2} \times 8\frac{1}{2}$, photocopied and saddle-stapled or perfect-bound, glossy card stock cover, b&w photo, includes occasional b&w sketches of original artwork. They receive about 250 poems a year, accept approximately 10-20%. Press run is 250 for about 100 subscribers of which 7 are libraries, 10 shelf sales; 50 distributed free to authors, reviewers and inquiries. Subscription: $10. Sample: $5 plus $1.50 postage/handling. Make checks payable to Power of Poetry/DSPT.

How to Submit: Submit 3-5 poems at a time. No previously published poems; simultaneous submissions OK. E-mail submissions OK. "Do not mail submissions to publisher's address. Contact general editor via e-mail for current address or send written inquiries to Dominican School." Reads submissions December through March only. Time between acceptance and publication is 3-6 months. Poems are circulated to an editorial board. "Poems reviewed by writers and/or scholars in field of creative writing/literature." Send SASE for guidelines. Responds in up to 6 months. Pays 1 copy/poem. Acquires first rights.

Book/Chapbook Needs & How to Submit: Power of Poetry publishes 1 chapbook of spiritual poetry through their annual competition. Chapbooks are usually 24 pgs., and are included as part of *Ruah*. "Poets should e-mail editor for contest guidelines and submission address or write to Dominican School." Reading fee: $10. Deadline: December 15. Replies to queries in 3-6 weeks; to mss in 3-6 months. Winner receives publication in a volume of *Ruah* and 25 author's copies (out of a press run of 250).

Advice: "*Ruah* is a gathering place in which new poets can come to let their voice be heard alongside of and in the context of 'more established' poets. The journal hopes to provide some breakthrough experiences of the Divine at work in our world."

$ ◻ ◎ RURAL HERITAGE (Specialized: rural, humor), 281 Dean Ridge Lane, Gainesboro TN 38562-5039, phone (931)268-0655, e-mail editor@ruralheritage.com, website www.ruralheritage.com, founded 1976, editor Gail Damerow.

Magazine Needs: *Rural Heritage* uses poetry related to rural living. "We are interested in action-oriented rather than image-oriented verse that offers insight into human nature and/or working with livestock, especially draft animals. Traditional meter and rhyme only. Poems must have touch of humor or other twist. Please, no comparisons between country and city life and no religious, political or issues-oriented material." As a sample the editor selected this poem, "Easy Choice" by John M. Floyd:

> *"You get rid of that/Plow horse right now,"/Said Jim's wife,/"Or I want a divorce."/So he put the old nag/On a boat to Mau Mau,/And then plowed a few rows/With his horse.*

RH is magazine-sized, bimonthly, using b&w photos, graphics and ads, 4-6 poems/issue. Circulation is 4,600. Subscription: $24. Sample: $7.

How to Submit: Submit up to 3 poems at a time, one/page. Prefers short poems (12 lines or less). "Previously published poems are OK if we are told where and when. Simultaneous submissions must be withdrawn before we publish. We welcome submissions via e-mail—one verse per message please. Don't forget your snail mail address so we'll know where to send the check if your verse is accepted." Time between acceptance and publication is 4-6 months. "We often group poems by theme, for example plowing, threshing and so forth according to season. Verse may also be coupled with an article of similar theme such as plowing, mule teams, etc." Send SASE for guidelines or obtain via website. Responds ASAP. Pays on publication, $5 and up (depending on length) and 2 copies. Buys first English language rights.

Advice: "We receive too much modern poetry (free verse), not enough traditional (true meter & rhyme), not enough humor. We get too much image poetry (we prefer action) and most poems are too long—we prefer 12 lines or less."

$ ◻ ◎ SACHEM PRESS (Specialized: translations, bilingual), P.O. Box 9, Old Chatham NY 12136-0009, founded 1980, editor Louis Hammer.

Book/Chapbook Needs: Sachem, a small press publisher of poetry and fiction, both hardcover and flat-spined paperbacks. The editor wants to see "strong, compelling, even visionary work, English-language or translations." He has published poetry by Cesar Vallejo, Yannis Ritsos, 24 leading poets of Spain (in an anthology), Miltos Sahtouris and himself. The paperbacks average 120 pgs. and the anthology of Spanish poetry contains 340 pgs. Each poem is printed in both Spanish and English, and there are biographical notes about the authors. The small books cost $6.95 and the anthology $11.95.

How to Submit: No new submissions, only statements of projects, until January 2001. Submit mss January through April only. Royalties are 10% maximum, after expenses are recovered, plus 50 author's copies. Rights are negotiable. Book catalog is free "when available," and poets can purchase books from Sachem "by writing to us, 33⅓% discount."

◎ SACRED JOURNEY: THE JOURNAL OF FELLOWSHIP IN PRAYER (Specialized: religious), 291 Witherspoon St., Princeton NJ 08542, phone (609)924-6863, fax (609)924-6910, founded 1950, contact Editor.

Magazine Needs: *SJ* is an interfaith bimonthly "concerned with prayer, meditation and spiritual life" using short poetry "with deep religious (or spiritual) feeling." It is 48 pgs., digest-sized, professionally printed, saddle-stapled with glossy card cover. They accept about 2% of submissions received. Press run is 10,000. Subscription: $16. Sample free.

How to Submit: Submit 5 poems at a time, double-spaced. Simultaneous submissions and "sometimes" previously published poems OK. Cover letter preferred. Responds in 2 months. Pays 5 copies.

$ ◎ ST. ANTHONY MESSENGER (Specialized: religious), 1615 Republic St., Cincinnati OH 45210-1298, website www.americancatholic.org, poetry editor Susan Hines-Brigger.

Magazine Needs: *St. Anthony Messenger* is a monthly 56-page magazine, circulation 359,000, for Catholic families, mostly with children in grade school, high school or college. In some issues, they have a poetry page that uses poems appropriate for their readership. Their poetry needs are limited but poetry submissions are always welcomed. As a sample here is "A Valentine for Darby" by Jean M. Syed:

> *Why do I love you, my potbellied love?/Not for your pregnant form or shiny pate./Were these on tender*
> *those decades ago,/would I have been so indiscriminate/as to let you win my heart? No princess/from*
> *passion ever took a frog to mate.*

How to Submit: "Submit seasonal poetry (Christmas/Easter/nature poems) several months in advance. Submit a few poems at a time; do not send us your entire collection of poetry. We seek to publish accessible poetry of high quality." Send regular SASE for guidelines and 9 × 12 SASE for free sample. Pays $2/line on acceptance. Buys first worldwide serial rights. *St. Anthony Messenger* poetry occasionally receives awards from the Catholic Press Association Annual Competition.

$ ▢ ◎ ST. JOSEPH MESSENGER AND ADVOCATE OF THE BLIND (Specialized: religious), 537 Pavonia Ave., P.O. Box 288, Jersey City NJ 07303, founded 1898, poetry editor Sister Mary Kuiken, C.S.J.P.

Magazine Needs: *St. Joseph Messenger* is semiannual, (16 pgs., 8 × 11). They want "brief but thought-filled poetry; do not want lengthy and issue-filled." Most of the poets they have used are previously unpublished. They receive 400-500 submissions a year, use approximately 50. There are about 2 pgs. of poetry in each issue. Circulation 15,000. Subscription: $5.

How to Submit: Sometimes comments on rejections. Publishes theme issues. Send SASE for guidelines, free sample and upcoming themes. Responds within 2 weeks. Pays $10-25/poem and 2 copies.

ST. MARTIN'S PRESS, 175 Fifth Ave., New York NY 10010. Prefers not to share information.

N ◖ SALMAGUNDI, Skidmore College, Saratoga Springs NY 12866, phone (518)580-5186, founded 1965, edited by Peggy Boyers and Robert Boyers.

> Work published in *Salmagundi* has been selected for inclusion in the 1995, 1996 and 1997 volumes of *The Best American Poetry*.

Magazine Needs: *Salmagundi* has long been one of the most distinguished quarterlies of the sciences and humanities, publishing poets such as Frank Bidart, Robert Pinsky, Sharon Olds, Gail Mazur, Louise Glück and W.D. Snodgrass. Each issue is handsomely printed, thick, flat-spined, priced at $5-10. Editors here tend to use more lyric free verse than any other style, much of it accessible and usually under 50 lines. Although the magazine is hefty, poems compete with prose (with the latter dominating). They use about 10-50 pages of poetry in each issue, receive about 1,200 submissions a year, use approximately 20 and have a 12- to 30-month backlog. Circulation is 5,400 for 3,800 subscribers of which about 900 are libraries. Subscription: $18/year, $30/2 years. Sample: $6.

How to Submit: Submissions not accompanied by SASE are discarded. "Phone calls are only welcome to inquire about submissions *already sent.*" Reads mss November through April only. Responds in 3 months. Pays 6 copies. Send books for review consideration.

✓ $ ◖ SALMON RUN PRESS; NATIONAL POETRY BOOK AWARD, P.O. Box 672130, Chugiak AK 99567-2130, e-mail salmonp@aol.com, founded 1991, editor/publisher John E. Smelcer.

Book/Chapbook Needs: Salmon Run publishes 2-3 books/year. They want "quality poetry by established poets, any subject, any style. No poetry that is not representative of the highest achievement in the art." They have published Galway Kinnell, Ursula K. Le Guin, X.J. Kennedy, Molly Peacock, Denise Levertov, Denise Duhamel, Philip Levine, Daniel Bourne and Luis Omar Salinas. As a sample the editor selected these lines from Philip Levine's "Peter's Gift":

MARKET CONDITIONS are constantly changing! If you're still using this book and it is 2002 or later, buy the newest edition of *Poet's Market* at your favorite bookstore or order directly from Writer's Digest Books (800)289-0963 or www.writersdigest.com.

> *My friend Peter found a strange newcomer/in the walnut tree. Late June,/near dusk, the soft light*
> *hanging on,/he stills us, and at first I catch nothing,/and then the soft voice, the bubbling.*

Their books are flat-spined and professionally printed on heavy, natural-colored paper with glossy color covers.
How to Submit: Query first with sample poems and cover letter with brief bio. Previously published poems and simultaneous submissions OK. Usually comments on rejections. Replies to queries within 1-3 weeks, to mss in 1-2 months. Pays 10% royalties, sometimes advances and a negotiable number of author's copies.
Also Offers: They also sponsor a pamphlet series ("by invitation only") and the National Poetry Book Award for book-length mss of 48-96 pgs. $10 reading fee and SASE required. Entries must be postmarked by December 30. The winning ms will be published in book form, nationally distributed and receive $1,000 prize.

[N] ⊘ SALT FORK REVIEW, P.O. Box 310, Tonkawa OK 74653, phone (580)628-6431, e-mail saltforkrevie w@yahoo.com, founded 1999, editor-in-chief Paul Bowers, poetry editor Todd Fuller, managing editor Amy Wilson.
Magazine Needs: Appearing biannually, *Salt Fork Review* is "a regional journal that seeks to publish high-quality poetry, literary fiction and nonfiction. We want image-driven poetry that employs either a narrative or lyrical tendency, or both, and seeks to entertain readers. No sing-song, cliché-filled poems that rely on philosophical grandstanding to teach morals of love, death, religion, etc." They have published poetry by Ron McFarland, Lisa Lewis, Walt McDonald, Eric Nelson and William Hathaway. The editors say *SFR* is 32-48 pgs., tabloid-sized, saddle-stapled with full-color cover, includes photos and artwork. They receive about 500 poems a year, accept approximately 5-10%. Publish 20-25 poems/issue. Press run is 500 for 50 subscribers of which 20 are libraries, 300 shelf sales; 50 distributed free. Single copy: $5; subscription: $8/year. Sample (including guidelines): $4.
How to Submit: Submit 3-5 poems at a time. Line length for poetry is 14 minimum, 200 maximum. No previously published poems; simultaneous submissions OK. E-mail submissions OK. Cover letter strongly preferred. "Poetry must be typewritten, single spaced, with author's name at the beginning of each poem." Reads submissions August 15 through May 15 only. Time between acceptance and publication is 6-9 months. Seldom comments on rejections. Responds in 3 months. Sometimes sends prepublication galleys. Pays 2 copies. Acquires first North American serial rights. Reviews books of poetry in 500 words, single book format. Open to unsolicited reviews. Poets may also send books for review consideration to poetry editor.
Advice: "Read as much contemporary work as possible and immerse yourself in the classics of your culture and the cultures of others."

☑ ⊘ SALT HILL; SALT HILL POETRY PRIZE; SALT HILL SHORT SHORT FICTION PRIZE; SALT HILL HYPERTEXT PRIZE, English Dept., Syracuse University, Syracuse NY 13244, phone (315)443-1984, website www-hl.syr.edu/cwp, founded 1994, editor Caryn Koplik, contact poetry editor.
   ▧ Poetry published in *Salt Hill* has also been included in *The Best American Poetry 1998.*
Magazine Needs: *Salt Hill*, published biannually, features "high-quality contemporary writing including poetry, fiction, essays, book reviews and artwork." They want "high quality original work, from four lines to four pages, to free verse and prose poems. We like to see the kind of intellectual and emotional engagement we feel is representative of a mature poetic imagination. Experimental work is welcome." They do not want "badly written sentimental work without soul." They have published poetry by Bei Dao, Daniela Crăsnaru, Bill Knott and Eléna Rivera. As a sample the editor selected these lines from "2 Bachelard" by Michael Burkard:

> *Days go by. 2 Bachelard begins to feel like a street. I/stare at this weak brown slip called a receipt*
> *with its clear/but incomplete scrawl and an entire world of passion and/rain and the inner and outer*
> *city returns to me. Yes, a/street. A sign. A smell. A love, a life, a love of life when/you could not let go*
> *of either.*

The editor says *Salt Hill* is 120-150 pgs., 5½×8½, perfect-bound, with art, photography and ads. They receive about 3,000 poems a year, accept approximately 2%. Press run is 1,000. Subscription: $15. Sample: $8.
How to Submit: Submit 5 poems at a time. No previously published poems; simultaneous submissions OK. Cover letter preferred with a brief bio. Time between acceptance and publication is 2-8 months. Seldom comments on rejections. Send SASE for guidelines. Responds in up to 6 months. Pays 2 copies. Buys one-time rights. Reviews books or chapbooks of poetry or other magazines in 900-3,000 words and/or essay reviews of single/ multi book format. Open to unsolicited reviews. Send books for review consideration to Book Review Editor, at the above address.
Also Offers: Sponsors annual *Salt Hill* Poetry Prize, awarding $500 1st Prize and publication, $100 2nd Prize and publication and $50 3rd Prize and publication. Submit unpublished poems with name, address and phone on each. Reading fee is $5 for up to 150 lines (1-3 poems); $3 extra for every additional 100 lines. Include SASE. Postmark deadline May 1. Also sponsors Salt Hill Hypertext Prize, awarding $500 1st Prize and web publication, $100 2nd Prize and web publication, 3rd Prize web publication. See website for details. Reading fee: $10. Address envelope to Web Contest. Send url address, or work as an attachment to jsparker@mailbox.syr.edu, or address envelope with floppy disks to Web Editor (disks will not be returned). Deadline: January 31.

[N] ◯ ◎ SAMSARA (Specialized: suffering/healing), P.O. Box 367, College Park MD 20741-0367, website www.members.aol.com/rdfgoalie/sammain.htm, founded 1993, editor R. David Fulcher.

Magazine Needs: *Samsara* is a biannual publication of poetry and fiction dealing with suffering. "All subject matter should deal with suffering/healing." They have published poetry by Michael Foster and Jeff Parsley. *Samsara* is 80 pgs., 8½×11, neatly typeset and stapled down the side with a colored card stock cover and b&w art. They receive about 150 poems a year, accept approximately 7%. Press run is 200 for 35 subscribers. Single copy: $5.50. Subscription: $10.

How to Submit: Reprints acceptable if 3 years since publication; simultaneous submissions OK, but "if it is a simultaneous submission, a cover letter should be provided explaining this status." Seldom comments on rejections. Send SASE for guidelines. Responds in 2 months. Pays 1 copy. Acquires first North American serial rights.

Also Offers: Website includes writer's guidelines, names of editors, reading schedule and the current submissions status (open or closed) of the magazine.

Advice: "Make me feel anguish, pain and loss—and then some hope—and you'll probably get into *Samsara*."

N ◯ **SANSKRIT**, UNC Charlotte, Cone University Center, Charlotte NC 28223, phone (704)547-2326, fax (704)547-3394, e-mail sanskrit@email.uncc.edu, website www.uncc.edu/life/sanskrit or www.uncc.edu/life/smp/smp_sanskrit.html, founded 1965, editor Jason Hughes.

Magazine Needs: *Sanskrit* is a literary annual using poetry. "No restrictions as to form or genre, but we do look for maturity and sincerity in submissions. Nothing trite or sentimental." They have published poetry by Kimberleigh Luke-Stallings. As a sample the editor selected these lines from "The World Will Always Be With Us" by Kristina Wright:

> *The blues, the scent of lilacs on the tongue, tiny cherries/softly push from my mouth like the first buds*
> *still straining,//Though once I walked stupid-faced: shambling through dairy/products, putrid flowers,*
> *the confusion of menus, guns, women/skinny as switches on scratch and sniff pages, children with/*
> *tremulous liquid hearts like firing glass vases, . . .*

Their purpose is "to encourage and promote beginning and established artists and writers." It is 60-65 pgs., 9×12, flat-spined, printed on quality matte paper with heavy matte card cover. Press run is 3,500 for about 100 subscribers of which 2 are libraries. Sample: $10.

How to Submit: Submit up to 15 poems at a time. Simultaneous submissions OK. Fax and e-mail submissions OK (include in body of message). Cover letter with 30-70 word bio required. Submission deadline is the first Friday in November. Editor comments on submissions "infrequently." Responds in 2 months. Pays 1 copy.

Also Offers: Website includes an online format at www.uncc.edu/life/sanskrit, writer's guidelines and information about student media is available at www.uncc.edu/life/smp/smp_sanskrit.html.

$ ◱ **SARABANDE BOOKS, INC.; THE KATHRYN A. MORTON PRIZE IN POETRY**, 2234 Dundee Rd., Suite 200, Louisville KY 40205, phone (502)458-4028, fax (502)458-4065, e-mail sarabandeb@aol.com, website www.SarabandeBooks.org, founded 1994, editor-in-chief Sarah Gorham.

Book/Chapbook Needs: Sarabande Books publishes books of poetry and short fiction. They want "poetry of superior artistic quality. Otherwise no restraints or specifications." They have published poetry by Michael Burkard, Belle Waring, Baron Wormser and Afaa Michael Weaver.

How to Submit: Query with 10 sample poems during the month of September only. No fax or e-mail submissions. SASE must always be enclosed. Previously published poems OK if acknowledged as such. Simultaneous submissions OK "if notified immediately of acceptance elsewhere." Seldom comments on rejections. Responds to queries in 3 months, to mss (if invited) in 6 months. Send SASE or visit website for guidelines. Pays 10% royalties and author's copies.

Also Offers: The Kathryn A. Morton Prize in Poetry is awarded to a book-length ms (at least 48 pgs.) submitted between January 1 and February 15. $15 handling fee and entry form required. Send SASE for guidelines beginning in November or obtain via website. Winner receives a $2,000 cash award, publication and a standard royalty contract. All finalists are considered for publication. "At least half of our list is drawn from contest submissions." Entry fee: $15. Reads entries January 1 through February 15 only. Competition receives 1,200 entries. Most recent contest winner was Cate Marvin for "World's Tallest Disaster." Judge was Robert Pinsky. Website includes guidelines and application form for contest, interviews with authors, ordering information and general information on press.

◉ **SATURDAY PRESS, INC.**, Box 43548, Upper Montclair NJ 07043, phone (973)256-5053, fax (973)256-4987, e-mail saturdaypr@aol.com, founded 1975, editor S. Ladov. "We do not plan to read manuscripts in the foreseeable future."

✔ **$** ◎ **SCAVENGER'S NEWSLETTER; KILLER FROG CONTEST (Specialized: science fiction/fantasy, horror, mystery, writing)**, 833 Main, Osage City KS 66523-1241, phone (785)528-3538, e-mail foxscav1@jc.net, website www.cza.com/scav/index/html, editor Janet Fox.

Magazine Needs: *Scavenger's Newsletter* may seem an odd place to publish poems, but its editor, Janet Fox, uses 1-2 every month. The *Newsletter* is a booklet packed with news about science fiction and horror publications. Ms. Fox prefers science fiction/fantasy, horror and mystery poetry and will read anything that is offbeat or bizarre. Writing-oriented poetry is occasionally accepted but "poems on writing must present fresh ideas and viewpoints.

The twelve "creatures" depicted in G.W. Thomas's illustration should feel right at home on the January 2000 cover of *Scavenger's*. The newsletter out of Osage City, Kansas, features information about science fiction and horror publications. Editor and publisher Janet Fox says she chose Thomas's cover because "I thought it was a whimsical and funny take on science fiction." For *Scavenger*, Fox uses science fiction/fantasy, horror and mystery poetry of 10 lines or less as filler. Thomas, of Prince George, British Columbia, titled his illustration "Twelve Portraits of the Artist as Species of Alien and Unknown Origins." *Scavenger's* runs 22-28 pages and is produced through a quick printing shop.

Poetry is used as filler so it must be ten lines or under. I like poems with sharp images and careful craftsmanship." They have published poetry by K.S. Hardy, David C. Kopaska-Merkel and Holly Day. As a sample she selected this poem, "Quasi-ku" by Richard William Pearce:

> Godzilla roaring/Home—Tokyo—stomped again/That's it, I'm moving.

Scavenger's Newsletter is 22-28 pgs., printed at a quick printing shop for 800 subscribers. Subscription: $22/year; $11/6 months. Send 1st class. Sample (including guidelines): $2.50.

How to Submit: Submit 3-6 poems at a time. Previously published poems, submissions by e-mail (no attachments) and simultaneous submissions OK (if informed)—reprints if credit is given. Send SASE for guidelines or request via e-mail. At last report was "accepting about 1 out of 20 poems submitted. I am currently reading selectively. "I have made the notice 'reading selectively due to backlog' a permanent part of the guidelines, since I do usually have quite a bit of material on hand yet do not want to close to the exceptional piece." Responds in 1 month or less. Pays $2 on acceptance plus one copy. E-mail submissions may choose cash or subscription. Buys one-time rights. Staff reviews science fiction/fantasy/horror and mystery chapbooks, books and magazines only. Send materials for review to either: Jim Lee, 801 - 26th St., Windber PA 15963 or Steve Sawicki, 186 Woodruff Ave., Watertown CT 06795.

Also Offers: "I hold an annual 'Killer Frog Contest' for horror so bad or outrageous it becomes funny. There is a category for horror poetry. Has been opening April 1, closing July 1 of each year. Prizes are $50 each in four categories: poetry, art, short stories and short short stories." The last contest had no entry fee but entrants wanting the anthology pay $4.50. Winners list available for SASE. Website features guidelines, information about *Scavenger's Newsletter*, Killer Frog Contest information and other projects.

☘ ✔ ⊘ **SCHOLASTIC CANADA LTD.; NORTH WINDS PRESS**, 175 Hillmount Rd., Markham, Ontario L6C 1Z7 Canada, website www.scholastic.com, founded 1971, contact Jane Snape.

Book/Chapbook Needs: Publishes entertaining, high-quality novels and picture books for children. "A good story is prerequisite; very little poetry published. We publish 2 picture books per year that feature poetry."

How to Submit: "However, we are not currently accepting unsolicited mss. Accepting query letters only."

$ ▢ ◎ **SCIENCE FICTION POETRY ASSOCIATION; STAR*LINE (Specialized: science fiction, horror); THE RHYSLING ANTHOLOGY**, 1300 Kicker Rd., Tuscaloosa AL 35404, phone (205)553-2284, e-mail dragontea@earthlink.net, website dm.net/~bejay/sfpa.htm, founded 1978, editor David Kopaska-Merkel.

Magazine Needs: The Association publishes *Star*Line*, a bimonthly newsletter and poetry magazine. They are "open to all forms—free verse, traditional forms, light verse—so long as your poetry shows skilled use of the language and makes a good use of science fiction, science, fantasy, horror or speculative motifs." The Association also publishes *The Rhysling Anthology*, a yearly collection of nominations from the membership "for the best science fiction/fantasy long and short poetry of the preceding year." Also accepts poetry written by children. The magazine has published poetry by Lawrence Schimel, Kendall Evans, Charlie Jacob, Terry A. Garey and Timons Esaias. The digest-sized magazine and anthology are saddle-stapled, photocopied, with numerous illustrations and decorations. They have 250 subscribers of which 1 is a library. Subscription: $13/6 issues. Sample: $2. Send requests for copies/membership information to John Nichols, Secretary-Treasurer, 6075 Bellevue Dr., North Olmstead OH 44070. Submissions to *Star*Line* only. They receive about 300-400 submissions a year, use approximately 80—mostly short (under 50 lines).

How to Submit: Send 3-5 poems/submission, typed. No simultaneous submissions, no queries. E-mail submissions OK "as part of the e-mail message, no attachments." Include brief cover letter. Responds in 1 month. Pays 5¢/line plus 1¢/word and a copy. Buys first North American serial rights. Reviews books of poetry "within the science fiction/fantasy field" in 50-500 words. Open to unsolicited reviews. Poets may also send books for review consideration to Todd Earl Rhodes, 735 Queensbury Loop, Winter Garden FL 34787-5808.

Also Offers: Website includes guidelines, editor's address, ordering and subscription address and links to *Rhysling Anthology* winners list.

☑ $ ◎ **SCIENCE OF MIND (Specialized: spirituality/inspirational)**, 3251 W. Sixth St., P.O. Box 75127, Los Angeles CA 90020-5096, phone (213)388-2181, fax (213)388-1926, website www.scienceofmind.com, founded 1927, editor-in-chief Kenneth Lind. Send all poetry mss to editorial associate Sylvia Delgado, sdelgado@scienceofmind.com.

Magazine Needs: *Science of Mind*, published monthly, "is a correlation of laws of science, opinions of philosophy, and revelations of religion applied to the needs and aspirations of humankind. A practical teaching, it helps thousands of people experience health, happiness, peace and love." They want "poems inspirational and spiritual in theme and characterized by an appreciation of *Science of Mind* principles. Average length is 8-12 lines. Maximum length is 25-30 lines." They do not want "religious poetry, stuff about Christ and redemption." *Science of Mind* is 112 pgs., digest-sized, web offset printed, perfect-bound with 4-color cover and color ads. They receive about 200 poems a year, accept approximately 6-8. Press run is 78,000 for 55,000 subscribers, 15,000 shelf sales. Single copy: $2.95; subscription: $24.95. Sample: $5.

How to Submit: Submit maximum of 3 poems at a time. No previously published poems; simultaneous submissions OK. No fax submissions. Cover letter preferred. "Only accepts will be contacted. Allow 3 months. Manuscript will not be returned." Time between acceptance and publication is 1 year ("each issue has a theme, so we may keep a poem until the right theme comes along"). Poems are read by the editorial associate, and if approved, sent to the editor for final decision. Publishes theme issues. Responds "not soon at all—most are rejected right away, but acceptances may take months." Pays $25 and 10 copies. Buys first North American serial rights.

◑ ◎ **SCORE MAGAZINE; SCORE CHAPBOOKS AND BOOKLETS (Specialized: form)**, 1015 NW Clifford St., Pullman WA 99163, phone (509)332-1120, e-mail orion@pullman.com, poetry editors Crag Hill and Spencer Selby.

Magazine Needs: Score Chapbooks and Booklets is a small press publisher of visual poetry in the annual magazine *Score*, booklets, postcards and broadsides. They want "poetry which melds language and the visual arts such as concrete poetry; experimental use of language, words and letters—forms. The appearance of the poem should have as much to say as the text. Poems on any subject; conceptual poetry; poems which use experimental, non-traditional methods to communicate their meanings." They don't want "traditional verse of any kind—be it free verse or rhymed." They have published poetry by Karl Kempton, John Vieira, Bruce Andrews, Larry Eigner and Pete Spence. They say that it is impossible to quote a sample because "some of our poems consist of only a single word—or in some cases no recognizable words." *Score* is 48-72 pgs., magazine-sized, offset printed, saddle-stapled, using b&w graphics, 2-color matte card cover. Press run is 200 for 25 subscribers, of which 6 are libraries, about 50-60 shelf sales. Sample: $10.

How to Submit: We strongly advise looking at a sample copy before submitting if you are not familiar with visual poetry. Previously published poems OK "if noted." No simultaneous submissions. Send SASE for guidelines. Pays 2 copies. Open to unsolicited reviews. Poets may also send books for review consideration.

Book/Chapbook Needs & How to Submit: For chapbook consideration send entire ms. No simultaneous submissions. Almost always comments on rejections. Pays 25% of the press run. They subsidy publish "if author requests it."

🌐 ☑ ◐ ◎ **SCOTTISH CULTURAL PRESS; SCOTTISH CONTEMPORARY POETS SERIES (Specialized: nationality)**, Unit 13d, Newbattle Abbey Business Annexe, Newbattle Rd., Dalkeith EH22 3LJ Scotland, United Kingdom, phone +44(0)131 660 6366, fax +44(0)131 660 6414, e-mail scp@sol.co.uk, founded 1992, directors Avril Gray and Brian Pugh.

Book/Chapbook Needs: Scottish Cultural Press publishes all styles of poetry. Poet should be Scottish or have strong Scottish connections and previously published in magazines, etc. Publishes 8-12 paperbacks/year. They do not want "new poets and/or modernistic visual poetry." They have published poetry by Valerie Gillies, George Bruce and Iain Crichton-Smith. Books are usually 64 pgs., A5, "burst-bound," with 2-color cover.

How to Submit: Submit 5-10 poems at a time. Previously published poems and simultaneous submissions OK. E-mail submissions OK. Cover letter required and must include bio of poet and indication of whether material is available on disk. Time between acceptance and publication is up to 9 months. Poems are circulated to an editorial board. Seldom comments on rejections. Replies to queries in 1 month; to mss in 3 months. Pays 10% of net income royalties and 20 author's copies (out of a press run of 1,000).

🍁 ☑ ◐ **SCRIVENER**, 853 Sherbrooke St. W., Montreal, Quebec H3A 2T6 Canada, phone (514)398-6588, fax (514)398-8146, e-mail scrivener@post.com, founded 1980.

Magazine Needs: *Scrivener* is an annual review of contemporary literature and art published in March by students at McGill University. With a circulation throughout North America, *Scrivener* publishes the best of new Canadian and American poetry, short fiction, criticism, essays, reviews and interviews. "*Scrivener* is committed to publishing the work of new and unpublished writers." *Scrivener* is perfect-bound, 8½×7, 120 pgs., with 25 pages of b&w photography printed on coated paper. Text and graphics are printed in b&w duotone cover. Subscription: $9 Canadian in Canada, $11 Canadian in US and $15 Canadian anywhere else. Prices include postage.

How to Submit: January 15 deadline for submissions; contributors encouraged to submit in early fall. Send 5-10 poems, one poem/page; be sure that each poem be identified separately, with titles, numbers, etc. Submissions require SASE for return. Comments or questions regarding back issues or submissions may be sent to Scrivener@ post.com. Scrivener only operates fully between September and April. Responds in 6 months. Pays 1 copy (multiple copies available upon request).

☑ $ ▢ ◯ **SCROLL PUBLICATIONS; SCROLL ORIGINAL ARTIST MAGAZINE**, P.O. Box 562, Swink CO 81077, phone (970)247-2054, e-mail scrollpubl@ria.net, website www.scrollpublications.com, founded 1990, editor Cherylann Gray.

Magazine Needs: *Scroll Original Artist Magazine* contains "humor, comics, slogans, music, short stories, fiction/nonfiction, artwork, recipes and poetry. We are strictly devoted to preserving the works and dreams of the original artist." They want poetry of any form or style, on any subject; length, no more than 30 lines. Nothing profane or vulgar. Also accepts poetry written by children. They have published poetry by Daniel Gray and Jenny Jacobs. As a sample the editor selected these lines from "Grandmothers" by Eve Mackintosh:

> *Grandmothers are rocks thrown into deep wells/Each brick fitted painstakingly to form/Solid*
> *foundations for dream castles created/by her children and offspring.*

The editor says *Scroll* is 75-80 pgs., 8½×11½, soft paperback, includes art, ads. They receive about 500 poems a year, accept approximately 65%. Press run is 150. Single copy: $6; subscription: $20. Sample: $4. Make checks payable to Cherylann Gray.

How to Submit: Submit up to 5 poems at a time. Reading fee: $4/5 poems. Previously published poems and simultaneous submissions OK. Cover letter preferred. Time between acceptance and publication is 3-6 months. Poems are circulated to an editorial board. Often comments on rejections. Publishes theme issues occasionally. Send large SASE for guidelines and upcoming themes. Responds in 2 months. Always sends prepublication galleys. Pays 1 copy. Acquires first or one-time rights. Reviews chapbooks of poetry. Open to unsolicited reviews. Poets may also send books for review consideration.

Book/Chapbook Needs & How to Submit: Scroll Publications publishes 3 chapbooks and 3 anthologies/ year. Query first, with 3-4 sample poems and a cover letter with brief bio and publication credits. Replies to queries in 2 months; to mss in 3 months. Pays 40-50% royalties and 50 author's copies (out of a press run of 200).

Also Offers: Sponsors biannual contest. Awards prizes of $250, $100 and $50 plus publication. Submit up to 7 poems, 30 lines maximum, with large SASE.

Advice: "We want poetry that's strong in nature, life and real experiences, thoughts and dreams."

Ⓝ ⊕ ◪ **SEAM**, P.O. Box 3684, Danbury, Chelmsford CM3 4GP, United Kingdom, founded 1994, editors Maggie Freeman and Frank Dullaghan.

Magazine Needs: *Seam* appears twice a year (in January and July) to publish "good contemporary poetry." They want "high quality poems that engage the reader in any length." They have published poetry by Kevin Crossley, U.A. Fanthorpe, Hugo Williams and Myra Schneider. *Seam* is 62 pgs., A5, folded with b&w cover photo. They receive about 2,000 poems a year, accept approximately 5%. Press run is 300. Subscription: £6 a year, £10 overseas. Sample: £3, £5 overseas.

How to Submit: Submit 5-6 poems at a time; each poem on 1 sheet of paper (A4 size). No poems previously published in UK or simultaneous submissions. Sometimes comments on rejections. Pays 1 copy.

⊕ ◪ **SECOND AEON PUBLICATIONS**, 19 Southminster Rd., Roath, Cardiff CF2 S4T Wales, phone/ fax 01222-493093, e-mail peter.finch@dial.pipex.com, founded 1966, poetry editor Peter Finch. Does not accept unsolicited mss.

☑ ▢ ◯ ◪ **SEEDHOUSE**, P.O. Box 883009, Steamboat Springs CO 80477, phone/fax (970)879-6978, e-mail seedhouse98@yahoo.com, website www.seedhousemag.org, founded 1998, editor-in-chief Barbara Block.

Magazine Needs: *Seedhouse* is "a bimonthly literary magazine for modern writers and poets. Accepts poetry, essays, short stories, nonfiction and b&w artwork and photography." They want "any good poetry. No juvenile work." Also accepts poetry written by children ages 15 and over. They have published poetry by Michael White, Colorado Award Winner, and Mary Crow, Poet Laureate of Colorado. As a sample the editor selected these lines from "Cliff Dwellers" by Ron Chappell:

> *still they roam the hidden reaches/ . . . archaic margins of my mind/and they call me, seek to know*
> *me/from an age beyond some border/where the eons gather stardust/from a people lost in time.*

Seedhouse is 16 pgs., magazine-sized, saddle-stapled, includes b&w art/graphics. Press run is 1,000 for 500 subscribers. Single copy: $2.75; subscription: $15. Sample: $3.50. Make checks payable to *Seedhouse Magazine*.

How to Submit: Submit 3 poems at a time. Line length for poetry is 80 maximum. No previously published poems; simultaneous submissions OK. E-mail and disk submissions in Word Perfect or MS Word OK. Cover letter preferred. "We prefer typed submissions, double-spaced, in an easy to read font. Include name, address, phone, and three-sentence bio." Often comments on rejections. Publishes theme issues occasionally. Send SASE for guidelines and upcoming themes. Responds in 3 months. Pays 2 copies. Acquires one-time rights.

Also Offers: Sponsors an annual summer writing contest for short stories and poetry. 1st Place winners: $50 plus 1-year subscription; 2nd Place winners: $30; 3rd Place: $20. Website includes writer's guidelines, editor's names, upcoming themes, contest guidelines, subscription information and titles and authors by issue.

Advice: "Proofread your work carefully. Be sure to retain original."

🔰 ✅ 🖥 ⭕ **SEEDS POETRY MAGAZINE; HIDDEN BROOK PRESS; SEEDS POETRY CON-TEST**, 412-701 King St. W., Toronto, Ontario M5V 2W7 Canada, e-mail hiddenbrookpress.com, website www.hiddenbrookpress.com/homepage.htm, founded 1994, publisher/editor Richard M. Grove.

Magazine Needs: *SEEDS* is an online publication dedicated to being an accessible venue for writers, no matter what their status is in the publishing world. It doesn't matter whether you've ever been published or not. We publish well-crafted poetry from around the world, so send us any style of poetry you love to write. Send us your newly written or previously published work but be sure it is your absolute top shelf, best stuff. Don't save it for the bottom drawer or the future. We do not appreciate obscure, self-indulgent word games. We are not very interested in reading rhymed verse though we do on occasion publish such poetry if it suits us personally. We are not at all interested in reading about one-night stands, love-lorn angst or the teen heart throb. Save this for your bottom drawer. Religious dogma and spiritually sappy work are usually not our cup of tea but we have published some interesting references to God, the universe and spiritual epiphanies. Our goal is to publish well-written, memorable work whether it is humorous, traumatic, nature poems, cityscapes or just the insight or outlook about life. Push your poetry to the edge but not too far over the edge for us. Oh and keep the four letter words to a minimum. We have published very few of them."

How to Submit: Submit "any number of poems by e-mail or ASCII-text file on disk with hard copy." Line length for poetry is 3-200 maximum. Previously published poems and simultaneous submissions OK. "Work, if accepted, is filed to fit with future themes, styles and formats of other works. Authors will be notified as to whether or not the editor is interested in keeping work on file." Obtain guidelines via website. Responds "as soon as possible."

Also Offers: Sponsors the *SEEDS* Poetry Contest, awards $100, $50 and $25 plus publication. Entry fee: $12 for 6 poems. "Send as many sets of 3 by the same author as you like on white paper, single spaced, font size 12 pt. (no fancy fonts) with your name, mailing address, phone and e-mail address on the back of each sheet. Please no cover letter, bio, comments or pleadings. After you have mailed your hard copy with your submission fee, then and only then, e-mail your submission in the body of the e-mail." Deadline: May 1 and October 1. Also sponsors *No Love Lost* and *The Open Window* poetry anthology contests. For *No Love Lost*, submit poems of love, hate, lust, desire, passion, jealousy and ambivalence, brotherly, sisterly, parental love, and love of country, city. Deadline: January 1. For *The Open Window*, send any style, theme and length. Deadline: June 1. For *No Love Lost* and *The Open Window* contests, send 5 poems, previously unpublished, of any styles, any length. Submission fee: $15/£7 includes purchase of book. Authors retain copyright. 1st, 2nd, 3rd Prizes plus 10 honorable mentions will be chosen plus up to 300 poems published. Send your submissions with a SASE or SAE with IRCs to Hidden Brook Press. Electronic and hard copy submissions required. All non-Canadian destinations pay in US dollars or British sterling if from Great Britain. For overseas submissions add $1 US or £1.

Advice: "The paper-based *SEEDS* and the website *SEEDS* are two different poetry publications containing a different selection of poems and published at different times of the year."

🔲 ⭕ **SEEKING THE MUSE: INSPIRED WORKS OF CREATIVITY**, D&K Publications, P.O. Box 650, Cerro Gordo IL 61818-0650, phone (217)763-3311, e-mail jagusch@one-eleven.net, website http://sites.netscape.net/jagusch/homepage, founded 1999, editor/publisher Kris Jagusch.

Magazine Needs: "*Seeking the Muse* is a semiannual anthology published in December and June by D&K Publications. Each issue features black & white artwork, poetry, fiction, fiction for children, fillers and personal essays on any theme, as well as reviews of materials geared toward kick-starting or maintaining the writer's creativity. Each issue accepts work that is inspired, as well as inspirational to other writers. We are looking for poetry that is creative, well-written and which details an individual moment that illuminates the universal. Clarity is important so the reader can understand the poem. We do not want poems that are sing-songy or which serve

FOR EXPLANATIONS OF THESE SYMBOLS, SEE THE INSIDE FRONT AND BACK COVERS OF THIS BOOK.

only to tell about an individual's painful moment without offering substance others can relate to. Please eschew obfuscatory scrivenery (avoid foggy writing)." They have published poetry by Najwa Salam Brax, Patricia G. Rourke and Nancy Furstinger. As a sample the editor selected these lines from "Dream of Ancients" by Cassondra Leigh Givans:

> *If, in exercise of our hours, we live/But as the dream of our creators—/Our hopes, the end of theirs,*
> *and our deeds,/the shadow of their own—will they, on waking,/Leap to their desks with emboldened*
> *hearts to pen/Our birth, their intellects afire for our beginning?*

STM is 52-64 pgs., 5½×8½, typeset and attractively printed, perfect-bound with cardstock cover, includes b&w line drawings. They receive about 200 poems a year, accept approximately 10%. Publish 10-15 poems/issue. Press run is 100 for 75 subscribers; 25 distributed free to authors and publishers. Single copy: $5 US, $6.50 Canadian and UK; subscription: $10 US, $13 Canadian and UK. Sample: $6. Make checks payable to D&K Publications.

How to Submit: Submit up to 5 poems at a time. Line length for poetry is 100 maximum (including stanza breaks). Previously published poems and simultaneous submissions OK. E-mail submissions OK ("if contained within the body and not as an attachment.") Cover letter preferred. "Standard manuscript format. Cover letters that include biographical information are appreciated. Feel free to 'let it all hang out' in the cover letter; we like to know who we're working with. Special consideration is given to works that explore, in a new and interesting way, the publication's theme of inspiration and the Muse." Reads submissions January 1 through December 1 only. Submit seasonal poems 2 months in advance. Time between acceptance and publication is 1 month. Often comments on rejections. Publishes theme issues occasionally. Send SASE for guidelines and upcoming themes. Responds in 1 month. Pays 1 copy per accepted piece. Acquires one-time serial rights.

SEEMS, P.O. Box 359, Lakeland College, Sheboygan WI 53082-0359, phone (920)565-1276 or (920)565-3871, fax (920)565-1206, e-mail kelder@excel.net, website www.lakeland.edu/faculty/~elder/seemswe b.htm, founded 1971, editor Karl Elder.

Magazine Needs: *Seems* is published irregularly (34 issues in 29 years). This is a handsomely printed, nearly square (7×8¼) magazine, saddle-stapled, generous with white space on heavy paper. Two of the issues are considered chapbooks, and the editor, Karl Elder, suggests that a way to get acquainted would be to order *Seems #14, What Is The Future Of Poetry?* for $5, consisting of essays by 22 contemporary poets, and "If you don't like it, return it and we'll return your $5." *Explain That You Live: Mark Strand with Karl Elder* (#29) is available for $3. There are usually about 20 pgs. of poetry/issue. Elder has published poetry by Kim Bridgford, William Greenway, William Heyen, Mary MacGowan and Terry Savoie. He said it was "impossible" to select 6 illustrative lines, but for an example of his own recent work see *The Best American Poetry 2000* published by Scribner. Print run is 350 for 200 subscribers of which 20 are libraries. Single copy: $4; subscription: $16/4 issues.

How to Submit: There is a 1- to 2-year backlog. "People may call or fax with virtually any question, understanding that the editor may have no answer." No simultaneous submissions. Responds in up to 3 months. Pays 1 copy. Acquires first North American serial rights. Returns rights upon publication.

Also Offers: Website currently consists of a home page with basic information, including images of the covers of two issues.

Advice: "We'd like to consider more prose poems."

SENECA REVIEW, Hobart and William Smith Colleges, Geneva NY 14456-3397, phone (315)781-3392, fax (315)781-3348, website www.hws.edu/~senecareview/, founded 1970, editor Deborah Tall, associate editor John D'Agata.

Poetry published in *Seneca Review* has also been included in the 1997 volume of *The Best American Poetry* and in the 1998 Pushcart Anthology.

Magazine Needs: *Seneca Review* is a biannual. They want "serious poetry of any form, including translations. No light verse. Also essays on contemporary poetry and lyrical nonfiction." They have published poetry by Seamus Heaney, Rita Dove, Denise Levertov, Stephen Dunn and Hayden Carruth. *Seneca Review* is 100 pgs., 6×9, professionally printed on quality stock and perfect-bound with matte card cover. You'll find plenty of free verse here—some accessible and some leaning toward experimental—with the emphasis on voice, image and diction. All in all, poems and translations complement each other and create a distinct editorial mood each issue. They receive 3,000-4,000 poems a year, accept approximately 100. Press run is 1,000 for 500 subscribers of which half are libraries, about 250 shelf sales. Subscription: $11/year, $20/2 years, $28/3 years. Sample: $5.

How to Submit: Submit 3-5 poems at a time. No simultaneous submissions or previously published poems. Reads submissions September 1 through May 1 only. Responds in up to 3 months. Pays 2 copies and a 2-year subscription.

Also Offers: Website includes guidelines, excerpts from current issue, profile of editors, available back issues, subscription info, info for advertisers and book stores.

SENSATIONS MAGAZINE, 2 Radio Ave., A5, Secaucus NJ 07094, website www.sensationsmag. com, founded 1987, publisher/executive editor David Messineo.

Magazine Needs and How to Submit: "In 2001, *Sensations Magazine* will release 4 issues: spring, summer, fall and winter, each with a full-color cover. Entry fee: $2/poem. Those who submit the maximum number—6 poems—get one of these 4 issues on its publication. Best poem gets $3.25/line—the highest 'per line' rate for any American literary magazine. 'Detailed critiques' provided only on 6-poem sets at no additional charge. Do not put your name on poem, put on separate sheet with titles. Enclose SASE posted with 99¢ for return of poems. Submit entry fees payable to David Messineo. Material for the year will all be judged at one time, then split into four issues. Poems may be on any theme, but we're interested in receiving only your 'signature pieces'—your most sensational, unpublished poems. Submission deadline: January 15, 2001 postmark date. Submissions from outside the U.S. encouraged; fees must be paid using international money order. All poets should include an e-mail address, if they have one! Good luck!"

Advice: Mr. Messineo says, "If you merely want a publication credit to add to a 'comma-list' in your bio, or don't care how your work is presented in publication, we're not for you. If you would appreciate having your poetry critiqued on up to 20 different categories, or would just like to be treated with personal courtesy and decency instead of as 'one among thousands' for a change, it's definitely worth your time to send an SASE to our address for the current submission requirements. Purchase of a back issue, as always, is recommended; rates and availability will be included with all inquiries we receive. Good luck!"

SERPENT & EAGLE PRESS, 10 Main St., Laurens NY 13796, phone (607)432-2990, founded 1981, poetry editor Jo Mish. They are currently not accepting poetry submissions.

SEVEN BUFFALOES PRESS; AZOREAN EXPRESS; BLACK JACK; VALLEY GRAPEVINE; HILL AND HOLLER ANTHOLOGY SERIES (Specialized: rural, regional, anthologies), Box 249, Big Timber MT 59011, founded 1973, editor Art Coelho.

Magazine Needs & How to Submit: The editor says, "I've always thought that rural and working class writers, poets and artists deserve the same tribute given to country singers." These publications all express that interest. For all of them Art Coelho wants poetry oriented toward rural and working people, "a poem that tells a story, preferably free verse, not longer than 50-100 lines, poems with strong lyric and metaphor, not romantical, poetry of the heart as much as the head, not poems written like grocery lists or the first thing that comes from a poet's mind, no ivory tower, and half my contributors are women." He has published poetry by R.T. Smith, James Goode, Leo Connellan and Wendell Berry. *The Azorean Express* is 35 pgs., 5½×8½, side-stapled. It appears twice a year. Circulation 200. Sample: $7.75. Submit 4-8 poems at a time. No simultaneous submissions. Responds in 1 month. Pays 1 copy. *Black Jack* is an anthology series on Rural America that uses rural material from anywhere, especially the American West; *Valley Grapevine* is an anthology on central California, circulation 750, that uses rural material from central California; *Hill and Holler*, Southern Appalachian Mountain series, takes in rural mountain lifestyle and folkways. Sample of any postpaid: $7.75.

Book/Chapbook Needs & How to Submit: Seven Buffaloes Press does not accept unsolicited mss but publishes books solicited from writers who have appeared in the above magazines.

Advice: "Don't tell the editor how great you are. This one happens to be a poet and novelist who has been writing for 30 years. Your writing should not only be fused with what you know from the head, but also from what you know within your heart. Most of what we call life may be some kind of gift of an unknown river within us. The secret to be learned is to live with ease in the darkness, because there are too many things of the night in this world. But the important clue to remember is that there are many worlds within us."

THE SEWANEE REVIEW, University of the South, Sewanee TN 37383-1000, phone (931)598-1246, e-mail rjones@sewanee.edu, website www.sewanee.edu/sreview/home.html, founded 1892, thus being our nation's oldest continuously published literary quarterly, editor George Core.

Magazine Needs: Fiction, criticism and poetry are invariably of the highest establishment standards. Many of our major poets appear here from time to time. *SR* has published poetry by Gladys Swan, Wendell Berry, Donald Hall, Anthony Hecht and Mark Jarman. Each issue is a hefty paperback of nearly 200 pgs., conservatively bound in matte paper, always of the same typography. Truly a magazine open to all styles and forms, issues we critiqued featured formal sequences, metered verse, structured free verse, sonnets, and lyric and narrative forms—all accessible and intelligent. Circulation: 3,200. Sample: $7.25.

How to Submit: Submit up to 6 poems at a time. Line length for poetry is 40 maximum. No simultaneous submissions. No electronic submissions. "Unsolicited works should not be submitted between June 1 and August 31. A response to any submission received during that period will be greatly delayed." Responds in 6 weeks. Pays 60¢/line, plus 2 copies (and reduced price of $4 for additional copies). Also includes brief, standard and essay-reviews.

Also Offers: Presents The Aiken Taylor Award for Modern American Poetry to established poets. Poets *cannot* apply for this prize. Website includes submission guidelines, subscription costs, selections from the magazine and links to useful references, publishers, etc.

Advice: "Please keep in mind that for each poem published in *TSR*, approximately 250 poems are considered."

SHADES OF DECEMBER, P.O. Box 244, Selden NY 11784, e-mail eilonwy@innocent.com, website www2.fastdial.net/~fc2983, founded 1998, poetry editor Alexander C.P. Danner, fiction editor Brandy L. Straus.

Magazine Needs: Published quarterly, *Shades of December* "provides a forum that is open to all forms of writing (poetry, prose, drama, etc.). Topics and tones range from the academic to the whimsical. We are open to any genre and style. No trite greeting-card verse." They have published poetry by Joe Lucia, Anne O'Malley, Jonathan Russell and Emily Rivard. As a sample the editor selected this poem, "From: Poetry To: Entropy" by Carl Marcum:

> Even asleep in your bed you're spinning/at hundreds of miles an hour./Only your covers and a
> misplaced faith in gravity/keep you from waking light years/away from yourself.

SOD is 64 pgs., digest-sized, neatly printed and saddle-stapled with colored cardstock cover, uses b&w graphics. Single copy: $3; subscription: $11. Sample: $3. Make checks payable to Alexander C.P. Danner.

How to Submit: Submit 2-6 poems at a time. No previously published poems; simultaneous submissions OK. Cover letter preferred. E-mail submissions OK. "Cover letter should include brief 50-word bio listing previous publications/noteworthy facts. Include SASE. All electronic submissions should be in an IBM-recognizable format (any version MS Word, Corel Word Perfect)." Time between acceptance and publication is 1-4 months. Seldom comments on rejections. Publishes theme issues occasionally. Send SASE for guidelines or obtain via e-mail or website. Responds in 6 weeks. Sometimes sends prepublication galleys. Pays 2 copies. Acquires one-time rights.

Also Offers: Website includes guidelines, subscription/ordering information, upcoming themes and sample pieces.

SHARING MAGAZINE (Specialized: religious, Christian healing), 6807 Forest Haven, San Antonio TX 78240, phone/fax (210)681-5146, founded 1932, editor Marjorie George.

Magazine Needs: *Sharing* is published monthly by the Order of St. Luke, a Christian healing ministry. They want poetry "on the subject of Christian healing only." The editor says *Sharing* is 32 pgs., 5½×8½, offset printed. They receive about 50 poems a year, accept approximately 25%. Press run is 9,000. Single copy: $1.75; subscription: $12/year.

How to Submit: Submit up to 4 poems at a time. Previously published poems and simultaneous submissions OK. Cover letter preferred. E-mail and disk submissions OK. Send SASE for guidelines. Responds in 1 month. Pays 5 copies. Acquires first or one-time rights.

Advice: "We are a very limited market and specific to poems on the topic of Christian healing."

SHATTERED WIG REVIEW, 425 E. 31st, Baltimore MD 21218, phone (410)243-6888, website www.nor mals.com/~normals/, founded 1988, contact Sonny Bodkin.

Magazine Needs: *SWR* is a semiannual using "everything in particular. Prefer sleaking nurse stories, absurdist trickles and blasts of Rimbaud. Exploring the thin line between reality and societal hallucination." They have published poetry by Gary Blankenburg, Cynthia Hendershot and Dan Raphael. As a sample the editor selected these lines from "Answering" by John M. Bennett:

> Seems like falling over chair, rings I skull-clapped/that stoney wall he dandruffs in, dithering before's/
> slump in the socket, an (eye slucked back in)/what I doubled seeing, like "crawling over air, sinks/I"
> dreaming my lid-blink closed . . . (so the far down/dull flat seems, like's phoney) all night looking

SWR is approximately 70 pgs., 8½×8½, photocopied, side-stapled with card stock covers with original artwork, art and graphics also inside. They receive about 10 submissions a week, accept about 20%. Press run is 300 for 100 subscribers of which 10 are libraries, 100 shelf sales. Subscription: $9 (2 issues). Sample: $4.

How to Submit: Previously published poems and simultaneous submissions OK. Seldom comments on rejections. Responds within 1 month. Pays 1 copy. Acquires one-time rights. Occasionally reviews books of poetry in 100 words. Open to unsolicited reviews. Poets may also send books for review consideration. The editor says there are no requirements for contributors except "that the contributor include us in their nightly prayers."

SHEMOM (Specialized: motherhood), 2486 Montgomery Ave., Cardiff CA 92007, e-mail peggyfrench@home.com, founded 1997, editor Peggy French.

Magazine Needs: "Appearing 2-4 times a year, *Shemom* celebrates motherhood and the joys and struggles that present themselves in that journey. It includes poetry, essays, book and CD reviews, recipes, art and children's poetry. Open to any style, prefer free verse. We celebrate motherhood and related issues. Haiku and native writing also enjoyed. Love to hear from children." As a sample the editor selected these lines from her poem "The Christmas Tree":

> It sits there/beautiful/pure/inviting us to stop/for a short while and reflect/and take stock of the good
> things/that are ours/forget about the homework for a minute/the dirty dishes/unwrapped presents/and
> just savor the holiday warmth.

The editor says *Shemom* is a 10-20-page zine. They receive about 20 poems a year, accept approximately 100%. Press run is 50 for 30 subscribers. Single copy: $3; subscription: $12/4 issues. Sample: $3.50. Make checks payable to Peggy French.

How to Submit: Submit 3 poems at a time. Previously published poems and simultaneous submissions OK. E-mail submissions OK. "Prefer e-mail submission, but not required if material is to be returned, please include a SASE." Time between acceptance and publication is 2-3 months. Responds in 1 month. Pays 1 copy. Acquires one-time rights.

$⬤ SHENANDOAH; THE JAMES BOATWRIGHT III PRIZE FOR POETRY, Troubadour Theater, 2nd Floor, Washington and Lee University, Lexington VA 24450-0303, phone (540)463-8765, e-mail lleech@wlu.edu, website www.wlu.edu/~shenando, founded 1950, editor R.T. Smith.

⬛ Poetry published in *Shenandoah* has been included in the 1997 volume of *The Best American Poetry*.

Magazine Needs: Published at Washington and Lee University, it is a quarterly literary magazine. They have published poetry by Mary Oliver, Ted Kooser, W.S. Merwin and Marilyn Hacker. As a sample the editor selected "Penumbra" by Betty Adcock:

> And something as cold as winter's breath/tightens in her, as later the asthma's vise/will tighten—hands
> on the throat, the truth.

The magazine is 140 pgs., 6×9, perfect-bound, professionally printed with full-color cover. Generally, it is open to all styles and forms. Circulation is 1,900. Subscription: $22/year; $35/2 years; $45/3 years. Sample: $5.

How to Submit: All submissions should be typed on one side of the paper only. Your name and address must be clearly written on the upper right corner of the ms. Include SASE. Reads submissions September 1 through May 30 only. Responds in 3 months. Payment includes a check, 1-year subscription and 1 copy. Buys first publication rights. Staff reviews books of poetry in 7-10 pages, multi-book format. Send books for review consideration. Most reviews are solicited.

Also Offers: Sponsors The James Boatwright III Prize For Poetry. A $1,000 prize awarded annually to the author of the best poem published in *Shenandoah* during a volume year. Website includes guidelines, samples, editors and subscription form.

N ⬤ ⬤ SHIP OF FOOLS; SHIP OF FOOLS PRESS, Box 1028, University of Rio Grande, Rio Grande OH 45674-9989, phone (614)992-3333 or (614)245-5353, founded 1983, editor Jack Hart, assistant editor Catherine Grosvenor, review editor James Doubleday.

Magazine Needs: *Ship of Fools* is "more or less quarterly." They want "coherent, well-written, traditional or modern, myth, archetype, love—most types. No concrete, incoherent or greeting card poetry." They have published poetry by Rhina Espaillat, Paula Tatarunis, Simon Perchik and Lyn Lifshin. As a sample the editors selected these lines by Elva Lauter:

> Sipping green tea,/I think, "Now I am there."/I will stay until stars/Streak my eyes/and the cup is
> empty.

They describe *Ship of Fools* as digest-sized, saddle-stapled, offset printed with cover art and graphics. Press run is 217 for 47 subscribers of which 6 are libraries. Subscription: $8/4 issues. Sample: $2.

How to Submit: No previously published poems or simultaneous submissions. Cover letter preferred. Often comments on rejections. Responds in 1 month. "If longer than six weeks, write and ask why." Pays 1-2 copies. Reviews books of poetry.

Book/Chapbook Needs & How to Submit: Ship of Fools Press publishes chapbooks but does not accept unsolicited mss.

◎ SHIRIM, A JEWISH POETRY JOURNAL (Specialized: ethnic), 4611 Vesper Ave., Sherman Oaks CA 91403, phone (310)476-2861, founded 1982, editor Marc Dworkin.

Magazine Needs: *Shirim* appears biannually and publishes "poetry that reflects Jewish living without limiting to specific symbols, images or contents." They have published poetry by Robert Mezcy, Karl Shapiro and Grace Schulmon. The editor says *Shirim* is 40 pgs., 4×5, desktop-published and saddle-stapled with card stock cover. Press run is 200. Subscription: $7. Sample: $4.

How to Submit: Submit 4 poems at a time. No previously published poems or simultaneous submissions. Cover letter preferred. Seldom comments on rejections. Publishes theme issues regularly. Responds in 3 months. Acquires first rights.

⬤ ⬤ SIDEWALKS, P.O. Box 321, Champlin MN 55316, founded 1991, editor Tom Heie.

Magazine Needs: *Sidewalks* is a semiannual anthology of poetry, short prose and art, published to promote the work of emerging and published writers and artists. They want "poetry that uses strong, original images and language, showing attention to craftsmanship, but not self-conscious; poetry that shows insight. No porno, kinky sex or rhyming verse." They have published poetry by Mark Vinz, Jay Meek, Michael Dennis Browne and Kenneth Pobo. As a sample the editor selected the last stanza of "The Winter Heart" by Mary Kay Rummel:

> She searches for the bear, remembering/how she'd watched her roll down the road/on round haunches.
> She knows they both/will wake with lust some morning/will walk on the ice in shoes of fire.

Sidewalks is 76-80 pgs., 5½×8½, professionally printed and perfect-bound with matte card cover and b&w art. They receive 600-800 poems a year, accept approximately 10%. Press run is 300 for 100 subscribers, 50 shelf sales. Single copy: $6; subscription: $9. Sample: $6.

How to Submit: Submit 3-6 poems at a time, name and address on each. No previously published poems or simultaneous submissions. Cover letter preferred. Deadlines: May 31 and December 31. Three readers read and vote on submissions; then a group meets to select the best work. Seldom comments on rejections. Send SASE for guidelines. Responds 1 month after deadline. Pays 1 copy. Acquires first rights.

Advice: "Sidewalks [are] those places where a child first meets the world, [a] place of discovery, of myth, power, incantation . . . a world in itself, places we continue to meet people, ignoring some, smiling at others, preoccupied, on our way somewhere, . . . [places] where we pass with just a glance or smile or protectively turn up our collar on a windy day, . . . paths to and from neighbors, to the corner grocery . . . paths that bring us home."

✓ ◯ ◿ **SIERRA NEVADA COLLEGE REVIEW**, P.O. Box 4269, Incline Village NV 89450, founded 1990, editor June Sylvester Saraceno.
Magazine Needs: *SNCR* is an annual literary magazine published in May, featuring poetry and short fiction by new writers. "We want image-oriented poems with a distinct, genuine voice. Although we don't tend to publish 'light verse,' we do appreciate, and often publish, poems that make us laugh. We try to steer clear of sentimental, clichéd or obscure poetry. No limit on length, style, etc." They have published poetry by Carol Frith, Simon Perchik, Taylor Graham and Maximilian Werner. As a sample the editor selected these lines from "The Small Town in the Heart" by Brendan McCormack:

> Closing in/on a red bead/on the red line of a white map/and a cloud goes by on the radio./Out of the
> last curve into the straightaway/the wind leans in behind you./There is a familiar comfort in the flow./
> The smell of wet leaves and cedar/gets in through a crack in the window.

The editor says *SNCR* is approximately 75 pgs., with cover art only. "We receive approximately 500 poems a year and accept approximately 50." Press run is 500. Subscription: $5/year. Sample: $2.50.
How to Submit: Submit 5 poems at a time. No previously published poems; simultaneous submissions OK. Include brief bio. Reads submissions September 1 through April 1 only. Sometimes comments on rejections. Responds in about 3 months. Pays 2 copies.
Advice: "We're looking for poetry that shows subtlety and skill."

[N] ⊕ ◎ **SILVER GULL PUBLISHING; NYARLATHOTEP MILK; GLASSHOUSE ELECTRIC** (Specialized: form/style, horror, science fiction), West Lodge, Higher Lane, Liverpool L9 7AB United Kingdom, founded 1996, editor J. Rogerson.
Magazine Needs: "*Glasshouse Electric* is a bimonthly broadsheet of all forms of experimental poetry, as well as ads and news items. Occasional supplements. We want all types of experimental poetry on any subject. Mainstream 'nongenre' poetry is not needed." They have published poetry by Steve Sneyd, Sam Smith, Andrew Darlington and Rupert Loydell. The editor says *GE* is 2-4 pgs., photocopied. They receive about 300 poems a year, accept approximately 60%. Press run is 100-200. Single copy free for SAE/IRC.
How to Submit: Submit 3-6 "camera-ready" poems at a time. No previously published poems or simultaneous submissions. Cover letter required. "One poem per page. Please state published history. No response without suitable stamps or IRCs (U.S. dollars okay, but at risk)." Time between acceptance and publication is 1-2 months. Seldom comments on rejections. Send SASE (or SAE and IRC) for guidelines. Pays 1 copy. Acquires first British serial rights. Staff reviews chapbooks of poetry and other magazines in 20-30 words, single book format. Open to unsolicited reviews. Send books for review consideration.
Magazine Needs & How to Submit: "*Nyarlathotep Milk* annually publishes horror/science fiction poetry, fiction and reviews. We use horror/science fiction poetry in any style." The editor says *NM* is 60-100 pgs., magazine-sized, photocopied and comb or perfect-bound with paper or card cover, includes b&w graphics and ads. They accept approximately 10% of poems received a year. Press run is 70-100 for 50 subscribers; 10-15 distributed free to reviewers (rest are mail order sales). Single copy: $10 (cash—at risk); subscription: $17/2 issues (cash—at risk). *Publication by invitation only.* "Poets may send samples of previously published work and history to be considered for future invitation."
Book/Chapbook Needs & How to Submit: Silver Gull Publishing publishes 1-3 chapbooks per year by British poets. Chapbooks are usually up to 32 pgs., A5, photocopied or saddle-stapled with paper or card cover, includes b&w graphics produced in-house. "Publication of unsolicited collections is rare. Query first with cover letter and samples. Must have reasonable published history—no unpublished poets." Replies to queries in 1-2 weeks. Pays 5 author's copies (out of a press run of 50). "We design book and pay all costs. Author receive 5 free copies for every 50 printed. No poems from previous collections." Write for catalogue.
Advice: "We are only interested in very original work, no re-hashes or regurgitations."

$ ◯ ◎ **THE SILVER WEB: A MAGAZINE OF THE SURREAL** (Specialized: science fiction, horror), P.O. Box 38190, Tallahassee FL 32315, fax (850)385-4063, e-mail annk19@mail.idt.net, founded 1989, editor Ann Kennedy.
Magazine Needs: *The Silver Web* is a semiannual publication featuring fiction, poetry, art and thought-provoking articles. They want "works ranging from speculative fiction to dark tales and all weirdness in between; specifically works of the surreal. We are looking for well-written work that is unusual and original. No genre clichés, that is, no vampires, werewolves, zombies, witches, fairies, elves, dragons, etc. Also no fantasy, sword and sorcery. Poems must use standard poetic conventions whether free verse or rhyming." They have published poetry by Glenna Holloway, Simon Perchik, Tippi N. Blevins and Jacie Ragan. As a sample we selected these lines from "Empty House" by Fabian Peake:

> You walk the pavement/of my street in your/scuffed black shoes,/dragging behind you/(on lengths of
> string/tied to your belt),/a hundred paintbrushes/dancing like drumsticks . . .

The Silver Web is 90 pgs., 8½×11, offset printed, perfect-bound with full-color cover and b&w photos, art and ads. They receive 10-20 poems a week, accept 10-20 a year. Press run is 2,000 for more than 300 subscribers. Subscription: $12. Sample: $7.20, $7.95 Canada and overseas.

How to Submit: Submit up to 5 poems at a time. Previously published poems OK, but note previous credit. Simultaneous submissions also OK. E-mail for queries and information only. "Cover letters are enjoyed but not essential. Provide an SASE with proper postage to ensure a response." Reads submissions January 1 through September 30 only. "You may receive a form rejection, but I will do my best to give personal comments as time allows." Send SASE for guidelines or request via e-mail. Responds in 2 months. Always sends prepublication galleys. Pays $10-50, 2 copies and discount on additional copies. Buys first or one-time rights.

☑ ☐ ◎ **SILVER WINGS/MAYFLOWER PULPIT (Specialized: religious, spirituality/inspirational); POETRY ON WINGS, INC.**, P.O. Box 1000, Pearblossom CA 93553-1000, phone (661)264-3726, e-mail poetwing@yahoo.com, founded 1983, published by Poetry on Wings, Inc., poetry editor Jackson Wilcox.

Magazine Needs: "As a committed Christian service we produce and publish *Silver Wings/Mayflower Pulpit*, a bimonthly poetry magazine. We want poems with a Christian perspective, reflecting a vital personal faith and a love for God and man. Will consider poems from 3-20 lines. Short poems are preferred. Poems over 20 lines will not even be read by the editor. Quite open in regard to meter and rhyme." Also accepts poetry written by children. They have published poetry by Patricia G. Rourke, June Gilchrist and Dr. J.W. McMillan. As a sample the editor selected these lines from "Refuge" by Lynn M. Olson:

> A solitary pelican dives below to feed his hungry belly/A fish from the depths of the ocean satisfies
> him/momentarily./The gentle rhythmic music of the ocean/consolesme./I search for a refuge from my
> pain./In a small cave within the tide pools/starfish dance among the rocks./I found heaven

Silver Wings/Mayflower Pulpit is 16 pgs., digest-sized, offset with cartoon-like art. Each issue contains a short inspirational article or sermon plus 15-20 poems. They receive about 1,500 submissions a year, use approximately 260. Circulation is 300 with 250 subscribers, 50 shelf sales. Subscription: $10. Sample: $2.

How to Submit: Submit typed ms, double-spaced. Include SASE. No previously published poems; simultaneous submissions OK. Time between acceptance and publication can be up to 2 years. Send SASE for guidelines and upcoming themes. Responds in 3 weeks, providing SASE is supplied. Pays 1 copy. "We occasionally offer an award to a poem we consider outstanding and most closely in the spirit of what *Silver Wings* seeks to accomplish." Acquires first rights.

Also Offers: Sponsors an annual contest. For theme and details send SASE.

Advice: "We have felt that the state of secular poetry today is thrashing in a stagnant pond out of which it cannot extract itself. We want to lift our poetry to a high road where God's sunlight is shining. We even encourage poets with little ability but having an upward mobile commitment."

◖ ☑ **SILVERFISH REVIEW; SILVERFISH REVIEW PRESS; GERALD CABLE POETRY CONTEST**, P.O. Box 3541, Eugene OR 97403, phone (541)344-5060, e-mail sfrpress@aol.com, website www.qhome.com/silverfish, founded 1979, poetry editor Rodger Moody.

Magazine Needs: *Silverfish* is a biannual (June and December) literary magazine. "The only criterion for selection of poetry is quality. In future issues, *Silverfish Review* will also showcase the short short story." They have published poetry by Chelsey Minnis, Denise Duhamel, Dick Allen, Ivan Arguelles, Gary Young, Robert Gregory, Kevin Bowen, Richard Jones, Floyd Skloot and Judith Skillman. The magazine is 48 pgs., digest-sized, professionally printed in dark type on quality stock, matte card cover with art. There are 30-34 pgs. of poetry in each issue. They receive about 1,000 submissions of poetry a year, use approximately 20, have a 6- to 12-month backlog. Circulation is 500. Subscription for institutions: $12; for individuals: $8. Sample: $4, single copy orders should include $1.50 for p&h.

How to Submit: Submit at least 5 poems to editor. No simultaneous submissions. Responds in about 3 months. Pays 2 copies and 1-year subscription, plus small honorarium when grant support permits. Reviews books of poetry. Open to unsolicited reviews. Poets may also send books for review consideration.

Also Offers: Silverfish Review Press sponsors the Gerald Cable Poetry Contest. A $1,000 cash award and publication by SRP is awarded annually to the best book-length ms or original poetry by an author who has not yet published a full-length collection. No restrictions on the kind of poetry or subject matter; translations not acceptable. A $20 reading fee must accompany the ms; make checks payable to Silverfish Review Press. Send SASE for rules. Website includes contest information and information on back of books published by SRP.

☑ ◯ **SIMPLYWORDS**, 605 Collins Ave., Centerville GA 31028, phone (912)953-9482 (between 10 a.m. and 5 p.m. only), e-mail simplywords@hotmail.com or simplywords@email.com, website http://welcome.to/simplywords, founded 1991, editor Ruth Niehaus.

FOR AN EXPLANATION of symbols used in this book, see the Key to Symbols on the front and back inside covers.

Magazine Needs: *SimplyWords* is a quarterly magazine open to all types, forms and subjects. "No foul language or overtly sexual works." They have published poetry by Marian Ford Parks, Najwa Salam Brax, Sarah Jensen and James Cannon. The editor says *SWM* is 20-30 pgs., magazine-sized, deskjet printed and spiral-bound, photo on cover, uses clip art. They receive about 500 poems a year, accept approximately 90%. Press run is 60-100 depending on subscriptions and single issue orders in house." Subscription: $18.50/year. Sample: $5.
How to Submit: Send SASE for guidelines before submitting. Line length for poetry is 28 maximum. "Name, address, phone number, e-mail and line count must be on each page submitted." SASE required. Reading fee: $1/poem. Time between acceptance and publication "depends on what issue your work was accepted for."
Also Offers: Sponsors a poetry contest with small cash prize. Winning poem is showcased on cover. Also uses 10-12 short stories a year.
Advice: "It is very important that you send for guidelines before you submit to any publication. They all have rules and expect you to be professional enough to respect that. So learn the ropes—read, study, research your craft. If you want to be taken seriously prove that you are by learning your chosen craft."

N ◎ SINISTER WISDOM (Specialized: lesbian, feminist), P.O. Box 3252, Berkeley CA 94703, founded 1976, editor Margo Mercedes Rivera.
Magazine Needs: *Sinister Wisdom* is a multicultural lesbian journal. The editor says, "We want poetry that reflects the diversity of lesbian experience—lesbians of color, Third World, Jewish, old, young, working class, poor, disabled, fat, etc.—from a lesbian perspective. No heterosexual themes. We will not print anything that is oppressive or demeaning to women, or which perpetuates negative stereotypes." The journal has published work by Gloria Anzaldúa and Betsy Warland. The editor says the quarterly magazine is 128-144 pgs., digest-sized, flat-spined, with photos and b&w graphics. Circulation is 3,500 for 1,000 subscribers of which 100 are libraries; newsstand sales and bookstores are 1,500. Single copy: $6; subscription: $20 US, $25 foreign. Sample: $7.50.
How to Submit: No simultaneous submissions. Time between acceptance and publication is 6 months to 1 year. Publishes theme issues. Send SASE for upcoming themes. Responds in up to 9 months. Pays 2 copies. Reviews books of poetry in 500-1,500 words, single or multi-book format.
Advice: "Send anything *other* than love poetry and want work by lesbians only."

◉ SITUATION, 10402 Ewell Ave., Kensington MD 20895, founded 1991, contact Mark Wallace and Joanne Molina.
Magazine Needs: *Situation* appears several times/year and is interested in "innovative work that explores how writing creates, dismantles, or restructures the possibility of identity. A poetry of situation. Works involving questions of race, class, gender or sexual preference are all encouraged." They want experimental or avant-garde poetry; "less likely to accept poetry in traditional forms." They have published poetry by Charles Bernstein, Sterling Plumpp, Joan Retallack and Stephen-Paul Martin. As a sample we selected these lines from "Arlem" by Renee Gladman:

> having decided on neither *extreme* because she is always/already in the middle I sat through
> intermission tapping my/foot to its duration. You ask me why I mourn the leaving/before you have left
> as if any answer would bring us closer/to the problem of poetry.

Situation is 24 pgs., $7 \times 8\frac{1}{2}$, neatly printed on bond paper, saddle-stapled, no cover. They receive about 200 submissions a year, accept approximately 15%. Press run is 200 for 100 subscribers of which 5 are libraries. Subscription: $10. Sample: $3. Make checks payable to Mark Wallace.
How to Submit: Submit 7 poems at a time. No previously published poems. Cover letter required. "All submissions must be accompanied by SASE." Time between acceptance and publication is usually 6 months. Seldom comments on rejections. Send SASE for guidelines or request via e-mail. Responds in 3 months. Sometimes sends prepublication galleys. Pays 2 copies. Acquires first rights.

🌐 ◖ SKALD, 2 Greenfield Terrace, Menai Bridge, Anglesey LL59 5AY Wales, United Kingdom, phone 1248-716343, founded 1994, contact Ms. Zoë Skoulding.
Magazine Needs: *Skald* appears approximately 3 times a year and contains "poetry and prose in Welsh or English. We focus on writers in Wales though submissions from elsewhere are welcome." They want "interesting and varied poetry in Welsh and English. Nothing didactic, sentimental or nostalgic." As a sample Ms. Skoulding selected these lines from "Life Story" by Malcolm Bradley:

> Unexplored eccentric swelling/fills my lunar skull./An atrocity of emptiness/leaves each glib cell/to
> the slow abstract/click of extinction.

Skald is 30-40 pgs., A5, professionally printed and saddle-stapled with textured card cover, contains b&w artwork. They receive about 300 poems a year, accept approximately 25%. Press run is 300 for 20 subscribers, 250 shelf sales; 20 distributed free to other magazines, art boards. Single copy: £3; subscription: £8/year (payments in sterling only).
How to Submit: Submit 2 poems at a time. No previously published poems or simultaneous submissions. Cover letter preferred. Time between acceptance and publication is 4 months. Often comments on rejections. Responds in 1 month. Pays 1 copy.

N ◖ SKIDROW PENTHOUSE, 44 Four Corners Rd., Blairstown NJ 07825, phone (908)362-6808 or (212)286-2600, founded 1998, editor Rob Cook, editor Stephanie Dickinson.

Magazine Needs: *Skidrow Penthouse* is published "to give emerging and idiosyncratic writers a new forum in which to publish their work. We are looking for deeply felt authentic voices, whether surreal, confessional, New York School, formal, or free verse. Work should be well crafted: attention to line-break and diction. We want poets who sound like themselves, not workshop professionals. We don't want gutless posturing, technical precision with no subject matter, explicit sex and violence without craft, or abstract intellectualizing. We are not impressed by previous awards and publications." They have published poetry by Walter Griffin, Gil Fagiani, Mary. Hebert, Anna Adams, Patrick McKinnon and Doug Dorph. As a sample the editor selected these lines from "The Hump" by Marc DePalo:

> To sit in a room and think about the walls, meditate on/the angles and the paint and the imperfections that/you'd never notice unless you had this much time/and this much patience and this much desperation/for a frigging epiphany even if it was just a paint crack or/a traffic light or a burned out bulb or a sudden crocus.

SP is 166 pgs., 5½×8½, professionally printed and perfect-bound with 2-color cover, includes original art and photographs as well as contest announcements, magazine advertisements. They receive about 500 poems a year, accept approximately 3%. Publish 35-40 poems/issue. Press run is 300 for 50 subscribers; 10% distributed free to journals for review consideration. Single copy: $10; subscription: $20. Sample (including guidelines): $7. Make checks payable to Rob Cook or Stephanie Dickinson.

How to Submit: Submit 3-5 poems at a time. Previously published poems and simultaneous submissions OK. "Include a legal sized SASE; also name and address on every page of your submission. No handwritten submissions will be considered." Time between acceptance and publication is 1 year. Seldom comments on rejections. Responds in 2 months. Pays 1 copy. Acquires one-time rights. Reviews books and chapbooks of poetry and other magazines in 1,500 words, single book format. Open to unsolicited reviews. Poets may also send books for review consideration.

Also Offers: "We're trying to showcase a poet in each issue by publishing up to 60 page collections within the magazine." Send SASE for details about chapbook competitions.

SKIPPING STONES: A MULTICULTURAL CHILDREN'S MAGAZINE; ANNUAL YOUTH HONOR AWARDS (Specialized: bilingual, children/teen, ethnic/nationality, nature/ecology, social issues), P.O. Box 3939, Eugene OR 97403, phone (541)342-4956, e-mail skipping@efn.org, website www.nonviolence.org/skipping/, founded 1988, editor Arun Toké.

Magazine Needs: *Skipping Stones* is a "nonprofit magazine published bimonthly during the school year (5 issues) that encourages cooperation, creativity and celebration of cultural and environmental richness." They want poetry by youth under 18; 30 lines maximum on "nature, multicultural and social issues, family, freedom . . . uplifting." No work by adults. As a sample we selected these lines from "The Sound and Rhythm of the Drum" by Alexander Harvey, age 10, from Washington, DC:

> The rhythm is as natural as laying eggs is to a chicken/My great ancestors of the past, all heard the rhythm of the drum./It's sounds are as beautiful/As a pack of wild horses running on the great plains.// Our ancestors have struggled to grow./When our ancestors spirits are low and bum/It lifts us up far into the sun./That's the rhythm and sound, of the drum.

SS is 8½×11, saddle-stitched, printed on recycled paper. They receive about 500-1,000 poems a year, accept approximately 10%. Press run is 3,000 for 1,700 subscribers. Subscription: $25. Sample: $5.

How to Submit: Submit up to 3 poems at a time. No previously published poems; simultaneous submissions OK. Cover letter preferred. "Include your cultural background, experiences and what was the inspiration behind your creation." Time between acceptance and publication is 3-9 months. Poems are circulated to a 3-member editorial board. "Generally a piece is chosen for publication when all the editorial staff feel good about it." Seldom comments on rejections. Publishes theme issues. Send SASE for guidelines and upcoming themes. Responds in up to 4 months. Pays 1 copy, offers 25% discount for more. Acquires all rights. Returns rights after publication, but "we keep reprint rights."

Also Offers: Sponsors Annual Youth Honor Awards for 7-17 year olds. Theme for Annual Youth Honor Awards is "Multicultural and Nature Awareness." Deadline: June 20. Entry fee: $3, includes free issue containing the winners. Send SASE for details.

SKYLARK (Specialized: themes), Purdue University Calumet, 2200 169th St., Hammond IN 46323, phone (219)989-2262, fax (219)989-2165, founded 1972, editor-in-chief Pamela Hunter, poetry editor Cathy Michniewicz.

Magazine Needs: *Skylark* is "a fine arts annual, one section (about 25 pages) of which is devoted to a special theme." *Skylark* publishes short stories, poetry, short essays, translations, illustrations and photographs. They are looking for "fresh voices, original images, concise presentation and honesty; poems up to 30 lines. No horror, nothing extremely religious, no pornography." They are also interested in receiving more prose poems and more well-crafted surrealistic poems. Also accepts poetry written by children, ages 5-18. They have published poetry by liony batista, Joanne M. Clarkson, Sandra Fowler, Matthew Thorburn and Charles B. Tinkham. As a sample the editor selected these lines from "Something" by Rich Mitchell:

> [Something] in the down of early snow/sweeps the dark and distant pines,/gathers on weary stone fences/silent and sable,/settles like fog.

Published in December, *Skylark* is 100 pgs., magazine-sized, professionally printed, perfect-bound, with four-color cover and numerous color illustrations inside the magazine. Publish 6 poems/issue. Press run is 900-1,000 for 50 subscribers of which 12 are libraries. Single copy: $8. Sample (back issues): $6.

How to Submit: Submit up to 6 poems at a time. "Cover letter encouraged. No previously published poems or simultaneous submissions. Inquire (with SASE) as to annual theme for special section." Fax submissions OK followed by SASE within 2 weeks. The theme for 2001 is "Education." Send SASE for themes and guidelines. Mss are read between October 15 and April 30. Responds in 3 months. Pays 1 copy/published poem. Acquires first rights. Editor may encourage rejected but promising writers.

Advice: "Send poems with greater coordination of form and content, sharper, more original imagery and a carefully-edited text."

SLANT: A JOURNAL OF POETRY, Box 5063, University of Central Arkansas, 201 Donaghey Ave., Conway AR 72035-5000, phone (501)450-5107, website www.uca.edu/english/Slant/HOMPAGE.html, founded 1987, editor James Fowler.

Magazine Needs: *Slant* is an annual using *only* poetry. They use "traditional and 'modern' poetry, even experimental, moderate length, any subject on approval of Board of Readers; purpose is to publish a journal of fine poetry from all regions of the United States and beyond. No haiku, no translations." Also accepts poetry written by children ("although we're not a children's journal.") They have published poetry by D.C. Berry and Susan Terris. As a sample the editor selected these lines from "Dream of the Face-Lift" by Lucille Lang Day:

> *My vanity is tall as a redwood,/loyal as a snow goose, so I get/a new face in time for the party./*
> *Carefully painting lips and eyelids,/I fear Eleanor Roosevelt./I would be seventeen.*

Slant is 125 pgs., professionally printed on quality stock, flat-spined, with matte card cover. They receive about 1,500 poems a year, accept approximately 70-80. Press run is 200 for 70-100 subscribers. Sample: $10.

How to Submit: Submit up to 5 poems of moderate length with SASE between September and mid-November. "Put name, address (including e-mail if available) and phone on the top of each page." No simultaneous submissions or previously published poems. Editor comments on rejections "on occasion." Allow 3-4 months from November 15 deadline for response. Pays 1 copy.

Also Offers: Website includes guidelines, editor/board of readers, table of contents from 1999 volume and index 1987-1996.

Advice: "I would like to see more formal verse."

SLATE & STYLE (Specialized: blind writers), Dept. PM, 2704 Beach Dr., Merrick NY 11566, phone (516)868-8718, fax (516)868-9076, e-mail LoriStay@aol.com, editor Loraine Stayer.

Magazine Needs: *Slate & Style* is a quarterly for blind writers available on cassette, in large print, Braille and e-mail, "including articles of interest to blind writers, resources for blind writers. Membership/subscription is $10 per year, all formats. Division of the National Federation of the Blind." Poems may be "5-36 lines. Prefer contributors to be blind writers, or at least writers by profession or inclination, but prefer poems not about blindness. No obscenities. Will consider all forms of poetry including haiku. Interested in new talent." They have published poetry by Stephanie Pieck, Louise Hope Bristow, Janet Wolff and Ken Volonte. As a sample the editor selected these lines from "To Matthew" by M.J. Lord:

> *I feel your hand reach out to me./A velvety soft palm and tiny fingers/reach through my skin,/grab my*
> *hand with an amazing strength./Your father lies beside me,/as he dreams of your premature birth.*

The print version is 28-32 pgs., magazine-sized, stapled, with a fiction and poetry section. Press run is 200 for 160 subscribers of which 4-5 are libraries. Subscription: $10/year. Sample: $2.50.

How to Submit: Submit 3 poems once or twice a year. No simultaneous submissions or previously published poems. Cover letter preferred. "On occasion we receive poems in Braille. I prefer print, since Braille slows me down. Typed is best." Fax submissions OK. Do not submit mss in July. Editor comments on rejections "if requested." Send SASE for guidelines. Responds in "two weeks if I like it." Pays 1 copy. Reviews books of poetry. Open to unsolicited reviews. Poets may also send books for review consideration.

Also Offers: They offer an annual poetry contest. Entry fee: $5/poem. Deadline: May 1. Write for details.

Advice: "Poetry is one of the toughest ways to express oneself, yet ought to be the easiest to read. Anything that looks simple is the result of much work."

SLIDE, 413 Brenda Dr., Wilmington NC 28409, phone/fax (910)395-4564, e-mail slide2000@usa.net, founded 1999, editor-in-chief Aimee Lind, managing editor Jess Waters.

Magazine Needs: *Slide* is published "to bring forward good art to our subscribers in a fashion that ensures a wide range of provocative original voices in each issue. *Slide* is looking for poems that illuminate something about ourselves, or how we live; art which keeps us buoyant in the mass culture. No erudite, cryptic, self-loathing, or otherwise insular poetry." The editor says *Slide* is 75 pgs., 6×9, perfect-bound with 80 lb. preset color cover. Press run is 3,000, 1,000 shelf sales; 2,000 distributed free to Wilmington area residents. Subscription: $11. Sample: $5.

How to Submit: Submit 3-5 poems at a time. No previously published poems; simultaneous submissions OK. E-mail and disk submissions OK. Cover letter preferred. "Disk and e-mail submissions must be in ASCII or Word Perfect format. Please include SASE with proper postage or IRC coupons." Reads submissions September 1 through May 31 only. Time between acceptance and publication is 1 year. Poems are circulated to an editorial board. Seldom comments on rejections. Publishes theme issues occasionally. Send SASE for guidelines and upcoming themes or obtain via e-mail. Responds in 4 months. Pays 5 copies. Acquires all rights. Returns rights upon publication. Reviews books of poetry in 500 words, single book format. Open to unsolicited reviews. Poets may also send books for review consideration.

Also Offers: "*Slide* occasionally publishes chapbooks, novels, novellas, plays, juried art shows, etc. in installment series. Artists should be aware of their eligibility to submit large pieces in confidence."

Advice: "Don't listen to anyone, send what is closest to your heart and mind."

☑ ◐ ◎ SLIPSTREAM (Specialized: themes), Box 2071, New Market Station, Niagara Falls NY 14301-0071, phone (716)282-2616 (after 5PM, EST), e-mail editors@slipstreampress.org, website www.slipstreampress.org, founded 1980, poetry editors Dan Sicoli, Robert Borgatti and Livio Farallo.

Magazine Needs: *Slipstream* is a "small press literary mag published in the spring and is about 90% poetry and 10% fiction/prose, with some artwork. The editors like new work with contemporary urban flavor. Writing must have a cutting edge to get our attention. We like to keep an open forum, any length, subject, style. Best to see a sample to get a feel. Like city stuff as opposed to country. Like poetry that springs from the gut, screams from dark alleys, inspired by experience." No "pastoral, religious, traditional, rhyming" poetry. They have published poetry by M. Scott Douglass, Lyn Lifshin, Douglas Goetsch, Gerald Locklin, Charles Bukowski, Jim Daniels, Gailmarie Pahmeier and Chrys Darkwater. As a sample the editors selected these lines from "Eunice and the Man Next Door" by Alison Pelegrin:

> *Just to see him work, she cut onions all day./By the time he took off his shirt/and hung it from the chain link fence,/she could have cried into the sink,/into the batch of gumbo she'd fixed.*

Slipstream appears 1-2 times a year in a 7 × 8½ format, 80-100 pgs., professionally printed, perfect-bound, using b&w photos and graphics. It contains mostly free verse, some stanza patterns. They receive over 2,500 submissions of poetry a year, use less than 10%. Press run is 500 for 400 subscribers of which 10 are libraries. Subscription: $15/2 issues and 2 chapbooks. Sample: $6.

How to Submit: Editor sometimes comments on rejections. Publishes theme issues. Send SASE for guidelines and upcoming themes. "Reading for a general issue through 2000." Responds in up to 2 months, "if SASE included." Pays 1-2 copies.

Also Offers: Annual chapbook contest has December 1 deadline. Reading fee: $10. Submit up to 40 pgs. of poetry, any style, previously published work OK with acknowledgments. Winner receives $1,000 and 50 copies. All entrants receive copy of winning chapbook and an issue of the magazine. Past winners have included David Chorlton, Sherman Alexie, Katharine Harer, Robert Cooperman, Leslie Anne Mcilroy, Serena Fusek, Rene Christopher and most recently Alison Pelegrin for "Dancing with the One-Armed Man." Website includes guidelines, announcements, samples of poetry, annual poetry chapbook winner, chapbook competition guidelines, audio/video information, back issues and order form.

Advice: "Do not waste time submitting your work 'blindly.' Sample issues from the small press first to determine which ones would be most receptive to your work."

☑ ◐ SMALL POND MAGAZINE OF LITERATURE, P.O. Box 664, Stratford CT 06615, phone (203)378-4066, founded 1964, editor Napoleon St. Cyr.

Magazine Needs: *SPML* is a literary triquarterly that features poetry . . . "and anything else the editor feels is interesting, original, important." Poetry can be "any style, form, topic, except haiku, so long as it is deemed good, but limit of about 100 lines." Napoleon St. Cyr wants "nothing about cats, pets, flowers, butterflies, etc. Generally nothing under eight lines." The magazine is 40 pgs., digest-sized, offset from typescript on off-white paper, with colored matte card cover, saddle-stapled, artwork both on cover and inside. Circulation is 300, of which about a third go to libraries. Subscription: $10/3 issues. Sample (including guidelines): $3 for a random selection, $4 current. "Free random back issue but send 77¢ postage; same quality, famous editor's comments."

How to Submit: The editor says he doesn't want 60 pages of anything; "dozen pages of poems max." Name and address on each page. No previously published poems or simultaneous submissions. Brief cover letter preferred. Time between acceptance and publication is within 3-15 months. Responds in up to 30 days. Pays 2 copies. Acquires all rights. Returns rights with written request including stated use. "One-time use per request." All styles and forms are welcome here. The editor usually responds quickly, often with comments to guide poets whose work interests him.

Ⓝ ◐ SMARTISH PACE, P.O. Box 22161, Baltimore MD 21203, website http://c5.tzo.com/smartish_pace, founded 1999 by editor Stephen Reichert.

Magazine Needs: Containing only poetry, *smartish pace* is published in the spring and fall. They have no restrictions on style or content of poetry. They have published poetry by Richard Jones, Stephen Sandy, Burton Raffel, Barry Spacks, Diane Thiel and Clarinda Harriss. As a sample the editor selected the opening lines of "How By Design" by Stephen Dunn:

> *I fingered the glassware, sat down alone/in a blue love seat,/consumer brain switched on, soul elsewhere like wind//that suddenly had enough of being where I was./Needing something,/I had left the incompleteness of my living room,//easy power of MasterCard in my wallet,/looking forward/to the carelessness of scrawling my name//because my name was clear, raised up, perfect.*

SP is about 80 pgs., 6×9, professionally printed and perfect-bound with color, heavy stock cover, original artwork appears on the cover of each issue. They receive about 1,500 poems a year, accept approximately 7%. Publish 50-60 poems/issue. Press run is 500 for 150 subscribers. Subscription: $12. Sample: $6.

How to Submit: Submit no more than 6 poems at a time. No previously published poems; simultaneous submissions OK. "Please provide prompt notice when poems have been accepted elsewhere. Cover letter with bio and SASE is required. Electronic submissions are encouraged and can be made at website." Submission deadlines: June 1 for fall issue, December 1 for spring issue. Submit seasonal poems 6 months in advance. Time between acceptance and publication is 3-12 months. Poems are circulated to an editorial board. "All poems are initially screened by editor Stephen Reichert and senior editor Daniel J. Todd. Promising poems are then considered by a four member editorial board." Send SASE for guidelines or obtain via website. Responds within 6 months. Pays 1 copy. Acquires first rights.

Also Offers: Website includes guidelines, editors and staff information, links to the editors' e-mails, link to submit poetry to *smartish pace*, previously published poets, poetry, back issues and ordering information.

GIBBS SMITH, PUBLISHER; PEREGRINE SMITH POETRY COMPETITION, P.O. Box 667, Layton UT 84041-0667, founded 1971, poetry series established 1988, poetry editor Gail Yngve.

Book/Chapbook Needs: They want "serious, contemporary poetry of merit." They have published *Perfect Hell* by H.L. Hix and *1-800-HOT-RIBS* and *Rock Farm* by Catherine Bowman. Books are selected for publication through competition for the Peregrine Smith Poetry Prize of $500 plus publication.

How to Submit: Entries are received in April only and require a $15 reading fee and SASE. Mss should be 48-64 typewritten pgs. "We publish only one unsolicited poetry ms per year—the winner of our annual Peregrine Smith Poetry Contest. For guidelines to the contest, interested poets should send a request with SASE through the mail." The winner of the 1999 contest was Peter Sears's *The Brink*. The judge for the series was Christopher Merrill.

SMITHS KNOLL, 49 Church Rd., Little Glemham, Woodbridge, Suffolk IP13 0BJ England, founded 1991, co-editors Roy Blackman and Smith Knoll.

Magazine Needs: *Smiths Knoll* is a magazine appearing 3 times/year. They look for poetry with honesty, depth of feeling, lucidity and craft. As a sample the editors selected these lines from "Cut Lip" by John Lynch:

> *The way she held out her hand/As if to say Daddy, what's this?//I hushed her, wiped her tears,/It's only*
> *blood I said//Later, on the motorway,/streams of tail-lights pouring red.*

Smiths Knoll is 60 pgs., A5, offset-litho, perfect-bound, with 2-color card cover. They receive 6,000-8,000 poems a year, "accept about one in forty." Press run is 500 for 350 subscribers. Single copy: £4.50; subscription: £12/3 issues (outside UK).

How to Submit: Submit up to 5 poems at a time to the co-editors. "We would consider poems previously published in magazines outside the U.K." No simultaneous submissions. Poems only. Doesn't commission work. "Cover letters should be brief: name, address, date, number of poems sent (or titles). We don't want life histories or complete publishing successes or what the poems are about. We do want sufficient IRCs for return of work. Constructive criticism of rejections where possible." Tries to respond within 1 month (outside UK). Pays £5 plus 1 copy/poem.

SNAPSHOTS; SNAPSHOT PRESS; TANGLED HAIR; SNAPSHOTS COLLECTION COMPETITION (Specialized: form/style), P.O. Box 35, Sefton Park, Liverpool L17 3EG United Kingdom, e-mail jb@snapshotpress.freeserve.co.uk, website www.mccoy.co.uk/snapshots, founded 1998, editor John Barlow.

Magazine Needs: Snapshots Press publishes two quarterly journals, *Snapshots* and *Tangled Hair*. *Snapshots* is published 3-4 times a year and *Tangled Hair* 2-3 times a year. *Snapshots* features high quality haiku and senryu by both new and internationally established haiku poets, each often being represented by a body of work. It also contains brief biographies on its contributors, and there is an award for the best poem in each issue, as voted for by subscribers. *Tangled Hair* is the first journal published in the UK to be devoted exclusively to tanka. Poems are printed one to a page for maximum effect. It also contains brief biographies on its contributors, and there is an award for the best poem in each issue, as voted for by subscribers." *Snapshots* has published poetry by Randy M. Brooks, Tom Clausen, A.C. Missias and Michael Dylan Welch. *Tangled Hair* has published poetry by Sanford Goldstein, Laura Maffei and Jane Reichhold. As a sample of work published in *Snapshots*, the editor selected this haiku by David Steele:

> *long weekend alone/the click of buttons/in the wash cycle.*

As a sample of work published in *Tangled Hair*, the editor selected this tanka by John Barlow:

> *hours/before daybreak—/the gap/between us/our bodies cannot warm*

The editor says *Snapshots* is 48-56 pgs., 4×6, professionally printed and perfect-bound with glossy card cover featuring a full-color photograph. *Tangled Hair*'s format is similar except it contains 64 pgs. and is 4×4. *Snapshots* receives about 5,000 poems a year (1,500 for *TH*), accept approximately 8% for each. Press run for both journals is 200. Subscription: $34. Sample of each publication: $10. Make checks payable to Snapshot Press. ("Checks accepted. U.S. banknotes preferred.")

How to Submit: For *Snapshots*, submit up to 20 haiku/senryu; for *Tangled Hair*, submit up to 12 tanka at a time. No previously published poems or simultaneous submissions. E-mail submissions OK. Cover letter required.

Submissions must be accompanied by a SAE and 2 IRCs. Time between acceptance and publication is up to 4 months. Sometimes comments on submissions. Send SAE and IRC for guidelines. Responds in 2 months. Always sends prepublication galleys. No payment. Acquires first rights.

Book/Chapbook Needs & How to Submit: Snapshot Press publishes 2-3 paperbacks and 4-8 chapbooks per year. Chapbooks are 32-40 pgs., 4×6, professionally printed, saddle-stitched with full-color glossy card covers. Order sample books by sending $9, or SAE and IRC for further details/order forms. One paperback and 4 chapbooks are selected biannually through the *Snapshots* Collection Competition. "No unsolicited manuscripts other than entries to *Snapshots* Collection Competition. All other material for anthologies and collections is solicited."

Also Offers: Sponsors two competitions: The *Snapshots* Collection Competition, for unpublished collections of haiku, senryu and tanka, held biennially. 1st Prize: $250 and publication of collection as a perfect-bound book; four runners-up: publication of collection as a full-color chapbook. The Haiku Calendar Competition is held annually (closing date July 31). Prize money: $500. Send SAE and IRC for rules/entry forms. Website includes information on Snapshot Press publications, articles, reviews, sample poems, submissions and subscription guidelines.

🌺 $⊘ SNOWAPPLE PRESS, P.O. Box 66024, Heritage Postal Outlet, Edmonton, Alberta T6J 6T4 Canada, founded 1991, editor Vanna Tessier.

Book/Chapbook Needs: Snowapple Press is an "independent publisher dedicated to writers who wish to contribute to literature." They publish 4-5 paperbacks/year. They want "contemporary, expansive, experimental and literary poetry." They have published poetry by Gilberto Finzi, Peter Prest, Vanna Tessier, Bob Stallworthy and Paolo Valesio. Books are usually 120-160 pgs., offset printed with #10 colored card cover with "art/graphics suitable to theme."

How to Submit: Submit 5 poems at a time, 14-75 lines each. Previously published poems and simultaneous submissions OK. Cover letter preferred. Reads submissions September through March 31 only. Time between acceptance and publication is 12-18 months. Poems are circulated to an editorial board. Replies in 3-4 weeks. Pays 10% royalty, $100 honorarium and 25 author's copies (out of a press run of 500).

Also Offers: Sponsors an occasional anthology contest. Send SASE (or SAE and IRC) with all correspondence. "Queries welcome for 10th anniversary 2001 Celebration Anthology."

✅ $⊘ ◎ SNOWY EGRET (Specialized: nature), P.O. Box 9, Bowling Green IN 47833, founded 1922 by Humphrey A. Olsen, contact editors.

Magazine Needs: They want poetry that is "nature-oriented: poetry that celebrates the abundance and beauty of nature or explores the interconnections between nature and the human psyche." As a sample they selected the middle and final lines of "Night Song" by Conrad Hilberry:

> All creatures/sleep,/except the fish./. . . all night long,/barracuda weave and angle/through the weeds,/ bluefins rise, flash/in the broken moonlight,/and dive again./Sharks graze old wrecks,/and marlins/ slice the dark.

Snowy Egret appears twice a year in a 60-page, magazine-sized format, offset, saddle-stapled, with original graphics. They receive about 500 poems a year, accept approximately 30. Press run is 800 for 500 subscribers of which 50 are libraries. Sample: $8; subscription: $12/year, $20/2 years.

How to Submit: Send #10 SASE for writer's guidelines. Responds in 1 month. Always sends prepublication galleys. Pays $4/poem or $4/page plus 2 copies. Buys first North American and one-time reprint rights. Open to unsolicited reviews. Poets may also send books for review consideration.

✅ ⊘ ◎ SO TO SPEAK: A FEMINIST JOURNAL OF LANGUAGE AND ART (Specialized: women/feminism), George Mason University, 4400 University Dr., MS 2D6, Fairfax VA 22030-4444, phone (703)993-3625, e-mail sts@gmu.edu, founded 1991, poetry editor Kaia Sand.

Magazine Needs: *So to Speak* is published 2 times a year. "We publish high-quality work about women's lives—fiction, nonfiction (including book reviews and interviews), b&w photography and artwork along with poetry. We look for poetry that deals with women's lives, but also lives up to a high standard of language, form and meaning. We are most interested in more experimental, high-quality work by new poets. There are no formal specifications. We like work that takes risks successfully. No unfinished/unpolished work." They have published poetry by Heather Fuller, Carolyn Forché, Allison Joseph, Allison Cobb, Gwyn McVay and Lyn Lifshin. As a sample they selected these lines from "Sister Cell" by Allison Cobb:

> close/vanish appear/kin knees sis/my toes is/divided half whole/live split to/cry sister/the pull

So To Speak is 120 pgs., digest-sized, photo-offset printed and perfect-bound, with glossy cover, includes b&w photos and art, ads. They receive about 300 poems a year, accept approximately 10%. Press run is 1,300 for 350 subscribers, 50 shelf sales; 500 distributed free to students/submitters. Subscription: $10. Sample: $5.

How to Submit: Submit 3-5 poems at a time. No previously published poems; simultaneous submissions OK. Cover letter preferred. Disk submissions OK. "Please submit poems as you wish to see them in print. We do have an e-mail address but do not accept e-mail submissions. Be sure to include a cover letter with contact info, publications credits, and awards received." Reads submissions all year, "but August 15 through November 1 and December 31 through April 15 are best." Time between acceptance and publication is 6-8 months. Seldom comments on rejections. Publishes theme issues occasionally. Send SASE for guidelines and upcoming themes.

Responds in up to 8 months. Pays 2 copies. Acquires one-time rights. Reviews books and chapbooks of poetry and other magazines in 750 words, single book format. Open to unsolicited reviews. Poets may also send books for review consideration.

Also Offers: *So to Speak* runs an annual poetry contest. Website includes submission guidelines, any upcoming contest info, contact info, links and samples/excerpts from journal. "Our 1999 judge was Lyn Lifshin."

Advice: "We are looking for poetry that, through interesting use of language, locates experiences of women."

$ ☐ ◯ ◢ ◎ THE SOCIETY OF AMERICAN POETS (SOAP); IN HIS STEPS PUBLISHING COMPANY; THE POET'S PEN; PRESIDENT'S AWARD FOR SUPERIOR CHOICE (Specialized: religious), P.O. Box 3563, Macon GA 31205-3563, phone (912)788-1848, e-mail DrRev@msn.com, founded 1984, editor Dr. Charles E. Cravey.

Magazine Needs: *The Poet's Pen* is a literary quarterly of poetry and short stories. "Open to all styles of poetry and prose—both religious and secular. No gross or 'X-rated' poetry without taste or character." Also accepts poetry written by children. They have published poetry by Henry Gurley, Kelly Martin, Mary Patton and Charles E. Cravey. As a sample the editor selected these lines from "Praise Song" by Norma Woodbridge:

> The mountains rise in harmony, as they press against the sky./The jet blue lake, serene and still, the
> forests sing nearby.//The snows send anthems in the air, they greet a new day's morn;/And deer run
> wild in freedom's path, the trilliums are born.//How great the wonder of our God, His majesty to sing;/
> The praises to His wondrous love, the gifts of joy to bring!

The Poet's Pen uses poetry primarily by members and subscribers, but outside submissions are also welcomed. Sample copy: $15. (Membership: $25/year.)

How to Submit: Submit 3 poems at a time, include name and address on each page. "Submissions or inquiries will not be responded to without a #10 business-sized SASE. We do stress originality and have each new poet and/or subscriber sign a waiver form verifying originality." Simultaneous submissions OK; previously published poems OK, if permission from previous publisher is included. Publishes seasonal/theme issues. Send SASE for upcoming themes or obtain via e-mail. Sometimes sends prepublication galleys. Editor "most certainly" comments on rejections.

Book/Chapbook Needs & How to Submit: In His Steps publishes religious and other books and publishes music for the commercial record market. Query for book publication.

Also Offers: Sponsors several contests each quarter which total $100-250 in cash awards. Editor's Choice Awards each quarter. President's Award for Superior Choice has a prize of $50; deadline is November 1. They also publish a quarterly anthology that has poetry competitions in several categories with prizes of $25-100.

Advice: "We're looking for poets who wish to unite in fellowship with our growing family of poets nationwide. We currently have over 850 poets and are one of the nation's largest societies, yet small enough and family operated to give each of our poets individual attention and pointers."

$ ◖ SOFT SKULL PRESS, INC., 98 Suffolk #3A, New York NY 10002, website www.softskull.com, founded 1992, editor Sander Hicks.

Book/Chapbook Needs: Soft Skull Press, Inc. "likes books that reinvent genre, like the poetic/political memoir of socialist poet Sparrow's 'Republican Like Me: A Diary of My Presidential Campaign.'" They publish 10 paperbacks and 2 hardbacks/year. They want poetry that is "angry, politically sharpened by struggle, honest, hard-working, post punk/hip hop-influenced beauty. No post-modern, ultra-subjective, bourgeois work." They have published poetry by Cynthia Nelson, John S. Hall, Tracie Morris and Sparrow. As a sample the editor selected these lines from a poem by Todd Colby:

> Ask the children/which member of their family/they would be willing to sacrifice for hot pig.

Books are usually 120 pgs., offset printed and perfect-bound, uses art.

How to Submit: Query first with 10-20 sample poems, cover letter, brief bio, publication credits and SASE. Don't query by e-mail! Previously published poems and simultaneous submissions OK. Time between acceptance and publication is 1 year. Poems are circulated to an editorial board. "Interns, volunteers, shareholders and comrades of press are on Editorial Board." Seldom comments on rejections. "If we like it but can't publish it, we'll say so." Replies to queries in 1 month; to mss in 6 months. Pays royalties of 6-8% plus advance of $10-100 and 25 author's copies (out of a press run of 1,500). Additional copies sold to author at 55% discount. Order sample books via website. See website for latest submission guidelines.

$ ◎ SOJOURNERS (Specialized: religious, political), 2401 15th St. NW, Washington DC 20009, phone (202)328-8842, fax (202)328-8757, website www.sojourners.com, founded 1975, poetry editor Rose Berger.

▨ The poetry section of *Sojourners* has received awards from the Associated Church Press and Evangelical Press Association.

Magazine Needs: *Sojourners* appears 6 times/year, "with approximately 40,000 subscribers. We focus on faith, politics and culture from a radical Christian perspective. We publish one or two poems/month depending on length. All poems must be original and unpublished. We look for seasoned, well-crafted poetry that reflects the issues and perspectives covered in our magazine. We highly discourage simplistic, rhyming poetry. Poetry using non-inclusive language (any racist, sexist, homophobic poetry) will not be accepted." *Sojourners* is about 70 pgs., magazine-sized, offset printed and saddle-stapled with 4-color paper cover, includes photos and illustrations throughout. They receive about 400 poems a year, accept approximately 6-8. Press run is 50,000 for 40,000 subscribers of which 500 are libraries, 2,000 shelf sales. Single copy: $4; subscription: $30. Sample: free.

How to Submit: Submit up to 3 poems at a time. Line length for poetry is 50 maximum. Cover letter with brief (3 sentences) bio required. Editor occasionally comments on submissions. Responds in up to 6 weeks. Pays $25/poem plus 5 copies. "We assume permission to grant reprints unless the author requests otherwise."

○ ◑ **SOMNILOQUY; SOMNILOQUY . . . ONLINE**, P.O. Box 720862, Orlando FL 32872-0862, phone (407)273-4942, e-mail editor@somniloquy.com, website www.somniloquy.com, founded 1996, managing editor Tracey Hessler.

Magazine Needs: *Somniloquy* is a "quarterly multi-genre journal which strives to published the best in prose and poetry." They want any style or format of poetry, 2 pages/poem maximum. No pornography or sexually explicit language. They have published poetry by Dave Taub, Kt. Frankovich and Liz Larraby. As a sample the editor selected these lines from "Child at a Grave" by Dave Taub:

> Knees bent to grasses and dust (to dust)/These solemn hours . . ./Deep to the eyes of youth./Searching
> for still younger days/shared from the womb/The breeze passing through the oaks and ashes (to ashes)/
> Here lies memories of a child's mind:/Yellow frock, fading sun/and crocuses around a small wooden
> cross/Naive enough to know only heaven.

Somniloquy is 52 pgs., 7×8½, desktop-published and side-stapled and taped with coated paper cover, uses computer-generated graphics. They receive about 500 poems a year, accept approximately 25%. Press run is 150 for 78 subscribers, 18 shelf sales. Single copy: $5; subscription: $16.97/year (4 issues). Sample (including guidelines): $6.26 (US). Make checks payable to T. Hessler RTWG.

How to Submit: Submit up to 3 poems at a time. Line length for poetry is 100 maximum. Previously published poems and simultaneous submissions only. Cover letter preferred. E-mail and disk submissions only. Reads submissions year-round; seasonal, 6 months in advance. Time between acceptance and publication is 3½ months. Poems are circulated to an editorial board. "Each of four editors reads and critiques each submission." Often comments on rejections. Send SASE for guidelines or obtain via e-mail or website. Responds in 2 months. Pays 1 copy. Acquires first North American serial rights. Reviews books of poetry in 500 words, single book format. Open to unsolicited reviews.

Also Offers: Website includes guidelines, editors' names, submission form, content from past issues, writers' links and message board.

Advice: "Send only finished, polished work which you consider your best."

✿ $ ♡ **SONO NIS PRESS**, P.O. Box 5550, Station B, Victoria, British Columbia V8R 6S4 Canada, phone (250)598-7807, fax (250)598-7866, e-mail sononis@islandnet.com, website www.islandnet.com/~sononis/, founded 1968, owner/publisher Diane Morriss.

Book/Chapbook Needs: Publishes 2 paperbacks/year. "We publish contemporary poetry, usually 2 mss a year, and 6-8 nonfiction titles (predominantly history)." They want "75 pages minimum; literature not limerick; connected or isolated poems acceptable. No rhyming ballads; haiku or religious verse." They have published poetry by Brian Brett, Linda Rogers and Sandy Shreve. As a sample the editor selected these lines from "Heaven Cake" in *Heaven Cake* by Linda Rogers:

> She is breaking her first/egg on the side of the metal bowl./It sounds like bedpans and nurses,/the girl
> who sat with Grandpa last night/holding his bruised hand in her own/until his old heart/stopped
> singing in hers.

Books are usually 80-120 pgs., 6×9 with laminated color cover.

How to Submit: Previously published poems OK, "if magazine publication only"; simultaneous submissions OK. Cover letter preferred. "Query letter preferred before submitting. Hard copy traditional submission only. No fax or e-mail submissions. Brief bio information and publication history helpful." Time between acceptance and publication is 14 months. Replies to queries in 2 months; to mss in 3 months. Pays "10% of suggested list for all books sold at normal discounts, 10% of net if deep discount," plus 10 author's copies (out of a press run of 600). For sample books, order direct or check local library.

Advice: "We are publishing only two poetry books a year—usually one established poet and one new poet. We never publish non-Canadians as the marketing is difficult. We are finding it harder and harder to publish limited market books. Promotion oriented authors are a bonus."

○ ○ ◑ **SOUL FOUNTAIN**, 90-21 Springfield Blvd., Queens Village NY 11428, phone/fax (718)479-2594, e-mail davault@aol.com, website www.TheVault.org, founded 1997, editor Tone Bellizzi.

ALWAYS include a self-addressed, stamped envelope (SASE) when sending a ms or query to a publisher within your own country. When sending material to other countries, include a self-addressed envelope and International Reply Coupons (IRCs), available at many post offices.

Magazine Needs: *Soul Fountain* appears 4 times a year and publishes poetry, art, photography, short fiction and essays. They are "open to all. Our motto is 'Fear no Art.' We publish all quality submitted work, and specialize in emerging voices. We are particularly interested in visionary, challenging and consciousness-expanding material." Also accepts poetry written by children, teens only. They have published poetry by Robert Dunn, Thomas Catterson, Jay Chollick and Paula Curci. *Soul Fountain* is 28 pgs., 8½×11, offset printed and saddle-stapled. Subscription: $10. Sample: $3.50. Make checks payable to Hope for the Children Foundation.
How to Submit: Submit 2-3 "camera-ready" poems at a time. No cover letters necessary. Previously published poems and simultaneous submissions OK. E-mail submissions OK (include in body of message). Time between acceptance and publication is 1 year. Pays 1 copy. "For each issue there is a release/party/performance, 'Poetry & Poultry in Motion,' attended by all poets, writers, artists, etc., appearing in the issue."
Also Offers: *Soul Fountain* is published by The Vault, "a not-for-profit arts project of the Hope for the Children Foundation; a growing, supportive community committed to empowering young and emerging artists of all disciplines at all levels to develop and share their talents through performance, collaboration and networking." Website includes submission guidelines.

N ⬤ SOUNDINGS EAST, Salem State College, Salem MA 01970, phone (978)542-6494, founded 1978, editor J.D. Scrimgeour.
Magazine Needs: "*SE* is published by Salem State College. We accept short fiction, creative nonfiction, short reviews and contemporary poetry. We publish both established and previously unpublished writers and artists. All forms of poetry welcome." *SE* appears twice a year, 64 pgs., digest-sized, flat-spined, b&w drawings and photos, glossy card cover with b&w photo. They receive about 500 submissions a year, use approximately 40-50. Press run is 2,000 for 120 subscribers of which 35 are libraries. Subscription: $10/year. Sample: $5.
How to Submit: Submit 5 poems at a time. Simultaneous submissions OK with notification. Be prompt when notifying *SE* that the work(s) was accepted elsewhere. Reads submissions September 1 through April 20 only. Fall deadline: November 20; spring: April 20. Responds within 4 months. Pays 2 copies. Rights revert to author upon publication.

⬛ ◎ SOUNDS OF A GREY METAL DAY; CREATIVE EXPRESSIONS PROJECT (Specialized: prisoners), % Jacqueline Helfgott, Dept. of Criminal Justice, Seattle University, 900 Broadway, Seattle WA 98122, phone (206)296-5477, fax (206)296-5997, e-mail jhelfgot@seattleu.edu, founded 1993, outside program coordinator/associate professor of criminal justice Jacqueline Helfgott, inside coordinator Patrick Bolt.
Magazine Needs: *Sounds of a Grey Metal Day* appears annually in November/December and publishes writing and art by prisoners and volunteers participating in the Creative Expressions Project. They welcome "poetry by prisoners about anything or poetry about prisons/imprisonment." Also accepts poetry written by children of incarcerated parents or relatives. *SGMD* is 75-85 pgs., magazine-sized, printed in "prison print shop" and saddle-stapled, textureed card stock cover, includes b&w drawings. Press run is 500. Single copy: $5. Make checks payable to Jackie Helfgott, money orders to CIPC.
How to Submit: Submit up to 3 poems at a time. No previously published poems or simultaneous submissions. Fax and e-mail submissions OK. Cover letter preferred. Disk submissions OK. Time between acceptance and publication varies. Poems are circulated to an editorial board. "Poems are circulated among committee of prisoners, volunteers, coordinators and selected by vote based on available space for outside submissions." Responds in 2 months. Pays 2 copies.

⬛ ⬜ ◨ ◎ THE SOUNDS OF POETRY; THE LATINO POETS' ASSOCIATION (Specialized: bilingual/foreign language, ethnic/nationality), 2076 Vinewood, Detroit MI 48216-5506, phone (313)843-2352, founded 1983, publisher/editor Jacqueline Rae Sanchez.
Magazine Needs: *The Sounds of Poetry* is published 3 times/year to "promote throughout the world an awareness (through poetry) that we are quite diverse, yet the same. We all love, hurt, laugh and suffer. We are open to all types of poetry with substance, grit, feeling; prefer one column and/or shorter poetry. Would like to see more feminist works. Always in need of fillers. Do not want to see fluff, insincere gibberish, foul language, nor porn, although light erotica is acceptable." Also accepts poetry written by children ages 14 and over. They have published poetry by t. kilgore splake, Gil Saenz, Jessica Sanchez, Rusty J. Street and Lladoow S. Shevshenko. As a sample the editor selected these lines from "In Search of Home" by Tumika Patrice Cain:

> *When I was hungry/You fed me with your words/Spooning me knowledge and widsom for breakfast/*
> *Whetting my carnal appetite in the twilight/Easing those yearnings/With whispered dialogue/Until my*
> *belly swelled with fullness*

The publisher says *SOP* is 24-32 pgs., digest-sized, saddle-stitched. "We use approximately 50-98 poems per issue representing at least 18 different states plus three or more other countries as well." Press run is 200. Subscription: $10. Sample: $4.50.
How to Submit: Submit 5 poems at a time. Previously published poems OK ("only if credit is listed on poem sheet submitted"); prefer no simultaneous submissions. Cover letter with titles of poems and bio preferred. "Type poems on an 8½×11 sheet of white paper, one poem per page unless submitting brief fillers (four titled fillers per sheet is OK), handwritten poems will be returned. Name, address and phone number should appear on each sheet submitted." Reads submissions January through October only. Time between acceptance and publication can be from several months to a couple years. Seldom comments on rejections. Publishes theme issues. Themes

for September 2000 (Michigan poems); June 2001 (Detroit poems). Send SASE for guidelines. Responds in up to 6 months. Pays 1 copy to contributor, 2 to subscriber. Poets may also send books for review consideration; "mark 'Review Copy' and enclose cover letter. We do not review excerpts of books/chapbooks."

Also Offers: "The Latino Poets' Association is a multicultural, multilingual, non-profit association whose 'purpose is to promote within the community and throughout the USA an appreciation and education of the writing/recitals of poetry by Latinos and those people who support the work of Latinos.' A person does not have to be Latino in order to join the L.P.A. Some L.P.A. poets write and recite only in Spanish, others write/recite in English, Spanish and French." Yearly membership: $25. Members have the opportunity to read at scheduled events. The LPA meets at the Bowen Branch Library-DPL, 3648 W. Vernor, Detroit MI, (313)297-9381. Send SASE for a schedule of L.P.A. events.

Advice: "Write poetry using the knowledge you have, research and expand, add your own feelings, emotions then take that same poetry to your ultimate heights. Write and rewrite until you are comfortable with your work. Attend poetry readings, listen closely to other poets as they read their material. Participate in open-mike readings, get feedback from other poets but ultimately use your own gut instincts."

SOUTH–A POETRY MAGAZINE FOR THE SOUTHERN COUNTIES; WANDA PUBLICATIONS, 61 West Borough, Wimborne, Dorset BH21 1LX England, phone (01202)889669, fax (01202)881061, e-mail wanda@wanda.demon.co.uk, founded 1972, administrator Mick Fealty.

Magazine Needs: *South* is published biannually "to give voice to poets writing in the South of England. As the magazine passes through the hands of seven editorial groups, our policy is open." They have published poetry by Ian Caws, Stella Davis, Finola Holiday, Elsa Corbluth and Brian Hinton. *South* is 68 pgs., 6×9, litho-printed and saddle-stapled with gloss laminated, duotone cover, includes photographs. They receive about 1,000 poems a year, accept approximately 10%. Press run is 400 for 200 subscribers of which 15 are libraries, 170 shelf sales; 15 distributed free to other magazines and reviewers. Single copy: £3.50; subscription: £6/2 issues, £11/4 issues. Make checks payable to Wanda Publications.

How to Submit: Submit 6 poems at a time. Previously published poems OK; no simultaneous submissions. Cover letter preferred. E-mail and disk submissions OK. Time between acceptance and publication is 5 months. Poems are circulated to an editorial board. "Each issue is selected by a different editorial group." Responds in 5 months. Pays 1 copy. Staff reviews books of poetry and other magazines in 400 words, multi-book format. Send books for review consideration.

SOUTH CAROLINA REVIEW, English Dept., 801 Strode Tower, Clemson University, Box 340523, Clemson SC 29634-0523, phone (864)656-3151 or 656-5399, fax (864)656-1345, founded 1968, editor Wayne Chapman.

Magazine Needs: *South Carolina Review* is a biannual literary magazine "recognized by the *New York Quarterly* as one of the top 20 of this type." They will consider "any kind of poetry as long as it's good. No stale metaphors, uncertain rhythms or lack of line integrity. Interested in seeing more traditional forms. Format should be according to new MLA Stylesheet." They have published poetry by Pattiann Rogers, J.W. Rivers and Claire Bateman. It is 200 pgs., 6×9, professionally printed, flat-spined and uses about 8-10 pgs. of poetry in each issue. Reviews of recent issues back up editorial claims that all styles and forms are welcome; moreover, poems were accessible and well-executed. Circulation is 600, for 400 subscribers of which 250 are libraries. They receive about 1,000 submissions of poetry a year, use approximately 10, have a 2-year backlog. Sample: $10.

How to Submit: Submit 3-10 poems at a time in an "8×10 manila envelope so poems aren't creased." No previously published poems or simultaneous submissions. "Editor prefers a chatty, personal cover letter plus a list of publishing credits." Do not submit during June, July, August or December. Publishes theme issues. Responds in 3 months. Pays copies. Staff reviews books of poetry.

SOUTH DAKOTA REVIEW (Specialized: regional, themes), University of South Dakota, Vermillion SD 57069, phone (605)677-5184 or 677-5966, fax (605)677-6409, e-mail bbedard@usd.edu, website www.usd.edu/SDR, founded 1963, editor Brian Bedard.

• *SDR* had 3 nominations for the Pushcart Prize in 1997.

SDR is a "literary quarterly publishing poetry, fiction, criticism, scholarly and personal essays. When material warrants, an emphasis on the American West; writers from the West; Western places or subjects; frequent issues with no geographical emphasis; periodic special issues on one theme, one place or one writer. Looking for originality, sophistication, significance, craft—i.e., professional work." They use 15-20 poems/issue. Press run is 500-600 for 450 subscribers of which half are libraries. Single copy: $6; subscription: $18/year, $30/2 years. Sample: $5.

How to Submit: Submit 3-6 poems at one time. Editor comments on submissions "occasionally." Publishes theme issues. Send SASE for guidelines. Responds in 2 months. Reads submissions year round. Pays in copies and 1-year subscription. Acquires first and reprint rights.

Advice: "We tend to favor the narrative poem, the concrete crafted lyric, the persona poem and the meditative place poem. Yet we try to leave some room for poems outside those parameters to keep some fresh air in our selection process."

☑ ◎ **THE SOUTH 666 BITCH (Specialized: form/style beat, gay, horror, erotica, psychic/occult, social issues)**, Box 3756, Erie PA 16508, founded 1997, editor "That Bitch".

Magazine Needs: *The South 666 Bitch* appears 2-4 times a year and is "eager to offend those (what be) easily offended! 'That Bitch' prefers pro-anti, pro-beat, pro-morbid, pro-street poetry; 3-40 lines." Does not want to see "anything pretentious." They have published poetry by R.L. Nichols, Jim Delavern, Laura Joy Lustig, Mark Sonnenfeld and Mr. Joseph Verrilli. The editor says *Bitch* is 6-8 pgs., 8½×11, photocopied and side-stapled with plenty of art and lots of ads. Accept approximately 2-10% of poems received. Press run is 36 for 2 subscribers. Sample: $1. Charges reading fee of $1/3 poems. Make checks payable to Robert L. Nichols.

How to Submit: Submit 3-6 poems at a time. Previously published poems and simultaneous submissions preferred. "Check your work for typos and uncorrect grammar (if unintentional)." Reads submissions January 2 through October 27 only. Time between acceptance and publication is 6 months. Seldom comments on rejections. Publishes theme issues occasionally. Halloween issue: October 30, 2000 deadline; possible Christmas issue: October 27, 2000 deadline. Responds in 6 months. Pays 1-2 copies.

Advice: " 'That Bitch' publishes only six poets per issue. Also: read Joe R and share da vibe!"

◖ ◎ **THE SOUTHERN CALIFORNIA ANTHOLOGY (Specialized: anthology); ANN STAN-FORD POETRY PRIZES**, c/o Master of Professional Writing Program, WPH 404, University of Southern California, Los Angeles CA 90089-4034, phone (213)740-3252, founded 1983.

Magazine Needs: *TSCA* is an "annual literary review of serious contemporary poetry and fiction. Very open to all subject matters except pornography. Any form, style OK." They have published poetry by Robert Bly, Donald Hall, Allen Ginsberg, Lisel Mueller, James Ragan and Amiri Baraka. The anthology is 144 pgs., digest-sized, perfect-bound, with a semi-glossy color cover featuring one art piece. A fine selection of poems distinguish this journal, and it has an excellent reputation, well-deserved. The downside, if it has one, concerns limited space for newcomers. Circulation is 1,500, 50% going to subscribers of which 50% are libraries, 30% are for shelf sales. Sample: $5.95.

How to Submit: Submit 3-5 poems between September 1 and January 1 only. No simultaneous submissions or previously published poems. All decisions made by mid-February. Send SASE for guidelines. Responds in 4 months. Pays 2 copies. Acquires all rights.

Also Offers: The Ann Stanford Poetry Prizes ($1,000, $200 and $100) have an April 15 deadline, $10 fee (5 poem limit), for unpublished poems. Include cover sheet with name, address and titles and SASE for contest results. All entries are considered for publication, and all entrants receive a copy of *SCA*.

☑ ◔ **SOUTHERN HUMANITIES REVIEW; THEODORE CHRISTIAN HOEPFNER AWARD**, 9088 Haley Center, Auburn University, Auburn AL 36849-5202, e-mail shrengl@auburn.edu, website www.aubur nedu/english/shr/home.htm, founded 1967, co-editors Dan Latimer and Virginia M. Kouidis.

Magazine Needs: *Southern Humanities Review* is a literary quarterly "interested in poems of any length, subject, genre. Space is limited, and brief poems are more likely to be accepted. Translations welcome, but also send written permission from the copyright holder." They have published poetry by Eamon Grennan, Donald Hall, Brendan Galvin, Susan Ludvigson, Andrew Hudgins, Bin Ramke and Fred Chappell. *SHR* is 100 pgs., 6×9, circulation 700. Subscription: $15/year. Sample: $5.

How to Submit: "Send 3-5 poems in a business-sized envelope. Avoid sending faint computer printout." No previously published poems or simultaneous submissions. No e-mail submissions. Responds in 2 months, possibly longer in summer. Always sends prepublication galleys. Pays 2 copies. Copyright reverts to author upon publication. Reviews books of poetry in approximately 750-1,000 words. Send books for review consideration.

Also Offers: Sponsors the Theodore Christian Hoepfner Award, a $50 award for the best poem published in a given volume of *SHR*.

Advice: "For beginners we'd recommend study and wide reading in English and classical literature, and, of course, American literature—the old works, not just the new. We also recommend study of or exposure to a foreign language and a foreign culture. Poets need the reactions of others to their work: criticism, suggestions, discussion. A good creative writing teacher would be desirable here, and perhaps some course work too. And then submission of work, attendance at workshops. And again, the reading: history, biography, verse, essays—all of it. We want to see poems that have gone beyond the language of slippage and easy attitudes."

☑ ◯ **SOUTHERN INDIANA REVIEW**, School of Liberal Arts, University of Southern Indiana, 8600 University Blvd., Evansville IN 47712, phone (812)465-1630, fax (812)465-7512, e-mail twilhelm@usi.edu, website www.usi.edu/libarts/english/review.htm, founded 1993, poetry editor Matthew Graham, fiction editor Thomas A. Wilhelmus, managing editor Jim McGarrah.

Magazine Needs: Published twice a year, *Southern Indiana Review* "celebrates the American heartland through poetry, fiction, nonfiction and artwork. We prefer originality, energy, and clarity, and we welcome both established and first-time writers. We publish poetry on any subject, in any form. No sentimental pieces." They have published poetry by Liam Rector, Ellen Bryant Voigt, Heather McHugh and Allison Joseph. *SIR* is 110 pgs., 6×9, professionally printed and perfect-bound with 4-color glossy cover, includes b&w photos and art. They receive about 2,500 poems a year, accept approximately 10%. Press run is 375. Subscription: $10. Sample: $6.

How to Submit: No previously published poems; simultaneous submissions OK. Cover letter preferred, include titles and brief bio. "An e-mail address is helpful." No e-mail submissions. Fax and disk submissions OK.

Reads submissions October through December. Time between acceptance and publication is 6 months. Seldom comments on rejections. Send SASE for guidelines or obtain via website. Responds in 3 months. Sometimes sends prepublication galleys. Pays 1 copy. Open to unsolicited reviews.

Also Offers: "*Southern Indiana Review* is a direct spinoff of Rope Walk Writers Retreat, a writing workshop conducted each summer in New Harmony, Indiana." Write for more information or request via e-mail.

◑ SOUTHERN POETRY REVIEW; GUY OWEN POETRY PRIZE, Advancement Studies, Central Piedmont Community College, Charlotte NC 28235, phone (704)330-6002, fax (704)330-6455, editor Ken McLaurin, founded 1958.

Magazine Needs: *SPR* a semiannual literary magazine "with emphasis on effective poetry. There are no restrictions on form, style or content of poetry; length subject to limitations of space." They have published work by R.T. Smith, Colette Inez, Dabney Stuart, Peter Cooley and Susan Ludvigson. *Southern Poetry Review* is 80 pgs., 6×9, handsomely printed on buff stock, flat-spined with textured, one-color matte card cover. Circulation is 1,000. Subscription: $8/year. Sample: $3.

How to Submit: Queries answered with SASE. Submit up to 3-5 poems at a time. Reads submissions September 1 through May 31 only. Pays 1 copy. Acquires first-time rights. Staff reviews books of poetry. Send books for review consideration.

Also Offers: Also sponsors the annual Guy Owen Poetry Prize of $500. Entry fee is an $8 subscription; submission must be postmarked in April. Submit 3-5 poems with SASE.

Advice: "This is the type of literary magazine to settle back with in a chair and read, particularly during dry creative spells, to inspire one's muse. It is recommended as a market for that reason. It's a tough sell, though. Work is read closely and the magazine reports in a timely manner."

✓ $◑ THE SOUTHERN REVIEW, 43 Allen Hall, Louisiana State University, Baton Rouge LA 70803-5005, phone (225)388-5108, fax (225)388-5098, e-mail bmacon@lsu.edu, website www.lsu.edu/guests/wwwtsm, founded 1935 (original series), 1965 (new series), poetry editors James Olney and Dave Smith.

⚑ Work published in this review has been included in the 1995, 1996, 1998 and 1999 volumes of *The Best American Poetry* and in *The Beacon's Best of 1999*.

Magazine Needs: *The Southern Review* "is a literary quarterly that publishes fiction, poetry, critical essays and book reviews, with emphasis on contemporary literature in the U.S. and abroad, and with special interest in southern culture and history. Selections are made with careful attention to craftsmanship and technique and to the seriousness of the subject matter. We are interested in any variety of poetry that is well crafted, though we cannot normally accommodate excessively long poems (say 10 pgs. and over)." They have published poetry by Norman Dubie, Margaret Gibson, Seamus Heaney, Yusef Komunyakaa, Susan Ludvigson and Robert Penn Warren. The beautifully printed quarterly is massive: 6¾×10, 240 pgs., flat-spined, matte card cover. They receive about 6,000 submissions of poetry a year. All styles and forms seem welcome, although accessible lyric and narrative free verse appear most often in recent issues. Press run is 3,100 for 2,100 subscribers of which 70% are libraries. Subscription: $25. Sample: $8.

How to Submit: "We do not require a cover letter but we prefer one giving information about the author and previous publications." Prefers submissions of up to 4 pgs. Send SASE for guidelines. Responds in 2 months. Pays $20/printed page plus 2 copies. Buys first North American serial rights. Staff reviews books of poetry in 3,000 words, multi-book format. Send books for review consideration.

Also Offers: Website includes guidelines, subscription information, current table of contents, relevant addresses, names, etc.

⊕ ◑ ◎ SOUTHFIELDS; SOUTHFIELDS PRESS; VENNEL PRESS; AU QUAI (Specialized: ethnic/nationality), 8 Richmond Rd., Staines, Middlesex TW18 2AB England, founded 1994, co-editors Richard Price, David Kinloch and Raymond Friel.

Magazine Needs: *Southfields* is a biannual journal that publishes "Scottish poetry of a wide range of styles and commitments, articles on key Scottish writing of any period, independent poetry from other countries, translations into the languages of Scotland, occasional art criticism, memoir and cross-genre prose. They want "Scottish poetry of a wide range of styles and commitments, but independent poetry from other countries, too. We do not want to see poetry which suggests the poet has not read an issue of the magazine before." They have published poetry by Gael Turnbull, Haryette Mullen, Fiona Templeton and Angela McSeveney. As a sample the editor selected these lines from "Compressor" by Richard Price:

> *A mash of half-bricks, off-cuts of board, glaur. The first foam of alyssum./Bungalows crating up the fields. Skelfy yellow rafters dreeping girls. Finished halls./A gripped man-hole lid, a lazy boy. A bath of petrol, a cigarette's disfigurement, teenage inferno./Twenty years later: a carpenter, a father, a face saved.*

The editor says *Southfields* is 72-84 pgs., magazine-sized, offset litho printed and perfect-bound, cover varies, occasional ads. They receive about 300 poems a year, accept approximately 15%. Press run is 200. Single copy: $10 (US); subscription: $20 (US). Sample: $8 (US). Make checks payable to Southfields Press.

How to Submit: Submit 3-6 poems at a time. No previously published poems or simultaneous submissions. Cover letter preferred. Time between acceptance and publication is 2 months. Poems are circulated to an editorial board. "If the first editor likes a poem enough it is sent to the second editor, etc." Seldom comments on rejections.

Responds in 2 months. Sometimes sends prepublication galleys. Pays 1 copy. Acquires first rights. Reviews books and chapbooks of poetry and other magazines in up to 1,500 words, single or multi-book format. Open to unsolicited reviews. Poets may also send books for review consideration to Richard Price.

Book/Chapbook Needs & How to Submit: Under Vennel Press, they publish Scottish and independent poetry from other countries; under the Au Quai imprint, translations. They have published *In the Metaforest* by Peter McCarey, Vennel Press, 2000. They publish 0-1 paperbacks and 1-5 chapbooks/year. Query first with a few sample poems and cover letter with brief bio and publication credits. Replies to queries in 2 weeks; to mss in 2 months. Pays 10% author's copies. Order sample books/chapbooks by sending $20 payable to Vennel Press.

$ ⊘ SOUTHWEST REVIEW; ELIZABETH MATCHETT STOVER MEMORIAL AWARD, 307 Fondren Library West, P.O. Box 750374, Southern Methodist University, Dallas TX 75275-0374, phone (214)768-1037, founded 1915, editor Willard Spiegelman.

⬛ Poetry published in *Southwest Review* has been included in the 1995 and 1998 volumes of *The Best American Poetry.*

Magazine Needs: *Southwest Review* is a literary quarterly that publishes fiction, essays, poetry and interviews. "It is hard to describe our preference for poetry in a few words. We always suggest that potential contributors read several issues of the magazine to see for themselves what we like. But some things may be said: We demand very high quality in our poems; we accept both traditional and experimental writing, but avoid unnecessary obscurity and private symbolism; we place no arbitrary limits on length but find shorter poems easier to fit into our format than longer ones. We have no specific limitations as to theme." They have published poetry by Adrienne Rich, Amy Clampitt, Albert Goldbarth, Leonard Nathan, Molly Peacock and Charles Wright. The journal is 6×9, 144 pgs., perfect-bound, professionally printed, with matte text stock cover. They receive about 1,000 submissions of poetry a year, use approximately 32. Poems tend to be lyric and narrative free verse combining a strong voice with powerful topics or situations. Diction is accessible and content often conveys a strong sense of place. Circulation is 1,500 for 1,000 subscribers of which 600 are libraries. Subscription: $24. Sample: $6.

How to Submit: No simultaneous submissions or previously published work. Send SASE for guidelines. Responds within a month. Always sends prepublication galleys. Pays cash plus copies.

Also Offers: The $250 Elizabeth Matchett Stover Memorial Award is awarded annually for the best poems, chosen by editors, published in the preceding year.

◪ ◎ SOUTHWESTERN AMERICAN LITERATURE (Specialized: regional), Center for the Study of the Southwest, Southwest Texas State University, San Marcos TX 78666, phone (512)245-2232, fax (512)245-7462, e-mail mb13@swt.edu, website www.english.swt.edu/css/cssindex.htm, founded 1971, editor Dr. Mark Busby, editor Dr. Dick Heaberlin.

Magazine Needs: *Southwestern American Literature* is "a biannual scholarly journal that includes literary criticism, fiction, poetry and book reviews concerning the Greater Southwest. While we are a regional journal, we enjoy seeing poetry of all subject matters, not just about tumbleweeds, longhorns and urban cowboys." They have published poetry by Naomi Shihab Nye, Alberto Rios, Alison Deming and Simon J. Ortiz. As a sample the editor selected these lines from "Light" by Simon J. Ortiz:

> Out to mail a letter at the corner mailbox,/morning moment, the sunlight caught/me striding loosely uphill. I cannot mistake/this morning for what it is: sunshine/air quick and rich in spirit, alert in my eye.

The editors say *SAL* is 100-125 pgs., 6×9, professionally printed and perfect-bound with 80 lb. embossed bond cover. They receive about 200 poems a year, accept approximately 10%. Press run is 300 for 225 subscribers of which 80 are libraries. Subscription: $14/year. Sample: $7.

How to Submit: Submit 3 poems at a time. No previously published poems; simultaneous submissions OK. Cover letter preferred. "Two copies of manuscript should be submitted along with SASE." No e-mail submissions. Time between acceptance and publication is 2-6 months. Poems are circulated to an editorial board. "Each poem that is accepted has been recommended by at least two members of our editorial board." Seldom comments on rejections. Publishes theme issues occasionally. Obtain guidelines via e-mail. Responds in 6 weeks. Pays 1 copy. Acquires all rights. Returns rights upon publication. Staff reviews books of poetry in 500-1,000 words, single or multi-book format. Send books for review consideration.

◪ SOU'WESTER, Box 1438, Southern Illinois University, Edwardsville IL 62026, phone (618)650-3190, founded 1960, managing editor Fred W. Robbins, associate editor Nancy Avdoian.

Magazine Needs: *Sou'wester* appears twice a year. "We lean toward poetry with strong imagery, successful association of images, and skillful use of figurative language." They have published poetry by R.T. Smith, Susan Swartwout and William Jolliff. There are 30-40 pgs. of poetry in each 6×9, 100-page issue. The magazine is professionally printed, flat-spined, with textured matte card cover, circulation is 300 for 500 subscribers of which 50 are libraries. They receive 3,000 poems (from 600 poets) each year, use approximately 36-40, have a 4-month backlog. Subscription: $10/2 issues. Sample: $5.

How to Submit: Simultaneous submissions OK. Does not read during August. Rejections usually within 4 months. Pays 2 copies. Acquires all rights. Returns rights. Editor comments on rejections "usually, in the case of those that we almost accept."

Advice: "Read poetry past and present. Have something to say and say it in your own voice. Poetry is a very personal thing for many editors. When all else fails, we may rely on gut reactions, so take whatever hints you're given to improve your poetry, and keep submitting."

THE SOW'S EAR POETRY REVIEW, 19535 Pleasant View Dr., Abingdon VA 24211-6827, phone (540)628-2651, e-mail richman@preferred.com, founded 1988, managing editor Larry Richman, graphics editor Mary Calhoun.

Magazine Needs: *The Sow's Ear* is a quarterly. "We are open to many forms and styles, and have no limitations on length. We try to be interesting visually, and we use graphics to complement the poems. Though we publish some work from our local community of poets, we are interested in poems from all over. We publish a few by previously unpublished poets." They have published poetry by Kathryn Stripling Byer, Andrea King Kelly, Luci Shaw, Floyd Skloot and R.T. Smith. *TSE* is 32 pgs., 8½×11, saddle-stapled, with matte card cover, professionally printed. They receive about 2,000 poems a year, accept approximately 100. Press run is 600 for 500 subscribers of which 15 are libraries, 20-40 shelf sales. Subscription: $10. Sample: $5.

How to Submit: Submit up to 5 poems at a time with SASE. No previously published poems; simultaneous submissions OK if you tell them promptly when work is accepted elsewhere. Enclose brief bio. No e-mail submissions. Send SASE or e-mail for guidelines. Responds in up to 6 months. Pays 2 copies. Buys first publication rights. Most prose (reviews, interviews, features) is commissioned.

Also Offers: They offer an annual contest for unpublished poems, with fee of $2/poem, prizes of $1,000, $250 and $100, and publication for 15-20 finalists. For contest, submit poems in September/October, with name and address on a separate sheet. Submissions of 5 poems/$10 receive a subscription. Include SASE for notification. 1998 Judge: Maggie Anderson. They also sponsor a chapbook contest in March/April with $10 fee, $1,000 1st Prize, publication, 25 copies and distribution to subscribers; 2nd Prize $200 and 3rd Prize $100. Send SASE or e-mail for chapbook contest guidelines.

Advice: "Four criteria help us to judge the quality of submissions: Does the poem make the strange familiar or the familiar strange or both? Is the form of the poem vital to its meaning? Do the sounds of the poem make sense in relation to the theme? Does the little story of the poem open a window on the Big Story of the human situation?"

[N:] $ ◯ ◿ ◎ SPACE AND TIME (Specialized: science fiction/fantasy, horror), 138 W. 70th St. (4B), New York NY 10023-4468, founded 1966, poetry editor Linda Addison.

Magazine Needs: *Space and Time* is a biannual that publishes "primarily science fiction/fantasy/horror; some related poetry and articles. We do not want to see anything that doesn't fit science fiction/fantasy/weird genres." They have published poetry by Lyn Lifshin, Susan Spilecki, Mark Kreighbaum and Cynthia Tedesco. As a sample we selected these lines from "Dark Waiting" by Catherine Mintz:

> *An unceasing rain/lamp light gold in the gutters./I refold bat wings.*

The issue of *Space and Time* we received was about 100 pgs., 5½×8½, perfect-bound. However, they are reformatting to 48 pgs., 8½×11, web press printed on 50 lb. stock and saddle-stitched with glossy card cover and interior b&w illustrations. They receive about 500 poems a year, accept approximately 5%. Press run is 2,000 for 200 subscribers of which 10 are libraries, 1,200 shelf sales. Single copy: $5; subscription: $10. Sample: $6.25.

How to Submit: Submit up to 4 poems at a time. No previously published poems or simultaneous submissions. Time between acceptance and publication is 3-9 months. Often comments on rejections. Poets may send SASE for guidelines "but they won't see more than what's here." Responds in up to 6 weeks, "longer if recommended." Pays 1¢/word ($5 minimum) plus 2 copies. Buys first North American serial rights.

[✓] ◿ SPILLWAY, P.O. Box 7887, Huntington Beach CA 92615-7887, phone (714)968-0905, founded 1991, editors Mifanwy Kaiser and Mark Bergendahl.

Magazine Needs: *Spillway* is a biannual journal, published in March and September, "celebrating writing's diversity and power to affect our lives. Open to all voices, schools and tendencies. We usually do not use writing which tells instead of shows, or writing which contains general, abstract lines not anchored in images. We publish poetry, translations, reviews, essays and b&w photography." They have published poetry by John Balaban, Sam Hamill, Richard Jones and Susan Terris. *Spillway* is about 176 pgs., digest-sized, attractively printed, perfect-bound, with 2-color or 4-color card cover. Press run is 2,000. Single copy: $8; subscription: $14/2 issues, $24/4 issues. Sample (including guidelines): $10. Make checks payable to *Spillway*, Mifanwy Kaiser.

How to Submit: Submit 3-6 poems at a time, 10 pages total. Previously published work ("say when and where") and simultaneous submissions ("say where also submitted") OK. Cover letter including brief bio and SASE required. "No cute bios—we need professional ones." Responds in up to 6 months. Pays 1 copy. Acquires one-time rights. Reviews books of poetry in 500-2,500 words maximum. Open to unsolicited reviews and essays, 10 pages maximum. Poets may also send books for review consideration.

Advice: "We have no problem with simultaneous or previously published submissions. Poems are murky creatures—they shift and change in time and context. It's exciting to pick up a volume, read a poem in the context of all the other pieces and then find the same poem in another time and place. And, we don't think a poet should have to wait until death to see work in more than one volume. What joy to find out that more than one editor values one's work. Our responsibility as editors, collectively, is to promote the work of poets as much as possible—how can we do this if we say to a writer you may only have a piece published in one volume and only one time?''

SPIN; POETRY ORBITAL WORKSHOPS, % Postal Agency, Ngakawau, Buller, New Zealand, phone 03 7828608, founded 1986, contact Leicester Kyle.

Magazine Needs: *SPIN* appears 3 times/year, March, July, November, and publishes poetry. "We have no hard and fast rules but appreciate poetry that excels in its form and content. No stereotyped, imitative or boring work." They have published poetry by George Gott, Catherine Maur, John O'Connor and Joanna Weston. As a sample the editor selected these lines from "Like Florida" by David Gregory:

> No new ways of telling time,/winking heart monitor digitals,/cruel and precise./Autumn is made
> apocryphal;/she extends herself south,/ahead of the shadows.

SPIN is 72 pgs., A5, photocopied and saddle-stitched with light card cover. They receive about 600 poems a year, accept approximately 25%. Press run is 150 for 110 subscribers of which 6 are libraries. Single copy: NZ 6.50; subscription: NZ 18. Sample: NZ 4.50.

How to Submit: "We expect contributors to subscribe/purchase. We are unable to supply contributors copies." Submit approximately 6 poems at a time. No previously published poems or simultaneous submissions. Cover letter preferred. "All submissions returned at each publication." Time between acceptance and publication is 1 month. Sometimes comments on rejections. Publishes theme issues. Responds within 3 months. Reviews books of poetry in 1-page (or more), or in multi 3-4 line notices. Open to unsolicited reviews. Poets may also send books for review consideration.

Also Offers: Subscription covers (optional) membership in poetry orbital workshops. "Each workshop or 'orbit' comprises four or five poets who by post submit poems to each other for reading and comment." Send SASE (or SAE and IRC) for details.

SPINDRIFT, Shoreline Community College, 16101 Greenwood Ave. N., Seattle WA 98133, phone (206)546-5864, founded 1962, faculty advisor varies each year, currently Carol Orlock.

Magazine Needs: *Spindrift* is open to all varieties of poetry except greeting card style. They have published poetry by Lyn Lifshin, Mary Lou Sanelli, James Bertolino, Edward Harkness and Richard West. *Spindrift*, an annual, is 125 pgs., handsomely printed in an 8″ square, flat-spined. Circulation is 500. Single copy: $6.50. Sample: $5.

How to Submit: "Submit two copies of each poem, six lines maximum. Include SASE and cover letter with 2-3 lines of biographical information including name, address, phone number, e-mail address and a list of all materials sent. We accept submissions until February 1; editorial responses are mailed by March 15." Send SASE for guidelines. Pays 2 copies. All rights revert to author upon publication.

Advice: "Read what the major contemporary poets are writing. Read what local poets are writing. Be distinctive, love the language, avoid sentiment."

SPINNING JENNY, Black Dress Press, P.O. Box 213, New York NY 10014, website www.blackdresspress.com, founded 1994, first issue Fall 1995, editor C.E. Harrison.

Magazine Needs: *Spinning Jenny* appears once a year. They have published poetry by Denise Duhamel, Matthew Lippman, Michael Loncar, Sarah Messer and a play by Jeff Hoffman. As a sample the editor selected these lines from "Infidelity" by Michael Morse:

> The stranger takes off his shirt,/and in your own good mind it's the kiss.//When you lean forward and
> close the eyes,/the stars and their just torments/wheel off to the somewhere-else.

SJ is 96 pgs., 5¼×9¼, perfect-bound with heavy card cover. "We accept less than 5% of unsolicited submissions." Press run is 1,000. Single copy: $6; subscription: $12/2 issues. Sample: $6.

How to Submit: No previously published poems; simultaneous submissions not encouraged. E-mail submissions OK (include in body of message). Seldom comments on rejections. Send SASE for guidelines. Responds within 2 months. Pays contributor copies. Authors retain rights.

Also Offers: Website includes guidelines, address/contact information and subscription info.

THE SPIRIT THAT MOVES US; THE SPIRIT THAT MOVES US PRESS, P.O. Box 720820-PM, Jackson Heights, Queens NY 11372-0820, phone (718)426-8788, e-mail msklar@mindspring.com, founded 1974, poetry editor Morty Sklar.

Magazine Needs & How to Submit: *"The Spirit That Moves Us* will be continuing its *Editor's Choice* series and publishing regular issues only occasionally. *Editor's Choice* consists of selections from other literary

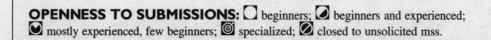

OPENNESS TO SUBMISSIONS: ☐ beginners; ◐ beginners and experienced; ◑ mostly experienced, few beginners; ◎ specialized; ⊘ closed to unsolicited mss.

magazines and small presses, where we choose from nominations by the editors of those magazines and presses." They have published poetry by Steve Kowit, Naomi Shibab Nye, Wendell Berry and Dorothy Allison. As a sample the editor selected these lines from "Everybody Says Hello" by Bob Jacob:

> Sometimes when the trees out back/Talk to one another/And the sky rumbles just before rain,/I'll stand at the window and listen./Sometimes, everybody says hello.

That poem appeared in *The Day Seamus Heaney Kissed My Cheek in Dublin* by Bob Jacob, which they offer as a sample for $8 plus $1 postage (regularly $12 plus $1.50 postage) or their *15th Anniversary Collection* for $6 and free shipping. Publishes theme issues. Send SASE for upcoming themes and time frames.

Advice: "Write what you would like to write, in a style (or styles) which is/are best for your own expression. Don't worry about acceptance, though you may be concerned about it. Don't just send work which you think editors would like to see, though take that into consideration. Think of the relationship between poem, poet and editor as personal. You may send good poems to editors who simply do not like them, whereas other editors might."

N **■** **○** **◎** **SPISH (Specialized: fish stories, poetry related to fishing)**, % Progressive, 5785 Yucca Lane North, Minneapolis MN 55446, e-mail spishmagazine@aol.com, website www.spish.com, founded 1999, attn: editors.

Magazine Needs: *Spish* is an electronic magazine featuring fish stories, poetry, art and photography. Appears "as we find time to produce it. We publish alternative, edgy, humorous poetry and short prose with a tie to fishing; along the lines of Brautigan, Bukowski or Jim Harrison. We aren't likely to publish rhyming or greeting card verse. If we have to read it twice to 'get it,' it probably won't make it." They have published poetry by Charlie Bukowski, Bill Meissner and Michael Hall. As a sample the editor selected this poem, "The Ice Fisherman" by Michael Hall:

> They sit on stools/like cats/staring into a mouse hole./Thinking perhaps,/about the unpaid loan/or the unfaithful wife,/praying/that there's something/down there/that will get them through/another winter.

How to Submit: Submit 3-5 poems at a time. Previously published poems and simultaneous submissions OK. E-mail submissions preferred (in body of message with "Submissions" in subject line.) Include brief bio (less than 3 sentences). Time between acceptance and publication is 1-4 months. Poems are circulated to an editorial board. Often comments on rejections. Obtain guidelines via website. Responds in 1 month. Acquires one-time rights and anthology rights.

Also Offers: Website includes poetry and stories, art and photography, submission guidelines, about the editors, past issues and links.

Advice: "Spend more time focusing on the story rather than the language. Write something that will be fun to read!"

◎ **SPITBALL: THE LITERARY BASEBALL MAGAZINE; CASEY AWARD (Specialized: sports/ recreation)**, 5560 Fox Rd., Cincinnati OH 45239, phone (513)385-2268, founded 1981, poetry editor William J. McGill.

Magazine Needs: *Spitball* is "a unique literary magazine devoted to poetry, fiction and book reviews exclusively about baseball. Newcomers are very welcome, but remember that you have to know the subject. We do and our readers do. Perhaps a good place to start for beginners is one's personal reactions to the game, a game, a player, etc. and take it from there." The 96-page, digest-sized biannual is computer typeset and perfect-bound. They receive about 1,000 submissions a year, use approximately 40. "Many times we are able to publish accepted work almost immediately." Circulation is 1,000 for 750 subscribers of which 25 are libraries. Subscription: $12. Sample: $6. "We now require all first-time submitters to purchase a sample copy for $6. This is a one-time only fee, which we regret but economic reality dictates that we insist those who wish to be published in *SB* help support it, at least at this minimum level."

How to Submit: "We are not very concerned with the technical details of submitting, but we do prefer a cover letter with some bio info. We also like batches of poems and prefer to use several of same poet in an issue rather than a single poem." Pays 2 copies.

Also Offers: "We sponsor the Casey Award (for best baseball book of the year) and hold the Casey Awards Banquet every January. Any chapbook of baseball poetry should be sent to us for consideration for the 'Casey' plaque that we award to the winner each year."

Advice: "We encourage anyone interested to submit to *Spitball*. We are always looking for fresh talent. Those who have never written 'baseball poetry' before should read some first probably before submitting. Not necessarily ours."

⊕ **✓** **○** **SPLIZZ**, 4 St. Marys Rise, Burry Port, Carms SA16 OSH Wales, e-mail amanda@stmarys4.freeserve.co.uk, founded 1993, editor Amanda Morgan.

Magazine Needs: *Splizz*, published quarterly, features poetry, prose, reviews of contemporary music and background to poets. They want "any kind of poetry. We have no restrictions regarding style, length, subjects." However, they do not want "anything racist or homophobic." They have published poetry by writers from throughout the world. The editor says *Splizz* is 40-44 pgs., A5, saddle-stapled with art and ads. They receive about 200-300 poems a year, accept approximately 90%. Press run is 150 for 35 subscribers. Single copy: £1.30, 5 IRCs elsewhere; subscription: £5 UK, £10 elsewhere. Sample: £1.30 UK, 5 IRCs elsewhere. Make checks payable to Amanda Morgan (British checks only).

How to Submit: Submit 5 poems, typed submissions preferred. Include SAE with IRCs. Previously published poems and simultaneous submissions OK. Cover letter required with short bio. Time between acceptance and publication is 2-4 months. Often comments on rejections. Charges criticism fee: "Just enclose SAE/IRC for response, and allow one to two months for delivery." Send SASE (or SAE and IRC) for guidelines. Responds in 2 months. Sometimes sends prepublication galleys. Reviews books or chapbooks of poetry or other magazines in 50-300 words. Open to unsolicited reviews. Poets may also send books for review consideration. E-mail for further enquiries.

Advice: "Beginners seeking to have their work published, send your work to *Splizz*, as we specialize in giving new poets a chance."

THE SPOON RIVER POETRY REVIEW (Specialized: regional, translations); EDITORS' PRIZE CONTEST, 4240/English Dept., Illinois State University, Normal IL 61790-4240, website www.litline. org/spoon, founded 1976, editor Lucia Getsi.

Magazine Needs: *SRPR* is a "poetry magazine that features newer and well-known poets from around the country and world." Also features 1 Illinois poet/issue at length for the magazine's Illinois Poet Series. "We want interesting and compelling poetry that operates beyond the ho-hum, so-what level, in any form or style about anything; language that is fresh, energetic, committed, filled with a strong voice that grabs the reader in the first line and never lets go." They also use translations of poetry. They have published poetry by Stuart Dybek, Amy Boeder, Leslie Andrienne Miller, Allison Joseph, Sheryl St. Germain and Dave Smith. *SRPR* appears biannually, 128 pgs., digest-sized, laser set with card cover using photos, ads. They receive about 3,000 poems a month, accept approximately 1%. Press run is 1,500 for 700 subscribers, of which 100 are libraries and shelf sales. Subscription: $15. Sample (including guidelines): $10.

How to Submit: "No simultaneous submissions unless we are notified immediately if a submission is accepted elsewhere. Include name and address on every poem." Do not submit mss May 1 through September 1. Editor comments on rejections "many times, if a poet is promising." Responds in 2 months. Pays a year's subscription. Acquires first North American serial rights. Staff reviews books of poetry. Send books for review consideration.

Also Offers: Sponsors the Editor's Prize Contest for previously unpublished work. One poem will be awarded $1,000 and published in the fall issue of *SRPR*, and two runners-up will receive $100 each and publication in the fall issue. Entries must be previously unpublished. Entry fee: $16, including 1-year subscription. Deadline: April 15. Write for details. Recent winners were Judith Westley and Aleida Rodríguez. Website includes guidelines, cover pictures, contest guidelines, subscription information and poems.

SPOUT MAGAZINE, P.O. Box 581067, Minneapolis MN 55458-1067, founded 1989, editors John Colburn and Michelle Filkins.

Magazine Needs: *Spout* appears approximately 3 times/year providing "a paper community of unique expression." They want "poetry of the imagination, poetry that surprises. We enjoy the surreal, the forceful, the political, the expression of confusion." No light verse, archaic forms or language. They have published poetry by Simon Perchik, Sheila E. Murphy, Lyn Lifshin and Jeffrey Little. As a sample the editor selected these lines from "Ode to Serge Chaloff" by Jeffrey Little:

> i want to lie down in the reeds by a muddy creek bed/w/a pack of jujubes & a staple gun & build for
> myself/a universe truly capable of grace . . .

The editor says *Spout* is 40-60 pgs., saddle-stapled, card stock or glossy cover is a different color each issue. They receive about 400-450 poems a year, accept approximately 10%. Press run is 200-250 for 35-40 subscribers, 100-150 shelf sales. Single copy price: $4; subscription: $12. Sample: $4.

How to Submit: Submit up to 6 poems at a time. Previously published poems and simultaneous submissions OK. Cover letter preferred. Time between acceptance and publication is 2-3 months. Poems are circulated to an editorial board. "Poems are reviewed by two of three editors, those selected for final review are read again by all three." Seldom comments on rejections. Send SASE for guidelines. Responds in 4 months. Pays 1 copy.

SPRING: THE JOURNAL OF THE E.E. CUMMINGS SOCIETY (Specialized: membership/subscription), 33-54 164th St., Flushing NY 11358-1442, phone (718)353-3631 or (718)461-9022, fax (718)353-4778, editor Norman Friedman.

Magazine Needs: *Spring* is an annual publication designed "to maintain and broaden the audience for Cummings and to explore various facets of his life and art." They want poems in the spirit of Cummings, primarily poems of one page or less. Nothing "amateurish." They have published poetry by John Tagliabue, Ruth Whitman, M.L. Rosenthal, William Jay Smith and Theodore Weiss. *Spring* is about 180 pgs., 5½×8½, offset and perfect-bound with light card stock cover. Press run is 700 for 200 subscribers of which 15 are libraries, 450 shelf sales. Subscription or sample: $17.50.

How to Submit: No previously published poems or simultaneous submissions. Fax submissions OK. Cover letter required. Reads submissions January through March only. Seldom comments on rejections. Responds in 6 months. Pays 1 copy.

Advice: "Contributors are encouraged to subscribe."

☑ ◎ **SPRING TIDES (Specialized: children)**, Savannah Country Day School, 824 Stillwood Dr., Savannah GA 31419-2643, phone (912)925-8800, fax (912)920-7800, e-mail Houston@savcds.org, website www.savcd s.org, founded 1989, contact Connie Houston.

Magazine Needs: *Spring Tides* is an annual literary magazine by children 5-12 years of age. "Children from ages five through twelve may submit material. Please limit stories to 1,200 words and poems to 20 lines. All material must be original and created by the person submitting it. A statement signed by the child's parent or teacher attesting to the originality must accompany all work." *ST* is 28 pgs., digest-sized, attractively printed and saddle-stapled with glossy card cover, includes b&w and 4-color art. Press run is 500; given to student at SCDS and sold to others. Single copy: $5.

How to Submit: Simultaneous submissions OK. SASE required. "Poems with or without illustrations may be submitted." Reads submissions January through August only. Poems are circulated to an editorial board. Always comments on rejections. Send SASE for guidelines. Responds in 4 months. Pays 1 copy.

☑ $ ◎ **SPS STUDIOS, INC., publishers of Blue Mountain Arts® (Specialized: greeting cards)**, Dept. PM, P.O. Box 1007, Boulder CO 80306-1007, fax (303)447-0939, e-mail bma@rmi.net, founded 1971, contact editorial staff.

Book/Chapbook Needs: SPS Studios publishes greeting cards, calendars, prints and mugs. They are looking for poems, prose and lyrics ("usually nonrhyming") appropriate for publication on greeting cards and in poetry anthologies. "Poems should reflect a message, feeling or sentiment that one person would want to share with another. We'd like to receive creative, original submissions about love relationships, family members, friendships, philosophies and any other aspect of life. Poems and writings for specific holidays (Christmas, Valentine's Day, etc.) and special occasions, such as graduation, anniversary and get well, are also considered. Only a small portion of the material we receive is selected each year and the review process can be lengthy, but be assured every manuscript is given serious consideration."

How to Submit: Submissions must be typewritten, 1 poem/page or sent via e-mail. Enclose SASE if you want your work returned. Simultaneous submissions "discouraged but OK with notification." Submit seasonal material at least 4 months in advance. Send SASE for guidelines or request via e-mail. Responds in up to 6 months. Pays $200/poem for the worldwide, exclusive right, $25/poem for one-time use in an anthology.

Advice: "We strongly suggest that you familiarize yourself with our products before submitting material, although we caution you not to study them too hard. We do not need more poems that sound like something we've already published. Overall, we're looking for poetry that expresses real emotions and feelings."

◻ ◢ **SPUNK**, Box 55336, Hayward CA 94545, phone (415)397-2596, founded 1996, editor Violet Jones.

Magazine Needs: Appearing 2 times a year, *Spunk: The Journal of Spontaneous Creativity* contains "writings and artwork of every nature. We are an outlet for spontaneous expressions only. Save the self-satisfied, over-crafted stuff for *The New Yorker*, please." Also accepts poetry written by children. They have published poetry by Errol Miller, B.Z. Niditch and C.C. Russell. *Spunk* is 30-50 pgs., 5½ × 8½, photocopied and side-stapled with light card cover, b&w art only, ads. They receive about 800-1,000 poems a year, accept approximately 10%. Press run is 500; all distributed free to anyone who really, really wants them. Sample: $2. No checks.

How to Submit: Submit any number of poems at a time. No previously published poems or simultaneous submissions. Cover letter preferred. "Just make us happy we opened the envelope—how you do this is up to you." Time between acceptance and publication is 6-12 months. Poems are circulated to an editorial board. "Our extremely small staff gets together now and then, we drink large amounts of coffee/tea and work through the 'in' pile until we have a zine." Often comments on rejections. Publishes theme issues occasionally. Send SASE for guidelines and upcoming themes. Responds in up to 1 year. Pays 1 copy. Acquires first North American serial rights. Staff occasionally reviews books and chapbooks of poetry and other magazines in 100-500 words, single book format. Send books for review consideration. "Our review section has expanded, we run reviews every issue now."

Advice: "*Spunk* is 30 pages of pure vim. Send us a shot in the dark if you like, but *Spunk* is always worth the postage (to see it in the flesh), and then you can see what we publish. Keep doin' what you doin' . . ."

Ⓝ ⊕ $ ◻ ◢ ◎ **STAND MAGAZINE; NORTHERN HOUSE; STAND MAGAZINE BIENNIAL POETRY COMPETITION (Specialized: translations)**, School of English, University of Leeds, Leeds LS2 9JT England, phone +44 (0)113 233 4794, fax +44 (0)113 233 4791, e-mail stand@english.novell.lee ds.ac.uk, website saturn.vcu.edu/~dlatane/stand.html, contact: editorial assistant, US editor: David Latané, Department of English, VCU, Richmond VA 23284-2005, e-mail dlatane@vcu.edu.

Magazine Needs: *Stand*, founded by Jon Silkin in 1952, is a highly esteemed literary quarterly. *Stand* seeks more subscriptions from US readers and also hopes that the magazine will be seriously treated as an alternative platform to American literary journals. The New Series edited by Michael Hulse and John Winsella has published poems by such poets as Michael Hamburger, Wole Souinka, Penelope Shuttle, Peter Porter, Ruth Padel and Christopher Hope. *Library Journal* calls *Stand* "one of England's best, liveliest and truly imaginative little magazines." Among better-known American poets whose work has appeared here are John Ashbery, Mary Jo Bang, Brian Henry and Michael Mott. Poet Donald Hall says of it, "among essential magazines, there is Jon Silkin's *Stand*, politically left, with reviews, poems and much translation from continental literature." Its current format is 9²⁄₁₀ × 6 (portrait), flat-spined, 128 pgs., professionally printed on smooth stock with matte color cover and uses ads. Circulation is 4,500 for 2,800 subscribers of which 600 are libraries. Subscription: $29. Sample: $11.

How to Submit: Cover letter required with submissions, "assuring us that work is not also being offered elsewhere." Publishes theme issues. Always sends prepublication galleys. Pays £25/poem (unless under 6 lines) and 1 copy (⅓ off additional copies). Buys first world serial rights for 3 months after publication. If work(s) appear elsewhere *Stand*/Northern House must be credited. Reviews books of poetry in 3,000-4,000 words, multi-book format. Open to unsolicited reviews. Poets may also send books for review consideration.

Also Offers: Sponsors the *Stand* Magazine Biennial Poetry Competition during even-numbered years. 1st Prize: £1,500. Send SASE (or SAE and IRC) for rules. Website includes the history of the magazine, current competition winners, and entry forms to download, subscription details, contents lists and cover images, information about the editors and poetry links.

STELLALUNA-POETRY CIRCLE (Specialized: satanic/occult), (formerly *Endemoniada*), e-mail canela_21@aol.com or Lucifera777@yahoo.com, website www.angelfire.com/pa3/stellaluna, contact Olga and 'Lucifera' Elena León. Bilingual-Spanish and English.

Needs: StellaLuna-Poetry Circle is a site dedicated to sharing poetry of all kinds. "Specifically we enjoy occult, vampiric, romantic, radical, traditional, passionate, dreamy, demonik, angelik, wiccan, pagan. We invite anyone who writes their own poetry to add their creation to our poetic temples. We prefer poems that are short and appeal to a mature audience. We also have an area to discuss poetry, and we have an area to add links to other poetic sites. We are very open to submissions. This is a ying yang experiment. Try it out." As a sample the editors selected these lines by Stan (Incarnedine):

> *Leaves may fall and wings may struggle/Though nature damns restraint,/In their spheres, their destined bubbles,/Every beast will see its way.*

How to Submit: "Once you enter the site you may post your poem in the area called 'Temple of Poetry.' You can post it yourself; it's very easy. The Spanish version and the English version are not translations of each other, they are different so if you speak both languages, visit both. One or two poems at a time please. There are not payments. You may link your personal poetry website to our site to help boost your visits."

THE WALLACE STEVENS JOURNAL (Specialized), Liberal Arts, Clarkson University, Box 5750, Potsdam NY 13699-5750, phone (315)268-3967, fax (315)268-3983, e-mail duemer@clarkson.edu, founded 1977, poetry editor Prof. Joseph Duemer.

Magazine Needs: *The Wallace Stevens Journal* appears biannually using "poems about or in the spirit of Wallace Stevens or having some relation to his work. No bad parodies of Stevens' anthology pieces." They have published poetry by David Athey, Jacqueline Marcus, Charles Wright, X.J. Kennedy, A.M. Juster and Robert Creeley. As a sample the editor selected these lines from "A Holograph Draft" by Richard Epstein:

> *Dear Sir:/I have received your letter of/the 26th. The offer it contains,/that in exchange for ~~mermaids~~ a warranty deed/to 1464 we drop our claim/for 16,000 ~~blackbirds~~ dollars, will not do./Our client has decided to obtain/~~a pair of scarlet boots~~ a writ of execution to be served/at his discretion. I remain, most truly,/~~the Rajah of Molucca~~ blithely yours/your obedient servant, Wallace Stevens*

The editor describes it as 80-120 pgs., 6 × 9, typeset, flat-spined, with cover art on glossy stock. They receive 200-300 poems a year, accept approximately 15-20. Press run is 900 for 600 subscribers of which 200 are libraries. Subscription: $25, includes membership in the Wallace Stevens Society. Sample: $4.

How to Submit: Submit 3-5 poems at a time. "We like to receive clean, readable copy. We generally do not publish previously published material, though we have made a few exceptions to this rule. No fax or e-mail submissions, though requests for information are fine." Responds in up to 10 weeks. Always sends prepublication galleys. Pays 2 copies. Acquires all rights. Returns rights with permission and acknowledgment. Staff reviews books of poetry. Send books for review consideration "only if there is some clear connection to Stevens." *The Wallace Stevens Journal* is published by the Wallace Stevens Society.

Advice: "Brief cover letters are fine, even encouraged. Please don't submit to *WSJ* if you have not read Stevens. We like parodies, but they must add a new angle of perception. Most of the poems we publish are not parodies but meditations on themes related to Wallace Stevens and those poets he has influenced. Those wishing to contribute might wish especially to examine the Fall 1996 issue which has a large and rich selection of poetry."

STICKS; STICKS ANTHOLOGY (Specialized: form), P.O. Box 399, Maplesville AL 36750-0399, press founded 1989, mini-anthology 1991, editor/publisher Mary Veazey.

Magazine Needs: *Sticks*, appearing irregularly, is "a mini-anthology of mostly short poems. All styles, subjects." The editor has published poetry by X.J. Kennedy and Richard Kostelanetz. As a sample she selected this poem, "Poem Responds to an Emergency" by Bob Grumman:

> *It took Poem less than 3 minutes/to break open the toilet/but he was too late:/only the porch-steps,/a few crevices of sparrowing/and the orange popsicle/were left of/her daylights.*

Sticks is a 4¼ × 5½, saddle-stapled or saddle-sewn booklet, professionally printed on Mohawk Superfine paper, 32 pgs. Press run is about 200. *Sticks* I through IV available for $3 each; sewn binding by request.

How to Submit: Submit up to 3 poems at a time. "As with any anthology, previously published material is encouraged and welcomed. While many poems are first-time publications, others are selected from chapbooks; a few are 'recycled' from the past? No guidelines." Does not usually comment on rejections. Responds in 1 month or so. Pays 10 copies. Featured poets may receive 15-50 copies.
Advice: "Please devise a Renaissance persona to submit to this anthology: ladies and gentlemen who view poetry as a part of the refined lifestyle, as almost a handwritten manuscript passed from friend to friend. Like Ben Jonson, be interested not only in the careful craftsmanship of writing but also in good criticism and the distribution and preservation of writing of lasting value. If you're in a rush, get ye to the shimmering internet and leave us bookworms to our fine paper and dip pens! 'Read not the Times, Read the Eternities,' said Thoreau."

STILL WATERS PRESS (Specialized: women), 459 S. Willow Ave., Galloway NJ 08201-4633, website www.netcom.com/~salake/StillWatersPoetry.html, founded 1989, editor Shirley Lake.
Book/Chapbook Needs: Still Waters is a "small press publisher of poetry chapbooks and poet's handbooks (contemporary craft). Especially interested in works by, for and about women. We prefer poetry firmly planted in the real world, but equally mindful of poetry as art. The transformation from pain to perseverance, from ordinary to extraordinary, from defeat to triumph, pleases us. But we reject Pollyanna poetry immediately. Nothing sexist, in either direction, nothing sexually erotic. No rhymed poetry unless you're a master of form who can meticulously avoid strange manipulations of syntax simply to achieve end-rhyme. No patriarchal religious verse. Preferred length: four lines to two pages per poem. Form: no restrictions—we expect content to dictate the form." They have published *Suzy and Her Husbands*, by Edward Mast and *Moving Expenses*, by Lori Shpunt. The press publishes 4-8 chapbooks/year, averaging 28 pgs. Sample chapbooks: $5; writer's guide booklets: $3.
How to Submit: Send SASE for guidelines, then query. Simultaneous submissions and previously published poems OK. Always sends prepublication galleys. Pays 10% of the press run. Royalties on second and subsequent press runs. Acquires first or reprint rights.
Also Offers: They hold 2 annual chapbook contests, each with $10 reading fee. Awards include publication and free author's copies. Send SASE for detailed guidelines.
Advice: "Read other poets, contemporary and traditional. Attend workshops, establish rapport with local peers, attend readings. Keep your best work in circulation. Someone out there is looking for you."

STONE SOUP, THE MAGAZINE BY YOUNG WRITERS AND ARTISTS; THE CHILDREN'S ART FOUNDATION (Specialized: children), P.O. Box 83, Santa Cruz CA 95063, phone (831)426-5557, fax (831)426-1161, e-mail editor@stonesoup.com, website www.stonesoup.com, founded 1973, editor Ms. Gerry Mandel.
Stone Soup has received both Parents' Choice and Edpress Golden Lamp Honor Awards.
Magazine Needs: Stone Soup publishes writing and art by children through age 13; they want to see free verse poetry but no rhyming poetry, haiku or cinquain. *Stone Soup*, published 6 times/year, is a handsome 7×10 magazine, professionally printed on heavy stock with 4-6 full-color art reproductions inside and a full-color illustration on the coated cover, saddle-stapled. A membership in the Children's Art Foundation at $32/year includes a subscription to the magazine. The editor receives 5,000 poetry submissions a year, uses approximately 12. There are 2-4 pgs. of poetry in each issue. Circulation is 20,000 for 13,000 subscribers, 5,000 to bookstores, 2,000 other. Sample: $5.
How to Submit: Submissions can be any number of pages, any format. Include name, age, home address and phone number. Must send SASE for response. No simultaneous submissions. No e-mail submissions. Criticism will be given when requested. Send SASE for guidelines or obtain via e-mail or website. Responds in 1 month. Pays $25, a certificate and 2 copies plus discounts. Buys all rights. Returns rights upon request. Open to reviews by children. Children through age 13 may also send books for review consideration.
Also Offers: Website features writer's guidelines, sample issue, philosophy, and related materials featuring children's writing and art.

STORY LINE PRESS; NICHOLAS ROERICH POETRY PRIZE, Three Oaks Farm, P.O. Box 1240, Ashland OR 97520-0055, phone (541)512-8792, fax (541)512-8793, e-mail mail@storylinepress.com, website www.storylinepress.com, Story Line Press founded 1985, executive director Robert McDowell.
Books published by Story Line Press have recently received such prestigious awards as The Lenore Marshall Prize, The Whiting Award and The Harold Morton Landon Prize.
Book/Chapbook Needs: Story Line Press publishes each year the winner of the Nicholas Roerich Poetry Prize ($1,000 plus publication and a paid reading at the Roerich Museum in New York; a runner-up receives a full Story Line Press Scholarship to the Wesleyan Writers Conference in Middletown, CT [see listing in Conferences and Workshops section]; $20 entry and handling fee). The press also publishes books about poetry and has published collections by such poets as Alfred Corn, Annie Finch, Donald Justice, Mark Jarman and David Mason.
How to Submit: Deadline for Nicholas Roerich Poetry Prize competition is October 31st. Send SASE for complete guidelines.
Also Offers: Story Line Press annually publishes 10-15 books of poetry, literary criticism, memoir, fiction and books in translation. Query first. Website includes catalog, contest guidelines, online orders, sample books and e-mail links.

⬛ ⬜ **THE STORYTELLER**, 2441 Washington Rd., Maynard AR 72444, phone (870)647-2137, website www.angelfire.com/ar/coolwriters, founded 1996, editor Regina Williams.

Magazine Needs: *The Storyteller*, a quarterly magazine, "is geared to, but not limited to new writers and poets." They want "any form up to 40 lines, any matter, any style, but must have a meaning. Do not throw words together and call it a poem. Nothing in way of explicit sex, violence, horror or explicit language. I would like it to be understood that I have young readers, ages 9-18." Also accepts poetry written by children of all ages. As a sample the editor selected this poem by Bryan Byrd:

> *This is the land of my memories:/Where forgotten river towns leak slowly into the Mississippi;/ Crumbling and ivy covered,/They jealously watch the trains and barges go by.*

Storyteller is 64 pgs., 8½×11, desktop-published and saddle-stapled with colored light card cover, original pen & ink drawings on cover, ads. They receive about 300 poems a year, accept approximately 40%. Press run is 600 for over 500 subscribers. Subscription: $20. Sample: $6 (if available).

How to Submit: Submit 2 poems at a time, typed and double-spaced. Previously published poems and simultaneous submissions OK, "but must state where and when poetry first appeared." Cover letter preferred. Reading fee: $1/poem. Time between acceptance and publication is 9 months. Poems are circulated to an editorial board. "Poems are read and discussed by staff." Often comments on rejections. Offers criticism service for $5/poem. Publishes theme issues occasionally. Send SASE for guidelines and upcoming themes. Responds in up to 5 weeks. Acquires first or one-time rights. Reviews books and chapbooks of poetry by subscribers only. Open to unsolicited reviews. Poets may also send books for review consideration to associate editor Ruthan Riney.

Also Offers: Sponsors a quarterly contest. "Readers vote on their favorite poems. Winners receive copy of magazine and certificate suitable for framing." Website includes guidelines, editors' names and sample poetry.

Advice: "I want to read what comes from your heart, whether good or bad. This is probably the easiest place to get your work in print—if it is well written. Thrown together words will not find a place in *The Storyteller*."

🔘 **STOVEPIPE, A JOURNAL OF LITTLE LITERARY VALUE; SWEET LADY MOON PRESS; SOCIETY OF UNDERGROUND POETS**, P.O. Box 1076, Georgetown KY 40324, e-mail troyteegarden@w orldradio.org, founded 1995, editor Troy Teegarden, reader of poetry Kate Teegarden.

Magazine Needs: *STOVEPIPE* is a quarterly journal of poetry, short fiction and b&w art. They are "open to most anything, but we suggest you order a copy of *STOVEPIPE* first. We extremely dislike forced rhyme poetry, cheesy Hallmark-esque lines and religious rants." They have published poetry by Guy Gonzalez, Jeff Worley and J. Todd Dockery. As a sample we selected these lines from "Impenetrable" by Sherrie Bennett:

> *She wants me to be soft, like velvet/able to bend around the edges/But I'm hard like nails,/I go straight into the matter/Holding on to what I know is solid*

STOVEPIPE is 24-60 pgs., 5½×8½, offset-printed and saddle-stapled with card stock cover, includes b&w art and photos. Accept approximately 10% of poems received. Press run is 250 for 25 subscribers of which 5 are libraries, 50 shelf sales. Subscription: $10, "includes free chapbook." Sample: $2 US; $2.50 Can/Mex; $3.50 world. Make checks payable to Troy Teegarden.

How to Submit: Submit 3-5 poems at a time. Simultaneous submissions OK. Must be informed of simultaneous submissions. "Please include an informal cover letter and short bio with all submissions." Time between acceptance and publication is usually 1-3 months. Often comments on rejections. Responds in 1 month. Pays 1 year subscription.

Book/Chapbook Needs & How to Submit: Sweet Lady Moon Press publishes 2-4 chapbooks/year—"if we like it, we publish it." Chapbooks are usually 60 pgs., 5½×8½, offset printed and saddle-stapled with heavy card stock cover, includes b&w art and photos. "We usually solicit the poets we'd like to publish, but are open to a sample of five poems and cover letter with bio." Replies to queries in 1 month. Payment varies. Obtain sample chapbooks by writing for free catalog (include SASE).

Also Offers: Sponsors The Society of Underground Poets (SoUP), a weekly one-hour radio show broadcast on WRVG from Georgetown, KY and broadcast in Real Audio on the web. More info at www.worldradio.org. "We are interested in poetry along with music, spoken word performances, taped recordings of poets and writers reading their works and lots of other stuff. We regularly interview national award-winning poets along with writers and editors from the smallest of presses. We also receive large amounts of books from established publishers and review them on the show right beside the latest issue of your zine or chapbook. Also featured each week is a regular section called News from the Writing World, put together by Heather Blakeslee at *Poets & Writers*, where we keep you updated on the latest news from around the globe. Send us your best stuff and we'll get it on the air." Send SASE for more information.

Advice: "Send us your best stuff. We enjoy reading poetry and short prose all year round."

USE THE GENERAL INDEX, located at the back of this book, to find the page number of a specific publisher. Also, publishers that were listed in last year's edition but not included in this edition are listed in the General Index with a notation explaining why they were omitted.

☑ $ ◪ **THE STRAIN**, 11702 Webercrest, Houston TX 77048, poetry editor Norm Stewart Jr.

Magazine Needs: *The Strain* is a monthly magazine using "experimental or traditional poetry of very high quality." They do not include sample lines of poetry here as they "prefer not to limit style of submissions."

How to Submit: Simultaneous submissions and previously published poems OK. Guidelines issue: $5 and 8 first-class stamps. Pays "no less than $5. We would prefer you submit before obtaining the guidelines issue which mostly explains upcoming collections and collaborations." Send books for review consideration.

☑ ◯ ◪ ◎ **STRUGGLE: A MAGAZINE OF PROLETARIAN REVOLUTIONARY LITERA-TURE (Specialized: political, ethnic/nationality, gay/lesbian/bisexual, socialism, workers' social issues, women/feminism, anti-racism)**, P.O. Box 13261, Detroit MI 48213-0261, phone (313)273-9039, e-mail timhall11@yahoo.com, founded 1985, editor Tim Hall.

Magazine Needs: *Struggle* is a "literary quarterly, content: the struggle of the working people and all oppressed against the rich. Issues such as: racism, poverty, women's rights, aggressive wars, workers' struggle for jobs and job security, the overall struggle for a non-exploitative society, a genuine socialism." The poetry and songs they use are "generally short, any style, subject matter must criticize or fight—explicitly or implicitly—against the rule of the billionaires. We welcome experimentation devoted to furthering such content. We are open to both subtlety and direct statement." They have published poetry by Vincent Obregon, Howard L. Craft, Pamela Bond and Calokie. As a sample the editor selected these lines from "naming things after heroes" by Cynthia Hatten:

> *a puerto rican lady/shouted/you been here for/three years/where'd yous get your/training/*
> *www.bullshit.bureaucracy*

Struggle is 36 pgs., digest-sized, photocopied with occasional photos of artwork, short stories and short plays as well as poetry and songs. Subscription: $10 for 4 issues. Sample: $2.50. Make checks payable to "Tim Hall—Special Account."

How to Submit: Submit up to 8 poems at a time. E-mail submissions OK (no attachments). Accepted work usually appears in the next issue. Editor tries to provide criticism "with every submission." Tries to respond in 4 months. Pays 2 copies.

Advice: "Show passion and fire. Humor also welcome. Prefer powerful, colloquial language over academic timidity. Look to Neruda, Lorca, Brecht, Bly, Whitman, Braithwaite, Pietri, Tupac Shakur, Aimé Césaire. Experimental, traditional forms both welcome. Especially favor: works reflecting rebellion by the working people against the rich; works against racism, sexism, militarism, imperialism; works critical of our exploitative culture; works showing a desire for—or fantasy of—a non-exploitative society; works attacking the Republican New Stone Age and the Democrats' surrender to it."

$ ◎ **STUDENT LEADERSHIP JOURNAL (Specialized: students, religious)**, Dept. PM, P.O. Box 7895, Madison WI 53707-7895, phone (608)274-4823 ext. 425 or 413, website www.ivcf.org/slj, editor Jeff Yourison.

Magazine Needs: *Student Leadership* appears 3 times/year and is a "magazine for Christian student leaders on secular campuses. We want poetry with solid Biblical imagery, not preachy or trite. Also, we accept little rhymed poetry; it must be very, very good." *Student Leadership* is 32 pgs., magazine-sized, full color, with no advertising, 70% editorial, 30% graphics/art. Press run is 8,000 going to college students in the US and Canada. Subscription: $12. Sample: $4.

How to Submit: No simultaneous submissions. Previously published poems OK. "Would-be contributors should read us to be familiar with what we publish." Best time to submit mss is March through July ("We set our year's editorial plan"). Editor "occasionally" comments on rejections. Send SASE for guidelines. Responds in 3 months. Time between acceptance and publication is 1-24 months. Pays $25-50/poem plus 2 copies. Buys first or reprint rights.

Advice: "Try to express feelings through images and metaphor. Religious poetry should not be overly didactic, and it should never moralize!"

⊕ ☑ ◪ ◎ **STUDIO, A JOURNAL OF CHRISTIANS WRITING (Specialized: religious, spirituality)**, 727 Peel St., Albury, New South Wales 2640 Australia, phone/fax 61 2 6021 1135, e-mail pgrove@bigpond.com, founded 1980, publisher Paul Grover.

Magazine Needs: *Studio* is a quarterly journal publishing "poetry and prose of literary merit, offering a venue for previously published, new and aspiring writers, and seeking to create a sense of community among Christians writing." The journal also publishes occasional articles as well as news and reviews of writing, writers and events of interest to members. In poetry, the editors want "shorter pieces but with no specification as to form or length (necessarily less than 200 lines), subject matter, style or purpose. People who send material should be comfortable being published under this banner: *Studio, A Journal of Christians Writing.*" They have published poetry by John Foulcher and other Australian poets. *Studio* is 36 pgs., digest-sized, professionally printed on high-quality recycled paper, saddle-stapled, matte card cover, with graphics and line drawings. Circulation is 300, all subscriptions. Subscription: $40 (Aud) for overseas members. Sample available (airmail to US) for $8 (Aud).

How to Submit: Submissions must be typed and double-spaced on one side of A4 white paper. Simultaneous submissions OK. Name and address must appear on the reverse side of each page submitted. Cover letter required; include brief details of previous publishing history, if any. SASE (or SAE with IRC) required. Response time is

2 months and time to publication is 9 months. Pays 1 copy. Acquires first Australian rights. Reviews books of poetry in 250 words, single format. Open to unsolicited reviews. Poets may also send books for review consideration.

Also Offers: The magazine conducts a biannual poetry and short story contest.

Advice: "The trend in Australia is for imagist poetry and poetry exploring the land and the self. Reading the magazine gives the best indication of style and standard, so send a few dollars for a sample copy before sending your poetry. Keep writing, and we look forward to hearing from you."

N ◻ ◯ STUDIO ONE, Haehn Campus Center, College of St. Benedict, St. Joseph MN 56374, e-mail studio1@csbsju.edu, founded 1976, editor changes yearly.

Magazine Needs: *Studio One* an annual literary and visual arts magazine appearing in May is designed as a forum for local, regional and national poets/writers. They have no specifications regarding form, subject matter or style of poetry submitted. However, poetry no more than 2 pgs. stands a better chance of publication. Also accepts poetry written by children. They have published poetry by Bill Meissner, Eva Hooker and Larry Schug. As a sample the editor selected these lines from "Jewels for Waking" by Tiffaney Dawn Dressen:

> *Do not touch me/when I sleep/my bones are breaking/into sapphires frozen/deep arctic blue*

The editor says *Studio One* is 50-80 pgs., soft cover, typeset. It includes 1-3 short stories, 22-30 poems and 10-13 visual art representations. They receive 600-800 submissions a year. No subscriptions, but a sample copy can be obtained by sending a self-addressed stamped manilla envelope and $6 for p&h.

How to Submit: Previously published poems and simultaneous submissions OK. E-mail submissions OK (include in body of message). Deadline: February 1 for spring publication. Seldom comments on rejections. Pays 1 copy. Send stamped, addressed postcard for confirmation of submissions received and SASE for results only.

✿ ✔ ◯ SUB-TERRAIN; ANVIL PRESS; LAST POEMS POETRY CONTEST, P.O. Box 1575, Bentall Centre, Vancouver, British Columbia V6C 2P7 Canada, phone (604)876-8710, fax (604)899-2667, e-mail subter@portal.ca, website www.anvilpress.com, founded 1988, poetry editor Paul Pitre.

Magazine Needs: Anvil Press is an "alternate small press publishing *sub-TERRAIN*—a socially conscious literary quarterly whose aim is to produce a reading source that will stand in contrast to the trite and pandered— as well as broadsheets, chapbooks and the occasional monograph." They want "work that has a point-of-view; work that has some passion behind it and is exploring issues that are of pressing importance (particularly that with an urban slant); work that challenges conventional notions of what poetry is or should be; work with a social conscience. No bland, flowery, uninventive poetry that says nothing in style or content." As a sample the editor selected these lines from "Eidetic" by Quentin Tarantino:

> *In fluid and electrics the alligator brain holds it all/rigid, refined and encyclopedic, the chemical well/*
> *contains a green bathing suit, improbable sex acts,/inclusive results from the elector of nineteen eighty-*
> *six/a bowl of stinging Thai soup and the origin of scars/all held static and wet in the ancient clock,*
> *the first mind.*

Sub-TERRAIN is 40 pgs., 7½ × 10½, offset printed, with a press run of 3,000. Subscription: $15. Sample: $5.

How to Submit: Submit 4-6 poems at a time. Simultaneous submissions OK; no previously published poems. No fax or e-mail submissions. Responds in up to 6 months. Pays money only for solicited work; for other work, 3-issue subscription. Acquires one-time rights for magazine. "If chapbook contract, we retain right to publish subsequent printings unless we let a title lapse out-of-print for more than one year." Staff occasionally reviews small press poetry chapbooks.

Book/Chapbook Needs & How to Submit: For chapbook or book publication submit 4 sample poems and bio, no simultaneous submissions. No fax or e-mail submissions. "Only those manuscripts accompanied by a self-addressed stamped envelope (SASE) will be considered. But I must stress that we are a co-op, depending on support from an interested audience. New titles will be undertaken with caution. We are not subsidized at this point and do not want to give authors false hopes—but if something is important and should be in print, we will do our best. Response time can, at times, be lengthy; if you want to be assured that your manuscript has been received, include a self-addressed stamped postcard for notification." Editor provides brief comment and more extensive comments for fees.

Also Offers: Sponsors Last Poems Poetry Contest for "poetry that encapsulates North American experience at the close of the 20th Century." Submit up to 4 poems. Entry fee: $15. Deadline: January 31. Winner announced March 1. Prize: $250, plus publication in Spring issue. Entrants receive a 4-issue subscription. Send SASE (or SAE and IRC) for more information.

Advice: "It is important that writers intending to submit work have an idea of what work we publish. Read a sample copy before submitting."

✔ ◯ SULPHUR RIVER LITERARY REVIEW, P.O. Box 19228, Austin TX 78760-9228, phone (512)292-9456, founded 1978, reestablished 1987, editor/publisher James Michael Robbins.

Magazine Needs: *Sulphur River* is a semiannual of poetry, prose and artwork. They have "no restrictions except quality." They do not want poetry that is "trite or religious or verse that does not incite thought." They have published poetry by Willie James King, Walter McDonald, James Scofield, Laurel Speer and Carol Frith. *SRLR* is digest-sized, perfect-bound, with glossy cover. They receive about 2,000 poems a year, accept approximately 4%. Press run is 400 for 200 subscribers, 100 shelf sales. Subscription: $12. Sample: $7.

How to Submit: No previously published poems or simultaneous submissions. Often comments on rejections, although a dramatic increase in submissions has made this increasingly difficult. Responds in 1 month. Sometimes sends prepublication galleys. Pays 2 copies.

Also Offers: "*Sulphur River* also publishes full-length volumes of poetry; latest book: *Wooden Windows* by Willie James King."

Advice: "Poetry is, for me, the essential art, the ultimate art, and there can be no compromise of quality if the poem is to be successful."

$ 🗂 ◳ SUMMER STREAM PRESS, P.O. Box 6056, Santa Barbara CA 93160-6056, phone (805)962-6540, founded 1978, poetry editor David D. Frost.

Book/Chapbook Needs: Publishes a series of books (Box Cars) in hardcover and softcover, each presenting 6 poets, averaging 70 text pgs. for each poet. "The mix of poets represents many parts of the country and many approaches to poetry. The poets previously selected have been published, but that is no requirement. We welcome traditional poets in the mix and thus offer them a chance for publication in this world of free-versers. The six poets share a 15% royalty. We require rights for our editions worldwide and share 50-50 with authors for translation rights and for republication of our editions by another publisher. Otherwise all rights remain with the authors." Also accepts poetry written by children. They have published poetry by Virginia E. Smith, Sandra Russell, Jennifer MacPherson, Nancy Berg, Lois Shapley Bassen and Nancy J. Wallace.

How to Submit: To be considered for future volumes in this series, query with about 12 sample poems, no cover letter. Replies to query in 6 months, to submission (if invited) in 1 year. Previously published poetry and simultaneous submissions OK. Editor usually comments on rejections. Always sends prepublication galleys. Pays 6 copies plus royalties.

Advice: "We welcome both traditional poetry and free verse. However, we find we must reject almost all the traditional poetry received simply because the poets exhibit little or no knowledge of the structure and rules of traditional forms. Much of it is rhymed free verse."

✅ $ ◳ THE SUN, 107 N. Roberson St., Chapel Hill NC 27516, website www.thesunmagazine.org, founded 1974, editor Sy Safransky.

Magazine Needs: *The Sun* is "noted for honest, personal work that's not too obscure or academic. We avoid traditional, rhyming poetry, as well as limericks, haiku and religious poetry. We're open to almost anything else: free verse, prose poems, short and long poems." They have published poetry by Stuart Kertenbaum, Chris Bursk, Barbara Hendryson, Alison Luterman and Sarah Pemberton Strong. As a sample the editor selected these lines from "Walking on Eggshells" by Sybil Smith:

> It seems to me/we don't see/the delicacy of creation/but crash around/in metal boots/blind to all the
> levels of destruction./If we thought of cells,/if we thought of molecules,/every moment, every day,/the
> awe would tame us.

The Sun is 48 pgs., magazine-sized, printed on 50 lb. offset, saddle-stapled, with b&w photos and graphics. Circulation is 50,000 for 48,000 subscriptions of which 500 are libraries. They receive 3,000 submissions of poetry a year, use approximately 36, have a 1- to 3-month backlog. Subscription: $34. Sample: $5.

How to Submit: Submit up to 6 poems at a time. Poems should be typed and accompanied by a cover letter. Previously published poems OK, but simultaneous submissions are discouraged. Send SASE for guidelines. Responds within 3 months. Pays $50-200 on publication plus copies and subscription. Buys first serial or one-time rights.

Ⓝ 🖰 ◳ SUNLIGHT & MOONBEAMS, Dept. of English, Ball State University, Muncie IN 47306, phone (765)285-8580, e-mail tkoontz@gw.bsu.edu, website www.bsu.edu/english/cwp/sun, founded 2000, editor Peggy Rice, editor Tom Koontz.

Magazine Needs: *Sunlight & Moonbeams* is an online magazine designed "to provide artistically excellent poetry for children. We invite professional poets to submit their work for publication. We publish poems for young children and for young adults. No poetry with weak artistry or prejudiced thought."

How to Submit: Submit 1-6 poems at a time. No previously published poems or simultaneous submissions. E-mail and disk submissions OK. Cover letter required with SASE, brief bio and other pertinent info. Reads submissions September 1 through April 31 only. Time between acceptance and publication is 1 month. Seldom comments on rejections. Publishes theme issues. Obtain guidelines and upcoming themes via website. Responds in 1 month. Acquires first rights. Reviews books of children's poetry in single and multi-book format. Send books for review consideration to Peggy Rice.

Also Offers: Website also includes a room for Poetry Goes to School, "a program in which Ball State University students teach poetry to elementary school children using classical poetry." Also included is an interactive room where children can create poems of their own; as well as rooms for parents and teachers.

◳ SUNSTONE, 343 N. 300 W., Salt Lake City UT 84103-1215, phone (801)355-5926, founded 1974, poetry editor Dixie Partridge.

Magazine Needs: Appearing 6-8 times a year, *Sunstone* publishes "scholarly articles of interest to an open, Mormon audience; personal essays; fiction; and poetry." They want "both lyric and narrative poetry that engages the reader with fresh, strong images, skillful use of language and a strong sense of voice and/or place. No didactic poetry, sing-song rhymes or in-process work." They have published poetry by Susan Howe, Anita Tanner, Robert Parham, Ryan G. Van Cleave, Robert Rees and Virgil Suarez. As a sample the editor selected these lines from "Sonora" by Georganne O'Connor:

> . . . the wind's hot breath steals the air from your chest/and every bead of sweat from your skin./From the canyon floor, I see hills/robbed of rain, studded with giant saguaro,/the sentinels. They have seen us coming./In the accordian folds of their flesh,/elf owl rests, insulated from heat. . . .

Sunstone is 96 pgs., 8½×11, professionally printed and saddle-stapled with a semi-glossy paper cover. They receive over 500 poems a year, accept 40-50. Press run is 10,000 for 8,000 subscribers of which 300 are libraries, 700 shelf sales. Subscription: $36/8 issues. Sample: $4.95.

How to Submit: Submit up to 5 poems with name and address on each poem. "We rarely use poems over 40 lines." No previously published poems or simultaneous submissions. Time between acceptance and publication is 18 months or less. Seldom comments on rejections. Send SASE for guidelines. Responds in 3 months. Pays 3 copies. Acquires first North American serial rights. Open to unsolicited reviews. Poets may also send books for review consideration. "Address to *book review editor—poetry*, not to poetry editor."

Advice: "Poems should not sound like a rewording of something heard before. Be original; pay attention to language, sharp imagery. Contents should deepen as the poem progresses. We've published poems rooted strongly in place, narratives seeing life from another time or culture, poems on religious belief or doubt—a wide range of subject matter."

SUPERIOR POETRY NEWS (Specialized: translations, regional, humor); JOSS (Specialized: spirituality/inspirational/psychic/occult); SUPERIOR POETRY PRESS, P.O. Box 424, Superior MT 59872, founded 1995, editors Ed and Guna Chaberek.

Magazine Needs: *Superior Poetry News* appears 4 times a year and "publishes the best and most interesting of new poets, as well as established poets, we can find. Also, we encourage lively translation into English from any language." They want "general, rural, Western or humorous poetry; translations; 40 lines or under. Nothing graphically sexual; containing profanity." Also accepts poetry written by children, but it has to be very good or unusual for the age level. They have published poetry by makyo, Roberts Mūks, Cae Pitharoulis and Charles L. Wright. As a sample the editor selected these lines from "Amrita" by Roberts Mūks, translated from Latvian:

> Birds and other flying things die quietly/making no noise about life/and death, no last words/leaving no trace

SPN is 12-20 pgs., 8½×5, photocopied and saddle-stapled with handcrafted cover, "relevant artwork accepted, ads open to subscribers (1 free per issue)." They receive about 500 poems a year, accept approximately 25%. Press run is 75 for 50 subscribers; 3-5 distributed free to libraries. Single copy: $1.50; subscription: $4. Sample: $2.

How to Submit: Submit 3-5 poems at a time. Previously published poems and simultaneous submissions OK (if stated). Cover letter with short bio preferred. Time between acceptance and publication is 1-3 months. Seldom comments on rejections, "but will if requested." Send SASE for guidelines. Responds in 1 week. Pays 1 copy. Acquires first rights. Staff reviews books and chapbooks of poetry and other magazines in 50-100 words, single book format. Send books for review consideration with return postage (overseas contributors please include two IRCs).

Magazine Needs & How to Submit: Superior Poetry Press also publishes *JOSS: A journal for the 21st century.* Published twice a year, *JOSS* features "all material which serves to project and uplift the human spirit for the great adventure of the next one hundred years. Writers of New Age, holistic, occult, prophetic material as well as visionary writers and poets in mainstream religious, philosophical, scientific and social disciplines are encouraged to submit." Subscription: $6/year. Sample: $3.50. Submit poems of up to 40 lines in length; articles 400 words maximum. Pays 1 copy.

SUZERAIN ENTERPRISES; LOVE'S CHANCE MAGAZINE; FIGHTING CHANCE MAGAZINE (Specialized: romance, horror, mystery, science fiction), P.O. Box 60336, Worcester MA 01606, founded 1994, editor/publisher Milton Kerr.

Magazine Needs: *Love's Chance Magazine* and *Fighting Chance Magazine* are each published 3 times/year to "give unpublished writers a chance to be published and to be paid for their efforts." *Love's Chance* deals with romance; *Fighting Chance* deals with dark fiction, horror and science fiction. "No porn, ageism, sexism, racism, children in sexual situations." They have published poetry by Gary McGhee, David A. Ross, Carol MacAllister and Jacqui Burnett. As a sample the editor selected these lines from "The Derelict Mind" by Vincent Page:

> After the last page,/after searching through the looking glass,/with desperation,/hushed clatter of I Ching sticks/gave way to ebony, mocha/chocolate brown snow dancing ballerinas/who didn't have time for chat rooms./Gazelle girls/never fog bound in island lore,/too busy for starship worship./ Publicized victories/left no time for pondering/why alone is such a long word

Both magazines are 15-30 pgs., 8½×11, photocopied and side-stapled, computer-designed paper cover. Both receive about 500 poems a year, accept approximately 10%. Press runs are 100 for 70-80 subscribers. Subscription: $12/year for each. Samples: $4 each. Make checks payable to Suzerain Enterprises.

How to Submit: For both magazines, submit 3 poems at a time. Line length for poetry is 20 maximum. Previously published poems and simultaneous submissions OK. Cover letter preferred. "Proofread for spelling

errors, neatness; must be typewritten in standard manuscript form. No handwritten manuscripts." Time between acceptance and publication is 6-12 weeks. Often comments on rejections. Send SASE for guidelines. Responds in 6 weeks. Acquires first or one-time rights.
Advice: "Proofread and edit carefully. Read and write, then read and write some more. Keep submitting and don't give up."

○ ◑ **SWEET ANNIE & SWEET PEA REVIEW**, 7750 Highway F-24 W, Baxter IA 50028, phone (515)792-3578, fax (515)792-1310, e-mail anniespl@netins.net, founded 1995, editor/publisher Beverly A. Clark.
Magazine Needs: *SA&SPR*, published quarterly, features short stories and poetry. They want "poems of outdoors, plants, land, heritage, women, relationships, olden times—simpler times." They do not want "obscene, violent, explicit sexual material, obscure, long-winded materials, no overly religious materials." They have published poetry by Anne Carol Betterton, Mary Ann Wehler, Susan Clayton-Goldner, Celeste Bowman, Dick Reynolds and Brenda Serotte. As a sample the editor selected these lines from "Brooding the Heartlands" by M.L. Liebler:

> There were those days/Lonesome out on/The Dakota Plains. Lonesome/In my prairie rose daydreams—/
> memories brooding across the heartland.

SA&SPR is 30 pgs., 5¼×8½, offset printed, saddle-stapled, bond paper with onion skin page before title page, medium card cover, and cover art. They receive about 200 poems a year, accept approximately 25-33%. Press run is 50 for 75 subscribers; 25-35 distributed free to contributors. Subscription: $24. Sample: $7. Make checks payable to Sweet Annie Press.
How to Submit: Submit 6-12 poems at a time. "Effective 2001, reading fee $5/author submitting. Strongly recommend ordering a sample issue prior to submitting and preference is given to poets and writers following this procedure and submitting in accordance with the layout used consistently by this Press." No previously published poems; simultaneous submissions OK. No e-mail submissions. Cover letter preferred with personal comments about yourself and phone number. Time between acceptance and publication is 6-9 months. "We select for theme first, select for content second; narrow selections through editors." Often comments on rejections. Publishes theme issues. Themes for 1999-2000 were Eclectic Woman, Eclectic Man, About Him!, Olden Times and Celebrating Gaia. Send SASE for guidelines and upcoming themes. Responds in 6 months or sooner. Pays 1 copy. Acquires all rights. Returns rights with acknowledgment in future publications. Will review chapbooks of poetry or other magazines of short length, reviews 500 words or less. Open to unsolicited reviews. Poets may also send books for review consideration.

◑ **SYCAMORE REVIEW**, Dept. of English, Purdue University, West Lafayette IN 47907, phone (765)494-3783, fax (765)494-3780, e-mail sycamore@expert.cc.purdue.edu, website www.sla.purdue.edu/academic/engl/sycamore/, founded 1988 (first issue May, 1989), editor-in-chief Numsiri C. Kunakemakorn, poetry editor changes each year; submit to Poetry Editor.
Magazine Needs: "We accept personal essays, short fiction, drama, translations and quality poetry in any form. We aim to publish many diverse styles of poetry from formalist to prose poems, narrative and lyric." They have published poetry by Mark Halliday, Dean Young, Bill Knott, Charles H. Webb, Kathleen Pierce and Catherine Bowman. The magazine is semiannual in a digest-sized format, 160 pgs., flat-spined, professionally printed, with matte, color cover. Press run is 1,000 for 500 subscribers of which 50 are libraries. Subscription: $12; $14 outside US. Sample: $7. Make checks payable to Purdue University (Indiana residents add 5% sales tax.)
How to Submit: Submit 3-6 poems at a time. Name and address on each page. No previously published poems except translations; simultaneous submissions OK, if notified immediately of acceptance elsewhere. No submissions accepted via fax or e-mail. Cover letters not required but invited; include phone number, short bio and previous publications, if any. "We read September 1 through March 31 only." Guidelines available for SASE. Responds in 4 months. Pays 2 copies. Acquires first North American rights. After publication, all rights revert to author. Staff reviews books of poetry. Send books to editor-in-chief for review consideration.
Also Offers: Website includes current issue information, writer's guidelines, online versions of out-of-print editions, back issue information and subscription information.
Advice: "Poets who do not include SASE do not receive a response."

○ **SYMBIOTIC OATMEAL; SYMBIOTIC PRESS, SYMBIOSIS PRESS, SLAP-DASH-UGLY CHAPBOOK SERIES**, P.O. Box 14938, Philadelphia PA 19149, founded 1997, editor Ms. Juan Xu.
Magazine Needs: *Symbiotic Oatmeal* is published 2 times a year and contains poetry, art and fun." They want poetry of "any style under three pages, would like to see more work from Asian Americans. No poor taste, poorly written work." They have published poetry by Giovanni Malito, Yen Li, John Sweet and Michael Hafer. As a sample the editor selected these lines from "Zodiac" by Joseph Farley:

THE SUBJECT INDEX, located at the back of this book, can help you select markets for your work. It lists those publishers whose poetry interests are specialized ◎ .

> *There is a morning out there,/beyond the horizon,/waiting for prayers/to call it out of darkness/and light the world*

SO is about 6 pgs., magazine-sized, photocopied and side-stapled. They receive about 50 poems a year, accept approximately 25%. Press run is 100. Single copy: $2 cash or 6 first-class stamps.

How to Submit: Submit 5 poems at a time. Previously published poems and simultaneous submissions OK. Cover letter required. Disk submissions OK. "Disk submissions must be on a diskette formatted in DOS and in WordPerfect format." Time between acceptance and publication is 1-5 months. Seldom comments on rejections. Offers criticism service. "I have a M.A. in English. If someone wants me to read a book manuscript, proof and give feedback I will need compensation of $25 or more, depending on length." Responds in 3 months. Pays 1 copy.

Book/Chapbook Needs & How to Submit: Symbiotic Press/Symbiosis Press publishes chapbooks. However, "Don't query about chapbooks. Projects are lined up until 2000."

$◓ SYNAESTHESIA PRESS; SYNAESTHESIA PRESS CHAPBOOK SERIES, P.O. Box 1763, Tempe AZ 85280-1763, phone (602)280-9092, e-mail synaepress@aol.com, website synaesthesiapress.com, founded 1995, editor Jim Camp.

Book/Chapbook Needs: Synaesthesia Press wants to publish "work seldom seen elsewhere." Under the Synaesthesia Press Chapbook Series, they publish 4 chapbooks/year. The editor has "no real specifications to form/style; I want to read fresh poetry that stimulates the reader." He does not want to see "the same garbage most little mags publish." They have published poetry by Jack Micheline, Tszurah Litzky, Roxie Powell and Steve Fisher. Chapbooks are usually 16 pgs., digest-sized, offset/hand press printed, sewn-wrap binding, 80 lb. cardstock cover.

How to Submit: Submit 16 poems at a time. Previously published poems and simultaneous submissions OK. Cover letter preferred. Time between acceptance and publication is 6 months. Replies to queries in 1 month. Pays honorarium of $200 and 6 author's copies (out of a press run of about 250). Order sample chapbooks by sending $15.

Advice: "Don't quit—submit!"

◖ ◓ SYNCOPATED CITY, P.O. Box 2382, Providence RI 02906, e-mail samuelgray@bigfoot.com, founded 1995, editor Liti Kitiyakara, poetry editors Margaret Balch-Gonzalez, Jerry Fogel and Milton Mannix.

Magazine Needs: *Syncopated City*, published quarterly, strives "to provide an outlet for the expression of creativity." They want "poetry of any subject and style; generally 50 lines or less, but will consider longer poems if truly outstanding." They do not want greeting card verse or untitled work. They have published poetry by John Grey, Hugh Fox, Lorette Thiessen and Ryan G. Van Cleave. As a sample the editor selected these lines from "Maybe Birds Would Carry It Away" by Christopher Woods:

> *But she won't open the locket./She can't./Maybe it's been too long./The hair might dissolve in the air./*
> *Maybe birds would carry it away.*

Syncopated City is 60 pgs., 5½×8½, photocopied, saddle-stapled with cardstock cover, original b&w artwork and ads. They receive about about 800 poems a year, accept approximately 20%. Press run is 150-200, mostly shelf sales, about 10% subscriptions including the Rockefeller Library at Brown University; 20-25 distributed free to reviewers and contributors. Subscription: $15. Sample: $4. Make checks payable to Gerald Fogel.

How to Submit: Submit up to 3 poems at a time, preferably under 50 lines, with full name on every page. Previously published poems and simultaneous submissions OK "if notified and poet retains rights." E-mail submissions OK ("attach file"). Cover letter preferred. Time between acceptance and publication is 6-12 months. Often comments on rejections. Send SASE for guidelines. Responds in up to 6 months. Pays 1 copy, additional copies half price. Acquires one-time rights.

Advice: "Quality is important, but it is equally important to make us think, make us feel. Don't feel it's necessary to conform—originality is important. We lean toward poetry that is more art than craft. Don't be afraid to be original, evoke thoughts and feelings."

⊕ ⊘ TAK TAK TAK, BCM Tak, London WC1N 3XX England, founded 1986, editors Andrew and Tim Brown. *Tak Tak Tak* appears occasionally in print and on cassettes. "However, we are currently not accepting submissions."

⊕ $◻◓ TAKAHE, P.O. Box 13335, Christchurch 8001 New Zealand, phone (03)359-8133, founded 1990, poetry editor Bernadette Hall.

Magazine Needs: "*Takahe* appears three to four times a year, and publishes short stories and poetry by both established and emerging writers. The publisher is the Takahe Collective Trust, a nonprofit organization formed to help new writers and get them into print. While insisting on correct British spelling (or recognized spellings in foreign languages), smart quotes, and at least internally consistent punctuation, we, nonetheless, try to allow some latitude in presentation. Any use of foreign languages must be accompanied by an English translation." No style, subject or form restrictions. Length: "A poem can take up to two pages, but we have published longer." They have published poetry by John O'Connor, John Allison, Sarah Quigley, Mark Pirie and Kapka Kassabova.

The editor says *Takahe* is 60 pgs., A4. They receive about 250 poems a year, accept approximately 30%. Press run is 340 for 250 subscribers of which 30 are libraries, 40 shelf sales. Single copy: $NZ6; subscription: $NZ24 within New Zealand, $NZ32 elsewhere.
How to Submit: Previously published poems OK; no simultaneous submissions. Cover letter required. IBM compatible disk submissions OK. Time between acceptance and publication is 4 months. Often comments on rejections. Send SASE for guidelines. Responds in 4 months. "Payment varies but currently NZ$30 total for any and all inclusions in an issue plus 2 copies." Acquires first or one-time rights.

■□◎ TALE SPINNERS; MIDNIGHT STAR PUBLICATIONS (Specialized: rural/pastoral), R.R. #1, Ponoka, Alberta T4J 1R1 Canada, phone (403)783-2521, founded 1996, editor/publisher Nellie Gritchen Scott.
Magazine Needs: *Tale Spinners* is a quarterly " 'little literary magazine with a country flavour,' for writers who love country and all it stands for." The editor wants poetry, fiction, anecdotes, personal experiences, etc. pertaining to country life. Children's poetry welcome." No scatological, prurient or sexually explicit or political content." She has published poetry by Joshua Michael Stewart, Justin Newman, Betty Lou Hebert, Jim Dewitt, Errol Miller, Jay Robinson and C. David Hay. As a sample the editor selected these lines from "Quest For Happiness" by Melvin Sandberg:
> *I've combed this globe from pole to pole,/by trail and boulevard,/But found what I was looking for/*
> *Right in my own back yard.*

TS is 48 pgs., 5½×8, photocopied and saddle-stapled with light cardstock cover, uses clip art or freehand graphics. They receive about 100 poems a year, accept approximately 80%. Press run is 75 for 50 subscribers. Subscription: $18. Sample: $4.
How to Submit: Submit up to 6 poems at a time. Previously published poems OK. Cover letter ensures a reply. Foreign submissions send SAE and IRC. "Short poems preferred, but will use narrative poems on occasion." Time between acceptance and publication is 3 months. Often comments on rejections. Responds in 2 weeks. Pays 1 copy.
Book/Chapbook Needs & How to Submit: Midnight Star Publications publishes chapbooks and soft cover novels as well as collections of poetry and fiction. Query first, with a few sample poems and a cover letter with brief bio and publication credits.

◐ TALKING RIVER REVIEW, Lewis-Clark State College, 500 Eighth Ave., Lewiston ID 83501, phone (208)799-2307, founded 1994, contact poetry editor.
Magazine Needs: *Talking River Review*, published biannually, considers itself a "high-quality literary magazine." They want "any length, any style, any subject. We print one long poem each issue (up to 15 pages). Send your best work." They do not want "sexist, racist or simple-minded poetry." They have published poetry by Stephen Dunn, Robert Wrigley and Dorianne Laux. As a sample the editor selected these lines from "Poverty" by Pattiann Rogers:
> *The lament wasn't in the stiff/whips of willow or the ice-captures/on pondweed and underwater tubers,/*
> *as we expected. No moan rose/from the frost-blackened spikelets/of bluejoint or twisted cattail.*

The editor says *Talking River Review* is 150 pgs., perfect-bound with color cover and some color art. They receive about 3,000 poems a year, accept less than 5%. Press run is 600 for 350 subscribers of which 50 are libraries, 100 shelf sales; 150 distributed free to students/contributors. Single copy: $6; subscription: $12. Sample: $5.
How to Submit: Submit up to 5 poems at a time. No previously published poems; simultaneous submissions OK. Cover letter preferred. Reads submissions September 1 through March 1 only. Time between acceptance and publication is 4 months. "Faculty advisor picks poems for board to consider; majority rules." Often comments on rejections. Send SASE for guidelines. Responds in up to 3 months. Sometimes sends prepublication galleys. Pays 1-year subscription and 2 copies. Acquires first rights.

Ⓝ ◐ ◎ TAMEME (Specialized: bilingual, regional), 199 First St., #335, Los Altos CA 94022, website www.tameme.org, founded 1999, contact poetry editor.
Magazine Needs: "*Tameme* is an annual literary magazine dedicated to publishing new writing from North America in side-by-side English-Spanish format. *Tameme*'s goals are to play an instrumental role in introducing important new writing from Canada and the United States to Mexico, and vice versa, and to provide a forum for the art of literary translation. By 'new writing' we mean the best work of serious literary value that has been written recently. By 'writing from North America' we mean writing by citizens or residents of Mexico, the United States and Canada." *Tameme* is open in regard to poetry. The say, "surprise us." They have published poetry by Alberto Blanco, Jaime Sabines, T. Lopez Mills, Marianne Toussaint and WD Snodgrass. They say *Tameme* is 225 pgs., 5½×8½. They receive about 200 poems a year, accept approximately 1%. Press run is 2,000. Subscription: $14.95. Sample: $14.95. Make checks payable to Tameme, Inc.
How to Submit: Previously published poems and simultaneous submissions OK. Cover letter preferred. Include SASE for reply. "If the work you submit has been published elsewhere, be sure to indicate where and when and who holds the copyright. If the work has not been previously published, *Tameme* reserves the right to publish it twice, once in the magazine and again in any future anthology of work that has appeared in *Tameme*. If the work has not been translated, it will be translated by an experienced literary translator chosen by *Tameme*'s editors. Time between acceptance and publication is 4 months. Poems are circulated to an editorial board. Seldom

comments on rejections. Send SASE (or SAE and IRC) for guidelines or obtain via website. Responds in 4 months. Always sends prepublication galleys. Pays 2 copies. Acquires first North American serial rights or one-time rights.

Also Offers: Website includes overview, content, contributors notes, purchase information and guidelines.

Advice: "Submissions via e-mail are not wanted. Poems cannot be read properly online. Do your work justice—send it snail mail with SASE."

$ 🖂 TAMPA REVIEW, Dept. PM, University of Tampa, 401 W. Kennedy Blvd., Tampa FL 33606-1490, founded 1964 as *UT Poetry Review,* became *Tampa Review* in 1988, editor Richard Mathews, poetry editors Kathryn Van Spanckeren and Donald Morrill. Send poems to Poetry Editor, *Tampa Review*, Box 19F, The University of Tampa, Tampa FL 33606-1409.

Magazine Needs: *Tampa Review* is an elegant semiannual of fiction, nonfiction, poetry and art (not limited to US authors) wanting "original and well-crafted poetry written with intelligence and spirit. We do accept translations, but no greeting card or inspirational verse." They have published poetry by Richard Chess, Naomi Shihab Nye, Jim Daniels and Stephen Dunn. As a sample the editors selected these lines from "Stranger" by Pattiann Rogers:

> The corridors and implications/Of my place, shaped by cat present/And gone, shapes cat lost and
> recovered./Strange reordering strangeness—come/Next time, wolf, butterfly, sloth, slug, wraith, wind.

TR is 72-96 pgs., 7½×10½ flat-spined, with acid free text paper and hard cover with color dust jacket. They receive about 2,000 poems a year, accept approximately 50-60. Press run is 1,000 for 175 subscribers of which 20 are libraries. Sample: $5.

How to Submit: Submit 3-6 poems at a time, typed, single-spaced. No previously published poems or simultaneous submissions. Unsolicited mss are read between September and December only. Send SASE for guidelines. Responds by mid-February. Sometimes sends prepublication galleys. Pays $10/printed page plus 1 copy and 40% discount on additional copies. Buys first North American serial rights.

◖ ⦿ TAPROOT LITERARY REVIEW; TAPROOT WRITER'S WORKSHOP ANNUAL WRITING CONTEST, P.O. Box 204, Ambridge PA 15003, phone (724)266-8476, e-mail taproot10@aol.com, founded 1986, editor Tikvah Feinstein.

Magazine Needs: *Taproot* is an annual publication, open to beginners. "We publish some of the best poets in the U.S. *Taproot* is a very respected anthology with increasing distribution. We enjoy all types and styles of poetry from emerging writers to established writers to those who have become valuable and old friends who share their new works with us." Writers published include Rochelle Mass, T. Anders Carson, Rachel Oliver, Marlene Meehl and Elizabeth Howkins. As a sample the editor selected these lines from "The Vantage Point of Paralysis" by Wendy Smyer Yu:

> I will watch death crawl slowly toward the hollow of my throat./He will devour my vision and my
> voice,/leaving only a card pace of nightmares/strung up against a blue-eyed sky.

The review is approximately 95 pgs., offset printed on white stock with one-color glossy cover, art and no ads. Circulation is 500, sold at bookstores, barnesandnoble.com, amazon.com, readings and through the mail. Single copy: $6.95; subscriptions $7.50. Sample: $5.

How to Submit: Submit up to 5 poems, "no longer than 30 lines each." Nothing previously published or pending publication will be accepted. Cover letter with general information required. E-mail submissions OK. "We would rather have a hard copy. Also, we cannot answer without a SASE." Submissions accepted between September 1 and December 31 only. Send SASE for guidelines. Sometimes sends prepublication galleys. Pays 2 copies. Open to receiving books for review consideration. Send query first.

Also Offers: Sponsors the annual Taproot Writer's Workshop Annual Writing Contest. 1st Prize: $25 and publication in *Taproot Literary Review*; 2nd Prize: publication; and 3rd Prize: publication. Submit 5 poems of literary quality, any form and subject except porn. Entry fee: $10/5 poems (no longer than 35 lines each), provides copy of review. Deadline: December 31. Winners announced the following March.

Advice: "We publish the best poetry we can in a variety of styles and subjects, so long as it's literary quality and speaks to us."

☑ ⦿ TAR RIVER POETRY, English Dept., East Carolina University, Greenville NC 27858-4353, fax (252)328-4880, website www.ecu.edu/journals, founded 1960, editor Peter Makuck, associate editor Luke Whisnant.

Magazine Needs: "We are not interested in sentimental, flat-statement poetry. What we would like to see is skillful use of figurative language." *Tar River* is an "all-poetry" magazine that accepts dozens of poems in each issue, providing the talented beginner and experienced writer with an excellent forum that features all styles and forms of verse. They have published poetry by Mark Jarman, Susan Ludvigson, Linda McCarriston, Albert Goldbarth, Jonathan Holden, Laurence Lieberman and Elizabeth Dodd. As a sample the editors selected these lines from "Salt Marsh" by Deborah Cummins:

> Let's dwell/among these undulant horizontals,/these lucent pools, small grassy islands/combed by white
> egrets./I want to add my obbligato/to the white-throated sparrow's/five-noted pleading . . .

Tar River appears twice yearly and is 60 pgs., digest-sized, professionally printed on salmon stock, some decorative line drawings, matte card cover with photo. They receive 6,000-8,000 submissions a year, use approximately 150-200. Press run is 900 for 500 subscribers of which 125 are libraries. Subscription: $10. Sample: $5.50.

How to Submit: Submit 3-6 poems at a time. "We do not consider previously published poems or simultaneous submissions. Double or single-spaced OK. Name and address on each page. We do not consider mss during summer months." Reads submissions September 1 through April 15 only. Editors will comment "if slight revision will do the trick." Send SASE for guidelines. Responds in 6 weeks. Pays 2 copies. Acquires first rights. Reviews books of poetry in 4,000 words maximum, single or multi-book format. Poets may send books for review consideration.

Also Offers: Website includes writer's guidelines, editors, sample poems and subscription info.

Advice: "Read, read, read. Saul Bellow says the writer is primarily a reader moved to emulation. Read the poetry column in *Writer's Digest*. Read the books recommended therein. Do your homework."

"TEAK" ROUNDUP (Specialized: subscribers); WEST COAST PARADISE PUBLISHING, P.O. Box 2093, Sardis Station Main, British Columbia V2R 1A5 Canada, phone (604)824-9528, fax (604)824-9541, e-mail wcpp@telus.net, editors Yvonne and Robert G. Anstey.

Magazine Needs: *"Teak" Roundup* is an international quarterly open to the work of subscribers only. They publish work from authors and poets across North America and beyond. Also accepts poetry written by children. As a sample the editors selected these lines from "A Joyous Moment" by Martin Goorhigian:

> Let the rivers flow/Through verdant lands/Where flocks browse/Carelessly beneath/The endless sun/
> And flowers bloom for eternity.

TR is 52 pgs., A5, offset printed, saddle-stapled, medium card cover with clip art, photos and ads. Subscription: $17 Canadian, $13 US, $24 overseas. Sample: $5 Canadian, $3 US, $8 overseas.

How to Submit: Accepts work from subscribers only. Submit 3-5 poems at a time. Line length for poetry is 40 maximum, but "good work makes room for exceptions." Fax submissions and e-mail OK (query only). SASE (or SAE with IRC) required for response. Publishes theme issues. Send SASE for guidelines and upcoming themes. No payment. "It is our goal to become a paying market when circulation makes it feasible." Responds in 1 week.

Also Offers: West Coast Paradise Publishing also publishes books and chapbooks. Send SASE for catalog.

TEARS IN THE FENCE, 38 Hodview, Stourpaine, Nr. Blandford Forum, Dorset DT11 8TN England, phone 0044 1258-456803, fax 0044 1258-454026, e-mail westrow@cooperw.fsnet.co.uk, founded 1984, general editor David Caddy.

Magazine Needs: *Tears in the Fence* is a "small press magazine of poetry, fiction, interviews, articles, reviews and graphics. We are open to a wide variety of poetic styles. Work that is unusual, perceptive, risk-taking as well as imagistic, lived and visionary will be close to our purpose. However, we like to publish a variety of work." They have published poetry by Edward Field, Lisa Glatt, Fred Voss, Lynne Hjelmgaard and K.M. Dersley. As a sample they selected these lines from "Dog-fox" by David Caddy:

> Whether to be a cock above a shit-heap,/a pig playing around with mud and root,/the drunken man
> talks to the dog-fox/pulling its nocturnal threads closer, tighter,/peeling away growth-rings, ghosts,
> monsters,/trying to say what really matters from here.

Tears in the Fence appears 3 times/year. It is 112 pgs., A5, docutech printed on 110 gms. paper and perfect-bound with matte card cover and b&w art and graphics. It has a press run of 700, of which 389 go to subscribers. Subscription: $18/3 issues. Sample: $7.

How to Submit: Submit 6 typed poems with IRCs. Cover letter with brief bio required. Publishes theme issues. Send SASE (or SAE and IRC) for upcoming themes. Responds in 3 months. Time between acceptance and publication is 8-10 months "but can be much less." Pays 1 copy. Reviews books of poetry in 2,000-3,000 words, single or multi-book format. Open to unsolicited reviews. Send books for review consideration.

Also Offers: The magazine is informally connected with the East Street Poets literary promotions, workshops and publications. They also sponsor an annual pamphlet competition open to poets from around the world. Also publishes books. Books published include *Hanging Windchimes In A Vacuum*, by Gregory Warren Wilson, *Heart Thread* by Joan Jobe Smith and *The Hong Kong/Macao Trip* by Gerald Locklin.

Advice: "I think it helps to subscribe to several magazines in order to study the market and develop an understanding of what type of poetry is published. Use the review sections and send off to magazines that are new to you."

TEBOT BACH, P.O. Box 7887, Huntington Beach CA 92615-7887, phone (714)968-0905, editors/publishers Mifanwy Kaiser and Mark Bergendahl.

Book/Chapbook Needs & How to Submit: Tebot Bach (Welsh for "little teapot") publishes books of poetry. Titles include *48 Questions* by Richard Jones, *The Way In* by Robin Chapman and *Written in Rain: New and Selected Poems 1985-2000* by M.L. Liebler. Query first with sample poems and cover letter with brief bio and publication credits. Include SASE. Replies to queries and mss, if invited, in 1 month. Time between acceptance and publication is 1-2 years. Write to order sample books.

N ☐ ◎ TEEN VOICES (Specialized: teen, women), P.O. Box 120-027, Boston MA 02112-0027, phone (617)262-2434, fax (617)262-5937, e-mail womenexp@teenvoices.com, website www.teenvoices.com, founded 1988, first published 1990.

Magazine Needs: *Teen Voices*, published quarterly, is a magazine written by, for and about teenage girls. Regular features are family, cultural harmony, surviving sexual assault, teen motherhood and all other topics of interest to our writers and readers. As a sample the editor selected these lines from "Nakedness" by Elizabeth Circo:

> *Wandering through the salmon pink room of/her childhood/She reminisces, smiling wistfully at the thought of/herself/at the innocent age of four/a precocious free spirit—*

The editor says *Teen Voices* is 72 pgs., with glossy cover, art and photos. "We accept 10% of the poems we receive, but can't afford to publish all of them timely." Press run is 25,000. Single copy: $3; subscription: $20. Sample: $5. Make checks payable to *Teen Voices*.

How to Submit: Submit any number of poems with name, age and address on each. No previously published poems; simultaneous submissions OK. Fax submissions and e-mail submissions included in body of message OK. Cover letter preferred. "Confirmation of receipt of submission sent in 6-8 weeks." Poems are circulated to a teen editorial board. Pays 3 copies. Open to unsolicited reviews.

$ ◙ TEMPORARY VANDALISM RECORDINGS; FREEDOM ISN'T FREE, P.O. Box 6184, Orange CA 92863-6184, e-mail tvrec@yahoo.com, website www.csulb.edu/~rroden, founded 1991 (Temporary Vandalism Recordings), 1994 (*Freedom Isn't Free*), editors Robert Roden and Barton M. Saunders.

Magazine Needs: *Freedom Isn't Free*, is published biannually. "Form, length, style and subject matter can vary. It's difficult to say what will appeal to our eclectic tastes." They do not want "strictly rants, overly didactic poetry." They have published poetry by M. Jaime-Becerra, Daniel McGinn, Jerry Gordon, Margaret Garcia and S.A. Griffin. As a sample the editor selected these lines from "The Woman Next Door" by Duane Locke:

> *Under her dark hair,/a white bowl/of ashes from burnt poppies.//She is afraid/she'll hear her clothes drop/and become apples.//She is afraid/her hands will turn into magpies/and have shadows.//She is afraid her mirror might vanish./She only bares her breasts to mirrors.*

FIF is 32 pgs., 4¼×5½, saddle-stapled, photocopied with colored card cover and some ads. They accept less than 15% of poems received. Press run is 500. Sample: $1. Make checks payable to Robert Roden.

How to Submit: Submit 5 neatly typed poems at a time. Previously published poems and simultaneous submissions OK. E-mail submissions OK. Cover letter preferred. Time between acceptance and publication is 3 months. "Two editors' votes required for inclusion." Seldom comments on rejections. Responds in up to 6 months. Pays 2 copies. Acquires one-time rights.

Book/Chapbook Needs & How to Submit: Temporary Vandalism Recordings strives "to make the world safe for poetry (just kidding)." They publish 3 chapbooks/year. Chapbooks are usually 40 pgs., photocopied, saddle-stapled, press run of 100 intially, with reprint option if needed. Submit 10 sample poems, with SASE for response. "Publication in some magazines is important, but extensive publishing is not required." Replies in 3 months. Pays 50% royalty (after costs recouped) and 5 author's copies (out of a press run of 100). For sample chapbooks send $5 to the above address.

⊕ ◙ 10TH MUSE, 33 Hartington Rd., Newtown, Southampton, Hants SO14 0EW England, founded 1990, editor Andrew Jordan.

Magazine Needs: *10th Muse* "is the leading international forum for nonist poetics. Nonism is the only contemporary experimental genre which is progressive and radical in outlook. Nonists overturned the conservatism of the experimental milieu by embracing nonexperimental traditions within the experimental aesthetic. That which was 'hidden' within the experimental milieu became simultaneously realised and superseded within nonism." They have published poetry by Peter Riley, Andrew Duncan, Dr. Charles Mintern, Ian Robinson, John Welch and Peter Russell. As a sample the editor selected these lines from "Glass Losing Equable Temperature" by Andrew Duncan:

> *The love I live for/is lost in rage/and I destroy/what I need protected/and stand guilty/of what was stolen from me*

10th Muse is 48-72 pgs., A5, photocopied, saddle-stapled, with card cover, no ads. Press run is 200. "U.S. subscribers—send $8 in bills for single copy (including postage)."

How to Submit: Submit up to 6 poems. Include SASE (or SAE with IRCs). Often comments on rejections. Responds in 3 months. Pays 1 copy. Staff reviews books of poetry. Send books for review consideration.

Advice: "Poets should read a copy of the magazine first."

⊕ ◙ TERRIBLE WORK; TERRIBLE WORKPRESS, 21 Overton Gardens, Mannamead, Plymouth, Devon PL3 5BX United Kingdom, founded 1993, contact Tim Allen.

Magazine Needs: *Terrible Work*, published annually, features "poetry/art/reviews illustrating the variety of non-mainstream work." They want "post-modern, neoL=anguage, primitive, surreal, speculative, minimal, computer, visual—all of high quality." They do not want "traditional formal, mainstream free verse, message, mystical or reactionary. We are particularly interested in publishing work by the most accomplished American and Canadian poets." They have published poetry by Tina Darragh, Bruce Andrews, Rosmarie Waldrop and Sheila E. Murphy. As a sample the editor selected this poem, "miniature" by Oliver Ahern:

the steaming pie is reluctant to leave the ground/it is given a helping hand by a man who lacks patience//point out that man to me/is he here in the park with all the other men?

Terrible Work is 100 pgs., A4, professionally printed and saddle-stapled with b&w card cover, includes b&w graphics. They receive about 1,000 poems a year, accept less than 10%. Press run is 400 for 2,500 subscribers, including some US university libraries. The remainder are sold through poetry readings and shelf sales. Single copy: $8 airmail (cash) or $14/2. (Editor says that he is often willing to swap an issue for similarly inclined US published magazine or book.)

How to Submit: Submit up to 10 pgs. at a time. No previously published poems or simultaneous submissions in UK "but not too concerned with same in USA and Canada." Time between acceptance and publication is up to 1 year. Responds in up to 3 months. Pays 1 copy. Reviews books of poetry or other magazines. Poets may also send books for review consideration.

TEXAS REVIEW; TEXAS REVIEW PRESS; X.J. KENNEDY POETRY COMPETITION, Sam Houston State University, Dept. of English and Foreign Languages, Huntsville TX 77341-2146, website www.shsu.edu/~eng_www/trp.html, founded 1976, contact Paul Ruffin.

Magazine Needs: *The Texas Review*, published biannually, is a "scholarly journal publishing poetry, short fiction, essays and book reviews." They have published poetry by Donald Hall, X.J. Kennedy and Richard Eberhart. *The Texas Review* is 152 pgs., digest-sized, offset printed, perfect-bound, bond paper with 4-color cover and ads. Press run is 1,000 for 500 subscribers of which 250 are libraries. Single copy: $12; subscription: $24. Sample: $5. Make checks payable to Friends of *Texas Review*.

How to Submit: No previously published poems or simultaneous submissions. Include SASE. Reads submissions September 1 through June 1 only. Time between acceptance and publication is 6 months. Poems are circulated to an editorial board. Seldom comments on rejections. Responds in a few months. Pays 1 year subscription and 1 copy (may request more). Acquires all rights. Returns rights "for publication in anthology." Open to unsolicited reviews.

Also Offers: Sponsors the X.J. Kennedy Poetry Competition. Winning mss will be published. For contest guidelines send SASE specifying "for poetry/fiction contest guidelines." Website includes catalog, contest guidelines and editors.

TEXAS TECH UNIVERSITY PRESS (Specialized: series), P.O. Box 41037, Lubbock TX 79409-1037, phone (806)742-2982, fax (806)742-2979, e-mail ttup@ttu.edu, website www.ttup.ttu.edu, founded 1971, editor Judith Keeling. Does not read unsolicited manuscripts.

THALIA: STUDIES IN LITERARY HUMOR (Specialized: subscribers, humor), Dept. of English, University of Ottawa, Ottawa, Ontario K1N 6N5 Canada, phone (613)230-9505, fax (613)565-5786, e-mail jtaverni@aixl.uottawa.ca, editor Dr. J. Tavernier-Courbin.

Magazine Needs: *Thalia* appears twice a year using "humor (literary, mostly). Poems submitted must actually be literary parodies." The editor describes it as $7 \times 8\frac{1}{2}$, flat-spined, "with illustrated cover." Press run is 500 for 475 subscribers. Subscription: $25 (US funds) for individuals, $27 (US funds) for libraries. Sample: $8 up to volume 11, $15 and $20 for volume 12-15 respectively (double issues).

How to Submit: Contributors must subscribe. Simultaneous submissions OK but *Thalia* must have copyright. Will authorize reprints. Publishes occasional theme issues. Query for guidelines and upcoming themes. "Queries via phone, fax or e-mail OK. Fax submissions OK. However, submissions must be in hard copy." Editor comments on submissions. Responds in 4 months. Reviews books of poetry. "Send queries to the editor concerning specific books."

THEMA (Specialized: themes), Thema Literary Society, P.O. Box 8747, Metairie LA 70011-8747, e-mail thema@mindspring.com, website www.litline.org/html/THEMA.html, founded 1988, editor Virginia Howard, poetry editor Gail Howard. Address poetry submissions to: Gail Howard.

Magazine Needs: *Thema* is a triannual literary magazine using poetry related to specific themes. "Each issue is based on an unusual premise. Please, please send SASE for guidelines before submitting poetry to find out the upcoming themes. Upcoming themes (and submission deadlines) include: 'Safety in Numbers' (11-1-00), 'What Sarah (or Edward) Remembered' (3-1-01), 'The Third One' (7-1-01). No scatological language, alternate life-style, explicit love poetry." Also accepts poetry written by children, but quality counts. Poems will be judged with all others submitted. They have published poetry by John Grey, Gail C. Forman, Liza Hyatt and Barbara J. Mackay. As a sample the editor selected these lines from "The Father" by Kate Harris:

From the top of the shadowed stair/I see him,/pacing behind the gray mesh/screen,/patterning it like a quilt/whose reds and blues were destined to run.

Thema is 200 pgs., digest-sized, professionally printed, with matte card cover. They receive about 400 poems a year, accept approximately 8%. Press run is 500 for 270 subscribers of which 30 are libraries. Subscription: $16. Sample: $8.

How to Submit: Submit up to 3 poems at a time with SASE. All submissions should be typewritten and on standard $8\frac{1}{2} \times 11$ paper. Submissions are accepted all year, but evaluated after specified deadlines. Send SASE for guidelines and upcoming themes. Editor comments on submissions. Pays $10/poem plus 1 copy. Buys one-time rights.

Also Offers: Website includes writer's guidelines, table of contents of current issue, subscription information and a list of back issues.

N $ ◻ ◎ THESE DAYS (Specialized: mainstream Christian), 100 Witherspoon St., Louisville KY 40202-1396, e-mail kaysno@worldnet.att.net, founded 1969, editor Kay Snodgrass.

Magazine Needs: "*These Days* is a quarterly magazine of daily devotions and devotional resources published by the Presbyterian Church (USA) in partnership with the Cumberland Presbyterian Chuch, The Presbyterian Church in Canada, The United Church of Canada, and the United Church of Christ. We publish only short religious poetry of high quality that has a contemporary but not erudite feel. We especially need church holiday and seasonal poems. We do not want to see nonreligious, nonliterary, obscure work or poetry that is outdated in form." They have published poetry by Anne Shotwell, Katherine Stewart, Sara A. DuBose, Richard Nystrom, Gordon E. Jowers and Ruth Hunt. The editor says *These Days* is 104 pgs., 8½×11, offset printed and stapled with soft, glossy cover, includes full color cover art. They receive about 500 poems a year, accept approximately 1%. Publish 1 poem/issue. Press run is 200,000 for 195,000 subscribers. Subscription: $5.70 regular print, $8-10 large print; Canada: $8.56 regular, $10.70 large print. Sample: 77¢ postage and 5×7 envelope.

How to Submit: Submit 5 poems maximum at a time. Line length for poetry is 3 minimum, 15 maximum. Previously published poems OK. Cover letter preferred. "Please include a SASE for reply and return of submissions. Electronic submission is acceptable." Submit seasonal poems 8 months in advance. Time between acceptance and publication is 1 year. Seldom comments on rejections. Send SASE for guidelines. Responds in 3 months. Pays $10 for cover poems and 5 copies. Acquires one-time rights.

Advice: "Study the publication thoroughly. If possible, subscribe and do the devotions daily."

☑ ◖ THIN COYOTE; LOST PROPHET PRESS, 2657 Grand St. NE, Minneapolis MN 55408, phone (612)781-6224, founded 1992, publisher/editor Christopher Jones, co-editor Maggie McKnight.

Magazine Needs: *Thin Coyote* is a quarterly magazine "churning up whirlwinds of creative endeavor by the planet's scofflaws, mule skinners, seers, witchdoctors, maniacs, alchemists and giant-slayers. Get in touch with your inner shapeshifter and transcribe his howls, growls and wails. No singsong rhyming crap; no greeting card devotional stuff or I'll come over to your house and put a terrible hurtin' on you." They have published poetry by Jonis Agee, John Millett, Pat McKinnon and Paul Weinman. As a sample the editor selected these lines from "invading dusk" by Laura Joy Lustig:

> jaded/with no snooze/because someone/is beside me/making me look/at myself/making shy nipples/
> pink gumballs/(because love/don't make me come)

TC is 40-60 pgs., 8½×11, docutech printed and perfect-bound with b&w cardstock cover, includes b&w photos and ads. They receive about 1,200 poems a year, accept approximately 5-10%. Press run is 300 for 30 subscribers of which 20 are libraries, 270 shelf sales. Single copy: $5; subscription: $15. Sample: $5. Make checks payable to Christopher Jones/*Thin Coyote*.

How to Submit: Submit 5 poems at a time. Previously published poems and simultaneous submissions OK. Cover letter preferred. Time between acceptance and publication is 2-4 months. Often comments on rejections. Send SASE for guidelines. Responds in 2 months. Pays 1 copy. Acquires first or one-time rights. Reviews books and chapbooks of poetry and other magazines. Open to unsolicited reviews. Poets may also send books for review consideration to Christopher Jones.

Book/Chapbook Needs & How to Submit: Lost Prophet Press publishes "primarily poetry, some short stories." They publish 2-3 chapbooks/year. Chapbooks are usually 30-40 pgs., 5½×8, offset printed and saddle-stapled with cardstock cover, includes art. Query first, with a few sample poems and a cover letter with brief bio and publication credits. Replies to queries in 1 month; to mss in 2 weeks. Pays advance or 25% of run.

◖ THIRD COAST, Dept. of English, Western Michigan University, Kalamazoo MI 49008-5092, phone (616)387-2675, fax (616)387-2562, website www.wmich.edu/thirdcoast, founded 1995, contact poetry editors.

Magazine Needs: *Third Coast* is a biannual national literary magazine of poetry, prose, creative nonfiction and translation. They want "excellence of craft and originality of thought. Nothing trite." They have published poetry by Chase Twichell, Robin Behn, Ed Ochester, Carolyn Kizer, Nance Van Winckel, Philip Levine and Tomaž Šalamun. As a sample they selected these lines from "Banishing the Angels" by Dana Levin:

> And then the cloud passed and a light came rushing down the steps/of the subway, and blazed up
> against the phone booth standing in the corner,/and inside it was a girl talking on the phone, all lit
> up amid the grime/of the subway, and when I saw her I wanted her to be/an angel, I wanted her with
> wings inside the station, to say/"the angel on the phone" and see it softly beating, old newspapers at
> its feet

THE GEOGRAPHICAL INDEX, located at the back of this book, can help you discover the publishers in your region. Publishers often favor poets (and work) from their own areas.

Third Coast is 140 pgs., 6×9, professionally printed and perfect-bound with a 4-color cover with art. They receive about 2,000 poems a year, accept 3-5%. Press run is 1,000 for 100 subscribers of which 20 are libraries, 350 shelf sales. Single copy: $6; subscription: $11/year, $20/2 years, $29/3 years.

How to Submit: Submit up to 5 poems at a time. Poems should be typed and single-spaced, with the author's name on each page. Stanza breaks should be double-spaced. No previously published poems or simultaneous submissions. No electronic submissions. Cover letter with bio preferred. Poems are circulated to assistant poetry editors and poetry editors; poetry editors make final decisions. Seldom comments on rejections. Send SASE for guidelines. Responds in 4 months. Pays 2 copies and 1-year subscription. Acquires first rights.

Also Offers: Website includes table of contents from past issues, poetry samples, names of editors and writer's guidelines.

THE THIRD HALF LITERARY MAGAZINE; K.T. PUBLICATIONS, 16, Fane Close, Stamford, Lincolnshire PE9 1HG England, phone (01780)754193, founded 1987, editor Mr. Kevin Troop.

Magazine Needs: *TTH* appears "as often as possible each year." The editor wants "meaningful, human and humane, funny poems up to 40 lines. Work which actually says something without being obscene." They have published poetry by Lee Bridges (Holland), Ann Keith (Amsterdam), Toby Litt (Prague) and Edmund Harwood, Michael Newman, Louise Rogers and Steve Sneyd (Britain). *TTH* is up to 100 pgs., A5, perfect-bound, illustrated, printed on white paper with glossy cover. Press run is over 200.

How to Submit: Submit 6 poems at a time. No simultaneous submissions. Cover letter and suitable SAE required. Publishes theme issues. Send SAE with IRCs for guidelines and upcoming themes. Responds ASAP. Pays 1 copy. *The Third Half* is priced at £4.95 each, £5.50 by post in UK, £8 overseas.

Book/Chapbook Needs & How to Submit: K.T. Publications also publishes other books in a Minibooks Series, for use in the classroom. Individual booklets vary in length and are perfect-bound with glossy covers. "Procedure for the publication of books is explained to each author; each case is different."

13TH MOON (Specialized: women), English Dept., University at Albany, State University of New York, Albany NY 12222, phone (518)442-4181, e-mail moon13@csc.albany.edu, website www.albany.edu/english/Moon, founded 1973, editor Judith Emlyn Johnson.

Magazine Needs: *13th Moon* is a feminist literary magazine appearing yearly (one double issue). Beyond a doubt, a real selection of forms and styles is featured here. For instance, free verse has appeared with formal work, concrete poems, long poems, stanza patterns, prose poems, a crown of sonnets and more. *13th Moon* is a 6×9, flat-spined, handsomely printed format with glossy card cover, using photographs and line art. Press run is 1,500 for 70 subscribers. Subscription: $10. Sample: $15.

How to Submit: Submit 3-5 poems at a time. No previously published poems or simultaneous submissions. Reads submissions September 1 through May 30 only. Publishes theme issues. Send SASE for guidelines and upcoming themes. Themes include "special issues on women's poetics, one focusing on poetry, one on narrative forms." Pays 2 copies. Acquires first North American serial rights.

Also Offers: Website includes writer's guidelines, names of editors, poetry and a price list for back issues.

THISTLEDOWN PRESS LTD. (Specialized: regional), 633 Main St., Saskatoon, Saskatchewan S7H 0J8 Canada, phone (306)244-1722, fax (306)244-1762, e-mail thistle@sk.sympatico.ca, website www.thistledown.sk.ca, founded 1975, editor-in-chief Patrick O'Rourke.

Book/Chapbook Needs: Thistledown is "a literary press that specializes in quality books of contemporary poetry by Canadian authors. Only the best of contemporary poetry that amply demonstrates an understanding of craft with a distinctive use of voice and language. Only interested in full-length poetry mss with 53-71 pgs. minimum." They published *Wormwood Vermouth*, *Warphistory* by Charles Noble and *Zhivago's Fire* by Andrew Wreggitt.

How to Submit: Do not submit unsolicited mss. Canadian poets must query first with letter, bio and publication credits. No e-mail or fax queries or submissions. Submission guidelines available upon request. Replies to queries in 2-3 weeks, to submissions (if invited) in 3 months. No authors outside Canada. No simultaneous submissions. "Please submit quality laser-printed or photocopied material." Always sends prepublication galleys. Contract is for 10% royalty plus 10 copies.

Advice: "Poets submitting mss to Thistledown Press for possible publication should think in 'book' terms in every facet of the organization and presentation of the mss: Poets presenting mss that read like good books of poetry will have greatly enhanced their possibilities of being published. We strongly suggest that poets familiarize themselves with some of our poetry books before submitting a query letter."

THORNY LOCUST, P.O. Box 32631, Kansas City MO 64171-5631, founded 1993, e-mail kofler@toto.net, editor Silvia Kofler, associate editor Celeste Kuechler.

Magazine Needs: *Thorny Locust*, published quarterly, is a "literary magazine that wants to be thought-provoking, witty and well-written." They want "poetry with some 'bite' e.g., satire, epigrams, black humor and bleeding-heart cynicism." They do not want "polemics, gratuitous grotesques, sombre surrealism, weeping melancholy or hate-mongering." They have published poetry by B.Z. Niditch, Phyllis Becker, Simon Perchik and Brian Daldorph. As a sample the editor selected these lines from "For Carl Sagan" by David Ray:

You devised on our behalf/. . . the machinery of our bodies/diagrammed. Our DNA/. . . It may be Light years yet/before we're heard . . ./in a place so distant . . ./Yet when you summarize/our life in math and chemistry . . ./You take the fear away from chaos/. . . and now/You've set out for the stars to see/ how much is worth your sending back.

Thorny Locust is 28-32 pgs., 7×8½, desktop-published, saddle-stapled with medium cover stock, drawings and b&w photos. They receive about 350-400 poems a year, accept approximately 35%. Press run is 150-200 for 30 subscribers of which 6 are libraries; 60 distributed free to contributors and small presses. Single copy: $4; subscription: $15. Sample: $3. Make checks payable to Silvia Kofler.

How to Submit: Submit 3 poems at a time. "If you do not include a SASE with sufficient postage, your submission will be pitched!" No previously published poems; simultaneous submissions OK. Cover letter preferred. Poetry and fiction must be typed, laser-printed or in a clear dot-matrix." Time between acceptance and publication is 1-2 months. Seldom comments on rejections. Send SASE for guidelines. Responds in 3 months. Pays 1 copy. Acquires one-time rights.

Advice: "Never perceive a rejection as a personal rebuke, keep on trying. Take advice."

○ ◑ ◎ **THOUGHTS FOR ALL SEASONS: THE MAGAZINE OF EPIGRAMS (Specialized: form, humor),** % editor Prof. Em. Michel Paul Richard, 478 NE 56th St., Miami FL 33137-2621, founded 1976.

Magazine Needs: *TFAS* "is an irregular serial: designed to preserve the epigram as a literary form; satirical. All issues are commemorative." Rhyming poetry and nonsense verse with good imagery will be considered although most modern epigrams are prose. As a sample the editor selected this poem by Rex E. Moser:

> *If Shakespeare had two IBMs/And I a humble quill/Would I produce artistic gems/And he this awful swill?*

TFAS is 80 pgs., offset from typescript and saddle-stapled with full-page illustrations, card cover. The editor accepts about 20% of material submitted. Press run is 500-1,000. There are several library subscriptions but most distribution is through direct mail or local bookstores and newsstand sales. Single copy: $6 (includes postage and handling).

How to Submit: Submit at least 1 full page of poems at a time, with SASE. Simultaneous submissions OK, but not previously published epigrams "unless a thought is appended which alters it." Editor comments on rejections. Publishes 1 section devoted to a theme. Theme for September 2000 was "The Third Millenium." Send SASE for guidelines. Responds in 1 month. Pays 1 copy.

N ❖ ○ 3 CUP MORNING; SOMETIMES I SLEEP WITH THE MOON . . . ELECTRONIC PUB-LICATION, 1372 Grantley Rd., Chesterville, Ontario K0C 1H0 Canada, fax (613)448-1478, e-mail abraxis@ccai.com, founded 1999, editor H. Moodie, webzine editor Mirri Moon.

Magazine Needs: Published bimonthly, *3 cup morning* is "a platform for the beginning and novice poet to showcase their work. We firmly believe that seeing your work in print is the single greatest encouragement needed to continue. Every poet should have the opportunity to see their work in print—at least once anyway." They accept all types of poetry, haiku, traditional, experimental, free form, etc. No violence, hate, profanity or graphic sex. They have published poetry by Robert Hogg, Valerie Poynter, J. Kevin Wolfe, Mary-Ann Hazen, Angela Contino Donshes and Ward Kelly. As a sample the editor selected these lines from "God's Imagination" by J. Kevin Wolfe:

> *And the Universe so laughs/at each new clever twist God puts/into his mundane assembly line job/of cramming priceless impeccable vapor/into cheap flawed bottles;/that even God chuckles.*

The editor says *3 cup morning* is 20 pgs., 5½×8½, photocopied and saddle-stapled with card cover, includes art/graphics. Publish about 15 poems/issue. Press run is approximately 100 copies. Subscription: $30. Sample: $5. Make checks or money order payable to H. Moodie.

How to Submit: Submit 5-8 poems at a time with $5 reading fee. Line length for poetry is 3 minimum, 40 maximum. Previously published poems and simultaneous submissions OK. E-mail and disk submissions OK. Cover letter preferred. "All work must be neatly typed on white paper with your name and address on every page. SAE with an IRC must be included if you want to have work returned or a review of your work sent to you. Would prefer to have an e-mail address to send critique to. Electronic submissions must be sent in plain text or html." Submit seasonal poems 1 month in advance. Time between acceptance and publication is 2 months. Poems are circulated to an editorial board. "All poetry is read as it is received and is given a final review on Wednesday mornings when all the staff read the poems and have a say." Often comments on rejections. Obtain guidelines via website. Pays 1 copy. Acquires one-time rights.

Also Offers: Website includes "writer's guidelines and how to submit guidelines and past issues of the magazine." They also publish *Sometimes I Sleep With the Moon*, an online publication.

▣ "We look for poetry that is very visual. Poetry you can touch and feel and taste. Creative, experimental, fantasy, etc." Contact: Mirri Moon at mirri@abraxis-publications.com.

Advice: "Poetry should elicit a strong response from the reader. Anger, desire, sadness, happiness, a desire to raid the fridge, go swimming, whatever. Always aim for the response. Write from the heart, the soul, the very depths of being. This is your legacy left behind—make it count! Write as if your very life depended on it. Write voraciously and about everything. Never look back."

☑ ◻ ◙ **360 DEGREES**, 517 N. Graham St. 3F, Charlotte NC 28202, founded 1993, managing editor Karen Kinnison.

Magazine Needs: *360 Degrees* is a biannual review, containing literature and artwork. "We are dedicated to keeping the art of poetic expression alive." They say they have "no real limits" on poetry, "only the limits of the submitter's imagination." However, they do not want to see "greeting card verse, simplified emotions or religious verse." Also accepts poetry written by children. They have published poetry by Sean Brendan-Brown, Rochelle Holt and Lyn Lifshin. As a sample the editor selected these lines from "Where Heroes Gather" by David Demarest:

> *"It is the encounter of a lifetime,/the endless struggle, like Sisyphus and his rock,/where the sun confronts the moon's sad and silent side/and rises again the better for it,/free, perhaps, yet forever locked within dark gates."*

360 Degrees is 40 pgs., digest-sized, neatly printed and saddle-stapled. They receive about 1,000 poems a year, accept approximately 80. Press run is 500 for 100 subscribers and one library. Subscription: $15. Sample: $5.

How to Submit: Submit 3-6 poems at a time. Include SASE. No previously published poems; simultaneous submissions OK. "Just let us know if a particular piece you have submitted to us has been accepted elsewhere." Cover letter preferred. Seldom comments on rejections. Send SASE for guidelines. Responds within 3 months. Pays 1 copy.

Advice: "We are a small, but excellent review. Most of the poems we accept not only show mastery of words, but present interesting ideas. The mastery of language is something we expect from freelancers, but the content of the idea being expressed is the selling point."

$ ◙ **THE THREEPENNY REVIEW**, P.O. Box 9131, Berkeley CA 94709, phone (510)849-4545, founded 1980, poetry editor Wendy Lesser.

◙ Work published in this review has also been included in the 1995 and 1998 volumes of *The Best American Poetry*.

Magazine Needs: *Threepenny Review* "is a quarterly review of literature, performing and visual arts, and social articles aimed at the intelligent, well-read, but not necessarily academic reader. Nationwide circulation. Want: formal, narrative, short poems (and others). Prefer under 100 lines. No bias against formal poetry, in fact a slight bias in favor of it." They have published poetry by Thom Gunn, Frank Bidart, Seamus Heaney, Czeslaw Milosz and Louise Glück. There are about 9-10 poems in each 36-page tabloid issue. They receive about 4,500 submissions of poetry a year, use approximately 12. Press run is 10,000 for 8,000 subscribers of which 150 are libraries. Subscription: $20. Sample: $10.

How to Submit: Submit up to 5 poems at a time. Do not submit mss June through August. Send SASE for guidelines. Responds in up to 2 months. Pays $100/poem plus year's subscription. Buys first serial rights. Open to unsolicited reviews. "Send for review guidelines (SASE required)."

◻ **THE THRESHOLD; CROSSOVER PRESS**, P.O. Box 101362, Pittsburgh PA 15237, phone (412)559-2269, fax (412)364-3273, e-mail lazarro@aol.com, website members.aol.com/lazarro/threshold/home.htm, founded 1996, editor D.H. Laird, poetry editor Monique Wetli.

Magazine Needs: "*The Threshold* is a quarterly magazine for writers by writers. We're not interested in trends or what is marketable. We want imaginative, thoughtful poetry. Open to all styles and subject matter." They have published poetry by Frank Anthony and Elena Geil. As a sample the editor selected these lines from "The Cellest" by Ace Boggess:

> *As if a potent aphrodisiac, an inducement to tranquil euphoria, I hear one of them sigh./Careful, meandering streams of thought echo from the subconscious, the id, demanding relegation./My thoughts, no doubt, are theirs.*

The Threshold is 48 pgs., magazine-sized, attractively printed and saddle-stitched with cardstock cover with b&w illustration, includes b&w illustrations. They receive about 100 poems a year, accept approximately 10%. They publish approximately 4 poems/issue. Press run is 500 for 100 subscribers, 300 shelf sales. Sample copy: $5.95; subscription: $19.95. Make checks payable to Crossover Press.

How to Submit: Submit up to 4 poems at a time. No previously published poems; simultaneous submissions OK. Cover letter preferred. "Poets should provide a brief biography." Time between acceptance and publication is 4 months. Publishes theme issues occasionally. Send SASE for guidelines. Responds in up to 6 months. Pays 1 copy. Acquires one-time rights.

Also Offers: Website includes guidelines, editor's name, excerpts from poetry and short story collections.

Advice: "Good writers are a dime a dozen. Good story tellers are priceless!"

◻ **THUMBPRINTS**, Thumb Area Writer's Club, P.O. Box 27, Sandusky MI 48471, founded mid-1980s, co-editor/president S.R. Elwood, co-editor Ron Curell.

Magazine Needs: *Thumbprints* appears monthly "to give writers a chance to be published." They want "any style of poetry, 40 lines maximum." No "vulgar language or sex of any kind. No satanic or witchcraft poetry." They have published poetry by Janet Murphy. The editor says *Thumbprints* is 8-10 pgs., 8½ × 11, photocopied and corner stapled with original art on cover. They receive about 300 poems a year, accept approximately 98%. Press run is 30-60 copies depending on submissions. Subscription: $10. Sample: $1. Make checks payable to Thumb Area Writer's Club.

How to Submit: Submit up to 5 poems at a time. Include SASE with all submissions. Line length for poetry is 40 maximum. Previously published poems and simultaneous submission OK. Cover letter preferred. Time between acceptance and publication is 1-2 months. Often comments on rejections. Publishes theme issues occasionally. Send SASE for guidelines and upcoming themes. Pays 1 copy. Author retains all rights.

✓ ▣ ◯ **THUNDER RAIN PUBLISHING; CORP.; L'INTRIGUE WEB MAGAZINE; THUNDER RAIN WRITER AWARD**, P.O. Box 1000, Livingston LA 70754, phone (225)686-2002, fax (225)686-2285, e-mail rhi@thunder-rain.com, website www.thunder-rain.com, founded 1996, managing editor Katherine Christoffel, associate editor Phyllis Jean Green, webmaster Mike Blezien.
Magazine Needs: *L'Intrigue* is an annual literary arts magazine with periodical updates. Accepts quality work by beginning and established poets. Accepts submissions of poetry, fiction, nonfiction, feature stories, and reviews on all literary material throughout the year. Welcomes information on literary events. They have published *Mixing Cement* by Peter Tomassi. As a sample they selected these lines from "At Howard's House" by M.W. Anderson who received the Thunder Rain Writer Award 1999:

> After dark we sit on the front porch in/Old wicker-back rocking chairs/Drinking Jack Daniels from mason jars/As we speak, warm whiskey mist escapes/Into winter darkness and mixes with/Chilled wind and drizzling rain.

They receive about 100 poems a year, accept approximately 25%.
How to Submit: Simultaneous submissions OK. Short bio preferred. E-mail and fax submissions OK. Send SASE for response to receipt or visit website. Acquires first North American serial rights. Copyright remains with author.
Also Offers: Sponsors the annual Thunder Rain Writer Award of $100 for all genre published in *L'Intrigue*. Winner notified in January of following year.

◐ **TIA CHUCHA PRESS**, P.O. Box 476969, Chicago IL 60647-2304, phone (773)377-2496, fax (773)296-0968, e-mail guild@charlie.cns.iit.edu, website www.nupress.nwu.edu/guild, founded 1989, director Luis J. Rodriguez.
Magazine Needs: They publish 2-4 paperbacks a year, "multicultural, lyrical, engaging, passionate works informed by social, racial, class experience. Evocative. Poets should be knowledgeable of contemporary and traditional poetry, even if experimenting. Ours is a culturally diverse, performance-oriented publishing house of emerging socially-engaged poetry. There are no restrictions as to style or content—poetry that 'knocks us off our feet' is what we are looking for." They have published *Talisman* by Afaa Michael Weaver and *You Come Singing* by Virgil Suarez. As a sample the editor selected these lines from "Eating in Anger" in *Fallout* by Kyoko Mori:

> My friend lived with a man who ate/peanut butter when they fought. She/found the spoons in his pockets, sticky/inverted mirrors in which her angry/words blurred backwards. . . .

How to Submit: Submit complete ms of 50 pages or more with SASE ("preferably 60-100 pages"). "We publish only in English, but will look at bilingual editions if they are powerful in both languages." Simultaneous submissions OK, if notified. Only original, unpublished work in book form. "Although, we like to have poems that have been published in magazines and/or chapbooks." Deadline: June 30. Do not submit via fax. Reads submissions during the summer months. Pays 5 copies.
Advice: "We are known for publishing the best of what is usually spoken word or oral presentations of poetry. However, we like to publish poems that best work on the page. Yet, we are not limited to that. Our authors come from a diversity of ethnic, racial and gender backgrounds. Our main thrust is openness, in forms as well as content. We are cross-cultural, but we don't see this as a prison. The openness and inclusiveness is a foundation to include a broader democratic notion of what poetry should be in this country."

⬀ $◯ ◐ **TICKLED BY THUNDER, HELPING WRITERS GET PUBLISHED SINCE 1990**, 14076-86A Ave., Surrey, British Columbia V3W 0V9 Canada, e-mail thunder@istar.ca, website www.home.istar.ca/~thunder, founded 1990, publisher/editor Larry Lindner.
Magazine Needs: *Tickled by Thunder*, appears 4 times/year, using poems about "fantasy particularly, about writing or whatever. Require original images and thoughts. Keep them short (up to 40 lines)—not interested in long, long poems. Nothing pornographic, childish, unimaginative. Welcome humor and creative inspirational verse." They have published poetry by Laleh Dadpour Jackson and Helen Michiko Singh. It is 24 pgs., digest-sized, published on Macintosh. 1,000 readers/subscribers. Subscription: $12/4 issues. Sample: $2.50. Send SASE (or SAE and IRC) for guidelines.
How to Submit: Include 3-5 samples of writing with queries. No e-mail submissions. Cover letter required with submissions; include "a few facts about yourself and brief list of publishing credits." Responds in up to 6 months. Pays 2¢/line to $2 maximum. Buys first rights. Editor comments on rejections "80% of the time." Reviews books of poetry in up to 300 words. Open to unsolicited reviews. Poets may also send books for review consideration.
Also Offers: They offer a poetry contest 4 times/year. Deadlines: the 15th of February, May, August and October. Entry fee: $5 for 1 poem; free for subscribers. Prize: cash, publication and subscription. We publish chapbooks. "We are interested in student poetry and publish it in our center spread: *Expressions*." Send SASE (or SAE and IRC) for details. Website includes writer's guidelines and names of editors.

☑ ◎ **TIGHTROPE; SWAMP PRESS**, 15 Warwick Rd., Northfield MA 01360, founded 1977, chief editor Ed Rayher.

Magazine Needs: *Tightrope*, appearing 1-2 times a year, is a literary magazine of varying format. They have published poetry by Robert Bensen and Gian Lombardo. Circulation is 300 for 150 subscribers of which 25 are libraries. Subscription: $10/2 issues. Sample: $6.

How to Submit: Submit 3-6 poems at a time. No simultaneous submissions. Time between acceptance and publication is 6-12 months. Sometimes comments on rejections. SASE required. Responds in 2 months. Pays "sometimes" and provides 2 copies. Acquires first rights.

Book/Chapbook Needs & How to Submit: *The editor is not presently accepting unsolicited submissions for chapbook publication.* Swamp Press is a small press publisher of poetry and graphic art in limited edition, letterpress chapbooks. Swamp Press has published books by Edward Kaplan, editor Ed Rayher, Alexis Rotella (miniature, 3×3, containing 6 haiku), Sandra Dutton (a 4 foot long poem), Frannie Lindsay (a 10×13 format containing 3 poems), Andrew Glaze, Tom Haxo, Carole Stone and Steven Ruhl. Pays 5-10% of press run and, if there is grant money available, an honorarium (about $50). Send SASE for catalog.

$ ◎ **TIMBERLINE PRESS**, 6281 Red Bud, Fulton MO 65251, phone (573)642-5035, founded 1975, poetry editor Clarence Wolfshohl.

Book/Chapbook Needs: "We do limited letterpress editions with the goal of blending strong poetry with well-crafted and designed printing. We lean toward natural history or strongly imagistic nature poetry but will look at any good work. Also, good humorous poetry." They have published *Ozark Meandering* by Jim Bogan; *Water Breathing Air* by Walter Bargen; *flurries* by LeRoy Gorman. Sample copies may be obtained by sending $5, requesting sample copy, and noting you saw the listing in *Poet's Market*. Responds in under 1 month. Pays "50-50 split with author after Timberline Press has recovered its expenses."

How to Submit: Query before submitting full ms.

■ ○ ◎ **TIMBOOKTU (Specialized: ethnic/nationality)**, P.O. Box 933, Mobile AL 36601-0933, e-mail editor@timbooktu.com, website www.timbooktu.com, founded 1996, editor Memphis Vaughan, Jr.

Magazine Needs: *TimBookTu* is a biweekly online journal. They want "positive, creative and thought-provoking poetry that speaks to the diverse African-American culture and the African diaspora." They have published poetry by Zamoundie Allie, Jamal Sharif, John Riddick, Rodney Coates, Michael Rodriguez and Richard "Rip" Parks. They receive about 500 poems a year, accept approximately 90%.

How to Submit: Submit 3 poems at a time. Previously published poems and simultaneous submissions OK. E-mail and disk submissions OK. Cover letter preferred. Time between acceptance and publication is 2 weeks. Always comments on rejections. Send SASE for guidelines. Responds in 2 weeks. Poets may send books for review consideration.

▨ ○ ◎ **TIME FOR RHYME (Specialized: form/style)**, P.O. Box 1055, Battleford, Saskatchewan S0M 0E0 Canada, phone (306)445-5172, founded 1995, editor Richard W. Unger.

Magazine Needs: *Time for Rhyme*, published quarterly, aims to "promote traditional rhyming poetry. Other than short editorial, contents page, review page, PoeMarkets (other markets taking rhyme), this magazine is all rhyming poetry." They want "any rhyming poetry in any form up to about 32 lines on nearly any subject." They do not want "obscene (4-letter words), pornographic, profane, racist or sexist. No e.e. cummings' style either." They have published poetry by Elizabeth Symon, Sharron R. McMillan, Anthony Chalk and J. Alvin Speers. *Time for Rhyme* is 32 pgs., 4×5½, photocopied, hand-bound with thread, hand press printed cover, with clip art, handmade rubber stamps, letterpress art and ads. They receive several hundred poems a year, accept approximately 10%. Subscription: $12. Sample: $3.25.

How to Submit: "Preference given to subscribers, however, no requirements." Previously published poems OK ("But must ensure poet retained rights on it. Prefer unpublished"). No simultaneous submissions. Cover letter preferred, list titles submitted and if first submission here give brief list of publications poet has been published in. No poems published yet? Send some general information." Often comments on rejections. Send SASE (or SAE and IRC) for guidelines. "Americans submitting can save money by sending SAE and $1 US bill (cheaper than IRC). Please no SASE with U.S. stamps." Responds ASAP. Pays 1 copy. Acquires first North American serial rights—will consider second serial rights. Staff reviews books/magazines containing mostly or all rhyming poetry. Reviews vary in length but up to about 100 words. Send books for review consideration.

Advice: "Though non-rhyming poetry can be excellent, *Time for Rhyme* was created to be a platform for poets who prefer rhyme and as a source for those who prefer to read it. Old-fashioned values popular here too. Might be best to read a back issue before submitting."

◎ ◎ **TIME OF SINGING, A MAGAZINE OF CHRISTIAN POETRY (Specialized: religious, themes)**, P.O. Box 149, Conneaut Lake PA 16316, e-mail timesing@toolcity.net, website www.toolcity.net/~timesing/, founded 1958-1965, revived 1980, editor Lora H. Zill.

Magazine Needs: *Time of Singing* appears 4 times a year. "We tend to be traditional. We like poems that are aware of grammar. Collections of uneven lines, series of phrases, preachy statements, unstructured 'prayers,' and trite sing-song rhymes usually get returned. We look for poems that 'show' rather than 'tell.' The viewpoint is unblushingly Christian—but in its widest and most inclusive meaning. Moreover, it is believed that the vital message of Christian poems, as well as inspiring the general reader, will give pastors, teachers, and devotional leaders rich current sources of inspiring material to aid them in their ministries. Would like to see more forms. They have published poetry by Tony Cosier, John Grey, Luci Shaw, Bob Hostetler, Evelyn Minshull, Frances P. Reid and Charles Waugaman. As a sample the editor selected these lines from "Stone Pillars" by Elizabeth Howard:

> Manoah brought his broken/body home. We grieved/two wheat straws leaning/into each other for succor,/but one pale day, joy/crept onto the hearth,/legs as spindly/as a grasshopper nymph's/on a frosty morning.

Time of Singing is 40 pgs., digest-sized, offset from typescript with decorative line drawings scattered throughout. The bonus issues are not theme based. They receive over 800 submissions a year, use about 175. Circulation is 300 for 150 subscribers. Single copy: $6; subscription: $15 US, $18 Canada, $27 overseas. Sample: $4.

How to Submit: Submit up to 5 poems at a time, single-spaced. "We prefer poems under 40 lines, but will publish up to 60 lines if exceptional." Simultaneous submissions and previously published poems OK. E-mail submissions OK, include in body of message. Time between acceptance and publication is 6-12 months. Editor comments with suggestions for improvement if close to publication. Publishes theme issues "quite often." Send SASE for guidelines and upcoming themes. Responds in 2 months. Pays 1 copy.

Also Offers: Sponsors several theme contests for specific issues. Send SASE for guidelines and upcoming themes. Website includes writer's guidelines, poetry samples, subscription information and names.

TO' TO' POS: AN ANNUAL ANTHOLOGY OF POETRY FOR THE INTERNATIONALLY MINDED (Specialized: themes), (formerly *To Topio*), 712 NW 13th St., Corvallis OR 97330, phone (541)753-9955, e-mail weaverroger@hotmail.com, founded 1996, founder Roger Weaver, contact editor.

Magazine Needs: *To' To' Pos* is published annually (Summer/Fall). "The landscape, site or locality that *To' To' Pos* refers to is global, so we welcome quality poetry from all over the world and in any language, so long as it is accompanied by an English translation approved by the author and so indicated with the author's legible signature." They have published *From Roots to Branches* edited by Chris Pine. As a sample the editors selected these lines from "The Free Song" by Gerard Bocholier, translated by J. Krause:

> Becoming simple obsesses us,/Writing smooth like water,/Speaking peony or sparrow,/Finding one's rhyme under light.

The editors say *To' To' Pos* is 50-100 pgs., digest-sized, perfect-bound with card cover. Subscription: $6.

How to Submit: Submit up to 6 poems or pages with name and address on each page. No previously published poems; simultaneous submissions OK. Cover letter preferred. Reads submissions September 1 through April 15 only. Poems are circulated to an editorial board with two editors agreeing on the acceptances. Seldom comments on rejections. Publishes theme issues. Theme for issue #4 was Incarceration. Send SASE for guidelines and upcoming themes. Pays 1 copy. Acquires one-time rights.

Also Offers: "Poetry Enterprises provides copyrighted but free materials for poets and artists, students and teachers. Send a SASE and request for information on traditional poetry, free verse or prose poetry."

TORRE DE PAPEL (Specialized: ethnic/nationality), 111 Phillips Hall, Iowa City IA 52242-1409, phone (319)335-0487, e-mail torredepapel@uiowa.edu, website www.uiowa.edu/~spanport, founded 1991, editor Eduardo Gúizar Alvarez.

Magazine Needs: Appearing 3 times a year, *Torre de Papel* is a "journal devoted to the publication of critical and creative works related to Hispanic and Luso-Brazilian art, literature, and cultural production. We are looking for poetry written in Spanish, Portuguese, or languages of these cultures; translations of authors writing in these languages; or poems in English representative of some aspect of Hispanic or Luso-Brazilian culture." They do not want to see "poetry for children; no religious or esoterical work." As a sample the editor selected these lines from David William Foster and Daniel Altamiranda's translation of "Cadáveres" by Néstor Perlongher:

> Along the tracks of a train that never stops/In the wave of a sinking ship/In a small wave, vanishing/
> On the wharves the steps the trampolines the piers/There are Corpses

The editor says *Torre de Papel* is 110 pgs., 8¾ × 11½. Press run is 200 for 50 subscribers of which 19 are libraries. Single copy: $7; subscription: $21. Sample: $10.

How to Submit: Submit up to 5 poems at a time. No previously published poems or simultaneous submissions. E-mail submissions OK, include as attached file. Cover letter with brief bio required. Include e-mail address. Submit 3 copies of each poem and a Macintosh or IBM diskette of the work. Reads submissions September through April only. Poems are circulated to an editorial board for review. "We send creative work to three readers of our advisory board for comments. However, since we publish articles and stories as well, space for poetry can be limited." Responds in 6 months. Pays 1 copy.

THE CHAPBOOK INDEX, located at the back of this book, lists those publishers who consider chapbook mss. A chapbook, a small volume of work (usually under 50 pages), is often a good middle step between magazine and book publication.

☑ $ ◎ **TOUCH (Specialized: religious, teens, themes)**, P.O. Box 7259, Grand Rapids MI 49510, phone (616)241-5616, founded 1970, managing editor Sara Lynne Hilton.
Magazine Needs: *Touch* is a 24-page edition "written for girls 9-14 to show them how God is at work in their lives and in the world around them. *Touch* is theme-oriented. We like our poetry to fit the theme of each issue. We send out a theme update biannually to all our listed freelancers. We prefer short poems with a Christian emphasis that can show girls how God works in their lives." They have published poetry by Janet Shafer Boyanton and Iris Alderson. As a sample the editor selected this poem, "Thanks for Funny Things," by Lois Walfrid Johnson:

> Thank You for funny things,/for the bubbling feeling of/giggles that fill my insides,/push up,/and spill
> over/in a shout of joy!/Thank You, Lord./Thank You!

Touch is published 9 times a year, magazine-sized. *Keeping In-Touch* newsletter is published in the summer. They receive 150-200 submissions of poetry/year, use 1 poem in each issue, have a 6-month backlog. Circulation is 15,500 subscribers. Subscription: $12.50 US, $15 Canada, $20 foreign. Sample and guidelines: $1 with 8×10 SASE.
How to Submit: Poems must not be longer than 20 lines—prefer much shorter. Simultaneous submissions OK. Query with SASE for theme update. Responds in 2 months. Pays $10-15 and copies.

☑ ☺ ◎ **TOUCHSTONE LITERARY JOURNAL (Specialized: bilingual/foreign language, form/ style, translations); PANTHER CREEK PRESS**, P.O. Box 8308, Spring TX 77387-8308, e-mail guidamj@fle x.net or panthercreek3@hotmail.com, website www.axnjxn.com, founded 1975, poetry editor William Laufer, managing editor Guida Jackson. (Mail for book projects should be sent to Panther Creek Press, P.O. Box 130233, Panther Creek Station, Spring TX 77393-0233, attn: Guida Jackson.)
Magazine Needs: *Touchstone Literary Journal* is an annual appearing in December that publishes "experimental or well-crafted traditional form, including sonnets, and translations. No light verse or doggerel." They have published poetry by Walter Griffin, Walter McDonald, Paul Ramsey and Janice Whittington. *Touchstone* is 100 pgs., digest-sized, flat-spined, professionally printed in small, dark type with glossy card cover. Subscription: $7.50. Sample: $4.
How to Submit: Submit 5 poems at a time. "Cover letter telling something about the poet piques our interest and makes the submission seem less like a mass mailing." Sometimes sends prepublication galleys. Pays 2 copies. Reviews books of poetry. Open to unsolicited reviews. Poets may also send books for review consideration to Review Editor.
Book/Chapbook Needs & How to Submit: Panther Creek Press also publishes an occasional chapbook. Send SASE for chapbook submission guidelines. "We previously published a book-length epic, *Kingdom of the Leopard: An Epic of Old Benin* by Nigerian poet chi chi layor. We are open to new projects. Query first, with SASE. Absolutely no mail is answered without SASE."
Also Offers: Website includes guidelines, names of editors, sample poetry, display of current titles and ordering information.

$ ☐ **TRADITION MAGAZINE**, P.O. Box 492, Anita IA 50020, phone (712)762-4363, founded 1976, editor Bob Everhart.
Magazine Needs: *Tradition* is a bimonthly "house magazine for our non-profit association devoted to preservation of pioneer music. Poetry needs to be related to pioneer music." The editor says *Tradition* is 56 pgs., magazine-sized, staple bound. They receive about 5 poems a year, accept approximately 50%. Press run is 2,500 for 2,000 subscribers. Subscription: $20. Sample: $3.75. Make checks payable to NTCMA.
How to Submit: Submit 2 poems at a time. Previously published poems and simultaneous submissions OK. Cover letter preferred. Time between acceptance and publication is 3 months. Publishes theme issues. Responds in 3 months. Pays $1/poem and 5 copies. Buys one-time rights. Reviews books of poetry and other magazines in multi-book format. Open to unsolicited reviews. Poets may also send books for review consideration to.

☐ ◎ **TRANSCENDENT VISIONS (Specialized: psychiatric survivors, ex-mental patients)**, 251 S. Olds Blvd. 84-E, Fairless Hills PA 19030-3426, phone (215)547-7159, founded 1992, editor David Kime.
Magazine Needs: *Transcendent Visions* appears 1-2 times a year "to provide a creative outlet for psychiatric survivors/ex-mental patients." They want "experimental, confessional poems; strong poems dealing with issues we face. Any length or subject matter is OK but shorter poems are more likely to be published. No rhyming poetry." They have published poetry by Lyn Lifshin, Chuck Mitchell, Gale Tolf, Chriss-Spike Quatrone and Paul Weinman. As a sample the editor selected these lines from "It (Fear)" by Gloria del Vecchio:

> What has happened to the rat?/Is it on some remote street with its/mouth and anus ruining space?/
> Suddenly, out of the chimney/the rat leaps into the room and/climbs up the paintings of large women.

TV is 24 pgs., 8½×11, photocopied and corner-stapled with paper cover, b&w line drawings. They receive about 100 poems a year, accept approximately 20%. Press run is 200 for 50 subscribers. Subscription: $6. Sample: $2. Make checks payable to David Kime.
How to Submit: Submit 5 poems at a time. Previously published poems and simultaneous submissions OK. Cover letter preferred. "Please tell me something unique about you, but I do not care about all the places you

insider report

A poet brings Europe to the world

Photo by Tihomir Pinter

Iztok Osojnik

Iztok Osojnik—poet, novelist, essayist, editor, translator, painter and mountain climber—is something of a Renaissance man. Born in Slovenia, the northernmost republic of the former Yugoslavia, Osojnik is vice president of the Slovene Writer's Association and director of the annual Vilencia poetry festival, which brings together writers from all over the world in celebration of Slovenian and regional literatures and to cultivate alliances among the literary communities of the world.

"My aim is to present central Europe to the world and to present the world to central Europe," says Osojnik. "I want to keep Vilencia as a forum for introducing different cultures and different national literatures, to make it the best informed and best equipped literary festival in this area and to serve the needs of central Europe."

A sense of community is important to Osojnik who, like so many others, has been affected by the breakup of the former Yugoslavia, a subject that has found its way into his poetry. "Of course I reacted to what was going on in the Balkans. I felt completely lost when I realized there was a slaughter going on. In a situation like that, you try to be honest—try to see if there's anything you can do besides just crying out of pain and helplessness," he says.

For Osojnik, writing has always been a means of rejuvenation, of accessing "spiritual potential." He says, "When I was three, maybe four years old, I remember looking at a leaf and trying to figure out where the sameness between the word 'leaf' and the thing I held in my hand came from. That was a really poetic experience. Of course, I didn't know it at the time, though looking back I definitely recognize that as the beginning. Years later, I read a poem by Li Po that basically said, I'm sitting here, I'm writing this down and it's infinity. And there I was, reading this poem 1,100 years later in the Slovenian language and it was infinity. I couldn't believe it."

Osojnik has published more than sixteen collections of verse, including *Mirrors in the Time of War* (DZS, Ljubljana, 1994); *Hewn Stones* (Obzorja, Maribor, 1995); *A Shepherd of Silence* (Poetry Miscellany Chapbooks, 1996); *Postcards for Darja* (DZS, Ljubljana, 1997); *New Born Stars* (with Uros Zupan, Poetry Miscellany Chapbooks, 1998); *Spleen in Berlin* (DZS, Ljubljana, 1999); and *Some Things Happen for the First Time* (Lumen Books, 2000). His poems have been translated into English, German, Hungarian, Italian, Hebrew, Serbian, Croatian, Galician, Czech and Macedonian.

"I'm very grateful when people translate my work," says Osojnik. "Robert Frost said that poetry is what gets lost in translation. I understand this because I translate other poets into my own language and there's always something that doesn't come through in translation. But the very moment you start translating me, it's you—it's your poem, and even if it's not so good according to my standards or anybody's standards, it was you who put some effort into translating it, and it's your person in there, and I respect that."

"Dead Poet's Society"

I climbed the Parnassus. Wearing only
Adidas shoes and shorts.
I stood on its barren peak at eight in the evening.
Among the rocks. Captivated by the vistas.
I rock climbed the steep slabs.
Scrambled up among prickly thorn-bushes and goats.
Deep behind me, in the gorge of Delphi,
the temple of Apollo glowed in the evening dusk.
I came upon a barely visible ancient path.
Cut into stone. The rustling of grasses. Goat's droppings.
A sweaty body. Wind whispering in the silence.
I returned to the valley. Pensive. Wind-blown. Emotional.
Daydreamed about you. Just like a classical
Greek hero. I watched the mountain's top. Sang softly.

(translated by Sonja Kravanja; reprinted by permission of the author)

For Osojnik, poets translating each other's work is another step in fostering an international community of writers. "I live here in central Europe, but I'm a planetary being. Whatever I do is on the planetary level—on the cosmic level if you want. The Portuguese poet Pessoa said his world was as large as the sky above his village—that's my world and it's cosmic in this sense because I'm open to everything."

"Everything" includes mastering several languages, exploring the "possible" through a variety of mediums, and reading voraciously. "When you put in a lot of effort and you study a lot—not for the sake of walking around and saying I know this and that, but because there's this struggle in you, this hunger—your mind comes to its full potential," says Osojnik. "You can read things that are easy, but then you're finished and you throw it away and think, ah, I read another book. But what do you do then? You need another book. But you can also do this the other way around—you take a very difficult book and you spend days, weeks, months, years, just going through it."

This drive—this curiosity—feeds Osojnik's writing. "I have an incredible production. It comes out all the time, even to the point where I have to stop myself. I start with the first sentence and write the first poem, then the second one comes, then the third and the fourth—they just go, go, go, go. When I stop I'm like a volcano, I feel like a blowing mountain."

In actuality, Osojnik is a world-class mountain climber. His ascents include Kilimanjaro, Mt. Everest, summits in the Andes and the Rockies and just about every peak in the Alps. "Climbing is definitely a school for life. It opens your eyes and gives you a 'supranatural' perspective on the world. It brings you in touch with the universe—the winds, the cold, the open space, with a mountain as a living being. It develops a persistence, a feeling for reality, an orientation, and correct judgment of what is important and what is not. It builds up a real friendship among climbers—one never gets that close to another person in everyday life. You learn about responsibility for other people and to go on and on without stopping or complaining, depending solely on yourself. These things are all very close to, or are even the essence of, literature or literary creation," he says.

"You have to discipline yourself and concentrate not to lose the thread," Osojnik explains. "What you do is walk on the dark side. All the time you walk on the dark side, you have what I call 'not-knowledge.' You let this not-knowledge sit upon your words and you just go with it. Half of you controls this full potential and the other half controls the language, and this is very difficult because language has its own logic."

Because of this logic in language, Osojnik often argues against the misuse of metaphors in poetry. "For me, poetry really goes beyond metaphor. It is experience itself—experience brought up through language. In mathematics, when you come to the end of the formula, you can't just introduce something that is illogical. It has to have an inner consequence, otherwise it doesn't work. The same is true with the poetry when, instead of working really hard on a particular passage, you snap a metaphor in there and jump across. That's too easy." Osojnik and "easy" do not mix well.

"Usually I write by hand, then I copy everything into the computer," he explains. "When the time comes to polish a poem I cut things, break things—I hate rhythm. I hate melody. I hate harmony and rhymes. For me, it's like this—the very moment something starts to repeat itself, it's gone.

"If you develop language as a tool, an existential tool, it enables you to open up these inner-personal existential spiritual experiences—I'm not talking about a mystique, I'm talking about something plain, straight, real—then you surprise yourself—you're surprising yourself all the time."

—*Michelle Moore*

have been published." Time between acceptance and publication is 3 months. Responds in 3 weeks. Pays 1 copy of issue in which poet was published. Acquires first or one-time rights. Staff reviews books and chapbooks of poetry and other magazines in 20 words. Send books for review consideration.

Also Offers: "I also publish a political zine called *Crazed Nation*, featuring essays concerning mental illness."

TRESTLE CREEK REVIEW (Specialized: regional), English Dept. North Idaho College, 1000 W. Garden, Coeur d'Alene ID 83814, phone (208)769-3384, fax (208)769-5918, founded 1982-83, poetry editor Andrea Carter et al.

Magazine Needs: *Trestle Creek* is a "2-year college creative writing program production. Purposes: (1) expand the range of publishing/editing experience for our small band of writers; (2) expose them to editing experience; (3) create another outlet for serious, beginning writers. We're fairly eclectic but prefer poetry on the Northwest region, particularly the innermountain West (Idaho, Montana, etc.). We favor poetry strong on image and sound, and country vs. city; spare us the romantic, rhymed clichés. We can't publish much if it's long (more than two pgs.)." This publication features both free and formal verse by relative newcomers. They have published poetry by Sean Brendan-Brown, E.G. Burrows, Ron McFarland and Mary Winters. As a sample the editor selected these lines from "under my skin" by Rande Mack:

> there are targets taking shape in the brains/of the yellowstone wolves—there are edges/over which they'll never know they've stumbled

TCR is a 57-page annual, digest-sized, professionally printed on heavy buff stock, perfect-bound, matte cover with art. Press run is 500 for 6 subscribers of which 4 are libraries. The editors receive 100 submissions a year, use approximately 30. Sample: $5.

How to Submit: Submit before March 1 (for May publication), no more than 5 pgs. No previously published poems or simultaneous submissions. Fax submissions OK. Responds by March 30. Pays 2 copies.

Advice: "Be neat; be precise; don't romanticize or cry in your beer; strike the surprising, universal note. Know the names of things."

◐ ◎ **TRI LINGUA (Specialized: ethnic/nationality, translations)**, P.O. Box 24927, New Orleans LA 70184-4927, e-mail trilingua@aol.com, website members.aol.com/TriLingua, founded 1999, editor Anne Marie Giovingo.

Magazine Needs: Published annually, *Tri Lingua* is "a place for American, French and Italian poets and writers to present their work in side-by-side translation. *Tri Lingua* also publishes poems without translation and invites readers to submit translations." They want "poems of any length or form, also short stories and essays which reflect the individual and respect and explore the language. Translations of published and unpublished works of other poets are also welcomed. No poems in their first stages of revision." The editor says *Tri Lingua* is about 48 pgs.

How to Submit: Submit 3-6 typed poems at a time. Previously published poems and simultaneous submissions OK, "if clearly stated in the cover letter." E-mail submissions OK, "if queried first." Cover letter with brief bio required. Include SASE or IRCs for returns. Time between acceptance and publication is 1-6 months. Seldom comments on rejections. Send SASE (or SAE and IRC) for guidelines or obtain via e-mail or website. Responds in 4 months. Sometimes sends prepublication galleys. Pays 1 copy. Acquires first and reprint rights. Staff reviews books of single and multi-book format. Send books for review consideration.

Also Offers: Website includes submission guidelines.

N ◐ ◎ **TRICYCLE: THE BUDDHIST REVIEW (Specialized: religious)**, 92 Vandam St., #3, New York NY 10013, phone (212)645-1143, fax (212)645-1493, e-mail editorial@tricycle.com, website www.tricycle. com, founded 1991, contact poetry editor.

Magazine Needs: "*Tricycle* is a nonsectarian quarterly review exploring the influence of Buddhism in the West. We look for poetry that attempts to explore the subject matter that the magazine explores—the influence of Buddhism and Western culture on each other." They have published poetry by Jane Hirshfield, Chase Twichell, Thich Nhat Hanh, Ko Un, Muso Soseki and the Sixth Dalai Lama. They say *Tricycle* is 136 pgs., 8½×11, web offset printed, perfect-bound, 100 lb. cover stock, includes contemporary and traditional illustrations and photography, 30% ads. They receive about 50 poems a year, accept approximately 15%. Publish 1-2 poems/issue. Press run is 60,000 for 40,000 subscribers of which 250 are libraries, 16,000 shelf sales; 300 distributed free to media, authors, artists. Single copy: $7.50; subscription: $24/year.

How to Submit: Submit 5 poems at a time. Previously published poems and simultaneous submissions OK. E-mail submissions OK. Cover letter required. Submit seasonal poems 5 months in advance. Time between acceptance and publication is 5 months. Poems are circulated to an editorial board. Seldom comments on rejections. Publishes theme issues occasionally. Obtain guidelines and upcoming themes via website. Responds in 5 months. Pays 1 copy. Acquires one-time rights. Staff reviews books of poetry and other magazines in single and multi-book format. Send books for review consideration to Editorial Department.

■ Website contains original content not found in the print edition. "We tend to publish more poetry on our website than in the magazine."

◐ **TRIQUARTERLY MAGAZINE; TRIQUARTERLY BOOKS/NORTHWESTERN UNIVERSITY PRESS**, 2020 Ridge Ave., Evanston IL 60208-4302, phone (847)491-7614, fax (847)467-2096, website www.triq uarterly.nwu.edu, editor Susan Hahn.

■ Work appearing in *TriQuarterly* has been included in *The Best American Poetry* (1995, 1996 and 1997) and the *Pushcart Prize* anthology.

Magazine Needs: *TriQuarterly* magazine "accepts a wide range of verse forms and styles of verse (long poems, sequences, etc.) with the emphasis solely on excellence, and some issues are published as books on specific themes." They have published poetry by Tom Sleigh, Carl Phillips, Edward Hirsch, Campbell McGrath, Susan Stewart and Theodore Weiss. *TriQuarterly*'s three issues per year are 200 pgs., 6×9, professionally printed and flat-spined with b&w photography, graphics, glossy card cover. There are about 40 or more pgs. of poetry in each issue. They receive about 3,000 poems a year, use approximately 60, 1 year backlog. Press run is 5,000 for 2,000 subscribers of which 35% are libraries. Single copy: $11.95; subscription: $24. Sample: $5.

How to Submit: No simultaneous submissions. No fax or e-mail submissions. Reads submissions October 1 through March 31 only. Sometimes works with poets, inviting rewrites of interesting work. Responds in 3 months. Always sends prepublication galleys. Pays 2 copies, additional copies available at a 40% discount. Acquires first North American serial rights. "We suggest prospective contributors examine sample copy before submitting." Reviews books of poetry "at times."

Book Needs & How to Submit: TriQuarterly Books (an imprint of Northwestern University Press) publishes 8-10 books/year of fiction and poetry. They have published poetry by William Meredith, Pimone Triplett and Muriel Rukeyser. Query with up to 10 sample pages of poetry with SASE, "but we cannot consider unsolicited manuscripts without a prior query." Send SASE for additional information.

✓ ◐ ◎ **TROUBADOUR; TOWERS AND RUSHING, LTD. (Specialized: style, rhyme)**, P.O. Box 691745, San Antonio TX 78269-1745, phone/fax (210)696-1363, e-mail publisher@towersandrushing.com, website www.towersandrushing.com, *Troubadour* founded 1997, Towers and Rushing Ltd. founded 1986, publisher/editor Dr. Ron Ribble.

Magazine Needs: *Troubadour*, published annually (March), "showcases the very best of contemporary rhyme and its poetic practitioners." They want "excellently crafted, accessible rhyming poetry. No forced rhyme or inversion, no epics, no self-pitying or self-indulgent verse, no useless profanity, mush or schlock, no kindergarten jingles or doggerel." They have published poetry, in their former semiannual publication, by Richard Moore, Henry Fischer, Richard Wakefield, Adam Berlin, Alexander Long, Margaret Mantle, Ed Wier, Brook Wiese and Gale White. As a sample the editor selected these lines from "The Complex" by 1999 Pushcart nominee Charles Rafferty:

> . . . *The shadows didn't move./He drank until he heard the morning knock/of pipes, the jangle of some distant clock.*

Troubadour is 150-200 pgs., 8½ × 5½, perfect-bound, with soft laminate cover. Past issues have included interviews or exchanges with Robert Goulet, Paul Scofield, J.D. McClatchy, X. J. Kennedy, Richard Moore and Nils Clausson. Single copy: $12. Sample copies of the former semiannual *Troubadour* can be instructive for prospective contributors and are available at $3 postpaid until supplies are exhausted.
How to Submit: Submit no more than 3 poems at a time with name and address. Line length for poetry is 32 maximum. No previously published poems. Simultaneous submissions OK, but must be so marked. Cover letter preferred with "whether poet has been published before or not and a little bit about the poet but keep in mind that poems will be selected for their merit not because of the poet's esteemed history: the greatest of poets have written more bad than good poems. SASE required or no response." No electronic submissions. Poetry accepted for consideration between July and December. Time between acceptance and publication is 2-4 months. Pays 1 copy for one-time rights. Contributors can purchase up to 6 additional copies at 40% off the cover price.
Also Offers: Website includes editors names and guidelines.
Advice: "We have interviewed folks like Rita Dove, Richard Moore, Robert Pinsky, Robert Hass, Gerald Stern, X.J. Kennedy and J.D. McClatchy. All assert that being a good reader is a necessary but not sufficient prerequisite for being a good poet. Before submitting be certain you understand what 'good' poetry is. Sampling the journal you intend to submit to is probably the best way to know whether or not you create what they hunger for."

$ ⊘ ◎ TRUE ROMANCE (Specialized: women); STERLING MACFADDEN, 233 Park Ave. S., New York NY 10003, editor Pat Vitucci.
Magazine Needs: *True Romance* is a monthly magazine publishing "subjects of interest to women—family, careers, romance, tragedy, personal crises." They want "poems that express a unique point of view. Poems that address topics. No Hallmark greeting cards." The editor says *TR* is 76 pgs., magazine-sized.
How to Submit: Submit 3 poems at a time. Line length for poetry is 8 minimum, 24 maximum. No previously published poems or simultaneous submissions. Send SASE for guidelines before submitting. Responds in 3 months. Pays $10-40. Buys all rights.

✓ ⊘ ◎ TSUNAMI INC.; THE TEMPLE, GU SI, EL TEMPLO (Specialized: foreign language), P.O. Box 100, Walla Walla WA 99362-0033, phone (509)529-0813, e-mail tsunami@innw.net, website www.tsunami-inc.net, founded 1995, editor Charles Potts, contact Stephen Thomas.
Magazine Needs: *The Temple, Gu Si, El Templo* is a quarterly tri-lingual poetry magazine. It contains poems in Chinese, Spanish and English; also news, reviews and events. They want "signature poems exhibiting artistic control, intellectual rigor, emotional commitment and a command of subject matter. No rhymes, haiku; formalist, overly clever or academic work." They have published poetry by Teri Zipf, John Oliver Simon, Jim Bodeen and Sharon Doubiago. As a sample the editor selected these lines from "The Wheel" by Stephen Thomas:

> *My daddy made me reinvent the wheel . . ./on the lathe which I'd invented more than once/and would again. The spoke wire/trembled like a martyr,/as I drew it out from the/extruder in the hissing workshop air.*

The Temple is 80 pgs., 7 × 10, web press printed on newsprint and saddle-stapled, includes ads for books and other magazines. They receive about 5,000 poems a year, accept approximately 1%. Press run is 5,000 for 300 subscribers of which 10 are libraries; 600 distributed free to poets at festivals. Subscription: $20. Sample: $5. Make checks payable to Tsunami Inc. "Familiarity is critical, poets must buy and read a sample first or be a subscriber."
How to Submit: Submit 3-5 poems at a time. Previously published poems OK; no simultaneous submissions. E-mail submissions OK. Cover letter preferred. "Send poems in 9 × 12 envelopes." Send Chinese mss to Denis Mair, 9200 Glendon Way, Rosemead CA 91770. Time between acceptance and publication is 1-3 months. Seldom comments on rejections. Send SASE for guidelines. Responds in 2 months. Pays 10 copies. Acquires first North American serial or one-time rights. Reviews books and chapbooks of poetry and other magazines in single or multi-book format. Open to unsolicited reviews. Poets may also send books for review consideration.
Book/Chapbook Needs: Tsunami Inc. publishes 3 paperbacks/year. Books are published by invitation only.

♣ ⊕ SENDING TO A COUNTRY other than your own? Be sure to send International Reply Coupons (IRCs) instead of stamps for replies or return of your manuscript.

Also Offers: Website includes guidelines, names of editors, sample poems and covers of books.
Advice: "Beginners send one to three poems, large envelope, SASE for reply. Know the contents of the magazine to date: we publish original poetry in Spanish and Chinese with English translations."

TUCUMCARI LITERARY REVIEW (Specialized: cowboy, form/style, humor, regional, social issues, memories, nostalgia), 3108 W. Bellevue Ave., Los Angeles CA 90026, founded 1988, editor Troxey Kemper.
Magazine Needs: *Tucumcari* appears every other month. "Prefer rhyming and established forms, including sonnet, rondeau, triolet, kyrielle, villanelle, terza rima, limerick, sestina, pantoum and others, 2-100 lines, but the primary goal is to publish good work. No talking animals. No haiku. No disjointed, fragmentary, rambling words or phrases typed in odd-shaped staggered lines trying to look like poetry. The quest here is for poetry that will be just as welcome many years later as it is now." They have published poetry by Jill Williams, Helen McIntosh Gordon, Mary Gribble, Michael L. Newell, Jim Boone and Ruth Daniels. As a sample the editor selected these lines from "Reflection" by Esther B. Swensen:

> *The youth I lost/so long ago/returns in you;/and should I look/in your clear eyes,/I see reflected there/*
> *the unlined me,/that was before.*

The magazine is 48 pgs., digest-sized, saddle-stapled, photocopied from typescript, with card cover. Press run is 150-200. Subscription: $12, $20 for overseas. Sample: $2, $4 for overseas.
How to Submit: Submit up to 4 poems at a time. Simultaneous submissions and previously published poems OK. Sometimes comments on rejections. Send SASE for guidelines. Responds within 1 month. Pays 1 copy. Acquires one-time rights.
Advice: "Writing is welcomed from amateurs, in-betweens and professors/scholars. Many college professors and writing teachers submit rhyming poems here. They say they're sick of non-rhyme junk. Oddly, some of the work by amateurs is more interesting than erudite, obscure allusions to Greek/Roman mythology personages and events—more honest, earnest and heart-felt. The main measure of acceptability is: Is it interesting? Is it good? What counts is what it says not whether the work is handwritten on lined notebook paper or presented on expensive computer-generated equipment/paper which often is very difficult to read. *TLR* often is overstocked with material, but if something arrives that I like, I will make room for it. I publish two or three extra or bonus issues a year (free to subscribers) trying to use up the backlog."

TURKEY PRESS, 6746 Sueno Rd., Isla Vista CA 93117-4904, founded 1974, poetry editors Harry Reese and Sandra Reese. "We do not encourage solicitations of any kind to the press. We seek out and develop projects on our own."

TURNSTONE PRESS LIMITED (Specialized: regional), 607-100 Arthur St., Winnipeg, Manitoba R3B 1H3 Canada, phone (204)947-1555, fax (204)942-1555, e-mail editor@turnstonepress.mb.ca, website www.TurnstonePress.com, founded 1976, contact acquisitions editor-poetry.
Books published by Turnstone Press have won numerous awards, including the McNally Robinson Book of the Year Award, the Canadian Author's Association Literary Award for Poetry and the Lampert Memorial Awards.
Book/Chapbook Needs: "Turnstone Press publishes Canadian authors with special priority to prairie interests/themes." They publish 2 paperbacks/year. They have published poetry by Di Brandt, Catherine Hunter, Patrick Friesen and Dennis Cooley. Books are usually 5½ × 8½, offset printed and perfect-bound with quality paperback cover.
How to Submit: Query first with 10 sample poems and cover letter with brief bio and publication credits. Previously published poems and simultaneous submissions OK. Cover letter preferred. "Please enclose SASE (or SAE with IRC) and if you want the submission back, make sure your envelope and postage cover it." Time between acceptance and publication is 1 year. Poems are circulated to an editorial board. "The submissions that are approved by our readers go to the editorial board for discussion." They receive more than 1,200 unsolicited mss a year, about 10% are passed to the editorial board. Replies to queries in 3 months; to mss in 4 months. Pays royalties of 10% plus advance of $200 and 10 author's copies.
Also Offers: Website includes writer's guidelines, list of books and samples of writing.
Advice: "Competition is extremely fierce in poetry. Most work published is by poets working on their craft for many years."

24.7; RE-PRESST, 30 Forest St., Providence RI 02906, founded 1994, poetry editor David Church. Currently not accepting submissions.

TWILIGHT ENDING, 21 Ludlow Dr., Milford CT 06460-6822, phone (203)877-3473, founded 1995, editor/publisher Emma J. Blanch.
Magazine Needs: *Twilight Ending* appears 3 times/year publishing "poetry and short fiction of the highest caliber, in English, with universal appeal." They have featured the work of poets from the US, Canada, Europe, Middle East, Japan and New Zealand. They want "poems with originality in thought and in style, reflecting the latest trend in writing, moving from the usual set-up to a vertical approach. We prefer unrhymed poetry, however we accept rhymed verse if rhymes are perfect. We look for the unusual approach in content and style with clarity. No haiku. No poems forming a design. No foul words. No translations. No bio. No porn." The editor says *TE*

is 5½×8½, "elegantly printed on white linen with one poem with title per page (12-30 lines)." They receive about 1,500 poems a year, accept approximately 10%. Press run is 120 for 50 subscribers of which 25 are libraries. Sample: $6 US, $6.50 Canada, $7 Europe, $8 Middle East, Japan and New Zealand. Make checks payable to Emma J. Blanch.

How to Submit: Submit only 3-4 poems at a time, typed, single spaced. No previously published poems or simultaneous submissions nor poems submitted to contests while in consideration for *Twilight Ending*. Include white business envelop for reply (overseas contributors should include 2 IRCs). No fax or e-mail submissions. "When accepted, poems and fiction will not be returned so keep copies." Submission deadlines: mid-December for Winter issue, mid-April for Spring/Summer issue, mid-September for Fall issue. No backlog, "all poems are destroyed after publication." Often comments on rejections. Send SASE for guidelines. Responds in 1 week. Pays nothing—not even a copy. Acquires first rights.

Advice: "If editing is needed, suggestions will be made for the writer to rework and resubmit a corrected version. The author always decides; remember that you deal with experts."

✓ ◐ TWO RIVERS REVIEW; ANDERIE POETRY PRESS, 215 McCartney St., Easton PA 18042, e-mail tworiversreview@juno.com (guidelines/inquiries only), website http://pages.prodigy.net/memmer/trr.html, founded 1998, editor Philip Memmer.

Magazine Needs: *Two Rivers Review* appears biannually and "seeks to print the best of contemporary poetry. All styles of work are welcome, so long as submitted poems display excellence." They have published poetry by Billy Collins, Christopher Buckley, Naomi Shihab Nye, Olga Broumas and Len Roberts. As a sample the editor selected these lines by Narda Bush:

> For her,/love has always been a burden. Something/scraped from the underbellies of saints and/careless
> dreamers. The boxed coffin/of a stranger, pulled by a mismatched team/to a pauper's grave.

The editor says *TRR* is 48-52 pgs., digest-sized, professionally printed on cream-colored paper, with card cover. Subscription: $12. Sample: $6. "Poets wishing to submit work may obtain a sample copy for the reduced price of $4."

How to Submit: Submit no more than 4 poems at a time with cover letter and SASE. No previously published poems. Simultaneous submissions OK, "but please inform the editor in the cover letter." No electronic submissions. Responds nearly always within 6 weeks. Acquires first rights.

Also Offers: Sponsors annual poetry contest with deadline in December. Send SASE or visit website for details. Website includes guidelines, sample poems, contest info and subscriptions info.

✂ ○ ◐ TYRO PUBLISHING, 194 Carlbert St., Sault Ste. Marie, Ontario P6A 5E1 Canada, fax (705)942-3625, e-mail tyro@sympatico.ca, founded 1984, editor Stan Gordon.

Book/Chapbook Needs: They now publish only book-length collections and only on compact disc with recorded readings. They have published *Brutal Beauty* by Ryan Tilley; *The Artist* by Dan Lukiv; and *The Vulnerable Poems* by J.C. Geddes.

How to Submit: "Send for guidelines to poetry editor Chris Belsito by e-mail only at mansion@mail.com." Always sends prepublication galleys.

N $ ◐ U.S. CATHOLIC; CLARETIAN PUBLICATIONS, 205 W. Monroe St., Chicago IL 60606, phone (312)236-7782, e-mail editors@uscatholic.org, website www.uscatholic.org, founded 1935, literary editor Maureen Abood.

Magazine Needs: "Published monthly, *U.S. Catholic* engages a broad range of issues as they affect the everyday lives of Catholics." They have no specifications for poetry, but do not necessarily want poems religious in nature. No light verse. They have published poetry by Naomi Shihab Nye. The editor says *U.S. Catholic* is 51 pgs., 8½×11, printed in 4-color and stapled, includes art/graphics. They receive about 1,000 poems a year, accept 12 poems. Publish 1 poem/issue. Circulation 50,000. Subscription: $22.

How to Submit: Submit 3 poems at a time. Line length for poetry is 50 maximum. No previously published poems; simultaneous submissions OK. Cover letter preferred. Always include SASE. Time between acceptance and publication is 3 months. Poems are circulated to an editorial board. Seldom comments on rejections. Send SASE for guidelines. Responds in 3 months. Pays $75. Acquires first North American serial rights.

N ◐ ◎ THE U.S. LATINO REVIEW (Specialized: ethnic, ecology, political, social issues), PMB #359, 82-04 Lefferts Blvd., Kew Gardens NY 11415, e-mail andrescastro@aol.com or editor@uslatinoreview.org, website www.uslatinoreview.org, founded 1999, editor Andres Castro.

Magazine Needs: "*USLR* is a biannual literary review for Latinos, our friends, and critics. It is indeed a labor of love dedicated to promoting the best we as a community of creative artists have to offer. We expect truth, excellence and passion from ourselves and contributors. We include poetry, short short story, essay, sketch art and other forms considered if queried. Submissions of all content and form are considered, but writers and artists should understand that we heavily favor work that focuses concretely on the urgent social, political, economic and ecological issues of our time. We stress that *USLR* is not exclusionary—we are won over easily by care, craft and conscience. Hate to say, but if you are going to be egocentric you better send a masterpiece." They have published poetry by Alma Luz Villianueva, L.S. Asekoff, Jack Agüeros and Michael Castro. As a sample we selected these lines from "Always Things Pressing Flat" by Lorraine Lopez:

damp palms mash my brother's/cowlick to his scalp. I remember/always her pushing things down/so that they would stay. You,/girls, she would say if we rose/to storm, shouldn't be angry.//never lose your temper. Never shout/nor punch. Don't shove, don't bite./never rattle windows, slam doors. You/girls, you have your outlet, your release.//I know your brother shattered that/plate. Yes, he throws those/ chingasos pretty hard. And sometimes/he pushes you down the stairs./every day he cries and curses and blows/snot bubbles like a bull in the ring.

USLR is 64 pgs., 5½ × 11½, professionally printed on 24 lb. stock and flat-spined with glossy card cover, includes black ink sketch art/prints. They receive about 500 poems a year, accept approximately 8-10%. Press run is 500 for 50 subscribers, 400 shelf sales. Single copy: $6 US; subscription: $12 US. Make checks payable to Andres Castro.

How to Submit: Submit 3-5 poems at a time. Previously published poems and simultaneous submissions OK. E-mail submissions OK, in body of e-mail/no file attachments. Cover letter preferred. "SASE must accompany submissions. A short bio is requested but not necessary for contributors page." Time between acceptance and publication is 1-6 months. Poems are circulated to an editorial board. "Editor does early screening and poems forwarded to editorial board of at least three others for final selection." Often comments on rejections. Send SASE for guidelines. Responds in 2 months. Sends prepublication galleys if requested. Acquires first rights.

Also Offers: Website includes writer's guidelines, names of editors, poetry, interviews, etc.

Advice: "Please, send your best."

☑ ◉ **U.S. 1 WORKSHEETS; U.S. 1 POETS' COOPERATIVE**, P.O. Box 127, Kingston NJ 08528-0127, founded 1973, managing editor Winifred Hughes.

Magazine Needs: *U.S. 1 Worksheets* is a literary annual, double issue December or January, circulation 400, which uses high-quality poetry and fiction. "We use a rotating board of editors; it's wisest to query when we're next reading before submitting. A self-addressed, stamped postcard will get our next reading period dates (usually in the spring)." They have published poetry by Alicia Ostriker, Elizabeth Anne Socolow, Jean Hollander, Frederick Tibbetts, Lois Marie Harrod, James Haba, Charlotte Mandel and David Keller. *U.S. 1 Worksheets* is 72 pgs., 5½ × 8½, saddle-stapled, with color cover art. "We read a lot but take very few. Prefer complex, well-written work." Subscription: $7, $12/2 years.

How to Submit: Submit 5 poems at a time. Include name, address and phone number in upper right-hand corner. No simultaneous submissions; rarely accepts previously published poems. Requests for sample copies, subscriptions, queries, back issues, and all mss should be addressed to the editor (address at beginning of listing). Pays 1 copy.

Ⓝ 🌐 $ ◉ **ULITARRA**, P.O. Box 195, Armidale NSW 2350 Australia, phone +61 2 6772-9135, founded 1992, co-editor Michael Sharkey.

Magazine Needs: *Ulitarra* is published biannually. "We focus on new writing by Australian writers. We also accept international submissions. The aim is quality." They want interesting poetry on any subject; any style. They do not want "poetry that is clumsily derivative; sentimental verse; poems addressed to pet animals or toys." They have published poetry by Brian Henry, Geraldine McKenzie, Coral Hull, Nicolette Stasko, Peter Porter and Elizabeth Smither. As a sample the editor selected this poem, "A Passing Thought" by Vera Newsom:

> *Reading their verse,/I'm lost for words—/it is their coolness/fascinates./All is wit/and wryness.*

The editor says *Ulitarra* is 170 pgs., 5½ × 8½, offset printed and perfect-bound with color, chromolux cover, includes art/graphics and ads. They receive about 3,000-4,000 poems a year, accept approximately 2%. Publish 30 poems/issue. Press run is 600 for 300 subscribers of which 100 are libraries, 150 shelf sales. Subscription: $19 (Australian). Sample: $10 (Australian).

How to Submit: Submit 2-3 poems at a time. Line length for poetry is 1 minimum, 200 maximum. No previously published poems or simultaneous submissions. Cover letter preferred. Include name and address on each page. Include SAE and IRC. Reads submissions February through May and September through November only. Time between acceptance and publication is up to 1 year. Poems are circulated to an editorial board. "Poems are read, and short listed ones are re-read by 2-4 editorial staff." Often comments on rejections. Responds in 1 month. Sometimes sends prepublication galleys. Pays $40 (Australian) and 1 copy. Acquires first rights. Staff reviews books and chapbooks of poetry and other magazines in 500 plus words, multi-book format. Send books for review consideration.

Also Offers: Sponsors the annual Robert Harris Poetry Prize of $1,000 (Australian). Deadline: April 30 each year. "To enter, buy a copy of the January issue."

Advice: "Buy or borrow a copy of whatever magazine you intend to submit work to. Read it carefully."

◻ ◎ **THE ULTIMATE UNKNOWN (Specialized: science fiction, horror)**, P.O. Box 219, Streamwood IL 60107-0219, e-mail ralitsa@sprynet.com, website www.wimall.com/cassini, founded 1995, editor David D. Combs.

Magazine Needs: *The Ultimate Unknown*, published quarterly, is a "literary magazine of science fiction, horror and the future." They want "science fiction, horror, future and politics of 20-30 lines, any style or meter." They do not want "profanity of any kind or excessive violence." They have published poetry by John Grey. *The*

Ultimate Unknown is 100 pgs., photocopied, saddle-stitched with color cover, art and ads. They receive about 50 poems a year, accept approximately 75%. Press run is 250 for 100 subscribers, 10 shelf sales; 50 distributed free to authors, advertisers and reviewers. Subscription: $14. Sample: $4. Make checks payable to Combs Press. **How to Submit:** "I encourage the author to subscribe, but this is not required, and only done after the acceptance." Submit any number of poems, each on a separate piece of paper with name and address. Previously published poems and simultaneous submissions OK. Cover letter preferred. Time between acceptance and publication is 3-6 months. "All poems are judged on an individual basis and accepted for their own merits." Always comments on rejections. Publishes theme issues. Send SASE for guidelines and upcoming themes. Responds in 3 months. Pays 1 copy. Acquires first North American serial or one-time rights. Staff reviews books or chapbooks of poetry or other magazines in 1-3 paragraphs. Send books for review consideration.
Advice: "We are very open to new poets. We give full credit to all poets."

$ **ULTRAMARINE PUBLISHING CO., INC.**, P.O. Box 303, Hastings-on-Hudson NY 10706-1817, phone (914)478-1339, fax (914)478-1365, e-mail washbook@sprynet.com, founded 1974, editor C.P. Stephens.
Book/Chapbook Needs: "We mostly distribute books for authors who had a title dropped by a major publisher—the author is usually able to purchase copies very cheaply. We use existing copies purchased by the author from the publisher when the title is being dropped." Ultramarine's list includes 250 titles, 90% of them cloth bound, one-third of them science fiction and 10% poetry.
How to Submit: Authors should query before making submissions; queries will be answered in 1 week. No queries/submissions via fax. Simultaneous submissions OK, but no disks. The press pays 10% royalties. "Distributor terms are on a book-by-book basis, but is a rough split."

UNDERSTANDING MAGAZINE; DIONYSIA PRESS LTD., 20 A Montgomery St., Edinburgh, Lothion EH7 5JS Great Britain, phone (0131)4787247, fax (0131)4770754, e-mail denise.smith@cabl einet.co.uk, founded 1989, contact Denise Smith.
Magazine Needs: *Understanding Magazine*, published 1-2 times/year, features "poetry, short stories, parts of plays, reviews and articles." They want "original poetry." They have published poetry by Susanne Roxman and Ron Butlin. As a sample we selected these lines from "Private Axis" by Thom Nairn:

> *The circles grow relentlessly,/His passage, inscrutably centrifugal/On this terminal cycle to silence.*

The editor says *Understanding* is A5 and perfect-bound. They receive 2,000 poems a year. Press run is 1,000 for 500 subscribers. Single copy: £4.50; subscription: £9. Sample: £3. Make checks payable to Dionysia Press.
How to Submit: Submit 5 poems at a time. No previously published poems; simultaneous submissions OK. E-mail and fax submissions OK. Time between acceptance and publication is 6-10 months. Poems are circulated to an editorial board. Often comments on rejections. Responds in 6 months. Always sends prepublication galleys. Pays 1 copy. Acquires all rights. Returns rights after publication. Staff reviews books or chapbooks of poetry or other magazines. Send books for review consideration.
Book/Chapbook Needs & How to Submit: Dionysia Press Ltd., publishes 14 paperbacks and chapbooks of poetry/year. "Sometimes we select from submissions or competitions." They have published *The Sand Garden* by Thom Nairn; *The Stone Moon* by D. Zervanou; *Poems* by T. Cloudsley; *Technique* by Gavin Bowd; *Sailing the Sands* by James Andrew; and *The Feeble Lies of Orester Chalkiopoulos* by Andreas Mitsou. Books are usually A5, perfect-bound, hard cover with art. Query first, with a few sample poems and cover letter with brief bio and publication credits. Replies to queries in 2-6 months. Pays author's copies. "We usually get arts council grants or poets get grants for themselves." For sample books or chapbooks, write to the above address.
Also Offers: Sponsors poetry competitions with cash prizes. Send SASE for guidelines.

$ **UNIVERSITY OF ALBERTA PRESS**, Ring House 2, Edmonton, Alberta T6G 2E1 Canada, phone (780)492-3662, fax (780)492-0719, e-mail u.a.p.@ualberta.ca, website www.ualberta.ca/~uap, founded 1969, managing editor Leslie Vermeer.
Book/Chapbook Needs: "The University of Alberta Press is a scholarly press, generally publishing nonfiction plus some literary titles." They publish 1-2 paperback poetry titles per year. They are looking for "mature, thoughtful work—nothing too avant-garde. No juvenile or 'Hallmark verse.'" They have published poetry by E.D. Blodgett, Alice Major, Bert Almon, Fred Wah, Monty Reid and Nigel Darbasie.
How to Submit: Query first, with 10-12 sample poems and cover letter with brief bio and publication credits. "Do not send complete manuscript on first approach." Previously published poems and simultaneous submissions OK. E-mail and disk submissions OK. Time between acceptance and publication is 6-10 months. Poems are circulated to an editorial board. "The process is: acquiring editor to editorial group meeting to two external reviewers to press committee to acceptance." Seldom comments on rejections. Replies to queries in 2 months. Pays royalties of 10% of net plus 10 author's copies. See website to order sample books.

THE OPENNESS TO SUBMISSIONS INDEX at the back of this book lists all publishers in this section by how open they are to submissions.

Also Offers: Website includes contact information and description of publishing program.

⬤ **UNIVERSITY OF CENTRAL FLORIDA CONTEMPORARY POETRY SERIES**, % English Dept., University of Central Florida, Orlando FL 32816-1346, phone (407)823-2212, founded 1968, poetry editor Judith Hemschemeyer.
Book/Chapbook Needs: Publishes two 50- to 80-page hardback or paperback collections each year. "Strong poetry on any theme in the lyric-narrative tradition." They have published poetry by Robert Cooperman, Katherine Soniat and John Woods.
How to Submit: Submit complete paginated ms with table of contents and acknowledgement of previously published poems. Simultaneous submissions OK. "Please send a reading fee of $7, a SASE for return of ms, and a self-addressed postcard for acknowledgment of receipt of ms." Reads submissions September through April only. Responds in 3 months. Time between acceptance and publication is 1 year.

⬤ **THE UNIVERSITY OF CHICAGO PRESS; PHOENIX POETS SERIES**, 5801 Ellis Ave., Chicago IL 60637, phone (773)702-7700, fax (773)702-9756, website www.press.uchicago.edu, founded 1891, poetry editor Randolph Petilos.
Book/Chapbook Needs: The University of Chicago Press publishes scholarly books and journals. "We may only publish four books in Phoenix Poets per year, and perhaps two or three books of poetry in translation per year. We occasionally publish a book of poems outside Phoenix Poets, or as a reprint from other houses." They have published poetry by Alan Shapiro, Tom Sleigh, David Ferry and Bruce Smith.
How to Submit: By invitation only. No unsolicited mss.

⬤ **UNIVERSITY OF GEORGIA PRESS; CONTEMPORARY POETRY SERIES**, 330 Research Dr., Suite B100, University of Georgia, Athens GA 30602-4901, phone (706)369-6135, fax (706)369-6131, e-mail mnunnell@ugapress.uga.edu, website www.uga.edu/ugapress, press founded 1938, series founded 1980, series editor Bin Ramke, poetry competition coordinator Margaret Nunnelley.
Book/Chapbook Needs: Through its annual competition, the press publishes 4 collections of poetry/year, 2 of which are by poets who have not had a book published, in paperback editions. They have published poetry by Marjorie Welish, Arthur Vogelsang, C.D. Wright, Martha Ronk and Paul Hoover.
How to Submit: "Writers should query first for guidelines and submission periods. Please enclose SASE." There are no restrictions on the type of poetry submitted, but "familiarity with our previously published books in the series may be helpful." No fax or e-mail submissions. $15 submission fee required. Make checks payable to University of Georgia Press. Manuscripts are *not* returned after the judging is completed.
Also Offers: Website includes competition guidelines.

✅ ⬤ **UNIVERSITY OF IOWA PRESS; THE IOWA POETRY PRIZES**, 119 West Park Rd., 100 Kuhl House, Iowa City IA 52242-1000, fax (319)335-2055, e-mail sharon-rebouche@uiowa.edu, website www.uiowa.edu/~uipress.
Book/Chapbook Needs: The University of Iowa Press offers annually The Iowa Poetry Prizes for book-length mss (50-150 pgs.) by poets who have already published at least one full-length book in an edition of at least 500 copies. Winners will be published by the Press under a standard royalty contract. Winning entries for 2000 were *Isolato* by Larissa Szporluk and *A Point Is That Which Has No Part* by Liz Waldner. (This competition is the only way in which this press accepts poetry.)
How to Submit: Mss are received annually in May only. All writers of English are eligible, whether citizens of the US or not who have published at least one book of poetry (a minimum of 50 pages in an edition of at least 500 copies). Poems from previously published books may be included only in mss of selected or collected poems, submissions of which are encouraged. Simultaneous submissions OK if press is immediately notified if the book is accepted by another publisher. $15 reading fee is charged; stamped, self-addressed packaging is required or mss will not be returned. Include name on the title page only. Single copy: $10.95 plus postage. "Visit us at www.uiowa.edu/~uipress."
Advice: "These awards have been initiated to encourage poets who are beyond the first-book stage to submit their very best work."

✅ ⬤ **THE UNIVERSITY OF MASSACHUSETTS PRESS; THE JUNIPER PRIZE**, P.O. Box 429, Amherst MA 01004-0429, phone (413)545-2217, fax (413)545-1226, website www.umass.edu/umpress, founded 1964.
Book/Chapbook Needs: The press offers an annual competition for the Juniper Prize, in alternate years to first and subsequent books. In even-numbered years (2000, 2002, etc.) only subsequent books will be considered: mss whose authors have had at least one full-length book or chapbook of poetry published or accepted for publication. Such chapbooks must be at least 30 pages, and self-published work is not considered to lie within this "books and chapbooks" category. In odd-numbered years (1999, 2001, etc.) only "first books" will be considered: mss by writers whose poems may have appeared in literary journals and/or anthologies but have not been published, or been accepted for publication, in book form. They have published *The Anchorage: Poems* by

Mark Wunderlich; *The Double Task* by Gray Jacobik; *El Coro: A Chorus of Latino and Latina Poetry* edited by Martín Espada; and *Fugitive Red* by Karen Donovan. "Poetry books are approximately $14 for paperback editions and $24 for cloth."

How to Submit: Submissions must not exceed 70 pgs. in typescript. Include paginated contents page; provide the title, publisher and year of publication for previously published volumes. A list of poems published or slated for publication in literary journals and/or anthologies must also accompany the ms. Such poems may be included in the ms and must be identified. "Mss by more than one author, entries of more than one ms simultaneously or within the same year, and translations are not eligible." Entry fee: $10 plus SASE for return of ms or notification. Entries must be postmarked not later than September 30. The award is announced in April/May and publication is scheduled for the following spring. The amount of the prize is $1,000 and is in lieu of royalties on the first print run. Poet also receives 12 copies in one edition or 6 copies each if published in both hardcover and paperbound editions. Fax, call or send SASE for guidelines and/or further information to the above address. Entries are to be mailed to Juniper Prize, University of Massachusetts, Amherst MA 01003.

Also Offers: Website includes historical information about the press, guidelines, staff listing, our books-in-print and seasonal catalogs, and excerpts from recently published books.

UNIVERSITY OF WISCONSIN PRESS; BRITTINGHAM PRIZE IN POETRY; FELIX POLLAK PRIZE IN POETRY, 2537 Daniels St., Madison WI 53718-6772, Brittingham Prize inaugurated in 1985, poetry editor Ronald Wallace.

Book/Chapbook Needs: The University of Wisconsin Press publishes primarily scholarly works, but they offer the annual Brittingham Prize and the Felix Pollak Prize, both $1,000 plus publication. These prizes are the only way in which this press publishes poetry. Send SASE for rules. Qualified readers will screen all mss. Winners will be selected by "a distinguished poet who will remain anonymous until the winners are announced in mid-February." Past judges include Charles Wright, Gerald Stern, Mary Oliver, Donald Finkel, Donald Justice, Lisel Mueller, Henry Taylor, Carolyn Kizer, Philip Levine, Rita Dove, Donald Hall and Robert Bly. Winners include Stefanie Marlis, Judith Vollmer, Renée A. Ashley, Tony Hoagland, Stephanie Strickland, Lisa Lewis, David Clewell, Bob Hicok, Lynn Powell, Dennis Trudell, Juanita Brunk, Olena Kalytiak Davis, Betsy Sholl, Frank X. Gaspar and Charles Harper Webb.

How to Submit: For both prizes, submit between September 1 and October 1, unbound ms volume of 50-80 pgs., with name, address and telephone number on title page. No translations. Poems must be previously unpublished in book form. Poems published in journals, chapbooks and anthologies may be included but must be acknowledged. There is a non-refundable $20 reading fee which must accompany the ms. (Checks to University of Wisconsin Press.) Mss will not be returned. Enclose SASE for contest results.

Advice: "Each submission is considered for both prizes (one entry fee only)."

UNLIKELY STORIES: A COLLECTION OF LITERARY ART, 209 West Dixie Ave., Marietta GA 30060, phone (770)422-9731, e-mail unlikely@flash.net, website http://go.to/unlikely, founded 1998, editor Jonathan Penton.

Magazine Needs: "*Unlikely Stories* is a monthly online publication containing poetry, fiction and nonfiction which falls under my own highly subjective definition of 'literary art.' I especially like work that has trouble finding publication due to adult, offensive or weird content." They want "any subject matter, including those normally considered taboo. I like informal poetry, but am open to formal poetry that demonstrates an understanding of good meter. No emotionless poetry, lies. 'I'll love you forever' is a lie; spare me." They have published poetry by Scott Holstad, Wendy Carlisle, Laurel Ann Boyer and Elisha Porat. As a sample the editor selected these lines from an untitled poem by Shari Nettles:

> even the little white flowers/in the yard/trembled when they heard you scream.

They receive about 500 poems a year, accept approximately 30%.

How to Submit: Submit 3 or more poems at a time. Previously published poems and simultaneous submissions OK. Cover letter preferred. E-mail and disk submissions OK. "*Unlikely Stories* is designed to promote acquaintanceship between readers and authors therefore, only multiple submissions will be accepted. I greatly prefer to see a bio; there is no maximum length." Time between acceptance and publication is 1 month. Often comments on rejections, if requested. Send SASE for guidelines or obtain via e-mail or website. Responds in up to 6 weeks. Acquires one-time rights.

Also Offers: "If a contributor asks me a question, or for editorial or business advise. I'll answer. I have edited full manuscripts for a fee." Website includes entire content, guidelines, contact information, complete content, interviews with select artists and bookstore.

Advice: "Write from the heart, if you must, but write from that part of you which is unique."

UNMUZZLED OX, 43B Clark Lane, Staten Island NY 10304, or Box 550, Kingston, Ontario K7L 4W5 Canada, phone (212)226-7170, founded 1971, poetry editor Michael Andre.

Magazine Needs & How to Submit: *Unmuzzled Ox* is a tabloid literary biannual. Each edition is built around a theme or specific project. The editor says, "The chances of an unsolicited poem being accepted are slight since I always have specific ideas in mind." They have published poetry by Allen Ginsberg, Robert Creeley and Denise Levertov. As a sample the editor selected these lines from "CL" by Daniel Berrigan:

> *Let's be grandiose, it's a game/Let's climb a balcony/Let's issue a manifesto//Why, we're turning things*
> *on their head/we're making history/we're—//Harmless.*

Only unpublished work will be considered, but works may be in French as well as English." Subscription: $20.

⟦N⟧ ◑ UNO MAS MAGAZINE, P.O. Box 1832, Silver Spring MD 20915, e-mail unomasmag@aol.com, website www.unomas.com/, founded 1990, contact poetry editor.

Magazine Needs: *UNo Mas*, published quarterly, features "general culture, music, fiction, essays, photography, art." They want "general poetry of short to medium length." They have published poetry by Sparrow. As a sample the editor selected these lines from "Krishna Harry and His Voice" by Kristine Durden:

> *pulling me across a river bed/baptism of sound/floating on ripples/riding each dip and wave/like dream*
> *flying*

The editor says *UNo Mas* is 50 pgs., 8½ × 11, offset-printed with a glossy 2-color cover. They receive about 100-150 poems a year, accept approximately 20-25%. Press run is 3,000 for 40 subscribers and which 1 is a library, most are shelf sales; 100 distributed free to advertisers. Single copy: $2.50; subscription: $9. Sample: $3. Make checks payable to Jim Saah.

How to Submit: Submit up to 5 poems with name on each page. Previously published poems and simultaneous submissions OK. Cover letter preferred with SASE. Accepts faxed submissions. E-mail submissions OK. Time between acceptance and publication is 3-6 months. Poems are circulated to an editorial board, "if we like it, we publish it." Seldom comments on rejections. Send SASE for guidelines. Responds in up to 6 weeks. Sometimes sends prepublication galleys. Pays 3 copies. Acquires one-time rights. Staff reviews books or chapbooks of poetry. Send books for review consideration.

Also Offers: Website includes fiction, poetry samples, reviews, interviews, photography and articles. Contact Ron Saah.

✓ ◯ ◪ ◎ UPSOUTH (Specialized: regional, religious), 323 Bellevue Ave., Bowling Green KY 42101-6133, phone (502)843-8018, e-mail galen@ky.net, website www.expage.com/page/upsouth, founded 1993, editor Galen Smith.

Magazine Needs: "*Upsouth* is a quarterly international newsletter for Southern and Catholic writers. We ask for tasteful poems, columns, essays, etc. No works of non-Christian views will be accepted. But the works do not necessarily have to be religious or spiritual to be accepted. Our intention is to be a creative outlet for spiritual or inspirational works, but *Upsouth* also has an interest in Southern culture and its literary figures and their writings, too. We do accept works from writers and poets from other regions of the U.S. and other parts of the world. We also accept works from non-Catholic writers and writers with other religious beliefs." They have published poetry by Rory Morse, Joyce Bradshaw and Leah Maines. As a sample the editor selected these lines from "Dear Heavenly Father" by Raymond Flory:

> *This day,/in this place/hold me once again./May I feel the touch*

Upsouth is 12-16 pgs., 8½ × 11, photocopied and corner-stapled, includes clip art. They receive about 100 poems a year, accept approximately 10%. Press run is 75 for 50 subscribers of which 10 are libraries, 10 shelf sales. Subscription: $8. Sample: $2. "We are more likely to publish your poem if you subscribe."

How to Submit: Submit 3 poems at a time. Line length for poetry is 21 maximum. Include SASE. Previously published poems and simultaneous submissions OK. Cover letter preferred. Seldom comments on rejections. Publishes theme issues occasionally (related to the seasons). Send SASE for guidelines. Responds in up to 2 months. Pays 1 copy. Author retains all rights. Reviews books and chapbooks of poetry and other magazines in 250 words. Open to unsolicited reviews. Poets may also send books for review consideration.

Also Offers: Website includes current info about the newsletter, editor's biographical information and editor's favorite links.

Advice: "We like for you to subscribe to *Upsouth*. We consider you as a friend and write you personal and encouraging letters. Our motto is 'your writing can change the world!' "

♣ ✓ ◯ URBAN GRAFFITI, P.O. Box 41164, Edmonton, Alberta T6J 6M7 Canada, e-mail cogwheels@worldgate.com, founded 1993, editor Mark McCawley.

Magazine Needs: Appearing 2 times a year, *Urban Graffiti* is "a litzine of transgressive, discursive, post-realist writing concerned with hard-edged urban living, alternative lifestyles, deviance—presented in their most raw and unpretentious form." They want "free verse, prose poetry; urban themes and subject matter; transgressive, discursive, post-realist and confessional work. No metaphysical, religious or Hallmark verse." They have published poetry by Lyn Lifshin, Carolyn Zonailo, Beth Jankalo, Daniel Jones and Allan Demeule. As a sample the editor selected these lines from "Extremities" by Martin O'Rourke:

> *still, watching you sleep, I wonder./What other deep cuts are you hiding?/If only I could slip inside*
> *your skin/as easily as your breath and remove them./If only I had healer's touch,/I could wipe them*
> *clean away.*

The editor says *Urban Graffiti* is 28 pgs., magazine-sized, photocopied and saddle-stapled with paper cover, includes art/graphics. They receive about 100 poems a year, accept 10-15%. Press run is 250. Single copy: $5; subscription: $10/3 issues. Make checks payable to Mark McCawley.

How to Submit: Submit 5-8 poems at a time. No previously published poems or simultaneous submissions. E-mail submissions OK. Cover letter "with creative bio" required. Time between acceptance and publication is

6-12 months. Seldom comments on rejections. Send SASE for guidelines. Responds in up to 6 months. Pays 5 copies. Acquires first North American serial and first anthology rights. Reviews books and chapbooks of poetry and other magazines in 500-1,000 words, multi-book format. Poets may also send books for review consideration.
Advice: "If it's raunchy, realistic, angry, sarcastic, caustic, funny, frightening, brutally honest . . . then that's what we're looking for at *UG*."

☑ ◉ **URBAN SPAGHETTI: LITERARY ARTS JOURNAL**, P.O. Box 5186, Mansfield OH 44901-5186, phone (419)524-8527, e-mail editor@urban-spaghetti.com, website www.urban-spaghetti.com, founded 1998, contact Cheryl Dodds.
Magazine Needs: "*Urban Spaghetti* is a biannual literary arts journal located in mid-Ohio featuring poetry, short stories and artwork from around the world. Our focus extends a hand to new poets who share a sense of social responsibility in their writing, and offer a fresh presentation and language which challenges us." They want "quality verse. All styles are accepted, but please send your best. Rhymed verse has its place. However, that place is not *Urban Spaghetti*." They have published poetry by David Citino, Adrie Kussorow, Duane Locke, B.Z. Niditch, Marge Piercy and Andrea Potos. As a sample we selected these lines from "Slogans" by Philip Avery:

> He's folding into madness/The way his mother used to be/Asking questions of his feet/Does the ocean
> rush ashore/Or push the land away/Does the sky turn black/When there's nothing left to see/And what
> time is dinner served/When there's nothing left to eat

US is 90-200 pgs., digest-sized, offset litho printed and perfect-bound with slick 90 lb. paper cover, includes b&w photos and drawings. They receive about 1,200 poems a year, accept approximately 10%. Press run is 500. Single copy: $10; subscription: $17.
How to Submit: Line length for poetry is 100 maximum. Simultaneous submissions (with notification) OK. Cover letter and bio preferred. E-mail submissions OK. "All poetry submitted to *Urban Spaghetti* will be considered for publication and must be accompanied by SASE. Non-accepted submissions will be returned if proper postage and envelope are provided." Reads submissions February through May for the Summer issue and August through November for the Winter issue. However, *US* accepts submissions throughout the year. Seldom comments on rejections. Publishes theme issues occasionally. Send SASE for guidelines. Responds in 2 months. "Sooner if e-mail address is provided." Pays 2 copies. Copyright reverts to author upon publication.
Also Offers: Website includes guidelines, editors, list of previously published writers, sample poetry and links.

⊕ ☑ ◉ ◉ **URTHONA MAGAZINE (Specialized: religious, Buddhism)**, 3 Coral Park, Henley Rd., Cambridge CB1 3EA United Kingdom, phone 01223 566567, fax 01223 566568, e-mail urthonawindhorse.freeserve.co.uk, website www.ziplink.net/~vajramat/urthona.html, founded 1992, contact poetry editor.
Magazine Needs: *Urthona*, published biannually, explores the arts and western culture from a Buddhist perspective. They want "poetry rousing the imagination." They do not want "undigested autobiography, political, or New-Agey poems." They have published poetry by Peter Abbs, Robert Bly and Peter Redgrove. As a sample the editor selected these lines from "The Shower" by Ananda:

> And somewhere there is gold,/and a song almost getting started/in the street we're leaving by://
> something like tenderness, how/the spring light races and dies/over the washed squares

Urthona is 60 pgs., A4, offset printed, saddle-stapled with 4-color glossy cover, b&w photos, art and ads inside. They receive about 300 poems a year, accept approximately 40. Press run is 900 for 50 subscribers of which 4 are libraries, 500 shelf sales; 50 distributed free to Buddhist groups. Subscription: £8.50 (surface), £11.50 (airmail)/2 issues; £15 (surface), £22 (airmail)/4 issues. Sample (including guidelines): £3.50.
How to Submit: Submit 6 poems at a time. No previously published poems or simultaneous submissions. Cover letter preferred. Fax and e-mail submissions (included in body of message) OK. Reads submissions January through July only. Time between acceptance and publication is 6-8 months. Poems are circulated to an editorial board and read and selected by poetry editor. Other editors have right of veto. Responds in 2 months. Pays 1 copy. Acquires one-time rights. Reviews books or chapbooks of poetry or other magazines in 600 words. Open to unsolicited reviews. Poets may also send books for review consideration.
Also Offers: Sponsors annual contest with £150 1st Prize, £80 2nd Prize and five 3rd Prizes of a 2-year subscription. Submit any number of poems with a £1.50/poem entry fee. Poems must be no longer than 40 lines; 1 poem/page. Put name, address and phone on separate sheet only. Entries not returned. Deadline: January 15.

☑ ◉ **UTAH STATE UNIVERSITY PRESS; MAY SWENSON POETRY AWARD**, Logan UT 84322-7800, phone (801)797-1362, fax (801)797-0313, e-mail mspooner@press.usu.edu, website www.usu.edu/~usupress, founded 1972, poetry editor Michael Spooner, publishes poetry only through the May Swenson Poetry Award competition annually. They have published *May Out West* by May Swenson; *Plato's Breath* by Randall Freisinger; *The Hammered Dulcimer* by Lisa Williams; *Necessary Light* by Patricia Fargnoli. See website for details.

◉ **VEGETARIAN JOURNAL; THE VEGETARIAN RESOURCE GROUP (Specialized: children/teens, vegetarianism)**, P.O. Box 1463, Baltimore MD 21203, website www.vrg.org, founded 1982.
Magazine Needs: The Vegetarian Resource Group is a publisher of nonfiction. *VJ* is a bimonthly, 36 pgs., 8½ × 11, saddle-stapled and professionally printed with glossy card cover. Circulation is 20,000. Sample: $3.
How to Submit: "Please no submissions of poetry from adults; 18 and under only."

Also Offers: The Vegetarian Resource Group offers an annual contest for ages 18 and under, $50 savings bond in 3 age categories for the best contribution on any aspect of vegetarianism. "Most entries are essay, but we would accept poetry with enthusiasm." Postmark deadline: May 1. Send SASE for details.

VEHICLE PRESS; SIGNAL EDITIONS (Specialized: regional), P.O. Box 125 Station Place du Parc, Montreal, Quebec H2W 2M9 Canada, phone (514)844-6073, fax (514)844-7543, e-mail vpress@cam.org, website www.vehiculepress.com, poetry editor Michael Harris, publisher Simon Dardick.
Book/Chapbook Needs: Vehicle Press is a "literary press with a poetry series, Signal Editions, publishing the work of Canadian poets only." They publish flat-spined paperbacks and hardbacks. They have published *White Stone: The Alice Poems* by Stephanie Bolster (winner of the 1998 Governor-General's Award for Poetry); *Facts* by Bruce Taylor and *Keep It All* by Yves Boisvert, translated by J. Cowan. As a sample they selected these lines by Michael Harris:

> These last years have left us/to marvel at lesser things—/at the mile-after-mile of roadside show:/the
> courtly scorpion at her brittle minuet;/the lolloping rabbit with her slow semaphore of ears;/a vulture
> folding his thin shadow up like an umbrella/over some fluttering rag of skin on the ground;/the roadkill
> and carcasses like footnotes/and glossary to our disquisition.

They publish Canadian poetry which is "first-rate, original, content-conscious."
How to Submit: Query before submitting.

THE VERNALIST; INVOLUTE PRESS, P.O. Box 406752, Louisville KY 40204, phone (502)585-3905, e-mail the_vernalist@hotmail.com, founded 1998, editor/publisher James Welch.
Magazine Needs: "*The Vernalist* is an annual journal of new growth in poetry and writing published each spring." They want "poetry and criticism (critical response), innovative, pertinent poetic thought of varying style and form preferably of unconventional dynamics, ranging in complexity from the lyric to the 'problematic.' " They do not want "poetry that lacks imagination or spiritually devoid poetry, self-centered or heterogenous group-centered such as 'feminist,' 'Beat,' 'neo-beat,' 'afro-centric' or performance/sound poetry." They have published poetry by Elizabeth Robinson, Ezra Mark, Lisa Samuels, Will Alexander, Elizabeth Willis and Kenneth Warren. As a sample the editor selected the lines from "The Net" by Catherine Arnold:

> In the other life,/I collect difficult thoughts;/Their ungivingness holds me/In the upright position./Every
> atom beating at my skull./As the world beats/As the bird beats shell against wall . . ./Shattering the
> involutions: Breaking the animal packed in its disintegrating hall.

The Vernalist is 90-100 pgs., 5½ × 8½, laser typeset and perfect-bound with light card cover, includes b&w art. They receive about 200 poems a year, accept approximately 20%. Publish 50 plus poems/issue. Subscription: $12. Sample: $6. Make checks payable to James Welch, *The Vernalist*.
How to Submit: Previously published poems and simultaneous submissions OK. E-mail and disk submissions OK. Cover letter with short bio and SASE preferred. Reads submissions January 1 through April 1 only. Time between acceptance and publication is 9 months. Poems are circulated to an editorial board. "Approximately six poets and writers review and concur." Publishes theme issues occasionally. Send SASE for guidelines and upcoming themes. Responds in 3 months. Pays copies per request. Reviews books and chapbooks of poetry and other magazines in 1,000 words, single and multi-book format. Open to unsolicited reviews. Poets may also send books for review consideration.
Book/Chapbook Needs & How to Submit: "Involute Press publishes new work that is linguistically innovative and contributes to spiritual development or the development of language." They publish 1-2 paperbacks and 2 chapbooks per year. "Poets should send at least 3 sample poems along with bio and publishing preferences/specifications for chapbooks. We reserve the right to print excerpts from the chapbooks or their entirety in the journal." Replies to queries in 2 weeks; to mss in 2 months. Payment varies. May offer author-subsidy arrangement, "depending on available funding."
Advice: "All styles are good except the boring style"—Voltaire.

VERSE, Plymouth State College, Plymouth NH 03264, fax (603)535-2584, founded 1984, editors Brian Henry and Andrew Zawacki.
Poetry published in this journal also appeared in the 1997 volume of *The Best American Poetry*.
Magazine Needs: *Verse* appears 3 times/year and is "an international poetry journal which also publishes interviews with poets, essays on poetry and book reviews." They want "no specific kind; we look for high-quality poetry. Our focus is not only on American poetry, but on all poetry written in English, as well as translations." They have published poetry by August Kleinzahler, Charles Wright, Heather McHugh, John Ashbery, James Tate, Gary Soto, Tomaz Salamun, Karen Volkman, Medbh McGuckian and Simon Armitage. As a sample the editor included these lines from "The Definition of Swan" by Geoffrey Nutter:

> One that resembles or emulates a swan/may be rightly called a "Swan," or more precisely,/"one who
> emulates a swan." We may say that he is swan-like./If he is long-necked and beautiful, or if he flies
> strongly/when once started, or sleeps in mim,/we may put him to sleep in a swannery./To "swan" is
> to wander aimlessly.

Verse is 128-256 pgs., digest-sized, professionally printed and perfect-bound with card cover. They receive about 5,000 poems a year, accept approximately 100. Press run is 1,000 for 600 subscribers of which 200 are libraries, 200 shelf sales. Subscription: $15 for individuals, $27 for institutions. Current issue $6. Sample: $5.

How to Submit: Submit up to 5 poems at a time. No previously published poems; simultaneous submissions OK. Cover letter required. Time between acceptance and publication is 3-9 months. Responds in 4 months. Often comments on rejections. "The magazine often publishes special features—recent features include Scottish poetry, Latino poets, prose poetry, women Irish poets, and Australian poetry." Always sends prepublication galleys. Pays 2 copies plus a one-year subscription. Open to unsolicited reviews. Poets may also send books for review consideration.

[N] [◐] VICTORY PARK, JOURNAL OF THE NEW HAMPSHIRE INSTITUTE OF ART, 148 Concord St., Manchester NH 03104-4858, phone (603)623-0313, ext. 520, fax (603)641-1832, founded 1996, senior editor Linda Butler.
Magazine Needs: "*Victory Park* is a biannual literary and visual arts publication. Content includes fiction, poetry, critical and visual essays on the arts and popular culture." They do not want poetry that is children/young adult-directed. They have published poetry by Wes McNair, Patricia Fargnoli, Rick Agran, Catherine Fraga, Catherine O'Brian and Joan Aleshire. The editor says *VP* is 94-112 pgs., 5½×8½, offset printed and perfect-bound with 4-color cover, includes art/graphics and ads. They receive about 800 poems a year. Publish 10-12 poems/issue. Press run is 1,000 for about 500 subscribers of which 60% are libraries, 20% shelf sales. Single copy: $10; subscription: $16/year. Sample: $5.
How to Submit: Submit 5 poems at a time. No previously published poems; simultaneous submissions OK. Cover letter preferred. "Include SASE, name/address/telephone number/titles on cover page. Envelope should be addressed to: Poetry Editor." Reads submissions December through March 15 (spring issue); June through September 15 (fall issue) only. Time between acceptance and publication is 4 months ("depending on date of receipt.") Poems are circulated to an editorial board. "Blind reading by associate poetry editors; final decisions made by poetry editor and senior editor." Seldom comments on rejections. Publishes theme issues occasionally. Send SASE for guidelines. Responds in 4 months. Pays 2 copies. Acquires first North American serial rights.

VIKING; PENGUIN PUTNAM INC., 375 Hudson St., New York NY 10014. Prefers not to share information.

[N] [$] [◐] [◎] THE VINCENT BROTHERS REVIEW (Specialized: themes), 4566 Northern Circle, Riverside OH 45424-5733, founded 1988, editor Kimberly A. Willardson.
• For 1999 and 2000, *TVBR* won grants from the Montgomery County Arts and Cultural District.
Magazine Needs: *TVBR* is a journal appearing 3 times/year. "We look for well-crafted, thoughtful poems that shoot bolts of electricity into the reader's mind, stimulating a powerful response. We also welcome light verse and are thrilled by unusual, innovative subjects and styles. We do not accept previously published poems, simultaneous submissions, or any type of bigoted propaganda. Sloppy mss containing typos and/or unintentional misspellings are automatically rejected. *TVBR* publishes at least two theme issues/year—poets should send us a SASE to receive details about our upcoming themes." They have published poetry by Deanna Pickard, Simon Perchik, Robert Paschell, Jonathan Levant, Fredrick Zydek and James Brooks. As a sample the editor selected these lines from "Getaway" by Susan Jelus:

> Drops of rain/on the window above the sharpwing/are driven back into tiny raging rivers/by the force
> of the takeoff/through grey soup/into pure white light

TVBR is 96-120 pgs., digest-sized, perfect-bound, professionally printed with matte card cover. Press run is 450. They have 250 subscribers of which 10 are libraries. Subscription: $15 individual, $18 institutions. "Subscribers from Canada add $4, overseas add $10." Sample: $7.95. Back issue: $5 (saddle stitched); $6 (perfect bound).
How to Submit: Submit up to 6 poems at a time, name and address on each page. Note in cover letter "where author read or heard about *TVBR*." No previously published poems; simultaneous submissions OK "but not preferred." Does not read poems in November or December. Poems are read by editor and two outside editors. Themes are "Cats and Dogs," Deadline: October 31, 2000; and "On the Job," Deadline: January 31, 2001. Often comments on rejections. Publishes theme issues. Send SASE for guidelines and upcoming themes. Responds in 3 months "usually." Always sends prepublication galleys. Pays $5-40/poem and 2 copies. Acquires one-time rights. Reviews books of poetry in 3,500 words maximum, single or multi-book format. Open to unsolicited reviews. Poets may also send books for review consideration.
Also Offers: Sponsors annual poetry contest: $200 for 1st and $100 for 2nd. Send SASE for details.
Advice: "Don't send your poetry to a magazine you haven't read. Subscribe to the little magazines you respect—they contain the work of your peers and competitors. Proofread your poetry carefully and read it aloud before sending it out."

[$] [♥] THE VIRGINIA QUARTERLY REVIEW; EMILY CLARK BALCH PRIZE, 1 West Range, Charlottesville VA 22903, phone (804)924-3124, fax (804)924-1397, founded 1925.

THE BOOK PUBLISHERS INDEX, located at the back of this book, lists those publishers who consider full-length book collections.

Magazine Needs: *The Virginia Quarterly Review* uses about 15 pgs. of poetry in each issue, no length or subject restrictions. Issues have largely included lyric and narrative free verse, most of which features a strong message or powerful voice. The review is 220 pgs., digest-sized, flat-spined, circulation 4,000.
How to Submit: Submit up to 5 poems and include SASE. "You will *not* be notified otherwise." No simultaneous submissions. Responds in 3 months or longer "due to the large number of poems we receive." Send SASE for submission details; do not request via fax. Pays $1/line.
Also Offers: They also sponsor the Emily Clark Balch Prize, an annual prize of $500 given to the best poem published in the review during the year.

☑ $ ◎ **VISTA PUBLISHING, INC. (Specialized: nurses)**, 422 Morris Ave., Suite 1, Long Branch NJ 07740, phone (732)229-6500, fax (732)229-9647, e-mail info@vistapubl.com, website www.vistapubl.com, founded 1991, contact Carolyn S. Zagury.
Book/Chapbook Needs: Provides "a forum for the creative and artistic side of our nursing colleagues." Publishes 10 paperback/year. They want "poetry written by nurses, relating to nursing or healthcare." They have published *Broken Butterflies* by Jodi Lalone and *Drifting Among the Whales* by Carol Battaglia. Books are usually 100 pgs., 6×9, trade paper, perfect-bound with illustrations if appropriate and 4-color cover.
How to Submit: Submit complete typed ms. "We are interested only in poetry collections with an average of 100 poems." No previously published poems; simultaneous submissions OK. Cover letter preferred. Has backlog to Fall 2000. Time between acceptance and publication is 2 years. Often comments on rejections. Replies in 3 months. Pays "percentage of profits."
Also Offers: Website includes contact information and a list of all current titles with prices and ordering information.

N ⊕ $ ○ ◑ ◎ **VOICEWORKS MAGAZINE (Specialized: children/teen/young adult)**, 156 George St., 1st Floor, Melbourne, Victoria, North Fitzroy 3065 Australia, phone (03)9416-3305, fax (03)9419-3365, e-mail vworks@vicnet.net.au, website www.glasswings.com.au/voiceworks, founded 1985, editor Craig Garrett.
Magazine Needs: *Voiceworks* appears 4 times a year to publish "young," "new," "emerging" writers under 25 years of age. "We have no specifications for poetry. Only the poets must be under 25 years of age. No racist, stollen or libelous work." The editor says *Voiceworks* is 80 pgs., 8½×11, perfect-bound, includes art/graphics and ads. They receive about 400 poems a year, accept approximately 14%. Publish 14 poems/issue. Press run is 1,000. Single copy: $5; subscription: $25/year. Sample: $3. Make checks payable to Express Media/*Voiceworks Magazine*.
How to Submit: Submit no more than 8 poems at a time. No previously published poems; simultaneous submissions OK. E-mail and disk submissions OK. Cover letter required. "We need a short bio and SASE (or SAE and IRC). If giving a disk or submitting by e-mail save the file as a Rich Text format." Reads submissions January 4 through 11, April 4 through 11, July 4 through 11 and October 4 through 11 only. Time between acceptance and publication is 2 months. Poems are circulated to an editorial board. "We all read the submissions, make comments and decide what to publish." Often comments on rejections. Publishes theme issues. Send SASE (or SAE and IRC) for guidelines and upcoming themes or obtain via e-mail or fax. Responds in 2 months. Pays $50. Poets retain rights. Staff reviews books and chapbooks of poetry and other magazines. Send books for review consideration.

■ ○ **VOIDING THE VOID**, % E.E. Lippincott, 8 Henderson Place, New York NY 10028, phone (212)628-2799, e-mail eelipp@aol.com, website www.vvoid.com, founded 1997, editor-in-chief E. E. Lippincott.
Magazine Needs: *Voiding The Void* is "a monthly existential-esque reader." Their poetry needs are "very open, if author feels the work is in keeping with *Voiding The Void*'s themes of 'tangibility' and amusement value." They have published poetry by Bryon Howell, Sue Batterton and Paul D. McGlynn. As a sample the editor selected these lines by Charles O'Hay:

> It is better to do one thing catastrophically/than to do a hundred acceptably./Disaster/done well/can
> set the experts chattering for decades

VTV appears both on hard copy (b&w, 8-page tabloid format) and on the web. They receive about 500 poetry submissions a year, accept approximately 95%. First press run is about 150 for approximately 100 subscribers. Single copy: 1 first-class stamp; subscription: $3.96/year. Make checks payable to E.E. Lippincott.
How to Submit: Submit up to 5 poems at a time. Simultaneous submissions OK. Cover letter preferred. E-mail and disk submissions OK. Time between acceptance and publication is 1-3 months. Always comments on rejections. Publishes theme issues occasionally. Obtain guidelines and upcoming themes via post, e-mail or website. Responds in 2 months. Pays 5 copies. Acquires one-time rights. Reviews books of poetry. Open to unsolicited reviews. Poets may also send books for review consideration.
Also Offers: Website includes writer's guidelines, correspondence information, e-mail access to editor, all back issues as well as the main display of the current issue of the hard copy.

N ○ ◎ **VORTEX OF THE MACABRE; DARK GOTHIC (Specialized: vampires, magical/occult themes)**, 1616 E. Barringer St., Philadelphia PA 19150-3304, e-mail serae37378@netzero.net, founded 1996, editor/publisher Ms. Cinsearae.

Magazine Needs: The editor publishes two biannual magazines, *Dark Gothic* and *Vortex of The Macabre*. "*Dark Gothic* is a vampire themed zine of dark, erotic and romantic poetry, art and short stories. *Vortex of the Macabre* publishes weird, insane, gross poetry and art, reviews, and short-short stories. If it's twilight-zoneish, tales from the crypt-ish, insane, kooky or just plain weird, I want it! Freestyle, prose, it doesn't matter since poetry is an art. No line limits here. No fuzzy-bunny stuff!" They have published poetry by William P. Robertson, C. David Hay and Douglas M. Stokes. As a sample the editor selected this untitled piece by Scott Falk:

> Rent limb from limb/the corpse is still/a shade comes forth/and eats its fill/Imbibing on death's nectar/ ensuring his survival/The death of one/is the life of another.

The publications are 20-30 pgs. (*DG*), 40-70 pgs. (*VOTM*), 8½×11, photocopied and side-stapled with b&w paper cover, includes "art of an eerie or morbid tone," also ads. They receive about 80-90 poems a year, accept approximately 95%. Press run is 100. Subscription: $14 for both, otherwise $9 for *VOTM*, $6 for *DG*. Sample: $4.50 for *VOTM*, $3 for *DG*. Make checks payable to Ms. Cinsearae S. "Purchase of copy is strongly encouraged. I sometimes get things too grossly obscene and almost criminal sounding! Also, contributors must send SASE with any works."

How to Submit: Submit 5 poems at a time. Previously published poems and simultaneous submissions OK. E-mail and disk submissions OK. Cover letter preferred. "Poems should be single-spaced, as well as any short stories submitted to *Dark Gothic*. Send 'friendly' cover letter about you; I don't care all that much about your 'credentials.' " Time between acceptance and publication is 5 months. Often comments on rejections. Publishes theme issues occasionally. Send SASE for guidelines and upcoming themes or obtain via e-mail. Responds in 3 months. Pays 1 copy. Acquires one-time rights. Reviews books and chapbooks of poetry and other magazines in up to 174 words. Open to unsolicited reviews. Poets may also send books for review consideration to the editor, % *VOTM* only.

Advice: "Don't give up! If writing is your one time love, persue it! Don't give it up for anyone or anything. Believe in yourself and your work. No one has the power to make you happy but you."

N ▨ ▢ ◎ VQ (Specialized: volcanoes), 8009 18th Lane SE, Lacey WA 98503, phone (360)455-4607, e-mail jmtanaka@webtv.net, website http://community.webtv.net/JMTanaka/VQ, founded 1992, editor Janet Tanaka.

Magazine Needs: *VQ* is an "interest" publication for professional and amateur volcanologists and volcano buffs. They want "any kind of poetry as long as it is about volcanoes and/or the people who work on them." They do not want "over-emotive, flowery stuff or anything not directly pertaining to volcanoes." Also accepts poetry written by children. They have published poetry by Dane Picard and C. Martinez. As a sample the editor selected these lines from "Farewell Observatory" by C. Scarpinati, translated from Italian by Claude Grandpey:

> A coat of fire shrouded your shoulders/and your sides, as tho' you were cold./Your masks, walls of iron/didn't collapse.

Subscription: $25; free on the Internet.

How to Submit: Submit any number of poems. E-mail and disk submissions (in body of message) OK. Previously published poems with permission of the original copyright holder and simultaneous submissions OK. Time between acceptance and publication is 3-6 months. Always comments on rejections. "I try not to outright reject, preferring to ask for a rewrite." Send SASE for guidelines. Responds in 1 month. Pays 3 copies. "Contributors may copyright in the usual fashion. But there is as yet no mechanism on the Internet to keep users honest. We also need written permission to publish on the Internet." Reviews books or chapbooks of poetry or other magazines by guest reviewers. Open to unsolicited reviews. Poets may also send books for review consideration if they are about volcanoes.

☑ $◎ WAKE FOREST UNIVERSITY PRESS (Specialized: bilingual/foreign language, ethnic/ nationality), P.O. Box 7333, Winston-Salem NC 27109, phone (336)758-5448, fax (336)758-5636, e-mail wfupress@wfu.edu, website www.wfu.edu/wfupress, founded 1976, director and poetry editor Dillon Johnston.

Book/Chapbook Needs: "We publish only poetry from Ireland. I am able to consider only poetry written by native Irish poets. I must return, unread, poetry from American poets." They have published *Collected Poems* by John Montague; *Ghost Orchid* by Michael Longley; *Selected Poems* by Medbh McGuckian; and *The Wake Forest Book of Irish Women's Poetry*. As a sample the editor selected the poem "Nights Thoughts" from *The Yellow Book* by Derek Mahon:

> windows flung wide on briny balconies/above an ocean of roofs and lighthouse beams;/like a storm lantern the wintry planet swings.

How to Submit: Query with 4-5 samples and cover letter. No simultaneous submissions. Replies to queries in 1-2 weeks, to submissions (if invited) in 2-3 months. Sometimes sends prepublication galleys. Publishes on 10% royalty contract with $500 advance, 6-8 author's copies. Buys North American or US rights.

Advice: "Because our press is so circumscribed, we get few direct submissions from Ireland. Our main problem, however, is receiving submissions from American poets, whom we do not publish because of our very limited focus here. I would advise American poets to read listings carefully so they do not misdirect to presses such as ours, work that they, and I, value."

$ ⬤ ◎ THE WAR CRY (Specialized: religious), 615 Slaters Lane, P.O. Box 269, Alexandria VA 22313, phone (703)684-5500, fax (703)684-5539, e-mail warcry@usn.salvationarmy.org, website http://publications.salv ationarmyusa.org, founded 1880, editor-in-chief Lt. Colonel Marlene Chase.

Magazine Needs: *The War Cry*, appearing biweekly, publishes "reports, commentary and testimonies that proclaim the gospel of Jesus Christ and His power to change lives today." They want "Christian poetry, any style, 16 lines maximum." As a sample the editor selected these lines from "Merciful Heavens!" by Ruth Glover:

> *Today my skies are clear;/The night is gone,/And all my midnight sighs/And foolish fears/Have faded*
> *with the dawn;*

The editor says *The War Cry* is 24 pgs., with photos and graphics. Press run is 300,000. Sample available for SASE.

How to Submit: Submit up to 6 poems at a time. Previously published poems and simultaneous submissions OK. Fax and e-mail submissions OK, for e-mail include as attached file (Word or WordPerfect) or in body of message. Cover letter preferred. Time between acceptance and publication varies. "Poems are screened by an editor who acts as a 'first reader,' then good ones are passed on to the editor-in-chief." Seldom comments on rejections. Publishes theme issues. Send SASE for guidelines and upcoming themes. Responds in up to 1 month. Pays $10-65 and 1 complimentary copy. Buys one-time and reprint rights.

Also Offers: Website features writer's guidelines, interviews and forums.

⬤ WARTHOG PRESS, 29 South Valley Rd., West Orange NJ 07052, phone (973)731-9269, founded 1979, poetry editor Patricia Fillingham.

Book/Chapbook Needs: Warthog Press publishes books of poetry "that are understandable, poetic." They have published *From the Other Side of Death* by Joe Lackey; *Wishing for the Worst* by Linda Portnay; and *Hanging On* by Joe Benevento.

How to Submit: Query with 5 samples, cover letter and SASE. "A lot of the submissions I get seem to be for a magazine. I don't publish anything but books." Simultaneous submissions OK. Ms should be "readable." Comments on rejections, "if asked for. People really don't want criticism." Pays copies, but "I would like to get my costs back."

Advice: "The best way to sell poetry still seems to be from poet to listener."

▧ $ ◎ WASCANA REVIEW, Dept. of English, University of Regina, Regina, Saskatchewan S4S 0A2 Canada, phone (306)585-4302, fax (306)585-4827, e-mail kathleen.wall@uregina.ca, website www.uregina.ca/English/wrhome/htm, founded 1966, editor Kathleen Wall.

Magazine Needs: *Wascana Review* appears twice a year publishing contemporary poetry and short fiction along with critical articles on modern and post-modern literature. "We look for high-quality literary poetry of all forms. No haiku or doggerel. No long poems. No concrete poetry." They have published poetry by Beth Goobie, Robert Cooperman, Lea Littlewolfe and Susanna Roxman. The editor says *WR* is a trade-sized paperback, 75-100 pgs., no art/graphics, no ads. They receive about 200-300 submissions a year, accept under 10%. Press run is 400 for 192 subscribers of which 134 are libraries, 100 shelf sales. Subscription: $10/year, $12 outside Canada. Sample: $5.

How to Submit: No previously published poems or simultaneous submissions. Cover letter required. SASE (or SAE and IRCs) necessary for return of mss. "Poems are read by at least two individuals who make comments and/or recommendations. Poetry editor chooses poems based on these comments. Poets may request information via e-mail. But no faxed or e-mailed submissions, please." Poets may also send SASE for guidelines and upcoming themes. Often comments on rejections. Publishes theme issues. Send SASE for guidelines. Responds within 6 months. Pays $10/page plus contributor's copy and 1-year subscription. Buys first North American serial rights. Reviews books of poetry in both single and multi-book format.

Also Offers: Website includes information on guidelines and special issues.

Advice: "*WR* will be featuring special issues from time to time. Poets should watch for news of these in upcoming editions."

Ⓝ ⬤ WASHINGTON REVIEW; FRIENDS OF THE WASHINGTON REVIEW OF THE ARTS, INC., P.O. Box 50132, Washington DC 20091-0132, phone (202)638-0515, website www.washingtonreview.c om, founded 1974, literary editor Heather Fuller.

Magazine Needs: *Washington Review* is a bimonthly journal of arts and literature published by the Friends of the Washington Review of the Arts, Inc., a nonprofit, tax-exempt educational organization. They publish local Washington metropolitan area poets as well as poets from across the US and abroad. "We have eclectic tastes but lean with more favor toward experimental work." *WR* is tabloid-sized, using 2 of the large pgs. each issue for poetry, saddle-stapled on high-quality heavy stock. Press run is 2,000 for 700 subscribers of which 10 are libraries. Sample: $2.50.

How to Submit: Cover letter with brief bio and SASE required with submissions. Pays 5 copies. Reviews books of poetry in 1,000-1,500 words, single format—multi-book "on occasion." Open to unsolicited reviews of books of poetry only. Poets may also send books for review consideration.

Also Offers: The review offers a $300 annual prize for the best poem published in the span of a year. Website includes an archive of poetry, fiction, reviews and interviews published in the print journal.

WASHINGTON SQUARE, A JOURNAL OF THE ARTS, 19 University Place, Third Floor, New York University Graduate Creative Writing Program, New York NY 10003, founded 1994 as *Washington Square* (originally founded in 1979 as *Ark/Angel*), editor Jennifer Keller.

Magazine Needs: Published semiannually, *Washington Square* is "a non-profit literary journal publishing fiction, poetry and essays by new and established writers. It's edited and produced by the students of the NYU Creative Writing Program." They want "all poetry of serious literary intent." They have published poetry by Marilyn Chin, Paul Muldoon, W.S. Merwin, Sharon Olds and Philip Levine. The editor says *WS* is 128 pgs. Press run is 1,000. Subscription: $12. Sample: $6.

How to Submit: Submit up to 6 poems at a time. No previously published poems; simultaneous submissions OK if noted. Time between acceptance and publication is 1-6 months. Poems are circulated to an editorial board. "The poetry editors and editorial staff read all submissions, discuss and decide which poems to include in the journal." Sometimes comments on rejections. Send SASE for guidelines or obtain via website. Responds in up to 6 weeks. Acquires first North American serial rights. Sometimes reviews books and chapbooks of poetry and other magazines in 300 words. Open to unsolicited reviews. Poets may also send books for review consideration.

WATER MARK PRESS, 138 Duane St., New York NY 10013, founded 1978, editor Coco Gordon. Currently they do not accept any unsolicited poetry.

● Note: Please do not confuse Water Mark Press with the imprint Watermark Press, used by other businesses.

WATERWAYS: POETRY IN THE MAINSTREAM (Specialized: themes); TEN PENNY PLAYERS (Specialized: children/teen/young adult); BARD PRESS, 393 St. Paul's Ave., Staten Island NY 10304-2127, phone (718)442-7429, fax (718)442-4978, e-mail water@tenpennyplayers.org, website www.ten pennyplayers.org, founded 1977, poetry editors Barbara Fisher and Richard Spiegel.

Magazine Needs: Bard Press "publishes poetry by adult poets in a magazine [*Waterways*] that is published 11 times/year. We do theme issues and are trying to increase an audience for poetry and the printed and performed word. The project produces performance readings in public spaces and is in residence year round at the New York public library with workshops and readings. We publish the magazine *Waterways*, anthologies and chapbooks. We are not fond of haiku or rhyming poetry; never use material of an explicit sexual nature. We are open to reading material from people we have never published, writing in traditional and experimental poetry forms. While we do 'themes,' sometimes an idea for a future magazine is inspired by a submission so we try to remain open to poets' inspirations. Poets should be guided however by the fact that we are children's and animal rights advocates and are a NYC press." They have published poetry by Ida Fasel, Kit Knight, Terry Thomas and Will Inman. *Waterways* is 40 pgs., 4¼×7, photocopied from various type styles, saddle-stapled, using b&w drawings, matte card cover. They use 60% of poems submitted. Press run is 150 for 58 subscribers of which 12 are libraries. Subscription: $20. Sample: $2.60.

How to Submit: Submit less than 10 poems for first submission. Simultaneous submissions OK. E-mail submissions OK. Send SASE for guidelines for approaching themes. "Since we've taken the time to be very specific in our response, writers should take seriously our comments and not waste their emotional energy and our time sending material that isn't within our area of interest. Sending for our theme sheet and for a sample issue and then objectively thinking about the writer's own work is practical and wise. Manuscripts that arrive without a return envelope are not sent back." Editors sometimes comment on rejections. Responds in less than a month. Pays 1 copy. Acquires one-time publication rights.

Book/Chapbook Needs & How to Submit: Chapbooks published by Ten Penny Players are "by children and young adults only—*not by submission*; they come through our workshops in the library and schools. Adult poets are published through our Bard Press imprint, *by invitation only*. Books evolve from the relationship we develop with writers we publish in *Waterways* and whom we would like to give more exposure."

Also Offers: They hold contests for children only.

Advice: "We suggest that poets attend book fairs. It's a fast way to find out what we are publishing. Without meaning to sound 'precious' or unfriendly, the writer should understand that small press publishers doing limited editions and all production work inhouse are working from their personal artistic vision and know exactly what notes will harmonize, effectively counterpoint and meld. Many excellent poems are sent back to the writers by *Waterways* because they don't relate to what we are trying to create in a given month."

WAY STATION MAGAZINE, 1319 S. Logan-MLK, Lansing MI 48910-1340, founded 1989, managing editor Randy Glumm.

Magazine Needs: *Way Station*, published occasionally, strives "to provide access and encourage beginning writers, while courting the established." They want "emerging cultures, world view, humanity direction, relationships—try all. No rhyme unless truly terrific." They do not want "religious or openly militant gay or lesbian poetry. Use common sense and discretion." They have published poetry by Charles Bukowski, Diane Wakoski, Stuart Dybek, Ethridge Knight and Terri Jewell. *Way Station* is 52 pgs., 8½×11, offset printed, saddle-stitched with heavy card cover, b&w art, photos and ads. They receive about 300 poems a year, accept approximately 20-30%. Press run is 1,000 for 35 subscribers of which 2 are libraries, 200 shelf sales; 500 distributed free to potential advertisers, readers, libraries and universities. Subscription: $18. Sample: $6.

How to Submit: Submit 5 poems with name and address on each page and $5 processing fee (returned if work is rejected). Previously published poems and simultaneous submissions OK. Cover letter preferred. Time between acceptance and publication is 1-2 months, sometimes longer. "If not struck immediately, I then put it aside and re-read later 3-4 times. I might also circulate if through a panel of volunteer readers." Often comments on rejections. Send SASE for guidelines. Responds in 2 months. Pays 2 copies. Acquires one-time or first North American serial rights. Reviews books or chapbooks of poetry or other magazines "if I have time." Open to unsolicited reviews. Poets may also send books for review consideration.

Advice: "It's best to check out your own work. Get advice from coaches, instructors prior to submitting. Also get sample copies of magazines you intend to submit to—this can only help you."

N **$** ☑ **WēBER STUDIES—VOICES AND VIEWPOINTS OF THE CONTEMPORARY WEST**, 1214 University Circle, Weber State University, Ogden UT 84408-1214, phone (801)626-6473, founded 1983, editor Sherwin W. Howard.

☑ Poetry published here has appeared in *The Best American Poetry 1996.*

Magazine Needs: *Wēber Studies* appears 3 times/year and publishes fiction, poetry, criticism, personal essays, nonfiction and interviews. It is an interdisciplinary journal interested in relevant works covering a wide range of topics. They want "125 lines maximum, including line spaces (stanza breaks). We will only publish 125 lines total of a poet per issue." They do not want "poems that are flippant, prurient, sing-song or preachy." They have published poetry by Mark Strand, Janet Sylvester, Ingrid Wendt and Katharine Coles. As a sample the editor selected these lines from "Rhapsody for the Good Night" by David Lee:

> *nightbird/and the hum of pickup tires/on hardscrabble/I listen//behind the mockingbird behind the wind/behind the sound a taproot makes/working its way down to water/past that I can hear them/they can hear me too/if they want to*

Wēber Studies is 120 pgs., 7½×10, offset printed on acid-free paper, perfect-bound, with 2-3 color cover, occasional color plates and exchange ads (with other journals). They receive about 150-200 poems a year, accept approximately 30-40. Press run is 800-1,000 for 600 subscribers of which 70-100 are libraries; 75 distributed free to on-campus faculty. Subscription: $20, $20 institutions. Sample: $7-8.

How to Submit: Submit 3 poems, 2 copies of each (one without name). No previously published poems; simultaneous submissions OK. Cover letter preferred. Time between acceptance and publication is 12-15 months. Poems are selected by an anonymous (blind) evaluation. Seldom comments on rejections. Publishes theme issues. Send SASE for guidelines and upcoming themes. Responds in up to 6 months. Always sends prepublication galleys. Pays $10-15/page; depending on fluctuating grant monies. Buys all rights. Copyright reverts to author after first printing.

Also Offers: Cash award given every three years for poems published in *Wēber Studies*. Only poetry published in *Wēber Studies* during 3-year interval considered.

Advice: "This journal is referred by established poets—beginners not encouraged."

☑ **$** ◎ **WELCOME HOME; MOTHERS AT HOME, INC. (Specialized: mothers, parenting, families, children)**, 8310A Old Courthouse Rd., Vienna VA 22182, e-mail mah@mah.org, website www.mah.org, founded 1984, manuscript coordinator Diane Bognan.

Magazine Needs: *Welcome Home* is a monthly publication of "support and encouragement for at-home mothers." They want "poetry about the experience of parenting. Nothing long or obscure." *WH* is 32 pgs., digest-sized, professionally printed and saddle-stapled with paper cover, includes original art and photos. They receive about 240 poems a year, accept approximately 8%. Press run is 16,000 for 14,000 subscribers of which 200 are libraries. Subscription: $18. Sample: $2. Make checks payable to *Welcome Home.*

How to Submit: Previously published poems and simultaneous submissions OK. Cover letter preferred. Disk submissions OK. "We prefer paper mailed to the office." Time between acceptance and publication is 6 months or more. Poems are circulated to an editorial board. Seldom comments on rejections. Responds in 1 month. Pays $10 and 5 copies. Acquires one-time rights.

Also Offers: Website includes writer's guidelines and samples.

N ○ ◎ **THE WELL TEMPERED SONNET (Specialized: form/style)**, 87 Petoskey St., Suite 120, New Hudson MI 48165, e-mail jamiet@ameritech.net, founded 1998, publisher/editor James D. Taylor II.

Magazine Needs: "Appearing biannually, *TWTS* publishes only compositions in sonnet form and caters to those who love and appreciate the form Shakespeare made famous. No erotica, blasphemy, vulgarity or racism." The editor says *TWTS* is magazine-sized, desktop-published and spiral-bound with attractive, heavy stock cover, sometimes includes art/graphics. Subscription: $20/year. Make checks payable to James Taylor. "We encourage submissions requesting subscriptions, details included in guidelines."

How to Submit: Submit 6 poems at a time. Previously published poems OK; no simultaneous submissions. E-mail and disk submissions OK. Seldom comments on rejections. Publishes theme issues occasionally. Send SASE for guidelines. Responds ASAP. Always sends prepublication galleys.

Also Offers: "We encourage and try to provide the means for interaction between other sonnetiers."

Advice: "A well composed sonnet is a piece of art. Understanding word usage is important in the development of the sonnet, as important as colors to a painter."

N □ ⦾ ◎ WELLSPRING: A JOURNAL OF CHRISTIAN POETRY (Specialized), e-mail wellspring@poetrypages.com, website www.angelfire.com/wa2/wellspring, founded 1999, editor Deborah Beachboard.
Magazine Needs: *Wellspring* is an online journal featuring quality Christian poetry by various authors. Poems are published on an ongoing basis. I am looking for quality Christian poetry that touches every aspect of Christian living—from the worship of God to the activities of daily life. No pornography, no senseless violence, nothing New Age." They have published poetry by Joyce Freeman-Clark, Nancy Spiegelberg, H. Arlequin, Robert K. Meyer II and Jean Calkins. As a sample the editor selected these lines from "A Farmer's Prayer" by Jane F. Hutto:

> Perhaps I'll go today, dear Lord,/A tramping 'cross some fresh-tilled soil,/Then sit beside a tree-lined
> stream/To contemplate Your graciousness,/And dream . . .

They accept approximately 60% of poems received a year.
How to Submit: Submit 5 poems at a time. Previously published poems and simultaneous submissions OK. E-mail submissions OK. Cover letter preferred. "Currently I am accepting submissions by e-mail only. When submitting, indicate it is for *Wellspring*. Include e-mail address and name with each poem submitted." Submit seasonal poems 1 month in advance. Time between acceptance and publication is 2 weeks. Seldom comments on rejections. Obtain guidelines via website. Responds in 2 weeks. Sometimes sends prepublication galleys. Acquires one-time rights.
Also Offers: Website includes complete guidelines, author biographies, poets' news items, the editor's statement of faith, ABC's of salvation, and other items of interest. "All poetry accepted is published online."
Advice: "Heartfelt poetry is wonderful, but quality poetry will show an understanding of the craft of poetry. Learn how to incorporate poetic device into your poetry even when writing free verse!"

$ ⦿ WESLEYAN UNIVERSITY PRESS, 110 Mt. Vernon, Middletown CT 06459, phone (860)685-2420, founded 1957, editor-in-chief Suzanna Tamminen.
Book/Chapbook Needs: Wesleyan University Press is one of the major publishers of poetry in the nation. They publish 4-6 titles/year. They have published poetry by James Dickey, Joy Harjo, James Tate and Yusef Komunyakaa.
How to Submit: Send query and SASE. Considers simultaneous submissions. Send SASE for guidelines. Responds to queries in 6-8 weeks, to mss in 2-4 months. Pays royalties plus 10 copies. Poetry publications from Wesleyan tend to get widely (and respectfully) reviewed.

⦿ WEST ANGLIA PUBLICATIONS, P.O. Box 2683, La Jolla CA 92038, editor Helynn Hoffa, publisher Wilma Lusk.
Book Needs: West Anglia Publications wants only the best poetry and short stories and publishes 1 paperback/year. They want "contemporary poems, well wrought by poets whose work has already been accepted in various fine poetry publications." They have published poetry by Gary Morgan, Robert Wintringer and John Theobald. As a sample the editor selected these lines from "Obedient As Dogs" in *Rings of Saturn, Selected and New Poems, 1999* by Kathleen Iddings:

> We stutter to the rimless surface./No smell of parsley or almond,/no slit of starlight/nor sheen of
> whispering stream.//A stereo fugue/shrieks like a dying dream./Wardens of the wind swing from a
> gibbet./locked in a cross-grained knot.

Books are usually approximately 75-100 pgs., 5½×8½, perfect-bound. Sample book: $10 plus $1.50 postage and handling.
How to Submit: Query with 6 poems, cover letter, professional bio and SASE.

⚏ $ ⦿ ◎ WEST COAST LINE (Specialized: ethnic/nationality, gay/lesbian/bisexual, love/romance/erotica, nature/rural/ecology, regional, social issues, women/feminism), 2027 EAA, Simon Fraser University, Burnaby, British Columbia V5A 1S6 Canada, phone (604)291-4287, fax (604)291-4622, e-mail wcl@sfu.ca, website www.sfu.ca/west-coast-line, founded 1990, editor Miriam Nichols, managing editor Jennifer Conroy.
Magazine Needs: *West Coast Line* is published 3 times/year and "favors work by both new and established Canadian writers, but it observes no borders in encouraging original creativity. Our focus is on contemporary poetry, short fiction, criticism and reviews of books." They have published poetry by Erin Mouré, Shok Mathur and Lydia Kwa. The magazine is 144 pgs., 6×9, handsomely printed on glossy paper and flat-spined. They receive about 500-600 poems a year, accept approximately 20. Approximately 40 pages of poetry/issue. Press run is 800 for 500 subscribers of which 350 are libraries, 150 shelf sales. Single copy: $10; subscription: $25.
How to Submit: Submit poetry ". . . in extended forms; excerpts from works in progress; experimental and innovative poems; to 400 lines." No previously published poetry or simultaneous submissions. E-mail submissions OK. Time between acceptance and publication is 2-8 months. Publishes theme issues. Send SASE for guidelines or request via e-mail. Responds in 4 months. Pays $8 (Canadian)/printed page plus a 1-year subscription and 2 copies. Mss returned only if accompanied by sufficient Canadian postage or IRC.
Advice: "We have a special concern for contemporary writers who are experimenting with, or expanding the boundaries of, conventional forms of poetry, fiction and criticism. That is, poetry should be formally innovative. We recommend that potential contributors send a letter of inquiry before submitting a manuscript."

The 18th Anthology cover of *West Wind Review* features "Tassajara Baths" by Sheila Lewis. Craig Wilson, managing editor, says one reason for choosing this piece is "its ability to draw you in." Wilson notes that a sense of "openness" in Lewis's cover art reflects his publication's tone and philosophy. A working artist for over 20 years, Lewis combines a career in counseling with art, working for the State of Oregon as a child and family therapist. *West Wind Review* is 224 pages of poetry, fiction and art in digest-sized format, flat-spined and handsomely printed.

✔ ◯ **WEST WIND REVIEW**, 1250 Siskiyou Blvd., Ashland OR 97520, phone (541)552-6518, e-mail westwind@student.sou.edu, founded 1980, editor Craig Wright, contact poetry editor.

Magazine Needs: *West Wind Review* publishes an annual anthology each spring in May. They are "looking for sensitive but strong verse that celebrates all aspects of men's and women's experiences, both exalted and tragic. We are looking to print material that reflects ethnic and social diversity." They have published poetry by Casey Kwang, Virgil Suarez, Pamela Steed Hill and Sean Brendan Brown. As a sample the editor selected these lines from "after the burnin moon" by Clarissa Armstrong:

> *given to daydreams that make her go weak in the knees; of her/limbs wrapped 'round Rooney's back*
> *like writhing white snakes,/of pushing a carriage full of sky-eyed babies; and her/own secret garden*
> *of bushes budding paper money in Spring. Of/babies bawling soft as lambs in the wake of wet-woolen*
> *sleep*

The anthology is usually 224 pgs., digest-sized, handsomely printed and perfect-bound. They receive about 1,200 submissions a year, publish 50-60 poems, 10 short stories and 16 pgs. of art. Press run is 500. Sample: $10.

How to Submit: Submit up to 5 poems. Manuscripts should have poet's name and address on first page." Include SASE. No previously published poems; simultaneous submissions OK. Cover letter required with name, address, phone number and a brief bio. No e-mail submissions. Deadline: November 15 for publication in late May. Send SASE for guidelines. Responds in March. Pays 1 copy.

Also Offers: Offers $50 award for best poem.

Ⓝ ⬆ ◎ **THE WESTCOAST FISHERMAN (Specialized: commercial fishing)**, 1496 W. 72nd Ave., Vancouver, British Columbia V6P 3C8 Canada, phone (604)266-8611, fax (604)266-6437, e-mail fisherman@west-coast.com, website www.west-coast.com, founded 1986, editor David Rahn.

Magazine Needs: *TWF*, published monthly, is "a nonpolitical, nonaligned publication serving the commercial fishing industry of Canada's west coast." They want "brief pieces, related to commercial fishing, pieces by fisherman most welcome. Seasonal poems welcome, e.g., salmon in summer, herring in spring, etc." They have published poetry by Tim Bowling. *TWF* is 56-64 pgs., 8½×11, professionally printed on 2-color newsprint, saddle-stapled, with full-color glossy cover, art, photos and ads. They receive about 20-40 poems a year, accept approximately 6. Press run is 7,000-8,000 for 5,600 subscribers; 1,550 distributed free. Subscription: $30 Canadian plus $2.10 GST. Sample: $3.95. Make checks payable to Westcoast Publishing Ltd.

How to Submit: Submit any number of poems. Previously published poems and simultaneous submissions OK. Cover letter preferred with "previous publishing history of poems (i.e., to whom it's already been sold)." Time between acceptance and publication could be as long as 1 year. "Poems held on file until an appropriate time and space becomes available." Send SASE (or SAE and IRC) for guidelines. Responds in 3 months. Pays $25/poem plus up to 10 copies. Buys one-time rights. Reviews books or chapbooks of poetry in 700 words. Open to unsolicited reviews. Poets may also send books of poetry on commercial fishing for review consideration.

🌐 💲 🔷 **WESTERLY; PATRICIA HACKETT PRIZE**, Centre for Studies in Australian Literature, University of Western Australia, Nedlands 6907, Australia, phone (08)9380-2101, fax (08) 9380-1030, e-mail westerly@uniwa.uwa.edu.au, website www.arts.uwa.edu.au/westerly, founded 1956, editors Dennis Haskell and Delys Bird, poetry editor Marcella Polain.

Magazine Needs: *Westerly* is a literary and cultural annual publishing quality short fiction, poetry, literary critical, socio-historical articles and book reviews with special attention given to Australia and the Indian Ocean region. "We don't dictate to writers on rhyme, style, experimentation, or anything else. We are willing to publish short or long poems. We do assume a reasonably well-read, intelligent audience. Past issues of *Westerly* provide the best guides. Not consciously an academic magazine." The annual magazine is 200 pgs., 5½×8½, "electronically printed," with some photos and graphics. Press run is 1,200. Subscription: $16 (US) airmail, $16 by e-mail.

How to Submit: Submit up to 6 poems at a time. Fax and e-mail submissions OK ("but replies may only be made for acceptances.") "Please do not send simultaneous submissions. Covering letters should be brief and nonconfessional." Time between acceptance and publication is 3 months. Publishes occasional theme issues. Responds in 3 months. Pays minimum of $30 plus 1 copy. Buys first publication rights; requests acknowledgment on reprints. Reviews books of poetry. Not open to unsolicited reviews. Poets may also send books to Reviews Editor for review consideration.

Also Offers: The Patricia Hackett Prize (value approx. $500) is awarded in March for the best contribution published in *Westerly* during the previous calendar year. Website includes details of past issues, subscription form and current issue.

Advice: "Be sensible. Write what matters for you but think about the reader. Don't spell out the meanings of the poems and the attitudes to be taken to the subject matter—i.e., trust the reader. Don't be swayed by literary fashion. Read the magazine if possible before sending submissions."

⭕ 📷 **WESTERN ARCHIPELAGO REVIEW (Specialized: ethnic/nationality, regional)**, P.O. Box 803282, Santa Clarita CA 91380, phone (213)383-3447, e-mail adorxyz@aol.com, founded 1999, editor Jovita Ador Lee.

Magazine Needs: *WAR* "publishes verse with a focus on the civilizations of Asia and the Pacific. All types of verse considered." As a sample the editor selected these lines (poet unidentified):

> Angel of Death, the High Priestess dances,/Turning in her silk;/Servant of the temple, covered in black
> robes,/Black cloth of Bali.

The editor says *WAR* is 12 pgs., 5½×8½, with glossy cover. Press run is 100. Subscription: $26. Sample: $7. Make checks payable to GoodSAMARitan Press

How to Submit: Submit 3 poems at a time. Previously published poems and simultaneous submissions OK. E-mail, fax and disk submissions OK. Cover letter with SASE required. Reads submissions September to June. Time between acceptance and publication is 6 weeks. Poems are circulated to an editorial board. Send SASE for guidelines. Responds in 6 weeks. Acquires all rights. Does not return rights. Reviews books and chapbooks of poetry and other magazines in 100 words. Poets may send books for review consideration.

☑ 💲 🔷 **WESTERN HUMANITIES REVIEW**, University of Utah, 255 S. Central Campus Dr., Room 3500, Salt Lake City UT 84112-0494, phone (801)581-6070, fax (801)585-5167, e-mail whr@lists.utah.edu, founded 1947, managing editor Jenny Mueller.

🔽 Poetry published in this review has been selected for inclusion in the 1995 and 1998 volumes of *The Best American Poetry*.

Magazine Needs: *WHR* is a semiannual publication of poetry, fiction and a small selection of nonfiction. They want "quality poetry of any form, including translations." They have published poetry by Philip Levine, Bin Ramke, Lucie Brock-Broido, Timothy Liu and Pattiann Rogers. *WHR* is 96-125 pgs., 6×9, professionally printed on quality stock and perfect-bound with coated card cover. They receive about 900 submissions a year, accept less than 10%, publish approximately 60 poets. Press run is 1,100 for 1,000 subscribers of which 900 are libraries. Subscription: $14 to individuals in the US. Sample: $8.

How to Submit: "We do not publish writer's guidelines because we think the magazine itself conveys an accurate picture of our requirements." No previously published poems; simultaneous submissions OK. No fax or e-mail submissions. Reads submissions October 1 through May 31 only. Time between acceptance and publication is 1-4 issues. Managing editor makes an initial cut then the poetry editor makes the final selections. Seldom comments on rejections. Occasionally publishes special issues. Responds in up to 6 months. Pays $5/published page and 2 copies. Acquires first serial rights.

Also Offers: They also offer an annual spring contest for Utah poets. Prize is $250.

🔳 💲 📷 **WESTERN PRODUCER PUBLICATIONS; WESTERN PEOPLE (Specialized: regional)**, P.O. Box 2500, Saskatoon, Saskatchewan S7K 2C4 Canada, phone (306)665-3500, fax (306)934-2401, e-mail people@producer.com, founded 1923, managing editor Michael Gillgannon.

Magazine Needs: *Western People* is a magazine supplement to *The Western Producer*, a weekly newspaper, circulation 100,000, which uses "poetry about the people, interests and environment of rural Western Canada." The magazine-sized supplement is 16 pgs., newsprint, with color and b&w photography and graphics. They receive about 500 submissions of poetry a year, use 60-70. Sample free for postage (2 oz.)—and ask for guidelines.

How to Submit: Submit up to 3 poems at a time, 1 per page. Name, address and telephone number in upper-left corner of each page. Responds within 2 weeks. Pays $15-50/poem.
Advice: "It is difficult for someone from outside Western Canada to catch the flavor of this region; almost all the poems we purchase are written by Western Canadians."

◐ WESTVIEW: A JOURNAL OF WESTERN OKLAHOMA, 100 Campus Dr., SWOSU, Weatherford OK 73096, phone (580)774-3168, founded 1981, editor Fred Alsberg.
Magazine Needs: *Westview* is a biannual publication that is "particularly interested in writers from the Southwest; however, we are open to work of quality by poets from elsewhere. We publish free verse, prose poems and formal poetry." They have published poetry by Miller Williams, Walter McDonald, Robert Cooperman, Alicia Ostriker and James Whitehead. *Westview* is 44 pgs., magazine-sized, saddle-stapled, with glossy card cover in full-color. They receive about 500 poems a year, accept approximately 7%. Press run is 700 for 300 subscribers of which about 25 are libraries. Subscription: $10/2 years. Sample: $4.
How to Submit: Submit 5 poems at a time. Cover letter including biographical data for contributor's note requested with submissions. "Poems on 3.5 computer disk are welcome so long as they are accompanied by the hard copy and the SASE has the appropriate postage." Editor comments on submissions "when close." Mss are circulated to an editorial board; "we usually respond within two to three months." Pays 1 copy.

⊕ ▯ ◐ WEYFARERS; GUILDFORD POETS PRESS, 1 Mountside, Guildford, Surrey GU2 5JD United Kingdom (for submissions), 9, White Rose Lane, Woking, GU22 7JA United Kingdom (for subscriptions), phone (01483)504566, founded 1972, administrative editor Martin Jones.
Magazine Needs: They say, "We publish *Weyfarers* magazine three times a year. All our editors are themselves poets and give their spare time free to help other poets." They describe their needs as "all types of poetry, serious and humorous, free verse and rhymed/metered, but mostly 'mainstream' modern. Excellence is the main consideration. Any subject publishable, from religious to satire. Not more than 45 lines." Also accepts poetry written by children. They have published poetry by Kenneth Pobo and Richard Ball (US), Michael Henry and Susan Skinner. As a sample the editors selected these lines from "The Lonely Places" by R.L. Cook:

> . . . Set in the rim of the globe, spots on the atlas,/Stern, hard & desolate,/Far from the bedlam towns,
> these lonely places,/Have waited & will wait,//Till they are left, one day, to the cold-eyed seabirds,/
> Gannet, guillemot, gull,/And the last croft, crumbling covered by the bracken,/And the wild sheep's
> skull . . .

The digest-sized, saddle-stapled format contains about 31 pgs. of poetry (of a total of 36 pgs.). They receive about 1,200-1,500 poems a year, accept approximately 125. The magazine has a circulation of "about 300," including about 200 subscribers of which 5 are libraries. Sample (current issue): $6 in cash US or £2.50 UK.
How to Submit: Submit up to 6 poems, one poem/sheet. No previously published poems or simultaneous submissions. Closing dates for submissions are end of January, May and September. Usually comments briefly on rejections. Pays 1 copy.
Also Offers: "We are associated with Surrey Poetry Center, which has an annual Open Poetry Competition. The prize-winners are published in *Weyfarers*."
Advice: "Always read a magazine before submitting. And read plenty of modern poetry."

$ ▯ ◐ WHETSTONE; WHETSTONE PRIZE, P.O. Box 1266, Barrington IL 60011-1266, phone (847)382-5626, fax (847)382-3685, editors Sandra Berris, Marsha Portnoy and Jean Tolle.
Magazine Needs: *Whetstone* appears annually in late November and publishes poetry, short fiction, novel excerpts and creative nonfiction. "We favor the concrete over the abstract, the accessible over the obscure. We like poets who use words in ways that transform them and us, whose images add a new dimension, whose meaning goes beyond first impression." Also accepts poetry written by children but work competes with adult submissions with same high standards. They have published poetry by Helen Reed and Bruce Guernsey. As a sample an editor selected these lines by Jennifer Richter:

> Tell me something I don't know/is the kind of thing he'll never say, so she stays

It is 96 pgs., digest-sized, professionally printed, perfect-bound with semi-gloss card cover. Press run is 850 for 200 subscribers of which 5 are libraries, 600 shelf sales. Subscription: $8.50 postage paid; back issues $5. Sample (including guidelines): $5. Make checks payable to BAAC.
How to Submit: Submit up to 7 poems at a time. Responds in 4 months. Always sends prepublication galleys. Pays 2 copies plus a monetary amount that varies. Buys first North American serial rights.
Also Offers: Awards the Whetstone Prize of $500 for the best poetry or fiction in each issue and additional prizes as well, including the new annual $250 Georgiana MacArthur Hansen Poetry Prize.

MARKETS THAT WERE listed in the 2000 edition of *Poet's Market* but do not appear this year are listed in the General Index with a notation explaining why they were omitted.

WHISKEY ISLAND MAGAZINE, English Dept., Cleveland State University, Cleveland OH 44115, phone (216)687-2056, fax (216)687-6943, e-mail whiskeyisland@popmail.csuohio.edu, website www.csuohio.edu/whiskey_island, founded 1968, student editors change yearly, contact poetry editor.

Magazine Needs: *Whiskey Island* appears biannually in January and July and publishes poetry, fiction, nonfiction and an interview each issue. They want "advanced writing. We want a range of poetry from standard to experimental and concrete poetry. Thought provoking." They have published poetry by Vivian Shipley, Kathleene West, Claudia Rankine, Patricia Smith and Dennis Saleh. As a sample the editor selected these lines from "Pigeon Bones & a Pair of Pants" by Ben Gulyas:

> he is . . . in his dreams/a man, mad with the deep blue of wooden corners/under a high eclipse where
> moon & sun/make dark luminous love/he is a man mad with something that breaks him open/and
> makes him sing—

Whiskey Island Magazine is 86-120 pgs., 6 × 9, professionally printed and perfect-bound with glossy stock cover and b&w art. They receive 1,000-1,500 poetry mss a year, accept approximately 6%. Press run is 1,200 for 200 subscribers of which 20 are libraries, about 200 shelf sales. Subscription: $12, $20 overseas. Sample: $5. Make checks payable to *Whiskey Island Magazine*.

How to Submit: Submit up to 10 pgs. of poetry at a time. Include SASE for reply/ms return. Include name, address, e-mail, fax and phone number on each page. No previously published poems or simultaneous submissions. Include cover letter with brief bio. Fax submissions OK. E-mail submissions OK for mss outside of US. Send as Rich Text format (.RTF) or ASCII files. Reads submissions September through April only. "Poets may fax inquiries and work that runs a few pages (longer submissions should be mailed). They may e-mail requests for submission and contest information." Poems are circulated to an editorial committee. Send SASE for guidelines or obtain via website. Responds within 4 months. Pays 2 copies, and 1 year subscription.

Also Offers: Sponsors an annual poetry contest. 1st Prize: $300; 2nd Prize: $200; 3rd Prize: $100. Entry fee: $10. Entries accepted October 1 through January 31. Query regarding contest for 2000. "Our website provides writer's guidelines, contest information, a history of the publication, and will, in the future, include poetry and fiction."

Advice: "Include SASEs and your name, address and phone for reply. List contents of submission in a cover letter."

WHITE EAGLE COFFEE STORE PRESS; FRESH GROUND (Specialized: anthology), P.O. Box 383, Fox River Grove IL 60021-0383, e-mail wecspress@aol.com, website http://members.aol.com/wecspress, founded 1992.

Magazine Needs & How to Submit: *Fresh Ground* is an annual anthology, appearing in November, that features "some of the best work of emerging poets. We're looking for edgy, crafted poetry. Poems for this annual are accepted during May and June only."

Book/Chapbook Needs: White Eagle is a small press publishing 5-6 chapbooks/year. "Alternate chapbooks are published by invitation and by competition. Author published by invitation becomes judge for next competition." They are "open to any kind of poetry. No censorship at this press. Literary values are the only standard. Generally not interested in sentimental or didactic writing." They have published poetry by Timothy Russell, Connie Donovan, Scott Lumbard, Linda Lee Harper, Scott Beal and Jill Peláez Baumgaertner. As a sample the editors included these lines from "Volunteer" in *The Wide View* by Linda Lee Harper:

> Her Head-Start students love her bosom plush as a divan./They celebrate and grieve there, noodle/
> their faces deeper, deeper, dangerous comfort./But she holds their fears close as if to absorb them/into
> her girth like calories from so much pasta,/each little rigatoni head, a child's dread allayed.

Sample: $5.95.

How to Submit: Submit complete chapbook ms (20-24 pgs.) with a brief bio, 125-word statement that introduces your writing and $10 reading fee. Previously published poems and simultaneous submissions OK, with notice. No electronic submissions. Competition deadlines: March 30 for spring contest; September 30 for fall contest. Send SASE for guidelines. "Each competition is judged by either the author of the most recent chapbook published by invitation or by previous competition winners." Seldom comments on rejections. Responds 3 months after deadline. All entrants will receive a copy of the winning chapbook. Winner receives $200 and 25 copies.

Also Offers: Website includes guidelines.

Advice: "Poetry is about a passion for language. That's what we're about. We'd like to provide an opportunity for poets of any age who are fairly early in their careers to publish something substantial. We're excited by the enthusiasm shown for this press and by the extraordinary quality of the writing we've received."

WHITE PELICAN REVIEW, P.O. Box 7833, Lakeland FL 33813, founded 1999, editor Nancy J. Wiegel.

Magazine Needs: *White Pelican Review* is a biannual literary journal dedicated to publishing poetry of the highest quality. They want "expertly-crafted, imaginatively-powerful poems rich in insight, music and wit. No pornography." They have published poetry by Fred Chappell, Aleida Rodríguez and Peter Meinke. As a sample the editor selected these lines from "Leaving Rabies" by Thérèse Halscheid:

> and his fur was matted/over his body/curved, in a way/of a stone,/wet curved stone/the kind you think/
> skims five times across water/before sinking,

The editor says *WPR* is approximately 48 pgs., digest-sized, photocopied from typescript and saddle-stapled with matte cardstock cover. They receive about 3,000 poems a year, accept approximately 3%. Press run is 250 for 80 subscribers of which 25 are libraries. Subscription: $8.

How to Submit: Submit 3-5 poems at a time. No previously published poems or simultaneous submissions. Cover letter and SASE required. "Please include name, address and telephone number on each page. No handwritten poems." Time between acceptance and publication is 3 months. Poems are circulated to an editorial board which reviews all submissions. "All editors review all submissions." Seldom comments on rejections. Send SASE for guidelines. Responds in 6 months. Pays 1 copy. Acquires one-time rights.

◐ **WHITE PINE PRESS; THE WHITE PINE PRESS POETRY PRIZE**, P.O. Box 236, Buffalo NY 14201, e-mail wpine@whitepine.org, website www.whitepine.org, founded 1973, editor Dennis Maloney, managing director Elaine LaMattina.

Book/Chapbook Needs & How to Submit: White Pine Press publishes poetry, fiction, literature in translation, essays—perfect-bound paperbacks. "*At present we are accepting unsolicited mss only for our annual competition, The White Pine Poetry Prize.* This competition awards $1,000 plus publication to a book-length collection of poems by a US author. Entry fee: $20. Deadline: December 1. Send SASE for details." No e-mail submissions. They have published *The Four Questions of Melancholy* by Tomaž Šalamun; *Pretty Happy!* by Peter Johnson; and *Bodily Course* (winner of the Poetry Prize) and *Treehouse* by William Kloefkorn. Send for free catalog.

Also Offers: Website includes writer's guidelines, poetry contest guidelines, list of current and backlist titles.

❧ ◐ **WHITE WALL REVIEW**, 63 Gould St., Toronto, Ontario M5B 1E9 Canada, founded 1976, editors change every year.

Magazine Needs: *White Wall Review* is an annual, appearing in May, "focused on publishing clearly expressed, innovative poetry. No style is unacceptable." They have published poetry by Vernon Mooers and David Sidjak. As a sample the editors selected these lines from "The Journal of Robert Delaunay" by John Allison:

> 1912: The poet gives the Orphic Word. And/the veil is torn asunder, an open Mystery/now before us:
> Light. All is Light.//Paris, City of Light. Roof-line and gable are/luminous intersections of thought;
> my mind/a mordant, holding the image.

WWR is between 90-144 pgs., digest-sized, professionally printed and perfect-bound with glossy card cover, using b&w photos and illustrations. Press run is 250. Subscription: $9 in Canada, $9.50 in US and elsewhere. Sample: $5.

How to Submit: Submit up to 5 poems at a time. A critique composed of 5 editors' comments is available for $5. "Please do not submit between January and August of a given year." Cover letter required; include short bio. Responds "as soon as we can (usually in April or May)." Pays 1 copy. They say, "Poets should send what they consider their best work, not everything they've got."

☐ ◉ **TAHANA WHITECROW FOUNDATION; CIRCLE OF REFLECTIONS (Specialized: animals, ethnic, nature, spirituality/inspirational)**, 2350 Wallace Rd. NW, Salem OR 97304, phone (503)585-0564, e-mail tahana@open.org, website www.open.org/tahana, founded 1987, executive director Melanie Smith.

Magazine Needs & How to Submit: The Whitecrow Foundation conducts one spring/summer poetry contest on Native American themes in poems up to 30 lines in length. Deadline for submissions: May 31. No haiku, Seiku, erotic or porno poems. Fees are $2.75 for a single poem, $10 for 4. Winners, honorable mentions and selected other entries are published in a periodic anthology, *Circle of Reflections*. Winners receive free copies and are encouraged to purchase others for $4.95 plus $1 handling in order to "help ensure the continuity of our contests." As a sample Melanie Smith selected these lines by David E. Sees:

> Alas . . ./I see/I hear . . ./my grandchild/move and speak . . ./the only thing native/is the complexion/
> of his skin . . . his eyes and hair . . ./alas . . . forgive/this lonely tear

Obtain guidelines via e-mail. Reviews books of poetry for $10 reading fee (average 32 pages).

Also Offers: Website includes veterans page, alcohol/drug, mental health alerts.

Advice: "We seek unpublished Native American writers. Poetic expressions of full-bloods, mixed bloods and empathetic non-Indians need to be heard. Future goals include chapbooks and native theme art. Advice to new writers: Keep writing, honing and sharpening your material; don't give up—keep submitting."

☐ ☐ ◐ ◉ **WHOLE NOTES; WHOLE NOTES PRESS (Specialized: children, translations)**, P.O. Box 1374, Las Cruces NM 88004-1374, *WN* founded 1984, Whole Notes Press founded 1988, editor Nancy Peters Hastings.

Magazine Needs: *WN* appears twice a year and tends toward close observation of the natural world, the beauty of nature and a poetry which affirms the human spirit. "All forms will be considered." Also accepts poetry written by children. As a sample the editor selected these lines from "Over Dangerous Wet Rocks" by Joyce Odam:

> Once you led me over dangerous wet rocks/into the sea-edge of a dwindling summer.//We were not
> there/to honor time or its commitments;//we were there for something/or our loss and of our finding.//

WN is 32 pgs., digest-sized, "nicely printed," staple bound, with a "linen 'fine arts' cover." They receive about 800 poems a year, accept approximately 10%. Press run is 400 for 200 subscriptions of which 10 are libraries. Subscription: $6. Sample: $3.

How to Submit: Submit 3-5 poems at a time. Some previously published poems used; no simultaneous submissions. Responds in 2 months. Pays 1 copy.

Book/Chapbook Needs & How to Submit: Whole Notes Press publishes 1 chapbook/year by a single poet. They have published chapbooks by Dan Stryk (*A Sea Change*), Robert Dorsett (*Threshold*) and Roy Scheele (*To See How it Tallies*). For 20-page chapbook consideration, submit 3-5 samples with bio and list of other publications. Pays 25 copies of chapbook. Editor sometimes comments on rejections.

Advice: "In the fall of each even-numbered year I edit a special issue of *WN* that features writing by young people (under 21). Overall, we'd like to see more translations and more poems about rural experiences."

N $ ◎ WICKED MYSTIC (Specialized: horror), Dept. WD, 532 La Guardia Pl. #371, New York NY 10012, phone (718)638-1533, e-mail scheluchin@wickedmystic.com, website www.wickedmystic.com, founded 1990, editor Andre Scheluchin.

Magazine Needs: *Wicked Mystic* is a quarterly of hardcore horror poetry and short stories. They want "psychological horror, splatter-gore, erotic, death, gothic themes, etc. No safe, conventional, conservative poetry." They have published poetry by Michael A. Arnzen, John Grey and James S. Dorr. *Wicked Mystic* is 100 pgs., magazine-sized, perfect-bound, with heavy stock colored cover and display ads. They receive about 1,000 poems a year, use approximately 5%. Press run is 10,000 for 4,500 subscribers of which 50 are libraries. Subscription: $23/4 issues. Sample: $5.95.

How to Submit: Submit typed poems, no longer than 30 lines. No previously published poems or simultaneous submissions. Cover letter required. Often comments on rejections. E-mail queries OK. Responds within 2 months. Pays 1 copy and $5/poem. Acquires first North American serial rights.

◐ ◎ WILLOW SPRINGS (Specialized: translations), 705 W. First Ave., MS-1, Eastern Washington University, Spokane WA 99201, phone (509)623-4349, fax (509)623-4238, founded 1977.

Magazine Needs: "We publish quality poetry and fiction that is imaginative, intelligent, and has a concern and care for language. We are especially interested in translations from any language or period." They have published poetry by James Grabill, Michael Heffernan, Robert Gregory and Patricia Goedicke. *Willow Springs*, a semiannual, is one of the most visually appealing journals being published. It is 128 pgs., 6×9, professionally printed, flat-spined, with glossy 4-color card cover with art. They receive about 4,000 poems a year, accept approximately 1-2%. Editors seem to prefer free verse with varying degrees of accessibility (although an occasional formal poem does appear). Press run is 1,500 for 700 subscribers of which 30% are libraries. Subscription: $10.50/year, $20/2 years. Sample: $5.50.

How to Submit: Submit September 15 through May 15 only. "We do not read in the summer months." Include name on every page, address on first page of each poem. Brief cover letter saying how many poems on how many pages preferred. No simultaneous submissions. Send SASE for guidelines. Responds in up to 3 months. Pays 2 copies plus a copy of the succeeding issue, others at half price, and cash when funds available. Acquires all rights. Returns rights on release. Reviews books of poetry and short fiction in 200-500 words. Open to unsolicited reviews. Poets may also send books for review consideration.

Also Offers: They have annual poetry and fiction awards ($200 and $250 respectively) for work published in the journal.

Advice: "We like poetry that is fresh, moving, intelligent and has no spare parts."

N ○ WINDOW JOURNAL, 32 Eden Ave., West Newton MA 02465, phone (617)965-0152, e-mail editor @open-window.com, website www.open-window.com, founded 1998, editor William Coveleskie.

Magazine Needs: "Published biannually, *window* is an avenue to introduce writers to the world and the world to writers. Each issue contains works from around the world. We want poetry of any style, on any subject; prefer free verse, minimalistic, imagistic, experimental poetry. Nothing prejudiced, fanatical with no respect to form, sexual. No forced rhyme, greeting card verse." They have published poetry by David Sutherland, Lisa Finan and Dr. Robert James Berry. As a sample the editor selected these lines from "Indigo" by Shannon L. Stevens:

> *Artifacts from distant times,/recorded on blood-stained sheets of parchment,/folded twice, and placed*
> *beside:/a single leaf of late October;/a ragged, crimson patch of quilt;/and a shard of carnival glass.*

window is 40-50 pgs., digest-sized, professional inkjet printing on color copy, saddle-stapled with semi-transparent vellum and cardstock cover, includes b&w art/graphics. They receive about 160 poems a year, accept approximately 60%. Press run is 200 for 150 subscribers of which 15 are libraries. Subscription: $7/year. Sample: $4. Make checks payable to William Coveleskie.

How to Submit: Submit 1-3 poems at a time. Line length for poetry is 60 maximum. Previously published poems and simultaneous submissions OK. E-mail and disk (IBM format) submissions OK. "For mailed submissions: send SASE; original works only; name and address on each page. For electronic submissions: original works only; name and address in footer; text formatted in body of e-mail." Reads submissions November 1 through February 1 and April 1 through September 1 only. Time between acceptance and publication is 2-4 months. Often comments on rejections. "If a work is submitted for feedback only, a fee for an in-depth critique will apply." Publishes theme issues occasionally. Send SASE for guidelines and upcoming themes or obtain via website. Responds in 3 months. Pays 1 copy. Acquires one-time rights.

Also Offers: Website includes name of editor, mission statement, submission guidelines (usps and e-mail), "my desk," a word from the editor, all past issues, feature area, subscription methods.

Advice: "Read and write, then read and write again. Challenge yourself and your best works."

☀ ✔ ◑ **WINDSOR REVIEW**, English Dept., University of Windsor, Windsor, Ontario N9B 3P4 Canada, phone (519)253-3000 ext. 2290, fax (519)971-3676, e-mail uwrevu@uwindsor.ca, founded 1965, poetry editor John Ditsky.

Magazine Needs: *Windsor Review* appears twice a year and features poetry, short fiction and art. "Open to all poetry but no epics." They have published poetry by Ben Bennani, Walter McDonald, Larry Rubin and Lyn Lifshin. It is professionally printed, 100 pgs., digest-sized. They receive about 500 poems a year, accept approximately 15%. Press run is 400. Subscription: $19.95 (+7% GST) individuals, $29.95 (+7% GST) institutions (Canadian); $19.95 individuals, $29.95 institutions (US). Sample: $7.

How to Submit: Submit 5-10 poems at a time, typed. No simultaneous submissions. Queries via e-mail, poetry submissions via fax OK. No e-mail submissions. Responds in 6 weeks. Pays 1 copy.

✔ ▣ ◑ **WINGS MAGAZINE, INC.**, e-mail tomjones1965@juno.com, website www.nywcafe.com/wings/, founded 1991, publisher/poetry editor Thomas Jones.

Magazine Needs: *Wings* is an exclusively online publication. "We want to publish the work of poets who are not as widely known as those published in larger journals but who nevertheless produce exceptional, professional material. We also publish personal essays, fiction and plays." They want "poetry with depth of feeling. No jingly, rhyming poetry. Rhyming poetry must show the poet knows how to use rhyme in an original way. Poetry on any theme, 80 lines or less, any style." As a sample the editor has selected these lines from "The Southern Ocean" by Robert James Berry:

> The wind blusters big waves/Glacial spring is coming//If you listen to the ocean's measured voice/In
> the wide pale eyes of Wakatipu//Sky father and earth mother/are making footsteps on the sea

They receive about 500 poems a year. "No requirements but we encourage poets to check out our website and get an idea of the kind of material we publish."

How to Submit: Submit up to 5 poems at a time. Previously published poems OK. "We take submissions through e-mail only. Send e-mail to the above juno address. Copy and paste the poem and bio into the e-mail message. The bio should be five lines or less." Always responds to submissions. Responds in 2 months. Staff reviews books and chapbooks of poetry in single book format. Send inquiries to pamwings@juno.com.

Also Offers: "Our needs are eclectic. Content can be on any topic as long as the poet shows mastery of subject matter and craft, as well as penetration into depths." Also, published a Best of Wings CD-ROM. Website includes poetry, short stories, personal essays, plays, archives, book reviews, books (in archives) and name of editors.

Advice: "We don't want doggerel. We want sincere, well-crafted work. Poetry has been reduced to second class status by commercial publishing, and we want to restore it to the status of fiction (novels) or plays."

Ⓝ ◑ ◎ **WINSLOW PRESS (Specialized: children/teen/young adult)**, 115 E. 23rd St., 10th Floor, New York NY 10010, phone (212)254-2025, fax (212)254-2410, e-mail winslow@winslowpress.com, website www.winslowpress.com, founded 1997, editorial assistant Sarah Nielsen.

Book/Chapbook Needs & How to Submit: Winslow Press publishes children's books and young adult novels. "Winslow Press is a new company, and while we are open to publishing poetry, we haven't published any as of yet. Please keep in mind, we are a children's book publisher, thus no adult material will be considered." Send SASE for submission guidelines.

Also Offers: Website includes Winslow's virtual library of books, plus games, links, activities and teachers' guides.

✔ ◑ ◎ **WISCONSIN ACADEMY REVIEW (Specialized: regional)**, 1922 University Ave., Madison WI 53705, phone (608)263-1692, fax (608)265-3039, e-mail review@wisconsinacademy.org, website www.wisc.edu/wisacad/, founded 1954, contact editor.

Magazine Needs: The *Wisconsin Academy Review* "publishes articles on scientific and cultural life of Wisconsin and provides a forum for Wisconsin (or Wisconsin background) artists and authors. Publishes original poetry." They want "good poetry of any kind; traditional meters acceptable if content is fresh. We rarely accept poems over 65 lines." They have published poetry by Credo Enriquez, Jean Feraca, Felix Pollak, Ron Wallace, Sara Rath and Lorine Niedecker. The *Review* is a 48-page quarterly, magazine-sized, professionally printed on glossy stock, glossy card color cover. Press run is 1,700 for 1,200 subscribers of which 100 are libraries. They use 3-6 pgs. of poetry/issue. They receive about 150 submissions a year, accept approximately 24. They have a 6- to 12-month backlog. Sample: $3.

How to Submit: Submit 5 pages maximum, double-spaced, with SASE. Must include Wisconsin connection if not Wisconsin return address. Poems not returned unless requested. Responds in 4 months. Pays 3 copies. Staff reviews books of poetry with Wisconsin connection only. Send related books for review consideration.

Also Offers: Website includes name of editor and writer's guidelines.

Advice: "We will consider traditional or experimental poetry but not light verse or sentimental rhymes."

✔ ◯ ◑ **WISCONSIN REVIEW; WISCONSIN REVIEW PRESS**, 800 Algoma Blvd., University of Wisconsin-Oshkosh, Oshkosh WI 54901, phone (920)424-2267, founded 1966, contact poetry editor.

Magazine Needs: *Wisconsin Review* is published 3 times/year. "The poetry we publish is mostly free verse with strong images and fresh approaches. We want new turns of phrase." They have published poetry by Stephen Perry, Lyn Lifshin, Karla Huston, Herman Asarnow, Cathryn Cofell, Shoshauna Shy and Troy Schoultz. As a sample the editor selected these lines from "False Candles" by Fernand Roqueplan:

> *Here's our town, rundown/without smiths or merlot. Rust blighted with apples/and our local vintner*
> *Ingo Rosado salted his vines/instead of surrendering to Gallo./Love begs real candlelight. Zoned/*
> *seaside cottages as sensual as high-rises/where lovers share through sheetrock walls/kinship to the*
> *thousand others/booming back in symphony.*

The *Review* is 80-100 pgs., 6×9, elegantly printed on quality white stock, glossy card cover with color art, b&w art inside. They receive about 1,500 poetry submissions a year, use approximately 75; 40-50 pgs. of poetry in each issue. Press run is 1,600 for 40 subscribers of which 20 are libraries. Single copy: $4; subscription: $10.
How to Submit: Submit mss September 15 through May 15. Offices checked bimonthly during summer. Submit up to 4 poems at a time, one poem/page, single-spaced with name and address of writer on each page. Simultaneous submissions OK, but previously unsubmitted works preferable. Cover letter required; include brief bio. Mss are not read during the summer months. Send SASE for guidelines. Responds in up to 9 months. Pays 2 copies.

✓ ◯ ◲ ◎ **THE WISHING WELL (Specialized: membership, women/feminism, lesbian/bisexual)**, P.O. Box 178440, San Diego CA 92177-8440, phone (858)270-2779, e-mail laddiewww@aol.com, website www.wishingwellwomen.com, founded 1974, editor/publisher Laddie Hosler.
Magazine Needs: *The Wishing Well* is a "contact magazine for women who love women the world over; members' descriptions, photos, letters and poetry published with their permission only; resources, etc., listed. I publish writings only for and by members so membership is required." 1-2 pgs. in each issue are devoted to poetry, "which can be up to 8″ long—depending upon acceptance by editor, 3″ width column." It is 7×8½, offset printed from typescript, with soft matte card cover. It appears bimonthly and goes to 100 members, 200 nonmembers. A sample is available for $5. Membership in *Wishing Well* is $35 for 3-5 months, $60 for 5-7 months, $120 for 15 months.
How to Submit: Membership includes the right to publish poetry, a self description (exactly as you write it), to have responses forwarded to you, and other privileges. E-mail submissions OK (if included in body of message) for members only. Personal classifieds section, 50¢/word for members and $1/word for nonmembers.
Also Offers: Website includes membership application and introductory letter describing membership with *The Wishing Well*.

Ⓝ $ ◲ ◎ **WITNESS (Specialized: themes)**, Oakland Community College, Orchard Ridge Campus, 27055 Orchard Lake Rd., Farmington Hills MI 48334, phone (248)471-7740, founded 1987, editor Peter Stine.
  ⚑ Poetry published here has also been included in the 1995 volume of *The Best American Poetry*.
Magazine Needs: *Witness* is a biannual journal of poetry, fiction and essays which often publishes special issues centered around themes. They want "poetry that highlights the role of the writer as witness to his/her times. No real specifications, except nothing wildly experimental." They have published poetry by John Balaban, Mary Oliver, Alicia Ostriker and Mark Doty. *Witness* is 192 pgs., 6×9, professionally printed and perfect-bound with coated card cover with full-color photo and b&w photos inside. They receive about 500 poems a year, accept approximately 5%. Press run is 2,800 for 400 subscribers of which 60 are libraries, 1,200 distributed to bookstores. Subscription: $15/1 year, $28/2 years. Sample: $9; upcoming special issues are announced inside.
How to Submit: Submit up to 4 poems, typed and single-spaced, with stanza breaks double-spaced. No previously published poems; simultaneous submissions OK. Cover letter required. Seldom comments on rejections. Publishes theme issues. Send SASE for guidelines and upcoming themes. Responds in 3 months. Pays $10/page plus 2 copies. Buys first serial rights.

◎ **WOODLEY MEMORIAL PRESS (Specialized: regional)**, English Dept., Washburn University, Topeka KS 66621, phone (785)234-1032, e-mail zzlaws@washburn.edu, website www.wuacc.edu/reference/woodley-press/index.html, founded 1980, editor Robert Lawson.
Book/Chapbook Needs: Woodley Memorial Press publishes 1-2 flat-spined paperbacks a year, about half being collections of poets from Kansas or with Kansas connections, "terms individually arranged with author on acceptance of ms." They have published *Looking for the Pale Eagle* by Stephen Meats, *Killing Seasons* by Christopher Cokinos, and *Gathering Reunion* by David Tangeman. As a sample the editor selected these lines from "The Drowning" in *The Gospel of Mary* by Michael Page:

> *I hear/there's a gospel of Mary./It is a fragment/and she is naturally saddened.*

Samples may be individually ordered from the press for $5.
How to Submit: Replies to queries in 2 weeks, to mss in 2 months. Time between acceptance and publication is 1 year.
Also Offers: Website features descriptions of books, board members' short bios and writers' guidelines.

◐ ◎ **WORCESTER REVIEW; WORCESTER COUNTY POETRY ASSOCIATION, INC. (Specialized: regional)**, 6 Chatham St., Worcester MA 01609, phone (508)797-4770, website www.geocities.com/Paris/LeftBank/6433, founded 1973, managing editor Rodger Martin.

Magazine Needs: *WR* appears annually "with emphasis on poetry. New England writers are encouraged to submit, though work by other poets is used also." They want "work that is crafted, intuitively honest and empathetic, not work that shows the poet little respects his work or his readers." They have published poetry by May Swenson, Robert Pinsky and Walter McDonald. *WR* is 160 pgs., 6×9, flat-spined, professionally printed in dark type on quality stock with glossy card cover. Press run is 1,000 for 300 subscribers of which 50 are libraries, 300 shelf sales. Subscription: $20 (includes membership in WCPA). Sample: $5.

How to Submit: Submit up to 5 poems at a time. "I recommend three or less for most favorable readings." Simultaneous submissions OK "if indicated." Previously published poems "only on special occasions." Editor comments on rejections "if ms warrants a response." Publishes theme issues. Send SASE for guidelines and upcoming themes. Responds in up to 9 months. Pays 2 copies. Buys first rights.

Also Offers: They have an annual contest for poets who live, work, or in some way (past/present) have a Worcester County connection or are a WCPA member.

Advice: "Read some. Listen a lot."

N **◻** **◎** **WORD DANCE (Specialized: children/teen)**, P.O. Box 10804, Wilmington DE 19850, phone (302)894-1950, fax (302)894-1957, e-mail playful@worddance.com, website www.worddance.com, founded 1989, director Stuart Unger.

Magazine Needs: "Published quarterly, *Word Dance* magazine encourages the love of reading and writing in a nonthreatening, playful environment. It was created to give young people a quality vehicle for creative expression, a place where their voices can be heard. It includes short stories, poems and artwork by kids in kindergarten through Grade 8." *Word Dance* features haiku, but accepts all forms of poetry. As a sample we selected this haiku by Ernie Blais:

> In the early dawn/The insects were gathering/Food for their new born.

The editor says *WD* is 32 pgs., 6×9, professionally printed and saddle-stapled, two-color card cover, includes two-color drawings. Subscription: $18/year US, $23 Canada, $28 other countries.

How to Submit: They accept poetry for four of their six sections. Field Trip accepts poems and stories about family and school trips; World Word accepts poems and short stories about the environment, war and peace, endangered species, etc.; for Haiku Corner send your Haiku poetry; Grab Bag accepts poems and short stories about any topic. "*Word Dance* receives many submissions for the Grab Bag section of the magazine, so competition is greater in this category. We recommend that students contribute to the other sections of the magazine to increase their chances of getting published." No previously published poems or simultaneous submissions. "Our submission form must be included with each submission." Obtain via magazine, website or call or write. Submission deadlines: February 25, May 25, August 25, November 25. Time between acceptance and publication is 6-9 months. Poems are circulated to an editorial board. Send SASE for guidelines or obtain via website. Copies are available at cost.

Also Offers: Website includes samples of writing and art, subscription information, submission guidelines, word games and links for kids.

Advice: "A subscription is suggested to see examples of work. We are a nonprofit organization. Parents and teachers are encouraged to help their child/student revise and edit work."

▣ **◿** **WORD SALAD; WORD SALAD POETRY CONTEST**, 3224 N. College Rd., PMB 107, Wilmington NC 28405, e-mail whealton@wordsalad.net, website wordsalad.net, founded 1995, publisher Bruce Whealton, editors Lynn Krupey and Jean Jones.

Magazine Needs: Published quarterly on the Web, *Word Salad* "continuously accepts original poetry. Although we do not restrict ourselves to one subject area or style, the Web allows us to receive a large number of poems and select the highest quality and we offer a world wide exposure. We are open to any form, style or subject matter; length should be no more than two typed pages. We especially like poetry dealing with oppressed/vulnerable populations, i.e., persons with mental illness, the poor/homeless. No greeting card verse or forced rhyme; most love poems unless you have something original to say. We invite gay/lesbian/bisexual poetry." They have published poetry by Scott Urban and Martin Kirby. As a sample we selected these lines from "Denial" by Paula Martin:

> Her every thought, word, and action/Consumed by the/Food That she will not face—/Unknowingly
> digesting/Her very soul/As the meal/Remains untouched/and we all stand by,/Silverware in hands,/
> Ready to help her/Eat,/If only she would take/The first bite

They receive about 1,200 poems a year, accept approximately 10%.

How to Submit: Submit 2 poems at a time. No previously published poems or simultaneous submissions. Cover letter preferred. E-mail and disk submissions OK. "We receive 200-300 poems per quarter and publish 20-30. Most of the submissions are received via e-mail. We ask that poets read the submission guidelines on the Web." Time between acceptance and publication is about 3 months. Seldom comments on rejections. Publishes theme issues occasionally. Obtain guidelines and upcoming themes via website. Responds in about 3 months. Sometimes sends prepublication galleys. Open to unsolicited reviews.

Also Offers: Sponsors annual poetry contest. See website for announcements. Winners are announced May 31. "*Word Salad* is linked to a directory of online resources related to writing and creativity. Additionally, we have a web-based chat program that allows live chat discussions."

⬤ THE WORD WORKS; THE WASHINGTON PRIZE, P.O. Box 42164, Washington DC 20015, e-mail wordworks@shirenet.com, website www.writer.org/wordwork/wordwrk1.htm, founded 1974, editor-in-chief Hilary Tham.

Book/Chapbook Needs: Word Works "is a nonprofit literary organization publishing contemporary poetry in single author editions usually in collaboration with a visual artist. We sponsor an ongoing poetry reading series, educational programs, the Capital Collection—publishing metropolitan Washington, D.C. poets, and the Washington Prize—an award of $1,500 for a book-length manuscript by a living American poet." Previous winners include *Following Fred Astaire* by Nathalie Anderson; *Tipping Point* by Fred Marchant; *Stalking the Florida Panther* by Enid Shomer; *The CutOff* by Jay Rogoff; and *Spinoza's Mouse* by George Young. Submission open to any American writer except those connected with Word Works. Send SASE for rules. Entries accepted between February 1 and March 1. Postmark deadline is March 1. Winners are announced at the end of June. They publish perfect-bound paperbacks and occasional anthologies and want "well-crafted poetry, open to most forms and styles (though not political themes particularly). Experimentation welcomed." As a sample the editors selected these lines from "Furnace Greens" in *Last Heat* by Peter Blair:

> I saw a hot strip of sheet metal jump the rolls/and sidewind across the floor/like a red snake. I saw the full moon rippled/into rags of light above a furnace stack.//I did the mill slouch, my boot up/on a stack of slabs, my forearms on my knee,/sitting without a chair, leaning/without a wall, looking like I didn't care./I drove home with explosions ringing in my ears, my lips blackened by soot,/eyebrows and nose hairs singed.

"We want more than a collection of poetry. We care about the individual poems—the craft, the emotional content and the risks taken—but we want manuscripts where one poem leads to the next. We strongly recommend you read the books that have already won the Washington Prize. Buy them, if you can, or ask for your libraries to purchase them. (Not a prerequisite.)" Most books are $10.

How to Submit: "Currently we are only reading unsolicited manuscripts for the Washington Prize." Simultaneous submissions OK, if so stated. Always sends prepublication galleys. Payment is 15% of run (usually of 1,000). Send SASE for catalog to buy samples. Occasionally comments on rejections.

Also Offers: Website includes a history of the Word Works; guidelines for the Washington Prize; list and description of books; ordering instructions; book descriptions; how to apply for the Miller Cabin Poetry Series and Young Poets Competition; trip for writers to Tuscany, Italy; membership info; how to volunteer; and list of staff members.

Advice: "Get community support for your work, know your audience and support contemporary literature by buying and reading the small press."

$⊚ WORDSONG; BOYDS MILLS PRESS (Specialized: children/teen/young adult), 815 Church St., Honesdale PA 18431, phone (800)490-5111, website www.boydsmillspress.com, founded 1990, manuscript coordinator Beth Troop, editor-in-chief Dr. Bernice E. Cullinan.

⬙ Wordsong's *Been to Yesterdays* received the Christopher Award and was named a Golden Kite Honor Book.

Book/Chapbook Needs: Wordsong is the imprint under which Boyds Mills Press (a *Highlights for Children* company) publishes books of poetry for children of all ages. They want quality poetry which reflects childhood fun, moral standards and multiculturalism. We are not interested in poetry for adults or that which includes violence or sexuality or promotes hatred." They have published *Fly With Poetry* by Avis Harley and *Wild Country* by David L. Harrison. As a sample the editor selected these lines from "My Name Is Jorge":

> My name is Jorge./I know that my name is Jorge./But everyone calls me/George./George./What an ugly sound!/Like a sneeze!/George!

How to Submit: "Wordsong prefers original work but will consider anthologies and previously published collections. We ask poets to send collections of 25-45 poems with a common theme; please send complete book manuscripts, not single poems. We buy all rights to collections and publish on an advance-and-royalty basis. Wordsong guarantees a response from editors within one month of our receiving submissions or the poet may call us toll free to inquire. Please direct submissions to Beth Troop, manuscript coordinator." No fax or e-mail submissions. Always sends prepublication galleys.

Also Offers: Website includes info on books, book reviews, author bios, Boyds Mills Press staff and author tours.

Advice: "Poetry lies at the heart of the elementary school literature and reading program. In fact, poetry lies right at the heart of children's language learning. Poetry speaks to the heart of a child. We are anxious to find poetry that deals with imagination, wonder, seeing the world in a new way, family relationships, friends, school, nature and growing up."

VISIT THE WRITER'S DIGEST WEBSITE at www.writersdigest.com for books on craft, hot new markets, daily market updates, writers' guidelines and much more.

✓ ○ **WORM FEAST!; TAPE WORM; VIDEO WORM; FREAKIN' EINSTEN, WORKIN' CLASS ZERO; KNIGHTMAYOR PRODUCTIONS**, P.O. Box 7030, Fallschurch VA 22046, e-mail llori@knightmay or.com, website www.knightmayor.com or www.mailbomb.com, founded 1981, editor Llori Steinberg.

• Knightmayor's paper-based zines are going electronic. Check out their website for the specific changes.

Magazine Needs: *WoRM fEASt!* is an underground monthly. *Tape WoRM* is an audio magazine with music, poetry, comedy and more. *Video WoRM* is a video endeavor with movies, visual art, animation, music videos, news events and more. Send SASE for details. *Freakin' Einstein, Workin' Class Zero* features "essays, 'you work for nothing get paid nothing rants.' " For *Wf* they want "as strange as humanoids can get; no traditional verse, no rhyme (unless it's way off the keister), no haiku, no love poems unless one-sided and morbid/dark and unusually sickening; and no Christian poetry." They have published poetry by Gregory K.H. Bryant, Fire Bridgewater, Greg Bryant, Abby Alice, Bill Shields and Vinnie Van Leer.

How to Submit: Send 1 poem at a time. Previously published poems OK. Cover letter with SASE required; "don't have to be professional, just state the facts and why you're interested in submitting. We respond as quickly as we can." E-mail submissions OK. Sometimes sends prepublication galleys. Send SASE or visit website for submission guidelines. Pays 1 copy. Reviews books of poetry. Open to unsolicited reviews. Poets may also send books for review consideration.

Book/Chapbook Needs & How to Submit: "We publish chapbooks for poets' personal use. You buy and you sell." Cost is $100 for 100 chapbooks of under 15 pgs. each.

Also Offers: Sponsors contests. Send SASE for details. "We also run the zene site mailbomb.com."

Advice: "We want everything from serious to sick, profound to profane, from sane to insane, from graceful to gory—get it?"

N ○ ○ ◎ **THE WRITE WAY (Specialized: writing); TAKING CARE OF YOURSELF (Specialized: health concerns); ANN'S ENTERPRISES**, P.O. Box 220102, Glenwood FL 32722, e-mail Igev9@aol.com, founded 1988, editor Ann Larberg.

Magazine Needs: *TWW* is a quarterly using poems of up to 20 lines on the theme of writing. As a sample the editor selected "Limerick Lamentation" by Donna Bickley:

> Composing a limerick's not easy/Although my attempts make me queasy,/I jot down a line, I stretch
> for a rhyme./Reaching as far as it pleases me.

TWW is a 6-page newsletter with articles on writing and ads. Single copy: $3; subscription: $6. Sample free with SASE.

How to Submit: Nonsubscribers must include $1 reading fee and SASE with submissions (up to 5 poems). Do not submit in summer. Reads submissions January 1 through June 30 only. E-mail submissions included in body of message OK; 20 line limit. Publishes theme issues: winter, writing (the writing life); spring, nature; summer, travel; fall, greeting card rhymed verse. Send SASE for upcoming themes. Responds in 6 weeks. Pays 1 copy. Open to unsolicited reviews. Poets may also send books for review consideration.

Also Offers: They publish an annual holiday poetry edition. Deadline for annual holiday issue is November 15. *Taking Care of Yourself*, a 4-page newsletter of well-being, is also published quarterly and accepts 1-2 short poems/issue on the theme of health. Sample free with SASE. Pays copies.

○ ○ **THE WRITER; POET TO POET**, 120 Boylston St., Boston MA 02116-4615, website www.channel1 .com/thewriter, founded 1887.

Magazine Needs: This monthly magazine for writers has a quarterly instructional column, "Poet to Poet," to which poets may submit previously unpublished work for possible publication and comment. Single copy: $4 back issues; $2.75 newsstand; subscription: $29 (introductory offer: 5 issues for $12).

How to Submit: Submit up to 3 poems, no longer than 30 lines each, name and address on each page, 1 poem to a page. Send SASE for guidelines only; do not send SASE with submission. There is no pay and mss are not acknowledged or returned. Acquires first North American serial rights.

N ○ **WRITER TO WRITER**, P.O. Box 2336, Oak Park IL 60303, e-mail blcroft@aol.com, founded 1995, editors Norman Hane and Barbara Croft.

Magazine Needs: "Published biannually, *Writer to Writer* exists to provide a forum in which poets and writers may express themselves in whatever ways seem meaningful to them. *WTW* also seeks sophisticated articles on poetic technique. We want literary poetry, no light verse or poetry about poetry; open to any form. We look for interesting use of language." They have published poetry by Gary Gildner, Eric Pankey, Jennifer Atkinson and Douglas K. Currier. The editors say *WTW* is 8½ × 11, photocopied and stapled with cardstock cover. They receive about 700 poems a year, accept approximately 3%. Publish 7-10 poems/issue. Press run is 150 for 50 subscribers. Subscription: $10. Sample: $5.

How to Submit: Submit 3-4 poems at a time. Line length for poetry is 50 maximum. No previously published poems; simultaneous submissions OK. Cover letter preferred. SASE required. Time between acceptance and publication is 2-4 months. Often comments on rejections. Send SASE for guidelines. Responds in 3 weeks. Pays 2 copies plus 1-year subscription. Acquires first rights. Reviews books of poetry and other magazines in 600 words. Open to unsolicited reviews. Poets may also send books for review consideration to Norman Hane, poetry editor.

Advice: "Send your best with no hype or sales pitch."

$🗌 WRITER'S BLOCK MAGAZINE; WRITER'S BLOCK CONTEST, P.O. Box 32, 9944-33 Ave., Edmonton, Alberta T6N 1E7 Canada, founded 1994, editor Shaun Donnelly.

Magazine Needs: *Writer's Block Magazine* appears biannually and publishes assorted fiction, nonfiction and poetry. They want poetry of any form, length or subject matter. *WBM* is 48 pgs., digest-sized, professionally printed and saddle-stapled with 4-color card cover. They receive about 500 poems a year, accept approximately 12. Press run is 10,000 for 500 subscribers, 2,000 shelf sales; 7,500 distributed free to Edmonton neighborhoods. Single copy: 3.50; subscription: $12/2 years. Sample: $5.

How to Submit: Submit 3 poems at a time. Previously published poems and simultaneous submissions OK. Cover letter preferred. Time between acceptance and publication is 6 months. Always comments on rejections. Send SASE (or SAE and IRC) for guidelines. Responds in 2 months. Pays $25. Buys first North American serial rights.

Also Offers: Sponsors the biannual Writer's Block Contest for novice poets. Entry deadlines are March 1 and September 1. Awards $75 plus publication to the best poem.

✓ $🗌 ◎ WRITERS' CENTER PRESS; THE FLYING ISLAND; WRITERS' CENTER OF INDIANA (Specialized: regional), P.O. Box 88386, Indianapolis IN 46208, phone (317)955-6336, fax (317)955-6450, founded 1979, executive director Todd Watson.

Magazine Needs: Writers' Center Press publishes *The Flying Island*, a biannual of fiction, poetry, reviews and literary commentary by those living in or connected to Indiana. They want poetry of high literary quality; no stylistic or thematic restrictions. They have published poetry by Jared Carter, Alice Friman, Yusef Komunyakaa and Roger Mitchell. *TFI* is 24 pgs., perfect-bound, includes artwork, graphics and photography. They receive about 1,000 poems a year, accept approximately 5%. Press run is 1,000 for 500 subscribers. Subscription: $10. Sample: $4.

How to Submit: Submit 2 copies of up to 3 poems. If non-Indiana resident, cover letter must explain Indiana connection. Previously published poems OK, but not encouraged. Simultaneous submissions OK, if so advised. Brief bio required. Often comments on rejections. Send SASE for guidelines. Responds in 6 months. Pays $5 minimum for previously unpublished work. Buys first North American serial rights.

Advice: "Balance solitary writing time by getting involved in a writing community. We frequently recommend rejected writers join a poetry workshop."

✓ 🗌 WRITER'S EXCHANGE; R.S.V.P. PRESS; NEW MARKETS, 100 Upper Glen Dr., Blythewood NC 29016-7806, e-mail eboone@aol.com, website http://members.aol.com/writernet/wrinet.htm, founded 1983, editor Gene Boone.

Magazine Needs: *Writer's Exchange* published quarterly, "is a small press magazine for writers and poets that covers the small press and its ever-changing array of diverse publications. The editor seeks articles on writing-related topics, particularly those that relate to small press writers and poets, such as how-to techniques for writing various types of poetry (from haiku to sonnets!), personal experiences about writing groups, conferences, writing courses, etc." He wants "poetry in various forms, including free verse, light verse, sonnets, tanka, haiku and other fixed-forms. Length: 3-35 lines. Topics of interest include relationships, personal experience, nature, etc. How-ever, what the editor is most interested in is what interests the poet, the subjects he or she choses to write about, these are the poems that will convey the uniqueness of the poet. What the editor does not want to see: poems that preach or "say" what the poet feels about problems facing our society. Take homelessness, for example. Show what the homeless person sees through his or her eyes and that will show your feelings as well and help to evoke a response, sometimes a deep, emotional reaction in the reader. I like writing that is upbeat or at least positive, enlightening or inspiring, especially humorous poetry about every day life, writing, etc. I will not consider material that is anti-religious, racist or obscene." He has published poetry by Victor Chapman, Najwa Salam Brax, Sarah Jensen and Edd McWatters. As a sample he selected these lines by Diane L. Krueger:

> all my hopes and dreams/feel possible once more with/resurgence of dreams . . . hopes/and . . . belief
> in our tomorrows

WE is 36 pgs., digest-sized, saddle-stitched, with a full-color cover. He accepts about half or more of the poetry received. Press run is 250. Subscription: $12. Sample: $3.

How to Submit: Submit no more than 8 poems at a time with SASE. "I prefer typed mss, one poem per page, readable. Poets should always proofread mss before sending them out. Errors can cause rejection." Previously published poetry OK; no simultaneous submissions. E-mail submissions *not* encouraged. "Electronic and disk-based submissions are not being accepted at this time. Please send manuscripts in standard, paper format, with your name and address on every page and a SASE for reply." Cover letter appreciated; list "prior credits, if any, and other details of writing background, such as writing interests." Time between acceptance and publication is 4 months. Send SASE for guidelines, request via e-mail or visit the website. Responds in 1 month. Pays 1 copy. Acquires one-time rights. Staff reviews books of poetry. Send books for review consideration.

Also Offers: They offer cash awards for quarterly contests sponsored through the magazine. Send SASE for current rules. In 1995 they began publishing *New Markets*, a newsletter featuring information on small press and New Age markets. Send SASE for details. The newsletter may become a column feature in *WE* when a new Paying Small Press Markets column is added to the magazine. *The Best of New Markets*, a compilation of the first six issues, is available for $3.95 postpaid. *Remembrance*, formerly a paper-format journal, is now published as an electronic ezine online at http://members.aol.com/eboone/remember/htm. *Remembrance Online* features poetry about unforgettable people (living and deceased), memorable moments, special places, and perfekt pets. Send SASE for complete guidelines. Same address as Writer's Exchange. The editor says he comments on rejections, "if I feel it will benefit the poet in the long run, never anything too harsh or overly discouraging." Website features guidelines for *WE* and other small press publications, including paying publications and others. Website includes WriterNet http://members.aol.com/writernet/wrinet.htm (the Writer's Exchange website) which features columns on writing techniques by established writers and poets: Mary H. Sayler, Mickey Clark, Diane L. Krueger, Lois Green Stone. Also features writing markets for those involved in the small press. Our sister website, WebBase1, features links to Research, Reference and other material of interest to writers and others at http://members.aol.com/webbase1/index1.html.

Advice: "Support the small press publications you read and enjoy. Without your support these publications will cease to exist. The small press has given many poets their start. In essence, the small press is where poetry lives!"

N 🌐 ◑ ◎ **WRITERS FORUM (INDIA) (Specialized: membership); THE QUEST**, C-1, Harmu Housing Colony, Ranchi 834012 India, founded 1987, editor Dr. Ravi Nandan Sinha.

Magazine Needs: *The Quest* is published biannually in June and December and contains "critical articles on Indian writing in English, book reviews and poetry." They want poetry of "all kinds—maximum length 24 lines. No bad wooden verse." They have published poetry by Eugenio Montale (Nobel laureate from Italy), Ada Aharoni (Israel), Diana Rubin (USA) and Igor Mikhailusenko (Russia). As a sample the editor selected these lines from "Sahara" by Mary Remorino (Argentina):

> For I am not the flower/spreading out its fragrance . . ./For I am not the grass/lying down on the greenness/then . . . I am wailing/For I am not the tree/squandering out its shadows

The editor says *Quest* is 72 pgs., 5½×9, offset printed, "flexiback" binding, paperback cover, ads. They receive about 800 poems a year, accept approximately 15%. Press run is 2,000 for 1,160 subscribers of which 236 are libraries. Subscription: $15 per year, $150 (life). Sample: $5. Make checks payable to "Editor, *The Quest*."

How to Submit: Submit 3 poems at a time. No previously published poems or simultaneous submissions. Cover letter required. "Handwritten material is not accepted. International Reply Coupons must accompany submission/inquiry." Time between acceptance and publication is 2 months. Seldom comments on rejections. Send SASE for guidelines. Responds in 2 months. Pays 2 copies. Acquires first rights. Staff reviews books and chapbooks of poetry and other magazines in 250 words, single book format. Send books for review consideration.

◎ **WRITER'S GUIDELINES & NEWS MAGAZINE (Specialized: writing); INDEPENDENT PUBLISHING CO.**, P.O. Box 18566, Sarasota FL 34276-1566, phone (941)924-3201, fax (941)925-4468, e-mail writersgn@aol.com, founded 1988, editor-in-chief Ned Burke, associate editor Carrillee Collins.

Magazine Needs: *WG&N* is "the friend of the writer. Our quarterly magazine offers regular reviews of small press publications, articles on playwriting, travel writing, overseas markets, pals with pens, hot off the press new items, markets, contests, magazine listings, market news, poetry, fiction and much more." They want "poetry with a writing slant. No erotica." They have published poetry by Joan Stanley and Errol Miller. As a sample the editor selected this poem, "Paper Clip Capes" by Angie Monnens:

> The editor must collect them/I'm sure of this one fact,/For when my work's rejected . . ./He never sends them back.

WG&N is 52 pgs., magazine-sized, offset printed and saddle-stapled with glossy paper cover, includes art/graphics and ads. They receive about 100 poems a year, accept approximately 25%. Press run is 2,500 for 1,000 subscribers, 500 shelf sales. Subscription: $19.95/year. Sample: $5. Make checks payable to Independent Publishing Co.

How to Submit: Submit up to 4 poems at a time. Line length for poetry is 24 lines maximum. No previously published poems or simultaneous submissions. Cover letter preferred. "SASE is a must for reply. Bio info desired." Time between acceptance and publication is 4-6 months. Seldom comments on rejections. Send SASE for guidelines. Responds in up to 4 months. Pays 2 copies. Acquires one-time rights. Reviews books and chapbooks of poetry and other magazines in 500 words, single book format. Open to unsolicited reviews. Poets may also send books for review consideration.

Also Offers: The Independent Publishing Co. offers printing to self-published authors.

Advice: "We are always seeking new and innovative writers."

☑ **$** ◐ ◻ ◑ **WRITERS' JOURNAL**, P.O. Box 394, Perham MN 56573-0394, phone (218)346-7921, fax (218)346-7924, e-mail writersjournal@wadena.net, website www.writersjournal.com, founded 1980, poetry editor Esther M. Leiper.

Magazine Needs: *Writers' Journal* is a bimonthly magazine "for writers and poets that offers advice and guidance, motivation, inspiration, to the more serious and published writers and poets." Esther Leiper has 2 columns: "Esther Comments," which specifically critiques poems sent in by readers, and "Every Day with Poetry," which discusses a wide range of poetry topics, often—but not always—including readers' work. She says, "I enjoy a variety of poetry: free verse, strict forms, concrete, Oriental. But we take nothing vulgar, preachy or sloppily written. Since we appeal to those of different skill levels, some poems are more sophisticated than others, but those accepted must move, intrigue or otherwise positively capture me. 'Esther Comments' is never used as a negative force to put a poem or a poet down. Indeed, I focus on the best part of a given work and seek to suggest means of improvement on weaker aspects." Also accepts poetry written by school-age children. They have published poetry by Lawrence Schug, Diana Sutliff and Eugene E. Grollmes. *Writers' Journal* is 64 pgs. (including paper cover), magazine-sized, professionally printed, using 4-5 pgs. of poetry in each issue, including columns. Circulation is 26,000. They receive about 900 submissions a year, use approximately 25 (including those used in Esther's columns). Single copy: $3.99; subscription: $19.97/year (US), Canada/Mexico add $15, Europe add $30, all others $35. Sample: $5.

How to Submit: "Short is best: 25-line limit, though very occasionally we use longer. Three to four poems at a time is just right." No query. Responds in up to 5 months. Pays $5/poem plus 1 copy.

Also Offers: The magazine also has poetry contests for previously unpublished poetry. Submit up to 6 poems on any subject or in any form, 25 line limit. "Submit in duplicate, one with name and address, one without." Send SASE for guidelines only. Deadlines: April 30, August 30 and December 30. Reading fee for each contest: $2 first poem, $1 each poem thereafter. Competition receives 1,000 entries a year. Winners announced in *The Writers' Journal.*

WRITING FOR OUR LIVES; RUNNING DEER PRESS (Specialized: women, feminism), 647 N. Santa Cruz Ave., The Annex, Los Gatos CA 95030-4350, founded 1991, editor/publisher Janet McEwan.

Magazine Needs: Appearing once a year in November, "*Writing For Our Lives* serves as a vessel for poems, short fiction, stories, letters, autobiographies and journal excerpts from the life stories, experiences and spiritual journeys of women." They want poetry that is "personal, women's real life, life-saving, autobiographical, serious—but don't forget humorous, silence-breaking, many styles, many voices. Women writers only, please." They have published poetry by Sara V. Glover, Kennette Harrison, Sara Regina Mitcho and Eileen Tabios. As a sample the editor selected these lines from "To the Great Blue Heron" by Joyce Greenberg Lott:

> Teach me how to swallow without chewing,/To hold a fish in my gullett until its scales become wings//
> Show me how to puff down into a secret/So only those who know me can find me/Teach me how to
> open my wings and fly,/unexpected and perfect, a crone in the sky.

Writing For Our Lives is 80-92 pgs., 5¼×8¼, printed on recycled paper and perfect-bound with matte card cover. They receive about 400 poems a year, accept approximately 5%. Press run is 700. Subscription: $15.50/2 issues. (CA residents add 8.25% sales tax). Back issues and overseas rates available, send SASE for info. Sample: $8, $11 overseas.

How to Submit: Submit up to 5 typed poems with name and phone number on each page. Previously published poems ("sometimes") and simultaneous submissions OK. Include 2 SASEs; "at least one of them should be sufficient to return manuscripts if you want them returned." Closing date is August 15. Usually responds in 3 days, occasionally longer. "As we are now shaping 2-4 issues in advance, we may ask to hold certain poems for later consideration over a period of 18 to 24 months." Seldom comments on rejections. Send SASE for guidelines. Pays 2 copies, discount on additional copies and discount on 1-year subscription. Acquires first world-wide English language serial (or one-time reprint) rights.

Advice: "Our contributors and circulation are international. We welcome new writers, but cannot often comment or advise. We do not pre-announce themes. Subscribe or try a sample copy—gauge the fit of your writing with *WFOL*—support our ability to serve women's life-sustaining writing."

WRITING ON THE EDGE (Specialized: writing/teaching writing), Campus Writing Center, UC Davis, One Shields Ave., Davis CA 95616, phone (530)752-2147, e-mail jdboe@ucdavis.edu, website www.english.ucdavis.edu/compos/woe/default.html, founded 1989, editor John Boe (queries), managing editor Margaret Eldred (submission requirements).

Magazine Needs: *Writing on the Edge* appears 2 times a year. "Our primary audience is college composition teachers but *WOE* is only partly academic in nature. We publish articles, personal essays, interviews, experimental writing, fiction, poetry and cartoons about writing and teaching writing." They want any poetry related to their specialty. Prefer poems under three pages. They have published poetry by Richard Hague, Robert Grudin and Michael Steinberg. As a sample the editor selected these lines from "Poetry Barbie" by Liz Ahl:

> She's mastered Haiku, with its tiny cup full/of syllables, but can't understand iambic/pentameter. I tell
> her it's because she has no/heartbeat. I press her tiny ear to my wrist/so she can listen to my pulse,
> and in minutes,/she's tossing off sonnets English and Italian,/about the wretchedness of being young,/
> plastic, and in love://My soul is plastic, hollow is my head/Each day I die but I am never dead.

WOE is about 104 pgs., digest-sized, professionally printed and perfect-bound with matte card cover. They receive about 20 poems a year, accept approximately 20%. Press run is 600 for 350 subscribers of which 50 are libraries; 50 distributed free to editors, contributors. Subscription: $20. Sample: $10. Make checks payable to Regents of the University of California.

How to Submit: Submit up to 3 poems at a time. Previously published poems and simultaneous submissions OK. E-mail submissions in attached file OK. Cover letter preferred. "Omit name and address from manuscripts. Keep cover letters short. Include SASE." Time between acceptance and publication is 1-2 years. Poems are circulated to an editorial board. "We send poems to reviewers; if they like the poems or if their reactions are mixed, the editors arrive at a concensus." Often comments on rejections. Publishes theme issues occasionally. Responds in 6 months. Pays 2 copies. Authors retain all rights.

Also Offers: Website includes names of editors, writer's guidelines and tables of contents.

N 🌐 📀 **WRITING ULSTER**, Room 12G11, University of Ulster at Jordanstown, Shore Rd., Newtownabbey, County Antrim BT37 0QB N. Ireland, phone (44)1232-366460, fax (44)1232-366824, e-mail w.lazenbatt@ulst.ac.uk, website www.ulst.ac.uk/homepage.html, founded 1990/91, editor Bill Lazenbatt.
Magazine Needs: *Writing Ulster* is published annually. They want "shorter pieces; lyrical; 'Irish' or 'American' themes especially welcome. Some sequences or shorter poems are acceptable. No long narrative pieces." They have published poetry by Paul Muldoon, Brendan Kenelly, Fred Johnston, Frank Ormsby and Michael Foley. As a sample the editor selected these lines (poet unidentified):

> *The dark neighborhoods under the sapphire and silver/of silent flight paths, and the day nearly over./*
> *Huge white unflappable fish pause to feed at international/arrivals, frost scratching the eyes and fins./*
> *The night almost starting and we're already at the mercy/of Hollywood myths: festering basements,*
> *body parts in the trash,/the fast food, brown paper, under-the-counter culture./And you lapsing into*
> *American to ask, "How's everything?"*

The editor says *WU* is 210-240 pgs., 5½×8½, soft cover, includes photographs and line drawings. They receive about 40 poems a year, accept approximately 40%. Publish 10-20 poems/issue. Press run is 500. Sample: £5. Make checks payable to University of Ulster.
How to Submit: Submit 2-3 poems at a time. E-mail submissions OK. Cover letter preferred. Reads submissions "usually January through April for publication later that year." Time between acceptance and publication is 6-8 months. Poems are circulated to an editorial board. "Selection is made by at least two, possibly three, readers." Publishes theme issues. Responds in up to 6 weeks. Pays 5-10 copies as requested. Acquires one-time rights. Staff reviews books of poetry in 700-1,000 words, single book format. Send books for review consideration.
Also Offers: Website includes cover picture, contents, addresses.

📀 **XANADU; POETIMES; LONG ISLAND POETRY COLLECTIVE**, % LIPC, P.O. Box 773, Huntington NY 11743, founded 1979, editors Lois V. Walker, Mildred Jeffrey, Sue Kain and Weslea Sidon.
Magazine Needs: *Xanadu* is an annual publishing "serious poems including prose poems, and an occasional adventuresome essay on contemporary poetry or critical theory." They want "well-crafted quality poems. Nothing inspirational, obscene or from beginners." They have published poetry by L.L. Harper, Hugh Fox, Hillel Schwartz and Ruth Moon Kempher. As a sample the editors selected these lines from "Autumn" by EG Burrows:

> *First cold slows flies/though the spider weaves/more brilliant mazes/hung with grace notes./Webs*
> *ornament/the double glass*

Xanadu is 64 pgs., 5½×8½, perfect-bound with b&w CS1 cover stock cover. Press run is 300 for 100 subscribers of which 5 are libraries. Sample: $7.
How to Submit: Submit 3-5 poems, typed, with your name and address on each page and #10 SASE. Include a brief bio. No previously published poems; simultaneous submissions OK. Poems must be typed. Seldom comments on rejections. Send #10 SASE for guidelines. Responds in up to 6 months. Pays 1 copy. Acquires first North American serial rights.
Also Offers: The Long Island Poetry Collective also publishes *Poetimes*, a bimonthly newsletter edited by Gillian Henderson that includes an extensive calendar of poetry events on Long Island, contests, market listings and poetry by its members. Subscription: $20/year, includes membership in LIPC and subscription to *Xanadu*.
Advice: "We would be glad to look at more quality post-modernist and formalist poetry."

N 📀 **XAVIER REVIEW**, Box 110C, Xavier University, New Orleans LA 70125, phone (504)483-7303, fax (504)485-7917, e-mail rskinner@xula.edu, founded 1961, editor Thomas Bonner, Jr, managing editor Robert E. Skinner.
Magazine Needs: *Xavier Review* is a biannual that publishes poetry, fiction, nonfiction and reviews (contemporary literature) for professional writers, libraries, colleges and universities. They want writing dealing with African/Americans, the South and the Gulf/Caribbean Basin. They have published *I Am New Orleans* by Marcus Christian; *Three Poets in New Orleans* by Lee Grue and poetry by Biljiana Obradovic and Patricia Ward. Press run is 500.
How to Submit: Submit 3-5 poems at a time with SASE. Pays 5 copies.

✔️ 📀 ◎ **XCP: CROSS-CULTURAL POETICS (Specialized: anthropology)**, % College of St. Catherine-Mpls, 601 25th Ave., South Minneapolis MN 55454, website bfn.org/~xcp, founded 1997, editor Mark Nowak.
• *Xcp* is a member of the Council of Literary Magazines and Presses.

TO RECEIVE REGULAR TIPS AND UPDATES about writing and Writer's Digest publications via e-mail, send an e-mail with SUBSCRIBE NEWSLETTER in the body of the message to newsletter-request@writersdigest.com, or sign up online at www.writersdigest.com.

Magazine Needs: *Xcp: Cross-Cultural Poetics* is published biannually. About *Xcp*, *The Poetry Project Newsletter* said, "Welcome to a writer's manual on how to detonate the Master-Axis of Big Brother Narratives." They have published poetry by Amiri Baraka, Diane Glancy, Juan Felipe Herrera and Edwin Torres. *Xcp* is 175 pgs., 6×9, perfect-bound, includes ads. Subscription: $18/2 issues individuals, $40/2 issues institutions (outside US add $4). Sample (including guidelines): $10. Make checks payable to College of St. Catherine.
How to Submit: Submit 6-8 poems at a time. No previously published poems or simultaneous submissions. Cover letter preferred. Time between acceptance and publication is 1-4 months. Seldom comments on rejections. Publishes theme issues. Responds in up to 2 months. Always sends prepublication galleys. Pays 2 copies. Acquires first rights. Reviews books of poetry in 1,500-2,000 words, single or multi-book format. Open to unsolicited reviews. Poets may also send books for review consideration.
Advice: "We advise all potential contributors to read several back issues (cover to cover) before submitting work." Sample copies also available from Small Press Distribution, 1-800-869-7553.

YALE UNIVERSITY PRESS; THE YALE SERIES OF YOUNGER POETS COMPETITION,
P.O. Box 209040, New Haven CT 06520-9040, phone (203)432-0900, website www.yale.edu/yup/, founded 1919, poetry editor (Yale University Press) Nick Raposo.
Book/Chapbook Needs & How to Submit: The Yale Series of Younger Poets Competition is open to poets under 40 who have not had a book previously published. Submit ms of 48-64 pgs. in February. Entry fee: $15. Send SASE for rules and guidelines. Poets are not disqualified by previous publication of limited editions of no more than 300 copies or previously published poems in newspapers and periodicals, which may be used in the book ms if so identified. Previous winners include Richard Kenney, Carolyn Forché and Robert Hass.

$ YANKEE MAGAZINE; YANKEE ANNUAL POETRY CONTEST, P.O. Box 520, Dublin NH 03444-0520, phone (603)563-8111, founded in 1935, poetry editor (since 1955) Jean Burden.
Magazine Needs: Though it has a New England emphasis, the poetry is not necessarily about New England or by New Englanders. They want to see "high-quality contemporary poems in either free verse or traditional form. Does not have to be regional in theme. Any subject acceptable, provided it is in good taste. We look for originality in thought, imagery, insight—as well as technical control." They do not want translations or poetry that is "cliché-ridden, banal verse." They have published poetry by Maxine Kumin, Liz Rosenberg, Josephine Jacobsen, Nancy Willard, Linda Pastan, Paul Zimmer and Hayden Carruth. As a sample the editor selected these lines from "Planting the Impatiens on St. Norbert's Day" by Joan Vayo:

> three Saturdays ago/the dogwood foamed//gone green now/I see white shells of it/in the impatiens/I
> rest around its roots

The monthly is 6×9, 144 pgs., professionally printed, saddle-stapled, using full-color and b&w ads and illustrations, with full-color glossy paper cover. They receive over 30,000 submissions a year, accept about 50-60 poems, use 4-5 poems/monthly issue. They have a national distribution of more than 700,000 subscribers. Single copy: $2.99. Subscription: $24.
How to Submit: Submit up to 6 poems at a time, up to 32 lines each, free verse or traditional. No previously published poems or simultaneous submissions. "Cover letters are interesting if they include previous publication information." Submissions without SASE "are tossed." Editor comments on rejections "only if poem has so many good qualities it only needs minor revisions." Responds in up to 6 weeks. Approximately 18-month backlog. Pays $50/poem, first North American magazine rights.
Also Offers: Sponsors an annual poetry contest judged by a prominent New England poet and published in the February issue, with awards of $150, $100 and $50 for the best 3 poems in the preceding year.
Advice: "Study previous issues of *Yankee* to determine the kind of poetry we want. Get involved in poetry workshops at home. Read the best contemporary poetry you can find."

YEFIEF, P.O. Box 8505, Santa Fe NM 87504-8505, phone (505)753-3648, fax (505)753-7049, e-mail arr@i magesformedia.com, founded 1993, editor Ann Racuya-Robbins.
Magazine Needs: *Yefief* is a serial imprint of Images For Media that was originally designed "to construct a narrative of culture at the end of the century." They want "innovative visionary work of all kinds and have a special interest in exploratory forms and language. There is no set publication schedule." They have published poetry by Michael Palmer, Simon Perchik and Carla Harryman. *Yefief* is 250 pgs., printed on site and perfect-bound with color coated card cover with color and b&w photos, art and graphics inside. Initial artbook press run is 500. Single copy: $24.95. Write for information on obtaining sample copies.
How to Submit: Submit 3-6 poems at a time. Previously published poems and simultaneous submissions OK. Responds in 2 months. Pays 2-3 copies. Open to unsolicited reviews. Poets may also send books for review consideration.

YEMASSEE; YEMASSEE AWARDS, Dept. of English, University of South Carolina, Columbia SC 29208, phone (803)777-2085, website www.cla.sc.edu/ENGL/index.html, founded 1993, editor Lisa Kerr.
Magazine Needs: *Yemassee* appears semiannually and "publishes primarily fiction and poetry, but we are also interested in one-act plays, brief excerpts of novels, essays, reviews and interviews with literary figures. Our essential consideration for acceptance is the quality of the work; we are open to a variety of subjects and writing styles." They accept 10-25 poems/issue. "No poems of such a highly personal nature that their primary relevance

is to the author; bad Ginsberg." They have published poetry by Kwame Dawes, Virgil Saurez, Phoebe Davidson, Pamela McClure and Catherine Davidson. *Yemassee* is 60-80 pgs., 5½ × 8½, professionally printed and saddle-stitched, quality uncoated cover stock, one-color cover graphic, no ads. They receive about 400 poems a year, accept approximately 10%. Press run is 750 for 63 subscribers, 10 shelf sales; 275-300 distributed free to English department heads, creative writing chairs, agents and publishers. Subscription: $6 for students, $15 regular. Sample: $4. Make checks payable to Education Foundation/English Literary Magazine Fund.

How to Submit: Submit up to 5 poems at a time. Line length for poetry is fewer than 50, "but poems of exceptional quality are considered regardless of length." No previously published poems. Cover letter required. "Each issue's contents are determined on the basis of blind selections. Therefore we ask that all works be submitted, without the author's name or address anywhere on the typescript. Include this information along with the title(s) of the work(s) in a cover letter. For longer submissions, please include an approximate word count." Reads submissions October 1 through November 15 and March 15 through April 30. Time between acceptance and publication is 2-4 months. "Staff reads and votes on 'blind' submissions." Seldom comments on rejections. Send SASE for guidelines. Responds in up to 10 weeks after submission deadline. Pays 2 copies with the option to purchase additional copies at a reduced rate. Acquires first rights.

Also Offers: Sponsors the *Yemassee* Awards when funding permits. Awards $400/issue, usually $200 each for poetry and fiction. Website includes writer's guidelines, editor's names, sponsor's names, table of contents and cover of most recent issues.

$⬚◎ YES! A JOURNAL OF POSITIVE FUTURES (Specialized: nature/rural/ecology, social issues, themes), P.O. Box 10818, Bainbridge Island WA 98110, phone (206)842-0216, fax (206)842-5208, e-mail yes@futurenet.org, website www.futurenet.org, founded 1996, associate editor Tracy Rysavy.

Magazine Needs: "Published quarterly, *Yes!* supports active citizen engagement in creating a just, sustainable and compassionate world. We help people find, inform and inspire one another to make a difference on issues that count for the long-term future of people and the planet. We're seeking poetry that relates to our overall purpose of creating a just, sustainable and compassionate world. No 'Hallmark' verse." Also accepts poetry written by children. They have reviewed the works of Joy Harjo and Martín Espada. As a sample the editor selected these lines from "Eagle Poem" by Joy Harjo:

> Remember the sky that you were born under/Know each of the star's stories./Remember the moon,
> know who she is. I met her/in a bar once in Iowa City./Remember the sun's birth at dawn, that is the/
> strongest point of time.

The editor says *Yes!* is 64 pgs., magazine-sized, sheet-fed printed, includes b&w photos and illustrations. They receive about 20 poems a year, accept approximately 10%. Press run is 15,000 for about 9,000 subscribers; about 1,500 distributed free to organizations and activists. Subscription: $24. Sample: $6.

How to Submit: Submit up to 5 poems at a time. Previously published poems and simultaneous submissions OK. Cover letter required. Fax and e-mail submissions OK (for e-mail include in body of message). "Send SASE; become familiar with our content before submitting." Time between acceptance and publication is 3-6 months. Seldom comments on rejections. Publishes theme issues. Send SASE for guidelines and upcoming themes or obtain via e-mail or website. Responds in 3 months. Always sends prepublication galleys. Pays $20-30 honorarium plus 2 copies plus subscription. Buys all rights. Reviews books of poetry in 300-1,000 words, single book format. Open to unsolicited reviews. Poets may also send books for review consideration.

Also Offers: Website includes sample articles, guidelines, interviews, names of editors, book reviews, letter to the editor and news of the nonprofit organization/publisher.

Ⓝ ⊕ ◑ YOMIMONO, 113-6 Ninokoshi, Kitakawamukai, Aza, Hiroshima, Matsushige-cho, Itano-gun, Tokushima-ken 771-0220 Japan, phone/fax (+81)886-99-7574, e-mail kammy@mxs.meshnet.or.jp, founded 1992, editor Suzanne Kamata.

Magazine Needs: Published annually, *Yomimono* is "an eclectic mix of poetry, fiction, essays, interviews and artwork from around the world. We're pretty open but we tend to favor innovative and international work. We like complicated yet accessible. Be concrete. No mediocre haiku, poems about drug trips, airy philosophizing, sappy love poems, rhyming verse." They have published poetry by Leza Lowitz, John Gribble, Sibyl James and Kate Krautkramer. As a sample the editor selected these lines from "Life Is Difficult, Part One" by Peter Bakowski:

> The heart on my sleeve/is at the dry cleaner's/a flock of tea-bags/just circled the house/and the kettle
> won't boil/says it wants to be/a poet.

The editor says *Yomimono* is 66 pgs., magazine-sized, desktop-published and perfect-bound, cover varies, includes b&w illustrations and photos. They receive about 100 poems a year, accept approximately 10%. Press run is 150. Single copy: $5; subscription: $10. Sample: $4. Make checks payable to Suzanne Kamata.

How to Submit: Submit up to 5 poems at a time. Previously published poems and simultaneous submissions OK. E-mail submissions OK. SASE or SAE and IRC required for reply. Time between acceptance and publication is up to 1 year. Poems are circulated to an editorial board. "Poems are discussed among three editors." Often comments on rejections. Responds in 6 months. Pays 3 copies. Acquires one-time rights. Reviews books and chapbooks of poetry and other magazines in 50-1,000 words, single and multi-book format. Open to unsolicited reviews. Poets may also send books for review consideration.

🌐 ◎ **YORKSHIRE JOURNAL (Specialized: regional)**, Ilkley Rd., Otley, West Yorkshire LS2 3JP England, phone (01943)467958, fax (01943)850057, e-mail sales@smith-settle.co.uk, founded 1992, editor Mark Whitley.

Magazine Needs: *Yorkshire Journal* is a quarterly general interest magazine about Yorkshire. They want poetry no longer than 25 lines with some relevance to Yorkshire. They have published poetry by Vernon Scannell, Anna Adams, Ted Hughes, Andrew Motion and Simon Armitage. As a sample the editor selected these lines from "The Herdwick Ram" by Leslie Quayle:

> As I unlatched the barn door's creaking hasp,/The grey ewes gathered, hungering, at my back,/Dawn's
> sallow glimmer pricked the tine and cusp/Of hawthorn crowns and slipped across the beck./He wasn't
> in the clamour for fresh hay,/Nor by the mistal, so I went to seek,/Hurrying through the damp grass,
> till I saw/The great, slumped shadow against the lambing creep.

Mr. Whitley says *YJ* is 120 pgs., highly illustrated. They receive about 200 poems a year, accept approximately 10%. Press run is 3,000 for 700 subscribers, 2,300 shelf sales. Subscription: £12. Sample: £2.95. Make checks payable to SMITH Settle Ltd.

How to Submit: Submit up to 6 poems at a time. Previously published poems and simultaneous submissions OK. Fax and e-mail submissions OK (for e-mail include in body of message). Cover letter required including biographical information. Has a large backlog. Time between acceptance and publication varies. Sometimes comments on rejections. Send SASE (or SAE and IRC) for guidelines. Responds within 1 month maximum. Pays 1 copy.

🄽 🌐 ◯ ◎ **YOUNG WRITER; YOUNG WRITER SUMMER ANTHOLOGY (Specialized: children/teen)**, Glebe House, Church Rd., Weobley, Herefordshire HR4 8SD England, phone/fax (01544)318901, e-mail youngwriter@enterprise.net, website www.mystworld/com.youngwriter, founded 1995, editor Kate Jones, editorial assistant Dela Whiting.

Magazine Needs: *Young Writer* appears 3 times a year "to inspire, nurture and educate young writers of all abilities and to support teachers working with them. It contains prose and poetry, fiction and nonfiction by young people." They want poetry by children under 18. "No poetry unsuitable to publish in magazine for readers under 18." They have published poetry by Rebecca Lawrence, Sarah Carlin, Alice Smith, Peter Ranscombe, Philip Nash and Melanie Hobbs. As a sample the editor selected this poem, "Floppy Hat" by Claire Hughes (age 13):

> Your floppy hat lies covered in cobwebs/Untouched for years./It holds the shape of your head./It has
> been strewn carelessly into its new home,/And then forgotten./Its very presence there creates a
> spectre . . ./of our past.

The editor says *YW* is 32 pgs., 8½×11, 4 color printing on high quality paper, saddle-stitched with self-cover, includes art/graphics. They receive about 1,000 poems a year, accept approximately 20%. Publish approximately 40 poems/issue. Press run is 10,000 for subscribers (individuals, schools and libraries), book club sales and shelf sales; 150 distributed free to publishers/authors. Single copy: £2.75 plus £1.24 p&h; subscription: £7.50 plus £2 p&h in Europe; £4 p&h, further afield; p&h free in UK; £4 p&h to US. Sample is free. (Send IRCs to cover postage to the US.)

How to Submit: Line length for poetry is 4-5 minimum, 40 maximum. Previously published poems and simultaneous submissions OK. E-mail and disk (Apple compatible) submissions OK. Cover letter preferred. Time between acceptance and publication is up to 1 year. Poems are circulated to an editorial board. "Read everything, short-list pieces that ring true, then balance the magazine." Often comments on rejections. Send SASE (or SAE and IRC) for guidelines or obtain via website. Responds in 1 month. Acquires one-time rights. Reviews books and chapbooks of poetry and other magazines in up to 50 words, single and multi-book format. Open to unsolicited reviews. Poets may also send books for review consideration. "Books should be suitable for readers under 18."

Also Offers: Also published an annual anthology of poetry and prose by writers 18 and under. Sponsors annual award competitions. Details on request. Website includes "a taste of the magazine plus editor's choice of children's writing, plus 'what's new?' newsboard and guidelines."

Advice: "We look for honesty and the ring of truth. We expect a level of competence in handling language. Both serious and humorous pieces considered. All material should be appropriate for our readership of children, though tough subjects may be tackled."

🌐 ✔ ◯ **ZINE ZONE**, 47 Retreat Place, London E9 6RH United Kingdom, phone (0207)739-1557, fax (0207)684-2053, e-mail getzz@zinezone.co.uk, founded 1992, contact "editorial."

Magazine Needs: *Zine Zone* appears 8 times a year and publishes "a chaotic mix of illustrative works with poetry, short stories, music reviews, etc." For their poetry wants, they say, "anything goes. Although, we mostly publish obscure unpublished poets and students." As a sample they selected these lines from "Laughing at Nothing" by Steve Andrews (Wales):

> Doing something ordinary is only an act;/There's freedom of expression in the ethers./I was talking to
> a Neanderthal face/And inspecting rooms on a personal pilgrimage,/Running like a child under smiling
> Heavens,/Laughing at nothing is too much for some it seems.

They say *ZZ* is 52 pgs., A4, photocopied and stapled with b&w paper cover, b&w graphics. They receive about 200 poems a year, accept approximately 50-70%. Press run is 500 for 120 subscribers. Single copy: £1.95 ($3 US); subscription: £18/8 copies, £11/4 copies. Sample: £3 ($5 US).

How to Submit: Previously published poems and simultaneous submissions OK. Cover letter preferred. Fax, e-mail and disk submissions (text format) OK. Time between acceptance and publication is 2 months. Reviews books and chapbooks of poetry and other magazines, single book format. Open to unsolicited reviews.

Also Offers: "Poetry nights organized in and around London (UK) where poets read their work to an audience."

$ ☑ ZOLAND BOOKS INC., 384 Huron Ave., Cambridge MA 02138, phone (617)864-6252, fax (617)661-4998, e-mail info@zolandbooks.com, website www.zolandbooks.com, founded 1987, publisher Roland Pease.

Book/Chapbook Needs: Zoland is a "literary press: fiction, poetry, photography, gift books, books of literary interest." They want "high-quality" poetry, not sentimental. They have published poetry by Kevin Young, Bill Berkson, Joel Sloman and Ange Mlinko. They publish 15 books/year, flat-spined, averaging 104 pgs.

How to Submit: Query with 5-10 sample poems, bio, publications and SASE. Sometimes sends prepublication galleys. Pays 5-10% royalties plus 5 copies. Buys all rights.

Also Offers: Website includes reviews, frontlist, backlist and amazon.com links.

▣ ☑ ZUZU'S PETALS QUARTERLY ONLINE, P.O. Box 4853, Ithaca NY 14852, phone (607)844-9009, e-mail info@zuzu.com, website www.zuzu.com, founded 1992, editor T. Dunn.

Magazine Needs: "We publish high-quality fiction, essays, poetry and reviews on our award-winning website, which was featured in *USA Today Online*, *Entertainment Weekly*, and *Web Magazine*. Becoming an Internet publication allows us to offer thousands of helpful resources and addresses for poets, writers, editors and researchers, as well as to greatly expand our readership. Free verse, blank verse, experimental, visually sensual poetry, etc. are especially welcome here. We're looking for a freshness of language, new ideas and original expression. No 'June, moon and spoon' rhymed poetry. No light verse. I'm open to considering more feminist, ethnic, alternative poetry, as well as poetry of place." They have published poetry by Ruth Daigon, Robert Sward, Laurel Bogen, W.T. Pfefferle and Kate Gale. As a sample the editor selected these lines from "San Francisco Earthquake" by Kathryn Young:

> Padre Pablo, in the dream I could understand/how the angels of death like wild birds/can be entertained
> with kind gestures/like strangers, how white their teeth,/how warm and dark their skin

ZPQO averages 70-100 pgs., using full-color artwork, and is an electronic publication available free of charge on the Internet. "Many libraries, colleges, and coffeehouses offer access to the Internet for those without home Internet accounts." They receive about 3,000 poems a year, accept approximately 10%. A copy of *Zuzu's Petals Poetry Buffet*, a sample of writing from the past 4 years is available for $5.

How to Submit: Submit up to 4 poems at a time. Previously published poems and simultaneous submissions OK. "Cover letters are not necessary. The work should speak for itself." Submissions via e-mail are welcome, as well as submissions in ASCII (DOS IBM) format on 3½″ disks OK. Include e-mail submissions in the body of the message. Seldom comments on rejections. Send SASE for guidelines or request via e-mail. Responds in up to 2 months. Acquires one-time electronic rights. Staff reviews books of poetry in approximately 200 words. Send books, galleys or proofs for review consideration.

Also Offers: Website includes full text of *Zuzu's Petals Quarterly*, writer's guidelines, over 10,000 helpful addresses, over 7,000 arts links, online discussion salon, updated literary news, poetry videos.

Advice: "Read as much poetry as you can. Support the literary arts: Go to poetry readings, read chapbooks and collections of verse. Eat poetry for breakfast, cultivate a love of language, then write!"

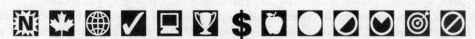

**FOR EXPLANATIONS OF THESE SYMBOLS,
SEE THE INSIDE FRONT AND BACK COVERS OF THIS BOOK.**

Contests & Awards

The opportunities for poets to receive recognition and publish their work are growing via the route of contests and awards. And while this section of *Poet's Market* is considerably smaller than Publishers of Poetry, it contains 34 new entries within its approximately 150 "markets."

Here you will find a wide range of competitions—from contests with modest prizes sponsored by state poetry societies, colleges or even cities to prestigious awards offered by private foundations. Among the various contests and awards included in this section are those that offer publication in addition to their monetary prizes. But even if publication is not included, the publicity generated upon winning some of these contests can make your name more familiar to editors.

SELECTING CONTESTS

Whether you're submitting one poem to a quarterly contest sponsored by a journal or an entire manuscript to an award offered by a book publisher, you should never submit to contests and awards blindly. Because many contests require entry fees, blind submissions will just waste your time. As in the Publishers of Poetry section, each listing here contains one or more Openness to Submissions symbols in its heading. These symbols will not only help you narrow the list of contests and awards to those open to your experience level, but they can also help you evaluate your chances of winning.

The ▢ symbol, for instance, is given to contests that welcome entries from beginning or unpublished poets. While most contests require entry fees, or membership in the sponsoring organization, they typically are not exploitative of poets, beginning or otherwise. Keep in mind, however, that if a contest charges a $5 entry fee and offers $75 in prizes, the organizers only need 15 entries to cover the prizes. Even though fees may also go toward providing a small honorarium for the judge, 100 entries will surely net the organizers a tidy profit—at the expense of the participating poets. Be careful when deciding which contests are worth your money.

The ◑ symbol precedes the name of general literary contests, usually for poets with some experience. This symbol may also precede awards for recently published collections, such as the Colorado Book Awards and the Pulitzer Prize in Letters, or fellowships designed for poets of "demonstrated ability," such as the Guggenheims. And competitions like the Stan and Tom Wick Poetry Prize, a contest open to poets writing in English who have not yet published a full-length collection, are listed under this symbol. If you're just beginning, start building a reputation by publishing in periodicals, then try your hand at these competitions.

Of all the symbols, perhaps the most useful is ◎, which designates specialized contests and awards. That is, you—or your poetry—must meet certain criteria to be eligible. Some contests are regional, so only poets from a certain area may enter. For example, the Montalvo Biennial Poetry Competition offers $2,000 in prizes to poets residing in California, Nevada, Oregon and Washington. Also, fellowships and grants offered by state and provincial arts councils are only open to residents of the particular state or province. Some of these programs are detailed here. For those not found, see the list of State and Provincial Grants following this section.

Other contests are limited to certain groups, such as women or students. For instance, the Frank O'Hara Award Chapbook Competition offers $500 and publication to gay, lesbian or bisexual poets. Also, the Senior Poet Laureate Poetry Competition offers an annual award to American poets age 50 or older.

A few contests are for translations only. Still others are limited to poets writing in certain forms or on certain subjects. If you write haiku, for example, consider the Penumbra Poetry &

Haiku Competition. One award limited to a certain subject is The Trewithen Poetry Prize, which only considers work dealing with rural themes. Competitions that primarily consider themselves specialized are often open to both beginning and established poets.

Also noteworthy are several other symbols often found at the beginning of a listing. These symbols are included to convey certain information at a glance. The 🅽 symbol identifies new listings, the 🌐 symbol denotes international listings, the 🍁 symbol indicates Canadian listings, and the ☑ symbol signifies a change in a listing's address, phone number, e-mail address or contact name.

In addition to the listings in this section, there are contests and awards (particularly those sponsored by journals) mentioned in listings in other sections of this book. For those, you should refer to the list of Additional Contests & Awards at the end of this section and consult the listings noted there for details. (See the General Index for the listings' page numbers.)

Once you've narrowed the contests and awards you want to enter, treat the submission process just as you would if you were submitting to a magazine: Always send a SASE for more information. Many contests want you to submit work along with their specific entry form or application. Others offer guidelines detailing exactly how they want poetry submitted. Also, deadlines for entries are often subject to change and if your work arrives after the deadline date, it will automatically be disqualified. Finally, obtain copies of recent winning entries for any contest you are considering. This will give you a good idea of the kind of work the judges appreciate. However, this may not apply if the judges change each year.

DISCOVER OTHER RESOURCES

Besides this section of *Poet's Market*, there are other sources of information on competitions. In fact, some good places to locate contests are in your own city or town. Many bookstores and libraries post announcements for local contests on their bulletin boards. Calling a nearby college's English department may provide you with the scoop on regional competitions. And, many poetry groups publish newsletters containing information on competitions that are available to nonmembers. Finally, don't forget to check websites and the classified ads of community arts/entertainment papers for those contests currently seeking entries.

For more information on the national level, *Poets & Writers Magazine* (see the listing in the Publications of Interest section) includes calls for entries for numerous contests and awards along the margins of its pages. In addition, the magazine also includes a Grants and Awards section listing recent winners of poetry and fiction prizes of $500 or more and prestigious nonmonetary awards in fiction and poetry. Reading the winners' work is a good way to determine the type of poetry these competitions are seeking.

Other publications containing information on contests and awards include the *Writer's Chronicle* published by Associated Writing Programs (see listing in the Organizations section), *Grants and Awards Available to American Writers* (published by the PEN American Center; see PEN's listing in Organizations), *The Writer* (published by The Writer, Inc., 120 Boylston St., Boston MA 02116), *Writer's Digest* magazine and the annual directory *Writer's Market* (both published by Writer's Digest Books). Check local bookstores for these publications or order copies directly from the publisher.

For detailed information on selecting and submitting to contests, read Chapter Three: Entering Contests in Michael J. Bugeja's *Poet's Guide* (Story Line Press, 1995). The chapter also includes essays from some well-known poets on their experiences with and opinions on competitions.

⬛**AKRON POETRY PRIZE**, The University of Akron Press, 374B Bierce Library, Akron OH 44325-1703, phone (330)972-5342, fax (330)972-5132, e-mail press@uakron.edu, website www.uakron.edu/uapress/poetryprize.html, award director Elton Glaser, offers annual award of $1,000 plus publication. Submissions must be unpublished and may be entered in other contests (with notification of acceptance elsewhere). Submit 60-100 pages maximum, typed, double-spaced, postmarked between May 15 and June 30, with SASE for results. Mss will not be returned. Do not send mss bound or enclosed in covers. Send SASE for guidelines. Inquiries via fax and e-mail OK. Entry fee: $25. Deadline: entries are accepted May 15 through June 30 only. Competition receives about 500 entries. Most recent contest winners were Dennis Hinrichsen, Beckian Fritz Goldberg and Jeanne E. Clark. Judge for the 2000 prize was Mary Oliver. Winner will be announced in September. Copies of previous winning books may be obtained by contacting UAP or through your local bookstore. The University of Akron Press "is committed to publishing poetry that, as Robert Frost said, 'begins in delight and ends in wisdom.' Books accepted must exhibit three essential qualities: mastery of language, maturity of feeling, and complexity of thought."

THE AMY AWARD (Specialized: women, form, regional), Guild Hall of East Hampton, 158 Main St., East Hampton NY 11937, phone (516)324-0806, fax (516)324-2722, website www.guildhall.org, established in 1996, offers annual honorarium plus a reading with a well-known poet in the *Writers at Guild Hall* series. Submissions may be entered in other contests. Submit 3 lyric poems of no more than 50 lines each, with name, address and phone on each page. Enclose SASE and bio. Entrants must be women 30 years of age or under residing on Long Island or in the New York metropolitan region. Send SASE for guidelines and deadline. Most recent award winner was Susan Pilewski. Entrants will be notified of winner via their SASE approximately 2 months after contest deadline. Guild Hall is the East End of Long Island's leading cultural center. It hosts, besides major museum, theater, and musical events, the *Writers at Guild Hall* series. Readers have included Tom Wolfe, Kurt Vonnegut, Joseph Brodsky, Maxine Kumin, Allen Ginsberg, Sharon Olds, John Ashbery, E.L. Doctorow, Eileen Myles and Linda Gregg.

ANDREAS-GRYPHIUS-PREIS; NIKOLAUS-LENAU-PREIS (Specialized: foreign Language), Die Künstlergilde e.V., Hafenmarkt 2, D-73728, Esslingen a.N., Germany, phone 0711/3969 01-0. "The prize is given annually to German-speaking authors who are dealing with the particular problems of the German culture in eastern Europe or to the best published literary works (which may be poems) that promote understanding between Germans and eastern Europeans." Prizes awarded: 1 Grand Prize of DM 25,000; 1 prize of DM 7,000. Submissions judged by a 7-member jury. They also sponsor the Nikolaus-Lenau-Preis for German-speaking poets. The prize is named in honor of Nikolaus Lenau, "a poet who facilitated understanding with the people of eastern Europe." The prize of DM 11,000 is awarded for published poems. Write for details.

ARIZONA STATE POETRY SOCIETY ANNUAL CONTEST, Penelope, Box 261, Gilbert AZ 85299, phone (480)507-8359, established in 1967, president Karen Odle. Contest for various poetry forms and subjects. Prizes range from $10-100; 1st, 2nd and 3rd place winners are published in the winter edition of *The Sandcutters*, the group's quarterly publication, and names are listed for honorable mention winners. Contest information available for SASE. Fees vary. Deadline: August 31. Competition receives over 1,000 entries a year. "ASPS sponsors a variety of monthly contests for members. Membership is available to anyone anywhere."

ARKANSAS POETRY DAY CONTEST; POETS' ROUNDTABLE OF ARKANSAS, phone (501)321-4226, e-mail vernalee@lpt.net, over 25 categories, many open to all poets. Brochure available in June; deadline in September; awards given in October. For copy send SASE to Verna Lee Hinegardner, 605 Higdon, Apt. 109, Hot Springs AR 71913.

ART COOP FELLOWSHIP IN POETRY, % Charli Valdez, 725 Ashland, Houston TX 77007, e-mail art_coop@yahoo.com, website www.geocities.com/~cottonwood, established in 1996, director Charli Buono de Valdez, offers annual fellowship in poetry open to poets everywhere. Awards cash prize (not less than $250) and publication. Pays winners from other countries by cashiers check. Include cover sheet, bio and list of publications. Send SASE for guidelines or visit website. Inquiries via e-mail OK. Entry fee(s): $5 for first poem, $2 each thereafter. Does not accept entry fees in foreign currencies. "For flat $10 fee and SASE, feedback on poems provided." Deadline: May 31. Competition receives 20 entries a year.

$ "ART IN THE AIR" POETRY CONTEST, Inventing the Invisible/"Art in the Air" Radio Show, 3128 Walton Blvd., PMB 186, Rochester Hills MI 48309, fax (248)693-7344, e-mail lagapvp@aol.com, website www.inventingtheinvisible.com, established in 1991, award director Margo LaGattuta, offers biannual award of 1st Prize: $100; 2nd Prize: $50; and 4 Honorable Mentions. Pays winners from other countries by check. ("All winners read poems on the radio.") Submissions may be entered in other contests. Submit 3 poems maximum in any form, typed, single-spaced, limit 2 pages per poem. Send SASE for guidelines or visit website. Inquiries via fax or e-mail OK. Entry fee(s): $5 for up to 3 poems. Accepts entry fees in foreign currencies. Deadlines: October 30, 2001 and April 30, 2001. Competition receives over 600 entries a year. Most recent contest winners include Simone Muench, Marilyn Krysi, Julie Moulds, Elizabeth Rosner, Bill Rudolph, Jenny Brown and Wyatt Townley (1998). Judges were Mary Jo Firth Gillett and Margo LaGattuta. Winner(s) will be announced 2 months after deadline. Copies of previous winning poems or books may be obtained by sending an SASE to the Inventing the Invisible address. " 'Art in the Air' is an interview radio show on WPON, 1460 AM, in Bloomfield Hills, MI, hosted by Margo LaGattuta. The theme is creativity & the creative process, especially featuring writers both local and national. Send only your best work—well crafted and creative. Judges look for excellence in content and execution."

◎ **ARTIST TRUST; ARTIST TRUST GAP GRANTS; ARTIST TRUST FELLOWSHIPS (Specialized: regional)**, 1402 Third Ave., Suite 404, Seattle WA 98101, phone (206)467-8734, fax (206)467-9633, e-mail info@artisttrust.org, website www.artisttrust.org, program director Heather Dwyer. Artist Trust is a nonprofit arts organization that provides grants to artists (including poets) who are residents of the state. Inquiries via fax and e-mail OK. Competition receives 1,000 entries a year. Most recent contest winners include Donna Miscolta, Thomas Gribble and Bruce Beasley. It also publishes, three times a year, a journal of news about arts opportunities and cultural issues. Website includes applications and other grant/publication opportunities.

◻ ◢ ◎ **ARTS RECOGNITION AND TALENT SEARCH (ARTS) (Specialized: students)**, National Foundation for Advancement in the Arts, 800 Brickell Ave., Suite 500, Miami FL 33131, phone (800)970-ARTS, fax (305)377-1149, e-mail nfaa@nfaa.org, established in 1981, program coordinator Dena Willman. "ARTS is a national program designed to identify, recognize and encourage young people who demonstrate excellence in dance, music, music/jazz, music/voice, theater, film and video, visual arts, photography and writing. Any eligible artist applying to the program will have access to approximately $3 million in scholarship opportunities from more than 100 leading colleges, universities and conservatories that subscribe to NFAA's Scholarship List Service. NFFA will invite a total of 125 artists to participate in 'ARTS Week 2001' in January in Miami-Dade County, Florida. ARTS Week is a once-in-a-lifetime experience consisting of performances, master classes, workshops, readings, exhibits and enrichment activities with renowned artists and arts educators. All expenses are paid by NFAA, including airfare, hotel, meals and ground transportation. As a resulte of their ARTS Week activities, participants will earn cash awards of $3,000 (Level 1), $1,500 (Level 2), $1,000 (Level 3), $500 (Level 4) and $100 (Level 5). NFAA will nominate up to 50 of the top ARTS award recipients to the White House Commission on Presidential Scholars for consideration as US Presidential Scholars in the Arts. Twenty ARTS awardees will ultimately be chosen for this prestigious award and be invited to Washington, DC for National Recognition Week in June. There, they will receive the Presidential Scholars medallion in a ceremony hosted by the White House and participate in many other exciting events." Submissions may be entered in other contests. Submit up to 6 poems in up to but not more than 10 pgs. Open to high school seniors and young people aged 17 or 18 by or on December 1 of the award year. Interested students should contact their guidance counselor for an ARTS 2001 application, call (800)970-ARTS, or apply online at our website, www.ARTSawards.org. Inquiries via fax and e-mail OK. Entry fee: $25 (June 1 early application deadline). The final deadline is October 2, 2000 and requires a $35 processing fee. Competition receives over 8,000 entries a year. Winners are announced by December 30 by mail. Website includes applications, deadlines and updates.

◼ ◯ ◢ **THE BACKWATERS PRIZE**, The Backwaters Press, 3502 N. 52nd St., Omaha NE 68104-3506, phone (402)451-4052, e-mail gkosm62735@aol.com, established in 1998, award director Greg Kosmicki, offers annual prize of $1,000 plus publication, promotion and distribution. "Submissions may be entered in other contests and this should be noted in cover letter. Backwaters Press must be notified if manuscripts are accepted for publication at other presses." Submit up to 80 pages on any subject, any form. "Poems must be written in English. No collaborative work accepted. Parts of the manuscript may be previously published in magazines or chapbooks, but entire manuscript may not have been previously published." Manuscript should be typed (or word processed) in standard poetry format—single spaced, one poem per page, one side only. Send SASE for guidelines only. Entry fee(s): $20. Does not accept entry fees in foreign currencies. Send postal money order or personal check. Deadline: postmarked by June 1 of each year. Competition receives 200-250 entries a year. Most recent contest winner was Sally Allen McNall (1999). Judge was Greg Kuzma. Winner will be announced in *Poets & Writer's* "Recent Winners." Copies of previous winning books may be obtained by writing to the press. "The Backwaters Press is a nonprofit press dedicated to publishing the best new literature we can find. Send your best work."

✓ ◎ **BAY AREA BOOK REVIEWERS ASSOCIATION AWARDS (BABRA); FRED CODY AWARD (Specialized: regional)**, 1450 Fourth St., #4, Berkeley CA 94710, phone (510)525-6752, established in 1981, contact Joyce Jenkins, offers annual awards which recognize "the best of Northern California (from Fresno north) fiction, poetry, nonfiction, and children's literature." Submissions must be previously published. Submit 3 copies of each book entered. Open to Northern California residents. Send SASE for guidelines. Deadline: December 1. BABRA also sponsors the Fred Cody Award for lifetime achievement given to a Northern California writer who also serves the community; and gives, on an irregular basis, awards for outstanding work in translation and publishing. The Cody Award winner for 1998 was Maxine Hong Kingston.

◼ ⊕ ◎ **BBC WILDLIFE MAGAZINE POET OF THE YEAR AWARDS (Specialized: nature)**, *BBC Wildlife Magazine*, Broadcasting House, Whiteladies Rd., Bristol BS8 2LR United Kingdom, phone +44(0)117 973 8402, fax +44(0)117 946 7075, e-mail wildlife.magazine@bbc.co.uk, established in 1994, award director Nina Epton, offers annual prize of £500, publication in *BBC Wildlife Magazine* plus the poem is read on BBC radio 4's "Poetry, Please" program. Runners-up receive cash prizes plus publication in *BBC Wildlife Magazine*. Pays winners from other countries by international money order. Submissions must be unpublished. Submit 1 poem on the natural world in any form, 50 lines maximum. Send SASE (or SAE and IRC) for guidelines only. Inquiries via fax or e-mail OK. "No entry fees, but entry form appears in magazine, so you have to buy magazine to enter." Deadline varies from year to year. Competition receives 1,500-2,000 entries a year. Most recent award winner was Matthew Barton (1997). Judges were Simon Rae (poet), Lavinia Greenlaw (poet), Gareth Owen (poet), Philip Gross (poet), Nick Davies (natural history broadcaster and novelist), Tim Dee (head of BBC literary unit), Rosamund Kidman Cox (editor of *BBC Wildlife Magazine*). Winner announced in *BBC Wildlife Magazine*. "Contact us for information before sending a poem in."

BECH PUBLICATIONS WRITING COMPETITION, BECH Publications (Ballarat East Community House), P.O. Box 2038, Ballarat Mail Centre, Ballarat, Victoria 3354 Australia, phone/fax (03)53314107, e-mail bech@netconnect.com.au, website www.yarranet.net.au/cedric/balleast/hom.htm, established in 1998, award director Maureen Taylor, offers annual prizes (Australian dollars) in 3 categories. Poetry: open to 60 lines—$150, $80. Short Story: open to 2,000 words—$150, $80. Prose: theme to 750 words—$100, $80. Submissions must be unpublished. Submit any number of poems. Send SASE (or SAE and IRC) for entry form and guidelines. Inquiries via fax or e-mail OK. Entry fee: (AUS) $4/entry. Does not accept entry fees in foreign currencies. Send International Bank Exchange rate or 3 IRCs plus 1 additional IRC for results. Competition receives approximately 300 entries a year. Judges were David Farnsworth, Ruth Strachan and Vicky Lowe. Winners announced by mail and the Internet. "Ballarat East Community House sponsors the BECH Publications Writing Competitions and has done so since 1998. It is a provider of Adult Community Education and vocational training and education with the State of Victoria Australia. Judges are hand-picked professional writers or dedicated wordsmiths with judging experience. The competition is open to all. We encourage everyone to 'have a go.' "

GEORGE BENNETT FELLOWSHIP, Phillips Exeter Academy, 20 Main St., Exeter NH 03833-2460, website www.exeter.edu, established in 1968, selection committee coordinator Charles Pratt. Provides a $6,000 fellowship plus room and board to a writer with a ms in progress. The Fellow's only official duties are to be in residence while the academy is in session and to be available to students interested in writing. The committee favors writers who have not yet published a book-length work with a major publisher. Send SASE for application materials or obtain via website. Deadline: December 1. Competition receives 150 entries. Recent award winners were Gina Apostol (1997-1998), Lysley Tenorio (1998-1999) and Ilya Kaminsky (1999-2000). Website includes a description of fellowship, application form and application instructions.

BEST OF OHIO WRITERS WRITING CONTEST (Specialized: regional), Ohio Writer Magazine, P.O. Box 91801, Cleveland OH 44101, offers annual contest for poetry, fiction and creative nonfiction. Prizes: $150 1st Prize, $50 2nd Prize, plus publication for first-place winner in a special edition of *Ohio Writer*. Submit up to 3 typed poems, no more than 2 pages each. Open to Ohio residents only. "Entries will be judged anonymously, so please do not put name or other identification on manuscript. Attach a 3×5 card with name, address, city, state, zip, and day and evening phone number. Manuscripts will not be returned." Entry fee: $5 for subscribers, $10 for nonsubscribers. (With $10 entry fee, you will receive subscription to *Ohio Writer*.) Deadline: June 30. Judges have included Larry Smith, editor of *Bottom Dog Press*; Richard Hague, author of *Milltown Natural*; Ron Antonucci, editor of *Ohio Writer*; Sheila Schwartz, author of *Imagine a Great White Light*. Winners will be announced in the September/October issue of *Ohio Writer*. (See listing for *Ohio Writer* in Publications Useful to Poets.)

BLUE NOSE POETRY POETS-OF-THE-YEAR COMPETITION, Blue Nose Poetry, 204 Horsenden Lane S, Perivale, Greenford, Middlesex UB6 7NU United Kingdom, phone 0208 997 2127, e-mail bluenose@athelstar.netkonect.co.uk, website www.netkonect.co.uk/~athelstar/, coordinator Helen Kenworthy, established in 1988, offers annual contest. £1,000 in prize money will be distributed at the discretion of the judges plus publication in an anthology. Poems may have been previously published in a magazine or journal but *not* in a collection or anthology. Send SASE for entry form and guidelines or obtain via website. Does not accept entry fees in foreign currencies. Send "checks made out to the sterling amount." Postmark deadline: April 25. Competition receives around 1,000 entries. Most recent winners were Roselle Angwin and Alexis Evans. Website includes program of events including competitions and workshops.

BLUESTEM PRESS AWARD, Bluestem Press, Emporia State University, English Dept., Box 4019, website www.emporia.edu/bluestem/index.htm, Emporia KS 66801-5087, phone (316)341-5216, fax (316)341-5547, established in 1989, editor/contest coordinator Philip Heldrich, offers annual award of $1,000 and publication for an original book-length collection of poems. Submissions must be unpublished and may be entered in other contests (with notification). Submit a typed ms of at least 48 pages on any subject in any form with a #10 SASE for notification. Send SASE for guidelines. Inquiries via e-mail OK. Entry fee: $18. Deadline: March 1. Competition receives 500-700 entries a year. Recent award winner was Mary Crockett Hill. Judge was Mark Cox. Winner will be announced in May. Copies of previous winning poems or books may be obtained by contacting the Bluestem Press at the above number. Enter early to avoid entering after the deadline. Also, looking at the different winners from past years would help. Manuscripts will *not* be accepted after the deadline and will not be returned. Website includes guidelines, announcements, previous winners and booklist.

THE BOARDMAN TASKER AWARD (Specialized: mountain literature), The Boardman Tasker Charitable Trust, 14 Pine Lodge, Dairyground Rd., Bramhall, Stockport, Cheshire SK7 2HS United

Kingdom, fax (0161)439-4624, established in 1983, secretary Dorothy Boardman, offers prize of £2,000 to "the author or authors of the best literary work, whether fiction, nonfiction, drama or poetry, the central theme of which is concerned with the mountain environment. Entries for consideration may have been written by authors of any nationality but the work must be published or distributed in the United Kingdom between November 1, 2000 and October 31, 2001. (If not published in the U.K., please indicate name of distributor.) The work must be written or have been translated into the English language." Submit ms in book format. "In a collection of essays or articles by a single author, the inclusion of some material previously published but now in book form for the first time will be acceptable." Submissions accepted from the publisher only. Four copies of entry must be submitted with application. Inquiries via fax OK. Deadline: August 1, 2001. Competition receives about 20 entries. Most recent winner was *The Totem Pole—and a Whole New Adventure* by Paul Pritchard, published by Constable.

N ⊘ BOLLINGEN PRIZE, Beinecke Rare Book and Manuscript Library, Yale University, P.O. Box 208240, New Haven CT 06520-8240, a biennial prize of $50,000 to an American poet for the best poetry collection published during the previous two years, or for a body of published poetry written over several years. **By nomination only.** "All books of poetry by American poets published during the two-year period are automatically considered." Judges change biennially. Prize awarded in February of odd-numbered years.

✦ ◎ BP NICHOL CHAPBOOK AWARD (Specialized: regional), 316 Dupont St., Toronto, Ontario M5R 1V9 Canada, phone (416)964-7919, fax (416)964-6941, established in 1985, $1,000 (Canadian) prize for the best poetry chapbook (10-48 pgs.) in English published in Canada in the preceding year. Submit 3 copies (not returnable) and a brief curriculum vitae of the author. Inquiries via fax OK. Deadline: March 31. Competition receives between 40-60 entries on average. Most recent winner was P. K. Page.

✔ ◎ CALIFORNIA BOOK AWARDS OF THE COMMONWEALTH CLUB OF CALIFORNIA (Specialized: regional), 595 Market St., San Francisco CA 94105, phone (415)597-6700, fax (415)597-6729, e-mail cwc@sirius.com, website www.commonwealthclub.org, established in 1931, senior director Jim Coplan, contact book awards jury. Annual awards "consisting of not more than two gold and eight silver medals" for books of "exceptional literary merit" in poetry, fiction and nonfiction (including work related to California and work for children), plus 2 "outstanding" categories. Submissions must be previously published. Submit at least 3 copies of each book entered with an official entry form. (Books may be submitted by author or publisher.) Open to books, published during the year prior to the contest, whose author "must have been a legal resident of California at the time the manuscript was submitted for publication." Send SASE for entry form and guidelines or obtain via website. Competition receives approximately 50 poetry entries a year. Most recent award winners were B.H. Fairchild and Chana Bloch. Website includes entry form, guidelines and list of previous winners.

✔ ◎ THE CENTER FOR BOOK ARTS' ANNUAL POETRY CHAPBOOK COMPETITION, 28 W. 27th St., 3rd Floor, New York NY 10001, phone (212)481-0295, e-mail info@centerforbookarts.org, established in 1995, award director Sharon Dolin, offers $500 cash prize, a $500 reading honorarium and publication of winning manuscript in a limited edition letterpress printed and handbound chapbook. Pays winners from other countries in US dollars. Submissions may be entered in other contests. Submit no more than 500 lines or 24 pgs. on any subject, in any form. Mss must be typed on one side of $8\frac{1}{2} \times 11$ paper. Send SASE for guidelines. Entry fee: $15/ms. Postmark deadline: December 1. Competition receives 500-1,000 entries/year. Most recent contest winner was Donald Pratt. Judges were Sharon Dolin and Gerald Stern. Winner will be contacted mid-April by telephone. Each contestant receives a letter announcing the winner. Copies of previous winning books may be obtained by sending $45. Reading fee is credited toward the purchase of the winning chapbook. "Center for Book Arts is a non-profit organization dedicated to the traditional crafts of bookmaking and contemporary interpretations of the book as an art object. Through the Center's Education, Exhibition and Workspace Programs we ensure that the ancient craft of the book remains a viable and vital part of our civilization."

N ◯ CNW/FFWA FLORIDA STATE WRITING COMPETITION, Florida Freelance Writers Association, P.O. Box A, North Stratford NH 03590-0167, phone (603)922-8338, e-mail contest@writers-editors.com, website www.writers-editors.com, established in 1978, award director Dana K. Cassell, offers annual awards for nonfiction, fiction, children's literature and poetry. Awards for each category are: 1st Place-$75 plus certificate, 2nd Place-$50 plus certificate, 3rd Place-$25 plus certificate, plus Honorable Mention certificates. Submissions must be unpublished. Submit any number of poems on any subject in traditional forms, free verse, religious or childrens. Send SASE for entry form and guidelines or visit website to print out entry form. Inquiries via e-mail OK. Entry fee: $3/poem (members), $5/poem (nonmembers). Deadline: March 15. Competition receives 350-400 entries a year. Competition is judged by writers, librarians and teachers. Winners will be announced on May 31 by mail and on website. "See list of previous winners and tips for poetry on website."

◎ COLORADO BOOK AWARDS (Specialized: regional), Colorado Center for The Book, 2123 Downing, Denver CO 80205, phone (303)839-8320, fax (303)839-8319, e-mail ccftb@compuserve.com, website www.aclin.org/~ccftb, executive director Christiane Citron, offers annual award of $500 plus promotion for books published in the year prior to the award. Submissions may be entered in other contests. Submit 6 copies of each book entered. Open to residents of Colorado. Send SASE for entry form and guidelines or obtain via e-mail or website. Entry fee: $30. Deadline: December 15. Competition receives 60 entries a year. Most recent award winner was Carolyn Evans Campbell. Winner will be announced at a ceremony/dinner in the spring. "We are a nonprofit organization affiliated with the Library of Congress Center for The Book. We promote the love of books, reading and literacy. We annually sponsor the Rocky Mountain Book Festival which attracts tens of thousands of people. It's free and includes hundreds of authors from throughout the country. We are located in the home of Thomas Hornsby Ferril, Colorado's late former poet laureate. This historic landmark home is used as a literary center and a tribute to Ferril's life and work."

INA COOLBRITH CIRCLE ANNUAL POETRY CONTEST (Specialized: regional), 2712 Oak Rd., #54, Walnut Creek CA 94596, treasurer Audrey Allison, has prizes of $10-50 in each of several categories for California residents and out-of-state members only. Three poems per contestant, but no more than 1 poem in any one category. Poems submitted in 2 copies, include name, address, phone number and member status on 1 copy only. Enclose a 3×5 card with name, address, phone number, category, title, first line of poem and status as member or nonmember. Members of the Ina Coolbrith Circle pay no fee; others pay $2 for each poem (limit 3). Send SASE for details. Deadline is August.

ABBIE M. COPPS POETRY COMPETITION; GARFIELD LAKE REVIEW, Dept. of Humanities, Olivet College, Olivet MI 49076, phone (616)749-7678, established in 1965, contest chairperson Laura A. Maas. Annual contest awarding $150 prize and publication in the *Garfield Lake Review*. $2/poem entry fee for unpublished poem up to 100 lines. Submit unsigned, typed poem, entrance fee, and name, address and phone number in a sealed envelope with the first line of the poem on the outside. Deadline: February 1.

COUNCIL FOR WISCONSIN WRITERS, INC. (Specialized: regional), Box 55322, Madison WI 53705. Offers annual awards of $500 or more for a book of poetry by a Wisconsin resident, published within the awards year (preceding the January 13 deadline). Competition receives 250 entries/year. Entry form and entry fee ($10 for members of the Council, $25 for others) required.

CREATIVE WRITING FELLOWSHIPS IN POETRY (Specialized: regional), Arizona Commission on the Arts, 417 W. Roosevelt St., Phoenix AZ 85003, phone (602)255-5882, fax (602)256-0282, e-mail general@arizonaarts.org, website http://az.arts.asu.edu/artscomm, literature director Jill Bernstein, offers biennial prizes of $5,000-7,500. Poetry fellowships awarded in odd-numbered years. Submissions can be previously published or unpublished, and can be entered in other contests. Submit 10 pgs. maximum on any subject. Open to Arizona residents over 18 years old. To request an application form, contact the Literature Director at (602)229-8226 or via e-mail. Entry deadline is in September of the year prior to the award. Website includes competition guidelines.

CRUMB ELBOW PUBLISHING POETRY CONTESTS (Specialized: themes), P.O. Box 294, Rhododendron OR 97049, phone (503)622-4798, established in 1996, award director Michael P. Jones, offers annual awards of publication and tearsheets from book, "for both established poets and beginners to introduce their work to new audiences by having their work published in a collection of poetry. We are always looking for complete manuscripts. Send SASE. Also need works for an anthology. Send at least six poems with a SASE. Would like to see b&w illustrations (pen/ink) accompany the poems." Crumb Elbow sponsors 7 contests all having different themes. They are the Scarecrow Poetry Harvest Contest (deadline August 1), Old Traditions & New Festivities: Winter Holiday Poetry Contest (deadline October 1), Natural Enchantment: Henry David Thoreau Poetry Contest (deadline February 1), Centuries of Journeys: History & Folk Traditions Poetry Contest (deadline April 1), Onward to the New Eden! Oregon Trail Poetry Contest (deadline January 1), Westward! Historic Trails Poetry Contest (deadline November 1), and Beyond the Shadows: Social Justice Poetry Contest (deadline June 1). Submissions may be entered in other contests. Submit at least 3 poems or verses. All submissions should be typed and accompanied by SASE. Send SASE for entry form and guidelines. Entry fees range from $2 for 3 poems to $15 for 22-30 poems. The award director says, "Have fun with your creativity. Explore with your words and don't be afraid of themes or to try something different." Crumb Elbow also publishes *The Final Edition* and *Wy'East Historical Journal*. Write for more information.

DANCING POETRY CONTEST, Artists Embassy International, 704 Brigham Ave., Santa Rosa CA 95404-5245, phone/fax (707)528-0912 (for fax, call first after 5 p.m.), e-mail jhcheung@aol.com, established in

1993, contest chair Judy Cheung. Annual contest awarding three Grand prizes of $100, five 1st Prizes of $50, 10 Second Prizes of $25, 25 3rd Prizes of certificates. The 3 Grand prize winning poems will be danced, choreographed, costumed, premiered and videotaped at the annual Dancing Poetry Festival at Palace of Legion of Honor, San Francisco. Natica Angilly's Poetic Dance Theater Company will perform the 3 Grand Prize-winning poems. Pays winners from other countries in international money orders with US value at the time of the transaction. Submissions must be unpublished or poet must own rights. Submit 2 copies of any number of poems, 40 lines maximum (each), with name, address, phone on one copy only. Foreign language poems must include English translations. Include SASE for winners list. Send SASE for entry form. Inquiries via e-mail OK. Entry fee: $5/poem or $10/3 poems. Does not accept entry fees in foreign currencies. Send international money order in US dollars. Deadline: June 15. Competition receives about 500-800 entries. Most recent contest winners include Alden Dean, Joseph Hunt and Mary Hope Whitehead. Judges for upcoming contest will be members of Artists Embassy International. Artist Embassy International has been a non-profit educational art organization since 1951, "Furthering intercultural understanding and peace through the universal language of the arts."

◖ ◓ **THE DOROTHY DANIELS ANNUAL HONORARY WRITING AWARD**, The National League of American Pen Women, Inc.—Simi Valley Branch, P.O. Box 1485, Simi Valley CA 93062, established in 1980, award director Diane Reichick. Annual award with 1st Prize of $100 in each category: poetry, fiction, nonfiction. Submissions must be unpublished. Submit any number of poems, 50 lines maximum each, on any subject in free verse or traditional. Manuscript must not include name and address. Include cover letter with name, address, phone, title and category of each entry; and line count for each. Poem must be titled and typed on 8½×11 white paper, single- or double-spaced spaced and one poem per page. Send SASE for guidelines. Entry fee: $3/poem. Deadline: July 30. Competition receives 1,500 entries a year. Recent award winner was Eileen Malone. Judges were 3 poets from their Pen Women branch. Send SASE for winners list; announced by mail on or before November 1. The National League of American Pen Women, a non-profit organization head-quartered in Washington, DC, was established in 1897 and has a membership of more than 7,000 professional writers, artists and composers. The Simi Valley Branch, of which noted novelists Dorothy Daniels and Elizabeth Forsythe Hailey are Honorary Members, was founded in 1977. "Request rules and follow them carefully—always include SASE."

◖ ◓ **EMILY DICKINSON AWARD IN POETRY**, Universities West Press, P.O. Box 22310, Flagstaff AZ 86002-2310, phone (520)213-9877, website www.popularpicks.com, contact Jane Armstrong, offers annual award of $1,000 and publication. "All finalists and semifinalists will be published in an anthology of poems by Universities West Press." Submissions must be unpublished. Submit up to 3 poems, total entry not to exceed 6 pgs., on any subject, in any form or style. Include short bio statement. Students and employees of Northern Arizona University may not enter. Send SASE for complete guidelines or visit website. Entry fee(s): $10. Make checks or money orders payable to Universities West Press. Postmark deadline: August 31. Judges include Andrew Hudgins, Barbara Anderson, Barbara Hamby and Angela Ball.

◖ **MILTON DORFMAN NATIONAL POETRY PRIZE**, % Rome Art & Community Center, 308 W. Bloomfield St., Rome NY 13440, phone (315)336-1040, fax (315)336-1090, e-mail racc@borg.com, contact Deborah H. O'Shea. Annual award for unpublished poetry. Prizes: $500, $200 and $100. Entry fee: $5/poem (American funds only; $10 returned check penalty); make checks payable to: Rome Art & Community Center. Contest opens July 1. Deadline: November 1. Include name, address and phone number on each entry. Poems are printed in Center's Newsletter. Competition receives about 1,000 entries a year. Judge to be announced. Winners notified by February 1, 2001. Send SASE for results. Website includes information on upcoming events at the Rome Art & Community Center.

Ⓝ ⊕ ◖ ◓ ◎ **DTCT OPEN POETRY AWARD (Specialized: themes)**, David Thomas Charitable Trust, Inverwick House, P.O. Box 6055, Nairn 1V12 5YB Scotland, phone (01667)453351, fax (01667)452365, established in 1990, award director David St. John Thomas, offers annual £1,000 prize split into 4 categories plus £250 for "Winner of Winners." Cash prize paid by sterling cheque/draft only. Submissions must be unpublished. Submit any number of poems any form; subject changes each year. Send SASE (or SAE and IRC) for entry form only. Inquiries via fax OK. Entry fee: £2.50 in sterling. Or IRCs to the value. Does not accept entry fees in foreign currencies. Deadline: January 15, 2001. Competition receives over 1,000 entries a year. Most recent award winner was Beryl Haigh. Judges are Alison Chesholm and Denis Corti. Winners will be announced March 15, 2001.

Ⓝ ⊕ ◖ **DUNCTON COTTAGE SHORT STORY AND POETRY COMPETITION**, Duncton Cottage Bird and Animal Sanctuary, 12 Hylton Terrace, Rookhope, Weardale, County Durham DL13 2BB United Kingdom, phone +44(0)1388 517005, fax +44(0)1388 517041, e-mail farplace@hotmail.com, established in 1999, offers annual cash prizes as a percentage of entry fees. Poems can be any subject and in any style. Please include SASE or SAE with IRC. Send SASE for entry form and guidelines. Inquiries via fax and e-mail OK. Entry fee: £5 for up to 2 poems, £1.50 each additional poem. Entry fees must be in UK sterling. Make checks payable to Duncton Cottage Bird & Animal Sanctuary. "For blind or partially sighted entrants, we will accept entries on cassette or on Word-compatible disk."

T.S. ELIOT PRIZE, The Poetry Book Society, Book House, 45 East Hill, London SW18 2Q2 United Kingdom, phone (020)8874 6361, fax (020)8877 1615, e-mail info@poetrybooks.co.uk, website www.poe trybooks.co.uk, established in 1993, award director Clare Brown, offers annual award for the best poetry collection published in the UK/Republic of Ireland each year. Prize is £5000 (donated by Mrs. Valerie Eliot) and "winning book is bound in Moroccan leather." Pays winners from other countries via publisher. Submissions must be previously published. Send SASE for entry form and guidelines. **Book/ms must be submitted by publisher** and have been published (or scheduled to be published) the year of the contest. Inquiries via fax and/or e-mail OK. Deadline: early August. Competition receives 100 entries a year. Most recent contest winner was Ted Hughes. Winners will be announced in January.

T.S. ELIOT PRIZE FOR POETRY; TRUMAN STATE UNIVERSITY PRESS, 100 E. Normal, Kirksville MO 63501-4221, phone (660)785-7199, fax (660)785-4480, e-mail tsup@truman.edu, website www2.t ruman.edu/tsup/, established in 1984, director, Paula Presley. Offers annual award of $2,000, publication, and 10 copies first prize. All entrants will receive a copy of the winning book. Submit 60-100 pages, include 2 title pages, 1 with name, address, phone and ms title; the other with only the title. Individual poems may have been previously published in periodicals or anthologies, but the collection must not have been published as a book. Include SASE if you wish acknowledgement of receipt of your ms. Mss will not be returned. Send SASE for guidelines. Inquiries via fax and e-mail OK. Entry fee: $25. Deadline: October 31. Competition receives 600 entries a year. Most recent contest winners were Harvey L. Hix, 2000; David Keplinger, 1999; Rhina Espaillat, 1998. Website includes T.S. Eliot Prize guidelines, past winners and judges, also books and order form. Truman State University Press also publishes critical books about poetry or poets, as well as hardcover and paperback originals and reprints.

EMERGING LESBIAN WRITERS AWARD (Specialized: lesbian), Astraea National Lesbian Action Foundation, 116 E. 16th St., New York NY 10003, phone (212)529-8021, fax (212)982-3321, e-mail grants@astra ea.org, website www.astraea.org, offers an annual award of $10,000 to "support the work of emerging lesbian writers." Submit 10-15 pgs. of collated poetry. "You may only submit in one category (fiction or poetry) per year." Open to US residents who have published "at least one piece of writing (in any genre) in a newspaper, magazine, journal or anthology; but not more than one book. Your work should include some lesbian content (broadly defined)." Submit 3 copies of ms with completed cover sheet and 1-paragraph bio. SASE required for entry form and guidelines. Inquiries via fax and e-mail OK. Entry fee: $5. Deadline: March 8. Most recent award winners include Elena Georgiou and Cheryl Whitehead. Applications are judged by a panel of lesbian writers who remain anonymous until after the competition. Applicants are notified by mail after June 30. Website includes general information and grant guidelines.

$ THE WILLIAM FAULKNER CREATIVE WRITING COMPETITION/POETRY CATEGORY, The Pirate's Alley Faulkner Society, Inc., 632 Pirate's Alley, New Orleans LA 70116, phone (504)586-1612, fax (504)522-9725, e-mail faulkhouse@aol.com, website www.wordsandmusic.org, established in 1993, award director Rosemary James, offers annual publication, The Double Dealer Redux Cash Prize $750; gold medal; trip to New Orleans from any Continental US city. "Foreign nationals are ineligible unless they reside in the U.S. Winners must be present at annual meeting to receive award." Submissions must be unpublished. Submit 1 poem on any subject in any English language form. US and Canadian citizens, US residents only. Send SASE or visit website for entry form and guidelines. Inquiries via fax and/or e-mail OK. Entry fee(s): $25 per entry. "We do not accept entries from other countries." Deadline: April 15. Competition receives 1,000 (for 5 categories) entries a year. Most recent contest winner was Andy Young (1998). Judge was James Nolan. Winners will be announced by letter and phone on September 1. "Competition is keen. Send your best work." Website includes competition guidelines, entry form, information about annual Writers' Conference and Words and Music.

FLORIDA INDIVIDUAL ARTIST FELLOWSHIPS (Specialized: regional), Florida Division of Cultural Affairs, Dept. of State, The Capitol, Tallahassee FL 32399-0250, phone (850)487-2980, fax (850)922-5259, e-mail vohlsson@mail.dos.state.fl.us, website www.dos.state.fl.us, arts administrator Valerie Ohlsson, annually offers an undetermined number of fellowships in the amount of $5,000 each. "The Individual Artist Fellowship Program is designed to recognize practicing professional creative artists residing in Florida through monetary fellowship awards. The program provides support for artists of exceptional talent and demonstrated ability to improve their artistic skills and enhance their careers. Fellowships may be awarded in the following discipline categories: dance, folk arts, interdisciplinary, literature, media arts, music, theatre and visual arts and crafts." Submissions can be previously published or unpublished. Submit 3-5 representative poems, single or double-spaced. "Reproductions of published work may not be submitted in published format. Open to Florida residents of at least 18 years of age who are not enrolled in undergraduate or graduate programs. Eight copies of the work sample must be included with 8 copies of the application form. Write for entry form and guidelines. Inquiries via fax and e-mail OK. Deadline: February 1 for 2000 (2001 not yet determined). Competitions receive 500 entries. Most recent winners were Richard Blanco, Michael Cleary, Michael Hettich and Allan Peterson. They also publish the *Dept. of State, Division of Cultural Affairs Informational Memo*, a newsletter of "information of concern to writers at state, regional, national and international levels." Website includes general information about the Florida Department of State, Division of Cultural Affairs.

⊘ **FOSTER CITY INTERNATIONAL WRITERS' CONTEST**, Foster City Arts & Culture Committee, 650 Shell Blvd., Foster City CA 94404. Yearly competition for previously unpublished work. $10 entry fee. Awards $250 each first prize for rhymed or blank verse and $125 for each honorable mention. Send SASE for instructions. Deadline: October 31. Awards announced January 15.

☑ ◯ ⊘ **GLIMMER TRAIN'S APRIL POETRY OPEN**, Glimmer Train Press, 710 SW Madison St., #504, Portland OR 97205, phone (503)221-0836, fax (503)221-0837, e-mail linda@glimmertrain.com, website www.glimmertrain.com, established in 1998, co-editor Linda Burmeister Davies, offers annual prizes. 1st Place: $500, publication in *Glimmer Train Stories* and 20 copies of that issue; 2nd Place: $250; 3rd Place: $100. Pays winners from other countries by check in US dollars. Submissions must be unpublished and may be entered in other contests. Submit up to 3 poems with no subject or form restrictions. "Name, address and phone number need to appear on all submitted poems." Entry fee(s): $10 for up to 3 poems (sent together). Does not accept entry fees in foreign currencies. Will accept Visa or Mastercard. Postmark deadline: April 30. Competition receives several hundred entries a year. Most recent contest winners were George Manner and Andrea King Kelly. Judged by the editors of Glimmer Train Press. Winners will be contacted by September 1. Glimmer Train Press publishes the quarterly *Glimmer Train Stories*, circulation 13,000. Website includes poetry presentation, top 25 winners of past contests, glimpses into issues of *Glimmer Train Stories* and *Writers Ask*.

☑ ◯ ⊘ **GLIMMER TRAIN'S OCTOBER POETRY OPEN**, Glimmer Train Press, 710 SW Madison St., #504, Portland OR 97205-2900, phone (503)221-0836, fax (503)221-0837, e-mail linda@glimmertrain.com, website www.glimmertrain.com, established in 1998, co-editor Linda Burmeister Davies, offers annual prizes. 1st Place: $500, publication in *Glimmer Train Stories* and 20 copies of that issue; 2nd Place: $250; 3rd Place: $100. Pays winners from other countries by check in US dollars. Submissions must be unpublished and may be entered in other contests. Submit up to 3 poems with no subject or form restrictions. "Name, address and phone number need to appear on all submitted poems." Entry fee(s): $10 for up to 3 poems (sent together). Does not accept entry fees in foreign currencies. Will accept Visa or MasterCard. Postmark deadline: October 31. Competition receives "several hundred" entries a year. Most recent contest winners were George Manner and Andrea King Kelly. Judged by the editors of Glimmer Train Press. Winners will be contacted by March 1. Glimmer Train Press publishes the quarterly *Glimmer Train Stories*, circulation 13,000. Website includes poetry presentation, top 25 winners of past contests, glimpses into issues of *Glimmer Train Stories* and *Writers Ask*.

☑ ⊘ **GRANDMOTHER EARTH NATIONAL AWARD**, Grandmother Earth Creations, P.O. Box 241986, Memphis TN 38124, phone (901)682-6936, fax (901)682-8274, e-mail grmearth@gateway.net, website www.grandmotherearth.com, established in 1994, award director Frances Cowden, offers annual award of $1,250 with varying distributions each year. $1,250 minimum in awards for poetry and prose $200 first, etc., plus publication in anthology; non-winning finalists considered if permission is given. Send published or unpublished work. Submissions may be entered in other contests. Submit at least 3 poems, any subject, in any form. Include SASE for winners list. Send 2 copies with name and address on one copy and on a 3×5 card. Send SASE or visit website for guidelines. Entry fee: $10/3 poems, $2 each additional poem. Entry fee includes a copy of the anthology. Deadline: July 15. Most recent award winner was Kitty Yeoger and others. Judge was Clouita Rice, Voices International and others. Winner will be announced on October 1 at the Mid-South Poetry Festival in Memphis. Copies of previous winning poems or books may be obtained by writing the above address.

☑ $⊘ **THE GREAT BLUE BEACON POETRY CONTEST**, The Great Blue Beacon, 1425 Patriot Dr., Melbourne FL 32940, phone (321)253-5869, e-mail ajircc@juno.com, established in 1997, award director A.J. Byers, offers prizes approximately 3 times/year, as announced, of 1st: $25; 2nd: $15; 3rd: $10. "Winning poem to be published in The Great Blue Beacon (amounts will be increased if sufficient entries are received.)" *The Great Blue Beacon* is a quarterly newsletter for all writers. Sample copy: $1 and 55¢ stamp or (IRC). Subscription: $10/year, students $8; outside the US $14. Submissions must be unpublished and may be entered in other contests. Submit up to 3 poems maximum on any subject in any form. "Submit two typed copies of each entry. On one copy, place your name, address and telephone number on the upper left-hand corner of the first page. No name or address on the second copy." Send SASE for guidelines. Inquiries via e-mail OK. Entry fee(s): $3/poem ($2 for subscribers to *The Great Blue Beacon*). Does not accept entry fees in foreign currencies. Accepts entry fees from other countries in US dollars. Competition receives 200-300 entries a year. Most recent contest winner was Anne White (1999). Winner(s) will be announced approximately 2 months after deadline date. "Contestants must send SASE or e-mail address with entry to receive notification of results. Submit your best work—no more than 24 lines/poem."

☑ ⊘ **GREAT LAKES COLLEGES ASSOCIATION NEW WRITERS AWARD**, GLCA, English Department, Denison University, Granville OH 43023, phone (740)587-5740, fax (740)587-5680, director Linda Krumholz, offers annual award to "the best first book of poetry and the best first book of fiction among those **submitted by publishers**. The winning authors tour several of the Great Lakes Colleges reading, lecturing, visiting classes, doing workshops, and publicizing their books. Each writer receives an honorarium of at least $300 from each college visited, as well as travel expenses, hotel accommodations and hospitality. Usually, one winner (fiction) tours in the fall, and the other winner (poetry) tours in the spring, following the competition."

Submissions must be previously published. Submit 4 copies of galleys or the printed book plus a statement stating author's agreement to commit to the college tour. Send SASE for guidelines. Inquiries via fax OK. Deadline: February 28. Competition receives about 60 entries for poetry, 45 for fiction a year. Most recent award winners were *A Gram of Mars* (fiction) by Becky Hagenston (published by Sarabande Books) and *Shells* by Craig Arnold (published by Yale University Press). Website includes director information, and our dates for current winners.

☐ ◎ **GREEN RIVER WRITERS' CONTESTS (Specialized: themes, forms)**, 1043 Thornfield Lane, Cincinnati OH 45224, established in 1991, contact contest chairman, offers 7 contests for poetry on various themes and in various forms. Entry fees range from $5-8 for nonmembers. Does not accept entry fees in foreign currencies. Send check or money order. Prizes range from $5-300. Pays winners from other countries by check. Send SASE for rules. Deadline: October 31. Competition receives 600 entries. Most recent contest winners include Sandra Lake Lassen and Donna Jean Tennis.

☑ ◎ **GROLIER POETRY PRIZE; ELLEN LA FORGE MEMORIAL POETRY FOUNDATION, INC.**, 6 Plympton St., Cambridge MA 02138, phone (617)547-4648, website www.grolierpoetrybookshop@com puserve.com, established in 1974, award director Louisa Solano. Contact Grolier Poetry Bookshop. The Grolier Poetry Prize is open to all poets who have not published either a vanity, small press, trade or chapbook of poetry. Two poets receive an honorarium of $200 each. Pays winners from other countries by money order. Up to 4 poems by each winner and 1-2 by each of 4 runners-up are chosen for publication in the *Grolier Poetry Prize Annual*. Opens January 15 of each year; deadline May 1. Submissions must be unpublished and may not be simultaneously submitted. Submit up to 5 poems, not more than 10 double-spaced pages. Submit one ms in duplicate, without name of poet. On a separate sheet give name, address, phone number and titles of poems. Only 1 submission/contestant; mss are not returned. $6 entry fee includes copy of *Annual*, checks payable to the Ellen La Forge Memorial Poetry Foundation, Inc. Does not accept entry fees in foreign currencies. Send money order. Enclose self-addressed stamped postcard if acknowledgement of receipt is required. Winners and runners-up will be selected and informed in early June. For update of rules, send SASE to Ellen La Forge Memorial Poetry Foundation before submitting mss. Competition receives approximately 500 entries. Most recent award winners include Maggie Dietz, Natasha Trethewey and Babo Kamel. The Ellen La Forge Memorial Poetry Foundation sponsors an annual intercollegiate poetry reading and a reading series, generally 10/semester, held on the grounds of Harvard University. Poets who have new collections of poetry available are eligible. Honoraria varies. Such poets as Philip Levine, Susan Kinsolvink, Donald Hall and Molly McQuade have given readings under their auspices. The small foundation depends upon private gifts and support for its activities.

◙ **GUGGENHEIM FELLOWSHIPS**, John Simon Guggenheim Memorial Foundation, 90 Park Ave., New York NY 10016, phone (212)687-4470, fax (212)697-3248, e-mail fellowships@gf.org, website www.gf.org. Guggenheims are awarded each year to persons who have already demonstrated exceptional capacity for productive scholarship or exceptional creative ability in the arts. The amounts of the grants vary. The average grant in 2000 was 34,800. Most recent award winners for poetry were David Baker, Rigoberto Gonzalez, Linda Gregerson, Brooks Haxton, Tony Hoagland, Eric Pankey and Bruce Smith (2000). In 2000, there were 182 winners awarded fellowships in the US. Application deadline: October 1.

◙ **HACKNEY LITERARY AWARDS; BIRMINGHAM-SOUTHERN COLLEGE WRITER'S CONFERENCE**, Birmingham-Southern College, Box 549003, Birmingham AL 35254, phone (205)226-4921, fax (205)226-3072, e-mail dcwilson@bsc.edu, website www.bsc.edu. This competition, sponsored by the Cecil Hackney family since 1969, offers $10,000 in prizes for novels, poetry and short stories as part of the annual Birmingham-Southern Writer's Conference. Send SASE for Hackney guidelines. Novels postmarked by September 30. Poems and short stories must be postmarked by December 30. Writing Today Writer's Conference winners are announced and prizes awarded, March 16-17, 2001.

◎ **J.C. AND RUTH HALLS; THE DIANE MIDDLEBROOK; AND ANASTASIA C. HOFFMANN FELLOWSHIPS IN POETRY (Specialized: MFA or equivalent degree in creative writing)**, Wisconsin Institute for Creative Writing, English Dept., 600 North Park St., Madison WI 53706, website polyglot.lss.wisc. edu/english, established in 1986, director Jesse Lee Kercheval. Annual fellowships will pay $23,000 for one academic year. Applicants will teach one creative writing class per semester at U. of Wisconsin and give a public reading at the end of their stay. Submissions may be entered in other contests. Submit 10 poems maximum on any subject in any form. Applicants must have an MFA or equivalent degree in creative writing. Applicants cannot have published a book (chapbooks will not disqualify an applicant). Send SASE for guidelines. Deadline: last day of February. Competitions receive 200 entries a year. Most recent winners were Rich Hilles and Amy Quan Barry. Judges were faculty of creative writing program. Results will be sent to applicants by May 1. Winners announced in *Poets & Writers* and *AWP Chronicle*. "The Halls fellowships are administered by the Program in Creative Writing at the University of Wisconsin-Madison. Funding is provided by the Jay C. and Ruth Halls Writing Fund and the Carl Djerassi and Diane Middlebrook Fund through the University of Wisconsin Foundation."

⊕ ✓ ◎ **FELICIA HEMANS PRIZE FOR LYRICAL POETRY (Specialized: membership, students)**, The University of Liverpool, P.O. Box 147, Liverpool L69 38X England, phone (0151)794 2458, fax (0151)794 3765, e-mail wilderc@liv.ac.uk, established in 1899, contact registrar, University of Liverpool, offers annual award of £30. Submissions may be entered in other contests. Submit 1 poem. Open to past or present members and students of the University of Liverpool. Send SASE for guidelines only. Inquiries via fax and e-mail OK. Deadline: May 1. Competition receives 12-15 entries. Judges were "the two professors of English Literature in the University." The winner and all other competitors will be notified by mail in June.

◑ **THE HODDER FELLOWSHIP**, The Council of the Humanities, 122 E. Pyne, Princeton University, Princeton NJ 08544, phone (609)258-4713, e-mail humcounc@princeton.edu, website www.princeton.edu/~hum counc, is awarded to a humanist in the early stages of a career. The recipient has usually written one book and is working on a second. Preference is given to applicants outside academia. "The Fellowship is designed specifically to identify and nurture extraordinary potential rather than to honor distinguished achievement." **Candidates for the Ph.D. are not eligible.** The Hodder Fellow spends an academic year in residence at Princeton working on an independent project in the humanities. Stipend is approximately $45,600. Submit a résumé, sample of previous work (10 pgs. maximum, not returnable), a project proposal of 2 to 3 pgs., and SASE. Guidelines available on website. The announcement of the Hodder Fellow is made in February by the President of Princeton University. Postmark deadline: November 1.

✓ ◑ **HENRY HOYNS FELLOWSHIPS**, Creative Writing Program, 219 Bryan Hall, P.O. Box 400121, University of Virginia, Charlottesville VA 22904-4121, phone (804)924-6675, fax (804)924-1478, e-mail lrs9e@v irginia.edu, website www.engl.virginia.edu/cwp, are fellowships in poetry and fiction of varying amounts for candidates for the M.F.A. in creative writing. Sample poems/prose required with application. Inquiries via e-mail OK. Deadline: January 1. Competition receives 300-400 entries. Website includes general information, applications and faculty biographies.

◎ **INDIVIDUAL ARTIST GRANTS (Specialized: regional)**, Cultural Arts Council of Houston/Harris County, 3201 Allen Parkway, Houston TX 77019, phone (713)527-9330, fax (713)630-5210, website www.cachh. org. Offers awards to Houston, Harris County visual artists, writers, choreographers and composers selected through an annual competition. The program offers awards in three categories: Artist Project, General Artist Fellowship and Emerging Artist Fellowships. Fellowship awards for writers are awarded every other year (2000), but encouraged to apply for project grants on off-years. Write for deadline date, application forms and guidelines. All information available on the website.

Ⓝ ⊕ ◯ **IRISH FAMINE COMMEMORATIVE LITERARY PRIZE**, Australian-Irish Heritage Association, P.O. Box 1583, Subiaco, West Australia 6904 Australia, phone (6108)09 381 8306, fax (6108)09 382 1283, e-mail aiha@ireland.com, website www.cyanus.uwa.edu.an/~koslis, established in 1997, award director Joe O'Sullivan, offers annual awards in 3 categories: short fiction, essay, poetry. Winner in each category will receive AUS $250. Best entry overall will receive additional AUS $250. Submissions must be unpublished. Submit unlimited number of poems on the theme "Separation" any form—100 lines maximum. The theme does not necessarily have to relate to the Irish Famine. Send SASE (or SAE and IRC) for complete guidelines or visit website. Inquiries via fax and e-mail OK. Entry fee(s): AUS $5/entry, will be donated to Community Aid Abroad/OXFAM to relieve world hunger. Accepts entry fees in foreign currencies. Deadline: December 31, 2000. Competition receives 150-200 entries a year. Judge was Professor (Sister) Veronica Brady. Winner(s) will be announced in March 2001. Copies of previous winning poems are published on the Internet. "AIHA conserves and publishes our Irish heritage. Contest commemorates famine in a practical way by donating entry fees in their entirety to OXFAM for relief of world hunger. Enter and help a good cause."

✓ ◎ **THE JAPAN FOUNDATION ARTIST FELLOWSHIP PROGRAM (Specialized: US residents with Japanese affiliations)**, The Japan Foundation New York Office, 152 W. 57th St., 39th Floor, New York NY 10019, phone (212)489-0299, fax (212)489-0409, e-mail yuika_goto@jfny.org, website www.jfny.org, director general Mr. Masaya Usuda, program assistant Yuika Goto, offers annual fellowships of 2-6 months in Japan (during the Japanese fiscal year of April 1 through March 31) for "accredited professional writers, musicians, painters, sculptors, stage artists, movie directors, etc." Submissions may be entered in other contests. Open to citizens or permanent residents of the US. "Affiliation with a Japanese artist or institution is required. Three letters of reference, including one from the Japanese affiliate must accompany all applications." Inquiries via fax and e-mail OK. Deadline: December 1. Competition receives 20-30 entries a year. Website includes program descriptions and award announcements.

$ ◎ **JAPANESE LITERARY TRANSLATION PRIZE (Specialized: translation of Japanese classical or modern literature into English)**, Donald Keene Center of Japanese Culture, Columbia University, 507 Kent Hall, New York NY 10027, phone (212)854-5036, fax (212)854-4019, website: www.columbia.edu/ cu/ealac/dkc, established in 1981, offers annual $2,500 prize for translation of a work of Japanese classical literature into English and a $2,500 prize for translation of a work of Japanese modern literature into English. "Special attention is given to new or unpublished translators and citizens of all nationalities are eligible."

Submissions may be entered in other contests. Submit 6 copies of book-length ms or published book. Send SASE for entry form and guidelines. Inquiries via fax OK. Deadline: March 1. Competition receives 20-25 entries a year. Most recent award winners were Jay Rubin (modern Japanese literature) and Hiroaki Sato (classical Japanese literature). Judge(s) were Donald Keene, Hortense Calisher, Howard Hibbett, Bonnie Crown and Robert Gottlieb. Website includes mission and history, calendar of events, scholarly activities, translation prizes and corporate sponsors.

JOHANN-HEINRICH-VOSS PRIZE FOR TRANSLATION, German Academy for Language and Literature, Alexandraweg 23, 64287 Darmstadt, Germany, phone (06151)40920, fax (06151)409299, e-mail deutsche.akademie@t-online.de, president Prof. Dr. Christian Meier, is an annual award of DM 20,000 for outstanding lifetime achievement for translating into German, **by nomination only**.

KEATS SHELLEY MILLENNIUM PRIZE, The Keats-Shelley Memorial Association, The Folio Society, 44 Eagle St., London WC1R 4FS England, awards £3,000 in prizes and publication to an essay on any aspect of Keats' or Shelley's work or life and/or a poem on the "Romantic theme of Time." Submissions must be unpublished, original work in English. May enter both categories but only once. Send SASE (or SAE and IRC) for complete guidelines. Entry fee(s): £5 sterling for single entry, £3 for second entry in other category. Entry fees from other countries should pay via international money order made payable to the Keats-Shelley Memorial Association or with sterling bank note. Deadline: April 30. Prize winners will be notified in early June. A presentation ceremony will be held in London in early July. "All first-time serious entrants who are not already friends of the KSMA will become Honourary Friends for one year receiving the annual Keats-Shelley Review, free newsletters, invitations to events, etc."

BARBARA MANDIGO KELLY PEACE POETRY CONTEST, Nuclear Age Peace Foundation, PMB 121, 1187 Coast Village Rd. #1, Santa Barbara CA 93108-2794, phone (805)965-3443, fax (805)568-0466, e-mail wagingpeace@napf.org, website www.wagingpeace.org, established in 1996, offers an annual series of awards "to encourage poets to explore and illuminate positive visions of peace and the human spirit." Awards $500 to adult contestants, $250 to youth (13 to 18), $250 to youth (12 and under) and honorable mentions in each category. Pays winners from other countries in US currency. Submissions must be unpublished and may be entered in other contests. Submit up to 3 poems on "positive visions of peace and the human spirit" in any form. Send 2 copies; maximum of 40 lines per poem. Put name, address, phone number and age in upper right hand corner of one copy. Send SASE for guidelines or download from website. Entry fee: $5/1 poem, $10/2-3 poems. Free for youth. Does not accept entry fees in foreign currencies but will accept US money order. Postmark deadline: July 1. Competition receives over 500 entries. Recent contest winner was Phyllis Cobb. Judged by a committee of poets. Winners will be announced through press release and mail notification by October. The Foundation reserves the right to publish the winning poems. "Nuclear Age Peace Foundation is a nonprofit peace and international security-related organization, focusing on the abolition of nuclear weapons, the strengthening of international law, the empowerment of youth, and the responsible and sustainable use of technology." To poets thinking about entering their contest they say, "Be creative and positive."

THE STEPHEN LEACOCK MEDAL FOR HUMOUR (Specialized: humor, regional), Stephen Leacock Associates, P.O. Box 854, Orillia, Ontario L3V 3P4 Canada, fax (705)325-9955, contact Marilyn Rumball (corresponding secretary), award chairman Judith Rapson, for a book of humor in prose, verse, drama or any book form—by a Canadian citizen. "Book must have been published in the current year and no part of it may have been previously published in book form." Submit 10 copies of book, 8 × 10 b&w photo, bio and $25 entry fee. Prize: Silver Leacock Medal for Humour and Laurentian Bank of Canada cash award of $5,000. Deadline: December 31. Competition receives 40-50 entries. The 1998 winner was *Barney's Version* by Mordecai Richler. The committee also publishes *The Newspacket* 3 times/year.

THE LEAGUE OF MINNESOTA POETS CONTEST, 432 Tyrol Dr., Brainerd MN 56401-2920, contact Joan Wiesner. Offers 19 different contests in a variety of categories and 3 prizes from $10-125 for poems up to 55 line limit. Nationally known judges. Nonmember fees: $1/poem per category; $2/poem, limit 6/Grand Prize category. Members fee: $3/18 categories; $1/poem, limit 6/Grand Prize category. Deadline: July 31. Winners are not published.

A LOVE AFFAIR LITERARY CONTEST, ABAC Arts Station, 2802 Moore Hwy., ABAC 45, Tifton GA 31794-2601, phone (912)386-3558, fax (912)391-2526, established in 1989, award director Liz Carson Reed, offers annual awards of $500 total. "Entries not accepted from outside USA." Submissions must be unpublished and may be entered in other contests. Submit any number of poems on any subject, in any form, no entry longer than 2 pgs., single-spaced. "No names on submissions. Identify with social security number. Include name, address, phone number and social security number on cover sheet." Send SASE for guidelines. Inquiries via fax and/or e-mail OK. Entry fee(s): $7 for up to 2 poems. Deadline: February 14, 2001. Competition receives 50 entries a year. The judge for upcoming awards will be Liz Carson Reed. "One 1st, 2nd and 3rd place winner announced during A Love Affair Festival events; first week in May." "Affinity Health Group and ABAC Arts Station sponsor numerous artistic activities and artists in a 5-county area. This is a literary contest. High quality poetry of any genre is desired."

MARIN ARTS COUNCIL INDIVIDUAL ARTIST GRANTS (Specialized: regional), 251 N. San Pedro Rd., San Rafael CA 94903, phone (415)499-8350, fax (415)499-8537, e-mail alison@marinarts.org, website www.marinarts.org, established in 1987, grants coordinator Alison DeJung, offers biennial grants starting at $2,000 to residents of Marin County, CA only. Submissions must have been completed within last 3 years. Submit 10 pgs. on any subject in any form. Open to Marin County residents only—"must have lived in Marin County for one year prior to application, be 18 or over and not in an arts degree program." Send SASE for entry form and guidelines. Inquiries via fax and/or e-mail OK. Winners will be announced June of each year. "The Marin Arts Council offers grants to individual artists (living in Marin County) in 13 different categories. Deadlines and categories alternate each year. Call for more information." Competition receives 50-100 entries. Website includes general info about the Marin Arts Council and the grants program. "Guidelines and application not online yet but will be soon."

MATURE WOMEN'S GRANTS (Specialized: women), National League of American Pen Women, 1300 17th St., Washington DC 20036-1973, phone (978)443-2165 established in 1976, award director Mary Jane Hillery, offers biennial (even-numbered years) award of $1,000 each for the categories of arts, letters and music for women aged 35 and older. Must be US citizen. Submit 3 poems. Previously published submissions OK. Include SASE for information or winners list. Open to women over the age of 35 during the calendar year of the award. "Women who enter may never have been a member of the Pen women." Include letter stating age, creative purpose and how you learned of the grant. Send SASE for guidelines during odd-numbered years. Entry fee: $8. Deadline: January 1 of the even-numbered year. Competition receives 160 entries in art, 140 in letters and 7-8 in music a year. Winner will be announced March 15.

MELBOURNE POETS UNION ANNUAL POETRY COMPETITION (Specialized: regional), Melbourne Poets Union, P.O. Box 7589, Melbourne, Victoria 3004 Australia, established in 1995, offers annual prize of $1,000. Pays winners from other countries "with a cheque in foreign currency, after negotiation with winner." Submissions must be unpublished. Submit unlimited number of poems on any subject in any form. "Open to Australian residents living in Australia or overseas." Send SASE (or SAE and IRC) for entry form and guidelines. Entry fee(s): AUS $4/poem. Accepts entry fees in foreign currencies. Deadline: October 27. Competition receives over 500 entries a year. Judge was Jennifer Strauss. Winner(s) will be announced on the last Friday of November. "The $1,000 prize money comes directly from entry money, the rest going to paying the judge and costs of running the competition."

MID-LIST PRESS FIRST SERIES AWARD FOR POETRY, Mid-List Press, 4324 12th Ave. S., Minneapolis MN 55407-3218, phone (612)822-3733, fax (612)823-8387, e-mail guide@midlist.org, website www.midlist.org, established in 1990, senior editor Lane Stiles. "The First Series Award for Poetry is an annual contest we sponsor for poets who have never published a book of poetry. The award includes publication and a $500 advance against royalties." Individual poems within the book ms can be previously published and can be entered in other contests. Submit at least 60 single-spaced pages. "Note: We do not return manuscripts. Other than length we have no restrictions, but poets are encouraged to read previous award winners we have published." Recent award winners include Adam Sol, Jennifer O'Grady, Donald Morrill, Dina Ben-Lev, Neva Hacker, Jeff Worley, Neil Shepard, Douglas Gray, Stephen Behrendt, J.E. Sorrell and Mary Logue. Submissions are circulated to an editorial board. Send #10 SASE for guidelines or print from website. "Guidelines for the 2001 award will be available after July 1, 2000." Entry fee: $20. Accepts submissions October 1 through February 1. Competition receives about 300 entries/year. "The First Series Award contest is highly competitive. We are looking for poets who have produced a significant body of work but have never published a book-length collection. (A chapbook is not considered a 'book' of poetry.)" No fax or e-mail inquiries.

VASSAR MILLER PRIZE IN POETRY, Univeristy of Missouri, English Dept., Tate 103, Columbia MO 65211, phone (573)882-6421, fax (573)882-5785, established in 1991, award director Scott Cairns, offers annual award of $1,000 and publication by the University of North Texas Press. Submit 50-80 pgs., include an additional title page without the name of the poet and #10 SASE for winners list. Send SASE for guidelines.

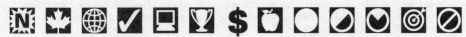

FOR EXPLANATIONS OF THESE SYMBOLS, SEE THE INSIDE FRONT AND BACK COVERS OF THIS BOOK.

Entry fee: $20. Make checks payable to UNT Press. Entries are read September 1 through November 30 only. Most recent award winner was Constance Merritt. Judge was Eleanor Wilner. Winner will be announced by March 15.

✔ ◎ **MILTON CENTER POETRY FELLOWSHIP (Specialized: religious)**, The Milton Center, 3100 McCormick Ave., Wichita KS 67213-2097, phone (316)942-4291 ext. 326, fax (316)942-4483, e-mail miltonc@n ewmanu.edu, established in 1986, award director Essie Sappenfield, offers annual residential fellowship of $1,225/ month stipend to complete first book-length work while in residence in Wichita, Kansas (September through May). Submissions must be unpublished. Submit 10 poems on any subject or in any form. Open to poets of "Christian commitment." Send SASE for entry form and guidelines. Inquiries via fax and e-mail OK. Entry fee: $15. Does not accept entry fees in foreign currencies. Send check or money order. Deadline: March 1. Competition receives 200 entries. Most recent award winners were Lisa Goett and John Jenkinson. Winner will be announced in mid April. Notification is by letter, phone or e-mail. "The Milton Center promotes excellence in Christian writing. Write well and have mature work habits. Don't worry about doctrinal matters, counting Christian symbols, etc. What you believe will automatically show up in your writing."

Ⓝ ◯ ◑ **MISSISSIPPI VALLEY POETRY CONTEST**, sponsored by North American Literary Esca- drille, P.O. Box 3188, Rock Island IL 61204, phone (319)359-1057, president Max J. Molleston, annually offers prizes of approximately $1,700 for unpublished poems in categories for students (elementary, junior and senior high), adults, Mississippi Valley, senior citizens, jazz, religious, humorous, rhyming, haiku, ethnic and history. Fee: $5 for up to 5 poems; 50 lines/poem limit. Fee for children: $3 for up to 5 poems. Does not accept entry fees in foreign currencies. Send check or US dollars. Professional readers read winning poems before a reception at an award evening in mid-October. Deadline: September 1. Competition receives 1,000-2,000 entries.

◎ **MONEY FOR WOMEN (Specialized: women/feminism)**, Barbara Deming Memorial Fund, Inc., P.O. Box 630125, Bronx NY 10463, administrator Susan Pliner, biannually awards small grants of up to $1,000 to feminists in the arts "whose work addresses women's concerns and/or speaks for peace and justice from a feminist perspective." Pays winners from other countries with a US check. Send SASE for application form. Applicants must be citizens of US or Canada. Application fee: $10. Does not accept entry fees in foreign currencies. Must send check drawn on US bank or cash (US). Deadlines: December 31 and June 30. Competition receives 350 entries a year. Most recent award winners were Christina Hutchins, Honoreé E. Jeffers and Natasha Trewethey. Winners announced in May and October. Also offers the Gertrude Stein Award for outstanding work by a lesbian, and the "Fannie Lou Hamer Award" for work which combats racism and celebrates women of color.

◎ **MONTALVO BIENNIAL POETRY COMPETITION (Specialized: regional)**, Villa Montalvo, P.O. Box 158, Saratoga CA 95071-0158, phone (408)961-5818, fax (408)961-5850, e-mail kfunk@villamontalvo.org (artist residencies only), website www.villamontalvo.org, director artist residency program Kathryn Funk, offers biennial awards (in odd-numbered years only) "to recognize the talent and efforts of those engaged in the poetic arts, both established and emerging." 1st Prize: $1,000 plus an artist residency at Villa Montalvo, California's historic estate for the arts, 2nd Prize: $500, 3rd Prize: $300, 8 Honorable Mentions: $25 each. Residency provides a furnished, self-sufficient apartment for one month. Submissions must be unpublished. "Open to all forms of poetry in English from residents of California, Nevada, Oregon and Washington." Send SASE for guidelines only. Entry fee: $10 for 3 poems. Postmark deadline: October 1, 2001. Competition receives about 250 entries. Most recent winners include Parthenia M. Hicks, Dawn McGuire, M.D. and Edward Smallfield. Judge for 1999 was Denise Duhamel. The judge for 2001 has not yet been chosen. Winners will be notified by December 15, 1999, and will be honored in an awards ceremony and reading at Villa Montalvo. Website includes information pertaining to all activities at Montalvo, including artist residencies, the gallery, outreach programs and performing arts series information.

◎ **MONTANA ARTS; MARY BRENNEN CLAPP MEMORIAL POETRY CONTEST (Specialized: regional)**, P.O. Box 1872, Bozeman MT 59771, biannual contest. Open to Montana poets or former Montana poets only, for 3 unpublished poems up to 100 lines total. Awards prizes of $50, $40, $30 and $20. Submit 3 poems and cover letter. Send SASE for guidelines. Deadline March in even-numbered years.

Ⓝ ◑ **JENNY MCKEAN MOORE WRITER IN WASHINGTON**, Dept. of English, George Washington University, Washington DC 20052, phone (202)994-6515, fax (202)994-7915, e-mail dmca@gwu.edu, website www.gwu.edu/~english, provides for a visiting lecturer in creative writing about $48,000 for 2 semesters. Apply by November 15 with résumé and writing sample of 25 pgs. or less. Awarded to poets and fiction writers in alternating years. Website includes some initial description of program, course description, readings schedule, other info.

◑ **SAMUEL FRENCH MORSE POETRY PRIZE**, English Dept., 406 Holmes, Northeastern University, Boston MA 02115, e-mail grotella@lynx.neu.edu, website www.casdu.neu.edu/~english/morse.htm, editor Prof. Guy Rotella, for book publication (ms 50-70 pgs.) by Northeastern University Press and an award of $1,000.

Inquiries via e-mail OK. Entry fee: $15. Deadline of August 1 for inquiries, September 15 for single copy of ms. Ms will not be returned. Open to US poets who have published no more than 1 book of poetry. Competition receives approximately 400 entries a year. Most recent award winners include Michelle Boisseau, Charles Webb and Jeffrey Greene. Website includes contest rules.

NASHVILLE NEWSLETTER POETRY CONTEST, P.O. Box 60535, Nashville TN 37206-0535, editor/publisher Roger Dale Miller. Founded 1977. Reporting time 6-10 weeks. Published quarterly. Sample copy: $3. Awards prizes of $50, $25 and $10 plus possible publication in newsletter, and at least 50 Certificates of Merit. Pays winners from other countries with check in US funds. Any style or subject up to 40 lines. One unpublished poem to a page with name and address in upper left corner. Send large #10 SASE for more information and/or extra entry forms for future contests. Entry fee: $5 for up to 3 poems. Must be sent all at once. Does not accept entry fees in foreign currencies but will accept check/money order in US funds. "All other nonwinning poems will be considered for possible publication in future issues." Competition receives over 700 entries a year. Recent contest winners include Alfred D. Hawkins, Dan Goldstein and James Lee Miller.

NATIONAL BOOK AWARD, National Book Foundation, 260 Fifth Ave., Room 904, New York NY 10001, phone (212)685-0261, e-mail natbkfdn@mindspring.com, website www.nationalbook.org, award directors Neil Baldwin and Meg Kearney, offers annual grand prize of $10,000 plus 4 finalist awards of $1,000. Submissions must be previously published and **must be entered by the publisher**. Send SASE for entry form and guidelines. Entry fee: $100/title. Deadline: July 10.

NATIONAL POETRY SERIES ANNUAL OPEN COMPETITION, P.O. Box G, Hopewell NJ 08525, established in 1978, between January 1 and February 15 considers book-length mss (approximately 48-64 pgs.). Entry fee: $25. Mss will not be returned. The 5 winners receive $1,000 each and are published by participating small press, university press and trade publishers. Send SASE for complete submissions procedures. Competition receives over 1,500 entries a year. Most recent winners were Tenaya Darlington, Eugene Gloria, Corey Marks, Dionisio Martinez and Standard Schaefer (1999).

NATIONAL WRITERS UNION ANNUAL NATIONAL POETRY COMPETITION, P.O. Box 2409, Aptos CA 95001, e-mail joelmobius@aol.com, website www.mbay.net/~NWU, chair Don Monkerud, contact poetry contest coordinator. See National Writers Union listing under Organizations. The 2000 competition is sponsored by Santa Cruz/Monterey Local 7 of the NWU. Entry fee: $4/poem. Prizes: $500, $300, $200, plus publication in union newsletter. Possible additional 1st place publication in *Poetry Flash*. For rules, see website. Send SASE for rules beginning in April. Deadline: December 1. Competition receives 1,000 entries a year. Judge for 2000 was Adrienne Rich. Website includes information about local and national events, and links for writers.

NEUSTADT INTERNATIONAL PRIZE FOR LITERATURE; WORLD LITERATURE TODAY, University of Oklahoma, 110 Monnet Hall, Norman OK 73019-4033, phone (405)325-4531, fax (405)325-7495, website www.ou.edu/worldlit/, editor Dr. William Riggan. Award of $40,000 given every other year in recognition of life achievement or to a writer whose work is still in progress; **nominations from an international jury only**. Most recent award winner was Nuruddin Farah (Somalia) 1998. Website includes general information on *World Literature Today* and the Neustadt Prize.

NEW MILLENNIUM AWARD FOR POETRY, New Millennium Writings, P.O. Box 2463, Knoxville TN 37901, e-mail donwill@aol.com, website www.mach2.com, contact editor Don Williams, offers 2 annual awards of $1,000 each. Pays winners from other countries by money order. Submissions must be previously unpublished but may be entered in other contests. Submit up to 3 poems, 5 pages maximum. No restrictions on style or content. Include name, address, phone number and a #10 SASE for notification. Manuscripts are not returned. Send SASE for guidelines. Entry fee: $15. Make checks payable to New Millennium Writing. Does not accept entry fees in foreign currencies. Send money orders drawn on US banks. Deadlines: June 11 and November 15. "Two winners and selected finalists will be published." Most recent award winners include Claire Bateman and Madeline Marcotte. Competition receives 2,000 entries a year. Website includes publication of winners, table of contents, photos of contributors, contest guidelines, cover graphics, how to order past issues, subscription information and much more.

NEW YORK FOUNDATION FOR THE ARTS (Specialized: regional), 155 Avenue of the Americas, 14th Floor, New York NY 10013, phone (212)366-6900, ext. 365, website www.nyfa.org, established in 1971, senior program officer Jennifer Feil, offers fellowships of $7,000 every other year for poets who are at least 18 and have resided in New York State for 2 years prior to application. No students are eligible for fellowships. Submit up to 10 pages of poetry (at least 2 poems), 3 copies of a 1-page résumé, and an application form. Call for application form in June or request via fax and/or e-mail. Postmark deadline is October 4. Competition receives 350 entries a year. Website includes history of Nyfa, services info, fellowship info, guidelines (applications can be downloaded), visual artist information, hotline which gives listings of resources for visual artists.

☑ ○ **NEW YORK UNIVERSITY PRIZE FOR POETRY**, New York University Press, 70 Washington Square S., New York NY 10012, phone (212)998-2575, fax (212)995-3833, e-mail nyupress.infor@elmer5.bobst. nyu.edu, website www.nyupress.nyu.edu, contact prize coordinator, established in 1990, offers annual award of a $1,000 honorarium, plus book publication. Send SASE for guidelines. Inquiries via e-mail OK. Most recent award winner was Veronica Patterson. Winners will be notified in Fall, 2000. Website includes guidelines and information on previous winners.

○ **NEWBURYPORT ART ASSOCIATION ANNUAL SPRING POETRY CONTEST**, 12 Charron Dr., Newburyport MA 01950, e-mail espmosk@juno.com, established in 1990, contest coordinator Rhina P. Espaillat, awards prizes of $200, 1st; $100, 2nd; and $50, 3rd; plus Honorable Mentions. Submit any number of unpublished poems; no restrictions as to length, style or theme. Open to anyone over 16 years old. Send 2 copies of each poem, one without identification, one bearing your name, address and telephone number, typed on 8½ × 11 paper with SASE for notification of contest results. Send SASE for guidelines. Entry fee: $3/poem. Make checks payable to Newburyport Art Association. Postmark deadline: March. Prizes will be awarded at a ceremony in May. "In 1999, we received 473 entries from 31 states." Winners were Jeff Holt, Carolyn Raphael and Alfred Dorn. The judge was David Berman. The judge for 2000 was Diana Der-Hovanessian.

Ⓝ ⊕ ◎ NSW PREMIER'S LITERARY AWARD "THE KENNETH SLESSOR PRIZE" (Special- ized: regional), NSW Ministry for the Arts, P.O. Box 5341, Sydney, NSW 2001 Australia, e-mail ministry@arts. nsw.gov.au, website www.arts.nsw.gov.au, established in 1980, offers annual award of AUS $15,000 for a book of poetry published in the previous year (i.e., for the 2001 contest, book must have been published between December 1, 1999 and November 23, 2000). Submissions must be previously published and may be entered in other contests. Submit 4 copies of published book. Open to Australians only. Write for entry form and guidelines. Inquiries via fax and e-mail OK. Competition receives 150 entries a year. Most recent award winner was Jennifer Maiden (2000). Judged by a panel of 16. Winners will be announced in May. "Obtain copy of guidelines before entering."

○ ○ ◎ **FRANK O'HARA AWARD CHAPBOOK COMPETITION; THORNGATE ROAD PRESS (Specialized: gay/lesbian/bisexual)**, Campus Box 4240, English Dept., Illinois State University, Normal IL 61790-4240, phone (309)438-7705, fax (309)438-5414, e-mail jmelled@ilstu.edu, website www.litline .org/html/thorngate.html, established in 1996, award director Jim Elledge, offers annual award of $500, publica- tion and 25 copies. All entrants receive a copy of winning chapbook. Submissions may be a combination of previously published and unpublished work and may be entered in other contests. Submit 16 pages on any topic, in any form. Another 4 pages for front matter is permitted, making the maximum total of 20 pages. Poets must be gay, lesbian or bisexual (any race, age, background, etc.). One poem/page. Send SASE for guidelines. Inquiries via e-mail OK. Entry fee: $15/submission. Deadline: February 1. Competition receives 200-300 entries. Most recent contest winner was *Amateur Grief* by Ron Mohring. Judge is a nationally-recognized gay, lesbian or bisexual poet. Judge remains anonymous until the winner has been announced. Winners will be announced by April 15 in various media—both lesbigay and "straight" in focus. Copies of previous winning books may be obtained by sending $6 to the above address made out to Thorngate Road. "Thorngate Road publishes at least two chapbooks annually, and they are selected by one of two methods. The first is through the contest. The second, the Berdache Chapbook Series, is by invitation only. "We published chapbooks by Kristy Nielsen, David Trinidad, Reginald Shepherd, Karen Lee Osborne, and Maureen Seaton in the Berdache series." Although the contest is only open to gay, lesbian, bisexual and transgendered authors, the content of submissions does not necessarily have to be gay, lesbian, bisexual or transgendered."

☑ ◎ **OHIOANA BOOK AWARDS; OHIOANA POETRY AWARD—(Helen and Laura Krout Memorial); OHIOANA QUARTERLY; OHIOANA LIBRARY ASSOCIATION (Specialized: re- gional)**, Ohioana Library Association, 65 S. Front St., Suite 1105, Columbus OH 43215-4163, phone (614)466- 3831, fax (614)728-6974, e-mail ohioana@winslo.state.oh.us, website www.oplin.lib.oh.us/ohioana, contact Linda Hengst. Ohioana Book Awards given yearly to outstanding books. Up to 6 awards may be given for books (including books of poetry) by authors born in Ohio or who have lived in Ohio for at least 5 years. The Ohioana Poetry Award of $1,000 (with the same residence requirements), made possible by a bequest of Helen Krout, is given yearly "to an individual whose body of work has made, and continues to make, a significant contribution to poetry, and through whose work as a writer, teacher, administrator, or in community service, interest in poetry has been developed." Nominations to be received by December 31. Competition receives several hundred entries. *Ohioana Quarterly* regularly reviews Ohio magazines and books by Ohio authors. It is available through member- ship in Ohioana Library Association ($25/year). Website includes information about the Ohioana Library Associa- tion, the Ohioana Awards and the Award recipients.

Ⓝ ○ **PANHANDLE PROFESSIONAL WRITERS**, P.O. Box 19303, Amarillo TX 79114, website www.u sers.arn.net/~ppw, contact contest chairman, open to all poets, 2 categories (rhymed, unrhymed) any subject or form, 50 lines maximum. Cash awards. Fee $7.50/poem. Other categories include short stories, book-length nonfiction, book-length fiction and nonfiction article. Send SASE for contest rules. Deadline: postmarked on or before March 15, 2001. Competition receives 100-200 entries. Most recent winners include Pauline Robertson,

Lynn Lewis, Marianne McNeil Logan, Jean Ravenscroft, Margaret Schultz and Lynn Olson. Website includes details about summer conference and upcoming meetings, history of the organization, membership information, contact information and useful links.

PAUMANOK POETRY AWARD COMPETITION; THE VISITING WRITERS PROGRAM, SUNY Farmingdale, Farmingdale NY 11735, e-mail brownml@farmingdale.edu, website www.farmingdale.edu/ CampusPages/ArtsSciences/EnglishHumanities/paward.html, established 1990, director Dr. Margery Brown. The Paumanok Poetry Award Competition offers a prize of $1,000 plus an all-expense-paid feature reading in their 2000-2001 series. They will also award two runner-up prizes of $500 plus expenses for a reading in the series. Pays winners from other countries in US dollars. Submit cover letter, 1-paragraph literary bio, up to 5 poems of up to 10 pgs. (published or unpublished), and $12 entry fee postmarked by September 15. Make checks payable to SUNY Farmingdale Visiting Writers Program (VWP). Does not accept entry fees in foreign currencies. Send money order in US dollars. Send SASE for results. Results will be mailed by late December. Send SASE for guidelines or obtain via their website. Inquiries via e-mail OK. Competition receives over 600 entries. Most recent contest winners include Sue Ellen Thompson (winner), Gailmarie Pohmeler and Nick Flynn (runners-up). Poets who have read in their series include Hayden Carruth, Allen Ginsberg, Linda Pastan, Marge Piercy, Joyce Carol Oates, Louis Simpson and David Ignatow. The series changes each year, entries in 1998 for the 1999-2000 series, so entries in the 1999 competition will be considered for the 2000-2001 series, and so on. Website includes Paumanok Poetry Award guidelines and other links to information on the Visiting Writers Program.

JUDITH SIEGEL PEARSON AWARD (Specialized: women), Wayne State University/Family of Judith Siegel Pearson, 51 W. Warren, Detroit MI 48202, phone (313)577-2450, contact Deborah Currie, offers an annual award of up to $250 for "the best creative or scholarly work on a subject concerning women." The type of work accepted rotates each year: poetry, 2002; fiction, 2000; plays and nonfictional prose, 2001. Submissions must be unpublished. Submit 4-10 poems on 20 pgs. maximum. Open to "all interested writers and scholars." Send SASE for guidelines. Deadline: March 1. Competition received 75 entries in 1999. Most recent contest winners were Eliza Garza and Natasha Saje (poetry). Winner announced in April.

PEN CENTER USA WEST LITERARY AWARD IN POETRY (Specialized: regional), PEN Center USA West, 672 S. Lafayette Park Place, #41, Los Angeles CA 90057, phone (213)365-8500, fax (213)365-9616, e-mail pen@pen-usa-west.org, website www.pen-west-usa.org, awards coordinator Christina Apeles, offers annual $1,000 cash award to a book of poetry published during the previous calendar year. Open to writers living west of the Mississippi. Submit 4 copies of the entry. Send SASE for entry form and guidelines. Inquiries via fax and e-mail OK. Entry fee: $20. Deadline: December 29, 2000. Recent award winner was B.H. Fairchild. Judges were Jim Kinsoe, Thom Gunn and Killarney Clary. Winner will be announced in a spring press release and then honored at a ceremony in Los Angeles. Website includes entry forms, guidelines, press releases, membership info and program info.

PENNSYLVANIA POETRY SOCIETY ANNUAL CONTEST, 801 Spruce St., West Reading PA 19611-1448, phone (610)374-5848, e-mail aubade@juno.com, website www.homestead.juno.com/aubade/index. html, contact contest chairman. The deadline for the society's annual contest is January 15. Grand prize category awards 3 prizes of $100, $50, $25 and three poems may be entered at $2 each for members and nonmembers alike. 17 categories are open to all poets; nonmembers pay $1.50/poem; categories 2-12 and 17-21, one poem/ category. Categories 13-16 are for members only. PPS members pay $2.50 total for entries in categories 2-21, inclusive. For information send SASE or check website. Also sponsors the Pegasus Contest for PA Students in grades 5-12. For information send SASE to Anne Pierre Spangler, contest chairman, 1685 Christine Dr., R.D. #2, Lebanon PA 17042. *"Pegasus contest for students is open only to Pennsylvania students!"* Deadline for the Pegasus contest is March 1. The Charles Ferguson Environmental Contest deadline is September 15 and the Carlisle "Kids 'N Critters" contest deadline is October 31. For information send SASE. The society publishes a quarterly newsletter containing pages of poetry by members and an annual *Prize Poems* soft cover book, containing prize-winning poems. Prize winning Pegasus poems are published in a booklet sent to schools which enter. PPS membership dues are $15/year. Make check payable to PPS, Inc. and mail to Richard R. Gasser, Treasurer, at the above address.

PENUMBRA POETRY & HAIKU COMPETITION (Specialized: form), Tallahassee Writers' Association, P.O. Box 15995, Tallahassee FL 32317-5995, e-mail available via website, website www.twaonline.o rg, established 1987, editor Carole Timin, offers cash prizes plus publication in and one copy of a chapbook of winners and finalists. Prizes: $100, $30 and $20 for poetry; $50, $20 and $10 for haiku. Pays winners from other countries by US check. Submission must be unpublished. No simultaneous submissions. Two categories: (1) poetry of up to 50 lines (shorter poetry is of equal value) and (2) 3-line haiku. Poems must be typed on 8½×11 paper; haiku on 3×5 cards. Send 2 copies of each entry. On the back of one copy only, write author's name, full address, telephone, e-mail and source of contest information. Send 1-paragraph bio with personal information and publications. Send SASE for complete guidelines or obtain via website. Entry fee: $5/poem, $3/ haiku. Does not accept entry fees in foreign currencies. Send us check or money order. Deadline: June 30. Competition receives 500-600 entries a year from US, Canada, Europe and others. Most recent winners were

Nancy Kangas (poetry) and Roberta Beary (haiku). Past judges: Lola Haskins and P.V. LeForge. Sample copy of *Penumbra* chapbook with over 50 pgs. of top winners and finalists available for $7.50. Website includes information on the Tallahassee Writers' Association, guidelines for the Penumbra competition, e-mail contact to editor andd purchasing information.

◎ **PEW FELLOWSHIP IN THE ARTS (Specialized: regional)**, The University of the Arts, 230 S. Broad St., Suite 1003, Philadelphia PA 19102, phone (215)875-2285, fax (215)875-2276, established in 1991, award director Melissa Franklin. Call or write for application and guidelines (available in mid-September). Must be a Pennsylvania resident of Bucks, Chester, Delaware, Montgomery or Philadelphia county for at least two years; must be 25 or older. Matriculated students, full or part-time, are not eligible. Deadline: December of the preceding year. Most recent judge was a panel of artists and art professionals. Winner will be announced by letter. "The Pew Fellowships in the Arts provides financial support directly to artists so they may have the opportunity to dedicate themselves wholly to the development of their artwork for up to 2 years. Up to 12 fellowships of $50,000 each (in 3 different categories) awarded each year."

✓ ◎ **THE RICHARD PHILLIPS POETRY PRIZE**, The Phillips Publishing Co., 2721 N.E. Stephens, Roseburg OR 97470, founded 1993, award director Richard Phillips, Jr. Annual award of $1,000 open to all poets. Submit 48-page ms, published or unpublished poems, any subject, any form. Include $15 reading fee/ms, payable to Richard Phillips Poetry Prize. Mss are not returned. Send SASE for guidelines. Postmark deadline: January 31. "Winner will be announced and check for $1,000 presented by March 31." Publication is the following September. Competition receives approximately 100 entries. Most recent prize winners were: Patricia Lang (2000), Paul Davidson (1999) and Jana Klenburg (1998). "There are no anthologies to buy, no strings attached. The best manuscript will win the prize."

◖ ◎ **POETIC POTPOURRI QUARTERLY CONTESTS**, P.O. Box 13, Lattimore NC 28089, award director Dennis Norville, offers quarterly awards of $75, $50, $25 and three Honorable Mentions. Submissions may be previously published and may be entered in other contests. Submit any number of poems on any subject in any style. "No porn! Put name and address on each page. Send SASE for guidelines." Entry fee: $2 for the first poem, $1 each additional poem. Postmark deadlines: March 31, June 30, September 30 and December 31. Send SASE with your entry if you want a winners' list. Winners will be announced within one month after contest deadlines.

✓ ◎ **THE POETRY CENTER BOOK AWARD**, 1600 Holloway Ave., San Francisco CA 94132, phone (415)338-2227, fax (415)338-0966, e-mail newlit@sfsu.edu, website www.sfsu.edu/~newlit/, established in 1980, business manager Eli Coppola. Method for entering contest is to submit a published book and a $10 entry fee. Does not accept entry fees in foreign currencies. Send money order in US dollars. "Please include cover sheet noting author's name, book title(s), name of person or publisher issuing check and check number." Book must be published and copyrighted during the year of the contest and submitted by December 31. Competition receives 200-250 entries. Most recent award winner was Elaine Equi for *Voices Over* (1998). Translations and anthologies are not accepted. Books should be by an individual writer and must be entirely poetry. Prize (only one) is $500 and an invitation to read for the Poetry Center. No entry form is required. Recent winners include Alicia Ostriker and Robert Wrigley. "The Poetry Center and American Poetry Archives at San Francisco State University was founded in 1954. Its archives is the largest circulating tape collection of writers reading their own work in the United States."

⚑ ◖ **POETRY FOREVER; MILTON ACORN PRIZE FOR POETRY; ORION PRIZE FOR POETRY; TIDEPOOL PRIZE FOR POETRY**, Poetry Forever, P.O. Box 68018, Hamilton, Ontario L8M 3M7 Canada, phone (905)312-1779, fax (905)312-8285, administrator James Deahl. Poetry Forever sponsors 3 annual contests for poets everywhere—the Milton Acorn Prize, the Orion Prize and the Tidepool Prize. Each contest awards 50% of its entry fees in 1st, 2nd and 3rd Place prizes. The top 3 poems also receive broadsheet publication. For all 3 contests, poems may be no longer than 30 lines. "Poems should be typed or neatly printed and no longer than 30 lines. Photocopied submissions OK." Send SASE or e-mail address to receive winners' list. Entry fee(s): $3/poem. Make checks payable to Poetry Forever. Deadlines: May 15 (Milton Acorn), June 15 (Orion Prize), July 15 (Tidepool Prize). "The purpose of the contests is to fund the publication of full-size collections by the People's Poet Milton Acorn (1923-1986), Ottawa poet Marty Flomen (1942-1997) and Hamilton poet Herb Barrett (1912-1995)." Recent winners include David Henderson (Orion Prize), Josh Auerbach (Milton Acorn) and Ronnie Brown (Tidepool Prize).

Ⓝ ◖ ◎ ◎ **THE POETRY SOCIETY OF VIRGINIA ANNUAL CONTESTS (Specialized: forms)**, 11027 Becontree Lake Dr., Apt. 303, Reston VA 20190, contest chairperson Lori C. Fraind, e-mail PoetryInVa@aol.com, offers 18 contests in various categories including: the Bess Gresham Memorial (garden or gardeners); Brodie Herndon Memorial (the sea); Judah, Sarah, Grace and Tom Memorial (inter-ethnic amity); Cenie H. Moon Prize (women); Karma Deane Ogden Memorial (PSV members only); and the Edgar Allan Poe Memorial. (All of the previous contests are open to any form, have limits of 32-48 lines, and some have specific subjects as noted.) The following group of contests require specific forms: the J. Franklin Dew Award (series of

3-4 haiku), Carleton Drewry Memorial (lyric or sonnet about mountains), Handy Andy Prize (limerick), Emma Gray Trigg Memorial (lyric, 64-line limit, PSV members only), Nancy Byrd Turner Memorial (sonnet). The last group of contests are open to elementary, middle school and high school students only: Elementary School Prize (grades 1-5, any form or subject, 24-line limit), Middle School Prize (grades 6-8, any form or subject, 24-line limit), High School Prize (grades 9-12, any form or subject, 32-line limit). All poems are open to nonmembers except those noted above. Cash prizes range from $10-100. Contest information available for SASE. Inquiries via e-mail OK. Entry fees: Adults, $2/poem; $1/high school entry; no fee for elementary school entries. Send **all entries** to Lori C. Fraind at the address above. Deadline for all contests is January 19. Competitions receive about 300 entries a year.

☑ ◢ ◎ **POETS' CLUB OF CHICAGO HELEN SCHAIBLE INTERNATIONAL SHAKESPEAR-EAN/PETRARCHAN SONNET CONTEST; THE INTERNATIONAL NARRATIVE CONTEST (Specialized: form)**, 3715 Chimney Hill Dr. Valparaiso IN 46383, chairman Bernard Hillila. The Helen Schaible International Shakespearean/Petrarchan Sonnet Contest is open to anyone **except** members of Poets' Club of Chicago. Submit only 1 entry of either a Shakespearean or a Petrarchan sonnet, which must be original and unpublished and must not have won a cash award in any contest sponsored previously by the Club. Write for rules, include SASE, no earlier than March. No entry fee. Prizes of $50, $35 and $15 plus 2 honorable mentions. Postmark deadline: September 1. Most recent contest winners include Peter Erickson, Mary Raymond and Jane Schlesinger. Winners will be notified by October 15. Send SASE with entry to receive winners' list. Also sponsors The International Narrative Contest, awarding annually a $75 first prize and a $25 second prize. Submissions must be unpublished. Submit 2 copies of 1 narrative poem, any form, any subject, of up to 40 lines to chairperson, Judith Korzonko, 14912 S. Mission Ct., Oak Forest IL 60452. Send SASE for guidelines. Entry must be typed on 8½ × 11 paper, single-spaced. Put name of contest and title of poem in the upper right-hand corner of both copies, and name and address in the upper left-hand corner on only one copy. No entry fee. Postmark deadline: September 1. Winners will be notified by October 15. The Poets' Club of Chicago meets monthly at the Harold Washington Library to critique original poetry which the members read at various venues in the Chicago area and publish in diverse magazines and books. Members also conduct workshops at area schools and libraries by invitation.

◻ ◎ **POETS' DINNER CONTEST (Specialized: regional)**, 2214 Derby St., Berkeley CA 94705-1018, phone (510)841-1217, contact Dorothy V. Benson. Since 1927 there has been an annual awards banquet sponsored by the ad hoc Poets' Dinner Committee, usually at Spenger's Fish Grotto (a Berkeley Landmark). Three typed copies of original, unpublished poems in not more than 3 of the 8 categories [Humor, Love, Nature, Beginnings & Endings, Spaces & Places, People, Theme (changed annually) and Poet's Choice] are submitted anonymously without fee, and the winning poems (Grand Prize, 1st, 2nd, 3rd) are read at the banquet and honorable mentions awarded. **Contestant must be present to win.** Cash prizes awarded; Honorable Mention receives books. The event is nonprofit. Send SASE for contest rules. Deadline is in January. Competition receives about 300 entries. Recent contest winners include Gayle Eleanor (Grand Prize); 1st Prizes, Alice Masek, Stephen Sadler, Marian Brown, Tammy Durston, William Landis and Gloria Kennedy.

Ⓝ ◢ **THE POETS' PRIZE**, The Poets' Prize Committee, % the Nicholas Roerich Museum, 319 W. 107th St., New York NY 10025, phone (212)864-7752, fax (212)864-7704, contact Daniel Entin, award directors Robert McDowell, Frederick Morgan and Louis Simpson. Annual cash award of $3,000 given for a book of verse by an American poet published in the previous year. The poet must be an American citizen. Poets making inquiries will receive an explanation of procedures. Inquiries via fax OK. Books may be sent to the committee members. A list of the members and their addresses will be sent upon request with SASE.

☑ ◢ **PULITZER PRIZE IN LETTERS**, % The Pulitzer Prize Board, 709 Journalism, Columbia University, New York NY 10027, phone (212)854-3841, fax (212)854-3342, e-mail pulitzer-feedback@pulitzer.org, website www.pulitzer.org, contact the Pulitzer Prize board. Offers 5 prizes of $5,000 each year, including 1 in poetry, for books published in the calendar year preceding the award. Inquiries via fax and e-mail OK. Submit 4 copies of published books (or galley proofs if book is being published after November), photo, bio, entry form and $50 entry fee. July 1 deadline for books published between January 1 and June 30; November 1 deadline for books published between July 1 and December 31. Competition receives 150 entries a year. Recent award winner was Mark Strand for *Blizzard of One* published by Alfred A. Knopf. Website includes downloadable entry form and guidelines, bios and photos of winners from 1995 to present and an archive of past winners.

Ⓝ ◻ **QUINCY WRITERS GUILD WRITING CONTEST**, P.O. Box 433, Quincy IL 62306, e-mail chillebr@adams.net, established in 1990, contact contest coordinator, offers annual award for original, unpublished poetry (serious poetry and light poetry), fiction and nonfiction. Cash prizes based on dollar amount of entries. 1st, 2nd and 3rd Place will be awarded in all categories. Send SASE for guidelines. Inquiries via e-mail OK. Entry fee: $2/poem; $4/nonfiction or fiction piece. Entries accepted from January 1 through April 1. Competition receives 110-125 poems. Recent contest winners include "Lovesick," by Dorothy Bizer; "I Love My Sister—but . . .," by Marjorie Millison and "The Affair," by Ellaraine Lockie. The Quincy Writers Guild meets monthly and consists of Quincy-area writers working in various genres.

QWF LITERARY AWARDS; QUEBEC WRITERS' FEDERATION, (Specialized: regional, translations), (formerly QSPELL), 1200 Atwater Ave., Montreal, Quebec H3Z 1X4 Canada, phone (514)933-0878, fax (514)934-2485, e-mail qspell@total.net, website www.qwf.org, contact Award Director, offers annual awards of $2,000 each for poetry, fiction and nonfiction and translation. Also offers a $1,000 first book award. Submissions must be previously published. Open to authors "who have lived in Quebec for at least 3 of the past 5 years." Submit a book published between October 1 of the preceding year and September 30 of the current year. "Books should have at least 48 pgs." Write for entry form. Inquiries via fax and e-mail OK. Entry fee: $10/title. Deadline: May 31. Finished proofs: August 15. Competition receives approximately 50 entries. Most recent award winners were Bruce Taylor (poetry), Elyse Gasco (fiction), Elaine K. Naves (nonfiction) and Sheila Fischman (translation). Poetry judges were NourBese Philip, Carolyn Souaid and John Steffler. Winners will be announced in November. "QWF was formed in 1988 to honor and promote literature written in English by Quebec authors." QWF also publishes *QWRITE*, "a newsletter offering information and articles of interest to membership and the broader community."

RAINMAKER AWARDS IN POETRY, *Zone 3*, Austin Peay State University, P.O. Box 4565, Clarksville TN 37044, phone (931)221-7031, fax (931)221-7393, managing editor Susan Wallace, offers annual awards of 1st Place $500, 2nd Place $300 and 3rd Place $100. Winning poems will also be featured in *Zone 3*. Submissions must be unpublished. Submit no more than 3 poems with SASE. Entry fee is 1 year's subscription (2 issues) to *Zone 3*: $8. "Submitters who prefer not to subscribe will be considered for publications but will not be included in the competition." Postmark deadline: January 1. Winner(s) will be announced in the Fall/Winter 2002 issue of *Zone 3*.

REDWOOD ACRES FAIR POETRY CONTEST, P.O. Box 6576, Eureka CA 95502, phone (707)445-3037, fax (707)445-1583, offers an annual contest with various categories for both juniors and seniors with entry fee of 50¢/poem for the junior contests and $1/poem for the senior contests. Deadline: May 25. Competition receives 200 entries.

MARY ROBERTS RINEHART AWARDS, Mail Stop Number 3E4, English Dept., George Mason University, Fairfax VA 22030-4444, phone (703)993-1180, e-mail bgompert@gmu.edu, contact Barb Gomperts or William Miller. Three grants of $2,000 each are awarded in spring for the best nominated manuscript in fiction, nonfiction and poetry. "Grants are made only for unpublished works by writers who have not yet published a book or whose writing is not regularly appearing in nationally circulated commercial or literary magazines. Writers may see a grant in only one category in any given year; an author not granted an award one year may apply in succeeding years, but once a writer receives an award, he or she may not apply for another, even in a different genre. Grant recipients are not required to be United States citizens but only works in English will be read, and awards are made only in US dollars." **A writer's work must be nominated in writing by an established author, editor or agent**. Nominations must be accompanied by a sample of the nominee's work, 10 pages of individual or collected poems and 30 pgs. of fiction or nonfiction. Postmark deadline: November 30. "Grants will be announced early in the following March on the awards web page (www.gmu.edu/departments/writing/winner.html). Candidates who wish to receive a printed announcement should submit a #10 SASE." Competition receives over 200 entries. Send SASE for guidelines.

ROANOKE-CHOWAN POETRY AWARD (Specialized: regional), North Carolina Literary and Historical Association, 4610 Mail Service Center, Raleigh NC 27699-4610, phone (919)733-9375, fax (919) 733-8807, website www.lib.unc.edu/ncc/onl/litawards.html, contact Jerry C. Cashion, offers annual award for "an original volume of poetry published during the twelve months ending June 30 of the year for which the award is given." Open to "authors who have maintained legal or physical residence, or a combination of both, in North Carolina for the three years preceding the close of the contest period." Submit 3 copies of each entry. Deadline: July 15. Competition receives about 15 entries. Recent award winners were Stephen Knauth, Kathryn Stripling Byer and James Seay. Winner will be announced during the annual meeting in November.

ANNA DAVIDSON ROSENBERG AWARD, FOR POEMS ON THE JEWISH EXPERIENCE (Specialized: ethnic), Judah L. Magnes Museum, 2911 Russell St., Berkeley CA 94705, website www.jfed.org/magnes/magnes, established in 1987, offers prizes of $100, $50 and $25, as well as honorable mentions, for up to 8 pgs. of 1-3 unpublished poems (in English) on the Jewish Experience. "This award is open to all poets. You needn't be Jewish to enter." There is also a Youth Commendation for poets under 19, a Silver Award if 65 or over, and a New/Emerging Poet Award. Do not send poems without entry form; write between April 1 and July 15 for form and guidelines (enclose SASE). Deadline: August 31. No electronic entries of any sort. Competition receives 250-450 entries a year. Recent winners include Doren Robbins, Alicia Ostriker, Myra Sklarew and Julia Levine. The Magnes Museum is the third largest Jewish museum in the country and sponsors numerous programs in the arts and literature.

THE CONSTANCE SALTONSTALL FOUNDATION FOR THE ARTS GRANTS (Specialized: regional), P.O. Box 6607, Ithaca NY 14851-6607, phone/fax (607)277-4933, e-mail artsfound@clarityconnect.com, program manager Lee-Ellen Marvin, offers grants of $5,000 and residencies at the Saltonstall Arts

Colony awarded to visual and literary artists. Poets submit up to 15 pages. Must be 21 years or older and resident of the central and western counties of New York state. Send SASE for application form. Deadline: December 1. Winners are announced April 30.

◎ **SAN FRANCISCO FOUNDATION; JOSEPH HENRY JACKSON AWARD; JAMES D. PHELAN AWARD (Specialized: regional, young adult)**, % Intersection for the Arts, 446 Valencia St., San Francisco CA 94103, phone (415)626-2787, fax (415)626-1636, e-mail intrsect@wenet.net, website www.wenet.net/~intrse ct, contact awards coordinator. The Jackson Award ($2,000), established in 1955, will be made to the author of an unpublished work-in-progress in the form of fiction (novel or short stories), nonfictional prose, or poetry. Applicants must be residents of northern California or Nevada for three consecutive years immediately prior to the deadline date of January 31, and must be between the ages of 20 and 35 as of the deadline. The Phelan Award ($2,000), established in 1935, will be made to the author of an unpublished work-in-progress in the form of fiction (novel or short stories), nonfictional prose, poetry or drama. Applicants must be California-born (although they may now reside outside of the state), and must be between the ages of 20 and 35 as of the January 31 deadline. Mss for both awards must be accompanied by an application form, which may be obtained by sending a SASE. The award judge will use a name-blind process. Mss should be copied on the front and back of each page and must include a separate cover page that gives the work's title and the applicant's name and address. The applicant's name should only be listed on the cover page; do not list names or addresses on the pages of the ms. Applicants may, however, use the mss title and page numbers on the pages of the ms. Mss with inappropriate identifying information will be deemed ineligible. Three copies of the ms should be forwarded with one properly completed current year's official application form to the address listed above. Entries accepted November 15 through January 31. Competitions receive 200 entries. Most recent contest writers include Matthew Iribarne (Joseph Henry Jackson Award), Eleni Sikelianos (James D. Phelan Award) and Joelle Fraser (Nonfiction Award). "Guidelines and application forms are available through the scholarship provider service, www.fastweb.com."

N ⊕ ◑ **AILEEN & ALBERT SANDERS MEMORIAL TROPHY**, 33 Alledge Dr., Woodford, North-amptonshire NN14-4JQ Great Britain, fax (01832)732406, established in 1995, award director Ivan Sanders, offers annual open poetry competition. Prizes: 1st Prize: annual trophy, certificate and publication; 2nd to 10th Prize: certificate and publication; best overseas poem entered receives certificate and publication; 11th to 25th Prize: publication. All entrants: free "AAS" anthology. Submissions must be unpublished and may be entered in other contests. Submit up to 5 poems maximum on any subject in any form/style. "Poems must be in English and no longer than 30 lines excluding title and lines between stanzas. Each poem should be typed on a separate A4 size page, and must not bear the author's details. Any poem bearing either the author's name or address is automatically disqualified, without refund of the entry fee. Poems may not be amended, and will not be returned. Retain copies of your work!" Send SASE (or SAE and IRC) for entry form and guidelines. Inquiries via fax OK. Entry fee: £5 (total). "All entries must be accompanied by a completed entry form and entry fee. This may be photocopied. Each entrant is eligible to have more than 1 poem published. Cheques/postal orders/bank drafts should be crossed and made payable to Ivan Sanders. No cheques/bank drafts drawn on overseas accounts are acceptable due to high U.K. bank charges. Overseas entrants (only) are allowed to pay by International Postage Coupons if preferred. (Entry fee 11 or 23 coupons.)" Deadline: January 31, 2001. Competition receives 750 entries a year. "The AAS committee and helpers prepare a short list of poems for the judge, who has discretion on whether or not to examine any or all of the other entries. The trophy is retained by the winner on a May to May basis, and this may not be removed from the U.K." Most recent award winner was Iain Morland. Judge for upcoming award will be Joy Hendry, editor of *Chapman*, Scotland's leading literary magazine. "Winner will be announced 2-3 weeks after close of competition by post to entrants providing a SAE." Anthologies are post free. Additional copies £5. Ivan Sanders says, "Read the rules. Submit in good time. Your work must be interesting/entertaining, as well as well written."

◻ ◑ ◎ **SARASOTA POETRY THEATRE PRESS; EDDA POETRY CHAPBOOK COMPETI-TION FOR WOMEN; SARASOTA POETRY THEATRE CHAPBOOK COMPETITION; ANIMALS IN POETRY; SPRING POETRY CHAPBOOK PRIZE FOR MEN (Specialized)**, P.O. Box 48955, Sara-sota FL 34230-6955, phone (941)366-6468, e-mail soultalk@aol.com, website augment.sis.pitt.edu/jms/, estab-lished in 1994-1998, award director Scylla Liscombe, offers 4 annual contests for poetry with prizes ranging from $25 1st Prize plus publication in an anthology to $100 1st Prize plus 25 published chapbooks. Honorable Mentions also awarded. Pays winners from other countries in copies. Send SASE for guidelines or visit website. Entry fees range from $4/poem to $10/ms. Competition receives an average of 200 entries a year. Judges for contests are the staff of the press and ranking state poets. Winners are notified by mail. "Sarasota Poetry Theatre Press is a division of Soulspeak/Sarasota Poetry Theatre, a non-profit organization dedicated to encouraging poetry in all its forms through the Sarasota Poetry Theatre Press, Therapeutic Soulspeak for at-risk youth and the Soulspeak Performance Center. We are looking for honest, not showy, poetry; use a good readable font. Do not send extraneous materials." Send SASE for details.

◻ ◎ **CLAUDIA ANN SEAMAN POETRY AWARD (Specialized: students)**, The Community Foun-dation of Dutchess County, 80 Washington St., Suite 201, Poughkeepsie NY 12601, phone (914)452-3077, fax (914)452-3083, established in 1983, offers annual award of $500 (1st Prize). Submissions may be entered in other contests. Submit 1 or 2 poems on any subject or in any form. Open to students in grades 9-12. "Entry must contain student and school names, addresses, and phone numbers and the name of the English or writing teacher." Send SASE for entry form and guidelines. Inquiries via fax OK. Deadline: June 1. Most recent award winner was Vanessa Kogan. Judged by "a panel of judges, including Donna Seaman (Claudia's sister)." Winner announced in September each year at the Barnes & Noble in Manhattan. Copies of previous winning poems may be obtained by contacting The Community Foundation (by phone or in writing). "The Community Foundation is a nonprofit organization serving Dutchess County, NY; it administers numerous grant programs, scholarship funds, and endowment requests. This is an excellent opportunity for young, previously unpublished poets to earn recognition for their work. Since there's no fee, there is little to lose; realize, however, that a national contest will have more entries than a regional competition."

◻ ⬤ ◎ **SENIOR POET LAUREATE POETRY COMPETITION (Specialized: senior citizen)**, Goodin Communications & Penny Peephole Publications, Chapbook Dept., P.O. Box 6003, Springfield MO 65801, e-mail goldenword@aol.com, website http://hometown.aol.com/goldenword/index.html, established in 1993, co-sponsors Wanda Sue Parrott and Vera-Jane Goodin, offers annual award to "American poets age 50 and older. Top winner will receive $60 and the Senior Poet Laureate title. Cash awards will also be given 1st Place winners in nine poetry categories. Pays winners from other countries by money order. The top 55 winning poems will be published in *Golden Words* chapbook of poems by leading older American poets." Submit any number of poems; 32 lines or less (unless specified otherwise); 1/page. Categories are haiku, short poem (12 lines or less), nostalgic, long poem (over 32 lines), sonnet, love, inspirational, light verse and western/pioneer/ tall tales poem. Send SASE for entry form and guidelines. Inquiries via e-mail OK. Entry fee: $1/poem. Does not accept entry fees in foreign currencies. Send money order. Deadline: August 1. Competition receives 1,000 entries a year. Most recent contest winner was Emery L. Campbell. Winners will be announced in October. The top winning poems from the 9 categories and the new Senior Poet Laureate's poem will also be published in *Hodgepodge* literary magazine.

◻ **SKY BLUE WATERS POETRY CONTESTS**, Sky Blue Waters Poetry Society, 232 SE 12th Ave., Faribault MN 55021-6406, phone (507)332-2803, contact Marlene Meehl. The society sponsors monthly contests with prizes of $40, $30, $20, $10 plus 3 paid honorable mentions at $5 each. Pays winners from other countries by check. Also sponsors semiannual awards in March and September with 1st Prize of $50, 2nd Prize $40, 3rd Prize $30, 4th through 10th Prizes $10. Simultaneous submissions are permitted. Submit any number of poems on any subject. Guidelines available for SASE. Entry fee: $2 first poem, $1 each additional poem. Does not accept entry fees in foreign currencies. Send check or money order. All winning poems (monthly and semiannual) automatically entered in The Best of the Best Contest to be judged each January. No fee required. 1st Prize $50, 2nd Prize $30, 3rd Prize $20. Winners will be announced by mail one month following deadline date. "The Sky Blue Waters Poetry Society is a group of Southern Minnesota poets who exist for the sheer 'love of writing.' Most members agree that writing is not just a love but a necessity. Keep writing. Keep submitting. Today's creation will be tomorrow's winner."

☑ ◐ **SLAPERING HOL PRESS CHAPBOOK COMPETITION**, Hudson Valley Writers' Center, 300 Riverside Dr., Sleepy Hollow NY 10591, phone (914)332-5953, e-mail info@writerscenter.com, established in 1990, co-editors Stephanie Strickland and Margo Stever, offers annual award of $500 plus 10 author's copies. Submissions must be from poets who have not previously published a book or chapbook. Submit 24 pages of poems with acknowledgements, any form or style, SASE and $10 reading fee. "Manuscript should be anonymous with second title page containing name, address and phone." Send SASE for guidelines. "See *Poets & Writers* for deadline, usually in the late spring." Competition receives 300-400 entries. Most recent contest winner was Andrew Krivac, *Islands*. Copies of previous winning books may be obtained by requesting order form.

☑ ◻ ◐ **KAY SNOW WRITING AWARDS**, Willamette Writers, 9045 SW Barbur Blvd., Suite 5A, Portland OR 97219-4027, phone (503)452-1592, fax (503)452-0372, e-mail wilwrite@teleport.com, website www.willamettewriters.com, established in 1986, award director Liam Callen, offers annual 1st Prize of $300, 2nd Prize of $150, 3rd Prize of $50 and publication of excerpt only, in December issue of *The Willamette Writer*. Pays winners from other countries by postal money order. Submissions must be unpublished. Submit 1-5 pages on any subject in any style or form, single spaced, one side of paper only. Send SASE for entry form and guidelines. Entry fee: $10 for members of Willamette Writers; $15 for nonmembers. Does not accept entry fees in foreign currencies. Only accepts a check drawn on a US bank. Deadline: May 15. Inquiries via fax and e-mail OK. Competition receives 150 entries. Most recent award winner was Andrejika Hough. Winners will be announced July 31. "Write and send in your very best poem. Read it aloud. If it still sounds like the best poem you've ever heard, send it in."

◪ ◐ **SOCIETY FOR CREATIVE WRITERS POETRY CONTEST**, % The English Dept., KSU, Manhattan KS 66506, phone (785)532-2398, e-mail scwm@oz-online.net, website www.geocities.com/writeron/cont2 000.html, established in 1993, award director Dr. William Adams, offers annual prizes. 1st Prize-50% of Prize Fund, trophy, poet laureate; 2nd Prize-30% of Prize Fund; 3rd Prize-20% of Prize Fund. (One dollar of every entry goes into Prize Fund.) All 3 winners also receive free copies of the April issue of literary magazine *Club*.

Submissions may be entered in other contests. Poems should be typed, 52 lines maximum. Send SASE for guidelines or visit website for information. Inquiries via e-mail OK. Entry fee(s): $3 per poem. Postmark deadline: February 28, 2001. Competition receives 120 entries a year. Most recent contest winner was Elbert McNeil M.D. (2000). Contest judged by members of the Society then faculty of Kansas State University. Winners will be announced around the end of March. Copies of previous winning poems may be obtained by sending SASE. "The Society for Creative Writers is a club for people interested in all forms of creative writing. Make sure you follow all the guidelines. Call or e-mail if you have questions or concerns."

[N] ◯ SOCIETY OF MIDLAND AUTHORS LITERARY AWARD, P.O. Box 10419, Chicago IL 60610-0419, website www.midlandauthors.com, established in 1915, award director Carol Jean Carlson, offers plaque with cash award at annual banquet. Submissions must be previously published. Submit 3 copies of published book. "Poets must reside in Illinois, Michigan, Indiana, Minnesota, Iowa, Ohio, Wisconsin, Nebraska or Missouri to enter." Visit website for information. Deadline: March 1. Competition receives 25-50 entries a year. Most recent award winner was *Thirty-Seven Years From the Stone* by Mark Cox (1999). Judges for upcoming award will be Kathryn Dohrmann, Richard Jones and Timothy Muskat. Winner announced in their newsletter *Literary License* and on the website. "The Society of Midland Authors is an 85-year-old literary association promoting the work of midwestern authors, poets and playwrights."

[N] ◯ THE SOUL OF THE POET AWARD, Grammar Bytes, 3044 Shepherd of Hills, PMB 519, Branson MO 65616, e-mail contest@grammarbytes.com, website www.grammarbytes.com, established in 1997, award director Shane Jeffries, offers biannual award. 1st Prize $250, 2nd Prize $100, 3rd Prize $25 plus honorable mention certificate. Pays winners from other countries by International Money Order. Submissions may be entered in other contests. Submit up to 30 pages of poems on any subject in any form. "All entries must be in English. All entries may be single or double-spaced but must be on standard 8½ × 11 paper. Clean photocopies are accepted. Do not send originals." Send SASE for guidelines or visit website for information. Inquiries via e-mail OK. Entry fee(s): $10 for up to 30 pages. Does not accept entry fees in foreign currencies. Send International Money Orders. Postmark deadlines: December 31, 2000 and June 30, 2001. Competition receives about 300 entries a year. Most recent award winner was David Glaser. "Previous winners select semifinalists, then a committee of 3 prominent writers will make final decision." Winners contacted via mail by February 15, 2001 for December 31 deadline and by September 12, 2001 for June 30 deadline. Send SASE for list of winners. "Grammar Bytes is dedicated to helping writers learn the proper usage of the English language by assisting in copyediting and proofreading. Great writing is great writing, regardless of style, technique or subject. Submit your best work and stay positive. The Soul of the Poet Award was created to aid writers in their journey toward ultimate literary goals—whatever they might be."

◯ SPAWN POETRY CONTEST, SPAWN (Small Publishers Artists and Writers Network), P.O. Box 2653, Ventura CA 93002-2653, contact Mary Embree, offers annual prizes of $100, $50 and $25 for poetry in rhymed and non-rhyming categories. Entries accepted from October 1 through December 31. Entry fees: $5 for SPAWN members, $10 for nonmembers. Send SASE for guidelines.

◪ WALLACE E. STEGNER FELLOWSHIPS, Creative Writing Program, Stanford University, Stanford CA 94305, phone (650)725-1208, fax (650)723-3679, e-mail gay.pierce@forsythe.stanford.edu, website www.stanford.edu/dept/english/cw/, administrator Gay Pierce, 5 in poetry, $15,000 plus tuition of over $6,000, for promising writers who can benefit from 2 years instruction and criticism at the Writing Center. Previous publication not required, though it can strengthen one's application. Deadline: Postmarked by the first working day after December 1. Inquiries via fax and e-mail OK. Competition receives 1,000 entries a year. Most recent winners were Gabrielle Calvocoressi, Matthew Doherty, Susan Kim, Mong-Lan Anne Pham and Brian Teare.

[N] ◪ ◎ STEPHAN G. STEPHANSSON AWARD FOR POETRY (Specialized: regional), (formerly Writers' Guild of Alberta Book Awards), Writer's Guild, 11759 Groat Rd., Edmonton, Alberta T5M 3K6 Canada, phone (780)422-8174, fax (780)422-2663, e-mail wga@oanet.com, website www.writersguild.ab.ca, awarded in six categories, including poetry. Awards $500 and leather bound copy of book. Eligible books will have been published anywhere in the world between January 1 and December 31. Their authors will have been a resident in Alberta for at least 12 of the 18 months prior to December 31. Contact the WGA head office for registry forms. Unpublished manuscripts are not eligible, except in the drama category. Anthologies are not eligible. Five copies of each book to be considered must be mailed to the WGA office no later than December 31. Submissions postmarked after this date will not be accepted. Exceptions will be made for any books published between the 15th and 31st of December. These may be submitted by January 15. Three copies will go to the three judges in that category; one will remain in the WGA library; and one will be placed in a WGA book display around the province. Works may be submitted by authors, publishers, or any interested parties. Inquiries via fax and e-mail OK. Competition receives varied amount of entries. Most recent contest/award winner was Monty Ried. Writers Guild publishes *WestWord* magazine "offering how-to-articles, a market and announcement section and issues related to all forms of writing." Website includes awards info, job/market listing, general information on WGA, program information and directory of writers.

N ⊕ ○ THE TABLA POETRY COMPETITION, Tabla/The Tabla Book of New Verse, Dept. of English, University of Bristol, 3-5 Woodland Rd., Bristol BS8 1TB England, fax (0117)928 8860, e-mail stephen.james@bristol.ac.uk, website www.bris.ac.uk/tabla, established in 1991, award director Dr. Stephen James, offers annual poetry competition. Prizes are 1st: £500, 2nd: £200, 3 runners-up: £100 each plus publication. Cash prizes are paid in UK sterling only. Submissions must be unpublished. Submit any number of poems on any subject in any form and any length. Poems must be typed on one side only; no names on poems to be judged. Send SASE (or SAE and IRC) for entry form and guidelines. Inquiries via fax and e-mail OK. "One free entry with purchase of *Tabla Book of New Verse* (£6 UK); all other entries: £3 UK each. "Book costs £7 (Eur), £8 (rest of world) to cover postage. Only UK standing fees and payments accepted." Deadline: September 30, 2000. Competition receives about 1,100 entries a year. Most recent contest winner was Philip Gross (1999). Judge was John Burnside. Judge for upcoming contest will be Anne Stevenson. Winners are announced by mail and on the website by late October each year. Send a SASE (or SAE and IRC) or visit the website for more details.

◐ ◎ TOWSON UNIVERSITY PRIZE FOR LITERATURE (Specialized: regional), Towson University, College of Liberal Arts, Towson MD 21252, phone (410)830-2128, award director Dean of the College of Liberal Arts, offers annual prize of $1,500 "for a single book or book-length manuscript of fiction, poetry, drama or imaginative nonfiction by a young Maryland writer. The prize is granted on the basis of literary and aesthetic excellence as determined by a panel of distinguished judges appointed by the university. The first award, made in the fall of 1980, went to novelist Anne Tyler." The work must have been published within the three years prior to the year of nomination or must be scheduled for publication within the year in which nominated. Open to Maryland residents under 40 years of age. Submit 5 copies of work in bound form or in typewritten, double-spaced ms form. Send SASE for entry form and guidelines. Deadline: May 15. Competition receives 8-10 entries. Most recent contest winners were Ned Balbo and Charles Marsh.

⊕ ○ ◐ ◎ THE TREWITHEN POETRY PRIZE (Specialized: rural), Trewithen Poetry, Chy-An-Dour, Trewithen Moor, Stithians, Truro, Cornwall TR3 7DU England, established in 1995, award secretary D. Atkinson, offers annual award of 1st Prize £300, 2nd Prize £150, 3rd Prize £75, plus 3 runner-up prizes of £25 each and publication in *The Trewithen Chapbook*. Pays winners from other countries by "sterling cheque" or draft only. Submissions may be entered in other contests "*but* must *not* previously have won another competition." Submit any number of poems on a rural theme in any form. Send SASE for entry form. Entry fee: £3 for the first poem and £2 for each additional poem. Does not accept entry fees in foreign currencies. Send "sterling cheque" or draft only. Deadline: October 31. Competition receives 1,000-1,500 entries. Most recent contest winners were Glenda Beagen and Roger Elkin. Judged by a panel of 3-4 working poets who remain anonymous. Winners will be announced at the end of December by results sheet and through poetry magazines and organizations. Winning poems published biennially in March/April. Copies of *The Trewithen Chapbook* may be obtained by using order form on entry form or by writing direct to the secretary enclosing a SAE with IRC. "We are seeking good writing with a contemporary approach, reflecting any aspect of nature or rural life in any country."

N ◐ KATE TUFTS DISCOVERY AWARD; KINGSLEY TUFTS POETRY AWARD, Claremont Graduate University, 160 E. 10th St., Suite B7, Claremont CA 91711-6165, phone (909)621-8974, fax (909)621-8390, established in 1992, 1993, award coordinator Betty Terrell. Kate Tufts Discovery Award offers annual award of $5,000, Kingsley Tufts Poetry Award offers annual award of $75,000 for a book published between September 15, 1999 and September 15, 2000. Submit 5 books. For both contests, pays winners from other countries by check. Send SASE for entry forms and guidelines or visit website for information. Inquiries via fax OK. Deadline: September 15. Kingsley Tufts Competition receives up to 500 entries a year. Most recent award winner was Robert Wrigley (2000).

N ⊕ ◐ V.B. POETRY PRIZE, Look and Learn Productions Limited, 20, Clifton House, Club Row, London E2 7HB United Kingdom, phone +44(20)7390759, e-mail looklearn@aol.com, website www.looklearn.com, established in 1999, award director Nicholas Morgan, offers annual cash prizes of 1st Prize £400, 2nd Prize £100, 3rd Prize £50. Pays winners from other countries by international money order. Submissions must be unpublished. Submit any number of poems on any subject in no more than 40 lines (including title). Poems must be in English. "Name of poet must not appear on ms. Poems must be typed on one side only of A4 sheet; no stapled sheets. Poems only accepted with entry form." Send SASE (or SAE and IRC) for entry form and guidelines or visit website for information. Inquiries via e-mail OK. Entry fee(s): £3 for each of the first two poems; subsequent entries are £1.50 each. Does not accept entry fees in foreign currencies. Send international money order. Deadline: March 31, 2001. Competition receives 200 entries a year. Most recent award winners were Joanna D. Nicolas, Esther Morgan, Khan Singh Kumar (1999). Judge was Ana Laura Lopez de la Torre. Winners announced in June in writing and on website. "We are a film and video productions company (i.e., we are looking for scripts). We also run an artist's shop including artist's books and may be interested in new talent."

⊕ $ ◐ VER POETS OPEN COMPETITION, Ver Poets, Haycroft, 61/63 Chiswell Green Lane, St. Albans, Hertfordshire AL2 3AL United Kingdom, phone (01727)867005, established in 1974, award director May Badman, offers annual prizes of £500, £300, 2 £100 prizes and a free copy of anthology "Vision On" to all winners and 30 selected poems. Pays winners from other countries in sterling by cheque. Submissions must be unpublished. Submit any number of poems on any subject, "open as to style, form, content. Poem must be no more than 30 lines excluding title, typed on white A4 sheets. Entry forms provided, pseudonyms to be used on poems." Send SASE for entry form and guidelines. Entry fee(s): £2.50 per poem. Accepts entry fees in foreign currencies. Deadline: April 30. Competition receives approximately 1,000 entries a year. Most recent contest winner(s) were Seán Body, Fiona Shackleton and André Mangeot (1999). Judge was Edward Storey. Winner(s) announced at an "Adjudication & Tea" event in June each year. "We have local and postal members, meet regularly in St. Albans, study poetry and the writing of it, try to guide members to reach a good standard, arrange 3 competitions per year with prizes and anthologies for members only. Plus the annual open competition. We do expect a high standard of art and skill. We make a gift to a charity each year."

VISITING FELLOWSHIPS FOR HISTORICAL RESEARCH BY CREATIVE AND PER-FORMING ARTISTS AND WRITERS (Specialized: American history and culture), American Antiquarian Society, 185 Salisbury St., Worcester MA 01609-1634, phone (508)755-5221, fax (508)754-9069, e-mail jdm@mwa.org, established in 1994, award director James David Moran, offers annual award of "a stipend of $1,200/four-week period of residency in Worcester, MA. Plus an allowance for travel." Submissions may be entered in other contests. "The contest is for a fellowship to do research in a national library of American history and culture. The library is devoted to pre-twentieth century materials." Send SASE for entry form and guidelines. Inquiries via fax and e-mail OK. Deadline: October 5. Competition receives 60 entries. Most recent award winners were Christopher Cokinos, nonfiction writer; Tom Dunn, playwright; Cornelia Nixon, novelist/short story writer; and Barbara Weisberg, children's writer and producer (1998). Winners will be announced in December. "Founded in 1812, as the country's first national historical organization, the American Antiquarian Society is both a learned society and a major independent research library. The AAS library today houses the largest and most accessible collection of books, pamphlets, broadsides, newspapers, periodicals, sheet music and graphic arts material produced through 1876 in what is now the United States, as well as manuscripts and a substantial collection of secondary works, bibliographies, and other reference works related to all aspects of American history and culture before the twentieth century." To poets thinking about entering the contest the director says, "learn about the collections in the library; consult *Under Its Generous Dome, A Guide to the Collections and Programs of the American Antiquarian Society*."

THE W.D. WEATHERFORD AWARD (Specialized: regional), Berea College, CPO 2166, Berea KY 40404, phone (606)986-9341, ext. 5140, contact chairman, for the published work (including poetry) which "best illuminates the problems, personalities, and unique qualities of the Appalachian South." Work is nominated by its publisher, by a member of the award committee or by any reader. The award is for $500 and sometimes there are special awards of $200 each. Deadline: December 31 of the year work was published.

WESTERN AUSTRALIAN PREMIER'S BOOK AWARDS (Specialized: regional), Library & Information Service of W.A., Alexander Library Bldg., Perth Cultural Centre, Perth, Western Australia 6000 Australia, phone (61 8)9427 3330, fax (61 8)9427 3336, e-mail jham@liswa.wa.gov.au, website www.liswa. wa.gov.au/pba.html, established in 1982, award director Ms. Julie Ham, offers annual poetry prize of AUS $5,000 for a published book of poetry. Winner also eligible for Premier's Prize of AUS $20,000. Submissions must be previously published. Open to poets either born in Western Australia, resident in Western Australia, or has been resident in Western Australia for at least 10 years at some stage. Write for entry form and guidelines or visit website. Inquiries via fax and e-mail OK. No entry fee. Deadline: September 30 each year. Competition receives about 10-15 entries in poetry category a year (120 overall). Most recent award winners were Tracy Ryan's *The Willing Eye*, John Kinsella's *The Hunt* and Fay Zwicky's *The Gatekeeper's Wife* (1998). Judges were Dr. David Black, Andre Malan, Terri-ann White, Jill Midolo. Winners announced in February each year (i.e., February 2001 for 2000 awards) at a presentation dinner given by the Premier of Western Australia. "The contest is organized by the Library and Information Service of Western Australia, with money provided by the Western Australian State Government to support literature."

WHITING WRITERS' AWARDS; MRS. GILES WHITING FOUNDATION, 1133 Avenue of the Americas, 22nd Floor, New York NY 10036-6710, director Barbara K. Bristol. The Foundation makes awards of $35,000 each to up to 10 writers of fiction, nonfiction, poetry and plays chosen by a selection committee drawn from a list of recognized writers, literary scholars and editors. Recipients of the award are selected from nominations made by writers, educators and editors from communities across the country whose experience and vocations bring them in contact with individuals of unusual talent. The nominators and selectors are appointed by the foundation and serve anonymously. **Direct applications and informal nominations are not accepted by the foundation.**

STAN AND TOM WICK POETRY PRIZE, Wick Poetry Program, Kent State University, P.O. Box 5190, Kent OH 44242-0001, phone (330)672-2067 or (330)672-2676, e-mail acone@kent.edu, website www.kent.edu:80/english/wick/WickPoetry.htm, established in 1994, award director Maggie Anderson, offers annual award of $2,000 and publication by The Kent State University Press. Submissions must be unpublished as a whole and may be entered in other contests. Submit 48-68 pages of poetry. Open to poets writing in English who have not yet published a full-length collection. Entries must include cover sheet with poet's name, address, telephone number and title of ms. Send SASE for guidelines. Entry fee: $15. Does not accept entry fees in foreign currencies. Send money order or US check. Deadline: May 1, 2001. Competition receives 700-800 entries. 1999 contest winner was Honoreé Fanonne Jeffers. Judge for 2000 contest was Li-Young Lee. Website includes contest guidelines and reading series schedule.

✓ ◎ **THE RICHARD WILBUR AWARD (Specialized: nationality)**, Dept. of English, University of Evansville, 1800 Lincoln Ave., Evansville IN 47722, phone (812)479-2963, offers an annual award of $1,000 and book publication to "recognize a quality book-length manuscript of poetry." Submissions must be unpublished ("although individual poems may have had previous journal publications"), original poetry collections and "public domain or permission-secured translations may comprise up to one-third of the manuscript." Submit ms of 50-100 typed pages, unbound, bound or clipped. Open to all American poets. Mss should be accompanied by 2 title pages: one with collection's title, author's name, address and phone number and one with only the title. Include SASE for contest results. Send SASE for guidelines. Entry fee(s): $20/ms. Postmark deadline: December 1. Competition receives 300-500 entries. Most recent contest winner was A.E. Stallings. Judge for last contest was Mary Jo Salter. The winning ms is published and copyrighted by the University of Evansville Press.

⊘ **OSCAR WILLIAMS & GENE DERWOOD AWARD**, New York Community Trust, 2 Park Ave., New York NY 10016, is an award given annually to nominees of the selection committee "to help needy or worthy artists or poets." **Selection Committee for the award does not accept submissions or nominations.** Amount varies from year to year.

🄽 ◻ **WINTER WOOD POETRY AWARD**, Heather's Teddy Bear Organization, Inc., 16 Oakdale Rd., Terryville CT 06786, established in 1999, offers annual awards of $100 (1st Prize), $50 (2nd Prize), and $25 (3rd Prize). Submissions must be unpublished and may be entered in other contests. Submit any number of poems on any subject in any style/form. Line length is 20 maximum per poem. Send SASE for complete guidelines. Entry fee(s): $5/poem. Make checks payable to The Heather's Teddy Bear Organization, Inc., "a nonprofit organization, 501-(c)(3)." Deadline: submissions must be postmarked no earlier than January 1, 2001 and no later than June 30, 2001. Judges are Sue Bacon, Linda Foster, Nancy Giudice, Lisa Lavoie, Garth Pelton. Winners announced in July. Send SASE for list of winners.

◑ ◎ **WISCONSIN ARTS BOARD FELLOWSHIPS (Specialized: regional)**, Wisconsin Arts Board, 101 E. Wilson St., 1st Floor, Madison WI 53702, phone (608)264-8191, fax (608)267-0380, e-mail mark.fraire@a rts.state.wi.us, website www.uwc.arts.state.wi.us, award director Mark Fraire, offers fellowships to "recognize the significant contributions of professional artists." Open to Wisconsin residents who are *not* fulltime students in the fine arts. Write for entry form and guidelines. Inquiries via fax and e-mail OK. Deadline: September ("call for exact date").

◑ ◎ **WORLD ORDER OF NARRATIVE AND FORMALIST POETS (Specialized: subscription, form)**, P.O. Box 580174, Station A, Flushing NY 11358-0174, established in 1980, contest chairman Dr. Alfred Dorn. This organization sponsors contests in at least 15 categories of traditional and contemporary poetic forms, including the sonnet, blank verse, ballade, villanelle, free verse and new forms created by Alfred Dorn. Prizes total at least $5,000 and range from $20 to $300. Only subscribers to *The Formalist* will be eligible for the competition, as explained in the complete guidelines available from the contest chairman. "We look for originality of thought, phrase and image, combined with masterful craftsmanship. Trite, trivial or technically inept work stands no chance." Postmark deadline for entries: November 28, 2000. Competition receives about 3,000 entries. Recent contest winners include Brian E. Drake, Rachel Hadas, Len Krisak, Roy Scheele, Melissa Cannon, Joseph Salemi, Deborah Warren, Albert Sterbak, Carolyn Raphael and Rhina P. Espaillat. (For more information on *The Formalist*, see their listing in the Publishers of Poetry section.)

🄽 ◻ ◑ **WRITERS AT WORK FELLOWSHIP COMPETITION**, Writers at Work, P.O. Box 540370, North Salt Lake UT 84054-0370, phone (801)292-9285, fax (801)294-5417, website www.ihi-env.com/watw.ht ml, contact Lisa Peterson, offers annual awards of $1,500 and $500 plus publication in *Quarterly West* (1st Place only). Submissions must be unpublished and can be entered in other contests, "but must be withdrawn if they win another contest." Submit 6 poems, 10 pgs. maximum, subject and form open. Entry must include 2 #10 SASEs and cover letter stating name, address, phone number, genre and title of ms. "No names on mss." Mss will not be returned. Open to any writer who has not published a book-length volume of original work. Obtain guidelines via their website. Inquiries via fax OK. Entry fee: $15/entry (make check payable to Writers at Work). Postmark deadline: March 15. Competition receives 1,200 entries a year.

🌐 ✓ 💲◻ ◑ **THE WRITERS BUREAU POETRY AND SHORT STORY COMPETITION**, The Writers Bureau, Sevendale House, 7 Dale St., Manchester M1 1JB England, phone (0161)228 2362, fax (0161)228 3533, e-mail comp@writersbureau.com, website www.writersbureau.com, established in 1994, offers annual prizes of £500, £250, £125, £75, £50, plus publication of the first places in Freelance Market News. Submissions must be unpublished. "Any number of entries may be sent. There is no set theme or form. Entries must be typed, and no longer than 40 lines." Send SASE for entry form. Inquiries via fax or e-mail OK. Accepts entry fees in foreign currencies as bank drafts in US currency. Deadline: July 31, 2000. Judge for last contest was Alison Chisholm. Winner(s) will be announced in September. "The Writers Bureau is a distance learning college offering correspondence courses in Journalism, Creative Writing and Poetry."

THE W.B. YEATS POETRY PRIZE FOR AUSTRALIA AND NEW ZEALAND, Beyond Ben Bulben, 6 Samuel Close, Berwick, Victoria 3806 Australia, website www.geocities.com/benbulben.geo, established in 1996, award director Declan Foley, offers annual contest with awards of Aus $300 1st Prize, $100 2nd Prize and commendation certificates. Submissions must be unpublished; open theme with unlimited entries. Poets must be permanent residents of Australia or New Zealand. "Type poem on A4 paper, no identification of author on poem. Attach separate paper with name and address. Include stamped addressed envelope (or SAE and IRC) for results. Send SASE (or SAE and IRC) for guidelines or visit website. "Postal entries only accepted. Entry fee(s): $5 for first poem, each additional entry $4. Does not accept entry fees in foreign currencies. Send Australian currency only. Deadline: December 31. Competition receives approximately 300 entries a year. Most recent contest winner was Aileen Kelly (1998). Judges were Dr. Kevin Brophy and Dr. Judith Rodriguez. "Two judges are invited each year." Winners announced "by phone first in February and by competition results published immediately." Copies of previous winning poems may be obtained by sending $5 and SASE (or SAE and IRC) to Beyond Ben Bulben. They also publish a thrice yearly newsletter on W.B. Yeats and his Circle.

THE W.B. YEATS SOCIETY ANNUAL POETRY COMPETITION, W.B. Yeats Society of New York, National Arts Club, 15 Gramercy Park S, New York NY 10003, phone (212)780-0605, website www.YeatsSociety.org, offers $250 cash prize for 1st Place, $100 cash prize for 2nd Place, and optional honorable mentions. Open to beginner as well as established poets; winners are invited to read their winning entries at the Taste of the Yeats Summer School, held each April in New York. They are also inducted as Honorary Members of the Society, a 501 (c)(3) charitable organization established in 1994, Andrew McGowan president. Judges have included poets Eamon Grennan, L.S. Asekoff, Campbell McGrath and Billy Collins. Annual deadline for submissions is February 15. No entry form is required. Submit any number of unpublished poems in any style or form, up to 50 lines each, typed on letter-size paper without poet's name. Enclose reading fee ($7 for first poem, $6 per additional poem) and attach a 3×5 card to each entry containing the poem's title along with the poet's name, address and phone/fax/e-mail numbers. Winners are selected by March 31 and announced in April. Winning entries and judge's report are posted on the Society's website.

Additional Contests & Awards

The following listings also contain information about contests and awards. See the General Index for page numbers, then read the listings and send SASEs (or SAEs and IRCs) for specific details about their offerings.

Creative With Words Publications
  (C.W.W.)
Creativity Unlimited Press®
Cricket
Crucible
Cumberland Poetry Review
Current Accounts
Cutbank
Davidson County Writers' Guild
Dead Metaphor Press
Defined Providence
Denver Quarterly
Dim Gray Bar Press
Doggerel
Driftwood Review, The
1812
Ekphrasis
Emerald Coast Review
Emotions Literary Magazine
Envoi
Epoch
Experimental Forest Press
Explorations
Fauquier Poetry Journal
Federation of British Columbia
  Writers
Field
Firewater Press Inc.
First Step Press
Five Points
Floating Bridge Press
Florida Review, The
Flyway
Formalist, The
Frogmore Papers
Frogpond
Funny Paper, The
Garnet
Gathering of the Tribes, A
Gentle Survivalist, The
George & Mertie's Place
Georgia Poetry Society
Gerbil
Graffiti Rag
Grain
Grasslands Review
Greater Cincinnati Writers' League
Greensboro Review, The
GSU Review
Guild Complex
Haiku Headlines: A Monthly News-
  letter of Haiku and Senryu
Half Tones to Jubilee
Harpweaver, The
Haypenny Press
Headlock Press
Heartlands Today, The
Heaven Bone Magazine
Heist Magazine
Helicon Nine Editions
Hellas
Hippopotamus Press
Hobo Poetry & Haiku Magazine
Hodgepodge Short Stories & Poetry
Hubbub
Hunger Magazine
Images Inscript
Indian Heritage Publishing
Indiana State Federation of Poetry
  Clubs
Inklings
Inkwell Magazine
International Quarterly

Interpreter's House
Iowa Review, The
Italian Americana
Kalliope
Kentucky State Poetry Society, The
Kestrel
Kit-Cat Review, The
LAIRE, Inc., the
La Jolla Poet's Press
Laurels
League of Canadian Poets, The
Leapings Literary Magazine
Ledbury Poetry Festival
Ledge, The
Linkway Magazine
Literal Latté
Literary Focus Poetry Publications
Literary Moments
Live Poets Society, Maine
Lone Stars Magazine
Lotus Press, Inc.
Louisiana Literature
Lucidity
Lullwater Review
Luz en Arte y Literatura
MacGuffin, The
Mad Poets Review
Magnolia Quarterly, The
Mail Call Journal
Malahat Review, The
Mammoth Books
Manitoba Writers' Guild Inc.
Many Mountains Moving
Marlboro Review, The
Maryland Poetry Review
Massachusetts State Poetry Society,
  Inc.
Medicinal Purposes Literary Review
Mekler & Deahl, Publishers
Mid-America Press, Inc., The
Mid-American Review
Midwest Poetry Review
Miller's Pond
Minority Literary Expo
Missing Fez, The
Mississippi Poetry Society, Inc.
Mississippi Review
Missouri Review
Mkashef Enterprises
Modern Haiku
mojo risin'
Mother Earth International Journal
(m)öthêr TØñgué Press
Mount Olive College Press
Muse Journal
Muse's Kiss Webzine
Mystery Time
Nassau Review
National Federation of State Poetry
  Societies, Inc.
National League of American Pen
  Women, Inc.
National Writers Association
Nebraska Review, The
Nerve Cowboy
Nevada Poetry Society
New Delta Review
New Era Magazine
New Issues Press
New Letters
New Mirage Quarterly, The
New Press Literary Quarterly, The
New Renaissance, The

New Rivers Press
New Song, A
New Writer, The
Newport University Writers' Confer-
  ence & Contest, Christopher
Nimrod
96 Inc Magazine
Northeast Corridor
Northern Stars Magazine
Northwords
Nostalgia
Notre Dame Review
Oak, The
Ohio State University Press/The Jour-
  nal Award in Poetry
Opened Eyes Poetry & Prose
  Magazine
Oracle Poetry
Orange Willow Review
Orbis
Oregon State Poetry Association, The
Our Journey
Outrider Press
Ozark Creative Writers Conference
Pacific Coast Journal
Painted Bride Quarterly
Palanquin
Paris Review, The
Parnassus Literary Journal
Passager
Passages North
Paterson Literary Review, The
Pavement Saw
P.D.Q. (Poetry Depth Quarterly)
PEN American Center
PEN Center USA West
Pearl
Peer Poetry Magazine
Pegasus Review, The
Pennwriters Annual Conference
People's Press, The
Peregrine
Phoebe (VA)
Piano Press
Pif Magazine
Pig Iron
Pikeville Review
Pitt Poetry Series
Plainsongs
Pleiades
Plowman, The
Poems & Plays
Poet Lore
Poetic License Poetry Magazine
Poetic Page
Poetic Realm
Poetic Voices Journal
Poetry
Poetry Forum
Poetry Ireland Review
Poetry Life
Poetry Miscellany, The
Poetry Northwest
Poetry Nottingham International
Poetry Review
Poetry Society of America
Poetry Society of Virginia, The
Poets at Work
Poets Corner
Poet's Fantasy
Poets' League of Greater Cleveland
Poets' Roundtable
Potato Hill Poetry

Potomac Review
Potpourri
Pottersfield Portfolio
Prairie Schooner
Pudding House Publications
Pygmy Forest Press
Quantum Leap
Quarter After Eight
Quarterly Review of Literature
   Poetry Book Series
Queen Street Quarterly
Raintown Review, The
RB's Poets' Viewpoint
Red Crow
Red Hen Press
River City
River Oak Review
River Styx Magazine
Riverstone
Rockford Review, The
Romantics Quarterly
Rosebud
Ruah
Salmon Run Press
Salt Hill
San Diego State University Writers
   Conference
Sandhills Writers Conference, The
Sarabande Books, Inc.
Scavenger's Newsletter
Scroll Publications
Seedhouse
Seeds Poetry Magazine
Shenandoah
Silver Wings/Mayflower Pulpit
Silverfish Review
Sinipee Writers Workshop
Skidrow Penthouse
Skipping Stones
Slate & Style
Slipstream
Smith Publisher, Gibbs

Snapshots
Snowapple Press
So To Speak
Society of American Poets (SOAP),
   The
Songwriters and Poets Critique
South Dakota State Poetry Society
Southern California Anthology, The
Southern Humanities Review
Southern Poetry Review
Southwest Review
Southwest Writers Workshop
Sow's Ear Poetry Review, The
Spitball
Spoon River Poetry Review, The
Stand Magazine
Still Waters Press
Story Line Press
Storyteller, The
Studio
sub-TERRAIN
Taproot Literary Review
Tears in the Fence
Texas Review
Texas Tech University Press
Thunder Rain Publishing
Tickled by Thunder
Time of Singing
Troubadour
Ulitarra
Understanding Magazine
University of Arizona Poetry Center
University of Georgia Press
University of Iowa Press
University of Massachusetts Press,
   The
University of Wisconsin Press
Unterberg Poetry Center of the 92nd
   Street Y, The
Urban Spaghetti
Urthona Magazine
Utah State Poetry Society

Vegetarian Journal
Victoria School of Writing
Virginia Quarterly Review, The
Washington Review
Washington Square
Waterways
Weber Studies
West Wind Review
Westerly
Western Humanities Review
Weyfarers
Whetstone
Whiskey Island Magazine
White Eagle Coffee Store Press
White Pine Press
Whitecrow Foundation, Tahana
Willow Springs
Wings Magazine, Inc.
Wisconsin Fellowship of Poets
Wisconsin Regional Writers'
   Association Inc.
Worcester Review
Word Salad
Word Works, The
World-Wide Writers Service, Inc.
WoRM fEASt!
Write Way, The
Writer's Block Magazine
Writers' Center Press
Writer's Exchange
Writers' Federation of Nova Scotia
Writers Guild of Alberta
Writers' Journal
Writers' Union of Canada, The
Writing Today
Yale University Press
Yankee Magazine
Yeats Society of New York, W.B.
Yemassee
Young Writer

State & Provincial Grants

Arts councils in the United States and Canada provide assistance to artists (including poets) in the form of fellowships or grants. These grants can be substantial and confer prestige upon recipients; however, **only state or province residents are eligible**. Because deadlines and available support vary annually, query first (with a SASE).

UNITED STATES ARTS AGENCIES

Alabama State Council on the Arts, *201 Monroe St., Montgomery AL 36130-1800. (334)240-3269. E-mail: staff@arts.state.al.us. Website: www.arts.state.al.us.*

Alaska State Council on the Arts, *411 W. Fourth Ave., Suite 1-E, Anchorage AK 99501-2343. (907)269-6610. E-mail: info@aksca.org. Website: www.aksca.org.*

Arizona Commission on the Arts, *417 W. Roosevelt, Phoenix AZ 85003. (602)255-5882. E-mail: general@arizonaarts.org. Website: az.arts.asu.edu/artscomm/.*

Arkansas Arts Council, *1500 Tower Bldg., 323 Center St., Little Rock AR 72201. (501)324-9766. E-mail: info@dah.state.ar.us. Website: www.arkansasarts.com.*

California Arts Council, *1300 I St., Suite 930, Sacramento CA 95814. (916)322-6555. E-mail: cac@cwo.com. Website: www.cac.ca.gov/.*

Colorado Council on the Arts and Humanities, *750 Pennsylvania St., Denver CO 80203-3699. (303)894-2617. E-mail: coloarts@artswire.org. Website: www.state.co.us/govusdir/arts/.*

Connecticut Commission on the Arts, *755 Main St., 1 Financial Plaza, Hartford CT 06103. (860)566-4770. Website: www.cslnet.ctstateu.edu/cca/.*

Delaware State Arts Council, *Carvel State Office Building, 820 N. French St., Wilmington DE 19801. (302)577-8278. E-mail: delarts@artswire.org. Website: www.artsdel.org/about/delaware.htm.*

District of Columbia Commission on the Arts & Humanities, *410 Eighth St. NW, 5th Floor, Washington DC 20004. (202)724-5613. E-mail: dccah@erols.com. Website: www.capaccess.org/ane/dccah/.*

Florida Arts Council, *Division of Cultural Affairs, Florida Dept. of State, The Capitol, Tallahassee FL 32399-0250. (850)487-2980. Website: www.dos.state.fl.us/dca/.*

Georgia Council for the Arts, *530 Means St. NW, Suite 115, Atlanta GA 30318-5793. (404)651-7920.*

Hawaii State Foundation on Culture & Arts, *44 Merchant St., Honolulu HI 96813. (808)586-0300. E-mail: sfca@sfca.state.hi.us. Website: www.state.hi.us/sfca.*

Idaho Commission on the Arts, *P.O. Box 83720, Boise ID 83720-0008. (208)334-2119. E-mail: bgarrett@ica.state.id.us. Website: www2.state.id.us/arts.*

Illinois Arts Council, *100 W. Randolph, Suite 10-500, Chicago IL 60601. (312)814-6750. E-mail: info@arts.state.il.us. Website: www.state.il.us/agency/iac.*

Indiana Arts Commission, *402 W. Washington St., Indianapolis IN 46204-2741. (317)232-1268. E-mail: arts@state.in.us. Website: www.state.in.us/iac/.*

Iowa Arts Council, *600 E. Locust, Capitol Complex, Des Moines IA 50319-0290. (515)281-4451.*

Kansas Arts Commission, *Jay Hawk Tower, SW 700 Jackson, Suite 1004, Topeka KS 66603. (785)296-3335.*

Kentucky Arts Council, *31 Fountain Place, Frankfort KY 40601-1942. (502)564-3757.*

Louisiana State Arts Council, *P.O. Box 44247, Baton Rouge LA 70804-4247. (225)342-8180. E-mail: arts@crt.state.la.us. Website: www.crt.state.la.us/arts/.*

Maine Arts Commission, *55 Capitol St., 25 State House Station, Augusta ME 04333-0025. (207)287-2724. E-mail: jan.poulin@state.me.us. Website: www.mainearts.com.*

Maryland State Arts Council, *175 West Ostend Street, Suite E, Baltimore MD 21230. (410)767-6555. E-mail: tcolvin@mdbusiness.state.md.us. Website: www.msac.org/.*

Massachusetts Cultural Council, *120 Boylston St., 2nd Floor, Boston MA 02116. (617)727-3668. E-mail: web@art.state.ma.us. Website: www.massculturalcouncil.org/.*

Michigan Council for Arts & Cultural Affairs, *P.O. Box 30705, Lansing, MI 48909. (313)256-3735. E-mail: artsinfo@cis.state.mi.us. Website: www.commerce.state.mi.us/arts/home.htm.*

Minnesota State Arts Board, *Park Square Court, 400 Sibley St., Suite 200, St. Paul MN 55101-1928. (651)215-1600. E-mail: msab@state.mn.us. Website: www.state.mn.us/ebranch/msab.*

Mississippi Arts Commission, *239 N. Lamar St., Suite 207, Jackson MS 39201. (601)359-6030. E-mail: vlindsay@arts.state.ms.us. Website: www.arts.state.ms.us/.*

Missouri Arts Council, *111 N. Seventh St., Suite 105, St. Louis MO 63101-2188. (314)340-6845. E-mail: mhunt01@mail.state.mo.us. Website: www.missouriartscouncil.org.*

Montana Arts Council, *P.O. Box 202201, Helena MT 59620-2201. (406)444-6430. E-mail: mac@state.mt.us. Website: www.art.state.mt.us.*

Nebraska Arts Council, *3838 Davenport St., Omaha NE 68131-2329. (402)595-2122. E-mail: nacart@synergy.net. Website: www.gps.k12.ne.us/nacuswebussite/nac.htm.*

Nevada State Council on the Arts, *602 N. Curry, Carson City NV 89703. (702)687-6680. Website: www.clan.lib.nv.us/docs/ARTS.*

New Hampshire State Council on the Arts, *40 N. Main St., Concord NH 03301-4974. (603)271-2789. Website: www.state.nh.us/nharts.*

New Jersey State Council on the Arts, *P.O. Box 306, 225 W. State St., Trenton NJ 08625. (609)292-6130. E-mail: njsca@arts.sos.state.nj.us. Website: www.artswire.org/Artswire/njsca/.*

New Mexico Arts Division, *228 E. Palace Ave., Santa Fe NM 87501. (505)827-6490.*

New York State Council on the Arts, *915 Broadway, New York NY 10010. (212)387-7000. E-mail: pinfo@nysca.org. Website: www.nysca.org.*

North Carolina Arts Council, *Department of Cultural Resources, Raleigh NC 27699-4632. (919)733-4834. Website: www.ncarts.org/home.html.*

North Dakota Council on the Arts, *418 E. Broadway, Suite 70, Bismarck ND 58501-4086. (701)328-3954. E-mail: comserv@state.nd.us. Website: www.state.nd.us/arts/index.html.*

Ohio Arts Council, *727 E. Main St., Columbus OH 43205. (614)466-2613. E-mail: wlawson@mail.oac.ohio.gov. Website: www.oac.ohio.gov/.*

Oklahoma Arts Council, *P.O. Box 52001-2001, Oklahoma City OK 73152-2001. (405)521-2931. E-mail: okarts@arts.state.ok.us. Website: www.oklaosf.state.ok.us/~arts/.*

Oregon Arts Commission, *775 Summer St. NE, Floor 2, Salem OR 97310. (503)986-0088. E-mail: oregon.artscomm@state.or.us.*

Pennsylvania Council on the Arts, *Room 216, Finance Bldg., Harrisburg PA 17120. (717)787-6883. E-mail: gmeluso@state.pa.us. Website: artsnet.heinz.cmu.edu/pca/.*

Institute of Puerto Rican Culture, *P.O. Box 9024184, San Juan PR 00902-4184. (787)725-5137.*

Rhode Island State Council on the Arts, *95 Cedar St., Suite 103, Providence RI 02903. (401)222-3880. E-mail: info@risca.state.ri.us. Website: www.risca.state.ri.us/.*

South Carolina Arts Commission, *1800 Gervais St., Columbia SC 29201. (803)734-8696. E-mail: guinnjea@state.sc.us. Website: www.state.sc.us/arts/.*

South Dakota Arts Council, *800 Governors Dr., Pierre SD 57501. (605)773-3131. E-mail: sdac@stlib.state.sd.us. Website: www.state.sd.us/state/executive/deca/sdarts/sdarts.htm.*

Tennessee Arts Commission, *401 Charlotte Ave., Nashville TN 37243-0780. (615)741-1701. Website: www.arts.state.tn.us/index.html.*

Texas Commission on the Arts, *P.O. Box 13406, Austin TX 78711-3406. (512)463-5535. E-mail: front.desk@arts.state.tx.us. Website: www.arts.state.tx.us/.*

Utah Arts Council, *617 E. South Temple, Salt Lake City UT 84102-1177. (801)236-7555.*
Website: www.dced.state.ut.us/arts/index.html.

Vermont Arts Council, *136 State St., Drawer 33, Montpelier VT 05633-6001. (802)828-3291.*
E-mail: info@arts.vca.state.vt.us. Website: www.state.vt.us/vermont-arts/.

Virgin Islands Council on the Arts, *41-42 Norre Gada, P.O. Box 103, St. Thomas VI 00804. (340)774-5984.*
E-mail: vicouncil@islands.vi.

Virginia Commission for the Arts, *Lewis House, 2nd Floor, 223 Governor St., Richmond VA 23219.*
(804)225-3132. E-mail: vacomm@artswire.org. Website: www.artswire.org/~vacomm/.

Washington State Arts Commission, *P.O. Box 42675, Olympia WA 98504-2675. (360)753-3860.*
E-mail: wsac@artswire.org.

West Virginia Arts Commission, *Cultural Center, 1900 Kanawha Blvd. E., Charleston WV 25305-0300.*
(304)558-0220. Website: www.wvlc.wvnet.edu/culture/arts.html.

Wisconsin Arts Board, *101 E. Wilson St., 1st Floor, Madison WI 53702. (608)266-0190.*
E-mail: artsboard@arts.state.wi.us. Website: www.arts.state.wi.us.

Wyoming Arts Council, *2320 Capitol Ave., Cheyenne WY 82002. (307)777-7742.*
Website: commerce.state.wy.us/cr/arts/index.htm.

CANADIAN PROVINCES ARTS AGENCIES

Alberta Foundation for the Arts, *901 Standard Life Centre, 10405 Jasper Ave., 9th Floor, Edmonton, Alberta T5J 4R7. (780)427-6315. E-mail: afa@mcd.gov.ab.ca. Website: www.affta.ab.ca.*

British Columbia Arts Council, *800 Johnson St., 5th Floor, Victoria, British Columbia V8V 1X4. (250)356-1728.*

The Canada Council, *350 Albert St., P.O. Box 1047, Ottawa, Ontario K1P 5V8. (613)566-4414.*
Website: www.canadacouncil.ca/.

Manitoba Arts Council, *525-93 Lombard Ave., Winnipeg, Manitoba R3B 3B1. (204)945-2237.*
E-mail: manart1@mb.sympatico.ca. Website: www.artscouncil.mb.ca.

New Brunswick Department of Economic Development, Tourism & Culture, *Arts Branch, P.O. Box 6000, Fredericton, New Brunswick E3B 5H1. (506)453-3984. Website: www.gov.nb.ca/edt/index.htm.*

Newfoundland & Labrador Arts Council, *P.O. Box 98, St. John's, Newfoundland A1C 5H5. (709)726-2212.*
E-mail: nlacmail@newcomm.net. Website: www.nlac.nf.ca/.

Nova Scotia Arts Council, *1660 Hollis St., Suite 302, P.O. Box 1559, CRO, Halifax, Nova Scotia B3J 2Y3.*
(902)422-1123.

Ontario Arts Council, *151 Bloor St. W., 6th Floor, Toronto, Ontario M5S 1T6. (416)961-1660.*
E-mail: info@arts.on.ca. Website: www.arts.on.ca/.

Prince Edward Island Council of the Arts, *115 Richmond, Charlottetown, Prince Edward Island C1A 1H7.*
(902)368-4410. Website: www.peisland.com/arts/council.htm.

Saskatchewan Arts Board, *3475 Albert St., Regina, Saskatchewan S4S 6X6. (306)787-4056.*

Yukon Arts Branch, *Box 2703, Whitehorse, Yukon Y1A 2C6. (867)667-8589. E-mail: arts@gov.yk.ca.*
Website: www.artsyukon.com.

Resources
Conferences & Workshops

Conferences and workshops are valuable resources for many poets, especially beginners. A conference or workshop serves as an opportunity to learn about specific aspects of the craft, connect with and gather feedback from other poets and writers, listen to submission tips from editors, and revel in a creative atmosphere that may stimulate one's muse.

In this section you'll find listings for 60 conferences and workshops—17 of which are new to this edition. All listings contain information indicating to whom the event is open, its general purpose, and areas of concentration. Some, such as the Catskill Poetry Workshop, are specifically geared to poets. Most, however, are more general conferences with offerings for a variety of writers, including poets.

A "typical" conference may have a number of workshop sessions, keynote speakers and perhaps even a panel or two. Topics may include everything from writing fiction, poetry, and books for children to marketing one's work. Often a theme, which may change from year to year, will be the connecting factor.

Other conferences and workshops cover a number of topics but have a primary focus. For example, the Mount Hermon Christian Writers Conference offers sessions on poetry, fiction, article writing and writing for children, but is geared toward authors interested in the Christian writing market. There are also events especially for women writers, Appalachian writers and Jewish writers.

Despite different themes or focuses, each listing in this section details the information poets need to determine which conference suits them best. To provide quick access to that information, we've included subheads with key terms to identify the type of information immediately following the subhead. For example, the subhead **Purpose/Features** contains information on a conference's general purpose, who may attend the event, scheduled themes and panels, offerings specifically available for poets, and speakers who have either attended or are scheduled to attend. The **Costs/Accommodations** subhead precedes information regarding the conference fee as well as any additional costs for food or housing, the availability of transportation to and from the event, and information on overnight accommodations. The subhead **Additional Info** details information on individual critiques, contests sponsored during a conference, and how to obtain brochures and registration forms.

In addition to subheads, you may find symbols at the beginning of a listing. These symbols are intended to provide certain information at a glance. The ⬛ symbol signifies listings new to this edition, the 🌐 symbol indicates international listings, the ⬛ symbol denotes Canadian listings and the ☑ symbol indicates a change in a listing's address, phone number, e-mail address or contact name.

It is important to note, however, that conference and workshop directors were still in the organizing stages when contacted. Consequently, some listings include information from last year's events simply to provide an idea of what to expect this year. For more up-to-date details, including current costs, send a SASE to the conference and workshop directors a few months before the dates listed.

BENEFITING FROM CONFERENCES

Without a doubt, attending conferences and workshops is beneficial. First, these events provide opportunities to learn more about the poetic craft. Some even feature individual sessions with workshop leaders, allowing you to specifically discuss your work with others. If these one-on-one sessions include critiques (generally for an additional fee), we have included this information, as mentioned above, under **Additional Info**.

Besides learning from workshop leaders, you can also benefit from conversations with other attendees. Writers on all levels often enjoy talking to and sharing insights with others. A conversation over lunch may reveal a new market for your work, or a casual chat while waiting for a session to begin can acquaint you with a new resource.

Also, if a conference or workshop includes time for open readings and you choose to participate, you may gain feedback from workshop leaders and others. For some, however, just the relief from the solitude of writing can make a conference or workshop worthwhile.

Another reason conferences and workshops are valuable is the opportunity they provide to meet editors and publishers who often have tips about marketing work. The availability of these individuals, however, does not necessarily mean they will want to read your latest collection of poems (unless, of course, they are workshop leaders and you have separate meetings scheduled with them).

Although editors and publishers cannot give personal attention to everyone they meet, don't be afraid to approach them. If they weren't interested in speaking to writers, they wouldn't have agreed to attend the conference. However, if the editor or publisher's schedule is too full to allow discussion of your work, ask if you may follow up with a letter after the event. This will give you the benefit of his or her undivided attention and, perhaps, develop into a contact in the poetry field.

SELECTING A CONFERENCE OR WORKSHOP

When selecting a conference or workshop to attend, keep your goals in mind. If you want to learn how to improve your craft, for example, consider one of the events entirely devoted to poetry or locate a more general conference where one-on-one critique sessions are offered. If you're looking for more informal feedback, choose an event that includes open readings. If marketing your work seems like an ominous task, register for a conference that includes a session with editors. And if you also have an interest in other forms of writing, an event with a wide range of workshops is a good bet.

Of course, also take your personal resources into consideration. If both your time and funds are limited, search for a conference or workshop within your area. Many events are held during weekends and may be close enough for you to commute. On the other hand, if you want to combine your family vacation with time spent meeting other writers and working on your craft, consider workshops such as those sponsored by The Writers' Center at Chautauqua. In either case, it is important to at least consider the conference location and learn about other enjoyable activities in the area.

Still other factors may influence your decision. Events sponsoring contests, for instance, may allow you to gain recognition and recoup some of your expenses. Similarly, some conferences and workshops have financial assistance or scholarships available. Finally, many are associated with colleges or universities and offer continuing education credits. When available, these options are included in the listings. Again, send a SASE for more details.

For other conferences and workshops, see *The Guide to Writers Conferences* (by ShawGuides, available at website http://www.shawguides.com or through our website http://www.writersdiges t.com); *Writers Conferences: An Annual Guide to Literary Conferences* (Poets & Writers, Inc., 72 Spring St., New York NY 10012, website http://www.pw.org); or the May issue of *Writer's*

Digest magazine (available on newsstands or directly from the publisher at 1507 Dana Ave., Cincinnati OH 45207, website http://www.writersdigest.com). You may also want to check the bulletin boards at libraries and bookstores for local events.

AMERICAN CHRISTIAN WRITERS CONFERENCES, P.O. Box 110390, Nashville TN 37222, phone (800)21-WRITE, director Reg Forder. Annual 2-day events founded 1981. 30 conferences/year. Held throughout the year in cities including Houston, Boston, Minneapolis, Chicago, St. Louis, Detroit, Atlanta, Miami, Phoenix and Los Angeles. Usually located at a major hotel chain like Holiday Inn. Average attendance is 50-80.
Purpose/Features: Open to anyone. Conferences cover fiction, poetry, writing for children.
Costs/Accommodations: Cost is $89-149, participants are responsible for their own meals. Accommodations include special rates at host hotel.
Additional Info: They also sponsor an annual Caribbean Christian Writers Conference Cruise each November. Send SASE for brochures and registration forms.

APPALACHIAN WRITERS WORKSHOP, P.O. Box 844, Hindman KY 41822, phone (606)785-5475, fax (606)785-3499, e-mail hss@tgtel.com, director Mike Mullins. Annual 5-day event founded 1977. Usually held at the end of July or beginning of August. Location: Campus of Hindman Settlement School in Knott County, KY. "The campus is hilly and access for housing is limited for physically impaired, but workshop facilities are accessible." Average attendance is 60-70.
Purpose/Features: Open to "anyone regardless of sex, age or race." Conference is designed to promote writers and writing of the Appalachian region. It covers fiction, poetry, writing for children, dramatic work and nonfiction. Offerings specifically available for poets include daily sessions on poetry, individual critique sessions and readings. Staff has included Lee Smith, Hal Crowther, George Ella Lyon, James Still and Barbara Smith.
Costs/Accommodations: Cost for workshop is approximately $350 for room, board and tuition. Information on overnight accommodations is available for registrants. Accommodations may include special rates at area hotels "once our facilities are filled."
Additional Info: Submit mss for individual critiques in advance. Send SASE for brochures and registration forms. Inquiries via fax or e-mail OK.

ART WORKSHOPS IN GUATEMALA, 4758 Lyndale Ave. S., Minneapolis MN 55409-2304, phone (612)825-0747, fax (612)825-6637, e-mail info@artguat.org, website www.artguat.org, director Liza Fourré. Annual 10-day educational travel program founded 1995. Workshops are held in Antigua, the old colonial capital of Guatemala. "It's a delightful small town with an international ambience. Very inspiring for writers." 2001 dates: January 19-28. Class limit is 10 students.
Purpose/Features: Offerings specifically available for poets include "Poetry/Snapshots in Words" with Rose-ann Lloyd. "Antigua provides daily inspiration for artists and has been an educational and cultural center for centuries."
Costs/Accommodations: Cost is approximately $1,725 includes "air transportation from US, tuition, lodging in a beautiful old colonial home, a hearty breakfast, ground transport, and some pretty interesting field trips." Offers the "Buddy Discount. If you've already attended one of our workshops and tell a friend who decides to take a workshop too, you'll get $50 off the tuition of your next workshop." Lodging and classes are held in a private colonial style home. Overflow goes to nearby hotels.
Additional Info: Call, write, e-mail or fax for more information. Complete information also found on website.

ASPEN SUMMER WORDS WRITING RETREAT AND LITERARY FESTIVAL (formerly Aspen Writers' Conference), P.O. Drawer 7726, Aspen CO 81612, phone (970)925-3122 or (800)925-2526, fax (970)920-5700, e-mail Aspenwrite@aol.com, website www.aspenwriters.org, executive director Julie Comins. Founded 1976. Three-day writing retreat, followed by three-day literary festival. Held the third week of June. Location: The Aspen Institute, Aspen Meadows campus or other site in Aspen. Average attendance is 100 for the festival and 50 for the retreat.
Purpose/Features: Open to all writers. Retreat includes intensive workshops in poetry, fiction, memoir and essay. Offerings specifically available for poets include poetry workshops, craft lectures and readings by faculty and participants. Faculty at last conference were Carol Muske (poetry); Ron Carlson (fiction); and Madeline Blais (memoir and essay).
Costs/Accommodations: Cost for retreat is $325; cost for the Literary Festival is $150; cost for both is $475. Transportation to and from on-site lodging and event is available. Information on overnight accommodations is available for registrants. Cost of on-site accommodations was $55/person/day double occupancy or $110/person/day single occupancy.
Additional Info: "We accept poetry manuscripts in advance that will be discussed during workshop." Send SASE for brochure and registration form or request via phone or e-mail. Include mailing address with all e-mail requests for brochures/registration forms. Inquiries via fax and e-mail OK. Website includes general information about Aspen Writers' Foundation, (including history); all programs; registration forms; information about photos of past presenters; and links to visiting Aspen.

AUSTIN WRITERS' LEAGUE SPRING AND FALL WORKSHOPS, 1501 W. Fifth St., Suite E-2, Austin TX 78703, phone (512)499-8914, fax (512)499-0441, e-mail awl@writersleague.org, website www.writersleague. org, executive director Jim Bob McMillan. Biannual workshops founded 1982. "Workshops are usually three- or six-hour sessions. Intensive classes last from 10-15 weeks and meet for three hours each week." Usually held weekends in March, April, May and September, October, November. Location: Austin Writers' League Resource Center/Library. Registration limited.

Purpose/Features: Open to all writers, beginners and advanced. Workshops cover fiction, poetry, writing for children, nonfiction, screenwriting, book promotion/marketing, working with agents/publishers, journal writing, special interest writing, creativity, grantwriting, copyright law and taxes for writers. Offerings specifically available for poets include at least 2 workshops during each series. Poetry presenters have included Ralph Angel, Rosellen Brown, Reginald Gibbons and Marion Winik. Past speakers have included Sandra Scofield, Sue Grafton, Peter Mehlman, Gregg Levoy, Lee Merrill Byrd and several New York agents and editors. "Occasionally, presenters agree to do private consults with participants. Also, workshops may incorporate hands-on practice and critique."

Costs/Accommodations: Cost is $35-75. Members get discount.

Additional Info: Requirements for critiques are posted in workshop brochure. Send SASE for brochures and registration forms or request via fax or e-mail (include mailing address). The Austin Writers' League publishes *The Austin Writer*, a monthly publication of prose and poetry selected from submissions each month. Poetry guidelines for other publications, awards and grants programs, and market listings are available through the League library.

N AUTUMN AUTHORS' AFFAIR, 1507 Burnham Ave., Calumet City IL 60409, phone (708)862-9797, e-mail vadew9340@aol.com, president Nancy McCann. Annual 3-day event founded 1983. The 2000 conference will be held October 2000. Average attendance is 200-275. Open to anyone.

Purpose/Features: Conference covers fiction, but Professor Charles Tinkham of Purdue University-Calumet, called "the poet of the people," usually gives a poetry workshop "covering the entire realm" of writing poetry. "We have between 40-75 published authors and qualified speakers at the conference."

Costs/Accommodations: Saturday-only and weekend packages, including most meals, are available. Information on overnight accommodations is also available. Send SASE for brochures and registration forms which include the cost of each package, special hotel rates and itinerary.

Additional Info: Inquiries via e-mail OK.

✓ BREAD LOAF WRITERS' CONFERENCE, Middlebury College, Middlebury VT 05753, phone (802)443-5286, fax (802)443-2087, e-mail blwc@middlebury.edu, website www.middlebury.edu/~blwc, administrative coordinator Carol Knauss. Annual 11-day event founded 1926. Usually held in mid-August. Average attendance is 230.

Purpose/Features: Conference is designed to promote dialogue among writers and provide professional critiques for students. Conference usually covers fiction, nonfiction and poetry.

Costs/Accommodations: Cost for the last conference was $1,690, including tuition, room and board. Fellowships and scholarships for the conference are available. "Candidates for fellowships must have a book published. Candidates for scholarships must have published in major literary periodicals or newspapers. A letter of recommendation, application and supporting materials due by April 1. Awards are announced in June for the conference in August." Taxis to and from the airport or bus station are available.

Additional Info: Individual critiques are also available. Sponsors the Bakeless Literary Publication Prizes, an annual book series competition for new authors of literary works in poetry, fiction and creative nonfiction. Send SASE for details. Send for conference brochures and application forms or obtain via website. Inquiries via fax and e-mail OK.

N 🌐 BRISTOL POETRY FESTIVAL, 20-22 Hepburn Rd., Bristol B52 8UD United Kingdom, phone (0044)117 9426976, fax (0044)117 9441478, e-mail festival@poetrycan.demon.co.uk, website www.poetrycan.de mon.co.uk, festival director Hester Cockcroft. Annual event founded 1996. 2000 dates were October 5-31. Location: "The festival takes place across the city of Bristol in a variety of venues." Average attendance is about 6,000.

Purpose/Features: Open to "everyone who is interested, from practicing poets to the general public. The festival aims to celebrate the best in local, national and international poetry in all its manifestations, with events for everyone including performances and workshops, competitions and exhibitions, public poetry interventions, community work and cross art form and digital projects." Offerings specifically available for poets include master classes from famous poets, workshops on poetry writing and performance, debates and competitions.

Costs/Accommodations: Cost varies. "Discounts are available for students, elderly people, the unwaged or the disabled."

Additional Info: Contest sponsored as part of festival. "Entry requirements vary, but competitions are always open to everyone and an entrance fee per poem is payable." Prizes include a modest cash award and publication. Judge is a "well known poet." Visit website for additional information. Inquiries via fax and e-mail OK. "Bristol

Poetry Festival is organized and funded by Bristol's Poetry Development Agency, the Poetry Can, which is based at the same address and managed by the same personnel." Website includes information about the festival, the Poetry Can, projects, employment opportunities, plus links to a range of useful websites on poetry.

N CANYONLANDS WRITERS RIVER TRIP, P.O. Box 68, Moab UT 84532, phone (435)259-7750, fax (435)259-2335, e-mail cfinfo@canyonlandsfieldinst.org, website www.canyonlandsfieldinst.org, contact registrar. Annual 5-day event founded 2000. Usually held in May on the San Juan or Colorado River. Attendance is a maximum of 16.
Purpose/Features: Open to all. Workshop covers instruction/critique on writing about relationships to the natural world while floating down observing anazazi ruins and red rock walls.
Costs/Accommodations: Cost is $500, includes instruction, lodging, all river meals.

CATSKILL POETRY WORKSHOP, Hartwick College, Oneonta NY 13820, phone (607)431-4448, fax (607)431-4457, e-mail frostc@hartwick.edu, website www.hartwick.edu/osp, director Carol Frost. Annual week long event. 2000 dates were July 1-8. Location: Hartwick College, a small, private college in the Catskill Mountain area. Average attendance is 25-30.
Purpose/Features: Open to "talented adult writers." Workshops cover poetry only. Offerings specifically available to poets include "traditional meters, free verse lineation and uses of metaphor; individual instruction."
Costs/Accommodations: Cost for 2000 was $799, including meals. Housing available in on-site facilities.
Additional Info: Send SASE for brochures and registration forms. Inquiries via fax and e-mail OK. Website includes information about the workshop, a list of the faculty and information about fees, credits and scholarships.

N THE COLLEGE OF NEW JERSEY WRITERS CONFERENCE, College of New Jersey, Department of English, P.O. Box 7718, Ewing NJ 08628-0718, phone (609)771-3254, e-mail write@tcnj.edu, director Jean Hollander. Annual 1-day event founded 1981. Usually held in April at the College of New Jersey campus. Average attendance is 800.
Purpose/Features: Open to anyone. Conference covers all genres of writing. "We usually have a special presentation on breaking into print." Twenty separate workshops as well as readings are offered. Recent featured speaker was John Updike.
Costs/Accommodations: Cost was $40 for day session; additional cost for workshops and evening session. Discounts available for students. Information on overnight accommodations is available for registrants.
Additional Info: Writers of poetry, drama, journalism, literature for the young, nonfiction and fiction may submit ms to be critiqued in writing by workshop leaders. Poetry and short story contest sponsored as part of conference. 1st Prize: $100; 2nd Prize: $50. Judges are workshop leaders and a special panel from the English Dept. Write or call for brochures and registration forms. Inquiries via e-mail OK.

N COLORADO MOUNTAIN WRITERS' WORKSHOP, P.O. Box 85394, Tucson AZ 85754, phone (520)206-9479, e-mail megfiles@compuserve.com, director Meg Files. Annual 5-day event founded 1999. 2000 dates were July 17-21. Location: Glenwood Springs, CO, on the mountaintop campus of Colorado Mountain College. Average attendance is 50.
Purpose/Features: Open to all writers, beginning and experienced. "The workshop includes sessions on writing and publishing fiction, nonfiction and poetry, as well as manuscript workshops and individual critiques and writing exercises." Faculty includes Sheila Bender, Jack Heffron, Meg Files and Joanne Greenberg. Other special features include "a beautiful high-country site, extensive and intensive hands-on activities, individual attention, and a supportive atmosphere."
Costs/Accommodations: Cost is $300; dorm rooms and meals are available on site.
Additional Info: Individual critiques are available. Submit 5 poems in advance to Meg Files.

☑ DESERT WRITERS WORKSHOP, P.O. Box 68, Moab UT 84532, phone (435)259-7750, fax (435)259-2335, e-mail cfinfo@canyonlandsfieldinst.org, website www.canyonlandsfieldinst.org, contact registrar. Annual 3-day event founded 1985. Usually held the first weekend in November at a ranch in the foothills of the LaSal Mountains. Attendance is a maximum of 33.
Purpose/Features: Open to all. Workshop covers 3 categories—fiction, nonfiction and poetry—and focuses on relationship to natural world.
Costs/Accommodations: Cost is $525, including meals, instruction and lodging.
Additional Info: Individual critiques are also available. "Participants will be able to mail some samples to their instructor before the workshop for critique." Send SASE for brochures and registration forms.

USE THE GENERAL INDEX, located at the back of this book, to find the page number of a specific publisher. Also, publishers that were listed in last year's edition but not included in this edition are listed in the General Index with a notation explaining why they were omitted.

☑ **DOWN EAST MAINE WRITER'S WORKSHOPS**, P.O. Box 446, Stockton Springs ME 04981, phone (207)567-4317, fax (207)567-3023, e-mail redbaron@agate.net, website www.maineweb.com/writers/, director Janet J. Barron. Annual 3-day events founded 1993. Usually held last part of July and first part of August. 2000 dates were June 23, 24, 25; July 14, 15, 16, and August 11, 12, 13. "The conference/workshop facility is a historic, 200 year-old writer's studio in the heart of a tiny, sleepy village in mid-coastal Maine. It is comfortable, within 100-or-so yards of Penobscot Bay, and handicapped-accessible."

Purpose/Features: "Our workshops are small, intimate gatherings, limited to 10 participants. These workshops are actually constructed around each student's needs and writing levels as evidenced by their responses to a comprehensive questionnaire sent them upon their registration. In other words, our enjoyable workshops are truly geared to and for each of the individuals who enroll in the intense, interactive and experiential, hands-on classes. The DownEast Maine Writer's Workshop's main purpose is to help aspiring writers understand the world of writing for publication. Each summer, a conference is held on "How to Get Your Writing Published," and sometimes one or more other subjects are treated in a 3-day workshop. Among these topics are: Poetry, Fiction, Nonfiction, Humor, Scriptwriting, Getting Published in the Children's Market and Creative Writing (fiction and nonfiction).

Costs/Accommodations: Cost for each 2000 conference was $295. Lunch is included in this cost. However, participants are responsible for their own dinners. "Local B&Bs and Inns provide full breakfasts." Discounts are available: 10% for AARP members, 10% for two people registering together, or 10% for early registration (at least 60 days before workshop). Information on overnight accommodations is available. Accommodations include special rates at area Bed & Breakfasts and Inns.

Additional Info: Individual critiques are also available during and immediately after each day's workshops or after workshops by fax or e-mail. Send SASE for brochures and registration forms or obtain via fax, e-mail or website. Inquiries via fax and e-mail OK. "The DownEast Maine Writer's Workshop's website contains comprehensive information re: the DEMWW's Director, what our three-day workshops are all about, dates and details of the annual conferences, editorial help novice writers can tap into when they need assistance, and the textbook used in the workshops and that also is available to all who have an interest in the writing world. In addition, we treat all participants as the special people that they are. We support them, encourage them, and inspire them. While communicating with them the realities of getting published in today's mega-competitive publishing environment, we motivate them to find the editors who will invite them to submit their work, then show them how to fill those editor's wish-lists."

EASTERN KENTUCKY UNIVERSITY CREATIVE WRITING CONFERENCE, Case Annex 467, Richmond KY 40475-3140, phone (606)622-5861, e-mail engbrown@acs.eku.edu, website www.english.eku.edu/conferences, co-directors Dorothy Sutton and Harry Brown. Annual 5-day event founded 1964. Usually held Monday through Friday of the third week in June. Location: Eastern Kentucky University. Average attendance is 15.

Purpose/Features: Open to poetry and fiction. The conference provides lectures, workshops and private conferences with visiting writers to "help writers increase their skills in writing poetry and fiction." A ms of 4-8 poems (8 pgs. maximum) must be submitted by May 15 and accepted before enrollment in conference is allowed. Offerings specifically available for poets include workshop discussions and individual conferences. Visiting writers have included David Citino, X. J. Kennedy, Donald Justice, Greg Orr, Maggie Anderson and Sena Naslund.

Costs/Accommodations: Cost for the last conference was $92 undergraduate and $133 graduate (in-state fees), $252 undergraduate and $369 graduate (out-of-state fees); participants are responsible for their own meals, available on campus. Cost for housing in on-site facilities was $56/week single occupancy, $40/week double occupancy. "Must bring your own sheets, pillow, blanket."

Additional Info: Send SASE for brochure or request via e-mail. Website also includes the brochure which lists the visiting writers and their bios, schedule of events, registration information, cost, etc.

☑ **FISHTRAP**, P.O. Box 38, Enterprise OR 97828, phone (541)426-3623, e-mail rich@fishtrap.org, website www.fishtrap.org, director Rich Wandschneider. Holds 3 annual 3- to 4-day events. Founded 1988. 1999 dates were Winter Fishtrap—February 19-21; Summer Workshop—June 28 through July 1; Summer Gathering—July 2-4. Location: "Winter site is a meeting room attached to a motel at Wallowa Lake, Oregon (off season); summer site is an old Methodist church camp." Average attendance is 50 for Winter Fishtrap ("always sold out"); 8 workshops (12 people/workshop) for Summer Workshop; 90 for Summer Gathering.

Purpose/Features: Open to anyone. "Fishtrap's goal is to promote good writing and clear thinking about the West. Also to encourage and promote new writers. There are always craft workshops on fiction, poetry, nonfiction; sometimes in children's writing, playwriting, radio, etc." Offerings specifically available for poets included a poetry workshop. Themes for 2000 were "Living and Writing on the Edge" (winter) and "West of Where?" (summer). Instructors for 2000 were Ursula Le Guin, Molly Gloss, Luis Urrea and Kim Stafford.

Costs/Accommodations: Cost for winter Fishtrap was $215-320 includes meals (higher price includes lodging); Summer Workshop was $220, Gathering was $175, meals and lodging available at $32/day at camp. Lodging also available at nearby motels.

Additional Info: Awards 5 fellowships annually. Send SASE or e-mail for brochures and registration forms. Each year the selected writings of workshop students and workshop instructors are published in an anthology. Website includes general information, information on writers retreat, fellowships and is updated with dates and instructors/presenters.

THE FLIGHT OF THE MIND, WOMEN'S WRITING WORKSHOPS, 622 SE 29th Ave., Portland OR 97214, phone (503)236-9862, fax (503)233-0774, e-mail soapston@teleport.com, website www.teleport.com/~soapston/FLIGHT/, director Judith Barrington. Annual events founded 1983. Usually held at the end of June, beginning of July. Two workshops in summer for 7 days each at "a rustic retreat center on the wild McKenzie River in the foothills of the Oregon Cascades." Average attendance is 70 women/workshop in 5 different classes.
Purpose/Features: Open to women writers. Workshops cover fiction, poetry, essays, memoirs, special-topic classes (e.g., "landscape and memory") with a feminist philosophy. In 2000 workshop leaders included Grace Paley, Dorianne Laux, Allison Joseph and Aleida Rodriguez.
Costs/Accommodations: Cost for workshop (including tuition, all meals and room) was $595-785. Scholarships available.
Additional Info: Participants are selected on the basis of work submitted. Peer critique groups form at workshop. Send first-class stamp for brochure and registration forms. Inquiries via e-mail OK. Website includes programs, bios of teachers (after December 2000).

FLORIDA CHRISTIAN WRITERS CONFERENCE, 2600 Park Ave., Titusville FL 32780, phone (407)269-6702 ext. 202, fax (407)383-1741, e-mail writer@digital.net, website www.kipertek.com/writer, director Billie Wilson. Annual 4-day event founded 1988. 2001 dates: January 25-29. Location: retreat center setting—conferee housing at motel. Meals, workshops and all general sessions held at retreat center. Average attendance is 200.
Purpose/Features: Open to all writers. "The conference has an instructional and marketing thrust. All genres are usually covered—49 workshops. Publishers and editors from over 35 publishing houses attend. Writers may submit manuscripts to the editors and publishers for critique and sale." Offerings specifically available for poets include 2 workshops plus marketing opportunities. Speakers/Teachers at last conference were Janis Whipple (Broadman & Holman Publications), Jeannie Harmon (Chariot Victor), Holly Miller (Clarity plus Saturday Evening Post), Kay Hall (Cross & Quill), Rachel Hoyer (Concordia Publishing House), Bonnie Jensen (DaySpring Cards), Mary Lou Redding (The Upper Room plus Devo'Zine).
Costs/Accommodations: Cost for 2000 was $515 for single occupancy, meals and tuition; $425 for double occupancy, meals and tuition; $300 for meals and tuition only. Discounts are available through early registration and scholarships. Transportation to and from the event is provided. "We provide shuttles from the Orlando International airport. Also, we provide transportation to and from the motel to the retreat center." Airport shuttle cost is $40/person. Information on overnight accommodations is available for registrants. Individual critiques also available.
Additional Info: "Each conferee may submit four manuscripts (five poems constitutes one manuscript) for critique. No fee." Send SASE for brochures and registration forms.

✓ **FOOTHILL WRITERS' CONFERENCE**, 12345 El Monte Rd., Los Altos Hills CA 94022-4599, phone (650)949-7316, fax (650)949-7375, e-mail ksw@mercury.fhda.edu, conference directors Jim Whearty and Kim Wolterbeek. Annual 6-day event founded 1975. Usually held the end of June/beginning of July. Location: Foothill College in Los Altos Hills. 2000 dates: June 2-27.
Purpose/Features: Open to everyone. Conference includes panel discussions and manuscript workshops; poetry one-on-one sessions; and poetry and prose readings. Past panels have included publishing on the World Wide Web, translating life experience into story, the use of silence in poetry and memoirs in non-Western society. Offerings specifically available for poets included a one-on-one manuscript workshop.
Costs/Accommodations: Cost for conference was $75, included enrollment fees and admission to faculty afternoon and evening readings, intensive writing workshops, and lectures and panels by faculty (college credit available). Participants are responsible for their own meals.
Additional Info: Individual poetry critiques available on a first come, first served basis. "Sign up posted on the first day of conference." Send SASE for brochures and registration forms. Inquiries via e-mail OK.

🔲 **FRONTIERS IN WRITING**, P.O. Box 19303, Amarillo TX 79114, website http://users.arn.net/~ppw, contact conference director. Usually held in Amarillo TX. Dates: June 8-9, 2001. Registration deadline: June 6. Average attendance is 100.
Costs/Accommodations: Cost for 1999 conference was $80 for Panhandle Professional Writers members and $115 for nonmembers. Send SASE for brochures and registration forms.

🔲 **HARVARD SUMMER WRITING PROGRAM**, 51 Brattle St., Dept S810, Cambridge MA 02138, phone (617)495-4024, fax (617)495-9176, e-mail summer@hudce.harvard.edu, website www.summer.harvard.edu. Annual 8-week event. 2001 dates: June 25 through August 17. Location: Harvard University. Average attendance is 700.
Purpose/Features: Open to all levels, from beginner to published author. Course offerings include creative, expository and professional writing. Offerings specifically available for poets include beginning poetry, intermedi-

ate poetry and graduate level poetry courses. Other special features include small classes, undergraduate and graduate credit, individual conferences, access to the Writing Center at Harvard, visiting writers, a reading series and a literary magazine. Instructors are writers, editors, and faculty members from Harvard as well as other universities.

Costs/Accommodations: Cost for 2000 conference was $1,700/course (2 courses is considered full-time), plus $2,900 for room and board (dormitory housing).

Additional Info: Enquiries via e-mail OK. Their catalog, courses, program policies and registration materials are available via the website.

HAYSTACK WRITING PROGRAM, Summer Session, School of Extended Studies, Portland State University, P.O. Box 1491, Portland OR 97207, phone (800)547-8887 ext. 4027 or (503)725-4186, fax (503)725-4840, e-mail herrinm@pdx.edu, website www.haystack.pdx.edu, director Maggie Herrington. Annual summer program founded 1969. One-week and weekend courses over the four weeks of the program. Classes are held in the local school of this small coastal community; some evening lectures and other activities. Average attendance is 10-15/class; 400 total.

Purpose/Features: Open to all writers. One-week workshops cover fiction, poetry, mystery, screenplay and nonfiction.

Costs/Accommodations: Cost for workshops is $125-450; participants pay for their own lodging and meals. Accommodation options range from camping to luxury hotels; listing provided upon registration.

Additional Info: Write for brochures and registration forms. Inquiries via fax and e-mail OK.

N: HIGHLAND SUMMER WORKSHOP, P.O. Box 7014, Radford University, Radford VA 24142, phone (540)831-5366, fax (540)831-5004, e-mail jasbury@runet.edu, director Grace Toney Edwards. Annual 2-week event founded 1977. Held the first 2 weeks in June. Location: Radford University campus. Average attendance is 20-25.

Purpose/Features: Open to everyone. "The conference, a lecture-seminar-workshop combination, is conducted by well-known guest writers and offers the opportunity to study and practice creative and expository writing within the context of regional culture." Topics covered vary from year to year. Poetry, fiction and essays (prose) are generally covered each year. The last workshop was led by Robert Morgan and Richard Hague. This year's leaders will be David Huddle and Joyce Dyer.

Costs/Accommodations: Cost for the conference ranged from $433-1075 plus $16/day for meals. Individual meals may also be purchased. On-site housing costs range from $19-28/night. On-site accommodations are available at Norwood Hall. Accommodations are also available at local motels.

Additional Info: Send SASE for brochures and registration forms. Inquiries via fax or e-mail OK.

N: HOFSTRA UNIVERSITY SUMMER WRITERS' CONFERENCE, Hofstra University, U.C.C.E., Hempstead NY 11549, phone (516)463-5016, fax (516)463-4833, e-mail Kenneth.A.Henwood@hofstra.edu, website www.hofstra.edu, director Kenneth Henwood. Annual 10-day event founded 1972. Usually starts the Monday after July 4th. Location: Hofstra University. Average attendance is 50-60.

Purpose/Features: Open to all writers. Conference covers fiction, nonfiction, poetry, children's writing, stage/screenwriting and, on occasion, one other area (science fiction, mystery, etc.). Guest speakers (other than the workshop leaders) "usually come from the world of publishing." There are also "readings galore and various special presentations."

Costs/Accommodations: Cost for 2000 conference was $400/workshop, $625 for 2. Additional fee of $375 for air-conditioned dorm room during conference. For those seeking credit, other fees apply.

Additional Info: Individual critiques are also available. "Each writer receives a half hour one-on-one with each workshop leader." They do not sponsor a contest, but "we submit exceptional work to various progams sponsored by Writers Conferences and Festivals." Write for brochures and registration forms (available as of April). Inquiries via fax and e-mail OK. Website includes descriptions of workshops, faculty bios, conference information and registrations form.

☑ INDIANA UNIVERSITY WRITERS' CONFERENCE, Ballantine Hall 464, Indiana University, Bloomington IN 47405, phone (812)855-1877, fax (812)855-9535, e-mail btenre@indiana.edu, website php.india na.edu/~iuwc/, director Romayne Ruginas. Annual week-long event founded 1940. Usually held the last week in June at the university student union. Average attendance is 100.

Purpose/Features: Open to all. Conference covers fiction and poetry. Offerings specifically available for poets included workshops and classes. Speakers at last conference included Rodney Jones (poetry) and Jesse Lee Kercheval (fiction).

Costs/Accommodations: Cost for the last conference was $200 for conference and classes, $300 for conference, classes and workshop; plus $25 application fee. Information on overnight accommodations is available for registrants. "Rooms available in the student union or in a dorm."

Additional Info: Individual critiques are also available. Submit 10 pgs. of poetry in advance. "All manuscripts are considered for scholarships." Send SASE for brochures and registration forms.

✓ **IOWA SUMMER WRITING FESTIVAL**, University of Iowa, 100 Oakdale Campus, W310, Iowa City IA 52242-5000, phone (319)335-4160, fax (319)335-4039, e-mail amy-margolis@uiowa.edu, website www.uiowa.edu/~iswfest, coordinator Amy Margolis. Annual event founded 1987. Held each summer in June and July for six weeks, includes one-week and weekend workshops at the University of Iowa campus. Average attendance is 150/week.
Purpose/Features: Open to "all adults who have a desire to write." Conference offers courses in nearly all writing forms. In 2000, offerings available for poets included 21 poetry classes for all levels. Speakers were Marvin Bell, Michael Dennis Browne, Timothy Liu, Jane Mead, James McKean and Kathryn Rhett.
Costs/Accommodations: Cost for 2000 conference was $175 for a weekend course and $390-420 for a one-week course. Participants are responsible for their own meals. Accommodations available at the Iowa House and the Sheraton. Housing in residence hall costs about $28/night.
Additional Info: Participants in week-long workshops will have private conference/critique with workshop leader. Send for brochures and registration forms. "Requests for info are accepted via phone, fax or e-mail." Website includes complete catalog of courses, faculty, workshop descriptions, registration forms, schedules, etc.

THE IWWG SUMMER CONFERENCE, The International Women's Writing Guild, P.O. Box 810, Gracie Station, New York NY 10028, phone (212)737-7536, fax (212)737-9469, e-mail dirhahn@aol.com, website www.iwwg.com, executive director Hannelore Hahn. Annual week-long event founded 1978. Usually held the second Friday in August through the following Friday. Location: Skidmore College in Saratoga Springs, NY. Average attendance is 450.
Purpose/Features: Open to all women. Sixty-five workshops offered. "At least four poetry workshops offered for full week."
Costs/Accommodations: Cost is $750 for conference program and room and board.
Additional Info: "Critiquing available throughout the week." Send SASE for brochures and registration forms or request via e-mail (include mailing address for response). The International Women's Writing Guild's bi-monthly newsletter publishes and features hundreds of outlets for poets. See listing in Organizations.

N KEY WEST WRITERS' WORKSHOP, 5901 College Rd., Key West FL 33040, phone (305)296-9081, ext. 302, fax (305)292-5155, website www.firn.edu/cc/fkcc, director Irving Weinman. One 5-day and 4 weekend events founded 1996. Usually held from early December or late January to early May at "the conference room of Key West's historic Old City Hall—a modernized 1890's landmark building in the heart of the old town. Subsidiary activities (introductory get-together and optional Literary Walking Tour) also held in Old Town, Key West." Average attendance is limited to 15 for poetry weekends, "or smaller if poet workshop leader wishes."
Purpose/Features: Open to all. However, "not for beginners." Workshops purpose is to "bring the best writers (some of whom live in Key West) into an intimate workshop setting with serious writers at all but beginning stages of their writing careers. Workshops to date have been offered in poetry, short fiction, essay, feature journalism and (5-day) novel/screenplay outlining." Offerings specifically available to poets have included weekend workshops with Richard Wilbur and John Ashbery.
Costs/Accommodations: Cost is $250/weekend; participants are responsible for their own meals; discounts are available "but, as yet, only to local county residents." Information on overnight accommodations is available.
Additional Info: Send SASE for brochures and registration forms. Inquiries via fax OK. "Interested poets will be put on our brochure mailing list."

N ⊕ LEDBURY POETRY FESTIVAL, Church St., Ledbury, Herefordshire HR8 1DH United Kingdom, phone +44(0)1531 634156, fax +44(0)1531 631193, e-mail prog@poetry-festival.com, website www.poetry-festival.com, festival manager Blanca Rey-Surman. Annual 2-week event founded 1987. 2001 dates: June 30 to July 8. 2000 dates were June 29 to July 9. Location: "Various venues in Ledbury (e.g., church, halls, schools). Ledbury is a small medieval market town. The town nestles in the wooded and rolling hills of Southeast Hereford-shire. Accessible by rail, bus and car." Average attendance is 24,000.
Purpose/Features: Open to poets and "literature-interested writers and readers." Festival covers poetry for adults, children and the elderly; also related music and drama events, walks and tours. Offerings include workshops, readings, The Poetry Place Platform, and a poetry slam. Speakers at last conference were Tom Paulin, Carol Ann Duffy, Simon Armitage and Alastair McGowan.
Costs/Accommodations: Costs vary; participants are responsible for their own meals. Discounts available to students (20%). Information on overnight accommodations is available. Accommodations include special rates at area hotels.
Additional Info: Contest sponsored as part of festival. Prizes include 1st Prize-£100, 2nd Prize-£50; junior (12-16) £50 book token, children (5-11) £50 book token. Judge for 2000 was Carol Ann Duffy (Poet Laureate nominee). Send SASE (or SAE and IRC) for brochures and registration forms. Inquiries via fax and e-mail OK.

LIGONIER VALLEY WRITERS CONFERENCE, P.O. Box B, Ligonier PA 15658, phone (724)537-3341, fax (724)537-0482. Annual 3-day event founded 1986. Usually held in July. 2000 dates were July 7-9. "This is a relaxing, educational, inspirational conference in a scenic, small town." Average attendance is 80.

Purpose/Features: Open to anyone interested in writing. Conference covers fiction, creative nonfiction and poetry.

Costs/Accommodations: Cost for conference is approximately $200. Participants are responsible for their own dinner and lodging. Information on overnight accommodations is available for registrants.

Additional Info: Send 9×6 SASE for brochures and registration forms. "We also publish *The Loyalhanna Review*, a literary journal, which is open to participants."

✓ **THE LITERARY FESTIVAL AT ST. MARY'S**, St. Mary's College of Maryland, St. Mary's City MD 20686, e-mail msglaser@osprey.smcm.edu, website www.smcm.edu/academics/litfest, contact Dr. Michael S. Glaser. An annual event held during the last 2 weekends in May. Approximately 18 guest poets and artists participate in and lead workshops, seminars and readings. Concurrent with the festival, St. Mary's College offers 2-week intensive writing workshops in poetry and fiction and a 10-day writer's community retreat.

Purpose/Features: The poetry and fiction workshop engages the participants in structured writing experiences. Intended for anyone with a serious interest in writing. They offer 4 college credits or may be taken as non-credit courses. The retreat, designed for the serious writer, offers individual plans for writing alone or in conjunction with other participants..

Additional Info: For applications or more information on these workshops or the festival, please write to Michael S. Glaser at the above address. Inquiries via e-mail OK. Website includes dates, events and participants.

✓ ◯ ◙ **MANHATTANVILLE'S WRITERS' WEEK**, Manhattanville College, 2900 Purchase St., Purchase NY 10577, phone (914)694-3425, fax (914)694-3488, e-mail dowdr@mville.edu, website www.manhattanville.edu, dean—graduate and profession studies, Ruth Dowd, RSCJ. Annual 5-day event founded 1983. Usually held the last week in June at the Manhattanville College campus (June 26-30, 2000) "suburban surroundings 45 minutes from downtown Manhattan." Average attendance is mroe than 90.

Purpose/Features: Open to "published writers, would-be writers and teachers of creative writing. The conference offers workshops in five genres: fiction, short story, creative nonfiction, poetry, screenwriting, children's/young adult literature. There is also a special workshop in The Writers' Craft for beginners." Offerings specifically available for poets include a poetry workshop conducted by Marie Howe. "In past years we have had such distinguished poet/workshop leaders as Mark Doty, Stephanie Strickland and Honor Moore. We generally feature a lecture by a distinguished writer."

Costs/Accommodations: Cost for conference is $560. Participants are responsible for their own meals. Information on overnight accommodations is available. "Rooms in the residence halls are available or students may choose to stay at area hotels. Housing in on-site facilities costs $25-30/night."

▨ **MIDLAND WRITERS CONFERENCE**, Grace A. Dow Memorial Library, 1710 W. St. Andrews, Midland MI 48640, phone (517)837-3435, fax (517)837-3468, e-mail ajarvis@vlc.lib.mi.us, conference coordinator Ann Jarvis. Annual 1-day event founded 1979. 1999 date was June 14. Location: Grace A. Dow Memorial Library in Midland, MI. Average attendance is 100.

Purpose/Features: Open to any writer, published or unpublished. Conference includes sessions that vary in content. The keynote speaker was Peggy Noonan. "We always have a well-known keynoter. In the past we have had Judith Viorst, Kurt Vonnegut, David McCullough, P.J. O'Rourke, Dave Barry and Pat Conroy." In 1999, presenters included Lev Raphael (Mystery Author), Jan Wahl (Children's Author), Steve Raphael (Newsletters) and Cynthia Sterling (Literary Agent).

Costs/Accommodations: Cost for conference was $50 until 2 weeks prior to the event ($60 after that). For students, senior citizens and handicapped participants, cost was $40 until 2 weeks prior to the event ($50 after that). Information on overnight accommodations is available for registrants.

Additional Info: Send for brochures and registration forms or request via e-mail (include mailing address for response). Brochures mailed in late April.

▨ **MISSISSIPPI VALLEY WRITERS CONFERENCE**, 3403 - 45th St., Moline IL 61265, phone (309)762-8985, e-mail kimseuss@aol.com, founder/director David R. Collins. Annual week-long event founded 1973. Usually held the second week in June at the Liberal Arts College of Augustana College. Average attendance is 80.

Purpose/Features: Open to all writers, "beginning beginners to polished professionals." Conference provides a general professional writing focus on many genres of writing. Offers week-long workshop in poetry. Evening programs as well as daily workshops are included.

Costs/Accommodations: Cost for conference was $25 registration, $50 one workshop, $90 two workshops, $40 each additional workshop. Conferees may stay on campus or off. Board and room accommodations are available at Westerlin Hall on Augustana campus, 15 meals and 6 nights lodging approximately $200.

MARKETS THAT WERE listed in the 2000 edition of *Poet's Market* but do not appear this year are listed in the General Index with a notation explaining why they were omitted.

Additional Info: Individual critiques are also available. Submit up to 10 poems. Awards presented by workshop leaders. Send SASE for brochures and registration forms. Inquiries via e-mail OK.

✔️ **MOUNT HERMON CHRISTIAN WRITERS CONFERENCE**, P.O. Box 413, Mount Hermon CA 95041, phone (831)335-4466, fax (831)335-9413, e-mail dtalbott@mhcamps.org, website www.mounthermon.o rg, director of specialized programs David R. Talbott. Annual 5-day event founded 1970. Always held Friday through Tuesday over Palm Sunday weekend. 2001 dates: April 6-10. Location: Full hotel-service-style conference center in the heart of the California redwoods. Average attendance is 250-300.
Purpose/Features: Open to "anyone interested in the Christian writing market." Conference is very broad-based. Always covers poetry, fiction, article writing, writing for children, plus an advanced track for published authors. Offerings specifically available for poets have included several workshops on poetry, plus sessions on the greeting card industry plus individual one-hour workshops on poetry. "We usually have 35-40 teaching faculty. Faculty is made up of publishing reps of leading Christian book and magazine publishers, plus selected freelancers." Other special features have included an advance critique service (no extra fee); residential conference, with meals taken family-style with faculty; private appointments with faculty; and an autograph party. "High spiritual impact."
Costs/Accommodations: Cost for 1999 conference was $730 deluxe; $610 standard; $520 economy; including 13 meals, snacks, on-site housing and $300 tuition fee. No-housing fee: $450. $15 airport, Greyhound or Amtrack shuttle from San Jose, CA.
Additional Info: Send SASE for brochures and registration forms. Inquiries via fax and e-mail OK.

✔️ **NAPA VALLEY WRITERS' CONFERENCE**, Napa Valley College, 1088 College Ave., St. Helena CA 94574, phone (707)967-2900, fax (707)967-2909, e-mail writecon@admin.nvc.cc.ca.us, website www.napacomed. org/writersconf, contact Mark Wunderlich, managing director Anne Evans. Annual week-long event founded 1981. Usually held the last week in July or first week in August at Napa Valley College's new facility in the historic town of St. Helena, 30 minutes north of Napa in the heart of the valley's wine growing community. Average attendance is 48 in poetry and 48 in fiction.
Purpose/Features: "The conference has maintained its emphases on process and craft, featuring a faculty as renowned for the quality of their teaching as for their work. It has also remained small and personal, fostering an unusual rapport between faculty writers and conference participants. The poetry session provides the opportunity to work both on generating new poems and on revising previously written ones. Participants spend time with each of the staff poets in daily workshops that emphasize writing new poems—taking risks with new material and forms, pushing boundaries in the poetic process." The 1999 poetry faculty was Mark Doty, Lynn Emannuel, Jane Hirshfield and David Lehman. "Participants register for either the poetry or the fiction workshops, but panels and craft talks are open to all writers attending. Evenings feature readings by the faculty that are open to the public and hosted by Napa Valley wineries."
Costs/Accommodations: Cost is $475, not including meals or housing. There are some limited partial scholarships, depending on donations. A list of valley accommodations is mailed to applicants on acceptance and includes at least one reduced-rate package. "Through the generosity of Napa residents, limited accommodations in local homes are available on a first-come, first-served basis."
Additional Info: All applicants are asked to submit a qualifying ms with their registration (no more than 5 pgs. of poetry or 10-15 pgs. of fiction) as well as a brief description of their background as a writer. Application deadline: June 1. Send SASE for brochures and registration forms. Inquiries via fax and/or e-mail OK. Website includes dates for next year's conference, faculty, format and application process.

CHRISTOPHER NEWPORT UNIVERSITY WRITERS' CONFERENCE & CONTEST, 1 University Place, Newport News VA 23606, phone (757)594-7158, fax (757)594-8736. Annual 2-day event founded 1981. Usually held in early April. 1999 dates were April 9-10. Location: the Christopher Newport University Student Center. Average attendance is 110.
Purpose/Features: Open to "all writers, any age, professional or amateur." Covers fiction, nonfiction, poetry, publishing, juvenile fiction, memoirs, romance, grammar and scriptwriting. Conference is designed "to educate, entertain, network, support and enrich."
Costs/Accommodations: Cost for 1999 was $70, including lunches; discounts are available to senior citizens and students. Information on overnight accommodations is available.
Additional Info: Contest sponsored for poetry, nonfiction, fiction and juvenile writing as part of conference. Judges are "different each year; authors, professors in each field." Send SASE for brochures and registration forms. Also publishes *The Voyager* ($5/year) which "contains information regarding the planning of the conference, other contest information in the region and accomplishments of past presenters."

✔️ **NORTHWEST OKLAHOMA WRITERS WORKSHOP**, 118 Lookout, Enid OK 73701, phone (580)237-6535, fax (580)237-2744, e-mail enidwriters@yahoo.com, website www.scribequill.com/enidwrtiers.ht ml, workshop coordinator Bev Walton-Porter. Annual 1-day event (9 AM to 3:30 PM) founded 1991. Usually held in April. Location: Cherokee Strip Conference Center, 123 W. Maine, Enid OK 73701. Average attendance is 40-50.

Purpose/Features: Open to writers of all genres. The workshop provides general writing instruction. Offerings specifically available for poets include a section on poetry. Speaker at last workshop was Annie Jones.
Costs/Accommodations: Cost is $45, including meals, discounts are available for early registration ($40 if registered a week before the workshop).
Additional Info: Send SASE for brochures and registration forms or obtain via website. Inquiries via fax and e-mail OK. The workshop is sponsored by the Enid Writers Club which publishes *EWC Times*, a quarterly newsletter for writers. Website includes information about writers club, writing samples, writing resources, information on contests/workshop and bookstore. Inquiries via e-mail OK.

N OAKLAND UNIVERSITY WRITERS' CONFERENCE, College of Arts and Sciences, 231 Varner Hall, Oakland University, Rochester MI 48309-4401, phone (248)370-3125, fax (248)370-4280, e-mail gjboddy@ oakland.edu, website www.oakland.edu/contin-ed/writersconf/, director Gloria J. Boddy. Annual 1½-day event founded 1961. 1999 dates: October 15-16. "The Oakland University Writers' Conference is conducted in the university student center, in meeting rooms and large dining/meeting areas, plus adjoining classroom buildings with lecture halls." Average attendance is 400-500.
Purpose/Features: Open to beginning through professional adult writers. "No restrictions as to geographic area." The conference is designed to "help writers develop their skills, to provide information (and contact) for getting published; to provide a current picture of publishing markets; to furnish a venue for networking. All genres of writing are covered." The conference offers "critiques, both one-on-one and group, on Friday. On Saturday, 36 concurrent sessions dealing with all aspects of writing in a variety of genres are available in four time slots. A well-known professional writer speaks at lunch. A panel of the major speakers answers questions in the concluding session."
Costs/Accommodations: Cost for 1999 conference is $38-48 for Friday critiques; $75 for Saturday conference plus $12 for lunch. "Discounts are not offered." Information on overnight accommodations is available for registrants.
Additional Info: Work must be submitted, in advance, for individual critiques. Brochures and registration forms available each September 1 prior to the October conference.

N OZARK CREATIVE WRITERS CONFERENCE, 6817 Gingerbread Lane, Little Rock AR 72204-4738, phone (501)565-8889, fax (501)565-7220, e-mail pvining@aristotle.net, conference counselor Peggy Vining, founded 1968. Annual 3-day event. Held second full weekend in October at the Inn of the Ozarks in Eureka Springs, Arkansas. 2000 dates; October 12-14.
Purpose/Features: Open to all writers.
Costs/Accommodations: Registration fee is $50 prior to September 1. "Eureka Springs is a resort town so register early for lodging (say you are with OCWI). Eighty rooms are blocked at the Inn of The Ozarks for the conference."
Additional Info: Various writing contests sponsored as part of conference. Sizeable monetary awards given for all types of writing. Send #10 SASE for brochure after April 1.

N PENNWRITERS ANNUAL CONFERENCE, RR2 Box 241, Middlebury Center PA 16935, phone (570)376-3361/2821, fax (570)376-2674, e-mail cjhoughtaling@usa.net, website http://pennwriters.org, treasurer C.J. Houghtaling. Annual 3-day event founded 1987. 2001 dates: May 18-20. Location: Grantville Holiday Inn, Grantville PA (near Hershey). Average attendance is 200.
Purpose/Features: Open to all writers novice to multi-published. Covers nonfiction and poetry. Offers workshops/seminars, appointments with agents and editors, autograph party, contests—all multi-genre oriented. Theme for 2001 conference is "A Way With Words."
Costs/Accommodations: Cost for 2001 conference is $130, includes some meals. A special dinner event costs $35. "Scholarship awards are presented to Pennwriter members who are winners in our annual writing contests." Transportation to and from airport/train station arranged with advance notice. Information on overnight accommodations is available. Housing in on-site facilities costs $82 per room double occupancy.
Additional Info: Contest sponsored as part of conference. Entries limited to 1 page, typed or handwritten (must be legible). Send SASE for brochures and registration forms or via website. Inquiries via fax and e-mail OK. "The Pennwriters Annual Conference is sponsored by Pennwriters, Inc., a nonprofit organization with goals to help writers get published." Website includes mission statement, bulletin board, events calendar and details, Board of Director's bios, chat room, store and membership form.

✓ PIMA WRITERS' WORKSHOP, Pima College, 2202 W. Anklam Rd., Tucson AZ 85709, phone (520)206-3020, fax (520)206-6020, e-mail mfiles@pimacc.pima.edu, director Meg Files. Annual 3-day event founded 1987. 2000 dates were May 26-29. Location: Pima College's Center for the Arts, "includes a proscenium theater, a black box theater, a recital hall, and conference rooms, as well as a courtyard with amphitheater." Average attendance is 200.
Purpose/Features: Open to all writers, beginning and experienced. "The workshop includes sessions on all genres (nonfiction, fiction, poetry, writing for children and juveniles, screenwriting) and on editing and publishing, as well as manuscript critiques and writing exercises." Faculty included David Citino, Karla Kuban, Victoria

Lipman, Nancy Mairs, Howard Meibach, Robert J. Serling, Sherri Szeman, Jacqueline Woodson and others, including 2 agents. Other special features include "the accessibility to writers, agents and editors; and the workshop's atmosphere—friendly and supportive, practical and inspirational."

Costs/Accommodations: Cost is $65; participants are responsible for their own meals. Information on overnight accommodations is available.

Additional Info: Individual critiques also available. Submit 3 poems in advance to Meg Files. Inquiries via fax or e-mail OK.

☑ **POETRY ALIVE! SUMMER RESIDENCY INSTITUTE FOR TEACHERS**, 20 Battery Park, Suite 505, Asheville NC 28801, phone (800)476-8172 or (828)232-1045, fax (828)232-1045, e-mail poetry@poetryaliv e.com, website www.poetryalive.com, director Allan Wolf. Annual 6-day event founded 1990. 2000 dates were June 18-24, July 16-22, July 23-29. Location: University of North Carolina at Asheville. Average attendance is 20/session.

Purpose/Features: Open to anyone. Themes or panels for conference have included "creative writing (poetry), reader response techniques, poem performance techniques and teaching." Speakers at last conference were Allan Wolf (performance poetry, writing) and Cheryl Bromley Jones (reader response, writing). Other special features include a trip to Connemara, the Carl Sandburg Home Place, and dinner out at the Grove Park Inn.

Costs/Accommodations: Cost for the 2000 conference was $700, including meals and housing in on-site facilities; discounts available to local commuters "who don't pay the cost of food and lodging." Transportation to and from the event is not provided. "We provide transportation from the airport."

Additional Info: Call or write for brochures and registration forms. Inquiries via fax and e-mail OK. "This workshop is designed specifically for teachers or any poets interested in working with students in the schools or as an educational consultant." Inquiries via fax OK. Website includes photos, descriptions, dates and prices.

[N] 🌐 🖉 **THE POETS' HOUSE/TEACH NAH'EIGSE**, Clonbarra, Falcarragh, Donegal Ireland, phone (00353)74 65470, fax (00353)74 65471, e-mail phouse@iol.ie, website members.tripod.com/~poetshouseireland, director Janice Fitzpatrick Simmons. Annual 10-day events, offered 3 times/summer, founded 1990. Usually held July through August in "a large performance area and classroom library in a traditional Irish cottage (refurbished)." Average attendance is 12-20/session.

Purpose/Features: Open to "all interested in writing poems and in Irish poetry; to apply send three poems." Conference is designed to "bring Irish and American poets together." Offerings specifically available to poets include a morning lecture, afternoon workshop and an evening reading by the poet of the day. "Poets on summer faculty may talk about what they wish." Faculty has included Sherod Santos, Billy Collins, Paul Durcan, John Montague, Medbh McGuckian, Eamon Grennan, Paula Meehan, Theo Dorgan and Bernard O'Donoghue.

Costs/Accommodations: Cost for 2000 was £450; summer program participants are responsible for their own meals. Information on overnight accommodations is available.

Additional Info: Individual critiques are also available. Submit 10 poems in advance to the directors. Send SASE for brochures and registration forms. Inquiries via fax OK. "We also offer an M.A. in Creative Writing (poetry) validated and awarded by Lancaster University." Cost £6,150 per annum (tuition only).

🏕 **SAGE HILL WRITING FALL POETRY COLLOQUIUM**, P.O. Box 1731, Saskatoon, Saskatchewan S7K 3S1 Canada, phone/fax (306)652-7395, e-mail sage.hill@sk.sympatico.ca, website www.lights.com/sagehill, executive director Steven Ross Smith. Annual 21-day event founded 1995. Usually held the first 3 weeks in October at "the peaceful milieu of St. Peter's College, adjoining St. Peter's Abbey, in Muenster, 125 kilometers east of Saskatoon."

Purpose/Features: Open to poets, 19 years of age and older, who are working in English. The colloquium offers "an intensive three-week workshop/retreat designed to assist poets with manuscripts-in-progress. Each writer will have established a publishing record in books or periodicals and will wish to develop his/her craft and tune a manuscript. There will be ample time for writing, one-on-one critiques, and group meetings to discuss recent thinking in poetics. Eight writers will be selected. Writers in and outside Saskatchewan are eligible." The instructor for the 2000 colloquium is Tim Lilburn.

Costs/Accommodations: Cost was $875, including tuition, accommodations and meals. "A university registration fee of $25 will be added if taking this course for credit." Transportation from Saskatoon can be arranged as needed. On-site accommodations included in cost.

Additional Info: Send SASE for brochures and registration forms. Website includes program information, scholarship information, tuition, course outlines, faculty profiles, application information and down-loadable application forms. Application deadline is July 30, 2000.

🏕 **SAGE HILL WRITING SUMMER EXPERIENCE**, P.O. Box 1731, Saskatoon, Saskatchewan S7K 3S1 Canada, phone/fax (306)652-7395, e-mail sage.hill@sk.sympatico.ca, website www.lights.com/sagehill, executive director Steven Ross Smith. Annual 7-day and 10-day events founded in 1990. Usually held the end of July through the beginning of August. The Summer Experience is located at St. Michael's Retreat, "a tranquil facility in the beautiful Qu'Appelle Valley just outside the town of Lumsden, 25 kilometers north of Regina." Average attendance is 54.

Purpose/Features: Open to writers, 19 years of age and older, who are working in English. No geographic restrictions. The retreat/workshops are designed to "offer a special working and learning opportunity to writers at different stages of development. Top quality instruction, a low instructor-writer ratio, and the rural Saskatchewan setting offers conditions ideal for the pursuit of excellence in the arts of fiction, poetry, playwriting, and creative nonfiction." Offerings specifically available for poets include a poetry workshop and poetry colloquium. The faculty in 2000 includes Dennis Cooley, Myrna Kostash and Daniel David Moses.

Costs/Accommodations: Cost for the last conference was $595, includes instruction, accommodations and meals. Limited local transportation to the conference is available. "Van transportation from Regina airport to Lumsden will be arranged for out-of-province travellers." On-site accommodations offer individual rooms with a writing desk and washroom.

Additional Info: Individual critiques offered as part of workshop and colloquium. Writing sample required with application. Application deadline: April 25, 2000.. Send SASE for brochures and registration forms. Website includes program information, scholarship information, tuition, application information and down-loadable application forms.

SAN DIEGO STATE UNIVERSITY WRITERS CONFERENCE, 5250 Campanile Dr., San Diego CA 92182-1920, phone (619)594-2517, fax (619)594-8566, e-mail jwahl@mail.sdsu.edu, website www.ces.sdsu.edu, extension director Jan Wahl. Annual 3-day event founded 1984. 2001 dates: January 19-21. Location: Double Tree Hotel, San Diego Mission Valley, 7450 Hazard Center Dr., San Diego. Average attendance is 350.

Purpose/Features: Open to writers of fiction, nonfiction, children's, poetry and screenwriting. "We have participants from across North America." The conference offers numerous workshops in fiction, nonfiction, general interest, children's, screenwriting, magazine writing and poetry. Speakers at last conference included Paul Breznick (senior editor, William Morrow), Tracy Sherrod (senior editor, Bantam Books), Tom Miller (senior editor, John Wiley and sons) and Joe Veltre (associate editor, St. Martins Press). Other special features include networking lunch, editor/agent appointments and novel writing workshops.

Costs/Accommodations: Cost is $225-300, including 1 meal, discounts are available for early registration. Transportation to and from the event is provided by the Doubletree Hotel. Information on overnight accommodations is available. Accommodations include special rates at The Doubletree Hotel.

Additional Info: Individual critiques are also available. See brochure for details. Contest sponsored as part of conference. "Editors and agents give awards for favorite submissions." Send SASE for brochures and registration forms or obtain via website. Inquiries via fax or e-mail OK. Website includes complete conference brochure posted November prior to January conference.

N: SAN JUAN WRITERS WORKSHOP, P.O. Box 68, Moab UT 84532, phone (435)259-7750, fax (435)259-2335, e-mail cfinfo@canyonlandsfieldinst.org, website www.canyonlandsfieldinst.org, contact registrar. Annual 4-day event usually held in March. Based out of the Recapture Lodge in scenic Bluff, Utah. Attendance is a maximum of 24.

Purpose/Features: Open to all. Workshop focuses on small group sessions discussing a sense of place and developing writing skills, related to natural history and community life.

Costs/Accommodations: Cost is $440, includes instruction, lodging and meals.

☑ THE SANDHILLS WRITERS CONFERENCE, Augusta State University, Augusta GA 30904, phone (706)737-1500, fax (706)667-4770, e-mail akellman@aug.edu, website www.aug.edu/langlitcom/sand_hills_conference, conference director Anthony Kellman. Annual 3-day event founded 1975. Facilities are handicapped accessible. Usually held the third weekend in March. 2000 dates: March 23-25. Average attendance is 100.

Purpose/Features: Open to all aspiring writers. Conference designed to "hone the creative writing skills of participants and provide networking opportunities. All areas are covered—fiction, poetry, children's literature, playwriting, screenwriting and writing of song lyrics, also nonfiction." Offerings specifically available to poets include craft lectures, ms evaluations and open readings. Speakers for next conference are Pulitzer Prize winner Robert Olen Butler (keynote) and New York literary agent Jane Dystel. Other faculty will give craft sessions and readings in poetry, fiction, nonfiction, children's literature, playwriting and songwriting.

Costs/Accommodations: Cost for 1999 was $156, including lunches; participants are responsible for dinners only. Information on overnight accommodations is available.

Additional Info: Individual critiques are also available. Submit 6 poems with a limit of 15 pages. Contest sponsored as part of conference. "All registrants who submit a manuscript for evaluation are eligible for the contest determined by the visiting authors in each respective genre." Send SASE for brochures and registration forms. Inquiries via fax and e-mail OK.

SEWANEE WRITERS' CONFERENCE, 310 St. Luke's Hall, 735 University Ave., Sewanee TN 37383-1000, phone (931)598-1141, e-mail cpeters@sewanee.edu, website www.sewanee.edu/Writers_Conference/home.html, conference coordinator Cheri B. Peters. Annual 12-day event founded 1990. Held the last 2 weeks in July at The University of the South ("dormitories for housing, Women's Center for public events, classrooms for workshops, Sewanee Inn for dining, etc."). Attendance is about 105.

Purpose/Features: Open to poets, fiction writers and playwrights who submit their work for review in a competitive admissions process. "Genre, rather than thematic, workshops are offered in each of the three areas."

In 2000, faculty members included fiction writers Tony Earley, Barry Hannah, Diane Johnson, Alice McDermott, Erin McGraw, Claire Mssud, Padgett Powell and Francine Prose; poets Andrew Hudgins, Mary Jo Salter, Dave Smith and Mark Strand; and playwrights Laura Maria Censabella and Romulus Linney. Other speakers included editors, agents and additional writers.

Costs/Accommodations: Cost for conference was $1,205, including room and board. Each year scholarships and fellowships based on merit are available on a competitive basis. "We provide free bus transportation from the Nashville airport on the opening day of the conference and back to the airport on the closing day."

Additional Info: Individual critiques are also available. "All writers admitted to the conference will have an individual session with a member of the faculty." A ms should be sent in advance after admission to the conference. Write for brochure and application forms. No SASE necessary. Inquiries via e-mail OK.

SINIPEE WRITERS WORKSHOP, Continuing Education, Loras College, Dubuque IA 52004-0178, phone (319)588-7139, fax (319)588-7964, e-mail lcrosset@loras.edu, director Linda Crossett. Annual 1-day event founded 1986. Usually held the third or fourth Saturday in April on the campus of Loras College, Dubuque, IA. Average attendance is 50-100.

Purpose/Features: Open to anyone, "professional or neophyte," who is interested in writing. Conference covers fiction, poetry and nonfiction.

Costs/Accommodations: Cost for the last workshop was $60 pre-registration, $65 at the door. Scholarships covering half of the cost are traditionally available to senior citizens and to full-time students, both college and high school. Cost includes handouts, coffee and donut break, lunch, snacks in afternoon and book fair with authors in attendance available to autograph their books. Information on overnight accommodations is available for out-of-town registrants.

Additional Info: Annual contest for nonfiction, fiction and poetry sponsored as part of workshop. There is a $5 reading fee for each entry (article/essay of 1,500 words, short story of 1,500 words or poetry of 40 lines). 1st Prize in each category is $100 plus publication, 2nd Prize $50 and 3rd Prize $25. Competition receives 50-100 entries. Entrants in the contest may also ask for a written critique by a professional writer. The cost for critique is an additional $15/entry. Send SASE for brochures and registration forms.

SOCIETY OF THE MUSE OF THE SOUTHWEST (S.O.M.O.S.), P.O. Box 3225, Taos NM 87571, phone (505)758-0081, fax (505)758-4802, e-mail somos@laplaza.com, website http://somostaos.org, contact administrator. Founded 1983. "We offer readings, special events and workshops at different times during the year, many during the summer." Length of workshops vary. Held at various sites in Taos. Average attendance is 10-50.

Purpose/Features: Open to anyone. "We offer workshops in various genres—fiction, poetry, nature writing, etc." Past workshop speakers have included Denise Chavez, Alfred Depew, Marjorie Agosin, Judyth Hill, Robin Becker and Robert Westbrook. Other special features include writing in nature/nature walks and beautiful surroundings in a historic writer's region.

Costs/Accommodations: Cost for workshops range from $30-175, excluding room and board. Information on overnight accommodations is available.

Additional Info: Send SASE for brochures and registration forms. Inquiries via fax or e-mail OK. Website includes description of event. "Taos has a wonderful community of dedicated and talented writers who make SOMOS workshops rigorous, supportive and exciting." Also publish *Chokecherries*, an annual anthology. Website includes upcoming events and soon "streaming audio" with poets reading their own works/words.

SOUTHAMPTON COLLEGE WRITERS CONFERENCE, 239 Montauk Hwy., Southampton NY 11968, phone (631)287-8349, fax (631) 287-8253, e-mail summer@southampton.liu.edu, website www.southampton.liu.edu, summer director Carla Caglioti. Annual 10-day to 2-week events founded 1976. 2000 dates were June 28-July 6. "The Writers Conference is held at Southampton College of Long Island University. The College is located in the heart of the Hamptons, one of the most beautiful and culturally rich resorts in the country. The campus occupies an attractive 110-acre site in the gently sloping Shinnecock Hills with views of the Atlantic Ocean, Shinnecock Bay and Peconic Bay." Average attendance is 45.

Purpose/Features: Open to writers, graduate students and upper-level undergraduate students. Conference covers poetry, fiction, short story and nonfiction. Theme for 2000 conference was "Writing for Love" and

**FOR EXPLANATIONS OF THESE SYMBOLS,
SEE THE INSIDE FRONT AND BACK COVERS OF THIS BOOK.**

"Writing for Money." Offerings specifically available for poets include a poetry workshop. Speakers at last conference were William Heyen, John Dufresne, June Spence, Robert Leuci, Annette Gordon-Reed, Susan Choi, Carter Coleman and Robert Reeves.

Costs/Accommodations: Cost was $580; participants are responsible for their own meals, discounts are available. "Each additional workshop is at the reduced rate of $350." Information on overnight accommodations is available. Housing in on-site facilities costs $230 to share a room with another participant, $340 for a single.

Additional Info: Send SASE for brochures and registration forms or obtain via website. Inquiries via fax or e-mail OK. "We have a College website which contains information on the Writers Conference under its summer offerings. Visitors should go to to the index and click on 'Summer' and then 'Writer's Conference.' "

☑ ◻ ◐ **SOUTHWEST WRITERS WORKSHOP**, 8200 Mountain Rd., NE, Suite 106, Albuquerque NM 87110, phone (505)265-9485, fax (505)265-9483, e-mail swriters@aol.com, website www.southwestwriters. org, contact contest chair. Annual 3- to 4-day event founded 1982. 2000 dates: September 21-24. Location: Marriott Hotel, Albuquerque. Average attendance is 500.

Purpose/Features: Open to all writers. Workshop covers all genres, focus on getting published—over 20 editors, agents and producers as presenters. "As part of the conference, SWW has an annual writing contest with a category for poetry. Contest judges are editors and agents." Recent contest winnders were Judith Buffaloe, Leroy Stradford and Kathryn Stevens. Other special features include preconference sessions on first 2 days of conference, appointments with editors, agents, producers and publicists.

Costs/Accommodations: Cost is $180-260. Early Bird discount if registered by July 15. Information on overnight accommodations is available. Accommodations include special rates at area hotels.

Additional Info: Individual critiques are also available through entry in annual contest. Submit poems with a limit of 50 lines in advance with $18 (member), $23 (nonmember) fee. Each must have separate entry form and fee. Send for entry form and rules. Send SASE for brochures and registration forms or obtain via website. Inquiries via fax or e-mail OK. Website includes contest rules, past winners, prize information, registration forms, conference registration forms and membership information.

SQUAW VALLEY COMMUNITY OF WRITERS POETRY WORKSHOP, 10626 Banner Lava Cap, Nevada City CA 95959, phone (530)274-8551 or 583-5200, e-mail svcw@oro.net, website www.squawvalleywriters.org, executive director Brett Hall Jones. Annual 7-day event founded 1969. 2000 dates were July 22-29. The workshop is held in The Squaw Valley Ski Corporation's Lodge. Squaw Valley is located in the Sierra Nevada near Lake Tahoe. "The workshop takes place in the off-season of the ski area. Participants can find time to enjoy the Squaw Valley landscape; hiking, swimming, river rafting and tennis are available." Average attendance is 64.

Purpose/Features: Open to talented writers of diverse ethnic backgrounds and a wide range of ages. "The Poetry Program differs in concept from other workshops in poetry. Our project's purpose is to help our participants to break through old habits and write something daring and difficult. Workshops are intended to provide a supportive atmosphere in which no one will be embarrassed, and at the same time to challenge the participants to go beyond what they have done before. Admissions are based on quality of the submitted manuscripts." Offerings include regular morning workshops, craft lectures and staff readings. "The participants gather in daily workshops to discuss the work they wrote in the previous 24 hours." 2000 staff poets: Lucille Clifton, Robert Hass, Galway Kinnell, Sharon Olds and Li-Young Lee.

Costs/Accommodations: Cost was $595, included regular morning workshops, craft lectures, staff readings and dinners. Scholarships are available. "Requests for financial aid must accompany submission/application, and will be granted on the perceived quality of manuscript submitted and financial need of applicant." Transportation to workshop is available. "We will pick poets up at the Reno/Lake Tahoe Airport if arranged in advance. Also, we arrange housing for participants in local houses and condominiums on the valley. Participants can choose from a single room for $375/week or a double room for $250/week within these shared houses. We do offer inexpensive bunk bed accommodations on a first come, first served basis."

Additional Info: Individual conferences are also available. "Only work-in-progress will be discussed." Send SASE for brochures and registration forms or request via e-mail (include mailing address for response). Inquiries via e-mail OK. Website also includes content of brochure. "We also publish an annual newsletter."

STEAMBOAT SPRINGS WRITERS CONFERENCE, P.O. Box 774284, Steamboat Springs CO 80477, phone (970)879-8079, e-mail freiberger@compuserve.com, director Harriet Freiberger. Annual 1-day event founded 1981. Usually held the third weekend in July. The conference site is a "renovated train station, the Depot is home of the Steamboat Springs Arts Council—friendly, relaxed atmosphere." Average attendance is 35-40 (registration limited).

Purpose/Features: Open to anyone. Conference is "designed for writers who have limited time. Instructors vary from year to year, offering maximum instruction during a weekend at a nominal cost." Speakers for 1999 included fiction writer Robert Greer, editor-in-chief of *High Plains Literary Review*, and Renate Wood, published poet, instructor at University of Colorado and on the faculty of MFA Program for Writers at Warren Wilson College.

Costs/Accommodations: Cost for 1999 was $35 (before May 29), including lunch. "A variety of lodgings available. Special discounts at Steamboat Resorts."

Additional Info: Send SASE for brochures and registration forms. Inquiries via e-mail OK. The conference is affiliated with *Seedhouse*, "a new publication with rapidly expanding circulation encourages submissions from unpublished writers. It is a 'not-for-profit' and 'no advertisement' publication." (See complete listing for *Seedhouse* in the Publishers of Poetry section of this book.)

☑ **SUMMER WRITING PROGRAM AT THE UNIVERSITY OF VERMONT**, 322 S. Prospect St., Burlington VT 05401, phone (800)639-3210, fax (802)656-0306, e-mail dlusk@pop.uvm.edu, website uvmce.uvm.edu:443/sumwrite.htm, director Daniel Lusk. Annual event founded 1994. Usually held during the month of July on the University of Vermont's campus, located in Burlington and close to Lake Champlain; room and board available on campus." Average attendance is 75-100.
Purpose/Features: Open to all qualified writers. "Workshops designed to provide supportive, non-competitive, demanding environments that focus on constructive criticism and encouragement. Less intensive lecture option offers seminars, small group sessions, and readings intended for new writers and those who prefer to work at their own pace." Workshop and lecture options covers fiction, poetry, autobiographies and nonfiction. The 1999 program featured Stephen Dunn, Gary Margolis, Philip Baruth, Pamela Painter, David Bradley, Joyce Johnson, David Huddle, Bill Roorbach and Leslie Ullman.
Costs/Accommodations: Costs for 1999 were $850 (workshop option), $200 (lecture option); residency fee of $700 includes private room and meals.
Additional Info: Inquiries via e-mail OK. No program in Summer 2000.

SWT SUMMER CREATIVE WRITING CAMP, Dept. of English, Southwest Texas State University, San Marcos TX 78666, phone (512)245-2163, fax (512)245-8546, e-mail swl3@swt.edu, website www.English.swt.edu/Camp.html, director Steve Wilson. Annual week-long event founded 1989. Usually held the last week in June. "The camp is held on the campus of the 21,000-student Southwest Texas State University, which is also home to a nationally recognized Master of Fine Arts program in creative writing. SWTSU is located in Central Texas, roughly twenty miles from Austin." Attendance is limited to 20 participants.
Purpose/Features: Open to all high school students. "Because the camp is for high school students, we ask that participants take workshops in both fiction and poetry. In addition to our standard workshops in poetry, we offer workshops in revision, and each camper takes part in one-on-one tutorials with the poetry workshop leaders. On the final day of the writing camp, campers present a public reading of their writing for friends, family and people from the local community."
Costs/Accommodations: Cost is $250, including meals. All campers stay in SWT residence halls. Costs included in program fee.
Additional Info: Send SASE for brochures and registration forms. "Our application deadline is April 15 of each year." Inquiries via fax or e-mail OK. "Our writing camp is quite competitive, so we encourage interested poets to send their best work." Website includes "an overview of our program, application details and links to information about SWT and San Marcos."

N **TAOS ART SCHOOL**, P.O. Box 2588, 432 Este Es Rd., Taos NM 87571, phone (505)758-0350, fax (505)758-4880, e-mail tas@laplaza.org, website www.taosartschool.org, founder/director Ursula Beck. Annual week-long events founded 1995. Workshops held every week from June through October. Location: in and around Taos. Average attendance is 10-12 students/workshop.
Purpose/Features: Open to writers and artists. "This college-credited school is about using the Arts as a language for the interrelatedness of all things. We represent a community of artists, philosophers, writers, sculptors, architects and scholars searching for the spiritual dimensions of Art and the artistic dimensions of the Spirit. We specialize in authentic Native American courses taught on site." Offerings specifically available to poets include workshops on creativity, yoga and poetry.
Costs/Accommodations: Cost for 1999 was $350; participants are responsible for their own meals, discounts are available. Information on accommodations is available. Accommodations include special rates at area hotels.
Additional Info: Write for brochures and registration forms. Inquiries via fax and e-mail OK. Website includes class schedule with tuition information and registration information.

N ⊕ **TŶ NEWYDD WRITERS' CENTRE**, Taliesin Trust, Llanystumdwy, Cricieth, Gwynedd LL52 0LW Wales, Great Britain, phone 01766 522811, fax 01766 523095, e-mail tynewydd@dial.pipeoc.com, director Sally Baker, founded 1990. 4½-day courses held throughout the year. Courses run Monday evening through Saturday morning at Tŷ Newydd, "a house of historical and architectural interest situated near the village of Llanystumdwy. It was the last home of Lloyd George, the former British prime minister. It stands in landscaped gardens and has fine views over Cardigan Bay towards the mountains of Meirionnydd." Average attendance is 12/course.
Purpose/Features: Open to anyone over 16 years of age. Courses are designed to "promote the writing and understanding of literature by providing creative writing courses at all levels for all ages. Courses at Tŷ Newydd provide the opportunity of working intimately and informally with two professional writers." Courses specifically for poets, of all levels of experience and ability, are offered throughout the year.
Costs/Accommodations: Cost for a 4½-day course is £320 (inclusive), some weekend courses available, cost is £125 (inclusive). Transportation to and from Centre is available if arranged at least a week in advance. Participants stay at Tŷ Newydd House in shared bedrooms or single bedrooms. "Vegetarians and people with

special dietary needs are catered for but please let us know in advance. Course participants help themselves to breakfast and lunch and help to prepare one evening meal as part of a team. Participants should bring towels and their own writing materials. Some typewriters and word processors are available."
Additional Info: Send SASE for brochures and registration froms. Inquiries via fax and e-mail OK.

☑ **UND WRITERS CONFERENCE,** University of North Dakota, Department of English, Grand Forks ND 58202-7209, phone (701)777-2768, e-mail jmckenzi@badlands.nodak.edu, website www.und.nodak.edu, director/professor James McKenzie. Annual 4- to 5-day event founded 1970. 2000 dates: March 20-24. "The conference takes place in the UND student Memorial Union, with occasional events at other campus sites, especially the large Chester Fritz Auditorium or the North Dakota Museum of Art." Average attendance is 3,000-5,000. "Some individual events have as few as 20, some over 1,000."
Purpose/Features: All events are free and open to the public. "The conference is really more of a festival, though it has been called a conference since its inception. The conference has a history of inviting writers from all genres. The conference's purpose is public education, as well as a kind of bonus curriculum at the University. It is the region's premier intellectual and cultural event." Theme for 2000 conference was "Writing War." Individual panel topics are "Vietnam Shadows," "Imagining the Enemy," "Who is the Enemy?" and "Writing War: Reflections and Responses." Faculty for 2000: Louis Simpson (poetry, memoir); Barbara Sonneborn (film); Tessa Bridal and Robert Olen Butler (fiction); Helen Fremont (memoir); Ha Jin (poetry, fiction); Eavan Boland (poetry, memoir); Arnold Isaacs (journalism); John Balaban (poetry, fiction, memoir). "They read, participate in panels and otherwise make themselves available in public and academic venues." Speakers at last conference were Joseph Bruchac, Robert Clark, Mark Doty, Galway Kinnell, Ruhama Veltfort and Terry Tempest Williams. Other special features include open-mike student/public readings every morning, informal meetings with writers, autograph sessions and dinners, receptions.
Additional Info: Send SASE for brochures. Inquiries via fax OK. Website includes biographies of visiting writers and complete conference schedule.

UNIVERSITY OF WISCONSIN-MADISON'S SCHOOL OF THE ARTS AT RHINELANDER, 715 Lowell Center, 610 Langdon St., Madison WI 53703-1195, fax (608)265-2475, e-mail kgb@mail.dcs.wisc.edu, website www.dcs.wisc.edu/lsa, administrative coordinator Kathy Berigan. Annual 5-day event founded 1964. Held July 24-28, 2000. Held at a local junior high school. Average attendance is 300.
Purpose/Features: Open to all levels and ages. Offerings specifically available for poets include poetry workshops and related workshops in creativity.
Costs/Accommodations: Cost for 2000 workshop ranged from $130-345. Information on overnight accommodations is available for registrants.
Additional Info: Write for brochures and registration forms.

🍁 ☑ **VICTORIA SCHOOL OF WRITING,** Box 8152, Victoria, British Columbia V8W 3R8 Canada, phone (250)595-3000, e-mail viewrite@islandnet.com, website www.islandnet.com/vicwrite/, registrar Margaret Dyment. Annual 4-day event founded 1996. 2000 dates were July 18-21. Location: "Residential school in natural, parklike setting. Easy parking, access to university, downtown." Average attendance is 100.
Purpose/Features: "A three- to ten-page manuscript is required as part of the registration process, which is open to all. The general purpose of the workshop is to give hands-on assistance with better writing, working closely with established writers/instructors. We have workshops in fiction, poetry and work-in-progress; plus two other workshops which vary." Offerings specifically available for poets include one of the intensive 4-day workshops (12 hours of instruction and one-on-one consultation). In 2000, this workshop was led by Don MacKay (Governor General's Award 1991).
Costs/Accommodations: Cost for 2000 workshop was $475 Canadian; includes 4 lunches and 1 dinner. Other meals and accommodations are available on site. "For people who register with payment in full before May 1, the cost is $435 Canadian."
Additional Info: Contest sponsored as part of conference. Most recent contest winners were Sara Cassidy, Betsy Trumpener and Sarah Pollard. Competition receives approximately 200 entries. Send SASE for brochures and registration forms. Inquiries via e-mail OK. Website includes bios of instructors, some workshop information, registration form, course descriptions and contest winners.

☑ **WESLEYAN WRITERS CONFERENCE,** Wesleyan University, Middletown CT 06457, phone (860)685-3604, fax (860)685-2441, e-mail agreene@wesleyan.edu, website www.wesleyan.edu/writing/conferen .html, director Anne Greene. Annual 5-day event founded 1956. Usually held the last week in June on the campus of Wesleyan University. The campus is located "in the hills overlooking the Connecticut River, a brief drive from the Connecticut shore. Wesleyan's outstanding library, poetry reading room, and other university facilities are open to participants." Average attendance is 100.
Purpose/Features: "Open to both experienced and new writers. The participants are an international group. The conference covers the novel, short story, fiction techniques, fiction-and-film, poetry, literary journalism and memoir." Special sessions recently included "Reading of New Fiction," "The Writers Life," "Writing Memoirs," and

"Publishing." Offerings specifically for poets included manuscript consultations and daily seminars with Pulitzer Prize-winner William Meredith and Honor Moore and Ha Jin. Other faculty included Madison Smartt Bell, Chris Offutt, Roxana Robinson, Jonathan Schell, and Amy Bloom.

Costs/Accommodations: Cost in 1999, including meals, was $680 (day rate); $795 (boarding rate). "Wesleyan has scholarships for journalists, fiction writers, nonfiction writers and poets. Request brochure for application information." Information on overnight accommodations is available. "Conference participants may stay in university dormitories or off campus in local hotels."

Additional Info: Individual critiques are also available. Registration for critiques must be made before the conference. Inquiries via fax and e-mail OK. Website includes overview of conference, information on schedule and faculty, scholarship information, rates and registration form.

☑ **WHIDBEY ISLAND WRITERS' CONFERENCES**, 5456 Pleasant View Lane, Freeland WA 98249, phone (360)331-6714, fax (360)331-6714, e-mail writers@whidbey.com, website www.whidbey.com/writers, director Celeste Mergens. Annual weekend event founded 1997. Usually held the first weekend in March at the South Whidbey High School's state-of-the-art facility, except for Friday's Author Fireside Chats, which are held in private residencies within the community." 2001 dates: March 2-4. Average attendance is 250.

Purpose/Features: Open to writers of every genre and skill level. Conference covers fiction, nonfiction, poetry, children's and screenwriting. Offerings specifically available for poets include workshops, panels and readings. Speakers at last conference included poets Pattiann Rogers, Maurya Simon, Bart Baxter and Susan Zwinger. Other special features include "Author Fireside Chats which are opportunities to meet and learn from the faculty in personable home settings with groups of 20 or less. Participants spend the day focusing on their chosen genre."

Costs/Accommodations: Cost for 2001 conference is $258, includes 3 meals, volunteer discounts available. "Rideshare board available through our website." Information on overnight accommodations is available. Accommodations include special rates at "local B&B's, as well as roommate share lists and dorm-style accommodations as low as $10/night.

Additional Info: Individual critiques are also available. Submit 8 poems with a limit of 2 poems/page by February 15. Send SASE for brochures and registration forms or obtain via website. Inquiries via e-mail OK. The conference is sponsored by the Whidbey Island Writers' Association. Website includes information about the conference, the presenters, accommodations, links to Whidbey Island information, registration forms, how-to best prepare to make the most of agent/editor/publisher meetings and conference opportunities. "This conference has been designed to offer personable interaction and learning opportunities. We consider all presenters and participants to be part of the 'team' here. We emphasize practical application strategies for success as well as workshop opportunities. We try to invite at least one poetry publisher per year (Copper Canyon Press in 1999)."

WINTER POETRY & PROSE GETAWAY IN CAPE MAY, 18 North Richards Ave., Ventnor NJ 08406, phone (609)823-5076, e-mail wintergetaway@hotmail.com, website www.wintergetaway.com, founder/director Peter E. Murphy. Annual 4-day event founded 1994. 2001 dates: January 12-15. "The Conference is held at the Grand Hotel on the Oceanfront in Historic Cape May, New Jersey. Participants stay in comfortable rooms with an ocean view, perfect for thawing out the muse. Hotel facilities include a pool, sauna, and whirlpool, as well as a lounge and disco for late evening dancing for night people." Average attendance is 150.

Purpose/Features: Open to all writers, beginners and experienced, over the age of 18. "The poetry workshop meets for an hour or so each morning before sending you off with an assignment that will encourage and inspire you to produce exciting new work. After lunch, we gather together to read new drafts in feedback sessions led by experienced poet-teachers who help identify the poem's virtues and offer suggestions to strengthen its weaknesses. The groups are small and you receive positive attention to help your poem mature. In late afternoon, you can continue writing or schedule a personal tutorial session with one of the poets on staff." Previous staff included Renee Ashley, Robert Carnevale, Cat Doty, Stephen Dunn, Kathleen Rockwell Lawrence, Charles Lynch, Peter Murphy, Jim Richardson and Robbie Clipper Sethi. There are usually 10 participants in each poetry workshop and 5 in each of the prose workshops. Other special features include extra-supportive sessions for beginners.

Costs/Accommodations: Cost for 2000 conference was $355, includes breakfast and lunch for 3 days, all sessions as well as a double room; participants are responsible for dinner only. Discounts are available. "Early Bard Discount: Deduct $25 if paid in full by November 15, 2000." Single-occupancy rooms are available at additional cost.

Additional Info: Individual critiques also available. "Each poet may have a 20-minute tutorial with one of the poets on staff." Write for brochures and registration forms. "The Winter Getaway is known for its challenging, yet supportive atmosphere that encourages imaginative risk-taking and promotes freedom and transformation in the participants' writing."

☑ **WISCONSIN REGIONAL WRITERS' ASSOCIATION INC.**, 510 W. Sunset Ave., Appleton WI 54911-1139, phone (920)734-3724, fax (920)734-5146, e-mail wrwa@lakefield.net, website www.inkwells.net/wrwa. Biannual conferences. Held first Saturday in May and last weekend in September at various hotel-conference centers around the state. Average attendance is 100-150.

Purpose/Features: Open to all writers, "aspiring, amateur or professional." All forms of writing/marketing presentations rotated between conferences. "The purpose is to keep writers informed and prepared to express and market their writing in a proper format." Poetry covered formally once a year. A book fair is held at the fall conference where members can sell their published works. A banquet is also held at the fall conference Saturday and Sunday, September 23 and 24, 2000, where the Jade Ring writing contest winners from 6 categories receive awards. Winners of two additional writing contests also receive awards at the spring conference. Most recent contest winner was Jackie Langetieg.

Costs/Accommodations: Spring conference is approximately $35-40, the 2-day fall conference approximately $40-60. Conferences also include Saturday morning buffet, the fall conference offers a hors d'oeuvres buffet at the Book Fair and entertainment at the Jade Ring Banquet. Meals (Saturday luncheon and dinner) are at an additional cost. Information about overnight accommodations is available for registrants. "Our organization 'blocks' rooms at a reduced rate."

Additional Info: Sponsors 3 writing contests/year. Membership in the WRWA and small fee are required. Send SASE for brochures and registration forms. "We are affiliated with the Wisconsin Fellowship of Poets and the Council of Wisconsin Writers. We also publish a newsletter, *Wisconsin Regional Writer*, four times a year for members." Website includes conference information, including a registration form; membership application; local club network; links to numerous other writers websites; link to upcoming speakers.

THE WRITERS' CENTER AT CHAUTAUQUA, P.O. Box 408, Chautauqua NY 14722, phone (617)964-8773, e-mail writer999@mindspring.com, co-directors Clara Silverstein and Carol Hicks. Annual event founded 1988. Held 9 weeks in summer from late June to late August. Participants may attend for 1 week or more. "We are an independent, cooperative association of writers located on the grounds of Chautauqua Institution." Average attendance is 60 for readings and speeches, 15 for workshops.

Purpose/Features: Readings and speeches are open to anyone; workshops are open to writers (or auditors). The purpose is "to make creative writing one of the serious arts in progress at Chautauqua; to provide a vacation opportunity for skilled artists and their families; and to help learning writers improve their skills and vision." Workshops are available all 9 weeks. Poetry Works meets 2 hours each day. In 2000, leaders included Richard Foerster, Kathleen Aguero, Wendy Mnookin, Lia Purpura, Geraldine Connolly, Bruce Bennett, Gregory Donovan, Michael Waters and Jim Daniels. Prose Works offers 2 hours a day in fiction and nonfiction, writing for children and Young Writers' Workshops. Poets are welcome to explore other fields. Other special features include 2 speeches a week and 1 reading, usually done by the Writers-In-Residence.

Costs/Accommodations: Cost is $100/week. Participants are responsible for gate fees, housing and meals and "may bring family; sports, concerts, activities for all ages. A week's gate ticket to Chautauqua is $180/adult (less if ordered early); housing cost varies widely, but is not cheap; meals vary widely depending on accommodations—from fine restaurants to cooking in a shared kitchen." Access is best by car or plane to Jamestown, NY. Contact the center for housing options.

Additional Info: Individual critiques are also available. Information published in spring mailing. Send SAE with 2 first-class stamps for brochures and registration forms. Inquiries via fax or e-mail OK. "We offer retroactive scholarship to one poet per summer. He or she is elected by workshop peers." The center also offers 4 workshops for children. "We now aid in the publication of poetry, creative nonfiction and fiction in two area newspapers (*The Post-Journal* and *The Dunkirk Observer*) via the coordination of two Saturday literature pages for the papers' joint Saturday magazine. The readership is 85,000. We have published poets from the likes of Lewis Turco and Marjorie Agosin to a 'beginning' 97-year-old nursing home resident. We seek excellence, general audience appeal and are limited to publishing regional writers and poets."

N WRITERS' CONFERENCE AT OAKLAND UNIVERSITY, 261 Varner Hall, Rochester MI 48309-4401, phone (248)370-3125, fax (248)370-4280, e-mail gjbody@oakland.edu, website www.oakland.edu/contened/writersconf/, director Gloria J. Boddy. Annual 1½-day event founded 1961. 2000 dates were October 20-21. Location: Oakland University campus. Average attendance is 350.

Purpose/Features: Open to all writers, all experience levels, all genres. "Conference provides an opportunity to exchange ideas and perfect writing skills by meeting with agents, editors and successful writers. The program features private and group manuscript evaluations, a choice of 40 presentations and a luncheon keynote speaker.

Costs/Accommodations: Cost for 2000 conference is $85 plus $12 for meals. Information on overnight accommodations is available. Accommodations include special rates at area hotels.

Additional Info: Individual critiques are also available. Submit up to 10 pages of poems with $58 fee. Write for brochures and registration forms or obtain via website. Inquiries via fax and e-mail OK. This conference is co-sponsored by the Oakland University College of Arts and Sciences and Detroit Women Writers. "Detroit Women Writers welcomes published authors to their membership. They function as a networking/support group for each other and host readings/workshops." Website includes brochure, speaker bios, schedule of events, registration info.

N WRITING TODAY, Birmingham-Southern College, Box 549003, Birmingham AL 35254, phone (205)226-4921, fax (205)226-3072, e-mail mross@bsc.edu, website www.bsc.edu, director of special events Martha Ross. Annual 2-day event founded 1978. 2000 dates were April 7-8. Location: Birmingham-Southern College campus. Average attendance is 400-500.

Purpose/Features: Open to "everyone interested in writing—beginners, professionals and students. Conference topics vary year to year depending on who is part of the faculty." Speakers at the last conference were Pat Conroy, Connie May Fowler, Richard North Patterson and David Sedaris.

Costs/Accommodations: Cost for 1999 conference was $120 before deadline ($125 after deadline), including lunches. Cost for a single day's events was $60, including luncheon. Either day's luncheon was $25. $10 cancellation fee. Information on overnight accommodations is available for registrants. Accommodations include special rates at area hotels.

Additional Info: Individual critiques are also available. In addition, the Hackney Literary Awards competition is sponsored as part of the conference. The competition, open to writers nationwide, offers $5,000 ($2,500 state level, $2,500 national level) in prizes for poetry and short stories and a $5,000 award for the novel category. Send SASE for conference information and see the listing for the Hackney Literary Awards in Contests and Awards. Send SASE for brochure or obtain via website.

YOSEMITE: ALIVE WITH POETRY, The Yosemite Association, Yosemite Field Seminars, P.O. Box 230, El Portal CA 95318, phone (209)379-2321, fax (209)379-2486, e-mail yose_yosemite_association@nps.gov, website www.yosemite.org, seminar coordinator Penny Otwell. Annual 3-day event. 2000 dates: October 13-15. Location: Yosemite Valley in Yosemite National Park. Average attendance is 8-10.

Purpose/Features: Open to "both emerging poets and those who are perhaps already published." Seminar is designed to "explore the exquisite fall scenery of Yosemite Valley through poetry. The seminar combines poetry writing tehniques with interesting, short hikes to areas that offer enticing fall color. Time is planned for free-writing exercises as well as for solitude to reflect and to write personal poems. Each day will feature a hike of no more that two miles, and will end with a friendly, informal group poetry reading and discussion. The instructor, poet-naturalist Kristina Rylands, will be available to help students throughout the seminar. A group anthology will be compiled by the instructor at a later day for mailing to each interested student."

Costs/Accommodations: Cost is $195 ($185 for Yosemite Association members); participants are responsible for their own meals. "Cabins are pre-reserved for students, and run about $54/night. We also offer free camping."

Additional Info: Call for brochures. "The Yosemite Association is a non-profit organization dedicated to educating the public about Yosemite. We publish books, offer 68 field seminars, and give funding to the National Park Service from our book sales. We welcome new members and will honor the member fee for those individuals just joining." Website includes course description for Alive With Poetry and 60 other seminars, along with a web camera live photo of the Yosemite Valley.

Organizations

The organizations listed in this section offer encouragement and support to poets and other writers through a wide variety of services. They may sponsor contests and awards, hold regular workshops or open-mike readings, or release publications with details about new opportunities and area events. Many of these groups provide a combination of these services to both members and nonmembers.

The PEN American Center, for instance, holds public events, sponsors literary awards, and offers grants and loans to writers in need. Poets seeking financial assistance should contact the arts council in their state or province (see State & Provincial Grants on pages 498-500).

Many organizations provide opportunities to meet and discuss work with others. Those poets with access to the Internet can connect with other poets from around the world through various online writing groups. The National Federation of State Poetry Societies, Inc., the National Writers Association and the Canadian Poetry Association are all national organizations with smaller affiliated groups which may meet in your state or province. And for those seeking gatherings more local or regional in focus, there are organizations such as the Davidson County Writers' Guild, the Ozark Poets, Virginia Writers Club and Writers Collective.

In addition to local and regional associations, there are organizations that focus on helping certain groups of writers. For instance, the International Women's Writing Guild supports women writers through various national and regional events and services.

For organizations close to home, check for information at a library or bookstore, or contact the English department at a nearby college. Your local branch of the YMCA is also a good source for information on writing groups and programs. In fact, the YMCA National Writer's Voice Project sponsors both open-mike readings and readings by nationally known writers in various YMCAs throughout the country. For more information, contact your local YMCA or the Chicago-based offices of the National Writer's Voice Project at (800)USA-YMCA, ext. 515, website www.YMCA.net.

If you are unable to find a local writer's group, however, start one by placing an ad in your community newspaper or posting a notice on a library or bookstore bulletin board. There are sure to be others in your area who would welcome the support, and the library or bookstore might even have space for your group to meet on a regular basis.

To locate some of the larger organizations (or representative samples of smaller groups), read through the listings that follow. Then send a SASE to those groups that interest you to receive more details about their services and membership fees. Also refer to the list of Additional Organizations at the end of this section, as well as the Publications of Interest section on pages 540-545.

ACADEMI–YR ACADEMI GYMREIG/THE WELSH ACADEMY, Mount Stuart House, 3rd Floor, Cardiff, Wales CF10 5FQ United Kingdom, phone 029 2047 2266, fax 029 2049 2930, e-mail post@academi.org, website www.academi.org, chief executive Peter Finch. Founded in 1959 to "promote literature in Wales and to assist in the maintaining of its standard." The Welsh National Literature Promotion Agency and Society of Writers is open to "the population of Wales and those outside Wales with an interest in Welsh writing." Currently has 2,000 total members. Levels of membership available are associate, full and fellow. Offerings available for poets include promotion of readings, events, conferences, exchanges, tours; employment of literature development workers; publication of a bimonthly events magazine; publication of a literary magazine in Welsh (*Taliesin*) and another (*NWR*) in English. Sponsors conferences/workshops and contests/awards. Publishes *A470: What's On In Literary Wales*, a magazine appearing 6 times a year that contains information on Welsh literary events. Also available to nonmembers for £15 (annual subscription). Members and nationally known writers give readings that are open to the public. Sponsors open-mike readings for members and the public. Membership dues are £15/ year. Send SASE for additional information or obtain via website. Inquiries via fax OK.

☑ **ADIRONDACK LAKES CENTER FOR THE ARTS**, P.O. Box 205, Rte. 28, Blue Mountain Lake NY 12812, phone (518)352-7715, fax (518)352-7333, e-mail alca@telenet.net, program coordinator Daisy Kelley. An independent, private, nonprofit educational organization founded in 1967 to promote "visual and performing arts through programs and services, to serve established professional and aspiring artists and the region through educational programs and activities of general interest." Open to everyone. Currently has 1,300 members. Levels of membership available are individual, family and business. Offerings available for poets include workshops for adults and children, reading performances, discussions and lectures. Offers a "comfortable, cozy performance space—coffeehouse setting with tables, candles, etc." Computers available for members and artists. Publishes a triannual newsletter/schedule that contains news, articles, photos and a schedule of events. "All members are automatically sent the schedule and others may request a copy." Sponsors a few readings each year. "These are usually given by the instructor of our writing workshops. There is no set fee for membership, a gift of any size makes you a member." Members meet each July. Send SASE for additional information. Inquiries via fax and e-mail OK.

Ⓝ **THE AMERICAN POETS' CORNER, THE CATHEDRAL CHURCH OF ST. JOHN THE DIVINE**, Cathedral Heights, 1047 Amsterdam Ave. at 112 St., New York NY 10025, phone (212)316-7500, website www.stjohndivine.org/Cathedral, contact Dept. of Public Education, initiated in 1984 with memorials for Emily Dickinson, Walt Whitman and Washington Irving. It is similar in concept to the British Poets' Corner in Westminster Abbey, and was established and dedicated to memorialize this country's greatest writers. A Board of Electors comprised of thirteen eminent poets and writers choose one deceased author each year for inclusion in The American Poets' Corner. The Cathedral is also home to the Muriel Rukeyser Poetry Wall, a public space for posting poems, which was dedicated in 1976 by Ms. Rukeyser and the Cathedral's Dean. Send poems for the Poetry Wall to the above address.

☑ Ⓟ **ARIZONA AUTHORS ASSOCIATION; ARIZONA LITERARY MAGAZINE; ARIZONA AUTHORS NEWSLETTER**, P.O. Box 87857, Phoenix AZ 85080-7857, phone (623)780-0053, fax (623)780-0468, e-mail vijayaschartz@az.rmci.net, website http://home.rmci.net/vijayaschartz/azauthors.htm, president Vijaya Schartz, contact contest coordinator. Founded in 1978 to provide education and referral for writers and others in publishing. State-wide organization. Currently has 250 total members. Levels of memberships available are Published, Unpublished (seeking publication), Professional (printers, agents and publishers) and Student. Sponsors conferences, workshops, contests, awards. Sponsors annual literary contest with 4 categories: poetry, short story, essay and novel. Awards publication in *Arizona Literary Magazine* and $100 1st Prize in each category. Pays winners from other countries by international money order. Does not accept entry fees in foreign currencies. Submissions must be unpublished and may be entered in other contests. Submit any number of poems on any subject of up to 42 lines. Send SASE for entry form and guidelines. Entry fee: $10/poem. Submission period: January 1 through July 1. Competition receives 1,000 entries a year. Most recent contest winners include Philip A. Buonpastore, Marlene E. Meehl, Abraham Burickson, Liza Guzman and Stella Pope Duarte. Judges are Arizona authors. Winners will be announced by November 15. Publishes *Arizona Literary Magazine*. Also publishes *Arizona Authors Newsletter*. Membership dues are $45. Members meet bimonthly. Send SASE for additional information. Inquiries via fax and e-mail OK. Guidelines available on website.

☑ **ASSOCIATED WRITING PROGRAMS; WRITER'S CHRONICLE; THE AWP AWARD SERIES**, Tallwood House, MS 1E3, George Mason University, Fairfax VA 22030, phone (703)993-4301, fax (703)993-4302, e-mail awp@gmu.edu, website http://awpwriter.org, founded 1967. Offers a variety of services to the writing community, including information, job placement assistance, writing contests, literary arts advocacy and forums. Annual individual membership is $57; placement service extra. For $20/6 issues you can subscribe to the *Writer's Chronicle* (formerly *AWP Chronicle*), containing information about grants and awards, publishing opportunities, fellowships, and writing programs. They have a directory, *The AWP Official Guide to Writing Programs*, of over 250 college and university writing programs for $25.95 (includes shipping). Also publishes the *AWP Job List* magazine, approximately 20 pgs., that contains employment opportunity listings for writers in higher education, editing and publishing. Also publishes *The Director*, approximately 12 pgs. that contains information on writers' conferences and festivals. The AWP Award Series selects a volume of poetry (48 pg. minimum) each year ($10 entry fee for members; $20 for nonmembers) with an award of $2,000 and publication. Deadline: February 28. Send SASE for submission guidelines. Query after November. Competition receives approximately 1,400 entries. Inquiries via fax and e-mail OK. Most recent contest winners include Bonnie Jo Campbell, Edward Kleinschmidt Mayes and Michael Martone. Their placement service helps writers find jobs in teaching, editing and other related fields. Website includes information on AWP's core services, contest guidelines, conference information and links to other writer's organizations and creative writing programs.

🌐 **ASSOCIATION OF CHRISTIAN WRITERS**, 73 Lodge Hill Rd., Farnham, Surrey GU10 3RB England, phone/fax (01252)715746, e-mail christian-writers@dial.pipex.com, website dspace.dial.pipex.com/christian-wri ters/, administrator Warren Crawford. Founded in 1971 "to inspire, train, equip and encourage Christian writers." National charity with regional affiliations open to "anyone who affirms and practises the Christian faith and writes for pleasure or profit." Currently has 1,000 total members. Levels of membership available are New Writers (exploring), Noncommercial Writers, Intermediate (few pieces published) and Experienced Writers (regularly published). Offerings available for poets include "market news in quarterly magazine, poetry adviser for personal manuscript critiques, postal workshops with other poets and poetry competitions." Sponsors 3 training days/year and annual contests. Publishes *Candle and Keyboard*, a quarterly magazine. Membership dues are £15 sterling/ year. Send SASE for additional information. Inquiries via fax or e-mail OK.

☑ **THE AUTHORS GUILD, INC.**, 330 W. 42nd St., New York NY 10036, phone (212)564-5904, fax (212)564-8363, e-mail staff@authorsguild.org, website www.authorsguild.org, executive director Paul Aiken. Founded in 1912, it "is the largest association of published writers in the United States. The Guild focuses its efforts on the legal and business concerns of published authors in the areas of publishing contract terms, copyright, taxation and freedom of expression. The Guild provides free 75-point book and magazine contract reviews to members and makes group health insurance available to its members. The Guild also sponsors Backinprint.com, a service that allows members to republish and sell their out-of-print books. Writers must be published by a recognized book publisher or periodical of general circulation to be eligible for membership. We do not work in the area of marketing mss to publishers nor do we sponsor or participate in awards or prize selections." Also publishes the *Bulletin*, a quarterly journal for professional writers. Write, call or e-mail for information on membership.

ℕ AUTHORS LEAGUE FUND, 330 W. 42nd St., New York NY 10036. Makes interest-free loans to published authors and professional playwrights in need of temporary help because of illness or an emergency. No grants.

THE BEATLICKS, 1016 Kipling Dr., Nashville TN 37217, phone (615)366-9012, fax (615)366-4117, e-mail beatlick@bellsouth.net, website www.geocities.com/SoHo/Studios/9307/beatlick.html, editor Joe Speer. Founded in 1988 to "promote literature and create a place where writers can share their work." International organization open to "anyone interested in literature." Currently has 200 members. "There is no official distinction between members, but there is a core group that does the work, writes reviews, organizes readings, etc." Offerings available for poets include publication of work (they have published poets from Australia, Egypt, India and Holland), reviews of books and venues, readings for local and touring poets and a poetry hotline. "We have also hosted an open mic reading in Nashville since 1988. We have read in bars, bookstores, churches, libraries, festivals, TV and radio. We produce an hour show every Friday on public access TV. Poets submit audio and video tapes from all over. We interview poets about their work and where they are from." Publishes *Beatlick Poetry News* (bimonthly). The *Beatlick Poetry News* is a networking tool, designed to inform poets of local events and to bring awareness of the national scene. "We include poems, short fiction, art, photos, and articles about poets and venues." Submit short pieces, no vulgar language. "We try to elevate the creative spirit. We publish new voices plus well-established talents." Subscription: $12/year. Members meet twice a month. Send SASE for additional information. Inquiries via fax and e-mail OK. "We promote all the arts." Website includes poetry, fiction, articles, events calendar and Beatlick products.

ℕ BERGEN POETS, 180-G1 Summit Ave., Summit NJ 07901, phone (908)277-6245, fax (908)277-2171, president Ms. Roberta L. Greening, founded in 1969 to "bring together poets and friends of poetry in our area, help the individual in writing and appreciation of poetry, and add to the cultural life of the community." Open to anyone in the community interested in poetry. "Our base is in Bergen County, New Jersey. However, our members extend from New York to Florida." Currently has 40 members. Offerings available to poets include a free monthly workshop at Borders Books. Meets the 3rd Thursday of each month. Publishes a quarterly newsletter. Sponsors open-mike readings following featured members' readings. Annual membership dues are $15 and include newsletter, meeting announcements and eligibility to be published in cooperative anthology. Send SASE for additional information. "Bergen Poets is one of the oldest poetry organizations in the state of New Jersey."

ℕ ♥ BLACK CULTURAL CENTRE FOR NOVA SCOTIA, 1149 Main St., Dartmouth, Nova Scotia B2Z 1A8 Canada, phone (902)434-6223, or (800)465-0767, fax (902)434-2306, e-mail mail@bccns.com, website www.bccns.com, Founded in 1983 "to create among members of the black communities an awareness of their past, their heritage and their identity; to provide programs and activities for the general public to explore, learn about, understand and appreciate black history, black achievements and black experiences in the broad context of Canadian life. The centre houses a museum, reference library, small auditorium and workshops."

♥ BURNABY WRITERS' SOCIETY, 6584 Deer Lake Ave., Burnaby, British Columbia V5G 3T7 Canada, contact person Eileen Kernaghan, founded 1967. Corresponding membership in the society, including a newsletter subscription, is open to anyone, anywhere. Yearly dues are $30. Sample newsletter in return for SASE with Canadian stamp. The society holds monthly meetings at The Burnaby Arts Centre (located at 6450 Deer Lake Ave.), with a business meeting at 7:30 followed by a writing workshop or speaker. Members of the society stage regular public readings of their own work. Sponsors a contest for poetry open to British Columbia residents. Competition receives about 200-400 entries a year. Recent contest winners include Mildred Tremblay, Frank McCormack and Kate Braid. Send SASE for details. Inquiries by e-mail OK.

✓ **THE WITTER BYNNER FOUNDATION FOR POETRY, INC.**, P.O. Box 10169, Santa Fe NM 87504, phone (505)988-3251, fax (505)986-8222, e-mail bynner@mciworld.com, director Steven Schwartz. The foundation awards grants, ranging from $1,000 to $15,000, exclusively to nonprofit organizations for the support of poetry-related projects in the area of: 1) support of individual poets through existing nonprofit institutions; 2) developing the poetry audience; 3) poetry translation and the process of poetry translation; and 4) uses of poetry. The foundation "may consider the support of other creative and innovative projects in poetry." Letters of intent are accepted annually from September 1 through January 1; requests for application forms should be submitted to Steven Schwartz, executive director, at the address above. Applications if approved must be returned to the Foundation postmarked by February 1. Inquiries via fax and e-mail OK.

✓ ✓ **THE CANADA COUNCIL FOR THE ARTS; GOVERNOR GENERAL'S LITERARY AWARDS**, P.O. Box 1047, 350 Albert St., Ottawa, Ontario K1P 5V8 Canada, phone (613)566-4414, ext. 5576, fax (613)566-4410, e-mail josiane.polidori@canadacouncil.ca, website www.canadacouncil.ca. Established by Parliament in 1957, the Canada Council for the Arts "provides a wide range of grants and services to professional Canadian artists and art organizations in dance, media arts, music, theatre, writing, publishing and the visual arts." The Governor General's Literary Awards, valued at $10,000 (Canadian) each, are given annually for the best English-language and best French-language work in each of seven categories, including poetry. Books must be first-edition trade books written, translated or illustrated by Canadian citizens or permanent residents of Canada and published in Canada or abroad during the previous year (September 1 through the following September 30). Collections of poetry must be at least 48 pgs. long and at least half the book must contain work not published previously in book form. In the case of translation, the original work must also be a Canadian-authored title. Books must be submitted by publishers with a Publisher's Submission Form, which is available from the Writing and Publishing Section. Send SASE for guidelines and current deadlines. Inquiries via fax and e-mail OK. Website includes information sheet and application forms, as well as downloadable historical listings of award nominees and winners.

✓ **CANADIAN CONFERENCE OF THE ARTS (CCA)**, 130 Albert St., Suite 804, Ottawa, Ontario K1P 5G4 Canada, phone (613)238-3561, fax (613)238-4849, e-mail cca@mail.culturenet.ca, website www.cultur enet.ca/cca, is a national, nongovernmental, not-for-profit arts service organization dedicated to the growth and vitality of the arts and cultural industries in Canada. The CCA represents all Canadian artists, cultural workers and arts supporters, and works with all levels of government, the corporate sector and voluntary organizations to enhance appreciation for the role of culture in Canadian life. Each year, the CCA presents awards for contribution to the arts. Regular meetings held across the country ensure members' views on urgent and ongoing issues are heard and considered in organizing advocacy efforts and forming Board policies. Members stay informed and up-to-date through *Blizzart*, a newsletter, which is published 4 times a year, and receive discounts on conference fees and on all other publications. Membership is $30 (plus GST) for Canadian individual members, $35 for US members and $45 for international members. Website includes CCA activities and information.

CANADIAN POETRY ASSOCIATION; POEMATA; THE SHAUNT BASMAJIAN CHAPBOOK AWARD; THE HERB BARRETT AWARD, P.O. Box 22571, St. George PO, Toronto, Ontario M5S 1V8 Canada, phone (905)312-1779, fax (905)312-8285, e-mail ad507@freenet.hamilton.on.ca or cpa@wwdc.com, website www.mirror.org/grouips/cpa, national coordinator Wayne Ray. Founded in 1985, "to promote all aspects of the reading, writing, publishing, purchasing and preservation of poetry in Canada. The CPA promotes the creation of local chapters to organize readings, workshops, publishing projects, readings and other poetry-related events in their area." The CPS's bimonthly magazine, *Poemata*, features news articles, chapter reports, poetry by new members, book reviews, markets information, announcements and more. Membership is open to anyone with an interest in poetry, including publishers, schools, libraries, booksellers and other literary organizations, for $30/year. Seniors and students: $20. Send SASE for membership form. Also sponsors The Shaunt Basmajian Chapbook Award, awarding $100 (Canadian) and publication, plus 50 copies. Submissions may be entered in other contests. Submit up to 24 pgs. of poetry, in any style or tradition. Mss must be typed, single-spaced with title on each page. A separate sheet should give the title and the author's name and address. Simultaneous submissions OK. Send SASE for guidelines. Entry fee: $15 (Canadian). All entrants receive a copy of the winning chapbook. Annual deadline: March 31. Sponsors The Herb Barrett Award, with 3 prizes of $75, $50 and $25 (Canadian), and publication in anthology. Submit haiku no more than 4 lines long. Mss must be typed or printed, 1 poem/page, on letter-size paper with no identifying marks. Name, address and phone, with titles or first lines, should be on a separate sheet of paper. Submissions will not be returned. Send SASE for guidelines. Entry fees: $10 (Canadian)/1-2 poems $15 (Canadian)/3 or more poems. Each entrant will receive a copy of the anthology. Deadline: November 30. *Poemata* publishes articles, book reviews and essays related to writing. Sample newsletter: $3. Request information via e-mail. Make checks payable to Canadian Poetry Association.

✓ COLUMBINE STATE POETRY SOCIETY OF COLORADO, P.O. Box 461131, Denver CO 80246, phone (303)465-0883, e-mail wagil@aol.com, secretary/treasurer Anita Gilbert. Founded in 1978 to promote the writing and appreciation of poetry throughout Colorado. State-wide organization open to anyone interested in poetry. Currently has 72 total members. Levels of membership available are: Members at Large who do not participate in the local chapters, but who belong to the National Federation and the State level; and members who belong to the national, state and local chapter, in Denver, Colorado. Offerings for the Denver Chapter include weekly workshops and monthly critiques. Sponsors contests, awards for students and adults. Sponsors the Annual Poets Fest where members and nationally-known writers give readings and workshops that are open to the public. Also sponsors a chapbook contest in alternate years under Riverstone Press. Most recent winner in 1999 was Claire Keyes. Membership dues are $10 state and national, $25 local, state and national. Members meet weekly. Send SASE for additional information. Inquiries via e-mail OK. No fax inquiries.

✓ DAVIDSON COUNTY WRITERS' GUILD, Arts Council for Davidson County, 23 W. Second Ave., Lexington NC 27292, phone (336)248-2551, fax (336)248-2000, e-mail fraziers@lexcominc.net, president Eric Frazier. Founded in 1972 to "encourage creative writing; to bring together writers and those interested in writing; to share ideas and inspiration and to critique original pieces; to provide resources and programs to help develop writing talents; to provide opportunities to have writing talents recognized; and to promote writing through contests for children, youth and adults." A county-wide organization open to any interested person 16 years of age and older. Currently has 15 active members. Membership benefits include "monthly meetings that offer 6-7 opportunities to read original work and occasional guest speakers conducting workshops—including poetry-related topics. The Guild's monthly meetings are conducted in a conference room above Frazier's Bookstore." Sponsors 3 annual writing contests—Adult, High School and Youth. "Winning and runner-up entries are published for the High School and Youth Contests in a book entitled *Ventures in Writing.*" Competition receives over 300 entries a year. Members give readings that are open to the public. Sponsors open-mike readings. Memberships dues are $15/year. Members meet monthly. Send SASE for additional informational. Inquiries via fax and e-mail OK.

N ⊕ THE EASTERN SUBURBS POETRY GROUP-N.S.W., Off Oxford St. Complex, Bondi Junction, N.S.W. Australia, phone (02)96992129, e-mail merlyn@easy.com.au, coordinator/founder Merlyn Swan. Founded in 1988 to provide "a platform for poets to express themselves, the publishing of group's contributions, improvement of skills through themes set by group and occasional workshops." Open to "anyone interested in writing and/or listening to poetry." Currently has 50 core members. "Many others come in and out for the occasional meeting." Benefits for poets include having audience reaction and comments; an annual Public Reading; meeting and communicating with fellow poets/writers; chance to enhance skills; meeting and tackling new ideas. "We meet every first Friday of the month at Church in the Market Place. The Waverley Library sponsors our annual festival." Also sponsors conferences/workshops. Members give readings that are open to the public. Sponsors open-mike readings for members. "We have an annual festival, and poets who have attended three meetings in the year can read a couple or more poems." Membership dues are $3/attendance. Send SASE (or SAE and IRC) for additional information. Inquiries via e-mail OK.

N ✉ FEDERATION OF BRITISH COLUMBIA WRITERS, M.P.O. Box 2206, Vancouver, British Columbia V6B 3W2 Canada, phone (604)683-2057, fax (604)683-8269, e-mail fedbcwrt@pinc.com, website swifty.com/bcwa. The federation "is a nonprofit organization of professional and emerging writers of all genres." They publish a journal of markets, awards and literary news/events; act as "a network centre for various other provincial writer's organizations; host, promote and organize workshops, readings, literary competitions and social activities; distribute directories which are distributed to schools, businesses, and organizations which may request the services of writers; and represent writers' interests to other professionally related organizations." Inquiries via fax OK.

✓ GEORGIA POETRY SOCIETY; BYRON HERBERT REECE CONTEST; EDWARD DAVIN VICKERS CONTEST; CHARLES B. DICKSON CHAPBOOK CONTEST; GEORGIA POETRY SOCIETY NEWSLETTER, P.O. Box 371123, Decatur GA 30037-1123, phone (404)289-9428, president Herbert W. Denmark. Founded in 1979 to further the purposes of the National Federation of State Poetry Societies, Inc. in securing fuller public recognition of the art of poetry; to stimulate a finer and more intelligent appreciation of poetry; and to provide opportunity for study of and incentive for practice in the writing and reading of poetry. State-wide organization open to any person who is in accord with the objectives listed above. There are no restrictions as to age, race, religion, color, national origin or physical or mental abilities. Currently has 190 total members. Levels of membership available are Active, fully eligible for all aspects of membership; Student, same as Active except they pay lower dues, do not vote or hold office, and must be full-time enrolled students through college level; Lifetime, same as Active but pay a one-time membership fee the equivalent of approximately 15 years dues, receive free anthologies each year, and pay no contest entry fees. Offerings available for poets include affiliation with NFSPS. At least one workshop is held annually, contests are throughout the year, some for members only and some for general submissions. Workshops deal with specific areas of poetry writing, publishing, etc. Contests include the Byron Herbert Reece Contest, Edward Davin Vickers Contest, Charles B. Dickson Chapbook Contest (members only) and many ongoing or one-time contests, with awards ranging from $250 downwards. Most recent contest winner: June Owens won 1st Place ($250) in the 1999 Ed Vickers award. Entry fees and deadlines vary. Does not accept entry fees in foreign currencies. Send US dollars or money orders. Send SASE for complete guidelines. Publishes *Georgia Poetry Society Newsletter*, a quarterly. Also available to nonmembers on request. Readings are held annually to celebrate National Poetry Day (October) and National Poetry Month (April) in public forums such as libraries; some are with specified poets reading their own poetry or works of famous poets, and some are open-mike readings. At each quarterly meeting (open to the public) members have an opportunity to read their own poems. Current annual membership dues are Active: $20; Family: $35; Student: $10; Lifetime: $300. Members meet quarterly. "Our bylaws require rotation in office. We sponsor an active and popular Poetry in the Schools project, conducting workshops or readings in schools throughout the state by invitation. We also sponsor the annual Margery Carlson Youth Awards contest in all Georgia schools and winning poems are submitted to the Manningham Youth Awards contest of NFSPS. Our membership ranges from 9 to 93 years of age." Also sponsors The Octavio Paz Spanish Language Poetry Writing Contest with prizes of $50, $25, $10. Entry fee: $1/poem. Deadline: June 15.

✓ **GREATER CINCINNATI WRITERS' LEAGUE**, 2735 Rosina Ave., Latonia KY 41015, phone (606)491-2130, e-mail karenlgeo@hotmail.com, president Karen George. Founded in 1930s "to promote and support poetry and those who write poetry in the Cincinnati area and the attainment of excellence in poetry as an art and a craft. We believe in education and discipline, as well as creative freedom, as important components in the development of our own poetry and open, constructive critique as a learning tool." Regional organization open to anyone interested in and actively writing. Currently has 35 total members. Offerings available for poets include a monthly meeting/workshop or critique. Critics are published poets, usually faculty members from local universities, who critique poems submitted by members. The group also joins in the critique. Sponsors workshops, contests, awards with monetary awards, and an anthology published every 2 years. Members give readings that are open to the public or sponsor open-mike readings at bookstores and other locations. Membership dues are $25. Members meet monthly. Send SASE for additional information.

✓ **GUILD COMPLEX**, 2936 N. Southport, Suite 210, Chicago IL 60657, phone (773)296-1108, ext. 18, fax (773)528-5452, e-mail guildcomplex@earthlink.net, website www.nupress.nwu.edu/guild, executive director Julie Parson-Nesbitt. Founded in 1989 to "serve as a forum for literary cross-cultural expression, discussion and education, in combination with other arts. We believe that the arts are instrumental in defining and exploring human experience, while encouraging participation by artists and audience alike in changing the conditions of our society. Through its culturally inclusive, primarily literary programming, the Guild Complex provides the vital link that connects communities, artists and ideas. Over 10,000 people attend at least one of our events each year." Offerings available for poets include "over 140 literary events each year—workshops, featured readings, open-mikes, youth focused events, contests, multimedia literary festivals and a yearly writers conference. Our twice weekly featured readings range from the solo voice to book release parties to festivals combining poetry with video or music." Events are held at The Chopin Theater in Chicago. Sponsors "a women writers conference (also open to men) each fall, and offers writing workshops with locally and nationally known writers throughout the year. We also sponsor the Gwendolyn Brooks Open Mike Award each spring ($500 prize), and Tia Chucha Press, the publishing wing of Guild Complex, which publishes four full-length manuscripts of poetry per year." (See listing in Publishers of Poetry section.) Also publishes semi-monthly calendar of events sent "to everyone on a mailing list, not just members." Locally or nationally known writers give readings that are open to the public. Sponsors open-mike readings. "We present biweekly events featuring poets, writers, performance poets and storytellers. Our Tuesday night events are youth-focused, and our Wednesday night events are for general audiences. Open-mikes precede most of these events." Basic membership is $30. Send SASE for additional information. Inquiries via fax and e-mail OK. Website includes event listings, contact info and Tia Chucha Press info.

INDIANA STATE FEDERATION OF POETRY CLUBS; THE POETS RENDEZVOUS CONTEST; THE POETS SUMMER STANZAS CONTEST; THE POETS WINTERS FORUM CONTEST; INDIANA POET, 808 E. 32nd St., Anderson IN 46016, phone (765)642-3611, contact ISFPC president. Founded in 1941 to unite poetry clubs in the state; to educate the public concerning poetry; and to encourage poet members. State-wide organization open to anyone interested in poetry. Currently has 151 total members. Offerings available for poets include 2 conventions each year, and membership in NFSPS. Sponsors conferences, workshops. Sponsors The Poets Rendezvous Contest. Offers more than $1,000 in prizes for poems in more than 25 categories. Entry fee: $5. Deadline: August 15. Sponsors the Poets Winters Forum and The Poets Summer Stanzas contests, with prizes of $25, $15 and $10 with 3 honorable mentions. Entry fee: $1/poem. Does not accept entry fees in foreign currencies. Deadlines: January 15 and June 15 (respectively). Send SASE for details. Competitions receive 150-200 entries. Publishes *Indiana Poet*, a bimonthly newsletter. Members or nationally known writers give readings that are open to the public. Membership dues are $10/year (includes national membership). Members meet monthly in various local clubs. Send SASE for additional information.

INTERNATIONAL WOMEN'S WRITING GUILD, P.O. Box 810, Gracie Station, New York NY 10028, phone (212)737-7536, fax (212)737-9469, e-mail dirhahn@aol.com, website www.iwwg.com, contact Hannelore Hahn, founded 1976, "a network for the personal and professional empowerment of women through writing." The Guild publishes a bimonthly 32-page journal, *Network*, which includes members' needs, achievements, contests, and publishing information. A manuscript referral service introduces members to literary agents. Other activities and benefits are annual national and regional events, including a summer conference at Skidmore College (see listing under Conferences and Workshops); "regional clusters" (independent regional groups); round robin manuscript exchanges; and group health insurance. Membership in the nonprofit Guild costs $35/year in the US and $45/year foreign. Inquiries via fax and/or e-mail OK. Website includes membership services, calendar of events, profiles of members, etc.

JUST BUFFALO LITERARY CENTER, 2495 Main ·St., Buffalo NY 14214, phone (716)832-5400, fax (716)832-5710, e-mail justbflo@aol.com, executive director Ed Taylor, founded 1975. It offers readings, workshops, master classes, an annual competition for Western New York writers, Spoken Arts Radio broadcasts on National Public Radio affiliate WBFO, and Writers-in-Education programs for school-age populations. Just Buffalo acts as a clearinghouse for literary events in the Greater Buffalo area and offers diverse services to writers and to the WNY region. "Although we do not accept submissions for publication, we will review works for possible author readings."

THE KENTUCKY STATE POETRY SOCIETY; PEGASUS; KSPS NEWSLETTER, 3289 Hunting Hills Dr., Lexington KY 40515, contact/editor Miriam Woolfolk. Founded in 1966 to promote interest in writing poetry, improve skills in writing poetry, present poetry readings and poetry workshops, and publish poetry. Regional organization open to all. Current membership about 250. Affiliated with The National Federation of State Poetry Societies. Offerings available for poets include association with other poets, information on contests and poetry happenings across the state and nation; annual state and national contests; national and state annual conventions with workshops, selected speakers and open poetry readings. Sponsors workshops, contests, awards. Membership includes the bimonthly *KSPS Newsletter*. Also includes a quarterly newsletter, *Strophes*, of the NFSPS; and the KSPS journal, *Pegasus*, published 3 times yearly: a spring/summer and fall/winter issue which solicits good poetry for publication, and a Prize Poems issue of 1st Place contest winners in over 40 categories. Members or nationally-known writers give readings that are open to the public. Dues for students $5; adults $15; senior adults $10. Other categories: Life; Patron; Benefactor. The 2000 Annual Awards/Workshop is planned for October at Ken Lake State Park in Western Kentucky. Send SASE for additional information.

⚡ THE LEAGUE OF CANADIAN POETS; POETS IN THE CLASSROOM; WHO'S WHO IN THE LEAGUE OF CANADIAN POETS; POETRY MARKETS FOR CANADIANS; LIVING ARCHIVES SERIES; NATIONAL POETRY CONTEST; GERALD LAMPERT MEMORIAL AWARD; PAT LOWTHER MEMORIAL AWARD; CANADIAN YOUTH POETRY COMPETITION, 54 Wolseley, 3rd Floor, Toronto, Ontario M5T 1A5 Canada, phone (416)504-1657, fax (416)504-0096, e-mail league@ican.net, website www.poets.ca, contact Edita Petrauskaite, founded 1966. The League's aims are the advancement of poetry in Canada and promotion of the interests of professional, Canadian poets. Information on full, associate student and supporting membership can be obtained via e-mail, website or by sending a SASE for the brochure, League of Canadian Poets: Services and Membership. The League publishes 6 newsletters; *Poets in the Classroom*, on teaching poetry to children; a directory called *Who's Who in The League of Canadian Poets* that contains a picture, bio, publications and "what critics say" about each of the members; Living Archives Series, chapbooks of feminist studies in Canada; and *Poetry Markets for Canadians* which covers contracts, markets, agents and more. The League's members go on reading tours, and the League encourages them to speak on any facet of Canadian literature at schools and universities, libraries or organizations. The League has arranged "thousands of readings in every part of Canada"; they are now arranging exchange visits featuring the leading poets of such countries as Great Britain, Germany and the US. The League sponsors a National Poetry Contest with prizes of $1,000, $750 and $500; the best 50 poems published in a book. Deadline: November 1. Entry fee: $6/poem.

**FOR EXPLANATIONS OF THESE SYMBOLS,
SEE THE INSIDE FRONT AND BACK COVERS OF THIS BOOK.**

Poems should be unpublished, under 75 lines and typed. Names and addresses should *not* appear on poems but on a separate covering sheet. Please send SASE for complete rules, info on judges, etc. Open to Canadian citizens or landed immigrants only. The Gerald Lampert Memorial Award of $1,000 is for a first book of poetry written by a Canadian, published professionally. The Pat Lowther Memorial Award of $1,000 is for a book of poetry written by a Canadian woman and published professionally. Write for entry forms. The league also sponsors a Canadian chapbook manuscript competition with prizes of $1,000, $750 and $500. Submit 15-24 pg. ms with $12 entry fee. Deadline: December 1. Also sponsors The Canadian Youth Poetry Competition. Prizes: $250, $350, $500. Deadline: November 15. Contact the League for full guidelines. "The League markets members books through a direct mail flyer."

N LIVE POETS SOCIETY, MAINE, P.O. Box 265, Liberty ME 04949, phone/fax (207)342-5017, contact Lynne Kaplowitz. Founded in 1989 to establish and maintain a venue for poetry in mid-coast Maine. State-wide organization. Currently has 60 total members. Members or nationally known writers give readings that are open to the public. Membership dues are Minstrel $10; Bard $25; Laureate $50. Members meet monthly. Send SASE for additional information.

N 🍁 LIVING SKIES FESTIVAL OF WORDS, 88 Saskatchewan St. E., Moose Jaw, Saskatchewan S6H 0V4 Canada, phone (306)691-0557, fax (306)693-2994, e-mail word.festival@sk.sympatico.ca, website www3.sk .sympatico.ca/praifes, operations manager Lori Dean. "Founded in 1996, the purpose/philosophy of the organization is to celebrate the imaginative uses of languages. The Festival of Words is a registered nonprofit group of over 150 volunteers who present an enjoyable and stimulating celebration of the imaginative ways we use language. We operate year-round bringing special events to Saskatchewan, holding open microphone coffee houses for youth and culminating in an annual summer festival in July which features activities centered around creative uses of language. National organization open to writers and readers. Currently has 142 total members. Offerings available for poets include "The Festival of Words programs which include readings by poets, panel discussions and workshops. In addition, poets attending get to share ideas, get acquainted and conduct impromptu readings. The activities sponsored are held in the Moose Jaw Library/Art Museum complex, as well as in various venues around the city (e.g., local restaurants/lounges)." Sponsors workshops. "Workshops are offered as part of the Festival of Words which is held in July on a yearly basis. We are also associated with *FreeLance* magazine which is a publication of the Saskatchewan Writers' Guild. This publication features many useful articles dealing with poetry writing and writing in general." Also publishes *The Word*, a newsletter appearing approximately 6-7 times a year that contains news of Festival events, fund-raising activities, profiles of members, reports from members. Also available to nonmembers. First issue is free. Members and nationally known writers give readings that are open to the public. Sponsors open-mike readings for members and for the public. Membership dues are $5. Send SASE for additional information or obtain via website. Inquiries via fax and e-mail OK. Website includes excerpts from the newsletter, past presenters featured, news of upcoming events, and news of Festival 2000.

MAINE WRITERS & PUBLISHERS ALLIANCE (MWPA), 12 Pleasant St., Brunswick ME 04011-2201, phone (207)729-6333, fax (207)725-1014, founded 1975. MWPA is "a nonprofit organization dedicated to promoting the value of literature and the art of writing by building a community of writers, readers, and publishers within Maine. The membership currently includes over 1,700 writers, publishers, librarians, teachers, booksellers and readers from across Maine and the nation." For an individual contribution of $35 per year members receive discounts on MWPA programs and books, and *Maine in Print*, a bimonthly compilation of calendar events, updated markets, book annotations, interviews with Maine authors and publishers, articles about writing and more. The alliance distributes selected books about Maine and by Maine authors and publishers, and it maintains a bookstore and reference library at its office in Brunswick. "Also offers more than 70 writing and publishing workshops annually and an annual fall writing retreat.

🍁 MANITOBA WRITERS' GUILD INC., 206-100 Arthur St., Winnipeg, Manitoba R3B 1H3 Canada, phone (204)942-6134, fax (204)942-5754, e-mail mbwriter@escape.ca, website www.mbwriter.mb.ca. Founded in 1981 to "promote and advance the art of writing, in all its forms, throughout the province of Manitoba." Regional organization open to "any individual with an interest in the art of writing." Currently has 430-500 members. Levels of membership are Regular and Student/Senior/Fixed income. Programs and services include: the Manitoba Workshop Series, intensive one-day sessions conducted by professional writers; Open Workshops, monthly sessions held in the fall and winter; an Annual Spring Conference, a 1-day event which includes panel discussions, readings, performances and special events; the Mentor Program, a limited number of promising writers selected to work one-on-one with experienced mentors; the Manitoba Writing and Publishing Awards which include the McNally Robinson Book of the Year Award and the John Hirsch Award for Most Promising Manitoba Writer, all awards are to "recognize and celebrate excellence in Manitoba writing and publishing"; the Café Reading Series, a weekly series showcasing emerging and established local writers; the Writers' Resource Centre, containing information about writing, publishing, markets, as well as Canadian periodicals and books by Manitoba authors; and a studio offering writers comfortable, private work space. Also now sponsors the Winnipeg International Writers Festival in the fall. Published 6 times/year, their newsletter, *WordWrap*, includes feature articles, regular columns, information on current markets and competitions, and profiles of Manitoba writers.

They also publish *The Writers' Handbook*, the Guild's "comprehensive resource manual on the business of writing." Membership fees are $45 Regular, $25 Student/Senior/Fixed Income. Send SASE for additional information.

MASSACHUSETTS STATE POETRY SOCIETY, INC.; BAY STATE ECHO; THE NATIONAL POETRY DAY CONTEST; THE GERTRUDE DOLE MEMORIAL CONTEST, 64 Harrison Ave., Lynn MA 01905, president Jeanette C. Maes. Founded in 1959, dedicated to the writing and appreciation of poetry and promoting the art form. State-wide organization open to anyone with an interest in poetry. Currently has 200 total members. Offerings available for poets include critique groups. Sponsors workshops, contests. Sponsors The National Poetry Day Contest, with prizes of $25, $15 and $10 (or higher) for each of 30 categories. Pays winners from other countries with US currency. Entry fee: $5. Deadline: August 1. Competition receives approximately 1,800 entries a year. Also sponsors The Gertrude Dole Memorial Contest, with prizes of $25, $15 and $10. Entry fee: $3. Deadline: March 1. Also sponsors the Poet's Choice Contest, with prizes of $50, $25 and $15. Entry fee: $3/poem. Deadline: November 1 and the Naomi Cherkofsky Memorial Contest, with prizes of $50, $30 and $20. Entry fee: $3/poem. Deadline: June 30. Does not accept entry fees in foreign currencies. Send SASE for guidelines. Competitions receive 300-500 entries a year. Publishes a yearly anthology of poetry and a yearly publication of student poetry contest winners. Publishes *Bay State Echo*, a newsletter, 5 times/year. Members or nationally-known writers give readings that are open to the public. Sponsors open-mike readings. Membership dues are $10/year. Members meet 5 times/year. Send SASE for additional information.

Ⓝ MISSISSIPPI POETRY SOCIETY, INC., 5713 Belle Fontaine, Ocean Springs MS 39564-9084, state president Brenda B. Finnegan ("This changes annually when new officers are installed"). Founded in 1932 "to foster interest in the writing of poetry through a study of poetry and poetic form; to provide an opportunity for, and give recognition to, individual creative efforts relating to poetry; and to create an audience for poetry; and suggest or otherwise make known markets and contests for poetry to its members." Statewide organization, affiliated with the National Federation of State Poetry Societies, consisting of three branches open to "anyone who writes poetry or is interested in fostering the interests of poetry." Currently has 108 total members. Offerings available for poets include monthly meetings, annual contests and an annual awards banquet. "The state also holds a Mini-Festival in the fall and an annual Spring Festival each spring. The Mini-Festival is a one-day event (plus Night-Owl readings at a get-together the night before); and the Spring Festival is two days, plus the Night-Owl event the night before. We also have noted speakers and sponsor contests at these events." The state publishes the newsletter *Magnolia Muse* on a bimonthly basis while the branches publish a newsletter of the same name on a monthly basis. "The state organization also publishes journals of all winning poems each year, and often of other special contests. There are occasionally 'featured poets,' and two or three of their poems are featured in an issue of *Magnolia Muse*." Members or nationally-known writers give readings that are open to the public. Membership dues are $20. Members meet monthly at branches, semiannually at the state level. Send SASE for additional information.

☑ MOUNTAIN WRITERS SERIES, Mountain Writers Center, 3624 SE Milwaukee Ave., Portland OR 97202, phone (503)236-4854, fax (503)232-4517, e-mail pdxmws@aracnet.com, website www.aracnet.com/~pdx mws, office manager Jennifer Grotz, program coordinator Michael Robins. Founded in 1973, "Mountain Writers Series is an independent non-profit organization dedicated to supporting writers, audiences and other sponsors by promoting literature and literacy through artistic and educational literary arts events in the Pacific Northwest." The Center is open to both members and nonmembers. Currently has about 100 total members. Levels of membership available are Contributing ($100), Supporting ($500), Patron ($1,000), Basic ($50), Student/Retired ($25) and Family ($75). "Poets have access to our extensive poetry library, resource center and space as well as discounts to most events. Members receive a seasonal newsletter as well. Poets may attend one-day workshops, weekend master classes, five-week and ten-week courses about writing." Authors who participated in 1999-2000 season included Yusef Komunyakaa, C.K. Williams, Billy Collins, Sandra Alcosser, Mark Doty, Karen Swenson and Lynn Emanuel. "The Mountain Writers Center is an 100-year-old Victorian house with plenty of comfortable gathering space, a reading room, visiting writers room, library, resource center, garden and Mountain Writers Series offices." Sponsors conferences/workshops. Publishes the *Mountain Writers Center Newsletter*. Also available to nonmembers for $12/year. Sponsors readings that are open to the public. "Nationally and internationally known writers are sponsored by the Mountain Writers Series Northwest Regional Residencies Program (reading tours) and the campus readings program (Pulitzer Prize winners, Nobel Prize winners, MacArthur Fellows, etc.). Send SASE for additional information or visit website. Inquiries via fax and e-mail OK.

☑ NATIONAL FEDERATION OF STATE POETRY SOCIETIES, INC.; STEVEN'S MANUSCRIPT COMPETITION, Membership Chairperson: Sy Swann, 2736 Creekwood Lane, Ft. Worth TX 76123, phone (817)292-8598 or (605)768-2127, fax (817)531-6593, e-mail JFS@flash.net, contest chairperson Claire Van Breeman Downes, 1206 13th Ave. SE, St. Cloud MN 56304. Founded in 1959, "NFSPS is a nonprofit organization exclusively educational and literary. Its purpose is to recognize the importance of poetry with respect to national cultural heritage. It is dedicated solely to the furtherance of poetry on the national level and serves to unite poets in the bonds of fellowship and understanding." Any poetry group located in a state not already affiliated but interested in affiliating with NFSPS may contact the membership chairperson. Canadian groups may also apply.

"In a state where no valid group exists, help may also be obtained by individuals interested in organizing a poetry group for affiliation." Most reputable state poetry societies are members of the National Federation and advertise their various poetry contests through the quarterly bulletin, *Strophes*, available for SASE and $1, editor Linda Banks, 2912 Falls Church Lane, Mesquite, TX 75149. Beware of organizations calling themselves state poetry societies (however named) that are not members of NFSPS, as such labels are sometimes used by vanity schemes trying to sound respectable. Others, such as the Oregon State Poetry Association, are quite reputable, but they don't belong to NFSPS. NFSPS holds an annual meeting in a different city each year with a large awards banquet, addressed by a renowned poet and writer. They sponsor 50 national contests in various categories each year, including the NFSPS Prize of $1,500 for 1st Prize; $500, 2nd; $250, 3rd; with entry fees ($3 for the entire contest for members, $5 for NFSPS Award; $1/poem for nonmembers and $5 for NFSPS Award, up to 4 poems/ entry). All poems winning over $15 are published in their anthology *ENCORE*. Rules for all contests are given in a brochure available from Linda Banks at *Strophes* or Claire Van Breeman Downes at the address above; you can also write for the address of your state poetry society. They also sponsor the annual Steven's Manuscript Competition with a 1st Prize of $1,000 and publication, 2nd Prize $500; October 1 deadline; contact Amy Zook, 3520 St. Rd. 56, Mechanicsburg OH 43044. Scholarship information is available from Pj Doyle, 4242 Stevens Ave., Minneapolis MN 55409. Inquiries via fax and e-mail OK.

⊠ NATIONAL LEAGUE OF AMERICAN PEN WOMEN, INC., 1300 17th St. NW, Washington DC 20036-1973, phone (202)785-1997, fax (202)452-6868, e-mail nlapw1@juno.com, website http://members.aol. com/penwomen/pen.htm, national scholarship chair Mary Jane Hillery. Founded in 1897 to promote women in the creative arts. National organization open to professional women in the creative arts. Currently has 4,500 total members. Levels of membership are: "full members, those who provide proof of payment for creative work— writers, artists, composers; associate members, those in the creative arts who have not supplied proof of payment for sufficient works." Offerings available for poets include opportunities for publication and cash prizes in contests. "The National Headquarters is in Northwest Washington DC within walking distance of the White House and many DC landmarks and memorials. It is a converted mansion in which Robert Tood Lincoln and his family lived for several months. We are near DuPont Circle with bookstores, computer center." Sponsors conferences/workshops and contests/awards. "A penwoman publishes *The Pen Woman*, a quarterly magazine in which previously published poems are published for greater exposure." Members and nationally known writers give readings that are open to the public. Membership dues are $30 to NLAPW, branch dues vary. Send SASE for additional information or obtain via website. Inquiries via fax and e-mail OK. Also sponsors a biennial $1,000 grant for which nonpen women poets are qualified to enter. Send SASE for flyer.

THE NATIONAL POETRY FOUNDATION; SAGETRIEB; PAIDEUMA, University of Maine, 5752 Neville Hall, Room 302, Orono ME 04469-5752, phone (207)581-3813, fax (207)581-3886, e-mail sapiel@maine .edu, website www.ume.maine.edu/~npf/, contact publications coordinator. "The NPF is a nonprofit organization concerned with publishing scholarship on the work of 20th century poets, particularly Ezra Pound and those in the Imagist/Objectivist tradition. We publish *Paideuma*, a journal devoted to Ezra Pound scholarship, and *Sagetrieb*, a journal devoted to poets in the imagist/objectivist tradition, as well as books on and of poetry. NPF occasionally conducts a summer conference." Sample copies: $8.95 for *Paideuma* or *Sagetrieb*. Send SASE for information or obtain and inquire via e-mail or website.

NATIONAL WRITERS ASSOCIATION; AUTHORSHIP, 3140 S. Peoria, #295, Aurora CO 80014, phone (303)841-0246, fax (303)751-8593, website www.nationalwriters.com, executive director Sandy Whelchel, founded 1937. National organization with regional affiliations open to writers. Currently has 3,000 total members. Levels of membership available are Published Writers and Other Writers. They have an annual Summer Conference where workshops/panels etc. are available to all attendees, including poets. Also offer a yearly poetry writing contest with cash awards of $100, $50 and $25. Pays winners from other countries by US check. Entry fee: $10/ poem. Accepts entry fees in foreign currencies. Deadline: October 1. Most recent contest winner was Jane Carpenter, Denver, Colorado. Send SASE for judging sheet copies. Publishes *Authorship*, an annual magazine. Also available to nonmembers for $18. Memberships dues are Professional $85; others $65. Members meet monthly. Send SASE for additional information. Inquiries via fax and/or e-mail OK. Contest forms available on website.

NATIONAL WRITERS UNION, 113 University Place, 6th Floor, New York NY 10003, phone (212)254- 0279, e-mail nwu@nwu.org, website www.nwu.org, contact Corrina Marshall. Offers members such services as a grievance committee, contract guidelines, health insurance, press credentials, car rental discounts, and caucuses and trade groups for exchange of information about special markets. Members receive *The American Writer*, the organization's newsletter. Membership is $95 for those earning less than $5,000/year; $155 for those earning $5,000-25,000; and $210 for those earning more than $25,000.

☑ NEVADA POETRY SOCIETY, P.O. Box 7014, Reno NV 89510, phone (775)322-3619, president Sam Wood. Founded in 1976 to encourage the writing and critiquing of poetry. State-wide organization. Currently has 30 total members. Levels of membership available are Active and Emeritus. Offerings available for poets include membership in the National Federation of State Poetry Societies, including their publication *Strophes*; monthly challenges followed by critiquing of all new poems; lessons on types of poetry. Members of the society are occasionally called upon to read to organizations or in public meetings. Membership dues are $10 (this includes membership in NFSPS). Members meet monthly. "We advise poets to enter their poems in contests before thinking about publication."

THE OREGON STATE POETRY ASSOCIATION, % President David Hedges, P.O. Box 602, West Linn OR 97068, phone (503)655-1274. Founded in 1936 for "the promotion and creation of poetry," the association has over 400 members, $18 dues, $12 (65 and older), $5 (18 and under), publishes a quarterly *OSPA Newsletter*, biannual *Verseweavers* chapbook, and annual *Cascadia* chapbook of Oregon student poetry. Sponsors contests twice yearly, October during Fall Poetry Conference and April during Spring Poetry Conference, with total cash prizes of $700 each (no entry fee to members, $3/poem for nonmembers; out-of-state entries welcome). Pays winners from other countries by International Money Order. Does not accept entry fees in foreign currencies. Send International Money Order. Themes and categories vary; special category for New Poets. Competition receives 1,400 entries a year. Most recent contest winners include Ross Coppock, June Foye, Melanie Green, Alice Hardesty, Ruth F. Harrison, Glenna Holloway, Rita Mazur, Lynn Veach Sadler and Shirley Willard. For details write to OSPA, contest chair Joan Henson, 6071 SW Prosperity Park Rd., Tualatin OR 97062, phone (503)638-7488 after July 1 and January 15 each year. The association, a member of the National Federation of State Poetry Societies, Inc. (NFSPS), sponsors workshops, readings and seminars around the state and an annual contest for students (K-12).

OZARK POETS AND WRITERS COLLECTIVE, P.O. Box 3717, Fayetteville AR 72702, phone (501)521-0119, e-mail bjmoossy@aol.com, chairperson Brenda J. Moossy. Founded reading series in 1993, incorporated in 1995, "to support and promote community involvement in Ozark literary arts; to encourage an appreciation of local writers by providing access to their work through readings, publications, workshops and other events; to ensure that the experience of writing and reading remain a vital part of life in the Ozarks." Regional organization open to any interested poets and writers. "Most participants come from the Ozarks, which encompasses parts of Arkansas, Missouri and Oklahoma." Offerings available for poets include slams with cash prizes and reading series and open mic. "OPWC also runs a weekly column in the *Northwest Arkansas Times* with space to showcase local and not so local poets, provide information about upcoming readers and events, and invite comment about the feast of poetry and all its flavors. *The Fayetteville Free Weekly* runs a monthly column showcasing the monthly featured reader." Nationally and locally known writers give readings that are open to the public. The readings are held on the last Wednesday of each month and are immediately followed by an open-mike session. "Slams are held on the second Tuesday of every month. Poets on Tour, the performing arm of the OPWC, is available for performances nationwide. They were recently added to the Arts on Tour Roster of the Arkansas Arts Council, becoming the first performance poetry troupe to do so." Board members meet quarterly; interested poets and writers may attend the meetings. Send SASE for additional information. Inquiries via e-mail OK.

PEN AMERICAN CENTER; PEN WRITERS FUND; PEN TRANSLATION PRIZE; GRANTS AND AWARDS, 568 Broadway, New York NY 10012, phone (212)334-1660, website www.pen.org. PEN American Center "is the largest of more than 100 centers which comprise International PEN, founded in London in 1921 by John Galsworthy to foster understanding among men and women of letters in all countries. Members of PEN work for freedom of expression wherever it has been endangered, and International PEN is the only worldwide organization of writers and the chief voice of the literary community." Its total membership on all continents is approximately 10,000. The 2,700 members of the American Center include poets, playwrights, essayists, editors, novelists (for the original letters in the acronym PEN), as well as translators and those editors and agents who have made a substantial contribution to the literary community. Membership in American PEN includes reciprocal privileges in foreign centers for those traveling abroad. Branch offices are located in Cambridge, Chicago, Portland/Seattle, New Orleans and San Francisco. Among PEN's various activities are public events and symposia, literary awards, assistance to writers in prison and to American writers in need (grants and loans up to $1,000 from PEN Writers Fund). Medical insurance for writers is available to members. The quarterly *PEN Newsletter* is sent to all members and is available to nonmembers by subscription. The PEN Translation Prize is sponsored by the Book-of-the-Month Club, 1 prize each year of $3,000 for works published in the current calendar year. They publish *Grants and Awards* biennially, containing guidelines, deadlines, eligibility requirements and other information about hundreds of grants, awards and competitions for poets and other writers: $15. Send SASE for booklet describing their activities and listing their publications, some of them available free.

N PEN CENTER USA WEST, 672 S. Lafayette Park Place #41, Los Angeles CA 90057, phone (213)365-8500, fax (213)365-9616, e-mail pen@pen-usa-west.org, website www.pen-usa-west.org. "Founded in 1952,

---

SENDING TO A COUNTRY other than your own? Be sure to send International Reply Coupons (IRCs) instead of stamps for replies or return of your manuscript.

PEN Center USA West strives to protect the rights of writers around the world, to stimulate interest in the written word, and to foster a vital literary community among the diverse writers living in the western U.S. The organization, therefore, has two distinct, yet complimentary aims: one fundamentally literary and the other having a freedom of expression mandate." Regional organization open to "poets, playwrights, essayists, novelists (for the original letters in the acronym, 'PEN'), as well as television and screen writers, critics, historians, editors, journalists and translators." Currently has 960 full members plus 16 associate members. Levels of membership are Full membership ("open to published or produced writers who have demonstrated work of substantial literary value and who meet the membership criteria in one or more categories") and Associate membership ("open to writers whose body of work only partially fulfills a criteria for full membership and to professionals, such as publishers, booksellers, literary presenters, and creative writing teachers, whose work ultimately benefits and promotes literature and writers"). Benefits of Full membership include invitations to PEN special events, workshops, seminars, and readings; participation on PEN committees; listing in and a copy of PEN's Member Directory; involvement in PEN's Freedom-to-Write activites; invitations to Members' Only events. Benefits of Associate membership include discounted admission to educational panels and seminars; invitations to PEN special events; involvement in Freedom to Write advocacy efforts; copies of *PEN News* and other publications such as *Author Access*. Sponsors conferences/workshops and contests/awards. Publishes *PEN News*, a bimonthly newsletter that contains updates on programs and general announcements. Members and nationally known writers give readings that are open to the public. Membership dues are $65 Full, $50 Associate. Send SASE for additional information or obtain via website. Inquiries via fax and e-mail OK. Website includes description of all programs, staff list, Freedom to Write alerts, awards/contest information.

PITTSBURGH POETRY EXCHANGE, P.O. Box 4279, Pittsburgh PA 15203, phone (412)481-POEM. Founded in 1974 as a community-based organization for local poets, it functions as a service organization and information exchange, conducting ongoing workshops, readings, forums and other special events. No dues or fees. "Any monetary contributions are voluntary, often from outside sources. We've managed not to let our reach exceed our grasp." Their reading programs are primarily committed to local and area poets, with honorariums of $25-75. They sponsor a minimum of three major events each year in addition to a monthly workshop. Some of these have been reading programs in conjunction with community arts festivals, such as the October South Side Poetry Smorgasbord—a series of readings throughout the evening at different shops (galleries, bookstores). Poets from out of town may contact the exchange for assistance in setting up readings at bookstores to help sell their books. Contact Michael Wurster at the above address or phone number.

THE POETRY LIBRARY, South Bank Center, Royal Festival Hall, London SE1 8XX United Kingdom, phone (0171)921 0943/0664, fax (0171)921 0939, e-mail poetrylibrary@rfh.org.uk, website www.poetrylibrary.org.uk, poetry librarian Mary Enright. Founded in 1953 as a "free public library of 20-century poetry. It contains a comprehensive collection of all British poetry published since 1912 and an international collection of poetry from all over the world, either written in, or translated into English. As the United Kingdom's national library for poetry, it offers loan and information service and large collections of poetry magazines, tapes, videos, records, poem posters and cards; also press cuttings and photographs of poets." National center with "open access for all visitors. Those wishing to borrow books and other materials must be residents of U.K." Offerings available for poets include "Library and information service; access to all recently published poetry and to full range of national magazines; only source of international poetry, including magazines; and information on all aspects of poetry." Offers browsing facilities and quieter area for study; listening facilities for poetry on tape, video record and CD. Adjacent to "Voice Box" venue for literature readings. Nationally known writers give readings that are open to the public. "Separate administration for readings in 'The Voice Box'—a year-round program of readings, talks and literature events for all writing. Poetry library does not arrange readings." Send SASE for additional information. Inquiries via fax and e-mail OK. "Our focus is more on published poets than unpublished. No unpublished poems or manuscripts kept or accepted. Donations welcome but please write or call in advance."

POETRY SOCIETY OF AMERICA; POETRY SOCIETY OF AMERICA AWARDS, 15 Gramercy Park, New York NY 10003, phone (212)254-9628, fax (212)673-2352, website www.poetrysociety.org, managing director Caroline Crumpacker, founded in 1910, is a nonprofit cultural organization in support of poetry and poets, member and nonmember, young and established, which sponsors readings, lectures and workshops both in New York City and around the country. Their Peer Group Workshop is open to all members and meets on a weekly basis. They publish *Crossroads: A Journal of the Poetry Society of America*, approximately 40 pgs., letter-sized. Send a SASE for contest guidelines. The following are open to members only: Alice Fay Di Castagnola Award ($1,000); *Writer Magazine*/Emily Dickinson Award ($250); Cecil Hemley Memorial Award ($500); Lucille Medwick Memorial Award ($500); Lyric Poetry Award ($500). Nonmembers may enter as many of the following contests as they wish, no more than 1 entry for each, for a $5 fee: Louise Louis/Emily F. Bourne Student Poetry Award, $250 for students in grades 9-12; George Bogin Memorial Award, $500 for a selection of 4 to 5 poems which take a stand against oppression; Robert H. Winner Memorial Award, $2,500 for a poem written by a poet over 40, still unpublished or with one book. (All have a deadline of December 21; awards are made at a ceremony and banquet in late spring.) The Society also has 2 book contests open to works submitted by publishers only. They must obtain an entry form, and there is a $10 fee for each book entered. Book awards are: Norma Farber Award, $500 for a first book; William Carlos Williams Award, a purchase prize of $500-1,000 for a book of poetry published by a small, nonprofit or university press, by a permanent resident of the US—translations not eligible. The Shelley Memorial Award of $5,000-7,500 and The Frost Medal $2,500 are by nomination only. For necessary rules and guidelines for their various contests send #10 SASE between October 1 and December 21. Inquiries via fax OK. Rules and awards are subject to change. Membership: $40. Inquiries via fax OK. Website includes information and calendar for awards and seminars; information on journal; postcards to send; discussion groups, etc.

☑ **THE POETRY SOCIETY OF VIRGINIA**, 616 Maple Ave., Richmond VA 23226-2648, phone (804)282-2753, e-mail smithjron@aol.com, president Ron Smith. Founded in 1923 to "encourage excellence in the writing, reading, study and appreciation of poetry." State-wide organization open to "anyone who supports the purpose of the society." Currently has 330 total members. Levels of membership available are Single, Family, Sustaining and Life. Offerings available for poets include annual contest, regional meetings with readings and guest poets. "We have collected published works of past and present poets; located at the library in Richmond." Sponsors annual contest. "There are categories for all poets 18 years of age and older, categories restricted to members only, and categories for school students. There are modest entry fees for poets who are not members of the Society. There are no entry fees for elementary and middle school students." Publishes a newsletter 6 times/year. Also available to nonmembers. Members and nationally known writers give readings that are open to the public. Sponsors open-mike readings. Membership dues are $20 and $300 for Life membership. Members meet in March, April, May, September, October and November. Send SASE for additional information.

POETS & WRITERS, INC. See listing under Publications of Interest.

☑ **POETS HOUSE: THE REED FOUNDATION LIBRARY; THE POETRY PUBLICATION SHOWCASE; DIRECTORY OF AMERICAN POETRY BOOKS; POETRY IN THE BRANCHES; NYC POETRY TEACHER OF THE YEAR**, 72 Spring St., New York NY 10012, phone (212)431-7920, fax (212)431-8131, e-mail info@poetshouse.org, website www.poetshouse.org, founded 1985, managing editor Jane Preston. Poets House is a 35,000-volume (noncirculating) poetry library of books, tapes and literary journals, with reading and writing space available. This comfortably furnished literary center is open to the public year-round. Over 30 annual public events include 1) poetic programs of cross-cultural and interdisciplinary exchange, 2) readings in which distinguished poets discuss and share the work of other poets, 3) workshops and seminars on various topics led by visiting poets, and 4) an annual $1,000 award for the designated NYC Poetry Teacher of the Year. In addition, Poets House continues its collaboration with public library systems, Poetry in The Branches, aimed at bringing poetry into NYC neighborhoods—through collection-building, public programs, seminars for librarians, and poetry workshops for young adults (information available upon request). Finally, in April Poets House hosts the Poetry Publication Showcase—a comprehensive exhibit of the year's new poetry releases from commercial, university, and independent presses across the country. Related Showcase events include receptions, panel discussions, and seminars which are open to the public and of special interest to poets, publishers, booksellers, distributers and reviewers. (Note: Poets House is not a publisher.) Following each Showcase, copies of new titles are added to the library collection and an updated edition of the *Directory of American Poetry Books*—edited by Poets House and available by mail is compiled. "Poets House depends, in part, on tax-deductible contributions of its nationwide members." Membership levels begin at $40/year, and along with other graduated benefits each new or renewing member receives a free copy of the most current directory. Inquiries via fax and e-mail OK. Website includes general information about their library, programs and resources; also contains a calendar of events.

☒ **POETS' LEAGUE OF GREATER CLEVELAND**, P.O. Box 91801, Cleveland OH 44101, phone (216)932-8444, executive director Darlene Montonaro. "Founded in 1974 to foster a supportive community for poets and to expand the audience for poetry among the general public." Conducts a monthly workshop where poets can bring their work for discussion. Publishes a monthly calendar of literary events in NE Ohio; a bimonthly magazine, *Ohio Writer*, which includes articles on the writing life, news and markets; and two chapbooks a year featuring an anthology of work by area poets. "The PLGC also sponsors a dramatic reading series, *Poetry: Mirror of the Arts*, which unites poetry and other art forms performed in cultural settings; and *Writers & Their Friends*, a literary showcase of new writing (all genres), performed dramatically by area actors, media personalities and performance poets." Membership dues are $25/year, includes subscription to *Ohio Writer* Magazine. Send SASE for information.

POETS THEATRE, 30 East Lake Rd., Cohocton NY 14826, e-mail bobrien4@juno.com, website www.members.tripod.com/~poetstheatre/index.html, director Beatrice Obrien, founded 1981. Sponsors readings and performances with limited funding from Poets & Writers. For a mostly conservative, rural audience. A featured poet, followed by open reading. Sponsors a summer Poetry Festival and an annual Poets Picnic in September. Meets second Thursday frequently as announced on web page. Inquiries via e-mail OK.

☑ **POETS-IN-THE-SCHOOLS**. Most states have PITS programs that send published poets into classrooms to teach students poetry writing. If you have published poetry widely and have a proven commitment to children, contact your state arts council, Arts-in-Education Dept., or other writing programs in your area to see whether you qualify. Three of the biggest programs are Teachers & Writers Collaborative, Inc., 5 Union Square W., Seventh Floor, New York NY 10003-3306, phone (212)691-6590, e-mail info@twc.org, website www.twc.org, which requires poets in its program have some prior teaching experience; California Poets-in-the-Schools, 870 Market St., Suite 1148, San Francisco CA 94102, phone (415)399-1565, e-mail info@cpits.org, website www.cpits.org; and Writers & Artists in the Schools, COMPAS, 304 Landmark Center, 75 W. Fifth St., St. Paul MN 55102, phone (651)292-3254, website www.compas.org, which includes both Minnesota-based writers and artists in their program.

SCOTTISH POETRY LIBRARY; SCHOOL OF POETS; CRITICAL SERVICE, 5 Crichton's Close, Edinburgh EH8 8DT Scotland, phone (0131)557-2876, director Robyn Marsack, librarian Penny Duce. A reference information source and free lending library, also lends by post and has a travelling van service lending at schools, prisons and community centres. The library has a computerized catalogue allowing subject-based searches and indexes of poetry and poetry magazines. The collection comprises over 20,000 items of Scottish and international poetry. The School of Poets is open to anyone; "at meetings members divide into small groups in which each participant reads a poem which is then analyzed and discussed." Meetings normally take place at 7:30 p.m. on the second Tuesday of each month at the library. They also offer a Critical Service in which groups of up to 6 poems, not exceeding 200 lines in all, are given critical comment by members of the School: £15 for each critique (with SAE). Publishes the *Scottish Poetry Index*, a multi-volume indexing series, photocopied, spiral-bound, that indexes poetry and poetry-related material in selected Scottish literary magazines from 1952 to present and an audio CD of contemporary Scottish poems *The Jewel Box* (January 1999).

SMALL PUBLISHERS ASSOCIATION OF NORTH AMERICA (SPAN), P.O. Box 1306, Buena Vista CO 81211, phone (719)395-4790, fax (719)395-8374, e-mail span@spannet.org, website www.spannet.org, executive director Marilyn Ross. Founded in 1996 to "advance the image and profits of independent publishers and authors through education and marketing opportunities." Open to "authors, small- to medium-sized publishers and the vendors who serve them." Currently has 1,300 total members. Levels of membership available are regular and associate vendor. Offerings available for poets include marketing ideas. Sponsors annual conference. Publishes *SPAN Connection*, "a 24-page monthly newsletter jam-packed with informative, money-making articles. Also available to nonmembers for $8/issue. Membership dues are $95/year (Regular), $120/year (Associate Vendor). Send SASE for additional information or visit website. Inquiries via fax OK.

SONGWRITERS AND POETS CRITIQUE, 2804 Kingston Ave., Grove City OH 43125, e-mail spcmusic@ yahoo.com, website www.freeyellow.com/members2/spcmusic, founded in 1985, treasurer Pat Adcock. A non-profit association whose purpose is to serve songwriters, poets and musicians in their area. The president of the organization says, "We have over 200 members from the U.S. and Canada at several levels of ability from novice to advanced, and try to help and support each other with the craft and the business of poetry and songs. We have published writers and recorded artists. We share information about how to pitch, send and package a demo and who to send it to. We also have a songwriting contest for member writers." Annual dues are $30. For more information send a #10 SASE, e-mail or visit website. Website includes upcoming events, newsletters, membership application, members' winning songs and poems (in Real Audio format), and links.

SOUTH DAKOTA STATE POETRY SOCIETY; PASQUE PETALS, Box 398, Lennox SD 57039, (605)647-2447, membership chair Verlyss V. Jacobson. Founded in 1926 to provide a place for members to publish their poetry. Regional organization open to anyone. Currently has 200-225 total members. Levels of membership available are Regular, Patron, Foreign, Student. Sponsors conferences, workshops and 2 annual contests, one for adults and one for students, with 12 categories. Deadlines: August 15 for adults, February 1 for students. Publishes the magazine *Pasque Petals* 6 times/year. Membership dues are $20 regular, $30 patron, $5 students. Members meet biannually. Send SASE for additional information.

THE THURBER HOUSE; JAMES THURBER WRITER-IN-RESIDENCE, 77 Jefferson Ave., Columbus OH 43215, phone (614)464-1032, fax (614)228-7445, officially opened in 1984. Listed on the National Register of Historic Places, The Thurber House is a literary center, bookstore and museum of Thurber materials. Programs include writing classes for children, author readings, Thurber celebrations and an art gallery. The Thurber House sponsors a writer-in-residence program that brings 2 journalists, a playwright, a poet or a fiction writer to spend a season living and writing in The Thurber House while teaching a course at The Ohio State University. Each writer will receive a stipend and housing in the third-floor apartment of Thurber's boyhood home. Please send a letter of interest and a curriculum vitae to Michael J. Rosen, literary director before December 15. Please note that The Thurber House is *not* a publishing house and does not accept unsolicited material. No inquiries via e-mail. Inquiries via fax OK.

UNIVERSITY OF ARIZONA POETRY CENTER, 1216 N. Cherry Ave., Tucson AZ 85721-0410, phone (520)321-7760, fax (520)621-5566, e-mail poetry@u.arizona.edu, website www.coh.arizona.edu/poetry/, director Alison Deming. Founded in 1960 "to maintain and cherish the spirit of poetry." Open to the public. The Center is located in 3 historic adobe houses near the main campus and contains a nationally acclaimed poetry collection that includes over 35,000 items. Programs and services include: a library with a noncirculating poetry collection and space for small classes, poetry-related meetings and activities; facilities, research support, and referral information about poetry and poets for local and national communities; the Free Public Reading Series, a series of 12 to 18 readings each year featuring poets, fiction writers, and writers of literary nonfiction; a guest house for residencies of visiting writers and for use by other University departments and community literary activities; a 1-month summer residency at the Center's guest house offered each year to an emerging writer selected by jury; and poetry awards, readings, and special events for undergraduate and graduate students. Publishes a biannual newsletter. Send SASE for additional information. "We do not have members, though one can become a 'Friend' through a contribution to our Friends of the Poetry Center account." Inquiries via fax and e-mail OK. Website includes info about programs and events, newsletter and guidelines.

THE UNTERBERG POETRY CENTER OF THE 92ND STREET Y; "DISCOVERY"/THE NATION POETRY CONTEST, 1395 Lexington Ave., New York NY 10128, phone (212)415-5759. Offers annual series of readings by major literary figures (weekly readings October through May), writing workshops, master classes in fiction and poetry, and lectures and literary seminars. Also co-sponsors the "Discovery"/*The Nation* Poetry Contest. Deadline in January. Competition receives approximately 2,000 entries a year. Most recent contest winners include John Poch, Gabriel Gudding, Yerra Sugarman and Martin Walls. Send SASE for information. "No phone queries, please."

UTAH STATE POETRY SOCIETY; POET TREE, Utah Arts Council & NEA, 7685 Dell Rd., Salt Lake City UT 84121-5221, phone (801)943-4211, e-mail rosieo4@juno.com, website www.spectre.com/usps, treasurer Rosalyn Ostler. Founded in 1950 to secure a wider appreciation of the poetry arts and to promote excellence in writing poetry. State-wide organization. Membership is open to all citizens of the State of Utah and to interested people from any other state in the union, without consideration of age, race, regional, religious, educational or other backgrounds. Currently has about 250 members. Sponsors conferences, workshops, contests, awards. USPS publishes, biannually, work of members in a chapbook anthology. Publishes *Poet Tree*, a biannual newsletter. Publishes one winning manuscript annually. Members or nationally-known writers give readings/workshops that are open to the public. Chapters meet at least once a month, with open readings, critiques, lessons. Annual Awards Festival includes open reading. Membership dues are $20/year ($15 for students) including membership in National Federation of State Poetry Societies and their newsletter *Strophes*, copy of the Book of the Year and other publications, and full contesting privileges. Send SASE for information. "We welcome all potential members." Website includes general membership information; information on workshops, contests and activities; and a complete online version of *Poet Tree*.

VIRGINIA WRITERS CLUB, P.O. Box 300, Richmond VA 23218, phone (804)648-0357, fax (804)782-2142, editor/administrator Charlie Finley. Founded in 1918 "to promote the art and craft of writing; to serve writers and writing in Virginia." State-wide organization with 7 local chapters open to "any and all writers." Currently has 350 total members. Offerings available for poets include networking with other poets and writers, discussions on getting published, workshops and a newsletter. Publishes *The Virginia Writer*, a newsletter appearing 5 times/year. Nationally known writers give readings that are open to the public. Membership dues are $25/year. Members meet 5 times/year plus workshops and monthly chapter meetings. Send SASE for additional information. Inquiries via fax OK.

☑ **WISCONSIN FELLOWSHIP OF POETS; MUSELETTER**, 8605 County Rd. D, Forestville WI 54213-9716, e-mail slocumss@gateway.net, vice president Peter Sherrill, president Sheryl Slocum. Founded in 1950 to secure fuller recognition of poetry as one of the important forces making for a higher civilization and to create a finer appreciation of poetry by the public at large. State-wide organization open to current and past residents of Wisconsin who write poetry acceptable to the Credentials Chairperson. Currently has 415 total members. Levels of memberships available are Associate, Active, Student and Life. Sponsors biannual conferences, workshops, contests and awards. Publishes "Wisconsin Poets' Calendar" poems of Wisconsin (resident) poets. Also publishes *Museletter* a quarterly newsletter. Members or nationally-known writers give readings that are open to the public. Sponsors open-mike readings. Membership dues are Active $15, Associate $10, Student $7.50, Life $100. Members meet biannually. Send SASE for additional information to WFOP Vice President Peter Sherrill, 8605 County Rd. D, Forestville WI 54213. Inquiries via e-mail OK.

N WOODLAND PATTERN, P.O. Box 92081, 720 E. Locust St., Milwaukee WI 53212, phone (414)263-5001. Executive director Anne Kingsbury calls it "a semi-glamorous literary and arts center." Kingsbury regards the center as a neighborhood organization; it includes a bookstore that concentrates on contemporary literature, much of it small press, much of it poetry, and also on multicultural children's literature. It also incorporates a multipurpose gallery/performance/reading space, where exhibitions, readings, a lecture series, musical programs and a reading and study group are held. The *Woodland Pattern Newsletter*, mailed free to 2,800 people, contains an annotated calendar and pieces about visiting writers.

N ⊕ THE WORDSMITHS (CHRISTIAN POETRY GROUP), 493 Elgar Rd., Box Hill North, Victoria 3129 Australia, phone (03)9890 5885, leader Jean Sietzema-Dickson. "Founded in 1987 to provide a meeting place where poets who, because of their Christian conviction, found themselves often uncomfortable in secular groups. We have met regularly since 1987, and early on decided that is was no use being closet writers. In 1988 (September) we started talking about publishing. Our concern as a group has been to encourage the development of excellence in our writing and to speak out with a distinctive voice." Open to "anyone who, knowing we are predominantly a Christian group, is happy to come along. We now have members who have not committed themselves to share our belief but who share our ethos." Currently has 30 total members, mostly from the greater Melbourne area. Offerings available for poets include monthly workshops, occasional guests poets and "a 'Quiet Day' once a year when we meet from 10-4 to spend some time together in silence, writing." Sponsors conferences/workshops. "We also have a publishing arm, Poetica Christi Press, and have published 4 group anthologies and 3 works of individual poets. We started with a chapbook in 1990." Also publishes *Wordsmiths Newsletter*, appearing "roughly" bimonthly. Also available to nonmembers for AUS $3. Members and nationally known writers give readings that are open to the public. Sponsors open-mike readings for members and the public. Membership dues are $15/year or $2/visit. Send SASE (or SAE and IRC) for additional information.

☑ **WORDTECH COMMUNICATIONS**, 1474 Yellowglen Dr., Cincinnati OH 45255, e-mail wordtech@fuse.net, website home.fuse.net/wordtech, editor Kevin Walzer. Founded in 1998. "We are a production house specializing in helping poets self-publish. The current system of publishing poetry—competitions charging reading fees—needs reform. Our method allows poets to take charge of their own work and deliver their work to an audience at reasonable prices. Whitman and other great poets self-published. Today's poets should not be ashamed to follow their example. Poets should send entire manuscript with SASE and cover letter outlining their background and publishing needs. We will review the manuscript to determine if we can work with the poet. The poet pays for production costs and receives all copies of the book to market. We charge for design, editing, critiquing if requested, and similar services. We keep our costs low to allow poets to recoup their investments. We request a limited number of books for archival purposes." Send SASE for additional information. Inquiries via e-mail OK.

☑ **WORLD-WIDE WRITERS SERVICE, INC. (3WS); WRITERS INK; WRITERS INK PRESS; WRITERS UNLIMITED AGENCY, INC.**, 233 Mooney Pond Rd., P.O. Box 2344, Selden NY 11784, phone (631)451-0478, fax (631)451-0477, e-mail axelrodthepoet@yahoo.com, website www.poetrydoctor.com or worldwidewriters.com, director Dr. David B. Axelrod, founded in 1976, Writers Ink Press founded 1978. "World-Wide Writers Service is a literary and speakers' booking agency. With its not-for-profit affiliate, Writers Unlimited Agency, Inc., it presents literary workshops and performances, conferences and other literary services, and publishes through Writers Ink Press, chapbooks and small flat-spined books as well as arts editions. **We publish only by our specific invitation at this time.**" *Writers Ink* is "a sometimely newsletter of events on Long Island, now including programs of our conferences. We offer 3 conferences a year: Healing Power of Writing, Long Island Literature Conference, Florida Writing Workshop and Poetry Conference. We welcome news of other presses and poets' activities. Review books of poetry. We fund raise for nonprofit projects and are associates of Long Island Writers Festival and Jeanne Voege Poetry Awards as well as the Key West Poetry Writing, January Workshops and Writing Therapy Trainings throughout the year in various locations. Arts Editions are profit productions employing hand-made papers, bindings, etc. We have editorial services available at small fees. Also inquire if appropriate. We are developing new Internet services (see our websites and e-mail address listed above) from online editing to college credit courses (University of New York certified); contests; books for sale; general information and advice for poets and writers." Also sponsors a new contest beginning in 2000. Most recent contest winner was George Wallace.

THE WRITER'S CENTER; WRITER'S CAROUSEL; POET LORE, 4508 Walsh St., Bethesda MD 20815, phone (301)654-8664, fax (301)654-8667, e-mail postmaster@writer.org, website www.writer.org, founder and artistic director Allan Lefcowitz, executive director Jane Fox, founded 1976. This is an outstanding resource for writers not only in Washington DC but in the wider area ranging from southern Pennsylvania to North Carolina and West Virginia. The Center offers 260 multi-meeting workshops each year in writing, word processing, and graphic arts. It is open 7 days a week, 10 hours a day. Some 2,300 members support the center with $30 annual donations, which allows for 7 paid staff members. There is a book gallery at which publications of small presses are displayed and sold. The center's publication, *Writer's Carousel*, is a 24-page magazine that comes out 6 times a year. They also sponsor 80 annual performance events, which include presentations in poetry, fiction and theater. The Center is publisher of *Poet Lore*—110 years old in 1999 (see listing in the Publishers of Poetry section). Their website has news and information about the Washington metropolitan literary community. Inquiries via e-mail OK. No fax inquiries.

☑ ☑ **WRITERS' FEDERATION OF NOVA SCOTIA; ATLANTIC POETRY PRIZE; ATLANTIC WRITING COMPETITION; EASTWORD**, 1113 Marginal Rd., Halifax, Nova Scotia B3H 4P7 Canada, phone (902)423-8116, fax (902)422-0881, e-mail talk@writers.ns.ca, website www.writers.ns.ca. Founded in 1975 "to foster creative writing and the profession of writing in Nova Scotia; to provide advice and assistance to writers at all stages of their careers; and to encourage greater public recognition of Nova Scotian writers and their achievements." Regional organization open to anybody who writes. Currently has 500 total members. Offerings available for poets include resource library with over 1,200 titles, promotional services, workshop series, annual festivals, manuscript reading service, and contract advice. Sponsors the Atlantic Writing Competition, for unpublished works by beginning writers, and the Atlantic Poetry Prize, for the best book of poetry by an Atlantic Canadian. Publishes *Eastword*, a bimonthly newsletter containing "a plethora of information on who's doing what, markets and contests, and current writing events and issues." Send SASE for additional information or obtain via website. Inquiries via fax and e-mail OK.

N **WRITERS GUILD OF ALBERTA**, 11759 Groat Rd., Edmonton, Alberta T5M 3K6 Canada, phone (780)422-7184, fax (780)422-2663, e-mail wga@oanet.com, website www.writersguild.ab.ca, executive director Miki Andrejevic or program coordinator Renate Donnovan. Founded in 1980 "to provide a community of writers which exists to support, encourage and promote writers and writing; to safeguard the freedom to write and read; and to advocate for the well-being of writers." Provincial organization open to emerging and professional writers. Currently has 750 total members. Offerings available for poets include workshops/conference, bimonthly newsletter with market section, and the Stephan Stephansson Award for Poetry. Sponsors conferences/workshops and contests/awards. Also publishes a bimonthly magazine that includes articles on writing, poems and a market section. Available to nonmembers for $60 Canadian/year. Members and nationally known writers give readings that are open to the public. Sponsors open-mike readings for members. Obtain additional information via website. Inquiries via fax and e-mail OK. Website includes directory of writers, job and market listings, workshop/conference information.

N **WRITERS INFORMATION NETWORK**, The Professional Association for Christian Writers, P.O. Box 11337, Bainbridge Island WA 98110, phone (206)842-9103, fax (206)842-0536, e-mail writersinfonetwork@juno.com, website www.bluejaypub.com/win, director Elaine Wright Colvin. Founded in 1983 "to provide a much needed link between writers and editors/publishers of the religious publishing industry, to further professional development in writing and marketing skills of Christian writers, and to provide a meeting ground of encouragement and fellowship for persons engaged in writing and speaking." International organization open to anyone. Currently has 1,000 members. Offerings available for poets include market news, networking, editorial referrals, critiquing and marketing/publishing assistance. Sponsors conferences and workshops around the country. Publishes a 32- to 36-page bimonthly magazine, *The Win-Informer* containing industry news and trends, writing advice, announcements and book reviews. The magazine will also consider "writing-related poetry, up to 24 lines, with inspirational/Christian thought or encouragement. We accept first rights only." Sample copy: $5. Membership dues are $35. Send SASE for additional information.

THE WRITERS ROOM, 10 Astor Place, 6th Floor, New York NY 10003, phone (212)254-6995, fax (212)533-6059, website www.writersroom.org. Founded in 1978 to provide a "home away from home" for any writer who needs a place to work. It is open 24 hours a day, 7 days a week, offering desk space, storage and comraderie at the rate of $185/quarter. It is supported by the National Endowment for the Arts, the New York State Council on the Arts, the New York City Department of Cultural Affairs and private sector funding. Call for application or download from website.

THE WRITERS' UNION OF CANADA, 24 Ryerson Ave., Toronto, Ontario M5T 2P3 Canada, phone (416)703-8982, fax (416)703-0826, e-mail twuc@the-wire.com, website www.swifty.com/twuc, founded 1973. Dedicated to advancing the status of Canadian writers. The Union is devoted to protecting the rights of published authors, defending the freedom to write and publish, and serving its members. National organization. Open to poets who have had a trade book published by a commercial or university press; must be a Canadian citizen or landed immigrant. Currently has over 1,300 total members. Offerings available for poets include contact with peers, contract advice/negotiation, grievance support and electronic communication. Sponsors conferences and workshops. Sponsors Annual General Meeting, usually held in May, where members debate and determine Union policy, elect representatives, attend workshops, socialize, and renew friendships with their colleagues from across the country. Publishes *The Writers' Union of Canada Newsletter* 9 times/year. Membership dues are $180/year. Regional reps meet with members when possible. Send SASE (or SAE and IRC) for additional information. For writers not eligible for membership, the Union offers, for a fee: publications on publishing, contracts, awards and more; a Manuscript Evaluation Service for any level writer; Contract Services, including a Self-Help Package, a Contract Evaluation Service, and a Contract Negotiation Service; and three annual writing competitions for developing writers. Inquiries via fax and/or e-mail OK. Website includes general information about publishing, members web pages and competition information.

N **W.B. YEATS SOCIETY OF NEW YORK**, National Arts Club, 15 Gramercy Park S, New York NY 10003, phone (212)780-0605, website www.YeatsSociety.org, president Andrew McGowan. Founded in 1990 "to promote the legacy of Irish poet and Nobel laureate William Butler Yeats through an annual program of lectures, readings, poetry competition and special events." National organization open to anyone. Currently has 400 total members. Offerings available for poets include an annual poetry competition and *Poet Pass By!*, an annual "slam" of readings, songs and music by poets, writers, entertainers. Also sponsors conferences/workshops. Members and nationally known writers give readings that are open to the public. Sponsors open-mike readings for members and the public. Membership dues are $15/year. Members meet monthly, September to June. Send SASE for additional information or obtain via website.

Additional Organizations

The following listings also contain information about organizations. See the General Index for page numbers.

Alden Enterprises
Anthology of New England Writers, The
Arkansas Poetry Day Contest
Asian Pacific American Journal
Austin Writers' League Spring and Fall Workshops
Baltimore Review, The
Bay Area Poets Coalition (BAPC)
Borderlands
Bristol Poetry Festival
British Haiku Society
California Quarterly
CNW/FFWA Florida State Writing Competition
Colorado Book Awards
Common Threads
Comstock Review, The
Connecticut River Review
Coolbrith Circle Annual Poetry Contest, Ina
Council for Wisconsin Writers, Inc.
Current Accounts
Dickey Newsletter, James
Emerald Coast Review
Faulkner Creative Writing Competition/Poetry Category, The William
FreeFall Magazine
Frogpond
Grolier Poetry Prize
Handshake
HQ Poetry Magazine
Intro

IWWG Summer Conference, The
Jewish Women's Literary Annual
Keats Shelley Millennium Prize
Kwil Kids Publishing
Laurels
Mad Poets Review
Magnolia Quarterly, The
Maryland Poetry Review
Midwest Villages & Voices
Milton Center Poetry Fellowship
New Orleans Poetry Forum
Newburyport Art Association Annual Spring Poetry Contest
96 Inc Magazine
Northwest Oklahoma Writers Workshop
Oracle Poetry
Outrider Press
Pennsylvania Poetry Society Annual Contest
Pennwriters Annual Conference
Peregrine
Poem
Poetic Hours
Poetry Harbor
Poetry Ireland Review
Poetry Kanto
Poetry Nottingham International
Poetry Review
Poetry USA
Poets' Club of Chicago International Shakespearean/Petrarchan Sonnet Contest
Poets' Roundtable

Pudding House Publications
QWF Literary Awards
Red Herring
Rockford Review, The
Romantics Quarterly
Science Fiction Poetry Association
Seaman Poetry Award, Claudia Ann
Society for Creative Writers Poetry Contest
Society of American Poets (SOAP), The
Society of Midland Authors Literary Award
Soul of the Poet Award, The
Sounds of Poetry, The
SPIN
Thumbprints
Ver Poets Open Competition
Washington Review
Weyfarers
Whitecrow Foundation, Tahana
Wisconsin Regional Writers' Association Inc.
Worcester Review
Word Works, The
Writers' Conference at Oakland University
Xanadu
Yeats Society Annual Poetry Competition, The W.B.

Publications of Interest

The publications in this section are designed to help poets with all aspects of writing and publishing poetry. While few are actual markets, many detail new publishing opportunities in addition to providing information on craft, advice on marketing, or interviews with poets and writers.

Poets & Writers Magazine, in fact, is one of the most useful resources for both poets and fiction writers. In addition to informative articles and interviews, it includes calls for submissions and contests and awards. *Writer's Digest*, on the other hand, covers the entire field of writing and features market listings as well as a monthly poetry column by Michael J. Bugeja, author of *The Art and Craft of Poetry* (Writer's Digest Books, 1994) and *Poet's Guide: How to Publish and Perform Your Work* (Story Line Press, 1995).

Other publications, such as *Rain Taxi Review of Books*, include reviews of poetry books and chapbooks or reviews of small press magazines. These reviews provide further insight into the different markets.

For poets seeking resources more regional in focus, several of the listings in this section are publications that include, among other items, markets, news and events for specific areas of the United States and Canada. For example, *First Draft* publishes information of interest to Alabama writers.

Finally, for those interested in various publishing opportunities, this section also includes information about other market directories as well as materials on self-publishing. And, in addition to the listings that follow, you will find other useful publications noted in Additional Publications of Interest on page 545.

To determine which of these publications may be most useful to you, read sample issues. Many of these books and periodicals may be found in your local library or located on newsstands or in bookstores. If you are unable to locate a certain magazine, order a copy from the publisher. For books, send a SASE with a request for the publisher's catalog or order information.

N **🌐** **THE BBR DIRECTORY**, P.O. Box 625, Sheffield S1 3GY United Kingdom, e-mail directory@bbr-online.com, website www.bbr-online.com/directory, editor/publisher Chris Reed, founded 1996, "is a monthly e-mail newssheet for everyone involved with or interested in the small press. Providing accurate and up-to-date information about what's happening in independent publishing all over the world, the *BBR Directory* is the ideal starting point for exploring the small press and for keeping tabs on who exactly is publishing what, and when." To subscribe, send a blank e-mail to directory-subs-on@bbr-online.com or sign up through our website. Inquiries via e-mail OK. *BBR* also has a special website of resources for writers at www.bbr-online.com/writers. Website contains "a fully searchable archive of every issue of the *BBR Directory*, plus a free Message Board facility where readers can post their publishing news for immediate viewing by other visitors to the website, network with other writers, or discuss issues relevant to small press and independent publishing."

N **BOOK MAGAZINE**, 4645 N. Rockwell, Chicago IL 60625, e-mail feedback@bookmagazine.com, website www.bookmagazine.com, editor Jerome Kramer, associate editor Adam Langer, founded 1998, is a bimonthly "magazine for the reading life. It covers new book releases (including poetry), news about authors, books being made into movies, teen book reviews, children's books and authors." Occasionally publishes original poetry. "We are always looking for good material." It is about 80 pgs., 8½×11, professionally printed and perfect-bound with 4-color, glossy paper cover, includes 4-color photos. Poets may send books for review consideration. Single copy: $4.95; subscription: $20/year. Inquiries via e-mail OK.

R.R. BOWKER; LITERARY MARKET PLACE; BOOKS IN PRINT, 121 Chanlon Rd., New Providence NJ 07974, phone (888)269-5372, e-mail info@bowker.com, website www.bowker.com. *LMP* is the major trade directory of publishers and people involved in publishing books. It is available in most libraries, or individual copies may be purchased (published in September each year). *BIP* is another standard reference available in most libraries and bookstores. Bowker publishes a wide range of reference books pertaining to publishing. Write for their catalog.

Get America's #1 Poetry Resource Delivered to Your Door—and Save!

Finding the right outlets for your poetry is crucial to publishing success. With constant changes in the industry, it's not always easy to stay informed. That's why every year poets trust the newest edition of *Poet's Market* for the most up-to-date information on the people and places that will get their poetry published (over 1,800 editors and publishers are included). This definitive resource also features insider tips from successful poets and editors that will further increase publishing opportunities.

2002 Poet's Market will be published and ready for shipment in August 2001.

Through this special offer, you can reserve your 2002 *Poet's Market* at the 2001 price—just $23.99. Order today and save!

Turn over for more books to help you get your poems published!

More Great Books to Help You Write and Publish Your Poetry!

Writing Personal Poetry
by Sheila Bender
Using this warm, encouraging instruction, you'll learn how to peel away your inhibitions and get in touch with your deepest feelings, then sculpt rich and meaningful poems. Whether you desire to write first poems, better poems or more poems, this book is designed to help you with a lifelong commitment to poetry.
#10595/$14.99/208 p/pb

Word Painting: A Guide to Writing More Descriptively
by Rebecca McClanahan
In this extraordinary guide instruction is combined with engaging word exercises to help elevate your writing to a new level of richness and clarity. You'll also find 75 creativity exercises and examples from award-winning writers.
#10709/$18.99/256 p/pb

You Can Write Poetry
by Jeff Mock
Discover how to express your thoughts and feelings using the rich, descriptive language of poetry. Through dozens of examples and "practice sessions," you'll learn about poetry's styles and structures, then create your own poems filled with texture and emotion.
#10571/$12.99/128 p/pb

The Art & Craft of Poetry
by Michael J. Bugeja
Nurture your poetry-writing skills with inspiration and insight from the masters of the past and present. From idea generation to methods of expression, you'll find everything you need to create well-crafted poetry!
#10392/$19.99/352 p

Creating Poetry
by John Drury
Definitions, examples, and hands-on exercises show you how to use language text, subject matter, free and measured verse, imagery, and metaphor to create your own wonderful works!
#10209/$18.99/224 p

The Poet's Handbook
by Judson Jerome
With expert instruction, you'll unlock the secrets of using figurative language, symbols, and concrete images. Plus, you'll discover the requirements for lyric, narrative, dramatic, didactic, and satirical poetry!
#01836/$14.99/224 p/pb

The Poetry Dictionary
by John Drury
This comprehensive book uncovers the rich and complex language of poetry with clear, working definitions. Several different poems are used to demonstrate the evolution of the form, making *The Poetry Dictionary* a unique anthology. It's a guide to the poetry of today and yesterday, with intriguing hints as to what tomorrow holds.
#48007/$18.99/352 p

CANADIAN POETRY, English Dept., University of Western Ontario, London, Ontario N6A 3K7 Canada, phone (519)661-3403, ext. 83403 or 85834, fax (519)661-3776, website www.arts.uwo.ca/canpoetry, editor Prof. D.M.R. Bentley, founded 1977. A biannual journal of critical articles, reviews and historical documents (such as interviews). It is a professionally printed, scholarly edited, flat-spined, 150-page journal which pays contributors in copies. Subscription: $15. Sample: $7.50. **Note that they publish no poetry except as quotations in articles.** Also offer Canadian Poetry Press Scholarly Editions, DocuTech printed, perfect-bound, containing scholarship and criticism of Canadian poetry. Send SASE for details.

DUSTBOOKS; INTERNATIONAL DIRECTORY OF LITTLE MAGAZINES AND SMALL PRESSES; DIRECTORY OF POETRY PUBLISHERS; SMALL PRESS REVIEW; SMALL MAGAZINE REVIEW, P.O. Box 100, Paradise CA 95967, phone (530)877-6110, fax (530)877-0222, e-mail dustbooks @desi.net, website www.dustbooks.com. Dustbooks publishes a number of books useful to writers. Send SASE for catalog. Among their regular publications, *International Directory* is an annual directory of small presses and literary magazines, over 6,000 entries, a third being magazines, half being book publishers, and the rest being both. There is very detailed information about what these presses and magazines report to be their policies in regard to payment, copyright, format and publishing schedules. *Directory of Poetry Publishers* has similar information for over 2,000 publishers of poetry. *Small Press Review* is a bimonthly magazine, newsprint, carrying current updating of listings in *ID*, small press needs, news, announcements and reviews—a valuable way to stay abreast of the literary marketplace. *Small Magazine Review*, which began publication in June, 1993, is included within *Small Press Review* and covers small press magazines. Inquiries via fax and e-mail OK.

ESSENTIAL MEDIA DISCOUNT COUNTERCULTURE CATALOG, P.O. Box 661245, Los Angeles CA 90066-1245, phone (310)574-1554, fax (310)574-3060, e-mail underground@essentialmedia.com, website www.essentialmedia.com, editor Kevin Segall, founded 1996, is a biannual "catalog and guide to the best of alternative culture—fiction, poetry, cult videos, CDs, comics, small press magazines and assorted oddities." Devotes 5% of its pages to poetry. It is 44 pgs., 8½×11, offset printed and saddle-stitched. Reviews books and chapbooks of poetry and other magazines—"we write reviews for everything we carry." Poets may send books for review consideration. Single copy: $2. Inquiries via fax and e-mail OK. Website includes entire catalog.

FIRST DRAFT: THE JOURNAL OF THE ALABAMA WRITERS' FORUM, The Alabama Writers' Forum, Alabama State Council on the Arts, 201 Monroe St., Montgomery AL 36130-1800, phone (334)242-4076 ext. 233, fax (334)240-3269, e-mail awf1@arts.state.al.us, website www.writersforum.org, editor Jeanie Thompson, founded 1992, appears 4 times a year, publishing news, features, book reviews, and interviews relating to Alabama writers. "We do not publish original poetry or fiction." It is 28 pgs., 8½×11, professionally printed on coated paper and saddle-stitched with b&w photos inside and a full color cover. Lists markets for poetry, contests/awards and workshops. Sponsored by the Alabama Writers' Forum, "the official literary arts advocacy organization for the state of Alabama." Reviews books of poetry, fiction, and nonfiction by "Alabama writers or from Alabama presses." Subscription: $25/year plus membership. Sample: $3.

FREELANCE MARKET NEWS, Sevendale House, 7 Dale St., Manchester M1 1JB England, phone (+44)0161 228 2362, fax (+44)0161 228 3533, e-mail fmn@writersbureau.com, website writersbureau.com, editor Angela Cox, founded 1968, is "a monthly newsletter providing market information for writers and poets." Regular features are market information and how-to articles. It is 16 pgs., A4. Lists markets for poetry, contests/awards and conferences/workshops. Associated with The Writers College which offers correspondence courses in poetry. Occasionally reviews books or chapbooks of poetry. Subscription: £29. Sample: £2.50. Inquiries via fax and e-mail OK.

THE GREAT BLUE BEACON, 1425 Patriot Dr., Melbourne FL 32940, phone (321)253-5869, e-mail ajircc@juno.com, editor/publisher Andy J. Byers, founded 1996, is "a quarterly newsletter for writers of all genres and skill levels. It contains writing tips, book reviews, humor, quotations and contest/publisher information." Occasionally publishes poetry but only through their periodic contests. It is 8 pgs., 8½×11, desktop-published and unbound. Poets may send books for review consideration. Single copy: $4; subscription: $10, $8 for students, $14 outside US. Sample: $1 plus 2 first-class stamps or IRC. Inquiries via e-mail OK.

**FOR EXPLANATIONS OF THESE SYMBOLS,
SEE THE INSIDE FRONT AND BACK COVERS OF THIS BOOK.**

🌐 **HANDSHAKE; THE EIGHT HAND GANG**, 5 Cross Farm Station Rd., Padgate, Warrington, Cheshire WA2 0QG England, contact John Francis Haines, founded 1992, is published irregularly to "encourage the writing of genre poetry, to provide a source of news and information about genre poetry, to encourage the reading of poetry of all types, including genre, and to provide an outlet for a little genre poetry." It is 1 A4 pg., printed on front and back. Lists markets for poetry and contests/awards. Single copy available for SAE and IRC.

🌐 **LIGHT'S LIST**, 37 The Meadows, Berwick-Upon-Tweed, Northumberland, TD15 1NY England, phone (01289)306523, editor John Light, founded 1986, is an annual publication "listing some 1,300 small press magazines publishing poetry, prose, market information, articles and artwork with address and brief note of interests. All magazines publish work in English. Listings are from the United Kingdom, Europe, United States, Canada, Australia, New Zealand, South Africa and Asia." It is 58 pgs., A5, photocopied and saddle-stitched with card cover. Lists markets for poetry. Single copy: $6 (air $7).

LITERARY MAGAZINE REVIEW, Dept. of English Language and Literature, The University of Northern Iowa, Cedar Falls IA 50614-0502, phone (319)273-2821, fax (319)273-5807, e-mail grant.tracey@uni.edu, editor Grant Tracey, founded 1981. A quarterly magazine (digest-sized, saddle-stitched, about 48-64 pgs.) that publishes critiques, 2-5 pgs. long, of various literary magazines, plus shorter "reviews" (about ½ page) of new journals during a particular year. Single copies: $5; subscriptions: $13.50/year. Request copies via e-mail.

N 🌐 **MERSEYSIDE ARTS MAGAZINE**, P.O. Box 21, Liverpool L19 3RX England, phone (0151)427 8297, fax (0151)291 6280, e-mail ms.arts.mag@cableinet.co.uk, editor Bernard F. Spencer, founded 1995, the publication is a bimonthly "local news and information magazine that caters to writers/poets, theatre arts, fine arts, photography, music and dance, film, video and digital media." Devotes roughly 15% to poetry and regularly features reviews, events, diary dates and competitions. *Merseyside* is between 44-52 pgs., A4, lithographed and saddle-stitched. Lists markets for poetry, contests/awards, conferences/workshops and readings. Associated with the Northwest Arts Board. Reviews books and chapbooks of poetry and other magazines. Poets may send books for review consideration. Single copy: £1 plus £1.89 postage. Inquiries via fax and e-mail OK.

MINNESOTA LITERATURE, One Nord Circle, St. Paul MN 55127, phone (651)483-3904, fax (651)766-0144, e-mail mnlit@aol.com, editor Mary Bround Smith, founded 1975. *ML* appears 10 times a year (September through June), providing news and announcements for Minnesota writers. Regularly features "Minnesota literary events such as readings, lectures, workshops, conferences and classes; news of publications written by Minnesotans or published in Minnesota; and opportunities for writers, such as grants, awards and want-ads." It is 8½ × 11, 8 pgs. (two 11 × 17 sheets folded), unbound. Subscription: $10 for 10 issues. Sponsors annual reading for creative writing nominees of Minnesota Book Awards. Publishes biennial bibliography of Minnesota publishers and literary publications.

N **OHIO WRITER**, P.O. Box 91801, Cleveland OH 44101, phone (216)932-8444, editor Ron Antonucci, is a bimonthly newsletter for Ohio writers or those connected with Ohio. It is 16-24 pgs., professionally printed on off-white stock, containing news and reviews of Ohio writing events, publications and regional opportunities to publish. Subscription: $15/year, $20 for institutions. It also sponsors an annual contest for Ohio writers. Competition receives about 300 entries. See the Best of Ohio Writers Writing Contest listing in the Contests and Awards section. Also accepts poems on writing, the writing life, etc. Payment on publication, $5-50.

PARA PUBLISHING, Box 8206-880, Santa Barbara CA 93118-8206, phone (805)968-7277, orders (800)727-2782, fax (805)968-1379, e-mail danpoynter@parapublishing.com, website www.parapublishing.com. Author/publisher Dan Poynter publishes how-to books on book publishing and self-publishing. *Writing Nonfiction: Turning Thoughts Into Books* shows you how to get your book out. *The Self-Publishing Manual, How to Write, Print and Sell Your Own Book* is all about book promotion. Poynter also publishes *Publishing Contracts on Disk, Book Fairs* and 45 Special Reports on various aspects of book production, promotion, marketing and distribution. *Free* book publishing information kit. The website has over 500 pages of valuable book writing, publishing and promoting information. This is a good way to sample Para Publishing's offerings. Inquiries via fax and e-mail OK.

PERSONAL POEMS, % Jean Hesse, 56 Arapaho Dr., Pensacola FL 32507, phone (850)492-9828, Jean Hesse started a business in 1980 writing poems for individuals for a fee (for greetings, special occasions, etc.). Others started similar businesses, after she began instructing them in the process, especially through a cassette tape training program and other training materials. Send SASE for free brochure or $20 plus $4.50 p&h (make checks payable to F. Jean Hesse) for training manual, *How to Make Your Poems Pay.*

POETRY CALENDAR, 611 Broadway #905, New York NY 10012, phone (212)260-7097, fax (212)475-7110, editor and publisher Dallas Galvin, founded 1975. "*Poetry Calendar* is a monthly magazine that combines reviews, interviews, excerpts, and essays along with the only comprehensive literary listing in New York City.

Thirteen-thousand copies are distributed each month, providing a complete schedule of poetry and fiction readings, performances, lectures, exhibits, workshops and related activities." It is 32-40 pgs., 8½×11, newsprint, glued. Subscription: $20. Copies free at newsstands.

THE POETRY CONNECTION, 13455 SW 16 Court #F-405-PM, Pembroke Pines FL 33027, phone (954)431-3016, editor/publisher Sylvia Shichman. *The Poetry Connection*, a monthly newsletter, provides information in flyer format. Poets, writers and performing artists receive information on how to sell their poetry/books, poetry and performing artists publications and contests, and obtain assistance in getting poetry published, plus info on how to win cash for your talent and mailing list rental. *TPC* has information on writing for greeting card directories, poetry and performing artists publications, plus info on a directory, that lists poetry contests with cash awards. Subscription: $20. Sample (including guidelines): $7. Make checks payable to Sylvia Schichman. Also sponsors The Magic Circle, a poetry publicity distribution network service. "Join the Magic Circle and have your bio and one poem sent directly to editors and publishers. 50 copies: $30 or 100 copies $60. Send large SASE for information. The Magic Circle will distribute your flyers in a reciprocal exchange. For information, please enclose a large SASE and write to: Sylvia Shichman."

☑ **POETS & WRITERS, INC.; A DIRECTORY OF AMERICAN POETS AND FICTION WRITERS; LITERARY AGENTS; POETS & WRITERS MAGAZINE**, 72 Spring St., New York NY 10012, phone (212)226-3586 fax (212)226-3963 (California only), website www.pw.org; California office: phone (415)986-9577, fax (415)986-9575, subscription office (815)734-1123. Poets & Writers, Inc., was founded in 1970 to foster the development of poets and fiction writers and to promote communication throughout the literary community. A nonmembership organization, it offers information, support, and exposure to writers at all stages in their careers. It publishes the bimonthly *Poets & Writers Magazine*, which delivers to its readers profiles of noted authors and publishing professionals, practical how-to articles, a comprehensive listing of grants and awards for writers and special sections on subjects ranging from small presses to writers conferences. The Readings/Workshops Program supports public literary events through matching grants to community organizations. The Literary Horizons Program offers how-to-publish seminars, panel discussions, a lecture series and online seminars. The program also provides a publishing information packet free of charge and compiles the biennial, *A Directory of American Poets and Fiction Writers*, which lists contact information and publication credits for more than 7,400 published U.S. authors.

PUSHCART PRESS, P.O. Box 380, Wainscott NY 11975. Publishes a number of books useful to writers, including the Pushcart Prize Series—annual anthologies representing the best small press publications, according to the judges; The Editors' Book Award Series, "to encourage the writing of distinguished books of uncertain financial value"; *The Original Publish-It-Yourself Handbook*; and the Literary Companion Series. Send SASE for catalog.

RAIN TAXI REVIEW OF BOOKS, P.O. Box 3840, Minneapolis MN 55403, e-mail raintaxi@bitstream.net, website www.raintaxi.com, editor Eric Lorberer, founded 1996. "*Rain Taxi Review of Books* is a quarterly publication available free in bookstores nationwide. Our circulation is 20,000 copies. We publish reviews of books that are overlooked by mainstream media, and each issue includes several pages of poetry reviews, as well as author interviews and original essays." Devotes 20% of publication to poetry. "We review poetry books in every issue and often feature interviews with poets." *Rain Taxi* is 56 pgs., 8½×11, web offset printed on newsprint and saddle-stitched. Poets may send books for review consideration. Subscription: $10. Sample: $3. Inquiries via e-mail OK. Website includes a selection of the contents of each issue, full table of contents for current and back issues and information about the organization. "We DO NOT publish original poetry. Please don't send poems."

[N] **SHAW GUIDES, INC.**, 10 W. 66 St., #30H, New York NY 10023, phone (212)799-6464, fax (212)724-9287, e-mail info@shawguides.com, website www.shawguides.com, president Dorlene Kaplan, founded 1988, "to publish due stories of educational travel and creative career programs worldwide." Publishes material on an ongoing basis on their website. Their *Guide to Writers Conferences* includes detailed descriptions of over 500 conferences and workshops worldwide at http://writing.shawguides.com. Inquiries via fax and e-mail OK.

⊕ **SPRINGBOARD: WRITING TO SUCCEED**, 30 Orange Hill Rd., Prestwich M25 1LS England, e-mail leobooks@rammy.com, editor Leo Brooks, is published quarterly to help aspiring writers. It is 32 pgs., A5, desktop-published and saddle-stapled with paper cover, includes clip art. Lists markets for poetry and contests/awards. Sponsors quarterly competitions for subscribers. Subscription: £8/year. Inquiries via e-mail OK. "Subscription to the magazine brings the right to belong to one or more of the folios which it supports. These postal folios are made of groups of six to eight writers who pass their work round the group for mutual encouragement and constructive criticism."

WOMEN'S REVIEW OF BOOKS, Wellesley College, Wellesley MA 02481, website www.wellesley.edu/WCW/CRW/WROB/welcome.html, contact Robin Becker, founded 1983, *WROB* is a monthly review of works by and about women, in all fields, including some poetry reviews. The editor says *WROB* is 32 pgs., tabloid-sized (10×15), published on newsprint. Single copy: $4; subscription: $25. Sample copy is free.

N ⊕ WORDS & PICTURES, 134 Glasgow Rd., Perth, Perthshire PH2 0LX Scotland, e-mail elizabeth_gatland@email.msn.com, editor Elizabeth Wein, founded 1996, "is the quarterly regional newsletter for the British Isles branch of The Society of Children's Book Writers & Illustrators. It serves as a forum for the discussion of issues in the professional field of children's literature and an organ which publicizes SCBWI business and activities. Occasionally we have market listings for poetry, articles focusing on poetry, or announcements of events relating to poetry (for children)." It is 16-20 pgs., A5, photocopied, folded and saddle-stapled. Also lists markets for contests/awards and conferences/workshops. Single copy: $4; subsciption: $17. Inquiries via e-mail OK. "Include SASE with U.K. postage or International Postal Coupon, with inquiry. Sample copies of text only available with e-mail inquiry."

⧫ ✓ WORDWRIGHTS CANADA, P.O. Box 456 Station O, Toronto, Ontario M4A 2P1 Canada, fax (416)752-0689, e-mail susanio@sympatico.ca, website www3.sympatico.ca/susanio, director Susan Ioannou, publishes "books on poetics in layman's, not academic terms, such as *Writing Reader-friendly Poems: Over 50 Rules of Thumb for Clearer Communication*; and *The Crafted Poem: A Step-by-Step Guide to Writing and Appreciation* (rev. ed.)." They consider mss of such books for publication, paying $50 advance, 10% royalties and 5% of press run. They also conduct "Manuscript Reading and Editing Services, as well as The Poetry Tutorial correspondence course for writers." Request order form via mail, fax or e-mail to buy samples. Inquiries via fax or e-mail OK. Website includes services for writers, handbooks on writing, The Poetry Tutorial writer's correspondence course, links to Canadian writer's sites and organizations.

⊕ ✓ WRITERS' BULLETIN, Cherrybite Publications, Linden Cottage, 45 Burton Rd., Little Neston, Cheshire CH64 4AE United Kingdom, website www.helicon@globalnet.co.uk, editor Shelagh Nugent, founded 1997. "Published bimonthly, *Writers' Bulletin* aims to give writers the most reliable and up-to-date information on markets for fiction, nonfiction, poetry, photographs, artwork, cartoons, plus information on resources, courses and conferences, book reviews (books about writing), editors' moves, publishing news, address changes, advice and tips on writing. All markets are verified with the editor—no guesswork or second-hand information." It is about 28 pgs., saddle-stapled with colored paper cover. Lists markets for poetry, contests/awards and conferences/workshops. Reviews informational or instructional books for poets and writers. Single copy: £2.40 Europe, £3 USA sterling only, £2 UK. Will accept the equivalent in US dollars (cash). Inquiries via e-mail OK. "Because we are adding news right up to publication day, *Writers' Bulletin* has the most up-to-date information available in print."

WRITER'S DIGEST BOOKS; WRITER'S DIGEST, 1507 Dana Ave., Cincinnati OH 45207, phone (800)289-0963 or (513)531-2690, website www.writersdigest.com. Writer's Digest Books publishes a remarkable array of books useful to all types of writers. In addition to *Poet's Market*, books for poets include *Writing Personal Poetry* by Sheila Bender, *You Can Write Poetry* by Jeff Mock, *The Poet's Handbook* by Judson Jerome, *Creating Poetry* by John Drury, and *The Art and Craft of Poetry* by Michael J. Bugeja. Call or write for a complete catalog. *Writer's Digest* is a monthly magazine about writing with frequent articles and market news about poetry, in addition to a monthly poetry column.

N ⊕ WRITERS' NEWS, P.O. Box 168, Wellington St., Leeds LS1 1RF United Kingdom, phone +44(0113)2388333, fax +44(0113)2388330, e-mail liz.innes@ypn.co.uk, editor Derek Hudson, founded 1989, is a monthly magazine containing news and advice for writers. Devotes up to 10% to poetry and regularly features a poetry workshop, critiques, "method and type explained" and annual and monthly competitions. It is 28-56 pgs., A4, saddle-stitched. Lists markets for poetry, contests/awards, conferences/workshops and readings. Associated with the David Thomas Charitable Trust (P.O. Box 6055, Nairn 1V12 54B) which sponsors poetry competitions. Occasionally reviews books and chapbooks of poetry and other magazines. Poets may send books for review consideration. Subscription: £49.90 overseas. Sample: £4.50. Inquiries via fax and e-mail OK.

N ⊕ ZENE, TTA Press, 5 Martins Lane, Witcham, Ely Cambs CB6 2LB England, e-mail ttapress@aol.com, website www.tta-press.freewire.co.uk, contact Team Zene, founded 1994, is a bimonthly "definitive guide to the vast independent press, recognised throughout the world as the creative writer's bible when it comes to looking for markets not normally found in more staid, mainstream writers' magazines. *Zene* covers all kinds of fiction, nonfiction and poetry from all genres, from mainstream to fantasy, from science fiction to horror, from thriller to romance. Neither does *Zene* restrict its coverage to the U.K., with regular reports from across the globe: Ireland, America, Canada, Australia, New Zealand, Europe, South Africa . . . in fact, everywhere there are independent titles publishing in the English language!" It is 36 pgs., A5, lithographed and saddle-stitched. Lists markets for poetry, contests/awards, conferences/workshops and readings. Reviews poetry collections, anthologies and poetry magazines. Poets may send books for review consideration. Subscription: $24 including airmail (6 issues). Inquiries via e-mail OK. Website includes details of *Zene* plus other TTA Press publications, extracts, news, links and special offers.

Additional Publications of Interest

The following listings also contain information about instructive publications for poets. See the General Index for page numbers.

Academi
Acid Angel
Acumen Magazine
Alden Enterprises
American Poetry Review
Anthology of New England Writers, The
Arizona Authors Association
Artist Trust
Associated Writing Programs
Association of Christian Writers
Austin Writers' League Spring and Fall Workshops
Authors Guild, Inc., The
Bathtub Gin
Beatlicks, The
Beggar's Press
Best of Ohio Writers Writing Contest
Black Buzzard Press
Borealis Press
Byline Magazine
Canadian Conference of the Arts
Canadian Poetry Association
Canadian Writer's Journal
Cherrybite Publications
Connecticut River Review
Cyber Oasis
Dandelion Arts Magazine
Emerald Coast Review
Federation of British Columbia Writers
FreeXpresSion
Georgia Poetry Society
Great Blue Beacon Poetry Contest, The
Guild Complex
Indiana State Federation of Poetry Clubs
Interbang

International Women's Writing Guild
IWWG Summer Conference, The
Kentucky State Poetry Society, The
Kwil Kids Publishing
Leacock Medal for Humour, The Stephen
League of Canadian Poets, The
Ligonier Valley Writers Conference
Living Skies Festival of Words
Mad Poets Review
Maine Writers & Publishers Alliance
Manitoba Writers' Guild Inc.
Massachusetts State Poetry Society, Inc.
Muuna Takeena
Nashville Newsletter Poetry Contest
National Federation of State Poetry Societies, Inc.
National League of American Pen Women, Inc.
National Poetry Foundation, The
National Writers Association
National Writers Union
Nevada Poetry Society
New Writer, The
New Writer's Magazine
Newport University Writers' Conference & Contest, Christopher
Northeast Arts Magazine
Northwest Oklahoma Writers Workshop
Northwoods Press
Oak, The
Ohioana Book Awards
Oregon State Poetry Association, The
Parnassus
PEN American Center
Pequod
Poetic Realm

Poetic Space
Poetry Ireland Review
Poetry Society of America
Poets House: The Reed Foundation Library
Poets' League of Greater Cleveland
Poets' Roundtable
Re:Verse!
Scavenger's Newsletter
SimplyWords
Small Publishers Association of North America
South Dakota State Poetry Society
Squaw Valley Community of Writers Poetry Workshop
Steamboat Springs Writers Conference
Sunlight & Moonbeams
Time For Rhyme
University of Arizona Poetry Center
Verse
Virginia Writers Club
Wisconsin Fellowship of Poets
Wisconsin Regional Writers' Association Inc.
World-Wide Writers Service, Inc.
Write Way, The
Writer, The
Writer's Center, The
Writer's Exchange
Writers' Federation of Nova Scotia
Writer's Guidelines & News Magazine
Writers Guild of Alberta
Writers Information Network
Writers' Journal
Xanadu

Websites of Interest

The Internet can be a useful tool for crafting and publishing poetry. Doing searches for specific forms of poetry will bring up many sites catering to your forms of choice. The following list can be used as a starting point for investigating pertinent websites for poets. We have broken them into four categories: The Business, The Organizations, The Search, and The Craft.

THE BUSINESS
IRS: www.irs.ustreas.gov/basic/cover.html
  Information, forms and publications, plus comments and help.
U.S. Copyright Office: www.loc.gov/copyright
  General information and forms you can print.

THE ORGANIZATIONS
The following websites contain information about the organization, list poetry awards and contests, and provide links to other literary resources, conferences and workshops.
The Academy of American Poets: www.poets.org/index.cfm
The International Organization of Performing Poets: www.slamnews.com/iopp.htm
Poets & Writers: www.pw.org
Poetry Society of America: www.poetrysociety.org
Teachers & Writers Collaborative: www.twc.org
Zuzu's Petals Organizations of Interest: www.zuzu.com

THE SEARCH
The following are search directories providing literary links.
Electronic Poetry Center: http://epc.buffalo.edu
Factsheet Five—Electric 'Zines!: www.factsheet5.com
John Hewitt's Writer's Resource: www.poewar.com
John Labovitz's e-zine-list: www.meer.net/~johnl/e-zine-list
The Literary Arts WebRing: www.lit-arts.com/WebRing/RingIndex.html
LitLine: www.litline.org/litline.html
W3PX Poetry Exchange: www.w3px.com
The Poetry Forum World Wide Registry: www.poetryforum.org/registry.htm
Poetry Today Online: www.poetrytodayonline.com
Writers Write™—The Write Resource™: www.writerswrite.com/

THE CRAFT
These sites can serve as a source of inspiration when creating your poetry.
Alan Cooper's Homonym List: www.cooper.com/alan/homonym.html
The Albany Poetry Workshop: www.sonic.net/poetry/albany/
Richard Lederer's Verbivore Page: http://pw1.netcom.com/~rlederer/index.htm
Rhetorical Figures: www.uky.edu/ArtsSciences/Classics/rhetoric.html
Rhyming Dictionary: www.rhymezone.com
A Word a Day: www.wordsmith.org/awad/index.html
The Word Wizard: wordwizard.com/

PUBLICATIONS ACCEPTING E-MAIL SUBMISSIONS

The following publications accept e-mail submissions. See the General Index for their page numbers. For e-mail submission instructions, see the publication's listing or obtain a copy of its writer's guidelines.

A Small Garlic Press
Aardvark Adventurer, The
Abiko Annual with James Joyce FW
   Studies
Able Muse
Abundance
Acid Angel
Acorn, The
Adoration: Journal of Christian
   Poetry
African Voices
Ag-Pilot International Magazine
Allisone Press
Ambitious Friends
American Tanka
Amethyst & Emerald Publishing
Amherst Review, The
Ancient Paths
Anna's Journal
Appalachian Heritage
Architrave
Arkansas Review
Artisan, A Journal of Craft
Avocet
Babel
Bark, The
Bathtub Gin
Beacon Street Review
Bear Deluxe, The
Bell's Letters Poet
Bible Advocate
Black Bear Publications
Bookpress
Boston Poet, The
Brilliant Star
Broken Boulder Press
brown-bag Lunch Magazine
Brunswick Publishing Corporation
Bugle, Journal of Elk Country
Cafe Review, The
Canadian Journal of Contemporary
   Literary Stuff, The
Canadian Woman Studies
Canadian Writer's Journal
Caribbean Writer, The
Carpe Laureate Diem
Chaff
Challenger international
Children, Churches and Daddies
Communities: Journal of Cooperative
   Living
Companion in Zeor, A
Concrete Abstract
Cornerstone
Coteau Books
Creative Juices
Creative with Words Publications
Creativity Unlimited Press
Cross & Quill
Current Accounts
Curriculum Vitae Literary
   Supplement
Cyber Oasis
Dead Fun
Descanso Literary Journal
Desperate Act

Devil Blossoms
Dickey Newsletter, James
dig.
Dixie Phoenix
Dreams and Nightmares
Drinkin' Buddy Magazine, The
Dry Bones Press
Dwan
ECW Press
Edgar: Digested Verse
Edge City Review, The
Emotions Literary Magazine
English Journal
English Studies Forum
Enterzone
Ethereal Green
Exit 13
Experimental Forest Press
Fat Tuesday
Feather Books
Filling Station
Flarestack Publishing
Flesh and Blood
For Poetry.Com
Forklift, Ohio
Forum
4*9*1*Imagination
Freehand
FreeXpresSion
Frogpond
Funny Paper, The
Futures Magazine
G.W. Review
Gargoyle Magazine
Genewatch
Gentle Reader
Girl Cult Girlkulturezine
GLB Publishers
Golden Isis Magazine
Gotta Write Network Litmag
Green Bean Press
Hadrosaur Tales
Harlem Review, The
Harpweaver, The
Heaven Bone Magazine
Heliotrope
Herb Network, The
Hey, Listen!
Higginsville Reader, The
Hunger Magazine
Idiot, The
Illuminations
Images Inscript
Imago
Improvijazzation Nation
Inklings
Interface, The
InterLink BBS
Italica Press
Japanophile
Jewel Among Jewels Adoption
   Network, Inc.
Jewish Spectator
Jones Av.
Jones Journal, The David
Journal of Asian Martial Arts

Journal of Contemporary Anglo-
   Scandinavian Poetry
Journal of New Jersey Poets
Journal of the American Medical
   Association
Jupiter's Freedom
Karawane
Kimera
Koja
Konfluence
Kota Press
Kwil Kids Publishing
Laurels
Leapings Literary Magazine
Left Curve
Limestone Circle
Link & Visitor, The
Literal Latte
Literary Focus Poetry Publications
Lithuanian Papers
Little Brown Poetry
Lone Willow Press
Lummox Press
Luna Negra
Lungfull! Magazine
Maelstrom
Magma Poetry Magazine
Magnolia Quarterly, The
Mail Call Journal
Mandrake Poetry Review
Mattoid
Mature Years
Medicinal Purposes Literary Review
Mekler & Deahl, Publishers
Melting Trees Review
Mennonite, The
Midwifery Today
Milton Magazine, John
Mind Matters Review
Mind Purge
Mkashef Enterprises
Monas Hieroglyphica
Monkey Flower
Mudlark
Murderous Intent
Muse Journal
Muse's Kiss Webzine
Musicworks
Muuna Takeena
National Forum
Naturally
New Song
Nova Express
O!!Zone
Oasis
Octavo
Office Number One
Ohio Teachers Write
Opened Eyes Poetry & Prose
   Magazine
Our Family
Our Journey
Owen Wister Review
Pandaloon
Paper Wasp: A Journal of Haiku
Paperplates

Paris/Atlantic
Penwood Review, The
Pep Publishing
Piano Press
Pif Magazine
Pink Cadillac
Plaza, The
Poetry & Prose Annual
Poetry Forum
Poetry of the People
Poet's Fantasy
Poet's Haven, The
Portland Review
Portraits of the Heart
Potluck Children's Literary Magazine
Prague Revue
Presbyterian Record, The
Presence
Princeton University Press
Prism International
Prosodia
Pulsar Poetry Magazine
Queen Street Quarterly
Queen's Quarterly
Rabbit Hole Press, The
Rattapallax
Red Crow
Red Dancefloor
Red Moon Press
Red Owl Magazine
Red River Review
Red Rock Review
Renaissance Online Magazine
Response
Rio: A Journal of the Arts

Rising
River King Poetry Supplement
Ruah
Salt Fork Review
Sanskrit
Scavenger's Newsletter
Science Fiction Poetry Association
Scottish Cultural Press
Scrivener
Seedhouse
Seeking the Muse
Shades of December
Shemom
Slide
Smartish Pace
Snapshots
Somniloquy
Soul Fountain
Sounds of a Grey Metal Day
South
Spish
StellaLuna-Poetry Circle
Struggle
Studio One
Sunlight & Moonbeams
Syncopated City
Taproot Literary Review
Teak Roundup
Teen Voices
These Days
3 Cup Morning
Thunder Rain Publishing Corp.
TimBookTu
Time of Singing
Tri Lingua

Tricycle
Tsunami Inc.
U.S. Latino Review, The
University of Alberta Press
Unlikely Stories
Uno Mas Magazine
Urban Spaghetti
Urthona Magazine
Vernalist, The
Voiceworks Magazine
Voiding the Void
Vortex of the Macabre
War Cry, The
Waterways
Well Tempered Sonnet, The
Wellspring
West Coast Line
Westerly
Window Journal
Wings Magazine, Inc.
Wishing Well, The
Word Salad
WoRM feASt!
Write Way, The
Writing on the Edge
Writing Ulster
Yes! A Journal of Positive Futures
Yomimono
Yorkshire Journal
Young Writer
Zine Zone
Zuzu's Petals Quarterly Online
Writer's Center, The

Glossary of Poetic Forms & Styles

Abstract poem: uses sound, rhythm and rhyme to convey emotion. The words' meanings are secondary to their sound.

Acrostic: the first or last letter in a line, read downward, form a word, phrase or sentence.

Alphabet poem: uses letters of the alphabet as points of departure for lines or whole poems.

Ballad: stories commonly about fatal relationships. Stanzas are quatrains with four beats in lines 1 and 3; and three beats in lines 2 and 4, which also rhyme.

Ballade: three stanzas rhyming *ababbcbC* (capital "C" meaning a refrain) and an envoie (half the number of lines of a stanza) rhyming *bcbC*.

Beat poetry: an anti-academic school of poetry born in the '50s in San Francisco. It is fast-paced free verse resembling jazz. The language is irreverent and slangy.

Blank verse: unrhymed, usually with iambic pentameter.

Calligram: poems whose words on the page form a shape or object related to the poem.

Cento: poem made up of pieces from poems by other authors.

Chant: poem where one or more lines is repeated over and over.

Cinquain: five-line stanza; or poem of five lines with 2, 4, 6, 8 and 2 syllables, respectively.

Concrete poem: the words dramatize their meaning by where they appear on the page; make use of space and sound.

Dada: movement based on deliberate irrationality and rejection of traditional artistic values.

Epigram: short, witty, satirical poem or saying written to be easily remembered. Like a punchline.

Free verse: no regular beat or rhyme.

Ghazal: usually five to fifteen lines of long-lined couplets, customarily expressing mystical thoughts. The couplets are not connected, but separate units.

Haibun: a Japanese form where prose is mixed with verse, specifically haiku, often in diary or travel journal form.

Haiku: poem about how nature is linked to human nature. Only three short lines containing 17 syllables, generally arranged 5-7-5. Uses simple words and expression, almost no adjectives.

Language poetry: attempts to detach words from their traditional meanings so something new arises. The poetry tries to break away from what we already know about poetry to experiment.

Limerick: five lines rhyming *aabba*, with a bawdy or scatalogical theme. The stresses in the lines are 3-3-2-2-3.

Lune: three-line poem of 13 syllables (5-3-5).

Lyric: intimate poem where poet speaks in own voice or a monologue, expressing emotion.

Nonsense verse: doesn't make sense, but it's not gibberish. Poem is consistent, but wacky.

Pantoum: poem of any length in four-line stanzas. Lines 2 and 4 are repeated as lines 1 and 3 of the next stanza, and so on. Doesn't have to rhyme. Ideally, in the last stanza, lines 2 and 4 repeat the opening stanza's lines 1 and 3.

Prose poem: looks like prose, but reads like poetry. No rhyme or set rhythm. It's unlike regular prose because of its intense and condensed language.

Quatrain: a four-line stanza.

Renga: long, image-filled in alternating stanzas of three and two lines, customarily created by a big group of poets taking turns.

Rondeau: the repeating lines and rhyme give the poem the quality of a round. It's usually 15 lines that rhyme *aabba aabR aabbaR* ("R" is the refrain).

Senryu: like haiku, but about human nature, often humorous, using direct language.

Sequence: a series of poems, often numbered. The poems must be connected in some way e.g., by theme, subject, stanza form, or ongoing narrative.

Sestina: six unrhymed stanzas of six lines each. The words at the end of the first stanza's lines repeat at ends of other lines. Each subsequent stanza rearranges the previous stanza's end-words as 6, 1, 5, 2, 4, 3. Ends with a three-line stanza using all six end-words, two to a line.

Sijo: a Korean form of poetry, 44 to 46 syllables, usually on three lines.

Skeltonic verse: short lines whose rhymes continue as long as they work, then changes to another rhyme.

Sonnet: often written about love and/or philosophy. It's a 14-line poem in two parts: octave (eight lines) and a sestet (six lines). There are three types: the Petrarchan (or Italian) rhymes *abbaabba* and varies the last six lines (*cdcdcd* or *cdecde* or *cdedce* or *ccdccd* or *cddcdd* or *cddcee*); the Shakespearean rhymes *abab cdcd efef gg*; the Spenserian rhymes *ababbbcbccdcdee*.

Surrealism: literary and artistic movement stressing the importance of dreams, the unconscious, irrational thought, free associations and disturbing imagery.

Tanka: frequently about love, seasons, sadness, with strong images and poetic devices haiku avoids. Five lines, with lines 1 and 3 being shorter. Syllables per line are 5-7-5-7-7.

Triolet: eight lines, with two rhymes and two repeating lines. The first line is repeated as lines 4 and 7. Lines 2 and 8 are the same: *ABaAabAB* (capitals indicate repeated lines or refrains).

Villanelle: six stanzas. The first five are three lines long, the sixth is four lines long. The first and last lines of the first stanza repeat as the final line of the next four stanzas and are also the last two lines of the poem. Rhyme scheme of *aba* for first five stanzas.

Visual: a combination of text and graphics usually only reproduced photographically.

Glossary of Listing Terms

A3, A4, A5. Metric equivalents of 11¾×16½, 8¼×11¾ and 5⅞×8¼ respectively.

Anthology. A collection of selected writings by various authors.

b&w. black & white (photo or illustration).

Bio. A short biographical paragraph often requested with a submission.

Camera-ready. Poems that are completely prepared for copy camera platemaking.

Chapbook. A small book of under 50 pages of poetry. Such a book is less expensive to produce than a full-length book collection, though it is seldom noted by reviewers.

Contributor's copy. Copy of an issue of a magazine or published book sent to an author whose work is included.

Cover letter. Letter accompanying a submission; it usually lists titles of poems and gives a brief account of publishing credits and biographical information.

Cover stock. Heavier book or text paper used to cover a publication, often coated on one or both sides.

Digest-sized. Approximately 5½×8½, the size of a folded sheet of conventional printer paper.

Electronic magazine. Publication circulated solely via the Internet and e-mail.

E-mail. Mail that has been sent electronically using a computer and modem.

Flat-spined. What many publishers call "perfect-bound," glued with a flat edge (usually permitting readable type on the spine).

Font. A particular style or design of type; typeface.

Galleys. Typeset copies of your poem(s). You should proofread and correct any mistakes and return galleys to editors within 48 hours of receipt.

Honorarium. A small, token payment for published work.

IRC. International Reply Coupon, postage for return of submissions from another country. One IRC is sufficient for one ounce by *surface mail*. If you want an airmail return, you need one IRC for each half-ounce. Do not send checks or cash for postage to other countries: The exchange rates are so high it is not worth the inconvenience it causes editors. (Exception: Many Canadian editors do not object to U.S. dollars; use IRCs the first time and inquire.)

Magazine-sized. Approximately 8½×11, the size of conventional printer paper unfolded.

ms. manuscript; **mss.** manuscripts.

Multi-book review. Also known as an omnibus or essay review. A review of several books by the same author or by several authors, such as a review of four or five political poetry books.

Multiple submission. Submission of more than one poem at a time; most poetry publishers *prefer* multiple submissions and specify how many poems should be in a packet. Some say a multiple submission means the poet has sent another manuscript to the same publication before receiving word on the first submission. This type of multiple submission is generally discouraged (see Simultaneous submission).

Offset. A printing method in which ink is transferred from an image-bearing plate to a "blanket" and from the blanket to the paper.

p. Abbreviation for pence.

p&h. postage & handling.

Perfect-bound. See Flat-spined.

Publishing credits. A list of magazines having published a poet's work, or a list of a poet's published books.

Query letter. Letter written to a publisher to elicit interest in a manuscript or to determine if submissions are acceptable.

Rights. First North American serial rights means the publisher is acquiring the right to publish your poem first in a U.S. or Canadian periodical. All rights means the publisher is buying the poem outright. Selling all rights usually requires that you obtain permission to reprint your work, even in a book-length collection.

Royalties. A percentage of the retail price paid to an author for each copy of the book that is sold.

Saddle-stapled. What many publishers call "saddle-stitched," folded and stapled along the fold.

SAE. Self-addressed envelope.

SASE. Self-addressed, stamped envelope. *Every* publisher requires, with any submission, query or request for information, a self-addressed, stamped envelope.

Simultaneous submission. Submission of the same manuscript to more than one publisher at a time. Many magazine editors *refuse to accept* simultaneous submissions. Some book and chapbook publishers do not object to simultaneous submissions. In all cases, notify editors that the manuscript is being simultaneously submitted.

Subsidy press. See Vanity press.

Tabloid-sized. 11×15 or larger, the size of an ordinary newspaper folded and turned sideways.

Unsolicited manuscript. A manuscript an editor did not specifically ask to see.

Vanity press. A slang term for a publisher that requires the writer to pay publishing costs, especially one that flatters an author to generate business. These presses often use the term "subsidy" to describe themselves. Some presses, however, derive subsidies from other sources, such as government grants, and do not require author payment. These are not considered vanity presses.

Indexes
Chapbook Publishers

A chapbook is a slim volume of a poet's work, usually under 50 pages (although page requirements vary greatly). Given the high cost of printing, a publisher is more apt to accept a chapbook than an entire book from an unproven poet.

Some chapbooks are published as inserts in magazines. (The winner of The Tennessee Chapbook Prize, for instance, is published as an insert in *Poems & Plays*.) Others are separate volumes. A physical description (binding, method of printing, cover, etc.) is usually included in the market listings, but whenever possible, request submission guidelines and samples to determine the quality of the product.

You'll find many presses, particularly those that sponsor chapbook contests, charge reading fees. Avoid any over $10. (Some folks go as high as $15 for book-length manuscripts, but chapbooks are easier to produce.)

If your chapbook is published, by the way, you may still participate in "first-book" competitions. For more information about both chapbook and book publishing, read How to Publish Your Poetry Successfully, beginning on page 10.

Following are publishers who consider chapbook manuscripts. See the General Index for the page numbers of their market listings.

Hey, listen!
High/Coo Press
Horse Latitudes Press
Hunger Magazine
Ibbetson St. Press
Implosion Press
Indian Heritage Publishing
Inkwell, The
Insects Are People Two
Inverted-A, Inc.
K.T. Publications
Lake Shore Publishing
Lapwing Publications
Lateral Moves
Ledge, The
Lilliput Review
Limited Editions Press
Lone Willow Press
Longhouse
Low-Tech Press
Lucidity
Lummox Press
Luna Bisonte Prods
Luz en Arte y Literatura
Mad River Press
Malafemmina Press
Maryland Poetry Review
Mekler & Deahl, Publishers
Mid-American Review
Miller's Pond
Minority Literary Expo
(m)öthêr TØñgué Press
Nerve Cowboy
New Orleans Poetry Journal
    Press
New Song, A
Northeast
Oasis Books
Ohio Review, The

One Trick Pony
Onthebus
Outrider Press
Pacific Coast Journal
Painted Bride Quarterly
Palanquin
Paradoxism
Parting Gifts
Pavement Saw
Pearl
Pecan Grove Press
Peer Poetry Magazine
Pennywhistle Press
Peregrine
Philomel Books
Piano Press
Pirate Writings
Pitchfork
Plowman, The
Poems & Plays
Poetic License Poetry Magazine
Poetic Space
Poetry Forum
Poetry Harbor
Poetry Miscellany, The
Poets at Work
Poets' Roundtable
Prairie Journal, The
Pudding House Publications
Rag Mag
Raintown Review, The
Rattapallax
Raw Dog Press
Raw Nervz Haiku
Red Crow
Red Dragon Press
Red Moon Press
Riverstone
Round Table, The
Ruah
Sarasota Poetry Theatre Press

Score Magazine
Scroll Publications
Serpent & Eagle Press
Ship of Fools
Silver Gull Publishing
Slapering Hol Press Chapbook
    Competition
Slide
Slipstream
Snapshots
Southfields
Sow's Ear Poetry Review, The
Still Waters Press
Stovepipe
Symbiotic Oatmeal
Synaesthesia Press
Syncopated City
sub-TERRAIN
Tale Spinners
"Teak" Roundup
Temporary Vandalism
    Recordings
Thin Coyote
Third Half Literary Magazine,
    The
Tickled by Thunder
Tightrope
Time of Singing
Touchstone Literary Journal
Understanding Magazine
University of Massachusetts
    Press
Vernalist, The
Water Mark Press
Waterways
White Eagle Coffee Store Press
Whole Notes
WoRM fEASt!

Book Publishers Index

The following are magazines and publishers that consider full-length book manuscripts. See the General Index for the page numbers to their market listings.

Openness to Submissions Index

This index ranks all magazines, publishers, contests and awards contained in *Poet's Market* according to their openness to unsolicited submissions. Some markets are listed in more than one category. See the General Index for the page numbers of their corresponding listings.

☐ OPEN TO BEGINNING POETS

Aardvark Adventurer, The; Above the Bridge Magazine; Acumen Magazine; Advocate; African Voices; Ag-Pilot International Magazine; Aguilar Expression, The; Alden Enterprises; Alembic; Allegheny Review; Alligator Juniper; Allisone Press; Alms House Press; American Cowboy Poet Magazine, The; Amethyst & Emerald Publishing; Amethyst Review, The; Analecta; Angel News Magazine; Anna's Journal; Anthology; Appalachian Heritage; Apropos; Arachne, Inc.; Arizona State Poetry Society Annual Contest; Arkansas Poetry Day Contest; Art Coop Fellowship in Poetry; Atlantic Monthly, The; Axe Factory Review; Babel; babysue; Back Porch, The; Backwaters Prize, The; Barbaric Yawp; Bathtub Gin; Bay Area Poets Coalition; Bay Windows; Baybury Review; BECH Publications Writing Competition; Beauty for Ashes Poetry Review; Beggar's Press; Belhue Press; Bell's Letters Poet; Bible Advocate; Bibliophilos; Black Diaspora Magazine; Black Spring Press; Boston Poet, The; Brobdingnagian Times, The; Broken Boulder Press; Buddha Eyes; Button Magazine; Bytes of Poetry; California Quarterly; Calyx; Capper's; Carpe Laureate Diem; CC. Marimbo Communications; Chaff; Challenger international; Cherrybite Publications; Children, Churches and Daddies; Chiron Review; Christianity and the Arts; Claremont Review, The; Climbing Art, The; Clubhouse Jr.; CNW/FFWA Florida State Writing Competition; Cochran's Corner; Connections; core literary journal; Cosmic Trend; Country Folk; Creative Juices; Creative With Words Publications; Creativity Unlimited Press®; Crucible; Crumb Elbow Publishing Poetry Contests; Cycle Press; Dancing Poetry Contest; Dandelion Arts Magazine; Daniels Annual Honorary Writing Award, The Dorothy; Dead Fun; Dickinson Award in Poetry, Emily; Doggerel; Dorfman National Poetry Prize, Milton; Dream International Quarterly; Drinkin' Buddy Magazine, The; Dry Bones Press; DTCT Open Poetry Award; Duncton Cottage Short Story and Poetry Competition; Eagle's Flight; Eastern Caribbean Institute; 1812; Enterzone; Experimental Forest Press; Feather Books; Fiddlehead, The; Fire; First Step Press; Flarestack Publishing; Flint Hills Review; Footprints; 4*9*1 Imagination; Free Focus; Freehand; FreeXpresSion; frisson: disconcerting verse; Funny Paper, The; Gentle Reader; Gentle Survivalist, The; Girl Cult Girlkulturzine; GLB Publishers; Glimmer Train's April Poetry Open; Glimmer Train's October Poetry Open; Gotta Write Network Litmag; Graffiti Rag; Grasslands Review; Green River Writers' Contests; GSU Review; Hadrosaur Tales; Haiku Headlines; Hanging Loose Press; Hard Row to Hoe; Haypenny Press; Herb Network, The; Hey, listen!; Hiram Poetry Review; Hodgepodge Short Stories & Poetry; Home Times; Horse Latitudes Press; Hunted News, The; Ibbetson St. Press; Implosion Press; Improvijazzation Nation; In 2 Print Magazine; Indian Heritage Publishing; Inklings; Inkwell Magazine; Inkwell, The; Insects Are People Two; Interbang; Interface, The; InterLink BBS; Irish Famine Commemorative Literary Prize; Jewel Among Jewels Adoption Network, Inc.; Jewish Spectator; Jones Av.; Jupiter's Freedom; K.T. Publications; Karawane; Kawabata Press; Keats Shelley Millennium Prize; Kelly Peace Poetry Contest, Barbara Mandigo; Kestrel; Kit-Cat Review, The; Kota Press; Kumquat Meringue; Kuumba; Kwil Kids Publishing; Lake Shore Publishing; Lapwing Publications; Laurels; League of Minnesota Poets Contest, The; Leapings Literary Magazine; Libra Publishers, Inc.; Lime Green Bulldozers; Limestone Circle; Linkway Magazine; Literally Horses; Literary Focus Poetry Publications; Literary Moments; Lochs Magazine; Lone Stars Magazine; Lonzie's Fried Chicken™ Literary Magazine; Lucid Moon; Lummox Press; Luna Negra; Lynx Eye; Magma Poetry Magazine; Magnolia Quarterly, The; Malafemmina Press; Maryland Poetry Review; Maypole Editions; Mediphors; Micropress New Zealand; Mid-America Press, Inc., The; Mind Purge; Minority Literary Expo; Missing Fez, The; Möbius; Monas Hieroglyphica; Monkey Flower; Mystery Time; Nashville Newsletter Poetry Contest; National Writers Union Annual National Poetry Competition; Nebo: A Literary Journal; Neovictorian/Cochlea, The; Nerve Cowboy; New Era Magazine; New Millennium Award for Poetry; New Mirage Quarterly, The; New Orleans Poetry Forum; New Rivers Press; New Writer's Magazine; New York Foundation for the Arts; New York University Prize for Poetry; Newsletter Inago; Night Roses; Nimrod; 96 Inc Magazine; Nite-Writer's International Literary Arts Journal; Northern Stars Magazine; Nuthouse; Oak, The; Offerings; O'Hara Award Chapbook Competition, Frank; Ohio Teachers Write; Old Red Kimono, The; Onset Review, The; Opened Eyes Poetry & Prose Magazine; Oracle Poetry; Orbis; Our Journey; Outer Darkness; Outrider Press; Oyez Review; Pacific Coast Journal; Palo Alto Review; PandaLoon; Panhandle Professional Writers; Paper Wasp; Parnassus Literary Journal; Partners Writing

Group; Passager; Path Press, Inc.; Pearson Award, Judith Siegel; Penmanship; Penumbra Poetry & Haiku Competition; People's Press, The; Pep Publishing; Pipe Smoker's Ephemeris, The; Pirate Writings; Pitchfork; Plowman, The; Poem du Jour; Poetcrit; Poetic Hours; Poetic Potpourri Quarterly Contests; Poetic Realm; Poetic Space; Poetic Voices Journal; Poetry Explosion Newsletter, The; Poetry Forever; Poetry Forum; Poetry Harbor; Poetry International; Poetry Miscellany, The; Poetry of the People; Poets at Work; Poets Corner; Poets' Dinner Contest; Poet's Fantasy; Poet's Haven, The; Poets' Podium; Poets' Roundtable; Portraits of the Heart; Potato Hill Poetry; Potluck Children's Literary Magazine; Prairie Journal, The; Prakalpana Literature; Premiere Generation Ink; Puckerbrush Press, The; Purple Patch; Quadrant Magazine; Quantum Leap; Rabbit Hole Press, The; Radiance; RB's Poets' Viewpoint; Red Herring; Red Owl Magazine; Red River Review; Red Rock Review; Redwood Acres Fair Poetry Contest; Rising; River King Poetry Supplement; Rockford Review, The; Rocky Mountain Rider Magazine; Romantic Outsider; Romantics Quarterly; Rose Tinted Windows; Rowan Books; Ruah; Rural Heritage; St. Joseph Messenger and Advocate of the Blind; Sanskrit; Sarasota Poetry Theatre Press; Scroll Publications; Seaman Poetry Award, Claudia Ann; Seedhouse; Seeds Poetry Magazine; Senior Poet Laureate Poetry Competition; Shemom; Sidewalks; Sierra Nevada College Review; Silver Web, The; SimplyWords; Skald; Skipping Stones; Sky Blue Waters Poetry Contests; Skylark; Smiths Knoll; Snow Writing Awards, Kay; Society of American Poets (SOAP), The; Society of Midland Authors Literary Award; Somniloquy; Soul Fountain; Soul of the Poet Award, The; Sounds of Poetry, The; Southern Indiana Review; SPAWN; SPIN; Spish; Splizz; Stand Magazine; Storyteller, The; Struggle; sub-TERRAIN; Superior Poetry News; Suzerain Enterprises; Sweet Annie & Sweet Pea Review; Symbiotic Oatmeal; Syncopated City; Tabla Poetry Competition, The; Takahe; Tale Spinners; Taproot Literary Review; "Teak" Roundup; Texas Review; Thalia; Third Half Literary Magazine, The; Thoughts for All Seasons; 3 Cup Morning; Threshold, The; Thumbprints; Thunder Rain Publishing; Tickled by Thunder; TimBookTu; Time For Rhyme; Tradition Magazine; Transcendent Visions; Trewithen Poetry Prize, The; Tyro Publishing; Ultimate Unknown, The; Understanding Magazine; Unlikely Stories; Upsouth; Urban Graffiti; Vernalist, The; Voiceworks Magazine; Voiding The Void; Vortex of the Macabre; Waterways; Way Station Magazine; Well Tempered Sonnet, The; Western Archipelago Review; Whitecrow Foundation, Tahana; Whole Notes; Window Journal; Winter Wood Poetry Award; Wisconsin Review; Wishing Well, The; Write Way, The; Writer, The; Writers At Work Fellowship Competition; Writer's Block Magazine; Writers Bureau Poetry and Short Story Competition, The; Writer's Exchange; Writers' Journal; Yeats Poetry Prize for Australia and New Zealand, The W.B.; Young Writer; Zine Zone

☑ OPEN TO BEGINNING & EXPERIENCED POETS

Aardvark Adventurer, The; Abbey; Abiko Annual; Able Muse; About Such Things; Abundance; ACM (Another Chicago Magazine); Acorn, The; Acorn Whistle; Acumen Magazine; Adastra Press; Adept Press; Adoration; Adrift; Aethlon; Affable Neighbor; African Voices; Ag-Pilot International Magazine; Aguilar Expression, The; Aim Magazine; Akron Poetry Prize; Akros Publications; Alabama Literary Review; Alaska Quarterly Review; Albatross; Alden Enterprises; Alice James Books; Alligator Juniper; Amelia; American Dissident, The; American Literary Review; American Poets & Poetry; Amethyst & Emerald Publishing; Amethyst Review, The; Amherst Review, The; Analecta; Anamnesis Press; Ancient Paths; Andreas-Gryphius-Preis; Angelflesh; Anhinga Press; Anthology; Anthology of New England Writers, The; Apalachee Quarterly; Aphasia Press; Appalachia; Appalachian Heritage; Aquarius; Architrave; Arizona State Poetry Society Annual Contest; Arjuna Library Press; "Art in the Air" Poetry Contest; Art Times; Artisan; Arts Recognition and Talent Search; Ascent; Asher Publishing, Sherman; Asheville Poetry Review; Atlanta Review; Atom Mind; Aura Literary/Arts Review; Aurorean, The; Axe Factory Review; Babel; Back Porch, The; Backwaters Prize, The; Baltimore Review, The; Barbarian Press; Barbaric Yawp; Barnwood Press; Barrow Street; Bathtub Gin; Bay Area Poets Coalition (BAPC); Bay Windows; Baybury Review; Beacon Street Review; Bear Star Press; Beatnik Pachyderm, The; Beauty for Ashes Poetry Review; Bellingham Review, The; Bellowing Ark; Bell's Letters Poet; Beloit Poetry Journal, The; Bennett Fellowship, George; Bibliophilos; Birch Brook Press; Birmingham Poetry Review; Bitter Oleander, The; BKMK Press; Black Bear Publications; black bough; Black Buzzard Press; Black Moon; Black Moss Press; Black Warrior Review; Blackwater Press; Blind Man's Rainbow, The; Blood and Fire Review; Blue Collar Review; Blue Light Press; Blue Nose Poetry Poets-of-the-Year Competition; Blue Unicorn; Blue Violin; Bluestem Press Award; Bogg Publications; Bombay Gin; Bookpress; Borderlands; Bordighera, Inc.; Boston Poet, The; Bottomfish; Boulevard; Brando's Hat; Breakfast All Day; Briar Cliff Review, The; BrickHouse Books, Inc.; Bridge, The; Bright Hill Press; Brilliant Corners; Brobdingnagian Times, The; Broken Boulder Press; Brown Bottle, The; brown-bag Lunch Magazine; Brownstone Review, The; Brunswick Publishing Corporation; Buddha Eyes; Buffalo Bones; Bugle, Journal of Elk Country; Burning Bush, The; Bytes of Poetry; California Quarterly; Calypso Publications; Camellia; Canadian Journal of Contemporary Literary Stuff, The; Capilano Review, The; Carolina Quarterly, The; Catamount Press; CC. Marimbo Communications; Cedar Hill Publications; Center for Book Arts' Annual Poetry Chapbook Competition, The; Chachalaca Poetry Review; Challenger international; Chariton Review, The; Chattahoochee Review, The; Cherrybite Publications; Chiron Review; Christian Century, The; Christian Science Monitor, The; Christianity and the Arts; Chrysalis Reader; Cider Press Review; Cimarron Review; Clackamas Literary Review; Clay Palm Review; Cleveland State University Poetry Center; Climbing Art, The; Clutch; Coal City Review; Coe Review, The; Cold Mountain Review; Collages & Bricolages; Colorado Review; Columbia; Comstock Review, The; Concho River Review; Concrete Abstract; Conduit; Confluence; Confluence Press; Confrontation Magazine; Connecticut Poetry Review, The; Connecticut Review; Connecticut River Review; Contemporary Verse 2; core literary journal; Corona; Coteau Books; Cottonwood; Countermeasures; Crab Orchard Review; Cream City Review; Creative Juices; Creative Writing Fellowships in Poetry; Cross-Cultural Communications; Crucible; Cumberland Poetry Review; Current Accounts; Curriculum Vitae Literary Supplement; Cutbank; Cyber Literature; Cyber Oasis; Dancing Poetry Contest; Daniel and Company, Publisher, John; Daniels Annual Honorary Writing Award, The Dorothy; Dark Regions; Dead End Street Publications; Dead Metaphor Press; Debut Review; Defined Providence; Denver Quarterly; Descanso Literary Journal; Descant; Desperate Act; Dickinson Award in Poetry, Emily; Didactic, The; dig.; Dirigible; Distillery, The; Dixie Phoenix; Doc(k)s; Dolphin-Moon Press; Dreams and Nightmares; Dry Creek Review, The; DTCT Open Poetry Award; Dwan; Eagle's Flight; ECW Press; Eckerd College Review; Edgar; Edge City Review, The; 1812; Ekphrasis; Eliot Prize for Poetry, T.S.; Emotions Literary Magazine; Emrys Journal; English Journal; Enterzone; Epicenter; Ethereal Green; Evangel; Event; Explorations; Family of Man Press; Farrar, Straus & Giroux/Books for Young Readers; Fat Tuesday; Faulkner Creative Writing Competition/Poetry Category, The William; Faultline; Fauquier Poetry Journal; Fiddlehead, The; Field; filling Station; Fine Madness; Firewater Press Inc.; Firm Noncommittal; First Class; First Step Press; 5 AM; Five Points; Flaming Arrows; Flarestack Publishing; Flesh and Blood; Flint Hills Review; Florida Individual Artist Fellowships; Florida Review, The; Flyway; Footprints; Formalist, The; Foster City International Writers' Contest; 4*9*1 Imagination; Fourteen Hills; Fox Cry Review; Free Lunch; FreeFall Magazine; FreeXpresSion; Fugue; Funny Paper, The; Future Tense Press; Futures Magazine; G.W. Review; Garnet; Gathering of the Tribes, A; Gentle Reader; Gentle Survivalist, The; George & Mertie's Place; Georgia Review, The; Gettysburg Review, The; Ginger Hill; Ginninderra Press; Girl Cult Girlkulturzine; GLB Publishers; Glimmer Train's April Poetry Open; Glimmer Train's October Poetry Open; Golden Isis Magazine; Gotta Write Network Litmag; Graffiti Rag; Graffito; Grain; Grandmother Earth National Award; Grasslands Review; Gravity Presses; Graywolf Press; Great Blue Beacon Poetry Contest, The; Great Lakes Colleges Association New Writers Award; Green Hills Literary Lantern; Green's Magazine; Greensboro Review, The; Grolier Poetry Prize; Guggenheim Fellowships; Gulf Coast; Gulf Stream Magazine; Hackney Literary Awards; Haight Ashbury Literary Journal; Haiku Headlines; Half Tones to Jubilee; Handshake Editions; Hanging Loose Press; Hanover Press, Ltd.; Harlem Review, The; Harpweaver, The; Hawaii Pacific Review; Hawai'i Review; Hayden's Ferry Review; Haz Mat Review; Headlock Press; Heartlands Today, The; Heaven Bone Magazine; Heist Magazine; Heliotrope; Hellas; Hellp!; Higginsville Reader, The; Hippopotamus Press; Hiram Poetry Review; Hobo Poetry & Haiku Magazine; Hodder Fellowship, The; Hollins Critic, The; Home Planet News; House of Anansi Press; Hoyns Fellowships, Henry; HQ Poetry Magazine; HU; Hunger Magazine; Hunted News, The; Ibbetson St. Press; Iconoclast, The; Illuminations; Images Inscript; Imago; Implosion Press; In the Grove; Indiana Review; Indigenous Fiction; Inklings; Inkwell, The; Interbang; Interface, The; Interim; International Poetry Review; International Quarterly; Interpreter's House; Inverted-A, Inc.; Iota; Iowa Review, The; Jewish Currents; Jones Av.; Jones Journal, The David; Journal of Contemporary Anglo-Scandinavian Poetry; Journal of New Jersey Poets; Journal of the American Medical Association (JAMA); Junction Press; Jupiter's Freedom; K.T. Publications; Kaeden Books; Karamu; Karawane; Kavya Bharati; Kawabata Press; Keats Shelley Millennium Prize; Kenyon Review, The; Kerf, The; Kestrel; Kimera; Kiosk; Kit-Cat Review, The; Koja; Konfluence; Kota Press; Krax; Kumquat Meringue; Kwil Kids Publishing; LAIRE, Inc., the; Lapwing Publications; Lateral Moves; Laurels; Ledge, The; Left Curve; Libido; Licking River Review, The; Light; Lilliput Review; Limestone Circle; Limited Editions Press; Links; Lintel; Listening Eye, The; Literal Latté; Literary Review, The; Literature and Belief; LitRag; Little Brown Poetry; Lochs Magazine; London Magazine; Lone Stars Magazine; Longhouse; Loonfeather Annual; Los; Louisiana Literature; Louisiana Review, The; Louisville Review, The; Love Affair Literary Contest, A; LSR (Latino Stuff Review); LUNGFULL! Magazine; Lucid Moon; Lucid Stone, The; Lucidity; Lullwater Review; Lummox Press; Luna Negra; Lynx Eye; MacGuffin, The; Mad Poets Review; Maelstrom; Magazine of Speculative Poetry, The; Magma Poetry Magazine; Magnolia Quarterly, The; Mail Call Journal; Main Street Rag Poetry Journal; Malahat Review, The; Mammoth Books; Mandrake Poetry Review; Manhattan Review, The; Mankato Poetry Review; Manoa; Many Mountains Moving; Marlboro Review, The; Maryland Poetry Review; Marymark Press; Massachusetts Review, The; Matchbook; Mattoid; Medicinal Purposes Literary Review; Mediphors; Medusa's Hairdo; Melbourne Poets Union Annual Poetry Competition; Mellen Poetry; Melting Trees Review; Michigan State University Press; Mid-America Press, Inc., The; Mid-American Review; Mid-List Press First Series Award for Poetry; Midwest Poetry Review; Midwest Quarterly, The; Milkweed Editions; Miller's Pond; Milton Magazine, John; Mind Purge; Minnesota Review, The; Missing Fez, The; Mississippi Review; Missouri

Review; Mkashef Enterprises; MM Review; Möbius; Modern Poetry In Translation; Monkey Flower; Morse Poetry Prize, Samuel French; Mount Olive College Press; Mudlark; Muse Journal; Muse's Kiss Webzine; Nanny Fanny; National Book Award; National Enquirer; National Poetry Series Annual Open Competition; Nebraska Review, The; Nedge; Nerve Cowboy; New Delta Review; New England Review; New Issues Press; New Laurel Review, The; New Letters; New Mirage Quarterly, The; New Orleans Review; New Orphic Review; New Press Literary Quarterly, The; New Renaissance, The; New Writer, The; New Writer's Magazine; New York Quarterly; Newburyport Art Association Annual Spring Poetry Contest; Nexus; Nightsun; Nimrod; 96 Inc Magazine; Nite-Writer's International Literary Arts Journal; No Exit; Nomad's Choir; Northeast Corridor; Northern Stars Magazine; Northwest Review; Northwoods Press; Northwords; Nostalgia; Notre Dame Review; Nova Express; Oasis; Oasis Books; Offerings; Offerta Speciale; Office Number One; O'Hara Award Chapbook Competition, Frank; Ohio State University Press/ The Journal Award in Poetry; Ohio Teachers Write; One Trick Pony; Onset Review, The; Onthebus; Opened Eyes Poetry & Prose Magazine; Oracle Poetry; Orange Willow Review; Osiris; Our Journey; Outerbridge; Outrider Press; Owen Wister Review; Oxygen; P.D.Q. (Poetry Depth Quarterly); Pacific Coast Journal; Pacific Enterprise Magazine; Paintbrush; Painted Bride Quarterly; Palanquin; Palo Alto Review; Panda-Loon; Paperplates; Paris/Atlantic; Parnassus Literary Journal; Parting Gifts; Partisan Review; Partners Writing Group; Passager; Passages North; Paterson Literary Review, The; Paumanok Poetry Award Competition; Pavement Saw; Pearl; Pecan Grove Press; Peer Poetry Magazine; Pegasus; Pembroke Magazine; Penmanship; Pennine Platform; Pennsylvania English; Penny Dreadful; Penwood Review, The; People's Press, The; Peregrine; Perspectives; Perugia Press; Phillips Poetry Prize, The Richard; Phoebe (NY); Phoebe (VA); Piano Press; Pif Magazine; Pig Iron; Pikeville Review; Pine Island Journal of New England Poetry; Pink Cadillac; Pinyon Poetry; Pirate Writings; Pitchfork; Pitt Poetry Series; Plainsongs; Plastic Tower, The; Plaza, The; Pleiades; Plowman, The; Poem; Poem du Jour; Poems & Plays; Poet Lore; Poetcrit; Poetic Potpourri Quarterly Contests; Poetry & Prose Annual; Poetry Bone; Poetry Center Book Award, The; Poetry Explosion Newsletter, The; Poetry Forum; Poetry Harbor; Poetry International; Poetry Ireland Review; Poetry Kanto; Poetry Miscellany, The; Poetry Northwest; Poetry Nottingham International; Poetry Review; Poetry USA; Poets at Work; Poets' Club of Chicago International Shakespearean/Petrarchan Sonnet Contest; Poets' Podium; Porcupine Literary Arts Magazine; Portland Review; Potato Hill Poetry; Potluck Children's Literary Magazine; Potomac Review; Potpourri; Pottersfield Portfolio; Prague Revue, The; Prairie Journal, The; Prairie Schooner; Prairie Winds; Pride Imprints; Primavera; Prism International; Prosodia; Provincetown Arts; Puckerbrush Press, The; Pudding House Publications; Pulitzer Prize in Letters; Pulsar Poetry Magazine; Purple Patch; QED Press; Quadrant Magazine; Quantum Leap; Quarter After Eight; Quarterly Review of Literature Poetry Book Series; Quarterly West; Queen Street Quarterly; Queen's Quarterly; Rag Mag; Rainmaker Awards in Poetry; Ralph's Review; Rattapallax; Rattle; Raw Dog Press; RE:AL; Red Cedar Review; Red Deer Press; Red Dragon Press; Red Hen Press; Red Herring; Red Owl Magazine; Red River Review; Red Rock Review; Renaissance Online Magazine; Response; Re:Verse!; Rhino; Rialto, The; Rio; Rio Grande Review; Rivelin Grapheme Press; River City; River King Poetry Supplement; River Oak Review; River Styx Magazine; Riverrun; Riverstone; Roanoke Review; Rocket Press; Rockford Review, The; Rocky Mountain Rider Magazine; Romantics Quarterly; Ronsdale Press; Room of One's Own; Rosebud; Rosenberg Award, Anna Davidson; Rowan Books; Sachem Press; Salt Fork Review; Salt Hill; Saltonstall Foundation for the Arts Grants, The Constance; Sanders Memorial Trophy, Aileen & Albert; Sarabande Books, Inc.; Sarasota Poetry Theatre Press; Score Magazine; Scrivener; Seam; Seedhouse; Seeking the Muse; Seems; Seneca Review; Senior Poet Laureate Poetry Competition; Sensations Magazine; Sewanee Review, The; Shades of December; Shattered Wig Review; Shenandoah; Ship of Fools; Sidewalks; Sierra Nevada College Review; Silverfish Review; Situation; Skidrow Penthouse; Skipping Stones; Skylark; Slant; Slapering Hol Press Chapbook Competition; Slide; Slipstream; Small Pond Magazine of Literature; Smartish Pace; Smiths Knoll; Snapshots; Snow Writing Awards, Kay; Snow-apple Press; Snowy Egret; So To Speak; Society for Creative Writers Poetry Contest; Society of American Poets (SOAP), The; Somniloquy; Soul Fountain; Soundings East; Sounds of Poetry, The; South; South Carolina Review; Southern Humanities Review; Southern Poetry Review; Southern Review, The; South-fields; Southwest Review; Southwestern American Literature; Sou'wester; Sow's Ear Poetry Review, The; SPIN; Spillway; Spindrift; Spinning Jenny; Spirit That Moves Us, The; Spout Magazine; Spunk; Stand Magazine; Stegner Fellowships, Wallace E.; Still Waters Press; Story Line Press; Stovepipe; Strain, The; Struggle; Studio; Studio One; Sulphur River Literary Review; Summer Stream Press; Sun, The; Sunlight & Moonbeams; Sunstone; Superior Poetry News; Sweet Annie & Sweet Pea Review; Sycamore Review; Synaesthesia Press; Syncopated City; Takahe; Talking River Review; Taproot Literary Review; Tar River Poetry; Tears in the Fence; Temporary Vandalism Recordings; Texas Review; Thema; These Days; Thin Coyote; Third Coast; Third Half Literary Magazine, The; 13th Moon; Thorny Locust; Thoughts for All Seasons; 360 Degrees; Threepenny Review, The; Tia Chucha Press; Tickled by Thunder; Tightrope; Time of Singing; To' To' Pos; Torre De Papel; Towson University Prize for Literature; Trestle Creek Review; Trewithen Poetry Prize, The; Tri Lingua; Tricycle; TriQuarterly Magazine; Troubadour; True Romance;

Tsunami Inc.; Tucumcari Literary Review; Tufts Discovery Award, Kate; Twilight Ending; Two Rivers Review; Tyro Publishing; U.S. Catholic; U.S. Latino Review, The; U.S. 1 Worksheets; Ulitarra; Ultramarine Publishing Co., Inc.; UNo Mas Magazine; Understanding Magazine; University of Central Florida Contemporary Poetry Series; University of Georgia Press; University of Massachusetts Press, The; Upsouth; Urban Spaghetti; Urthona Magazine; V.B. Poetry Prize; Ver Poets Open Competition; Vernalist, The; Victory Park; Visiting Fellowships for Historical Research; Voiceworks Magazine; War Cry, The; Warthog Press; Wascana Review; Washington Square; Way Station Magazine; Wĕber Studies; Wellspring; West Coast Line; West Wind Review; Westerly; Western Humanities Review; Westview; Weyfarers; Whetstone; Whiskey Island Magazine; White Eagle Coffee Store Press; White Pelican Review; White Pine Press; White Wall Review; Whole Notes; Wick Poetry Prize, Stan and Tom; Willow Springs; Windsor Review; Wings Magazine, Inc.; Winslow Press; Wisconsin Academy Review; Wisconsin Arts Board Fellowships; Wisconsin Review; Wishing Well, The; Witness; Worcester Review; Word Salad; Word Works, The; World Order of Narrative and Formalist Poets; Write Way, The; Writer, The; Writer to Writer; Writers At Work Fellowship Competition; Writers Bureau Poetry and Short Story Competition, The; Writers' Center Press; Writers Forum; Writers' Journal; Writing Ulster; Xanadu; Xavier Review; Xcp: Cross-Cultural Poetics; Yankee Magazine; Yeats Society Annual Poetry Competition, The W.B.; Yefief; Yemassee; Yomimono

◙ OPEN MOSTLY TO EXPERIENCED POETS, FEW BEGINNERS

A Small Garlic Press; Aabye; Abraxas Magazine; Acid Angel; Ambit; America; American Poetry Review; American Scholar, The; Amicus Journal, The; Antioch Review, The; Arjuna Library Press; Bacchae Press; Barbarian Press; Black Tie Press; Boa Editions, Ltd.; Bone & Flesh Publication; Boston Phoenix, The; Boston Review; Café Review, The; Canadian Dimension; Caveat Lector; Center Press; Chelsea; Chicago Review; City Lights Books; Clark Street Review; Coffee House Press; Commonweal; Conjunctions; Copper Canyon Press; Darengo; Debut Review; Descant; Devil Blossoms; Dial Books for Young Readers; Dickey Newsletter, James; Dim Gray Bar Press; Écrits des Forges; English Studies Forum; Epoch; European Judaism; Evansville Review, The; Expedition Press; Fire; First Things; Fish Drum; Flambard; For Poetry. Com; Forklift Ohio; Frogmore Papers; Galaxy Press; Gargoyle Magazine; Gecko; Grand Street; Green Bean Press; Habersham Review; Helicon Nine Editions; Holiday House, Inc.; Horizon; Hubbub; Hudson Review, The; Image; Indigenous Fiction; Iris; Journal, The; Kaeden Books; Kaimana; La Jolla Poet's Press; Laurel Review; Link & Visitor, The; Lips; Lone Willow Press; Long Shot; Loom Press; Matriarch's Way; Mekler & Deahl, Publishers; Mesechabe; Michigan Quarterly Review; Mind Matters Review; Mississippi Mud; mojo risin'; Muuna Takeena; Nassau Review; National Forum; New Criterion, The; New Yorker, The; New Zoo Poetry Review; North American Review; North Dakota Quarterly; Northeast; Northeast Arts Magazine; O!!Zone; Ocean View Books; Octavo; Ohio Review, The; Old Crow Review; Open Spaces; Orchises Press; Other Side Magazine, The; Panjandrum Books; Paris Review, The; Passeggiata Press; Pavement Saw; Pequod; Philomel Books; Planet; Ploughshares; Poetry; Poetry Life; Polyphonies; Prose Poem, The; Pygmy Forest Press; Raintown Review, The; Red Dancefloor Press; Red Moon Press; Salmagundi; Salmon Run Press; Smith Publisher, Gibbs; Soft Skull Press, Inc.; Sono Nis Press; Southern California Anthology, The; Spinning Jenny; Spoon River Poetry Review, The; StellaLuna-Poetry Circle; Stevens Journal, The Wallace; Sticks; Tameme; Tampa Review; Tebot Bach; 10th Muse; Terrible Work; Touchstone Literary Journal; University of Alberta Press; University of Iowa Press; Unmuzzled Ox; Utah State University Press; Vehicule Press; Verse; Virginia Quarterly Review, The; Wesleyan University Press; West Anglia Publications; Yale University Press; Zoland Books Inc.; Zuzu's Petals Quarterly Online

◎ SPECIALIZED—OPEN TO POETS FROM SPECIFIC AREAS OR GROUPS OR POEMS IN SPECIFIC FORMS OR ON SPECIFIC THEMES

Aardvark Adventurer, The; Abiko Annual With James Joyce FW Studies; Able Muse; Aboriginal SF; About Such Things; Above the Bridge Magazine; Acorn, The; Adoration; Adrift; Aethlon; African Voices; Ag-Pilot International Magazine; Aguilar Expression, The; Aim Magazine; Albatross; Alice James Books; Alive Now; Allegheny Review; Amelia; American Cowboy Poet Magazine, The; American Research Press; American Tanka; American Tolkien Society; American Writing; Amicus Journal, The; Amy Award, The; Analecta; Ancient Paths; Andreas-Gryphius-Preis; Angel News Magazine; Anna's Journal; Anthology of New England Writers, The; Antietam Review; Antipodes; Appalachia; Apropos; Arachne, Inc.; Arkansas Review; Artist Trust; Arts Recognition and Talent Search; Asian Pacific American Journal; Avocet; Babel; Barbarian Press; Bark, The; Bauhan, Publisher, William L.; Bay Area Book Reviewers Association Awards; Bay Windows; Baybury Review; BBC Wildlife Magazine Poet of the Year Awards; Beacon; Beacon Street Review; Bear Deluxe, The; Bear Star Press; Belhue Press; Bell's Letters Poet; Benjamin Franklin Literary and Medical Society, Inc.; Bennett & Kitchel; Best of Ohio Writers Writing Contest; Bible Advocate; Bibliophilos; Bilingual Review Press; Birch Brook Press; Birmingham Poetry Review; Bitter Oleander,

Geographical Index

Use this index to locate poetry-related publishers and events in your region. Much of the poetry published today reflects regional interests. In addition, publishers often favor poets (and work) from their own areas. We also include conferences and workshops in this index to help you easily find local happenings. Also, keep your neighboring areas in mind for other opportunities.

Here you will find the names of U.S. publishers, conferences and workshops arranged alphabetically within their state or territory. Following them are lists of publishers in Canada, the United Kingdom, Australia, France, Japan and other countries. See the General Index for the page numbers of their corresponding listings.

ALABAMA
Publishers of Poetry
Alabama Literary Review
Alden Enterprises
Aura Literary/Arts Review
Birmingham Poetry Review
Black Warrior Review
Catamount Press
Dreams and Nightmares
Inverted-A, Inc.
Melting Trees Review
Minority Literary Expo
National Forum
Poem
Science Fiction Poetry
  Association
Southern Humanities Review
Sticks
TimBookTu

Conferences & Workshops
Writing Today

ALASKA
Publishers of Poetry
Alaska Quarterly Review
Explorations
Salmon Run Press

ARIZONA
Publishers of Poetry
Alligator Juniper
Allisone Press
Anthology
Bilingual Review Press
Hayden's Ferry Review
Lucid Stone, The
Missing Fez, The
Newsletter Inago
Riverstone
Synaesthesia Press

Conferences & Workshops
Colorado Mountain Writers'
  Workshop
Pima Writers' Workshop

ARKANSAS
Publishers of Poetry
Arkansas Review
Cedar Hill Publications
Family of Man Press
Lucidity
Nebo
Slant
Storyteller, The

Conferences & Workshops
Ozark Creative Writers
  Conference

CALIFORNIA
Publishers of Poetry
Able Muse
Acorn, The
Adoration
Amelia
American Indian Studies
  Center
Amethyst & Emerald Publishing
Anamnesis Press
Aphasia Press
Arctos Press
Avocet
Bark, The
Bay Area Poets Coalition
Bear Star Press
Blue Unicorn
Bottomfish
Burning Bush Publications
California Quarterly
Caveat Lector
CC. Marimbo Communications
Center Press
Cider Press Review
City Lights Books
Clutch
Concrete Abstract
Creative With Words
  Publications (C.W.W.)
Creativity Unlimited Press®
Cyber Oasis

Daniel and Company, Publisher,
  John
Dark Regions
Drinkin' Buddy Magazine,
  The
Dry Bones Press
Ekphrasis
Emotions Literary Magazine
Enterzone
Epicenter
Faultline
For Poetry.Com
Fourteen Hills
Free Lunch
GLB Publishers
Golden Isis Magazine
Greenhouse Review Press
Haight Ashbury Literary
  Journal
Haiku Headlines
Harcourt, Inc.
Hard Row to Hoe
Idiot, The
In the Grove
Interbang
Jewish Spectator
Junction Press
Kerf, The
Konocti Books
Kuumba
La Jolla Poet's Press
Leapings Literary
  Magazine
Left Curve
Libra Publishers, Inc.
Los
Lummox Press
Luz en Arte y Literatura
Lynx Eye
Mandrake Poetry Review
Mind Matters Review
Mkashef Enterprises
Monkey Flower
Mother Earth International
  Journal

Moving Parts Press
New Mirage Quarterly, The
Onthebus
Oxygen
Pacific Coast Journal
Panjandrum Books
P.D.Q. (Poetry Depth Quarterly)
Pearl
Penwood Review, The
Piano Press
Poetry International
Poetry USA
Post-Apollo Press, The
Prometheus Press
Prosodia
Pygmy Forest Press
QED Press
Radiance
Rattle
Red Dancefloor Press
Red Hen Press
Ruah
Science of Mind
Shemom
Shirim
Silver Wings/Mayflower Pulpit
Sinister Wisdom
Southern California Anthology
Spillway
Spunk
Stone Soup
Summer Stream Press
Tameme
Tebot Bach
Temporary Vandalism
   Recordings
Threepenny Review, The
Tucumcari Literary Review
Turkey Press
West Anglia Publications
Western Archipelago Review
Wishing Well, The
Writing For Our Lives
Writing on the Edge

Conferences & Workshops
Foothill Writers' Conference
Mount Hermon Christian
   Writers Conference
Napa Valley Writers' Conference
San Diego State University
   Writers Conference
Squaw Valley Community of
   Writers Poetry Workshop
Yosemite: Alive with Poetry

COLORADO
Publishers of Poetry
Arjuna Library Press
Bible Advocate
Bombay Gin
Buffalo Bones
Clark Street Review
Climbing Art, The
Cloud Ridge Press

Clubhouse Jr.
Colorado Review
Dead Metaphor Press
Denver Quarterly
Dry Creek Review, The
Inklings
Many Mountains Moving
Ocean View Books
Passeggiata Press
Pep Publishing
Pinyon Poetry
Scroll Publications
Seedhouse
SPS Studios, Inc.

Conferences & Workshops
Aspen Summer Words Writing
   Retreat and Literary Festival
Steamboat Springs Writers
   Conference

CONNECTICUT
Publishers of Poetry
Clay Palm Review
Connecticut Poetry Review, The
Connecticut Review
Connecticut River Review
Creative Juices
Dirigible
Hanover Press, Ltd.
Haypenny Press
Intertext
Small Pond Magazine of
   Literature
Twilight Ending
Wesleyan University Press
Yale University Press

Conferences & Workshops
Wesleyan Writers Conference

DELAWARE
Publishers of Poetry
Möbius
Word Dance

DISTRICT OF COLUMBIA
Publishers of Poetry
American Scholar, The
G.W. Review
GeneWatch
Middle East Report
Sojourners
Washington Review
Word Works, The

FLORIDA
Publishers of Poetry
Abundance
American Poets & Poetry
Angel News Magazine
Anhinga Press
Apalachee Quarterly
Cycle Press

Eckerd College Review
Emerald Coast Review
Florida Review, The
4*9*1 Imagination
Gulf Stream Magazine
Half Tones to Jubilee
Home Times
International Quarterly
Jupiter's Freedom
Kalliope
Kings Estate Press
Literary Moments
LSR (Latino Stuff Review)
Magic Changes
Mudlark
National Enquirer
New Writer's Magazine
Nuthouse
Oasis
Poetry of the People
Silver Web, The
Somniloquy
Tampa Review
Thoughts for All Seasons
University of Central Florida
   Contemporary Poetry Series
White Pelican Review
Write Way, The
Writer's Guidelines & News
   Magazine

Conferences & Workshops
Florida Christian Writers
   Conference
Key West Writers' Workshop

GEORGIA
Publishers of Poetry
Anna's Journal
Atlanta Review
babysue
Blood and Fire Review
Carpe Laureate Diem
Chattahoochee Review, The
Classical Outlook, The
Dickey Newsletter, James
Five Points
Georgia Review, The
GSU Review
Habersham Review
Herb Network, The
LAIRE, Inc., the
Lullwater Review
Midwest Poetry Review
Old Red Kimono, The
Parnassus Literary Journal
SimplyWords
Society of American Poets, The
Spring Tides
University of Georgia Press
Unlikely Stories

Conferences & Workshops
Sandhills Writers Conference

Northwoods Press
Puckerbrush Press, The

Conferences & Workshops
DownEast Maine Writer's
Workshops

MARYLAND
Publishers of Poetry
Abbey
Antietam Review
Baltimore Review, The
Black Moon
BrickHouse Books, Inc.
Cochran's Corner
Dolphin-Moon Press
Feminist Studies
In the Family
Johns Hopkins University Press,
The
Maryland Poetry Review
Nightsun
Octavo
Open University of America
Press
Oracle Poetry
Passager
Pegasus Review, The
People's Press, The
Plastic Tower, The
Poet Lore
Potomac Review
Samsara
Shattered Wig Review
Situation
Smartish Pace
UNo Mas Magazine
Vegetarian Journal

Conferences & Workshops
Literary Festival at St. Mary's

MASSACHUSETTS
Publishers of Poetry
Aboriginal SF
Adastra Press
Agni
Albatross
American Dissident, The
Amherst Review, The
Appalachia
Atlantic Monthly, The
Aurorean, The
Bay Windows
Beacon Street Review
Boston Phoenix, The
Boston Poet, The
Boston Review
Button Magazine
Christian Science Monitor, The
Eidos Magazine
Godine, Publisher, David R.
Harvard Advocate, The
Houghton Mifflin Co.
Ibbetson St. Press

Loom Press
Mad River Press
Massachusetts Review, The
New Renaissance, The
96 Inc Magazine
Old Crow Review
Onset Review, The
Osiris
Partisan Review
Peregrine
Perugia Press
Ploughshares
Potato Hill Poetry
Provincetown Arts
Soundings East
Suzerain Enterprises
Teen Voices
Tightrope
University of Massachusetts
Press, The
Voiding The Void
Window Journal
Worcester Review
Writer, The
Zoland Books Inc.

Conferences & Workshops
Harvard Summer Writing
Program
Pine Island Journal of New
England Poetry
Whidbey Island Writers'
Conferences

MICHIGAN
Publishers of Poetry
Above the Bridge Magazine
Affable Neighbor
American Tolkien Society
Angelflesh
Bennett & Kitchel
Bridge, The
Clubhouse
Dead Fun
Driftwood Review, The
Ethereal Green
Expedition Press
Gazelle Publications
Graffiti Rag
Gravity Presses
Improvijazzation Nation
Japanophile
Literally Horses
Lotus Press, Inc.
MacGuffin, The
Michigan Quarterly Review
Michigan State University Press
New Issues Press
Northern Stars Magazine
Passages North
Perspectives
Poetic Page
Rarach Press
Red Cedar Review
Riverrun

Sounds of Poetry, The
Struggle
Third Coast
Thumbprints
Touch
Way Station Magazine
Well Tempered Sonnet, The
Witness

Conferences & Workshops
Midland Writers Conference
Oakland University Writers'
Conference
Writers' Conference at Oakland
University

MINNESOTA
Publishers of Poetry
Ascent
Coffee House Press
Conduit
Futures Magazine
Graywolf Press
Karawane
Kumquat Meringue
Liftouts Magazine
Loonfeather Annual
Lutheran Digest, The
M.I.P. Company
Mankato Poetry Review
Meadowbrook Press
Midwest Villages & Voices
Milkweed Editions
New Rivers Press
Once Upon A Time
Poetry Harbor
Rag Mag
Sidewalks
Spish
Spout Magazine
Studio One
Thin Coyote
Writers' Journal
Xcp: Cross-Cultural Poetics

Conferences & Workshops
Art Workshops in Guatemala

MISSISSIPPI
Publishers of Poetry
Bell's Letters Poet
Doggerel
Magnolia Quarterly, The
Mississippi Review

MISSOURI
Publishers of Poetry
BKMK Press
Boulevard
Chariton Review, The
Country Folk
Debut Review
Funny Paper, The
Gospel Publishing House
Green Hills Literary Lantern

Helicon Nine Editions
Hodgepodge Short Stories &
    Poetry
Laurel Review
Mid-America Press, Inc., The
Missouri Review
Nazarene International
    Headquarters
New Letters
Offerings
Paintbrush
Pleiades
River Styx Magazine
Thorny Locust
Timberline Press

MONTANA
Publishers of Poetry
Bugle
Corona
Cutbank
Poem du Jour
Rocky Mountain Rider Magazine
Seven Buffaloes Press
Superior Poetry News

NEBRASKA
Publishers of Poetry
Beggar's Press
Blind Horse Review, The
Lone Willow Press
Nebraska Review, The
Plainsongs
Prairie Schooner

NEVADA
Publishers of Poetry
Interim
Limited Editions Press
Pegasus
Red Rock Review
Sierra Nevada College Review

NEW HAMPSHIRE
Publishers of Poetry
Bauhan, Publisher, William L.
Bone & Flesh Publication
Brown Bottle, The
Little Brown Poetry
Northern Centinel, The
Red Owl Magazine
Verse
Victory Park
Yankee Magazine

NEW JERSEY
Publishers of Poetry
Adept Press
black bough
Companion in Zeor, A
Devil Blossoms
Edgar
Exit 13
Flesh and Blood

Hellp!
Higginsville Reader, The
Journal of New Jersey Poets
Kelsey Review
Lips
Literary Review, The
Long Shot
Lucid Moon
Maelstrom
Mail Call Journal
Marymark Press
Naturally
Paterson Literary Review, The
Princeton University Press
Quarterly Review of Literature
    Poetry Book Series
Sacred Journey
St. Joseph Messenger and
    Advocate of the Blind
Saturday Press, Inc.
Sensations Magazine
Skidrow Penthouse
Still Waters Press
U.S. 1 Worksheets
Vista Publishing, Inc.
Warthog Press
Wings Magazine, Inc.

Conferences & Workshops
College of New Jersey Writers
    Conference, The
Winter Poetry & Prose Getaway
    in Cape May

NEW MEXICO
Publishers of Poetry
American Research Press
Asher Publishing, Sherman
Atom Mind
Countermeasures
Gentle Survivalist, The
Hadrosaur Tales
Katydid Books
Paradoxism
Pennywhistle Press
RB's Poets' Viewpoint
Whole Notes
Yefief

Conferences & Workshops
Society of the Muse of the
    Southwest
Southwest Writers Workshop
Taos Art School

NEW YORK
Publishers of Poetry
Aardvark Adventurer, The
Adrift
Advocate
African Voices
Alms House Press
America
American Tanka
Amicus Journal, The

Antipodes
Arachne, Inc.
Architrave
Art Times
Asian Pacific American Journal
Bantam Dell Publishing Group
Barbaric Yawp
Barrow Street
Belhue Press
Birch Brook Press
Bitter Oleander, The
Black Diaspora Magazine
Black Spring Press
Black Thistle Press
Blueline
Boa Editions, Ltd.
Bomb Magazine
Bookpress
Bright Hill Press
Brownstone Review, The
Camellia
CC Motorcycle News Magazine
Chelsea
Columbia
Commonweal
Comstock Review, The
Confrontation Magazine
Conjunctions
Cross-Cultural Communications
Desperate Act
Dial Books for Young Readers
Dim Gray Bar Press
Earth's Daughters
Edgewise Press, Inc.
1812
Epoch
Farrar, Straus & Giroux/Books
    for Young Readers
Firebrand Books
First Things
Fish Drum
Free Focus
Frogpond
Futurific
Gathering of the Tribes, A
Gerbil
Grand Street
Green Bean Press
Grove Atlantic
Hanging Loose Press
Harlem Review, The
Haz Mat Review
Heaven Bone Magazine
Helikon Press
Holiday House, Inc.
Holt & Company, Henry
Home Planet News
Hudson Review, The
Hunger Magazine
Iconoclast, The
Inkwell Magazine
Italica Press
Jewish Currents
Jewish Women's Literary Annual
Kiosk

RE:AL
Red River Review
Rio Grande Review
Sharing Magazine
Southwest Review
Southwestern American
  Literature
Strain, The
Sulphur River Literary Review
Texas Review
Texas Tech University Press
Touchstone Literary Journal
Troubadour

Conferences & Workshops
Austin Writers' League Spring
  and Fall Workshops
Frontiers in Writing
SWT Summer Creative Writing
  Camp

UTAH
Publishers of Poetry
Literature and Belief
New Era Magazine
Of Unicorns and Space Stations
Quarterly West
Smith Publisher, Gibbs
Sunstone
Utah State University Press
Wēber Studies
Western Humanities Review

Conferences & Workshops
Canyonlands Writers River Trip
Desert Writers Workshop
San Juan Writers Workshop

VERMONT
Publishers of Poetry
Anthology of New England
  Writers, The
Longhouse
Marlboro Review, The
New England Review

Conferences & Workshops
Bread Loaf Writers' Conference
Summer Writing Program at the
  University of Vermont

VIRGIN ISLANDS
Publishers of Poetry
Caribbean Writer, The
Eastern Caribbean Institute

VIRGINIA
Publishers of Poetry
Black Buzzard Press
Blue Collar Review
Bogg Publications
Breakthrough Inc.
Brunswick Publishing
  Corporation
Chrysalis Reader
Dixie Phoenix

Edge City Review, The
Fauquier Poetry Journal
Gargoyle Magazine
Garnet
Hollins Critic, The
Intro
Iris
Limestone Circle
New Zoo Poetry Review
Orchises Press
Penmanship
Phoebe
Pocahontas Press, Inc.
Red Dragon Press
Red Moon Press
Reflect
Roanoke Review
Shenandoah
So To Speak
Sow's Ear Poetry Review, The
Virginia Quarterly Review, The
War Cry, The
Welcome Home
WoRM fEASt!

Conferences & Workshops
Highland Summer Workshop
Newport University Writers'
  Conference & Contest,
  Christopher

WASHINGTON
Publishers of Poetry
Ag-Pilot International Magazine
Babel
Bellingham Review, The
Bellowing Ark
Cleaning Business Magazine
Copper Canyon Press
Dead End Street Publications
Descanso Literary Journal
Fine Madness
Floating Bridge Press
Footprints
Frontiers
George & Mertie's Place
Heliotrope
Indigenous Fiction
Kimera
Kota Press
LitRag
Murderous Intent
Open Hand Publishing Inc.
Pif Magazine
Poetry Northwest
Poets Corner
Pride Imprints
Rose Alley Press
Score Magazine
Sounds of a Grey Metal Day
Spindrift
Tsunami Inc.
VQ
Wellspring
Willow Springs

Yes!

WEST VIRGINIA
Publishers of Poetry
Bibliophilos
Kestrel
Laurels

WISCONSIN
Publishers of Poetry
Abraxas Magazine
Acorn Whistle
Country Woman
Cream City Review
First Class
Fox Cry Review
Magazine of Speculative Poetry
Modern Haiku
Muse World Media Group
Neovictorian/Cochlea, The
Northeast
Pacific Enterprise Magazine
PandaLoon
Poet's Fantasy
Porcupine Literary Arts
  Magazine
Premiere Generation Ink
Rosebud
Seems
Student Leadership Journal
University of Wisconsin Press
Wisconsin Academy Review
Wisconsin Review

Conferences & Workshops
University of Wisconsin-
  Madison's School of the Arts
  at Rhinelander
Wisconsin Regional Writers'
  Association Inc.

WYOMING
Publishers of Poetry
Calypso Publications
High Plains Press
Owen Wister Review

CANADA
Publishers of Poetry
Amethyst Review, The
Antigonish Review, The
Arsenal Pulp Press
Barbarian Press
Black Moss Press
Borealis Press
Bread of Life Magazine, The
brown-bag Lunch Magazine
Canadian Dimension
Canadian Journal of
  Contemporary Literary Stuff
Canadian Literature
Canadian Woman Studies
Canadian Writer's Journal
Capers Aweigh Annual
  Anthology

Capilano Review, The
Challenger international
Church-Wellesley Review, The
Claremont Review, The
Contemporary Verse 2
Cosmic Trend
Coteau Books
Descant
dig.
ECW Press
Écrits des Forges
Emploi Plus
Event
Fiddlehead, The
filling Station
Fireweed
Firm Noncommittal
FreeFall Magazine
Girl Cult Girlkulturzine
Goose Lane Editions
Graffito
Grain
Green's Magazine
Guernica Editions Inc.
Harpweaver, The
House of Anansi Press
In 2 Print Magazine
Jones Av.
Kwil Kids Publishing
Link & Visitor, The
Malahat Review, The
Mekler & Deahl, Publishers
(m)öthër TØñgué Press
Muse Journal
Musicworks
New Orphic Review
On Spec
Our Family
Paperplates
Plowman, The
Poets' Podium
Pottersfield Portfolio
Prairie Journal, The
Presbyterian Record, The
Prism International
Queen Street Quarterly
Queen's Quarterly
Rabbit Hole Press, The
Raw Nervz Haiku
Red Deer Press
Ronsdale Press
Room of One's Own
Rowan Books
Scholastic Canada Ltd.
Scrivener
Seeds Poetry Magazine
Snowapple Press
Sono Nis Press
sub-TERRAIN
Tale Spinners
"Teak" Roundup
Thalia
Thistledown Press Ltd.
3 Cup Morning
Tickled by Thunder

Time For Rhyme
Turnstone Press Limited
Tyro Publishing
University of Alberta Press
Unmuzzled Ox
Urban Graffiti
Vehicule Press
Wascana Review
West Coast Line
Westcoast Fisherman, The
Western Producer Publications
White Wall Review
Windsor Review
Writer's Block Magazine

Conferences & Workshops
Sage Hill Writing Fall Poetry
    Colloquium
Sage Hill Writing Summer
    Experience
Victoria School of Writing

AUSTRALIA
Publishers of Poetry
Ambitious Friends
core literary journal
FreeXpresSion
Galaxy Press
Ginninderra Press
Heist Magazine
Hobo Poetry & Haiku Magazine
Imago
Lithuanian Paper
Mattoid
Paper Wasp
Quadrant Magazine
Studio
Ulitarra
Voiceworks Magazine
Westerly

FRANCE
Publishers of Poetry
Doc(k)s
Handshake Editions
Paris/Atlantic
Polyphonies

JAPAN
Publishers of Poetry
Abiko Annual With James Joyce
    FW Studies
Plaza, The
Poetry Kanto
Yomimono

UNITED KINGDOM
Publishers of Poetry
Aabye
Acid Angel
Acumen Magazine
Akros Publications
Ambit
Aquarius
Blackwater Press

Brando's Hat
Breakfast All Day
British Haiku Society
Carn
Chapman
Cherrybite Publications
Connections
Crescent Moon Publishing
Current Accounts
Dandelion Arts Magazine
Darengo
Dialogos
Enitharmon Press
Envoi
European Judaism
Feather Books
Fire
Firewater Press Inc.
First Offense
Flambard
Flarestack Publishing
Forum
Freehand
Frogmore Papers
Gairm
Gentle Reader
Handshake
Headlock Press
Hilltop Press
Hippopotamus Press
HQ Poetry Magazine
HU
Interpreter's House
Iota
Jones Journal, The David
Journal of Contemporary Anglo-
    Scandinavian Poetry
Kawabata Press
Kingfisher Publications PLC
Konfluence
Krax
K.T. Publications
Lapwing Publications
Lateral Moves
Links
Linkway Magazine
Lochs Magazine
London Magazine
Magma Poetry Magazine
Maypole Editions
Modern Poetry In Translation
Monas Hieroglyphica
New Writer, The
Tŷ Newydd Writers' Centre
Northwords
Oasis Books
Orbis
Partners Writing Group
Peer Poetry Magazine
Pennine Platform
Planet
Poetic Hours
Poetry Life
Poetry Nottingham International
Poetry Review

U.S. and Canadian Postal Codes

United States

AL	Alabama	MI	Michigan	VT	Vermont
AK	Alaska	MN	Minnesota	VI	Virgin Islands
AZ	Arizona	MS	Mississippi	VA	Virginia
AR	Arkansas	MO	Missouri	WA	Washington
CA	California	MT	Montana	WV	West Virginia
CO	Colorado	NE	Nebraska	WI	Wisconsin
CT	Connecticut	NV	Nevada	WY	Wyoming
DE	Delaware	NH	New Hampshire		
DC	District of Columbia	NJ	New Jersey	**Canada**	
FL	Florida	NM	New Mexico	AB	Alberta
GA	Georgia	NY	New York	BC	British Columbia
GU	Guam	NC	North Carolina	LB	Labrador
HI	Hawaii	ND	North Dakota	MB	Manitoba
ID	Idaho	OH	Ohio	NB	New Brunswick
IL	Illinois	OK	Oklahoma	NF	Newfoundland
IN	Indiana	OR	Oregon	NT	Northwest Territories
IA	Iowa	PA	Pennsylvania	NS	Nova Scotia
KS	Kansas	PR	Puerto Rico	ON	Ontario
KY	Kentucky	RI	Rhode Island	PEI	Prince Edward Island
LA	Louisiana	SC	South Carolina	PQ	Quebec
ME	Maine	SD	South Dakota	SK	Saskatchewan
MD	Maryland	TN	Tennessee	YT	Yukon
MA	Massachusetts	TX	Texas		
		UT	Utah		

Subject Index

Use this index to save time in your search for the best markets for your poetry. The categories are listed alphabetically and contain the magazines, publishers, contests and awards that buy or accept poetry dealing with specific subjects. Most of these markets have the ⓘ symbol before their listing titles.

Check through the index first to see what subjects are represented. Then look at the listings in the categories you're interested in. For example, if you're seeking a magazine or contest for your poem about "baseball," look at the titles under **Sports/Recreation**. After you've selected a possible market, refer to the General Index for the page number. Then read the listing *carefully* for details on submission requirements.

Under **Themes**, you will find those book and magazine publishers that regularly publish anthologies or issues on announced themes (if interested, send a SASE to these publishers for details on upcoming topics). **Regional** includes those outlets which publish poetry about or by poets from a certain geographic area; and the category **Form/Style** contains those magazines and presses that seek particular poetic forms or styles, such as haiku or sonnets or experimental work. Finally, those publishers listed under **Specialized** are very narrow in their interests—too narrow, in fact, to be listed in one of our other categories.

We do not recommend you use this index exclusively in your search for markets. Most magazines, publishers and contests listed in *Poet's Market* have wide-ranging poetry preferences and don't choose to be listed by category. Also, many of those who specialize in one subject are often open to others as well. Reading *all* the listings is still your best marketing strategy.

Animal: Bark, The; Bugle, Journal of Elk Country; Kerf, The; Literally Horses; Pygmy Forest Press; Ralph's Review; Rocky Mountain Rider Magazine; Whitecrow Foundation, Tahana

Anthology: Arctos Press; Asher Publishing, Sherman; Ashland Poetry Press, The; Asian Pacific American Journal; Bay Area Poets Coalition (BAPC); Birch Brook Press; Bytes of Poetry; Calypso Publications; Catamount Press; Coteau Books; Crescent Moon Publishing; Cross-Cultural Communications; Feather Books; Floating Bridge Press; Helicon Nine Editions; Kingfisher Publications PLC; Lake Shore Publishing; Literary Focus Poetry Publications; Meadowbrook Press; Mekler & Deahl, Publishers; New Mirage Quarterly, The; Northwoods Press; Outrider Press; PandaLoon; Passeggiata Press; Pennywhistle Press; Plowman, The; Poet's Fantasy; Prairie Journal, The; Pudding House Publications; Red Moon Press; Scroll Publications; Seeds Poetry Magazine; Seven Buffaloes Press; Society of American Poets (SOAP), The; Southern California Anthology, The; Spirit That Moves Us, The; Sticks; Waterways; White Eagle Coffee Store Press; Word Works, The; Young Writer

Bilingual/Foreign Language: Andreas-Gryphius-Preis (German); Babel (multicultural); Bibliophilos (French, German, Romanian); Bilingual Review Press (Spanish); Borderlands (multilingual); Carn (Celtic); Cló Iar-Chonnachta (Irish Gaelic); Cross-Cultural Communications (African, Asian, Cajun, Dutch, Finnish, Israeli, Italian, Scandinavian, Spanish, Swedish, Turkish, Yiddish); Doc(k)s (French); Dwan (Spanish); Écrits des Forges (French); Gairm (Scottish Gaelic); Horizontes (Spanish); Italica Press (Italian); LSR (Latino Stuff Review) (Spanish); Luz en Arte y Literatura (Spanish); M.I.P. Company (Russian); New Renaissance, The; Osiris (French, Italian, Polish, Danish, German); Plaza, The (Japanese); Poetry of the People (French, Spanish); Prakalpana Literature (Bengali); Princeton University Press (multilingual); Rarach Press (Czech); Sachem Press (Spanish); Skipping Stones; Sounds of Poetry, The (Spanish, French); Tameme (Spanish); To' To' Pos (Spanish); Touchstone Literary Journal (multicultural); Tsunami Inc. (Chinese, Spanish); Unmuzzled Ox (French); Wake Forest University Press (Irish Gaelic)

Horror: Dark Regions; Dead Fun; Edgar; Jupiter's Freedom; Magazine of Speculative Poetry, The; Mkashef Enterprises; Nova Express; Oak, The; On Spec; Outer Darkness; Penny Dreadful; Ralph's Review; Scavenger's Newsletter; Science Fiction Poetry Association; Silver Gull Publishing; Silver Web, The; Space and Time; Suzerain Enterprises; Ultimate Unknown, The; Wicked Mystic

Humor: Aardvark Adventurer, The; Country Woman; Dixie Phoenix; Feather Books; Firm Noncommittal; Funny Paper, The; Idiot, The; Krax; Leacock Medal for Humour, The Stephen; Libido; Lutheran Digest, The; Meadowbrook Press; Mississippi Valley Poetry Contest; Mystery Time; National Enquirer; New Writer's Magazine; New Yorker, The; Nuthouse; Outrider Press; Poetry of the People; Raw Dog Press; Rural Heritage; Superior Poetry News; Thalia; Thoughts for All Seasons; Tucumcari Literary Review

Love/Romance/Erotica: Aguilar Expression, The; Cosmic Trend; Crescent Moon Publishing; Eidos Magazine; Expedition Press; Forum; Implosion Press; Kuumba; Libido; M.I.P. Company; Mkashef Enterprises; Night Roses; Pep Publishing ("ethical multiple relationships"); Poetry Explosion Newsletter, The; Poetry of the People; Suzerain Enterprises; West Coast Line

Membership/Subscription: Apropos; Bell's Letters Poet; Cherrybite Publications; Cochran's Corner; Common Threads; Current Accounts; Cyber Literature; Dandelion Arts Magazine; Dickey Newsletter, James; Emshock Letter, The; Hemans Prize for Lyrical Poetry, Felicia; Herb Network, The; Hodgepodge Short Stories & Poetry; Intro; Laurels; Micropress New Zealand; Minority Literary Expo; Mystery Time; Pennsylvania Poetry Society Annual Contest; Poetcrit; Poetry Explosion Newsletter, The; Poetry Forum; Poetry Life; Poetry Nottingham International; Poets at Work; Poets' Roundtable; Quarterly Review of Literature Poetry Book Series; Society of American Poets (SOAP), The; Spring (e.e. cummings society); "Teak" Roundup; Thalia; Tickled by Thunder; Wishing Well, The; World Order of Narrative and Formalist Poets; Writers Forum

Mystery: Murderous Intent; Mystery Time; Oak, The; Outer Darkness; Pirate Writings; Queen's Mystery Magazine, Ellery; Scavenger's Newsletter; Suzerain Enterprises

Nature/Rural/Ecology: Albatross; Amicus Journal, The; Appalachia; Arachne, Inc.; Avocet; BBC Wildlife Magazine Poet of the Year Awards; Bear Deluxe, The; Bugle, Journal of Elk Country; Catamount Press; Climbing Art, The; Dickey Newsletter, James; Gentle Survivalist, The; Hard Row to Hoe; Heaven Bone Magazine; Herb Network, The; Houghton Mifflin Co.; Kerf, The; Lutheran Digest, The; Melting Trees Review; Night Roses; Northern Centinel, The; Open University of America Press; Poetry Explosion Newsletter, The; Poetry of the People; Pygmy Forest Press; Ralph's Review; Rural Heritage; Seven Buffaloes Press; Skipping Stones; Snowy Egret; Tale Spinners; Trewithen Poetry Prize, The; U.S. Latino Review, The; West Coast Line; Whitecrow Foundation, Tahana; Yes!

Political: Aim Magazine; Bibliophilos; Blue Collar Review; Canadian Dimension; Collages & Bricolages; Left Curve; Northern Centinel, The; Other Side Magazine, The; Pudding House Publications; Pygmy Forest Press; Sojourners; Struggle; U.S. Latino Review, The

Psychic/Occult: Allisone Press; Crescent Moon Publishing; Mkashef Enterprises; Ralph's Review; Superior Poetry News; Vortex of the Macabre

Regional: Above the Bridge Magazine (Michigan's Upper Peninsula); Acorn, The (Western Sierra); Alice James Books (New England); Amy Award, The (NYC, Long Island); Antietam Review (DC, DE, MD, PA, VA, WV); Antipodes (Australia); Arkansas Review (seven-state Mississippi River Delta); Artist Trust (WA); Bay Area Book Reviewers Association Awards (Northern CA); Baybury Review (Midwest); Beacon (Southwestern Oregon); Bear Star Press (Western and Pacific states); Best of Ohio Writers Writing Contest; Blackwater Press (UK); Blueline (Adirondacks); Borderlands (TX, Southwest); BP Nichol Chapbook Award (Canada); Briar Cliff Review, The (Midwest, Siouxland); Buffalo Bones (Western states); California Book Awards of The Commonwealth Club of California; Canadian Literature; Capers Aweigh Annual Anthology; Caribbean Writer, The; Cleveland State University Poetry Center (OH); Colorado Book Awards; Confluence Press (Northwestern US); Coolbrith Circle Annual Poetry Contest, Ina (CA); Coteau Books (Canada); Cottonwood (Midwest); Council for Wisconsin Writers, Inc.; Creative Writing Fellowships in Poetry (AZ); Cycle Press (Florida Keys); Dixie Phoenix; Dolphin-Moon Press; Driftwood Review, The (MI); Eastern Caribbean Institute; Emerald Coast Review; Fiddlehead, The (Atlantic Region); Fireweed: Poetry of Western Oregon; Floating Bridge Press (WA); Florida Individual Artist Fellowships; Goose Lane Editions (Canada); Guernica Editions Inc. (Canada, US); Habersham Review (GA); Heartlands Today, The (Midwest); High Plains Press; House of Anansi Press (Canada); HU (Ireland); Hunger Magazine; Imago (Queensland, Australia); In the Grove (CA, Central Valley); In 2 Print Magazine (Canada); Individual

Artist Grants (TX, Houston, Harris County); Interpreter's House (UK); Journal of New Jersey Poets; Kaimana (Pacific); Kelsey Review (Mercer County, NJ); Landfall (New Zealand); Leacock Medal for Humour, The Stephen (Canada); Long Island Quarterly; Lonzie's Fried Chicken℠ Literary Magazine (South); Loonfeather Annual (MN); Louisiana Literature; Louisiana Review, The; Marin Arts Council Individual Artist Grants; Melbourne Poets Union Annual Poetry Competition; Mid-America Press, Inc., The (AR, IA, IL, KS, MO, NE, OK); Middle East Report; Midwest Villages & Voices; Mississippi Valley Poetry Contest; Montalvo Biennial Poetry Competition (CA, NE, OR, WA); Montana Arts; (m)öthêr TØñgué Press (Canada); New Issues Press; New York Foundation for the Arts; Ninety-Six Press (Greenville, SC); North Carolina Literary Review; Northeast Corridor; Northwords (Northern Scotland); Now & Then (Appalachia); NSW Premier's Literary Award "The Kenneth Slessor Prize"; Ohioana Book Awards; On Spec (Canada); "Over The Back Fence" Magazine (OH); Passeggiata Press (Non-European, Non-American); Paterson Literary Review, The; PEN Center USA West Literary Award in Poetry; Pelican Publishing Company (LA); Pew Fellowship in the Arts (PA); Pine Island Journal of New England Poetry; Poetry Harbor (Upper Midwest); Poetry Ireland Review; Poets' Dinner Contest (CA); Potomac Review (MD); Prairie Journal, The (Canada); Puckerbrush Press, The (ME); Queen Street Quarterly; Queen's Quarterly (Canada); QWF Literary Awards (Quebec, Canada); Red Crow; Response; Review (Latin American); Revista/Review Interamericana (Puerto Rican, Caribbean, Hispanic, Latin America); Roanoke-Chowan Poetry Award (NC); Rocky Mountain Rider Magazine; Ronsdale Press (Canada); Rowan Books; San Francisco Foundation (CA, NV); Seven Buffaloes Press; South Dakota Review; Southwestern American Literature; Spoon River Poetry Review, The (IL); Stephansson Award for Poetry, Stephan G.; Superior Poetry News; Syncopated City; Tameme; Thistledown Press Ltd. (Canada); Towson University Prize for Literature (MD); Trestle Creek Review (innermountain West); Tucumcari Literary Review; Turnstone Press Limited (Canada); Upsouth (South); Vehicule Press (Canada); Weatherford Award, The (Appalachian South); West Coast Line (Canada); Western Archipelago Review (Asia, Pacific); Western Australian Premier's Book Awards; Western Producer Publications (Western Canada); Wisconsin Academy Review; Wisconsin Arts Board Fellowships; Woodley Memorial Press (KS); Worcester Review (New England); Writers' Center Press (IN); Yorkshire Journal

Religious: About Such Things; Adoration; Alive Now; Allisone Press; Ancient Paths; Angel News Magazine; Bible Advocate; Bread of Life Magazine, The; Brilliant Star; Christian Century, The; Christianity and the Arts; Clubhouse Jr.; Commonweal; Cornerstone Magazine; Crescent Moon Publishing; Cross & Quill; Encounter; European Judaism; Evangel; Expedition Press; Feather Books; Gospel Publishing House; Herald Press; Image; Jewish Currents; Jewish Spectator; Link & Visitor, The; Literature and Belief; Lutheran Digest, The; Mature Years; Mennonite, The; Milton Center Poetry Fellowship; Milton Magazine, John; Miraculous Medal, The; Nazarene International Headquarters; New Era Magazine; Oblates; Open University of America Press; Other Side Magazine, The; Our Family; Perspectives; Prayerworks; Presbyterian Record, The; Queen of All Hearts; Sacred Journey; Sharing Magazine; Silver Wings/Mayflower Pulpit; Society of American Poets (SOAP), The; Sojourners; St. Anthony Messenger; St. Joseph Messenger and Advocate of the Blind; Student Leadership Journal; Studio; These Days; Time of Singing; Touch; Tricycle; Upsouth; Urthona Magazine (Buddhism); War Cry, The

Science Fiction/Fantasy: Aboriginal SF; Allisone Press; Companion in Zeor, A; Dark Regions; Dreams and Nightmares; Gotta Write Network Litmag; Handshake; Hilltop Press; Jupiter's Freedom; Magazine of Speculative Poetry, The; Mkashef Enterprises; Nova Express; Oak, The; Ocean View Books; Of Unicorns and Space Stations; On Spec: More Than Just Science Fiction; Outer Darkness; Pirate Writings; Poetry of the People; Poet's Fantasy; Ralph's Review; Scavenger's Newsletter; Science Fiction Poetry Association; Silver Gull Publishing; Silver Web, The; Space and Time; Suzerain Enterprises; Ultimate Unknown, The

Senior Citizen: Funny Paper, The; Mature Years; Oak, The; Passager; Senior Poet Laureate Poetry Competition

Social Issues: Aguilar Expression, The; Aim Magazine; Allisone Press; Black Bear Publications; Blue Collar Review; Bridges; Carolina Wren Press; Christian Century, The; Collages & Bricolages; Haight Ashbury Literary Journal; Left Curve; Melting Trees Review; Northern Centinel, The; Other Side Magazine, The; Our Family; Paper Wasp; Pudding House Publications; Pygmy Forest Press; Skipping Stones; Struggle; Tucumcari Literary Review; U.S. Latino Review, The; West Coast Line; Yes!

Specialized: Ag-Pilot International Magazine; American Research Press; American Tolkien Society; Anna's Journal (childlessness issues); Beacon Street Review (graduate-level writers); Blindskills, Inc. (blind or visually impaired); Boardman Tasker Award, The (mountain literature); Breakthrough Inc.; Brilliant Corners (jazz-related literature); Carnegie Mellon Magazine; CC Motorcycle News Magazine; Classical Outlook, The (classics, Latin); Cleaning Business Magazine; Communities (intentional community living); Creative With Words Publications (C.W.W.); Dovetail; Dream International Quarterly; Dry Bones Press (nursing); Ekphrasis (ekphrastic verse); Exit 13 (geography/travel); 4*9*1 Imagination (neo-immanentist/sursymbolist); Futurific (optimistic poems of the future); GeneWatch; Golden Isis Magazine (pagan/ wiccan); Halls, J.C. and Ruth (MFA or equivalent degree in creative writing); Harvard Advocate, The (university affiliation); Heist Magazine (men); Herb Network, The; Insects Are People Two; Japan Foundation Artist Fellowship Program, The (US residents with Japanese affiliations); Japanese Literary Translation Prize; Jewel Among Jewels Adoption Network, Inc.; Jones Journal, The David; Journal of African Travel-Writing; Kaleidoscope (disability themes); Karawane (open mic/spoken word performers in Twin Cities area); Kavya Bharati; Mail Call Journal (American Civil War); Midwifery Today (childbirth); Milton Magazine, John (visual impairment); Minority Literary Expo; Musicworks; Naturally (family nudism and naturism); Northern Centinel, The; Ohio Teachers Write; Once Upon A Time; Open University of America Press (distance learning, English pedogogy); Our Family (family/marriage/parenting); Our Journey (recovery issues); O!!Zone (visual poetry, photography, collage); Pep Publishing ("ethical multiple relationships"); Piano Press; Pipe Smoker's Ephemeris, The; Potato Hill Poetry; Samsara; Slate & Style (blind writers); Sounds of a Grey Metal Day (prisoners); SPS Studios, Inc.; Spish; Spring (e.e. cummings society); StellaLuna-Poetry Circle; Stevens Journal, The Wallace; Struggle; Transcendent Visions (psychiatric survivors, ex-mental patients); Tucumcari Literary Review; Urthona Magazine (Buddhism); Vegetarian Journal; Visiting Fellowships for Historical Research (American history and cultural); Vista Publishing, Inc. (nurses); Vortex of the Macabre; VQ; Welcome Home (mothers, parenting, families, children); Westcoast Fisherman, The; Xcp: Cross-Cultural Poetics (anthropology)

Spirituality/Inspirational: Alive Now; Allisone Press; Angel News Magazine; Avocet; Chrysalis Reader; Crescent Moon Publishing; Dixie Phoenix; Gentle Survivalist, The; Heaven Bone Magazine; Lutheran Digest, The; New Song, A; Oak, The; Oblates; Our Family; Penwood Review, The; Presbyterian Record, The; Ruah; Science of Mind; Silver Wings/Mayflower Pulpit; Studio; Superior Poetry News; Whitecrow Foundation, Tahana

Sports/Recreation: Aethlon; CC Motorcycle News Magazine; Climbing Art, The; Journal of Asian Martial Arts; Pegasus Review, The; Spish; Spitball

Students: Allegheny Review; Analecta; Arts Recognition and Talent Search; Common Threads; Fiddlehead, The; Funny Paper, The; Hemans Prize for Lyrical Poetry, Felicia; Intro; League of Minnesota Poets Contest, The; Merlyn's Pen; Modern Haiku; Night Roses; Offerings; Pennsylvania Poetry Society Annual Contest; Potato Hill Poetry; Seaman Poetry Award, Claudia Ann; Student Leadership Journal

Themes: Alive Now; American Tolkien Society; Apalachee Quarterly; Ashland Poetry Press, The; Chrysalis Reader; Classical Outlook, The (classics, Latin); Collages & Bricolages; Columbia; Cosmic Trend; Creative With Words Publications (C.W.W.); Crumb Elbow Publishing Poetry Contests; Curriculum Vitae Literary Supplement; Descant; DTCT Open Poetry Award; Earth's Daughters; Event; Green River Writers' Contests; Haight Ashbury Literary Journal; Heartlands Today, The (Midwest); Hopscotch; Jewish Currents; Journal of the American Medical Association (JAMA); Kaleidoscope (disability themes); Kalliope; Lime Green Bulldozers; Magic Changes; Middle East Report; Now & Then (Appalachia); Our Family (family/ marriage/parenting); Paintbrush; Palo Alto Review; Partisan Review; Passager; Pig Iron; Poetic Realm; Poetry of the People; Prairie Journal, The; Rosebud; Skylark; Slipstream; South Carolina Review; South Dakota Review; Thema; Time of Singing; To' To' Pos; Touch; Unmuzzled Ox; Vincent Brothers Review, The; Waterways; Witness; Yes!

Translations: Abiko Annual With James Joyce FW Studies; Barbarian Press; Birmingham Poetry Review; Black Buzzard Press; Blue Unicorn; Borderlands; British Haiku Society; Carolina Quarterly, The; Chelsea; Chicago Review; Classical Outlook, The (classics, Latin); Collages & Bricolages; Cross-Cultural Communications; Cumberland Poetry Review; Darengo; Denver Quarterly; Dirigible; Dwan; Eagle's Flight; Field; Formalist, The; Frogpond; Guernica Editions Inc.; G.W. Review; Hunger Magazine; International Poetry Review; International Quarterly; Intertext; Japanese Literary Translation Prize; Johann-Heinrich-Voss Prize for Translation; Journal of African Travel-Writing; Journal of Contemporary Anglo-Scandinavian Poetry; Kalliope; Luz en Arte y Literatura (Spanish); Mandrake Poetry Review; Manhattan Review, The; Mid-American Review; Modern Poetry In Translation; New Laurel Review, The; New Native Press; New Renaissance, The; New Yorker, The; Oasis Books; Osiris (French, Italian, Polish, Danish, German); Paintbrush; Partisan Review; Passeggiata Press (Non-European, Non-American); Polyphonies; Post-Apollo Press, The; Princeton University Press; Quarterly Review of Literature Poetry Book Series; Quarterly West; Renditions; Review (Latin American); Rhino; Sachem Press (Spanish); Seneca Review; Spoon River Poetry

General Index

Markets and resources that appeared in the *2000 Poet's Market* but do not appear in this edition are identified by two-letter codes in parentheses explaining why these entries no longer appear.

The codes are: **(ED)—Editorial Decision; (NR)—No (or late) Response** to Requests for Updated Information; **(NS)—Not Accepting Submissions** (which include publishers who are overstocked as well as those who no longer publish poetry); **(OB)—Out of Business** (or, in the case of contests, cancelled); **(RR)—Removed by Request** (no reason given); and **(UF)—Uncertain Future** (which includes publishers who have suspended publication or are reorganizing their operation).

Markets that appeared in the 2000 edition of *Poet's Market*, but do not appear this year, are listed in this General Index with the following codes explaining why these entries were omitted: (ED)—Editorial Decision, (NS)—Not Accepting Submissions, (NR)—No (or late) Response to Request for Updated Information, (OB)—Out of Business, (RR)—Removed by Market's Request, (UF)—Uncertain Future.

Markets that appeared in the 2000 edition of *Poet's Market*, but do not appear this year, are listed in this General Index with the following codes explaining why these entries were omitted: (ED)—Editorial Decision, (NS)—Not Accepting Submissions, (NR)—No (or late) Response to Request for Updated Information, (OB)—Out of Business, (RR)—Removed by Market's Request, (UF)—Uncertain Future.

Markets that appeared in the 2000 edition of *Poet's Market*, but do not appear this year, are listed in this General Index with the following codes explaining why these entries were omitted: (ED)—Editorial Decision, (NS)—Not Accepting Submissions, (NR)—No (or late) Response to Request for Updated Information, (OB)—Out of Business, (RR)—Removed by Market's Request, (UF)—Uncertain Future.

Markets that appeared in the 2000 edition of *Poet's Market*, **but do not appear this year, are listed in this General Index with the following codes explaining why these entries were omitted: (ED)—Editorial Decision, (NS)—Not Accepting Submissions, (NR)—No (or late) Response to Request for Updated Information, (OB)—Out of Business, (RR)—Removed by Market's Request, (UF)—Uncertain Future.**

Markets that appeared in the 2000 edition of *Poet's Market,* **but do not appear this year, are listed in this
General Index with the following codes explaining why these entries were omitted: (ED)—Editorial
Decision, (NS)—Not Accepting Submissions, (NR)—No (or late) Response to Request for Updated
Information, (OB)—Out of Business, (RR)—Removed by Market's Request, (UF)—Uncertain Future.**

Markets that appeared in the 2000 edition of *Poet's Market*, but do not appear this year, are listed in this General Index with the following codes explaining why these entries were omitted: **(ED)**—Editorial Decision, **(NS)**—Not Accepting Submissions, **(NR)**—No (or late) Response to Request for Updated Information, **(OB)**—Out of Business, **(RR)**—Removed by Market's Request, **(UF)**—Uncertain Future.

Quadrant Magazine 354
Quale Press (RR)
Quantum Leap 354
Quarter After Eight 355
Quarterly Review of Literature Poetry Book Series 355
Quarterly West 355
Quebec Writers' Federation (see QWF Literary Awards)
Queen of All Hearts 356
Queen Street Quarterly 356
Queen's Mystery Magazine, Ellery 356
Queen's Quarterly 356
Quest, The (see Writers Forum/India)
Quincy Writers Guild Writing Contest, The 487
QWF Literary Awards 488

R

R.R. Bowker 540
R.S.V.P. Press (see Writer's Exchange)
Rabbit Hole Press, The 356
Radiance 357
Rag Mag 357
Ragan Prize, Sam (see Crucible)
Rain Crow Publishing (RR)
Rain Taxi Review of Books 543
Rainmaker Awards in Poetry 488
Raintown Review, The 358
Ralph's Review 358
Rambunctious Press (NR)
Rambunctious Review (NR)
Rarach Press 358
Raskolnikov's Cellar (see Beggar's Press)
Rattapallax 359
Rattapallax Press (see Rattapallax)
Rattle 359
Raw Dog Press 359
Raw Nervz Haiku 360
Raw Seed Review, The (NR)
Ray Poetry Award, David (see Potpourri)
RB's Poets' Viewpoint 360
RC's Stamp Hot Line (see Ralph's Review)
RE:AL 360
Reach (see Cherrybite Publications)
Readers' Choice Awards (see Prairie Schooner)
Reality Street Editions 361
Reater, The (NR)

Red Candle Press, The (NR)
Red Cedar Review 361
Red Crow 361
Red Dancefloor (see Red Dancefloor Press)
Red Dancefloor Press 361
Red Deer Press 362
Red Dot (NR)
Red Dragon Press 362
Red Felt Award, The (see The Missing Fez)
Red Hen Poetry Contest (see Red Hen Press)
Red Hen Press 362
Red Herring 362
Red Moon Anthology, The (see Red Moon Press)
Red Moon Press 363
Red Owl Magazine 363
Red Rampan' Broadside Series (see Red Rampan' Press)
Red Rampan' Press 364
Red Rampan' Review (see Red Rampan' Press)
Red River Review 364
Red Rock Poetry Award (see Red Rock Review)
Red Rock Review 364
Redbud Hill Press (see Red Crow)
Redwood Acres Fair Poetry Contest 488
Reece Contest, Byron Herbert (see Georgia Poetry Society)
Reed (UF)
Reeves Poetry Prize for Justice, The Jeremiah (NR)
Reflect 364
Reflections of You Journal (NR)
Reiman Publications (see Country Woman)
Rejected Quarterly, The (NR)
Renaissance Online Magazine 365
Renditions 365
Re:Print! (see Re:Verse!)
Re-presst (see 24.7)
Response 365
Re:Verse! 366
Review 366
Revista/Review Interamericana 366
RFD 366
Rhino 367
Rhyme Time (see Mystery Time)
Rhysling Anthology, The (see Science Fiction Poetry Association)

Rialto, The 367
Richmond Communications LLC (NR)
Rinehart Awards, Mary Roberts 488
Rio 367
Rio Grande Press (NR)
Rio Grande Review 367
Rising 368
Rising Star Publishers (see Oracle Poetry)
Rivelin Grapheme Press 368
River City 368
River King Poetry Supplement 368
River Oak Review 368
River Styx Magazine 369
Riverrun 369
Riverrun Press, Inc. (NS)
Riverstone 369
Riverstone Poetry Chapbook Award (see Riverstone)
Roanoke Review 370
Roanoke-Chowan Poetry Award 488
Roberts Award, Summerfield G. (NR)
Rocket Press 370
Rockford Review, The 370
Rockford Review, The, sample cover 370
Rockford Writers' Guild (see The Rockford Review)
Rocky Mountain Rider Magazine 371
Roerich Poetry Prize, Nicholas (see Story Line Press)
Romantic Hearts (OB)
Romantic Outsider 371
Romantics Poetry Group (see Romantics Quarterly)
Romantics Quarterly 371
Ronsdale Press 372
Room of One's Own 372
Rose Alley Press 372
Rose Poetry Competition, Reuben (NR)
Rose Tinted Windows 372
Rosebud 373
Rosenberg Award, Anna Davidson 488
Roth Residence in Creative Writing, Philip (NR)
Round Table, The 373
Rowan Books 373
Rowhouse Press (NR)
Ruah 373

Markets that appeared in the 2000 edition of *Poet's Market*, but do not appear this year, are listed in this General Index with the following codes explaining why these entries were omitted: **(ED)—Editorial Decision, (NS)—Not Accepting Submissions, (NR)—No (or late) Response to Request for Updated Information, (OB)—Out of Business, (RR)—Removed by Market's Request, (UF)—Uncertain Future.**